**NOVELL'S**

# Guide to NetWare® 6 Networks

NOVELL'S

Guide to NetWare® 6
Networks

JEFFREY F. HUGHES AND BLAIR W. THOMAS

Novell Press, San Jose

Wiley Publishing, Inc.

Novell's Guide to NetWare® 6 Networks
Novell Press
2211 North First Street
San Jose, CA 95131
Copyright © 2002 Novell, Inc.

Published by Wiley Publishing, Inc., Indianapolis, Indiana
Published simultaneously in Canada

For general information on our other products and services or to obtain technical support, please contact our Customer Care Department within the U.S. at 800-762-2974, outside the U.S. at 317-572-3993, or fax 317-572-4002.

Wiley also publishes its books in a variety of electronic formats. Some content that appears in print may not be available in electronic books.

*Library of Congress Cataloging-in-Publication Data:*
Library of Congress Control Number: 2001099742
ISBN: 0-7645-4876-X
Manufactured in the United States of America
10 9 8 7 6 5 4 3 2

Gamal Herbon, *Publisher, Novell Press, Novell, Inc.*
Novell Press is a trademark and the Novell Press logo is a registered trademark of Novell, Inc.

# Welcome to Novell Press

Novell Press, the world's leading provider of networking books, is the premier source for the most timely and useful information in the networking industry. Novell Press books cover fundamental networking issues as they emerge — from today's Novell and third-party products to the concepts and strategies that will guide the industry's future. The result is a broad spectrum of titles for the benefit of those involved in networking at any level: end user, department administrator, developer, systems manager, or network architect.

Novell Press books are written by experts with the full participation of Novell's technical, managerial, and marketing staff. The books are exhaustively reviewed by Novell's own technicians and are published only on the basis of final released software, never on prereleased versions.

Novell Press at Wiley Publishing is an exciting partnership between two companies at the forefront of the knowledge and communications revolution. The Press is implementing an ambitious publishing program to develop new networking titles centered on the current versions of NetWare, GroupWise, ZENworks, DirXML, and networking integration products.

Novell Press books are translated into several languages and sold throughout the world.

**Gamal Herbon** Publisher Novell Press, Novell, Inc.


# About the Authors

**Jeffrey F. Hughes,** Master Certified Novell Engineer, joined Novell in 1993. **Blair W. Thomas,** Master Certified Novell Engineer, joined Novell in 1986 as a system programmer and later moved to consulting. Blair has given presentations at more than 15 BrainShare events held throughout the United States and the world. Both authors were senior consultants for Novell Consulting Services and have designed and implemented NetWare 4, NetWare 5, and NetWare 6 sites around the globe. They have more than 25 years of combined networking experience. Jeffrey Hughes holds a B.S. degree in marketing from Brigham Young University. Blair Thomas holds a B.S. degree in computer science and an MBA from Brigham Young University.

# Credits

## Novell Press

**Publisher**
Gamal Herbon

## Wiley Publishing

**Acquisitions Editor**
Katie Feltman

**Project Editor**
Lane Barnholtz

**Technical Editor**
Kent Beck

**Copy Editors**
Lane Barnholtz
Ryan Rader

**Editorial Managers**
Ami Frank Sullivan
Kyle Looper

**Senior Vice President,
Technical Publishing**
Richard Swadley

**Vice President and Publisher**
Mary Bednarek

**Project Coordinator**
Dale White

**Graphics and Production Specialists**
Beth Brooks
Gabriele McCann
Jacque Schneider
Erin Zeltner

**Quality Control Technicians**
David Faust
John Greenough
Andy Hollandbeck

**Proofreading and Indexing**
TECHBOOKS Production Services

*For Wendy, Laurin, and McKenna.*
*This one's for you.*

*JFH*


*To Pam and Jessa, the bright stars in my life.*

*BWT*

# Preface

**N**etWare 6 is Novell's latest flagship product, based on all the best features of NetWare 4 and NetWare 5, adding significant enhancements based on Web technology, including Web Access (login via browse), iFolder, Internet Printing, Portal Services to manage servers, and universal, browser-based access to network resources. NetWare 6 incorporates NetWare Web Access, a convenient tool that gives users Web-based network access so that users no longer need a Novell client to connect to the network. With NetWare Web Access, users can log in to your network via any standard Web browser. Using their eDirectory user names and passwords, they can log in to the Web Access Portal and interface with your NetWare network. Because NetWare 6 is tightly integrated with eDirectory, the users see only the information they are authorized to view. This means that you can define the information and services each user sees, depending on each user's role in your organization.

Among its many exciting features, NetWare 6 offers enhancements to the eDirectory, including increased management capabilities, improved performance, powerful security, routing, Web publishing, and file and print services. The eDirectory is one of the most widely used directories in the industry. The directory allows you to organize network resources, provide easy access to those network resources, and centralize the administration of your network.

NetWare 6 revolutionizes file access and management by incorporating iFolder, which enables you to access personal files — from anywhere, at anytime — through virtually any Web-enabled device. NetWare 6 also includes Internet Printing (iPrint), which provides global access to all of your print resources through a standard Web browser. This enables you to support remote or traveling users. NetWare 6 already is making inroads in the industry as a powerful network platform coupled with a powerful directory to provide a secure, scalable, and flexible infrastructure that fulfills the needs of any size environment.

This book is your comprehensive design and implementation guide for NetWare 6. If you are moving from NetWare 4 or NetWare 5, you'll find this book a rich source of information as you make the transition. If you're implementing IP or moving from IPX to IP, this book will help you install and configure native IP on your servers. Topics covered in this book range from the fundamentals of NetWare 6 and its new features, to installation and maintenance, to managing the internal operations of the eDirectory. The information presented in this book will help you design, implement, maintain, and troubleshoot all aspects of NetWare 6 and related applications.

# What You'll Learn from Reading This Book

This book is written for all LAN administrators, system administrators, consultants, resellers, and any others who design, implement, and support NetWare 6 networks.

Using this book, you will learn basic to complex concepts regarding the feature set of NetWare 6. Whether your interest lies in accessing network resources using Web-based technology, in designing a NetWare 6 tree, or in understanding the requirements of your IP protocol, you will find this book to be the definitive source.

# How This Book Is Organized

This book is organized into five conceptual parts: "The Basics of NetWare 6," "Designing NDS eDirectory," "NetWare 6 Operations and Maintenance," "NetWare 6 Administration," and "Integrating Additional Services with NetWare 6."

**Part I: The Basics of NetWare 6** — Includes information on the NetWare 6 operating system, the eDirectory, installation of NetWare 6, and other new features. Novell's NetWare 6 installation and management utilities are covered so that readers can quickly install and configure NetWare 6. Part I also provides readers with a comprehensive look at eDirectory objects and how these objects are used to build a directory tree. An understanding of eDirectory objects is a prerequisite to utilizing the full potential of the directory. eDirectory naming conventions are covered in the last chapter of Part I.

**Part II: Designing NDS eDirectory** — Describes in great detail the steps required to design an eDirectory tree and covers design options for eDirectory trees, with many examples based on the fictitious ACME company. In addition, the design topics include a thorough discussion of partitioning and replicating an eDirectory tree. The last chapter of Part II provides clear explanations and examples of how to design an eDirectory tree for time synchronization.

**Part III: NetWare 6 Operations and Maintenance** — Provides a much-needed look at the internal operations of the eDirectory. We discuss directory operations that include partitioning, as well as managing eDirectory in a complex network environment. This section provides a thorough discussion on troubleshooting eDirectory. Effective troubleshooting requires an understanding of internal processes and the tools you can use to make adjustments to the directory. Refer to Chapter 9 for a detailed description on how to use the NetWare Remote Manager and the latest versions of the DSREPAIR and DSTRACE utilities during troubleshooting operations.

In addition, this section covers the new operating system features, security, eDirectory enhancements, hardware support, licensing, and third-party support. We conclude this section by discussing the tuning parameters you can use to maximize stability and performance of your NetWare 6 network.

**Part IV: NetWare 6 Administration** — Rounds out the many day-to-day aspects of NetWare 6 that you will need to know in order to upgrade, manage, and support your network. Topics include designing login scripts and access for NetWare 6, and providing a comprehensive security plan for your network.

In addition, Part IV discusses Internet Printing (iPrint), NetWare Distributed Print Services, and how to set up and configure printing for NetWare 5 and NetWare 6 networks. Part IV presents valuable information about preparing for a NetWare 6 upgrade, including creating an implementation schedule, gaining lab experience, and readying your NetWare 5 servers. Also covered are the upgrade options available to you, as well as the advantages and disadvantages of these options. The options include the new Novell Migration Wizard. Client migration options are also discussed in terms of the different approaches that are available to move workstations to Novell's software, including the Native File System.

**Part V: Integrating Additional Services with NetWare 6** — Discusses how you can integrate additional products with NetWare 6. These products include ZENworks, Novell Storage Services, Internet Access/FTP services, pure IP, iFolder, eGuide, and Storage Area Networks.

The four appendixes include valuable information that you can use as a handy reference:

- Appendix A describes the contents of the three CD-ROMs that accompany this book and explains their installation and use.

- Appendix B covers the eDirectory error codes. This listing of error codes helps you identify problems and determine resolution steps for directory-related issues.

- Appendix C provides information on the server console commands. This listing shows all the NetWare 6 utilities that run at the server console.

- Appendix D provides information on Novell's internal debugger, which can be used to diagnose NetWare 6 operating system problems.

## Special Features in This Book

Throughout this book we use the fictitious ACME company, which serves as the basis for many of the examples illustrated in the book. We chose as an eDirectory tree a large, worldwide company with wide area network (WAN) connections. Our intent is not to preclude smaller companies, but to demonstrate as realistically as possible the many features and concepts of NetWare 6.

Regardless of the size of your NetWare 6 installation, the design and installation strategies are the same. You may have fewer wide area connections or no WAN at all. As you read through the chapters (especially the design chapters), you will understand how to design a tree that meets your particular needs.

We also have, where appropriate, included Consulting Experience sidebars based on actual consulting visits with various customers. These Consulting Experience sidebars emphasize particular examples that demonstrate concepts and approaches to eDirectory design.

## The CD-ROM Set Accompanying This Book

Finally, this book includes three value-packed CD-ROMs: one containing a five-user version of the NetWare 6 operating system, another containing Digital Airlines Demo, and another containing NetWare 6 online documentation. If you are new to NetWare, we encourage you to install the NetWare 6 CD-ROM to learn and gain experience as you read through the book. Quick installation instructions for NetWare 6 are found in Appendix A, with comprehensive installation instructions detailed in Chapter 2.

## Sources

In the process of researching this book, we gratefully acknowledge the following Novell sources:

- Novell's NetWare 6 Online Documentation
- NetWare 6 Product Information (Novell's Web site at www.novell.com/products/netware)
- "Compatibility Mode Installation and Configuration" (*Novell AppNotes,* September 1998, Harinath Subramaniam)
- "DNS/DHCP Services Design Issues and Troubleshooting" (Novell White Paper, August 1998, Amitabh Sinha)
- "Novell Distributed Print Services" (Novell White Paper, August 1998, Hugo Parra)

# Acknowledgments

This book reflects the experience and information gathered from the members of Novell Consulting Services group and Novell as a whole. Blair wishes to thank in particular Carl Seaver, Kryt Nay, Todd Hogan, and Jim Sorenson. We also wish to thank Matt Keller and Steve Bearnson. All have been contributors in one way or another to this effort.

Thanks to all those in Novell Documentation, Novell Technical Support, and the NDS Engineering team for their knowledge of NetWare 6.

Thank you to Ryan Johnson of Novell Press, who has been our constant advocate in producing this book and in making Novell information available to our readers.

We thank Lane Barnholtz from Hungry Minds, who diligently worked with us to edit and re-edit this manuscript. Thanks for keeping up with all the little details of this book and keeping everything moving through production. Your help and experience have been invaluable. We also would like to thank all the others from the Hungry Minds team, including Ryan Rader, Ami Frank Sullivan, Kyle Looper, and Dale White, who have been instrumental with many editorial and production aspects of this book. We appreciate your support and encouragement.

Also, thanks to Katie Feltman at Hungry Minds, who has been supportive during this project. Her organizational skills have helped see this project to its completion.

We also would like to thank Kent Beck, who provided a careful technical review of this work. Kent's years of NetWare experience have been very helpful. Thanks for spending so much time working with us on this project.

Finally, as always, we thank our NetWare customers around the world who believe in NetWare and who push Novell's products to their limits. We continually press forward with your help to make these products the very best in the industry.

# Contents at a Glance

# Contents

## Part II    Designing NDS eDirectory    245

# The Basics of NetWare 6

# Introduction to NetWare 6

*"The only way round is through."* — Robert Frost

**N**etWare is still one of the world's most popular network operating systems. With NetWare 6, Novell has incorporated all the advantages of previous versions of NetWare and has added new features that build on its foundation to provide a distributed computing infrastructure. NetWare 6 increases productivity, reduces costs, and simplifies installing and maintaining your network.

Key to NetWare 6 is Novell Directory Services (NDS), now referred to as NDS eDirectory (we'll use NDS and eDirectory interchangeably throughout this book), which is a special-purpose name service that enables you to find and use network resources and data as a single integrated system. NDS provides this powerful operating system with the same speed and reliability that you've come to expect with NetWare 3, NetWare 4, and NetWare 5. NDS eDirectory reaches across all major platforms to provide a distributed directory service. No other directory can operate on as many platforms as NDS eDirectory. With the introduction of NetWare 6, you now have the ability to fully manage storage resources, security, and mixed-client environments with greater flexibility and scalability. NetWare 6 provides a reliable and secure foundation necessary for the eBusiness world.

Many corporations over the years have embraced and implemented NetWare as an integral part of everyday business computing solutions. Today, local and wide area networks are running business-critical applications once considered the sole domain of mainframe computers. More and more businesses are finding that they can operate more efficiently and cost-effectively on NetWare networks and still receive the same security and administrative benefits of larger systems.

With the advent of NetWare 6, NetWare has become even more powerful, scalable, and flexible, widening its lead over any other directory-based network operating system available. NetWare 6 is still the same powerful network operating system that NetWare has always been, but it has new features and services that make it more than just a local area network. For example, the need to connect remote and disparate devices to the network has increased dramatically over the past two years. The need for additional storage has also increased dramatically as more users need access to corporate information. Novell has met these challenges with the release of NetWare 6.

This book focuses on NetWare 6, but also includes information on NDS eDirectory, which is the backbone of NetWare 6. NDS eDirectory reaches across all major platforms to provide client integration, security, and scalability. Novell has even made huge strides lately in the file system with its introduction of iFolder, which enables you to synchronize, back up, and access your files and applications anywhere and at any time.

The following paragraphs summarize the essence of what NetWare 6 is and what it can do for you. But, you'll want to read subsequent chapters for more detailed information about this new, powerful operating system.

## Non-Stop Access to Your Files

With NetWare 6 there is no longer a need to be near your data files in order to access them. New to NetWare 6, *iFolder* provides the capability to synchronize, back up, and access your files and applications anywhere and at any time.

## Printing Via the Internet

Novell has always been a leader in providing networked printing capability. NetWare 6 brings even greater functionality to printing by utilizing Internet printing using the Internet printing protocol (IPP). Any printer can be transformed into an IPP printer and users can utilize the Web server aspects of the software to access any printer on the network. A user can also send a print job via HTTP and SSL encryption in a secure and safe manner.

## Greater Storage Capability

Novell's Storage Area Network (SAN) technology provides high-speed storage performance for NetWare servers. SAN technology allows you to dramatically expand the storage capability of your network. NetWare 6 includes free cluster software for up to two systems. Up to 32 NetWare servers may be formed into a cluster. These clusters can all be managed by the NetWare 6 operating system.

Novell Storage Services allows for unlimited disk volumes that can be up to 8TB (terabytes) in size. NSS uses a 64-bit interface and can keep track of huge numbers of objects in your network. The NSS file system keeps track of volumes, partitions, and the files differently and uses more server memory than before.

## Easy Network Management

NetWare 6 improves upon such tools as ConsoleOne and other java-based utilities to allow an administrator to easily manage any size network. Adding NetWare Remote Manager gives administrators greater flexibility for manager servers across an entire enterprise.

## Directory Services for Security and Management

eDirectory continues to evolve with greater scalability and greater management features, which makes its use in enterprise environments and e-business easier and more completely possible. Much will be discussed in this book with regards to eDirectory, its design, its installation, and its maintenance.

eDirectory provides management and security for network resources as well as a strong foundation for eBusiness.

Before understanding what NetWare 6 is, it helps to understand the purpose and function of a network operating system. From this starting point, we will begin a comprehensive look at the NetWare 6 operating system and its many features.

## Network Operating Systems

A network consists of resources, such as servers, workstations, printers, bridges, routers, gateways, and other peripheral computer equipment (CD-ROMs or jukeboxes, modems, and so on).

The network operating system (NOS) is software that communicates with each of these devices to form an integrated system. Some of the resources tied together by NDS eDirectory are shown in Figure 1.1.

**FIGURE 1.1:** *NDS eDirectory and the NetWare 6 OS tie together network resources from devices called servers.*

The primary role of the NOS and all the other resources on the network is to build an infrastructure that distributes information among all the network devices. The network components are the server and the client, and now include external storage and other mobile computing devices. The architecture that distributes the processing between these machines is called *distributed processing*. The following sections describe the server, the client, and how processing can be distributed between each.

## Servers

The *server* is the primary component in the distributed processing model. The server is the physical hardware device that runs the network operating system. In turn, the network operating system (NOS) is the software program that enables the local resources of the server to be shared among the network users. The NOS controls the following resources of the server:

- ► Memory
- ► File system (disk drives)
- ► CPU scheduling
- ► Input/output to shared network devices (CD-ROM, modems, and so on)
- ► Workstation connectivity and access to file system resources
- ► Loading and distributing application programs (including NDS eDirectory)

Figure 1.2 shows the local server resources that are managed by the NOS.

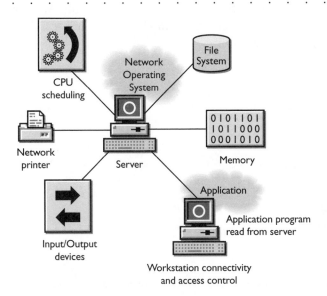

**FIGURE 1.2:** *The NOS manages the sharing of the server's local resources and coordinates directory synchronization.*

The NOS software either runs as a dedicated machine or can be distributed equally across all nodes on the network. A NOS that makes use of workstation-to-workstation communications in a peer-to-peer environment is an example of a *distributed NOS*. A NOS whose primary software runs on a dedicated hardware platform is a *centralized NOS*. NetWare 6 is an example of a centralized NOS in which the central node is called the server.

### Clients

The portion of the NOS that connects the workstations to the server is called the *client software*. The client software runs on the workstations and is the consumer of services provided by the NetWare server. It also enables the workstation to load applications or share resources from the server. Figure 1.3 illustrates the relationship between the NOS running at the server and the client software running at the workstation.

Workstations that load the client portion of the network operating system are often referred to as clients. NetWare 6 has greatly expanded on the concept of a client connecting to a server. As covered in this book, you can access information through various forms of a client or use no client at all. A Web browser can be used as a client. Also, the Apple iMac requires no client but connects to a NetWare 6 server out of the box through native protocols. NDS servers also act as clients of other NDS servers in the tree but not in the same way as a workstation. An NDS server may communicate with other NDS servers during login or when searching for a particular piece of directory information.

**FIGURE 1.3:** *Client software loads on the workstation and enables it to connect to the server.*

**In this book, we will use the terms *workstation* and *client* interchangeably. Technically, though, only the workstations that load the client software and make use of the services provided by the servers should be called clients.**

# Distributed Processing

*Distributed processing* occurs when the NOS coordinates the processing in a decentralized fashion. Applications running on the network are a type of distributed processing. For example, each workstation requests its own copy of an application from the operating system. The application is then loaded and run entirely on the workstation. The workstation runs the application independently, and the network operating system simply coordinates access to the shared resources. In the network, application processing can be distributed (client-based) or centralized (server-based) or both (client/server-based). Each of these methods offers advantages and disadvantages that make them right for certain applications and wrong for others.

### Client-Based Applications

The types of applications that run entirely on the workstation are called *client-based applications*. For example, all the clients may use the same word processing application, but separate copies of the application are executed in each workstation. A copy of the application is transmitted from the server to the client but is executed at the client workstation. In general, applications that are keyboard and display intensive with minimal disk I/O are well suited for the client.

Spreadsheets and word processing programs are examples of client-based applications because they are heavy users of the display and keyboard with infrequent disk or file access. There is no benefit in running any part of these applications outside the workstation once the program has been loaded into workstation memory from the server. Figure 1.4 illustrates client-based application processing in which the application is loaded from the server.

### Server-Based Applications

Applications that do all the processing locally at the server are known as *server-based applications*. These applications are usually specialized applications that execute only on the server. For example, backup/restore software needs to read the file system and write it to the local tape device (on the server) and may not need to transfer data across the network. Other types of backup software run as clients on a server and transfer files from other servers. Another example is network management software that controls or monitors the operation of the operating system. In addition, NetWare Loadable Modules are primarily server-based applications, although some have a client counterpart that does some of the processing. Figure 1.5 illustrates server-based application processing.

**FIGURE 1.4:** *Client-based application processing. The application is loaded from the server.*

**FIGURE 1.5:** *Server-based application processing*

## Client/Server-Based Applications

*Client/server-based applications* split the responsibility of the processing between the client and the server. The client and server work together to execute the application even though it is running on different machines. The fact that the parts of the application are running on different machines is entirely transparent to the user. The software that runs on the server is called the *back end* and manages the shared information. The client portion of the application is called the *front end* and allows communication and access to the server (or back end). Figure 1.6 illustrates client/server application processing.

**FIGURE 1.6:** *Client/server application processing*

An example of a newer client/server-based application is Novell's iFolder application. It consists of three components that work together. The first component, the iFolder client, allows access to current files on a personal computer. The iFolder client performs synchronization whenever it's connected to the network to keep all files up to date. The second component, the iFolder browser plug-in, provides secure authentication links to a central iFolder server. And the third component, the iFolder server, provides the necessary infrastructure for secure file synchronization and access. For more information on installing and configuring this product, refer to Chapter 20.

## What Is NetWare 6?

NetWare 6 offers the widest range of distributed applications or network services in the industry. In Figure 1.7, you can see that NetWare 6 provides file, print, directory service, database, communication (includes host connectivity), messaging, network management, software distribution, imaging, Web services, and telephony.

**FIGURE 1.7:** *NetWare 6 is defined as a complete range of network services.*

These network services are provided to users regardless of their type of desktop. The goal of NetWare has always been to tie different users running Windows, OS/2, Macintosh, UNIX, or Windows NT/Windows 2000 into a distributed information system, as shown in Figure 1.8.

NetWare 6 enables these diverse workstations to access NetWare services and perform distributed processing in their native environments. Figure 1.9 shows how users can choose the desktop system that best fits their needs and still share services and information with other network users using different platforms.

In addition to the integration of desktops, NetWare 6 also integrates larger host computers from vendors such as IBM, Digital, and Hewlett-Packard. Regardless of where information is located on the network, users can access host-based resources and information from their desktops.

Applications that can benefit from client/server-based implementation are database, communications, and transactional applications that require frequent access to disk storage. Consider a database that searches, sorts, generates reports, and so forth. The database will perform better if you place the database engine on the server (where disk I/O is intensive) and process the data entry and user interface at the client. The client simply passes the data request to the database engine, which performs the action and responds accordingly.

Another example would be an e-mail system in which the user reads and composes mail messages at the client and then passes the responsibility for delivery to a server process. Thus, while the server is delivering the messages to the other mail users, the client (or sender) can continue other activities.

**FIGURE 1.8:** *NetWare 6 connects desktops running Windows, OS/2, Macintosh, UNIX, and Windows NT/Windows 2000 operating systems.*

**FIGURE 1.9:** *NetWare 6 offers distributed processing among workstations running the DOS, Windows, OS/2, Macintosh, UNIX, and Windows NT/Windows2000 operating systems.*

▶ • • • • • • • • • • • • • • • • • • • • • • • • • • • • • • • ◀

## Novell Directory Services eDirectory

Novell Directory Services (also referred to as NDS eDirectory) is an ongoing effort from the company to provide a more scalable directory with greater functionality in each subsequent release. NDS eDirectory is currently on Release 8.6 and is on a different release schedule than that of the NetWare operating system. As a NetWare administrator you will at times be doing an upgrade of NDS eDirectory on the same platform of NetWare. NDS eDirectory is an information name service (database comes to mind) that organizes network resources—users, groups, printers, servers, volumes, and other physical network devices—into a hierarchical tree structure. Figure 1.10 illustrates the structure of an NDS tree. We will use many examples of NDS eDirectory trees in this book.

▶ • • • • • • • • • • • • • • • • • • • • • • • • • • • • • • • ◀

**FIGURE 1.10:** *The structure of an NDS tree*

The NDS tree, also known as the eDirectory tree, enables resources to be managed and displayed as a single enterprise view. By contrast, NetWare 3 provided only a server-centric view. You can manage the tree including objects and their various properties by providing varying degrees of security access, giving your network enormous flexibility as it expands and changes.

NDS eDirectory replaces the bindery found in NetWare 3 networks. A major difference between the two methods is that the Directory is distributed and can be replicated on multiple servers for increased fault tolerance and performance. The bindery in NetWare 3 is a flat structure in which resources belong to a single server. Compatibility with the bindery is still available in NetWare 6 for applications requiring bindery services.

For a detailed description of the newest features of eDirectory, see Chapter 10.

## NDS Provides a Single Point of Login

Users log into the network once using one username and password to access all authorized network resources. This means that users log into the network, and NDS will process other connections to NetWare 3 and NetWare 6 servers if the username and password are the same.

By contrast, NetWare 3 bindery users had to log into each network server individually with a username and password. This could mean that the users would have to provide a different ID and password for each additional server connection. Single-user login also makes your job easier as an administrator. You create each user account only once for all NetWare 6 servers in the Directory tree. Multiple user accounts on multiple servers are no longer needed in NetWare 6. This feature alone can save you hours of work. As you will see, NDS eDirectory serves as the central point of management, eliminating tedious duplication and increased administrative costs.

The addition of Novell's Single Sign-On to NetWare 5 and NetWare 6 has improved these versions over their predecessors. Novell's Single Sign-On allows users to only log in once and has NDS provide the login and authentication to other devices such as host systems and other platforms. For more information on Single Sign-On, refer to Chapter 17.

## NDS Provides Easy Administration

NetWare 6 consolidates most NDS administrative functions into easy-to-use utilities with graphical interfaces that greatly reduce the time you spend on network administration. The main Novell utility for administration is ConsoleOne. ConsoleOne is a Java-based utility that provides the same functionality as NWADMIN and considerably more.

While still used for some administration, NWADMIN is Novell's older utility that enables you to make changes to the Directory with an easy point and click of a mouse.

This object-oriented view of the NDS tree is what lets you perform many routine administrative functions easily. NDS objects, files, directories, and server functions can be controlled through the NWADMIN or ConsoleOne utilities. When users change departments, for example, you simply drag and drop the users to a new location to give them appropriate directory rights, or move users with the move command. Adding file system directory rights for a user in versions prior to NetWare 4 required a multilayered menu and a somewhat tedious process of adding each new user. With NetWare 5 and NetWare 6, all that is required to add directory rights is to drag the user's icon to the specific directory or object; the NWADMIN utility will ask you for a confirmation prior to completing the request.

## NDS eDirectory Is Scalable

NDS eDirectory is an object hierarchy that can be divided into smaller sections to be distributed to any number of network servers. We say it is "scalable" because one server can, but does not need to, contain all Directory information. With NDS eDirectory, the information can be distributed and also replicated on multiple servers to provide increased accessibility and reliability. Figure 1.11 shows how NDS eDirectory can be distributed across the servers in the network. Novell has demonstrated massive scalability of the directory by building a billion object tree. Although no organization will probably need to build a tree of that size, you can be assured that your directory has the capability to grow to any size needed. For more information on the scalability of the directory and design recommendations, see Chapter 5.

The process that divides the directory hierarchy into smaller pieces and makes eDirectory scale is called *partitioning*. Another process, known as *replication,* is the mechanism that makes the partition redundant. The partitions and replicas are completely transparent to users and can be scattered across multiple NetWare 6 servers. These features make NDS eDirectory a powerful facility for storing, accessing, managing, and using information about the network resources, regardless of where they are physically located. This means that your NDS tree can easily grow to meet the demands of your environment. Another benefit is that your NDS tree design can be easily modified to reflect both organizational and functional changes in your company.

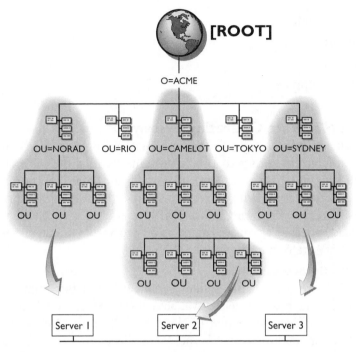

**FIGURE 1.11:** *NDS provides distribution of the information across the network servers.*

# NetWare 6 Features

NetWare 6 is the next generation of the NetWare operating system. Therefore, it inherits features from previous versions, namely those from NetWare 4.*x* and NetWare 5.*x* and even some from NetWare 3. This section examines the new and enhanced features of NetWare 6. The descriptions given in this chapter are brief, presenting only introductory information about each feature. Later chapters offer more in-depth information. The NetWare 6 features are categorized into the following sections:

- ► Operating system
- ► File and print systems
- ► Novell Directory Services (NDS)
- ► Network services

▸ Security

▸ Installation and upgrade

▸ Developer support

▸ Third-party add-ons

▸ Workstation/client support

## Changes to the NetWare Operating System

NetWare 6 offers many new changes to the core NetWare operating system. NetWare 6 is aimed at large enterprises that serve customers with 1,000 or more employees. The trend for these types of companies is toward large, centralized data centers known as server farms. With server farms comes the use of symmetric multiprocessing (SMP) server hardware. Most SMP servers use two CPUs to distribute the workload, but they can use as many as 32 processors in one server. Novell has designed NetWare 6 to make use of SMP.

### The NetWare 6 Multiprocessor Kernel

The core of the NetWare 6 operating system is a new kernel that supports multiple processors out of the box. This effort was actually started at the release of NetWare 5, but it has been expanded upon in NetWare 6. The new NetWare 6 kernel is called the NetWare multiprocessor kernel (MPK). The obvious benefit of having a multiprocessor kernel is that it automatically supports machines that have more than one processor. In fact, it supports single and multiple processors from the same kernel. This means that you can make better use of existing processors in your servers or add processors as needed to help speed up specific services.

The NetWare MPK can support a machine with as many as 32 processors. During installation, NetWare 6 automatically detects the number of processors by reading the multiple processor table in the machine's BIOS. It then determines which of the NetWare 6 Platform Support Modules (PSMs) match the hardware platform. A PSM is a hardware abstraction layer or interface that NetWare 6 uses to support different hardware dependencies.

In addition, the new multiprocessor kernel provides many new services and offers support for Java applications. The NetWare 6 operating system kernel adds these functions: memory protection, virtual memory, preemption, and application prioritization. Novell has included an enhanced version of NetWare 6 Cluster Services, which enables you to create clusters with up to 32 nodes for fault tolerance. An enhanced version of Novell Storage Services (NSS) is included with this release. NSS provides an object-oriented storage with 64-bit internal and external interfaces. Without NSS, the NetWare file system supports a 32-bit interface that limits files to

2GB, directory entries to 16 million per volume, and volumes per server to 64. For more information about NSS, see Chapter 10.

Although the server operating systems of NetWare 5 and NetWare 5.1 included some core components that were SMP enabled, not all components were SMP enabled. For example NetWare 5 provided SMP capability for C-Library (CLIB), RSA encryption, routing functions, and Multiple Link Interface Drivers (MLIDs).

NetWare 6 adds to the core set of functions that are already SMP-enabled. This includes MP-enabled versions of the IP stack, the NetWare Core Protocol (NCP) engine, Web and search engines, NDS eDirectory, and NSS.

### Memory Protection

The memory protection in NetWare 6 enables you to load any server applications in their own protected address spaces. The applications are then shielded from other applications and the operating system itself. The result is that failure of one application does not affect any of the other applications or processing of the operating system. You can use protected address spaces to run untried or troublesome applications. Any program or module loaded into a protected address space cannot corrupt the operating system or cause server abends (abnormal ends). The protected address space provides a safe place to run applications. All protected address spaces use virtual memory.

As mentioned, each application can be loaded into its own protected address space. A protected address space is a portion of cache server memory that has controlled communication with the server operating system. The protected address space is only a portion of cache memory that can be set aside, sometimes called user address spaces or ring 3. In contrast, the NetWare operating system does not run in a protected address space. The operating system address space is sometimes called ring 0 or the kernel address space.

In the first release of NetWare 5, only a few NetWare Loadable Modules (NLMs) or applications could be loaded into the protected memory space. NetWare 6 loads Java-based applications in protected mode by default. In addition, you can optionally load GroupWise 5.5, Lotus Notes (except for the debugging module), and Oracle 8. However, certain types of modules and programs cannot run in protected addresses. The protected address spaces run in ring 3; others must be loaded at ring 0 instead. Here is a list of common NLM programs and executables that cannot be loaded into a protected address space:

- SERVER.EXE
- LAN drivers
- Disk drivers
- MONITOR.NLM

### Virtual Memory

Virtual memory is a memory management scheme that provides the NetWare 6 operating system with the capability to allocate more than the actual physical memory of the server machine. It does this by using the disk as an extension of memory and by swapping code and data between physical memory and disk as necessary. When the data on disk is needed again, it is moved back into the physical memory. Because data is swapped on and off of the disk, the available memory can be used for a larger amount of data than its actual physical capacity would allow. Virtual memory provides NetWare 6 with a more efficient use of memory and lessens the likelihood that low memory conditions will cause an abend condition.

NetWare 6 moves the data out of physical memory to swap files on the hard drive if the data has been used infrequently. More specifically, the available memory is assessed to see which data items have been used less recently than the rest. How recently data has been used is determined by a bit in each field of the translation table that indicates whether the address space has been used since the last time it was checked. Data that has not been used for some time can be moved from memory to disk, thus, freeing memory for other uses.

As mentioned earlier, protected memory uses virtual memory. The reason is the memory management subsystem can allocate to each process a unique protected virtual address available to run the threads of the process. Thus, each process has a separate address space, so a thread in one process cannot view or modify the memory of another process. This architecture provides the protected memory for NetWare 6.

NetWare 6 loads a few applications or modules into virtual memory by default. One of these applications is the Java Virtual Machine (JVM). Any other modules that are loaded by the JVM will run in virtual memory. On the other hand, any modules and programs that cannot run in virtual memory can also not use protected memory because protected memory uses virtual memory. Here is a list of common NLM programs and executables that cannot be loaded into virtual memory:

- ► SERVER.EXE
- ► LAN drivers
- ► Disk drivers
- ► MONITOR.NLM
- ► Novell Storage Services (NSS)

As an example, the server operating system (SERVER.EXE) cannot run in virtual memory because it must always be resident in memory and cannot be swapped to disk. The same condition exists for all the other modules.

### Preemption

The NetWare 6 kernel has also been developed to support preemption, just like previous version of NetWare. *Preemption* eliminates the problems associated with applications running on the server as NLMs that have been written poorly and that monopolize the processor. In order to take advantage of preemption in NetWare 6, the application must be explicitly written or enabled by the developers to support the kernel's preemption.

### Application Prioritization

As previously mentioned, MPK enables you to support *application prioritization* or *load balancing,* which ensures optimal application distribution among processors. Application prioritization is implemented as part of the new NetWare 6 kernel, and the system administrator decides how to prioritize the applications running on your servers. You can specify the level of processor usage that you want to dedicate to each application.

By adjusting the amount of processor time dedicated to each application, you can tune the quality of service provided. In addition, both single-processor and multiple-processor machines can benefit from the flexibility of application prioritization. Thus, if a single processor machine has multiple applications, you can allow one application to have more CPU cycles than the others.

### The NetWare 6 GUI Console (ConsoleOne)

NetWare 6 enables the server console to appear in a graphical user interface (GUI) environment. Its appearance and operation are similar to those for programs in the X Window environment found on UNIX platforms. A GUI server environment permits use of a graphical interface to programs such as installation and Java applications at the server console. To use ConsoleOne, the server must have a VGA or higher video adapter board and a VGA or higher display monitor, along with a mouse.

**The GUI environment requires additional server RAM. It is not recommended to run the GUI environment on servers with less than 64MB of RAM.**

NOTE

### Hot Plug PCI

Just like NetWare 5 and NetWare 5.1, NetWare 6 supports the capability to upgrade or replace network interface cards while the server is running, easing server expansion and providing longer server uptime.

### I2O Support

I2O (Intelligent I/O) improves I/O throughput and server performance by relieving the CPU of interrupt-intensive tasks such as memory calls and system interrupts. I2O is an industry-driven software specification designed to provide a standards-based solution to offload input/output traffic from the central processing unit, and it enables hardware vendors to develop a single driver to work with all networking platforms. NetWare 6 provides I2O support for Ethernet- and SCSI-class devices and block storage, making server management easier while increasing application processing efficiency.

## Changes to the File and Print Systems

In addition to the changes that have been made to the operating system in NetWare 6, the file system has had some significant additions. This section describes the changes made to the file system, including those to the Novell Storage Services (NSS) and Storage Management Services (SMS).

### Novell Storage Services

Novell Storage Services (NSS) was new to the NetWare 5 file system and was designed to mount large server volumes in seconds, virtually eliminating the limits on the number or size of files that can be stored in volumes and directories. You can use NSS to quickly open and update large files, such as those found in databases.

**NOTE**

**NSS version 3.0 now supports SYS: volumes in addition to the data volumes that all previous versions of NSS support. NSS also supports file compression, as well as user and directory quotas. NetWare 6 can compress NSS files that are infrequently used or not used at all. You can limit the space a user consumes on an NSS directory and the space a directory consumes on an NSS volume. NSS 3.0 also supports the Transaction Tracking System (TTS).**

NSS is a 64-bit indexed storage system that allows for billions of volumes and directories. It allows up to 8-terabyte file sizes and 64-bit addressing with an extremely small memory footprint. Even more spectacular is the speed at which a volume can be remounted. Virtually any size volume can be mounted in seconds.

Novell Storage Services (NSS) eliminates several limitations that currently exist in the NetWare file system. NSS provides object-oriented storage with 64-bit internal and external interfaces. Without NSS, the NetWare file system only supports a 32-bit interface that limits file sizes to 2GB, maximum directory entries per volume to 16 million, and volumes per server to 64. With NSS, the NetWare file system can host a single 8TB (terabyte) file. This would be extremely useful for database applications. In addition, the NSS file system can support virtually unlimited directory entries (or number of files) per volume. During testing, a volume with 1 billion files was successfully created with three name spaces loaded. This demonstrates that the file system can support 3 billion directory entries on a single NetWare volume. Thousands of volumes can be created per server; however, the current NCP interface only supports 127 volumes per server.

In addition to larger volumes and more files, NSS supports much faster volume mount times. A normal NSS volume mounts in less than one second, regardless of size or number of files stored. If the NetWare 6 server crashes and a volume is not dismounted cleanly, when the server is brought back up, the volume will be restored and mounted in 15 seconds to one minute. This is the case for all NSS volumes on the server. By contrast, the older FAT-based file system is organized so that volume mount time increases with number and size of files.

These NSS features are available with NetWare 6:

▸ Up to 8-terabyte file sizes (a terabyte is equivalent to 8,192 gigabytes)

▸ Capability to create and access trillions of files in a single directory

▸ Faster volume mounting and repair

▸ Lower server memory requirements for mounting any size volume

NSS does not fully replace the default NetWare file system because of some current limitations. Future releases of NSS will address these issues. For example, NSS currently does not support the Transaction Tracking System (TTS), disk striping, disk mirroring, Hierarchical Storage Management (HSM), or Real Time Data Migration (RTDM).

NSS 3.0 is compatible with the traditional NetWare file system. NSS still only requires 32MB of RAM to mount, and you can migrate your data at your own pace.

### Storage Management Services (SMS)

Novell Storage Management Services (SMS) lets you back up, restore, and verify data stored on the network and on network clients. NetWare 6 SMS includes Enhanced SBACKUP, ensuring regular and complete backups of all the data on your network, including the NDS database, bindery data, GroupWise data, and client and server file systems.

### An Improved Backup Utility

NetWare 6 introduces a new GUI-based backup utility that allows for multiple and repetitive scheduling. This new backup utility is a replacement version of the SBACKUP utility. Using this utility, network administrators can perform backups across the network.

### Novell Distributed Print Services (NDPS)

Novell Distributed Print Services (NDPS) was released in NetWare 5, and NetWare 6 continues to enhance printing with support of the Internet Printing Protocol (IPP). NDPS is designed to simplify access and administration of network print services. NDPS is a distributed service that consists of client, server, and connectivity software components to seamlessly connect the applications to the network printers.

NDPS provides bidirectional communication between users and printers by downloading drivers for plug-and-print installation of new devices. NDPS enables users to easily locate network printers and can provide information such as printer and job status.

In the past, the Novell Distributed Print Services product has been offered as an add-on product that could be integrated into existing NetWare 4 networks. In NetWare 5 and NetWare 6, NDPS is included as the regular print services for the operating system. If you are satisfied with your current NetWare printing infrastructure, however, NetWare 6 will continue to support it. Then you can incrementally deploy NDPS at your own pace to gain the features and benefits.

NDPS gives users and administrators greater control over their printing. Features such as bidirectional feedback, print job status, automatic driver downloading, and event notification for printer status help simplify and streamline the usability and administration of network printing. NDPS provides the following major benefits, features, and printing capabilities:

▶ NDPS enables the network administrator to centrally manage printing services from a single location.

▶ Users submit print jobs directly to the printers; no print queues need to be created.

▶ NDPS supports bidirectional communications with the printers.

▶ Administrators can move, copy, delete, prioritize, and pause print jobs.

▶ Network administrators are able to monitor and control print jobs, and they can receive print alerts or event notifications through e-mail, pop-up windows, event logs, and other methods, such as beepers and faxes.

▸ Users can determine whether a printer is available or busy and can copy or move print jobs between network printers as necessary.

▸ A plug-and-print option enables you to quickly install printers that can be immediately used by everyone with setup rights.

▸ NDPS reduces the network traffic associated with Service Advertising Protocol (SAP) broadcast because direct-connect printer devices no longer require SAP.

▸ Any NDPS printer can be managed through a standard SNMP console using the standard printer management information base (MIB).

▸ NDPS supports the current NetWare queue-based printing environment. Therefore, it enables you to upgrade to NDPS as quickly or slowly as necessary.

## Novell Directory Services eDirectory

The latest version of NDS eDirectory includes the usual transitive synchronization, transitive vector, caching the replica changes, multiple objects per packet, randomized replica lists, distributive reference links, and WAN Traffic Manager. But its latest Version 8.6 is cross platform and platform independent. This means that NDS can be run on platforms other than NetWare, including the following:

▸ IBM AIX

▸ Linux

▸ Microsoft Windows 2000 Professional, Server, and Advanced Server

▸ Novell NetWare 5.*x*

▸ Novell NetWare 6

▸ Sun Solaris

▸ eDirectory 8.6 provides the following features. For a more complete description of eDirectory 8.6, see Chapter 5.

▸ Increased scalability and replication performance

▸ Hot-continuous backup

▸ Greater support of LDAP auxiliary classes

▸ Persistent searches

▸ Dynamic group management

▸ Novell Modular Authentication Services to support MD5 and SHA-1 passwords on top of the existing RSA PKI

### Transitive Synchronization and Transitive Vectors

The *transitive vector* is a newer structure that has been added to the partition root object for each partition. It is essentially a group of modification timestamps representing the values held by each replica. Each replica has one transitive vector. The transitive vector differs from the synchronized up to property in that it holds a group of timestamps for each replica, where synchronized up to only holds one value for each replica in the partition. Another major difference between the transitive vector and the synchronized up to property is that the transitive vector is synchronized between servers where synchronized up to is not synchronized.

Replica synchronization in NetWare 6 uses *transitive synchronization,* which is the method of using transitive vectors while synchronizing two NetWare 6 servers. Transitive synchronization uses the transitive vector instead of the synchronized up to property that was used in NetWare 4.

With NetWare 6, server replication no longer happens within a replica ring or list as it has in the past. Transitive synchronization works through the transitive vector. If a source server's transitive vector is more recent than a target server's vector, the source server does not need to synchronize with that target server. This procedure reduces synchronization traffic, freeing up bandwidth. It employs either the IPX or IP protocol.

Each time that replica synchronization is scheduled to run on the NetWare 6 server, transitive synchronization reads the transitive vector to determine which replicas it needs to synchronize with. Because each NetWare 6 server has a transitive vector, the process can immediately determine how up to date each of the other replicas are. Using transitive synchronization, a specific server does not have to contact each of the other servers in the partition to complete replica synchronization. After a successful synchronization, the target or destination server merges the transitive vector with that of the source server. In addition, the changes are guaranteed to converge across all replicas of a partition over time.

### The Replica Ring Is Randomized

After replica synchronization starts in NetWare 4, the replicas in the replica ring are contacted and updated in a sequential order. Therefore, the first replica in the replica ring is updated first, followed by the second one, and so on. Because the replica ring is identical on all the servers holding copies of this partition, the synchronization process updates all the replicas for each partition in the same order. This may have an undesirable effect if multiple servers are trying to synchronize with the same replica on the same server simultaneously. Because only one inbound synchronization is supported per partition (not per server), one of the synchronization processes will have to back off and attempt again at a later time. This situation only arises if synchronization tends to execute at approximately the same time on multiple servers.

To help alleviate this situation, NetWare 6 changes the sequence in which replicas are processed by randomizing the replica ring list before attempting to contact the first server. This greatly reduces the possibility that one of the servers will have to back off and attempt to resynchronize with a replica. By randomizing which replica receives the first update, transitive synchronization more quickly converges the data for each partition. As previously mentioned, transitive synchronization can converge the NDS data among all the replicas of a partition without having each replica talk to every other replica.

### Cache Object Changes

A new feature that caches changes to the NDS objects enhances the performance of replica synchronization. Remember that the changes or updates that affect the NDS objects include adding, deleting, moving, or renaming an object, as well as changing the properties or attributes of the object.

Using NetWare 4, NDS sequentially searched the entire object file, comparing timestamps to find the objects that have been updated since the last successful synchronization. Sequential searching effectively limited the size of the NDS partitions. When describing implementation of the NDS tree in NetWare 4 in previous versions of this book, we gave you a practical recommendation of 1,000–1,500 objects. In order to overcome this limitation, NetWare 6 eliminates the sequential search time by caching all changes to the objects. The capability to cache the objects in the NDS database greatly increases the speed of searching for and updating each replica and partition.

The object cache maintains a set of object IDs that have been modified since the last synchronization. The cache is populated by placing object IDs in the cache that have been modified as a result of client requests or inbound synchronization. Each cache entry has the modification time relative to the last synchronization. The cache that NDS maintains is for each partition that is stored on a server. The cache has a start time associated with it that identifies when the cache was built. Changes only need to be sent out if the transitive vector for the remote server is less than or equal to the transitive vector for the local server. The janitor process cleans up the cache periodically by removing the object IDs that have already been sent to all the replicas.

### Multiple Objects per Synchronization Packet

In order to help synchronize individual replicas faster, NetWare 6 supports more than one object in each communication packet. Formerly, NetWare 4 only allowed changes for one object in a single communication packet. By allowing multiple changes to different objects in a single packet, NetWare 6 reduces the total number of packets needed to synchronize replicas. If the number of changes between two replicas is small, all the updates between them can be accomplished in a single packet. Basically, this means that a partition can be synchronized in a minimum of one packet.

### Distributed Reference Links

NetWare 6 includes a new method for maintaining external references, called *distributed reference links* (DRLs). These links are more efficient than backlinks for renaming, moving, and deleting external references. The distributed reference links are more efficient because unlike backlinks, they are not tied to a specific NetWare server but instead reference the partition that stores the external reference object. By contrast, when a backlink is created it stores the NetWare server name and object ID for each external reference object.

As mentioned, the major downside to using backlinks is that they are tied to specific NetWare servers and not tied to the external reference object's location in the NDS tree. Backlinks result in each NetWare server's tending to have a connection to every other server in the NDS tree. In order to alleviate this problem, distributed reference links store the partition name and object ID where each external reference object exists. By storing the partition name, the individual NetWare servers can resolve the DRLs by using the NDS tree structure.

### Inheritable ACLs

Using the inheritable access control lists (ACLs), you can provide role-based assignments by assigning supervisor rights to operators or help desk staff to manage specific types of objects or resources. For example, you can assign rights to a group to manage only the printers, servers, or users. Using the new Password Administrator property, you can specify a help desk group to reset only the user's password.

Another new feature of NetWare 6 is its capability to display all the schema-defined properties in a single list in NWADMIN anywhere in the NDS tree. The properties that are shown are for all the objects in the schema. This gives you the ability to select any property at any level in the NDS tree. For example, you can give a group the rights to manage all users' telephone numbers at the O=Organizational level.

### The WAN Traffic Manager

The WAN Traffic Manager (WTM) enables you to manage NDS traffic across WAN links, reducing network costs and increasing performance benefits. The WAN Traffic Manager is a policy-based tool for managing the cost and congestion of WAN traffic. Its clients (such as NDS) request a policy decision before initiating WAN traffic. WTM, as a policy evaluator, checks administrator-supplied policies and attempts to match input criteria to one of them. If it finds a match, it runs the rest of the policy to see whether to allow the WAN traffic to proceed or to delay it. WTM is a valuable tool for networks that have significant congestion on their WAN links (for example, with ISDN or slow dial-up links), enabling administrators to control and manage bandwidth use and congestion.

### Catalog Services

NDS Catalog Services provides a method to store directory data in a non-partitioned format, indexed for rapid access. Directory information stored in catalog or index format is easily customized for searching, sorting, and reporting purposes. Distribution and replication of these indexes enable administrators to quickly access a "snap shot" of the complete network directory as opposed to performing a query across the entire network.

Catalog Services enables the development of applications that need rapid access to directory data in a centralized repository. These applications might include Contextless Login, NDS White Pages, fast lookup for Lightweight Directory Access Protocol (LDAP) gateways, and many others. One of these new Catalog Services applications, called Contextless Login, leverages the NDS catalog and enables users to authenticate from any point on the network simply by typing their login name and password, removing the need to know the location of their user object in the NDS tree.

Catalogs are stored as FLAIM databases within stream attributes in the NDS directory. Catalog databases can be scoped to include data from the entire directory tree or from one or more subtrees. The attributes stored in the catalog can be filtered according to user requirements. Catalog Services includes a dredger that reads the directory to build catalogs; an NWADMIN snap-in that controls the scope, filtering, time interval, and other aspects of catalog creation; and a set of query Application Program Interfaces (APIs) that support development of applications to find catalogs and read data from them.

### LDAP

NetWare 6 supports Lightweight Directory Access Protocol (LDAP) version 3, an industry-standard protocol that enables users to easily access X.500-based directories such as NDS. LDAP Services for NDS is a server-based interface between NDS and LDAP-compliant applications running optionally under Secure Sockets Layer (SSL). In NetWare 6, the performance of LDAP access to NDS has also been significantly enhanced, enabling unlimited scalability through NDS's advanced replication and management of back-end directory functions. NDS eDirectory does not need an LDAP 3 gateway to translate LDAP 3 into NDS. NDS eDirectory has incorporated the LDAP 3 protocol, and it processes the queries natively, providing even greater performance.

## Changes to the Network Services

Several new enhancements make the basic network services in NetWare 6 more flexible, manageable, and secure. The new network services included in NetWare 6 are Pure IP, Service Location Protocol (SLP), DNS/DHCP integration, the ZENworks Starter Pack, NetWare Licensing Services, and Internet Connectivity.

### Pure IP

New in NetWare 5 was Pure IP, which enabled NetWare to support TCP/IP in a pure sense. It does not encapsulate or tunnel IPX/SPX communications. Pure IP enables servers and clients to make NetWare Core Protocol (NCP) calls directly over the TCP/IP stack to be routed by any IP router on the network. Although NetWare 6 maintains support for IPX/SPX protocols, you now have the option of implementing a pure TCP/IP environment or using IPX/SPX alone or as part of a mixed TCP/IP and IPX/SPX environment. This is advantageous for customers who require a Pure IP environment because it eliminates multiple protocols and frees up valuable network bandwidth, while enabling them to control IP implementation at their own pace.

Novell severed the operating system's dependence on IPX/SPX and rewrote the IPX-only applications and utilities to support TCP/IP. As a result, NetWare 6 servers and workstations can use TCP/IP, IPX/SPX, or both. The major advantages of supporting Pure IP in NetWare are as follows:

- ▸ Consolidation to one protocol in your network
- ▸ More efficient use of LAN and WAN bandwidth
- ▸ A wider range of opportunities for remote user connectivity

Although Pure IP has major advantages, Novell is committed to retain backward compatibility to IPX/SPX. NetWare 6 ships with features that provide a seamless compatibility between IPX and IP-based technologies. NetWare 6's Compatibility Mode enables customers to move to an IP-Only environment without having to replace valuable IPX-based applications and without having to introduce disruptions into their network operations. In addition, NetWare 6 ships an IP Compatibility Mode Migration Gateway that enables you to move to an IP-Only network, incrementally if desired.

In essence, it is your choice whether to use IPX/SPX or TCP/IP as your network protocols. In order to install Pure IP, use the standard NetWare 6 installation program. During installation, select the protocols that you want your server to support. If you enable IPX/SPX, you must select an internal IPX address for the server, as you normally would. If you enable TCP/IP, you must select an IP address for the server.

### Service Location Protocol

Service Location Protocol (SLP) provides automatic resource discovery and registration over TCP/IP connections. Network resources such as servers and printers use SLP. SLP is more efficient than Service Advertisement Protocol (SAP) because it creates less ongoing network traffic than SAP. In addition, SLP enables network resources to carry extended description attributes. For example, a printer could be categorized as a "PostScript printer loaded with legal-sized paper used by Consulting."

### DNS/DHCP Integration

With NetWare 6 you can store Dynamic Host Configuration Protocol (DHCP) and Domain Name Service (DNS) information in the NDS database and can easily manage IP addresses. This feature provides centralized management of your IP addresses, replication, and fault tolerance of these addresses. You can easily import DNS and DHCP data, automate IP address assignments, and eliminate network problems associated with duplicate IP addresses. Dynamic DNS is also supported.

Domain Name Service (DNS) converts domain names (such as www. novell.com) to numerical IP addresses (such as 137.65.2.5). Because NetWare 6 integrates DNS with NDS, each user can automatically be assigned an appropriate DNS server upon login. For example, a mobile user in a distant location might be assigned a DNS server with a faster response time than for a desktop user in a local office.

Dynamic Host Configuration Protocol (DHCP) provides unique IP addresses upon request to users and network devices. Because NetWare 6 uses NDS to help automate DHCP services, you can store IP address in NDS. When a user logs into the network, DHCP consults NDS and provides an appropriate IP address for that user. DHCP eliminates the older methods of manually tracking and assigning IP addresses, and NDS ensures that DHCP provides managed IP addresses throughout the enterprise.

### The ZENworks Starter Pack

NetWare 6 is designed for use with the ZENworks Starter Pack, which includes Novell Application Launcher (NAL) and Workstation Manager as part of the NetWare 6 installation. NAL delivers applications to the user's desktop via NDS. Workstation Manager enables you to remotely manage and upgrade Windows 3.1, Windows 95/98, and Windows NT/Windows2000 workstations. ZENworks, which stands for Zero Effort Networking, is a bundle of management utilities that assists you in managing individual workstations in an enterprise.

The components of ZENworks enable administrators to solve a user's workstation problems without visiting the user's workstation. By adding workstation objects and workstation group objects to the NDS tree, administrators can manage the desktop configuration, distribute applications, and perform maintenance on the workstation through NDS.

With ZENworks installed, workstations are registered with NDS each time a user logs into the network. Registration enables administrators to look at a workstation object's details and centrally manage workstations through NDS.

**Features Available in the Full ZENworks Product**  Additional ZENworks functionality can be obtained by purchasing the full-featured product. Once you install ZENworks and the Novell Client provided on the ZENworks CD-ROM, you can take advantage of these additional features:

▶ **The Help Requester** — This application lets users send a message about a workstation problem to the administrator or Help Desk. The message automatically includes the workstation object's details stored in NDS. You can use the message and the workstation object in NWAdmin to solve the problem. This saves time and effort, especially when problem workstations are located on a WAN.

▶ **Workstation inventory** — ZENworks enables you to easily inventory and track all the configuration data for Windows workstations on the network.

▶ **Remote control of workstations** — By enabling remote control access on the network's workstations, you can connect to a workstation remotely and navigate the desktop to troubleshoot workstation problems without having to visit the workstation.

The full ZENworks product requires an additional purchase. For pricing and details, check out the ZENworks Web page at the following location:

`www.novell.com/products/zenworks`

Both the starter pack and the full version of the ZENworks product are discussed in detail in Chapter 19.

### NetWare Licensing Services

These two services simplify installation and licensing of new Novell products. Each works on the server to reduce the time and effort you must spend on installing and licensing. Common utilities and interfaces now standardize each of these tasks. NLS provides a single utility you can use to license all future NetWare products; ensures consistent, efficient, and rapid licensing for NetWare products; and permits licensing for all products conforming to NLS requirements.

### Internet Connectivity

NetWare 6 ships with the Novell Internet Access Server (NIAS) 4.1. NIAS provides routing between local and remote LANs, remote access to all company network resources (including e-mail and Internet access) through a modem or other connection, and remote service management of all connectivity services and servers from your workstation.

## Changes to Security

Several new security features come with NetWare 6, which builds upon the NetWare 4 and NetWare 5 existing security features. The new features have been integrated with Novell Directory Services (NDS) and help simplify administration of each new feature. They also provide security for improved Internet data integrity and privacy across public networks. The new security features include Public Key Infrastructure Services (PKIS), Novell International Cryptographic Infrastructure (NICI), Secure Authentication Services (SAS), and the audit system. This section discusses these new features, explains why they are important, and explains how they provide NetWare 6 with advanced security services.

### Public Key Infrastructure Services (PKIS)

NetWare 6 includes PKIS, which supports public key cryptography and digital certificates in a NetWare 6 environment. Digital certificates provide a method for checking the authenticity of keys used in a public key cryptographic session. In NetWare 6, PKIS enables you either to act as your own certificate authority or to use the services of third-party certificate authorities. Through PKIS, you can generate and sign various types of digital certificates and store and manage these certificates within NDS.

PKIS enables any designated NetWare 6 administrators to establish a Certificate Authority (CA) management domain within NDS. PKIS allows administrators to manage certificates and keys for Secure Sockets Layer (SSL) security for LDAP servers.

Certificate management includes services such as establishment of a CA local to your organization, certificate renewal, simplified certificate revocation with certificate suspension (without complex certificate revocation lists), creation of certificate signing requests (for use with external CAs), unlimited certificate minting services for applications, and using SSL in the NetWare environment (such as Novell LDAP Services for NDS).

Using PKIS, you can control the costs associated with obtaining key pairs and managing public key certificates. PKIS helps you create a local CA based on NDS that signs certificates for other services on the network. With PKIS you can also generate unlimited key pairs and issue unlimited public key certificates through the local CA at no charge.

NDS stores all keys and certificates that are generated by PKIS or obtained from external CAs. NDS's trusted directory features mean that public keys can be openly published while private keys are securely protected.

### Novell International Cryptographic Infrastructure (NICI)

NetWare 6 includes cryptographic services named Novell International Cryptographic Infrastructure (NICI). NICI enables developers to use the Controlled Cryptography Service (CCS) API to integrate cryptographic schemes with their applications. NICI also enables developers to write a single application that can be used in several countries, regardless of the differences in countries' cryptographic laws. For example, a developer could write a single application that uses 128-bit cryptographic keys when used within the United States and 40-bit cryptographic keys when used within countries that allow only keys of that length.

NICI is an infrastructure of network cryptographic services for worldwide consumption that supports strong cryptography and multiple cryptographic technologies. The NICI infrastructure has been developed in response to customer and internal Novell needs while complying with various national policies on the shipment and use of cryptography. Cryptography services on the NetWare platform provide fundamental security features such as confidentiality, integrity, authentication, and nonrepudiation.

The services are modular in nature, which enables new cryptographic engines, libraries, and policy managers to be dynamically added. The infrastructure is also tightly controlled, enforced through an integral OS loader that verifies modules before loading and controls access to modules only via standardized interfaces. A Novell SDK provides available cryptographic services.

NICI is the foundation for future network cryptographic services. It ensures that your product complies with international cryptography import and export laws through enforced region-specific cryptographic policies. NICI also provides for single, worldwide commodity vendor products and supports extensible, application-specific cryptographic libraries and interchangeable cryptographic technologies.

### Secure Authentication Services

NetWare 6 includes Secure Authentication Services (SAS), an infrastructure for supporting both existing and emerging authentication mechanisms, such as biometric and token-authentication systems. Through SAS, NetWare 6 also supports SSL version 3. Developers can use the SAS API to write applications that can establish encrypted SSL connections. (Developers can then use NICI to ensure that these SSL connections conform to the laws of each country in which the applications are used.)

Authentication is a fundamental component of a robust network service — it is how you identify yourself. Without authentication, you cannot secure a network. Novell's Secure Authentication Services (SAS) provides next generation authentication services, as well as an evolving industry authentication mechanism for the future. In NetWare 6, SAS provides Secure Sockets Layer (SSL) support. Server applications use the SAS API set to establish encrypted SSL connections.

SAS is built entirely on NICI. This means that the SAS service itself is based on a single executable file. Because no cryptography is included in the SAS NLM, you can ship a single NLM worldwide for easy administrator management and tracking. Also, any applications written to the SAS API can also be based on a single executable file.

In addition, applications written to the SAS application can go through a one-time and usually expedited export approval process. Novell has already received export approval for SAS and NICI. This means that application developers benefit from expedited export procedures.

PKIS also provides key management for the SSL services. Any application written to the SAS interface inherits the capability to have PKIS manage its certificates. NDS access control lists (ACLs) manage access to the private key that enables SSL. Because SAS is a network service, it has its own network identity. ACLs are set up on the SSL key object in such a way that only the SAS identity can read the private key. This guarantees that nonauthorized entities such as users, other server applications, and even the application built on top of SAS cannot gain access to and expose or subvert the private key.

### Auditing Services

NetWare 6 includes auditing services, which enable administrators to monitor users' access to an organization's network and to record this monitoring information in audit log files. You can create NDS objects to represent audit log files, and you can then manage these objects just as you manage other objects in the NDS tree. You can also grant rights to the NDS objects representing audit log files, just as you grant rights to other objects in the NDS tree. As a result, you can assign administrators to view and manage audit log files.

The audit system now takes advantage of exposed NDS audit services in the following ways:

▶ Audit log files are represented and managed as NDS objects.

▶ Access to the audit information and configuration is controlled by the standard NDS rights.

▶ Auditing is configured at the container and volume levels.

▶ The audit policy for a container or volume specifies what is audited within the volume or container and which users are audited.

The audit system is an essential element of the total NetWare security environment. You must have network audit integrity to ensure that the network is secure. Additionally, some industries, such as banking, require auditing to be done as part of business operations. The NetWare auditing system can monitor and record every relevant network transaction, which user performed the transaction, and when the transaction occurred.

NetWare provides audit data granularity. This includes which events are audited, control of audit configuration, and access to audit data.

## Changes to Installation and Upgrades

Several changes to the installation or upgrade utilities are available in NetWare 6. In addition, improved utilities are available to help you upgrade your clients. These new installation and upgrade tools enable you to chose the option that best reflects your organization's network structure or design.

### The NetWare 6 Installation Program (NWCONFIG.EXE and .NLM)

The NetWare 6 installation program is used either to install a new NetWare 6 server or to upgrade an existing NetWare 5 server to NetWare 6. Upgrading an existing NetWare 5 server to NetWare 6 is often called an *in-place upgrade*.

Novell also provides the NWDEPLOY.EXE utility to prepare your servers before beginning a migration to NetWare 6. NWDEPLOY can be run during the beginning a NetWare 6 install through the install screen when running an installation of NetWare 6. For more information about NWDEPLOY.EXE see Chapter 10.

### The Novell Upgrade Wizard

NetWare 6 still provides the Novell Upgrade Wizard, which moves the NetWare 3 source server's bindery (including print information) and file system to a destination NetWare 6 server. The utility is a wizard-based interface, which ensures ease of use for across-the-wire upgrades. The wizard can also detect potential conflicts and provide options to resolve them before the upgrade begins.

### Automatic Client Update

The Automatic Client Update (ACU) ships with NetWare 6. This utility is used to upgrade all varieties of NetWare clients. For example, you can upgrade NetWare 3 clients to NetWare 6 clients automatically from a central location.

## Changes to Developer Support

NetWare 6 caters to network developers by providing the world's fastest Java Virtual Machine (JVM) for running server-based Java applications and services. Following are several additional enhancements made to the NetWare 6 system.

### Java Support in NetWare 6

NetWare 6 supports Java applications running on the server. Java Virtual Machine (JVM), which is part of the NetWare 6 kernel, enables a wide range of Java-developed applications to serve your network and users. You can now develop Java-based applications for the Internet using Java and Java scripting.

This means that the Java support on NetWare 6 enables you to run Java applets on the server console, display Java applications in X Window–style formats — with full mouse and graphic support — and run multiple Java applications on the server while the server performs other tasks.

Java support in NetWare 6 is provided by JAVA.NLM. This NLM starts the Java engine, which enables Java applications to run. You can load Java support by calling JAVA.NLM at the server console prompt, and you can run Java applications using the APPLET console command.

### Scripting

NetWare 6 scripting and component services offer you choice, compatibility, and speed. NetWare 6 supports the major scripting languages available, including Perl 5, NetBasic, and JavaScript. In addition, NetWare 6 also ships with and supports the Common Object Request Broker Architecture (CORBA), ORB, JavaBeans for NetWare, and JavaScript.

## Third-Party Add-Ons

Several third-party products are included at no cost in NetWare 6. Novell includes these third-party products as part of the NetWare 6 package software in order to integrate them with NDS and take advantage of the security and services of NetWare 6. Some of the third-party products are listed in the sections that follow.

### IBM Websphere Web Server

The IBM WebSphere Application Server is a Java-based application environment that enables you to build, deploy, and manage Internet and intranet applications on NetWare. This product provides you with a robust way to deploy Web services on the fast, secure, and stable NetWare environment. There is a charge for the Advanced version of the software

### NetScape FastTrack Server

NetWare 6 provides a fully integrated version of the Netscape FastTrack server. This Web server used Netscape Web server code specifically adapted for maximum performance on a NetWare 6 platform along with integration to eDirectory. This integration with eDirectory makes the Web server easier to administer and more secure by restricting who can administer the Web server and what content the user can publish. The Netscape FastTrack server supports eDirectory, LDAP, Common Gateway Interface, CGI, PERL, and NetBasic.

### BTRIEVE

Even after years and years of use, the BTRIEVE key-indexed record management system still provides high-performance data handling and improved programming productivity. BTRIEVE enables an application to retrieve, insert, update, or delete records either by key value or by sequential or random access methods.

## Changes to Workstation/Client Support

Several new enhancements to the workstation or client appear in NetWare 6. Most notable is the support for Pure IP for each of the new clients that ship with NetWare 6. In addition, Novell's new clients are all based on the new and advanced NetWare Client 32 architecture, which departs from the NetWare DOS Requester software (the VLM-based client). Client 32 enables client software to run in protected mode and, in addition, requires less than 5KB of conventional memory while providing a larger cache. The Client 32 architecture, designed for robust connectivity and easy maintenance, provides the following features:

- ▸ Client 32 detects changes in a workstation's network environment and restores connections to the network when the relevant network service is restored. This makes Client 32 the most reliable NetWare client available. And when a computer loses its connection to the network, the computer continues to run without having to reboot.

▸ Client 32 caches frequently used data, such as file content and network information, resulting in less traffic on the network and faster response times on the client.

▸ Client 32 supports multiple Directory tree access and complete Novell Directory Services access.

The new clients based on this Client 32 code are NetWare Client 32 for DOS/Windows 3.x, NetWare Client 32 for Windows 95/98, NetWare Client 32 for Windows 2000, NetWare Client 32 for Windows NT, and NetWare Client for Macintosh.

### NetWare Client 32 for DOS/Windows 3.x

In addition to all the benefits of the Client 32 architecture, the NetWare Client 32 for DOS/Windows 3.x software provides these capabilities:

▸ The familiar graphical NetWare User Tools utility is available in Windows to enable network users to manage their network environment.

▸ Support for Novell's 32-bit Pure IP transport is included.

▸ The same Target Service Agent used to enable backup and restore on workstations using the NetWare DOS Requester software works on workstations using the Client 32 for DOS/Windows 3.x software.

NetWare Client 32 for DOS/Windows 3.x differs from the NetWare Client 32 for Windows 95/98 software in these ways:

▸ The core Client 32 component, NIOS, runs as an executable file rather than as a virtual device driver (VXD).

▸ NIOS uses a text configuration file (NET.CFG) rather than the registry.

▸ There is no graphical interface for changing configuration parameters. You have to edit the NET.CFG file manually and restart the client software to implement the changes.

### NetWare Client 32 for Windows 95/98

NetWare Client 32 for Windows 95/98 differs from the NetWare DOS Requester and the NetWare Client32 for DOS/Windows 3.x software in these ways:

▸ The core Client 32 component, NIOS, runs as a virtual device driver (VXD) rather than as an executable file.

▸ There is usually no STARTNET.BAT file. Windows 95/98 loads the client at startup.

▶ There is no NET.CFG file. Configuration settings are saved in the Windows 95/98 registry. Because configuration settings are saved in the registry, you can manage Client 32 parameters using the Windows 95/98 System Policies Editor.

▶ You can upgrade Windows 3.1x workstations to Windows 95/98 and NetWare Client 32 for Windows 95/98 in one installation process, called the *Batch Install*.

▶ Client 32 for Windows 95/98 is fully integrated into the Explorer and Network Neighborhood utilities. In addition, you can log into NetWare networks and run login scripts from the Windows 95 desktop environment.

▶ Client 32 for Windows 95/98 supports long filenames.

▶ Client 32 for Windows 95/98 supports the following industry standard protocols:

- Windows 95/98 implementations of TCP/IP, Winsock, Named Pipes, and NetBIOS

- The Windows 95/98 WSOCK32.DLL (supported by the Client 32 IPX protocol stack)

- Simple Network Management Protocol (SNMP)

- The Microsoft Client for Microsoft Networks

### NetWare Client 32 for Windows NT and Windows 2000

The NetWare Client for Windows NT brings the full power, ease of use, manageability, and security of NetWare 4, intraNetWare, and NetWare 6 to Windows NT workstations. It enables organizations to get the most from their NetWare networks through NT workstations.

With the NetWare Client for Windows NT, you can take full advantage of NetWare services, such as NDS, and realize the performance of the NetWare Core Protocols (NCPs).

### NetWare Client for Macintosh

The NetWare Client for Macintosh does not ship directly on the NetWare CD-ROMs. A third-party vendor provides the NetWare Client for Macintosh for NetWare.

The newer iMac can connect directly out of the box without any client software to a NetWare 6 server by utilizing the Novell NetWare Native file system software.

For detailed information about each of the NetWare clients and their installation and configuration instructions, please see Chapter 17.

## Summary

This chapter has provided you with brief descriptions of the features of NetWare 6, including the many new features that greatly enhance NetWare 6. NetWare 6 is scalable and enables you to add up to 32 CPUs for each SMP server. You can also link multiple NetWare 6 servers together in what is known as a cluster. NetWare 6 also provides enhanced storage services through NSS 3.0 and NetWare 6 is more flexible for large enterprises while offering the most secure and cost-effective network operating system available. For installation and configuration information, refer to the rest of the chapters in this book.

CHAPTER 2

# Installation and Management Utilities for NetWare 6

*"The question of common sense is always 'What is it good for?'—a question which would abolish the rose and be answered triumphantly by the cabbage."—J. R. Lowell*

The NetWare 6 operating system provides you with many utilities that help you install and manage your NetWare 6 servers. Your job as an administrator is made easier by being familiar with the utilities and their functions. This chapter focuses on just the installation and management utilities that are available in NetWare 6, and it does not attempt to cover the many smaller utilities available from Novell. For information on the other utilities, please refer to Novell's NetWare 6 documentation. The following installation and management utilities are covered in this chapter:

- ▶ INSTALL (INSTALL.BAT and INSTALL.EXE)
- ▶ NWCONFIG (formerly called INSTALL.NLM)
- ▶ NWADMIN
- ▶ NDS MANAGER
- ▶ MONITOR
- ▶ DSREPAIR
- ▶ DSTRACE
- ▶ DSMERGE
- ▶ ConsoleOne
- ▶ NLIST
- ▶ Miscellaneous server utilities
- ▶ Miscellaneous workstation utilities

## NetWare 6 Installation

The first utility that you need to become familiar with is the NetWare 6 INSTALL.BAT installation program. This installation program loads the server INSTALL.NLM program. Both of these installation programs are found on the NetWare 6 CD-ROM.

Before you install the NetWare 6 software, however, you need to make sure that the server meets the hardware requirements. Next, you need to prepare the server hardware by creating the proper disk partitions. Finally, you need to update NDS eDirectory running on any existing NetWare 4or NetWare 5 servers to the latest version. At the time of this printing, eDirectory is at version 8.5.1. Follow the NDS eDirectory install instructions only if you are installing the NetWare 6 server into an existing NDS tree.

If the NetWare 6 server being installed is the first NetWare server on the network, you want to take some time to consider how to design your NDS eDirectory tree. Please review Chapter 5 if this is your first NetWare installation. We have found that well-designed trees, including partitions, replicas, and time synchronization, are by far the easiest to manage and support. The design decisions you make before installation will affect how users interact with the network resources. Providing easy access to network resources and reducing costs are the ultimate goals when you install a network operating system.

## Server Hardware Requirements for NetWare 6

An important prerequisite to preparing for a NetWare 6 installation is to make sure that you have the proper server hardware. The server hardware needs to meet or exceed the minimum hardware requirements as given in the Novell manuals. Novell recommends the following minimum hardware configuration, although your needs will vary according to the applications running on your servers:

- A server-class PC with a Pentium II or higher processor
- A VGA or higher resolution display adapter (SVGA recommended)
- A DOS partition of at least 200MB, with 2GB of available space
- Available disk space outside the DOS partition — Standard NetWare products and WebSphere
- Application Server for NetWare — 2GB on volume SYS.

### RAM

- Standard NetWare products — 256MB
- WebSphere Application Server for NetWare — 256MB (512MB recommended) in addition to standard NetWare products
- A CD-ROM drive that can read ISO 9660-formatted disks; computers with bootable CD-ROM drives must fully support the El Torito specification
- A PS/2 or serial mouse is recommended, but not required

### Software and Other Requirements

- DOS 3.3 or later — DOS 7 is included on the NetWare 6 License/Cryptography diskette. Do not use the version of DOS that ships with the Windows NT or Windows 95/98 operating systems

- ▸ DOS CD drivers
- ▸ NetWare 6 Operating System CD-ROM (this book includes a 3-user version of NetWare 6)
- ▸ NetWare 6 License diskette
- ▸ Novell Client for DOS and Windows 3.1x (optional, for installation from a network)
- ▸ An IP address (contact your ISP, if necessary)
- ▸ An IP address of a DNS (contact your network administrator, if necessary)
- ▸ The name of your domain (contact your system administrator, if necessary)
- ▸ Network board and storage device properties (contact your computer hardware manufacturer, if necessary)

## Preparing the Server Hardware for NetWare 6

NetWare 6 requires a boot partition of at least 50MB (we recommend 100MB) to start the computer and load NetWare. The boot partition contains the NetWare startup and server files. To create and format a boot partition, complete the following steps:

**1.** If the computer already has an operating system installed, such as Windows, you should completely remove the operating system. Be sure to back up any data on this machine before removing the operating system.

**2.** Boot your computer with DOS 3.3 or later. If needed, you can boot from the NetWare 6 License disk (if separate from your operating system disk). DOS 7 and all required DOS utilities are included on the floppy disk. Do not use the version of DOS that ships with the Windows 95, Windows 98, or Windows NT operating system.

**3.** Use FDISK to create at least a 100MB active DOS partition: Type **FDISK**, create a primary DOS partition, and make it the active partition. The computer restarts.

**4.** Format and transfer DOS system files to the partition by changing to A: and typing **FORMAT C: /S**. Your disk drive is now ready to begin the NetWare 6 installation.

**5.** If you are installing from the NetWare 6 CD-ROM, make sure that the CONFIG.SYS file contains the settings of at least FILES=40 and BUFFERS=30.

**Consulting Experience**

The following recommendations for the server hardware are based on a more realistic configuration for running NetWare 6 in your production network. Our recommendations are as follows:

- ▸ A Pentium III class PC
- ▸ 256MB of RAM
- ▸ 10GB of hard disk space
- ▸ A 500MB partition for DOS
- ▸ A 24X speed CD-ROM drive
- ▸ A 3.5-inch drive
- ▸ A network card that is at least a 32-bit card
- ▸ An SVGA monitor and card
- ▸ Network cabling

Your computer should now have an active boot partition of at least 100MB. Continue the installation by accessing the installation files on the NetWare 6 CD-ROM.

## Preparing Your Existing Network for NetWare 6

If the new NetWare 6 server is going to be installed into an existing NetWare 4 or NetWare 5 network, review the following list of NetWare and NDS versions to ensure that you are running at least these version levels.

NDS eDirectory for NetWare can co-exist with the following NDS versions:

- ▸ NetWare 4.11 or 4.2 with NDS 6.09 or later
- ▸ NetWare 5 Support Pack 5 or later with Pre-NDS 8 7.46 or later
- ▸ NetWare 5 Support Pack 5 or later with NDS 8.35 or later
- ▸ NetWare 5.1 Support Pack 1
- ▸ Windows NT 4.0 Support Pack 4 or Windows 2000 with eDirectory 8.38 or later
- ▸ NDS eDirectory 8.5 on NetWare, Solaris, Linux, and Tru64 UNIX

### Updating the NDS Schema

When upgrading a NetWare 5.*x* server to NDS eDirectory, you must update the NDS schema by running DSREPAIR on the server that has the master replica of the [Root] partition.

If either of the following conditions exists, you must run DSREPAIR.NLM before installing the first NDS eDirectory server in your tree:

▸ Any NetWare 5 server in your NDS tree is running NDS 8 or NDS 8 NetWare Update.

▸ Your first installation of NDS eDirectory is on a NetWare 5 server that does not hold a writeable replica of the [Root] partition.

To update the NDS schema, follow these steps:

**1.** Copy the appropriate DSREPAIR.NLM file from the product CD-ROM (or downloaded and expanded file) to the SYS:\SYSTEM directory of the server that contains the master replica of the Tree partition. Use the following Table 2.1 as a guide for updating these versions.

TABLE 2.1

*Upgrading the NDS Schema*

| NETWARE VERSION | NDS VERSION | COPY |
| --- | --- | --- |
| 4.11 | 6.09 or later | \PATCHES\DSREPAIR \NW4X\DSREPAIR.NLM |
| 5.0 or later | NDS 7.46 or later | \PATCHES\DSREPAIR \NW5X\DSREPAIR.NLM |
| 5.0 or later | 8.11 or 8.17 | Not supported |
| 5.0 or later | 8.35 or later | \PATCHES\DSREPAIR \NWNDS8\DSREPAIR.NLM |

**2.** At the server console of the master replica of the [Root] partition, load DSREPAIR.NLM.

**3.** Select Advanced Options Menu ⇨ Global Schema Operations.

**4.** Enter the administrator's name (for example, .Admin.VMP) and password.

**5.** Select Post NetWare 5 Schema Update ⇨ Yes. DSREPAIR updates the schema and posts the results to the DSREPAIR.LOG file.

Ignore any errors associated with adding object classes. DSREPAIR.NLM is simply applying the Post NetWare 5 Schema Update changes to each object. Use

Table 2.1 as a reference and copy the appropriate patch version of DSREPAIR.NLM to each NetWare server in the NDS tree. This step ensures that the schema needed for NDS eDirectory is properly maintained when DSREPAIR.NLM is run in the future.

If you use an earlier version of DSREPAIR.NLM and select Rebuild Operational Schema, schema enhancements made by the Post NetWare 5 Schema Update will be lost. To resolve lost schema enhancements, run DSREPAIR.NLM according to Table 2.2, which follows.

T A B L E   2.2

*Running Earlier Versions of DSREPAIR*

| IF YOU ARE RUNNING DSREPAIR FROM HERE | DO THIS |
| --- | --- |
| A server that holds a writeable replica of the Tree partition | Reapply the Post NetWare 5 Schema Update to your NDS tree. |
| Any other server | Click Advanced Options ⇨ Global Schema Operations ⇨ Request Schema from Tree. |

**6.** Close DSREPAIR.NLM before installing NDS eDirectory on the server. If DSREPAIR.NLM is loaded, the server might not restart. Install the Support Pack as shown in Table 2.3.

T A B L E   2.3

*Installing the Support Pack*

| BEFORE INSTALLING NDS EDIRECTORY ON THIS SERVER | INSTALL THIS SUPPORT PACK |
| --- | --- |
| NetWare 5 | NetWare 5 Support Pack 5 |
| NetWare 5.1 | NetWare 5.1 Support Pack 1 or later |

Support packs are available from Novell at `Support.Novell.Com`. You can download a file or purchase a CD-ROM. Follow these instructions to load the support pack. If you download NW51SP1.EXE, the support pack might take several minutes to verify an ARJ-SECURITY envelope. After verification, the support pack creates an NW5SPX directory and places subdirectories and files there.

### Installing NDS eDirectory

If you are upgrading NDS, do the following:

1. In the AUTOEXEC.NCF file, comment out the lines that load virus scanners, database applications such as Sybase or Oracle, backup applications, and other programs that rely on files being continually open and volumes being mounted.

   • During the NDS eDirectory 8.5 installation, the software must dismount volumes so that trustee assignments can be migrated.

   • Be aware that virus scanners and other programs might be embedded inside other products, for example, ZENworks, ManageWise, and BorderManager.

   • Restart the server and verify that the programs and applications referred to in Step 1 are not running.

2. If you have an IP-only environment, load IPXSPX.NLM.

   • NWCONFIG.NLM looks in Btrieve for the product list. Btrieve subsequently requires IPX. Loading IPXSPX.NLM allows Btrieve to load. After you reboot the server, IPXSPX.NLM does not reload, so you have an IP-only environment again.

3. At the server console, load NWCONFIG.NLM.

4. Select Product Options ⇨ Install a Product Not Listed.

5. Press F3 (F4 if you're using RCONSOLE) and enter the path to the NDS files under the NW directory, for example, SYS:\NW.

   • Follow the prompts concerning license agreements, the README file, and tips.

   • After the files are copied, the server automatically restarts and begins to install components for ConsoleOne and Novell Certificate Server.

6. Enter the administrator's login name (for example, Admin.Acme).

   • So that the installation program can access the Security container and create a Server Certificate object, log in to the existing Security container object as a user with Supervisor rights.

**This window might close before you enter this information. If it does, toggle (Alt+Esc) to the window and enter the information. Otherwise, the installation will be incomplete.**

IMPORTANT

**7.** Follow the online instructions concerning the Certificate Server, LDAP, languages, components, and products to install.

**8.** After the installation is completed, restore the lines that you commented out in Step 1 and then click Yes to restart the server.

Repeat this procedure for each NetWare 5.*x* server that you want to upgrade to NDS eDirectory 8.5 for NetWare.

You can download an evaluation license from the NDS eDirectory Web page at `http://www.novell.com/products/nds/licenses/eval_85.html`.

Because the internal NDS identifiers change after upgrading to NDS eDirectory, the backlink process has to update backlinked objects for them to be consistent.

Backlinks keep track of external references to objects on other servers. For each external reference on a server, the backlink process ensures that the real object exists in the correct location and verifies all backlink attributes on the master of the replica. The backlink process occurs two hours after the database is open and then every 780 minutes (13 hours). The interval is configurable from 2 minutes to 10,080 minutes (7 days).

After you migrate to NDS, Novell Consulting recommends that you force the backlink to run by issuing a SET DSTRACE=*B command from the server console. Running the backlink process is especially important on servers that do not contain a replica.

**eDirectory Utilities**    When your servers are at DS 8.5.1, it is important that you are using the latest NDS support tools and not the older versions because the older versions are often not supported with the updated DS.

The following information outlines the prerequisites and steps for upgrading your existing NetWare 4.11 servers to the newer NDS version 5.99a:

**1.** Ensure that all NetWare 4.11 servers are at service pack IWSP5B before upgrading to DS 5.99a.

**2.** Ensure that time is synchronized across all servers.

**3.** Ensure that NDS is healthy, which means that no NDS errors (–6*xx* errors) appear on the DSTRACE screen.

**4.** Ensure that you have NDS ADMIN access rights to all areas of the NDS tree.

**5.** Ensure that all communication links are up.

**6.** Ensure that all servers remain up during this process.

After you have performed all the prerequisite steps, you need to manually upgrade NDS to version 5.99a on the server that houses the master replica of the [ROOT] partition in the NDS tree. After you do this, follow these steps for all other servers:

**I.** Create a batch file to copy all the files from DS411L.EXE to the appropriate directory on each NetWare 4.11 server. Please see the README file (from DS411L.EXE) for instructions on where the files should be placed. Because the upgrade requires unloading the old DS and reloading the new DS, you need to ensure that the DS.NLM 5.99a (and supporting NDS tools) are copied to all servers before this process is completed.

You may want to consider creating a batch file to revert to the old files, in the unlikely event of a problem.

**2.** Start the process of unloading and reloading DS.NLM on servers that have replicas on them first, and then move on to the ones that don't have replicas.

This unloading and reloading process can be accomplished with NDS Manager 1.25 (which is part of DS411L.EXE). This utility automates the update process so that you don't have to physically visit each server or RCONSOLE into the server. This makes the update process faster, with the goal of completing the unloading and reloading process before the next replication cycle.

**3.** After reloading the newer DS.NLM, run DSREPAIR to check for proper synchronization between replicas.

**NOTE**

**Due to the older version of DS (5.73) running on your NetWare 4.11 servers, we recommend that you complete the entire process within a 48-hour window. This upgrade is simple and can be completed within a 4-hour window, assuming that the previously described prerequisites are met.**

## Installing a NetWare 6 Server

The following sections describe in detail the step-by-step instructions for installing a new NetWare 6 server. These sections assume that you have completed the preparatory steps of acquiring the proper server hardware requirements, preparing the hardware, and updating NDS eDirectory on any existing NetWare 4 or NetWare 5 servers. In addition, these sections discuss how to install only the NetWare 6 server from the NetWare 6 CD-ROM.

### Begin the Installation

1. Insert the NetWare 6 CD-ROM into a CD-ROM drive installed as a DOS device or a network device. For information on setting up your CD-ROM, refer to your CD-ROM vendor documentation.

2. Change to the root of the CD-ROM drive and run the NetWare 6 INSTALL program by typing **INSTALL** at the root. The first several screens are the License Agreements. Read the agreements and press F10 to accept them.

3. Select the type of NetWare Server Installation from the main menu, as shown in Figure 2.1. You can select an Express installation or a Custom Installation. Express assumes various defaults and is a little faster, but for most cases you want to select the Custom Install so that you have control of each install step. The NetWare Express installation program guides you through a basic server installation using the following default values:

   - A 4GB volume SYS will be created
   - LAN and disk drivers will be auto discovered
   - The following default products will be installed:
   - NDPS

     - NetWare Enterprise Server
     - NetWare Administration Server NFS Server
     - IBM Websphere Application Server
   - Country Code: 1
   - Codepage:437
   - Video: Super VGA Plug N Play
   - Keyboard: United States
   - Mouse: PS/2

   Although the default settings work for most configurations, you can change or specify new settings for the server ID number, numbering scheme, server reboot options, and SET parameters. NetWare 6 can be installed either on a new computer, as an upgraded server, or as a pre-migration server. If you are performing a new server installation, select New Server. This option does not delete system partitions and other partitions such as DOS, UNIX, and Windows. The new server install *does* delete detected NetWare partitions containing volume SYS, and any other volumes that are part of that NetWare partition. If you want to keep volumes that are part of that NetWare partition, select the Upgrade option instead. Upgrading retains all your server data such as files, directory structure, partitions, and volumes. You also have the option to specify the destination of the server startup files. The startup directory is the directory on the DOS boot partition that contains the files to launch the NetWare 6 server. The pre-migration option simply prepares and installs a destination server for the Migration Wizard utility. For more information on the Migration Wizard utility, see that section later in this chapter.

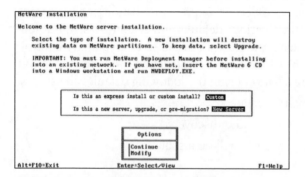

**FIGURE 2.1:** *The NetWare Server Installation main menu screen*

**NOTE**

**You must run the NetWare Deployment Manager before installing it into an existing network. If you have not done so, insert the NetWare 6 CD-ROM into a windows workstation and run NWDEPLOY.EXE.**

4. If you are upgrading from a previous version of NetWare, select the option Upgrade. An upgrade preserves all server data including files, directory structures, partitions, and volumes. Figure 2.2 illustrates the selection for Upgrading from NetWare 4.*x* or 5*x*.

▸ After you have selected the type of installation, select Continue to proceed with the install process. You are then presented with the following onscreen information:

• The Load Server at Reboot option defaults to Yes. This means that the proper command to start up the NetWare 6 server during reboot is added to AUTOEXEC.BAT and CONFIG.SYS. The old files are renamed and saved with a .00*X* extension. You can select No to prevent the commands from being added to each file and to prevent the server from booting automatically at startup.

```
NetWare Installation

Welcome to the NetWare server installation.

    Select the type of installation and specify the directory
    where the server startup files will be installed.

    A new installation will destroy data on existing NetWare partitions.

    Use the Tab or arrow keys to move between windows.
    To learn more about the installation, press F1.

    ┌─────────────────────────────────────────────────────────┐
    │ Is this a new server or an upgrade?  Upgrade from 3.1x or 4.1x │
    │                                                           │
    │ Startup directory              C:\NWSERVER               │
    └─────────────────────────────────────────────────────────┘

                    ┌─────────────┐
                    │  Options    │
                    ├─────────────┤
                    │ Continue    │
                    │ Modify      │
                    └─────────────┘
Alt+F10=Exit   F2=Advanced settings   F3=Response file   Esc=Back   F1=Help
```

**FIGURE 2.2:** *You can select Upgrade from NetWare 4.x or 5.x instead of installing a new NetWare 6 server in order to retain all of your server's data. Choosing this option keeps all the files, directories, NDS partitions, and replicas.*

### Select the Regional or Country Settings

**5.** After selecting the type of server installation that you want and setting or changing any of the default parameters, you are prompted to choose the appropriate country, code page, and keyboard mapping for your language and computer hardware. Selecting the regional or country setting is shown in Figure 2.3. In most cases, simply use the defaults.

```
NetWare Installation

Select the regional settings for the server.

            ┌──────────────────────────────────────┐
            │ Country:    001  (USA)                │
            │ Code page:  437  (United States English) │
            │ Keyboard:   United States             │
            └──────────────────────────────────────┘

                    ┌─────────────┐
                    │  Options    │
                    ├─────────────┤
                    │ Continue    │
                    │ Modify      │
                    └─────────────┘
Alt+F10=Exit            Esc=Back            F1=Help
```

**FIGURE 2.3:** *During the server installation, you need to choose the appropriate country, code page, and keyboard mapping for your language and computer hardware.*

**6.** Select the mouse and video display type for your computer's hardware. The mouse type and video display are not automatically detected by the installation program. If the default settings for each do not match your computer hardware, you need to identify the correct settings for each item. Please note that, although the NetWare 6 server supports either a PS/2 or serial mouse, no mouse is required.

You can select the mouse and video display using the information as displayed in Figure 2.4.

```
NetWare Installation

Select the mouse type and video mode for the server.



                    Mouse type:  PS/2

                    Video:       Super VGA




                    Options
                    Continue
                    Modify

Alt+F10=Exit          Esc=Back              F1=Help
```

**FIGURE 2.4:** *Select the mouse and video display types.*

As mentioned, the installation program does not automatically detect the type of video display installed with your computer system. However, the installation program is optimized to display with video display hardware that is VESA 2 compliant. Choose Standard VGA only if your video board does not support 256 colors.

At this point, if you select Continue, the NetWare file system copy begins and runs for several minutes while copying files to your server.

**Select a Platform Support Module**

**7.** The installation program automatically detects the device drivers that match the device types in your computer hardware. The different device types that the installation program supports include Platform Support Module (PSM), Hot Plug PCI, and other storage adapters. You also have the option to change any of the selections manually. Figure 2.5 shows the screen in the installation program that enables you to provide hardware device driver support.

A Platform Support Module (PSM) provides increased performance for multiprocessor computers. The installation program automatically detects PSM device drivers. If the install software does not detect a PSM, the server does not have or need a PSM driver. Some server hardware supports the Hot Plug PCI feature available in NetWare 5 and NetWare 6. If your computer supports this feature, the install program will detect it. Hot Plug enables you to insert and remove an adapter card while the server is powered on. The platform support module and Hot Plug support module are optional devices.

```
┌─────────────────────────────────────────────────────────────────┐
│ NetWare Installation                                              │
│                                                                   │
│ The following device drivers were detected for this server. Add, change, or │
│ delete device drivers as needed.                                  │
│                                                                   │
│  ┌ Device types ──────── Driver names ────────────────────────┐  │
│  │ Platform Support Module:   (optional)                       │  │
│  │                                                             │  │
│  │ HotPlug Support Module:    (optional)                       │  │
│  │                                                             │  │
│  │ Storage adapters:          AHA2940                          │  │
│  └─────────────────────────────────────────────────────────────┘ │
│                                                                   │
│                    ┌──────────────────┐                           │
│                    │     Options       │                          │
│                    ├──────────────────┤                           │
│                    │ Continue          │                          │
│                    │ Modify            │                          │
│                    └──────────────────┘                           │
│                                                                   │
│ Alt+F10=Exit  Esc=Back                             F1=Help        │
└─────────────────────────────────────────────────────────────────┘
```

**FIGURE 2.5:** *The installation program automatically detects the appropriate device drivers for the Platform Support Module, Hot Plug PCI, and Storage adapters. If you need to, you can easily change the drivers loaded.*

In addition to the PSM and Hot Plug PCI, the installation automatically detects and configures most storage adapters. The storage adapter requires a software driver called a disk driver to support the physical device. In previous versions of NetWare, disk drivers had .DSK file extensions. In NetWare 5 and NetWare 6, the .DSK device drivers are no longer supported. Instead, NetWare 5 and NetWare 6 use the NetWare Peripheral Architecture (NWPA), which replaces the .DSK with the Custom Device Module (CDM) and the Host Adapter Module (HAM). The storage adapter uses the HAM (.HAM file extension) as the interface between the computer and adapter card. The individual storage devices or drives use the CDM (.CDM file extension) as the interface between the drive and the HAM.

**NOTE** **The disk drivers with the .DSK drivers are no longer supported in NetWare 5 and NetWare 6. Instead, NetWare 5 and NetWare 6 use the capabilities of the NetWare Peripheral Architecture (NWPA). NWPA uses a host adapter module (HAM) and a custom device module (CDM).**

The installation program automatically detects many types of storage adapters, such as IDE and SCSI adapters. If your particular storage adapter is not detected, choose the appropriate driver from the drop-down list or copy it from a floppy disk. The CDMs and HAMs are obtained from the storage device or storage adapter manufacturer.

### Select a Storage Device and Network Board

**8.** The install program automatically detects many type of storage devices, such as IDE drives, SCSI drives, CD-ROM drives, and tape drives. Make sure that the devices installed in your server have been properly detected. If one or more of your devices have not been detected, choose the appropriate driver from the list provided or insert the driver from a floppy disk. To obtain a driver not provided on the NetWare 6 CD-ROM, check the hardware vendor's Web site for device driver downloads. To add a driver, select Modify in the Options box shown in Figure 2.6.

```
NetWare Installation

The following device drivers were detected for this server.  Add, change, or
delete device drivers as needed.


 ┌─ Device types ──────────── Driver names ──────────────────┐
 │                                                            │
 │  Storage devices:          SCSIHD                          │
 │                                                            │
 │  Network boards:           3C90X                           │
 │                                                            │
 │  NetWare Loadable Modules: (optional)                      │
 │                                                            │
 └────────────────────────────────────────────────────────────┘

                     ┌────────────────┐
                     │    Options     │
                     ├────────────────┤
                     │ Continue       │
                     │ Modify         │
                     └────────────────┘

 Alt+F10=Exit  Esc=Back                                F1=Help
```

**FIGURE 2.6:** *Device drivers for your server's hardware have been automatically detected. In order to add any missing drivers to your configuration, select Modify and choose the driver from a list.*

### Create a NetWare Partition and SYS: Volume

**9.** After the device drivers have been installed, you need to set up the NetWare partitions and volumes. You want to use the volumes to divide NetWare partitions into smaller sections. During the installation, NetWare automatically creates the first NetWare volume on your server as volume SYS. NetWare 6 requires a minimum SYS: volume of 350MB. You can modify the partition size by entering the desired size in megabytes. If you plan to have additional volumes on the NetWare partition, do not allocate the entire partition to the SYS: volume. In order to create NetWare partitions and volume SYS for your server, follow these directions:

**a.** If volume SYS already exists on the server, you will replace volume SYS when doing a new server installation. Removing an existing volume SYS is optional. After removing volume SYS during a new server installation, you must choose either to replace just the SYS:volume and its partition or to remove all NetWare volumes and NetWare/NSS partitions. Either option removes only NetWare partitions. Other types of partitions, such as DOS, Unix, and system/utility partitions, are not removed. Figure 2.7 shows the installation screen for removing existing NetWare volumes and partitions.

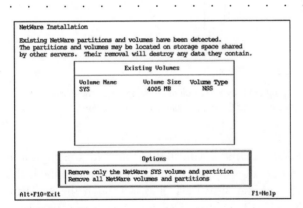

**FIGURE 2.7:** *The installation program detects an existing NetWare volume. You have the option to replace just the SYS: volume or all volumes.*

**b.** If no SYS: volume exists, the installation program guides you through creating one. First, you must create the NetWare partition that will host the volume. By default, NetWare tries to take all available space on the storage device and allocate it to the NetWare partition, unless you change the size. To modify the NetWare partition size, select the Modify option as shown in Figure 2.8. Select the device, and backspace over the current size. Type the new size and press Enter. Press F10 to save the settings and continue.

**NOTE**

**NSS volumes use disk space outside the NetWare partition. If you want to create NSS volumes, remember to reduce the size of the NetWare partition so that the appropriate amount of disk space is available for NSS volumes.**

```
NetWare Installation

         Volume SYS and Partition Properties
    Device:         SEAGATE ST32550N rev:0019 [V312-A0-D0:0]
    Filesystem Type:                    NSS
    NetWare Partition Size (MB):        1019.8
    Volume SYS Size (MB):               1015.9
    File Compression:                   Off
    NOTE: Press F1 for size recommendations.

              Options
              Continue
              Modify
    Alt+F10=Exit                        F1=Help
```

**FIGURE 2.8:** *The NetWare installation program tries to take all available space on the device and allocate it to the partition and volume. You can modify the size using the Modify option.*

In order to know how big the SYS: volume is, you should start with the minimum requirement for the NetWare 6 operating system. As previously mentioned, the operating system requires a SYS: volume of at least 2GB. Although the NetWare operating system requires only 350MB, volume SYS must be large enough to accommodate all of the NetWare products that you will installed. Table 2.4 outlines the absolute minimum requirements for the SYS: volume. In addition to the minimum sizes in the table, you should add as much as 200–300MB to the volume SYS size. This should prove optimal for most system operations.

| TABLE 2.4 | |
| --- | --- |
| NETWARE 6 PRODUCTS | MINIMUM VOLUME SYS SIZE |
| NetWare 6 operating system | 2GB |
| NetWare 6 with default products | 2GB |
| NetWare 6 with all products | 2GB |
| NetWare 6 with all products and documentation | 2GB |

Although default settings work for most installations, you might need to modify volume properties such as block size, file compression, data migration, and suballocation. To modify the properties of the SYS: volume, press F3=Volume Properties. A new screen appears, which enables you to change the block size and change or display status (mounted or unmounted), file compression, block suballocation, and data migration. Figure 2.9 shows an example of the volume properties screen.

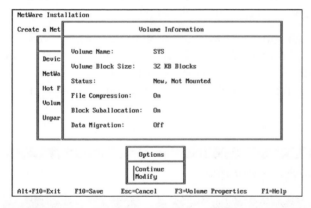

**FIGURE 2.9:** *The installation program enables you to modify the properties of the volumes.*

Although you can change the volume block size using the volume properties screen, the volume block size is automatically optimized for your server on the basis of the size of the volume. Typically, a larger block size optimizes the volume for large files.

File compression, by default, is automatically enabled. Enabling the compression feature maximizes disk space in NetWare 6. The only negative is that the file access for files that have been compressed is increased. Also note that some backup programs cannot back up compressed files.

Suballocation is also automatically enabled in NetWare 6. Suballocation enables more efficient use of disk space because it enables blocks to contain data from more than one file.

Data migration is automatically disabled. Data migration is used to identify inactive files and move them to near-line storage systems, such as optical disks. Inactive files are files that have not been opened for a specified amount of time.

### Choose Graphical Mode for the Installation Program

**10.** After you have set up all the initial hardware features, the NetWare 6 system files are copied to the SYS: volume. If you are installing from the network rather than from a CD-ROM, you are prompted to reconnect to the network. To continue the installation, enter the password for the user that originally logged in. After the initial copy, the NetWare 6 installation program continues in graphical display mode.

Although a mouse is recommended to navigate the graphical display, you can use the keyboard commands shown in Table 2.5. In general, you use the arrow keys on the numeric keypad for cursor movements. Before trying to use these keys, make sure that the NumLock (number lock) key is on to enable cursor movement from the keypad.

TABLE 2.5

*Graphical Keyboard Actions*

| KEYSTROKE | ACTION |
| --- | --- |
| Tab | Move focus to next element. |
| Shift+Tab | Move focus to previous element. |
| Enter | Select. |
| Up-arrow (keypad 8) | Move cursor up. |
| Down-arrow (keypad 2) | Move cursor down. |
| Right-arrow (keypad 6) | Move cursor right. |

| KEYSTROKE | ACTION |
| --- | --- |
| Left-arrow (keypad 4) | Move cursor left. |
| Hold Shift while pressing keypad | Accelerate cursor movement. |
| Keypad 5 | Select or click an object (for dragging). |
| Keypad + (plus) | Double-click an object (to drop). |
| Alt+F7 | Move to next window. |
| Alt+F8 | Move to previous window. |

### Name the NetWare 6 Server

**11.** The first dialog box that appears in the NetWare 6 graphical display of the installation program names the NetWare 6 server. The NetWare 6 server must be unique among all other servers in the NDS tree. The server name can have from 2 to 47 alphanumeric characters and can contain underscores and dashes, but no spaces. The first character cannot be a period. Figure 2.10 shows this dialog box.

**FIGURE 2.10:** *The NetWare 6 server is named using the graphical display mode in the installation program.*

### Install the NetWare File System

**12.** After you give the NetWare 6 server a name, you are ready to create volumes in addition to the SYS: volume, which has already been created. You can create either traditional volumes or NSS volumes. You can create additional volumes from available disk space on your hard drive.

The traditional NetWare volume supports all the normal NetWare 6 features including suballocation, compression, data migration, and the transaction tracking system (TTS).

Novell Storage Services (NSS) is a newer file system introduced in NetWare 5 and enhanced for NetWare 6 (NSS version 3.0) that offers increased flexibility with large files, name spaces, and storage devices. NSS 3.0, which ships with Netware 6, uses a 64-bit interface and supports files and volumes up to 8TB each. NSS 3.0 supports the following new features:

- Data shredding (U.S. Green Book File Security Standard)
- Opportunistic (OP)-lock support for client caching
- XML-based management (which enables you to use Perl or other scripting languages to build your own management utilities)
- File service protocol independence for Network File System (NFS)
- Modified file lists for better streaming speeds during backup
- Software to support Redundant Array of Independent Disks (RAID) 0 with ConsoleOne management
- Please see the Novell Storage Services section later in this chapter.
- The dialog box shown in Figure 2.11 is used to create NetWare volumes from free space on disk drives. Notice that the SYS: volume already exists because it was created in an earlier process.
- As mentioned, you can create additional volumes from any available free space on a storage device. Volume names can have between 2 and 15 characters. Valid characters include A through Z, 0 through 9, and the following characters: ! - @ # $ % & ( ). The volume name can't begin with an underscore or have two or more consecutive underscores.

In NetWare 6, you can divide a large disk drive installed in the server into several volumes during installation. Conversely, you can distribute a volume over multiple physical disk drives. Be aware, however, that creating a volume that spans two or more storage devices is never recommended. If a volume spans disk devices and one of the devices fails, all data on the entire volume could be lost. We typically recommend that you create volumes that match the physical size of the disk device.

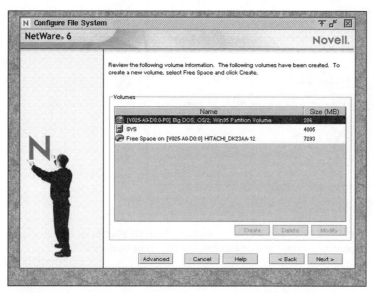

**FIGURE 2.11:** *You can create volumes from free space on disk drives. Using this utility, you can create either traditional NetWare volumes or NSS volumes. The NSS volumes were new in NetWare 5 and enhanced for NetWare 6 with NSS version 3.0.*

You can create traditional volumes from either traditional or unpartitioned free space as shown in Figure 2.12. In this example, we are creating a volume called VOL1.

To create a traditional volume, you simply select free space on the appropriate disk drive, select the volume type, and click the Create button. Next, type the name of the volume that you desire and click the OK button. To allocate only a portion of the free disk space to the volume, type the amount of space to use, and click the Apply to Volume button.

If you want to add more space to the volume, first make the volume include additional free space by selecting any additional free space on any disk device, type the amount of space to use on that device, and finally click the Apply to Volume button.

**FIGURE 2.12:** *The NetWare 6 installation program enables you to create volumes on the server. The volume called VOL1 is created as a traditional volume from the free space on the disk device.*

In addition to the traditional volumes, you can also create NSS volumes using this utility. In order to create the NSS volume, select the appropriate free space and click the Create button. Next select the Volume Type NSS option, type the name of the volume, and click OK.

If while creating the NSS volume you find that the Volume Type NSS option is not available, the selected free space is not available for NSS. This means that the disk device will not support the NSS file system. To continue, you need to go back to the previous screen and select another area of free space.

Figure 2.13 shows an example in the NetWare 6 installation program of creating an NSS volume.

In addition to creating new volumes for the NetWare 6 server, you can also modify the size of existing volumes, delete a volume, or mount volumes. When modifying the size of any existing volume, you can either increase or decrease it. To reduce the size of an existing volume, however, you must delete and re-create the volume. You can delete any volume you have created, except volume SYS. After a volume is deleted, all data on the volume is lost.

**FIGURE 2.13:** *You can create an NSS volume using the installation program. In order to create the NSS volume, select the appropriate free space and click the Create button. Next select the Volume Type NSS option, type the name of the volume, and click OK.*

In order for volumes to be accessed by NetWare 6, they must be mounted. Volumes can be mounted immediately or at the end of installation. If you created a traditional NetWare volume, the mounting time depends on its size. Figure 2.14 illustrates how new volumes can be mounted during the installation process. We recommend that you mount the volumes now if you plan to install additional products and services, such as the NetWare 6 documentation, on a volume other than volume SYS. You can also wait to mount volumes after the installation program completes, if you are installing products and services on volume SYS only.

### Install the Networking Protocols

The NetWare 6 server can be installed to support several different network protocol configurations. For example, the server can process Pure IP packets or IPX packets. In some cases, you may want to mix and match IP and IPX. If you are moving from NetWare 4 and IPX to NetWare 6 and Pure IP, you will want the compatibility of both protocols during the transition period. Therefore, you can set up your NetWare 6 server to install IP-Only, IPX-Only, or both protocols.

**FIGURE 2.14:** *The new volumes that you have created can be mounted either immediately or after the installation completes.*

NetWare 6 provides the NCPs to run on either IPX or IP. In a dual-stack environment, the NCP engine selects an IP connection before an IPX connection. If an IP connection is made, all of the NCP packets use the TCP transport for communication. One of the advantages of a protocol-independent system is that the system can support IP, IPX, or both concurrently. Thus, a significant opportunity exists for mixing and matching the multiple protocols to achieve migration goals.

In the NetWare 6 installation program, the protocols are assigned to network boards. Both the IPX and IP protocols can be assigned to a single network board, a fact that enables the server to communicate using IP and IPX. Figure 2.15 illustrates how you select the protocols to use during the installation process.

For IP-Only, you must have a unique IP address, a subnet mask, and a router or gateway address. Follow the onscreen install instructions. NetWare 6 automatically loads and binds the appropriate IP frame type for your network board. Passive support for IPX is still provided. The server responds to IPX requests but does not broadcast its service using IPX. For IPX-Only, follow the onscreen instructions. NetWare automatically loads and binds the appropriate IPX frame types for your network board. For IPX and IP together, likewise follow the onscreen instructions. Both protocols can be bound to a single network board. The server processes IP requests using Pure IP. The server also broadcasts and replies to IPX requests using IPX.

**FIGURE 2.15:** *The network protocols are assigned directly to the network boards. Both the IPX and IP protocols can be assigned to a single network board, a fact that enables the server to communicate using IP and IPX.*

### Set the Server's Time Zone

After you have selected the specific protocols that you want the server to use, you need to set the server's time zone in preparation for installing Novell Directory Services (NDS). In order to set the server's time zone, select the appropriate location where the server resides, as shown in Figure 2.16.

The server time and time zone are important in order to synchronize network events. Advanced time synchronization settings are available during the Customize section of the installation.

**FIGURE 2.16:** *The NetWare 6 installation program allows you to set the server's time zone by selecting the appropriate location where the server will reside physically.*

### Set Up or Install Novell Directory Services (NDS) eDirectory

Novell Directory Services (NDS) eDirectory is Novell's directory technology, which provides global access to all networking resources. Network resources such as servers and printers are presented hierarchically in an NDS tree. Users log into the NDS tree with a single login name and password instead of logging into specific servers. NDS allows users with the proper access rights to log into the network and view and access network resources.

A very important step during the installation of the NetWare 6 server is to set up NDS eDirectory. We recommend that, in order to complete this step, you understand the basic concepts relating to NDS eDirectory. These concepts include the NDS tree itself, NDS containers, and context. The NDS tree name is the top level of the available network resources and must be unique among other NDS tree names on the network. NDS container objects, much like subdirectories, contain network objects. The server can be installed into two types of container objects: Organization (O) and Organizational Unit (OU). The context, much like DOS directory paths, denotes the full path of a network object in the NDS tree. For example, a NetWare server might be installed into an Organizational Unit (OU) named Sales under the organization (O) named ACME. The context would be denoted as OU=SALES.O=ACME or SALES.ACME.

In order to install NDS eDirectory, you are offered the choice either to install the server into an existing NDS tree or to create a new NDS tree, as shown in Figure 2.17.

If you select an existing tree, the server is installed into an Organization or Organizational Unit object that already exists. The installation utility searches for all NDS eDirectory trees on your network. You must have Supervisor rights to a particular level in the tree in order to install the server there.

**FIGURE 2.17:** *During the installation process, you have a choice either to install the server into an existing NDS tree or to create a new NDS tree.*

In addition, if the NetWare 6 server being installed is going into an existing NetWare 4x or NetWare 5.x tree, it causes the schema to be updated with the latest NetWare 6 schema. Because the schema is being modified, you must have Supervisor rights at the [ROOT] of the existing NDS tree. You are prompted to enter the administrator name and password for the entire NDS tree.

Figure 2.18 shows what is needed to install the new NetWare 6 server into an existing NDS tree. Notice that you are required to provide the name and password for the user with administrator rights to the [ROOT] object of the tree.

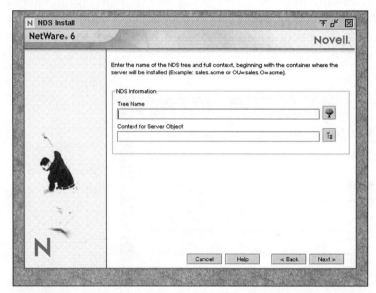

**FIGURE 2.18:** *If you have chosen to install the NetWare 6 server into an existing NDS tree, you are required to provide the tree name, the context for the server object, and the name and password for the user with administrative rights to the [ROOT] object of the tree.*

If you install the new NetWare 6 server into a new NDS tree, the installation prompts you to enter several pieces of information, as shown in Figure 2.19. For example, you must enter a new NDS tree name (in this case, the name is ACME_INC). The new NDS tree name must be unique in your network. Next, you enter the context or location for placement of the server object. Finally, you need to enter the name and password for a user with Supervisor rights at the O or OU where the server object will be installed.

**FIGURE 2.19:** *ACME_INC is the name of the new NDS tree in this example. In addition to the name, you are prompted to enter the context of the server object and the name and password for a user with Supervisor rights at the O or OU where the server object will be installed.*

When setting up a new NDS tree, be aware that the top level of the tree is the most important functionally because it serves as the foundation for the rest of the tree. The top of the tree is considered to be the first several levels of the tree and is generally based on the network infrastructure. For more information on NDS tree design, please refer to Chapter 5.

After you have entered the appropriate information, the new server is added to either the new or existing NDS tree. A message informs you that the install of NDS has been successful, as shown in Figure 2.20. The message also informs you that the new NDS tree has been created or the server has been installed.

**FIGURE 2.20:** *After you have entered and accepted the appropriate information to install the new server, an NDS summary screen is displayed. This is the case whether you installed the server using the new or existing NDS tree options.*

The NetWare 6 server object and volume objects have been installed in the container you specified. If you have created a new NDS tree, a user (default name ADMIN or whatever name you've specified) with Supervisor rights to the NDS tree is created in the O or Organizational container. It is important that you record the administrator password and other relevant information so that you can give Supervisor access to your network.

### License the NetWare 6 Server

The new NetWare 6 server must have a valid license in order to function properly. You can install the license from the NetWare 6 License disk or browse to a directory that contains NetWare 6 licenses. Figure 2.21 illustrates how you can install the license file for NetWare 6 server.

Although the server can be installed without a license, the unlicensed server allows only two user connections. If you choose to initially install the NetWare 6 server without the license, you can use the NetWare Administrator (NWADMIN) utility to install licenses at a later date.

**FIGURE 2.21:** *The NetWare 6 server license is installed from the NetWare 6 License disk that comes with the server software.*

**NOTE**

**Keep in mind that the license file for the three-user version found in this book is part of the NetWare 6 CD-ROM. There is no separate license file. After you are prompted for a license, hit F9 to continue with the install. You may be prompted with a message that the license did not install. Disregard the message. You will be able to connect three users to your test NetWare 6 server.**

### Install Other Networking Products

After you complete installation of the main server component, the NetWare 6 server installation is basically complete. However, you now have the option to select other networking products to install. The other networking products provide enhanced functionality, such as network management and Internet access, to NetWare 6. In order to install any of the optional networking products, select the appropriate check boxes next to the products that you want to be installed, as shown in Figure 2.22.

**FIGURE 2.22:** *The NetWare 6 installation program allows you to install additional networking products after the main server components have been installed. Although you can choose which products to install, installing the products that are already selected by default ensures that you include the features recommended for NetWare.*

After you have selected and accepted the additional networking products, a summary dialog box is presented, giving you the required space needed to install the products, as shown in Figure 2.23. Keep in mind that you will be required to enter additional parameters for each product you select beyond the defaults.

You can customize installation of many of the networking products for your networking environment. To customize the products and components, click the Customize button. For more information on customizing the additional networking products, refer to the later section, "Customizing the NetWare 6 Installation."

**FIGURE 2.23:** *The installation program shows you a summary dialog box for the additional networking products. This dialog box shows you the space requirements to install the products.*

### Complete the Server Installation

If you do not want or need to customize the additional networking products, basic server installation is now complete. Depending on which additional products you are installing, you may be prompted to insert additional CD-ROMs.

From the summary screen (shown in Figure 2.23), click the Finish button to begin installing NetWare 6 and additional products. After all files are copied, installation is completed, and a message is displayed. Figure 2.24 shows the Installation Complete dialog box.

After the files are copied, you need to reboot the NetWare 6 server by simply selecting or clicking the Yes button. NetWare 6 is automatically loaded after the computer reboots, or you can load it manually. To load the server manually, reboot the server by clicking Yes, change to the startup directory containing the NetWare server files (C:\NWSERVER), and type **SERVER**.

**FIGURE 2.24:** *The NetWare 6 server installation is complete after it copies all the files for the additional networking products. You need to reboot the server in order for the settings to take effect.*

## Customizing the NetWare 6 Installation

This section of the chapter describes how to set advanced options and customize installation of your new NetWare 6 server. Advanced options are available throughout the installation, and customization is available from the summary dialog box at the end of the installation program.

After you select the additional networking products and services to install, the installation program provides a summary dialog box with a Customize button. You need to select this button if you want to customize the installation of each product and service for your networking environment.

The products and services are contained in several major categories that are presented to you as shown in Figure 2.25. The customization options categories are as follows:

- The NetWare operating system
- The file system

- ▶ Network protocols
- ▶ Timesync
- ▶ NDS

**FIGURE 2.25:** *The installation program enables you to customize the additional products and services. In order to customize a product, select Customize at the bottom of the screen and click OK.*

### NetWare Operating System Properties

NetWare operating system properties include the STARTUP.NCF, CONFIG.SYS, AUTOEXEC.NCF, AUTOEXEC.BAT, SERVER PROPERTIES, and Language files. Keep in mind that on a new server install, the STARTUP.NCF and AUTOEXEC. NCF are not visible because they have not been created. You can access each file by selecting NetWare OS and the Configure button on the right side of your screen.

For example, the server's number can be modified at this point if needed. Changing the server ID number during customization places the new server ID number in the AUTOEXEC.NCF file. The new server ID number takes effect only after you reboot the server.

Using the this menu, you can customize NetWare 6 as shown in Figure 2.26.

**FIGURE 2.26:** *The Configure button is used to customize NetWare 6 to make a change to the server ID number.*

In addition to the NetWare OS settings, you can also provide settings for the NetWare 6 Services. These services include any of the additional functions you have elected to install, such as the NetWare Enterprise Web server, FTP server, and so on. Some have properties that can be modified here. For example, you can specify where you would like the Certificate Server object to be stored during this installation. Figure 2.27 illustrates how you can specify where to store the server certificate object. Select NetWare 6 Services⇨Novell Certificate Server⇨Configure to see this screen.

The file system option allows you view existing volumes and their components and to create new partitions if desired. You can also mount volumes from this page as shown in Figure 2.28.

**FIGURE 2.27:** *Using this utility, you can decide where to store the server certificate object.*

**FIGURE 2.28:** *The file system configuration option allows you to create, modify, and mount volumes on your NetWare server.*

The component screen for the NetWare Operating System lists the products and services that will be installed for each component. As shown in Figure 2.29, checking a box adds the entire component to the list of products and services to install. Unchecking a box removes the entire component from the list of products and services to be installed.

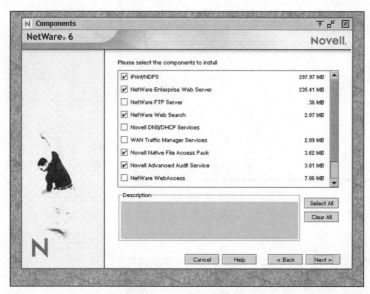

**FIGURE 2.29:** *The Component screen in NetWare Operating System install enables you to control which products and services will be installed for each component.*

### File System Properties

You are able to customize the NetWare file system — the physical and logical aspects of storing files on storage devices, such as a disk drive. The file system consists of partitions, volumes, and free space. You can customize the NetWare file system by performing these tasks:

▶ Viewing available free space

▶ Creating, modifying, and deleting partitions

▶ Creating, modifying, and deleting volumes

▶ Mounting volumes

Figure 2.30 shows the File System Properties dialog box.

**FIGURE 2.30:** *You are able to customize the NetWare file system — the physical and logical aspects of storing files on storage devices, such as a disk drive. The file system consists of partitions, volumes, and free space.*

Free space represents space available on storage devices for creating partitions and volumes. Several different types of free space can exist in NetWare. These include free space, NetWare partition free space, unpartitioned free space, and not partitioned free space. To create a traditional volume, you can use either free space or NetWare partition free space. To create an NSS volume, you can use free space, unpartitioned free space, or not partitioned free space.

As you know, partitions subdivide a physical storage device. Several types of server hardware can exist. For example, the server boot partition is typically formatted with DOS. The boot partition contains the files that load the NetWare operating system. In addition, the server always contains at least one traditional partition that holds the SYS:volume. This partition cannot be modified or deleted. The main purpose of the SYS:volume is to contain server system setup information.

Besides the boot partition and the partition used by the SYS:volume, you can create other partitions from any available free space on the server. You can create either standard (traditional) partitions or NSS partitions. The volumes in NetWare subdivide a partition. This means that the volumes are created within a partition. You can create two types of volumes:

▸ **Traditional volumes** — Traditional volumes can be created within NetWare (or NetWare traditional) partitions.

▸ **NSS volumes** — NSS volumes can be created within NetWare NSS partitions.

After you have created either a traditional or NSS partition, you then need to establish or create the NetWare volume from the partition. Traditional partitions can contain only traditional volumes. Likewise, NSS partitions can contain only NSS volumes. To create a traditional volume from a traditional partition, select the NetWare partition or traditional partition listed. Continue the process by clicking the New Volume button and naming the volume. Figure 2.31 gives you an example of creating traditional NetWare volumes from a partition.

**FIGURE 2.31:** *You can create a traditional volume from a traditional partition by first selecting the partition. You need to give the new volume a name.*

You can accept the default size of the volume or change the volume size by entering the amount of disk space. If required, increase the size of the volume by selecting another free space and clicking the Apply to Volume button.

In order to create an NSS volume, select the Unpartitioned free space and click New Partition. You need to give a name to the volume. The installation program attempts to take all the available free space and make it the volume. You can decide to accept the default size of the volume or change the volume size by entering the amount of disk space. Finish the process by clicking the Apply to Volume button. In addition, you can increase the size of the volume by selecting another free space and applying it to the volume. Figure 2.32 illustrates an example creating an NSS volume from the free space available on the server.

As always, in order for volumes to be accessed by NetWare, they must be mounted. Volumes can be mounted immediately or at the end of the customization or installation process.

**FIGURE 2.32:** *You can create an NSS volume by selecting the available free space on the server.*

### Network Protocols

NetWare 6 provides support for Internet Protocol (IP) and the Internetwork Packet Exchange (IPX) protocol. Figure 2.33 shows an example of configuring the network protocols. You can bind and configure either IPX or IP for the server.

**FIGURE 2.33:** *The installation program uses the Protocols Properties dialog box to customize the configuration of the IPX and IP network protocols.*

Although the basic installation selects the default IPX frame types for your network, you can decide which frame types the server will support. Each frame type that is used on the network is treated as a logical network segment and requires its own IPX network address, even though each frame type is using the same network board and physical cable segment. To add IPX frame types from the Protocols Properties dialog box, check the box of the desired frame type and enter the network address. This is the IPX address, which is a hexadecimal number of one to eight digits (1 to FFFFFFFE) that identifies a specific network cable segment.

In addition, you can customize the IP configuration by specifying an IP address, which identifies each device on the network. The address consists of 32 bits, which are represented as decimal values separated by periods, such as 145.45.67.89. If your server connects to the Internet, you must obtain a unique IP address. For information on receiving an IP address, contact your Internet service provider (ISP). IP addressing typically requires you to provide the subnet mask and router addresses.

Subnet masks enable you to break up your network into smaller networks. Your network could have too many nodes or could be too geographically diverse to manage as a single network. Dividing your network into smaller networks with their own addresses allows the network routers to filter and reduce the network activity seen by any of the nodes. However, this approach might not be appropriate on a large network that needs to appear to network administrators as a single network.

The router (gateway) is the address of the router that connects two different environments such as a LAN and the Internet. You can enter a specific router (gateway) address, or you can rely on the network to automatically find the nearest router. If you specify the address, remember that the router must exist on your network segment.

**IPX Compatibility**     NetWare 6 enables you to provide compatibility between legacy IPX services and new Pure IP services. This compatibility option, called IPX compatibility, is essential to an upgrade or migration process. It is also key in supporting a mixture of both IPX and IP services on the same wire. IPX compatibility, often called Compatibility Mode, consists of redirectors, a protocol Migration Agent (MA), a bindery population agent, and the Service Location Protocol (SLP). The combined use of these components creates the on-demand virtual IPX network within the IP network while allowing only IP packets to cross the wire. Moreover, Compatibility Mode provides continuity of communication between IP-based networks and IPX-based networks, and it supports SAP and RIP using SLP.

In order to enable IPX compatibility, you need to use the dialog box shown in Figure 2.34. When the appropriate box is checked, IPX compatibility is enabled to provide support for applications requiring IPX. Although the server does not broadcast services using RIP and SAP, NetWare 6 processes any IPX request that arrives at the server.

IPX compatibility uses a Compatibility Mode network number and allows you to load the Migration Agent on the server. The Compatibility Mode network number is an eight-digit hexadecimal number that identifies the IPX compatibility mode network. It functions as a virtual IPX network number. All compatibility devices, such as clients, servers, and Migration Agents, must use the same compatibility mode network number in order to communicate. The number must be unique among other numbers, such as the server ID number and the IPX network number. The default compatibility mode network number is FFFFFFFD.

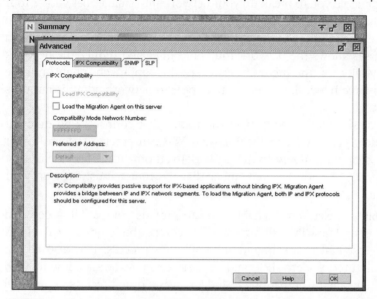

**FIGURE 2.34:** *The installation program provides IPX compatibility through the Protocols Properties dialog box. IPX compatibility provides a virtual IPX network within the IP network while allowing only IP packets to cross the wire.*

NetWare 6 provides the capability to regulate IP and IPX protocols using a Migration Agent. A Migration Agent regulates the protocol function on different network segments. If a Migration Agent is not enabled, packets will not be forwarded onto network segments communicating with a different protocol. The following are the two different configurations for the Migration Agent depending on the number of network boards in the server:

- **One network board** — If your server contains only a single network board, enabling Migration Agent causes IPX packets destined for other networks to be "tunneled" in IP packets.

- **Two network boards** — If your server contains two network boards, enabling Migration Agent causes the server to function as a gateway that filters or forwards the packets in each network environment. For example, a server acting as a Migration Agent can have one network board communicating with the IP network and another network board communicating with IPX. IPX requests destined to travel across the IP network are tunneled in IP packets. IP packets destined to travel across the

IPX network segment are tunneled in IPX packets. Separating the protocols on network segments reduces the traffic on both segments. IPX packets such as RIP and SAP are kept on the IPX segment, while IP packets remain on the IP segment.

**Domain Name Service (DNS)**    NetWare 6 has added support for Domain Name Service (DNS), which provides the functionality that matches text names, such as novell.com, with numbers used by computers, such as 145.45.67.89. For example, a workstation on a TCP/IP network uses the DNS to find the addresses to locate a NetWare server or other network resources. If you have an existing domain naming system already installed on your network, you want to enter its domain name and name server(s) in the setup screen shown in Figure 2.35. If you want to install Novell's DNS on your network, you must return to the Summary dialog box and install Novell DNS/DHCP Services in Other Products and Services.

**FIGURE 2.35:** *The NetWare Installation program enables you to set up and customize the DNS setting for the server.*

During setup of DNS, you are asked to supply the domain name. A *domain name* divides the Internet into functional categories. The top-level domains identify types of organizations, such as commercial (com), educational (edu), government (gov), international entities (int), U.S. military agencies (mil), network providers (net), and other organizations (org). Domain names can also use two-letter country codes to specify geographical locations such as United States (us) or United Kingdom (uk). Domain names are separated into individual levels with periods, such as sales.acme.com or norad.acme.co.us.

In addition to domain names, DNS manages domain name servers. A *name server* is a computer that translates names into IP addresses for other devices, such as workstations on the network. To obtain the name, NetWare 6 searches the IP address of each name server in the sequence entered into the Name Server field.

**iPrint/NDPS**    You can customize your configuration of iPrint/NDPS services by specifying the location of your NDPS resource database and selecting the print drivers to be installed. To configure iPrint/NDPS you can select the iPrint/NDPS option under the NetWare 6 Services dialog box shown in Figure 2.36. After selecting this option, select the Configure option on your screen.

**FIGURE 2.36:** *You can set up iPrint/NDPS services by using the customize option of the NetWare 6 install.*

NDS PropertiesThe first dialog box that appears when you select NDS Properties is an NDS summary page that details the current NDS installation (shown in Figure 2.37). It lists the NDS tree name, server context, and administrator name and context. This page is for informational purposes only; nothing can be changed or modified using it.

**FIGURE 2.37:** *The NDS Properties dialog box includes an informational summary detailing the current NDS eDirectory installation. It lists the NDS tree name, server context, and administrator name and context. You cannot change or modify any of the NDS settings from this screen.*

**SNMP Configuration**  Under the protocols heading you can configure devices for SNMP, as shown in Figure 2.38. The information to be sent when an event occurs can include the server name, hardware description, server location, and administrator name. Any or all of this information is recorded when an event occurs. You can also specify where to send the SNMP information, that is, which devices receive the information when an SNMP event occurs. Each device should be running an SNMP-compatible management utility such as the ManageWise utility.

You can specify IPX and IP destination addresses for the devices to receive the information, for example, the IPX or IP trap destination address. A device's IPX trap destination address includes the network and node numbers separated by a colon, such as 01010340:1233456789. The IP trap destination address is the IP address of the destination device in standard notation, such as 145.45.67.89.

**FIGURE 2.38:** *You can configure SNMP settings under the Protocols section, SNMP.*

Time SynchronizationThe NetWare installation program allows you to specify the type of time server you want the server to be. The purpose of a time server is to synchronize the reported time across the network and provide expiration dates and time stamps to establish the order of events taking place in NDS. Figure 2.39 shows an example of how you can establish the proper time server type for your server.

NetWare 6 distinguishes three types of time servers that provide network time: single-reference, reference, and primary. All other servers are called secondary time servers because they receive their time from the time providers. A single-reference time server is typically the first server in a network. The installation program automatically designates the first NetWare 6 server installed as a single-reference time server. The single-reference time server is then able to provide time to the entire network.

A primary time server is responsible for determining and setting the network time. A primary time server polls other primary and reference servers to determine the "average network time," which is then distributed to other requesting servers.

A network usually has only one reference time server. A reference time server provides a network time for all primary time servers to migrate to. It is used on larger networks where primary time servers are required.

**FIGURE 2.39:** *The NetWare installation program allows you to specify the type of time server you want the server to be.*

By default, all servers except the first server are designated as secondary time servers. The installation process of a typical NetWare 6 server automatically sets the server to be a secondary time server. The secondary time servers rely on other sources, such as a single-reference time server, to provide them with network time. A secondary time server can get the network time from another secondary time server or from a single-reference, reference, or primary time server.

**Novell Distributed Print Services (NDPS)** Novell Distributed Print Services (NDPS) is installed by default on each NetWare 6 server. An NDPS resource database (in the SYS:NDPS\REDIR directory) used by the NDPS Resource Management Service (RMS) is copied automatically to that server. The RMS is a central repository for network resources and services. It contains printer drivers, banners, printer definition (NPD) files, and possibly fonts.

If you choose to customize NDPS, you are asked whether you want to create a new Broker object on this server and whether you want the different brokered services to be enabled. In general, you want these services, including the resource database for the Resource Management Service, available for each broker that you create. If disk space is an issue on a specific server and you do not intend to create a Broker object on that server, be sure the Copy Resource Files box is not checked. This saves approximately 60MB of disk space on that server.

## The NWCONFIG Utility

The NWCONFIG utility allows you to perform many routine tasks on your NetWare 6 servers, ranging from loading and unloading drivers to removing and reinstalling NDS. The NWCONFIG utility is the former INSTALL utility found on NetWare 4.*x* versions. NWCONFIG includes all the functionality of INSTALL and additional functionality. In this section, we primarily highlight what is new to this utility and do not discuss every option it includes.

You can initiate the NWCONFIG utility by typing NWCONFIG at any NetWare 6 server console or through the RCONSOLE utility. An example of the main screen for NWCONFIG is shown in Figure 2.40.

**FIGURE 2.40:** *The NWCONFIG main screen*

With NWCONFIG, you can perform the following functions:

- ▸ **Driver Options** — Load/unload disk and network drivers and perform configuration of disk, storage, and network drivers.

- ▸ **Legacy Disk Options** — Configure NetWare partitions/volumes is now available under ConsoleOne under the Disk Management item of the Tools menu.

▶ **NSS Disk Options** — Configure NSS storage and volumes is now available under ConsoleOne under the Disk Management item of the Tools menu.

▶ **License Options** — Covers all capabilities of licensing including installation, removal, and set up of licenses.

▶ **Copy File Options** — Install NetWare system files. This option should not be used to install a different version of NetWare.

▶ **Directory Options** — Handle many different directory functions, including the following:

- Install Directory Services onto this server
- Remove Directory Services from this server
- Upgrade NetWare 3.*x* bindery information to the Directory
- Upgrade mounted volumes into the Directory
- Perform Directory backup and restore options
- Extend the schema

▶ **NCF files options** — Create and edit server startup files including the AUTOEXEC.NCF and STARTUP.NCF files and upgrade a v3.1*x* AUTOEXEC.NCF file.

▶ **Multi CPU Options** — Install and uninstall SMP functionality.

▶ **Product Options** — Install other product information.

# Novell Storage Services

Novell Storage Services (NSS) is a product that runs on your NetWare 5 or NetWare 6 server. NetWare 6 introduced NSS version 3.0. In addition to the traditional NetWare file system, administrators and users can now take advantage of Novell Storage Services, which offers more flexibility for storage and file management than previous versions of NetWare. Here are some of the advantages:

▶ NSS is ideal for systems with large files and volumes or large numbers of volumes, directories, and files. NSS allows up to an 8 terabyte file size and holds up to 8 trillion files in an NSS volume. You can also mount up to 255 NSS volumes on a server. You no longer need to worry about file or volume limitations; you are limited only by the capacity of your storage devices.

▶ With NSS, hard disk space can be fully utilized. Unused free space on all hard drives in unpartitioned space attached to your server or in NetWare volumes (including SYS) can be combined into a storage pool and used to create NSS volumes.

▶ NSS volumes mount rapidly and with less RAM than ever before. You can mount any number of NSS volumes and any size NSS volume with as little as 1MB RAM.

▶ NSS is now the default method for mounting CD-ROMs as volumes, offering much faster access to multiple CD-ROM drives installed in towers.

As future storage device types appear on the market, new NSS modules can be developed to recognize the devices for the pool. This means that no matter what type of device you have attached to your server, NSS will recognize it and be able to use the available free space for NSS volumes if the device can be written to.

NSS and the traditional NetWare file system run side by side. You can create up to 64 NetWare volumes or 256 NSS and NetWare volumes combined, including volume SYS. The choice is yours, as long as you have at least one NetWare volume, SYS, on each server.

Before creating an NSS volume, make sure you have met the following requirements:

▶ A server running NetWare 6.

▶ A minimum of 10MB space free for an NSS volume. If you have only one hard drive and you did not allocate enough free space in your NetWare partition and NetWare volume for NSS, reconfigure your drive to allow the required 10MB space.

▶ 1.5MB RAM (300 cache buffers) for loading the modules.

▶ 2MB memory (500 cache buffers) for running NSS.

You can then follow these instructions after loading the ConsoleOne utility from your NetWare 6 server.

**1.** Select Tools menu in the ConsoleOne utility. An example of this screen is shown in Figure 2.41.

**FIGURE 2.41:** *The NSS Configuration screen in the ConsoleOne Utility*

**2.** Select the Disk Management option. This option enables you to view and prepare free space for NSS configuration. It contains these options: Update Provider Information, Assign Ownership, Release Ownership, View Free Space, and Return to the Previous Menu.

NSS scans your devices to find free space for NSS to use, and it lists the free space on each device as a separate storage deposit object. You can also view free space. After NSS has taken free space, you can create your storage groups and NSS volumes.

**3.** Select NSS Volume Options. Before you enter the options, you must authenticate to NDS using Administrator rights. NSS Volume Options enables you to create one or more NSS volumes. The volume options are Create, Modify, Delete, View Volumes, and Return to the Previous Menu.

To create a single NSS volume from a single device, you select Create ⇨ NSS Volume, select a managed object marked Single, select a name for your volume, and then confirm your choice.

To create multiple NSS volumes in one storage group, first create the storage group by selecting Create ⇨ Storage Group and confirming your choice. You then select Create ➪ NSS Volume, select a managed object marked Group, select the volume size, select the name, and confirm your choice. For additional NSS volumes, you select NSS Volume again and repeat the steps, segmenting your volumes according to how much space you have in your storage group.

**4.** At the server console prompt, mount the newly created NSS volume by entering this command:

mount volume_name

where the volume_name is the name of the new NSS volume. You can use the mount all command if you prefer.

When you enter NSS volumes from the command line, you see the new NSS volume and an additional NSS_Admin volume — a read-only volume that contains configuration information describing NSS objects.

**NOTE** **CD-ROMs recognized by NSS are mounted automatically. In NetWare 6, this happens when the NetWare 6 version of the CDROM .NLM is loaded. The CD and CD-ROM utilities used in previous releases of NetWare are no longer supported.**

## Installing NetWare 6 Licenses

Novell License Services enables you to easily install additional licenses to your NetWare 6 server. After loading NWADMIN32 at your NetWare 6 server, follow these steps to install NetWare 6 licenses:

**1.** Select Tools ➪ Novell Licensing Services ➪ Add Licenses.

**2.** Select Add License File.

**3.** Select a path to the .NLF file that has the license. The default path is SYS:\LICENSE. However, your license may be on a floppy disk or CD-ROM.

**4.** Log in by entering the administrator's complete name and password.

**5.** At the Installable Licenses screen, select an envelope file. An envelope file contains one or more licenses. A sample envelope file is 42c1f1d.nlf.

**6.** Exit NWADMIN.

You can now view the installed licenses by using NLS Manager's Tree View or NetWare Administrator. An example of the NLS screen in NWADMIN by selecting Generate License Reports is shown in Figure 2.42.

**FIGURE 2.42:** *NetWare Licensing Services*

## Novell Directory Services

This option under NWCONFIG enables you to perform many NDS operations such as the installation and removal of Directory Services. It also enables you to move NetWare 3.*x* bindery information to the Directory and upgrade mounted volumes to the Directory. An example of this screen is shown in Figure 2.43.

**FIGURE 2.43:** *The Directory Services Options screen*

## NDS Backup and Restore

An important feature of the Directory Services screen is that of performing NDS maintenance. With this feature, you can back up and restore the NDS data files that are stored on your NetWare 6 server. This is helpful whenever you need to perform a hardware upgrade on a NetWare 6 server. Keep in mind that this is a separate process additional to doing a full backup of your NetWare 6 server. For more information on backup and restore through Novell's enhanced SBACKUP utility, see Chapter 18.

To initiate a backup of your NDS files before a hardware upgrade, you need to select the option that says Save Local DS Information Prior to Hardware Upgrade, as shown in Figure 2.44.

**FIGURE 2.44:** *The NDS backup and restore options*

After selecting this screen, you are prompted to perform a backup of the NDS files on this server. Doing so creates a temporary file called BACKUP.NDS that stores all NDS and replica information in that server's SYS:SYSTEM directory as well as disables NDS on this system until you perform your hardware upgrade and do a restore of the backup file. This screen is shown in Figure 2.45.

You then are prompted to log into the Directory Services Login/Authentication screen. Enter the administrator name and password; the system logs you into the Directory and creates the BACKUP.NDS file.

You can then exit the NWCONFIG utility and bring down the NetWare 6 server.

**FIGURE 2.45:** *Getting ready to back up NDS data*

After you make the changes to the hardware (or you've installed a new NetWare 6 server), you can load NWCONFIG again. Go to the Directory Services options and select the option that says Restore Local NDS Information after Hardware Upgrade, as shown in Figure 2.46. You can then specify the path to restore the information from.

**FIGURE 2.46:** *Restoring the NDS information to a NetWare 6 server*

NOTE

**You can also use this utility to perform a backup and restore after a hardware failure. Obviously, this requires that you have run the backup procedure beforehand and have stored the BACKUP.NDS file on another machine elsewhere.**

## Product Options

The last screen in the NWCONFIG utility is the Product Options screen. This option enables you to install new products to your NetWare 6 server. An example of this screen is shown in Figure 2.47.

**FIGURE 2.47:** *Installing other products on a NetWare 6 server*

# The ConsoleOne Utility

ConsoleOne is a newer Java-based tool for managing your network and its resources. ConsoleOne lets you manage the following:

- ▶ NDS eDirectory objects, schema, partitions, and replicas
- ▶ NetWare server resources

If you install other Novell products, additional capabilities are automatically snapped in to ConsoleOne. For example, if you install Novell eDirectory, the capability to configure the LDAP interface to eDirectory is automatically snapped in to ConsoleOne.

This section explains the basics of ConsoleOne including how to install and start ConsoleOne.

ConsoleOne is installed when you install NDS eDirectoy and NetWare 6. But, if you don't have it already installed, you can follow these instructions:

**I.** If a previous version of ConsoleOne is running on the Windows computer, exit it.

**2.** Insert the CD-ROM that contains ConsoleOne, or go to www.novell.com/downloads to download the free software.

**3.** Browse the CD-ROM or Web site until you find the available ConsoleOne packages, and select the package for Windows/NetWare.

**TIP**

**If you are using a CD-ROM that runs an installation program and you see an option to install just ConsoleOne, choose that option and skip to Step 5.**

**4.** If you are using the Web site, download and unzip the ConsoleOne files to a temporary area. If you are using a CD-ROM, skip this step.

**5.** Run the installation executable file (SETUP.EXE or CONSOLEONE.EXE). Follow the onscreen instructions to complete the installation.

### Starting ConsoleOne on Windows

If ConsoleOne is installed locally on the Windows computer, simply double-click the ConsoleOne icon on the desktop.

### Configuring ConsoleOne Accessibility

To make ConsoleOne accessible to Windows assistive technologies, you must install the Java Access Bridge. The Java Access Bridge is a technology used to expose the Java Accessibility API in a Windows DLL so that Windows assistive technologies can provide access to applications and applets running with a Java Virtual Machine on a Windows system and implementing the Java Accessibility API.

To set up the Java Access Bridge for use with ConsoleOne, follow these steps:

**1.** Download the Java Access Bridge from the Java Access Bridge Web site at www.sun.com.

**2.** Unpack the Java Access Bridge into the C:\ACCESSBRIDGE-1_0 directory and run the following command:

```
C:\ACCESSBRIDGE-1_0\INSTALLER\INSTALL
```

For more information on installing and configuring the Java Access Bridge, see the Java Access Bridge README.

### NetWare

If you install ConsoleOne on a NetWare server, you can run it locally on that server or remotely on a Windows computer with a drive mapped to that server.

Installing ConsoleOne on a NetWare server also allows other Novell products such as eDirectory to add needed snap-ins to your installation.

## Installing ConsoleOne on NetWare

1. Bring down Java and any Java applications that are running on the server, including the server GUI.

   You can do this by typing **JAVA -EXIT** at the console prompt.

2. Have all users who are currently running ConsoleOne remotely through a connection to the server exit their ConsoleOne sessions.

3. At a Windows workstation, map a drive letter to the root of the server's SYS: volume.

4. At the same workstation, insert the CD-ROM that contains ConsoleOne, or go to www.novell.com/download.

5. Browse the CD-ROM or Web site until you find the available ConsoleOne packages, and select the package for Windows/NetWare.

6. If you are using the Web site, download and unzip the ConsoleOne files to a temporary area. If you are using a CD-ROM, skip this step.

7. Run the installation executable file (SETUP.EXE or CONSOLEONE.EXE).

8. Follow the onscreen instructions to complete the installation. When you are prompted for the location to install to, select the drive that is mapped to the root of the server's SYS:volume.

**You must select a drive that is mapped to a letter, not a UNC path.**

IMPORTANT

## Starting ConsoleOne on NetWare 6

Remember these points when starting ConsoleOne on NetWare 6:

▶ To start ConsoleOne locally on a NetWare server, type **C1START** at the console prompt.

▶ To start ConsoleOne remotely from a Windows computer with a drive mapped to the NetWare server, see your Novell documentation.

▶ For help with navigating and performing basic tasks in ConsoleOne. If you encounter problems starting or using ConsoleOne, see your Novell documentation.

# The NetWare Administrator (NWADMN32.EXE) Utility

As mentioned in the first chapter, Novell provides two utilities for managing your NetWare 6 network. These utilities are ConsoleOne and NWADMIN. Both utilities have similar functionality, but Novell is moving toward ConsoleOne with more functionality in each subsequent release. However, some options, such as licensing, discussed earlier, are still found in NWADMIN.

The NetWare Administrator utility, or NWADMN32.EXE, is a Windows-based utility that makes changes to the Directory as easy as the point and click of a mouse. This utility is used by system administrators to manage objects in the NDS tree. Figure 2.48 shows the main window for the 32-bit NWADMIN utility, which has an executable filename of NWADMN32.EXE.

Because NWADMN32.EXE is a Windows-based utility, it enables you to graphically manage all objects and properties in the NDS tree, which you can create, change, or browse by selecting or clicking the individual NDS objects.

The NWADMIN utility is executed at a client workstation from Windows. With this utility, you can view, create, move, delete, and assign rights to the individual objects in the NDS tree. Typically, the individuals using NWADMIN will be system administrators with Supervisor rights over their container objects.

**FIGURE 2.48:** *The main window for the 32-bit NWADMIN utility (called NWADMN32.EXE)*

**TIP**

**You may limit access to the NWADMIN utility by moving the utility from the SYS:\PUBLIC subdirectory to another subdirectory that only administrators have access to. Most of your users will not need to use this utility.**

In order to execute this utility, you must have the NetWare DOS Requester, VLMs, or Client 32 software running on the workstation. Make sure that you have loaded the appropriate client software, or the NWADMIN utility will not load. (For more information on client software, see Chapter 18.) The 32-bit NWADMIN works with Novell's Client 32 for DOS/Windows and Windows 95/98.

You can use this utility to organize, manage, and browse the NDS objects that are contained in the tree by performing any of these functions:

- ► Create and manage NDS objects.
- ► Assign rights in the NDS tree and file system.
- ► Set up the print services.
- ► Display or browse object and property information stored in the tree.
- ► Set up and manage the NDS partitions and replicas through NDS Manager as a snap-in utility.

## Using NWADMIN to Create and Manage NDS Objects

You can use NWADMIN to create, delete, modify, rename, move, and get detailed information about NDS objects. In order to create an NDS object, you must first be logged into the tree as an individual who has rights, such as the ADMIN (or other administrative) user at the container where you want to create the object.

For example, in order to create the user CN=GWASHINGTON in the container OU=RIO.O=ACME, move to that container in the tree and select the Create option from the Object menu. Figure 2.49 shows the New Object dialog box that is displayed after the Create option is selected.

You can then select the User object from the list of objects, and you are presented with the Create User dialog box to fill out. Figure 2.50 shows the Create User dialog box for the user GWASHINGTON in the container RIO.ACME.

**FIGURE 2.49:** *The New Object dialog box in NWADMIN is displayed after the Create option is selected.*

**FIGURE 2.50:** *The Create User dialog box in NWADMIN for the user GWASHINGTON.RIO.ACME*

You can also use this utility to delete or rename any of the NDS objects. You can also move a selected NDS object from one location in the NDS tree to another. Figure 2.51 shows how the move operation for ALINCOLN might look. In this figure, we are moving CN=ALINCOLN from the ADMIN.RIO.ACME to AUDIT.ADMIN.RIO.O=ACME.

**FIGURE 2.51:** *The NWADMIN screen for moving CN=ALINCOLN from the ADMIN.RIO.ACME to AUDIT.ADMIN.RIO.ACME.*

## Using NWADMIN to Assign Rights to the NDS Tree and File System

This object-oriented look of the utility makes the assignment of rights much easier. Rights to users, groups, containers (OUs), files, and directories can be assigned by simply dragging and dropping one icon onto another.

For example, when a user changes departments, you simply drag and drop the user to give that user the appropriate rights or move the user with the move command. Figure 2.52 shows the operation of dragging and dropping one object onto another to give it rights.

The operation of dragging and dropping is also used to assign rights to the files and directories in the file system. You can bring up the Details dialog box for an object and assign file and directories rights there. For example, in Figure 2.53, the NDS group object called CN=COMMON in the container ADMIN.RIO.ACME is granted rights to the COMMON subdirectory stored on the server CAM-SRV1.

**FIGURE 2.52:** *The NWADMIN windows associated with the operation of dragging and dropping one object onto another to give it rights*

**FIGURE 2.53:** *The NDS group object called CN=COMMON in the container ADMIN.RIO.ACME is granted rights to the COMMON subdirectory stored on the server CAM-SRV1.*

Adding file system directory or object rights in previous versions of NetWare required a multilayered menu utility and a tedious process of adding each user. Now all that is needed to add file system directory rights is to drag the user's icon over to the specific directory or object, and NetWare simply asks you for a confirmation.

Because all the network resources in the NDS tree are represented by NWADMIN, managing multiple NetWare 6 servers is greatly simplified. Instead of managing a single server, you can focus your management efforts on a group of servers.

For more information on assigning rights, refer to Chapter 13.

## Using NWADMIN to Set Up the Print Services

The NWADMIN utility can also be used to set up and manage the printing environment. NWADMIN is a functional equivalent to the PCONSOLE utility in DOS. For example, in order to create a printer, select the desired container where the printer will be located. Select Create from the Option menu and then select Printer as the object to create. Figure 2.54 shows the dialog box that appears.

**FIGURE 2.54:** *Creating a printer object in NWADMIN*

From the screen shown in Figure 2.54, you can click the Define Additional Properties button to define characteristics of the printer. If you select the additional properties, the Printer dialog box appears.

In order to create a print queue and print server object, you follow the same steps that you used to create the printer object. However, you select Print Queue and Print Server, instead of Printer, as the objects to create. The dialog boxes that are presented are very similar.

**TIP**

**For the print queues, NetWare 6 creates a subdirectory immediately under the root of the volume called QUEUES. Under this subdirectory, the operating system creates a numbered directory that matches the ID number of the queue. If the directory is created remotely, it does not use the ID of the queue object at all.**

After all the corresponding print objects are created (printer, print queue, and print server), you can use NWADMIN to link them together. You perform this operation in a two-step process. First, you assign the print server to the print queue as shown in Figure 2.55. Second, you assign the printer to the print queue as shown in Figure 2.56.

**FIGURE 2.55:** *Using NWADMIN to assign the print server to the print queue*

**FIGURE 2.56:** *Using NWADMIN to assign the printer to the print queue*

You can check the status of the printing setup using a new feature of NetWare 6 that displays the print layout. This feature is called Print Layout Page and is shown in Figure 2.57.

**FIGURE 2.57:** *Using NWADMIN to display the Print Layout page*

## Using NDSMANAGER to Manage Partitions and Replicas

In order to manage your NDS partitions and replicas properly, you need to be able to perform several types of operations. These operations are Create Partition, Merge Partition, Move Subtree, Add Replica, Remove Replicas, Change Replica Type, and Abort Partition. You can also delete a server object after removing the replicas from the tree. You can perform all these operations using the NDS Manager utility.

**TIP**

**Be sure to review Chapter 9 before performing any partitioning operations. Chapter 9 gives specific detailed instructions on how to check and verify partition operations and their states. It is important not to start an additional partition operation before the first partition operation has completed.**

Figure 2.58 shows you the NDS Manager utility, which you is run as a stand-alone utility.

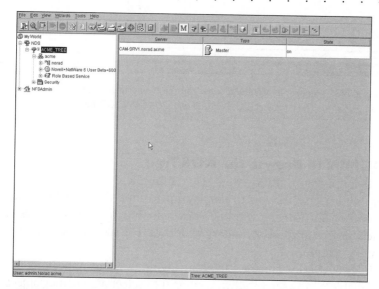

**FIGURE 2.58:** *The ConsoleOne utility controls the partitioning and replica placement of the NDS database.*

In Figure 2.59 you can see that the partitions are denoted with a small box icon to the left of the OU container object. In this example, OU=NORAD and OU=CAMELOT are partitions.

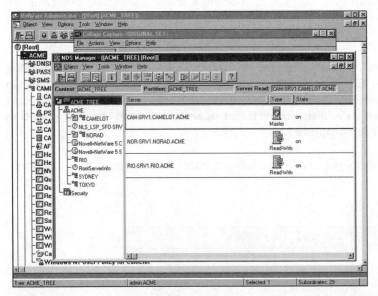

**FIGURE 2.59:** *Using the NDS Manager in NWADMIN, you can see the partitions denoted with a small box icon to the left of the OU container. OU=NORAD and OU=CAMELOT are shown as partitions.*

## Using NWADMIN to Browse the NDS Tree

The NetWare Administrator utility runs as a multiple-document interface (MDI) application, which enables you to display up to nine different browsing windows at one time. The primary window shown in Figure 2.60 provides a background for viewing one or more secondary windows. The secondary windows support that browsing feature.

The browsers in NWADMIN are the secondary windows that appear in the utility. To open or enable a browser window, you need to select a container object from the primary window and then select the Browse option from the Tools menu.

The new window is the browser window that displays the NDS objects from the selected container or current context. You can then select objects, directories, and files to perform the administrative tasks. Figure 2.61 shows an example of a browser window for the objects in the ACME tree.

**FIGURE 2.60:** *The main window for the NWADMIN utility*

**FIGURE 2.61:** *A browser window in NWADMIN for the ACME tree*

You can open up to nine browser windows to view the individual container objects. To view multiple browser windows at the same time, select the Tile option from the Windows menu. Figure 2.62 shows three browser windows tiled for the objects in the ACME tree.

The title for each of the browser windows displays the context of the container where the browser window is set. These titles help you remember and organize the browser windows on your screen.

**FIGURE 2.62:** *Three browser windows tiled for the objects in the ACME tree*

### Browsing the NDS Tree Using the Container Objects in NWADMIN

You can browse the NDS tree by walking through the container objects. The container objects can be browsed by expanding or opening them and displaying their contents. The following are several ways to expand the container objects within the NWADMIN utility:

▶ Double-click the object to expand the container to show its contents and the subordinate objects. If the container is expanded, you can collapse the container by double-clicking again.

▶ Select a container object in the tree and choose the Expand option from the View menu to expand the contents of the container. You can collapse the container using the Collapse option from the same menu.

▶ Select a container object and press the + key on the keypad of the keyboard. The container object will expand and show its contents. (The key with the + above the equal sign on your keyboard does not work for this operation.) You can collapse the container by pressing the − key on the keypad.

▶ Select a container object and press the right mouse button (or right-click). Select the Browse option from the short menu that appears. This option launches a new browser window with the contents of the container object. Figure 2.63 shows the short menu that appears after you press the right mouse button.

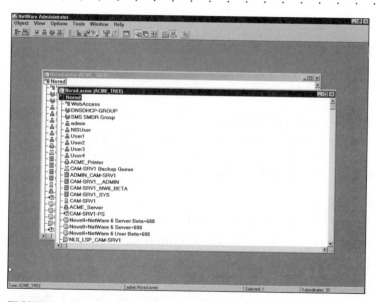

**FIGURE 2.63:** *A short menu appears when you press the right mouse button.*

Figure 2.64 illustrates several container objects that have been expanded for the ACME tree.

**FIGURE 2.64:** *Expanded container objects for the ACME tree*

### Browsing the Properties in NWADMIN

You can browse the properties for the individual object by opening the Object dialog box or selecting the Details option from the Object menu. You can open the Object dialog box using any of the following methods:

- ▶ Double-click the object.
- ▶ Select the object and then choose the Details option from the Object menu.
- ▶ Select the object and press the right mouse button. Choose Details from the short menu that appears.

The Object dialog box is organized or divided into pages that you select individually. The Identification page is the default or first page shown. Figure 2.65 shows the dialog box for an object in the ACME tree.

You can browse the specific information for an object by selecting the corresponding page. The page icons are located on the right-hand side of the Object dialog box and are specific to the type of object being displayed.

**TIP**

The pages in the Object dialog box are all part of the same dialog box. When you select a different page, you are still in the same dialog box. If you press OK or Cancel on any page, you are affecting the entire dialog box, not just the individual page. Pressing OK saves modifications to all the pages, and pressing Cancel exits the dialog box without saving any changes to any page. In order to move between pages of the dialog box, select the desired page.

**FIGURE 2.65:** *The Object or Details dialog box for an object in the ACME tree*

### Searching for Objects and Properties in NWADMIN

You can find object and property information in the NDS tree using the Search feature. You can perform this function without having to expand each of the container objects. The search operation checks each of the objects in the tree unless you restrict or narrow the search criteria.

For example, in Figure 2.66, the search criteria are set up to find all the users in the ACME tree that have the department property equal to City=SCOTTSDALE.

**NDS MANAGER (NDSMGR32.EXE) Utility**   The NDS Manager (NDSMGR32. EXE) utility is available in NetWare 6 to enable you to manage and monitor the NDS tree, NDS partitions, and replicas.

**FIGURE 2.66:** *The search criteria are set up to find all the users in the ACME tree that have the department property equal to City = Scottsdale.*

NDS Manager is a graphical hierarchical browser that offers many new features. These feature include these capabilities:

- ▶ Can run as a stand-alone application or as an integrated part of the NetWare Administrator utility (NWADMIN).

- ▶ Provides partitioning and replication capabilities for Novell's Directory Services.

- ▶ Provides the capability to repair the Directory from a client workstation running NDS Manager.

- ▶ Includes a version update capability so that any or all NetWare servers in a network can be updated to a newer version of the DS.NLM file.

- ▶ Provides context-sensitive help for synchronization errors detected by the Partition Continuity option.

As shown in Figure 2.67, NDS Manager is part of Novell's NetWare 6 product. This utility can be run as a stand-alone utility or snapped into the NWADMIN utility. In order to snap the NDS Manager into NWADMIN, you need to copy the NWSNAP32.DLL from the server's SYS:PUBLIC\WIN32 directory to SYS:\PUBLIC\WIN32\SNAPINS. The next time that the NWADMIN utility is executed, the NDS Manager utility becomes available from the Tools menu.

If you receive an Access Deny error while copying NWSNAP.DLL, you need to remove the read-only file attribute.

**FIGURE 2.67:** *You can run NDS Manager as a stand-alone utility or snap it into the NWADMIN Tools menu.*

Most operations can be performed from either the hierarchical Tree view or the list of partitions and servers. They are represented on the button bar by icons so that you can toggle between views of partitions and servers and views of the NDS trees.

The other view from which you work in NDS Manager is the Partition Continuity view, which enables you to view the condition of your tree and perform repair operations if necessary. Before using NDS Manager, you should access these views and become familiar with their features and options. An example of a server and partition view is shown in Figure 2.68.

As shown in Figure 2.69, after you select a particular partition, you can right-click the mouse or select the icons from the toolbar to pull up a series of options. The options shown in Figure 2.69 include these:

- **Information** — Displays information about the partition such as where the master replica is stored, the number of read/write replicas, and the time of the last replica synchronization (see Figure 2.70).

- **Check Synchronization** — Reads the partition synchronization status of the selected partition or partition list (see Figure 2.71).

- **Merge** — Merges the selected partition with its parent partition.

**FIGURE 2.68:** *You can view your NDS tree from two vantage points: partitions and the servers they are stored on, or servers and the partitions they contain.*

**FIGURE 2.69:** *Selecting an individual partition lets you query the partition for information or make changes to it, such as moves and merges.*

**FIGURE 2.70:** *Selecting the information option on a partition gives you useful information such as the last time the partition was synchronized.*

**FIGURE 2.71:** *You can easily check the synchronization status of a partition before starting any type of partitioning operation.*

- ▸ **Move** — Moves the selected container (partition) to a new context that you specify.

- ▸ **Abort Operation** — Attempts to abort a partition operation that has been initiated on the selected partition.

- ▸ **Partition Continuity** — Helps you identify whether any of a partition's replicas are experiencing synchronization errors. This operation is also known as "walking the replica ring," as shown in Figure 2.72.

- ▸ **Add Replica** — Enables you to create and add additional replicas for the partition. When adding a new replica, you need to select the server where the replica will be held.

After you run the Partition Continuity option, you are presented with the results of the check, mainly if all servers were able to "talk" in the replica list. This screen also provides another menu bar with the Repair option. Before running DSREPAIR, the utility prompts you as shown in Figure 2.73.

**FIGURE 2.72:** *The Partition Continuity check shows you the state of partitions stored on servers in your tree.*

**FIGURE 2.73:** *The REPAIR option runs DSREPAIR on the local server's NDS database and issues a warning before performing the operation.*

The REPAIR menu option enables you to perform the following DSREPAIR functions on your servers:

- **Synchronize Immediately** — Performs an immediate synchronization on every server that contains a copy of the replica selected for synchronization.

- **Receive Updates** — Deletes the Directory data of a replica and replaces it with data from the master replica of the partition. Choose this option if the replica is corrupted or has not received updated data for an extended period of time.

- **Send Updates** — Sends updates from one replica to another on the partition. When you send updates from a replica, the Directory data in that replica is broadcast from the server it resides on to all the other replicas of the partition, including the master replica. The other replicas combine the new information you sent with the data that they already have. If the replicas have data besides the data sent to them, they retain that data.

- **Information** — Provides information on partitions, replicas, servers, and synchronization errors.

- **Verify Remote Server IDs** — This operation verifies the following:
  - The remote server's name
  - The remote server's ID in a server's database
  - The remote ID, which is this server's ID as it is found in the remote server's database

  If any errors are detected, this operation attempts to repair the server IDs.

- **Repair Replica** — Repairs a replica on a server. Repairing a replica consists of checking the replica ring information on each server that contains a replica and validating the remote ID. This operation repairs only the chosen replica on the server you select.

- **Repair Network Addresses** — Repairs network addresses to ensure that the servers in your network are broadcasting correct addresses.

- **Repair Local Database** — Repairs local database records when your NDS database is corrupted. This operation resolves inconsistencies in the local Directory database so that it can be opened and accessed.

- **Assign New Master** — A repair feature that should be used only when the current master replica is corrupted, when the server on which the current master replica resides has lost data integrity, or when the server on which the current master replica resides has had an unrecoverable hard disk failure. Do not use this feature to change a replica type.

▶ **Remove Server** — Removes a server from an NDS tree.

**TIP**

**Misuse of the Remove Server operation can cause irrevocable damage to the NDS tree. If a server that is no longer in the tree appears in the replica ring, instead of using the Remove Server operation, perform a Delete Server operation to delete the server's object.**

▶ **Repair Volume Objects** — Checks the association of all the mounted volumes with Volume objects in the Directory. If the volume is not associated with a Volume object, this operation looks for one in the context of the NetWare Server object. If the volume is found, the Volume object is attached to the volume. If the volume is not found, this operation attempts to create one.

▶ **Abort Operation** — Attempts to abort a partition operation that has been initiated on the selected partition.

NDS Manager allows you as an administrator to perform the operations just listed from a single utility. After running DSREPAIR, you can view the error log for any synchronization errors or other errors that may have occurred during the repair. An example of the log file is shown in Figure 2.74.

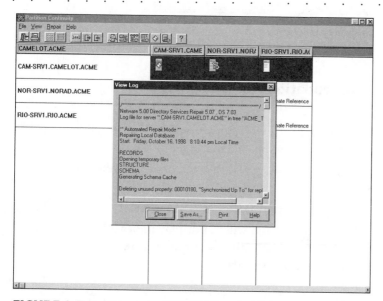

**FIGURE 2.74:** *After running DSREPAIR from the NDS Manager utility, you can view the error log file generated by DSREPAIR.*

One other useful feature of the NDS Manager utility checks versions of the DS.NLM and then updates the server with a later version if necessary. An example of viewing the DS.NLM version is shown in Figure 2.75.

**FIGURE 2.75:** *Prior to updating your servers to a newer version of the DS.NLM, you can check the version number through NDS Manager.*

## General Recommendations for Using NDS Manager

Keep in mind the following guidelines when using the NDS Manager utility:

- The NetWare Client 32 for DOS/Windows or Windows 95/98 is recommended when running NDS Manager.

- NDS Manager fully supports NDS v4.89a and above as well as DSREPAIR.NLM v4.31 and above.

- NDS Manager does not support DSREPAIR.NLM versions prior to 4.31.

- Partition and replica information will not display information for some fields if the information for the partition or replica is read from a server running NDS versions prior to 4.89a.

▶ The Partition Continuity Grid will not show any synchronization errors (even if they exist) for replicas stored on servers running NDS versions prior to 4.89a.

▶ When running NDS Manager on VLMs, be aware that VLMs default to a maximum of eight simultaneous connections to servers. This default can cause "Unable to attach" and "Unable to read" error messages (often in the form of statuses −321, x8801, and x8809) in NDS Manager. You can avoid this problem by upgrading to Client 32.

## The MONITOR Utility

The MONITOR utility (MONITOR.NLM) is a server-based utility that helps you easily manage and configure much of the system as well as observe network performance statistics. This utility uses a C-Worthy menu interface. The MONITOR utility NetWare 6 provides the ability to view and change each of the server's SET parameters.

The MONITOR utility's main startup screen is called the General Information screen. Figure 2.76 shows an example of the MONITOR's main screen, which includes general information about server performance. At the top of the General Information screen, you can view processor utilization, server up time, processor speed, server processes, and connections used (which typically represents the number of users logged in).

**FIGURE 2.76:** *The MONITOR main screen includes general information about server performance.*

As mentioned, the main menu in MONITOR provides you with a menu-driven interface to the system SET parameters available on the server. MONITOR has replaced the SERVMAN utility that shipped with previous versions of NetWare 4. Thus, SERVMAN is not included with the NetWare 6 operating system.

To get to the SET parameters, select the menu item called Server Parameters from the main menu. Other options from the main menu cover connection information, LAN configuration, storage information, volume information, and network information. After you have selected the Server Parameters, a list of categories (similar to the one displayed if you type **SET** at the server console) is displayed. At this point, you can select a specific category or area to view and edit. Figure 2.77 shows the Server Parameters screen, which enables you to select the category of SET parameters.

**FIGURE 2.77:** *The Server Parameters main screen enables you to select the categories of SET parameters. In this example, the Time category has been selected.*

An example of using the SET parameter in the MONITOR utility is shown in Figure 2.78. As shown, NetWare 6 includes a rich set of settable parameters governing time and time synchronization.

Using this section, you can configure the time on your NetWare 6 servers. You can accomplish most changes and configurations with the SET parameters by using the MONITOR utility. The SET parameters rarely need changing. However, some environments may require that you adjust some of them.

**FIGURE 2.78:** *The time parameters can be found in the Server section of MONITOR.*

## The **DSREPAIR** Utility

The DSREPAIR utility enables you to monitor NDS, check for errors, and correct problems in the name service on an individual server basis. The utility runs as a NetWare Loadable Module (NLM) at the server console. The utility is menu-driven and is written with the well-known C-worthy user interface.

You can run the DSREPAIR utility on any NetWare 6 server in the Directory tree. Additionally, the utility can either be loaded while at the server console or through access to a server via the RCONSOLE utility.

The DSREPAIR utility provides the following options:

- ▶ **Unattended Full Repair** — This feature automatically performs repair operations on the local NDS name service without operator assistance.

- ▶ **Time Synchronization** — This option checks the time synchronization for all servers that are known to the local server. You must monitor and correct time synchronization problems before performing any repair operation. A replica of the [ROOT] partition must be on the local server running DSREPAIR for this feature to contact all servers in the tree.

- ▶ **Report Synchronization Status** — This option lets you check the synchronization status of any partition on the server and the servers holding the association replicas.

- ▶ **View Repair Log File** — This option lets you view all the operations of the DSREPAIR utility by consulting a log file stored on your server. The default log file is SYS:SYSTEM\DSREPAIR.LOG. You should always view the log file after running the utility.

▶ **Advanced Options Menu** — The advanced options on this menu give you greater flexibility to manually control the repair of your NDS tree.

For more complete information or detailed instructions on the many options available in the DSREPAIR utility, please refer to Chapter 9.

## The DSTRACE Utility

In previous versions of NetWare 4, DSTRACE referred to a group of SET commands available at the server console. In NetWare 6, DSTRACE is a utility that executes as a NetWare Loadable Module (NLM) and that provides expanded monitoring capabilities over its predecessor. After it is loaded, you can use DSTRACE (also called the Novell Directory Services Trace Event Monitor) to monitor synchronization status and errors. DSTRACE is primarily used to determine and track the health of NDS as it communicates with the other NetWare 6 servers in the network.

You can use DSTRACE commands to accomplish the following:

▶ Monitor the status of NDS synchronization processes.

▶ View errors that occur during NDS synchronization.

The basic functions of DSTRACE are to view the status of the Directory Services trace screen in NetWare 6 and initiate limited synchronization processes. For more complete information or detailed instructions on how to establish the proper setting for the DSTRACE utility, please refer to Chapter 9.

## The DSMERGE Utility

The DSMERGE utility enables you to merge NDS trees into the same tree. DSMERGE.NLM provides the mechanism for combining two trees through four basic functions:

▶ Checks status of NetWare 6 servers in the Directory Tree before the merge.

▶ Checks time synchronization status of NetWare 6 servers before the merge.

▶ Renames a directory tree when necessary.

▶ Performs the merge of two trees when the previous criteria are satisfied.

The main screen of DSMERGE enables you to perform these operations; it is displayed in Figure 2.79.

**FIGURE 2.79:** *The main DSMERGE screen*

## Checking the Status of NetWare 6 Servers

Before and after the merge of two trees, it is important to check the status of your NetWare 6 servers. Before the merge, you want to check the versions of each NetWare 6 server and its current status. Table 2.6 lists the possible statuses and brief descriptions.

TABLE 2.6

*NetWare 6 Server Statuses*

| STATUS | DESCRIPTION |
|---|---|
| DS Locked | The server responds with an error message indicating that the NDS name service is locked and not accessible. |
| Inaccessible/Down | The server does not respond and is considered to be inaccessible. |
| Error <–N> | N is the Directory Services error code number. This status indicates that the server is not responding because of the error condition listed in the value N. |
| Wrong Tree | The server is responding with a tree name that does not match the tree name of the local server containing the master replica of [ROOT]. |
| UP | The server is up and functioning. |

The check phase of DSMERGE also ensures that the current server on which you are running this utility holds a replica of the [ROOT] partition. If it cannot find a replica of [ROOT], the operation aborts.

Next, the DSMERGE utility attempts to find all NetWare 6 servers in the tree by searching a list of servers to collect the server name, version of NDS, and tree name. If a server in the list cannot be found or has an incorrect tree name, the utility issues an error message. After all the servers have been contacted, the operation displays the list of servers onscreen and their statuses. An example of checking the servers before a DSMERGE operation is shown in Figure 2.80.

**FIGURE 2.80:** *DSMERGE checks the status of servers before the merge operation begins.*

## Checking Time Synchronization

Another important check that the DSMERGE utility performs is the status of time synchronization on all servers to be merged. Both trees must be synchronized, and they must refer to the same time source. After DSMERGE is loaded on a server containing a replica of the [ROOT] partition, you can initiate the time synchronization command as shown in Figure 2.81.

The option checks the time status of all servers for server name, NDS version, and the time synchronization status. If there is a time delta between a NetWare 6 server and the local server running DSMERGE, the difference is displayed as shown in Figure 2.82.

**FIGURE 2.81:** *The time synchronization status screen in the DSMERGE utility*

Your merged Directory tree must have only one reference or single-reference time source. If the two trees you are merging both have a reference or a single-reference server, you must assign one of them as a secondary server prior to initiating the merge.

```
NetWare 5.0 DS Merge Tree   2.00                NetWare Loadable Module
Tree name: ACME_TREE
Server name:  .CAM-SRV1.CAMELOT.ACME




           Time Synchronization Information For Tree: ACME_TREE

    Server name                       Type          In Sync       Time Delta
    .CAM-SRV1.CAMELOT.ACME            Single        YES                    0
    .NOR-SRV1.NORAD.ACME              Secondary     YES                    0
    .RIO-SRV1.RIO.ACME                Secondary     NO             -14:17:07



This list shows each server recorded in the tree's root partition along with
time synchronization information.
                              Up=Previous server            Alt+F10=Exit
Esc=Return to main menu       Down=Next server              F1=Help
```

**FIGURE 2.82:** *If time synchronization differs, the DSMERGE utility shows the time delta between servers.*

## Renaming a Directory Tree

Another useful feature found in the DSMERGE utility is the capability to rename an NDS tree. You must use this option if you are merging two trees that have the same name. Keep in mind that currently this is the only Novell utility that enables you to change the name of your NDS tree. You must load DSMERGE.NLM on the server that contains the master replica of the [ROOT] partition. The utility first verifies that you are running on the server containing the master replica of [ROOT].The master replica can calculate a list of servers that the utility can contact to change the names of servers holding a replica of [ROOT].

If a server in the list cannot be contacted, a warning message is issued. You can proceed to rename the tree if servers are unavailable, but you must enter a confirmation to continue the operation.

The operation actually begins by changing the name of the local tree's [ROOT] object to the new tree name. If an error occurs during this process, the operation is aborted. After the local server has changed the name of the [ROOT] object, a command is issued to change all servers in the local tree to the new tree name. Keep in mind that after this process has completed, many more synchronization activities are being performed in the background. When initiated, this process is irrevocable. After completion of the operation, you should check the status of the servers once again to verify that all servers have received the new name.

## Performing the Merge Operation

After you have checked and verified the status of your NetWare 6 servers, along with time synchronization, you are ready to perform the merge operation. After the completion of DSMERGE, you have a single tree with a common [ROOT]. The operation merges the selected source tree with a target tree. The end result is a tree with the target tree's name of [ROOT].

DSMERGE.NLM must be loaded on a server containing the master replica of [ROOT] of the source tree. The operation occurs in four phases:

### Phase 1: Merge Check

This check ensures that your source server running DSMERGE.NLM contains the master replica of the [ROOT] partition. If this check is successful, you see a screen similar to the one shown in Figure 2.83. This screen asks for the tree names of both the source and target trees along with their administrative names and passwords.

### Phase 2: Merge Preparation

This phase modifies the source tree partitions. The utility performs a schema comparison. If the schemas do not match, you need to use DSREPAIR to import a remote schema from the other tree. The utility also splits the [ROOT] partition from all other objects in the tree, making a partition that contains only the [ROOT] object. All other read/write or read-only replicas of [ROOT] are also removed from any servers in the tree. After this operation is completed, the utility can actually merge the trees. Keep in mind that the partitioning operations mentioned here could also be performed beforehand with the Partition Manager or PARTMGR utilities. The first two phases are displayed in the utility before you continue, as shown in Figure 2.84.

**FIGURE 2.83:** *The Merge Trees Information screen*

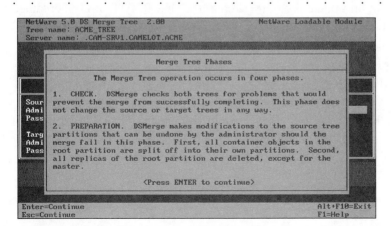

**FIGURE 2.84:** *The first phases of the DSMERGE process are displayed for information purposes and are followed by another screen showing the next two phases.*

### Phase 3: Merge Trees

After the first two phases are completed, the merge operation begins. Once again, the operation gathers the list of servers known by the source server. Each server in the source tree is contacted to obtain its server address and distinguished name in preparation for merging the source tree to the target tree.

The merge operation actually changes the name of the source tree [ROOT] object to that of the [ROOT] in the target tree. After this process occurs, the source server receives a new name and issues a command to change the tree names of all servers in the source tree.

### Phase 4: Merge Completion

The merge completion phase includes the continuation of renaming the tree and servers in the source tree. A copy of the target tree's [ROOT] replica is then copied over to the source server. This operation may take some time depending on the size of the target's [ROOT] replica. Any objects that are no longer needed are removed by the background synchronization processes.

Some manual tasks may have to be completed after the two trees are merged. These tasks would include placing copies of the [ROOT] replica where needed in your tree. You may have to restore any objects that were deleted before the DSMERGE utility was run. Because the source tree has had significant changes to the partitions below [ROOT], you have to use the Partition Manager or PARTMGR utilities to place partitions back again. Follow the guidelines discussed in Chapter 6.

Finally, you may have to check workstations that have the PREFERRED TREE statement set in their NET.CFG. Each workstation with the source tree name has to be changed to reflect the target tree name. You can accomplish this through the use of batch files or an update program, such as the UCUPDATE utility, contained in the user's container login script.


## The NLIST Utility

The NLIST utility in NetWare 6 enables you to browse the information in the NDS tree.

The NLIST utility enables any user to search and view information for most of the NDS objects, such as the following:

- ▶ AFP Server
- ▶ Alias
- ▶ Computer

- ▶ Directory Map
- ▶ Group
- ▶ Organization
- ▶ Organizational Unit
- ▶ Print Queue
- ▶ Print Server
- ▶ Printer
- ▶ Profile
- ▶ Server
- ▶ User
- ▶ Volume

You have several options for searching the Directory tree. Figure 2.85 displays one of the help screens for NLIST, which lists the display options for the objects in the tree.

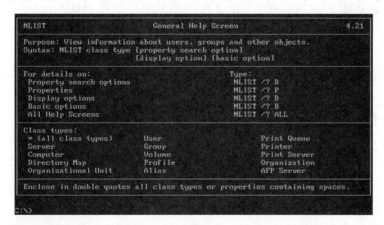

```
NLIST                        General Help Screen                      4.21

Purpose: View information about users, groups and other objects.
Syntax: NLIST class type [property search option]
                         [display option] [basic option]

For details on:                        Type:
  Property search options              NLIST /? R
  Properties                           NLIST /? P
  Display options                      NLIST /? D
  Basic options                        NLIST /? B
  All Help Screens                     NLIST /? ALL

Class types:
  * (all class types)    User              Print Queue
  Server                 Group             Printer
  Computer               Volume            Print Server
  Directory Map          Profile           Organization
  Organizational Unit    Alias             AFP Server

Enclose in double quotes all class types or properties containing spaces.

C:\>
```

**FIGURE 2.85:** *The NLIST help screen that lists the display options for the objects in the tree.*

You must enter the proper syntax for the NLIST utility to execute. The syntax is as follows:

```
NLIST [object type] [=object name] [/options]
```

Examples:

▸ **NLIST User /R /S** — Searches for all user objects in the tree starting at [ROOT].

▸ **NLIST Server /B** — Displays all the servers using bindery calls just like the NetWare 3 SLIST command.

You can also use NLIST to search for and display information about the properties for each of the objects. You use the WHERE and SHOW options in the command line to accomplish the browsing. For example, the syntax for the WHERE and SHOW options for an object is as follows:

```
NLIST object class [=object name] [WHERE
[property]operator [value]]
[SHOW property[,property . . .]]
```

Examples:

▸ **NLIST user=AEINSTEIN /D** — Displays all properties for the user AEINSTEIN in the ACME tree.

▸ **NLIST user WHERE "Security Equal To" EQ CAMELOT_ADMIN** — Shows all the users that are security equivalent to the CAMELOT_ADMIN organizational role relative to the current context in the ACME tree.

# NETBASIC

NETBASIC is a scripting language specifically designed for the NetWare environment. It creates BASIC language scripts that can be run on your server platform as interpreted BASIC programs and also compiled as NetWare Loadable Modules (NLMs) for server execution. NETBASIC ships with a suite of utility scripts and example programs demonstrating how the language is used. NETBASIC scripts can be written to query information from NDS as well as perform various management functions on your NetWare 6 servers. In fact, any Open Systems Architecture (OSA)–compliant component APIs are accessible, including the NetWare and Novell Directory Services APIs.

NETBASIC is licensed from HiTecSoft, Inc., and offers three basic features:

▸ The Network Management Extensions engine. This tool loads and unloads components such as NLMs and BASIC scripts from an operational server on demand.

▸ A BASIC script interpreter for NetWare 6 compatible with Visual Basic that enables an administrator to easily and quickly develop scripts for your servers, such as new utilities and automated tasks.

▸ BASIC scripting APIs for the Internet. With these APIs, an administrator can develop advanced Internet and intranet services, such as dynamic HTML pages and sites that access Novell services or Oracle databases.

NETBASIC provides the capability to create Web pages to output HTML source code. The output from a BASIC script is written to the Web server, which then routes the data back to the Web browser.

NETBASIC also provides a document management component known as DOC.NLM that enables you to write BASIC language scripts to generate HTML documents quickly and easily on the fly. You can then link a NETBASIC script to an HTML document.

## Miscellaneous Server Utilities

By way of reference, the NetWare 6 utilities can be separated into two categories: the server utilities and the workstation utilities. The server utilities enable you to change server parameters, monitor the load on the server, and control its allocation of resources. A server utility runs on the server console and executes as either a NetWare Loadable Module (NLM) or a Java program. In contrast, the workstation utilities for NetWare 6 are generally run from a DOS, Windows 3.*x*, Windows 95/98, Windows NT/2000 workstation. Menu-driven and graphical utilities are included. Like the server utilities, they enable you to manage the NetWare 6 server environment.

Typically, you can run the server utilities directly from the NetWare 6 server console using the LOAD <utility name> command. However, one of the major changes that NetWare 6 offers is the capability to execute a server utility without having to use the LOAD command. In NetWare 6, the LOAD command is completely optional.

Table 2.7 lists several but not all of the server utilities for NetWare 6 server. For a complete description of the server console commands, see Appendix C.

TABLE 2.7

*Server Utilities*

| UTILITY | DESCRIPTION |
|---|---|
| ACTIVATE SERVER | Loads the MSEngine for the NetWare 6 SFT III system, synchronizes the memory of both SFT III servers, and executes the MSSTART.NCF and MSAUTO.NCF scripts. |
| ATCON | Monitors the activity of AppleTalk network segments. |
| ATCONFIG | Configures NetWare for Macintosh after installation. |
| ATXRP | Works with PSERVER to send a print job to an AppleTalk network printer from a NetWare print queue. |
| BRGCON | Views bridge configuration information for a NetWare server for an OS/2 bridge. |
| CONLOG | Captures console messages generated by modules during system initialization and writes the messages to the default file, SYS:\ETC\CONSOLE.LOG, or to another file. |
| DSMERGE | Renames and merges Novell Directory Services (NDS) trees. |
| DSREPAIR | Maintains and repairs the NDS database on a server. |
| FILTCFG | Defines filters for the Internetwork Packet Exchange (IPX), TCP/IP, and AppleTalk protocols. |
| HALT | Used at a NetWare 6 SFT III server console to bring down an IOEngine on one SFT III server while leaving the other IOEngine running. |
| INETCFG | Defines an internetworking configuration for the IPX, TCP/IP, and AppleTalk protocols, simplifying the process of configuring local area networks using network and routing protocols supported by NetWare 6. |
| IPXCON | Monitors and troubleshoots IPX routers and network segments. |
| IPXPING | Sends an IPX ping packet to an IPX server or workstation to determine whether the node is reachable. |
| NPRINTER | Enables a printer attached to any server to be a network printer. |

| UTILITY | DESCRIPTION |
|---------|-------------|
| NUT | Used with NetWare 3.11 NLMs that require NUT's library. |
| NWSNUT | (NLM utility user interface) Provides a library of routines used by certain NLM programs, such as MONITOR or SERVMAN. |
| PING | Determines whether an IP node on the network is reachable and provides statistics about the route between nodes. PING sends an Internet Control Message Protocol echo request packet to an IP node and notifies you when it receives a reply. |
| RPL | (Remote Program Load) Enables remote booting of IBM PC–compatible diskless workstations that have network boards installed. |
| RTDM | (Real Time Data Migration) Enables data migration at the server console. |
| SBACKUP | Used to back up and restore specified NDS and file system data on a server, workstation, or service that you select. |
| TCPCON | Enables you to monitor activity in the TCP/IP segments of the network. |
| TIMESYNC | Controls time synchronization on servers running NDS. |
| TPING | (Trivial PING) Enables you to determine whether an IP node on the network is reachable. TPING requires a hostname parameter. |
| UNICON | Used at the server console to manage certain NetWare/IP products installed on a server, such as the NetWare Domain Name System (DNS) and the NetWare/IP Domain SAP/RIP Service (DSS). |

# Miscellaneous Workstation Utilities

As mentioned, you generally run the workstation utilities for NetWare 6 from a DOS, Windows 3.x, Windows 95/98, Windows NT, or OS/2 workstation. For example, the 32-bit NetWare Administrator utility (NWADMN32.EXE) enables you to manage your NDS tree by creating, moving, deleting, changing, and renaming objects and containers. In addition, the NDS Manager utility enables you to easily view and manipulate the NDS partition and replicas.

Table 2.8 lists many of the NetWare 6 workstation utilities. All of the workstation utilities are executed from a workstation that is logged into the NetWare 6 network. Some utilities (for example, CX and LOGIN) only require an attachment to a NetWare 6 server.

| TABLE 2.8 | |
|---|---|
| *NetWare 6 Workstation Utilities* | |

| UTILITY | DESCRIPTION |
|---|---|
| AUDITCON | Audits file system and NDS events on the network. |
| ATOTAL | Used to total the accounting charges on your network. |
| CX | Enables you to change your context in the Directory tree. |
| NCUPDATE | Updates any number of users' NET.CFG files with a new name context after a container object has been moved or renamed. |
| NDS Manager | Enables you to create, manage, and repair Directory partitions and replicas. This utility includes a superset of the features in the menu-based DSREPAIR utility and replaces the graphical Partition Manager utility available with previous releases of NetWare 4. |
| NetWare Administrator (NWADMIN) | A graphical utility that enables you to create and manage Directory objects, set up and manage network printing, manage partitions and replicas (via the integrated NDS Manager utility), and manage licensing services (via the integrated NLS Manager utility). NetWare Administrator incorporates all the functions available in FILER, NETADMIN, PARTMGR, and PCONSOLE. Includes the DSMigrate utility. |
| NetWare File Migration | A graphical utility that enables you to migrate files from NetWare 3.1*x* servers to NetWare 6 servers. The NetWare File Migration utility should be used after the NetWare 3.1*x* bindery has been migrated using DS Migrate. |
| NetWare Login | Used at a Windows 3.1*x* or Windows 95/98 workstation to access a NetWare Directory tree or server or to run a login script. |
| NetWare Print | Used at a Mac OS–based workstation to choose (Chooser Mac OS) and configure a Novell Directory Services printer or print queue. |
| NetWare Tools (OS/2) | Used to access network resources from an OS/2 workstation. NetWare Tools enable you to perform tasks such as mapping drives, managing printer connections, managing the Directory tree, managing server connections, displaying network users, and sending messages. |
| NetWare User Tools | Enables users to manage their network environment, including drive mappings, printing, sending broadcasts, and Directory access. |
| NetWare Volume Mounter (Mac OS) | Used at a Mac OS–based workstation to mount a NetWare volume. |

| UTILITY | DESCRIPTION |
| --- | --- |
| NLIST | Enables you to view information about files, directories, users, groups, volumes, servers, and queues. |
| NLS Manager | Used to manage NetWare Licensing Services (NLS). |
| NPATH | Enables you to determine the search sequence that NetWare uses to find message files so that you can troubleshoot why a user's workstation can't find a particular file, why the workstation is finding an incorrect version of a file, or why the workstation is displaying a foreign language. |
| NPRINTER | Enables a printer attached to a DOS, Windows 3.1x, or OS/2 workstation to be a network printer. |
| NPTWIN95 | Enables a printer attached to a Windows 95/98 workstation to be a network printer. |
| NWSTART (OS/2) | Starts NetWare Client for OS/2 on an OS/2 workstation if the DISCONNECT ON parameter is included in the NET.CFG file. The DISCONNECT ON parameter prevents NetWare Client for OS/2 from making a network connection when the workstation is started. |
| NWSTOP (OS/2) | Disconnects NetWare Client for OS/2 without turning off your computer. |
| NWXTRACT | Used to extract and copy files from the NetWare Installation CD-ROM to the network or to local drives. |
| Remote Console | Used to view and control one or more (Mac OS) server consoles from a Mac OS–based workstation. |
| SETUPDOC | Used at a Windows 3.1x workstation to install and delete document collections and DynaText viewers, configure viewers to access document collections in various ways, and create viewer icons at individual workstations. |
| ICE | Enables you to import data from an existing database into the NDS database. |
| /VER | Enables you to view the version number of a utility and the files that the utility requires. |
| WSUPGRADE | Enables you to upgrade the IPX LAN driver on the workstation to the corresponding Open Data-Link Interface (ODI) driver. |
| ZENworks | Enables you to manage and access network applications as Directory objects, providing advanced application control and access by network users. Also enables you to remotely manage desktops and take inventory. |

Several changes have been made to the DOS utilities. Table 2.9 lists the traditional DOS utilities that have been supported by previous versions of NetWare. The list indicates whether the DOS utility is currently supported in NetWare 6. Please refer to the Novell documentation for specific information about each of the supported DOS utilities.

TABLE 2.9

*DOS Utilities Supported by NetWare 6*

| DOS UTILITY | SUPPORTED IN NETWARE 6 |
| --- | --- |
| ADDICON | NO |
| ALLOW.BAT | NO |
| ATOTAL | YES |
| ATTACH.BAT | NO |
| AUDITCON | YES |
| BREQUEST | YES |
| BREQUTIL | YES |
| BROADCAST | YES |
| BROLLFWD | YES |
| CAPTURE | YES |
| CASTOFF.BAT | NO |
| CASTON.BAT | NO |
| CHKDIR.BAT | NO |
| CHKVOL.BAT | NO |
| COLORPAL | NO |
| CX | YES |
| DOSGEN | YES |
| DSPACE.BAT | NO |
| ENDCAP.BAT | NO |
| FILER | YES |

| DOS UTILITY | SUPPORTED IN NETWARE 6 |
| --- | --- |
| FLAG | YES |
| FLAGDIR.BAT | NO |
| GRANT.BAT | NO |
| LISTDIR.BAT | NO |
| LOGIN | YES |
| LOGOUT | YES |
| MAP | YES |
| MIGPRINT | NO |
| MIGRATE | NO |
| MENU_X.BAT | NO |
| MENUCNVT | NO |
| MENUEXE | NO |
| MENUMAKE | NO |
| MENURSET | NO |
| NCOPY | YES |
| NCUPDATE | YES |
| NDIR | YES |
| NETADMIN | NO |
| NETUSER | NO |
| NLIST | YES |
| NMENU.BAT | NO |
| NPATH | YES |
| NPRINT | YES |
| NPRINTER | YES |
| NVER | YES |
| NWDETECT | YES |
| NWLOG | YES |
| NWSTAMP | YES |

*continued*

| TABLE 2.9 |
| :---: |

*DOS Utilities Supported by NetWare 6 (continued)*

| DOS UTILITY | SUPPORTED IN NETWARE 6 |
| --- | --- |
| NWXTRACT | YES |
| PARTMGR | NO |
| PCONSOLE | NO |
| PRINTCON | NO |
| PRINTDEF | NO |
| PSC | NO |
| PURGE | YES |
| PUPGRADE | NO |
| RCONSOLE | YES |
| REBOOT.COM | YES |
| REMOVE.BAT | NO |
| RENDIR | YES |
| REVOKE.BAT | NO |
| RIGHTS | YES |
| SALVAGE.BAT | NO |
| SEND | YES |
| SESSION.BAT | NO |
| SETPASS | YES |
| SETTTS | YES |
| SLIST.BAT | NO |
| SMODE.BAT | NO |
| SYSCON.BAT | NO |
| SYSTIME | YES |
| TLIST.BAT | NO |
| TYPEMSG | YES |
| UIMPORT | YES |

| DOS UTILITY | SUPPORTED IN NETWARE 6 |
|-------------|------------------------|
| USERLIST.BAT | NO |
| VERSION.BAT | NO |
| VOLINFO.BAT | NO |
| WBROLL | YES |
| WHOAMI | YES |
| WNDBCNVT | YES |
| WSUPDATE | NO |
| WSUPGRD | NO |

· · · · · · · · · · · · · · · · · · · · · · · · · · ·

## Summary

The first job of a network administrator is to understand the tools that are available for his or her use. The NetWare 6 operating system provides you with many utilities that help you install and manage the NetWare 6 server. Your job is easier when you are familiar with the utilities and their functions.

# Novell Directory Services Objects and Attributes

> *"If two objects have the same logical form, the only distinction between them, apart*
> *from their external properties, is that they are different."* — *Ludwig Wittgenstein*

**N**ovell Directory Services (NDS) eDirectory consists of a collection of objects that follow a set of rules regarding how they are created and used. Familiarity with NDS objects and attributes and the ways in which they are used to build the NDS tree structure will enhance your use of NetWare 6. Understanding the structure of the NDS eDirectory schema will enable you to include additional objects by installing add-on or third-party applications. In addition, understanding the internal structure of NDS objects and the schema will give you greater flexibility in managing and designing your NetWare 6 network.

This chapter begins with a discussion of NDS objects and attributes (also referred to as properties). We next explain the NDS schema, including its components and rules, and how NDS objects are created. We discuss schema extensions to help you understand how additional object classes and attributes can be added, and how you can modify existing classes. We then explore the purpose and use of many individual NDS objects with examples of how you can use them effectively in your tree. The end of the chapter provides a discussion on the Schema Manager utility and its use. Where pertinent, we also include notes from our consulting experience to help you understand how different objects are used in actual customer environments.

# Introduction to NDS Objects and Attributes

As a network administrator, your primary responsibility is to maintain the servers, volumes, users, groups, printers, and other resources in the network. To help with this task, NDS enables you to view all network resources as objects within a distributed or network-wide name service, known as the NDS tree. You decide which network resources are created and placed as objects in the name service. These objects can include users, groups, printers, servers, volumes, computers, and so on.

Each entry in the NDS tree consists of an object and its attributes, or of data stored as a property. For example, the User object can have more than 150 attributes, some of which have multiple values. Although your installation will never use them all, you have a great deal of flexibility to utilize those that make sense for your company. Table 3.1 shows an example of a User object. This User object does not show all available attributes, but notice that some of its attributes have multiple values.

**TABLE 3.1**

*Examples of a User Object*

| OBJECT | PROPERTY | VALUE(S) |
|--------|----------|----------|
| User | Login Name | GWASHINGTON |
| | Given Name | George |
| | Last Name | Washington |
| | Title | President, Statesman, Farmer, Cherry Tree Killer |
| | Location | Washington, D.C., Mount Vernon |
| | Telephone | (not invented) |
| | Fax Number | (not invented) |
| | Description | President of the United States |

## NDS eDirectory Objects

NDS objects are the entities that store the information or data about each network resource. NDS objects represent both physical and logical entities on the network. Table 3.2 presents examples of both logical and physical network resources that can be represented by NDS.

**TABLE 3.2**

*Examples of logical and physical entities*

| LOGICAL ENTITIES | PHYSICAL ENTITIES |
|------------------|-------------------|
| User | Printer |
| Group | NetWare Server |
| Print Queue | Volume |

Because many NDS objects can be in a network, the objects are organized into a hierarchical structure called the NDS tree. A good analogy here is a file system. A file system is a hierarchy of subdirectories and files. A hierarchy is used because files are easier to manage in this structure, rather than storing them all at the same level. The same is true with NDS.

NDS classifies all objects as either container or leaf objects (noncontainer objects). Container objects are analogous to subdirectories in a file system, and leaf objects are analogous to files. Both are discussed in the following sections.

### Container Objects

Container objects are objects that are allowed subordinate objects. Container objects form the hierarchy of the NDS tree and are typically named after the locations, divisions, departments, and workgroups in your company. Container objects enable you to group other NDS objects together into a tree. A branch or subtree of the NDS tree consists of a container object and all the objects it holds, which can include other container objects.

Several types of container objects are defined for your use. The container object base classes are as follows:

▸ **TOP [ROOT]** — A special object at the top of the NDS tree.

▸ **Organization (O=)** — Represents the name of your company.

▸ **Organizational Unit (OU=)** — Represents locations, departments, divisions, or workgroups.

▸ **Country (C=)** — Represents a country with a two-letter country code.

▸ **State (S=)** — Represents a state. Not currently enabled.

▸ **Locality (L=)** — Represents a locality. Currently is enabled.

Although the NetWare 6 Directory defines five container objects, the current utilities display only the Organization (O=), Organizational Unit (OU=), Locality (L=), and Country (C=). The TOP [ROOT] class is supported, but only the NDS system can create it. Both the State and Locality containers are supported in the NDS schema, but they are not displayed in the NWADMIN utility. The OU serves the same purpose.

Figure 3.1 illustrates how container objects are the building blocks of the NDS tree. Container objects also help organize and manage the leaf objects or noncontainer objects.

### Leaf Objects (Noncontainer Objects)

Leaf objects are located at the ends of the NDS tree branches and don't contain any other subordinate objects. Leaf objects are used to represent network resources. Leaf objects for NetWare 6 include the following:

- ▸ AFP Server
- ▸ Application Object
- ▸ Alias
- ▸ Bindery Object
- ▸ Bindery Queue
- ▸ Computer
- ▸ Directory Map
- ▸ Group
- ▸ NCP Server
- ▸ CommExec
- ▸ External Entity

- ▸ Organization Role
- ▸ Queue
- ▸ Print Server
- ▸ Printer
- ▸ Profile
- ▸ User
- ▸ Unknown
- ▸ Volume
- ▸ Messaging Server
- ▸ Message Routing Group
- ▸ List

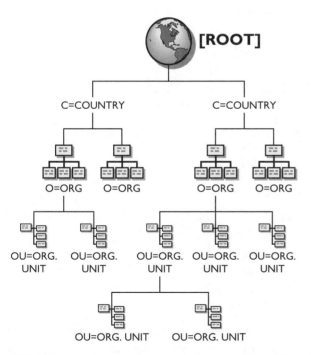

**FIGURE 3.1:** *The container objects are organized into a hierarchical structure called the NDS tree.*

You can place container objects and leaf objects in different arrangements in your NDS tree, according to your company's needs. Figure 3.2 illustrates how container objects organize leaf objects.

**FIGURE 3.2:** *Container objects organize leaf objects in the NDS tree.*

## NDS Attributes

The *attributes* of an object specify the type of information that that object can store. Different types of objects have different types of attributes. Thus, it can be said that the attributes define or describe the object. For example, a User object has, among many others, the following attributes: Login Name, Last Name, Group

Membership, Telephone, and Fax Number. On the other hand, a Printer object can have (among many others) the following attributes: Name, Network Address, Location, Print Server, and so on.

There are two categories of attributes for an object: mandatory and optional. *Mandatory attributes* are required during the object creation and cannot be circumvented or removed. NDS utilities enforce data entry for mandatory attributes. Typically, these attributes are necessary for operation. Many of the attributes that are mandatory are used to comply with the X.500 standard. For example, the last name of a User object is mandatory. Also, the host server property is mandatory when creating a Volume object.

**NOTE**

**The X.500 standard defines the basic structure for a directory tree and the inheritance classes. Novell's implementation of X.500 is similar to the 1988 and 1992 RFPs for directory trees.**

An object's *optional attributes* can be entered as the network administrator deems appropriate.

The value of a property is the data stored in that property. In most cases, users can read and write an object's attributes, although some attributes are not readable or writeable by the client. One property type may have a single value, whereas another may have multiple values. For example, the Telephone property of a User object can hold several different telephone numbers.

There is a specific syntax for the value of each property. One use of the syntax is to define the acceptable characters for the value field(s). See the next section, "The NDS Schema," for more details on the syntax (data types) for each property.

## The NDS Schema

The NDS schema contains the rules used to create and maintain each object and property in the Directory. The schema rules dictate the requirements, limits, and relationships of all objects and attributes that can exist in the Directory. NDS enforces these rules for each client request to change (add, delete, modify, and so on) an object or property.

The NDS eDirectory schema is automatically stored on every NetWare 6 server you install, even if you don't have administrator-defined NDS replicas stored on that server. The NetWare 6 installation automatically places the schema on the server because of the following reasons:

▸ The schema enables each server to create and maintain all NDS objects and attributes.

▸ The administration utilities require access to the schema during the creation of an object or objects.

The schema consists of three major components: object classes, attribute type definitions, and attribute syntaxes. Together, these three components establish the rules that control the creation of each particular object type in eDirectory. In Figure 3.3, you can see the relationship between these components. For instance, each object class is defined in terms of attribute or property definitions. The property types, in turn, are defined in terms of the property syntaxes. The property syntaxes are the data type of the values or information that can be stored in the property.

```
┌─────────────────────┐
│    Object Class     │
└─────────────────────┘
          ▲
┌─────────────────────────────┐
│   Attribute Definitions     │
│   (or Property Types)       │
└─────────────────────────────┘
          ▲
┌─────────────────────┐
│  Attribute Syntaxes │
└─────────────────────┘
```

**FIGURE 3.3:** *Relationship among the three components of the schema: objects, attributes, and attribute syntaxes*

For the most part, the objects defined in the base schema for NetWare 6 are taken from the X.500 specifications for appropriate objects in a directory service.

NetWare 6 defines additional objects that describe existing NetWare 3 bindery objects. You can also install other products, such as ZENworks, that will create new object classes, thereby extending your network's schema. Some objects in the schema currently have little use and are intended for future enhancements to the Directory.

## Object Classes

The *object class* defines the types of NDS objects that can be created and stored in eDirectory. A set of object class rules is used to create individual objects and to determine their characteristics. This means that every object in a tree belongs to an object class that specifies which attributes can be used, or must be used, as well as where objects can be created in relation to other objects. Figure 3.3 illustrates how object classes are constructed from property types. Keep in mind that object classes can refer to other object classes, as well.

The base schema that ships with NetWare 6 contains numerous classes. These object classes cannot be removed or deleted. Following is a list of some of the object classes stored in the schema:

- AFP Server
- Alias
- Application
- Bindery Object
- Bindery Queue
- CommExec
- Computer
- Country
- Device
- Directory Map
- External Entity
- Group
- List
- Locality
- Message Routing Group
- Messaging Server
- NCP Server

- Organization
- Organizational Person
- Organizational Role
- Organizational Unit
- Partition
- Person
- Printer
- Print Server
- Profile
- Queue
- Resource
- Server
- Top
- Unknown
- User
- Volume

Each object class in the schema is determined by the distinctive information held in five components. The five components or type of information that make up an object class definition are as follows:

- **Structure rules** — Defines the relationship of the objects in the Directory tree. The relationship is constructed based on two items: naming attributes (how the object is named) and containment class (which object classes the object can be subordinate to).

- **Super classes** — Builds the internal structure of the schema by relating the object classes to each other. Some object classes are simply the building blocks for the other object classes, or they are classes from which the object class inherits its definition.

- **Mandatory attributes** — The attributes listed in the mandatory property list for the object class are the attributes required during the object's creation and throughout the life of the object.

- **Optional attributes** — The attributes listed in the optional property list for the object class are the attributes that are not required but may be added.

- **Object class flags** — Five object class flags are either set to ON or OFF. The three remaining object class flags include the container flag, effective status, and nonremovable flag.

For example, the following is the definition of the Group object class:

| | |
|---|---|
| **Object class:** | GROUP |
| **Class flags:** | Effective Class |
| **Super classes:** | Top |
| **Named By:** | CN (Common Name) |
| **Containment:** | Organization |
| | Organizational Unit |
| **Mandatory attributes:** | CN |
| **Optional attributes:** | Description |
| | Full Name |
| | GID |
| | Locality Name |
| | Member |
| | *(and so forth)* |

The following is the definition of the Organization object class:

| | |
|---|---|
| **Object class:** | ORGANIZATION |
| **Class flags:** | Effective Class, Container Class |
| **Super classes:** | Top |
| **Named By:** | O (Organization Name) |
| **Containment:** | Country |
| | Locality |
| | Top |
| **Mandatory attributes:** | O |
| **Optional attributes:** | Description |
| | Detect Intruder |
| | E-mail Address |
| | Facsimile Telephone Number |
| | *(and so forth)* |

### Structure Rules

The *structure rules* for an object define the relationship between the objects in the NDS tree. The relationship between object classes is determined by two items: naming attributes and containment class. The *naming attributes* determine how the object is named. The *containment class* determines where the object may appear in the Directory tree relative to the other object classes. Both are discussed below.

**Naming Attributes**    The naming attributes determine how an object is named in the NDS tree. An object is identified in the tree by its common name and also by the names of all its parent containers. An object's name includes the object name type and a value, connected together with an equal (=) sign. Some object classes are container objects, whereas other objects are leaf objects (or noncontainer objects). Table 3.3 lists the object name types that are currently used in the naming property of the object class definition.

| TABLE 3.3 | |
|---|---|
| List of the object name types that are available for use in object name type definitions | |
| **NAME VALUE** | **NAME TYPE** |
| C | Country Name |
| L | Locality Name |
| S | State or Province Name |
| O | Organization Name |
| OU | Organizational Unit Name |
| CN | Common Name |
| BT | Bindery Type |

The first four name types — C=Country Name, L=Locality Name (S=State or Province), O=Organization Name, and OU=Organizational Unit Name — are all the container objects. The CN=Common Name and BT=Bindery Type are used for the leaf objects.

An object's leaf-most name is referred to as its partial name or relative distinguished name (RDN). For example, the user MTERESA in the ACME tree has an RDN of CN=MTERESA. If we refer to the user's distinguished name or full name, it would be defined as the RDN, MTERESA, plus the names of all the parent containers above the user MTERESA. The distinguished name would be written as follows:

```
CN=MTERESA.OU=FOOD.OU=SYDNEY.O=ACME
```

Therefore, the structure rules effectively control the formation of the distinguished names and relative distinguished names for each of the objects created in the NDS tree.

Nearly every object class has one or more object name types defined in the Naming portion of the object class definition, unless inherited by a super class. For example, the Organization object class is named by the "O" name type. The naming property of the Organizational Unit object class is defined as an "OU" name type. The Country object class has the "C" name type. It is mandatory that at least one naming property be defined or inherited.

The Named By property is not always a reflection of the class to which an object belongs. For example, leaf objects, such as User or Printer, are named by the Common Name (CN). The CN= name property does not by itself give you any indication to which class the object belongs.

An object class can allow for multiple object name types in the Named By property in the definition. In these cases, any one of the object name types can be used to name the object. For classes having multiple naming attributes, any combination of the naming attributes can be used. The property values are connected together by using the plus (+) sign.

A common occurrence of this peculiar naming convention occurs in the case of bindery objects. In the definition of the bindery object class, there are two object name type attributes called Bindery Type (BT) and Common Name (CN). A bindery object would then be defined as follows:

```
CN=ATPSUSER+BINDERY TYPE=83
```

The Locality object class definition also has a multivalued Named By property definition. It is named by either the name type L=Locality Name, or S=State or Province Name. Therefore, the RDN for a Locality object could appear as follows:

```
L=NORAD+S=COLORADO
```

**Containment Classes**   As we mentioned earlier in this chapter, some object classes are designed to contain other objects. The containment class list specifies where the individual object classes may appear in the NDS tree. Each object class has a definition or list of the container objects that it may be created in or subordinate to. This list, called the *containment class list*, builds the relationship between the object classes in the NDS tree.

An individual object can only reside or be created directly in a container that is located in its containment class list. For example, the Group object class can only be placed in or created subordinate to an Organization or Organizational Unit object. The containment class list for the Group object lists this relationship, as illustrated in the list of Group object classes previously shown. The following example for the Group object class is taken from the list of Group object classes:

| | |
|---|---|
| **Object class:** | GROUP |
| **Named By:** | CN (Common Name) |
| **Containment:** | Organization |
| | Organizational Unit |

The containment class list simply specifies that the Group objects can be placed under either the Organization or Organizational Unit objects in the tree. Therefore, the containment class specifies where an individual object may appear in the Directory tree. The schema prohibits objects from being created directly below or subordinate to container objects whose class definition is not in the new object's containment list.

The following is a list of the container objects that are used in the containment class lists for each of the object class definitions:

- ▶ Top
- ▶ Country
- ▶ Locality
- ▶ Organization
- ▶ Organizational Unit

The containment class dictates the structure of the NDS tree and changes as the tree expands toward the bottom. For example, the Organization and Country object classes are the only object definitions that have Top in their containment class list. The Top object class is implemented as the [ROOT] object in the tree. This means that only Organization and Country objects can be subordinate objects to [ROOT]. The Organization and Locality object class definitions are the only object classes that have the Country object listed in their containment class. Thus, Organization and Locality objects can only be subordinate objects to Country. Continuing down the tree, the Organizational Unit has the Organization, Locality, and Organizational Unit (itself) defined in its containment class.

As the tree expands toward the bottom, most of the leaf object class definitions have the containment class for both Organization and Organizational Unit. This means that most leaf objects will reside either within the Organization or Organizational Unit container objects.

### Super Classes

The internal structure of the schema is built using the super classes specification for the object class. The super classes help designate the structure of the schema internally and do not dictate the hierarchical structure for the NDS tree. As previously stated, the NDS tree structure is dictated by each object's definition of the containment class.

The super classes are the object class definitions in the schema from which other object classes may be constructed. A complete definition for an object class is derived from the components of the object class itself plus all the components of its super class objects. An example of the super class structure for a User object class is illustrated in Figure 3.4.

**Top**
Effective Class
| | |
|---|---|
| Super Classes: | (none) |
| Containment: | (none) |
| Named by: | (none) |
| Mandatory: | Object Class |
| Optional: | ACL |
| | Back Link |
| | Bindery Property |
| | Obituary |
| | Reference |

**Person**
Non-Effective Class
| | |
|---|---|
| Super Classes: | Top |
| Containment: | (none) |
| Named by: | (none) |
| Mandatory: | CN |
| | Surname |
| Optional: | Description |
| | Full Name |
| | See Also |
| | Telephone Number |

**Organizational Person**
Non-Effective Class
| | | |
|---|---|---|
| Super Classes: | Person | |
| Containment: | Organization | |
| | Organizational Unit | |
| Named by: | CN | |
| | OU | |
| Mandatory: | (none) | |
| Optional: | EMail Address | Postal Address |
| | Facsimile Telephone No. | Postal Code |
| | Locality Name | Postal Office Box |
| | OU | S |
| | Physical Delivery Office | SA |
| | Name | Title |

**Organizational User**
Effective Class
| | | | |
|---|---|---|---|
| Super Classes: | Organizational Person | Login Grace Remaining | Password Expiration |
| Containment: | (none) | Login Intruder Address | Time |
| Named by: | (none) | Login Intruder Attempts | Password Minimum |
| Mandatory: | (none) | Login Intruder Reset | Length |
| Optional: | Account Balance | Time | Password Required |
| | Allow Unlimited Credit | Login Maximum | Password Unique |
| | Group Membership | Simultaneous | Required |
| | Higher Privileges | Login Script | Password Used |
| | Home Directory | Login Time | Print Job Configuration |
| | Language | Message Server | Private Key |
| | Last Login Time | Minimum Account | Profile |
| | Locked By Intruder | Balance | Public Key |
| | Login Allowed Time Map | Network Address | Security Equals |
| | Login Disabled | Network Address | Server Holds |
| | Login Expiration Time | Restriction | Type Creator Map |
| | Login Grace Limit | Password Allow | UID |
| | | Change | |
| | | Password Allow | |
| | | Interval | |

**FIGURE 3.4:** *Super class structure for the User object class as defined in the schema*

The NDS Directory enables classes to inherit from other class objects in a unidirectional manner. This means that object class B can inherit from object class A, but object class A cannot inherit from object class B. The concept of inheritance among objects in the schema stipulates that an object class inherits the features of its super classes. This means that all the definitions of the super class objects are inherited in the new object class. If object class B inherits from object class A, B must receive all the definitions from A. The Directory does not have the capability to inherit only parts of the super class definition. A class may inherit from multiple super classes.

### Mandatory Attributes

The attributes listed in the mandatory property list for the object class are the only attributes that are required when the object is defined. If a property is mandatory, every object created from the class must have at least one assigned value for each mandatory property.

### Optional Attributes

The attributes listed in the optional property list for the object class are the attributes that are not required during the creation of the object. If a property is listed as optional, that property may or may not be created when the object is created.

### Object Class Flags

Several object class flags are set to either ON or OFF. These object class flags include the container flag, effective and noneffective status, and nonremovable flag, among others. All of these are discussed in this section.

**Container Flags**   The container flag is set to ON only for the object classes that are designated as the container object classes in the Directory tree. The container flag would be set to ON for the following object classes: Top, Country, Locality, Organization, and Organizational Unit.

The container flag is set to OFF for all the object classes that are the leaf objects in the schema or noneffective classes.

**Effective and Noneffective Status**   Each object class is categorized as an effective or noneffective class. Effective classes are visible in the utilities and are used to create new objects in your NDS tree.

Noneffective object classes are used as super classes to build the other object class information. Therefore, noneffective classes are used only in the definition of other objects and not to create objects in the Directory tree. The noneffective object classes are not visible using the management utilities; however; they are visible as effective classes. Noneffective object classes in the schema are used to create other object classes in the Directory tree. (Later in this section, each object is listed along with a notation of its effective or noneffective class.)

**Nonremovable Flag**   The nonremovable flag determines whether the object class can be removed from the schema definitions. The nonremovable flag is set to ON for all object classes that are defined in the base schema that is shipped with NetWare 6. The object classes added later to extend the schema have the nonremovable set to OFF.

## Property or Attribute Type Definitions

All the attributes found in eDirectory consist of an attribute type and an attribute value. The attribute identifies the nature of the information that will be stored by the property and dictates the syntax used to enter the value.

A property definition is based on special constraints and on a specific property syntax that determines the values the property can store. Attributes and their syntaxes have a one-to-one relationship. Approximately 142 available attributes are defined in the base NDS schema that ships with NetWare 6. Various combinations of these attributes apply to all object classes. You can view some of the available attributes or attributes for each object through the use of the NWADMIN utility. You can also use the Schema Manager utility that is discussed at the end of this chapter.

Following is a list of some of the attributes defined for the Group object class:

- Access Control List
- Authority Revocation
- Auto Start
- Back Link
- Bindery Property
- CA Public Key
- Certificate Validity Interval
- Common Name
- Default Queue
- Department
- Description
- Desktop
- E-mail Address
- Equivalent To Me
- Full Name

- GID
- Last Referenced Time
- Location
- Mailbox ID
- Mailbox Location
- Member
- Object Class
- Obituary
- Organization
- Other Name (other values of common name)
- Owner
- Reference
- Revision
- See Also

The property type definition consists of Property Syntax and Property Constraints, which are both discussed next.

## Attribute Syntax

The *attribute syntaxes* are predefined data types for values that will be stored in eDirectory. The NDS eDirectory schema is *extensible*, as discussed in the next section, meaning that you can create new object classes and attributes based on the property syntaxes. You can also add attributes to existing class definitions. Although the schema is extensible, the property syntaxes cannot be alternated. Currently, 28 static attribute syntaxes are defined in the schema. To view the syntax for a particular object, use the Schema Manager utility. Following is a list of some of the property syntaxes defined in the schema:

- Backlink
- Boolean
- Case Exact String
- Case Ignore List
- Case Ignore String
- Class Name
- Counter
- Distinguished Name
- E-mail Address
- Facsimile Telephone Number
- Hold
- Integer
- Interval
- Net Address

- Numeric String
- Object ACL
- Octet List
- Octet String
- Path
- Postal Address
- Printable String
- Replica Pointer
- Stream
- Telephone Number
- Time
- Timestamp
- Typed Name
- Unknown

## Property Constraints

*Property constraints* are all restrictions that affect the property values for each of the attributes. These constraints include whether the property values can have a single value or multiple values, whether the property values are immediately synchronized between replicas, or whether the property is hidden or nonremovable. The constraints also manage access control to the property value.

For example, a property can be constrained to allow only someone with sufficient rights to the object to add a property.

The attribute constraint also dictates the matching rules that are used when comparing two values of the same syntax. The primary matching rules are equality, substrings, and ordering. The equality rule searches for equal values of the attribute values and only applies if the property types are the same. The equality check can't compare unless the property is the same. Therefore, the syntax would be the same. The substring compares two string property values where a wildcard "*" can be used. The ordering rules compare for "less than," "equal to," and "greater than."

For a complete definition of the property syntax IDs, data formats, and matching rules, please refer to Novell's Software Developer's Kit (SDK) or the Schema Manager utility, which is discussed at the end of this chapter.

### Schema Structure

The NDS Base Schema consists of each object class along with its attributes or attributes and the property syntaxes. As shown in Figure 3.5, the schema structure can be represented as a pyramid in which the foundation consists of the property syntaxes. These property syntaxes are used to define a property; in turn, the property defines the object classes, and the object classes determine the schema structure.

**FIGURE 3.5:** *The schema structure is represented as a pyramid in which the foundation is the property syntaxes, which define the attributes. The attributes define the object classes, and the object classes determine the schema structure.*

## The Extensibility of the NDS Schema

NDS provides a mechanism for making changes or extensions to the schema. The purpose of this section is to give an overview of how this can be accomplished in your NetWare 6 environment. For specific information on Application Program Interface (API) functions and making API calls, see the NDS API Reference Manual from Novell. By using the client API, the schema can be expanded beyond the base schema, which Novell provides. Attributes can be added to existing object classes, or new object classes or attributes can be created.

The first step to extending the schema is to create new property definitions and/or new object class definitions. The extensions to the schema can be accomplished through the use of programming, with Novell's API calls designed for this purpose. After completing this task, you have modified the schema. All changes or extensions are automatically replicated on all NetWare 6 servers in the Directory tree.

Third-party applications also provide a means for extending the schema. Novell's NetWare Application Launcher, for example, makes an extension to the schema to define an Application icon. Prefixes for schema extensions can be registered with Novell Developer Support. This registry ensures that schema prefixes among vendors are not duplicated on the schema.

Any user performing modifications to the schema must have write rights (Supervisor rights) on the [ROOT] object. Before you create a new property or object class, determine first if the property or object class already exists in the schema. If you cannot find the property or object class you need or if the class is missing a property, you can then take the steps necessary to extend the schema.

Each time there are modifications to the schema, these changes are synchronized on all NetWare 6 servers in the tree. Synchronization requires no administrator intervention because it is part of the NDS background processes that occur. The schema synchronization occurs through the use of the trickle-down algorithm because the synchronization occurs from the top and proceeds downward.

**NOTE** The trickle-down algorithm is the approach used for schema synchronization where the schema on the master of [Root] is synchronized first and proceeds downward to all servers holding a copy of NDS eDirectory.

Therefore, the schema updates propagate across replicas of the same partition and downward in the tree structure from the [ROOT].

The trickle-down method causes a NetWare 6 server receiving an updated schema to build a distribution list in order to update servers that it knows about. It then checks all servers in its distribution list to determine if they have received an updated copy of the schema. If they have not received a copy, that server sends an updated copy of the latest schema to other servers. This process extends only down and across, not up. The Schema Manager utility (discussed at the end of this chapter in "The Schema Manager Utility" section) enables you to make extensions to the NDS schema.

# NDS Objects and Their Uses

You will discover, if you haven't already, that some NDS objects are used much more than others. Obviously, the User object is the most commonly used object in your tree. Some other leaf objects may never be used in your tree. That's okay. It's unlikely that any NetWare 6 networks will have a need for all the objects defined in NDS. However, they are in the schema for a general audience that may need them at some point.

To make your job easier, we have first grouped the objects in the following sections according to how they are used:

▸ **Required objects** — These are the objects that either you must define or are defined for you during the installation of NetWare 6.

▸ **Commonly used objects** — These objects include both the container and noncontainer objects, along with examples of how the objects can be used. These examples are based on actual consulting experiences.

▸ **Less commonly used objects** — These are the objects that may have less importance for you. Where appropriate, we have listed consulting recommendations with these objects, as well.

## Required Objects

The following objects are required in your NDS tree. When you install your first NetWare 6 server, these objects are present in your NDS tree. All of these objects require you to name them at some point in the NetWare 6 installation.

As shown in Figure 3.6 of Novell's installation utility, you are prompted for the name of the tree, organization, and organizational units. You can always come back later through ConsoleOne and create additional containers if needed.

**FIGURE 3.6:** *Novell's NetWare installation requires that you name all required objects during the installation.*

## Top and [ROOT] (Effective Class)

**Purpose** The Top object class is the super class of all other object classes in the schema. This object is also the container object for all other objects in the Directory hierarchy. The Top class is an effective class object. The only instance of the Top object is the [ROOT] object.

The [ROOT] object is at the top of your inverted tree structure. The [ROOT], from a visual standpoint in the utilities, is the starting point of your tree and branches downward, as shown in Figure 3.7. The name of the [ROOT] object is your tree name, although this name is not indicated or displayed in the utilities. When you install the first NetWare 6 server in a tree, you are prompted for a tree name, which means that you actually assign a name to the [ROOT] object. Each tree will contain one and only one [ROOT] object.

The [ROOT] object's name, which is the tree name, is broadcast on your network using the Service Advertising Protocol (SAP). If you have multiple trees running on the same network infrastructure, you must ensure that the names are unique.

**FIGURE 3.7:** *ACME tree structure shows the [ROOT] object at the top of the inverted tree structure.*

**Sample Uses** Choose a name for [ROOT] that clearly identifies the organization or company for the tree. Keep in mind that renaming the [ROOT] object or tree name can only be done with the DSMERGE.

[ROOT] is the only instance of the Top object class in the NDS tree. However, in the schema, all object classes must have the super class of Top defined, including any new classes created by extending the schema. Top is the only object that has no super class. All object classes inherit from the class Top. All object classes that you may define through schema extensions must contain the Top class.

· · · · · · · · · ·

**Consulting Experience**

Most companies simply use the same name as their company or Organization object and add a _TREE. For example, our tree name for ACME is ACME_TREE. The organization name is O=ACME. You want to choose a name that you can recognize as the tree name if you are using software analysis tools on your network and looking at server-to-server communications. Figure 3.8 illustrates how the NDS tree for ACME has been named.

[ROOT] (ACME_TREE)

O=ACME

OU=NORAD    OU=RIO    OU=CAMELOT    OU=TOKYO    OU=SYDNEY

OU=CHARITY OU=LABS OU=PR      OU=CHARITY OU=OPS OU=PR      OU=CHARITY OU=CRIME OU=PR

OU=CHARITY OU=ADMIN OU=PR      OU=CHARITY OU=HR OU=PR

**FIGURE 3.8:** *The NDS tree for ACME is named ACME_TREE.*

### Organization (Effective Class)

**Purpose**    This object class is used to define organization objects in the tree. An organization is located directly under the [ROOT] object or C=Country object. This object is used to define the name of a company, and you are required to define at least one organization in your NDS tree. Multiple O=Organization objects may be used directly below [ROOT] or Country as shown in Figure 3.9.

[ROOT]

O=ABC_INC                    O=XYZ_INC

OU=SFO  OU=LA  OU=SEA  OU=NY      OU=DAL  OU=ATL OU=MIA

**FIGURE 3.9:** *Multiple O=Organization objects defined for a large conglomerate company*

> **Consulting Experience**
>
> Most companies typically define only one Organization object in their NDS tree. If all your business units are connected with the same network, then a single Organization object more accurately represents your network. Your guideline for using multiple Organization objects is based on the network infrastructure in which you operate. For example, if you are a large conglomerate with varied businesses that have decided to communicate information together using NetWare 5 for the exchange of information, you can use multiple Organization objects, as shown in Figure 3.9. If each company is separately managed with a separate network infrastructure, you can create multiple Organization objects for each business unit under the [ROOT] object. You can also use the Organizational Unit objects to represent your business units.
>
> For more information on designing multiple Organization objects, see Chapter 5.

**Sample Uses**   The ACME tree is defined as the name of its organization, O=ACME. The organization represents the name of your company or organization and should be an overall descriptor of the business. If you are a member of a nonprofit group or university, the name of your Organization object can be the same name as your university or group.

### User (Effective Class)

**Purpose**   Obviously, the most common object in your tree, the User object, represents every user that is part of your NetWare 6 network. The User object is similar to the user object found in NetWare 3 environments, but it contains more attributes.

**Sample Uses**   During the installation of your first NetWare 6 server, you are prompted to assign a password for the first user ADMIN created on the network. This user, named ADMIN, has object Supervisor rights assigned to the [ROOT] object of your tree. Initially, the ADMIN user has all rights (NDS and File System) to the entire tree. At this point in your installation, it is the only object with such complete and extensive access to your network. The importance of maintaining the ADMIN user or another object with the same rights at [ROOT] is well-known. If you should delete this object without making other rights assignments, say to an organizational role, your access to the tree will be lost. Your options in this situation would be to reinstall NDS or to call Novell Technical Support to provide you reentrance into your tree.

### Consulting Experience

After you have installed the first couple of NetWare 6 servers, ensure that the ADMIN password is protected. The following steps will diminish the likelihood of losing access to your tree:

1. Your first NetWare 6 server installation prompts you for a password for the ADMIN user. Remember that the first password you assign to the NDS for ADMIN is also assigned to the bindery Supervisor object created by the NetWare Configuration utility. If you are doing a bindery upgrade, the supervisor's password is taken from the bindery. If the bindery supervisor's password does not exist, then the NDS ADMIN password is used. If you later change the ADMIN user's password, the bindery Supervisor password does not change. Choose a password that will not easily be guessed. Change your passwords periodically for greater security. You should also consider creating a secondary object with trustee rights to the [Root] object If the Admin object is corrupted or accidentally deleted, there is a backup user with the same rights in effect. You can hide this object from view by using an inherited rights filter.

2. Create an organizational role in the O=Organization level of your tree and assign this role object Supervisor rights at the [ROOT] object of your tree.

3. Do not make this organizational role object a security equivalent to the original ADMIN user. If the original ADMIN were to be deleted, your organizational role would have no access to the tree because the security equivalency would be lost. For more information on how to define security for organizational roles, refer to Chapter 13.

### NCP Server (Effective Class)

**Purpose**  A NetWare (NCP) server object is automatically created for any NetWare 6 server being installed or upgraded to NetWare 6. The server object holds key information, such as the network address and the version of NetWare you are running on that machine. This object type is used to represent any server that provides NetWare Core Protocol (NCP) transport and session services and that can represent either bindery or NDS-based NCP servers. This subclass of the Server object provides further definition of NCP services available on a particular server.

### Consulting Experience

Be sure to follow the naming standards presented in Chapter 4. This is a resource on which you will no doubt want to perform Directory queries. Consistent and appropriate naming help this process considerably

**Sample Uses**   The supported Services property can be used to list NCP-based features and services available for this network address. As part of an NDS search engine, you can search for available NCP services.

Another useful feature is the Operator property, which is used by an NCP server as an access control list. If a particular object is part of this access control list, that object can perform remote console operations. These remote operations do not mean using RCONSOLE; they have the capability to exercise the console APIs, which RCONSOLE does not use.

The server object is basically managed by NDS and requires little attention from the administrator.

### Volume (Effective Class)

**Purpose**   The server volume object is automatically created when you install a NetWare 6 server into the tree. A file server must have at least one volume called the SYS volume. The server may have additional volumes that are defined during the installation of NetWare 6. A volume object is created for each mounted volume during the installation. The naming convention is <file server name> _ <volume name>.

### Consulting Experience

NetWare 6 gives you flexibility to place print queues on any NetWare 6 volume. We recommend that you always create at least one other volume in addition to the SYS volume so that your print queue doesn't fill up the SYS volume and cause NDS to become disabled.

Use the volume restrictions to limit the size of your volumes before they fill up. You can also limit the disk space used on the Home Directory if you are short on space or want to limit each user on the volume.

**Sample Uses** This object type exists primarily to differentiate it from other types of resource objects and to allow greater flexibility for volume management, if needed. It is also used in MAP commands and is required by the FILER utility to grant file system rights.

## Commonly Used Objects

Following is a list of the most commonly used NDS objects. Most, if not all, of these objects will be used in your NDS tree. Small sites with perhaps one server may not use all of these objects. In fact, it is only necessary to make use of the objects that will best serve the purposes of your network environment.

> **The following objects are schema extensions for ZENworks These extensions occur during the installation of ZENworks automatically.**
>
> **NOTE**

### Application Object (Effective Class)

**Purpose** The purpose of this object is to define the application objects for the ZENworks for Desktops. This object has changed since the introduction of NetWare 4, when there used to be a different application object for each workstation operating system. For example, there was an application object for DOS, Windows 3.1, Windows 95, and Windows NT. Now just one application object represents programs that can be executed on all workstations.

**Sample Uses** You may want to create an application object for the application programs stored on a central server where all network users can access them. These applications can be DOS, Windows 3.1, Windows 95, Windows NT, and Windows 2000. In addition, you can create application objects that represent application programs loaded on each user's local drives or desktops. For more information on using the Novell's ZENworks for Desktops and ZENworks for Servers, refer to Chapter 20.

### Bindery Object (Effective Class)

**Purpose** This leaf object represents any object other than user, group, queue, profile, and print server created through bindery services. The bindery object has the format of Common Name + Object Type and is used to provide backward compatibility for bindery-oriented applications or utilities.

**Consulting Experience**

Do not delete a bindery object until you verify its purpose in the Directory. Some installation utilities create a bindery object that, if removed, will cause problems for the application. Always check first before deleting bindery objects that appear in your containers.

**Sample Uses**    You will see bindery objects appear after a migration from NetWare 3 to NetWare 6 if an object is not identifiable by NDS. Some applications create bindery objects to suit their particular purposes. For applications that still require the bindery services, a bindery object could exist in the tree. Although these objects appear in utilities, such as NWADMIN, they are nonmanageable from NWADMIN and are present only for information purposes.

### Organizational Unit (Effective Class)

**Purpose**    Nearly all NDS trees, except environments with a single NetWare 6 server, use Organizational Units. They are, however, optional. Organizational Units subdivide the tree into either locations or organizations, which could be departments, divisions, or workgroups. The Organizational Unit is also referred to as a container and contains the login script property, also known as the container login script. All users in a container will execute that container's script if it is available.

**Sample Uses**    As shown in Figure 3.10, the ACME tree uses containers to make logical divisions in the tree. Notice that the first level of OUs represent geographic sites based on the network infrastructure, and the subsequent levels represent the departments of ACME. Many trees will be designed in this fashion with several levels of nested organizational units. For more information on designing a NetWare 6 tree, see Chapter 5.

### Organizational Role (Effective Class)

**Purpose**    An Organizational Role object is typically used to define a role or position within an organization object or container object. The role is extremely useful because the object or file rights are granted to the role itself and not to the occupants who may belong to the role.

**[ROOT]**

O=ACME

OU=NORAD    OU=RIO    OU=CAMELOT    OU=TOKYO    OU=SYDNEY

OU=CHARITY    OU=OPS    OU=PR        OU=CHARITY    OU=CRIME    OU=PR

OU=FIN    OU=DIST        OU=BLUE    OU=WHITE

**FIGURE 3.10:** *The use of organizational units makes NDS tree subdivision clear and logical.*

**NOTE**

**This rule is different for object creation. For example, an object is created by a user assigned to the organizational role. The object creation rights to the new object go to the user creating the object, not to the organizational role.**

### Consulting Experience

Most companies use the Organizational Unit to represent geographic locations, divisions, and workgroups. You generally use an Organizational Unit to group common users and resources in the same container. Organizational Units should not be created to represent a single person or a single resource. They are used to provide access to a group of users in a particular part of the tree. NetWare 6 does provide the capability to move containers to new locations in the tree should your needs change.

**Sample Uses**     Organizational Roles are especially useful in maintaining subadministrators. The occupant can be moved in and out of the role quickly to facilitate short-term assignments. For example, if the regular administrator is absent for any length of time, another user can be moved into the role temporarily to manage the network. Implementing this object is just like implementing a group. The organizational role occupants derive their rights through security equivalence to the role object.

As shown in Figure 3.11, we have created an organizational role for each city contained in the ACME tree. This administrator will have rights to manage the entire container, such as adding and deleting users or servers.

**FIGURE 3.11:** *Organizational Roles created for the ACME tree*

### Group (Effective Class)

**Purpose**     This class is used to represent a set of users from any part of the NDS tree. The membership of the group is static and is only modified by your administrative action.

Groups function the same way they did in NetWare 3. There is little difference between using group objects and organizational unit (OU) objects. Both have the same function, which is to place common users close together. It is true that users who are members of both objects receive rights by security equivalence, but there are some differences. Because of security equivalence, any member of an OU receives whatever rights the OU possesses. Users inside groups also receive whatever rights the group possesses — and as with a container, there is no Inherited Rights Filter (IRF) provision. For more information on NDS security, refer to Chapter 13.

---

### Consulting Experience

The use of an organizational role is highly recommended as a way to administer rights in your network to various administrators in your network. You can more easily track who has received rights as administrators in your tree by checking who has been made an occupant of a role. Assigning rights to individuals through means other than the organizational role is not recommended because it is more difficult to track which individuals have been granted rights in your tree. After a few months or even weeks, you'll forget who has been assigned rights. For more details on setting up an organizational role for your tree, see Chapter 13.

---

Groups are used to differentiate rights within a particular Organizational Unit. Rather than create multiple subcontainers, you can simply use groups within a container for users who need a specific environment created.

**Sample Use**    In order to provide rights to a smaller subset of users in the CHARITY.SYDNEY.ACME OU, you can use a group. Figure 3.12 shows an organizational unit called OU=Charity that is populated with users and resources. Within this OU are two sets of users. Each group accesses different software on the server and needs different rights assignments. Within the container or OU login script (known as the system login script in NetWare 3), the IF MEMBER OF GROUP statements are used to determine which group a user belongs to for rights assignments. When each user logs into the network, the login script determines whether a user is a member of a group and sets the appropriate environment variables.

### Directory Map (Effective Class)

**Purpose**    The Directory Map object is a pointer that refers to a file system directory on a NetWare volume. It is used in login scripts or by the MAP command to point to a directory that contains a particular application.

**Sample Use**    Let's assume you have WordPerfect installed in a directory called WP60. If you were to upgrade your software to WordPerfect 6.1, you could choose to rename the subdirectory as WP61. You would also have to change every login script to reflect this change for the new subdirectory. Through the use of a directory map, you can eliminate making changes to your login scripts. Your directory map object is used in your login scripts and points to a subdirectory on a NetWare volume. Your only change is to have the directory map point to WP61. All container login scripts are left intact.

**FIGURE 3.12:** *The Organizational Unit OU=Charity with two groups created to differentiate users within the same container*

### Consulting Experience

Groups are great to use in a container to provide further differentiation of rights to a subset of users. We recommend that groups be used in a container instead of creating more containers. Additional containers would require the use of additional container login scripts. Limit the number of groups to fewer than 15 in a container login script, if possible. The more groups there are, the longer the container login script will be, and a slower login will occur. If you have 15 or more groups, however, you should create additional containers because the login script must check your users against each group membership list. Groups should be contained locally. Avoid the use of groups that contain users from multiple organizational units.

### Alias (Effective Class)

**Purpose**    An alias is another name for an object. An *alias* is an object that points to another object you specify in the Directory tree. An alias can point to either a container object (an object that holds other containers) or a noncontainer object (one that does not have any other containers).

**Sample Uses**    An alias is a name containing at least one relative distinguished name. As a network administrator, you may grant users access to a particular resource contained in another OU, such as a printer. For example, you can create an alias to reference that printer. The alias can be considered a relay to another object in a different part of the tree.

You can also alias one OU to another OU, giving one OU to the other OU's resources. It appears as though the alias places the alias's container inside the other container.

The object being aliased is known as the *primary object*. When you create an alias object, you may or may not name it with some indication that it is an alias to another object. For example, the name might include the word "alias," as in Alias_Blair.

### Print Server (Effective Class)

**Purpose**    The print server leaf object represents a server that takes print jobs out of a print queue and sends them to a network printer. This object is used in conjunction with the Printer and Print Queue objects. A print server object must be created for every actual print server that exists on the NetWare 6 network.

---

### Consulting Experience

Directory map objects are useful for providing a standard container login script on multiple servers. We recommend that you have standard file structures for all your NetWare 6 file servers so that you can facilitate easier use of directory maps. If you maintain a directory map for an application, you can make a change to the directory map pointer and have it be effective for many servers. The directory map requires that the administrator make each user security equivalent to the map object and for containers with large numbers of users. This could be a drawback, from an administration standpoint. However, to simplify this situation, you can grant rights to the container on the directory pointed to by the directory map.

**Consulting Experience**

The alias object is useful in moving subtrees or renaming containers so that you can easily make the transition. The alias can assist you in this migration path. In addition, the alias can be useful for some companies wanting to create mobile users who do not want to remember their user context. The alias can be created at the top of the tree below the Organization object, for example, to shorten the user's context. If user DAVID wants to log in to the network, he only needs to remember that his context is DAVID.Acme because that alias points to his actual context in the tree. This example is shown in Figure 3.13. Keep in mind that this example refers to a limited number of users, such as mobile users. We are not implying that you should alias every user in your tree.

**Sample Uses**    All NetWare 6 networks using printers will have at least one print server object. You can use this object to define which printers to assign to users, based on their position or location in the NDS tree. You can also define the print server operators.

**FIGURE 3.13:** *Mobile user DAVID has a shortened context through the use of aliasing.*

### Consulting Experience

You can place the Printer object along with the Print Queue object as high as possible in your NDS tree to support many users. If your printer is for only your container, then place the printer in your container. If more containers need access to the printer, place the object in the next highest level in your tree. Keep in mind that the placement of printers higher in the tree also adds overhead to NDS in terms of name resolution. We also recommend that you configure printers as network-direct printers in queue server mode as explained in Chapter 14.

### Printer (Effective Class)

**Purpose**   The Printer object is used in conjunction with the print server object. Use this object to manage a printer. The assignment for a print queue can be made within the object.

**Sample Uses**   You can attach printers to the network in several different ways—namely, directly to the network, to a printer port of a NetWare server, or to a printer port of a PC.

### Queue (Effective Class)

**Purpose**   This object represents a print queue defined on a NetWare 6 server. The queue actually represents the directories where the print jobs are sent to be serviced by a printer.

**Sample Uses**   Place the Print Queue object along with the Print object at the highest level possible in your tree to service the most users.

### Profile (Effective Class)

**Purpose**   The Profile object is used as a special purpose scripting object that is executed by LOGIN.EXE and is a shared login script after the execution of your container login script. The profile script can contain special drive mappings or environment settings that you want a select group of people to receive.

One of the attributes of a user object is the profile. When a user is first created using the NWADMIN utility, you can specify that the user be part of a profile. You can also add a user to a profile anytime after by going back and adding the profile to a user object's attributes.

**Consulting Experience**

All NetWare 6 print queues should be placed on a volume other than the SYS volume for greater fault tolerance of the server. A queue object must be created for NetWare 6 printing. A Print Queue object is assigned to a printer.

**Sample Uses**    A profile script has three notable uses:

▶ Creating a global login script

▶ Creating a location login script

▶ Creating a special function login script

**Creating Global Login Scripts**    NetWare 4 does not use a global system login script. Each Organizational Unit created will have its own login script, referred to as the OU login script. The order of execution of login scripts is as follows:

**1.** OU login script

**2.** Profile login script, if used

**3.** User login script

**4.** Default login script if no other script is available

Therefore, if you want to create a more global login script and include multiple Organizational Units, you could employ the profile object to set up a specific environment for a group of users. Keep in mind that this type of solution is expensive in terms of NDS overhead that will be created on your network.

**Consulting Experience**

Typically, the profile object is used as a global login script for a workgroup or organization. Keep in mind that the profile object executes from one container, although users may be participating from other containers and may see some performance issues if the script is executing over a wide-area connection. In addition, you will notice increased overhead of NDS traffic as NDS searches the tree to locate a particular object.

## Consulting Experience

Before deleting an unknown object, first check to make sure it is unnecessary. When you have verified that the object is unnecessary, remove it from your tree. There is no point in maintaining unknown and unused objects.

**Location Login Scripts**   A profile can also be used for determining allocation of resources based on location. For example, each department of a company may have three printers and three print queues. A profile enables you to assign a particular group of users to a specific print queue. You can use a profile login script to capture to a particular print queue, and the users will automatically capture to that print queue.

**Special Function Scripts**   A profile can be used as a special function script to assign users access for applications. For example, you can create a profile script that only administrators will use. This script may give these users a specific drive assignment to a help desk utility. In this scenario, you would move the help desk utility out of the SYS:Public directory into a new subdirectory you create called HELPDESK. When a user logs into the network, the admin Profile object is executed, and the user is assigned a drive mapping to the HELPDESK directory. Only users who execute the profile script will be assigned rights to access the help desk utility.

### Unknown (Effective Class)

**Purpose**   This object class represents any object created by the server to restore any object whose base class is currently undefined in the schema. Objects of this class type are created by only the server, not the client, and usually occur when a mandatory property of an object has been lost.

Unknown objects are created during synchronization of objects as placeholders when a mandatory property of an object has been lost and when an object class has been deleted and the server had an object of that class.

**Sample Uses**   NDS automatically creates this object. If an unknown object appears in your tree, check to see if some other object has been deleted. In the case of a deleted server object, the server's volume objects appear as unknown objects and must be deleted by an administrator. In other circumstances, an unknown object may appear temporarily as the NDS background processes work through a synchronization process.

## Less Commonly Used Objects

### AFP Server (Effective Class)

**Purpose**    The AFP Server object represents an AppleTalk Filing Protocol-based server that is part of your NetWare 6 network as a server node or router for connected Macintosh workstations.

**Sample Use**    This object serves only as a descriptor object and does not provide any management capability for your AFP server in a NetWare 6 environment. You can use this object for informational purposes about AppleTalk in your NetWare 6 environment.

### Bindery Queue (Effective Class)

**Purpose**    The Bindery Queue object represents a leaf object queue that has been placed in the Directory through an upgrade or migration to NetWare 6.

**Sample Use**    A bindery queue is used to support other queues upgraded from NetWare 3.

### Country (Effective Class)

**Purpose**    This object is used to define country entries in your NDS tree. The Country Name property is restricted to two characters as defined by the ISO3166 standard. Directory Services does not check to see if characters are correctly defined; it only determines whether two are present.

**Sample Uses**    For companies desiring to use the Country object, there are several considerations. First, the object must be placed directly below the [ROOT] object. Specifying this option during installation of NetWare 6 is shown in Chapter 16. Second, consider the ramifications of adding the Country object to your tree in terms of adding another layer to your tree and lengthening your users' context. Also, carefully plan your tree design so your users' context will be logical and will make sense. For example, assume you added the Country object to the ACME tree under [ROOT]. Because your company is global in nature, which country do you choose? If you decide that C=US, notice what the context would be for users not reporting under the US region. This example is shown in Figure 3.14.

### CommExec (Effective Class)

**Purpose**    The CommExec object is used to manage Novell's NetWare for SAA NetWare Loadable Module on a NetWare 6 Server.

**Sample Use**    This object is used only with NetWare SAA and provides management capabilities and rights privileges for the [ROOT] level of your NDS tree.

Distinguished name: CN=SIRKAY.OU=CHARITY.OU=TOKYO.O=ACME.C=US

**FIGURE 3.14:** *The Country object can cause your users' context to look different from the context you are actually trying to represent.*

### Locality (Effective Class)

**Purpose**    The Locality object is used to define geographic locations in the NDS tree, such as states, regions, or counties. The Locality object is currently not enabled by Novell's NWADMIN or NDS Manager utilities. Therefore, it is not visible through the current utilities. Programs are available to define and view this object class.

### Consulting Experience

Our recommendation is to avoid using the Country object in your tree. Even with emerging gateway technology to interconnect disparate directory databases, the gateway will handle the distinction between databases using and not using the Country object. The Country object is also not necessary for companies wanting to connect to a public data provider for Directory Services.

**Consulting Experience**

Although the Locality and State objects exist in the NDS schema, we do not recommend that you use them in implementing your NDS tree. The main reason is that these objects are not supported by the administrative utilities. For example, the current versions of NWADMN95 and NWADMNNT are not capable of creating new objects or of managing the Locality and State objects. We feel the O and OU objects will meet your needs as containers in the NDS tree.

The Locality and State objects were primarily developed for implementation by the telecommunication providers into their NDS trees.

**Sample Uses**   This object must be named by one or both of its attributes: L=Locality Name, and/or S=State or Province Name. Most companies will not need to use this object. Some Directory Services that provide connection services through NDS use the Locality object.

### Computer (Effective Class)

**Purpose**   This object class can represent computers used as NetWare servers and computers used as client workstations.

**Sample Use**   A key property of this object is the Operator, which can be used to identify individuals or groups that typically handle the daily hardware maintenance of this computer.

### Device (Noneffective Class)

**Purpose**   This object subclass is used to represent a physical device, such as a modem or printer that you want to have defined in your tree.

**Sample Uses**   One property contained in this object is the Locality Name, which can be used to identify the physical location of a device. In addition, as more devices become NDS enabled, the Device object may come into greater use for managing those objects.

### External Entity (Effective Class)

**Purpose**   This object is used to store information about nonnative NDS objects in the Directory tree.

**Sample Use**   Some situations may require that an NDS object have information about another object that does not exist on the Directory Tree. A messaging service, for example, can use the External Entity class to store information about e-mail users who exist on other systems outside of the NetWare 6 tree.

### List (Effective Class)

**Purpose**   This object is used to represent an unordered set of object names in the Directory. It could be a list of leaf objects or other objects that you want to group together logically, based on some type of search criteria.

**Sample Use**   The Member property is used to define the objects that are members of the list. The members can be any individual objects, even including Group objects. However, the key difference between this object and a group object is that membership in a list does not imply security equivalence as it does in a group. This object can be used to list objects logically for NDS searches.

### Message Routing Group (Effective Class)

**Purpose**   Closely related to the Messaging Server, the Message Routing Group object is used to represent a group of messaging servers that communicate with each other to transfer messages.

**Sample Use**   The Member property is used to define the messaging servers that belong to the Message Routing Group.

### Messaging Server (Effective Class)

**Purpose**   This object is used to represent messaging servers, such as Novell's Message Handling Service (MHS) servers, that may exist in the Directory tree.

**Sample Uses**   If you are using Novell's MHS services for NetWare 6, you will use this object. Important attributes, such as the Message Routing Group, Messaging Server Type, and Supported Gateway, will be configured to define the types of services provided for e-mail communications on your network.

### Organizational Person (Noneffective Class)

**Purpose**   This object defines anyone who either represents or is in some way associated with a particular organization, such as an employee. This object is part of two subclasses defined in the X.500 standard: Organizational Person and Residential Person.

**Sample Use**   The User object is a subclass of the Organizational Person. The user class inherits from the organizational person.

### Person (Noneffective Class)

**Purpose**   This object contains the more common attributes of the Organizational Person and Residential Person objects.

**Sample Uses**    The X.500 specification defines two subclasses of Person: Organizational Person and Residential Person. The current NetWare 6 schema does not include Residential Person. The separation of Person from Organizational Person has been done for future compatibility with X.500.

### Resource (Noneffective Class)

**Purpose**    This object class is used to identify the logical resources available on your network. The resource class is similar to the device class in that a device is a physical unit, and a resource is a nonphysical or logical unit.

**Sample Uses**    A useful property in this object is the Host Resource Name, which can be used if a host's local identification differs from a more global resource identification. If a resource is being used by multiple localities, you can define a Locality name, Organization name, and Organizational Unit name as separate identifiers. If you define appropriate values, you can initiate NDS searches for a particular resource name, locality, or organization.

# The Schema Manager Utility

The Schema Manager utility is found within the NDS Manager utility from the Object pull-down menu. It can also be found under the Tools menu in the ConsoleOne utility. For more information on how to use NDS Manager and ConsoleOne, refer to Chapter 2. Schema Manager allows those with Supervisor rights to the [Root] of a tree to view and customize all aspects of the schema of that tree.

You can use Schema Manager to do the following:

- ▶ View a list of all classes and attributes in the schema.
- ▶ View information on a property, such as its syntax and flags.
- ▶ Extend the schema by adding a class or a property to the existing schema.
- ▶ Create a new class by naming it and specifying applicable attributes, flags, containers to which it can be added, and parent classes from which it can inherit attributes.
- ▶ Create a property by naming it and specifying its syntax and flags.
- ▶ Add a property to an existing class.
- ▶ Compare the schemas of two trees and print the results.
- ▶ View or print a report on a selected class or property, or on the entire schema.
- ▶ View or print the extensions to the schema.

▸ Delete a class that is not in use or that has become obsolete.

▸ Delete a property that is not in use or that has become obsolete.

▸ Identify and resolve potential problems.

**Schema Manager is extremely powerful. An inexperienced user can cause serious damage to an NDS tree with this utility. Schema Manager requires Supervisor rights at the [Root] of the tree. Care should be**
WARNING **taken when providing access to this utility.**

As shown in Figure 3.15, the Schema Manager utility shows the existing object classes and attributes for that tree. The object classes are shown on the left of the screen, and the attributes on the right.

For example, if you double-click or right-click the User object, you will activate the Class Manager screen. This screen enables you to view all aspects of the User object, including mandatory attributes, optional attributes, naming attributes, containment classes, and class flags. An example of this screen is shown in Figure 3.16. To view class inheritance, click the Class Inheritance button within the Class Manager screen, as shown in Figure 3.17.

**FIGURE 3.15:** *The main screen of the Schema Manager utility shows the object classes and attributes for that tree.*

**FIGURE 3.16:** *The Class Manager option shows you all property aspects of the object and enables you to add new attributes.*

**FIGURE 3.17:** *An example of the Class Inheritance for the user class*

To add a new attribute (or property) to the object class, select the Add Attribute button in the Class Manager screen. As shown in Figure 3.18, a list of available attributes to select from appears, along with the object's current attributes. Simply select the attribute you wish to add to the object class and click OK. Doing so adds the attribute to the object class you have selected.

With Schema Manager, you also have the ability to add a completely new object class and/or attributes to your schema. You'll want to add a new class or attributes if you currently don't have such a class in your schema and want to represent that particular resource or property within NDS. The Schema Manager provides two wizards that walk you through the creation of a new object class and the creation of a new property. We will discuss the creation of a new object class using the wizard. The creation of a new property is basically the same process.

**FIGURE 3.18:** *Adding optional attributes to an existing object class*

To enable the Create Class Wizard, select Object ⇨ Create New Class. The wizard appears, as shown in Figure 3.19.

**FIGURE 3.19:** *Enabling the Create Class Wizard*

The first step in creating a new class is to select a name for your new object, as shown in Figure 3.20.

The next step is to select which class or classes the new class will inherit from. This basically means you are defining which attributes the object will receive through inheritance of other classes. When you move a class into the Available classes box, as shown in Figure 3.21, the new class is automatically assigned the same attributes as the class specified. You can then add attributes as needed to customize the new class.

**FIGURE 3.20:** *The first step in creating a new object class is to provide a name for the new object.*

**FIGURE 3.21:** *Selecting other classes from which you want the new class to inherit attributes*

Figure 3.22 shows where you select the class flags for this new class. You can select either Effective Class, Container Class, or both. These class flags control how this class is used. There are five class flags, but only two of them are user defined. Check this flag when you want to create an effective class, which can be used to create objects.

**FIGURE 3.22:** *Specifying the class flags for either effective class or container class*

Uncheck this flag when you want to create a noneffective class, which can be used as a placeholder for a group of attributes. A noneffective class cannot be used to create objects but can be specified as a class from which other classes can inherit attributes.

Check the container class flag when you want to make this a container class. When it is used to create objects, those objects will become container objects (such as "OU"). Do not check this flag for a leaf object.

The wizard then asks you to select the mandatory and optional attributes for this new class. Mandatory attributes are required at the time the user object is created. An example of selecting the mandatory attributes is shown in Figure 3.23. An example of selecting the optional attributes for a new class is shown in Figure 3.24.

**FIGURE 3.23:** *You can specify mandatory attributes for a new object class.*

**FIGURE 3.24:** *Selecting optional attributes for a new object class*

The last step in creating a new object class is to specify the containment classes for this object. This option enables you to specify to which containers the new object can be placed. An example of this screen is shown in Figure 3.25.

**FIGURE 3.25:** *Selecting the container classes for the new object class*

The last screen of the wizard shows a summary of the new object class, as shown in Figure 3.26. Be sure to check carefully the specifications of this new object before writing it to your NDS schema. If any part of the new object needs modification, you can go back through the screens to make changes. Once you select the Finish button, the new object class is created in your NDS schema, providing there are no syntax violations. If such errors do occur, you need to go back through the wizard screens to determine why the object cannot be created.

**FIGURE 3.26:** *Be sure to check the summary of the new class to be created.*

## Summary

This chapter presented a basis for understanding and using NDS objects in your tree along with the schema structure, which is the foundation of NDS. Extensions can be made to the schema to add new object classes or to add attributes to existing object classes.

With this information, you will be able to create a useful naming standard and to define appropriate objects for use within your tree.

# Directory Services Naming Conventions

*"It is impossible that every particular thing should have
a distinct peculiar name." — John Locke*

The concept of naming is closely tied to the Novell Directory Services (NDS) eDirectory structure. Object naming is fundamental to eDirectory because it provides a definition of the objects in the tree, as well as defining their relationships to the other objects in the tree. In addition, resource searching, a key function of the NDS eDirectory name service, is provided through the use of object naming within the Directory. Good naming provides improved search capabilities now and in the future as more applications take advantage of the Directory's capabilities.

NetWare 6 uses a set of rules known as the Directory *schema* to define the naming hierarchy for the entire NetWare 6 network. The schema is replicated across all NetWare 6 servers that exist in the same tree. By contrast, the very old NetWare 3 *bindery* is a flat naming structure that is defined by each individual NetWare 3 server, and it does not provide a hierarchy of bindery objects. This concept is depicted in Figure 4.1.

This section will first consider the basic elements provided within NDS for searching and locating objects within the Directory. These elements include the concepts of name types, distinguished names, relative distinguished names, contexts, typeful and typeless naming, and other methods of naming.

Next, we will discuss how to create a naming standard for your particular needs, including sample standards that can be implemented at your organization.

## NDS Naming Rules

eDirectory is a collection of objects that follow a set of rules regarding their creation, naming, and use. You can improve your tree design by becoming familiar with how each of the objects and attributes are used in building the NDS tree structure and how they should be named.

Understanding the schema helps you understand the internal rules of the objects, including the name types. Understanding the schema also helps you determine the necessity of creating additional objects through schema extensions or on existing NDS objects and attributes. Since its introduction, the types and number of objects and attributes has grown dramatically. Nearly every Novell application will make several extensions to the schema, as well as to any third party application installed on a NetWare 6 server.

**FIGURE 4.1** *A comparison between the NetWare 3 bindery and the NetWare 6 Directory*

Next, we will explain briefly the NDS eDirectory schema—its components, rules, and how the objects are created. For a more detailed understanding of the eDirectory schema refer to Chapter 3.

## The NDS eDirectory Schema

eDirectory consists of objects and attributes that are defined by a set of rules called the schema. The schema rules dictate the naming and relationship of the objects and attributes that can exist in the Directory.

The eDirectory schema is automatically stored on every NetWare 6 server you install, and any updates to the schema eventually are automatically synchronized to all NetWare 6 servers. The length of time to synchronize is a factor of the number of servers in your tree that need updating.

The schema consists of three major components: the object class, the attribute definitions, and the attribute syntaxes. These three components work together to establish the rules that control the creation of a particular object type in the Directory. For example, each object is defined in terms of the attribute definitions and other class definitions. The attribute definitions, in turn, are defined in terms of the attribute syntaxes. Attribute syntaxes are the data types of the attribute values and define the type and length of data. Figure 4.2 illustrates the relationship between the components of the schema. See Chapter 3 for additional information on attribute classes and syntaxes.

**FIGURE 4.2** *Relationship between the three components of the schema: attribute syntaxes, attribute definitions, and objects*

The *object class* defines the types of NDS objects that can be stored in the Directory. The object class comprises the rules for creating the individual objects and determining that object's set of characteristics. This means that every object in the tree belongs to an object class that specifies what attributes are used within the object. These attributes can be the user's name, phone number, work department, and so on.

The base schema that ships with NetWare 6 contains a predefined number of object classes. These object classes cannot be removed or deleted from the schema. You can, and will, add additional object classes to the schema with the addition of new applications.

Novell's Schema Manager utility makes extensions to the schema to add additional objects. See Chapter 3 for a complete listing of the schema extensions. Each of the object classes in the schema is defined by the relationship of the object's containment in the Directory tree. This relationship is constructed on the basis of the containment class rules.

## Object Name Types

Each object consists of a naming attribute and its value. The value is assigned by the administrator during the object creation in the Directory tree. An equals (=) sign connects the naming attribute to the value. The naming attribute determines how the object will be used in the Directory tree. Some objects are container objects, and other objects are leaf objects (or noncontainer objects). Table 4.1 lists the object name attributes that are assigned to each of the NDS objects. Generally, they are abbreviated.

TABLE 4.1

*List of the object name types that are assigned to each of the NDS objects*

| NAME ATTRIBUTE | NAME DESCRIPTION |
| --- | --- |
| C | Country Name |
| L | Locality Name |
| S | State or Province Name |
| O | Organization Name |
| OU | Organizational Unit Name |
| CN | Common Name (includes all leaf objects) |
| BT | Bindery Type |

**Consulting Experience**

As you may have noticed from the Novell utilities in the past, not all of the object class attributes of the container objects were available to you when building your NDS tree. For example, the class L=Locality Name and the S=State or Province Name did not show up in NWAdmin. These object classes were in the NDS schema for years, but they were not exposed by the utilities. The L=Locality class was placed in the schema for compatibility with the X.500 standard. Utilities, such as Nwadmin and ConsoleOne, now show these object classes.

The name types C=Country Name, L=Locality Name, O=Organization Name, and OU=Organizational Unit Name are naming attributes of container objects. The TOP class is also a container object (containing [ROOT]), although it is not visible to the Novell utilities. S=State or Province Name is not a base class. Bindery Type is a naming type for bindery objects that are migrated from NetWare 3 to NetWare 4, NetWare 5, or NetWare 6.

The name type CN=Common Name includes all the leaf objects or noncontainer objects. Therefore, if the object is a user, printer, server, or any other leaf object, it is named by the type CN. The following is a list of all the leaf objects you may use to represent the network resources in your NDS tree. These objects are all named with the "CN=".

- Audit
- AFP Server
- Bindery
- Bindery Queue
- Computer
- Directory Map
- Group
- NetWare Server
- NLS
- Organization Role
- Print Queue
- Print Server
- Printer
- Profile
- User
- Volume

Alias is not shown in this list because it is actually named by the object that it is referencing, such as an Organization, Organizational Unit, or Common Name.

## Distinguished Names

Each object in the tree is given a distinguished name during its creation. An object's *distinguished name* consists of the name of the object plus the names of each of the container objects between itself and the [ROOT] object of the NDS tree. The naming of the object determines the location or position of the object in the tree. The object name attribute, mentioned in the previous section, can be used to help define the distinguished name by specifying the object type for the distinguished name. The distinguished name, therefore, provides a global, complete, and unique name in the Directory tree.

For example, in Figure 4.3 in the ACME tree, the distinguished name for the user Abraham Lincoln is the user object name plus the names of all the containers in which he is a member. It can be viewed as a path back to the top or [ROOT] of the tree. Thus, the distinguished name for the user Abraham Lincoln begins with his common name, CN=ALINCOLN, followed by each of the containers in which he is a member, OU=AUDIT.OU=ADMIN.OU=RIO.O=ACME, back to the [ROOT] object. Therefore, the distinguished name is read from left (lowest level in the tree Common Name) to right (highest level [ROOT]).

The sequence for writing or displaying the distinguished name of an object is as follows:

```
CN=ALINCOLN.OU=AUDIT.OU=ADMIN.OU=RIO.O=ACME
```

The distinguished name can be separated into segments, and each segment of the object's name is separated by periods. Each segment of an object's name consists of two parts: CN=ALINCOLN where CN is the object name type (abbreviated CN for Common Name) and ALINCOLN is the object name value.

**TIP**

**The proper order for writing an object's distinguished name is the least-significant (object deepest in the tree) to the most-significant (object closest to the [ROOT]). The distinguished name is always written left to right.**

NDS will resolve the distinguished names regardless of their character case. For example, ALINCOLN's distinguished name could also be written as follows:

```
cn=alincoln.ou=audit.ou=admin.ou=rio.o=acme
```

as well as:

`CN=ALincoln.OU=Audit.OU=Admin.OU=Rio.O=Acme`

The preceding distinguished names for the user ALINCOLN are equivalent.

**FIGURE 4.3** *Each object in the ACME tree has a complete or distinguished name that is unique based on its object name plus the names of each of the container objects all the way back to [ROOT]. For example, CN=ALINCOLN.OU=AUDIT.OU=ADMIN.OU=RIO.O=ACME.*

Another example of a distinguished name in the ACME tree is for the print queue object known as HP4SI-PQ1. The HP4SI-PQ1 is found in the NDS tree in the container MEDICAL, which is in the container HR, which is in the container SYDNEY, which, in turn, is in container ACME. Figure 4.4 illustrates the distinguished name for this print queue object.

CN=ASchweitzer

CN=MRD-SRV1

CN=MRD-SRV2

CN=HP4SI-PQ1

CN=HP4SI-P1

**FIGURE 4.4** *The distinguished name for a print queue object in the ACME organization is CN=HP4SI-PQ1.OU=MEDICAL.OU=HR.OU=SYDNEY.O=ACME.*

## Consulting Experience

It can be cumbersome to use the distinguished name when referring to the NDS eDirectory objects. You should become familiar with the use of the *relative distinguished name*, which is defined as the leaf-most portion of the name in relation to its parent container. A *partial name* is another commonly used term and is defined as the name in relation to a container. For example, referring to Figure 4.5, LABS-SRV1.LABS is a partial name in relation to the container NORAD.ACME. The server object LABS-SRV1 is the relative distinguished name in relation to the container LABS.

Figure 4.5 shows the distinguished name for two NDS server objects. These server objects are as follows:

```
CN=LABS-SRV1.OU=LABS.OU=NORAD.O=ACME and
CN=WHITE-SRV1.OU=WHITE.OU=CRIME.OU=TOKYO.O=ACME
```

**TIP**

**Notice that the object [ROOT] is not used in any of the distinguished names. The [ROOT] object is always implied by the NDS eDirectory system. Therefore, you are not required to supply a [ROOT] object when entering a distinguished name.**

**FIGURE 4.5** *The distinguished names for the server object CN= LABS-SRV1.OU=LABS.OU=NORAD.O=ACME and the server object CN=WHITE-SRV1.OU=WHITE.OU=CRIME.OU=TOKYO.O=ACME*

# Relative Distinguished Names

A *relative distinguished name* (RDN) is the individual name assigned to an object, otherwise known as the value plus the object naming attribute. The relative distinguished name must be unique only in relation to its parent object. This means that there cannot be two objects in the same container using the same name.

In Figure 4.6 objects in the R&D department in the NORAD location of the ACME tree have relative distinguished names that are unique in relation to their parent object OU=R&D. The objects are CN=LDAVINCI (user), CN=R&D-SRV1 (server), CN=R&D-SRV1_SYS (volume), and CN=R&D-PSI.

**FIGURE 4.6** *The objects in the R&D container of the ACME tree have unique relative distinguished names.*

You can see in Figure 4.7 that you cannot create a second user object named CN=LDAVINCI in the same container R&D.LABS.NORAD.ACME. NDS naming does not permit duplicate object names in the same container, regardless of the object type.

**FIGURE 4.7** *Two objects within the same container cannot have the same relative distinguished name. There cannot be two objects named CN=LDAVINCI in the container R&D.LABS.NORAD.ACME.*

It may not always be obvious that objects of different types still need unique relative distinguished names in the container. For example, a user object and a group object cannot have the same relative distinguished name in the same container for the same reasons we just discussed.

The relative distinguished name only has to be unique in the parent container. The same object name can exist in the tree if the objects are located in different containers because the parent object has a different name, which causes the object to have a unique distinguished name. Thus, the objects with the same name in different containers have unique relative distinguished names in relation to their parents.

Figure 4.8 illustrates how two different printer objects in the ACME tree can have the same relative distinguished name but still have a unique distinguished name in the Directory. The two printer objects are as follows:

```
CN=HP4SI-P1 (in container OU=PR.OU=NORAD.O=ACME)
CN=HP4SI-P1 (in container OU=CHARITY.OU=TOKYO.O=ACME)
```

Both the printer objects named HP4SI-P1 are relative distinguished names in relation to their parent containers OU=PR.OU=NORAD.O=ACME and OU=CHARITY.OU=TOKYO.O=ACME, respectively.

▶ . . . . . . . . . . . . . . . . . . . . . . . . . . . . . ◀

### Consulting Experience

If you are migrating from NetWare 3, be aware that you will need to have a unique relative distinguished name for each of the objects that you will be moving to NetWare 6 and NDS eDirectory. The NetWare 3 bindery permits you to create objects with the same name as long as the object types are different. This rule does not apply to NetWare 6 and NDS eDirectory.

For example, it is common for an administrator in NetWare 3 to create a print queue object and the group that will use the print queue with the same name. This is an easy method to administer the printing setup, as this form of naming is legal in the NetWare 3 bindery. However, in NetWare 4, NetWare 5, and NetWare 6 each object in the container must have a unique relative distinguished name.

When preparing to migrate from NetWare 3 to NetWare 6, you must resolve any of these duplicate names. If you do not resolve the naming conflicts, the NetWare 6 migration utility will migrate the first object but not the second object with the same name.

### Consulting Experience

Although the relative distinguished names for user objects must be unique within one container in the tree, we highly recommend that you create a unique naming standard across the entire tree for all users. Having a global naming standard for users reduces name conflicts when users are created and subsequently moved to another container for any reason. Keep in mind that e-mail systems also require unique names, and most network administrators never allow duplicate names.

**FIGURE 4.8** *Two separate printer objects in the ACME tree can have the same relative distinguished name only if the printers are in different containers in the tree.*

Relative distinguished names are not just reserved for the leaf objects. All objects in the NDS tree have relative distinguished names in relation to their parent containers. For example, in the ACME tree, two OU=NORAD containers cannot exist under the O=ACME. However, in Figure 4.9, notice that two containers called CHARITY and PR are under each of the locations. This is acceptable to NDS eDirectory because each instance of the OU=CHARITY and OU=PR containers is unique in relation to its parent container.

Remember, combining each of the relative distinguished names with its parent object back to [ROOT] creates a distinguished name for the Directory object. Also, both the relative distinguished name and the distinguished name can be entered as *typeful* or *typeless* names as explained in the next two sections.

**FIGURE 4.9** *Each of the OU=CHARITY and OU=PR containers under each of the location OUs have relative distinguished names because they are unique under each of the locations.*

## Typeful Names

Using or placing the object name types in an object's distinguished name is referred to as *typeful naming*. A couple of examples of typeful names in the ACME tree are as follows:

```
CN=SIRKAY.OU=CHARITY.OU=TOKYO.O=ACME
```

or

```
CN=TOK-CHR-PS1.OU=CHARITY.OU=TOKYO.O=ACME
```

where the user SIRKAY and print server TOK-CHR-PS1 are in the Charity OU in the Tokyo location.

You can also refer to each of these objects independently as CN=SIRKAY, CN=TOK-CHR-PS1, OU=CHARITY, OU=TOKYO, and O=ACME.

Each of these objects has its object name type plus the object name; hence, the definition of typeful naming. Typeful names, such as the CN designator, help define the object's location in the hierarchy. The CN designator always indicates a leaf object and is the lowest object in the eDirectory hierarchy.

Typeful names are not required by the Novell utilities or NDS to indicate an object's complete name because you can use typeless names to write the complete name.. The Novell client software allows you to use typeless names because it parses the entered name with the appropriate name type.

The typeful naming method is not case sensitive. The following names from the earlier example are equivalent:

```
cn=sirkay.ou=charity.ou=tokyo.o=acme
```

is equivalent to

```
CN=SIRKAY.OU=CHARITY.OU=TOKYO.O=ACME
```

and

```
cn=tok-chr-ps1.ou=charity.ou=tokyo.o=acme
```

is equivalent to

```
CN=TOK-CHR-PS1.OU=CHARITY.OU=TOKYO.O=ACME
```

### Consulting Experience

Using typeful names can obviously be a lengthy method for indicating an object's distinguished name. Thus, this form of naming is not required or recommended for use with the command line utilities, especially LOGIN.EXE. It is cumbersome for the user to learn and use typeful naming. Typeful naming is only useful for documentation purposes.

## Typeless Names

*Typeless names* are object names that do not include the object name type in each segment. The typeless names for the examples mentioned earlier would be as follows:

```
SIRKAY.CHARITY.TOKYO.ACME
```

and

```
TOK-CHR-PS1.CHARITY.TOKYO.ACME
```

where the user SIRKAY and print server TOK-CHR-PS1 are in the Charity OU in the Tokyo location.

Notice that we have removed the object name type from each of the segments in the object. You can now refer to the objects as simply SIRKAY (where the CN= has been removed), TOK-CHR-PS1, CHARITY, TOKYO, and ACME. All the object name types have been removed.

Like the typeful naming method, typeless naming is not case sensitive. Again, using the examples given above, the following names are equivalent:

```
sirkay.charity.tokyo.acme
```

is equivalent to

```
SIRKAY.CHARITY.TOKYO.ACME
```

and

```
tok-chr-ps1.charity.tokyo.acme
```

is resolved in the same way as

```
TOK-CHR-PS1.CHARITY.TOKYO.ACME
```

**TIP**

**Typeless names are easier to use for both administrators and users because they are shorter and more intuitive. You will use the typeless naming more during your day-to-day operations. You should become familiar with it. You can also use this method of typeless naming for indicating either a relative distinguished name or a distinguished name.**

## Context

An object is identified in eDirectory by its distinguished name, which provides the dual benefits of uniqueness and location within the tree. An object's *context* is its position or location in the NDS tree. If two objects are in the same container, they have the same context because their parent container is identical. In NDS tree terms, the context can be defined as the name of the parent object.

For simplicity, NetWare 6 enables the client to shorten or abbreviate a complete object name through the use of a user context.

Figure 4.10 shows CDARWIN's context or location in the ACME tree. CDARWIN is in part of the Pollution department organizational unit (OU=POLL), in the R&D department (OU=R&D), in the LABS division (OU=LABS), in the NORAD office (OU=NORAD), under the ACME tree (O=ACME). The context for CDARWIN is OU=POLL.OU=R&D.OU=LABS.OU=NORAD.O=ACME.

FIGURE 4.10 *The context in the ACME tree for the user CN=CDARWIN is OU=POLL.OU=R&D.OU=LABS.OU=NORAD.O=ACME.*

**TIP**

**The best analogy for the context in NDS eDirectory is the "path" in the DOS file system. The path statement in DOS helps you quickly and automatically find files stored in specific subdirectories. In the same fashion, the context in NDS helps you find resources in specific NDS containers.**

Setting a context helps the user and administrator access NDS objects in the tree more easily. If a context is set, the user and administrator simply have to enter the relative distinguished name for the resource in the container where the context has been set. Figure 4.11 shows several contexts that exist on the ACME tree:

```
OU=OPS.OU=CAMELOT.O=ACME
OU=FIN.OU=OPS.OU=CAMELOT.O=ACME
OU=DIST.OU=OPS.OU=CAMELOT.O=ACME
```

## Simpler Logins

Using the information in Figure 4.11, in order for the user KINGARTHUR to log in using just the command syntax

```
LOGIN KINGARTHUR
```

he can set the name context variable in the workstation file NET.CFG to

```
Name Context = "OU=OPS.OU=CAMELOT.O=ACME"
```

The user KINGARTHUR could also use the Novell CX (Change ConteXt) utility to manually select the same context, although this is impractical. Keep in mind that the CX command is valid only during the current session. By selecting the correct context, the user can simply enter his user name at the LOGIN.EXE command line and NDS will look in the OU=OPS container for his name.

The alternative is not having a context set. This means that the user would have to know his distinguished name and be able to enter it in order to log in. For example, if the user KINGARTHUR did not set a context, he would have to enter the following during login:

```
LOGIN CN=KINGARTHUR.OU=OPS.OU=CAMELOT.O=ACME
```

or

```
LOGIN KINGARTHUR.OPS.CAMELOT.ACME
```

A context can only be set to a container object. This means that you can set a context to point to either an Organizational Unit (OU=), an Organization (O=), or the [ROOT] object. You cannot set a context to a leaf object.

**FIGURE 4.11** *Several contexts at different levels are shown in the ACME tree.*

A user can more easily identify an object in the tree if his or her context is set to the appropriate container in the tree. For example, if the user MERLIN wants to search for all printers in the OU=DIST in the OPS division in CAMELOT, he can set his context to OU=DIST.OU=OPS.OU=CAMELOT.O=ACME and search only there for the desired printer using the NWUSER utility.

The name context in NDS enables you to navigate the tree more easily. The bindery context (discussed in the next section) enables you to browse the same information as a bindery naming service, which is viewed as an entirely different context.

## Bindery Context

It's hard to believe after all these years that binderies are still in use in literally thousands of installations. NDS provides compatibility with NetWare 2 and NetWare 3 using a feature called bindery services. This feature enables bindery versions of NetWare and other bindery-based applications to access the NDS tree as if it were the bindery. Bindery services is accomplished by setting a bindery context on the server, which specifies the name of the NDS tree container(s) to search as the bindery.

**TIP**

**In order to set the bindery context on a server, you can, for example, enter** SET BINDERY CONTEXT = OPS.CAMELOT.ACME **at the server console. The server bindery context can also be set using the server-based SERVMAN utility.**

Before the release of NetWare 4, NetWare 5, and NetWare 6, object information was not available from a distributed directory. A NetWare 3 server stored only information related to its own server in the bindery. Therefore, applications were written that accessed each NetWare 3 server's bindery for a user name or other information. NDS provides bindery services that enable objects in a container to be accessed by bindery-based clients, as well as by NDS objects. When a bindery-based application makes bindery calls to the server, the server sees the objects in the container where the server bindery context is set.

**NOTE**

**In terms of bindery context on the server, NDS sees only the objects that previously existed in a NetWare 3 bindery as the bindery objects. These objects are limited to user, group, print queue, and print server.**

The default server bindery context is set to the container where the server was installed. You can change the context to another container or OU if you want. Previous versions of NetWare 4, up to and including NetWare 4.02, only permitted you to set a single context for your server. NetWare 5 and NetWare 6 enable you to set up to 16 contexts for a single server.

You can set multiple contexts by using the MONITOR utility as shown in Figure 4.12. This utility enables you to separate each context using a semicolon or a space as shown in this example.

**FIGURE 4.12** *Use the MONITOR utility to set multiple bindery contexts.*

## Leading Periods

The period (.) separates the individual name segments in distinguished names, relative distinguished names, and user contexts. Through the use of leading and trailing periods in the name sequence, you can quickly navigate to any object in the tree. This is useful for referencing objects located in other portions of the tree from a workstation console.

A name with a leading period instructs the client software to ignore the current context and start the search at the [ROOT] object. This means that any object name with a leading period will be treated as a distinguished name starting at the [ROOT] object.

For example, in Figure 4.13, the current context for a user is set to the following:

```
OU=R&D.OU=LABS.OU=NORAD.O=ACME
```

Using the Novell CX utility, you type the following command (notice the leading period at the beginning of the distinguished name):

```
CX .DIST.OPS.CAMELOT.ACME
```

which will be resolved to the container OU=DIST.OU=OPS.OU= CAMELOT.O=ACME by the NDS client. The leading period causes the name to be treated as a whole name, not a partial name. In other words, start at the [ROOT] and work down.

**FIGURE 4.13** *A view of the ACME tree and changing the context*

Using the leading period is simply a shortcut for navigating the tree from the command line utility of your workstation. There can be only one leading period in the object name on the command line.

Trailing Periods

A period after an object name (known as a *trailing period*) can be used to select a new context. The use of a single trailing period will move the current context up by one container in the tree. For instance, you can use the Novell CX (Change ConteXt) utility and type the following command at the DOS prompt (notice the single trailing period):

```
CX.
```

This command will automatically move you up one layer or container in the tree. Unlike leading periods, you can have as many trailing periods up to the number of relative distinguished names (RDNs) in the current context. If you want to move the current context up two layers in the tree, simply supply two trailing periods. You change the context in the tree one layer for every trailing period you supply at the end of the name.

In Figure 4.14, assume that the current context is

```
OU=DIST.OU=OPS.OU=CAMELOT.O=ACME
```

and you want to change the context to O=ACME. You simply type the following command (notice the three trailing periods):

```
CX...
```

Trailing periods can be used with relative distinguished names to indicate segments of the context to be replaced. The replacement occurs during the resolution of the full distinguished name.

In Figure 4.14, for example, assume that the current context is the following:

```
OU=DIST.OU=OPS.OU=CAMELOT.O=ACME
```

If you wanted to change your context to the OU=FIN container, which is under OU=OPS, you would simply type the following command (notice the trailing period):

```
CX OU=FIN.
```

For each trailing period in the RDN, one segment of the context is ignored. This starts at the least-significant segment (deepest in the tree) and proceeds to the most-significant segment or until the trailing periods are exhausted.

Again in Figure 4.14, assume the current context is as follows:

```
OU=DIST.OU=OPS.OU=CAMELOT.O=ACME
```

If you wanted to change your context to the OU=WHI container, which is under OU=LABS in the NORAD location, you would need to type the following command:

```
CX OU=WHI.OU=LABS.OU=NORAD...
```

**[ROOT]**

O=ACME

OU=NORAD    OU=RIO    OU=CAMELOT    OU=TOKYO    OU=SYDNEY

OU=CHARITY   OU=LABS   OU=PR     OU=CHARITY   OU=OPS   OU=PR

AEinstein

LABS-SRVI

LABS-SRVI-SYS

OU=R&D     OU=WHI

LDavinci     CBabbage

R&D-PSI    CANNONBJ-PI

KINGARTHUR

OPS-SRVI

OPS-SRVI-SYS

OPS-PSI

CANONBJ-PQI

CANONBJ-PI

CONTEXT IS:
OU=OPS.OU=CAMELOT.O=ACME
OU=FIN.OU=OPS.OU=CAMELOT.O=ACME
OU=DIST.OU=OPS.OU=CAMELOT.O=ACME

OU=FIN     OU=DIST

Guinevere     Merlin

FIN-PSI    HPIII-PI

**FIGURE 4.14** *Changing the context by using trailing periods*

# A Naming Standards Document

Creating a naming standards document need not be difficult or time consuming. The first step is to determine why such a standard should be created. The preceding sections of this chapter have demonstrated that naming is the structure of the Directory tree. As a basis or purpose for why the standard is important, consider the following:

▶ How can you provide a Directory structure for your employees that is flexible, easy to use, and meets today's business needs?

▶ How can you ensure that you provide a consistent Directory structure within all divisions, locations, and even operating companies?

▸ How can you communicate and implement a consistent standard that everyone will follow across an entire company?

The answers to these questions lie in creating a naming standards document that will force you to devise clear and easy-to-remember names and, thus, make the NDS database a more useful resource.

## Naming Guidelines

Create some naming guidelines before installing your first NetWare 6 server. Once an installation has begun, it becomes more difficult to implement a standard. At a minimum, you should determine how Organizational Units, Servers, and User objects will be defined. These will be the most widely created objects along with your printing objects.

If you have already implemented some existing naming standards, that's the place to start your review. Many companies already have some guidelines in place for defining their users' names. These guidelines are usually based on an e-mail standard. Review the standard and make modifications where necessary. If your company's network is small, you should still create naming guidelines because the network will most likely grow to include more users and resources, which will make naming more important. It's also easier to support a network with consistent naming.

Your naming guidelines need to be global in nature. You should strive to implement your naming guidelines consistently across the entire network so that all users and departments can readily and easily access resources anywhere on the LAN. Global naming guidelines can also help your administrators understand the purpose and use of all objects in the tree.

Most likely you will need input from others in your company in order to create some naming guidelines. You should gather information from the organizations within your company that must participate in forming the naming standard. This information may include input from e-mail administrators, network administrators, and mainframe personnel.

Usually an established host environment will have user naming standards in place. Review these standards as a basis for your NetWare 6 user naming guidelines. Some customers prefer to maintain their host user IDs on the LAN rather than create a new standard at the network level. Others can't wait to change their host user IDs!

Consider all other naming guidelines that you may already have in place from a NetWare 3 environment to determine how well they might fit into the NetWare 6 environment. Your NetWare 3 printers and servers may already have names defined that will work just fine after migration to a NetWare 6 tree. If your organization has sufficient or acceptable guidelines, there is no need to change them.

As mentioned previously, many sites already have e-mail addresses set up that require a user naming convention, such as the first initial and last name of the user (for example, TJEFFERSON for Thomas Jefferson).

Naming guidelines provide consistency across your network. If your naming standard is already consistent and firmly in place, you are in great shape and can move on to the next phase of designing your NDS tree. If you do not have an existing naming standard, you should consider establishing naming guidelines that meet the following goals:

▸ Make browsing and navigation of the NDS tree easier for the users.

▸ Make maintenance of the NDS tree easier for the administration staff.

▸ Make merging separate NDS trees easier.

▸ Keep the NDS object names unique, as required by certain services.

▸ Avoid special characters reserved by the operating systems.

Each of these guidelines is discussed in the following sections.

## Improve NDS Browsing and Navigation

Your primary objective for creating the naming guidelines is to provide the network user with a simple view of the network resources contained in the tree. You may not see the immediate need for good naming guidelines, but as more applications are written to take advantage of NDS and its searching capabilities, an uncomplicated naming standard will be needed.

Objects named with purpose and consistency will eventually provide you with a solid foundation that benefits your administrators, as well as your users. You will see that the system is much more efficient if users can quickly identify the network resources available to them and minimize the impact on searching NDS across multiple locations.

You should keep the names of all the objects short and simple, yet descriptive enough so that the user knows what the object is and the services it provides from its name. For example, the object name HP4SI-P1 is short, yet descriptive, and it lets the user know that this object is a Hewlett Packard 4si printer. The object name HP4SI-PQ1 is another example of a short name, but it is different from the previous example. The PQ1 suffix lets the user know that the object is the print queue that supports the printer (P1).

As you can see, there are many instances throughout the book where we have benefited from using the names of containers and network resources from the ACME tree. It has been helpful to have clear and simple names. Some examples of the naming guidelines for ACME are shown in Table 4.2.

TABLE 4.2

*Examples of the naming guidelines for ACME*

| OBJECT | ENTITY | STANDARD |
|---|---|---|
| [ROOT] | Tree Name | ACME_TREE |
| O=Organization | A Cure for Mother Earth | ACME |
| OU=Organizational Unit | Rio de Janeiro, Brazil | RIO |
| | Tokyo, Japan | TOKYO |
| | Sydney, Australia | SYDNEY |
| | Research and Development | R&D |
| | World Health Index | WHI |
| | Facilities | FAC |
| | Public Relations | PR |
| Users | George Washington | GWASHINGTON |
| | Thomas Jefferson | TJEFFERSON |
| | Leonardo da Vinci | LDAVINCI |
| | Albert Einstein | AEINSTEIN |
| Servers | Server in Labs | LABS-SRV1 |
| | Server in White | WHITE-SRV1 |
| | Server in NORAD/PR | NOR-PR-SRV1 |
| Printers | HP4si in NORAD/PR | HP4SI-P1 |
| Print Queues | Queue in NORAD/PR | HP4SI-PQ1 |

## Maintain Networks and NDS eDirectory

Consistent naming provides a framework for the network administrators to monitor and maintain the network and NDS. The administrators will be installing file servers, creating users and printers, modifying existing objects, and moving objects within the tree. The administrators will also set up all the user configuration files at the workstation to connect to NDS in the predetermined fashion. The administrator's job will be much easier if naming guidelines are in place.

## Merge NDS trees

The capability to merge multiple NDS trees is a feature introduced way back in NetWare 4.1. However, merging two trees within the company will be much easier if the trees are based on the same naming standards for container and leaf objects. The tree merge will be seamless to users because their workstation configuration files will not have to be modified, even though the NDS trees are merged.

## Keep NDS eDirectory Object Names Unique

Some of the tree objects are required to have unique object names in order for the network to work properly. For instance, the file server and print server objects stored in NDS broadcast their services using the Service Advertising Protocol (SAP). Although the file server and print server objects are not required to have unique names on the network, it is highly recommended in order to avoid confusion for users and administrators, especially when running any traces or doing troubleshooting.

Establishing the naming guidelines and publishing them to all network administrators in the company helps keep the NDS eDirectory objects unique, and hopefully saves you time to work on more valuable pursuits. As stated previously, it is recommended that the user objects have unique names throughout the network. This way users can be moved or new users added without conflict.

### Consulting Experience

All network devices on the network that communicate using the Service Advertising Protocol (SAP) should have unique object names in the entire network. Therefore, all file servers and print servers should have unique names on the wire. The maximum length of the names of the objects that use SAP is 47 characters. The space character is illegal for server names.

Not all the objects in the NDS tree will need unique names throughout the network. You decide which NDS objects have unique names. The SAP requires that file server object names be unique on the network.

## Avoid Special or Reserved Characters

NDS requires the use of the escape character with some characters. Therefore, we recommend you avoid using them in your naming guidelines. The characters are as follows:

- **Period (.)** — The period is used by NDS to separate the name segments of distinguished names. For example, the distinguished name for the user George Washington is

  `CN=GWASHINGTON.OU=ADMIN.OU=RIO.O=ACME`

- **Commas (,)** — The comma is allowed by NDS naming rules. However, it is confusing and generally should be avoided.

- **Plus (+)** — The plus sign is used by NDS to represent objects with multiple naming attributes, such as the bindery objects. A common use of the plus sign is for bindery objects placed in the NDS database. For example, a bindery object with the plus sign in the name is seen as CN=BinderyObject+Name. In the case of an Appletalk print server, it might appear as the following:

  `CN=AtpsQuser+83`

- **Equals (=)** — The equals sign is used by NDS to tie together name types and object names. For example, the object type O=Organization would appear as the following:

  `O=ACME`

- **Backslash (\)** — The backslash precedes the special characters above if they are used as part of an object name. For example, suppose you want to use the name *ACME Inc.*, which has a period at the end. In order to make it a legal NDS name, you would need to enter the following:

  `ACME Inc\.`

It is also recommended that you understand the following guidelines if you use spaces in any of the object names; you may want to use the underscore character instead. Spaces are used as delimiters for all the command line parameters. If you use spaces in the NDS object names and need to use the name with a command line utility, you will need to enclose the name in quotes.

For example, the user George Washington is named "George Washington" in NDS with a space separating the first and last name. In order to use the relative distinguished name with the LOGIN.EXE program, the name would have to be entered with quotes around it:

```
LOGIN "George Washington"
```

and not

```
LOGIN George Washington
```

If you were required to provide the full distinguished name during login, the name would then appear as follows:

```
LOGIN "GEORGE WASHINGTON.ADMIN.RIO.ACME"
```

You can also use the underscore character as a replacement for the space character because NDS interprets the space and underscore in the same way. In the example of the user George Washington, his name would appear as follows:

```
George_Washington
```

When the name is used during login, it would be entered without the quotation marks:

```
LOGIN George_Washington
```

You should also avoid the use of the forward slash (/) in your naming of any container or leaf object. Some Windows-based utilities will fail if you map permanent drives or capture a print queue. This is a Windows issue that does not permit the use of the forward slash in any object name.

## Producing a Naming Standards Document

Producing a naming standards document is not glamorous work, but it shouldn't require a great deal of time to complete, either. Here are some steps you can take to produce your naming standards document as quickly and efficiently as possible:

▸ Document the naming standard for each object to be used in the NDS tree.

▸ Provide an example for each object used.

▸ Specify attributes for each of the objects selected.

These steps are discussed in detail in the next section.

## Determining Object Naming Standards

In order to create the naming guidelines, review which NDS objects you will use in your NDS tree. Typically, these objects include organizational units, servers, users, printers, print queues, groups, organizational roles, directory maps, and profiles.

Other possible areas for naming consistency include the attributes associated with each object you define in the NDS tree. In short, any information you plan on using to search the NDS database needs a naming standard for consistency.

The naming standard for each of the objects used in the ACME tree is included in Table 4.3.

|   |   |
|---|---|
| **T A B L E   4.3** | |

*NDS object naming standard for the ACME tree*

| NDS OBJECTS | STANDARD |
|---|---|
| Users | First character of the first name plus the entire last name. All titles are spelled out. |
| Organization | Abbreviation of the company name. |
| Organizational Unit | Location, division, or department name. Abbreviate the names if they are over eight characters long. |
| NetWare Server | Department-SRV#. Exception is the Location-Department-SRV#, which is for the CHARITY and PR departments. The difference is because of the duplication of container names for all locations of CHARITY and PR. |
| Volumes | ServerName_VolumeName. |
| Print Server | Department-PS#. Exception is the Location-Department-PS#, which is for the CHARITY and PR departments. |
| Printer | PrinterType-P#. |
| Print Queue | PrinterType-PQ#. |
| Computer | No standard because it is not used. |

## Providing Example Objects

You may have noticed when reading Table 4.3 that there were no examples of the object naming standards. Remember, a picture is worth a thousand words. An example can convey the meaning of an entire written page. Therefore, include some brief examples in your naming guidelines document. As shown in Table 4.4, you can convey your meaning more quickly and easily by providing an example. Table 4.4 is simply a reprint of Table 4.3, but examples for each of the object's naming standard have been added for clarity.

TABLE 4.4

*NDS object naming standard for the ACME tree*

| NDS OBJECTS | STANDARD |
|---|---|
| Users | First character of the first name plus the entire last name. All titles are spelled out.<br>Examples: GWASHINGTON, SIRGAWAIN |
| Organization | Abbreviation of the company name, which is "A Cure for Mother Earth."<br>Example: ACME |
| Organizational Unit | Location, division, or department name. Abbreviate the names if they are over eight characters long.<br>Example: NORAD, R&D, ADMIN |
| NetWare Server | Department-SRV#. Exception is Location-Department-SRV#, which is for the CHARITY and PR departments.<br>Examples: LABS-SRV1, NOR-CHR-SRV1 |
| Volumes | ServerName_VolumeName.<br>Examples: LABS-SRV1_SYS, NOR-CHR-SRV1_SYS |
| Print Server | Department-PS#. Exception for the CHARITY and PR departments, which is Location-Department-PS#.<br>Examples: FAC-PS1, TOK-PR-PS1 |
| Printer | PrinterType-P#.<br>Examples: HP4SI-P1, CANONBJ-P2 |
| Print Queue | PrinterType-PQ#.<br>Examples: HP4SI-PQ1, CANONBJ-PQ2 |
| Computer | No standard because it is not used. |

## Specifying Object Class Attributes

For some installations, you may need to determine which attributes will be required for the selected objects. Some attributes are mandated by the NDS schema when you create the object. This means that if the mandatory attributes are not filled in, the NDS utilities will not create the object. For example, during the creation of a user object, you are required to specify the Login Name and Last Name attributes.

You may have additional attributes that you would like all your administrators to include when they create a new object. This type of information might include addresses, fax numbers, department names, and so on. Table 4.5 illustrates the naming standards for a user object with additional attributes you want filled in when the users are created. Not all the attributes for the user are represented in the table. Some attributes are required and a value must be entered at creation, while other attributes are optional and are left up to you to determine if they should be used. System attributes are those attributes that NDS automatically populates during the creation of the object.

### TABLE 4.5

NDS property naming standards for a user object in the ACME tree

| ATTRIBUTES | REQ/OPT/SYSTEM | STANDARDS |
|---|---|---|
| Login Name | Required | First character of the first name plus the entire last name. Add a middle initial to resolve name conflicts. |
| Given Name | Optional | First name of the user. |
| Last Name | Required | Last name of the user. |
| Full Name | Optional | First and last name of the user. |
| Generational Qualifier | Optional | SR, JR |
| Middle Initial | Optional | Middle initial of the user, if known. |
| Other Name | Optional | |
| Title | Optional | Job title. |
| Description | Optional | |
| Location | Optional | City or site location (NORAD, RIO). |
| Department | Optional | |
| Telephone | Optional | Business phone number with area code. |
| Fax Number | Optional | Fax phone number with area code. |
| Language | Optional | Preferred language of the user. |
| Network Address | System | |
| Default Server | Optional | Enter the same server as the home directory. |

| ATTRIBUTES | REQ/OPT/SYSTEM | STANDARDS |
|---|---|---|
| Home Directory | Optional | Enter the volume/ subdirectory/user path. |
| Require Password | Optional | Force the user to have a password. |
| Account Balance | Optional | |
| Login Script | Optional | Determined by the site administrators. |
| Print Job Configuration | Optional | Determined by site administrators. |
| Post Office Box | Optional | |
| Street | Optional | |
| City | Optional | |
| State or Province | Optional | |
| Zip Code | Optional | |
| See Also | Optional | |

## More Naming Standards Ideas

### User Accounts

When you create a naming standard, one of the first steps is to decide how to standardize your usernames. NetWare 6 allows usernames to be up to 64 characters long. However, a 64-character username is a long name and not easy to use.

In the example of ACME, the username was limited to the first character of the first name plus the entire last name. If duplicate names are within a single container, the middle initial is added to resolve the name conflict. This type of username may not be used globally because of the number of username conflicts.

Some companies have limited the length of the username to eight characters. This naming convention for the user accounts matches the naming of the user's DOS home directory. Because DOS is limited to just eight characters for subdirectory names, limiting the usernames to eight characters automatically matches the name of the DOS subdirectory assigned to the user. For example, if you use eight characters for the user Thomas Jefferson, his name could be defined as follows:

TJEFFERS

which is the first character of his first name and the first seven characters of his last name.

### Consulting Experience

Currently the Novell utilities do not enforce additional required attributes that you define as an administrator. However, we recommend a well-documented guideline in which you explain your reason for including a particular attribute. Your administrators will be more likely to adhere to the guideline if they understand the reasoning behind the inclusion of an object's attribute.

Another way to represent a user is to take the first six characters of his last name and the first two characters of his first name. This name would appear as follows:

JEFFERTH

Duplicate names can be handled by specifying a middle initial in one of the two names, such as the following:

TQJEFFER

(Thomas Q. Jefferson)
or

QJEFFETH

(Q. Jefferson Thomas)

**TIP**

**Remember, object names within the same container must be unique. Duplicate names are allowed only if the objects are in different containers. However, it is still recommended that you keep object names unique across the entire tree.**

### Organization and Organizational Unit Names

Your organization name should reflect your company name. The company name "A Cure for Mother Earth" is abbreviated as ACME. Thus, the O=Organization is called O=ACME. For the Organizational Units, the locations and departments with short but descriptive names are used. For instance, OU=SYDNEY and OU=TOKYO are examples of the location OUs. They could have been abbreviated to SYD and TOK, but their names are already short. Examples of the division and department Organizational Units are OU=R&D for the Research and Development department and OU=MRKT for the Marketing department.

**The tree name can be named with the company name plus _TREE. We have chosen ACME_TREE as our tree name for the ACME company and O=ACME for the organization. Notice that the difference between the tree name and the organization name is simply the addition of the "_TREE."**

### Server Names

Server names should be unique on the entire network because each server name is broadcast through the SAP (Service Advertising Protocol). You may wish to consider a server name that signifies a location and department.

For ACME, a NetWare server in the CHARITY department of NORAD is called NOR-CHR-SRV1, and a print server is called NOR-CHR-PS1. A server in the R&D department in NORAD is called SRV1. You may wonder why the naming standards seem different for different departments. Notice that the R&D department is a unique department within the ACME tree and that there is no need for the location name in the server name. However, the CHARITY and PR departments are not unique departments within the ACME tree. These two departments are placed as OUs beneath every location, and the servers in those containers should have the location name in order to be unique.

### Printer and Print Queue Names

Printers and print queue names do not have to be unique on the network. The department and location information is obtained by where the printer and print queue are placed in the tree. The distinguished name of the printer or print queue object is used to discover the location and department in which the printer is placed. Thus, the individual object name for the printer and print queue should show the function of the printer.

For example, in the ACME tree an HP4si printer is named HP4SI-P1, and the print queue that supports the printer is called HP4SI-PQ1. A Canon Bubble Jet printer is named CANONBJ-P2, and the print queue is named CANONBJ-PQ2. This type of naming provides users with fundamental information about the printer they will be using.

The user can obtain the location and department in which the printer has been placed from the distinguished name or location in the ACME tree. For example, a Canon Bubble Jet printer (CANONBJ-P1) in the Operations (OPS) department in Camelot (CAMELOT) has a distinguished name of CANONBJ-P1.OPS.CAMELOT. ACME.

The difference between the printer object and the print queue object is defined by the object suffix. For instance, the "P" is for the printer object and the "PQ" is for print queue object.

**NOTE**

A printer that connects directly to the network and services a print queue on the file server is called a *queue server*. A queue server is a special-purpose print server that needs to have a unique name to broadcast using **SAP**. All queue servers use **SAP** to advertise their services on the network.

# A Sample Naming Standard

The following table provides another example of how you can create a naming standard document that is simple but useful. Table 4.6 shows the document with the object type, the naming syntax, and an example. Keep in mind that although we have already demonstrated our naming standard in previous sections of this chapter, the following naming standard is another one for your review.

**TABLE 4.6**

*Sample of a Basic Naming Standard*

| OBJECT TYPE | SYNTAX | EXAMPLE |
|---|---|---|
| [ROOT] or Tree Name | AAAA_TREE | ACME_TREE |
| Organization | AAAA = Company Name | O=ACME |
| Organizational Units | XXXXXX,YYYYY<br>XXXXX = Location<br>YYYYY = Department | OU=RIO, OU=FIN |
| NetWare Servers | XXXYYZ## | RIO-ADM-F0I |
| Print Servers | XXXYYZ## | NOR-CHR-P04 |
| Volume Names | Server_Volume<br><br>XXX = Location<br>(NOR, RIO, CAM, TOK, SYD)<br><br>YYY = Department (LAB, CHR, PR, ADM, OPS, FIN) Z = Server type where: F=File Server, T=Test Server, P=Print Server, C=Comm Server, etc. ## = Quantity (01, 02, 03, . . . , 99) Volumes are SYS, APPS, DATA, USERS, SHARE | RIO-ADM-F0I_SYS |

| OBJECT TYPE | SYNTAX | EXAMPLE |
|---|---|---|
| Printers | YYYTTLL##P | FIN-LJPS01-P |
| Queues | YYYTTLL##Q | FIN-LJPS01-Q |
| Queue Server | YYYTTLL##QS<br>YY = Department<br>(LAB, CHR, PR, ADM, OPS, FIN, HR)<br>TT = Type of printer (LJ for LaserJet,<br>BJ for BubbleJet, PL for plotter)<br>LL = Language (PS for PostScript,<br>PC for PCL, and so on)<br>## = Number of printer,<br>queue, or queue server<br>(01, 02, 03, . . . , and so on)<br>P = Printer<br>Q = Queue<br>QS = Queue Server | FIN-LJPS01-QS |
| Group Help Desk | Function<br>Function (the activity that the group<br>will perform) | WP_Group |
| Organizational Roles | Name_Function<br>Function (the administrative activity<br>or role that the Organizational Role<br>performs) | RIO_Admin_OR |
| Profiles | Name_P<br>Name (the purpose of the Profile<br>object) | Mobile_P |
| Directory Maps | Directory Name<br>Directory Name (the DOS directory<br>name in which the application<br>has been installed) | WP61 |

# Network Addressing Standards

Network addresses are another important area of naming. Having a defined standard for internal network addresses and IP addresses is as important as NDS naming. This section provides some brief examples on defining standards for internal network addresses and IP addresses for your network.

## Server Internal Network Address

The IPX cable address defines the physical cable segment for your file servers. The cable segment may be your entire network, or you may have many segments based on locations in your network infrastructure. If you do not already have a standard for cable segments, you should implement one. A brief example of a cable segment standard is as follows:

XXXSSSSN

For example, 20025451 represents the Norad (200) facility building 2545, segment number 1, where

- ▸ XXX = Numeric value that represents a location, such as NOR, CAM, or TOK.
- ▸ SSSS = Numeric identifier for a wiring closet or building.
- ▸ N = Numeric value that represents a number for the specific segment. This value is useful if you have more than one segment in that location.

## IPX Network Address

Most sites using NetWare 3 have an IPX network address in place for the existing NetWare 3 servers. If you have an IPX network address, you can continue to use the same standard in NetWare 6. The important point is to maintain unique network addresses for all your NetWare servers because duplicate addresses will obviously cause great difficulties for your network. The IPX network address must be unique for the cable segment address, as well.

A sample network address may appear as the following convention:

ARRSSSSN

where

- ▸ A = Indicates that this is an internal IPX number.
- ▸ RR = Indicates a numeric value designating a state or other region.
- ▸ SSSS = Indicates a location.
- ▸ N = Indicates the server number, such as 1 to 10.

## IP Addressing

One of the newer features in NetWare 5 and NetWare 6 is native support for network connectivity and access in a "Pure IP" environment. This is accomplished by enabling the NetWare Core Protocol (NCP), which drives NetWare connectivity and access to be passed through the network via IP.

Implementing IP connectivity in a LAN environment can be a daunting task for most administrators. The variety of network devices using IP, such as LAN-to-host connectivity, printing, and Internet browsers, increases the complexity. Thus, an addressing standard is a requirement for implementing IP on your network.

The workstations, servers, host systems, gateways, and other network devices each must have a unique IP address to communicate. The IP addresses are 32-bit numbers that are structured and represented as twelve-digit numbers organized into four three-digit decimal numbers with the following format:

```
AAA.BBB.CCC.DDD
```

The first three fields have a possible range of numbers from 0 to 255, with the fourth field ranging from 1 to 254. The numbers in the IP address represent two parts: the network number and the host number. In IP terminology, *host* refers to a node on your network. The IP address class determines where in the address IP splits between the network and host numbers. Three IP classes deal with network and host numbers: class A, B, and C. Each class has different rules for how it assigns the network and node numbers.

Table 4.7 illustrates how the different IP address classes split the network and host numbers for IP.

TABLE 4.7

The different IP address classes split the network and mode numbers for IP

| IP ADDRESS CLASS | IP ADDRESS | NETWORK | #OST |
|---|---|---|---|
| Class A | A.B.C.D | A | B.C.D |
| Class B | A.B.C.D | A.B | C.D |
| Class C | A.B.C.D | A.B.C | D |

The IP address class can be determined by the value of the first digits (that is, the A digits). Class A addresses begin with 1–127. Class B addresses begin with a value from 128 through 191. Class C addresses begin with a number equal to or greater than 192. For example, the following IP address is a class C address because its first number is greater than 192:

```
195.001.001.187
```

In this example, the first three numbers form the network number:

195.001.001

The last number forms the host node number:

187

These variations of the IP addressing classes create a variety of possible configurations for the network and host numbers. Table 4.8 illustrates the range for both the network numbers and host numbers.

TABLE 4.8

*The IP classes create a variety of network and node addresses*

|  | CLASS A | CLASS B | CLASS C |
|---|---|---|---|
| Maximum number of networks | 127 | 16,384 | 2,097,152 |
| Maximum number of computers per network | 16,777,214 | 65,534 | 254 |
| Network number part | A | A.B | A.B.C |
| Network number range | 001–127 | 128.0–191.255 | 192.0.0–223.255.255 |
| Node number part | B.C.D | C.D | D |
| Node number range | 0.0.1–255.255.254 | 0.1.255.254 | 0–254 |
| Subnet mask | 255.0.0.0 | 255.255.0.0 | 255.255.255.0 |

### Subnet Masks

If your large network is large enough to use class A or B addresses, the network may be divided into subnets. A *subnet* is a segment of a network used to divide a network into more manageable groups. When using class A and B addresses, typically too many addresses are for networks and not enough for the nodes or computers. You can eliminate this problem by using subnets to divide the number of computers that can be placed on a network.

**IPv6 is currently in development. It will address the issue of creating additional IP addresses. NetWare 6 will support both the current IPv4 and IPv6 standards.**

NOTE

### IP Addressing Standards

Because IP addresses are unique, they must be assigned according to the type and class of your network. You should create an address standard accordingly. The basic addressing standards should include addresses for the company's backbone and major network infrastructure. A range of network addresses should be reserved for growth. You can develop standard IP addresses for departments, type of network media connecting the computers, and so on.

For workstations, as you assign node (host) numbers, it is a good idea to begin with the low end of the node number range and work up. You should reserve the number 0 and the number 255 and not use them as node assignments because they are sometimes used by TCP/IP. This means that you should start at 1 and go up to 254 when addressing all your workstations.

**NOTE** **Novell provides with NetWare 6 a Dynamic Host Configuration Protocol (DHCP) capability that enables workstations to be assigned an IP address dynamically from a pool of available addresses. See Chapter 10 for more information.**

If you connect your network to the Internet, you must get a DARPA Internet address from the Internet Network Information Center, called InterNIC. They can be contacted at www.internic.com.

With a naming standard in place, you are ready to begin the design of your NDS eDirectory tree. Remember that your naming standard will make administration of your tree easier, and it will provide you with consistent naming across your entire organization.

## Summary

We have reviewed the fundamentals of creating a naming standard for NDS, network addresses, and IP addresses. If you don't have a standard in place for these aspects of your network, now is the time create one. With a naming standard in place, you are now ready to move on to the more challenging (and exciting) aspect of designing your NDS tree.

# Designing NDS eDirectory

# NDS eDirectory Design

*"He that plants trees loves others beside himself."*
*— Thomas Fuller (Gnomolgia 1732)*

**A**fter you are familiar with NDS objects and have devised a naming standard, you are ready to design your NetWare 6 tree. This section outlines the steps involved in the design of your NDS tree and explores different design options that you can use depending on the size of your network. Once you have a design that meets your needs, you can begin the installation or upgrade to NetWare 6. NDS eDirectory is installed along with the first NetWare 6 server that you install. Although you can always make changes to your tree later, a properly designed tree almost never needs significant changes. Modifications may be necessary at some point to meet the needs of your changing organization. Because NetWare 6, along with NDS eDirectory version 8.5 and higher, includes NDS for non-NetWare platforms, we include design information about those systems, as well. At the time of writing this book Novell was shipping NDS eDirectory 8.6. Novell's eDirectory is supported on the following platforms:

- ▶ IBM AIX
- ▶ Linux
- ▶ Microsoft Windows 2000 Professional, Server, and Advanced Server
- ▶ Novell NetWare 5.x
- ▶ Novell NetWare 6
- ▶ Sun Solaris

· · · · · · · · · · · · · · · · · · · · · · · · · · · · · · · · · · ◀

# NDS Tree Design

When designing your NDS tree, the following three goals should drive the design decisions you make:

- ▶ Organize the network resources in your company for ease of access.
- ▶ Provide a blueprint for a consistent rollout and upgrade to NetWare 6.
- ▶ Provide flexibility to the design to reflect corporate changes.

## Number of NDS eDirectory Trees

Novell has generally recommended that organizations use a single tree for their production environment because eDirectory is used to represent your corporate resources. Novell, for example, uses a single production tree that crosses the entire globe.

Novell has also distinguished between a traditional tree and an eBusiness tree. There are some slightly different design considerations between the two trees as discussed in this chapter. The traditional tree is what has always been defined for the enterprise in terms of container layout and design. This tree is used primarily for file and print activities. The eBusiness tree takes into consideration massively scalable trees for web servers and includes web authentication and access to thousands, if not millions, of users.

Some organizations may need multiple trees and need to link them together. To link them together, you can use DirXML, Novell's solution for enterprise-wide directory integration. DirXML is a development solution using the Extensible Markup Language (XML) that enables multiple NDS eDirectory trees or other disparate directories to synchronize data among them. An administrator can define what information can be shared between directories and how it should be shared through connectors.

DirXML can also synchronize data between Microsoft Active Directory servers, iPlanet's Directory Server, Microsoft Exchange, and Lotus Notes. Independent software vendors (ISVs), internal developers, and Novell Consulting make use of the Novell DirXML Driver Toolkit to assist in the integration or to create custom drivers. For more information on DirXML see Novell's website at `www.novell.com/products/nds/products/nds`.

## Organize Network Resources

The primary objective for designing the NDS tree is to organize the network resources in your company for easy access. The power of a directory service is that it can group resources logically so that users can find them. The NDS tree should be arranged to reflect the location and placement of the network resources in the network. The network resources should also be placed in the tree to provide easy access to both users and administrators. The goal of the NDS tree design then is not to reproduce the organization chart of the company but to represent all users and resources in a way that enables them to work efficiently and easily. Notice in Figure 5.1 how users and resources are grouped together for ease of access. Some users need access to a particular printer or server, while a larger group (or the entire company) will need access to an e-mail server. The e-mail server can be placed higher in the tree so that all users needing that resource have easier access to it.

**FIGURE 5.1** *Resources and users are grouped near each other in the ACME tree. The OPS division has a NetWare 6 server dedicated for e-mail.*

## Provide a Blueprint for Consistent Rollout and Upgrade

Your blueprint for NDS installation includes naming standards, tree design, and upgrade strategies. With this information in hand, you will have a guide for the installation of all your NetWare 6 servers. For example, the tree design gives you the location where an NDS server should be installed. An administrator can review the naming standards and know exactly how a server should be named. During the rollout of NetWare 6, some companies may be forced to implement more than one NDS tree on the network, with the intent to merge them together in the future. Creating more than one NDS tree is much easier if the multiple trees are based on a similar NDS tree design and similar naming conventions.

In addition, your blueprint gives you a clear map of how to upgrade an entire corporation to NetWare 6. Initially, your upgrade will begin with a few servers and may eventually involve hundreds. Your design can be the master plan for upgrading all your servers to NetWare 6.

## Allow for Corporate Changes

Another objective of the NDS tree design is to provide flexibility for both users and administrators. This simply means that as the corporation changes, both organizationally and physically, you can facilitate those changes easily without making large modifications to your tree structure. For example, you may want a design that allows for easy moves of users and containers. Also, keep in mind that many companies buy or merge with other companies. This objective can be met by designing the NDS tree as described in the following sections.

These objectives seem trivial, but they become important when you consider all the NDS eDirectory design issues. One classic example that always seems to come up is that different groups or individuals in your organization will want the NDS tree designed to meet their specific needs or situation. These political issues can best be handled by referring to your design goals. For example, how does a particular design approach help you organize your network resources? In other words, if you have specific goals to fall back on, you can deal with the political issues by applying each issue against your design goals. Keep in mind that the network is installed to serve a business purpose and to drive costs down. Your job as an administrator is to see that this purpose is being met. If you design your NDS tree with this in mind, many of the political issues can be removed from this process.

### Consulting Experience

Politics should not get in the way of your tree design, but sometimes it does. During the design process, some individuals insist that they be represented as their own organizational units in the tree because of where they appear organizationally in their agency. They incorrectly assume that managerial positions or positions of authority should receive special attention in the design of the tree. As important as these individuals may be, they do not function as their own organizational units in the tree. Regardless of their titles, they are users and, thus, share resources with other individuals on the same floor or building.

# NDS eDirectory Tree Design Tasks

This section introduces the tasks associated with the NDS eDirectory tree design. The tasks or steps provide an easy-to-understand and effective method for designing your NDS tree. The tree design consists of five steps:

1. Gather your network and company documents.
2. Design your tree in the shape of a pyramid.
3. Design the top level of your tree.
4. Design the bottom level of your tree.
5. Make modifications to the tree based on your company's needs.

**X-REF**

**Modifications to your tree design may include any new products that you wish to add to NDS, such as Novell's ZENworks product. For more information on ZENworks, see Chapter 19. Also see the "NDS Design for ZENworks" section later in this chapter.**

While no absolute or exact way to design an NDS tree exists, some methods are definitely more efficient than others. Efficiency is achieved when the tree is stable and the design provides for the least amount of NDS traffic possible. Efficiency is also achieved when users can easily locate resources.

These design methods are presented in the following sections to help you design an efficient NDS eDirectory tree. The methods presented here have been developed by Novell Consulting and have been successfully implemented by hundreds of their large and small customers. The design guidelines presented here work for small and large companies regardless of any unique design requirements.

It is important to define what we mean by small and large companies. For the purposes of the examples given in this chapter, a small company consists of five or fewer servers (with no wide area network [WAN] connections) and fewer than 500 users. Certainly, there is no written law that this definition is always true; however, a network of this size has fewer design ramifications than a network with thousands of users and a complicated network infrastructure.

A large network then is anything with more than five servers with a WAN connection and more than 500 users. As you read through this chapter, you will be able to determine which category (small or large) you fall into. So, let's begin the design.

## Gather Corporate Documents

Some company information or documentation is necessary to help you initiate an NDS eDirectory tree design for your corporation. Typically, the most painful task in designing the NDS tree is gathering all these corporate documents. However, trying to design the tree without them is an even more painful task. These documents are the inputs into the NDS tree design process; try to obtain as many of them as you can. Each of the documents is used during a different phase of the design process, and some documents are more important than others. The following documents are listed and discussed below in order of importance.

### Wide Area Network Diagrams

The most important company document is the wide area network (WAN) layout or map. The WAN map is required before starting the NDS design for your company because it is used to design the top of the NDS tree. If your company has campus networks at one or more locations, documentation of the physical campus network is also needed.

Figure 5.2 shows the ACME WAN layout map. The WAN layout or physical layout usually consists of all your major hub locations that are interconnected with routers and bridges. Notice in ACME's WAN layout map that all five main sites are shown with their router connections and the speed of these links in kilobits per second. Your WAN layout map may look similar, or it may include the link speeds of your satellite offices.

Your WAN documentation may consist of more than one compact diagram. Don't worry if your documentation consists of many pages of information. The key here is to understand how your infrastructure is organized and where the major hub locations exist. These documents are necessary for the upper layer design of your tree, as we will explain. Most large companies have some sort of wide area network diagrams available. We recognize that a WAN network diagram is a document always in flux at most companies. However, try to obtain the latest WAN map from the staff that manages your network infrastructure.

If you have a small network (no WAN, five or fewer servers, fewer than 500 users), you may not have a WAN map, but you will probably have an organizational chart. Organizational charts are discussed at the end of this section and will be used for smaller network designs.

**FIGURE 5.2** *The ACME Physical WAN layout map includes important information, such as the major hub locations of its network, as well as router connections and link speeds.*

### Campus Network Maps

Along with your WAN layout maps, campus diagrams provide a further breakdown of locations of your hub sites. This type of documentation varies from company to company. Some companies show the entire hub and campus diagrams together; others separate the information because of the size of their network. A campus network map may show you a campus, such as the NORAD campus shown in Figure 5.3.

The ACME campus map for NORAD shows information such as a Fiber Distributed Data Interface (FDDI) ring and routers connecting this site's buildings. The campus diagram may also show buildings and their interconnections. Again, this information, along with the physical WAN map, describes your WAN/LAN infrastructure. This preliminary information is necessary to build the foundation for your NetWare 6 environment.

Labs Building (R&D, WHI)

Router

Router

512 Kb to RIO

512 Kb to CAMELOT

512 Kb to TOKYO

Router

Router

Router

Router

NORAD FDDI BACKBONE

Router

Router

Charity Building

Router

Router

Public Relations Building

**FIGURE 5.3** *The campus diagrams show a continuation of your physical WAN diagrams. Information can include connection types between buildings, such as FDDI, bridged token rings, 10baseT, fiber, and so on.*

### Site Lists

The next item to obtain for your tree design is a list of sites or locations of your network. Sometimes this information is included with your other documentation discussed previously. Large companies usually have a list of sites with their locations. For example, the ACME network has a site known as CAMELOT, which is shown as a single site on the WAN map for ACME. Further documentation, however, shows sites within the CAMELOT area, such as an operations center (OPS) located at the south end of the city and a public relations office (PR) center located in the downtown district. An office for charitable contributions (CHARITY) is also found at the downtown location. Figure 5.4 shows an example of the sites for the CAMELOT location.

### Resource Lists (File Servers, Printers, and Other Resources)

A resource list may be included with your LAN maps for each site. This list gives important information about the current servers and printers found in each region, site, building, or department. Table 5.1 shows the resource list for ACME with its servers, printers, and print queues. This information will later be used in your tree design for the placement of these resources.

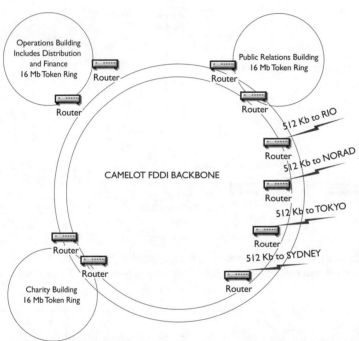

**FIGURE 5.4** *The CAMELOT site includes three buildings under its designation: Operations (OPS), Public Relations (PR), and CHARITY.*

**NOTE**

**Keep in mind that the information we are referring to in this resource list will be either NetWare 3, NetWare 4, or NetWare 5 server information or other operating systems that will be upgraded to NetWare 6. This resource list may also include server platforms where you intend to place a copy of NDS eDirectory. This list enables you to know beforehand where many object types need to be created in the NDS eDirectory tree. Notice also that some of the naming standards shown in the list can be used in your NetWare 6 environment while others may need some slight changes.**

T A B L E  5.1

*ACME Resource List*

| LOC/DIV | SERVER NAME | PRINTERS/QUEUES |
|---|---|---|
| <u>NORAD</u> | NOR-SRV1 | |
| CHARITY | NOR-CHR-SRV1 | HP4SI-PQ1<br>HP4SI-P1 |
| LABS | LABS-SRV1 | |
| R&D.LABS | R&D-SRV1<br>R&D-PS1 | HP4SI-PQ1<br>HP4SI-P1 |
| POLL.R&D.LABS | | HP4SI-PQ2<br>HP4SI-P2 |
| NUC.R&D.LABS | | HP4SI-PQ3<br>HP4SI-P3 |
| VR.R&D.LABS | | HP4SI-PQ2<br>HP4SI-P2 |
| WHI.LABS | WHI-SRV1<br>WHI-SRV2 | CANONBJ-PQ1<br>CANONBJ-P1 |
| WHI.LABS | WHI-SRV3<br>WHI-PS1 | |
| PR | NOR-PR-SRV1<br>NOR-PR-PS1 | HP4SI-PQ1<br>HP4SI-P1<br>CANONBJ-PQ2<br>CANONBJ-P2 |
| <u>RIO</u> | RIO-SRV1 | |
| CHARITY | RIO-CHR-SRV1<br>RIO-CHR-PS1 | HP4SI-PQ1<br>HP4SI-P1 |
| ADMIN | ADMIN-SRV1<br>ADMIN-SRV2<br>ADMIN-ADM-PS1 | CANONBJ-PQ1<br>CANONBJ-P1 |
| FAC.ADMIN | FAC-SRV1<br>FAC-PS1 | HP4SI-PQ1<br>HP4SI-P1 |
| AUDIT.ADMIN | AUDIT-SRV1 | HP4SI-PQ1<br>HP4SI-P2 |

*continued*

T A B L E  5.1

ACME Resource List (continued)

| LOC/DIV | SERVER NAME | PRINTERS/QUEUES |
|---|---|---|
| MRKT.ADMIN | MRKT-SRV1 | HPIII-PQ1<br>HPIII-P2 |
| PR | RIO-PR-SRV1<br>RIO-PR-PS1 | HP4SI-PQ1<br>HP4SI-P1<br>CANONBJ-PQ2<br>CANONBJ-P2 |
| <u>CAMELOT</u> | CAM-SRV1 | |
| CHARITY | CAM-CHR-SRV1<br>CAM-CHR-PS1 | HP4SI-PQ1<br>HP4SI-P1 |
| OPS | OPS-SRV1<br>OPS-PS1 | CANONBJ-PQ1<br>CANONBJ-P1 |
| FIN.OPS | FIN-SRV1<br>FIN-SRV2<br>FIN-SRV3<br>FIN-PS1<br>FIN-PS2 | HP4SI-PQ1<br>HP4SI-PQ2<br>HP4SI-P1<br>HP4SI-P2 |
| DIST.OPS | DIST-SRV1<br>DIST-SRV2 | HPIII-PS1<br>HPIII-PQ1<br>HPIII-P1 |
| PR | CAM-PR-SRV1<br>CAM-PR-PS1 | HP4SI-PQ1<br>HP4SI-P1 |
| <u>SYDNEY</u> | SYD-SRV1 | |
| CHARITY | SYD-CHR-SRV1<br>SYD-CHR-SRV1<br>SYD-CHR-PS1 | HP4SI-PQ1<br>HP4SI-P1 |
| HR | HR-SRV1<br>HR-SRV2<br>HR-PS1 | HP4SI-PQ1<br>HP4SI-P1 |
| MEDICAL.HR | MED-SRV1<br>MED-SRV2 | HP4SI-PQ1<br>HP4SI-P1 |
| FOOD.HR | FOOD-SRV1<br>FOOD-SRV2 | HP4SI-PQ2<br>HP4SI-P2 |
| SHELTER.HR | SHELT-SRV1<br>SHELT-SRV2 | HP4SI-PQ3<br>HP4SI-P3 |

| LOC/DIV | SERVER NAME | PRINTERS/QUEUES |
|---|---|---|
| PEACE.HR | PEACE-SRV1 | HPIII-PQ4 |
|  |  | HPIII-P4 |
| PR | SYD-PR-SRV1 | HP4S1-PQ1 |
|  | SYD-PR-PS1 | HP4S1-P1 |
| TOKYO | TOK-SRV1 |  |
| CHARITY | TOK-CHR-SRV1 | HP4S1-PQ1 |
|  | TOK-CHR-SRV1 | HP4S1-P1 |
|  | TOK-CHR-PS1 |  |
| CRIME | CRIME1-SRV1 | HP5-PQ1 |
|  | CRIME1-SRV2 | HP5-PQ1 |
|  | CRIME1-PS1 | HP4FI-P2 |
| BLUE.CRIME | BLUE-SRV1 | HPIII-PQ1 |
|  | BLUE-PS1 | HPIII-P1 |
| VIO.BLUE.CRIME | VIO-SRV1 | HP4SI-PQ2 |
|  | VIO-SRV2 | HP4SI-P2 |
| ENV.BLUE.CRIME | ENV-SRV1 | HP4S1-PQ3 |
|  |  | HP4S1-P3 |
| THEFT.BLUE.CRIME | THEFT-SRV1 | HP4SI-PQ4 |
|  |  | HP4SI-P4 |
| WHITE.CRIME | WHITE-SRV1 | CANONBJ-PQ1 |
|  | WHITE-SRV2 | CANONBJ-P1 |
|  | WHITE-PS1 |  |
| CYBER.WHITE.CRIME | CYBER-SRV1 | HPIII-PQ2 |
|  |  | HPIII-P1 |
| POL.WHITE.CRIME | POL-SRV1 | HP4SI-PQ3 |
|  |  | HP4SI-P3 |
| FIN.WHITE.CRIME | CRIMEI-FIN-SRV1 | HP4SI-PQ4 |
|  |  | HP4SI-P4 |
|  |  | HP4SI-P5 |
| PR | TOK-PR-SRV1 | HP4S1-PQ1 |
|  | TOK-PR-PS1 | HP4S1-P1 |

## Company Organizational Chart

The organizational chart is also an important document. It is the last piece of information that is helpful in designing your tree. Your company may have many pages of organizational charts or a single chart. Your main purpose in obtaining the organization chart is to determine what divisions, departments, or other groups need to be created at the bottom layer of your tree. Figure 5.5 shows ACME's organizational structure. It is the input from this structure that determines the lower layers of the NDS trees.

FIGURE 5.5 *The organizational structure for ACME provides information about departments, divisions, and workgroups that may need to be represented in your NDS tree structure.*

As you will see, the organizational chart is used only during the design of the bottom of the tree. After you have gathered the corporate documents, you are ready to start the planning of the NDS tree.

## Design Tree in the Shape of a Pyramid

The design of the NDS eDirectory tree should take the shape of a pyramid or inverted tree. This has been true since the first release of NDS. The pyramid design implies that you place most of the containers and objects at the bottom of the structure with fewer containers at the top. The pyramid design shape of the tree is logically split into two sections. First, you will design the top of the tree, with its appropriate containers, and then you will design the bottom of the tree. We will explain where the distinction is made between the top and the bottom of the tree.

Figure 5.6 illustrates how the pyramid design is split into the top and bottom sections of the tree.

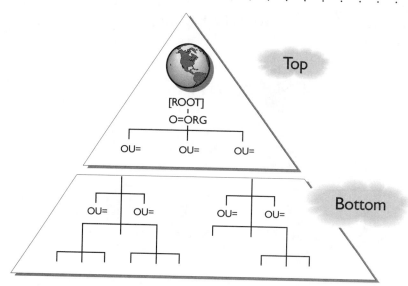

**FIGURE 5.6** *The NDS tree should be designed like a pyramid with a top and bottom portion of the tree.*

The advantage of a pyramid-shaped tree layout is that the top layers become the foundation (or static layers) upon which the bottom layers can be established. The bottom layers of the tree will be more dynamic, allowing for greater flexibility to change when your company changes. This design approach enables you to more easily make changes, such as moving users or subtrees.

Another advantage of the pyramid tree design is that the partitioning of the NDS database is more natural. The alternative to the pyramid design is to create a flat tree layout or structure that places all the objects in the top layers of the tree. As shown in Figure 5.7, a very flat and wide tree is not as an efficient design as a pyramid shape because of how NDS eDirectory communicates with its subordinate levels. NDS eDirectory provides enormous scalability, and some companies may have hundreds of branch offices and a headquarter location where a wide, flat design may be necessary. Later on, we explain ways to make this type of design more efficient. NDS eDirectory (starting with version 8.0) is massively scalable, but you still must take into consideration the speed of your WAN links and try to preserve precious WAN bandwidth where possible through proper design.

Novell has also (as of NDS eDirectory version 8) defined an eBusiness tree. This design typically has very few containers, usually an Organization container and possibly an OU, with thousands of users. This type of design does not really represent a pyramid shape, unless you start to have multiple locations. If that's the case then the pyramid design approach still makes sense.

[ROOT]

O=XYZ

OU=LOC1   OU=LOC2   OU=LOC3   . . .   OU=LOC149   OU=LOC150

**FIGURE 5.7** *A very flat and wide tree is not as efficient as designing an NDS eDirectory tree with the pyramid shape. The design in this figure shows 150 locations at one level.*

**An efficient NDS eDirectory tree will have more organizational units at the bottom and fewer at the top. Our recommendation is to have only 10 to 15 OUs at any given level in the tree. Even the largest companies with many branch offices will usually meet this requirement, as explained later in this chapter.**

TIP

Having all the objects in the top of the tree also makes the tree rigid for most large companies. A flat tree is not recommended primarily because of the way it has to be partitioned and replicated. Synchronization traffic of NDS eDirectory on all servers in the tree is increased with this type of approach. The tree partition and replica layout become extremely flat, which creates many subordinate reference replicas. Subordinate references are pointers between partitions and subordinate partitions. They are automatically created by NDS for tracking purposes. For more information about subordinate reference replicas, refer to the "NDS Partitions and Replicas" section later in this chapter.

As seen in Figure 5.8, the tree begins with the [ROOT] object at the top followed by the O=Organization object. After the O=Organization object(s), the next level is a layer of OU=Organization Unit(s). Typically, only a selected set of users and network resources is located in the top layers of the tree. For example, the ADMIN user object is located in the O=Organization object because the installation program automatically creates it.

**FIGURE 5.8** *The top of the tree includes the [ROOT] object, O=Organization, and the first layer of OUs. The first layer of OUs should be based on the network infrastructure.*

The bottom of the tree is defined by the local area network (LAN) and is based on the actual organization of your company from a departmental or divisional standpoint. In Figure 5.9, the bottom layers in the tree are most flexible if they represent the organizational structure of your company. This can be accomplished by using the divisions, departments, and workgroups in the corporation. The bottom layer OUs will hold the majority of your leaf objects, such as the users, file servers, printers, queues, and other network resources. This approach provides the greatest flexibility because when you make changes to a department you will only affect the container(s) of that department. The rest of the tree is left unchanged. In contrast, if you have organizations represented at the top of your tree and you make changes to an organization, these changes can possibly affect containers that are subordinate to the container you initially changed.

Both the top and the bottom of the tree are illustrated in Figure 5.10 and will be discussed in the following sections in greater detail.

BOTTOM OF THE TREE
– Based on the organization
of the company

**FIGURE 5.9** *The bottom of the tree is based on the organization of the company. These lower layers offer flexibility to the tree design for moves and other changes.*

Top
–WAN
– Geography
– Static

[ROOT]
|
O=ORG

OU=    OU=    OU=

Bottom

– LAN
– Organization
– Flexible

**FIGURE 5.10** *The top of the NDS tree is based on the WAN or locations of your company and becomes the static portion of the tree. The bottom of the tree is based on the LAN and organization of your company and gives you the flexibility to make moves and other changes.*

## Design Top Level of the Tree

The design of the top of the NDS tree is the foundation of the NDS tree. The rest of the tree branches downward from the top. As we mentioned earlier in this chapter, the top level of the tree includes the tree name, which is the [ROOT] object, the O=Organization object, and the first layer of OU=Organization Units which, for most companies, will be based on your WAN infrastructure and locations. Figure 5.11 illustrates how we are taking the information from the WAN diagrams and designing the upper layer of the tree.

As shown in Figure 5.12, a guideline for the maximum number of containers at each level is 50. Although this number is not a strict rule, we have found that most companies can maintain greater efficiency for NDS synchronization if they stay at or below this range. For companies with many branch offices exceeding this value, try to insert a level of regional organizational units one level above to distribute the load of branch offices under these regional containers.

Most companies can work within this guideline. However, for exceptionally large companies with thousands of branch offices (a national postal system, for example), you may have no choice but to exceed this recommendation. If you must, pay special attention to partitioning and replication guidelines as presented in Chapter 6.

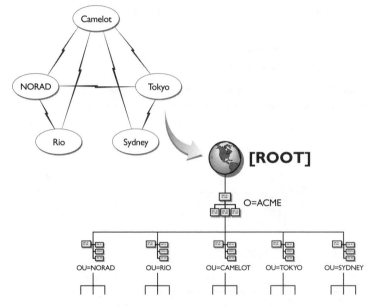

**FIGURE 5.11** *For the upper layer of the tree, match the major hub locations of your network to the first level of organizational units in your tree.*

### Tree Name or [ROOT] Object

The first entity that needs to be named in NDS is the tree itself. The tree name is also the name of the [ROOT] object, which is placed as the topmost object in your tree. The NDS tree name is displayed in many of the current NetWare utilities, such as MONITOR and NWCONFIG. The tree name you choose can represent the company name plus _TREE. For example, our company is called ACME, so we chose to name the tree ACME_TREE, as shown in Figure 5.13.

O=XYZ

OU=LOCI    OU=LOC2    OU=LOC3    . . .    OU=LOC49    OU=LOC50

With eDirectory, there is no limit to
the number of subordinate containers.

**FIGURE 5.12** *The number of subordinate containers is unlimited at each level in the tree. Beyond this number you should consider adding another level in your tree to distribute your containers.*

[ROOT] (ACME_TREE)

O=ACME

OU=NORAD    OU=RIO    OU=CAMELOT    OU=TOKYO    OU=SYDNEY

**FIGURE 5.13** *Another name for the [ROOT] object is ACME_TREE.*

The name of the tree should be a unique value on the network wire because the tree uses SAP to broadcast to the client or workstations where the tree can be found. SAP bootstraps clients and all applications requiring NDS to efficiently find the NDS database. If you need to install more than one physical NDS tree, make sure that the trees have different names. An example of this important point is illustrated in Figure 5.14.

The company name plus _TREE is recommended because it clearly identifies the tree SAP as an NDS tree when you DISPLAY SERVERS at a console. Be careful not to make this name too long. Also, the SAP does not support spaces in the name, which is advertised via SAP, and the NetWare 6 installation utility (NWCONFIG) does not let you place spaces in the tree name.

**TIP**

**The NDS tree always starts with the [ROOT] container object. In most discussions, however, the [ROOT] object is not counted as a layer in the tree.**

**NOTE**

**The object class definition in the schema that defines the [ROOT] is the object class TOP. The [ROOT] object is the only instance of the object class TOP and for this reason TOP is known as an effective class.**

**FIGURE 5.14** *You may have multiple trees on your network. Each NDS tree must have a unique name, such as ACME_TREE1 on Server1 or ACME_TREE2 on Server2.*

The [ROOT] object is parent to either the C=Country and/or O=Organization. Novell Consulting recommends that you use the O=Organization below [ROOT] rather than the C=Country object.

### To Use or Not to Use Country Objects

The C=Country designator is used to specify a particular country code based on the X.500 standard. Most companies are not required to use the country object for their corporate trees. Instead, they can create a separate tree used for connecting to the public data network or through a 32-bit client that can connect to multiple trees.

If you choose to use the Country object, keep in mind that it adds an additional layer to your NDS tree, and it also creates some rather odd distinguished names for your objects. Consider the example in Figure 5.15. If we were to add the Country object to the ACME tree, which country do we choose? Do we use multiple country codes? For our example, ACME is headquartered primarily in CAMELOT; therefore, our Country object will be C=UK for England in this example.

**FIGURE 5.15** *The use of the Country object can create some odd contexts in your tree.*

Let's look at some of the user's contexts that would be created in other locations if we used only the C=UK COUNTRY designator. Abe Lincoln resides in the RIO location, so his context would be as follows:

```
CN=ALINCOLN.OU=AUDIT.OU=ADMIN.OU=RIO.O=ACME.C=UK
```

User Sherlock Holmes in the TOKYO location would have the following context:

```
CN=SHOLMES.OU=CRIME.OU=TOKYO.O=ACME.C=UK
```

Now, if your names are supposed to adequately describe and identify a user's location in the tree, these examples are a little confusing and add more length to the context. Also, for some users who work in both the United Kingdom and the United States, it is difficult, if not impossible, to determine where in the tree they belong.

If you have already implemented the Country object in your tree, not to worry. It does not cause any serious consequences, but keep in mind the considerations just discussed.

### Locality

You also have the option to use the Locality container object in your tree design. This container conforms to the X.500 naming conventions and, if needed, can be implemented to represent your directory environment. Some government agencies may find this object useful, but, generally, most companies will have little need for it. The schema also support the State object, but its utilities to not display it either in NWADMIN or ConsoleOne.

### Organization Names

After the [ROOT] object at the top, you will provide the NDS tree with at least one O=Organization. At least one O=Organization object is required for all NDS trees. The subsequent layers in the tree (the OUs) will be placed directly below the O=Organization.

We recommend that you name the O=Organization the same name as your company or use an abbreviation. Most companies use an abbreviation for the company name because it is easier when you are typing an object's context. For example, our company is named ACME Intelligence Agency. In almost every case, the Organization layer in the tree contains only one O=Organization, which gives you a single object to represent the entire company. Figure 5.16 shows how we have named our organization to represent our company name ACME.

**FIGURE 5.16** *ACME is representative of our entire company and is used as our organization name in our NDS tree.*

Your company may want to use more than one O=Organization if your corporation has multiple companies that do not share the same network infrastructure. For example, the large conglomerate shown in Figure 5.17 uses multiple O=Organization objects because two separate companies (separate network infrastructures) are included in a single NDS tree.

**FIGURE 5.17** *A large conglomerate company with multiple O=Organization objects*

### Small Companies

In some cases with small companies, the tree design can easily be finished at this point because most servers, users, and other resources can be placed in the Organization container without creating any more containers. If you are the network manager responsible for all users, printers, and servers, you can simply group everyone in the same container, which can be the Organization container.

Figure 5.18 shows how a tree design can be simple for a small company. If ACME had only a few servers in a single location, its tree could appear as shown in the figure. You may still want to subdivide the tree a little more if you have separate groups.

O=ACME

CN=GWashington

CN=KingArthur

CN=ACME-SRV1

CN=ACME-SRV1_SYS

CN=ACME-SRV2

CN=ACME-SRV2_SYS

**FIGURE 5.18:** *Small companies can group all their resources in the organization container and avoid creating additional OUs if they have limited network administration needs.*

### Consulting Experience

We recommend that you not name the O=Organization the same name that you used for the NDS tree. For troubleshooting purposes, the NDS tree can be named with the company name plus _TREE (or other designator), and the O=Organization should be named with just the company name or an abbreviated company name. The ACME corporation would therefore be named O=ACME, with a tree name ACME_TREE.

### Geographic Design

As mentioned previously, the layer below the O=Organization is the first layer of OU=Organizational Units in the NDS tree. This layer of OUs is the most important layer of the NDS tree because it represents the geographic locations of your company. You can use your company WAN maps or WAN documentation to carefully design the contents of this layer, which becomes the foundation for the entire tree. This method is often referred to as the geographic design approach because you use your company's geographic or WAN location information for the design at the top of the tree.

The key to designing the top of the tree is to match the WAN infrastructure or locations of your company with the first OU layers or containers. Based on our experience at many sites, the design of the top of the tree should be completely based on the WAN infrastructure. You will have a successful NDS tree design if you follow the guideline of representing the sites of your company with the topmost OUs. Figure 5.19 and Figure 5.20 illustrate how the top layer of the ACME tree is designed based on the physical WAN layout of the company.

### Consulting Experience

A single NDS tree with two or more O=Organization objects is rarely used and is generally not recommended. This configuration is not often used because one of the design goals is to represent the entire corporation in the single tree with the same organization name. However, NDS operates either way without difficulty.

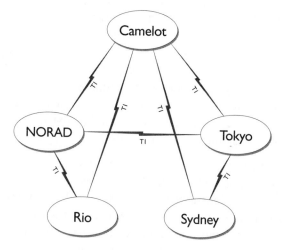

Physical WAN Layout for ACME

**FIGURE 5.19:** *Physical WAN layout for ACME*

[ROOT]

O=ACME

OU=NORAD    OU=RIO    OU=CAMELOT    OU=TOKYO    OU=SYDNEY

**FIGURE 5.20:** *Top layer of the tree design for ACME, which is based on the physical or geographic WAN sites*

If you are a small company (no WAN, 5 servers or fewer, fewer than 500 users), you can simply use the first Organization container you created to name your company. This container will hold all your objects, including printers, servers, and users. Administration of a single container is easy and requires little maintenance. You can also create a container beneath the Organization container and place the resources there.

In general, if your company has multiple geographic sites or locations, you should represent the locations in the NDS tree at the top of your tree. The organizational structure of departments, divisions, and workgroups will be placed under each of these locations. Keep in mind that one of our design goals is to design a flexible tree in which changes are easily made. As you might expect, there are a few exceptions to the practice of designing geographically:

▸ Companies with a single site or campus-connected network are not dependent upon the geographic design approach. Because this configuration does not have physical locations that can be placed under or created as OUs, you will skip the geographic design approach at the top of the tree and proceed directly to the departmental design approach. Some companies with few servers and users may not need to create additional containers. Rather, they can place all the NDS objects under the single O=Organization.

▸ For companies with WAN sites or locations connected with high speed links, such as T-3 or greater, the location OUs are less important because the limitation of the WAN has been removed. This is because WAN speeds are approaching LAN speeds. For the purpose of NDS tree design, the high-speed WAN connections really represent LAN bandwidths. However, we still recommend that you use the geographic design approach. See the section "Design Bottom Levels of the Tree" later in this chapter.

When considering a campus network layout, such as a research park or university, consider first the speed of the links between the buildings or floors of the campus network. The locations in the campus network, such as buildings, could be used to represent minor sites in the network infrastructure and in the NDS tree. The buildings in the campus network can be useful container objects if they help organize your network resources and the NDS tree. The ability to effectively organize network resources is one of your design goals. The ACME tree NORAD location, as shown in Figure 5.21, has used buildings named by function as its organizational units. Either design approach is acceptable. You must determine which one provides the best description of your environment.

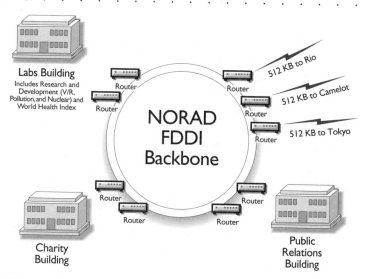

**FIGURE 5.21** *The ACME NORAD organization units are named based on their functions, which are also the building names, such as OU=CHARITY, OU=LABS, and OU=PR.*

If your company does not have a WAN infrastructure but only a LAN network, then you can skip the geographic design approach and go directly to the departmental design discussed later in this section.

### Consulting Experience

Many companies still choose to use geographic containers even though they have very high speed WAN links. One company, for example, has a metropolitan area network (MAN) running FDDI to connect 12 buildings together across a city. The basis for the company's decision to use geographic sites at the top of the tree was twofold. First, for administrative purposes, the company wanted a single administrator to support each site. The sites gave the tree a good place to break out security administration. Second, the company was installing an e-mail application on its servers at each geographic location. So, even though the company has high-speed links, it still chose to design geographically.

### Regional Layers

In some cases, it will be necessary to place regional containers directly below the O=Organization in the NDS tree to more fully distribute the total number of locations or geographic sites. Placing regional OUs under the O=Organization, but before the actual location OUs, increases NDS operating efficiency and gives the tree a closer pyramid shape.

As an example, consider the company ACME as we change the WAN layout to include more offices or cities around the world. We are changing ACME's WAN infrastructure only for this example. Figure 5.22 illustrates the offices or cities that are connected together via 56K links. Each of the cities added to the WAN layout is connected to its appropriate regional hub. Using the WAN infrastructure, we have designed a new tree, which includes regional OUs named North America (NA), South America (SA), Europe (EUR), Asia (ASIA), and Australia (AUST). These regional OUs group the appropriate cities and help keep the NDS tree design closer to a pyramid shape. See Figure 5.23 for the new ACME tree based on regional containers. Notice how the physical WAN layout in Figure 5.22 is driving the tree design in Figure 5.23.

**FIGURE 5.22** *Example of ACME with regions and cities. This is typically called a "hub and spoke" WAN infrastructure.*

**FIGURE 5.23** *Example of ACME tree with the regions and cities as the top layers*

If your network uses a WAN infrastructure with a number of physical sites or offices, you may want to create regional containers based on those WAN sites at the top layer, which will help distribute the individual offices. Having the regional OUs helps the NDS tree operate more efficiently during all phases of operation.

### Departmental Design Not Based on Your WAN

The departmental design approach can be used most efficiently at the top of the tree only if your company does not have a WAN infrastructure or other locations to consider. If your company has only a LAN-based network, you can skip the design of the top layers and go directly to the bottom layer design, which is based solely on the organization of the company. Novell defines this type of design as an e-business design as well.

If you do not have WAN links, you may consider designing your NDS tree by placing the departments, divisions, and workgroups at the top of the tree. This method is often called the departmental design approach and is not recommended for a company with a WAN infrastructure. Having the organizations placed at the top of the tree (when you have WAN links) is a less efficient tree design because any change to the top organizations ripples down the entire structure, including the site locations below.

Consider the example in Figure 5.24 in which we have designed the top of the tree organizationally with locations at the bottom. The first question you need to ask is, "Where do most network changes occur?" Most changes will occur in your organization. That's not to say that changes don't occur in geographic sites as well, but they are less frequent. Therefore, when you make changes to the tree, you want to impact as few people as possible. This is the third design goal of building flexibility into the tree design. In terms of other design elements, such as administration, partitions, replicas, network resource placement, login scripts, and bindery services, it is apparent that the organization layers at the bottom of the NDS tree more adequately address these factors.

**FIGURE 5.24** *The ACME tree with organizations at the top and geographic sites on the bottom is a less flexible way to design a tree in a network with WAN links and multiple locations. This is a poor tree design.*

## Design Bottom Levels of the Tree

You should design the bottom levels of the NDS eDirectory tree along the organizational lines of your company by using your company's organizational charts or similar documents. The bottom layers of the tree are made up of OU containers, which are based on the divisions, departments, workgroups, and teams under each of the various locations defined at the top of the tree. Figure 5.25 shows the ACME organization chart that we will use in our tree.

**FIGURE 5.25** *The ACME organization chart used in our NDS tree*

The bottom layers of the tree should represent the network resources located in the LAN network of the location or site. Because the LAN supports a greater bandwidth or throughput of information than the WAN, the design of the bottom layers is extremely flexible. You, as the designer and administrator, can shape the bottom of the tree to meet your specific needs.

We recommend that you design the bottom of the tree based on the organizational chart documents because the users and administrators are already familiar with that type of layout. Remember that the bottom section is flexible if it is designed around organizations. You will discover through experience that a tree designed with the organizations at the bottom of the tree can more easily adapt to the changing requirements of the corporation. Figure 5.26 shows the bottom layers of the ACME tree based on the organizational charts for each ACME site.

During the design of the bottom of the NDS tree, ensure that there is a place for every user and network resource currently in your company. Remember that the primary goal in designing the NDS tree is to organize the network resources, including the users. If you do not have a place for all the users or network resources, then you need to adjust your tree design. The bottom layers are typically the only ones affected. Refer back to Table 5.1 for the ACME resource list.

This list has information on servers and printers, and it provides you with helpful information for placing resources in your tree.

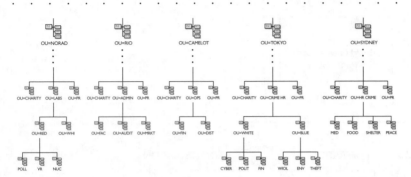

**FIGURE 5.26** *The ACME tree with the bottom layers of OUs based on the organizational charts of the company*

As mentioned earlier, the bottom containers or OUs in the tree are typically the divisions, departments, workgroups, and teams of your company. Do not include as containers any individuals that appear as division or department heads in your company's organizational charts. You simply want to identify the functional groups or departments; the individuals become the users in each container.

### The ACME Tree Design

Notice in Figure 5.27 that the top layers of the ACME tree are based solely on the WAN infrastructure and remain fairly stable or constant. Once the WAN infrastructure for ACME is considered in the design, the design effort shifts to the bottom of the tree. The bottom of the tree is based on the organizational chart for ACME. Most of the network resources will be placed in the bottom of the tree. Figure 5.27 illustrates a clear division between the top and bottom of the tree design phases in which the top is based on locations in the WAN and the bottom is based on the company's organizational information after crossing into the LAN infrastructure.

### Placing Network Resources

The placement of the network resources, such as servers or printers, in the tree can affect how you design the bottom layers. As you decide where to place the physical network resources in the tree, you should consider the needs of the users who will share these resources. If the network resources are organized according to divisions, departments, and workgroups, they should be placed in the same container with the users. However, if the network resources offer services to multiple departments in one site or location, you should place the resources in the location OU.

The placement of the network resources is an important design consideration for the bottom of the tree because the appropriate containers need to exist to place resources. If the OUs or containers do not exist, they need to be created. Remember that one of the primary goals for designing the NDS tree is to organize your network resources.

With your resource list in hand, you can place your resources in their appropriate locations in the NDS tree. In the rest of this section, we display illustrations of the ACME tree's five main sites. Included with each of these illustrations are some examples of how objects can be used in the ACME tree for the greatest impact and efficiency. Figure 5.28 shows the NORAD subtree with its resources.

**FIGURE 5.27** *The ACME tree has been designed and consists of two phases: the top and bottom of the tree.*

At the NORAD site, as well as all other sites, we have placed a central server at the top OU=NORAD. This server holds the master replica of the NORAD partition and can also function as an e-mail server for this location. The same process is repeated at all five sites.

**FIGURE 5.28** ACME NORAD Site

Notice that the naming standards follow a simple pattern based on our naming standards document. Servers are always defined by unique names across the entire tree because of the SAP requirement. Printers and print queues, however, can have the same name as long as they reside in different containers, such as HP4SI-P1, found in both OU=CHARITY and OU=POLL containers.

In Figure 5.29, the RIO location shows the placement of resources in each of the departments. It is not necessary to place all users in your tree using drawings such as these. We have included a user in each location as an example. The primary purpose of placing objects in this fashion is to determine their general placement in the tree. This gives you a better understanding of organizations and their resources.

In addition to creating user and server objects, you also will want to create some other objects. For the RIO location, as well as all major locations, you should consider creating an organizational role object as the site administrator. Grant supervisor rights at the site location, such as RIO, to the organizational role object. For example, create a role called ADMIN_RIO. You can then move a user or two in as occupants of the role. If you have multiple administrators managing organizations at the same site, you may want to create separate roles for each department.

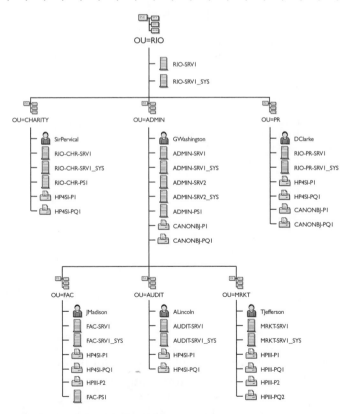

**FIGURE 5.29:** ACME RIO Site

Because CAMELOT is basically the center of activity for the ACME tree, you may want to maintain control over the ADMIN user object from this location. Change the password frequently and limit the number of users who know the password. An example of the CAMELOT site is shown in Figure 5.30.

**FIGURE 5.30** *ACME CAMELOT Site*

You can also use directory map objects to simplify the administration of your users. For example, the SYDNEY office uses directory maps in all their container login scripts. As versions of their specialized software change, the SYDNEY site administrator changes only the pointer of the directory map object to the new software version. This automatically enables all users in SYDNEY to see the new version of software because all container login scripts use the same directory map. An example of this site is shown in Figure 5.31.

**FIGURE 5.31** *ACME SYDNEY Site*

The TOKYO office has traveling users, as shown in Figure 5.32. We will create an alias for these users at the top of the tree at O=ACME. With the alias in place, a traveling user such as DHOLIDAY in the OU=THEFT only has to remember to log in as DHOLIDAY.ACME. This makes the login process much easier for users who travel but do not carry their own laptops.

**FIGURE 5.32** *ACME TOKYO Site*

### Creating Common Resource Containers

Some companies prefer to group similar resources in the same containers, such as a container for all servers, printers, and users. Keep in mind that this approach may work for smaller companies that do not have to group thousands of users in the same container or hundreds of servers together. This design approach works best with smaller companies that want to provide a simple grouping of resources.

**NOTE**

**Universities may also need to use this approach to designing an NDS tree because of the location of servers and users. If you are designing a tree for a university, create containers based on students' last names (that is, A-C, D-F) rather than lumping them all into one container. This will make for a little easier searching. However, NDS eDirectory will scale quite easily with a single container.**

## NDS Design for ZENworks

This section describes how you can fine-tune the design guidelines to efficiently accommodate the additional objects created by Zero Effort Networking (ZENworks) software, in particular, ZENworks for Desktops. The specific design guidelines do not require you to redesign your tree, but simply to add objects to containers in the existing design. ZENworks add additional objects to your NDS eDirectory tree, but this is not an issue because of the enormous scalability of the directory.

ZENworks is made up of several components: Novell Application Launcher (NAL), Workstation Manager, Inventory, and Remote Control. ZENworks enables you to create the following objects:

- Application objects
- Application folders
- Policy Packages
- Workstations (different from Computer object)
- Workstation Groups

In order to design your NDS tree with these objects, we recommend that you continue to follow the NDS guidelines as previously described. Nothing in your design should change. The only issue should be where to place the objects. Therefore, the main issues are as follows:

> ▸ Where do I place the new objects?

> ▸ Do I use existing department containers or the same container for each workstation user?

> ▸ Do I use containers called OU=APPLICATIONS, OU=WORKSTATIONS, OU=USERS, and so on to separate out these new objects?

To answer each of these questions, let's consider each product feature individually.

## Novell Application Launcher

Novell Application Launcher (NAL), with accompanying Application and Application Folder objects, enables you to quickly and easily distribute applications to users' workstations and to manage those applications as objects in the NDS eDirectory tree. Users access the applications that you assign to them using the Application Launcher Window and Application Launcher Explorer components. Place or create the application objects and the supporting group objects close to the users who will be accessing them.

The application folders are only used by the network administrators. The user never accesses an application folder object. Therefore, you can place the application folder objects in the most convenient location for the administrators. The information in the application folder is cached in each of the application objects that are linked to the application folder. This method reduces that NDS traffic needed to maintain the application folders with their enclosed applications. An example of where to place the application object folder using ConsoleOne is shown in Figure 5.33. This example shows placement of the folders near the network administrator.

For networks with multiple locations across a WAN, you should create the application objects in the NDS container that represents the physical site or location. For example, the application objects would be placed in the OU=SFO and OU=ATL containers if you had two locations. The reason for creating new application objects for each location is to achieve better scalability across the network. By following this approach, the users are associated with an application object that is local to them.

**NOTE**

**We recommend that you avoid designing ZENworks so that the users have to access the application objects across the WAN in remote partitions. Do not create one application for your entire network if it will be accessed from multiple locations across the WAN. A better**

approach is to create application objects in the same containers as the users. This approach keeps users going to a local object rather than increasing traffic across your WAN links. This assumes that the location of the application being referenced is also local to the user.

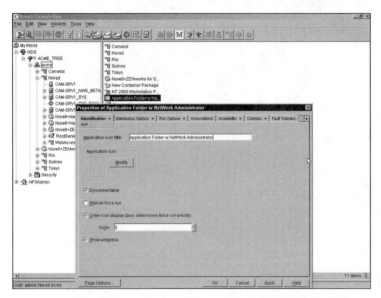

**FIGURE 5.33** *The user does not need to access the application folder, so place it in the same container with the network administrator.*

On the other hand, if your network is contained in a single LAN infrastructure, you could create just one application object per application program. In addition, you should create a different application object to reference each application server that is installed. If you have multiple application servers at one location or site, we recommend that you create a ZENworks application object for each different application object on each server. For example, if you have three servers holding applications that will be used by your users, create a ZENworks application for each program on each server. An example of this design approach is shown in Figure 5.34. You can use the following format to name the ZENworks application object:

```
<PROGRAM_NAME>-<SERVER_NAME>
```

```
                              [ROOT]

                              O=ACME

  OU=NORAD    OU=RIO    OU=CAMELOT   OU=TOKYO   OU=SYDNEY

              ─▢ RIO_APPSRV1
              ─▢ RIO_APPSRV2
              ─▢ RIO_APPSRV3
              ─▢ WP-RIO_APPSRV1
              ─▢ SS-RIO_APPSRV1
              ─▢ EM-RIO_APPSRV1
              ─▢ DB-RIO_APPSRV1
              ─▢ WP-RIO_APPSRV2
              ─▢ SS-RIO_APPSRV2
              ─▢ EM-RIO_APPSRV2
              ─▢ DB-RIO_APPSRV2
              ─▢ WP-RIO_APPSRV3
              ─▢ SS-RIO_APPSRV3
              ─▢ EM-RIO_APPSRV3
              ─▢ DB-RIO_APPSRV3
```

**FIGURE 5.34** *An example of three servers holding application objects for each application on each server*

Table 5.2 illustrates how you can create individual applications objects that represent the programs installed on each NetWare server.

TABLE 5.2

Example of how to create individual application objects in your NDS tree to represent the programs installed on each NetWare Application Server

| SERVER NAME | NETWARE SERVER HOLDING APPLICATION | MATCHING APPLICATIONS OBJECTS |
|---|---|---|
| RIO_APPSRV1 | Word Processing application<br>Spread Sheet application<br>E-mail application<br>Database application | WP-RIO_APPSRV1<br>SS-RIO_APPSRV1<br>EM-RIO_APPSRV1<br>DB-RIO_APPSRV1 |
| RIO_APPSRV2 | Word Processing application<br>Spread Sheet application<br>E-mail application<br>Database application | WP-RIO_APPSRV2<br>SS-RIO_APPSRV2<br>EM-RIO_APPSRV2<br>DB-RIO_APPSRV2 |
| RIO_APPSRV3 | Word Processing application<br>Spread Sheet application<br>E-mail application<br>Database application | WP-RIO_APPSRV3<br>SS-RIO_APPSRV3<br>EM-RIO_APPSRV3<br>DB-RIO_APPSRV3 |

This configuration enables you to set up and effectively use the fault tolerance and load balancing features built into the ZENworks product.

In order to manage these similar application objects pointing to different servers, use the new application object copy feature that is available in ZENworks. When creating a new application object, you are given the option to create it from an existing application object in the tree. After copying an application object, you need to change the source server, path, drive mapping, and others (as necessary). An example of creating an application object from an existing application object is shown in Figure 5.35

**NOTE**

**We recommend that you *do not* use a generic NDS object copy utility to create new application objects. Instead, always use the application object copy feature in ZENworks.**

**FIGURE 5.35** *Creating a new Application Object from an existing Application Object in NDS*

## Group Objects

Group objects in NDS are used for many different purposes. One use is to grant users rights to other resources. With ZENworks, groups are often created to grant multiple users rights and associate them to application objects. The group objects used to grant rights to the ZENworks application objects need to follow the same design guidelines as do the application and application folder objects themselves. Place the group objects in the same container with the associated application object.

Consider the following design rules for group objects:

▸ Create the group object in the same container as the associated application.

▸ If possible, avoid spanning group memberships across a WAN network.

▸ For the least amount of traffic, keep the users in the group in the same partition. The result is that you minimize external references and their associated network traffic.

An example of creating a group local to the users is shown in Figure 5.36.

**FIGURE 5.36** *Create groups that are close to users for the best NDS performance.*

## Application Object Associations

For ease of administration, you can associate or assign the application objects to a user, group, or container. When the Application Launcher Window or Application Launcher Explorer starts up, it searches for all associated applications from the user object. It next searches for application objects associated to groups to which the user is a member. And finally, depending on the Container Levels setting in the launcher configuration (known as the up-context), it searches for applications associated to the user object's parent containers. The up-context settings are as follows:

−1 Reads all parent containers to the top of the tree for associated applications

0 Does not read any parent; searching is turned off

1 Only reads the immediate parent container for associated applications

2 Reads only two levels up; parent and parent's parent associated applications

You can control the searching criteria used by changing the configuration in the Launcher Configuration property page in Configuration ⇨ Current Settings ⇨ Inherit Container Applications. An example of this configuration setting is shown in Figure 5.37.

**FIGURE 5.37** *Setting the search criteria for application associations in the Novell Application Launcher*

We recommend that for the best performance you use the following guidelines for establishing the associations to application objects:

▸ Set the searching to 0 or 1, which turns off searching or localizes the search just to the users' local container.

▸ You can set the searching to 2, if the parent and parent's parent are local to the user. Local means in the containers on the same LAN, not across the WAN network.

▸ Use the −1 (search to top of tree) setting sparingly; it should only be used on LAN-only networks.

▸ If user access is across the WAN, restrict the searching of groups. The group searching can be turned off.

Another design consideration is using the Application object's Schedule property page to let you control when users are delivered applications. This is useful in the scenario where you want to distribute a large Service Pack (operating system update) to all users. For example, you do not want a large update to occur at 8:00 a.m. when all network users are logging into the network. In addition, you may not want this distribution to occur on weekends when no technical support people are on-site. Or, on the other hand, maybe you do.

For these reasons, we recommend that you make the Application object available Monday through Friday, spreading the network traffic load throughout the day. This can be accomplished by configuring the system to download the Service Pack at 8:00 a.m. during user login; however, make sure to set the "Spread from Start Time" to 180 minutes. The application then becomes available on a random basis between the hours of 8:00 a.m. through 11:00 a.m. For more information, refer to context-sensitive Help on the Application object's Schedule property page.

## Workstations and Workstation Groups

ZENworks and the use of the Workstation objects could potentially double the total number of objects in your tree. How does this impact the current NDS tree design guidelines? The answer is that the new objects will not impact any of the current design guidelines. Because the Workstation Import Policy defines where the Workstation objects are created in your NDS tree, consider the following guidelines:

▸ Create the Workstation objects in the same container as the user object.

▸ Create the Workstation in a single-purpose container (OU= WORKSTATIONS), but this has limitations.

As a general rule, we recommend that you place the Workstation and Workstation Group objects with the accompanying users. Placing the Workstation objects with the users enables you to keep the NDS design flexible and efficient.

However, we recognize that the Workstation objects are not going to be accessed by the users, but instead by the client component itself. Therefore, the speed of access depends on the proximity of the physical workstation to the NDS partition and not the location of the user in the NDS tree.

Another aspect to consider is that the administrative staff will use the Workstation object to store the inventory for the physical machine. If your administrative staff is decentralized, with different groups handling different functions, you may want to create a separate container called OU= WORKSTATIONS to place the objects in. This type of design enables you to assign certain network administrators access to manage just the Workstation objects.

As the number of objects in the current partition grows, you can partition off just the OU=WORKSTATIONS container as its own partition. The use of OU=

WORKSTATIONS may be appropriate for some NDS trees only because the workstation objects are used exclusively by the network administrators and not the users. An example of using a container solely for Workstations is shown in Figure 5.38.

We typically *do not* recommend that you create resource specific containers to place similar resources together for the other network resources. For example, we *do not* recommend creating a separate container for all servers, users, printers, groups, organizational roles, applications, policies, and other resources. Figure 5.39 illustrates the bottom of the NDS tree using resource specific containers. This is typically not recommended except for the Workstation objects because eventually you may end up with all your users in one partition and their resources in another partition on another server. This reduces the efficiency of NDS.

**FIGURE 5.38** *Using a resource-specific container for OU=WORKSTATIONS*

**Consulting Experience**

Keep in mind that we recommend a separate container for workstation objects because these objects are used almost solely by the administrator. For all other resources (user objects, servers, and so on), we don't recommend the use of separate containers, as explained in further detail next.

**FIGURE 5.39** *An example of resource-specific containers at the bottom of the tree*

Keep in mind that this design may seem to work if all the containers are in the same partition. However, we do not recommend designing your NDS tree using these single-purpose containers for the following reasons:

▶ Reduces user speed of access.

▶ Bottom of the tree becomes more inflexible.

▶ Scalability at the bottom of the tree is limited.

▶ Further partitioning of containers reduces performance.

▶ Designed for the administrators and not users.

These problems are magnified if the site or location has thousands of users, workstations, and so on. As each OU is partitioned off, the performance and access is reduced. Partitions are created to help NDS scale across the servers, which typically means that each partition will reside on different servers. As the replicas are moved off each server, the user's resources (servers, printers, groups, applications, policies) become dispersed, reducing the speed of access.

In addition to the reduced access and flexibility, the network performance can be adversely affected with the higher number of external references that are created to track all the objects not physically residing on each server.

## Policy Packages

ZENworks offers several new objects known as Policy Packages that enable you to manage users' workstations remotely and in a consistent fashion. Several different types of Policy Packages can be created:

- ► Container Package
- ► WIN31 User Package
- ► WIN31 Workstation Package
- ► WIN95 User Package
- ► WIN95 Workstation Package
- ► WINNT User Package
- ► WINNT Workstation Package
- ► WIN2000 User Package
- ► WIN2000 Workstation Package

The Container Package is used to define how the client component searches in NDS for associated Policy Packages. The User Policy Packages are associated to either users, groups, or containers. The Workstation Policy Packages can be associated to either Workstations, Workstation Groups, or containers. It is not possible to assign several Policy Packages to the same user object.

We recommend that you place the Policy Package objects closest to the users or workstations that will be accessing it. For Policy Packages consider the following guidelines:

▶ Create the Container Policy Package at the highest level of the tree as needed. It should never exceed the location or site container.

▶ Create the User Policy Package in the same container as the users that will access it.

▶ Create the Workstation Policy Package in the same container as the workstations that will access it. If you have defined a single-purpose container for workstations (OU=WORKSTATIONS), place the policies in the same container.

If user access to the Policy Package is across the WAN, restrict the searching of groups. The group searching can be turned off using the Search Policy. Examples of where to place the policy packages are shown in Figures 5.40, 5.41, and 5.42.

**FIGURE 5.40** *Create the Container Policy Package at the highest level needed in your NDS tree.*

**FIGURE 5.41** *Create the User Policy Package local to the users that will use it.*

**FIGURE 5.42** *Create the Workstation Policy Package in the same container where the users will access it.*

# Additional Design Considerations

Some LAN administrators may try to design the NDS tree and simultaneously consider all the external factors that may affect the design of the tree. Considering all the factors at once is difficult because the tree will shift and change as you attempt to consider all the design inputs. Some of the most popular distractions are bindery services, partitioning, replication, and login scripts.

Experience has shown that designing the tree is simple if you base the top layers of the tree solely on the WAN infrastructure and the bottom layers according to your organizational information.

When you have completed your first draft design of the NDS tree, you are ready to apply some other design considerations as needed. This process greatly simplifies the tree design effort. It is interesting to note that the design considerations affect primarily the design of the bottom of the tree, not the top of the tree. This is acceptable because the greatest flexibility for changes in the design is supported at the bottom of the tree.

Again, our approach is to design the bottom level of the NDS tree aligned entirely to the organizations of your company. You can then apply the design considerations as needed. The following design considerations affect the bottom of the tree:

- ▸ Administration
- ▸ NDS partitions and replicas
- ▸ Login scripts
- ▸ Bindery services

**TIP** **Remember that these design considerations apply only to the bottom of the tree; they do not alter the top layers in the tree design. By reviewing each design consideration, you will see how these considerations apply only to the users and other network resources that are contained in the bottom layers.**

## Administration

One of the most important design considerations is how the NDS tree is going to be managed at your company. Are you going to manage the NDS tree as one Information System (IS) group (the centralized approach) or by several different IS groups in the company (the decentralized approach)?

### Centralized Management

In the centralized management approach, the entire NDS tree is controlled by one group in the company. This group manages all the additions and deletions of the NDS objects, partitioning, replication, and everything else related to the NDS database. Figure 5.43 shows how you can centrally manage your tree with one IS group having rights to the top of your tree and down. For more information regarding rights assignments, refer to Chapter 13.

**FIGURE 5.43** *A centralized management approach with a single group having rights to the entire tree*

### Decentralized Management

In the decentralized management approach, portions of the NDS tree are delegated to individuals or independent groups in the company for management. These individuals or groups may be administrators for each department or site administrators responsible for all the network resources in a particular location. All subadministrators should, however, adhere to your previously defined naming standards. Figure 5.44 illustrates how you can set up administration for the lower containers in your group. You will have a central IS staff managing the upper layers of the tree, with other administrators being responsible for their respective containers.

If the NDS tree is going to be centrally managed, it makes sense to further the tree design to the bottom layers. The central team that provides administration has control of all the objects in the tree from top to bottom.

However, if the tree is going to be decentrally managed, each department administrator or site administrator will decide independently how the tree is organized in that portion of the tree. The top administrators have full responsibility to create the tree down to the department or site and then relinquish control at that layer to each of the independent LAN administrators. Top administrators of the tree will still want to give design guidelines and suggestions to the bottom administrators on organizing the lower containers and grouping network resources. The following is a list of suggestions that you can give your administrators as guidelines. These ideas can also be mandated through the use of access controls as explained in Chapter 13.

**FIGURE 5.44:** *Creating a distributed administration approach by creating container administrators. Each subadministrator has rights to his or her own organizational unit.*

## Guidelines for Subadministrators

Here are some rules of thumb for subadministrators:

▸ Subadministrators should have sufficient security and access rights over their container(s) to create, delete, or change all objects within their subcontainer.

▸ Each subadministrator will carefully determine if more levels need to be created beneath their container before making changes.

▸ Subadministrators should maintain the naming standards as defined by the corporation at all levels in the NDS tree.

▸ Subadministrators should not further partition their OUs without the assistance of the central IS department. In some cases, the subadministrator will not be granted rights to do so.

> ▸ Subadministrators will inform the central IS staff before adding a new server into the corporate tree.

The depth of the tree or number of layers in the tree may be affected by whether your administration is centralized or decentralized. Remember, the recommendation is to build the NDS tree like a pyramid with fewer containers at the top and more containers at the bottom. Centralized administration may imply that a tree designed flat and wide would be easier to administer. If your company has only a few servers and users, you can build a shallow tree that is suited to centralized administration.

This may not be possible if your company is large with many servers, users, and geographic sites. In this case you will need to design the NDS tree with more layers, which means a deeper tree.

For decentralized management of NDS trees, individual administrators along with central administrators can determine the depth of their portion of the tree. Although there is no hard and fast rule regarding the total number of layers in the tree, the NDS tree is easier for the user to find information if the tree has three to five layers. Typically, even the largest companies can design a useful tree with five layers or fewer. Notice in Figure 5.45 that the ACME tree consists of five layers, not including [ROOT].

**FIGURE 5.45** The ACME tree consists of five layers, not including [ROOT].

**TIP** There is a logical limit to the number of layers in the tree you can access. For example, NDS has a limit of 255 characters for a distinguished name. Thus, the actual limit for the number of layers is dependent on the number of characters in the names of your objects. If your OU names are long, your tree will be unable to have as many layers as it would with shorter OU names. For example, if all the OU names were just two characters, you could have 51 layers (OU=US, 256/5 = 51). We recommend that you give the OUs in your tree short, descriptive names. See Chapter 4 for more information on naming standards.

## NDS Partitions and Replicas

The next design consideration you need to address is how you will split the NDS database into partitions. For this discussion, we will consider the size of the partition (total number of objects), the total number of replicas, and where in the tree the partition will be created. A container object is required for the creation of a partition and is designated the root-most object of the partition. Figure 5.46 shows a partition root called NORAD in the NORAD facility. The partition root is named NORAD because that is the starting point of that partition.

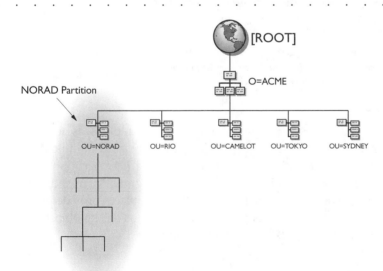

**FIGURE 5.46** *A partition root object is named NORAD in the ACME tree.*

When deciding where to create a partition, you should follow the physical network infrastructure. Like the top layer of the tree, the partitions of the tree should represent the WAN, making each site or location its own partition. The benefit of partitioning the NDS database according to the WAN is that the information needed by the local users stays inside that location. We have partitioned each of the location organizational units by site as illustrated in Figure 5.47.

**FIGURE 5.47** *Each site is its own partition and maintains its portion of the NDS database on its own servers within the site.*

The size of your partitions and the total number of replicas is a design consideration for the bottom of the tree. Typically, partition size is unlimited in a NetWare 6 environment. In Figure 5.48 we have created a new partition called OPS under CAMELOT because that location's partition has grown large and is still running a version of NetWare 4. More partitions in the right places provide greater efficiency in your tree design. Remember, a partition contains all the objects in a defined subtree, not just the objects in a single container.

**FIGURE 5.48** *A new partition is created in the OPS department. It is now a child partition of its parent named CAMELOT.*

The next consideration is the total number of replicas of a partition. If the number of replicas is greater than 50, consider creating additional partitions to reduce the total number of replicas. Novell recommends three replicas for each partition. The primary reason you would need more than three replicas of any partition is either for bindery services and improved access. Bindery services requires a writeable copy of the replica. Refer to the "Bindery Services" section later in this chapter. Improved access login and tree searching access can be achieved by placing a replica close to where the user reside.

Follow these server hardware guidelines for rolling out eDirectory on any platform as shown in Tables 5.3 and 5.4.

| T A B L E   5 . 3 | | | |

Hardware installation requirements for Novell eDirectory and server System requirements for NetWare, Windows NT, and Linux

| NDS OBJECTS | PROCESSOR | MEMORY | HARD DISK |
|---|---|---|---|
| 100K | Pentium III 450-470 Mhz (single) | 384 MB | 144MB |
| 1 million | Pentium III 450-700 MHz (Dual) | 2GB | 1.5 GB |
| 10 million | Pentium III 450-700 Mhz (2-4) | 2 GB+ | 15 GB |

| T A B L E   5 . 4 | | | |

Hardware installation requirements for Novell eDirectory and server system requirements for Solaris

| NDS OBJECTS | PROCESSOR | MEMORY | HARD DISK |
|---|---|---|---|
| 100K | Sun Enterprise 450 | 384 MB | 144MB |
| 1 million | Sun Enterprise 4500 | 2GB | 1.5 GB |
| 10 million | Sun Enterprise 4500 or higher with multiple processors | 2 GB+ | 15 GB |

Decide who is responsible for the partitioning of the NDS tree. If you manage the tree centrally, all the partitioning decisions are made by the central IS department. If the tree is decentralized, you may turn over the rights of partitioning the tree to each of the local site or facility administrators. Whichever way you decide to handle partitioning, make sure you decide before installation of NetWare 6 begins and make a company policy stating who will handle the partitioning.

## Login Scripts

Another design consideration for the bottom of the tree is designing how the users will access the information in the tree. For more information on designing NDS eDirectory login scripts see Chapter 12. The users will primarily access NDS through the use of login scripts. Remember, the users need login scripts to map network drives and applications, capture to print queues, and set other variables. Thus, the login scripts become an important design consideration. Typically, the users needing the same login script will be grouped together in the same OU container. You can then use the OU login script to provide users access to the NDS tree. Figure 5.49 shows a container login script that will be used by everyone in the container.

**FIGURE 5.49** *All users execute the login script in the container where they reside.*

You will separate the users that need different login scripts for the same reason. As you design the login scripts for your users, you are in fact designing the organization of the bottom level of the tree.

Another strategy for organizing the login scripts is to have the same login script for all users and copy it to multiple containers. In this manner, the user placement in the tree is not affected. However, this strategy requires that the network administrator be responsible for keeping all copies of the login script the same.

It is recommended that you use the OU container login script to replace the functionality of the NetWare 3 system login script. This helps you organize the bottom layers and containers in your tree.

## Consulting Experience

Partition size is no longer an issue with the release of NDS version 8. However, check your user and synchronization performance and use that as a guide if you are experiencing any performance issues. WAN links can still be a source of concern, and bandwidth can be conserved through proper design. These recommendations are also dependent upon the speed of your server hardware. Some slower servers may necessitate the need to limit the number of replicas placed on that server.

You can also use the profile login script whenever possible for configuring the users for access to resources that are more global in nature. The profile login script enables you to span a single login script across multiple OU containers and assign it to specific users. For example, the container SYDNEY has a profile script created for the HR departmen;. its subordinate departments of MEDICAL, FOOD, and SHELTER (as shown in Figure 5.50), all use the script. The script can reside in any container, and users from any container can execute it.

**FIGURE 5.50** *A profile script used by users from MEDICAL, FOOD, and SHELTER*

Through the login script, each user maps network drives to the appropriate network server and establishes access to specific network applications and services. Most login scripts depend on groups and directory map objects for these drive mappings. These groups and directory map objects must be accessible so that any users needing them can find them during login.

In order to simplify the mapping to generic network applications (ones needed by all network users), it is appropriate to place the applications in the same subdirectory structure on all the servers. In other words, use the same file structure for all servers. Then when a user maps the drive, he or she does not care which server responds.

For example, assume that each network user needs to have drive mappings to both a word processor and spreadsheet software. These two software packages are installed on all file servers in the same place on the file system (SYS:APPS\WP and SYS:APPS\QPRO). All servers that have a generic file system structure enable the users to map these applications, regardless of their location or the server to which they are physically attached. An example of how you can standardize your file system is shown in Figure 5.51.

**FIGURE 5.51** *A standard file system on all your NetWare 6 servers will make administration of your network easier.*

## Bindery Services

NDS provides compatibility with NetWare 2 and NetWare 3 using a feature called bindery services. This feature allows bindery versions of NetWare applications and other third-party software that requires the bindery to access the NDS database as if it were the bindery. For example, a client can use the NETX shell (NetWare 3 client) to log in to a NetWare 6 server and run any bindery-based application that may exist on a NetWare 4, NetWare 5, or NetWare 6 server.

Bindery services can be enabled through the server SET Server Bindery Context command. The server can select one OU, Organization, or Locality container, or many containers, as the bindery context. The server bindery context is simply the containers the server sees as the bindery. All the leaf objects in the NDS container(s) that are also objects in the NetWare 3 bindery (for example, users, groups, queues, print servers, and profiles) are seen as objects through the bindery Application Program Interfaces (APIs). The following figures show how you can set a server's bindery context(s). Figure 5.52 shows how you can use the MONITOR utility to set the bindery context(s). Figure 5.53 shows how you can verify that the bindery context(s) have been set on a server.

**FIGURE 5.52** *Using the MONITOR utility to set the server context at OU=CRIME.OU=TOKYO.O=ACME. This setting implies that the container "CRIME" is set as the bindery context.*

**FIGURE 5.53:** *Typing* **SET BINDERY CONTEXT** *at a NetWare 6 server console will display a server's bindery context(s) if the context has been set.*

**TIP**

Typing **SET BINDERY CONTEXT** at a server shows the string of contexts as valid or invalid. If you want to see only the valid (effective and active) contexts, you must type **CONFIG** at the server console.

Bindery services in NetWare 6 lets you select up to 16 containers as the server bindery context. The major requirement for bindery services is that the server must store at least a read/write replica of the partition where the bindery context is set. If a server has the maximum 16 bindery contexts set, the server would have to store 16 separate replicas just to support bindery services on all contexts. Figure 5.54 shows how we have set multiple bindery contexts on a server in TOKYO to search the organizational units of CRIME, BLUE, and WHITE when a bindery request is made.

**FIGURE 5.54:** *Multiple bindery contexts are separated by semicolons on a server in TOKYO, which views the CRIME, BLUE, and WHITE containers as its bindery.*

As you can see, placing replicas on servers to support bindery services increases the total number of replicas for each partition. This affects the tree design because you may be forced to split a partition to reduce the number of replicas. Bindery services is the principal reason for maintaining more than a few replicas of any partition. Refer back to the section "NDS Partitions and Replicas" earlier in this chapter.

Another design consideration is that you should place all the clients or users requiring bindery services from a particular file server in the OU container where you have set the server bindery context. This consideration can affect the NDS tree design at the bottom level because it may require you to combine users and resources of multiple departments or workgroups into one OU. You may need to separate users from the resources they don't use for the same reason. In any event, the organization of the bottom layers of the tree may be affected because the users and resources need to be arranged for bindery services.

Before you change the bottom of the tree design to accommodate bindery services, determine whether you even need bindery services for the servers. Remember, bindery services is an optional feature that does not have to be enabled at each server. You should determine if the clients are using NETX or applications that require bindery services. You could also identify the users and key applications and force them to use bindery services on specific servers.

With an NDS tree design roughed out, you are now ready to design for partitioning and replication.

**Consulting Experience**

Here is a brief list of some of the applications you may encounter that make bindery calls. Although this list is brief, you need to check all your applications to determine if they require the bindery.

- NetWare 3 Print Services
- Backup Utilities
- Host Connectivity Products
- Menuing Systems
- Network Management Utilities
- Database Software
- Other NetWare 3-Based Applications and Utilities

## Summary

This chapter presented the basics of NDS tree design for any size environment, regardless of the size of the network. Once you have your WAN information and other corporate documents in hand, you can design the top level of your NDS tree. Then you can move on to designing the bottom level of your tree by considering the effects of administration, partitions and replicas, login scripts, and bindery services. By following the guidelines presented here, you will have an NDS tree that is flexible enough to meet the changing needs of your company.

# Designing NDS eDirectory Partitions and Replicas

*"The beginning is the most important part of the work." — Plato*

**T**he NDS eDirectory tree information is stored on the servers in data files. These data files may either be centralized on one or two network servers or be distributed across all the network servers in the company. Although the eDirectory tree can be distributed to servers across the network, users are provided a single view of its resources. With eDirectory, the information is not only distributed but also replicated on multiple servers to provide increased reliability. Figure 6.1 shows how the directory might be distributed across a few servers in the network for the ACME company while still providing the user with a single view of the network resources.

**FIGURE 6.1** *NDS eDirectory provides distribution of the information across a few of the network servers for ACME while still providing the user with a single view of the network resources.*

**Consulting Experience**

In a small company, you can place all of its resources into a single O=Organization in the eDirectory tree structure for simplicity or create an OU under the O=Organization. The server installation can automatically create a container for you.

In a company with a small number of servers, the eDirectory tree information could be centralized with all the information residing on one or possibly two network servers. The benefit of having the data files centralized on just a couple of servers is that administration is easier. The eDirectory tree will perform efficiently as long as the total number of users and network resources for the entire company remains small.

Companies that have large networks with a large number of servers should split the eDirectory tree (or object hierarchy) into sections and distribute them to the appropriate network servers.

## NDS eDirectory Partitions

NDS eDirectory is represented as a hierarchical structure called a tree into which all the network resources are placed. Figure 6.2 illustrates how the database is viewed as a hierarchical tree. The directory partitions are also hierarchical and follow the same structure as the tree.

NDS eDirectory partitions are logical sections of the Directory tree. *Partitioning* is the process of splitting the Directory hierarchy or tree into smaller parts or subtrees. These subtrees can then be physically stored on your network servers as replicas of the partition. Partitioning the tree enables you to selectively distribute the tree information to the areas in the network that need the information. Figure 6.3 illustrates how the Directory hierarchy or tree for ACME can be split into partitions and placed on or copied to the network servers.

[ROOT]

ORGANIZATION(O)=ACME

OU=NORAD    OU=RIO    OU=CAMELOT    OU=TOKYO    OU=SYDNEY

- USERS
- GROUPS
- SERVERS
- PRINTERS
  o
  o
  o
- ETC

- USERS
- GROUPS
- SERVERS
- PRINTERS
  o
  o
  o
- ETC

- USERS
- GROUPS
- SERVERS
- PRINTERS
  o
  o
  o
- ETC

**FIGURE 6.2** *NDS eDirectory for ACME is viewed as a hierarchical structure called a tree.*

**TIP**

**When NDS eDirectory partitions are mentioned and described, you should not confuse them with file system partitions. A *partition* is a portion of the eDirectory tree and does not contain any file system information. A *file system partition*, on the other hand, has the capability to split a hard drive into logical segments for use by the operating system.**

**NDS eDirectory partitions and file system partitions serve different purposes and are not related in any way.**

Partitioning gives you the ability to scale the directory across the multiple network servers. Splitting up the tree into partitions and storing them on separate network servers will distribute the workload for each of the servers. In addition, the NetWare utilities enable you to select the servers in the network where you want to store the different partitions. This enables you to achieve better performance through targeted replica placement.

**FIGURE 6.3** *The NDS eDirectory tree for ACME has been partitioned and placed on or copied to the network servers.*

As mentioned earlier, the layout of the partitions is hierarchical, meaning that one partition is parent to subordinate or child partitions. When all partitions (parents and children) are connected together via the directory, they form a hierarchical map back to the [ROOT] object. Figure 6.4 illustrates how the individual partitions form a hierarchical map, often called a *partition map*.

## The Parent-Child Relationship between Partitions

The relationship between the individual partitions in the tree is a *parent-child relationship*. Where the boundaries between the partitions meet, the partition closer to the [ROOT] is considered the parent and the one farther away is the child.

TIP

The parent-child relationship is also described in terms of subordinate and superior partitions. A subordinate partition (or child) is the partition that is down the tree or farther from the [ROOT]. The superior partition (or parent) is the partition that is closer to the top of the tree than its subordinate partition.

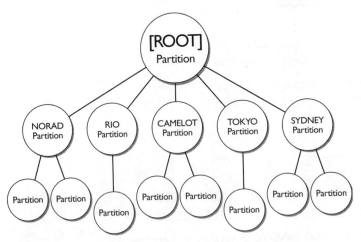

**FIGURE 6.4** *Individual partitions for the ACME tree form a hierarchical partition map.*

In the ACME partition map, the parent-child relationship between partitions is illustrated in Figure 6.5. In this example, the OU containers that have been partitioned at NORAD, RIO, CAMELOT, TOKYO, and SYDNEY are child partitions to the partition [ROOT], which is the parent. In the case of the CAMELOT partition, it is also a parent partition with the three subordinate partitions as the child partitions.

Partitioning can be compared to the responsibility of parents for keeping track of their children. When child partitions are created, their parent must maintain their locations. If the server does not hold both the parent and its child partitions, the directory will create a subordinate reference replica for each of the child partitions and will place it on the server. The subordinate reference (also known as a *Sub Ref*) is the pointer from the parent replica to the location of the child replica.

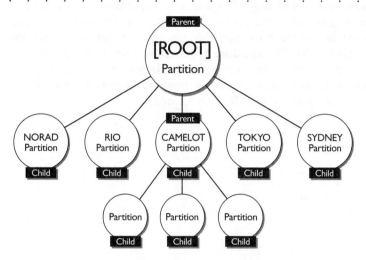

**FIGURE 6.5** *The parent-child relationship between the partitions in the ACME tree*

NDS eDirectory requires that the location of the subordinate partitions be linked with their parent to form a common set of information and a complete map of the tree. The users can then traverse the tree after login. The parent only needs to know the location of its child partitions if the child partitions are not stored on the same server as the parent. The subordinate reference topic is  discussed in more detail in the "Subordinate Reference Replicas" section later in this chapter.

If you should create new partitions below the CAMELOT partition, as illustrated in Figure 6.6, then CAMELOT becomes a parent partition to the newly formed partitions. Although CAMELOT is a new parent, it is still a child partition of [ROOT]. However, no grandparent relationship exists, in which a grandparent must know about grandchild partitions. Only the parent-child relationship exists among partitions in the directory.

**TIP**

**NDS eDirectory maintains the relationship between the parent and child partitions. If a server is holding a parent partition and is not storing the child partition, the directory creates a subordinate reference replica pointing to the child partition. This replica maintains the links throughout the directory itself. Again, the subordinate reference replicas are placed on servers where the parent partition is and the child partition is not. Therefore, any server holding a parent partition can end up storing subordinate reference replicas to child partitions.**

Servers can also end up holding a large number of subordinate reference replicas depending on how you design the partitions for your eDirectory tree—for example, creating or partitioning each of the organizational units beneath the [ROOT] partition. If you have too many partitioned organizational units that are immediately below the [ROOT], the directory creates subordinate reference replicas automatically for any servers holding a copy of the [ROOT] partition.

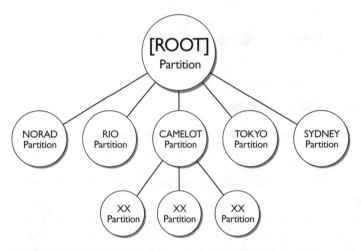

**FIGURE 6.6** *New partitions created below the CAMELOT partition*

Design your tree so that you minimize the degree to which each server holds subordinate reference replicas. Minimizing subordinate references will generate less communication traffic when replicas need to be synchronized.

## Partitioning Is Transparent to Users

Partitioning of the Directory's database is completely transparent to users, who can traverse the entire tree regardless of which server they are connected to. For example, a user sitting at a single workstation on the network sees the eDirectory tree as a single logical entity, even though the directory has been partitioned and distributed across the servers.

Although a specific server may not contain the complete set of directory data files for the network, users still have the ability to get the information they request through background processes that the directory establishes and maintains between the separate partitions.

## Partitioning Rules

The NDS eDirectory partitions follow these rules:

▶ The partition is named and requires a single container object at the top (or root) of the partition (not to be confused with the [ROOT] partition). The container object that is used as the start of the partition is called the *partition root object*. Only one partition root object exists for each partition, and it is the topmost container object. An example of partition root objects is shown in Figure 6.7.

▶ Two organizational unit containers at the same level cannot exist as a partition without a parent container. This rule is similar to the first rule. Figure 6.8 illustrates how two peer OUs in the ACME tree cannot be contained in the same partition.

▶ The partitions cannot overlap with any other part of the tree, meaning that one object will never reside in two partitions, as illustrated in Figure 6.9.

▶ The partition contains all of the information for the connected subtree. Each partition may be thought of as a section or subtree of the entire tree.

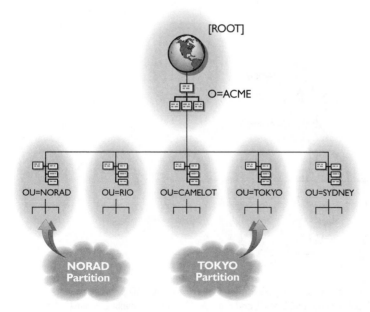

**FIGURE 6.7** *Several partition root objects in the ACME tree*

**FIGURE 6.8** *Two peer OUs in the ACME tree, such as OU=NOR and OU=RIO, cannot be contained in the same partition. A partition must have a single container object to define the top of the partition.*

**FIGURE 6.9** *Partition information cannot overlap. For example, the NORAD partition cannot contain information that is subordinate to OU=RIO, and the TOKYO partition cannot contain information that is subordinate to OU=SYDNEY. An object can exist in only one partition.*

## The [ROOT] Partition

During installation of the first eDirectory server, the [ROOT] partition for the tree is created automatically and placed on the NetWare 6 server. A copy (replica) of [ROOT] is placed on this server. In NetWare 6, the [ROOT] partition is the only partition that the installation program will create. Figure 6.10 illustrates the point at which the [ROOT] partition is created during installation of NDS eDirectory on the first NetWare 6 server. All other partitioning of the NDS database must be created by you or other system administrators. The [ROOT] partition cannot be removed unless you remove the directory from all the NetWare 6 servers, which is really removing the entire tree.

After the first server has been installed, you can add the objects necessary to build the tree structure for your company. In Figure 6.11, the ACME tree has been constructed using the NWADMIN utility to add the necessary container objects.

All the objects that have been added to the ACME tree are initially held by a single partition, called the [ROOT] partition. Figure 6.12 illustrates how the [ROOT] partition is holding all the objects in the eDirectory tree until further partitioning can take place. After installation, this partition resides only on the first NetWare 6 server installed.

Because there is only one copy of the [ROOT] partition, you should place the partition on other servers as they are installed in the system. The Novell Installation Program automatically creates additional copies of the partition as you add servers. For example, server NOR-SRV1 is installed into the tree and receives a read/write copy of the partition. Figure 6.13 shows that you will have two copies of the [ROOT] partition placed on the servers, NOR-SRV1 and CAM-SRV1.

Child partitions can be created from the [ROOT] partition by selecting a subordinate container object, typically an OU, as the top of the partition. A partition can have only one topmost container object (referred to as the *partition root object*).

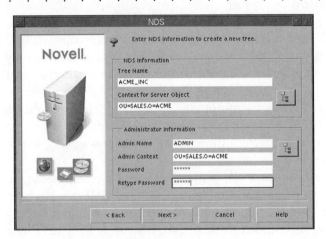

**FIGURE 6.10** *The [ROOT] partition is created automatically when the first NetWare 6 server is installed. In this example, the first server is the CAM-SRV1 server in CAMELOT, which holds the master replica of [ROOT].*

**FIGURE 6.11** *The ACME tree has been constructed by adding the necessary objects.*

**FIGURE 6.12** *The [ROOT] partition holds all the objects in the tree until further partitioning takes place.*

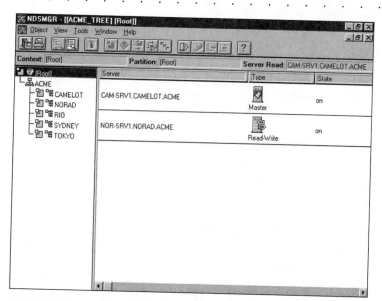

**FIGURE 6.13** *Using the NDS Manager utility, you can see two copies of the [ROOT] partition, NOR-SRV1 and CAM-SRV1, that have been placed on the servers for the ACME tree.*

When the partition is created, it takes its name from the topmost container object (partition root object). All the objects in the tree that are under the container object constitute the contents of the new partition. Creating a partition does not affect the child partition boundaries. Figure 6.14 shows the creation of the NORAD partition for the ACME tree. All the objects in the subtree under NORAD are included in the partition.

**FIGURE 6.14** *A new partition called NORAD is created for the ACME tree*

Creating a child partition from the parent partition is an operation called create partition in the NetWare utilities. The operation is fast and in most cases does not generate much traffic on your network, unless you have many replicas of the partition. The operation simply divides one partition into two partitions with all the information staying on the same server that contained the original partition. This create partition operation makes a new child partition on all the servers that had a copy of the parent partition. Figure 6.15 shows the NORAD partition being created from the [ROOT] partition.

It is recommended that the [ROOT] partition be kept small with only the [ROOT] object, O=Organization containers, and a few objects if necessary. For example, in order to keep the [ROOT] partition small for ACME, further partitioning needs to take place. As illustrated in Figure 6.16, if more partitions are created directly under the [ROOT] partition, then the [ROOT] partition holds only the topmost portions of the tree.

**FIGURE 6.15** *A conceptual view of a create partition operation to create the NORAD partition. This operation affects both original copies of the [ROOT] partition, which are stored on CAM-SRV1 and NOR-SRV1.*

**FIGURE 6.16** *The [ROOT] partition for the ACME tree should hold only the topmost portion of the tree.*

## Partition Design

Designing and partitioning your NDS eDirectory tree can be simple if you remember the reasons for creating a partition. You create a partition to scale the directory across your network servers. If your network is small, then you do not need to partition your tree.

The number one design criterion for partitioning is the physical layout of your network infrastructure—the WAN links and the network servers. Using this criterion, your main task is to partition the NDS eDirectory tree to localize the information. This means that you want to partition the directory to keep the NORAD information in NORAD, the RIO information in RIO, and so on. Figure 6.17 illustrates the physical WAN layout for the ACME company. Figure 6.18 shows how the ACME tree has been partitioned to support the physical WAN layout. Note that in our example the [ROOT] partition is small and includes only the [ROOT] and organization container objects. Keeping the [ROOT] partition small is recommended and will be discussed later in this chapter when we address replication design and placement.

**FIGURE 6.17** *The physical WAN network layout for the ACME company*

**FIGURE 6.18** *The ACME tree has been partitioned according to the WAN infrastructure.*

As illustrated in Figure 6.19, you can see that the NORAD partition and its object information have been be placed on the server in NORAD. The same is true for all the locations. By partitioning the NDS eDirectory tree based on your WAN network layout, you can keep the information local to each location and yet still find and use the resources throughout the entire tree.

**FIGURE 6.19** *NDS eDirectory distributes the information across the network servers for ACME. The NORAD partition is stored locally on the NORAD server. Each of the partitions is stored on its local server.*

## Guidelines for Creating Partitions

The following guidelines were developed to assist network administrators when designing a plan for partitioning and replication that provides a stable and efficient network.

The specific guidelines and recommendations for designing your partitions are as follows:

▶ Do not span a WAN link or physical locations with a partition. This design rule preserves bandwidth between servers and site locations. Extra traffic occurs during each of the normal synchronization operations. Spanning a partition across the WAN link, as shown in Figure 6.20, generally should be avoided.

▶ Keep the [ROOT] partition small. The [ROOT] partition should include only the [ROOT] object and the O=Organization object. Do not include additional containers in the [ROOT] partition other than the [ROOT] object and Organization=ACME object, as shown in Figure 6.21. This means that you should not include any other subordinate container OUs in the partition with the [ROOT] partition. As illustrated in Figure 6.21, you should avoid partitioning an individual location within the [ROOT] partition. [Root] should remain small in case you end up placing this partition on multiple servers.

▶ The top layers of the tree should be partitioned according to the locations in your company. Again, do not span a WAN link with the same partition. Partition locally wherever possible.

**TIP**

**These guidelines do not suggest that you partition every organizational unit in your tree. Partition locally and partition further at each site only if necessary.**

▶ The bottom layers of the tree should be split off into additional partitions only if there are special requirements. The special requirements are either a large partition (total number of objects is greater than 1 million), more than ten replicas of the same partition, or the need to break out an administrative subtree.

**FIGURE 6.20** *Do not span the WAN link, as shown in this example of the [ROOT] partition spanning the CAMELOT, RIO, and TOKYO sites.*

**FIGURE 6.21** *Do not include additional containers in the [ROOT] partition other than [ROOT] object and Organization=ACME. We recommend that you not leave the individual location information in the [ROOT] partition.*

▶ Do not create a partition for a location (even if it is across a WAN link) if there is no local server to store it on. This situation is common only with small remote offices that do not have servers at their local site. The users in this situation would access all the network services across the WAN infrastructure on a server located elsewhere. Access to the directory is no different. Figure 6.22 shows how these users at OU=DIST would still be part of a partition contained on a server in OU=DIST because they do not have their own server.

**Consulting Experience**

The guidelines presented here assume that your server hardware is fast, meaning Pentium-class PCs operating at 500 MHz or better. Keep in mind that the slowest server in the replica list tends to affect all synchronization activities of even the faster servers in the same partition. If you are operating on slower hardware, you should carefully read the recommendations throughout this section for partitioning guidelines.

[ROOT]

O=ACME

OU=NORAD    OU=RIO    OU=CAMELOT    OU=TOKYO    OU=SYDNEY

OU=CHARITY  OU=OPS  OU=PR

OU=FIN    OU=DIST

**Remote
Office**

**FIGURE 6.22** *Users will be part of a partition stored on another server if they do not have a local server in their office.*

## Partitioning the Top Layers

As mentioned earlier, the top layers in the tree should be partitioned according to the WAN infrastructure, as shown in Figure 6.23. Because the top layers of the tree should already be designed according to the WAN links, partitioning will naturally follow these boundaries.

Combining multiple geographic sites into one partition generates unnecessary traffic and consumes bandwidth on your system. If you try to span more than one location in a partition, then the information in the partition will synchronize with the other copies across the slower WAN links. This reduces the efficiencies of the network and defeats the purpose of trying to create a partition in the first place.

If you have implemented regional OU containers in your tree, then you should create a partition for each of the regional OUs and store that partition on a server separate from its parent partition. After the regional partitions are defined in your tree, you will need to create partitions at the locations under each of the regions

and store them on separate servers from their parents in order to distribute the
subordinate references to multiple servers.

**FIGURE 6.23** *The top layers of the ACME tree partitioned according to the WAN infrastructure*

## Partitioning the Bottom Layers

Because the design of the bottom of the tree is based on the divisions,
departments, and workgroups within each location of the WAN, the tree should
already be partitioned at the WAN site or location. Further partitioning may not
be needed. However, you may want to partition the directory simply to provide
administrators the responsibility for partitions lower in the tree. For example, if a
departmental or site manager wants the responsibility to manage his or her own
partitioning, then you need to plan the parent partitions accordingly. Also, the
rights needed to partition the NDS tree are effective write rights to the access
control list (ACL) of the top container object of the partition. There are several
ways to receive this privilege. One way is through the Supervisor object right to
the container object that defines the partition. You can also grant explicit write
rights to its ACL. Also, if a need exists to create a new partition from the parent
partition, then the administrator creating the child needs full rights to the parent.

In order to perform other partition operations, such as add/remove replica and
change replica type, you are required to have rights to the server object that is
being affected. For more information on security and rights, see Chapter 13.

# NDS Replicas

As mentioned earlier, NDS eDirectory is a global name service; it can be split into partitions and then distributed to any number of network servers. The feature that distributes eDirectory is called *partitioning,* and the characteristic that makes it redundant is called *replication.* An NDS eDirectory replica is the physical copy of a partition that is stored on a network server. An eDirectory partition can have multiple replicas or copies stored on different network servers. The group of replicas that exist for a particular partition is called a *replica list.*

It is important to remember that a partition is a logical structure, whereas the replica is a physical copy of the partition, as illustrated in Figure 6.24, where the [ROOT] partition for ACME is placed on servers NOR-SRV1, CAM-SRV1, and TOK-SRV1.

The fact that an eDirectory tree can be partitioned and replicated makes eDirectory a powerful facility for storing, accessing, managing, and using information about network resources, regardless of where they are physically located. Replication increases the availability of eDirectory so that any number of servers can be down and the users can still log in and access the network services.

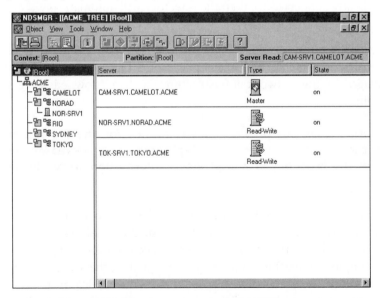

**FIGURE 6.24** *NDS eDirectory replicas for the [ROOT] partition are stored on different servers throughout the network. In this case, the [ROOT] partition for ACME is placed on servers NOR-SRV1, CAM-SRV1, and TOK-SRV1.*

## The Purpose of NDS eDirectory Replicas

Replication is a major feature and advantage of Directory Services. Replication of the eDirectory tree serves three primary purposes:

▶ **Fault tolerance** — Replication increases the availability of a partition (a section of the eDirectory tree) to the users because the partition now has more than one copy of its information. For example, if a server holding a replica of the partition becomes unavailable, then the users can use another copy or replica for authentication and updates.

▶ **Performance** — You can increase the performance of the directory access by proper physical placement of the replicas. Replication enables you to have multiple replicas of the partition and to place those replicas local to the users that need the information. Having a local replica decreases the time needed to authenticate, make changes, do searches, and extract the directory information.

▶ **Name resolution** — The mechanism that NDS eDirectory uses to locate the proper server is *name resolution* or *tree walking*. Users requesting the directory information have to first locate the server that stores the information. If the requested information is not found on the server that the user is already connected to, then the directory will automatically connect the user to the proper server.

The primary goal of replication is to eliminate the single point of failure for an NDS eDirectory partition. Having multiple replicas of a partition protects you against most outages in the network infrastructure, such as downed servers, routers, or WAN links.

**NOTE**    **NDS replication does not provide fault tolerance for the file system stored on the NetWare 6 servers. Replication only increases the availability of the NDS object and property information stored in the directory partition.**

The NetWare 6 installation program helps replicate the directory partitions for fault tolerance during installation of the server. When you are installing additional servers into the tree, the installation program tries to place up to three replicas for a partition. For example, the partition where you are installing the server has less than three total replicas. The installation places a read/write replica on the new server. Automatic replication applies only to the partition where the server object is being installed and does not affect other partitions in the tree. The purpose for doing this automatic replication is to support fault tolerance of the eDirectory database. If you are comfortable with the three automatic replicas placed during installation, then you may not need to change the replication of a partition for fault tolerance.

## Replica Types

Proper placement of replicas on the network servers is important to ensure proper operation of the directory. A server may contain a number of replicas if they are from different partitions. A server also does not have to contain any replicas. In order to understand where and when to place the replicas, you must understand the different types of replicas and their characteristics.

As stated earlier, each partition can have multiple replicas. And each replica will be one of the following four replica types: master, read/write, read-only, and subordinate reference.

### The Master Replica

The master (M) replica of a partition is always the first replica that is created; it can be changed as other replicas are added. Only one master replica can exist for each partition. The master replica provides these features:

- **Accepts client updates to the NDS object and attributes** — This is the ability to add, delete, and modify the objects in the partition.

- **Controls all partitioning operations** — These operations include splitting and joining partitions, moving objects and subtrees, adding and removing replicas, and repairing the replicas.

- **Conforms to the X.500 model** — This model enables clients to request the use of only the master replica.

NDS permits only one master replica per partition because the master replica controls all the partitioning operations. The master replica essentially locks the partition during any partition operation. Therefore, it ensures that only one operation is performed at a time. This mechanism provides the directory database integrity.

For example, in order to change the partition structure of the tree through either a create or merge partition operation, you must be able to contact the master for that partition. The master then works with the other replicas to complete the operation. If you are the system administrator, you must have sufficient rights to the partition before the directory will let you partition.

In addition, the master replica is equal to all other replicas during replica synchronization. Replica synchronization is a peer-to-peer mechanism, not a master-slave device.

The master replica provides complete access to the object and property information in the partition. This means that users can log in through this replica and make changes to the information in the replica. Changes include adding, deleting, and renaming NDS objects, or modifying the objects and the properties.

Figure 6.25 shows the master replicas for the [ROOT], CAMELOT, NORAD, RIO, TOKYO, and SYDNEY partitions of the ACME tree. The master replicas are stored on the server CAM-SRV1.

**FIGURE 6.25** *The master replicas for the [ROOT], CAMELOT, NORAD, RIO, TOKYO, and SYDNEY partitions of the ACME tree are stored on the server CAM-SRV1.*

### The Read/Write Replica

The purpose of the read/write (R/W) replica is to distribute the partition information across the NetWare 6 servers on the network for fault tolerance and performance. The read/write replica is used most often (especially in large networks with many servers) because any number of them can exist for any given partition. Although there is no limit to the number of read/write replicas per partition, we do recommend that you keep the number small and create a new read/write replica only when needed.

A read/write replica provides these features:

▶ **Accepts client updates to the NDS objects and properties** — Client updates include adding, deleting, and modifying the objects in the partitions.

▶ **Provides fault tolerance for the partition** — This means that the read/write replicas improve availability of the information stored in the partition.

▶ **Increases performance of the directory access by the physical placement of the read/write replicas** — The read/write replica enables you to have multiple replicas of the partition and to place those replicas local to the users who need the information.

Like the master replica, the read/write replica provides users complete access to the object and property information in the partition. A read/write replica also allows clients to make modifications. Because updates can be made to a read/write replica, users of the network can use the read/write replica to log in and make authentication requests.

In other NetWare 6 documentation, the read/write replica is often referred to as a secondary replica.

**TIP**

**The bindery services feature in NetWare 6 requires that at least a read/write or master replica of the partition containing the bindery context exist on the server where the services are needed.**

Figure 6.26 shows the read/write replicas for the [ROOT] partition of the ACME tree. There are a couple read/write replicas that are stored on the servers NOR-SRV1, and TOK-SRV1.

### The Read-Only Replica

The read-only (RO) replica, as the name implies, does not accept changes from users. The only way that a read-only replica discovers changes is through synchronization with the other replicas (read/write and master).

The read-only replica has these features:

▶ **Provides access to the NDS objects and attributes in the partition** — This replica does not accept client updates but does accept read requests from the clients.

▸ **Provides fault tolerance for the partition** — This means that the read-only replicas improve availability of the information stored in the partition.

▸ **Increases performance of the NDS access through its physical placement** — You can make these replicas local to the users who need the information.

**FIGURE 6.26** *The read/write replicas for the [ROOT] partition of the ACME tree are stored on the servers NOR-SRV1 and TOK-SRV1.*

Because a read-only replica cannot be updated, it cannot support login or authentication requests from users. For this reason, read-only replicas are seldom used or implemented into production. There are currently few reasons to implement read-only partitions.

**NOTE** When a network user logs into NDS, three properties of the user object are updated: Network Address, Login Time, and Last Login Time. In order for users to change or update these three properties, they must log into at least a read/write or master replica. The read-only replica cannot accept user logins because these properties cannot be updated. When a network user logs out of the directory, the Network Address property for the user object is modified.

One possible use of a read-only replica is when you are trying to provide users read access to the NDS information but not to update activity. For example, if you want to build an off-site disaster recovery center for your servers, you can implement a read-only replica, which will maintain itself through replica synchronization but not let any users connect to those servers.

**NOTE** Be aware that if you disable the login on a NetWare 6 server (in this case a server with a read-only replica), then the other NetWare 6 servers will be incapable of connecting to the server to perform replica synchronization. Disabling logins on a server with any replicas should be avoided because it discontinues the replica synchronization for that server.

### The Subordinate Reference Replica

A subordinate reference (SR) replica contains only one object — the topmost container object in the partition. The topmost object in the partition defines the partition and is called the *partition root object*. This container object stores partition information that links together the partitions in the tree. Subordinate reference replicas connect the parent partitions with their child partitions.

Subordinate reference replicas are created and managed by the directory and the servers. You do not need to manage them. NDS places a subordinate reference replica on a server that contains a replica of the parent but does not have the child replica. NDS places a subordinate reference replica for each child of the parent on that server. Figure 6.27 illustrates a partitioned tree and its subsequent replica placement on the network servers. Some of the servers have subordinate reference replicas.

Some of the servers in Figure 6.27 are storing subordinate reference replicas because the servers are holding the parent partition, but not the corresponding child partition. For example, TOK-SRV1 holds a copy of the [ROOT] partition but not the NORAD, CAMELOT, or RIO partitions. As a result, subordinate references are established on TOK-SRV1 to link the parent partition with its child partitions.

The subordinate reference replicas that connect the tree together are visible in Novell's NDS Manager utility and also in the DSREPAIR utility. Figure 6.28 displays all the replicas on the server NOR-SRV1. Notice the subordinate reference replica for the CAMELOT partition.

Because a subordinate reference replica does not contain all of the information for each of the objects in the partition, it cannot provide users access to the object and property information. A user cannot log in through this replica because there is no NDS object information to access.

**FIGURE 6.27** *The ACME tree is partitioned, and subordinate reference replicas are created whenever a parent partition exists on a server without a copy of a child partition.*

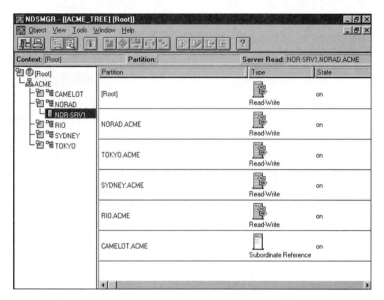

**FIGURE 6.28** *NDS Manager or ConsoleOne displays all of the read/write replicas on the server NOR-SVR1.*

# NDS Replication Design

One of the most important responsibilities of a directory administrator is to design the placement of the NDS replicas. The replication design includes the distribution and placement of replicas to the specific network servers for each of the partitions. Your replica design should provide fault tolerance for each partition.

Before you complete your replication design, you need to know some basic rules. These rules apply to all replicas and will help you understand how replicas are implemented or placed throughout the servers on the network.

- ▶ A partition can have multiple replicas, which are copies of a partition that can be stored on separate servers across your network, as explained in previous sections.

- ▶ A partition can only have one replica designated as the master. The other partitions will be read/write replicas or in some rare cases read-only replicas.

▶ Only one replica of a partition can be stored on any given server. A NetWare 6 server can hold multiple replicas from different partitions. It cannot hold two replicas of the same partition.

▶ All replicas will participate in the replica synchronization for a partition. All replicas are part of synchronization operations, regardless of replica type.

These rules are important because they describe the characteristics of replication. Knowing these rules will help you efficiently design the replica placement during implementation of your NetWare 6 network.

ConsoleOne is a Java-based administration tool that you can use to manage NDS eDirectory and third-party products on a variety of platforms, including Windows workstation and a NetWare server. With ConsoleOne you can also quickly browse large eDirectory trees, even those with containers holding thousands of objects. In a recent test, ConsoleOne took only two seconds to explore eDirectory containers that held 50,000 objects. ConsoleOne also enables you to manage server hardware components such as the server memory, hard drives, volumes, and network adapters.

## Guidelines for Replica Placement

These are the design guidelines for replica placement for any partition:

▶ Replicate for fault tolerance.

▶ Replicate locally.

▶ Replicate for bindery services.

▶ Replicate for improved name resolution.

We discuss each of these design considerations in detail in the following sections.

### Replicate for Fault Tolerance

A primary goal of replication is to eliminate the single point of failure for an NDS partition. Having multiple replicas of a partition on separate servers increases the availability of object information if one of the servers should become unavailable. In Figure 6.29, the NORAD and CAMELOT partitions have been replicated to multiple servers at their respective sites to provide fault tolerance for each partition. If one of the servers in the partition becomes unavailable, NDS will respond from the other server.

The NetWare 6 installation program automatically creates up to three NDS replicas for fault tolerance. When you install additional servers into the tree, the installation program places up to three replicas of the partition where the server is going to be located in the tree. If the partition where you are installing the server has fewer than three total replicas, the installation will place a read/write replica on the new server in that partition.

If the server being installed is upgraded or has an existing bindery, such as a NetWare 3.12 server, then the installation program will automatically convert the bindery to an NDS replica of the partition where the server is being installed. A NetWare 3.12 server being upgraded receives at least a read/write replica of the partition, even if three other replicas already exist for that partition.

**FIGURE 6.29** *The NORAD and CAMELOT partitions have been replicated to multiple servers on the network to provide fault tolerance for the directory.*

In Figure 6.30 the NORAD partition has been replicated automatically to the servers NOR-SRV1, NOR-CHR-SRV1, and LABS-SRV1 by the installation program. Because NOR-SRV1 contains the master replica of the [ROOT] partition, it also receive the master replica for the NORAD partition. The other servers will receive read/write replicas until there are at least three replicas for the NORAD partition. Notice that a fourth server (R&D-SRV1) has been installed into the partition but did not automatically receive a replica. The installation program assumes that the R&D-SRV1 is a new server that was not upgraded from NetWare 3.12 (meaning there was no bindery to convert to a replica).

Automatic replication applies only to the partition where the server object is being installed and does not affect other partitions in the tree. The purpose of automatic replication is to support fault tolerance of the NDS tree information. If you are comfortable with where the three automatic replicas were placed during installation, then you need not change the replicas of a partition for fault tolerance.

**FIGURE 6.30** *The installation program automatically replicates the NORAD partition to the first three servers: NOR-SRV1, NOR-CHR-SRV1, and LABS-SRV1. A fourth server (R&D-SRV1) was installed into the partition but did not receive an automatic replica.*

As a general guideline, you should always have both a master and two read/write replicas for every partition. At a minimum, we recommend two replicas, and three replicas are even better. Again, having two or three replicas eliminates any single point of failure in your network. By placing multiple replicas locally, you ensure that any NetWare 6 server with the same replica can fail without affecting the directory availability for your users.

### Replicate Locally

The best method to guarantee efficiency in the replication design is to replicate locally. This means placing all the replicas of a partition on local servers. You should not place a replica across a WAN link if you have servers available locally, meaning on the same side of your WAN link. If you follow this guideline, you can guarantee that users will retrieve their object information from the nearest available server. Figure 6.31 is an example of placing a replica that is not local to that partition.

**FIGURE 6.31** *You should always try to replicate locally by placing replicas of a partition on the servers at that location or site. Do not place a replica across a WAN link from the original partition.*

Ideally, you should place the replica containing a user's information on the server that stores the user's home directory. This may not always be possible, but it does improve the user's access to NDS objects and properties. For example, during the login process the user maps drives to volumes, captures to print queues, and accesses several of the user objects and properties. The directory executes each of these requests, regardless of where the replicas are stored. However, the login speed for the user will be increased if the user finds the requested information on his or her preferred server.

Again, the primary design consideration is that you replicate the NDS partition locally. For example, a partition is created for a specific location, and a master replica is placed on a server in that location. We recommend that you place your read/write replicas of the partition on different servers in the same physical location as the master replica. If you are forced to place the third replica across a WAN link because the location has only two servers, then we recommend that you not create the third replica if it is placed across the WAN link. This choice depends upon the level of fault tolerance you want to maintain.

The following questions are often asked, "What happens if the location or site has only one server? Do I still partition and replicate locally? How do I replicate for fault tolerance?" In the case of a remote site with just one server, you should still partition at that site and place the master replica on that server. A second replica of the partition can be placed on the nearest location for purposes of fault tolerance. Typically, the remote site with just one server contains a small number of user objects. Therefore, although we do not recommend replicating across your WAN, a small replica across your WAN in this case is your only alternative for replication. It is better to replicate a small partition across a WAN than to lose the directory information if the server ever goes down.

Figure 6.32 illustrates how a small remote office in the ACME tree should be replicated. Assume that a small remote site called OU=SLC is connected to the NORAD hub. The remote site of SLC has only one server (SLC-SRV1). You should create a small partition and replicate it to SLC1. You should also place a replica in the NORAD location on the server NOR-SRV1.

**FIGURE 6.32** *The remote site of SLC has only one server (SLC-SRV1). You should create a small partition called SLC and replicate it to the SLC-SRV1 and NOR-SRV1 servers in the NORAD location. It is more important to replicate for fault tolerance than to not replicate across the WAN links*

## Place Replicas to Support Bindery Services

As mentioned earlier, bindery services does require the placement of a read/write or master replica on the server that sets the bindery context. The bindery context set at the server is officially known as the *server bindery context*. Figure 6.33 illustrates how the NOR-SRV1 server needs to hold a read/write replica in order to set the server bindery context at OU=NORAD.

The server bindery context can be set at the server console by typing this command:

```
SET SERVER BINDERY CONTEXT = "OU=NORAD.O=ACME"
```

In Figure 6.34, all the objects in the NORAD container that are NetWare 3 bindery objects are viewed and accessed as if they are in a bindery. The NDS objects available through bindery services include the user, group, print queue, print server, profile, and bindery type objects. This list is included because these are the only objects that were defined in the NetWare 3 bindery. The new NDS objects, such as directory map, organizational role, computer, and alias, do not show up as bindery objects in your Directory.

In order for a NetWare 6 server to support bindery services, it must hold either a read/write or master replica of a partition where the server is installed. You will need to place read/write replicas on the network servers to support bindery services.

A NetWare feature known as bindery services enables the NetWare server to respond to the bindery calls made by the bindery-based utilities and applications. Bindery services lets these applications run on NetWare version 4, 5, and 6 without modifications. Bindery Services is supported for backwards compatibility to NetWare and is used less and less nowadays.

**FIGURE 6.33** *Setting the bindery services for partition NORAD requires that a read/write or master replica be stored on the NOR-SRVI server, which is where the server sets the server bindery context.*

**FIGURE 6.34** *Server NOR-PR-SRV1 has a bindery context set to "OU=PR.OU=NORAD.O=ACME."*

Bindery services is also required during a NetWare 3 to NetWare 6 server upgrade. For example, if you are upgrading a NetWare 3 server, a read/write replica of the partition is placed on the upgraded NetWare 6 server. The read/write replica is placed on the server regardless of whether there are already three replicas, as described earlier in the "Replicate for Fault Tolerance" section. The system assumes that because the server is being upgraded from NetWare 3, bindery services in NetWare 6 will be needed.

### Place Replicas for Improved Name Resolution

The mechanism the directory uses to find the object location is referred to as *name resolution*. If the object information is not stored locally, the server must search the Directory tree to find the other servers that have the object information. Every replica maintains a set of pointers to all the other replicas in the same partition. The directory uses these pointers to locate the partitions that are above and below in the Directory tree. With the name resolution mechanism, NDS can follow these pointers to locate the servers holding the requested data.

**Consulting Experience**

Do not replicate [ROOT] more than three times. Keep in mind your understanding of subordinate reference replicas. Each replica of [ROOT] you create will also create subordinate reference replicas. Spreading around more copies of a partition increases the number of subordinate references. For example, assume you have 10 child partitions created directly below [ROOT] because you have 10 locations. When you replicate [ROOT] three times, you will have 10 subordinate reference replicas on 3 separate servers for a total of 30 subordinate reference replicas. Add two more replicas of [ROOT] and you have 50 servers holding subordinate reference replicas.

TIP

**For improved speed of name resolution from one side of the tree to the other, you can replicate the [ROOT] partition in a couple of strategic locations, such as hub sites, so that users can search the tree faster. The [ROOT] partition should be small to keep directory traffic to a minimum. However, unlike with other partitions, you should not replicate [ROOT] more than three times.**

To speed access to the appropriate server, you can place replicas closer to that server to help the user find the requested information. For example, if you are trying to locate information from one side of the tree to the other, the partition that will help you is the [ROOT] partition. In this case, you can replicate the [ROOT] partition to that major hub site in your company. Replicating the [ROOT] partition is recommended only if it is set up as a small partition and you only replicate it a couple of times. "Small" means the [ROOT] partition should include just the [ROOT] object and the O=ACME object. See Figure 6.35 for an illustration of a small [ROOT] partition that is replicated across a WAN link.

[ROOT]
Partition

O=ACME

**FIGURE 6.35** *The [ROOT] partition can be replicated across the WAN links if it is created as a small partition containing just the [ROOT] object and O=ACME object.*

Figure 6.36 illustrates how the [ROOT] partition can be replicated to a few strategic locations in the WAN infrastructure to facilitate improved name resolution. In this case, we have placed a copy of [ROOT] in NORAD on the NOR-SRV1 server, in CAMELOT on the CAM-SRV1 server, and in TOKYO on the TOK-SRV1 server.

[ROOT]

O=ACME

[ROOT] – Master        [ROOT] – R/W        [ROOT] – R/W

NOR-SRV1        CAM-SRV1        TOK-SRV1

**FIGURE 6.36** *NDS replicas for the [ROOT] partition are stored on different servers throughout the network to improve name resolution.*

The small [ROOT] partition (containing few objects) is also fairly static, so [ROOT] may be replicated across the WAN links. However, do not go overboard on replicating this partition. Three replicas of the [ROOT] partition are usually sufficient.

We do not recommend that you replicate any other partition across the WAN infrastructure for the purpose of name resolution. Because [ROOT] is at the top of your tree and a lot of name resolution must traverse the [ROOT] partition, it makes sense to replicate [ROOT] only at key hub locations in your tree.

## Summary of NDS Partition and Replica Design Guidelines

The specific design rules for partitioning and replication of the directory can be separated into two different categories depending on your specific implementation requirements, your hardware, and your staff's knowledge level. The two categories defined for the partition and replica design rules are Quick Design and Advanced Design.

### Quick Design

The Quick Design rules for partitions and replicas are simple, basic rules that can be implemented in all companies and applied to almost every situation, regardless of the WAN or LAN infrastructure. Quick Design is highly recommended for designers and customers who want to operate their NDS tree structures as effectively as possible. These design rules minimize the impact of replica synchronization and provide a good foundation for overall performance.

The Quick Design rules provide everyone with an easy and safe method to design and implement NDS eDirectory in their network environments. If you use the recommendations that follow, you will be successful in designing the directory. The system will also be much easier to service and maintain.

Here are the specific Quick Design rules for partitioning and replication of NDS:

- ▸ Partition size — Unlimited objects
- ▸ Number of child partitions per parent — 150 partitions
- ▸ Number of replicas per partition — 150 replicas
- ▸ Number of replicas per server — 150 replicas
- ▸ Number of replicas per Replica Server — 300 replicas (see the next "Consulting Experience" sidebar)
- ▸ Minimum server hardware — Pentium III 500+ MHz with 1GB of RAM

Only a few situations will arise in which the Quick Design rules will not apply. For the few portions of the tree where these rules cannot be followed, we introduce the more costly Advanced Design rules.

### Advanced Design

The Advanced Design rules are simply greater numbers for each of the partition and replica areas. Because the requirements for these rules exceed the requirements given in the Quick Design rules, they are more costly in terms of the efficiency of replica synchronization on the servers. For this reason, we strongly recommend, if not require, that you or your staff completely understand the impact of the larger requirements. It is safe to say that the Advanced Design rules require that the individuals who maintain the system need to have a greater knowledge of NDS and NetWare 6.

For the most part, the Advanced Design rules are targeted at the consultant or administrator who understands the ramifications of moving past the Quick Design rules to the larger requirements.

The specific Advanced Design rules for partitioning and replication of NDS, shown in the following list, are the maximum values for each area and should never be exceeded. The Advanced Design rules are as follows:

- ▶ Partition size — Unlimited objects
- ▶ Number of child partitions per parent — 500 partitions
- ▶ Number of replicas per partition — 500 replicas
- ▶ Number of replicas per server — 500 replicas
- ▶ Number of replicas per Replica Server — 1000 replicas (see the next "Consulting Experience" sidebar)
- ▶ Minimum server hardware — Pentium IV 1+ GHz with 3GB of RAM

## Hardware Requirements for Replicas

Determining the hardware requirements is difficult because of each of the previous factors mentioned. A general example is that a basic installation of NDS eDirectory with the standard schema requires approximately 74 MB of disk space for every 50,000 users. Obviously, if you add a new set of attributes or utilize many user object attributes, the object size and disk space requirements will grow. If every user is impacted, then the amount of disk space, processor, and memory will also need to be increased.

## Consulting Experience

A *replica server* is a dedicated NetWare 6 server that just stores NDS replicas. This type of server is sometimes referred to as a *DSMASTER server*. This configuration has become popular with companies that have many single server remote offices. The replica server provides a place for you to store additional replicas for the partition of a remote office location.

The ultimate limiting factor for the number of replicas on any server is that replica synchronization on the server must be able to complete in 30 minutes or less. The factors that affect the time it takes to complete the synchronization include the following:

- ▶ CPU speed of the replica server
- ▶ Number of replicas
- ▶ Number of objects in each replica
- ▶ Size of each replica ring
- ▶ Location of replicas in the replica ring (local or remote)
- ▶ Speed of the WAN links connecting remote replicas
- ▶ RAM on replica server
- ▶ Frequency of inbound replica synchronizations

NDS eDirectory scales on a single processor and does not consume high amounts of processor power. Adding processors, however, will boost performance of eDirectory in an Intel environment. Table 6.1 and Table 6.2 will help you estimate the amount of hardware needed for particular installations:

| TABLE 6.1 | | | |
|-----------|---|---|---|
| *Intel-Based Implementations (NetWare, Windows NT, and Linux)* | | | |
| OBJECTS | PROCESSOR | MEMORY | HARD DISK |
| 100k | Pentium III 450-700 MHz (single) | 384MB | 144MB |
| 1 million | Pentium III 450-700 Mhz | 2GB | 1.5GB |
| 10 million | Pentium III 450-700 MHz | 2GB+ | 15GB |

| | TABLE 6.2 | | |
|---|---|---|---|
| | Unix-Based Implementation (Solaris) | | |
| OBJECTS | PROCESSOR | MEMORY | HARD DISK |
| 100k | Sun Enterprise 4500 | 384MB | 144MB |
| 1 million | Sun Enterprise 5500 | 2GB | 1.5GB |
| 10 million | Sun Enterprise 6500 with multiple processors | 2GB+ | 15GB |

## Managing NDS Partitions and Replicas

In order to manage your NDS partitions and replicas properly, you need to understand and use several types of operations. The NDS partition and replica operations are as follows: create partition, merge partition, move partition (subtree), add replica, remove replica, change replica type, and abort partition operation. These operations are discussed later in this section. There are two main utilities in NetWare 6, called NDS Manager and ConsoleOne that enable you to perform NDS partition and replica operations on the NDS tree.

As mentioned previously, ConsoleOne is a Java-based administration tool that you can use to manage NDS eDirectory and other third-party products on either a Windows workstation or at the NetWare server console. In addition to managing NDS eDirectory, ConsoleOne also allows you to manage the server hardware components such as the hard drives, LAN cards, and memory..

The NDS Manager utility is the Windows-based administration program. ConsoleOne can be used either on your Windows workstation or at the server console. This program is used by the system administrators to manage all NDS partitions and replicas. Figure 6.37 shows the NDS Manager main window.

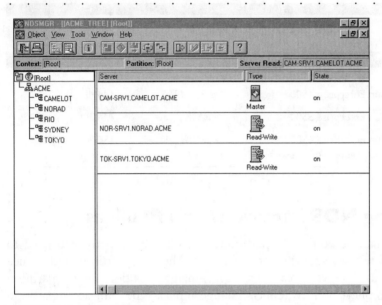

**FIGURE 6.37** *The NDS Manager utility controls the partitioning and replication of the NDS database.*

In Figure 6.38 you can see that the partitions are denoted with small box icons to the left of the OU container object. In this example, OU=CAMELOT and OU=NORAD are partitions.

## NDS Partition and Replica Operations

All partition and replica operations require that the master replica for the partition be available. As mentioned earlier, the master replica locks the partition before it starts the operation. The only partition operations that do not require the master replica to lock the partition are the add replica and remove replica operations.

All the replicas for a specific partition must be available in order to complete the operation. If a replica is not reachable, the directory system will wait until it is available.

If you are performing a merge partition operation, then you need to check the status of both the parent and child partitions involved in the merge. Again, you should check the status of the partitions before you start the merge operation.

### Consulting Experience

Before you start a partition operation, you should *always* check the status of the replicas of the partition. You can avoid many problems if you check the synchronization status of the replicas before you perform any partition operation. You can use DSREPAIR to check the status of the replicas and synchronization. Make sure that the synchronization is complete before starting a new operation on that partition. Figure 6.39 displays a status check of the replicas in DSREPAIR. For more information on specific interpretations of each of the items shown, you can refer to a discussion of the DSREPAIR utility in Chapter 10.

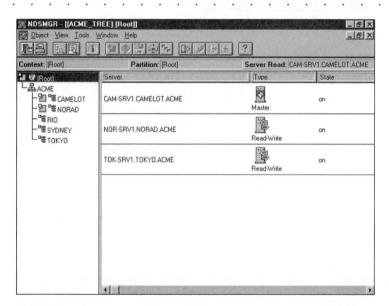

**FIGURE 6.38** *In the NDS Manager, the partitions are denoted with a small box icon to the left of the OU container. OU=CAMELOT and OU=NORAD are shown as partitions.*

Another operational guideline is that after you have started a partition operation, you should be patient and wait for all the synchronization to complete. As we've mentioned, the directory is a distributed and replicated system that is loosely consistent, and it may take time before the changes to the directory partition will be reflected across the network. Synchronization of a partition with many objects and replicas naturally take longer than synchronization with just a few objects.

**FIGURE 6.39** *Use DSREPAIR to check the status of the replicas before starting a partition operation.*

In addition to checking the partition status through the DSREPAIR utility, you can use the DSTRACE utility. Figure 6.40 shows the screen in DSTRACE to check after the synchronization completes. If the synchronization has errors, they will be displayed as shown in Figure 6.40.

If possible, we recommend that you centralize partition operations management. Only one person or a small group of people should be responsible for all of the partitioning and replication for your company. You might decide that only one workstation on the network should start the partition operations. In this way, you can eliminate the possibility that two people or two different workstations will be simultaneously making changes to the partitions.

### Consulting Experience

If your NetWare 6 servers are running the code release of DS.NLM, then you can use DSREPAIR to read the partition status after the partition operation. It will be more accurate than previous releases of DSREPAIR, which often generated the "partition busy" error message.

The next several sections discuss each of the partition and replica operations that can be performed. These operations include create new partition, merge partition, move partition or subtree, add replica, remove replica, change replica type, rebuild replicas, and abort partition operations.

**FIGURE 6.40** *The Replica screen in DSTRACE shows you when the synchronization has completed for a partition.*

### The Create Partition Operation

*Creating* a new partition is the same as creating a child partition from the parent partition. This operation is sometimes called a *partition split.* The terms *create* and *split* are used interchangeably. The operation is generally fast because it generates less network traffic than do other partition operations. The traffic is limited to changes to the replica pointers, synchronization, and partitioning control. Once again, however, if you have many replicas of the partition before the split, the directory also must contact each server holding a replica in order to perform the operation there.

The operation simply divides the partition into two, with all the information staying on the same servers where the operation originally started. This split operation creates a new child partition on all the servers that had a copy of the parent partition.

When the partition is created, the partition takes its name from the topmost container object (partition root object). All the objects in the tree that are under the container object form the contents of the new partition.

In the following examples, we have installed a third server in the tree, called TOK-SRV1. The result of installing the TOK-SRV1 server into the tree is that it will receive a read/write copy of the [ROOT] partition. Figure 6.41 shows how you can use the NDS Manager utility to create a new partition called the TOKYO partition for the ACME company. All the objects in the subtree under TOKYO are included in the partition.

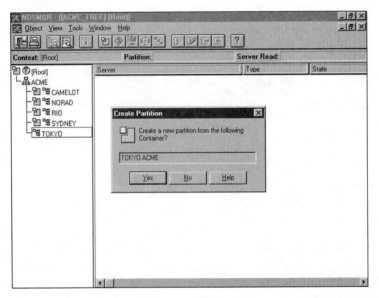

**FIGURE 6.41** *The OU=TOKYO container is created as a new partition for the ACME tree.*

Notice in Figure 6.42 that the create partition operation for TOKYO places copies of the new TOKYO partition on all the servers that originally had copies of the parent partition [ROOT]. You can remove the additional copies if they are not placed on the servers you want.

In Figure 6.42 the TOKYO partition and its information can be placed on the servers in TOKYO. The same is true for all the locations. By partitioning the NDS tree, you can keep the location information in each location and still find and use the resources throughout the entire NDS tree.

In order to perform the create partition operation, you must have rights to the top of the partition or the OU container that defines the partition. The effective rights needed are write rights to the ACL of the top container object that defines the partition. There are several ways to receive this privilege. You can be granted either the Supervisor object right or the explicit write property right to the ACL.

Either of these two rights will enable you to perform the create partition operations on the tree.

Figure 6.43 illustrates the rights needed to perform the future partition operation for the NORAD partition in the ACME tree. Notice that the user, AEinstein, has been given the Supervisor object right to the OU=NORAD. The OU=NORAD is the top of the partition and is referred to as the partition root object of the NORAD partition.

**FIGURE 6.42**  *The create partition operation placed copies of the new TOKYO partition on all the servers that originally had copies of the [ROOT] partition. These servers are NOR-SRVI, CAM-SRVI, TOK-SRVI.*

### The Merge Partition Operation

The operation used to combine a child partition with its parent is called a *merge*. This operation is also sometimes called a *partition join*. The terms *merge* and *join* are used interchangeably. This operation takes varying amounts of time and could generate network traffic, depending on which servers originally held the partitions.

The merge operation requires that each server holding a copy of the parent partition receive a copy of the child partition before the merge can take place. In return, each server holding a copy of the child partition must receive a copy of the parent before the merge can be completed. The merge operation attempts to move copies of either the parent or child partition to the appropriate servers as needed. After the copies have been successfully moved, the merge operation then joins the partitions together.

**FIGURE 6.43** *The user AEinstein has been assigned the rights needed to perform the create partition operation for the NORAD partition.*

It is strongly recommended that you manually place copies of the parent partition on all the servers with a child partition before you initiate the merge operation. In turn, you should place copies of each of the child partitions on the servers holding the parent partitions before you start the merge operation.

You will have greater success merging partitions if you manually place copies of the parent and child partitions on appropriate servers. In order to accomplish this task, you must know where each of the copies of the partitions is located. Refer to "The Partition and Replica Matrix" section later in this chapter.

If all the servers have copies of both the child and parent partitions before the merge operation begins, the merge will be quicker and encounter fewer problems, thus, enabling the operation to complete. Copies of both child and parent partitions also prevent large amounts of directory data from moving across the network during the operation. Network traffic occurs when you prepare for the merge by placing the appropriate replicas on the servers.

An example of a merge partition operation is illustrated in Figure 6.44, where the OPS partition is merged back with its parent partition CAMELOT. The utility will ask you to confirm the merge operation as shown.

In order to perform the merge partition operation, you must have rights to only the child partitions. The effective rights needed are the write rights to the ACL of the child partitions. There are several ways to receive these privileges. You can be granted either the Supervisor object right or the explicit write property right to the ACL property.

**FIGURE 6.44** *The OPS partition is merged back with its parent partition, CAMELOT.*

> **Consulting Experience**
>
> Check the synchronization status of all replicas in the partition with DSREPAIR before initiating any partition operation. All replicas must be available and functioning properly before you proceed with the partitioning.

Figure 6.45 illustrates the rights needed to perform the merge partition operation for the CAMELOT and OPS partitions in the ACME tree. Notice that the user, KingArthur, has been given the Supervisor object right to the OU=OPS container.

**FIGURE 6.45** *The user, KingArthur, has been assigned the rights needed to perform the merge partition operation for the OPS and CAMELOT partitions.*

### The Move Subtree Partition Operation

The operation used to move an OU container and its entire contents or subtree from one location in the NDS tree to another is called a *move subtree*. This operation is important when you reorganize the information in your NDS tree because it enables you to move the container objects in the NDS tree. In order for you to move an OU container, the following two conditions must exist:

▶ **The OU container object being moved must be a partition.** — This means that the OU container object must be a partition root object. You will need to create a partition from the OU container before moving it if one does not exist.

▶ **The partition or subtree you want to move cannot have any child partitions.** — You may be forced to merge child partitions with their parent in order to move the subtree.

This operation is essentially moving a partition from one location in the NDS tree to another location. This operation can generate network traffic depending on the servers on which the parent partitions were originally placed.

In Figure 6.46 we have assumed that the join operation did not occur or was aborted. The NDS Manager Move Partition screen for the OPS partition under the CAMELOT location is moved to another location in the NDS tree, in this case, under the NORAD.ACME container.

In order to perform the move partition (subtree) operation, you must have rights to all the partitions involved. The effective rights needed are the write rights to the ACL of the top container object that defines the partition. There are several ways to receive this privilege. You can be granted either the Supervisor object right or the explicit write property right to the ACL property.

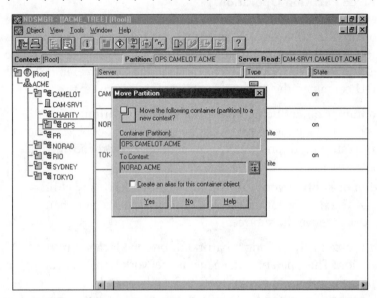

**FIGURE 6.46** *The OPS partition is moved to another location (under the NORAD.ACME) in the NDS tree.*

### The Add Replica Operation

The *add replica* operation is used to create a new copy of the partition information and store it on another server. Adding replicas to other network servers requires that all the data in the partition be copied to the new servers across the network. This operation causes network traffic. Because the amount of traffic is dependent on the number of objects in the partition, it is a good idea to schedule this operation during a low-use time in the network.

Figure 6.47 shows the NDS Manager dialog box used to perform an add replica operation. You first select a partition to which you want to add a replica. In this case the [ROOT] partition is selected. You then select the server on which the new replica will be placed.

**FIGURE 6.47** *Using the NDS Manager utility to add a new replica to the [ROOT] partition*

### The Remove Replica Operation

The *remove replica* partition operation is used to delete a copy of the partition information from a specific server. You might think that this operation to delete the replica happens quickly because it simply marks the information to be removed from the server. However, every object in the replica must now be set up as an external reference, that is, as a pointer to the real object in another replica on another server. With the creation of the external references, *backlinks*, which are pointers back to the external references, are established. Even though the backlinks are checked in the background process, the initial setup will take time. For a complete discussion on external references and backlinks, see Chapter 8.

Figure 6.48 shows the NDS Manager dialog box that is used to remove a replica of a partition. You first select a partition from which you want to remove the replica. In this case the [ROOT] partition is selected. You then select the server from which to remove the replica. In this example, we have selected the TOK-SRV1 as the replica to remove. The result is that only two replicas remain on the servers, CAM-SRV1 and NOR-SRV1.

**FIGURE 6.48** *Using the NDS Manager utility to remove the TOK-SRV1 replica from the [ROOT] partition*

### The Change Replica Type Operation

The *change replica type* operation can be performed when a specific type of replica needs to be changed. For example, if you want a different replica to be the master replica for the partition, you highlight which replica you want to be the new master, and NDS will change the type and propagate the change to the other replicas. In order to change the master replica, the target server must have a read/write or read-only replica.

Figure 6.49 shows the NDS Manager dialog box used to change the replica type for a partition. You first select a partition for which you want to perform the change replica type operation. In this case the [ROOT] partition is selected. You then select the server on which to change the replica type. We have selected the read/write replica on NOR-SRV1. We can now change its type to master. The result is that the master replica on CAM-SRV1 changes to a read/write replica.

**FIGURE 6.49** *Using the NDS Manager utility to change the replica type for the [ROOT] partition*

**TIP**

You are not allowed to change a master replica to read/write or read-only by selecting the server holding the master replica. The utility requires you to select either a read/write or read-only replica on another server and change it to the master replica.

### The Rebuild Replica Operation

There are a couple of ways you can rebuild the replica information for each of the partitions. The *rebuild replica* operation is used when the NDS information on the current server is not completely accurate or has become corrupt.

From the NDS Manager utility, there are two ways to update replica information. These two operations are called send updates and receive updates. Both of these functions are network intensive because they move all the partition data across the network to the servers. They are discussed in the sections that follow.

**Send Updates**   The *send updates* operation tries to send all the object information to all the other replicas in the ring. This operation synchronizes all the other replicas for the partition with the replica you have selected. You would perform this operation when the partition information on some of the servers is not complete or has become corrupted. By selecting the most current replica or the replica that has the best information, you can send its information to all the other replicas in the partition. You can use either NDS Manager (Send updates) or DSREPAIR (Send all objects to every replica in the ring).

Figure 6.50 shows an example of using NDS Manager to perform the send updates operation. In this example, the server CAM-SRV1, which is the master replica of the [ROOT] partition, is selected as the sending replica. The Send Updates operation will send the contents of the selected replica to all the other replicas in the partition.

**FIGURE 6.50** *The send updates replica operation. The CAM-SRV1 server, which holds the master replica of the [ROOT] partition, is selected as the sending replica. This operation sends the contents of the selected replica to all the other replicas in the partition.*

The receive updates operation synchronizes selected replicas with the information from the master replica. You would perform this operation when the partition information on one of the servers is not as complete as the master replica. This operation can be performed using both the NDS Manager and DSREPAIR utilities.

**Receive Updates**   The *receive updates* operation essentially marks the affected replica as a new replica. The operation begins adding the partition information to the replica again. Figure 6.51 shows an example of the receive updates operation using the DSREPAIR utility. In this example, the server named NOR-SRV1 receives the replica information from the master replica of the [ROOT] partition. (Notice that the "Send all objects to every replica in the ring" message is the send updates operation mentioned earlier.)

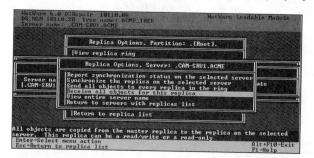

**FIGURE 6.51**   *The receive updates replica operation. The server named NOR-SRV1 receives the replica information from the master replica of the [ROOT] partition. This operation sends the contents of the master replica to the server holding the selected replica.*

**TIP**

**Check the synchronization status of all replicas in the partition with DSREPAIR before initiating any partition operation. All replicas must be available and functioning properly before you proceed with the partitioning.**

### The Abort Partition Operation

You have the ability to abort a partition operation that was previously started. The *abort partition* operation is valid only for certain partition operations, including create, merge, move subtree, and change replica type. The abort partition operation cannot be used on add replica or remove replica.

This feature is valuable not as an undo function but as a way to back out of partition operations that do not complete. For example, only one partition operation can take place at a time. As a result, if a partition operation starts and does not complete, no other partition operations can be started. A partition operation will wait indefinitely if one of the servers in the replica list of the partition becomes unavailable because of either a downed server or an unavailable communication link. This problem is manifested by "The master replica state is not on for the selected partition" message if you try to start another partition operation (see Figure 6.52). You can also check the status of the replicas using the NDS Manager utility.

**FIGURE 6.52** *The message displayed from NDS Manager if another partition operation is requested before the first partition operation is completed*

If you suspect that a partition operation is having difficulty completing, then either you can wait until the situation causing the problem is cleared up or you can abort the operation. To abort the partition operation, you can go to NDS Manager, select the partition, and press the Abort button. Figure 6.53 displays the abort partition operation in NDS Manager. In this example, the operation that has not completed is the change replica type operation because the replica state information shows each replica with Change Type 0. This means that the current change state of the replicas is 0. For more information and a complete list of the replica change states, see Chapter 8, "NDS eDirectory Internals and Operations."

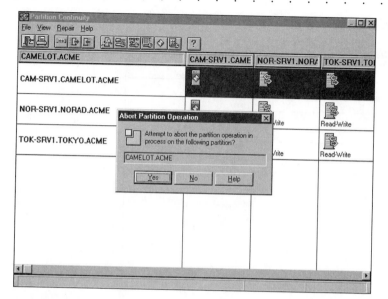

**FIGURE 6.53** *The Abort Partition Operation dialog box in NDS Manager*

To execute the abort operation, click Yes at the bottom of the dialog box.

After the partition operation aborts, the replicas involved will be turned back on as illustrated in Figure 6.54. In this example, each replica state has been set to ON, meaning that the partition is ready once again.

You can also abort a partition operation within the DSREPAIR utility. From the DSREPAIR main menu select the Advanced Options menu. From the Advanced Option menu select the Replica and Partition Operations menu. A list of all the partitions and replicas stored on the server is displayed. After you select the partition that is having problems, the Replica Options menu is displayed (see Figure 6.55). Down the menu is the Cancel Partition Operation selection. When you select this item, you will be asked to log into the directory as someone who has rights over the partition.

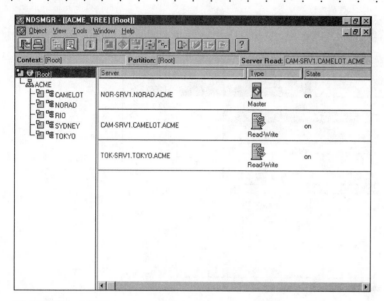

**FIGURE 6.54** *The replica states are turned back to ON after the partition operation is aborted.*

**FIGURE 6.55** *You can use DSREPAIR to abort or cancel a partition operation.*

## The Partition and Replica Matrix

The best method for keeping track of where partitions and replicas are stored in the directory is to create a partition and replica matrix. The matrix, as shown in Figure 6.56, helps you document the creation and replication of partitions.

The matrix helps you design and implement the partitions and replicas more efficiently. If you need to perform any partition operation, you have a quick and easy tool available.

| M - MASTER<br>R/W - READ/WRITE | RO - READ ONLY<br>SR - SUBORDINATE REF. | | PARTITIONS | | | | | |
|---|---|---|---|---|---|---|---|---|
| DESCRIPTION OF THE SERVER | | | [ROOT] | NORAD | RIO | CAMELOT | TOKYO | SYDNEY |
| NAME | LOCATION | NETWORK ADDRESS | | | | | | |
| | CAMELOT | ØBØØFADE | | | | | | |
| | NORAD | ØFFØBBØØ | | | | | | |
| | NORAD | ØFFØBBØØ | | | | | | |
| | RIO | ØØØØIØØØ | | | | | | |
| | TOKYO | ØØ22ØØØI | | | | | | |
| | SYDNEY | 2IØØIØØØ | | | | | | |

**FIGURE 6.56** *You should document your NDS partitions and replicas using a partition and replica matrix.*

## Replica Synchronization

Replication of the directory database is one of the major features of NDS eDirectory. However, because a partition can be distributed, any changes or updates to that partition take place on an individual replica, which in turn must pass the latest changes to all the other replicas of that partition. This process of ensuring that all the latest changes or updates to a particular partition are reflected in each of its replicas is called *synchronization*.

When updates and modifications are made to the directory, the fact that one of the replicas in a partition changes while the other replicas do not receive the updated information is known as *loose consistency*. Loose consistency simply means that all the replicas are not instantaneously changed as updates to NDS are made. So as the directory receives updates from users and administrators, all the replicas for the partition are not guaranteed to be completely converged or synchronized at any one time. However, to ensure the integrity of the database, NDS automatically synchronizes all the replicas for a specific partition. Figure 6.57 illustrates how the replicas for the [ROOT] partition will stay synchronized among the servers. This figure should be viewed only as a conceptual illustration.

For a complete discussion on how the replicas send and receive data for the partition, see Chapter 9. For information on Transitive Synchronization and Synchronized Up To Vector see the respecctive sections in Chapter 10.

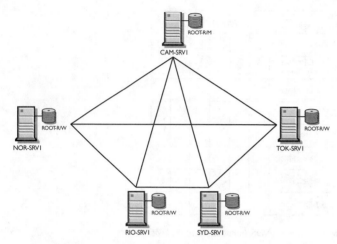

**FIGURE 6.57** *The NDS replicas synchronize with each other to maintain consistency of the [ROOT] partition information. The synchronization is loosely consistent because of the timing during the process.*

This synchronization, which runs in the background, introduces a new level of complexity to the network and the traffic it could generate. The information passed between the replicas during the synchronization exchange is limited to just the updates, thus, reducing the total amount of network traffic.

Because the synchronization process between replicas could impact the traffic on both the local LAN and WAN networks, you should decide where to place the replicas. You can also control which replicas in the partition will accept client updates by choosing the type of replica to place in service.

### Subordinate Reference Replicas

A special consideration applies to the distribution of subordinate reference replicas. The subordinate reference replicas participate in synchronization as much as the other types of replicas for the partition. However, the amount of information for the subordinate reference replicas is little. Nonetheless, the subordinate reference replicas change timestamps with the other replicas, and no object data is passed.

> · · · · · · · · · · · · · · · · · · · · · · · · · · · · · · ◄

**Consulting Experience**

In the example of 200 cities being partitioned off the [ROOT], the issue is not just the traffic among the replicas because little data is passed between a subordinate reference replica and the other replicas. The bigger concern is the effect that the large number of subordinate reference replicas has on partition operations and completion of partition operations. Remember, each replica of a partition must be contacted before a partition operation can be successfully completed. The other issue, once again, is supportability and repairability.

If you have done a careful job of designing your tree and partitions in a hierarchical layout, then a good distribution of the subordinate references will be automatically handled by the directory. If you have created only a few replicas per partition, then the subordinate references have been optimized and there is little else that you need to change.

Remember, the subordinate reference replicas are needed because they provide tree connectivity by linking the parent partitions with their child partitions. A subordinate reference replica is essentially a pointer down the tree to the next layer of partitions. Using the subordinate reference mechanism, NDS operates more efficiently because it does not have to place a full replica (master, read/write, and read-only) to provide the tree connectivity. The directory will place a subordinate reference replica on a server that contains a replica of the parent but does not have the child replica. Again, subordinate reference replicas are useful because eDriectory does not require you to connect the tree manually by placing full replicas.

Because the directory is responsible for maintaining the subordinate reference replicas, you, as administrators, need to know about their placement and impact on synchronization. Again, keep in mind that supportability and repairability play heavily into this equation. The more subordinate references, the more servers need to be contacted during a repair procedure.

A subordinate reference replica contains only one object, which is the topmost container object in the partition (typically an OU). This top container object, which is called the *partition root object*, stores the partition information that links the tree together. The partition root object holds a list of all the replicas in the partition (master, read/write, read-only, and subordinate references) that participate in replica synchronization. The greater the number of subordinate reference replicas, the larger their impact on synchronization. You should ascertain where the subordinate references are being created and, if possible, try to reduce them. By reducing the number of subordinate reference replicas, you will increase the performance of synchronization for each server. One way to reduce subordinate references is to reduce the number of replicas of the parent partition by reducing the number of servers that contain a copy of the parent partition. Another way to reduce subordinate reference replicas is to place the child partitions on the same servers as their parents. The second option is not always feasible.

### An Example of Subordinate References

A good example with which to illustrate subordinate reference replicas is the [ROOT] partition, which is at the top of the tree. The ACME tree is partitioned as shown in Figure 6.58. In this example, we have 200 cities or locations, each partitioned under the [ROOT] partition.

**FIGURE 6.58** *The ACME tree has over 200 cities, each partitioned under the [ROOT] partition.*

Consider what would happen each time you place a replica of the [ROOT] partition on a server. The directory would be forced to create 200 subordinate references replicas on that server, one for each of the child partitions. From the server's perspective, it now has to participate in each one of the 200 partitions' synchronization processes. This amount of work may overload one server, and as a result, the server will be incapable of keeping up with all the changes in the network. You can see the problem, especially as you add more replicas of the [ROOT] partition to other servers in the network.

The simplest way to eliminate this problem is to use a hierarchical design for your tree and partitions, which naturally distributes the subordinate references accordingly. For example, to fix the problem with the ACME tree in Figure 6.58, you simply need to change the design of the tree. By adding another layer of partitions or OUs directly under the [ROOT] partition, you can help distribute the subordinate reference replicas across more network servers. In Figure 6.59 we have added regional layer OUs and partitions in the ACME tree to help distribute the subordinate reference replicas. Each regional OU is its own partition.

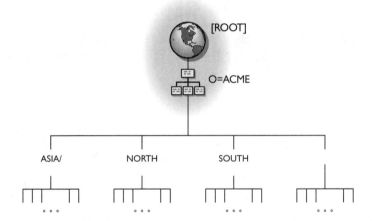

**FIGURE 6.59** *Adding a layer of regional OUs and partitions in the ACME tree design helps distribute the subordinate reference replicas.*

### The Effect of Subordinate References on Partitioning Operations

Partitioning operations constitute another issue that could affect the placement of the subordinate reference replicas. During any partitioning operation all the replicas in the replica list, including the subordinate reference replicas, must be contacted in order for the partitioning operation to complete. If, for any reason, the server with a replica is not available, then the partitioning operation will not complete. The operation will try to contact the replicas that are unavailable until they can be reached. The total number of subordinate references could affect the efficiency of the partitioning operation.

One design consideration discussed earlier is to distribute the number of subordinate references among more servers, thus, reducing the chance that a server containing subordinate references may not be up during partitioning operations.

You may be wondering why the subordinate reference replicas are contacted during a partition operation. Even though subordinate references do not contain all the partition information, they do contain the partition root object, which could change during the operation.

## Summary

Now with these partitioning and replication guidelines in place you can move to the last step in NDS design. This step is NDS time synchronization, which is the topic of the next chapter.

# NDS eDirectory Time Synchronization

*"Nothing puzzles me more than time or space; and yet nothing troubles*
*me less, as I never think about them." — Charles Lamb*

**A** step in your NDS tree design is to determine the time synchronization
configuration for your NetWare 6 servers. *Time synchronization* is the capability of
NetWare 6 servers to coordinate and maintain consistent time among all servers
in the NDS tree. Time synchronization is necessary to ensure that each Novell
Directory Service event receives an accurate timestamp.

A time synchronization configuration can be easily and quickly designed for a
NetWare 6 network of any size. For single-server or small-network environments
you can accept the defaults provided by NetWare 6's installation utility. This
configuration is commonly referred to as the *single reference configuration* or *default
configuration*. No steps are required of the LAN administrator because the setup is
handled completely by the NetWare 6 installation utility.

For larger networks with more servers or multiple sites, a configuration known
as a time provider group is recommended. The *time provider group* is designed to
provide greater fault tolerance and efficiency for communicating the time across
multiple servers and wide area networks. Both of these approaches are discussed
in this chapter.

Once NetWare time has been configured, little additional activity is required to
maintain this function. Time synchronization is both stable and dependable once
it has been configured. Both the single reference and the time provider group
design options are explained in this section, and background information about
how time synchronization functions in a NetWare environment is provided. In
addition, the SET commands that relate to time synchronization are discussed
here.

· · · · · · · · · · · · · · · · · · · · · · · · · · · · · · · · ·

## NDS Time Synchronization

Time synchronization services provided in NetWare 6 are the mechanism by
which network time is maintained on all NetWare 6 servers. If you are migrating
from NetWare 4.x or 5.x, you will already have time synchronization configured
and will not need to change the configuration when migrating to NetWare 6.
NetWare 6 uses the TIMESYNC NetWare Loadable Module (NLM) to coordinate
the time among servers on the network. TIMESYNC.NLM will maintain each
server's time to Universal Coordinated Time (UTC), which is the world time

standard. Local time is used as a reference from which servers can calculate their UTC value. Local time will either be ahead of or behind of the UTC value depending on your geographic location. Each time zone has an offset (+ or −) in relation to the UTC. For example, the United States' time zones are behind UTC, and most of Europe's time zones are ahead of UTC.

TIMESYNC.NLM is automatically loaded each time the server is started. Time synchronization is active only when TIMESYNC.NLM is loaded. Do not unload this module or you will create problems with resolutions of duplicate event collisions of NDS timestamps (discussed later).

A strict relationship applies between local time and UTC. Each server uses this relationship to maintain both UTC and local time counters. To the extent that an accurate time signal is available, both UTC and local time will be accurate, but TIMESYNC does not guarantee accuracy, only consistency. The difference between local time and UTC depends on the time zone and daylight saving time (DST) status of the server, as illustrated in this equation:

```
UTC = LOCAL TIME + (timezone offset) - (current daylight
adjustment)
```

For example, consider a server located in Provo, Utah. Provo uses mountain standard time during part of the year and mountain daylight time the rest of the year. Mountain standard time is behind UTC by seven hours. When mountain daylight time takes effect, local time is adjusted forward by one hour from mountain standard time. So local time for the server in Provo is behind UTC by seven hours when daylight saving time is not in effect and six hours when it is in effect:

```
UTC = LOCAL TIME + (7 hours) - (0 hours) [when DST is not in
effect]
UTC = LOCAL TIME + (7 hours) - (1 hour) [when DST is in
effect]
```

If you want to view time at a server's console, you can type **TIME** to display its status. Figure 7.1 shows how you can see the time information from the server, which displays the local server's time, as well as the UTC value.

The time information displayed includes the time zone string, the status of daylight saving time (including when it starts and ends), the UTC value, the local time, whether time synchronization is active, and whether the server's time is synchronized to the network. Using this information, you can easily detect whether the server is synchronized to the network time.

**FIGURE 7.1** *Time information is displayed at the server console by entering* **TIME.**

Once time is synchronized on all NetWare 6 servers, the Directory can accurately timestamp any network event; for example, adding a new user or assigning rights to a new administrator are both considered events. The timestamp ensures that as the Directory tree replicas are synchronized, the correct order of events will be applied during replica synchronization. Timestamps are discussed in detail in the next section.

### NDS Timestamps

Each event that occurs in NDS is marked with a timestamp, a unique value within an NDS partition. The timestamps are used to order the events or changes that occur on multiple servers. Timestamping events keep all NDS changes in their proper order. For more information regarding timestamps, refer to Chapter 8.

Timestamps within all the replicas of any partition are unique. As shown in Figure 7.2, the left portion of the timestamp shows the seconds since 1970 of the change based on UTC. This ensures that there are unique timestamps for any changes that are at least 1 second apart. The second portion of the timestamp shows the replica number. The replica number creates unique timestamps for changes occurring within the same second on different replicas. The last portion of the timestamp is called the *event counter*. The event counter is set to zero at the beginning of each second. It is incremented with each change on a particular replica when changes occur within the same second. This event counter further enables a unique timestamp for events occurring in rapid succession on the same replica within the same second.

NDS TIMESTAMP

| 32 BITS | 16 BITS | 16 BITS |
|---|---|---|
| Seconds since 1970 | Replica # | Event Counter |

64 BITS OR 8 BYTES

**FIGURE 7.2** *The components of an NDS timestamp*

The timestamp is a critical component in replica synchronization. When NDS updates a replica, it requests the timestamps from that replica to identify the data. The timestamp provides a unique value for the object and properties, which identifies the time and place of where the event originated. If the same object or property is updated on different replicas (or servers) at exactly the same second and event ID, the replica number between the servers would be different. NDS makes the updates using the greater or latest timestamp. When compared, timestamps are treated as 32-bit, 16-bit, and 16-bit unsigned with seconds as the most significant.

An example of an object being deleted will help explain how timestamps work. While the actual procedures and processes for deleting objects are more complex than described here, this simplified explanation should provide a sufficient understanding for our purposes. In general terms, whenever a client or workstation deletes an object or property from a replica on a server, the server does not immediately purge it from its local database. Instead, it issues a timestamp for the object or property and marks the object or property value as "not present" or deleted. After replica synchronization propagates the change to all other replicas, the janitor process purges the object or property. The janitor process is simply an NDS process that periodically scans the Directory for deleted objects and purges them.

NOTE

**To support accurate timestamps, the servers must maintain accurate time, and that time must be synchronized between the servers. Time synchronization provides the mechanism to ensure that each server is synchronized to the network time. You want accurate timestamps so that the order of modification is accurate. This means that the last modification timestamp is the winner.**

## External Time Sources

An accurate and automated time of day can also be provided by attaching your NetWare 6 server (reference or single reference) to an external time source service, such as a radio clock, an atomic clock, or the Internet (a time source provided by connecting to the Internet). Although not mandatory for the operation of a NetWare 6 network, the use of an external time source in larger network installations is highly recommended because it eliminates the manual task for a network administrator to verify time. In addition, the external time source provides an accurate time of day for your network, which is required by some NLMs or backup devices. The use of an external time source is shown in Figure 7.3.

FILE SERVER/TIME SERVER

**FIGURE 7.3** *Attach your time server to an external source for automatic time updates.*

## Time Server Types

Each NetWare 6 server is configured as a specific type of time server during installation. All NetWare 6 servers perform the same basic time functions, including the following:

- ▶ Provide UTC information to any client or NLM making the request
- ▶ Provide status information on time synchronization
- ▶ Make adjustments to correct discrepancies when time synchronization is active

A NetWare 6 server provides time to any client or NLM making a request for network time. For example, your backup or archival software may require accurate network time to know when to initiate a particular process or function. Client utilities may also query time from a NetWare 6 server of any type.

Regardless of the configuration, all NetWare 6 servers provide time status information. Through time synchronization, each NetWare 6 server knows the status of its clock with respect to the network.

All NetWare 6 servers are time servers and participate as either providers of time or consumers of time. The internal mechanism for querying the time is the same for all types of servers. There are three types of time providers: primary servers, reference servers, and single reference servers. Time providers coordinate time among themselves to determine the "official" network time. Time consumers are known as secondary servers and can request time from any of the three types of time providers. Time consumers will constitute the majority of your NetWare 6 servers. Figure 7.4 shows the categories of the time servers.

| TIME PROVIDERS | TIME CONSUMERS |
|---|---|
| Primary | Secondary |
| Reference | |
| Single Reference | |

**FIGURE 7.4** *Time servers are categorized into one of two classes: time providers and time consumers.*

Functionally, all NetWare 6 servers are similar in terms of how they are configured for time. In fact, reference and single reference servers are just special cases of primary servers. Each NetWare 6 server on the network is responsible for its own synchronization and status. This means that each server, at periodic intervals, polls other servers for time, makes any necessary adjustments, and waits for the next interval to repeat the process.

Because time synchronization is a server-centric operation, each server determines if its time is within an acceptable limit, known as the *synchronization radius*. A server is synchronized to the time on the network when its time is within the synchronization radius. If the server determines that its time is within the radius, it raises a time synchronization flag. This synchronization flag indicates that this server has a UTC value that can be used by NDS to accurately timestamp events on the network.

Secondary servers are the most common type of server, as they will synchronize to either a time provider or another secondary server.

### Secondary Time Servers

*Secondary time servers* rely on other sources to provide them with network time. A secondary server can query another secondary, single reference, reference, or primary time server for the network time.

The secondary server will be the most prevalent type of server on your network because most of your servers do not need to participate in determining network time. During the installation of your file servers, all servers except the first server are designated as secondary servers. The first server is automatically designated a single reference time server, as explained later in this section.

During installation of your file servers, all servers except the first server are designated as secondary servers. The first server is automatically designated a single reference time server, as shown in Figure 7.5. This is the default configuration. If the UTC value on the secondary time servers is within the synchronization radius, the synchronization flag can be raised.

The secondary server adjusts its clock to make up any difference in the time it receives from the network. Another server or servers will provide the network time during each polling interval. Therefore, any discrepancies in the secondary server's time will be resolved during each polling interval. The secondary servers can and do provide time to requesting client or server applications.

The secondary time servers do not participate in determining network time. These servers do not negotiate time with any other time servers. They simply get the network time from another source on the network and make the appropriate adjustments to their own clock during each polling interval. The secondary server raises its synchronization flag once its time discrepancy is less than the synchronization radius set for that server.

SINGLE
REFERENCE

SECONDARY TIME SERVERS

**FIGURE 7.5** *The secondary time servers will attempt to get their network time from the time providers. In this case, all the secondary time servers are communicating with a single time provider called a single reference time server.*

### Primary Time Servers

The *primary time servers* are responsible for determining and setting the network time. The primary time servers are classified as time providers because they distribute the network time to other requesting servers. The secondary servers will constitute the majority of the requesting servers needing network time.

In order to determine the network time, the primary server polls other primary and reference servers from its list of servers. This process determines the "official time" for the network because each primary server polls other primary servers to determine any discrepancies between its local clock and the calculated network time. If a difference exists, the primary server tries to adjust its clock to remedy the discrepancy.

Figure 7.6 illustrates how a primary time server polls the other time providers. In this case, the other time providers are primary servers. Each primary time server wakes up (at default ten-minute intervals) and polls the other time providers on the network during its polling process. In this example, time is requested from all other primary time servers and the reference server.

Like all time servers, a primary server will determine if its time is within its synchronization radius. If the server is within the radius, it raises its synchronization flag to indicate that synchronization has occurred.

During the polling, each primary time server has a weighting factor of one. This weighting factor means that all other primary servers will be given equal consideration during the polling interval. Each primary server will "wake up" on its polling interval and begin checking its time against other time providers.

For example, primary server A begins polling the other primary servers in the group. Its current network time is 10:15 a.m. After polling begins, primary server B returns a time of 10:20 a.m. and primary server C returns a time of 10:10 a.m. Because each server has a weighting factor of one, they are treated equally, and the two times are averaged together to produce a time of 10:15 a.m. An example of this process is shown in Figure 7.7.

The polling process is unique and operates independently for all time servers, as each server is responsible for its own network time. Although your servers may have the default polling interval of every ten minutes, each server will most likely be polling at different ten-minute intervals because each primary server checks its time against other time providers in the tree.

While primary servers alone can achieve network time, they need the help of a consistent time provider that never makes adjustments to its clock after polling. A special case of the primary server is the reference server, which sets time for the entire network.

**FIGURE 7.6** *A primary time server polls other time providers.*

**FIGURE 7.7** *Each primary time server wakes up and begins polling the other time providers during its polling process.*

### Reference Time Servers

A *reference time server* is a time provider that adds additional capability to a primary time server. The reference server works with other time providers, such as primary servers, to provide the network time. The difference between the reference server and a primary server is that the reference server will always believe that it has network time and will not adjust its internal clock. Therefore, you should place a reference server where you set network time and force all other primary servers to adjust their time to the reference server. The reference server participates in polling intervals just like the primary servers, but it does not adjust its clock.

The best configuration is to have one reference server with a few primary servers to provide accurate time. Figure 7.8 illustrates the configuration of one reference server and multiple primary time servers on the network.

Over time all NetWare 6 servers converge their internal clocks to the time of the reference server. On the other hand, the reference server never adjusts its clock. This naturally makes the reference server over time the point of reference for convergence.

During polling, the reference server has a weighting factor of 16. This means that all primary servers converge their time to that of the reference server because it has the greatest weighting in terms of time. You will typically want to have only one reference server on your network, as it is the definitive time source. The best configuration is to have one reference server with a few primary servers to provide accurate time. Design configuration options are discussed in the following section.

Primary servers work with the reference server to provide fault tolerance and multiple sources for time. The reference server must, like other primary servers, contact another source during polling in order to raise its synchronization flag. In addition, if the reference server should fail, multiple primary servers can still provide consistent network time to requesting servers and clients until you restore another reference server. Therefore, the reference server is the supreme authority for time, except when it is not accessible.

Like all time servers, a reference server will determine if its time is within the synchronization radius. If the server is within the radius, then it raises its time synchronization flag, which indicates that its time is acceptable for timestamping events.

**FIGURE 7.8** *The configuration of one reference server and multiple primary time servers on the network*

Because the reference server does not make an adjustment to its internal clock, you can connect it to an external source. Having an external clock accomplishes several important things. First, it provides an accurate and automated mechanism to check time. Some of your applications may require accurate time of day if they initiate a process, such as a backup, in the middle of the night. Second, an automated time source helps ensure that the reference server's clock is not drifting and consequently is keeping all other servers in your network with accurate time.

The server's own clock can be used as a time source, but time must be verified manually by an administrator to ensure that it is staying accurate and not drifting.

Ideally, the reference server can be connected to an external clock source to provide highly accurate time. Products are available that connect PCs to external time sources, such as a radio clock or modem, which can contact an outside source.

**TIP**

**For more information on external clock solutions you can contact Novell's Web server to download the TIMESG.TXT file. This file contains companies and their product names that support the external time source solution.**

Only one reference server should be used on the network. Multiple reference servers could be placed on the network, but they will not synchronize with each other.

### Single Reference Time Servers

The *single reference time server* is a standalone time provider for the entire network. The single reference is the default configuration and is established automatically during installation. The main difference between a reference server and a single reference server is that the single reference server can raise its synchronization flag without confirming its time with any other time providers. It does, however, go through the polling process like all NetWare 6 servers. In this case, the polling does not expect a response from any server. A response from another server would indicate that another time provider has been erroneously placed on the network. This condition would cause the single reference server to report an error to the console screen.

A single reference server should be the only time provider on the network. The rest of the time servers should be secondary servers. The secondary servers simply contact the single reference to get the network time. Figure 7.9 illustrates a single reference time server, with the others being secondary time servers.

A single reference server enables you to have all other servers remain as secondary servers, which will adjust their times to the single reference time during each polling cycle. Like the reference server, a single reference server can be connected to an external source to feed the network accurate time of day.

In addition, the single reference server's own clock, instead of an external source, can be used as the time source. Occasionally, it may be necessary to check the server's time against a reliable source because some of your applications, such as backup or archiving software programs, may require accurate network time.

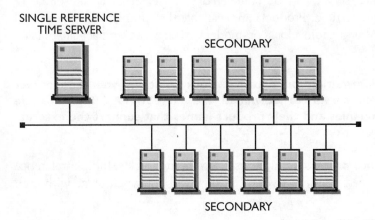

**FIGURE 7.9** *A single reference time server provides time to the secondary time servers.*

# Time Synchronization Design

Once you understand the different types of time servers, you are ready to look at which design option best suits your particular needs. This section provides you with the options available to design NDS time synchronization.

## Time Synchronization Configuration Options

Your NetWare 6 network may use two basic time server configurations for single reference (the default) or a time provider group. All other available configurations are variations of these two. As part of your NDS design, evaluate the time synchronization configurations and choose the one that best meets the needs of your company. Here are two important factors to consider:

> ▸ Is your network multisite-connected by a WAN? If it is, then we recommend always using the second option, that of a time provider group. A time provider group gives your network greater fault tolerance in a wide area network configuration by distributing the time providers to multiple locations.

▸ If your site consists of 30 or fewer NetWare 6 servers and is not connected by a WAN, the default option of single reference server will work extremely well. The LAN environment can easily contact a single reference server without crossing a WAN link. In addition, your servers can easily contact the single reference server without burdening the server.

Consider the configuration options discussed in the sections that follow in making your decision and use the MONITOR utility to make the necessary changes. This utility is run from a NetWare 6 server console by typing LOAD MONITOR. From the menu select Server Parameters and then select the Time option as shown in Figure 7.10.

**NOTE**

**NetWare 6 has moved the functionality of the SERVMAN utility found in NetWare 4 to the MONITOR utility for greater consolidation of utilities. You get the same functionality as you had with SERVMAN from NetWare 4.**

**FIGURE 7.10** *The main screen of the MONITOR utility with the Time option selected*

### The Default Option: A Single Reference Time Server

When the first NetWare 6 server is installed in the NDS tree, it is automatically configured as a single reference server. All additional NetWare 6 servers installed in the same tree are automatically configured as secondary servers. The Novell installation utility assumes that your installation will initially consist of two levels of servers: A single reference at the first level and secondary servers at the second level provide you with a default installation.

The advantages of the default configuration are that it is easy to understand and requires absolutely no advanced planning. In addition, no configuration files are needed, and the possibility of errors during time synchronization is considerably minimized.

In the default configuration, select a central file server that can be easily contacted by the other NetWare 6 servers in your network. Remember, the first NetWare 6 server you install is automatically configured as the single reference server, as shown in Figure 7.11. You can always designate another server as the single reference by using the NWCONFIG utility. Figure 7.12 shows an example of a single-reference time-server configuration setup.

SINGLE REFERENCE
TIME SERVER

SECONDARY TIME SERVERS

**FIGURE 7.11** *A single reference time configuration with only one server providing time to the entire network is shown. This configuration is suitable for a network that has fewer than 30 servers and is situated in one geographic location.*

A potential drawback of the default configuration is that if the single reference server should fail, the network has lost its only time provider. However, if this happens for only a short period of time (a day or less), there is little problem with the timestamping of events. All NetWare 6 servers should continue to maintain their time and continue to stamp NDS events. If your single reference is down for prolonged periods, we recommend that you designate a new server as the single reference to ensure that you have a source for time on your network. In order to designate a new server as the single reference, simply go to the server and make the change using NWCONFIG.

**FIGURE 7.12** *Use the NWCONFIG utility to designate another server as your single reference or to make other configuration changes.*

### The Custom Option: A Time Provider Group

The time provider group offers another design option. The time provider group requires one reference server and a minimum of two primary servers that will participate in the synchronization process to coordinate the network time. These time source servers form a time provider group that in turn provides time to the rest of the NetWare 6 servers.

The time provider group configuration works well for networks that have more than 30 NetWare 6 servers or that are situated in several locations in a wide area configuration. Figure 7.13 illustrates the placement of the time providers in the major hub sites of the ACME tree.

### Consulting Experience

Regardless of the size of your network, you can initially accept the single reference default until your installation grows beyond 30 servers or unless you immediately begin with NetWare 6 on both sides of a WAN. Also, if you choose the single reference server option, do not use any other time provider, such as a primary or a reference. A single reference is the only time source required on the entire network under this configuration.

▸ · · · · · · · · · · · · · · · · · · · · · · · · · · · · · · · · · · ◂

**FIGURE 7.13**  *The placement of the time providers in the major hub sites of the ACME tree*

The time provider group configuration option requires simple configuration adjustments for the few servers you want to designate as participants in the time provider group. One server will be designated as the reference, and a recommended two to seven servers may be designated as primary servers. Primary servers may be designated by using the NWCONFIG utility's Time Parameters screen, as shown in Figure 7.14.

In selecting your reference server, look for a centralized location in your network infrastructure. For example, if your WAN is designed like the ACME WAN with a hub-and-spoke design, your reference server should be centrally placed at the hub location. The primary servers should be distributed across your wide area links to the other hub locations. If your network is a large WAN, place your primary servers in just a few strategic locations. The rest of the installed file servers will be secondary servers. Figure 7.15 shows where the reference server and primary servers should be placed for network efficiency in the ACME tree.

**FIGURE 7.14** *Using the NWCONFIG utility to designate a primary server*

**FIGURE 7.15** *An example of time server designations for a hub-and-spoke infrastructure in the ACME tree*

It is highly recommended that you connect the reference server to an external time source to provide highly accurate time. Figure 7.16 shows an example of a time provider group in the ACME tree that is connected to an external time source. The ACME time provider group contains one reference server located in CAMELOT and four other primary servers located in NORAD, RIO, TOKYO, and SYDNEY. This configuration offers redundancy and the capability to balance the requests for the time.

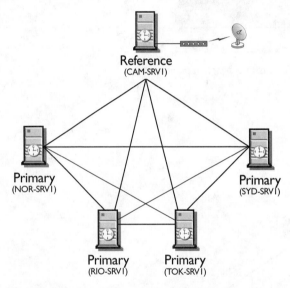

**FIGURE 7.16** *This time provider group configuration offers redundancy and the means to balance requests for the time.*

## Multiple Time Provider Groups

Some companies may need to use multiple time provider groups for redundancy in worldwide corporations. For example, we could create a time provider group at NORAD and also at CAMELOT so that time is distributed from each area rather than traversing a WAN. Multiple time provider groups require that your reference servers be connected to external clocks to converge their times. An example of multiple time provider groups is shown in Figure 7.17. Each reference is connected to an external source to provide accurate and automated time, thus ensuring that both groups are distributing the same time (or very close to it) for the entire tree.

**FIGURE 7.17** *An example of multiple time provider groups in the ACME tree*

## Time Synchronization Communication Options

Secondary time servers periodically request the time and need to communicate with time sources on the network. Time providers also need to find other time providers in order to determine the correct UTC.

NetWare 6 servers communicate time information using one of two methods: the Service Advertising Protocol (SAP) or configured lists. The following two sections discuss these two methods.

### Time Synchronization Using the Service Advertising Protocol

The SAP method is the default at installation and requires no intervention. As new NetWare 6 servers are designated primary providers, no custom configurations to the existing time servers or to new servers are required for time communication. Time providers such as a primary, reference, or single reference servers advertise their presence on the network using SAP by default.

SAP can cause a small amount of additional traffic on your network. Also, because SAP is self-configuring, a new time server that is unintentionally configured as a wrong type in the same tree could disrupt your time synchronization.

**TIP**

The time synchronization **SAP** type is **0x026B. If you have decided to use SAP for your time communication, you must not filter this packet type on any routers that connect your NetWare 6 servers together.**

### Time Synchronization Using Configured Lists

The use of a configured list enables you to specify exactly which servers should be contacted for a time provider group and to also make requests for time consumers. For all implementations using time provider groups, we recommend that you use a configured list instead of SAP as your communication option. The configured list option keeps time synchronization traffic to a minimum and also prohibits anyone from placing other time providers on your network that might cause problems with the network time. A server must obtain the configured list if it is to participate in network time for your tree. For the ACME tree we chose to use a time provider group along with a configured list that specifies the time servers in the time provider group. After the list is created, it is then distributed to all time servers in the group through the file called TIMESYNC.CFG.

The configured list is created by using the MONITORutility, selecting the Time option, and making the entries for each server name that you want to contact in your time provider group. The first step is to enable the configured list option as shown in Figure 7.18. Once it is set to ON, you can begin creating your configured list.

**FIGURE 7.18** *Using MONITOR to enable the configured list option for time communication*

The configured list entries use the server names separated by spaces, as shown in Figure 7.19 for the ACME tree. We have designated CAMELOT as their reference server location. All other major sites in our tree will contain one primary server to communicate with the reference server in CAMELOT.

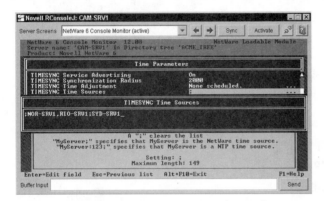

**FIGURE 7.19** *A configured list for the ACME time provider group is shown. This list is stored on each file server in the time provider group.*

Configured lists give you complete control of the time synchronization hierarchy. The configured list also reduces the SAP traffic on your network because SAP broadcasts are not used. Instead, the configured list specifies the source server by name to contact.

A proposed time synchronization configuration is found in the example that follows. In this example the corporate office is located in CAMELOT. The reference server in CAMELOT is linked to an external time source. This source server sets both the NetWare server clock and the hardware time-of-day clock. Primary servers are located in RIO, NORAD, SYDNEY, and TOKYO. These time sources will work together to determine the actual network time during each polling interval. The ACME tree is using the configured sources list so that all the servers can contact each other to determine the network time. In the example that follows, the TIMESYNC.CFG file is shown with its configured list.

**TIMESYNC.CFG for reference server in CAMELOT**
\# Configuration parameters for server CAM-SRV1

```
Configured Sources = ON
Directory Tree Mode = ON
Hardware Clock = ON
Polling Count = 3
Polling Interval = 10
Service Advertising = OFF
Synchronization Radius = 2000
Type = REFERENCE
```

\# Configured time source list server CAM-SRV1

```
Time Source = RIO-SRV1
Time Source = TOK-SRV1
Time Source = SYD-SRV1
Time Source = NOR-SRV1
Time Source = CAM-SRV1
```

**TIMESYNC.CFG for primary servers in RIO, TOKYO, NORAD, AND SYDNEY**
\# Configuration parameters for server TOK-SRV1

```
Configured Sources = ON
Directory Tree Mode = ON
Hardware Clock = ON
Polling Count = 3
Polling Interval = 10
Service Advertising = OFF
Synchronization Radius = 2000
Type = PRIMARY
```

\# Configured time source list from server TOK-SRV1

```
Time Source = CAM-SRV1
Time Source = RIO-SRV1
Time Source = SYD-SRV1
Time Source = NOR-SRV1
Time Source = TOK-SRV1
```

The secondary servers located in each geographic region would use the following TIMESYNC.CFG file. The server *xxxxx* indicates any secondary server located in the ACME tree:

**TIMESYNC.CFG for secondary servers**

# Configuration parameters from server *xxxxx*

```
Configured Sources = ON
Directory Tree Mode = ON
Hardware Clock = ON
Polling Count = 3
Polling Interval = 10
Service Advertising = OFF
Synchronization Radius = 2000
Type = SECONDARY
```

# Configured time source list from server *xxxxx*

```
Time Source = CAM-SRV1
Time Source = RIO-SRV1
Time Source = TOK-SRV1
Time Source = NOR-SRV1
Time Source = SYD-SRV1
```

In each geographic region, the time source list should be reordered to place the closest time provider first on the list. Next, place the lowest-cost (time and hops) providers, and finally the rest of the providers. This enables the secondary server to initially contact the closest available server to obtain the correct network time.

## Other Design Considerations

This section describes some time configurations that are less frequently implemented but are used mostly by corporations that have multiple offices around the world.

### Configuring Secondary Servers to Follow Other Secondary Servers

In some cases it may be necessary for secondary servers to receive their time from other secondary servers. For large companies this situation may occur as you try to limit the number of primary servers spread across your WAN network as time providers. Therefore, if you use the configured list option, you can configure secondary servers to obtain their time from other secondary servers that are obtaining their time from a primary server elsewhere. As shown in Figure 7.20, the ACME tree has secondary servers that follow other secondary servers.

CONFIGURED LIST
OPTION ONLY

Single Reference Server

Secondary Server

Secondary Servers

**FIGURE 7.20** *Secondary servers can be configured to follow other secondary servers if you use configured lists.*

Time providers such as primary servers will not follow a secondary server. You can only configure a secondary server to follow another secondary server. If your company has many sites, you should consider placing a primary server at a hub location with your secondary servers contacting the hub. If your SPOKE or REMOTE locations have multiple servers, you may want to designate one secondary server to contact the primary server for time on behalf of the other secondary servers. An example of this arrangement is shown in Figure 7.21.

TIP

**The total allowable time radius for the entire system is ten seconds. Therefore, keep the number of secondary servers following each secondary to a depth of only two to three servers. Any depth greater than two to three servers may lead to time synchronization errors, which are unacceptable for NDS.**

**FIGURE 7.21** *A hub-and-spoke arrangement with primary and secondary servers. At the remote or spoke locations, the secondary servers contact other secondary servers for their time.*

### Having More Than One Reference Server

Some organizations may require more than one reference server because of their dispersed locations. For example, you may want to have a time provider group in two different countries, rather than having time traffic cross over expensive or extremely busy wide area connections. As shown in Figure 7.22, you can have multiple reference servers as long as they are each connected to an external source. The external source is needed so that these reference servers can maintain the same time and not drift.

### Time Synchronization Traffic Considerations

Although the amount of time traffic is generally small, it may be useful to know what kind of a network load is generated by time synchronization. The actual workload is controlled by the number of time exchanges during each polling loop. You can take steps to further minimize the workload if you have bandwidth constraints on your network. The actual traffic load is determined by how many time exchanges you have configured for each polling loop.

**FIGURE 7.22** *Multiple reference servers can be used as long as they are connected to external time sources.*

The default is to make three time exchanges, each of which involves an NCP send/receive pair totaling 332 bytes of data. Thus, the default three exchanges involve six packets totaling 996 bytes of data.

Therefore, you can calculate the amount of traffic for each server during a specific polling interval with this equation:

```
NDS Traffic = (N - 1) * (Polling Count) * 332
```

where N = the number of providers to contact.

For example, let's assume that a network has five time providers in its group (one reference and four primary servers) and is using the default intervals of three send/receive exchanges every ten minutes for each server. You can determine the amount of traffic generated in this way:

```
(5 - 1) * (3) * (332) = 3,984 bytes/10 minutes/per time
source server
```

Each time source server would, at its own ten-minute interval, generate 3,984 bytes of traffic on your network. Obviously, the more primary servers you have, the more traffic will be generated on your network.

It is also possible, but not recommended, to change the polling interval to cut down on network traffic. The default polling interval is ten minutes. But as long as the server clock is not drifting and synchronization is maintained, that polling interval may be extended.

In situations where perhaps dozens of secondary servers would poll a single primary server across a slow LAN or WAN segment, it may be helpful to increase the polling period to even one or two hours. This would cut back on the network traffic and probably have little or no effect on synchronization, unless the server clocks drift by several seconds a day.

In fact, once a server has reached a stable state, the amount of network traffic attributed to time synchronization will probably be minuscule compared to the normal everyday traffic.

### Checking Time Synchronization Status

You can easily check the time synchronization status of all servers by using the DSREPAIR utility as shown in Figure 7.23. After typing LOAD DSREPAIR at the server's console, you can select Time Synchronization to check the status. Keep in mind that if you are running DSREPAIR on a server containing a copy of the [ROOT] partition, the Time Synchronization option will search all NetWare 6 servers in the entire tree beginning at ([ROOT]) and searching downward. If you do not want this to happen, run DSREPAIR on a server that does not hold a copy of the [ROOT] partition.

**FIGURE 7.23** Using DSREPAIR to obtain a status of time synchronization

## Adding New Time Servers

When you add a new server to an already synchronized network, time synchronization acts on two basic premises. First, it works from the notion that adding a server should not disrupt the network's time synchronization. Second, it assumes that if the new server's time doesn't agree with network time, the network time is more likely to be correct.

Therefore, the first act of time synchronization (for any server type) during boot-up is to set the server time to the time reported by the first time provider contacted. This is true even for reference and single reference servers that do not normally adjust their clocks.

When you bring up a server, make sure that time synchronizes properly and, if necessary, reset the time on reference and single reference servers manually. It is always a good idea to check the time after bringing up a server just to make sure that all the time parameters are set correctly and that the time is synchronized.

If you are currently using the default option of a single reference server and all other servers secondary, you can continue reading this section to make the change to a time provider group. This configuration requires you to change the time type on the server you want to designate as a reference server by using the MONITOR utility. An example of this is shown in Figure 7.24. Only one server will be designated as the reference server in our example.

**FIGURE 7.24** *An example of a server being designated as the reference time server*

The next step is to designate some server as a primary time server. Using the MONITOR utility again, you will change your selected server's type to primary. Repeat this procedure for all appropriate servers, but for no more than seven servers. You can have more than seven primary servers, but keep in mind that the more primary servers, the greater the amount of traffic on your network during each polling interval for time.

**TIP**

**Experience has shown that most companies can have stable time by using only three or four primary servers in the entire network. Only a few servers need to work with the reference server to determine time for the entire network. Also, consider that there should be only one server designated as the primary time provider per hub location.**

After you have made configuration changes for both the reference server and the primary servers, save the changes when prompted before exiting the MONITOR utility. An example of how this screen appears is shown in Figure 7.25.

**FIGURE 7.25** *Be sure to save changes to the TIMESYNC.CFG file before exiting the MONITOR utility.*

# Time Synchronization Operations

This section discusses how you can configure the time on your NetWare 6 servers and explains how to use the various SET parameters that are provided. In addition, you will learn the commands found in the MONITOR utility for adjusting the time parameters. Most changes and configurations with time can be accomplished by using the MONITOR utility, which is discussed in this section. The SET parameters will rarely need changing. However, some environments may require that you adjust some of them.

### Using the SET Parameters for Time Synchronization

NetWare 6 includes a rich set of settable parameters governing time synchronization. The time synchronization parameters can be set from the server console using the SET commands or through the menu-driven MONITOR utility. In addition, your current time synchronization SET parameters can be viewed from the server console by typing SET and then selecting the Time option as shown in Figures 7.26 and 7.27. The setting for time synchronization can be stored in a special configuration file called TIMESYNC.CFG. This file is located in the SYS:SYSTEM subdirectory of your NetWare 6 servers.

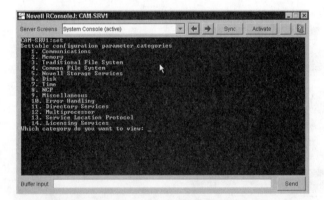

**FIGURE 7.26** *To view SET parameters at the server console, type SET.*

**TIP**

Do not place **TIMESYNC** parameters in the **AUTOEXEC.NCF** file because they will not work from that file. Only time synchronization parameters that start with the **TIMESYNC** label can be placed in the **TIMESYNC.CFG** file. Figure 7.28 illustrates an example of a **TIMESYNC.CFG** file.

**FIGURE 7.27** *To view the current settings for time synchronization, select the Time option. This figure is only a partial view of the time SET parameters.*

**FIGURE 7.28** *A sample TIMESYNC.CFG file*

The easiest way to modify the time synchronization parameters is to use the MONITOR utility. After you load MONITOR from the server console select Server Parameters and then the Time option. The screen for the time synchronization parameters is shown in Figure 7.29.

▶ • • • • • • • • • • • • • • • • • • • • • • • • • ◀

**FIGURE 7.29** *An example of the MONITOR utility as it is displayed after you select the Time option from Server Parameters. The Time Parameters screen enables you to modify many aspects of time.*

The function and use of each of the settable time synchronization parameters are discussed in the text that follows.

### TIMESYNC Add Time Source = <server name>
### Default: Empty

This option enables you to add the name of a particular NetWare 6 server or servers as potential time providers to your configured list. The server name that you enter here will be stored in the TIMESYNC.CFG configuration file. The TIMESYNC.CFG configuration file is updated if you choose the Update TIMESYNC.CFG option after exiting the time parameter screen. Duplicate entries are not accepted in the time sources list and will be ignored.

You will use this option only if you are using a configured list and want to add a new server to the configured list as a time provider.

The name of the NetWare 6 server is not the distinguished name. Instead, it is the least significant segment of its name. For example, a NetWare 6 server in the ACME tree has a distinguished name of CN=NOR-SRV1.OU=NORAD.O=ACME. The name entered in this field is simply NOR-SRV1.

To add the servers NOR-SRV1, CAM-SRV1, and TOK-SRV1 to the list of time sources in the TIMESYNC.CFG files, enter these lines:

```
SET TIMESYNC ADD TIME Source = NOR-SRV1
SET TIMESYNC ADD TIME Source = CAM-SRV1
SET TIMESYNC ADD TIME Source = TOK-SRV1
```

### TIMESYNC Configuration File = <volume:subdirectory\file>
### Default: SYS:SYSTEM\TIMESYNC.CFG

This parameter defines the path or location of the configuration file used by time synchronization. TIMESYNC.CFG is the default name for the configuration file that stores all the settings for time on your NetWare 6 server. There is little if any need to change the name of this file, and we recommend that you accept the default, TIMESYNC.CFG. This file can easily be copied to multiple NetWare 6 servers if needed.

If you want to store the TIMESYNC.CFG file in the SYS:SYSTEM\TIME subdirectory, issue this command:

```
SET TIMESYNC CONFIGURATION FILE = SYS:SYSTEM\TIME
```

### TIMESYNC Configured Sources = ON/OFF
### Default: OFF

This parameter determines whether the NetWare 6 server finds the time providers on the network using SAP or an existing configured list. A setting of OFF tells the server to listen to any time providers that are sending out SAP. A setting of ON tells the server to ignore SAP and to rely only on the configured lists set up in the TIMESYNC.CFG file. The server will only try to contact the time providers that are in its configured list. This parameter must be set to ON in order to support custom configured lists.

We recommend that, when you are using configured lists, each one of the secondary servers have a primary or reference server as the first member of its list. However, secondary servers may also be entered in the configured lists. This option enables a secondary server to get the time from other secondary servers in the event that the primary and reference time providers do not respond.

**TIP**

**If you want to view the list of servers that have been established as the time providers in the configured list on a particular server, you can type this command from that server's console: SET TIMESYNC TIME SOURCE =. Notice that the equal sign is required with no following parameters.**

### TIMESYNC Directory Tree Mode = ON/OFF
### Default: ON

This parameter controls the use of SAP in the NDS tree. A setting of ON, which is the default, tells the time server to ignore the SAP packets from servers that are not part of your NDS tree. A value of OFF enables the server to listen to all time SAP packets from any time provider on the network even if it is outside the same Directory Services tree.

When you leave this setting to ON, you maintain tighter control over the NDS tree of this server.

### TIMESYNC Hardware Clock = ON/OFF
### Default: ON

This parameter controls hardware clock synchronization to the software clock, which is maintained by NetWare 6 servers. A value of ON, which is the default, has a different meaning depending on the type of time server that is being used. The value of ON for the single and reference servers enables them to read their hardware clocks at the beginning of each polling loop and to set the software clocks accordingly. The capability of the single and reference time servers to read their hardware clocks and reset the software clocks provides the network with a basic external clock synchronization. In this case the hardware clock acts as an external time source. This is kind of a poor man's radio clock.

Set this parameter to OFF only if the single or reference servers use an external time source, such as an atomic or radio clock.

The value of ON for the primary and secondary servers means that the hardware clock is set to the time of the software clock after each polling process. This setting is useful because corrections made to the software clock during polling can be written to the hardware clock. Thus, the network time is reflected the next time the server is brought down and back up. Each time the server is booted, it reads the hardware clock.

All primary and secondary servers in the same Directory tree should use the same setting for this parameter.

### TIMESYNC Polling Count = <number (1 to 1,000)>
### Default: 3

This parameter determines how many time packets to exchange during polling. Increasing the number of packets adds more traffic to the network. We recommend that you leave the default value of 3, which works well in most cases. The only time you may want to change this value is when you have unreliable or erratic network communication links between the time servers.

The higher the value is set, the greater the amount of network traffic introduced. The lower the value, the less accurate the time information exchanged. Again, the default value of 3 is highly recommended.

### TIMESYNC Polling Interval = <number (10 to 2,678,400)>
### Default: 600 seconds (or 10 minutes)

This parameter determines the length of time between each polling. In the case of the default, every 600 seconds (or 10 minutes) the server polls the other time servers in the tree. After the initial installation of your NetWare 6 servers, you may want to increase this value to reduce the total number of polling traffic on the network. Just remember that time polling does not generate an inordinate amount of traffic on your network. We recommend that you leave the default setting if you keep the total number of time providers under ten. We also recommend that all the time servers in the same NDS tree have the same setting for this parameter.

Decreasing this parameter creates an increase in network traffic but higher time synchronization accuracy. Increasing this interval is recommended when the time servers have to cross a WAN link to get time.

### TIMESYNC Remove Time Source = <server name>
### Default: Empty

This option enables you to specify a server or servers to be removed from the time source list. The server name entered in this field will be removed from the configuration file if you exit and choose YES to update TIMESYNC.CFG option after updating and exiting the time parameter screen. This field returns a blank screen after you have specified a value in this field. If you try to delete an entry from the time sources list, which does not exist, the request will be ignored.

This option is the reverse of the TIMESYNC Add Time Source option. Here, too, the name of the NetWare 6 server is not the distinguished name. Instead, it is the least significant segment of its name. For example, a NetWare 6 server in the ACME tree has a distinguished name of CN=NOR-SRV1.OU=NORAD.O=ACME. The name entered in this field is simply NOR-SRV1.

This command is primarily used at the server console to remove a time provider that has gone down or become unavailable for any reason.

**TIP**

**If you are trying to add or remove a time source permanently, using either the TIMESYNC Add Time Source and TIMESYNC Remove Time Source parameters can be difficult because they do not give you any feedback on whether the instructions were successful. An alternative to using these fields is to edit the configuration file directly using any text editor.**

**TIMESYNC Reset = ON/OFF**
**Default: OFF**

This parameter resets all time parameters to the default values and clears the configured lists. A value of ON resets the time parameters and writes the configuration file after exiting from the MONITOR screen. Be careful — any changes you have made previously to the TIMESYNC.CFG file will be lost. For example, all the configured server lists are cleared and set back to the internal defaults. If you set the parameter to ON and press Enter, the values are reset and the parameter automatically returns to the default OFF value.

You should never have to reset the time parameters on a production server. This option is valuable for restoring the parameters as you experiment with them in a lab situation.

**TIMESYNC Restart Flag = ON/OFF**
**Default: OFF**

This parameter controls restart time synchronization. You can use this feature to restart time synchronization after you have created or changed the configuration parameters in the file. After this command is issued from the file server console, the parameter automatically resets to OFF.

**TIMESYNC Service Advertising = ON/OFF**
**Default: ON**

This parameter controls the time servers that are time providers advertising through SAP. When the parameter is ON, the single reference and primary time primary servers send out or advertise using SAP. Setting the value to OFF means that the time provider servers will not send out SAP. You will want to set this parameter to OFF when you use configured lists. Turning SAP off reduces the traffic on the network.

**TIMESYNC Synchronization Radius = <milliseconds (0 to 2,147,483,647)>**
**Default: 2,000 (or 2 seconds)**

This parameter controls the maximum time a server's clock is allowed to vary from network time and still be considered synchronized. The default of 2,000 milliseconds works well for most installations. This time parameter can be adjusted or increased to enable a wider margin of error for time synchronization between servers. However, increasing this value reduces the collision resolution occurring in NDS. A lower value causes the server to maintain tighter time synchronization. Because the tighter synchronization radius may be difficult or impossible to achieve, the time servers lose time synchronization. We recommend that you never set the synchronization radius under the 2,000 millisecond value.

If you need to change this parameter, you can do so through the NWCONFIG utility, as shown in Figure 7.30.

**FIGURE 7.30** *Changes to the synchronization radius can be made through the MONITOR utility.*

**TIMESYNC Time Adjustment = [+ | – ] hour:minutes:seconds [AT month/day/year hour:minutes:seconds [AM | PM] | [CANCEL]] Default: One hour from the current time or six polling intervals, whichever is longer**

This parameter enables time adjustments to be made to the network time. You should use this feature sparingly. Misuse of this parameter will affect the servers networkwide and could change the order of the NDS events. You should also use this parameter during the day, when it will not be excessively disruptive to the network operation.

You can use the optional AT parameters to schedule the time adjustment to take place in the future. For example, the command for a time adjustment schedule in the future might look like this:

```
SET TIMESYNC TIME ADJUSTMENT = +00:01:30 AT 4/6/99
```

11:00:00 PM the command will adjust network time ahead one minute and thirty seconds on April 6, 1999, at 11:00 PM. Use the CANCEL command to remove a previously scheduled time adjustment from taking place. For example, in order to cancel the time adjustment of +00:01:30, enter the following:

```
SET TIMESYNC TIME ADJUSTMENT = +00:01:30 CANCEL
```

If you do not use the optional AM or PM parameters, then NetWare 6 assumes a 24-hour (military time) clock. Use a plus sign (+) to indicate a time adjustment forward and a minus sign (–) to indicate a time adjustment backward.

This command would not normally be used in a time server configuration that is receiving its time from an external source. We recommend that you use this option only when a significant one-time correction must be made to the network time. You should perform the time adjustment operation on either reference or single reference time servers.

**TIP**

**The TIMESYNC Time Adjustment parameter can modify the network time only on primary, reference, and single reference time providers because they can affect the network time. This parameter should not be used with a secondary time server.**

**TIMESYNC Time Source = <server name>**
**Default: None**

This parameter is the same as the TIMESYNC Add Time Source parameter discussed previously. You can specify a server to be added to the configuration list. So you may ask, "Why are there two parameters that perform the same function?" This option makes more sense and is easier to enter at the server console command line. For example, you simply type the following:

```
SET TIMESYNC TIME SOURCE = <server name>
```

By entering this command at the server console, you are adding the server to your configuration list. Use the TIMESYNC Remove Time Server parameter to remove the servers from the configured list.

To reduce the confusion, we recommend that you use this parameter only at the server console and use the TIMESYNC Add Time Source parameter in the MONITOR utility.

**TIP**

**You can display the current list of time servers that has been established in the configuration list by entering the TIMESYNC Time Source = command at the server console. Notice that no server name is entered.**

**TIMESYNC Type = <time server type>**
**Default: Single (during the first installation of NetWare 6)**
**Secondary (during all subsequent installations)**

This parameter sets the time server type for the NetWare 6 server. The possible values are SECONDARY, PRIMARY, REFERENCE, and SINGLE (for single reference).

You can use this parameter to change the time server type for the NetWare 6 server on the fly. This value is placed in the TIMESYNC.CFG configuration file and is used when TIMESYNC.NLM is initialized as the server is booted or when the restart flag is used.

### TIMESYNC Write Parameters = ON/OFF
### Default: OFF

This parameter writes all the current time synchronization parameters to the TIMESYNC.CFG configuration file. The value of ON writes the parameters; the value of OFF does not write the parameters. This SET parameter is a trigger and automatically resets to OFF.

### TIMESYNC Write Value = <number>
### Default: 3

This parameter controls which parameters are written to the TIMESYNC.CFG configuration file by the Write Parameter ON/OFF action. The possible values are as follows:

- Write only the internal parameters
- Write only the parameters for TIMESYNC Add Time Source
- Write both internal and time source server parameters

### Default Time Server Type = <time server type>
### Default: Secondary

This parameter is used when the server first initializes because it is placed in the AUTOEXEC.NCF file. The value of this parameter is overridden by the TIMESYNC type parameter found in the configuration file. The default server type is used if the TIMESYNC configuration file is not present or is invalid. We recommend that you set the default time server type to the same value as the TIMESYNC Type value given previously. This reduces confusion and the potential for problems if the configuration file is lost for some reason.

### Time ZONE = <time zone string>
### Default: <NO TIME ZONE>

This parameter specifies the time zone where the server is located. The value is a time zone string indicating the abbreviated time zone name, the offset from UTC, and the alternative abbreviated name for daylight saving time. This parameter causes a UTC value to be recalculated from local time. To reduce confusion, we recommend that you set this parameter correctly for the actual physical server location.

The format for the time zone string is *xxx*N[*yyy*], where "*xxx*" is the time zone (MST = U.S. mountain standard time or EST = U.S. eastern standard time). The

"N" is the number of hours offset from UTC (7 = U.S. mountain or 5 = U.S. east coast). The "yyy," which is optional, indicates that daylight saving time is in effect (MDT = U.S. mountain daylight saving time or EDT = U.S. eastern daylight saving time). Thus, the time zone string for the U.S. mountain time zone is

```
MST7MDT
```

and that for the U.S. eastern time zone is

```
EST5EDT
```

### Daylight Saving Time Status = ON/OFF
### Default: OFF

This parameter indicates whether daylight saving time is in effect. Possible values are ON and OFF. If this parameter is set to ON, the DST (daylight saving time) parameter should be used. The status of this parameter may be changed at any time. However, changing the status does not change the local time, but it does cause UTC to be recalculated.

### Daylight Saving Time Offset = [+ | – ]hour:minute:seconds
### Default: +1:00:00

This parameter controls the offset applied to time calculations when daylight saving time is in effect. The offset, in seconds, is added to local time at the beginning of daylight saving time. A change causes UTC to be recalculated from local time.

### Start of Daylight Saving Time = <Month [Day | Day of Week] [Condition] hour:minute:seconds>
### Default: April Sunday First 2:00:00 AM

This parameter enables you to set up the local date and time or some simple rules for when the change from standard time to daylight saving time occurs. The following example sets the start of daylight saving time at 2:00 A.M. to the first Sunday of April (which is also the default):

```
SET START OF DAYLIGHT SAVING Time = (April Sunday First
2:00:00 AM)
```

### End of Daylight Saving Time = <Month [Day | Day of Week] [Condition] hour:minute:seconds>
### Default: October Sunday Last 2:00:00 AM

This parameter enables you to set up the local date and time or specify some simple rules for calculating when daylight saving time ends. The following example sets the end of daylight saving time at 2:00 A.M. on the last Sunday of October (which is also the default):

```
SET END OF DAYLIGHT SAVING Time = (October Sunday Last
2:00:00 AM)
```

The preferred method for setting the daylight saving time (DST) status is through the use of the SET Start of Daylight Saving Time command and the SET End of Daylight Saving Time command placed in the AUTOEXEC.NCF file during system initialization.

Note the two ways to indicate when DST should start or end:

▸ Specify an exact date when the change to daylight saving time occurs.

▸ Specify a rule for calculating the dates. The operating system recalculates the next change and automatically schedules it for the next year.

Both the start and the end dates and times for daylight saving time (DST) must be set before either date is actually scheduled.

### New Time with Daylight Saving Time Status = ON/OFF
### Default: OFF

This parameter controls the adjustment of local time when DST is in effect. This command is similar to the TIMESYNC Daylight Saving Time Status parameter, but when this value is set to ON it adjusts the local time by adding or subtracting the DST time offset without changing the UTC for the server. This is accomplished by changing the daylight saving time status and adjusting the local time by the daylight saving time offset, effectively leaving the UTC unchanged. This is designed to correct a DST error. If a supervisor arrives and sees that DST did not change when it should have, this command changes it.

**TIP**

**When changing daylight saving time information manually on a server, be aware that you may cause a UTC value to be recalculated from local time. The "SET New Time with Daylight Saving Time Status" command is expressly intended to avoid the recalculation of the UTC value and force local time to be recalculated instead. Use this command to change the daylight saving time status on a system that is otherwise correct and in time synchronization with the network.**

Attempting to accomplish the same thing by changing local time and then changing the daylight saving time status results in loss of time synchronization.

## Additional TimeSync SET Commands

The following NetWare 6 SET commands for time synchronization are not documented in Novell manuals. These SET commands can assist you in fine-tuning your environment even further. However, these parameters may or may not work in future versions of NetWare 6. We have documented them here so that you can have all of the options when working with time synchronization. We recommend that you not adjust these parameters unless you are solving a specific problem and understand the use of each parameter.

### TIMESYNC Immediate Synchronization = On/Off
### Default: Off

This parameter triggers time synchronization, which simply means that it starts polling. After the value has been set to ON, it automatically resets to OFF, which is the default. This parameter is sometimes useful for creating screen output after the debug flag has been set, rather than waiting for the synchronization process to awaken normally.

Note that this SET parameter does not speed up synchronization in any way; it simply wakes up the synchronization process. Normally the synchronization process responds within two seconds. Occasionally there may be a delay of several seconds (ten seconds or fewer) because of normal network overhead while attempting to reach the target server.

### TIMESYNC Short Interval = <number (10 to 600 seconds)>
### Default: 10

This parameter determines the shortest interval between pollings. This parameter is used when the server falls out of time synchronization. In such a case, it immediately polls the network more frequently to establish time synchronization more quickly. The default interval is every ten seconds. You may want to increase this value for expensive WAN links that should not monopolize all the bandwidth just to support time synchronization when it has been lost.

### TIMESYNC Maximum Offset = <number (10 to 16,777,215 seconds)>
### Default: 600

This parameter specifies the maximum amount of adjustment that the server tries to gain between pollings. The default is 600 seconds, or 10 minutes. The greater the value, the faster the time server adjusts itself toward the network time.

### TIMESYNC Correction Floor = <number (in milliseconds)>
### Default: 1

This parameter sets the minimum value in milliseconds that any NDS server must differ from before the correction is applied. Any adjustment must be larger than this value, or the correction is ignored. This value must always be less than the synchronization radius. If it is not less than the synchronization radius, then time synchronization will not be possible.

This parameter is undocumented or hidden so that system administrators will not change it without knowing the consequences. We highly recommend that you leave the default setting of one millisecond to support NDS.

The only reason to change this parameter would be to eliminate the correction for the one-tick jitters that sometimes occur. This may be an issue if other applications are present that depend on time being synchronized and that also are extremely sensitive to larger amounts of error correction over a ten-minute period.

### SET TIMESYNC Offset Ceiling = <number (0 to 315,532,800)>
### Default: 10 years

A time provider whose clock is too far behind network time will be unable to vote. This parameter sets the value that is used to determine if a server's clock is too far behind the network time. Again, if the time on a server is further away from the network time than this value, it will be ignored and the time of the network will not be adjusted based on that server.

## Timesync Debug Commands

NetWare 6 enables you to monitor the status of time synchronization on a server using the time synchronization debug commands. These commands are useful for debugging, testing, and fine-tuning the synchronization configuration. Note, however, that as undocumented commands they may or may not work in future versions of NetWare 6.

When executed, the debug commands start a separate time synchronization screen on the file server console. After the debug screen starts, information about the time synchronization function is written to the console. This information may be helpful when you are trying to determine if the servers are contacting each other in the manner that you expect for time synchronization. It is also educational to read the debug messages to see the way the system changes the times on each server to converge on the network time. To turn on the time synchronization debug screen and its information, type the following:

```
SET TIMESYNC DEBUG = 7    (turns on the debug screen)
SET TIMESYNC DEBUG = 0    (turns off the debug screen)
```

Figure 7.31 illustrates the time synchronization debug screen.

```
        offset.h = 00000000  offset.l = 0BF20F51
TIMESYNC: Polled server RIO-SRV1 (Primary/Chained Secondary)
        offset.h = 00000000  offset.l = 0DCB5F10

*** TIMESYNC: Unable to communicate with server TOK-SRV1! ***

*** TIMESYNC: Unable to communicate with server SYD-SRV1! ***

Uniform Adjustment Requested:  +0.0CDEB730
This server is configured as a REFERENCE
*** Time is synchronized ***
TIMESYNC: Polled server NOR-SRV1 (Primary/Chained Secondary)
        offset.h = 00000000  offset.l = FD12AFC0

TIMESYNC: Polled server RIO-SRV1 (Primary/Chained Secondary)
        offset.h = 00000001  offset.l = 0CFB95E6

*** TIMESYNC: Unable to communicate with server TOK-SRV1! ***

*** TIMESYNC: Unable to communicate with server SYD-SRV1! ***

Uniform Adjustment Requested:  +1.050722D3
This server is configured as a REFERENCE
*** Time is synchronized ***
```

**FIGURE 7.31** *The time synchronization debug screen*

TIP

**You can set the debug flag to values other than 7, but the results are not useful because each bit in the value controls a group of messages or disables output altogether. The debug information that appears onscreen is not particularly well formatted. Some portions are language enabled and may be translated.**

The following messages are examples of the type of information provided by the debug screen:

```
TIMESYNC: Polled server NOR-SRV1
Weight = 1, OFFSET.H = FFFFFFFF OFFSET.L = F1F06723
```

The most useful pieces of information are the name of the server (NOR-SRV1) and the weight (normally 0, 1, or 16). If time synchronization cannot actually exchange information with the other time server or if out-of-range data is detected, the weight will be zero. A weight of zero generally means that the server is not up or is not reachable across the network.

The values for OFFSET.H and OFFSET.L are the calculated deviation of the server's time from the target server's time. The values form a 64-bit signed number with an implied hexadecimal point separating the whole and fractional parts:

```
FFFFFFFF.F1F06723
```

This number means that this server is a fraction of a second ahead of NOR-SRV1. Another possibility that may occur is a weight of zero with nonzero offset values, indicating that the synchronization data is out of range (one server is more than ten years ahead of the other).

If this message does not appear at all, no time providers or sources are in this server's list. Either the configured time source list is empty or no SAP time sources can be found, or both. Of course, if you have disabled the use of SAP, the only possible cause is that the configured time source list is empty. You can check the state of the list by typing

```
SET TIMESYNC TIME SOURCE =
```

at the system console screen. Notice that the equal sign with no parameter following is required to return the list of time sources.

The next message is

```
Uniform Adjustment Requested = -0.0E0F98DD
Server type = 2
```

This message shows the actual time adjustment that needs to be applied to the clock during the next polling interval. The message also shows the time server types, which are 2 = Secondary, 3 = Primary, 4 = Reference, and 5 = Single.

The adjustment value is hexadecimal, but the sign is displayed so that the magnitude of the adjustment is easier to understand. In this case, the value 0.0E0F98DD (one tick) is significant to time synchronization. This server is ahead of NOR-SRV1 by one tick. It is common to see one-tick or one-half-tick errors that are caused by randomness between the two machines.

When the adjustment is +0.00000000, the servers are in exact synchronization, which really means that no error can be detected by the algorithm. It is also common to see this value stabilize at a very small negative value, such as −0.00000094, because of a small round-off error in the synchronization algorithm when slowing the clock. The error of 0.00000094 is 34 nanoseconds, much smaller than the resolution of the clock and nothing to worry about.

The next message,

```
Adjustment smaller than Correction Floor was ignored.
```

is mentioned because it is quite common. It means that the clock adjustment is so small that it is being ignored. Actually, the parameter that determines the cutoff point is called the TIMESYNC Correction Floor and is set to one millisecond by default.

## Troubleshooting Time Synchronization

When time for a server fails to synchronize to the network, the most probable reason is that there are no reachable time providers. Check the configuration information to be sure it is correct. Make sure that the time providers are running and are synchronized themselves. Remember that a secondary server will not be synchronized until its time providers are synchronized. If necessary, turn on the debug option and verify that the server is actually contacting a time provider.

If the time on the file server has been set far ahead, time synchronization may take a long time. Remember that the server should not move time backward. So, for example, it takes at least two hours of real time to lose two hours.

**TIP**

**Setting time backward on a server is not a good thing to do for most applications that require synchronized timestamps. If you set the time backward on a server that is participating in NDS, the system will generate synthetic time to account for the local time being set backward. You should always set the DOS time before booting the server, just to make sure that the hardware clock has the correct time. (For more information on synthetic time see the "Synthetic Time" section, later in this chapter.)**

Remember that time synchronization requires routing information to make contact with the time provider. Sometimes it takes awhile for routing information to get to a server, especially when the server has just been booted. Even though time synchronization normally happens quickly, wait a minute or two before jumping to conclusions. Also, try executing the DISPLAY SERVERS console command to see if the router knows the target server.

### Booting Time Servers

A rare condition exists when the only two time providers on a network are booted for the first time. Because the first actions of any server are to find a time provider and to set its own clock, determining which server will first set its clock from the other server (the first server polled sets the time) can be problematic. Once servers have synchronized, and as long as one time provider remains active, other time providers can be shut down and rebooted. The booting server will set its time to the network time. Because one server remains in operation, that server is not attempting to set its clock, and the rare condition does not exist.

Again, it is always a good idea to set the DOS time before booting a server to make sure that the hardware clock is correct and to minimize any possible time adjustment.

### NDS Time Not Synchronized

NDS may report this error message:

```
Time_Not_Synchronized Error -659 (FD6D)
```

Yet when users check the server's status with the TIME command, it reports that time is synchronized. What this error message actually means is that NDS has received a timestamp that is older than information already in the Directory. The server time has probably been set backward because of a dead CMOS battery or because the time was incorrectly set when the server was booted.

This error message occurs mostly on small networks that use the default time synchronization configuration. Note that it is an NDS error, not a TIMESYNC.NLM error.

### Correcting Local Time on a Server

Fortunately, once time information is correctly configured, there is little need to change it. When time synchronization is active, you need to be extremely cautious about changing local time information. If local time information is not configured correctly and time synchronization is active, the UTC will also be incorrect. Time synchronization attempts to adjust local time to correspond to network time, which will, in turn, control the UTC. Time synchronization may, therefore, fight efforts to correct poorly configured local parameters.

To avoid this problem, you have to unload the TIMESYNC NLM, configure the local time information correctly, and then reload the NLM.

**NOTE**

**The TIMESYNC NLM is automatically loaded when the NetWare server is booted.**

As an alternative to unloading TIMESYNC, use the following command after correctly setting the server time and creating a TIMESYNC.CFG configuration file:

```
SET TIMESYNC RESTART/FLAG = On
```

### Synthetic Time

When time synchronization is lost because the local time is set backward, NetWare 6 will continue to issue timestamps on the servers using synthetic time. When this situation occurs, the synthetic time message will appear on your server console screen, as shown in Figure 7.32, indicating that synthetic time is being used to create timestamps for the partitions on the server. Synthetic time is also issued when DS.NLM loads and time synchronization has not yet been established.

```
3-03-1998   7:29:02 pm:     DS-7.3-27
   Synthetic Time is being issued on partition ".T=ACME_TREE."

3-03-1998   7:29:51 pm:     DS-7.3-29
   Established communication with server .CAM-SRV1.CAMELOT.ACME

3-03-1998   7:31:02 pm:     DS-7.3-27
   Synthetic Time is being issued on partition ".T=ACME_TREE."

3-03-1998   7:31:41 pm:     DS-7.3-29
   Established communication with server .RIO-SRV1.RIO.ACME

3-03-1998   7:33:02 pm:     DS-7.3-27
   Synthetic Time is being issued on partition ".T=ACME_TREE."

3-03-1998   7:33:48 pm:     RSPX-4.12-28
   Remote console connection granted for 01010500:0080C7E2170B

NOR-SRV1:
```

**FIGURE 7.32** *Synthetic time is created when the time on the Reference or Single Reference servers is set backward. You will be notified with a server console message.*

Synthetic time is the process of creating timestamps from the most recent timestamp in NDS. Synthetic time takes the most recent timestamp and modifies just the event counter to create a new timestamp. This means that the time is not incremented, just the event counter. The event counter is a two-byte value that holds up to 65,535 events. Once the event counter rolls over, the number of seconds in the timestamp is incremented by one. Synthetic time continues until the real time of day catches up with the synthetic timestamps being used.

### Time Configurations for Cross Platforms

In addition to the Timesync.NLM for NetWare servers, other servers and workstations can use the Network Time Protocol (NTP). NTP is part of the UDP protocol suite and is part of TCP/IP. Any computer using NTP must also be running TCP/IP. The Internet can provide time from an NTP server on the Internet. NTP also is synchronized to the Universal Time Coordinated (UTC), the same as the Timesync.NLM can.

NTP also used a concept known as "stratum". A stratum-1 server has an attached time piece such as a radio clock or an atomic clock. A stratum-2 server gets time from a stratum-1 server, and so on.

For NetWare 5 and NetWare 6 servers you can load the NTP.NLM to implement NTP time synchronization. For NetWare 3, NetWare 4, UNIX, Windows NT, and TCP/IP workstations, third-party NTP time services are available. You can check the following Web site regarding time synchronization software:

http://tycho.usno.navy.mil

Regardless of the platform where you are installing NDS, you need to ensure that time is synchronized for all replicas.

### Solaris Time Synchronization

To set up a Solaris server as a Timesync server complete the following steps:

**1.** Enter the following lines in the file /etc/inet/ntp.conf:

```
Server 127.127.1.0
Fudge 127.127.1.0 stratum 0
```

**2.** Enter the following command to start the xntpd daemon:

```
/usr/lib/inet/xntpd
```

**3.** Enter the following:

```
ntptrace
```

You should see the following information after a few minutes

```
Localhost:stratum1, offset 0.000060. symch distance 0.01004
```

## Summary

Time synchronization is the method by which all the NetWare 6 servers maintain the same UTC value across the network. Although it is not directly part of NetWare Directory Services, time synchronization is used primarily by the Directory to maintain the order of events that occur. Because the computer hardware does not inherently maintain consistent time, time synchronization continually attempts to correct time variations.

Time servers are either time providers or time consumers. The time consumer is the secondary time server type, whereas the time providers are primary, reference, and single reference time servers. The time providers determine the official network time. Secondary time servers only attempt to stay synchronized with one other server.

The default configuration of a single reference for time synchronization is easy to understand and requires no advanced planning. The single reference default is a great place to start your installation. Depending on your needs you can keep the defaults or configure a time provider group as your needs change. A custom configuration or time provider group offers you complete control of the time synchronization hierarchy and enables you to build fault tolerance into the system. Time synchronization requires little maintenance once it has been configured.

You only need to determine which communication option works best in your environment. SAP is the default and adds little additional traffic to your network as long as you keep the number of configured primary servers at no more than seven. You can also use a configured list in place of SAP.

You can set many time synchronization parameters on a NetWare 6 server. Altering these parameters can enhance system performance for time on the network.

Once configured, time synchronization is stable and dependable. It is one of those features that almost never needs changing, unless your network changes in size or location.

# NetWare 6 Operations and Maintenance

# NDS eDirectory Internals and Operations

> *"The first rule of intelligent tinkering is to save
> all the parts."* — Paul R. Ehrlich

The main function of NDS eDirectory is to provide a name service. The name service groups network resources together in a hierarchical structure called a *tree*. Each network resource can be represented in the NDS tree as a single NDS object. The information about all the objects or network resources can be distributed across the servers in a network. In NDS eDirectory the object information and the rules to create and manage these objects are stored on the individual NetWare 6 servers in special data files. The data files associated with the directory are created during server installation.

With eDirectory, information is not only distributed but also replicated to provide increased reliability and accessibility. These features provide the Directory with the capacity to place the information close to the users for convenient access while enabling the job of the name service to be shared among the servers.

Because the information in the Directory can be distributed, the background processes that maintain the consistency of information are designed to support multiple servers. In order to support the operation between multiple servers, each server must be capable of establishing a connection and authenticating to the other NetWare 6 servers in the tree.

This chapter focuses on all NDS eDirectory concepts and the internal operations that take place within servers. This information will help you to better understand the "black box" called the Directory.

## First Server Installation

The best way to describe and examine the creation of eDirectory is to understand the installation procedure. We will discuss several basic concepts, including partitions, replicas, and bindery objects.

When you install the first NetWare 6 server and eDirectory, the installation program prompts you to enter the name of the tree, the server context, and the password for the ADMIN user, which is created by default.

The name of the NDS tree is important because it names the hierarchy in which each of the objects or network resources will reside. The name you choose for the tree must be a unique value on the network. For example, the name that we have selected for our sample tree is ACME_TREE.

**TIP**

**Each tree is identified by a name that can contain up to 32 ASCII characters. The tree name may contain only capital letters (A–Z), the digits (0–9), the hyphen (-), and the underscore (_) character. The tree name must not start or end with an underscore or a space. The tree name cannot have more than one underscore character in succession. This means that the NDS tree name cannot have back-to-back underscores. For example, "BAD__TREENAME" is illegal.**

**TIP**

**During the simple installation method for NetWare 6, the NDS tree name and the O=Organization container are named the same. In this case, the installation utility only prompts you for the password. This is the password for the ADMIN object.**

The server context you choose is significant for several reasons. First, it forms the initial tree structure. Second, it becomes the parent or container object for the server object itself and all of its volumes. Third, it becomes the place in the tree where the bindery services context may be set for the server.

During installation of the first server and of the eDdirectory, several events take place. The following elements are created as part of this process:

1. NDS eDirectory data files (partition, entry, value, and block files).

2. Internal NDS eDirectory partitions, which consist of the following:
   - System partition
   - Bindery partition
   - External reference partition
   - Schema partition

3. Base schema.

4. System objects, which consist of the following:
   - Data storage for nonreplicating server data (a Pseudo Server object)
   - Data storage for the NetWare 6 server's dynamic SAP type 4 server object

5. The first user-created partition, called the [ROOT] partition.

6. The [ROOT] object for the tree.

7. An object for each container object in the server's name.

8. The server object in the appropriate container.

9. A volume object for each server volume, using the naming convention of "file server name_volume name."

**10.** The ADMIN user.

**11.** The bindery Supervisor account, which initially uses the ADMIN password. If the server is upgraded from the NetWare 3 bindery, it uses the password of the Supervisor from the bindery.

These remaining events also take place:

▸ The ADMIN user is granted Supervisor object rights to the [ROOT] object.

▸ [PUBLIC] is given object Browse rights to the [ROOT] object.

▸ Upgrade of existing bindery objects to NDS eDirectory (if the server is being upgraded from NetWare 3).

The installation of the first server creates a single partition, named [ROOT], as the topmost object in the tree. The master replica of the [ROOT] partition is stored on the server. Each of the objects created by the installation of the first server is in the master replica of the [ROOT] partition. Figure 8.1 illustrates a logical view of the NDS tree for ACME after the first server CAM-SRV1 has been installed.

**FIGURE 8.1** *A logical view of the NDS tree for ACME after the first server CAM-SRV1 has been installed*

# The NDS eDirectory Program File (DS.NLM)

The NDS eDirectory program code is located in the DS.NLM file, which is placed in the SYS:SYSTEM directory during installation. This NLM file is loaded by the operating system during server bootup. The DS.NLM provides the directory name services on the server. The most important thing to remember is the build number for the NLM. For example, NetWare 6 ships with the build number DS 664.

The build number for DS.NLM can be found by running the NDIR.EXE program against the DS.NLM file. To find the build number for DS.NLM, enter the following:

```
NDIR DS.NLM /ver
```

You can also find the build number for DS.NLM by using the MODULES console command and looking at the entry for the NLM. In order to use the MODULES command, enter the following at the server console prompt and check the version of the DS.NLM that is loaded:

```
MODULES DS* or DS.NLM
```

One of the items shown by the MODULES command is the version of each module that is loaded at the server. See Figure 8.2.

**FIGURE 8.2** *You can check the build number for DS.NLM by using the MODULES command at the server console prompt. The version shown here is DS.NLM 7.03.*

Newer versions of the DS.NLM can be copied to the SYS:SYSTEM directory on your server system. You may want to save the older DS.NLM by renaming it.

In order to unload and reload the new DS.NLM from the SYS:SYSTEM directory without taking the server down, enter the following DSTRACE command:

```
SET DSTRACE = **
```

You can perform the reload of DS.NLM using the more conventional method by simply entering the following server console commands:

UNLOAD DS

and

LOAD DS

A new workstation utility called DUPGRADE automatically copies the newer DS.NLM to each of your NetWare 6 servers and performs the reload of the software. This utility is available from the Novell corporate Web site at www.novell.com.

## Locating a NetWare 6 Server

NDS eDirectory is a distributed name service by which a client can locate the network resources anywhere in the network. Once the client or workstation is attached to any NetWare 6 server, then all the servers work together to locate the requested service.

The NetWare 6 servers that contain NDS eDirectory replicas advertise the tree using the Service Advertising Protocol (SAP). Although the Service Location Protocol (SLP) has replaced SAP in Pure IP, SAP is still used for Internetwork Packet Exchange (IPX) communications. The SAP value contains two parts:

- **Service type** — 0x0278 hex (or 632 decimal). The SAP type is used to advertise the tree.

- **Service name** — The service name is 47 characters contained in two segments.

The first 32 characters of the Service Name are the NDS tree name. The tree is padded with underscore characters to take up the entire 32 characters, if necessary.

The other 15 characters of the Service Name are created from converting the server's network address. The server's network address contains the network address for the server, the internal IPX node number, and the NCP socket number in that order. The address is compressed to fit into the 15 bytes. The client connects to the server by reversing the compression and uses the address and socket numbers.

The workstation initially finds the first NetWare 6 server by broadcasting or making a service request indicating the Service Type 0x0278. Any server receiving this request that has NDS eDirectory replicas of the NDS tree will respond to the request.

By looking at the Service Name field, the workstation or client determines the NDS tree name supported by the server and uses that information in choosing a server to contact. If the workstation has a setting for the Preferred Tree in the NET.CFG, it looks for the name equal to that of the Preferred Tree. The workstation can then connect to the server at the address and socket number extracted from the Service Name field.

**TIP**

**The other Service Advertising Protocols (SAPs) that you need to support NetWare 6 are type 0x0004, 0x026B, and type 0x0107. A normal NCP server or file server uses the SAP type 0x0004. This type is used for the SAP and Routing Information Protocol (RIP) broadcasts between servers. The SAP type 0x026B is used by Time Synchronization. Time servers use SAP type 0x026B to communicate with other time providers. The SAP type 0x0107 is used to find remote servers using RCONSOLE. If you plan to support RCONSOLE, then you need to support SAP type 107, as well.**

**TIP**

**It is important that you do not establish a Routing Information Protocol filter between NetWare 6 servers. Each NetWare 6 server must be capable of seeing every other NetWare 6 server. This is especially true with NetWare 6 servers that do not have any NDS eDirectory replicas. Some people think that because a NetWare 6 server does not have replicas, it can be filtered out. The server needs to be capable of doing a service request for type 0x0278 to find the NDS tree. In addition, the clients or workstations need type 0x0278 to boot up.**

# NDS eDirectory Data Files

The physical representation of the NDS tree and its objects relates to the actual NDS eDirectory data files. The object and partition information is stored on the server in the data files under the SYS:_NETWARE directory, which is hidden by the operating system.

This directory is only visible through the RCONSOLE utility. After loading RCONSOLE and logging into the appropriate server, press ALT+F1 to bring up the main menu and then select the Scan Directory option. Figure 8.3 illustrates how to selectively scan SYS:_NETWARE using RCONSOLE. Figure 8.4 illustrates a view of the contents of the SYS:_NETWARE folder using RCONSOLE.

Five eDirectory files have the .DSD file extension, but a number of stream files may be used to support login script files, print job configurations, and so on. The stream files use the 8.3 DOS file-naming convention. However, they are distinguished from the others because their names consist of hexadecimal values only (0 to 9 and A to F). The directory uses the following files:

- Base file (0.DSB)
- Partition file (3.DSD)
- Entry file (0.DSD)
- Value file (1.DSD)
- Block file (2.DSD)
- Stream files (all have .DSD extensions)

**FIGURE 8.3** *Scanning the folder SYS:_NETWARE using RCONSOLE*

**FIGURE 8.4** *Viewing the contents of the folder SYS:_NETWARE using RCONSOLE*

New in NetWare 6 is the base file (0.DSB), whose purpose is simply to hold the names of all the .DSD files. The other files hold the object, property, and partition information stored in the directory. These files work together to provide the complete NDS tree information for each server. The relationship between each of the eDirectory data files is illustrated in Figure 8.5. This figure shows how the partition record points to the first object in the partition, which, in turn, points to specific property values.

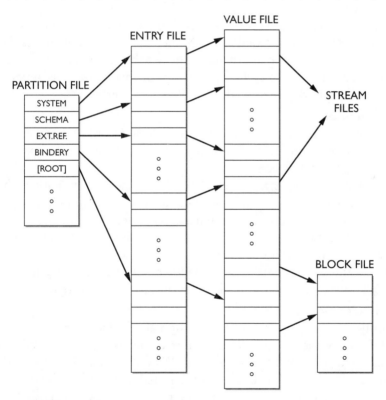

**FIGURE 8.5** *The eDirectory data files are related as shown here. Each partition record points to the first object in the partition, which, in turn, points to the specific property values.*

The filename and its description or purpose are presented in the following sections.

## The Partition File (3.DSD)

The partition file named 3.DSD contains a list of each of the partitions defined on the local server and within the local eDirectory database. The partition file holds a record for each partition. Each partition record points to the starting record within the entry file for the specific objects.

The following four eDirectory internal partitions are always stored on each NetWare 6 server: system partition, schema partition, external reference partition, and bindery partition. They are discussed in the paragraphs that follow.

### The System Partition

The first partition in the partition file is the system partition, which points or locates the Pseudo Server object, as well as the NameBase version. Data available from this partition is server-specific information, such as the name of the tree and the version of the database. Because the information in this partition is server-centric, it is not synchronized with any other NetWare 6 server.

### The Schema Partition

The second partition is the schema. The schema partition record locates the top of the schema objects for the directory. The schema itself is the set of rules for the structure of the NDS tree and objects.

The initial installation of the server creates the base schema that ships with NetWare 6. The schema can be extended to include other custom objects and properties. In order to keep all copies of the schema on all servers throughout the tree the same, the information or objects in the schema partition are synchronized by eDirectory with the other NetWare 6 servers.

To be more exact, this file contains the information to locate the schema objects in the entry (0.DSD) file. Nothing in this file is specifically synchronized.

### The External Reference Partition

The third partition in the partition file is the external reference partition. This partition record is used as the partition for the external reference objects stored on the server. An external reference is created for an NDS object that is not stored locally but needs an object ID on the local server. The external reference holds the object ID for the object that is external to this server.

The information in this partition is server-centric and is not synchronized with the other NetWare 6 servers. Again, to be more exact, this file contains just the information to locate the external reference objects in the entry file.

The external reference partition can be used to locate the top of the NDS tree, which refers to the [ROOT] object. Note that this partition is present even if the local database contains a copy of the [ROOT] partition.

### The Bindery Partition

The fourth partition is the bindery partition. The bindery partition locates the bindery server SAP name and associated properties or attributes. The information in this partition is server-centric and is not synchronized by the directory to the other NetWare 6 servers.

The bindery partition also holds the dynamic bindery information, which contains the Service Advertising Protocol (SAP) and Routing Information Protocol (RIP) data received by the server during normal operation in the NDS tree.

The partition file contains a representation for every user-created partition on the server. These are the partitions that the system administrators create by using the NetWare Administration utilities.

## The Entry or Object File (0.DSD)

The entry file contains the individual records of the directory objects that are created to form the NDS tree. In addition to these objects, this file contains the information for each of the schema, bindery, and external reference objects. The term "entry" is often used to refer to an eDirectory object. The object's name, its partition, and its parent within the NDS tree are among several pieces of data recorded in an individual entry.

One of the objects is the Pseudo Server object, which stores the information about the specific server. This object is not synchronized with the other NetWare 6 servers. The information held in the Pseudo Server object includes these items:

- The name of the NDS tree
- The server object's public key, which is used for authentication
- The server object's private key, which is used for authentication
- The synchronized up to vector for the schema partition
- The Remote ID list, which contains ID pairs consisting of a local ID and a remote ID (see "The Object ID" section later in this chapter)
- The Monitored Connection, which cleans up connections that the client has terminated improperly

## The Value, Block, and Stream Files

The property information can be stored in several different places within the internal structures of the directory. In order to store the property information in a variety of formats, NDS eDirectory uses the value (1.DSD), block (2.DSD), and stream files. The majority of the structured property information is stored in the value file. If an overload area is needed for any properties, then the overload is written to the block file. If the property is free-form with no defined structure, then it is stored in a stream file.

### VALUE.NDS (1.DSD)

The value file (1.DSD) contains the property or attribute records used by the objects contained within the entry file. There is an entry in this file for every attribute value, whether the attribute is single valued or multivalued. For example, some of the attributes for the user object in the directory are multivalue fields. If there are multiple values defined for the user, each additional value will have an entry in this file. The access control list (ACL) attribute, for example, is multivalued and may have many entries or values. Each of the values will have an entry in this file. The value file works in conjunction with both the block file and the stream files.

### BLOCK.NDS (2.DSD)

The block file (2.DSD) contains records that are used by the record in the value file. If the data entered into a value field of a property or attribute is large, it overflows into this file. For example, if an attribute value is large, the remaining information for that attribute is stored in the block file. Any given value record may have multiple records assigned in this file.

### Stream Files

The stream files are individual files that exist in the SYS:_NETWARE directory. These files contain the value information for attributes that are free form and of variable length. For example, the login scripts, printer control files, and print job definitions attributes are stored in stream files. The stream files use the 8.3 DOS filenaming convention. However, they are distinguished from the other files because their names consist of hexadecimal values only (0 to 9 and A to F). In addition, each stream file has a .DSD extension.

## The NDS eDirectory .TMP Data Files

A complete set of temporary NDS eDirectory data files is created when the DSREPAIR utility is executed. No .TMP files are created for any of the stream files. The temporary NDS data files are created by DSREPAIR when it is running and are used to perform all the changes against the partitions. At the end of the repair, these temporary (.TMP) files become the permanent eDirectory data files, unless you choose not to accept the repairs that were made. The current data files become .DOD files.

**TIP**

**DSREPAIR creates the .DOD set of data files. These .DOD files will be overwritten by DSREPAIR only after 72 hours. This feature helps the Novell Technical Support organization react to customer problems that may be recently caused. You can also proactively manage the backup of the .DOD set of data files for NDS (often referred to as the DIB). To accomplish this objective, you can use DSREPAIR–RC to back up your DS database in case you have problems and want to recover from the backed up DIBs.**

The .DOD files are stored on the server in the same place where the regular data files are stored under the SYS:_NETWARE directory. You can see these files by using the RCONSOLE utility and by selecting the Scan Directory option from the main menu. Figure 8.6 shows the .DOD files created by DSREPAIR.

**FIGURE 8.6** *RCONSOLE shows the .DOD files created by the DSREPAIR utility in the SYS:_NETWARE directory.*

# Timestamps

Because the directory hierarchy can be distributed or replicated across servers in a network, the information in each of the replicas can change without the other replicas immediately knowing about it. This form of synchronization is known as being loosely consistent.

The sequence of events that occurs within the directory can become confused unless a mechanism is provided to ensure that the events are updated to each replica as they actually happen. The term *event* is used to refer to a creation or modification to the eDirectory objects or properties.

The mechanism that ensures that the events are changed in sequence are the timestamps for each of the objects and properties. When an event occurs, the directory issues a new timestamp and associates the timestamp with the event. Synchronization between replicas of a partition uses the timestamps associated with every object and property or attribute to indicate the time the modification was made. For example, if the same object (same property) is modified by two different administrators at approximately the same time, both updates may not take place because the last timestamp wins the update.

The purpose of the timestamp in eDirectory is to ensure that the information stored in the directory will converge across all NetWare 6 servers over time.

There is a timestamp for each object when it is created, and one for when it is modified; the former is called the *object creation timestamp* and the latter the *last modification timestamp*. A timestamp also is issued for every change to a property value.

The timestamp value for objects and properties is unique within an NDS eDirectory partition because the timestamps are assigned by the replica where the objects exist. This provides an ordering of the events that occur across all the servers holding replicas of a partition. Figure 8.7 illustrates the timestamp structure, which has three parts or fields.

**FIGURE 8.7** *The structure for a timestamp attribute*

- ▶ **Seconds** — This is a four-byte value that stores UTC time in whole seconds since midnight, January 1, 1970. The whole seconds represent the actual time that the event (creation or modification) took place.

- ▶ **Replica Number** — This is a two-byte field that stores the replica number where the event occurred and where the timestamp was issued. Every replica of a partition is assigned a unique number when it is created. The master replica is responsible for assigning a number to the new replica. The replica number ensures a unique timestamp within a partition.

▶ **Event ID** — This is a two-byte field that stores the number of events that occurred during a second. Because computers are so fast, many events can occur within any one second. The event ID permits a timestamp to be issued for events that occur in one second. The event ID is a sequence number that starts at 0 and increments to 65565. The event ID is reset every second.

The timestamp is a critical component in the replica synchronization process. When the directory updates a replica, it requests the timestamps from that replica to identify the data. The timestamp provides a unique value for the object and properties that identify the time and place of the event's origin. If the same object or property is updated on different replicas (or servers) at exactly the same second and event ID, the replica number between the servers will be different. The directory makes the updates using the greater or latest timestamp. When compared, timestamps are treated as 32-bit, 16-bit, and 16-bit unsigned, with seconds as the most significant.

Whenever a client or workstation deletes an object or attribute from a replica on a server, the server does not immediately purge it from its local database. Instead, it issues a timestamp for the object or attribute and marks the object or attribute value as "not present" or deleted. After replica synchronization propagates the change to all other replicas, the janitor process purges the object or attribute (see the "Obituaries" section later in this chapter).

To support accurate timestamps, the servers must maintain accurate time and that time must be synchronized between the servers. Time synchronization provides the mechanism to ensure that each server is synchronized to the network time. You want accurate timestamps so that the order of modification is accurate, which means that the last modification timestamp is accepted.

# NDS eDirectory Structures for Objects and Properties

The NDS tree hierarchy is composed of directory objects and properties. The objects and properties are stored as records in the eDirectory data files. The pieces of the data stored for each object are shown in Figure 8.8. Each record has seven fields.

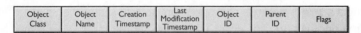

| Object Class | Object Name | Creation Timestamp | Last Modification Timestamp | Object ID | Parent ID | Flags |
|---|---|---|---|---|---|---|

**FIGURE 8.8** *The NDS eDirectory object*

- ▸ **Object class** — The object class is the base object class as defined in the schema for the object. A particular object type defines an object.

- ▸ **Object name** — The object name is the relative distinguished name of the object.

- ▸ **Creation timestamp** — The creation timestamp is issued to the object when it is created.

- ▸ **Last modification timestamp** — The last modification timestamp holds the timestamp of the last change received by this replica made to the object, whether it was the object itself or its associated properties.

- ▸ **Object ID** — The object ID is a unique ID given to the object by the server where the replica is held.

- ▸ **Parent ID** — The parent ID is the object ID of the parent container object to this object.

- ▸ **Flags** — The flags are present, not present, alias, partition root, created by reference, and so on.

**TIP** Sometimes the data contained in the object is called nonattribute object information because the information is stored with the object but not as attributes or properties.

The property or attribute shown in Figure 8.9 has four data items defined.

| Timestamp | Attribute Name | Attribute Flags | Value |
|---|---|---|---|

**FIGURE 8.9** *The properties or attributes of the object*

- ▸ **Timestamp** — The timestamp holds the timestamp of the creation time for the attribute.

- ▸ **Attribute name** — The attribute name specifies the name of the attribute. The syntax or data type can be determined using the attribute name.

▸ **Attribute flags** — The attribute flags control the states of the attribute.

▸ **Value** — The value is the actual information or data stored.

## An Object's Unique Name (Tuned Name)

An object's *tuned name* is the distinguished name of the object plus the creation timestamp for each of the parent container objects. The tuned name provides the directory with an absolutely unique ID structure for each of the objects. To illustrate the concept of a tuned name, we will use the following example. A system administrator decides to rename the user SIRGALAHAD to user GALAHAD. He or she then decides to create a new user called SIRGALAHAD. In order to guarantee that the directory knows that these two are separate objects, the concept of a tuned name is introduced. The tuned name is really a global unique name for the object.

A tuned name for an object is the distinguished name of the object with a little extra information. Each segment of the distinguished name is made up of a combination of the relative distinguished name bound with its creation timestamp. Remember that a distinguished name includes each parent object all the way back to and including [ROOT]. This means that the tuned name includes not only each relative distinguished name but also the creation timestamp for each relative distinguished name so that it can build the tuned name of the object.

As an example, the tuned name for the user SIRGALAHAD.CHARITY. CAMELOT.ACME would be as follows:

SIRGALAHAD (creation timestamp)
CHARITY (creation timestamp)
CAMELOT (creation timestamp)
ACME (creation timestamp)
[ROOT] (creation timestamp)

Including each creation timestamp for each object in the distinguished name removes any ambiguity about identifying the object. In the example, where SIRGALAHAD was created a second time under the same container, the first SIRGALAHAD differs from the second one created because of a difference in the creation timestamp.

The tuned name concept is used internally by the directory. You cannot see the tuned name for an object using the current administration utilities.

Although objects have a unique object name or tuned name, you cannot have two objects with the same distinguished name. This would happen if two objects with the same relative distinguished name were in the same container. If two objects with the same name are synchronized into the same container but with different creation timestamps, the directory must rename one of the objects. The naming convention used by eDirectory to rename one of the objects is *number_number.* For example, a duplicate object is renamed to 1_2.

### Object References

The values of some attributes in the directory are other NDS eDirectory objects. To truly understand objects in eDirectory, you need to understand how the objects are referenced. When an object stores another object as an attribute value it is said to have an object reference.

For example, a group object has a membership attribute, and the values of this attribute are NDS eDirectory objects. A printer object has an attribute whose values are other objects. The access control list is an example of an attribute for an object that stores other object IDs. The rights assignments for the directory are held in the access control list.

An object can also have its own object as one of its own attribute values. For example, a user object receives the read/write attribute for its own login script and print job configuration. The object becomes a trustee of itself.

To describe object references, we will use an example in the ACME tree. Consider Figure 8.10, where the user AEINSTEIN.LABS.NORAD.ACME is made security equivalent to the user KINGARTHUR.OPS.CAMELOT.ACME. The security equivalence attribute for AEINSTEIN has the value of the user to which he is security equivalent. In this case there is a value for KINGARTHUR.OPS.CAMELOT. ACME.

▶ • • • • • • • • • • • • • • • • • • • • • • • • • • • • ◀

### Consulting Experience

The rename problem has been noticed mostly in networks and servers that are migrating from NetWare 4.02 to NetWare 6. The reason is that NetWare 4.02 does not support tuned names and NetWare 6 requires them. In order to cure the problems experienced with renamed objects, run DSREPAIR, option number 8 on the NetWare 4.02 server before upgrading. Make sure that the DSREPAIR utility you run is the updated version for NetWare 4.02. This updated DSREPAIR utility is available on the Novell corporate Web site.

**FIGURE 8.10** *The user AEINSTEIN.LABS. NORAD.ACME is made security equivalent to the user KINGARTHUR.OPS.CAMELOT.ACME in the ACME tree.*

The object AEINSTEIN.LABS.NORAD.ACME is said to have an object reference to the object KINGARTHUR.OPS.CAMELOT.ACME. Internally, NDS stores the security equivalent attribute value as an object ID for the user KINGARTHUR. The client sees the value of the attribute as the distinguished name of the object.

A number of properties or attributes defined in the schema can contain object references. Some of these attributes are security equivalences, group membership, member, operator, and replica.

## The Object ID

One of the most important fields contained in the object structure is the object ID. Most of the operations that can be performed on the NDS objects require that the requesting client have or obtain the object ID. The object ID is a four-byte (32-bit) value that serves as a handle to the objects themselves.

Each object in a replica stored on a NetWare 6 server has a corresponding object ID on that server. The object ID is assigned on a per-server basis, which means that it is not a global ID and is valid only on the server that assigned it.

Because the object ID is server-centric, it is not replicated, except for the backlinks and replica pointer table. The backlinks are discussed in detail in the "External References and Backlinks" section. The replica pointer table is discussed in "The Replica Pointer Table" section.

Each server that stores a copy of the object will probably have a different object ID for the same object. Figure 8.11 illustrates how each NetWare 6 server has a different object ID for the user object stored in different replicas. In this example, KINGARTHUR in the ACME tree has different object IDs on servers CAM-SRV1 and OPS-SRV1.

**FIGURE 8.11** *Servers CAM-SRV1 and OPS-SRV1 have different object IDs for the user KINGARTHUR, which are stored in different replicas of the same partition.*

### Obtaining the Object ID

The object ID is used in most of the internal operations performed by Directory Services. The client must first obtain the object ID for the object before it can execute the operation. The client has several methods for obtaining the object ID.

The first method is known as *name resolution,* in which the client starts with the distinguished name of the object and makes the request to Directory Services to return the location and ID for the object. The name resolution method is used when logging into the network, capturing to printers, mapping network drives, and using NWADMIN or ConsoleOne to browse the tree. Each of the network resources is found using the name resolution process. The name resolution process is described in the "Name Resolution (Tree Walking) Operation" section. The second method for obtaining the object ID is for the client to start with the current context and list the objects available in that container. Using the utilities provided, the client can then select any object and receive information that is of interest. This procedure is often called *yellow pages* or *white pages.* .

This method of obtaining the object ID is used mainly within the NWADMIN, NAL, or ZENworks utilities. The user navigates through the tree listing all the objects. Depending on the utility, the user can set a filter to weed out unwanted object types. Filters are available by name patterns, NDS object classes, or modification timestamps. An example of how to navigate through the NDS tree is shown in Chapter 2 in the section "Searching for Objects and Properties in NWADMIN."

The third method for obtaining the object ID is for the client to execute a search. The search capabilities are powerful because you can select the objects by attribute values. The objects that match the value of the search criteria are returned. The search can be applied to the current container in the tree, or it can extend to the entire subtree.

### NDS eDirectory Operations That Use the Object ID

Once the client has obtained a valid object ID, it operates on an object by sending requests to the server where the object ID was obtained. Remember, the object ID is valid only on a per-server basis. The operating system also requires the object ID when performing operations. The file system, connection table, and other systems use this ID to identify the appropriate NDS object.

The most basic service provided is to read the detailed information about the object itself using the Read operation. The result of this operation is shown in NWADMIN when the Detail dialog box is opened for the object KINGARTHUR, as shown in Figure 8.12.

**FIGURE 8.12** *Detailed information for the KINGARTHUR object using the Read operation in NWADMIN*

Other operations are Add, Delete, Modify, Get Effective Rights, Compare, and many others. Each operation that can be performed against an NDS object is self-explanatory.

### Object IDs for Servers

The object ID for the NetWare server objects is stored in pairs consisting of a local server ID and a remote server ID. The server ID pairs are used as a shortcut for the server-to-server authentication that supports NDS operations, such as replica synchronization. An authenticating object ID for the server object is required and is used in the connection table of the server. Thus, a server stores an object ID for all the other NetWare 6 servers that the local server has authenticated to. The following list illustrates how each server holds a server ID pair, which includes object IDs for the local server and the remote server:

► The local server ID is the local ID held for the remote server.

► The remote server ID is the local server's ID on the specific remote server.

For example, the server ID pairs that are held by each of the servers CAM-SRV1 and NOR-SRV1 are shown in Figure 8.13. The server ID pairs are also shown on a server basis in DSREPAIR under the Advanced menu option. Figure 8.14 illustrates the server ID pairs stored in NOR-SRV1.

SERVER IDs

| LOCAL ID | REMOTE ID |
|----------|-----------|
| 01023000 | 89007601 |
|          |           |

CAM-SRV1

| LOCAL ID | REMOTE ID |
|----------|-----------|
| 89007601 | 01023000 |
|          |           |

NOR-SRV1

**FIGURE 8.13** *The server ID pairs are held by each of the servers CAM-SRV1 and NOR-SRV1 in the ACME tree.*

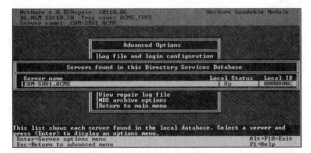

**FIGURE 8.14** *The server ID pairs are held by the server NOR-SRV1, as shown in the DSREPAIR utility.*

### Object IDs Used as File System Trustees

In order to maintain backward compatibility, the operating system uses the object ID rather than the object name to assign trustees for file system rights. The trustees of the file system are not stored in NDS; instead, they are stored in the same place as they are stored in NetWare 3, which is in the Directory Entry Table (DET). The Directory Entry Table is part of the file system. Figure 8.15 illustrates how assignments for the trustees of file system rights are made using the object ID. In this example, the user KINGARTHUR is assigned Read and File Scan rights to the SYS:APPS directory on the server CAM-SRV1.

**FIGURE 8.15** *The assignments for the trustees of file system rights are made using the object ID. KINGARTHUR is assigned Read and File Scan rights to the SYS:APPS directory on the server CAM-SRV1.*

# External References and Backlinks

The object ID discussed in the previous section is valid on the server as long as the object is stored in the replica on the server. Sometimes the server holds a temporary object ID for objects that are not stored locally. The temporary object ID is called an *external reference*. These external references work together with backlinks or distributive reference links to provide the distribution of the directory.

An external reference is created to reference an object that is not physically located on the local server. When a NetWare 6 server needs to reference information about an object that is not held in any local replicas, that server creates an external reference, which provides a local object ID for the real object on the other servers.

In order for eDirectory to keep track of all the external references created, each object can have a multivalued property called a *backlink*. The backlink points to the external reference with which it is associated. Each backlink value is periodically checked to verify that the associated external reference still exists. The backlink property of the object contains the name of the server that holds the external reference and the object ID that is assigned to the object on that server.

In order to understand how the external references and backlinks are used, you need to understand the object IDs on the server and when they are used. For example, the server needs the object IDs for use in the file system, connection table, and other systems.

In Figure 8.16, the object AEINSTEIN is contained in the NORAD partition, which is stored on server NOR-SRV1. The server CAM-SRV1 holds only a replica of the CAMELOT partition. Consider a situation in which AEINSTEIN maps a network drive to the server CAM-SRV1. The drive mapping forces the user to authenticate to CAM-SRV1, where a local object ID is needed by the connection table for assignment of file system rights.

**FIGURE 8.16** *The NORAD partition is stored on NOR-SRV1, and the CAMELOT partition is stored on CAM-SRV1.*

The user object for AEINSTEIN, which mapped a drive to CAM-SRV1, is not physically stored on the server, so it must create an external reference because a local object ID is needed to authenticate the real object. The real object is in the NORAD partition on the NOR-SRV1 server. The external reference created on the CAM-SRV1 server stores the object ID that is needed on the local server. In this case the object ID is 03 01 89 00 hex. Likewise, a backlink is created on the real object to track the external reference. Figure 8.17 illustrates the relationship of creating an external reference and backlink for the user object AEINSTEIN in the ACME tree.

**FIGURE 8.17** *An example of an external reference and backlink for the user object AEINSTEIN*

## The Purpose of External References

The purpose of the external reference is to be able to reference an object in the directory without requiring that object to be physically duplicated on the local server. The external reference architecture enables eDirectory to be distributed across the servers in the network while still being capable of referencing its objects. NDS eDirectory can reference all the objects in the directory without having to store a complete replica of each partition on each NetWare 6 server.

External references provide two major functions for NDS. First, they provide the directory with the capability to reference objects that are not local to the server. Second, they provide the complete skeleton of the tree structure and maintain an object's lineage "up" the tree. The external references are stored on a per-server basis on each NetWare 6 server in the external reference partition. Because the data in this partition is server-centric, it is not synchronized to other NetWare 6 servers in the network.

External references improve system performance by caching frequently accessed information. Currently, the directory caches only an object's public key. Because authentication requires the client's public key, it is cached on the external reference so that it does not have to be read each time. The external references that are created for the server objects also store the server's status and DS revision or build number.

An external reference is an object stored in the entry (0.DSD) file as part of the external reference partition and has these components:

▸ **Object ID** — A unique object ID issued by the local server for the real object

▸ **Relative distinguished name** — The real object's relative distinguished name

Whenever a server creates an external reference for an object in the NDS tree, it also creates external references for each of the parent containers, if needed. These are the parent containers that are in the distinguished name of the object all the way back to and including [ROOT]. An external reference for the parent container is needed only when it has not been previously created.

### The Purpose of Backlinks

The backlink property of an object is used by the directory system to enable easy maintenance of the external references of that object. When an object is renamed, moved, or deleted from the system, the backlinks aid in modifying the external references to that object to reflect the changes. This process provides data integrity for the directory. For example, when an object is renamed, moved, or deleted, the backlinks make it possible to change all external references to the object.

The format for the backlink property or attribute includes these values:

▸ **Object ID** — The object ID value that is issued for the external reference on the remote server. This value enables NDS to find the associated external reference or object ID on the remote server.

▸ **Distinguished name** — The remote server object's distinguished name in the NDS tree. This value identifies the server holding the external reference.

### Distributed Reference Links

NetWare 6 provides a method for maintaining external references called *distributed reference links (DRL)*. These links are more efficient than backlinks when renaming, moving, and deleting the external references. The distributed reference links are more efficient because, unlike backlinks, they are not tied to a specific

NetWare server; instead, they reference the partition that stores the external reference object. Alternatively, when a backlink (in NetWare 4) is created it stores the NetWare server name and object ID for each external reference object.

As mentioned, the major downside to using backlinks is that they are tied to a specific NetWare server and not tied to the external reference object's location in the NDS tree. The result of using backlinks is that each NetWare server tends to have a connection to every other server in the NDS tree. To alleviate this problem, distributed reference links have been added to NetWare 6 that store the partition name and object ID where each external reference object exists. By storing the partition name, the individual NetWare servers can resolve the DRLs by using the directory tree structure.

Like backlinks, the DRLs have a periodic process that checks to verify that the associated external reference still exists. This process that periodically checks the DRLs provides data integrity for the NDS database. The distributed reference link is implemented using a new "Used By" property of the object. The "Used By" property contains the distinguished name of the partition that holds the external reference and the object ID that is assigned to the object.

Although distribution reference links are fully implemented in NetWare 6, backlinks will not go away. During certain situations, the backlinks continue to be used to help maintain the external references. NetWare 6 uses both methods.

## Creating External References and Backlinks

The external references are created for a number of reasons. For example, at times a server requires information about an object that is not stored locally. Having this information helps the local server maintain an object ID for an object. NDS eDirectory creates the object ID for each object. The external reference object supplies an object ID for the server where the real object is not stored. An example is a server that needs to grant file system rights to an object that is not local. The server requires the object ID to make the trustee assignment.

The corresponding property to the external reference is the backlink. A new value for the backlink property is written on the object each time an external reference is created. The backlink property value is used by the directory to keep track of where the external references of an object are located.

External references are required for five different situations on a NetWare 6 server. For these situations, it is assumed that the actual object for which the external reference is created is not stored locally on the server. The five different methods or situations are as follows:

- Completing the distinguished names
- Authentication
- File system access control
- Dealing with attribute values that are objects
- Replica removal

**Complete the Distinguished Names**
The name field for the object stores only the relative distinguished name of the object. Each object also requires the object ID for the parent objects. Therefore, external references are created on the server to complete the skeleton up the NDS tree for each of the objects that it holds in its partitions. One external reference is created for each relative distinguished name in the complete name. This means that external references are created for each of the parent container objects that are not physically stored on the server.

For example, the server CAM-SRV1 in the ACME tree holds only the CAMELOT partition, which defines each of the objects for that subtree. In order to complete the distinguished naming for the objects in the partition, the O=ACME and [ROOT] objects must have external references. The real objects for each external reference are stored in the [ROOT] partition on the server NOR-SRV1. Figure 8.18 illustrates this example.

For each replica a server holds, it must know the distinguished name of the partition, which is defined by the partition [ROOT] object. This means that external references will be created to complete each relative distinguished name of the partition all the way back to the [ROOT] object.

Likewise, an external reference object cannot exist without the server knowing about every object in its distinguished name. The external reference objects themselves are stored as relative distinguished names, not simple distinguished names. This is true for every object, not just the external references. When a server creates an external reference, it most likely creates external references to complete the distinguished name of the object contained in the external reference. If an external reference for the parent containers of the object has been previously created, another reference is not needed.

[ROOT]

O=ACME

OU=NORAD    OU=RIO    OU=CAMELOT    OU=TOKYO    OU=SYDNEY

CAM-SRVI

OU=CHARITY    OU=OPS    OU=PR

OU=FIN    OU=DIST

OBJECTS
ACME
[ROOT]          Backlinks

EXTERNAL REFERENCES

| ACME | 07721429 |
|------|----------|
| [ROOT] | 07618429 |

NOR-SRVI

[ROOT]-M

CAM-SRVI

CAMELOT-M

**FIGURE 8.18** *External references are created on server CAM-SRVI for the O=ACME and [ROOT] objects. The external references are needed to complete the distinguished names of the objects in the partition CAMELOT.*

For example, in Figure 8.19, server RIO-SRV1 does not hold any NDS replicas in the ACME tree. The user object KINGARTHUR.OPS.CAMELOT.ACME is created as an external reference on the server RIO-SRV1. The server would need to create additional external references for each of the objects in the distinguished name of KINGARTHUR, including the [ROOT] object. [ROOT] is implied in every object name.

EXTERNAL REFERENCES

| KINGARTHUR | 0615360E |
|---|---|
| OPS | 02665801 |
| CAMELOT | 01008015 |
| ACME | 05225983 |
| [ROOT] | 18883608 |

RIO-SRV1
NO NDS REPLICAS

**FIGURE 8.19** *An example of an external reference created for the user KINGARTHUR on RIO-SRV1, as well as other external references created to complete the distinguished name for KINGARTHUR*

## Authentication

NDS eDirectory objects (typically users and servers) can authenticate themselves to a NetWare 6 server for access to specific network resources even though the objects are not stored locally on that server. The authentication mechanism needs an object ID defined for each object that authenticates, as well as an object ID for each security equivalence of the object.

The object ID is used in the server connection table to calculate the security privileges for the connection. One of the steps in authentication is the calculation of the object's security equivalences. The results of the calculation are stored in the object's entry of the connection table of the server. All security equivalences of the object that authenticate are included in the connection table. These security equivalences are stored in the server's connection table as object IDs and not as names.

For those objects that are not stored locally, an external reference is created that supplies an object ID to the connection table. This is true even for the other NetWare 6 servers that attach and authenticate for purposes of synchronizing replicas.

An example of this situation is illustrated in Figure 8.20. (This is the same example that was illustrated in Figures 8.16 and 8.17.) The user object AEINSTEIN maps a network drive to the server CAM-SRV1. Because AEINSTEIN is not physically stored on the server, it must create an external reference for the real object. The real object is in the NORAD partition on the NOR-SRV1 server. The external reference created on the CAM-SRV1 server stores the object ID that is needed on the local server. Likewise, the real object stores a backlink property value to track the external reference.

**FIGURE 8.20** *An example of an external reference and backlink for the user object AEINSTEIN in the ACME tree*

The server CAM-SRV1 will create an external reference for each of the other objects in the distinguished name of AEINSTEIN. These objects are OU=LABS, OU=NORAD, O=ACME, and [ROOT], as shown in Figure 8.21. The objects O=ACME and [ROOT] should already exist on the server CAM-SRV1 as external references because they are needed to complete the distinguished name of the objects in the CAMELOT partition.

**FIGURE 8.21** *An example of external references and backlinks for the objects OU=LABS, OU=NORAD, O=ACME, and [ROOT], which are part of the distinguished name for AEINSTEIN in the ACME tree*

### File System Access Control

An external reference object can be created to supply an object ID for the file system rights assignments. The assignment of file system rights is maintained by NetWare 6 using the object IDs. The object ID becomes the trustee for the files and directories rights assignments. The rights assignments for the file and directory system are stored in the Directory Entry Table. This control list stores the object ID for the user that has the rights.

If the object does not exist on the server, an external reference is created, which supplies the file system's Directory Entry Table with an object ID. For example, in Figure 8.22 a user KINGARTHUR can have file and directory rights to NOR-SRV1, even though the KINGARTHUR user object is not stored in a replica on the NOR-SRV1 server. In this example, KINGARTHUR is given Read and File Scan rights to the SYS:APPS directory on NOR-SRV1. The server requires an object ID for the user KINGARTHUR to place in the trustee list for the directory. An external reference is created for KINGARTHUR, but the real user object is stored on CAM-SRV1.

**FIGURE 8.22** The user KINGARTHUR is granted Read and File Scan rights to the directory SYS:APPS on the server NOR-SRV1. An external reference is created for the user and its parents.

External references are also created for OU=OPS, which is the parent object in the distinguished name of the user. The OU=CAMELOT object already exists on the server NOR-SRV1 in a subordinate reference replica for the CAMELOT partition. The objects O=ACME and [ROOT] are not created as external references because they are real objects on the server NOR-SRV1 in the [ROOT] partition.

### Attribute Values That Are NDS eDirectory Objects

The values of some attributes are other eDirectory objects. These values are known as *object references*. For example, a group object has a membership attribute, and the value of this attribute is an object. A printer object has an attribute whose values are objects. The access control list (ACL) is an example of an attribute for an object that stores other object IDs.

All object references are stored in the directory as object IDs. Thus, if an attribute references an object that is not stored locally, the server creates an external reference for that object. This means that external references are created on a server if the object is placed as the value of an attribute or property of another object.

### Replica Removal

When you remove a replica of a partition from a server, the directory will create an external reference for each object in the partition. Although each of the objects in the removed replica changes into an external reference, the directory marks each object with a zero modification timestamp. This means that the directory should check the external references at the next backlink interval to see if they are in use by the system. If the external references are not used, the system will clear them out as soon as possible.

## Maintaining External References

External references require updating when the real object is deleted, moved, or renamed, or when the security equivalence has changed. After successfully synchronizing all the replicas of a partition, the directory checks any object that has been renamed, moved, or deleted. The operation that deletes, moves, and renames an object adds obituary attribute values to that object. To maintain consistency between the external references and backlinks, there are backlink obituaries for every backlink attribute of the object.

At the end of a successful replica synchronization of a partition, a portion of the janitor process (known as the *purger*) processes the obituaries on the object in the partition. If NDS finds any backlink obituaries, it notifies the server that contains the object's external reference to update that external reference appropriately. The janitor process is discussed in more detail in Chapter 9.

Periodically, the directory checks the external references to see if the original object still exists. The NDS eDirectory feature that checks the validity of the external references and backlinks is called the *backlink process*. The backlink process is discussed in more detail in Chapter 9.

## Deleting External References

On each server, the directory deletes external references if they have not been accessed for a period of time, which is determined by a SET parameter called External Reference Life Span. The types of external references that will be deleted after a this period of time are the ones created for temporary use. For example, the external references created to support authentication should be removed by the directory after this period of time. In contrast, external references are permanent and should not be deleted if they are created as attribute values of an object (such as group membership) and external references created by the server.

The system administrator can use this directory SET parameter to set the number of hours after which the system deletes external references that are unused. The directory SET parameter that controls the life span for external references is set as follows:

```
SET NDS External Reference Life Span = 192
```

The value of this SET parameter is set in hours. The default value of 192 (hours) or eight days works well, and we recommend that you leave it. The range for this SET parameter is 1 to 384 (in hours). The default is set to eight days so that this operation does not occur in exactly one-week intervals.

When an external reference is accessed, it updates the modification timestamp to the current time. The process that removes the external references builds a list of unused external references by checking the modification timestamp of each external reference compared with the life span interval. Using the default value for this SET parameter, the process removes the external reference after eight days. The process that checks each server to see if the external references are still in use is called the *backlink process* or *backlinker*.

Each time the backlink process runs, the server checks each object ID associated with an external reference to make sure it is still in use. This means that the Directory Entry Tables for the file system need to be scanned, in a process that can be intensive. The janitor process then purges the deleted external references. For more information about the backlink and janitor processes, refer to Chapter 9.

When the directory removes an external reference, the server holding the external reference requests that the server holding the original object or real object delete the backlink attribute value associated with the external reference.

# Obituaries

The directory uses a special attribute of an object called an *obituary* to track renames, moves, and deletions of both objects and external references. Because the directory is loosely consistent, each NetWare 6 server needs a mechanism to keep track or record the instances of the objects. The purpose for the obituaries is to maintain consistency in the instances of objects across all the different replicas of a partition until synchronization is completed.

The obituaries help maintain consistency because each server cannot receive all updates simultaneously. This means that the servers may not hold the same information at a given time. For this reason, each server holds on to the latest set of information until all the other servers holding replicas for a partition receive the updates. The directory uses obituaries to coordinate or keep track of instances of objects.

## Obituary Attribute Values

When an object is moved, renamed, or deleted in the directory, the system adds a new obituary attribute value to the object. There is one obituary for each move, rename, or delete operation. There is an obituary for each backlink attribute and one for each server in the replica pointer table (replica ring). See the "Obituary Types" section later in this chapter for more on the various obituaries.

Because obituaries are attribute values of the object, they are synchronized to the other servers using the same mechanism that all replica synchronization uses. This means that obituaries for the objects are synchronized across replicas of a partition.

For example, when an object is deleted, the directory marks the object as not present, which means not visible to the clients. However, the object is retained in the name service until the removal is propagated to the other servers. The attribute values are removed, and the proper obituaries are established to indicate that the object is no longer logically present. In this case the obituary is of type "dead."

## Obituary Data

The obituary attribute for an object can be a multivalued attribute. The pieces of data for the obituary property or attribute are defined as a string. The obituary property or attribute is made up of the following pieces of data:

► **Obituary type** — Indicates the operation that has taken place on the object.

► **Obituary state** — An obituary goes through several different states as it is processed. The obituary state records the progress.

► **Old creation timestamp** — This is the creation time of the original object.

### Obituary Types

The type of obituary determines the operation being performed. The directory classifies the obituary type internally into two categories: primary and secondary. Typically, when an object is changed, the primary obituary is the mechanism that conveys the change to servers holding replicas of the object. The primary obituaries are used for the types restored, dead, and moved.

Secondary obituaries convey the change to servers holding external references of the changed object. Any given primary obituary can have several secondary obituaries.

The backlink obituary is the only secondary obituary currently in the system. It keeps external references synchronized with the real objects. All other obituaries are primary obituaries that keep track of changes made to the objects themselves.

The specific obituary types are as follows:

► 0 — Restored

► 1 — Dead

► 2 — Moved

► 3 — Inhibit move

► 4 — Old relative distinguished name

► 5 — New relative distinguished name

► 6 — Backlink

► 7 — Tree old relative distinguished name

► 8 — Tree new relative distinguished name

► 9 — Purge all

► 10 — Move subtree

### Obituary States

An obituary goes through several states. The sequence of states progresses as the servers process the operation.

The specific obituary states are as follows:

► 0 — Initial

► 1 — Notified

 ▸ 2 — OK to purge
 ▸ 4 — Purgeable

Figure 8.23 shows how obituaries are used when an object is renamed. The servers CAM-SRV1 and OPS-SRV1 hold a replica of the CAMELOT partition. The user object SIRGALAHAD in the CAMELOT partition is renamed to GALAHAD.

**FIGURE 8.23**  *The user object SIRGALAHAD in the CAMELOT partition is renamed to GALAHAD. The appropriate obituaries are established for each object.*

The rename operation for SIRGALAHAD to GALAHAD is started on the server CAM-SRV1, which establishes a New RDN obituary type for it. This obituary ensures that all servers can access the object using SIRGALAHAD, even if they have not been notified of the name change. The server then creates object GALAHAD and establishes an Old RDN obituary pointing back to the original object. Using this method, the object can be accessed either by the name SIRGALAHAD or GALAHAD while the rename is completed.

In order to complete the rename, each server holding a copy of the SIRGALAHAD object needs to be informed. In this case, the server OPS-SRV1 receives the rename update via normal replica synchronization. After all replicas have been completely synchronized, the servers can delete the SIRGALAHAD object and remove the obituaries. The rename is completed, as shown in Figure 8.24.

**FIGURE 8.24** *The object SIRGALAHAD has completed the rename to GALAHAD, and the obituaries have been removed.*

The process is a little more complicated than shown because the obituaries each go through all the state changes before the operation is completed. A more detailed discussion about the operation and how the obituaries function is included in Chapter 9.

# The Server Partition Table

Each NetWare 6 server maintains a list of the replicas that are physically stored in the server. This list is called the *server partition table*. You can think of the server partition table as the list of partitions that are stored on the server. The server partition table can be viewed using NDS Manager, ConsoleOne, or by using DSREPAIR under the Advanced Options menu from the Replica and Partition Operations menu. Figure 8.25 shows the server partition table on the server NOR-SRV1 as shown from the NDS Manager utility. The server NOR-SRV1 holds a replica of the partitions NORAD and [ROOT].

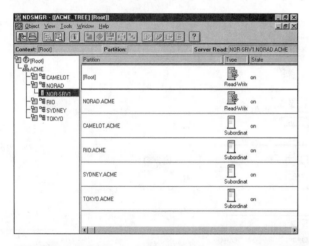

**FIGURE 8.25** *The server partition table on the server NOR-SRV1 as shown from the NDS Manager utility. The server NOR-SRV1 holds a replica of the partitions NORAD and [ROOT]. It also holds the subordinate reference for the CAMELOT, RIO, SYDNEY, and TOKYO partitions.*

The records for the server partition table are stored in the NDS eDirectory data file called 3.DSD. The following information is stored for each replica of a partition located on the server:

> ▸ **Partition name** — The distinguished name of the topmost object in the partition, which is called the *partition root object*

▸ **Replica type** — Master, read/write, read-only, and subordinate reference

▸ **Replica state** — The current state of the replica

▸ **Replica timestamp** — The next timestamp issued for the replica, including the timestamps that are issued for any modification on the replica

The replica state field contains the current state of the replica. This field is used as an attribute that is stored by each replica as defined in Table 8.1.

TABLE 8.1

*The Replica States Definitions*

| STATE | VALUE | DESCRIPTION |
|---|---|---|
| RS_ON | 0 | On |
| RS_NEW_REPLICA | 1 | New replica |
| RS_DYING_REPLICA | 2 | Replica in the process of being removed |
| RS_LOCKED | 3 | Locked |
| RS_CTR_0 | 4 | Change Replica Type, State 0 |
| RS_CTR_1 | 5 | Change Replica Type, State 1 |
| RS_TRANSITION_ON | 6 | Transition On State |
| RS_TRANSITION_MOVE | 7 | Transition Move State |
| RS_TRANSITION_SPLIT | 8 | Transition Split State |
| RS_SS_0 | 48 | Split, State 0 |
| RS_SS_1 | 49 | Split, State 1 |
| RS_JS_0 | 64 | Join, State 0 |
| RS_JS_1 | 65 | Join, State 1 |
| RS_JS_2 | 66 | Join, State 2 |
| RS_MS_0 | 80 | Move Subtree, State 0 |
| RS_MS_1 | 81 | Move Subtree, State 1 |
| RS_MS_2 | 82 | Move Subtree, State 2 |

# NDS eDirectory Partition Structure

An NDS eDirectory partition is created by selecting one container object (usually an organizational unit) as the top of the partition boundary or root of the partition. The distinguished name of the topmost object becomes the name of the partition. This object is also referred to as the *partition root object*.

**TIP**

**Do not confuse the partition root object with the [ROOT] object at the top of the NDS tree. The [ROOT] object is a special container object that defines the top of the NDS tree. The partition root object is just the topmost object in a particular partition.**

When a partition is created, the container object that is selected as the top of the partition has several new attributes added to support replica synchronization. The partition root object is the container object with additional properties or attributes defined that reveal the details of the partition's status and replica placement. These attributes are also used by the directory to synchronize the information between replicas of the partition.

The attributes of the partition root object that define the partition and support the eDirectory functions are defined as follows:

- ▶ **Replica pointer table** — This multivalued attribute stores the list of replicas for the partition.

- ▶ **Synchronized up to** — This multivalued attribute contains a timestamp for each replica in the replica pointer table. Every replica on which modifications have occurred should have a timestamp. Each timestamp indicates the value received from other replicas of the partition. It represents the time that the data is modified up to for that replica. This attribute is often referred to as the *synchronized up to vector*.

- ▶ **Partition creation timestamp** — This attribute is known as the *epoch*. Although this attribute is in the timestamp syntax, it does not hold a time value. Instead, it holds a counter that begins at 1 and increments by 1 for each new epoch. An epoch indicates when the repair timestamp is executed.

- ▶ **Inherited access control list** — This attribute contains access control information inherited from a parent partition. It is the summary of the access control lists to that point in the NDS tree.

▸ **Partition control** — This attribute tracks the progress of partition operations, such as splitting, joining, adding, and deleting replicas.

▸ **Replica up to** — This attribute contains a timestamp for each replica that is used to represent the purge time for replica. This is often called the *replica up to vector* because each replica has a timestamp. This attribute is a forerunner to the next release of NetWare 6. This attribute is localized to a particular server, which means that it is not synchronized to the other servers.

▸ **Partition status** — The status of the last synchronization effort. This value could show errors, if any. The partition status attribute is localized to the server and is not synchronized.

Each of these attributes is discussed in more detail in the following sections.

## The Replica Pointer Table

The replica pointer table stores or references all the servers having a replica of a given partition. The replica pointer table is often referred to as the *replica ring* or *replica list*. Each of these names is equivalent. In this book we refer to the attribute as the replica pointer table. The replica pointer table is an attribute of the partition root object. Each server with a replica of a particular partition has the replica pointer table.

The replica pointer table attribute is extremely important to the internal function of eDirectory. The values in this attribute are used to perform replica synchronization between NetWare 6 servers. For example, when the local replica receives an update from the client, the replica can find the physical location of the other replicas by using the information in the replica pointer table attribute.

The replica pointer tables for each server should be identical. If the replica pointer tables are not identical, your directory will not be capable of completing replica synchronization for the partition.

You can view the replica pointer table by using NDS Manager, ConsoleOne, or DSREPAIR. However, most administrators are more apt to use DSREPAIR because it will be the most accurate and up-to-date reference. Figure 8.26 displays the replica pointer table for the [ROOT] partition, as seen on NOR-SRV1 using the DSREPAIR utility under the Replica Ring option from the Replica and Partition Operations menu.

As mentioned earlier, the replica pointer table should be consistent across all servers that hold a copy of the partition. This means you should get the same results when viewing the replica ring using DSREPAIR, regardless of which server you execute it on.

The replica pointer table attribute contains a list of the replicas for a partition. For each replica on the server, the replica pointer table has an attribute, which contains the server name, replica type, replica state, replica number, and internal IPX address for each server holding replicas of that partition.

**FIGURE 8.26** *The replica pointer table for the [ROOT] partition as seen on NOR-SRV1 using the DSREPAIR utility*

The replica pointer table attributes are as follows:

▸ **Server name** — The server name is the distinguished name of the server where the replica is physically located.

▸ **Replica type** — The replica type indicates the capabilities of the replica. The replica type will have one of the following values: 0=Master; 1=Read/Write (Secondary); 2=Read-Only; and 3=Subordinate Reference.

▸ **Replica state** — This value is typically set to ON. During partition operations, a partition can go through several states. Some of the states include On, New, Dying, Split, and Join. The complete list of replica states is provided in Table 8.1.

▸ **Replica number** — The replica number is assigned when the replica is created by the master replica for the partition. Each replica for a partition has a unique number.

▸ **Partition root object ID** — This is the object ID of the partition root object on the server. The partition root object ID identifies the root-most NDS object of the partition. This value is valid only on the server that stores the local replica of the partition.

▸ **Number of addresses** — The network addresses for the server are held in this value. A server can be accessible over different protocols and will have different network addresses for each protocol. The number of addresses held in this value depends on the number of protocols supported by the server. The IPX internal network number is always held in this value, which indicates the server's last known address. The address has three parts, including the address type (IPX, IP, and so on), address length, and address data.

The example of a replica pointer table in Figure 8.27 might help you understand how it looks. For this example, assume that the servers CAM-SRV1, NOR-SRV1, and TOK-SRV1 all hold replicas of the [ROOT] partition. Also assume that the servers NOR-SRV1, LABS-SRV1, and RD-SRV1 hold replicas of the NORAD partition. A logical representation for the replica pointer table for the [ROOT] partition on server CAM-SRV1 in the ACME tree is shown in the figure.

| SERVER NAME | REPLICA TYPE | REPLICA STATE | REPLICA NUMBER | PARTITION ROOT OBJECT ID | ADDRESS |
|---|---|---|---|---|---|
| CAM-SRV1 | READ/WRITE | ON | 2 | 06001823 | NET ADDRESS/ NODE/SOCKET |
| NOR-SRV1 | MASTER | ON | 1 | 50112030 | NET/NODE/SOCKET |
| TOK-SRV1 | READ/WRITE | ON | 3 | 14830000 | NET/NODE/SOCKET |

**FIGURE 8.27** *The replica pointer table for the [ROOT] partition on server CAM-SRV1 in the ACME tree*

A logical representation for the replica pointer table for the NORAD partition on server NOR-SRV1 in the ACME tree is shown in Figure 8.28.

| SERVER NAME | REPLICA TYPE | REPLICA STATE | REPLICA NUMBER | PARTITION ROOT OBJECT ID | ADDRESS |
|---|---|---|---|---|---|
| NOR-SRV1 | MASTER | ON | 1 | 50112030 | NET/NODE/SOCKET |
| LABS-SRV1 | READ/WRITE | ON | 3 | 81233010 | NET/NODE/SOCKET |
| RD-SRV1 | READ/WRITE | ON | 2 | 61230010 | NET/NODE/SOCKET |
| CAM-SRV1 | SUBORDINATE REFERENCE | ON | 5 | 06182300 | NET/NODE/SOCKET |
| TOK-SRV1 | SUBORDINATE REFERENCE | ON | 4 | 14830000 | NET/NODE/SOCKET |

**FIGURE 8.28** *The replica pointer table for the NORAD partition on server NOR-SRV1 in the ACME tree*

## Synchronized Up To

The synchronized up to attribute is a multivalued attribute that contains a timestamp for each replica in the replica pointer table plus one timestamp for each replica on which modifications have been made. The timestamp indicates the last update and point in time that the local replica has received from other replicas of the partition. This attribute is often referred to as the *synchronized up to vector*.

The synchronized up to attribute is important to the normal operation of the directory because when using this list of timestamps, the replicas of the partition know what information to synchronize between servers. Because the synchronized up to attribute contains the timestamp for updates received for this replica up to a given time, other servers send updates only to this replica after that time. Synchronization tests against the synchronized up to attribute to determine if the other replicas on the other servers need updating. As mentioned earlier, this attribute is often referred to as the *vector* of timestamps for the server.

## The Partition Creation Timestamp

The partition creation timestamp is the attribute that determines the epoch for the partition. The epoch indicates what instance of the partition this is and which replica number is the master. The epoch value starts with 1 and increments by 1 each time the repair timestamp operation is executed. The repair timestamp operation essentially changes the instance of the partition.

During replica synchronization, epoch values are compared to ensure that obsolete information is not passed.

Normal partition and replica operations preserve this partition creation timestamp, although an administrator can change it indirectly by using DSREPAIR and executing the repair timestamp function. Refer to Chapter 10 before using this function to repair timestamps and declaring a new epoch.

The definitions of the partition creation timestamp attributes are given in the list that follows. The individual fields that make up the partition creation timestamp are the same as a regular timestamp. Although the data type or syntax of a timestamp is used, the parts of the timestamp are interpreted differently than those of a regular timestamp. The seconds, replica number, and event ID that make up the timestamp are defined as the following:

- **Seconds** — Holds the epoch counter, starting at 1 and incrementing sequentially by 1.

- **Replica number** — Holds the replica number for the local replica that assigns the epoch for the partition. This is the replica number that holds the master replica.

- **Event ID** — Not used.

## The Inherited Access Control List

The inherited access control list attribute contains the access control information inherited from all the previous parent partitions. The attribute is a summary or cumulative effect of all the access control lists inherited from parent containers down to the object's context in the tree.

The access control list attribute helps the server calculate the rights of the objects more quickly because the security information is local. This means that when calculating rights, the server does not have to go to other servers to find the security or rights information. A server should be capable of making access control decisions using only local information.

NDS eDirectory would be poorly designed if it forced the server to walk the tree and gather all the security or rights information for the users each time they accessed data. The inherited rights access control list attribute of the partition provides the capability of the server to look only at the local partition information to determine security rights all the way back to the [ROOT] object.

## Partition Control

The partition control attribute tracks the progress of partition operations. However, its primary job is to lock out further partition operations until the current one is completed. The partition operations are change replica type, move subtree, split or create partition, join or merge partition, and repair timestamps. The add replica and delete replica operations are not tracked by the partition control attribute.

Typically, the partition sequences through several states as the partition operation progresses. These states are the same states used for the replica states. (See the "Server Partition Table" section earlier in this chapter.)

Because each replica of a partition can have only one state, only one partition operation can be in progress at a time. The master replica of the partition controls the partition operations and acts as a traffic cop.

The partition operation in progress uses the partition control functions defined in Table 8.2.

TABLE 8.2

*The Partition Control Function Definitions*

| FUNCTION | VALUE | DESCRIPTION |
| --- | --- | --- |
| PC_IDLE | 0 | No operation in progress |
| PC_SPLITTING | 1 | Splitting |
| PC_SPLITTING_CHILD | 2 | Splitting child partition |
| PC_JOINING_UP | 3 | Child of two joining partitions |
| PC_JOINING_DOWN | 4 | Parent of two joining partitions |
| PC_MOVE_SUBTREE_SRC | 5 | Source of the move subtree |
| PC_MOVE_SUBTREE_DEST | 6 | Destination of the move subtree |
| PC_LOCKED | 7 | Partition locked |
| PC_REPAIRING_TIMESTAMPS | 8 | Timestamps being repaired |
| PC_CHANGING_REPLICATYPE | 9 | Replicas changing types |

## Replica Up To

New in NetWare 6 is a structure called the replica up to vector. The replica up to vector has been added to the partition root object of each partition. This attribute contains a timestamp for each replica that is used to represent the purge time for a replica. It is called the *replica up to vector* because there is a timestamp for each replica. This attribute is localized to a particular server, which means that it is not synchronized to the other servers.

Because replica up to is kept as a vector with an entry for each replica, the replica convergence can be achieved without having each replica talk to every other replica. The structure of the replica up to vector consists of received up to time stamps for all replicas in a given replica ring. The structure of the replica up to vector includes this information:

- ▶ **Flags** — Replica-specific information
- ▶ **Server** — The ID of the server that holds the replica
- ▶ **Received up to vector** — Time vector for the replica

One entry exists for each replica in the ring. However, subordinate reference replicas do not have an entry in the replica up to vector structure, which means that the subordinate reference replicas no longer participate with the normal replica synchronization.

Replica synchronization uses the replica up to time vector to determine which replicas it needs to synchronize with. Each server has a replica up to vector that keeps track of how up to date each replica is. After successful synchronization, the receiver merges the replica up to vector with the replica up to vector of the sender.

### Partition Status

The partition status attribute provides information about the success or failure of the last replica synchronization cycle. The attribute could contain the directory error codes, if necessary. For more information about the directory error codes, refer to Appendix B.

# Bindery Services

In previous versions of NetWare, information was not available from a distributed directory. Instead, each server in the network stored a database that contained information such as the name, object ID, and password of every user or object that had access to the services provided by that server. The bindery also included information about all the services provided by the server and network.

Because the servers in the network did not share or communicate this information, the user's or object's information was stored separately on every server to which it had rights. For example, if user BTHOMAS had rights to NetWare 3 servers called NCS, ENG1, and MKTG1, his information would be stored on each of the three NetWare 3 servers. Each time BTHOMAS wanted to access services on a different server, he would have to establish a connection and log into that server.

Starting with NetWare 4 and continuing with NetWare 6, the directory provides the network user with a single login to the entire network with access to additional network resources as needed. The user does not have to log into each server to gain the resources on that server. Instead, the directory automatically authenticates the user to the server. Authentication is completed seamlessly for the user.

However, in order for the directory to support backward compatibility for the bindery application and users, it provides the object information to these users through bindery services. These services are on a server-by-server basis. Bindery services enable the objects in a container to be accessed by both directory-enabled clients and bindery-based servers and clients.

Unlike the NDS tree, which is hierarchical, objects in the bindery have no hierarchical relationship (a flat structure), and these objects are specific to one server. To provide access for bindery users and clients, the directory imitates a flat structure for leaf objects within one or more container objects.

## The Server Bindery Context

The server bindery context is the name of the container object(s) where bindery services is set for the server. The server bindery context is also referred to as the *bindery path*. You can set the bindery context using a SET command at the console. In order to set the bindery context for the server NOR-SRV1 in the ACME tree, enter the following command at the server console prompt:

```
SET BINDERY CONTEXT = "OU=NORAD.O=ACME"
```

Bindery-based clients and servers can access the objects subordinate to the containers where the bindery context is set. Because NetWare 6 enables you to set multiple bindery contexts for the server, the handling of the invalid context error has changed. NetWare 6 cannot fail the entire SET command because one of the containers specified may be valid.

In order to see or verify the effective bindery path for a server, you should enter the following command at the server console prompt:

```
CONFIG
```

When you check the effective bindery path by using the CONFIG command, you will see the distinguished names of each container object listed on separate lines. Each container listed here is a valid bindery path. Objects created through bindery services are created as subordinate to the first effective (or valid) bindery path.

In previous versions of NetWare 4, you were limited to setting the bindery context at only one container object. With NetWare 4.11 (or later) and NetWare 6, you can set up to sixteen container objects as the bindery context.

## Multiple Bindery Contexts

When multiple bindery contexts have been defined, a client searches for a bindery object by looking through the containers in the order they appear in the list.

Setting multiple bindery contexts can create one potential problem, which is known as *eclipsing*. In NDS, two objects can have the same relative distinguished name, but the objects must be in different containers. For example, in Figure 8.29, two user objects are created in the ACME tree, each with the relative distinguished name JOHN. These objects exist in the OU=OPS and OU=PR containers. This example assumes that the server bindery context is set to both the OU=OPS and OU=PR containers in that order.

**FIGURE 8.29** *Two user objects are created in the ACME tree with the relative distinguished name JOHN. These objects exist in the OU=OPS and OU=PR containers.*

NDS eDirectory distinguishes between the two objects because their distinguished names are different. However, the bindery client sees only the object's relative distinguished name. If a bindery client searches for the object JOHN, it finds an object in OU=OPS first and stops searching, whether or not that is the object the client is looking for. In this situation, the client is unable to access the object JOHN in the OU=PR container. This effect is called *eclipsing* and occurs only in bindery services, not in NDS.

You can solve this problem by making sure that no two objects in the NDS tree have the same relative distinguished name. A good naming standard is important and should be enforced.

Eclipsing also occurs when a dynamic bindery object has the same name as a static bindery object, although this situation is rare. In such cases, the dynamic object always eclipses the static object.

## Objects in the Bindery

The bindery used in previous versions of NetWare enabled two categories of objects. These object classes are as follows:

- ▸ Static bindery objects
- ▸ Dynamic bindery objects

These object categories are specified by a flag on the object itself. The difference between the static and dynamic categories refers to the longevity expected for each of the objects rather than to a specific type of object.

### Static Bindery Objects

The static bindery objects consist of the normal user, group, print queue, print server, and profile objects defined in the bindery of NetWare 3. These objects are created permanently in the bindery until someone manually deletes them.

When migrated, the static bindery objects are stored in the container objects specified in the bindery context of the NetWare 6 server. If multiple containers are specified in the bindery context, the objects are migrated or placed in the first valid container in the bindery path.

The directory schema defines what attributes each object class has. Thus, it regulates the makeup or creation of each object class. The NetWare 3 bindery is not hierarchical and does not need to distinguish objects by classes. Therefore, the bindery does not have formal schema definitions. However, the bindery does enable specific object types. These object types are used to identify the object within the bindery. For example, objects of type 1 are user objects, and group objects are type 2.

Some of the well-known object types have direct counterparts in the directory schema and can be converted or mutated during installation, migration, or creation. The mutation occurs for object types from the bindery to the appropriate object class. For each bindery object type to be mutated, it must have all the mandatory attributes of the targeted object class and cannot have the same name as another object in the container.

The bindery object types that are mutated by the directory are as follows:

- ▸ User
- ▸ Group
- ▸ Print queue
- ▸ Print server
- ▸ Profile

For example, a client using a bindery-based application wants to create a user object called JOE on a NetWare 6 server in the NDS tree. The application makes a bindery API to create a user object. The request is made as follows:

```
CN=JOE+BinderyType = 1
```

The base object class is a bindery object type. The data is immediately converted to an NDS eDirectory user object class, and the name then becomes the following:

```
CN=JOE
```

**TIP**

**Not all the directory objects in the tree are available or visible to the bindery APIs. Bindery services applies only to leaf objects that are in the NetWare 3 bindery definitions, including the objects for user, group, print queue, print server, and profile. Also included is the bindery object base class CN=XXXX+BinderyType=643.**

### Dynamic Bindery Objects

The dynamic bindery objects are used for Service Advertising Protocol object names and information. This enables the advertising servers or services to have their objects added to the bindery as dynamic objects. For example, these objects are the file server and print server names that use SAP to become known on the network. In NetWare 6 additional services use SAP to become known, such as the NDS tree and time synchronization.

If the bindery is closed and reopened, these objects and their properties are automatically deleted. Figure 8.30 illustrates how the information from the network would be directed logically to the appropriate section of the bindery according to the type of information.

Figure 8.30 is a logical representation of the bindery services. In reality, the bindery does not have separate sections for dynamic and static information. All bindery information is stored in the bindery files. The properties of the dynamic objects are mostly network addresses.

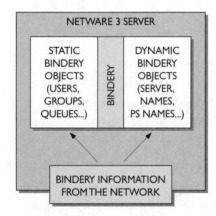

**FIGURE 8.30** *NetWare 3 bindery information from the network is directed to the appropriate section of the bindery according to the type of information.*

In order for NetWare 6 to be completely compatible with previous versions of NetWare, the dynamic bindery objects need to be supported. Because the bindery no longer stores objects in NetWare 6, the directory must provide this functionality.

The parent objects of dynamic bindery objects are not in the directory hierarchy. They are not associated with a specific parent container in the tree. Instead, the dynamic bindery objects are stored in the NDS eDirectory internal partition called the *Bindery partition.* These objects can be accessed by a bindery client or server and are not dependent on whether the bindery context is set for the server.

Figure 8.31 illustrates logically how the information from the network would be directed to the appropriate section of the directory to provide the same function as the bindery.

Figure 8.31, like Figure 8.30, is a logical representation of the directory. In reality, the directory does not have separate sections for the dynamic bindery object information. All the dynamic bindery objects are located physically adjacent to the other objects in the NDS eDirectory data files. See Figure 8.32 for an illustration of the object data file. The properties of the dynamic objects are mostly network addresses.

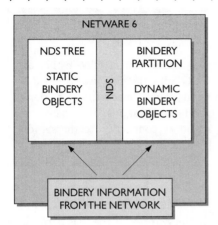

**FIGURE 8.3 I** *Information from the network is directed to the appropriate section of NDS to provide the same function as the bindery.*

ENTRY.NDS (OBJECT DATA FILE)

| USER | GROUP | DYNAMIC BINDERY | ORG. | DYNAMIC BINDERY | . . . | USER |
|------|-------|-----------------|------|-----------------|-------|------|

**FIGURE 8.32** *An example of the object data file in NDS eDirectory. Notice that the dynamic bindery objects are stored adjacent to all the other objects.*

## The Bindery Supervisor Account

The bindery Supervisor account is created during the installation of the server. The Supervisor is a server-centric account created on every NetWare 6 server. This account is created even when NDS eDirectory replicas are installed on that server or when a bindery services context is set on the server. However, the Supervisor user is only accessible if a valid bindery context is set for the server. This is true with the exception of the Server Console Lock and Unlock operation, which can be performed using the Supervisor password.

The Supervisor account is not seen as an object of the NDS tree because it is server-centric. The Supervisor user is stored in the bindery partition, which is one of the four partitions that exists even if an NDS eDirectory replica is not installed on the server.

**Consulting Experience**

Although it is possible to use the administrative utilities, such as NWADMIN, to create an object in the directory tree called SUPERVISOR, the new user is not the same Supervisor user seen in the bindery. Any modifications made to the bindery Supervisor account are limited to bindery-based modifications. The individual logging in as the Supervisor user has to have a bindery connection to the server and use the bindery-based utilities.

The Supervisor account has all rights to the individual server, which includes the objects and file system. This is the same as NetWare 3. If there is a bindery services context(s) set on the server, the Supervisor user will automatically have all rights to the bindery objects in the context(s). The Supervisor account has rights only to the objects that are also bindery objects. For example, these objects are users, groups, queues, print servers, and profiles. Because the Supervisor user does not show up in the NDS tree, you cannot log in as Supervisor using a directory connection. This means that the NWADMIN utility cannot be used by someone logged in as Supervisor. The Supervisor account can only access the objects using the SYSCON utility in NetWare 3.

The Supervisor account will always be assigned a password during creation. This was not the case in previous versions of NetWare 4 (specifically NetWare 4.01) because the individual installing the server was not required to have a password. The Supervisor user receives its password during creation under the following conditions:

▶ The server is a new NetWare 6 server that is not migrated from NetWare 3. The Supervisor is assigned the password of the user, typically the ADMIN user, which logs into the tree to perform the installation of the server.

▶ The server is being migrated from NetWare 3 to NetWare 6 using the INSTALL program. The Supervisor account information remains the same as before the upgrade. If the Supervisor account in NetWare 3 does not have a password, the password of the user (usually ADMIN) that logged in to the tree to do the installation is assigned to the bindery Supervisor in NetWare 6.

▸ The server is being migrated from NetWare 3 to NetWare 6 using the Novell Upgrade Wizard utility. When you migrate using the Upgrade Wizard utility, the NetWare 6 server is already installed and running. This means that the Supervisor account on the new NetWare 6 server is already created and has a password. The password is created according to the first condition in this list.

It is important that you safeguard the password for the Supervisor. The password that the Supervisor is assigned is not completely synchronized with the user that installs the new NetWare 6 server into the tree. If the ADMIN user ever changes its password, the password for the Supervisor account is not changed. The two accounts are completely separate after the initial installation.

## The DS Client

We typically think of clients as the workstation software that logs the user into the network and accesses the network services. However, each NetWare 6 server uses the built-in client software to attach and authenticate the server to the other NetWare 6 servers. Thus, the servers become clients of the other servers in the NDS tree. The client software used to support server-to-server connections is called the directory client or DS client.

Because the directory is distributed and replicated among any of the NetWare 6 servers in the network, one server may need the NDS eDirectory information stored by another server. This mechanism provides the interconnectivity needed to support all the multiple server operations and processes. The DS client is sometimes referred to as the *virtual client*. (This term is used mainly in DSTRACE.)

The NetWare 6 servers use the same protocol as the workstation software to establish and authenticate to the other servers. The authentication process is initiated as a background authentication procedure.

The connection made by the DS client between NetWare 6 servers is viewed in the MONITOR utility on the server. The connections made from server to server authenticate using the distinguished name of the NetWare 6 server object. These connections are marked with an asterisk (*) to indicate that the connection is not a licensed connection but rather an authenticated directory connection.

Figure 8.33 shows the DS client connections made between servers on the MONITOR screen for the servers CAM-SRV1 and NOR-SRV1 in the ACME tree.

**FIGURE 8.33** *These DS client connections are made between servers on the MONITOR screen for the servers CAM-SRVI and NOR-SRVI in the ACME tree.*

The messages related to the DS client can be viewed on the directory screen at the server console using the SET DSTRACE command VCLIENT (VC or virtual client). The command is entered as follows:

```
SET DSTRACE = +VCLIENT
```

The other NetWare 6 servers occupy not only many of the directory connections but also the NOT LOGGED IN connections that may be shown on the MONITOR screen. Other NetWare 6 servers perform the name resolution operation using the NOT LOGGED IN connection type and do not need to authenticate.

### Consulting Experience

If your servers are communicating using IPX, then it is very important that you do not filter the Routing Information Protocol (RIP) from your NetWare 6 network. If RIP is being filtered, the NetWare 6 servers will not be capable of finding each other to synchronize. The directory stores the addresses for the other NetWare 6 servers in its replica pointer table; however, it needs to find the route using RIP.

# Name Resolution (Tree Walking) Operation

NDS eDirectory's primary responsibility is to retrieve requested object or network resource information from the servers distributed across the network. The directory locates the object information using the operation or mechanism called *name resolution*. This operation walks the partitions of the NDS tree to locate objects or specific information requested by the user or client. Name resolution occurs when the client requests object information from the directory and the NetWare 6 servers. If the object information is not on the server to which the client is connected, the process will walk or navigate through the partitions on the other NetWare 6 servers to find the correct information. Name resolution is often called *tree walking*.

Name resolution starts with a distinguished name for an NDS object in the tree and attempts to obtain the object ID for the searched object on a specific server. The name resolution returns a list of addresses for servers that store the requested object information. Before we discuss the specific details associated with name resolution, we need to quickly review the concepts of NDS partitions and replicas.

## NDS Partition Review

As mentioned previously, the NDS tree can be divided into pieces or sub-trees called partitions and stored on the NetWare 6 servers as NDS replicas. Partitioning provides distribution of the directory information across the NetWare 6 servers.

Each partition is named by the container object at the root of the subtree called the partition root object. The partition root objects have additional properties or attributes that are used to find the directory information on other servers and keep it synchronized. These additional attributes are as follows:

- ▸ **Replica pointer table** — Stores the list of replicas for the partition
- ▸ **Synchronized up to** — Contains a timestamp for each replica in the replica pointer table
- ▸ **Partition creation timestamp** — Determines the epoch for the partition.

▶ **Inherited access control list** — Contains access control information inherited from the parent partitions

▶ **Partition control** — Tracks the progress of partition operations like splitting, joining, change replica type, and move subtree operations

▶ **Partition status** — Contains information regarding the last synchronization attempt

## Subordinate Reference Replica Review

Different types of replicas can be stored on the NetWare 6 servers. These replicas are the physical representation of the NDS tree. The replica type that helps the NDS tree stay physically connected is the subordinate reference replica. A subordinate reference replica is created by the directory on a server that holds a replica of the parent partition but not the child partitions.

The subordinate reference replica for a partition does not contain all of the objects in that partition. Instead, the subordinate reference contains only a copy of the partition root object (or the topmost object of the partition), including all its properties and attributes.

Because the subordinate reference replica holds a copy of the partition root object, it contains information such as the location of all the other replicas for the partition. An example of the contents of a subordinate reference replica for the partition CAMELOT, which is stored on server NOR-SRV1, is shown in Figure 8.34.

The replica pointer table property contains a list of the replicas for a partition. The list holds the server name, replica type, replica state, replica number, object ID for the partition root object, and addresses for each of the servers in the replica pointer table. Using this information, the subordinate reference replicas not only keep the NDS tree connected but also can aid in the procedure to resolve a name.

## Name Resolution Methods

The purpose of the name resolution or tree walking mechanism is to eliminate the necessity of the user's or client's awareness of the physical location of network resources. The term *name resolution* literally means resolving a name to an address; in this case, the address of the server where the requested object is stored.

**FIGURE 8.34** *A subordinate reference replica for the partition CAMELOT, which is stored on server NOR-SRV1, contains the replica pointer table for the partition.*

In Figure 8.35 the client or workstation requests information about an NDS object. Because the client is currently authenticated to the server CAM-SRV1, that server tries to fulfill the request. Unable to fulfill the request, CAM-SRV1 walks the tree on behalf of the client. In this case, CAM-SRV1 contacts the server NOR-SRV1. The server NOR-SRV1 returns its lack of success. CAM-SRV1 contacts RIO-SRV1, which responds negatively. This process continues until the requested object information is located on SYD-SRV1. The physical location information is returned to the client. The client, in turn, connects directly to SYD-SRV1 to read the object information.

**FIGURE 8.35** *The workstation makes a request for information about an object to the server CAM-SRV1. Then the server CAM-SRV1 contacts the other servers to find the object.*

The name resolution requests are made for only specific replica types. Even though the server may have the object information requested, it may not have the right type of replica to support the request made by the client. For example, the client wants to modify a certain object. If a read-only replica responds, it will not help. The replica type is an important part of the request for name resolution.

The name resolution operation is used to access resources and find object information during login and authentication. In other words, a client requesting information about an object is serviced by the server using the name resolution or tree walking process in the following ways:

- Object found on the local server
- Walk down the tree to locate the object
- Walk up the tree to locate the object
- Walk up and down the tree to locate the object
- Server without a replica

When the client makes the request for object information, the distinguished name of the object is always used. NDS eDirectory uses the individual relative distinguished name (RDN) to compare against the values at each server. Using this method, the directory will determine if the information is on the local servers or whether it needs to go to other servers holding information up or down the tree.

If the current NetWare 6 server contains a replica with the requested object information or target object, the directory completes the request by returning the physical location of the object information. In this case, the physical location of the object information is returned to the client. The physical location is the network address for the local server. If the directory determines that the name resolution operation will have to walk the tree (up or down), the local server acts as a proxy on behalf of the client to contact the other NetWare 6 servers.

Assuming that the object information exists down the tree from the information stored on the local server, the server will read the replica pointer table (replica ring) for the partitions that are down the tree. The server can use subordinate references replicas to locate the server(s) holding the child partition. In an interesting twist, the name resolution operation uses the attributes of the subordinate reference replicas to navigate up the tree to locate the servers that store replicas for the parent partition. The following sections discuss the details of each case.

### Object Found on the Local Server

When the client makes the request for object information, it passes the distinguished name to the server it is connected to. If the NetWare 6 server contains a replica with the requested object information or target object, the directory completes the request by passing the physical location of the object information back to the client. In this case, the physical location of the object information is the network address of the local server. The client then makes the read request for the specific object or property information.

For example, a workstation is connected to the server NOR-SRV1 in the ACME tree. The server NOR-SRV1 holds the master replicas of the NORAD and [ROOT] partitions, as illustrated in Figure 8.36.

**FIGURE 8.36** *The workstation is connected to the server NOR-SRV1 in the ACME tree. The server holds replicas of the NORAD and [ROOT] partitions.*

The workstation requests the location information about the user object AEINSTEIN.LABS.NORAD.ACME. The server NOR-SRV1 first checks to see if it has a copy of the requested object. Because NOR-SRV1 holds a replica (master replica) of the partition that contains the object information, it returns the physical location of the object information and the object ID back to the workstation. In this case, the physical location of the object information is the network address of NOR-SRV1. The workstation can then continue or complete the request (read, modify, and so on).

### Walk down the Tree to Locate the Object

If the object information is not found on the local server, the directory will determine that it needs to either walk down or up the tree based on the distinguished name of the object being requested. The direction that the directory searches, either up or down, is determined by using a partial match on the distinguished name.

The matching that occurs for the names is processed from the root to the leaf (top to bottom). Any given name is matched object by object or parent by parent, checking each of the subordinate objects. The name is processed in this fashion until the object is found, or the names do not match and there is not a subordinate object for the parent. The subordinate reference replicas are then read (if going down), and the process continues on the next server.

If the directory has determined that it must walk down the tree, the server that the workstation originally connected to uses the subordinate reference replicas of the name being located. Remember, the subordinate reference replicas are created on servers that have a copy of the parent partition but not the child partition. Therefore, each server that has a replica of a parent partition knows the location of each child partition using the subordinate reference replicas.

In this case, the subordinate reference replica of the partition is used to provide the best partial match to the distinguished name of the object requested. Using the DS client, the server connects to the nearest server holding a correct replica type of the child partition based on a least-cost route.

For example, the workstation is connected to the server NOR-SRV1 in the ACME tree. The ACME tree is partitioned at each of the major cities. The NORAD partition is further partitioned at OU=R&D and OU=WHI, as shown in Figure 8.37. The partitions [ROOT] and NORAD are held by the server NOR-SRV1. The servers R&D-SRV1 and WHI-SRV1 hold the master replicas of their respective partitions as illustrated.

A workstation sends a request to NOR-SRV1 for the information about the user object LDAVINCI.R&D.LABS.NORAD.ACME. NDS first checks it to see if it has a copy of the requested object. Because NOR-SRV1 does not hold the object information, DS must look on another server.

DS compares each segment of the distinguished name of the object with the information stored on the server. By comparing and matching the names available on the server, the name resolution operation determines whether the object information is subordinate to (down) the tree or up the tree.

**FIGURE 8.37** *The workstation is connected to the server NOR-SRV1 in the ACME tree. The server NOR-SRV1 holds replicas of the NORAD and [ROOT] partitions. The servers R&D-SRV1 and WHI-SRV1 hold the master replicas of their respective partitions.*

Determining that the object information is down the tree, the server that the workstation originally connected to walks the NDS tree as a proxy agent on behalf of the workstation. In this case, the NOR-SRV1 performs the proxy for the workstation. In order to locate the servers that contain the lower-level partitions, the server NOR-SRV1 uses the subordinate reference replicas that go down according to the name matched. In this case, the R&D subordinate reference replica is used. The server NOR-SRV1 reads the replica pointer table for the R&D subordinate reference replica, as shown in Figure 8.38.

| SERVER NAME | REPLICA TYPE | REPLICA STATE | REPLICA NUMBER | PARTITION ROOT OBJECT I.D. | ADDRESS |
|---|---|---|---|---|---|
| R&D-SRV1 | M | ON | 1 | 06040000 | Net Address/ Node/Socket |
| NOR-SRV1 | SR | ON | 2 | 14015016 | Net Address/ Node/Socket |

**FIGURE 8.38** *The replica pointer table for the R&D partition. The replica pointer table is an attribute of a replica. In this case, the replica is the subordinate reference replica stored on the server NOR-SRV1.*

Using this information, the NOR-SRV1 connects to the R&D-SRV1 using the DS client software (server-to-server connection). Because the server R&D-SRV1 holds the requested object information for LDAVINCI.R&D.LABS.NORAD.ACME, the tree walking phase is completed. The server R&D-SRV1 verifies to NOR-SRV1 that it has a copy of the object information. In turn, the server NOR-SRV1 returns the physical location of the object information back to the workstation. In this case, the physical location of the object information is the network address of R&D-SRV1. DS automatically authenticates the workstation to the server R&D-SRV1 to access or read the object information associated with the request.

Figure 8.39 logically illustrates the following name resolution steps that were performed for the preceding example:

1. The workstation makes a request to access specific object information. The server NOR-SRV1 receives the request.
2. The object information is not stored on the NOR-SRV1 server. The server checks the R&D subordinate reference replica and reads the replica pointer table for the R&D partition.
3. The server NOR-SRV1 makes a request for the object information to the server R&D-SRV1.
4. The server R&D-SRV1 sends a list of the physical locations of the object plus the object IDs. In this case, it is the server address of R&D-SRV1.

**5.** The list is returned to the workstation of the servers that contain the object location. In this case, the server R&D-SRV1 is the only server.

**6.** The directory automatically connects the workstation to server R&D-SRV1 to provide access to the object information.

**FIGURE 8.39** *Name resolution steps*

### Requested Object Information on Multiple Servers

Consider the preceding example in which the workstation is requesting object information for the user object LDAVINCI.R&D.LABS.NORAD.ACME. What would happen if the server WHI-SRV1 also holds a read/write replica for the R&D partition? In this case, the replica pointer table for the partition R&D would appear as shown in Figure 8.40.

If more than one server holds a replica or copy of the partition that contains the information, DS will take that into account. Once the object information is located and the list of servers that can satisfy the request is found, a referral list (list of server addresses) is built from the replica pointer table of the object's partition. The server builds the referral list and passes it back to the client. This client may be the DS client of the current NetWare 6 server performing the proxy for the workstation. Again, the referral list is the list of all the server addresses that have the requested replica type for the partition.

| SERVER NAME | REPLICA TYPE | REPLICA STATE | REPLICA NUMBER | PARTITION ROOT OBJECT I.D. | ADDRESS |
|---|---|---|---|---|---|
| R&D-SRV1 | M | ON | 1 | 06040000 | Net Address/ Node/Socket |
| NOR-SRV1 | SR | ON | 2 | 14015016 | Net Address/ Node/Socket |
| WHI-SRV1 | R/W | ON | 3 | 83621020 | Net Address/ Node/Socket |

**FIGURE 8.40** *The replica pointer table for the partition R&D with the WHI-SRV1 added. The WHI-SRV1 server has a read/write replica of the partition.*

When the current server has found the referral list of servers by proxy for the workstation, it passes the list to the workstation. Once this referral list is received by the workstation, it makes a Routing Information Protocol (RIP) request for each server in the referral list. The purpose of the RIP requests is to determine which server is the closest according to the least-cost route. The workstation is responsible for determining the costing for each server based on a least-cost algorithm (number of ticks).

### Walk up the Tree to Locate the Object

If the directory determines that it needs to walk up the tree, the servers use the replica pointer tables from the root-most partition stored on the server to find other NetWare 6 servers in the tree. In the previous example (walking down the tree), the subordinate references were used to locate object information lower in the tree. Actually, the subordinate reference replicas stored in the replica pointer table of a server can also be used to walk up the tree to find an object.

Remember, the replica pointer table for a replica contains all the server names, server addresses, replica types, and so on for a particular partition. Using the information contained in a replica pointer table of a partition, DS can determine not only where the child partitions are but also the names and addresses for the servers that hold copies of the parent partition.

DS creates a subordinate reference replica on a server that holds a replica of the parent partition but not the child partitions. Thus, it can be reasoned that a server holding a replica of the child partition has knowledge of the parent servers storing the subordinate references. To illustrate how the information in the replica pointer table can be used to walk up the tree, see Figure 8.41.

For this example, assume that a workstation is connected to the server R&D-SRV1. The workstation requests information about the user object ADMIN.ACME.

NDS first checks the server R&D-SRV1 to see if it has a copy of the requested object. Because R&D-SRV1 does not hold the object information, DS must look on another server.

[ROOT]

O=ACME

OU=NORAD    OU=RIO    OU=CAMELOT    OU=TOKYO    OU=SYDNEY

OU=CHARITY    OU=LABS    OU=PR

AEINSTEIN

OU=R&D    OU=WHI

NOR-SRV1

[ROOT]-M
R&D-SR
NORAD-M
RIO-SR
CAMELOT-SR
TOKYO-SR
SYDNEY-SR
WHI-SR

R&D-SRV1

R&D-M

WHI-SRV1

WHI-M
R&D-R/W

**FIGURE 8.41** *The server NOR-SRV1 in the ACME tree holds replicas of the NORAD and [ROOT] partitions with subordinate reference replicas as needed. The servers R&D-SRV1 and WHI-SRV1 hold the master replicas of their respective partitions. The server WHI-SRV1 holds a read/write replica for the R&D partition.*

DS compares names and determines that the object information is up the tree. The server R&D-SRV1 begins walking the NDS tree as a proxy agent on behalf of the workstation. In order to locate the servers that contain the upper-level information, the server reads the replica pointer table for the R&D partition, as shown in Figure 8.42.

| SERVER NAME | REPLICA TYPE | REPLICA STATE | REPLICA NUMBER | PARTITION ROOT OBJECT I.D. | ADDRESS |
|---|---|---|---|---|---|
| R&D-SRV1 | M | ON | 1 | 06040000 | Net Address/ Node/Socket |
| NOR-SRV1 | SR | ON | 2 | 14015016 | Net Address/ Node/Socket |
| WHI-SRV1 | R/W | ON | 3 | 83261020 | Net Address/ Node/Socket |

**FIGURE 8.42** *The replica pointer table for the partition R&D. The replica pointer table is the same on every server that stored a replica of the R&D partition. In this case, replicas are located on the servers R&D-SRV1 (master replica), WHI-SRV1 (read/write replica), and NOR-SRV1 (subordinate reference replica).*

The replica pointer is an attribute of the partition root object of a replica, which means that this information is available on every server that stores a replica of the partition. In this case, replicas are on the servers R&D-SRV1 (master replica), WHI-SRV1 (read/write replica), and NOR-SRV1 (subordinate reference replica).

By reading the replica pointer table, the server R&D-SRV1 sorts the server addresses according to least cost and contacts one. Either one of these addresses could have the object information. If the server WHI-SRV1 is contacted, then it reads its root-most partition and returns the referral list. In this case, WHI-SRV1 is no closer than R&D-SRV1. Next, the server NOR-SRV1 is contacted. NOR-SRV1 matches the name and finds the object. The location and object ID are returned in the referral list to R&D-SRV1. In turn, R&D-SRV1 sends the referral list to the client.

You may think that because the server NOR-SRV1 holds the subordinate reference replica, it would be given preference as the first server to contact. However, servers with subordinate reference replicas are not given preference over other servers in the replica pointer table of the server R&D.

### No Subordinate Reference Replicas for a Partition

It is possible for a NetWare 6 server to have replicas for a partition, and the partition not to have any subordinate reference replica types. This would be the case if all servers that held parent partitions also held the child partitions.

In this situation the server information in the replica pointer table guarantees a server with a parent partition. Remember, if the server with a parent partition does not hold the child partition, then a subordinate reference replica is created.

To illustrate this issue, consider the previous example but with a slight modification. Change the replica type on the server NOR-SRV1 from a subordinate reference replica to a read/write replica for the R&D partition, as shown in Figure 8.43.

**FIGURE 8.43** *The server NOR-SRV1 in the ACME tree holds replicas of the [ROOT], NORAD, and R&D partitions with subordinate reference replicas as needed. The servers R&D-SRV1 and WHI-SRV1 hold the master replicas of their respective partitions. In addition, the server WHI-SRV1 holds a read/write replica for the R&D partition.*

The station that is connected to the server R&D-SRV1 requests information about the user object AEINSTEIN.LABS.NORAD.ACME. NDS checks the R&D-SRV1 server to see if it has a copy of the requested object. R&D-SRV1 does not hold the object information, so NDS must find another server.

By comparing the names, the directory determines that the object information is up the tree. The server R&D-SRV1 performs the tree walking as the proxy on behalf of the workstation. In order to locate the servers that contain the upper-level information, the server reads the replica pointer table for the R&D partition, as shown in Figure 8.44.

| SERVER NAME | REPLICA TYPE | REPLICA STATE | REPLICA NUMBER | PARTITION ROOT OBJECT I.D. | ADDRESS |
|---|---|---|---|---|---|
| R&D-SRV1 | M | ON | 1 | 06040000 | Net Address/ Node/Socket |
| WHI-SRV1 | R/W | ON | 2 | 83261020 | Net Address/ Node/Socket |
| NOR-SRV1 | R/W | ON | 3 | 47819010 | Net Address/ Node/Socket |

**FIGURE 8.44** *The replica pointer table for the partition R&D. The replica pointer table is the same on every server that stored a replica of the R&D partition. In this case, replicas are on the servers R&D-SRV1 (master replica), WHI-SRV1 (read/write replica), and NOR-SRV1 (read/write replica). Notice that this partition has no subordinate references.*

NDS eDirectory reads the replica pointer table on the current server, which is R&D-SRV1. The closest server (least cost) in the replica pointer table is used.

R&D-SRV1 would connect to either server WHI-SRV1 or server NOR-SRV1 in the hope that they could offer more information about moving up the tree. If the server WHI-SRV1 is contacted, it could not offer more information about walking up the tree because of the replicas it stores. The WHI-SRV1 does not have a replica closer to the [ROOT] than R&D, so the referral list returned is discarded by R&D-SRV1.

If the server NOR-SRV1 is contacted, then you have found the server that holds the parent partition. The object information is found in the NORAD partition, and the name resolution sends back a referral list. In this fashion, the directory can walk up the tree using the replica pointer table, whether a subordinate reference replica exists or not.

### Walk up and down the Tree to Locate the Object

When DS needs to find information about an object that is located in the NDS tree in peer partitions, the name resolution operation walks up the tree to the nearest common parent and then back down.

For example, a workstation is connected to the server R&D-SRV1 in the ACME tree. The ACME tree is partitioned at each of the major cities. The NORAD partition is further partitioned at OU=R&D and OU=WHI, as shown in Figure 8.45. The partitions [ROOT] and NORAD are held by the server NOR-SRV1. The server CAM-SRV1 holds the master replica of the CAMELOT partition, while the servers R&D-SRV1 and WHI-SRV1 hold their respective partitions.

**FIGURE 8.45** *The workstation is connected to the server R&D-SRV1 in the ACME tree. The server NOR-SRV1 holds replicas of the NORAD and [ROOT] partitions. The server CAM-SRV1 holds the CAMELOT partition, while the servers R&D-SRV1 and WHI-SRV1 hold their respective partitions.*

Figure 8.46 logically illustrates the name resolution steps that are performed to resolve the name MERLIN.DIST.OPS.CAMELOT.ACME starting from the server R&D-SRV1:

**FIGURE 8.46** *These name resolution steps are performed to resolve the name MERLIN.DIST.OPS.CAMELOT.ACME starting from the server R&D-SRV1.*

**1.** A workstation makes a request for information about the user object MERLIN.DIST.OPS.CAMELOT.ACME. The server R&D-SRV1 receives the request. The server R&D-SRV1 performs the proxy on behalf of the workstation.

**2.** NDS eDirectory checks R&D-SRV1 first to see if it has a copy of the requested object by comparing names. Because R&D-SRV1 does not hold the object information, the directory must look on another server. In order to locate the servers that possibly contain the proper partitions, the server R&D-SRV1 uses the replica pointer table of the root-most partition on the server — in this case, the R&D partition.

**3.** R&D-SRV1 makes a proxy request for the object information to the server NOR-SRV1 because it is the only other server in the replica pointer table (replica ring).

**4.** The server NOR-SRV1 then determines (by comparing names) if the object information is found locally or if the directory needs to continue walking up or down the tree. The object information is not found locally on NOR-SRV1. And because the server NOR-SRV1 has a subordinate reference replica of the CAMELOT partition, it continues walking down the tree to find MERLIN.DIST.OPS.CAMELOT.ACME in the CAMELOT partition.

**5.** NOR-SRV1 sends a referral list (replica pointer table of the partition CAMELOT) of the servers that could possibly hold the object information back to R&D-SRV1. In this case, the referral list is the server address for CAM-SRV1.

**6.** R&D-SRV1 makes a proxy request for the object information to the server CAM-SRV1 because it contains the partition CAMELOT.

**7.** The server CAM-SRV1 determines (by comparing names) if the object information is found locally or if the directory needs to continue walking up or down the tree. The object information for MERLIN.DIST.OPS. CAMELOT.ACME is found locally on CAM-SRV1 in the CAMELOT partition.

**8.** CAM-SRV1 sends a referral list back to R&D-SRV1 of the servers that contain the object information. In this case, the list is the server address for CAM-SRV1.

**9.** The referral list is returned to the workstation for the servers that contain the object information, which includes the object ID. In this case, the server CAM-SRV1 is the only server.

**10.** The workstation contacts server CAM-SRV1 to provide access to the object information.

The DS client software provides the server-to-server connections for walking the trees. Because the server R&D-SRV1 did not hold the requested object information for MERLIN.DIST.OPS.CAMELOT.ACME, the tree walking was performed by the directory transparent to the user of the workstation.

### Server without an NDS Replica

If the workstation attaches to a server that has no NDS replicas, DS must locate another NetWare 6 server. When a server without replicas receives a request for object information, the server sends a service request for SAP type 0x0278 to the network. The SAP type 0x0278 is the NDS tree SAP. Another NetWare 6 server that is part of the NDS tree will respond.

NetWare 6 servers without replicas connect to the tree using SAP type 0x0278. The servers without replicas run the limber process (described later in "The Limber Process" section), check external references, and provide authentication services just like a server with NDS replicas.

### Caching to Support Authentication

The total time required to authenticate between NetWare 6 servers is reduced through caching important information. The reduction is a result of the NetWare 6 servers remembering the object IDs of each of the servers they connected to during previous authentications. Storing the object ID for the other servers enables the time required to authenticate to those servers to be reduced in the future.

The specific information cached is the object ID of the server object on the other (remote) server. For example, if NOR-SRV1 authenticates to R&D-SRV1, then NOR-SRV1 stores the object ID for the R&D-SRV1 and vice versa.

## NDS eDirectory Background Processes

The information for NDS eDirectory is loosely consistent, meaning that after a modification is made on a replica and before synchronization, the data will be different from one replica to another. Several NDS eDirectory background processes are implemented to ensure synchronization of directory data over a period of time. Most notable among these background processes is replica synchronization, which synchronizes the information between replicas of the NDS eDirectory partitions.

The other NDS eDirectory background processes run periodically and are responsible for a number of internal operations that keep the information on all servers in the directory tree consistent. All of these background processes execute automatically without user or administrator intervention. Many of these processes can be forced to execute immediately by using the SET parameters for DSTRACE. There are other SET parameters for the Directory that control the interval between execution for a few of the background processes.

### The Replica Synchronization Process

NDS eDirectory is a loosely consistent database, meaning that changes or updates can occur at various replicas and that not all the replicas may have the exact information at the same time. However, because the directory is loosely synchronized, an update made at one replica propagates to other replicas of the partition over time. The replicas work together to exchange the information to perform all updates. These changes are automatically sent to the other replicas of that partition by a background process called *replica synchronization*. Replica synchronization guarantees consistency of the information across all the replicas of a partition.

The updates or modifications that affect the NDS eDirectory data include adding, deleting, moving, or renaming an object, as well as changing the properties or attributes of an object. Replica synchronization passes only the data that has changed for each object or property between the replicas of the partition. Passing only the information that is updated ensures that the information sent is reduced and that network traffic for synchronization is kept to a minimum.

Replica synchronization is a background process that is event driven. Any modification to the eDirectory database activates replica synchronization. This means that replica synchronization is scheduled to run on a server after an object or property on that server has been updated. The process is scheduled according to the property or attribute being changed. Each property has a flag that determines if it is high convergence or not. The flag has the following settings:

▸ Fast synchronization (high convergence)

▸ Slow synchronization (not high convergence)

### Fast Synchronization

Fast synchronization is the normal synchronization, which is scheduled to occur ten seconds after a client update event occurs on the server. The changes or updates to objects that are made by the client are scheduled using fast synchronization. Synchronization scheduled for ten seconds after the first update that is received enables several subsequent modifications, if any, to be processed simultaneously.

### Slow Synchronization

When a user logs into the NDS tree, four properties or attributes of the user object are changed. These properties are as follows:

▸ Network address

▸ Last login time

▸ Current login time

▸ Revision count

Slow synchronization is login-related synchronization scheduled to occur 30 minutes after the login event. The properties or attributes that are used when a user logs in to the network are scheduled for slow synchronization.

The network address property added to the user objects when they log in indicates the physical workstation address from which the user is logging in. The last login time and current login time properties are modified to reflect the current status.

### How Legacy Replica Synchronization Works

Replica synchronization involves updating all the replicas for a specific partition with all the changes made to the partition since the last synchronization cycle. The process takes the replica pointer table (replica ring) and synchronizes each of these one at a time with the most recent changes. The process must contact the servers in the replica ring one at a time to complete a synchronization cycle for the partition. This type of synchronization is referred to as legacy because it occurs only between servers where one server is running NetWare 4 versions.

Every time replica synchronization starts, it processes each of the replicas in the replica ring in a sequential order. Therefore, the first replica is synchronized first, followed by the second one, and so on. Because the replica ring is identical on all the servers holding copies of this partition, synchronization affects all the replicas for each partition in the same order. This may have an undesirable effect of multiple servers trying to synchronize with the same replica on the same server simultaneously. Because only one inbound synchronization is supported per partition (not per server), one of the synchronization processes will have to back off and attempt again at a later time. This situation only arises if synchronization tends to execute at approximately the same time on multiple servers.

To help alleviate this situation, NetWare 6 changes the sequence in which replicas are processed by randomizing the replica ring list before attempting to contact the first server. This reduces the possibility that one of the servers will have to back off and attempt to resynchronize with a replica.

The subordinate reference replicas are included in synchronization for a partition because they are found in the replica pointer table for a partition. This means that each of the replicas, including the subordinate reference replicas, is contacted during the synchronization cycle. The subordinate reference replica contains only the partition root object, and its changes to that object are synchronized. The synchronized up to attribute of the partition root object changes frequently and is typically the only value synchronized for a subordinate reference replica.

After a server successfully sends all pending updates to a replica on another server, it proceeds to the next replica until all replicas have been updated. If the operation fails for any reason and is unable to update one or more replicas during the cycle, it reschedules synchronization to run at a later time. NetWare 6 uses transitive synchronization between servers if possible and handles synchronization differently. The next section describes the changes that NetWare 6 provides.

### Changes to Synchronization in NetWare 6

Features that help make NDS eDirectory more scalable across your network servers include transitive synchronization, transitive vector, caching the replica changes, multiple objects per packet, and randomized replica lists. These features reduce traffic across WAN infrastructures and enable you to more easily manage both the NDS tree contents and your network's overall system.

**Transitive Synchronization and Transitive Vector**   Replica synchronization in NetWare 6 uses transitive synchronization. Transitive synchronization uses the transitive vectors during synchronizing between two NetWare 6 servers. Transitive synchronization uses the transitive vector instead of the Synchronized Up To property that was used in NetWare 4.

The transitive vector is a new structure that has been added to the Partition Root object for each partition. It is essentially a group of modification timestamps representing the values held by each replica. One transitive vector exists for each replica. The transitive vector differs from the Synchronized Up To property because it holds a group of timestamps for each replica, whereas the Synchronized Up To property holds only one value for each replica in the partition. Another major difference between the transitive vector and the Synchronization Up To property is that the transitive vector is synchronized between servers, whereas the Synchronization Up To property is not synchronized.

As mentioned, the transitive vector structure is kept as a vector with an attribute for each replica. Using the transitive vector, synchronization can achieve convergence among the replicas of a partition without having all replicas talk to every other replica. The structure of the transitive vector consists of modification timestamps for all replicas in a given replica ring. The transitive vector has been added to the Partition Root object of each partition in NetWare 6, as described here:

| | |
|---|---|
| **Server ID** | Server ID that holds the replica |
| **Timestamp Vectors** | Timestamp vector for each replica in replica ring |

Each time that replica synchronization is scheduled to run on the NetWare 6 server, transitive synchronization reads the transitive vector to determine which replicas it needs to synchronize with. Because each NetWare 6 server has a transitive vector, the process can immediately determine how up-to-date each of the other replicas are. Using transitive synchronization, a specific server does not have to contact each of the other servers in the partition to complete replica synchronization. After a successful synchronization, the target or destination server merges the transitive vector with the transitive vector of the source server. In addition, the changes are guaranteed to converge across all replicas of a partition.

When a change occurs in an object or property, the replica synchronization is scheduled to run. When the synchronization executes, it determines which servers need to communicate by comparing the timestamps of the source and target servers in the transitive vector. The source server is the local server that received the update, and the target server is the destination server of replica synchronization. If the time is greater for the local server, then the replica updates are sent. The local or source server does not request the target server's timestamps. The timestamps for the target server are already local in the transitive vector. After all updates are sent, the source server sends its transitive vector values, which are merged into the transitive vector values of the target server.

As previously mentioned, this method of using the transitive vector during synchronizing between two NetWare 6 servers is called transitive synchronization. You may be wondering how the transitive vector works if the synchronization occurs on a replica ring with NetWare 6 servers and NetWare 4 servers. If a replica ring includes a mixed server environment, the two servers will synchronize using the NetWare 4 method of passing the Synchronized Up To vectors. After the synchronization has completed, either the transitive vector from the NetWare 6 server or the Synchronization Up To vector from the NetWare 4 server is merged.

**Replica Ring is Randomized**    In NetWare 4, when the replica synchronization starts, it contacts and updates each of the replicas in the replica ring in a sequential order. Therefore, the first replica in the replica ring is updated first, followed by the second one, and so on. Because the replica ring is identical on all the servers holding copies of this partition, the synchronization processes all the replicas for each partition in the same order. This may have an undesirable effect if multiple servers are trying to synchronize with the same replica on the same server simultaneously. Because only one inbound synchronization is supported per partition (not per server), one of the synchronization processes will have to back off and try again. This situation only arises if synchronization tends to execute at approximately the same time on multiple servers. To help alleviate this situation, NetWare 6 changes the sequence in which replicas are processed by randomizing the replica ring list before attempting to contact the first server. Randomization greatly reduces the possibility that one of the servers will have to back off and attempt to resynchronize with a replica. By randomizing which replica receives the first update, transitive synchronization more quickly converges the data for each partition. As previously mentioned, transitive synchronization can converge the NDS eDirectory data among all the replicas of a partition without having all replicas talk to every other replica.

**Cache Changes**    Using a new feature — caching the changes to the objects — enhances the performance of replica synchronization. Remember that the changes or updates that affect the objects include adding, deleting, moving, or renaming an object, as well as changing the properties or attributes of the object.

Using NetWare 4, NDS sequentially searches the entire object file, comparing timestamps to find the objects that have been updated since the last successful synchronization. The sequential searching effectively limits the size of the partitions. To overcome this limitation, NetWare 6 eliminates the sequential search time by caching all changes to the objects. The capability to cache the objects in the NDS database greatly increases the speed of searching for and updating each replica and partition.

The object cache maintains a set of object IDs that have been modified since the last synchronization. The cache is populated by placing object IDs in the cache that have been modified as a result of client requests, as well as by inbound synchronization. Each cache entry has the modification time relative to the last synchronization. The cache that NDS eDirectory maintains is for each partition stored on a server. The cache has a start time associated with it that identifies when the cache was built. Changes only need to be sent out if the transitive vector for the remote server is less than or equal to the transitive vector for the local server. The janitor process cleans up the cache periodically by removing the object IDs that have already been sent to all the replicas.

**Multiple Objects per Synchronization Packet**    To help synchronize individual replicas faster, NetWare 6 supports more than one object in each communication packet. Formerly, NetWare 4 only allowed changes for one object in a single communication packet. By allowing multiple changes to different objects in a single packet, NetWare 6 reduces the total number of packets needed to synchronize with other replicas. If the number of changes between two replicas is small, it is feasible that all the updates between the two replicas can be accomplished in a single packet. Basically, this means that a partition can be synchronized in a minimum of one packet.

### Scheduling Replica Synchronization

As mentioned in previous chapters, every object and property that exists in the directory has an associated timestamp. Objects have a creation timestamp and a last modification timestamp. Properties have a timestamp that indicates when they were last changed. The modification to a property or attribute value consists of deleting the old value and creating the new one. Thus, the timestamp associated with the property could be called a creation timestamp.

By way of review, each replica of a partition on a server maintains a property or attribute called the synchronized up to vector. The synchronized up to vector is a list of timestamps, one for each replica in the partition plus one for every modification. Synchronization examines the timestamp held in the synchronized up to attribute for each replica and determines if the information needs to be updated. The synchronized up to values for each replica of a partition can be viewed using either the NDS Manager or DSREPAIR utilities. Figure 8.47 shows the replica information for the CAMELOT partition, as shown in the NDS Manager utility.

Before starting replica synchronization and the first replica update, the server takes a snapshot of its own synchronized up to vector. The server saves the snapshot of these values in memory until all replicas have been contacted and successfully updated.

**FIGURE 8.47** *The replica information for the CAMELOT partition, as shown in the NDS Manager utility*

## Performing Replica Synchronization

The purpose of replica synchronization is to send any changes to the other servers that have a replica for a given partition. DSTRACE refers to this process as the *skulker*. Factors that determine whether synchronization is necessary are modifications or changes occurring with an associated timestamp. The transitive vector from the other servers in the replica pointer table of a partition is compared with the local transitive vector. If there are differences, the appropriate updates are made.

DS examines the replica pointer table (replica ring) for the local partition to locate the replicas of the partition. The timestamps in the synchronized up to vector are compared to determine the need to synchronize changes. Figure 8.48 shows a logical representation of the dialog that occurs each time the local server contacts one of the other servers in the replica pointer table.

**FIGURE 8.48** *The dialog that occurs between servers during replica synchronization*

Following are the specific operations and steps that are performed during replica synchronization:

1. The source (or local) server schedules its synchronization after it receives a modification or event. If the process is flagged as fast synchronization, the source server schedules synchronization at the current time plus 10 seconds. Otherwise, the source server schedules synchronization at the current time plus 30 minutes.

2. The source server reads its synchronized up to vector.

3. The source server reads the replica pointer table to determine which servers hold replicas of the partition being synchronized.

4. The source server sets a flag that this partition is currently performing an outbound synchronization. This prevents the DSREPAIR utility from simultaneously running multiple instances of synchronization for the same partition.

**5.** The source server connects and authenticates to a target server holding a replica to be synchronized. If the server cannot establish a connection, it displays a DS error –625 for the server and proceeds to the next replica.

**6.** The source server requests the timestamp synchronized up to vector from the target server.

**7.** The target server reads its own replica pointer table to determine whether the source server is in its replica ring. If not, the server returns a DS error –672 denying access.

**8.** The target server checks if the specified replica is already processing incoming synchronization requests from another server. If so, the server returns a DS error –692. If not, the server returns a start reply to the source server.

**9.** The target server sends the requested synchronized up to vector of timestamps to the source server.

**10.** The source server determines whether it needs to send updates by comparing its own synchronized up to values to that of the target server. If the timestamps for the source server are more recent than the target's timestamps, the synchronization will proceed. If the timestamps are not more recent, the source server completes the synchronization request with that server and begins synchronizing with the next replica in the ring. The source server then skips to Step 14.

**11.** The source server sends the updates with the values to be changed for each object.

**12.** The target server verifies that the objects sent from the source server should be updated. The target server compares the local timestamps for each of its objects with the one received from the source server.

**13.** The target server updates the appropriate object and property information. The source and target servers repeat the update procedure until all updates are sent and received. The servers then send a reply indicating success or failure.

**14.** The source server sends the target server an end synchronization message and includes the source server's own synchronized up to vector.

**15.** The target server merges the timestamp values into its own synchronized up to vector using the higher values of the two vectors.

**16.** The target server replies to the end synchronization request with a completion code indicating success or failure.

**17.** The source server checks if all the replicas have been processed (All Processed=Yes).

  **a.** If all the replicas have not been processed, then the source server either retries the synchronization for the replicas that were previously busy or reschedules the process for the partition if retries are exceeded.

  **b.** The source server creates the partition status attribute to indicate synchronization results.

  **c.** If all the replicas have been processed, the source server writes the synchronized up to vector that it began the process with to its replica up to vector for the partition.

**18.** The replica synchronization process is completed.

By default the replica synchronization process is scheduled to execute only when changes are received to the object or properties in the NDS tree. However, using a DSTRACE command you can force the process to start (even if there are no changes to be propagated). To manually start replica synchronization, enter the following DSTRACE command at the server console:

```
SET DSTRACE = *S
```

This setting checks to see if the partition has been marked as changed; if not, it won't do anything. The DSTRACE command or setting to force replica synchronization to exchange the timestamp (synchronization up to) is entered at the server console as follows:

```
SET DSTRACE = *H
```

### The Replica Synchronization Heartbeat

NDS eDirectory provides a trigger, or heartbeat, every 30 minutes to schedule replica synchronization. The heartbeat enables each NetWare 6 server to contact all of the other NetWare 6 servers that it has in its replica pointer tables. The heartbeat is checked in case the server has become disconnected from the network. The heartbeat starts replica synchronization for each partition that it holds.

The network administrator can adjust the heartbeat time interval using the SET command called the NDS inactivity synchronization interval. The default value for this parameter is 30 minutes, but you can set this parameter by entering the following command at the server console:

```
SET NDS INACTIVITY SYNCHRONIZATION INTERVAL = 60
```

A SET DSTRACE command may be used to initiate the heartbeat synchronization immediately. This command is entered as follows:

```
SET DSTRACE = *H
```

The SET DSTRACE command, SET DSTRACE = !H [time in minutes] may be used to change the default time interval parameter. Although you can change the default time interval using this SET parameter, we do not recommend it.

## The Inspector Process

DS uses the inspector process to verify that the object and property information in the NDS data files are valid. The inspector process specifically checks and verifies that the directory information stored on the server is formed correctly. If the information has anomalies, the inspector does not attempt to perform corrective action.

This process validates the object and property information, including the object name, class, timestamps, and references. It also checks to make sure that other objects reference the object correctly.

This process runs as needed with the flatcleaner process (described later in "The FlatCleaner Process" section). The network administrator can manually activate the inspector using a DSTRACE SET command. To start the inspector process, enter the following:

```
SET DSTRACE = +INSP
```

This process can be expensive in terms of CPU utilization and should not be executed manually on a server during normal working hours.

## The Limber Process

The limber process maintains tree and server connectivity. At specific times, each NetWare 6 server in the NDS tree checks its distinguished name and addresses. The limber process updates or modifies these values if necessary. The limber process checks the local server's entry to make sure that its distinguished name and address have not changed.

The limber process also ensures that if the relative distinguished name or internal IPX address is modified, the changes are replicated. The server name or IPX internal address can be changed in AUTOEXEC.NCF and then it can take effect when the server is restarted. The server name and IPX address are stored in the NDS server object created for the server.

If a server changes its name or address, the limber process is responsible for ensuring that the modifications are made to each replica pointer table in the partition. If the changes occur on the server with the master replica, the limber process changes its local address in the replica pointer table. If the changes occur on a server holding a nonmaster replica, the limber process tells the master replica. The limber process can initiate the backlink process, which does part of the checking for the limber process.

The limber process is initiated when each NetWare 6 server boots up or Novell Directory Services is restarted. The process is also initiated every three hours by default. The limber process can be event driven, meaning it starts when a server address is added, changed, or deleted. An address can be added for another protocol while the system is running.

The limber process verifies that the server has the correct tree name. If the tree name is changed, the limber process effects the change on the server. The tree name modification is performed by the server holding the master replica of the root partition. This server then sends the request to all the other servers in the tree. If the update request fails to reach a server, the limber process will eventually make sure that the change is received by the server after it becomes available.

The limber process can be started on a server manually by executing a SET DSTRACE command at the server console prompt. The command to schedule the limber process to start is as follows:

```
SET DSTRACE = *L
```

### The Backlink Process

When creating an external reference, the directory also schedules the creation of a backlink attribute for the object. Thus, the corresponding attribute to an external reference object is the backlink. The purpose of the backlink is to keep track of external reference objects on other servers.

The backlink process checks the local external reference objects that are on the server. It also verifies the backlink attribute values that have been created for the objects contained on the server.

DS periodically checks the external references to see if a reason continues for them to exist. If an external reference is not needed, the directory will mark it to be removed.

The backlink process also enables maintenance of the external references by periodically verifying the information stored in the backlink attribute of the object. Each backlink attribute holds the remote server name and object ID of the associated external reference. By default, the backlink process checks consistency automatically every 780 minutes (13 hours). The default value can be changed for the backlink process by setting the SET parameter called the NDS backlink interval, which is entered in minutes. In order to change the SET parameter at the server console, enter the following:

```
SET NDS BACKLINK INTERVAL = 900
```

The range for this parameter is 2 to 10080 minutes. The backlink interval can also be changed using DSTRACE by entering the following console command:

```
SET DSTRACE = !B [2-10080 minutes]
```

Using DSTRACE, the backlink process can be forced to execute immediately by setting the process flag. Enter the following DSTRACE server console command:

```
SET DSTRACE = *B
```

The backlink process will initiate sooner than the next regularly scheduled interval.

When an object is renamed, moved, or deleted, the backlinks make it possible for all the external references to that object to be changed. The backlink process has the responsibility to make the corresponding changes to the external references. Thus, the backlink process helps to maintain the integrity of external references by allowing them to be updated to reflect the changes made to the original objects.

Again, NetWare 6 has *distributed reference links,* which are a more efficient way to handle the renaming, moving, and deleting of external references. Although distribution reference links are fully implemented in NetWare 6, backlinks will not go away. Backlinks will also continue to be used to help maintain the external references. NetWare 6 uses both methods.

## The Janitor Process

The primary responsibility of the janitor process is to keep everything in the DS clean. This process enables the DS to efficiently reuse the storage or disk resources of the server. It accomplishes this task by performing several functions associated with the objects and properties in the NDS data files. The janitor process performs the following tasks:

▸ Purges the deleted objects and values from the data files

▸ Schedules the flatcleaners

▸ Updates the Inherited Rights ACLs for the partitions

▸ Alerts for synthetic time

### Purging Deleted Objects and Properties

Before the object or property value is purged, replica synchronization makes sure that the object or value to be deleted is completely synchronized with all the other replicas of the partition. This ensures that each replica knows the object is going to be deleted before removing or purging it.

The directory reads the replica up to attribute of the partition and compares it against each object timestamp to determine which objects and property values need to be purged. A property value can be purged from an object if both of the following conditions are met:

- The property value is marked as deleted or not present.

- The timestamp for the property is less recent than the purge time (the purge time is the same as the synchronized up to timestamp).

Once the janitor process has inspected all the property values for an object, it determines whether the entire object itself can be purged. The janitor process will purge any object that meets the following criteria:

- Object is marked as deleted or not present

- Object has no property values

NDS eDirectory also checks if the partition root object (the topmost object in the partition) has been renamed. If the container object has been renamed, the janitor notifies all external references of the partition root object of the new name. While scanning the partition, the janitor builds two lists:

- **The release object ID list** — This is a list of objects that have been marked as moved. For each object in the list, the master replica processes the obituaries for the move, which releases the move inhibit destination object.

- **The notify external reference list** — The server with the master replica builds a list of objects that have backlink obituaries to be processed. For each object in the list, the janitor uses this list to send synchronization messages to the associated external references. The messages specify the operation that must be performed on the external reference.

### Updating Inherited Rights ACLs

The janitor process determines the rights that should flow out through the inherited rights ACLs and updates the partitions. The inherited rights ACLs allow rights that are given at the higher levels in the tree to flow down from parent to child partitions. This enables all users to calculate all their rights in the entire tree from simply reading their local partition. The users do not need to walk the tree during login to calculate their rights.

By default, the janitor process is scheduled every hour (60 minutes). The default value can be changed by setting the SET parameter called NDS janitor interval, which is entered in minutes. In order to change the SET parameter at the server console, enter the following:

```
SET NDS JANITOR INTERVAL = 120
```

The range for this parameter is 1 to 10080 minutes. The janitor interval can also be changed using DSTRACE by entering the following console command:

```
SET DSTRACE = !J [1-10080 minutes]
```

### The Flatcleaner Process

The flatcleaner process purges or removes the objects in DS that are marked as deleted. The flatcleaner purges the expired dynamic bindery objects and external reference objects from the NDS data files. This process purges only the objects that have been marked as deleted or not present.

The flatcleaner process is scheduled by the janitor process. It is started after the flatcleaner interval has expired. By default the flatcleaner interval is one hour (60 minutes). The default value can be changed by setting the DSTRACE SET parameter at the server console as follows:

```
SET DSTRACE = !F (in minutes)
```

The flatcleaner can be forced to execute using a DSTRACE command at the server console as follows:

```
SET DSTRACE = *F
```

### The Schema Synchronization Process

The NDS eDirectory schema can be modified or changed by creating new object classes or property definitions. The schema can be modified by client software. Typically, this would happen when new software applications are installed that require specific new kinds of objects or attributes. The user installing the software must have sufficient access rights before it can make the modifications.

**TIP**

**For example, Novell's GroupWise software product has an optional feature that extends the NDS schema. The feature is a snap-in option to the NWADMIN utility, which enables the administrator to create GroupWise accounts at the same time a user object is created in the NDS tree.**

Schema changes are replicated or propagated among all the servers containing replicas. The schema is replicated using a similar synchronization process known as the replica synchronization process. Without this synchronization, the schema information on one server could become different from that on the other NetWare 6 servers in the tree.

Using schema synchronization, which is event driven, schema modifications are scheduled ten seconds after the change. The updates to the schema are propagated automatically from one server to another in much the same way as other directory updates. However, the schema synchronization differs in that partitions replicate according to the replica pointer table (replica ring), but schema synchronization occurs according to a trickle-down method. In this trickle-down method the schema synchronization or updates propagate in two directions:

- Across servers holding a replica of a given partition
- Downward in the partition tree

### Propagation across Replicas of a Partition

Like NDS objects, each schema object has a timestamp that indicates its last modification. The procedures for comparing and updating timestamps for the schema information between servers are the same as for any other objects.

To propagate the latest schema updated information among the replicas of a partition, a server uses schema synchronization with a few slight changes. NetWare 6 servers without replicas can add themselves to the list of servers contacted. The specific operations and steps that are performed during schema synchronization for the replicas of a partition are listed here:

1. The source server takes a snapshot of its own local synchronized up to attribute.

2. The source server reads all the replica pointer tables (replica rings) in order to make a list of target servers to be sent the schema updates. The distribution list can include NetWare 6 servers that do not have replicas. The reference replica to the source server is stripped from the list, as well as all subordinate reference replicas.

3. The source server pings each target server in the distribution list to determine the tree depth of the root-most replica on the target server. If the replica depth is less than the source server's depth, the target server is skipped.

4. A start synchronization request is then sent to the target server. The target server replies to the request by sending its synchronized up to vector.

5. The source server compares the synchronized up to vectors to determine if the schema updates should be sent.

6. The source server sends the updates to the schema.

7. The source server sends the target server an end synchronization request containing its own synchronized up to vector.

8. The target server merges the timestamp values into its own synchronized up to vector using the higher value of the two vectors.

9. The schema synchronization is terminated for a partition after the source server has contacted and updated all the target servers.

### Propagation Down to the Lower Partitions

In order to propagate the schema modifications down to lower partitions, the server where the modification is received starts schema synchronization with its partitions. Each time a target server receives a modification, it sends the modification to lower partitions, if any. It will never send the modification to partitions that are higher. The procedures for schema synchronization are described earlier in this chapter in the section "Propagation across Replicas of a Partition."

The trickle-down method of synchronizing the schema occurs when a target server receives the updated schema and builds its own list of servers for distributing the just-received schema to. The target first checks to see if the partition(s) is lower than the original partition (the partition where the modification is made). The procedures for updating the schema are performed across all replicas of a partition. In this way the schema updates are propagated downward to other partitions in the directory tree and across all replicas of the partition.

## Controlling Schema Synchronization

By default schema synchronization is scheduled to execute only when changes are made to the schema or after the expiration of the schema synchronization heartbeat. The default interval for the schema synchronization heartbeat is 4 hours (240 minutes). However, a DSTRACE command can force the process to start (even if no changes are to be propagated). To manually start schema synchronization, enter the following DSTRACE command at the server console:

```
SET DSTRACE = *SS
```

This flag starts the process, which will check to see if the schema on that server needs to be synchronized. This is the schema synchronization heartbeat.

You can disable schema synchronization altogether by entering the following DSTRACE command at the server console:

```
SET DSTRACE = !S   [0 = ON, Nonzero = OFF]
```

This flag both enables and disables the schema synchronization. The flag value of 0 enables the schema synchronization. A nonzero value disables the schema synchronization.

# NDS eDirectory Partition and Replica Operations

An administrator using the NDS Manager utility can make structural changes to the NDS tree. For example, the administrator can add and remove replicas, change replica types, create or merge partitions, or move subtrees.

The directory is a multithreaded system that enables the server to participate or perform multiple partition operations on different partitions on the server. A server can hold replicas of different partitions, and these replicas can be involved in their individual partition operations simultaneously on the server.

## Partition and Replica Operation Control and Status

All partition and replica operations are initiated by contacting the master replica for the partition. Because each partition can have only one operation in progress at a time, the master replica of the partition controls the operation. The master replica ensures that other partition operations are not started until the first operation is completed. The master replica is the traffic cop for partition operations.

The partition has certain attributes that are used to manage the partition operations. For example, some of the attributes used to help with the partition operation are replica pointer table, replica status, partition control, and partition status. As the operation proceeds through several states, each server involved records the activity of these states in the partition control and status attributes.

Most partition operations are processed in several major passes. In the first pass, all affected servers are contacted with the details of the change. They report errors, if any. If any errors are detected in the first pass, this means the operation did not start and the message is returned to the utility. If there are no errors, the second pass contacts all the servers with replicas of the partition to finalize the modification.

The following sections summarize the operations that create and manage the partitions and their replicas. The partition operations we will discuss include the following:

▶ Add replica

▶ Remove replica

▶ Change replica type

▶ Create (split) partition

▶ Merge (join) partition

▶ Move subtree or partition

## Add Replica Operation

The add replica operation causes a new replica for a partition to be added to the partition's replica point table. The major events that occur during the add new replica operation are listed here:

1. An administrator with the proper rights issues a request using the NDS Manager utility to add a new replica for the partition. DS client automatically authenticates the workstation to the server holding the master replica of the partition.

2. The administrator determines the replica type (read/write or read-only) and selects the target server that will store the new replica.

3. The server holding the master replica verifies the access rights of the user or administrator to the partition and destination server and checks that:

   a. The target server object exists in the NDS tree.

   b. The replica type requested is read/write or read-only.

   c. The partition is not involved in another partition operation.

4. The master replica server obtains the object ID for the partition root object on the target server.

5. The master replica assigns the first unused replica number to the new replica.

**6.** The master replica adds replica pointer table attribute values to the target server and sets the state for the new replica to RS_NEW_REPLICA. The master replica server adds the new replica created on the target server to its replica pointer table. This change to the replica pointer table will be synchronized out to the other replicas in the partition during the replica synchronization already scheduled.

**7.** The master replica schedules an immediate replica synchronization to begin downloading the contents of the partition to the target server.

**8.** The master replica server informs the client or workstation that the add new replica request was successful.

**9.** The replica state begins with the replica in the RS_NEW_REPLICA state. During this replica state:

 **a.** The target server accepts update requests from only the master replica.

 **b.** Clients cannot access the new replica; it is treated as not available.

**10.** After all the information is sent to the new replica, the master replica server changes its replica state attribute from RS_NEW_REPLICA to RS_TRANSITION_ON. The replica state attribute will be propagated to the other replicas of the partition by normal replica synchronization.

**11.** When the target server receives the replica state value of RS_TRANSITION_ON, it sends a request to the other replicas to obtain any updates more recent than those of the master replica.

**12.** The target server synchronizes with all other replicas of the partition as needed.

**13.** The target server then sends a request to the master replica server to change the replica state value to RS_ON.

**14.** The master replica server receives the request and sets the replica state for the new replica to RS_ON. The replica state attribute will be propagated to the other replicas of the partition by normal replica synchronization.

**15.** If needed, the master replica server sends a request to create the necessary reference replicas that are subordinate to the new replica. If the subordinate references replicas are created, the target server sends a request to the master of each child partition to update the replica pointer table to reflect the change.

**16.** Each change will be propagated to the other replicas of each partition by normal replica synchronization.

**17.** The add new replica operation is complete.

## Remove Replica Operation

The remove replica operation deletes a replica from a specific server, and it also removes it from the replica pointer table of the partition. The master replica cannot be removed. To remove a replica, a user must have managed rights at the partition root object and the server from which the replica is being removed. The major events that occur during the remove replica operation are listed here:

1. An administrator with the proper rights issues a request using the NDS Manager utility to remove a replica from a server. DS automatically authenticates the workstation to the server holding the master replica of the partition.

2. The administrator selects the target server from which the replica is being removed.

3. The master replica server verifies the access rights of the user or administrator to the partition and server and checks that:

   a. The master replica exists on that server.

   b. The replica state is RS_ON.

   c. The partition is not involved in another partition operation.

4. The master replica server changes the replica state to RS_DYING_REPLICA.

5. The change to the replica state is propagated to the other replicas of the partition through normal replica synchronization.

6. The target server knows that it has a replica whose state is RS_DYING_REPLICA. It checks to see if it holds the parent of the partition being removed.

7. If the target server holds a parent:

   a. It sends a request to the server holding the master replica to update the replica pointer table to reflect the change. This request indicates that the replica being removed from the target server is changed to a subordinate reference replica.

   b. The target server sends the pending changes to at least one other replica not being removed and whose replica state is RS_ON.

   c. The master replica server changes the replica type in the replica pointer table to subordinate reference for the target server replica.

   d. The master replica server changes the replica state to RS_ON.

**8.** If the target server does not hold the parent partition:

    **a.** The target server sends the pending changes to at least one other replica not being removed and whose replica state is RS_ON.

    **b.** The target server sends a request to the master replica server to remove the replica from the replica pointer table of the partition.

    **c.** The change to the replica pointer table will be propagated to the other replicas of the partition by normal replica synchronization.

**9.** The target server converts its objects in the removed replica to external reference objects. It sends a request to create a backlink to a server holding the real object for each external reference created.

**10.** All changes are propagated to the other replicas for the partition through replica synchronization.

**11.** The remove replica operation is complete.

## Change Replica Type Operation

The change replica type operation changes the type of any replica. The operation is started when an administrator decides to change the type of a replica on a specific server. The types of replicas that can be chosen are master, read/write, and read-only. You cannot change a replica to a subordinate reference. The subordinate reference replicas are maintained by the directory.

The change replica type operation differs when the operation assigns a new master replica. This section discusses changing both nonmaster replica types (read/write and read-only) and changing to a master replica. In order to change a replica to a master replica, the target server must hold a read/write or read-only replica of the partition.

The major events that occur during the change replica type operation of a nonmaster replica are listed here:

**1.** An administrator with the proper rights issues a request using the NDS Manager utility to change the replica type to either read/write or read-only. DS automatically authenticates the workstation to the server holding the master replica of the partition.

**2.** The master replica server checks the access rights of the user or administrator to the partition.

3. The master replica server changes the replica type in its copy of the replica pointer table.

4. The change to the replica pointer table will be propagated to the other replicas of the partition by normal replica synchronization.

5. The change replica type operation is complete.

The steps to change the Replica Type to a Master Replica are listed here:

1. An administrator with the proper rights issues a request using the NDS Manager utility to change the replica type to the master replica. DS automatically authenticates the workstation to the server holding the master replica of the partition. This server is called the source server.

2. The source server checks the access rights of the user or administrator to the partition.

3. The source server identifies the target server by using the partition control attribute's distinguished name field.

4. The source server sets the partition control attribute to PC_CHANGING_REPLICATYPE.

5. The source sets the replica state of each replica in the replica pointer table to RS_CRT_0.

6. The change to the partition control and replica pointer table attributes will be propagated to the other replicas of the partition using normal replica synchronization. This enables all the replicas in the partition to change the partition state to RS_CRT_0.

7. The source server sends a request to the target server to set the replica to the new master. This routine tells the target server that it is now the master replica of the partition.

8. The target server waits until its clock is ahead of the timestamps issued by the source (old master replica) server. It then issues new timestamps on the replica pointer table of this partition.

9. The target server removes its name from the partition control attribute's distinguished name field.

10. The target server is now the master replica and sets the partition state in the replica pointer table to RS_CRT_1.

11. The target server changes its replica type in the replica pointer table to read/write (secondary) for the source server.

**12.** The target server replies to the source indicating that the replica type has been successfully changed to master.

**13.** The change to the replica pointer table on the target server will be propagated to the other replicas of the partition using normal replica synchronization.

**14.** The source server changes its own replica type to read/write in the replica pointer table.

**15.** The source server changes its replica state to RS_CRT_1.

**16.** The changes made to the source server will be propagated to the other replicas of the partition using normal replica synchronization.

**17.** The source server changes its replica state to RS_ON.

**18.** The change will be propagated to the other replicas of the partition.

**19.** The change replica type operation is complete.

### Create (Split) Partition Operation

The create partition operation causes a partition (parent) to split and form a new child partition in the NDS tree. You can create any partition as long as it has a single container object as its partition root object. The major events that occur during the create partition operation are listed here:

**1.** An administrator with the proper rights issues a request using the NDS Manager utility to create a new partition in the NDS tree. DS automatically authenticates the workstation to the server holding the master replica of the partition.

**2.** The master replica server identifies the container object that will become the new partition root object where the partition is created.

**3.** When the master replica server changes the master replica of the partition where the split will occur, the following events take place:

    **a.** The access rights of the user or administrator to the partitions and servers involved are checked.

    **b.** The replica state in each of the replica pointer tables is set to RS_SS_0.

    **c.** The partition control attribute is set with the distinguished name of the new partition root object and sets the current operation, which is a split partition.

**4.** The changes made to the master replica will be propagated to the other replicas of the partition using normal replica synchronization.

**5.** The master replica server sends a request to each server holding a replica of the partition to perform a split procedure. The subordinate references replicas are not included.

**6.** The servers holding replicas of the partition then process the split request by taking the partition attributes and values from the parent to the partition root object of the child partition.

**7.** Each server returns a reply indicating success or failure to the split request.

**8.** The master replica server performs the split procedure on its own replica list.

**9.** The master replica server sets the replica state to RS_SS_1 (split state 1).

**10.** The replica state (RS_SS_1) is propagated from the master replica to each of the other replicas of the partition.

**11.** The master replica server advances the partition state and replica state to RS_ON for both the parent partition and new child partition.

**12.** The changes made to the master replica will be propagated to the other replicas of the partition.

**13.** The create or split partition operation is complete.

## Merge (Join) Partition Operation

The merge partition operation causes a child partition to be joined back together with its parent partition. This operation requires that both a parent and child partition already exists in the NDS tree structure.

At the beginning of the merge operation, the replicas for each of the two partitions do not have to be stored on the same servers. However, the operation first proceeds by copying a replica of either the parent or child partition to all the servers involved. This ensures that each server will have the replicas for both the parent and child partition.

The merge operation makes the replica pointer table the same for both the parent and child partitions, excluding the subordinate references from the parent's replica list. When the directory creates all the replicas of the new partition, it simply erases the partition boundary between the parent partition and the child partition.

▶ · · · · · · · · · · · · · · · · · · · · · · · · · · · · · · · ◀

### Consulting Experience

It is highly recommended that before executing a merge operation of a parent and child partition, manually place replicas of each partition on the servers that will be involved. If the replicas do not exist, the merge operation will place them for you. However, the merge operation will complete faster if you manually place the replicas in advance.

The major events that occur during the merge partition operation are listed here:

**1.** An administrator with the proper rights issues a request using the NDS Manager utility to merge a child partition with its parent. DS automatically authenticates the workstation to the server holding the master replica of the child partition.

**2.** The workstation sends the request to the server holding the child partition.

**3.** The master replica of the child partition locates the parent partition's master replica.

**4.** The master replica of the child partition verifies the access rights of the user or administrator to the partitions and servers involved and checks that:

    **a.** The request is valid.

    **b.** The child partition is not involved in another partition operation.

    **c.** The software versions on the servers involved support the merge operation. This means that all servers involved must be running the DS.NLM v 4.63 or later.

**5.** The master replica of child partition sends a request to the server holding the master replica of the parent partition to start the merge.

**6.** The master replica of the parent partition receives a request to start the merge operation and changes the master replica as follows:

    **a.** The replica state in the replica pointer tables and partition control attribute is set to RS_ JS_0.

    **b.** The partition control attribute also receives the distinguished name of the child partition root object.

    **c.** The current operation is set to PC_ JOINING_DOWN.

**7.** The changes made to the master replica will be propagated to the other replicas of the parent partition using normal replica synchronization.

**8.** The master replica of the parent partition replies to the server holding the master replica of the child partition the success or failure of the request to start the merge.

**9.** The master replica of the child partition receives the reply and changes the master replica as follows:

    **a.** The replica state in the replica pointer tables and partition control attribute is set to RS_ JS_0.

    **b.** The partition control attribute also receives the distinguished name of the parent partition root object.

    **c.** The current operation is set to PC_ JOINING_UP.

**10.** The master replica of the child partition replies to the client or workstation that the merge operation client is successful or not.

**11.** The changes made to the master replica will be propagated to the other replicas of the parent partition using normal replica synchronization.

**12.** The master replica servers for both the parent and child partitions check the replica pointer table (replica ring) to determine which servers must add replicas. Both a replica of the parent and child partitions are required before the merge can take place.

**13.** The master replica server sends a request to other servers as follows:

    **a.** Servers containing replicas of the child partition, but not the parent, receive new replicas of the parent with new replica numbers.

    **b.** Servers containing replicas of the parent partition, but not the child, receive new replicas of the child partition with new replica numbers. These do not include the servers containing subordinate reference replicas.

**14.** The master replica of the child partition advances the replica state to RS_ JS_1.

**15.** The master replica of the parent partition checks that the child partition state is PC_ JOINING_UP.

    **a.** If the state is not PC_ JOINING_UP, it sets the partition and replica states to RS_ON. This stops the partition merge procedure.

    **b.** If the state is PC_ JOINING_UP, it sends a request to all servers holding replicas of the two partitions to perform a merge procedure.

NOVELL'S GUIDE TO NETWARE 6 NETWORKS

16. The nonmaster server receives the request and erases the boundary between the partitions by placing all objects from both partitions into one partition.

17. The master replica of the parent partition then performs the merge procedure on itself.

18. The master replica of the parent partition sets the replica state of the new merged partition to RS_ JS_2.

19. The changes made to the master replica will be propagated to the other replicas of the parent partition.

20. The master replica of the child partition then performs the merge procedure on itself.

21. The master replica of the child partition sets the replica state of the new merged partition to RS_ JS_2.

22. The changes made to the master replica will be propagated to the other replicas of the parent partition.

23. The master replica of the child partition sets the replica state to RS_ON.

24. The master replica of the parent partition sets the replica types as follows:

    a. The master replica of the parent becomes the master replica of the merged partition.

    b. The master replica of the child partition becomes a read/write replica.

    c. All other replicas of the child partition become replicas of the new partition.

25. The changes made to the master replicas will be propagated to the other replicas of the partition using normal replica synchronization.

26. The merge or split partition operation is complete.


## Move Subtree or Partition Operation

NetWare DS allows you to move any subtree of the NDS tree as long as it is a partition. The subtree or partition being moved cannot have child partitions.

The move subtree operation moves a container with all its subordinate objects to another logical location in the NDS tree. The objects in the moved partition change their distinguished name but the relative distinguished name remains the same. The servers that hold replicas for the partition being moved remain the same during the operation. This means that the move is logical (in the NDS tree) and not physical.

In the following example, the NDS tree has three partitions (NORAD, CAMELOT, and OPS), which are involved in moving the subtree. Figure 8.49 illustrates the OPS partition being moved from CAMELOT.ACME (source) to NORAD.ACME (destination).

**FIGURE 8.49** *The OPS partition will be moved from CAMELOT.ACME (source) to NORAD.ACME (destination).*

The major events that occur during the move subtree operation are listed here:

1. An administrator with the proper rights issues a request using the NDS Manager utility to move the subtree or partition OPS from CAMELOT.ACME (source) to NORAD.ACME (destination). DS automatically authenticates the workstation to the server holding the master replica of the OPS partition.

2. The workstation sends the request to the server holding the master of the NORAD partition. This is the destination partition.

**3.** The master replica server of NORAD creates the following control list of information:

  **a.** The access rights of the user or administrator to the partitions and servers involved

  **b.** The operation's expiration time, which is set to one hour

  **c.** The partition root object ID for NORAD (the destination)

  **d.** The distinguished name of the server holding the master replica of OPS

  **e.** The new relative distinguished name of the moved object

**4.** If the expiration time passes before a moved object is received from the source server, the destination server purges its record of the move details and does not continue moving the partition.

**5.** The master replica of NORAD checks its ACL attribute to see that the administrator or client has create rights and that the partition is idle.

**6.** The client sends a message to finish the move to the master replica server of OPS.

**7.** The master replica server of OPS checks that its software version and all the other servers holding replicas of the OPS partition are at least DS v 4.63.

**8.** If the source and destination partitions are the same partition, then a PartitionOverlap flag is set.

**9.** At the request of the source server, the master replica of OPS sets the following:

  **a.** The replica state in the replica pointer table is set to RS_MS_0.

  **b.** The partition control function is set to PC_MOVE_SUBTREE_DEST.

  **c.** The partition control attribute also receives the distinguished name of the destination partition.

  **d.** An OBT_TREE_OLD_RDN is added to the source object if its relative distinguished name is being changed. This obituary records the old name of the partition being moved.

**10.** The master replica server of OPS sends the client a reply indicating success or failure.

**11.** The changes made to the master replica will be propagated to the other replicas of the CAMELOT partition using normal replica synchronization.

**12.** The master replica of NORAD sets the following:

   **a.** The replica states in the replica pointer table are set to RS_MS_0.

   **b.** Partition operation is set to PC_MOVE_SUBTREE_SRC.

   **c.** The partition control attribute also receives the distinguished name of the source partition.

   **d.** An OBT_TREE_OLD_RDN is added to the source object if its relative distinguished name is being changed. This obituary records the old name of the partition being moved.

**13.** The changes made to the master replica will be propagated to the other replicas of the NORAD partition.

**14.** The master replica of OPS builds a server notification list of servers that will participate in moving the subtree:

   **a.** Servers holding replicas of the CAMELOT partition

   **b.** Servers holding replicas of the NORAD partition

   **c.** Servers holding replicas of the OPS partition

   **d.** Servers holding external references to objects in the CAMELOT partition (as identified by backlinks)

**15.** The master replica server for OPS records the server notification list as an OBT_MOVE_TREE obituary for each server in the list.

**16.** If the PartitionOverlap flag was set in Step 8, then the master replica server for OPS sends a partition lock request to the server holding the master replica of the NORAD partition. This prevents other partition operations on the partitions while the subtree is being moved.

**17.** The master replica server for OPS sends a reply indicating success or failure. The client no longer participates in moving the subtree.

**18.** The master replica server for OPS will drive the completion of the move subtree operation.

**19.** The master replica server sends a request to every server in the server notification list to start the move subtree. This request is driven by the obituaries.

**20.** Each server on the notification list changes its replicas according to the new NDS tree structure. The change to each server depends on the replicas it holds.

**21.** The master replica server sends a request to each of the servers on the notification list to end the move operation.

**22.** Servers on the list set their obituary flags to OBF_PURGEABLE and return a reply.

**23.** The master replica sends a partition unlock request to the master replica of CAMELOT and also sends a partition unlock request to the server holding the master replica of NORAD if the PartitionOverlap flag was set.

**24.** The master replica server receiving the unlock request sets the partition state to RS_ON.

**25.** The master replica of OPS sets the replica states to RS_ON.

**26.** The changes made to the master replicas will be propagated to the other replicas of the appropriate partition.

**27.** The move subtree partition operation is complete.

## Summary

NDS eDirectory is a distributed and replicated system that has been designed to run on multiple servers across your network. In order to more effectively maintain and troubleshoot the directory, you need to understand the background processes, internal components, and overall architecture. This chapter has focused on these components and processes.

# Troubleshooting NetWare 6 and eDirectory

*"What we anticipate seldom occurs; what we least expected*
*generally happens." — Henrietta Temple*

**C**hapter 8 gave you a much better understanding of how the internal operations of NetWare 6 work together to provide an enterprise network system. In fact, you should make sure to read Chapter 8 before reading this chapter because the material covered here uses terms explained in that chapter. This chapter also deals with partition and replica operations. For the details on these concepts, you can refer back to Chapter 6 as well as Chapter 8.

Troubleshooting has been described as a combination of art, science, and luck. One reason troubleshooting tends not to be much fun is that administrators often do not know enough about the underlying technology to properly define network problems when they occur. Unfortunately, as networks grow larger and larger, they also become more complex. In a single server environment, troubleshooting is usually confined to tracking down the hardware or software module experiencing a problem. NetWare 6 continues to introduce improved repair utilities and procedures for maintaining your network. Make sure to keep informed about patches and announcements by checking Novell's Web site regularly. Novell is dedicated to providing the best operating system available in the industry.

This chapter describes NDS primarily from the point of view of supportability. Based on information gathered, in part, by the staff on Novell's technical support teams, this chapter explains how to maintain and troubleshoot NDS. Experience has shown that, if NDS operations are properly verified before and after being initiated, NDS management can be virtually error free. This chapter covers three key topics:

▶ Understanding and using the NetWare 6 troubleshooting and repair tools

▶ Performing and verifying partition operations

▶ Troubleshooting do's and don'ts

# Understanding and Using the Troubleshooting and Repair Tools

The following sections describe the NetWare 6 troubleshooting and repair tools: NetWare Remote Manager, iMonitor, DSREPAIR, and the DSTRACE SET commands. These utilities are very important tools you will use during normal maintenance and troubleshooting of NetWare 6 and the directory. By using a combination of these tools, you will be able to perform basic troubleshooting steps:

- Discover trouble areas in NetWare 6.
- Identify problems and view NetWare 6 settings and configuration.
- Identify the partition that is experiencing errors by using and understanding the DSTRACE SET parameters and using the DSREPAIR utility.
- Identify the replica(s) in the partition that have errors. Identify these errors by using the DSTRACE SET commands and the DSREPAIR utility.
- Identify the error and take the appropriate action. Appendix B lists the error codes and recommended remedies.

## NetWare Remote Manager

The NetWare Remote Manager (NRM) is a browser-based management utility that allows you to troubleshoot Netware 6 from any workstation that is equipped with a Web browser. NetWare Remote Manager uses encrypted password exchange via secure socket layer (SSL) that keeps the management connection secure. Using SSL also means that the login credentials to the utility are passed through and you don't need to log in directly to the utility. The NetWare Remote Manager provides complete server-specific information clearly and securely within the client browser. A monitoring page with a traffic signal icon (green, yellow, and red lights) immediately indicates the health of dozens of servers. With one click, a system administrator can select any specific server to see more detailed information or to make configuration changes.

You can use the NetWare Remote Manager for typical server management tasks such as mounting and dismounting volumes, managing server connections, and configuring SET parameters. The NetWare Remote Manager allows you to accomplish the following tasks:

- Mounting and dismounting volumes
- Accessing files on volumes and DOS partitions
- Managing server connections
- Configuring SET parameters
- Monitoring system resources
- Viewing server console screens

▸ Downing, restarting, or resetting a server

▸ Browsing the NDS tree and viewing partitions

In addition to typical server management functions, NRM provides tools that allow you to manage a server's health and resources by doing the following tasks:

▸ Checking the general server health status

▸ Viewing the status of all loaded modules, including memory usages for each NLM

▸ Viewing information about all hardware adapters, hardware resources, and processor data

▸ Monitoring the health of many server processes and resources

NetWare Remote Manager is supported by the PORTAL.NLM that is automatically loaded on the server and requires no setup or configuration. You can access or launch the NetWare Remote Manager in a Web browser from a Windows workstation. The minimum browser requirements are Netscape Navigator 4.5 or Microsoft's Internet Explorer 5. To launch NRM, enter the following information in the location or URL field:

```
https://10.0.0.10:8009 (CAM-SRV1's IP address)
```

In previous versions of NetWare 5.1, you could use an unsecured port of 8008. However, this is no longer supported because the NetWare Remote Manager uses SSL. Note that the "s" at the end of "http" gives it a secure connection and the 8009 designates the Secure Socket Layer port. Figure 9.1 shows the first screen that appears.

The first screen that is displayed in the utility shows server information and Volume Management, which shows you the volumes that the server currently has mounted. For more information about Volume Management, see the "Volume Management" section, later in this chapter.

### NetWare Remote Manager Features

NetWare Remote Manager provides far more than just minor configuration changes. Server console screens that allow a network administrator to control all server-based applications may be viewed through the browser. The directory tree and established partitions are displayed, and servers may be downed, restarted, or reset through the browser.

**FIGURE 9.1** *NetWare Remote Manager enables you to remotely troubleshoot the NetWare 6 server via a browser.*

The main page that appears after you first access the utility includes server information. The header section of the main page contains the following information:

▶ The server's name

▶ The NetWare version

▶ The version and date of SERVER.EXE

▶ Server Health Status (a traffic light health indicator shows the status of the server)

Notice that the Server Health Status light icon is showing red instead of green. This indicates a critical problem. A green light indicates that the overall status of the server is good. A yellow light indicates a suspect status. A red light indicates a bad status. In Figure 9.1, the status of the CAM-SRV1 server is red, indicating that the server is in trouble. If you click on the traffic light icon, you see the Server Health Monitor screen, which is the summary list of 17 troubleshooting hot spots.

If you are deep in the interface, you can access the main page by clicking the NetWare Remote Manager text in the header area. The configuration page enables you to adjust port numbers, start and stop the HTTP log file, and toggle settings for viewing hidden SET parameters and hidden console commands. You can also unload and reload the PORTAL.NLM and set up IP filtering to control access to Portal.

You can add text, graphics, and custom links to the front page to customize the main page by creating an HTML file named PRTLANNC.HTM and placing it in the server's SYS:\LOGIN directory. Any information in this file will appear at the bottom of the main page. Because this file will be included in the HTML code that generates the front page, do not include the <body> and </body> tags.

### Diagnose Server

NetWare Remote Manager provides a powerful capability that helps you monitor the health of the server and diagnose problems that occur. Diagnose Server is the first section that allows you to display the following screens of information:

- ▶ Health Monitor
- ▶ Profile/Debug
- ▶ Run Config

**Health Monitors**  The NetWare Remote Manager utility not only allows network administrators to manage their NetWare 6 servers through a Web browser interface; it can also act as a server health monitor, providing a list of 17 potential hot spots that could cause problems. This utility is a great tool to help troubleshoot and diagnose those trouble spots and help you find out actually what is causing problems. You can focus on six basic areas to diagnose and resolve poorly running servers:

- ▶ A program or NLM is hogging the server CPU
- ▶ A server module is using a large amount of memory
- ▶ An errant program is causing the server to abend
- ▶ A program is monopolizing server processes
- ▶ Users are filling up disk space on server volumes
- ▶ A file is locked and inaccessible to users

When you want to diagnose a server's health, the first place to start is the Health Monitors page under the Diagnose Server. Access this page by clicking either the Health Monitors tab or the health indicator next to the server name. This page provides the health status (green, yellow, or red) for all known components of the system, as well as current, peak, and maximum values. The peak value is the highest number that has been reached since the PORTAL.NLM was last loaded. Figure 9.2 shows the Health Monitor screen that provides a quick summary of the major components in the server.

**FIGURE 9.2** *Using the Health Monitor screen, you can see a quick summary of the current status for each of the major hardware components in the server.*

If any item in the list changes to yellow or red, the status light on the main page changes to reflect the problem. In the example shown in Figure 9.2, the Available Memory status displays Bad in red, and the Cache Performance status is yellow or Suspect. The Server Health status, reported by the status light next to the server name, is updated every five seconds, but the graphic refreshes only if the status has changed.

Click the info icon for a component-specific line item on the Server Health page to view an outline of information that includes the specific health criteria (thresholds) for green/yellow/red in that category. The outline also provides suggestions in some cases for what might be going wrong in that category if a yellow or red indicator is displayed.

The following items are tracked on the Server Health page:

- DS thread usage
- Work to do response time
- Allocated server processes
- Available server processes
- Abend/debug information (if the server has abended and recovered automatically)
- CPU utilization (for each processor, if there is more than one)
- Connection usage
- Available memory
- Virtual memory performance
- Cache performance
- DS status (loaded or open)
- Packet receive buffers
- Available ECB's
- LAN traffic
- Available disk space
- Available directory entries
- Disk throughput

The Multiple Server Monitor option in Portal enables you to monitor the health of any or all of the Portal servers on your network. Follow the link under Health Monitors to access a list of all Portal servers visible to the current server. Use the check boxes to indicate which servers you want to monitor. When you click the Build Server Monitoring page, you see a one-line display for each server, with a traffic light indicator (green/yellow/red) and the server name. From this page, you can click the server name to go to that server's front page or you can click the status light icon to jump directly to the target server's health page.

You can build a customized list of servers to monitor and update the page at an interval that you define. If any of the servers in your list turn yellow or red, you see it when the page refreshes. You can control the format of the Multi-Server health monitor page to some extent by specifying the number of columns to use (the default is 3), the time interval (in seconds) between health updates (the default is 10), and the length of the server name to display. The default is to display the full server name, but if you are monitoring many servers or if you've specified many columns, you may want to display only the first few characters of a server's name, for example.

If one of the traffic light icons turns black on the health monitor page, the current Portal server has lost communication with that particular server (if it is being rebooted, for example). If the server later re-establishes communication, the traffic light will be updated on the next page refresh.

**Profiling and Debug Information**    Under the Diagnose Server option, you can choose the Profile/Debug option. The initial display shows CPU utilization by thread. You can see the names of the threads currently in use in the system, as well as the percentage of the execution time that these threads are currently using. Click the thread name to view specific thread information. Click the percent value to see profile details. You can view Profile CPU execution details for an individual NLM by clicking the NLM name. Figure 9.3 shows the Profile and Debug screen that allows you to view the CPU utilization.

### Consulting Experience

Depending on the memory use on your workstation and the Web browser you are using, the health monitor page may yield unpredictable results if more than 40 servers are being monitored simultaneously. In some cases, you may have to shut down the browser if it stops responding in this situation.

**FIGURE 9.3** *You can use the Profile/Debug screen to view the CPU utilization by thread and percentage of execution time.*

Under the Execution Profile Data by Thread heading, you can see the Thread Name, the Thread ID, the Thread State, the Parent NLM of the thread, and the Execution Time. If you click on the execution time, you can see where this specific thread is actually spending its time running, broken down by procedure and percentage of time per procedure.

Under Additional Debug Operations, you can profile calls to a specific procedure, disassemble code, dump memory, and dump stack information at that location while the server is still running. This option enables you to view specific information about a thread that may be having a problem.

**Run Config**   Under the Diagnose Server option, you can choose the Run Config option that executes and displays a complete set of configuration information from the server. This option is useful in providing you information about the current configuration remotely. Figure 9.4 shows the Run Config screen that is available.

**FIGURE 9.4** *Using NetWare Remote Manager, you can remotely view the configuration information that is typically available only from the server console. This information allows you to view the current versions and settings.*

### Manage Server

In addition to monitoring and debugging server problems, you can use the NetWare Remote Manager for common server management tasks as well as mounting and dismounting volumes, managing server connections, and configuring SET parameters. Within the Manager Server section of the utility, you are given the following options:

- ▶ Volumes
- ▶ Console Screens
- ▶ Connections
- ▶ Set Parameters
- ▶ Schedule Tasks
- ▶ View Memory

▸ Config

▸ View Statistics

▸ Down/Restart

**Volumes**    The first set of information that is displayed is the Volume Management tab that provides you a list of the server's volumes, local drives, and disk partitions. From the Volume Management screen, you can set volume, directory, and file attributes, as well as copy, delete, rename, and create directories and files. In addition, the attributes and mount status of volumes are shown. From this page, you can expand the view of the volumes to browse the file system. You can view the file system on volumes on the server, access DOS partitions, browse directories and files, and view and change attributes of files, directories, and volumes. To browse a volume or partition, click the desired drive or volume. Click the directory names to move down the tree. Click the double dots to navigate up the tree. Figure 9.5 shows the information that is presented after you select the SYS: volume.

**FIGURE 9.5** *You can browse the file system on the server using NetWare Remote Manager. Remotely, you can browse up and down the file directory tree, and upload files from your workstation to the server.*

The View Volume Segment Info link is followed by a list of entries under the Volume Information table, such as whether the volume is mounted, the file system type, loaded name spaces, compression and sub-allocation information, and so on, as shown in the Table 9.1. The Description column contains available settings for the entries and a brief description of what they mean.

TABLE 9.1

*Volume Information*

| INFORMATION | DESCRIPTION |
| --- | --- |
| Volume Is Mounted | Yes/No. You can dismount volumes using the main Volume Management screen. |
| File System Name | NetWare Traditional File System or the Novell NSS File System. |
| Loaded Name Spaces | DOS, MAC, NFS, LONG. These are added automatically when the NSS File System is loaded. The traditional file system loads only DOS and LONG file name spaces automatically; the other name spaces must be loaded manually. |
| Read-Only | Tells you whether this volume is Read-Only, such as a CD-ROM volume running under NSS. This entry is set by the NetWare file system itself (the setting prevents the file system from trying to write to a CD-ROM) and cannot be changed. |
| Compression Status | On or Off. Settable from under the Volume Attributes column for Traditional File System volumes. After it is enabled, it cannot be disabled. |
| Sub-allocation | On or Off. Settable from under the Volume Attributes column for Traditional File System volumes. After it is enabled, it cannot be disabled. |
| Sub-allocation Unit Size | 512 bytes minimum size and cannot presently be changed. |
| Migration Status | On or Off. Settable from under the Volume Attributes column for Traditional File System volumes. Shows whether file migration is used on this volume. |
| Migrated Files | This entry displays Off or the number of migrated files. Shows how many files have been migrated to an HCSS (High-Capacity Storage System) unit. |
| Block Size | The size that blocks are set at on this volume. 64K blocks are used by NSS, but on traditional NetWare file system volumes, this is settable from 8K to 64K block size upon creation of the volume itself. |

*continued*

| | T A B L E   9 . 1 | |
| :--- | :--- | :--- |
| | *Volume Information (continued)* | |
| **INFORMATION** | **DESCRIPTION** | |
| Sectors Per Block | Number of sectors in a block, which depends on the block size selected. For 64K, the number of sectors is 128K. | |
| Total Blocks | Number of blocks in this volume, depending on the volume size. | |
| Free Blocks | Number of hard disk drive blocks that are presently free for use on this volume. Does not include blocks that are used through the Salvage system. | |
| FAT Blocks | Number of hard disk drive blocks that are presently in use for the File Allocation Table (FAT). | |
| Freeable Blocks In Salvage System | Number of volume blocks that at one time held data but have been deleted, and are salvageable through the FILER or the Portal utility, but have now aged long enough to be freed up for use if needed. If you have the Immediate Purge attribute set on this volume, this entry displays 0. | |
| Non-freeable Blocks In Salvage System | Shows the number of deleted files that haven't aged long enough through the Least Recently Used (LRU) algorithm to be regarded as available to be freed up for use if needed. Settable through the Minimum File Delete Wait Time and the File Delete Wait Time SET parameters. | |
| Directory Size, In Blocks | Shows the number of volume blocks that are presently in use for the Directory Entry Tables (DET). | |
| Total Directory Entries | Shows the total number of directory entries that are available for use on this volume. | |
| Used Directory Entries | Shows the number of directory entries that are presently in use on this volume. | |
| Extended Directory Space | Shows how much disk space has been allocated to store extraneous information, such as long names, name spaces, and other migration storage information. | |

Your access to directories and files on the NetWare partitions, as well as your ability to copy files to and from any given directory, are governed by the rights based on the credentials of the user who is logged in. This screen also allows you to delete or rename a directory or file. For directories, you can also create a new subdirectory (on NetWare volumes only). If your browser is set up to recognize a certain file extension (for example, .TXT), you can click a file of that type and view it directly. Otherwise, you can download any file to your local machine by clicking the filename.

If you have rights to write to the current directory that you're viewing, an Upload button enables you to copy a file from any other mapped drive to that directory. This utility allows the uploading of only one file at a time.

You can also mount or dismount any volumes. With admin rights, you can mount and dismount volumes by clicking the Mounted status column for a given volume. You are asked to confirm your choice before the volume is actually dismounted.

In addition to the ability to browse the file system, you can also navigate through files and directories on the server's DOS partition. Be aware that setting the Shareable attribute on a DOS file does not have any effect unless SHARE is loaded in DOS. Admin rights are required for access to the server's DOS partition. Figure 9.6 shows how to view the DOS partition through the NRM utility.

**FIGURE 9.6** *NetWare Remote Manager enables you to view, access, and upload files to the local partitions on the NetWare 6 server.*

In addition to managing the server's volumes, you can use the NRM utility to view and manage the disk partitions and hard disk components. Figure 9.7 shows the screen you use to manage the disk partitions and supporting hardware.

**FIGURE 9.7** *NetWare Remote Manager enables you to view and manage all aspects of the hard drive partitions and hardware components.*

**Console Screens**   The Console Screen page allows you to view all current server console screens. The System Console screen allows for simple command-line input such as entering the version command, or loading/unloading a module. The command-line input supports up to 32 characters. Some of the server screens are view-only and do not allow user input. When viewing one of the screens, you can control the refresh rate of this display by choosing a page refresh rate at the top of the window. Refresh is suspended when you click Command Line Input. Figure 9.8 shows how the NetWare Remote Manager enables you to view the server console screens.

**FIGURE 9.8** *You can view the current server console screens.*

**Connections**    Using the NetWare Remote Manager, you can view and manage the current server connections. You can even send broadcast messages from this interface remotely to all connected users. Between the two connection screens shown in Figure 9.9 and Figure 9.10, you can perform the following actions:

- View current connections
- Clear specific connections
- Clear all not logged in connections
- Broadcast messages to all users

For a specific connection, you can view the login time, connection number, network address, login status, files in use, and so on, and send a message to that specific connection. The connection information via the NetWare Remote Manager differs slightly from that displayed in the MONITOR.NLM. The NRM connection information screen includes information about Connection 0 and Monitor does not. Another difference is that Portal does not use the asterisk character to mark connections that don't count against the server's connection limit.

**FIGURE 9.9** *NetWare Remote Manager enables you to view the current server connections in all states.*

**FIGURE 9.10** *You can also send broadcast messages, clear "Not Logged In" connections, and view the number of licensed connections installed and used.*

**SET Parameters**   From the SET Parameters screen, you can view and change settings for any SET parameter for NetWare 6. From the main screen after you select the SET parameters option, you can see the major categories of the SET parameters, as shown in Figure 9.11.

**FIGURE 9.11**  *Using the NetWare Remote Manager, you can view all SET parameter categories that the server supports.*

After you select a category of SET parameters, you can view the current value, minimum and maximum values where appropriate, help descriptions, and (where applicable) the name of the NLM that owns the SET parameter. The settings can also be saved to a text file on the SYS: volume for reference. Figure 9.12 shows the screen that appears after you select the communication category of SET parameters.

**View Memory**   The System Memory Information screen enables you to view how the server memory has been allocated. This page includes total server memory and cache memory used, and it enables you to select other specific memory statistics on the server. In addition, you can view memory usage as a pie chart. You also see links to view statistics on Swap File, individual NLM memory usage, and Virtual Memory information. Figure 9.13 shows the server memory page that is available in NetWare Remote Manager.

**FIGURE 9.12** *Communication SET parameters in NetWare Remote Manager*

**FIGURE 9.13** *The server memory page enables you to view all aspects of current memory setting and usage.*

From the System Memory Information screen, click on NLM Memory to bring up a list of all NLMs that are using memory. The NetWare Loadable Modules Information screen appears, displaying clickable buttons to sort the memory listing by the following categories: Name (in alphabetical order), Code, Data, Alloc Memory, NLM Total (in bytes), and NLM Total. Clicking on the Alloc Memory category, for example, displays which NLMs are using the most memory, from highest to lowest. Figure 9.14 shows the NLM Memory screen that displays the memory allocated to each NLM.

**FIGURE 9.14** *Clicking on the NLM Memory button from the System Memory Information screen displays the server modules' memory usage in alphabetical order.*

Using the NetWare Remote Manager, you can view, manage, and troubleshoot other aspects of the server and its subsystem. For example, you can view pages that show current information for most of the system resources and system statistics. From the system statistics page, you can view the following statistics:

▶ **Network management information** — Enables you to see the current number of server processes, current cache buffers, active file handles, current connections, number of NLMs loaded, and server uptime (in ticks).

▶ **Kernel statistic information** — Enables you to view the current status of the internal process of the NetWare kernel that includes run queues and work-to-do lists.

▶ **LSL statistical information** — Enables you to view the current allocated Event Control Blocks (ECBs), free ECBs, and other communication parameters.

▶ **Media manager statistical information** — Enables you to view current disk statistics that include I/O request rate, data transfer rate, and disk reads and writes.

**Down Server Options**   The Down Server Options screen allows you or an Administrator user to down, restart, or reset (warm boot) the server. You are asked to confirm your choice before the action is taken. The Reset button does a warm boot on the server machine, so if your AUTOEXEC.BAT does not include the command to load the server, you lose access to the server. Figure 9.15 shows the Down Server Options page available in the NetWare Remote Manager.

### Application Management

You can use the NetWare Remote Manager to view and manage the applications of the server. Within the Application Management section of the utility, you are given the following options to view the current module list: You can sort the list by module name, code/data size, or memory usage by clicking the column heading. Click the memory value for an individual NLM to view detailed memory statistics for that module. Then click a module name for detailed information (flags, resources, memory use details, module dependency list, and so on) as well as an option to unload the NLM if no module dependencies exist. An entry field appears at the top of this page to load an NLM on the server.

The Application Management section also provides the ability to view and manage the server's address space and memory protection. The page that provides these features shows information about modules running in protected address spaces on the server. Click an address space name to view a listing of all NLMs loaded there. You can also load an individual module or execute an NCF to load several modules into the same protected address space.

**FIGURE 9.15** *The Down Server Options page enables you to remotely down, reset, and restart the server.*

In addition, you can manage the server's registry and Winsock implementation. The registry page allows you to view the entire NetWare Registry tree structure. The registry view is read-only. The page that manages Winsock 2 shows detailed information on Winsock Sockets and Global API counter information. You can close an individual socket by clicking the button at the bottom of the socket detail page.

### Hardware Management

You can use the NetWare Remote Manager to view and manage the server's hardware. Within the Hardware Management section of the utility, you can view and manage the hardware adapters. The Hardware Adapter page lists all storage and network adapters on the server. Click the individual adapter name for detailed information on each (device name, type, capacity, partition info, and so on). Statistical data and links to LAN and disk performance are also available. Figure 9.16 shows the Hardware Adapter page in NetWare Remote Manager.

**FIGURE 9.16** *The Hardware Adapter page enables you to view and manage the server hardware components.*

Within the Hardware Management section, you can view and manage the processor information page that enables you to view detailed information and the status of all processors available on the server. If more than one processor is present, you can stop and start processors individually (except for P0). You can also see the status of the server's hardware interrupts, slots, ports, DMA (if applicable), and shared memory. In addition, you can view the PCI device information page that provides details on each PCI device listed by HIN (hardware instance number) and gives links to additional details on the Status register and Command register for each.

## NDS Management

You can use the NetWare Remote Manager to view and manage the NDS tree and partitions. Within the NDS Management section of the utility, the Tree Walker enables you to view the current NDS tree. You can get details on and delete individual objects. Use the delete function with caution because the Admin user can delete any object including the Admin object itself. Figure 9.17 shows the NDS tree walker page within NetWare Remote Manager.

**FIGURE 9.17** *The Tree Walker page within NetWare Remote Manager enables you to view the current tree and its objects.*

The NetWare Remote Manager also enables you to view and manage the NDS Partitions. Figure 9.18 shows how you can view and manage the NDS partition using the NetWare Remote Manager.

**FIGURE 9.18** *You can view and manage the NDS partitions using the NetWare Remote Manager.*

## The iMonitor Utility

The NDS iMonitor utility provides monitoring and diagnostic capability to your NDS tree. It lets you look at all servers, partitions, replicas, and objects in your NDS tree. The iMonitor utility lets you monitor your servers and NDS from any location on your network where a Web browser is available. When iMonitor first comes up, it displays the Agent Summary page shown in Figure 9.19.

From the Agent Summary page, you can view the health of your NDS servers and view general information about your NDS tree, including synchronization information, agent process status, and the total servers known to your database. You can view the number and types of replicas you have and the length of time since they have been successfully synchronized. You can also view the number of errors for each replica type. If only one replica or partition is available to view, the heading is Partition Synchronization Status. If the Agent Synchronization Summary doesn't appear, you can view no replicas based on your identity. You can also view the status of processes that run on an agent without the administrator's intervention. When you have a problem or a piece of information, a status is recorded. The table increases or decreases, depending on the number of recorded statuses.

▶ • • • • • • • • • • • • • • • • • • • • • • • ◀

**FIGURE 9.19** *The NDS iMonitor startup page is called the Agent Summary page.*

In addition, the Agent Summary page shows the name of the server to which you're connected in blue at the top of the page. In this case, we're looking at a server called CAM-SRV1.ACME.ACME_TREE. You can use the hot links on the main page to examine information such as the partition synchronization status of your master and other replicas.

The icons along the top of the page are a tool bar and contain utilities such as Login, Agent Summary, and Repair. The left column contains links that you can use to go to different reports. On subsequent pages, the column also contains the filters that you can use to view report pages. Using the links, NDS iMonitor provides the following features:

- ▶ NDS health summary
- ▶ Synchronization information
- ▶ Known servers
- ▶ Agent configuration
- ▶ Hyperlinked DS Trace

- Agent information
- Error information
- Object/schema examiner
- Partition list
- Agent process status
- Agent activity
- Verb statistics
- Background process schedule
- DS Repair

The information that you are allowed to view in iMonitor is based on your identity. The information that you view in iMonitor shows what is happening on your server at that moment.

### The iMonitor Utility System Requirements

To use iMonitor, you need any HTML 3 browser, such as Netscape 4.06 or later or Internet Explorer 4 or later, and NDS eDirectory 8.5. The iMonitor utility runs on NetWare 6 and can be placed in AUTOEXEC.NCF. The workstation platform is Windows 98/NT/2000, Linux, Solaris, and Tru64 UNIX. For Windows 98/NT/2000, iMonitor loads automatically when NDS runs. For Linux, Solaris, and Tru64 UNIX, enter NDSIMONITOR -l at the server's system console to load the module. You can also use iMonitor to monitor NDS versions. You can use iMonitor to monitor the following versions of NDS:

- All versions of NDS for NetWare 4.11 or later
- All versions of NDS for Windows NT/2000
- All versions of NDS for UNIX

NDS iMonitor can be used in two different modes of operation: Direct mode and Proxy mode. No configuration changes are necessary to move between these modes. NDS iMonitor moves between these modes automatically, but you should understand them in order to successfully and easily navigate the NDS tree.

Direct mode is used when your Web browser is pointed directly at a TCP/IP address or DNS name on a machine running the iMonitor executable and reading only information on that machine's local NDS Directory Information Base (DIB). These features are server-centric; that is, they are available only to the iMonitor running on that machine. These features use local API sets that cannot be accessed remotely. Server-centric features in iMonitor include the DS Trace, DS Repair, and Background Process Schedule pages. When a machine is using direct mode, all iMonitor features are available on that machine. Key features of direct mode are as follows:

▶ Full server-centric feature set

▶ Reduced network bandwidth (faster access)

▶ Access by proxy still available for all versions of NDS

Proxy mode is used when your Web browser is pointed at an iMonitor running on one machine, but is gathering information from another machine. Because iMonitor uses traditional NDS non-server-centric protocols for non-server-centric features, all previous versions of NDS back to NDS v6 can be monitored and diagnosed. However, server-centric features use APIs that cannot be accessed remotely. While in proxy mode, if you wish to switch to direct mode for a different server, you can do so as long as it is a version of NDS in which iMonitor has shipped. If the server you are gathering information on by proxy has an iMonitor running, you see an additional icon button in the Navigator frame. When you move your mouse over the icon, you see a link to the remote iMonitor on the remote server. If the server you are gathering information on by proxy is an earlier version of NDS, no additional icon is shown and you will always have to gather information on that server by proxy until it is upgraded to a version of NDS that includes iMonitor. Key features of proxy mode are as follows:

▶ Not every server in the tree must be running NDS iMonitor in order to use most iMonitor features.

▶ Only one server is required to be upgraded.

▶ There is a single point of access for dial-in.

▶ You can access iMonitor over a slower-speed link while iMonitor accesses NDS information over higher-speed links.

▶ Previous NDS version information is accessible.

▶ Server-centric features are available only where iMonitor is installed.

### Accessing the iMonitor Utility

In order to access the iMonitor utility, open your Web browser on your workstation and run NDS iMonitor in two ways:

▶ Type the TCP/IP address and port of a server running NDS iMonitor in the address field, followed by /NDS (for example, `http://10.0.0.10:8008/NDS`).

▶ Through the NetWare Remote Manager (PORTAL.NLM) Portal screen, you select NDS iMonitor from the NDS Management menu in the left column.

You can use DNS names anywhere that you can also use a server's TCP/IP address or distinguished name in iMonitor.

If needed, the iMonitor utility uses HTTPS for secure iMonitor operations. If the default HTTP port on which iMonitor is listening is 80, the HTTPS port is 81. If the default HTTP port on which iMonitor is listening is 8008, the HTTPS port is 8009. For secure NDS iMonitor operations on Linux, Solaris, and Tru64 UNIX systems, you must create a Key Material object (KMO) in the server context. After creating the KMO, add it to the ndsimonitor configuration file. To do so, add the following line to the /usr/lib/imon/ndsimon.conf file, and then run the ndsimonitor utility:

```
SSLKey: KMO_name
```

Ensure that a space character appears after the colon character and before the KMO name.

### Anatomy of an iMonitor Page

Each iMonitor page is divided into three frames or sections: the Navigator frame, the Assistant frame, and the Data frame.

**Navigator Frame**  The Navigator frame is located across the top of the page. This frame shows the server name where the data is being read from, your identity, and the icons you can click to link to other screens, including online help, login, server portal, and other iMonitor pages.

**Assistant Frame**  The Assistant frame is located at the left side of the page. In this frame, you find additional navigational aids, such as links to other pages, items that help you navigate data in the Data frame, or other items to assist you with obtaining or interpreting the data on a given page.

**Data Frame**  The Data frame shows the detailed information about your servers that you request by clicking one of the links listed above. This is the only page you see if your Web browser does not support frames.

### Viewing Partition Synchronization Status

From the Agent Synchronization page, you can view the synchronization status of your partitions. You can filter the information by selecting from the options listed in the Assistant frame on the left side of the page. Figure 9.20 shows the partition information in iMonitor.

**FIGURE 9.20** *You can view the partition information for the server to which you are connected.*

The partition page provides server partition information that includes the partition, errors, last modified time, purge time, and replica state. From the Partitions page, you can view information about the replicas on the server with which you are communicating. You can filter the page by selecting from the options in the Assistant frame on the left side of the page. The Purge Time column is the data that has been deleted before it can be removed from the database because all replicas have seen not the deletion. The last modification time is the last-issued time stamp of data written to the database for the replica. This lets you see whether the time is in the future and if synthetic time is being used. If you select one of the partitions, you receive a second view with more detail for the partition, as shown in Figure 9.21.

**FIGURE 9.21** *When you select one of the partitions, you see a second view of more detailed information for the partition.*

### Viewing Server Connection Information

Using iMonitor, you can view the connection information for the server that you are connected to. Depending on the transport, protocol, configuration, and platform you are running on, you might not see ping information. You can view connection information for the server, including the server referral, time delta, and replica depth. The server referral is a set of addresses by which your server can be reached. Figure 9.22 shows the connection page in iMonitor.

### Controlling and Configuring the DS Agent

From the Agent Triggers page, you can control and configure the DS Agent. The functionality you have at this page depends on the rights of the current identity and the version of NDS you are looking at. You can use agent synchronization settings to disable or enable inbound or outbound synchronization. You can specify in hours the amount of time you want synchronization to be disabled. You can configure the amount of database cache used by the DS database engine.

Various cache statistics are also provided to assist you in determining whether you have an appropriate amount of cache available. Having an inadequate amount of cache may severely impact your system's performance.

**FIGURE 9.22** *The server connection page in iMonitor*

You can use background process settings to modify the interval at which certain background processes run. These settings are equivalent to the SET DSTRACE=!option command. Figure 9.23 shows the background process settings that enable you to control the background process of NDS on the server.

From the Background Process Schedule page, you can view the background processes that are scheduled, what their current state is, and when they are scheduled to run again. NDS iMonitor's Background Process Schedule is a server-centric feature. That is, it can be viewed only on a server where iMonitor is running. If you need to access the background process schedule on another server, you must switch to the iMonitor running on that server. As you upgrade more servers to NDS eDirectory 8.5, iMonitor's server-centric features will be more available to you. The background process status page is shown in Figure 9.24.

**FIGURE 9.23** *You can view and manage the background process for NDS using iMonitor.*

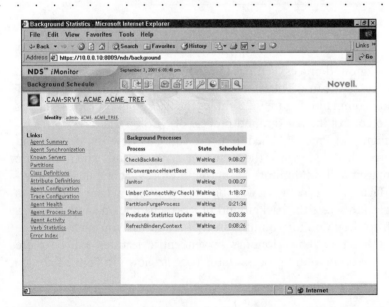

**FIGURE 9.24** *The current background process status, state, and schedule can be viewed using iMonitor.*

To access information on the Background Process Schedule page, you must be the equivalent of Administrator of the server or a console operator.

### Viewing Trace Option Information

From the Trace Configuration page, you can configure trace settings. NDS iMonitor's DS Trace is a server-centric feature. That is, it can be initiated only on a server where iMonitor is running. If you need to access this feature on another server, you must switch to the iMonitor running on that server. As you upgrade more servers to NDS eDirectory 8.5, iMonitor's server-centric features will be more available to you.

You can use agent triggers to initiate certain background processes. These triggers are equivalent to using the SET DSTRACE=* option command. You can use trace triggers to show the trace flags that must be set in order to display the specified DS Agent information in DS Trace. These triggers might write large quantities of information to trace. Generally, we recommend that these triggers be enabled only when instructed by Novell Technical Support. Figure 9.25 shows the trace triggers that are available in iMonitor.

**FIGURE 9.25** *Trace triggers that control DS Trace in iMonitor*

To access information on the Trace Configuration page, you must be the equivalent of Administrator of the server or a console operator. You can submit changes to Trace Options and Trace Line Prefixes. If DS Trace is off, click Submit to turn it on. If DS Trace is already on, click Submit to submit changes to the current trace.

Trace On/Off: You can turn DS Trace on or off by using this button. The button text changes based on the current DS Trace state. If DS Trace is on, the button text says Trace Off. Clicking it turns DS Trace off. When DS Trace is off, clicking Trace On is equivalent to clicking Submit.

These DS Trace options apply to the events on the local DS Agent where the trace is initiated. The options show errors, potential problems, and other information about NDS on your local server. Turning on DS Trace options can increase CPU utilization and might reduce your system's performance; therefore, DS Trace should generally be used for diagnostic purposes, not as a standard practice. These options are a more convenient equivalent of the SET DSTRACE=+option command. You can view a live run of DS Trace using iMonitor. Figure 9.26 shows how you can use the Trace Live page to view DS Trace information.

**FIGURE 9.26** *Using iMonitor, you can view the Trace Live page to view current DS Trace information.*

### Viewing Verb Count Activity

From the Verb Statistics page, you can determine activity or traffic patterns and troubleshoot problems in NDS. You can use this page to view the verbs and requests that are currently being handled by NDS. If you view this page on an older version of NDS, you might not see as much information as you would if you were running on DS build number 8500 or later. Figure 9.27 shows the Verb Statistics page in iMonitor.

**FIGURE 9.27** *The Verb Statistics page in iMonitor can be used to view activity and help you troubleshoot problems.*

From the Verb Statistics page, you can determine traffic patterns and potential system bottlenecks. You can use this page to view a running count of all verbs called and requests made since NDS was last initialized. This page also shows how many of those requests are currently active and the minimum, maximum, and average times (shown in milliseconds) required to process those requests. Background process, bindery, and standard NDS requests are tracked.

### Viewing NDS Server Errors

From the Error Index page, you can view information about the errors found on your NDS servers. The errors are separated into two fields: NDS-specific errors and other errors that might be of interest. Each error listed is hyperlinked to a description that contains an explanation, possible cause, and troubleshooting actions. Figure 9.28 shows the NDS Error Index page in iMonitor.

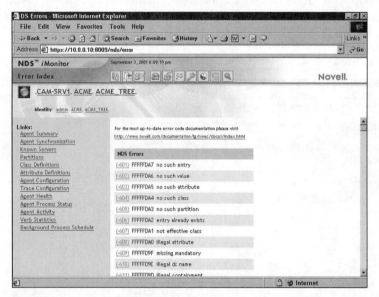

**FIGURE 9.28** *You can use the NDS Error Index page to view information about errors found on the NDS server.*

From the Error Index page, you can link to the latest Novell documentation on errors, technical information, and white papers.

### Viewing DS Repair Information

From the DS Repair page, you can view problems and back up or clean up your DIB sets. NDS iMonitor's DS Repair is a server-centric feature. That is, it can be initiated only on a server where iMonitor is running. If you need to access the DS Repair information on another server, you must switch to the iMonitor running on that server. As you upgrade more servers to NDS eDirectory 8.5, iMonitor's server-centric features will be more available to you. Other server-centric features include the DS Trace and Background Process Schedule pages. Figure 9.29 shows the DS Repair page.

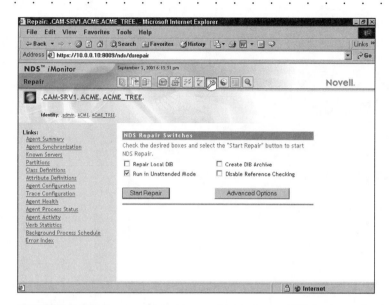

**FIGURE 9.29** *You can view problems and back up your NDS database using the DS Repair page.*

To access information on this page, you must be the equivalent of Administrator of the server or a console operator. You cannot access DSREPAIR.LOG until the operation is finished if the DSREPAIR utility is running or you have initiated a repair from the DS Repair page in iMonitor.

You can also use the DS Repair Advanced Switches to fix problems, check for problems, or create a backup of your database. You do not need to enter information in the Support Options field unless you are directed to do so by Novell Technical Support.

### Using iMonitor to Monitor and Configure Cache Settings

The best way to monitor and configure cache settings is to use iMonitor, which was released with eDirectory 8.5. Using iMonitor enables you to intuitively view information about the current cache settings, look at the statistics to determine possible adjustments, and make the appropriate settings. Best of all, you do this through an Internet browser for any operating system on the back end (NetWare, Windows NT/2000, or UNIX/Linux).

Figure 9.30 shows the Agent Configuration page that allows you to view the database cache. You can monitor and make changes to the cache settings for this server.

**FIGURE 9.30** *Under the Agent Configuration, you can see the database cache selections that show the Database Information and Database Cache statistics.*

The Agent Configuration page enables you to configure and monitor the cache segments being used by the NDS database subsystem. The information provided on this page helps you determine whether you have an adequate cache size and, if not, helps give you an idea how much you should have. For most applications of the directory, the default behavior and cache settings are adequate.

The Database Cache page is divided into three sections: Database Information, Database Cache Information, and Database Cache Configuration. The size of the database cache and associated files on the disk is in KB. Stream files are part of the associated files but are never cached. These should be subtracted from the DIB size to compute the size of the NDS database.

### The Database Cache Screen

The Database Cache page in iMonitor enables you to easily configure the eDirectory cache for a server. In fact, this is the preferred method to configure your cache. It enables you to adjust the cache for whatever server platform you are running, and it prevents you from making mistakes related to not being able to remember all the commands needed for adjusting the cache (for example, the DSTRACE functions under NetWare).

The following is an explanation of each of the settings on the Database Cache Configuration screen:

- **Dynamic Adjust** — This setting allows the NDS database to dynamically adjust the amount of system memory to be used for the cache, based on the amount it thinks it needs and the parameters specified below.

- **Cache Adjust Percentage** — This specifies the percentage of available memory allowed to be used for the record and block caches combined.

- **Cache Size Constraints** — While dynamically adjusting, NDS follows the constraints specified here: namely, use no less than the specified amount of memory for the cache, and use no more than the total amount of available memory minus the specified amount.

- **Hard Limit** — This setting allows the NDS administrator to specify the exact amount of system memory to be used for the cache.

- **Cache Maximum Size** — This is the size in KB of the record and block caches combined.

- **Block Cache Percentage** — This is the percentage of the system memory available for caching that should be allocated to the block cache. The remaining percentage is allocated to the record cache.

- **Cache Adjust Interval** — This interval applies only when Dynamic Adjust is set. It controls how often the cache size is adjusted based on the specified percentage and constraints.

- **Cache Cleanup Interval** — This setting controls how often unused old versions are removed from the cache.

- **Cache Settings Permanent** — When checked, any changes submitted via iMonitor are made permanent, overwriting any previously saved settings or system defaults.

If no cache settings have been previously specified as permanent, when the eDirectory 8.5 agent starts up, the cache is defaulted to a hard limit of 16MB for the first 10 minutes. Because the eDirectory agent usually loads when a server is rebooted, this default behavior allows other applications the opportunity to load and request system resources first. After 10 minutes, the default behavior is to switch to Dynamic Adjust mode based on the amount of available memory. The default values for Dynamic Adjust mode are as follows:

- Cache Adjust Percentage = 51%
- CacheSizeConstraints = > 16MB < (Total Available Memory - 24 MB)

For both Dynamic Adjust and Hard Limit, the default Block Cache Percentage = 50% and the default Cache Adjust and Cache Cleanup Intervals are 15 seconds.

## The DSREPAIR Utility

The DSREPAIR utility enables you to monitor the directory on each NetWare 6 server, check for errors, and correct problems in the name service on an individual server basis. The utility runs as a NetWare Loadable Module (NLM) at the server console. The utility is menu driven and is written with the well-known C-worthy user interface. These are the main functions of DSREPAIR:

- ▶ Correct or repair inconsistencies in the NDS database
- ▶ Check NDS partition and replica information and make changes where necessary
- ▶ Initiate replica synchronization

You can run the DSREPAIR utility on any NetWare 6 server. Additionally, the utility can either be loaded from the server console or through access to a server via the RCONSOLE utility. The DSREPAIR utility can be run remotely in this manner. Figure 9.31 illustrates the DSREPAIR utility main menu.

**FIGURE 9.31** *The DSREPAIR utility main menu*

The DSREPAIR utility provides the following options:

- ▶ **Single Object Repair** — This option resolves inconsistencies that may prevent access to the selected object. To perform this function, you need to provide the object ID.
- ▶ **Unattended Full Repair** — This feature automatically performs repair operations on the local NDS name service without operator assistance.

- **Time Synchronization** — This option checks the time synchronization for all servers that are known to the local server. You must monitor and correct time synchronization problems before performing any repair operation. A replica of the [ROOT] partition must be on the local server running DSREPAIR for this feature to contact all servers in the tree.

- **Report Synchronization Status** — This option lets you check the synchronization status of any partition on the server and the servers holding the association replicas.

- **View Repair Log File** — This option lets you view all the operations of the DSREPAIR utility by consulting a log file stored on your server. The default log file is SYS:SYSTEM\DSREPAIR.LOG. You should always view the log file after running the utility.

- **Advanced Options Menu** — The advanced options on this menu give you greater flexibility to manually control the repair of your NDS tree.

These options are discussed in the following sections.

### Single Object Repair

The Single Object Repair option enables you to target the repair operations to a selected object in the directory. The repair function attempts to resolve all inconsistencies in the object, which may be preventing the directory from accessing the data. This repair operation or function can be performed against objects in only the user-defined partitions and external reference partitions.

### Unattended Full Repair

The Unattended Full Repair option automatically performs all possible repair operations that do not require operator assistance. This option goes through five major repair procedures:

- It repairs the local NDS database, which locks the database during the repair operation so that no new database updates can occur until completed.

- It repairs any NCP server object's network address; the database is not locked during this operation.

- It verifies all remote NCP server object IDs; the database is not locked during this operation.

- It checks replica rings; the database is not locked during this operation.

- It authenticates every server in the ring and verifies information on the ring.

You can control which of the preceding items are checked or repaired by using the Repair Local DS Database option, which is described later in this chapter under the "Advanced Options Menu" section.

The log file records all the actions during the Unattended Full Repair operation. When the repair operations are completed, the log file is opened so that you can see what repairs were made and check the current state of the database. Figure 9.32 shows the log file after the Unattended Full Repair operation has been run on the ACME tree.

**FIGURE 9.32** *The log file after the time synchronization operation has been run on the ACME tree*

### Time Synchronization

The Time Synchronization option contacts every server known to the local server and requests information about time synchronization, Directory Services, and server status. The information is written to the log file. When the operation has completed, the log file is opened so that you can check the status of time synchronization plus other Directory Services information.

An explanation of each field in the log file that is returned after running Time Synchronization is provided in Table 9.2.

TABLE 9.2

*Fields in the DSREPAIR Log File or Time Synchronization*

| FIELD | CONTENT |
| --- | --- |
| Server Name | This is the distinguished name of the server responding to the request. |
| DS.NLM Version | This is the version of the DS.NLM running on the responding server. This information is valuable as a quick reference to see the versions of NDS running on the servers of your network. |

| FIELD | CONTENT |
|---|---|
| Replica Depth | The replica depth indicates how deep in the NDS tree, moving away from [ROOT], the first replica is on the responding server. Each server knows which replica is highest in the NDS tree. This value is the number being reported. A positive number indicates how many objects exist from the [ROOT] to the highest replica. A value of –1 indicates that no replicas are stored on the server. |
| Time Source | The time source is the type of time server that the responding server is configured to be. |
| Time is in Sync | This field indicates the time synchronization status of the responding time server. The possible values are Yes and No. The value displayed is the status of the synchronization flag for each server. This means that the server's time is within the time synchronization radius. Refer to Chapter 7 for more information on time synchronization. |
| Time Delta | This field reports the time difference, if any, from the time synchronization radius for each server. The time synchronization radius is two seconds by default, so you will probably not see a server with more than a two-second difference. If the value is larger, the Time is in Sync field is probably set to No. The maximum that the field can report is up to 999 minutes and 59 seconds. |

### Reporting Synchronization Status

The Report Synchronization Status option starts a replica synchronization process for all the partitions that have replicas on this server. This operation starts the synchronization process for all partitions and replicas. If you want to perform the same operation for individual partitions, you need to select the Replica and Partition Operations option from the Advanced Options menu.

The report synchronization status operation contacts each server in each of the replica lists stored on the server. A server does not attempt to synchronize to itself, so the status returned for a server's own replica is the value of "host."

The operation uses the log file to track the actions of the requests and displays any errors that occur. This operation is a quick and easy way to determine that the partitions and servers are communicating and synchronizing properly.

### Viewing the Repair Log File

The View Repair Log File option lets you view the DSREPAIR log file, which contains the results of the previously performed operations. The default log file is stored in SYS:SYSTEM\DSREPAIR.LOG. When DSREPAIR performs an operation, the results are written to this log file. A record of each succeeding operation is appended to the log file, which increases in size with each repair operation. The size of the log file is displayed on the title line in parentheses after the name of the file.

Using the Advanced Options menu in DSREPAIR (discussed next), you can set current file size, reset the log file, log output to a new file name, and append to an existing file.

### The Advanced Options Menu

The Advanced Options menu enables you to control the individual repair operations manually. You can also use it to monitor status and access diagnostic information about your NDS tree. These options provide advanced repair operations that you should execute only if you understand the procedures and how they function. The Advanced Options menu provides the options shown in Figure 9.33, several of which are identical to the main menu options.

**FIGURE 9.33** *The Advanced Options menu in DSREPAIR*

**Log File and Login Configuration**   This option lets you configure the log file and log into the Directory tree. Configuring the log file enables you to manage where DSREPAIR writes the information it gathers. You can turn the log file off, delete it, and change the name of the file itself. The file can be stored on any volume or DOS drive.

The login function presents a login screen that lets you enter an administrator user name and password. After you have logged in, the authentication information is maintained in server memory for all other repair operations that require an administrator to log in.

**Repair Local DS Database**   This option repairs the local NDS name service and performs the same function as the Unattended Full Repair option in the main menu. Figure 9.34 shows the Repair Local DS Database selection screen. You can select or deselect each item to turn it on or off for the unattended full repair.

**FIGURE 9.34** *The Repair Local DS Database selection screen*

During the repair operations, NDS is temporarily locked, preventing clients from logging in. Several items are checked during the repair operation. For example, the Directory tree structure is checked to ensure that all records are linked to the [ROOT] object and that the object and property records are linked. The partition records are checked for validity, and any errors are fixed. A check is made for invalid checksums and links between records, and any errors are fixed.

The repair operation creates a set of temporary NDS files that are used to perform all the changes.. At the end of the repair operation these temporary files become the permanent NDS files, unless you choose not to accept the repairs that were made.

**Servers Known to this Database**   This option displays all the servers that the local NDS knows about. Each server must contact all servers in the replica list during replica synchronization. The local server knows about only the servers it needs to contact. If the local server has a copy of the [ROOT] partition, the list of known servers most likely contains all the servers in the tree because of remote and local IDs.

Figure 9.35 shows the servers found in the directory database screen. This information shows servers from replica lists, servers from remote/local IDs, and NCP server objects in any partition.

The Local Status field displays the state of the server as seen from the local server. If the value for a server is Up, the remote server is active. However, if the value is Down, the local server cannot communicate with the other server.

**FIGURE 9.35** *The servers found in this directory database screen in DSREPAIR*

If you can select a server from the list, the Server Options menu shown in Figure 9.36 becomes available. This menu applies to the selected server.

**FIGURE 9.36** *The DSREPAIR Server Options menu*

The Server Options menu provides the following options:

▸ **Time Synchronization and Server Status** — This option contacts every server known to the local server and requests information about time synchronization, Directory Services, and server status. This option is the same as the Time Synchronization option on the main menu.

▸ **Repair All Network Addresses** — This option checks every server object known to this server and searches for the server's name in the local SAP table. If the address is found in the SAP table, this address is compared with the value stored by the local server. If the two addresses do not match, the address in the SAP table is assumed to be correct and the other addresses are changed to match it. This operation is performed if you select the Unattended Full Repair option from the DSREPAIR main menu.

▶ **Repair Selected Server's Network Address** — This option repairs the highlighted server's network address in replica rings and server objects in the local database. As shown in Figure 9.37, you see a log file displaying the results of this activity and any errors that may have been generated.

▶ **View Entire Server's Name** — This option enables you to view the server's distinguished name. Figure 9.38 shows a view of the server's full name from DSREPAIR.

**FIGURE 9.37** *The screen that is displayed when you select the Repair Selected Server's Network Address option in DSREPAIR*

**FIGURE 9.38** *The DSREPAIR View Entire Server's Name Options menu*

**Replica and Partition Operations**   You should become very familiar with the Replica and Partition Operations option on the Advanced Options menu. You will use this menu more than any other menu during the maintenance of NDS. When this option is selected, DSREPAIR displays a list of all the replicas stored on the server. This list applies only to the server on which you are running DSREPAIR. The menu option to view replicas is called Replicas Stored on This Server and is shown in Figure 9.39. Each replica is shown in list format, with the replica type (master, read/write, read-only, and subordinate reference) and replica state (ON, OFF, and so on).

**FIGURE 9.39** *The Replicas Stored on This Server menu in DSREPAIR*

From the Replicas Stored on This Server menu, you can select an individual replica or partition, which enables you to obtain more specific information and perform maintenance functions. After you select an individual replica or partition from the list, you see a larger Replica Options menu called Replica Options, Partition: *partition name*. Figure 9.40 shows this Replica Options menu, and you can see that the name of the partition is CAMELOT.ACME. This menu includes an extensive list of specific options and operations that enable you to perform specific diagnostic and repair functions. These operations apply only to the partition selected.

The Replica Options menu is the most heavily used menu in DSREPAIR because it enables you to monitor, diagnose, and repair specific problems with the replicas stored on a particular server. Several repair options in this menu require you to log in as a user who has rights to perform the operation. The utility makes you log in before running all of the important repair options as a final check that you are authorized to perform the operation.

The operations in this menu affect the entire partition and all of its replicas. This is one place where the DSREPAIR utility can start operations on the other servers through the use of a replica list.

**FIGURE 9.40** *The Replica Options menu in DSREPAIR for the CAMELOT.ACME partition*

If you want to affect only the replica that is stored on a specific server, select the View Replica Ring option, select a specific replica on any server, and then perform partition and replica operations on only that server.

The Replica Options menu supplies several additional options that you can execute for the partition and all of its replicas, as described next:

> ► **View Replica Ring** — This option provides another menu or list of all the servers that contain replicas for the selected partition. The menu that appears is called Replicas of Partition: *partition name*. A replica ring is equivalent to a replica list, which is a list of all the servers that hold replicas for a specific partition. The replica ring shows the replica type and replica state information for each server. You can choose a server or replica in this list and display the Replicas of Partition: *partition name* menu, as shown in Figure 9.41, which provides more functionality on the selected server. Figure 9.41 shows information for the CAMELOT.ACME partition.

```
NetWare 6.0 DSRepair  10110.06              NetWare Loadable Module
DS.NLM 10110.20  Tree name: ACME_TREE
Server name: .CAM-SRV1.ACME

┌──────────────────────────────────────────────────────┐
│          Replica Options, Partition: .ACME            │
├──────────────────────────────────────────────────────┤
│ View replica ring                                     │
│ Report synchronization status of all servers          │
├──────────────────────────────────────────────────────┤
│              Replicas Of Partition: .ACME             │
├──────────────────────────────────────────────────────┤
│  Server name           Replica type     Replica state │
│ .CAM-SRV1.ACME         Master           On            │
├───────────┬──────────────────────────────────────────┤
│ .Tokyo.ACME│ Cancel partition operation               │
│ .[Root].   │ Designate this server as the new master replica│
│            │ View entire partition name               │
│            │ Return to replica list                   │
└───────────┴──────────────────────────────────────────┘
This list shows each server that has a replica of the partition. Select a server
and press <Enter> to display an options menu.
 Enter=Ring options menu                         Alt+F10=Exit
 Esc=Return to replica menu                       F1=Help
```

**FIGURE 9.41** *The Replicas of Partition menu in DSREPAIR*

Selecting the View Replica Ring option displays the Replicas for Partition: *partition name* menu, which supplies the following options. These options affect only the selected partition:

▸ **Report Synchronization Status on the Selected Server** — This option checks the synchronization status of every server that has a replica of the selected partition. If all the servers with a replica response are synchronizing, the partition is functioning properly.

▸ **Synchronize the Replica on All Servers** — This option performs a synchronization of the selected partition on all servers that contain a replica and reports the status.

▸ **Repair All Replicas** — This option performs a repair of all replicas on this server. This option also checks and validates the information on each server that contains a replica, as well as the IDs of both the remote and local servers. This is the same information that is checked when you select the Unattended Full Repair option from the main menu. In other words, you can run an Unattended Full Repair or a Repair Local Database instead of choosing the Repair All Replicas option.

▸ **Repair Selected Replica** — This option performs a repair on only the highlighted replica. This option is the same as the Repair All Replicas option, except that it repairs only the selected replica. Before choosing this option, you can run an Unattended Full Repair or Repair Local Database, both of which are equivalent to this operation.

▸ **Repair Ring, All Replicas** — This option performs a repair on the replica ring of all the replicas displayed in the replica table. Repairing a replica ring consists of checking the replica ring information on each server that contains a replica of a given partition and validating remote ID information. It is recommended that you perform the Repair Local Database operation on the local NDS database within the last 30 minutes before executing this option.

▸ **Repair Ring, Selected Replica** — This option performs a repair on the replica ring of the selected replicas displayed in the replica table. Repairing a replica ring consists of checking the replica ring information on each server that contains a replica of a given partition and validating remote ID information. It is recommended that you perform the Repair Local Database operation on the local NDS database within the last 30 minutes before executing this option.

▶ **Schedule Immediate Synchronization** — This option causes the replica selected to begin the synchronization process immediately, so that the immediate synchronization occurs for all the replicas stored on this server. You can use this option to initiate synchronization activity if you want to view the Directory Services trace screen started by DSTRACE.

▶ **Cancel Partition Operation** — This option attempts to cancel a partition operation that was started for the selected partition. This operation talks to the master replica, which is responsible for the partition operations. Some partition operations may not be canceled if they have progressed too far. Other partition operations — such as the add replica partition operation — cannot be canceled.

▶ **Designate this Server as the New Master Replica** — This option designates the local replica of the selected partition as the new master. Each partition can have only one master replica, so the previous master replica is changed to a read/write replica.

This option is useful for designating a new master replica if the original one is lost. This situation may arise, for example, if the server holding the master replica has a hardware failure and will be down for a while or indefinitely.

▶ **View Entire Partition Name** — This option displays the full distinguished name of the selected partition.

**Check Volume Objects and Trustees**    This option checks the association of all mounted volumes on the current server with all mounted volumes for valid volume objects and valid trustees on the volumes. If a volume is not associated with its Volume object, DSREPAIR looks for a Volume object in the same context as the NetWare Server object. If the Volume object is found in the same context as the NetWare Server object, the Volume object is associated with the physical volume. However, if the Volume object is not found in the same context as the server, an attempt is made to create a Volume object. If the volume and Volume object association is established, DSREPAIR verifies the trustees of the Volume object.

This option requires you to log in as the ADMIN user or equivalent before performing this operation. As mentioned, all mounted volumes are searched for valid trustee ID numbers. A report is displayed that lists the invalid trustee ID numbers and then they are deleted from the volume.

**Check External References**    This option checks each external reference object on the server to locate a replica containing the object. If all servers that contain a replica of the partition where the object resides are inaccessible, the object is not found during the check and a warning message is issued. If the object cannot be found, a report is displayed with a warning.

**Global Schema Operations**    The Global Schema Operations option contains several schema operations that might be necessary to bring this server's schema into compliance with the master of [ROOT]. These operations should be used only as necessary. The local and unattended repair operations already verify the schema. The schema is a system of rules and definitions for object properties that establishes the content and format of each object and the object's relationships in the database.

After you select the Global Schema Operations option, you are provided with the following methods for managing the schema:

▸ **Request Schema from Tree** — You should choose this option to request the master replica of the root of the tree to synchronize its schema to this server. Any changes to the schema are propagated to this server from the master replica of the [ROOT] for the next 24 hours. If all servers request the schema from the master replica, network traffic can increase. Therefore, use this option with caution.

▸ **Import Remote Schema** — This option is used for equalizing the schema before merging two trees. Choose an NDS tree that contains the schema you want to add to the current tree's schema. After you choose a tree, the server that holds the master replica of the [ROOT] partition is contacted. The schema from that server is used to extend the schema on the current tree.

▸ **Reset Local Schema** — This option invokes a schema reset that clears the timestamps on the local schema and requests an inbound schema synchronization. In order to ensure that not all servers in the tree rest at once, this option is unavailable if executed from the master replica of the [ROOT] partition.

▸ **Post NetWare 5 Schema Update** — This option extends and modifies the schema for compatibility with post NetWare 5 directory changes. This option requires that this server contain a replica of the [ROOT] partition, and that the state of the replica must be ON.

▶ **Optional Schema Enhancements** — This option extends the schema containment rules and other schema enhancements. This option requires that this server contain a replica of the [ROOT] partition, and the state of the replica must be ON. In addition, all NetWare 4 servers in the tree must have an NDS version of at least DS.NLM version 6.01 or higher. Earlier versions of DS.NLM will not be able to synchronize.

**View Repair Log File**    The View Repair Log File option enables you to view and manage the log file created when you run the other DSREPAIR options. The default log file is SYS:SYSTEM\DSREPAIR.LOG. When DSREPAIR is loaded, the log file is opened and active. When repair operations are performed, the activity is appended to the log file. The size of the file is displayed within parentheses on the far right side of the title line. You can use this option to control the log file. For example, you can turn the log file off, turn it on again, change the filename, change its location, or delete the file by using the Log File Configuration option in the Advanced Options menu. You can place the log file on a NetWare volume or on a DOS drive.

**Create NDS Archive Set**    This option contains several features that enable you to create a copy of the NDS database stored on the current server for use in troubleshooting NDS and your NDS tree. The database archive set is useful only to a Novell technical support technician experienced in reading NDS dump file information. If you experience a problem with NDS on a specific server, creating a database archive records the state of the server's NDS database.

The database archive set can be written to only a local NetWare volume; DOS drives are not supported. Depending on the size of the NDS database, the resulting database archive set may be fragmented into multiple files if necessary. This operation requires the NDS database to be closed for the duration of the archiving procedure.

### Advanced DSREPAIR Switches

You can use one of several advanced switches as a load parameter to add functionality to DSREPAIR. These switches should be used only in advanced situations and by expert users that understand the impact. If you use these switches incorrectly, you could damage the directory beyond repair. The proper usage of the switches is DSREPAIR –X, where X is the individual switch.

Table 9.3 itemizes each DSREPAIR switch and describes how you can use it. These swtiches are undocumented and Novell does not guarantee that they will be supported for every version of the directory.

TABLE 9.3

*DSREPAIR Switches and Descriptions*

| SWITCH | DESCRIPTION |
|---|---|
| -A | Advanced mode that includes several additional options in the Advanced Options. The new options include: Declare new epoch, Promote subordinate reference to master, Destroy replica, and so on. |
| -L <log file name> | Specify an alternative location/name for the log file. Default is "SYS:SYSTEM\DSREPAIR.LOG". The path can be any NetWare volume or DOS drive, as in "A:TEMP.LOG". The path and filename specified must be DOS 8.3 format. |
| -U | Unattended mode. Repair runs the main menu unattended mode operations without user intervention, and unloads when completed. This operation also creates a status file called "<LOG FILE NAME>.DSM" by default that contains status information for the NDSMANAGER tool. |
| -RC | Create a database backup file (SYS:SYSTEM\DSREPAIR.DIB). |
| -P | Flag or mark all unknown class objects as referenced (a referenced object is not synchronized), so that they are updated on the next heartbeat. |
| -RD | Launch unattended repair of local database. |
| -XK2 | Highly destructive. Last resort operation that removes all replicas, partitions, and objects. This operation also leaves behind external references for all objects removed. |
| -XK3 | Destructive. Clears the backlink status of all external references. You need to SET DSTRACE=*B in order to force the backlink process to rebuild the backlinks. |

## DSTRACE SET Commands

In NetWare 6, DSTRACE referred to a group of SET commands available at the server console. DSTRACE was often referred to as a utility; however, it was really just a group of server SET commands. These SET commands were useful for monitoring how NDS was functioning. DSTRACE is a utility (a NetWare Loadable Module) that you can load and then use to monitor synchronization status and errors. DSTRACE starts a new screen on the server console called Directory Services that is used primarily to determine and track the health of NDS as it communicates with the other NetWare 6 servers in the network.

You can use DSTRACE commands to perform the following:

▸ Monitor the status of NDS synchronization processes.

▸ View errors that occur during NDS synchronization.

After you enable DSTRACE by typing DSTRACE, you can type HELP DSTRACE to see the list of options shown in Figure 9.42.

```
DSTRACE - Novell Directory Services Trace Event Monitor.

USAGE: DSTRACE {Options}

Options:
  {taglist}             List of qualified event tags.
  ON                    Enable tracing to target device.
  OFF                   Disable tracing to target device.
  FILE                  Change command target to log file.
  SCREEN                Change command target to trace screen.
  INLINE                Display events inline.
  JOURNAL               Display events on a background thread.
  FMAX={size}           Specify maximum disk file size.
  FNAME={name}          Specify disk file name.

Examples:
  DSTRACE INLINE
  DSTRACE SCREEN ON +AL +CB -FR
  DSTRACE FMAX=10240 FNAME=DBTRACE.LOG

Notes:
  All event type tags and keywords (except DSTRACE) may be shortened. To
  display the current configuration and a list of event tag names, enter
  'DSTRACE' with no options. The default tag qualifier is '+'.
CAM-SRV1:
```

**FIGURE 9.42** *To start the Directory Services screen, type DSTRACE at the server console. After DSTRACE is enabled, you can type HELP DSTRACE to view the Help screen.*

To enable DSTRACE for viewing and event logging, you need to type the following commands while at the Help screen. Table 9.4 lists the commands that you can enter using the DSTRACE syntax.

TABLE 9.4

*Basic DSTRACE Commands*

| COMMAND OPTION | DESCRIPTION |
| --- | --- |
| DSTRACE ON | Enable tracing to a target device. |
| DSTRACE OFF | Disable tracing to a target device. |
| DSTRACE FILE | Change command target to log file. |
| DSTRACE SCREEN | Change command target to trace screen. |

continued

TABLE 9.4

*Basic DSTRACE Commands (continued)*

| COMMAND OPTION | DESCRIPTION |
|---|---|
| DSTRACE INLINE | Display events inline. |
| DSTRACE JOURNAL | Display events on a background thread. |
| DSTRACE FMAX={size} | Specify maximum disk file size. |
| DSTRACE FNAME={name} | Specify disk filename. |

After you have enabled DSTRACE, you can specify what you would like to view. You can select a whole array of information to view by specifying the DSTRACE command followed by a tag list. Note that when you select a view, that item is highlighted on your server screen in blue. Those items that you have not selected are displayed in gray.

The tag list is shown in Figure 9.43.

**FIGURE 9.43** *The tag list is a list of items you can select for viewing/logging with DSTRACE.*

To enable a tag, you simply type DSTRACE followed by the item you wish to view. Keep in mind that you have the options of viewing the file on the console only, logging the item to a file, or doing both. A legend at the top of the screen tells you whether you are viewing, logging to a file, or both. For example, you can type **DSTRACE TIME** to show event times. To disable this view, type **DSTRACE –TIME**, or to abbreviate, type **DSTRACE –TI**. The first two letters of each tag work for disabling. You must always type **DSTRACE** in full.

**NOTE**

**DSTRACE** was originally developed and used by the Novell **NDS** engineers to help develop **NDS**. Novell technical support uses it to diagnose **NDS** errors and determine the health of the NetWare 6 system. The **DSTRACE** utility is also provided for the benefit of all administrators.

In NetWare 6, the DSTRACE screen displays the important information in color. Different colors highlight key events that occur during the synchronization process for the server. For example, partition names are displayed in blue, and success and error messages are displayed in green and yellow. However, not all problems appear color coded. The trace screen displays synchronization information for every replica stored on that server.

### Using DSTRACE

The quickest way to become familiar with the DSTRACE screen is to use it and learn what all the messages mean. Here is a standard set of DSTRACE commands that you can try:

```
DSTRACE   (load DSTRACE on the server)
DSTRACE+  <your preferred set tags or flags separated by
spaces>
DSTRACE SCREEN ON (Enables viewing on the screen)
DSTRACE FILE ON (Enables the events to be logged to a file)
```

DSTRACE has three main parts:

▶ Basic functions

▶ Debug messages

▶ Background process

### Basic Functions

The basic functions of DSTRACE are to view the status of the Directory Services trace screen in NetWare 6 and initiate limited synchronization processes. If you are familiar with NetWare 4, you notice that the DSTRACE screen has changed. However, you can still use the other DSTRACE options from NetWare 4.11 or 4.2.

### Debugging Messages

When the DSTRACE screen is enabled, the information displayed is based on a default set of filters. If you want to view more or less information than the default, you can manipulate the filters using the debugging message flags. The debugging messages help you determine the status of NDS and verify that everything is working well.

Each NDS process has a set of debugging messages. To view the debugging messages on a particular process, use a plus sign (+) and the process name or option. To disable the display of a process, use a minus sign (–) and the process name or option. Here are some examples:

```
SET DSTRACE = +SYNC (Enables the synchronization messages)
SET DSTRACE = -SYNC (Disables the synchronization messages)
SET DSTRACE = +SCMA (Enables the schema messages)
```

You can also combine the debugging message flags by using the Boolean operators & (which means AND) and | (which means OR). The syntax for controlling the debugging messages at the server console is as follows:

```
SET DSTRACE = +<trace flag> [<trace flag>]
```

or

```
SET DSTRACE = -<trace flag> [& <trace flag>]
```

Table 9.5 describes the trace flags for the debugging messages. You can enter abbreviations for each of the trace flags. These abbreviations or alternatives are listed within parentheses in the table.

**TABLE 9.5**

*Trace Flags for the Debugging Messages*

| TRACE FLAG | DESCRIPTION |
|---|---|
| ALL | Display all tags |
| ABUF | Display agent buffers. |
| ALOC | Display the memory allocation information. |
| AREQ | Display messages relating to inbound client requests and what action is requested. |
| AUMN | Display messages and information related to auditing. In many cases, this causes the server to pop into the debugger if auditing encounters an error. |
| AUNC | Audit NCP requests on this server. |
| AUSK | Audit skulker information. |
| AUTH | Display messages that are displayed while authenticating connections to the server. |

| TRACE FLAG | DESCRIPTION |
| --- | --- |
| BASE | Display a base set schema. |
| BLNK | Display messages related to verification of backlinks and external references. The backlink process resolves external references to make sure that a real object exists in NDS. For real NDS objects, the backlink process makes sure that an external reference exists for each backlink attribute. |
| BEMU | Display messages relating to Bindery Services (emulation). |
| CBUF | Display client buffer information. |
| CHNG | Change cache. |
| COLL | Display collisions. |
| DNS | Display Domain Name Server. |
| DRLK | Display distributed reference links. |
| DXML | Display dirXML events. |
| DVRS | DirXML drivers. |
| FRAG | Display fragger debug messages. The fragger breaks up and rebuilds DS NCP packets — which can be up to 64K — into packets that can be transmitted on the network. |
| INIT | Display messages that occur during the process of initializing or opening the local name service. |
| INSP | Display messages related to the inspector process, which verifies the DS name service and object integrity on the local server. The inspector is part of the janitor process. If errors are detected, it could mean that you need to run DSREPAIR. Be aware that messages reported by this process may not all be actual errors. For this reason, you need to understand what the messages mean. |
| JNTR | Display messages related to the janitor process. The janitor controls the removal of deleted objects. It also finds the status and version of NCP servers and other miscellaneous record management. |
| LDAP | Display LDAP information. |
| LMBR | Display messages related to the limber process, which verifies tree connectivity by maintaining the server name, address, and replicas. This involves verifying and fixing the server name and server address if it changes. |
| LOCK | Display messages related to name service locking information. |
| LOST | Display lost entries. |

*continued*

TABLE 9.5

Trace Flags for the Debugging Messages (continued)

| TRACE FLAG | DESCRIPTION |
| --- | --- |
| MISC | Miscellaneous information. |
| MOVE | Move. |
| NCPE | Display NCP Engine. |
| NMON | Display ndsmons. |
| PART | Display messages related to partitioning operations. This trace flag may be useful for tracking partition operations as they proceed. |
| PURG | Purger. |
| RECM | Display messages related to the name base transactions, such as rebuilding and verifying the internal hash table and iteration state handling. |
| RSLV | Display messages related to resolving name requests (tree walking). Resolve name resolves the name maps and object names to an ID on a particular server. |
| SAPM | Display Service Advertising packets. |
| SCMA | Display messages related to the schema being modified or synchronized across the network to the other servers. |
| SPKT | Display server packets. |
| SKLK | Display messages related to the synchronization process, which is responsible for synchronizing replicas on the servers with the other replicas on other servers. This is one of the most useful trace flags available. |
| STRM | Display messages related to stream attributes information. |
| SYNC | Display inbound synchronization information. |
| TAGS | Show entire list of event tags. |
| THRD | Display threads. |
| TIME | Display messages related to the synchronization or exchange of the timestamps between replicas. These messages display local and remote Synchronized Up To vectors, which contain the timestamps for the replica. |
| TVEC | Display time vector information. |

| TRACE FLAG | DESCRIPTION |
|---|---|
| VCLN | Display messages related to the virtual client, which handles the outbound server connections needed to pass NDS information. |
| WANM | Display WAN Traffic Manager information. |

### The Background Process

In addition to the debugging messages, which help you check the status of NDS, a set of commands forces the NDS background processes to run. To force the background process to run, you precede the command with an asterisk (*), as in the following example:

```
SET DSTRACE = *H
```

You can also change the status, timing, and control for a few of the background processes. To change these values, you must precede the command with an exclamation point (!) and enter a new parameter or value, as in the following example:

```
SET DSTRACE = !H 15 (parameter value in minutes)
```

Here is the syntax for each statement controlling the background processes of NDS:

```
SET DSTRACE = *<trace flag> [parameter]
```

or

```
SET DSTRACE = !<trace flag> [parameter]
```

▶ · · · · · · · · · · · · · · · · · · · · · · · · · · ◀

### Consulting Experience

As you use the debugging messages in DSTRACE, you will find that some of the trace flags are more useful than others. One of the favorite DSTRACE settings of Novell technical support is actually a shortcut:

```
SET DSTRACE = A81164B91
```

This setting turns on (by setting the appropriate bits) a group of debugging messages. Table 9.6 shows all the trace flags that are available for DSTRACE.

Table 9.6 lists the trace flags for the background processes, any required parameters, and the process that the trace flags will display.

**TABLE 9.6**

*Trace Flags for Background Processes*

| FLAG | PARAMETERS | DESCRIPTION |
| --- | --- | --- |
| *. | None | Unload and reload DS.NLM from the SYS:SYSTEM directory. For a short period of time, both DS.NLM and DSOLD.NLM will be loaded. This command is extremely useful when you are updating a version of DS.NLM. You can perform this operation during normal business hours without disrupting the users on that server. |
| *B | None | Force the backlink process to begin running. The backlink process can be traffic intensive, and you should probably wait until a slow time on the network before setting this command. |
| !B | Time (in minutes) | Set the backlink process interval used by NDS to check the backlink consistency. This command is the same as the NDS SET parameter NDS Backlink Interval, which is seen in the SERVMAN utility. The default is 1,500 minutes (25 hours). The range for this parameter is 2 to 10,080 minutes (168 hours). |
| *D | Replica rootEntryID | Abort the Send All Updates or *I. This command is used only when a Send All Updates or *I cannot complete (and is therefore endlessly trying to send the objects to all replicas). This situation usually occurs when one of the servers is inaccessible. |
| *F | None | Force the flatcleaner process, which is part of the janitor process. The flatcleaner purges or removes the objects marked for deletion in the name service. |
| !F | Time (in minutes) | Set the flatcleaner process interval, changing when the flatcleaner process automatically begins. The flatcleaner process purges or removes the deleted objects and attributes from the name service. The default interval for this process is 240 minutes (4 hours). The value entered must be greater than 2 minutes. |

| FLAG | PARAMETERS | DESCRIPTION |
| --- | --- | --- |
| *G | None | Give up on a server when too many requests are being processed. The process gives up on the server and sets the server status to down. |
| *H | None | Force the heartbeat process to start. This flag starts immediate communication to exchange timestamps with all servers in replica lists. This command is useful for starting the synchronization between servers so that you can observe the status. |
| !H | Time (in minutes) | Set the heartbeat process interval. This parameter changes when the heartbeat process begins. The default interval for this process is 30 minutes. |
| *I | Replica rootEntryID | Force the replica on the server. The command is issued to send a copy of all its objects to all other servers in the replica list. This command is the same as Send All Objects in DSREPAIR. |
| !I | Time (in minutes) | Set the heartbeat base schema interval. This parameter changes the schema heartbeat interval. The default interval for this process is 30 minutes. |
| !J | Time (in minutes) | Set the janitor process interval. This parameter changes when the janitor process executes. This command has the same function as SET command NDS Janitor Interval in the SERVMAN utility. The default interval is 2 minutes, with the limits of 1 to 10,080 minutes (168 hours). |
| *L | None | Start the limber process. The limber process checks the server name, server address, and tree connectivity of each replica. |
| *M | Bytes | Set the maximum size of the trace file in bytes, with a range of 10,000 to 10,000,000 bytes. |
| *P | None | Display the tunable parameters and their default settings. |
| *R | None | Reset the TTF file, which is the SYS:SYSTEM\DSTRACE.DBG file by default. This command is the same as the SET parameter NDS Trace File Length Set to Zero. |
| *S | None | Schedule the skulker process, which checks whether any of the replicas on the server need to be synchronized. |
| *SS | None | Force immediate schema synchronization. |

*continued*

| TABLE 9.6 | | |
|---|---|---|
| Trace Flags for Background Processes (continued) | | |
| **FLAG** | **PARAMETERS** | **DESCRIPTION** |
| !T | Time (in minutes) | Set the server UP threshold. This flag changes the server state threshold, which is the interval at which the server state is checked. The default interval is 30 minutes. |
| *U | Optional ID of server object | Force the server state to UP. If no server ID is specified, all servers in replica lists are set to UP. This command performs the same function as the SET parameter NDS Server Status. |
| !V | A list | List any restricted versions of the DS. If no versions are listed in the return, no restrictions exist. |
| !W | Time (in ticks) | Change the IPX Request in Process (RIP) delay. This is the length of time to wait after getting an IPX timeout before resending the packet. The default value is 15 ticks. The range is 1 through 2,000 ticks. |
| !X | Number of retries | Change the number of IPX retries for the DS (server-to-server) client. After the retry count has been exceeded, an NDS error −625 is displayed. The default value is 3. The range is 1 through 50. |
| !Y | Number | Factor the estimated trip delay. It is used in the equation: IPX Timeout = (T *Y) + Z. This is where T is equal to the ticks required to get to the destination server. The default is value 2. The range is 0 through 530. |
| !Z | Number | Add additional delay for the IPX timeout. To increase the timeout, change this parameter first. It is used in the equation: IPX Timeout = (T *Y) + Z. This is where T is equal to the ticks required to get to the destination server. The default value is 4. The range is 0 through 500. |

# Performing and Verifying Partition Operations

Due to the loosely connected nature of NDS, any kind of partition operation change needs to be synchronized to other replicas of the partition. Because partition operations are performed by the master replica of that partition, master replicas should be used to verify any partition operation. The example of the NDS partition operations in this chapter uses the tree and partition information in

Figure 9.44. The partitions are shown as circles. Figure 9.45 shows a view of the servers and their respective replicas. Some people prefer to view the different replicas of partitions stored on a particular server, whereas others prefer to view each partition and the servers on which they are stored.

**[Root]**

O=ACME

OU=NORAD    OU=RIO    OU=CAMELOT    OU=TOKYO    OU=SYDNEY

OU=CHARITY    OU=LABS    OU=PR

**FIGURE 9.44** *A partitioned view of the ACME tree*

| **CAM–SRV1** | **CAM–SRV2** | **CAM–SRV3** | **CAM–SRV4** | **CAM–SRV5** |
|---|---|---|---|---|
| [ROOT]–M | [ROOT]–RW | [ROOT]–RW | CAMELOT–RW | PR–RW |
| NORAD–M | CAMELOT–RW | CHARITY–RW | OPS–RW | |
| RIO–M | CHARITY–M | | | |
| CAMELOT–M | OPS–M | | | |
| TOKYO–M | PR–M | | | |
| SYDNEY–M | | | | |

**FIGURE 9.45** *A grouping of ACME servers and their partitions*

Before starting any NDS partition operation, remember that the relationship between partitions is a parent-child relationship. This entire section refers to the information in Figure 9.45. Notice in Figure 9.44 that the [ROOT] partition is a parent with five children — NORAD, RIO, CAMELOT, TOKYO, and SYDNEY. Notice that CAMELOT's parent partition is [ROOT]. The CAMELOT partition is also a parent partition with three child partitions: CHARITY, OPS, and PR. As shown in Figure 9.45, the tree includes the five servers CAM-SRV1, CAM-SRV2, CAM-SRV3, CAM-SRV4, CAM-SRV5. Most of the examples in this chapter concentrate on the CAMELOT partition and its subordinate child partitions. Table 9.7 shows the replica assignments for [ROOT], NORAD, RIO, CAMELOT, TOKYO, SYDNEY, CHARITY, OPS, and PR.

**NOTE**

**For discussion purposes only, we may place the replicas on the servers in a fashion that does not strictly follow our design recommendations. The examples used in this chapter do not imply a design recommendation for your replica placement; instead, these examples are simply used to explain the partition operations.**

TABLE 9.7

*Replica Assignments for [ROOT], NORAD, RIO, CAMELOT, TOKYO, SYDNEY, CHARITY, OPS, and PR. (M indicates a master replica, and RW indicates a read/write replica.)*

| [ROOT] | NORAD | RIO | CAMELOT | TOKYO | SYDNEY | CHARITY | OPS | PR |
|---|---|---|---|---|---|---|---|---|
| CAM-SRV1-M | CAM-SRV1-M | CAM-SRV1-M | CAM-SRV1-M | CAM-SRV1-M | CAM-SRV1-M | CAM-SRV2-M | CAM-SRV2-M | CAM-SRV2-M |
| CAM-SRV2-RW | CAM-SRV2-RW | CAM-SRV2-RW | CAM-SRV2-RW | CAM-SRV2-RW | CAM-SRV2-RW | CAM-SRV3-RW | CAM-SRV3-RW | CAM-SRV4-RW |
| CAM-SRV3-RW | CAM-SRV3-RW | CAM-SRV3-RW | CAM-SRV3-RW | CAM-SRV3-RW | CAM-SRV3-RW | CAM-SRV4-RW | CAM-SRV4-RW | CAM-SRV5-RW |

As mentioned previously, some people prefer to view the partitions and replica assignments by server. Using the same set of information that is shown in Table 9.7 and displaying or representing this information by server is illustrated in Table 9.8. Notice that each server is shown and then the partitions.

For each NDS partition, there is a replica list. In order to have a complete replica list for each partition, you have to consider the subordinate reference replicas (also known as subrefs) that are created automatically by NDS. When a server holds a copy of a partition such as a read/write (RW), read-only (RO), or master (M) of a parent partition, but does not hold the copy of the child partition, NDS automatically creates a subordinate reference, facilitating a link from the parent partition to the child partition. The link is necessary so that if the server holding the parent partition is queried about an object that exists on one of its child partitions, it knows which server to talk to. In other words, subordinate reference replicas are critical to the tree walking process, which is performed by the NetWare 6 servers. Therefore, including the subordinate reference replicas, the replica list just described will actually appear as shown in Table 9.9.

TABLE 9.8

Partition and Replica Assignments for Each of the Servers CAM-SV1, CAM-SRV2, CAM-SRV3, CAM-SRV4, and CAM-SRV5. (M indicates a master replica, and RW indicates a read/write replica.)

| CAM-SRV1 | CAM-SRV2 | CAM-SRV3 | CAM-SRV4 | CAM-SRV5 |
|---|---|---|---|---|
| [ROOT]-M | [ROOT]-RW | [ROOT]-RW | CHARITY-RW | PR-RW |
| NORAD-M | NORAD-RW | NORAD-RW | OPS-RW | |
| RIO-M | RIO-RW | RIO-RW | PR-RW | |
| CAMELOT-M | CAMELOT-RW | CAMELOT-RW | | |
| TOKYO-M | TOKYO–RW | TOKYO–RW | | |
| SYDNEY-M | SYDNEY-RW | SYDNEY-RW | | |
| | CHARITY-M | CHARITY-RW | | |
| | OPS-M | OPS-RW | | |
| | PR-M | | | |

TABLE 9.9

Replica List for Each Server. (M indicates a master replica, RW indicates a read/write replica, and SR indicates a subordinate reference replica.)

| CAM-SRV1 | CAM-SRV2 | CAM-SRV3 | CAM-SRV4 | CAM-SRV5 |
|---|---|---|---|---|
| [ROOT]-M | [ROOT]-RW | [ROOT]-RW | CHARITY- RW | PR-RW |
| NORAD-M | NORAD-RW | NORAD-RW | OPS-RW | |
| RIO-M | RIO-RW | RIO-RW | PR-RW | |
| CAMELOT-M | CAMELOT-RW | CAMELOT-RW | | |
| TOKYO-M | TOKYO-RW | TOKYO-RW | | |
| SYDNEY-M | SYDNEY-RW | SYDNEY-RW | | |
| CHARITY-SR | CHARITY-M | CHARITY-RW | | |
| OPS-SR | OPS-M | OPS-RW | | |
| PR-SR | PR-M | | | |

The following sections discuss the various partition operations that you can perform and explain how to properly verify their status and completion.

## Adding Replicas

The add replica operation adds a new replica to a partition's replica list and may be used fairly often by your administrators. Here are the steps involved in this operation:

1. The master replica of the partition adds the server name as New Replica to the replica list.

2. The master replica sends all the objects in the partition to the new replica. You have a NEW state until the master has successfully sent all changes to the new replica.

3. The master replica sets the state in the replica ring to TRANSITION ON.

4. All the other replicas begin synchronizing with the new replica.

5. The master replica sets the replica state to ON.

At this point, let's add a read/write replica of the CAMELOT partition to the CAM-SRV3 server. You should follow these steps to successfully carry out the add replica operation.

### Phase One

1. Run DSREPAIR and choose the Report Synchronization Status option. The CAMELOT partition has both parent and child partitions. Therefore, the placement of a read/write replica of CAMELOT on CAM-SRV3 causes the new replica to get involved in replica synchronization with servers that hold a replica of [ROOT] (the parent replica) and CHARITY, OPS, and PR (the child replicas). For this reason, you should check the synchronization status of the partition itself and of the child partitions. Use DSREPAIR to check the replica synchronization status.

2. Load DSREPAIR.NLM on the servers holding the master of CAMELOT and CHARITY, OPS, and PR partitions. In this case, CAM-SRV1 and CAM-SRV2 would need to be checked. In order to check the status of the replica synchronization, you need to choose the Report Synchronization Status option. An example of this report is shown in Figure 9.46.

### Consulting Experience

We are often asked "Is there something that we can do on a daily basis as a proactive measure to tell whether NDS is performing smoothly?" As a network administrator, you can follow the steps below to ensure that your NetWare 6 network is running smoothly. Take some time to learn and practice these steps. You should also follow these steps before you initiate any partition operations.

- ▶ Check the time synchronization status of the servers using DSREPAIR.
- ▶ Check to make sure that the servers are communicating properly. Use the replica synchronization option in DSREPAIR.
- ▶ Check to make sure that the replica synchronization process has completed for the partitions. You can use DSTRACE to do the checking.
- ▶ Check the replica state for each partition. Use DSREPAIR to check the replica states. If the state of the partitions is okay, you can initiate the partition operation that you choose. Make sure to check the state of all the partitions involved in the operation.
- ▶ Always check the log file in DSREPAIR for errors that may show up in the replica synchronization status.

**FIGURE 9.46** *A view of the Report Synchronization Status option*

This first phase verifies that no synchronization errors are on the partition itself, its parent, and its children. Only after you know that no errors exist should you initiate the add replica operation.

If any errors are reported by DSREPAIR's Report Synchronization Status option, you need to find out what they are before continuing with the add replica operation. For more information, refer to Appendix B for a listing of error codes and recommended actions.

**TIP**

**You can also use the Partition Status option in DSREPAIR to search for any errors. For example, you may see a –698 error indicating that the partition is busy synchronizing. This is normal unless the error continues indefinitely.**

### Phase Two

1. Set the DSTRACE screen on the master replica to monitor the operation. In this case, the server holding the master replica is CAM-SRV1.

2. Follow this step if the partition status shows an error or the status does not change. If no errors are shown in the report from Phase One, it is time to SET DSTRACE on the server holding the master replica of the partition as follows:

```
SET DSTRACE = ON      (Turn on debug trace screen. Press Alt+Esc
to see                                      the trace debug
screen.)
SET TTF = ON          (Open DSTRACE.DBG file)
SET DSTRACE = *R      (Reset DSTRACE.DBG to zero length)
SET DSTRACE = 1       (Turn off all the switches)
SET DSTRACE = +S      (Show detailed synchronization)
```

These steps capture the operations that the master replica must take to finish the add replica operation. The text file that holds the trace information is in the SYS: SYSTEM\DSTRACE.DBG file on the master.

### Phase Three

1. Issue the add replica operation using NDS Manager or ConsoleOne.

Figure 9.47 shows an example of adding a replica.

### Phase Four

1. Verify the partition operation from the back end.

2. After issuing the call from the NDS Manager utility, you need to check the master server that controls the back-end process. You have two ways to

verify that the add replica operation has completed: You can use DSTRACE, or you can use DSREPAIR and the Report Synchronization Status option. It is a good idea to use both methods to gather all possible information about the operation.

**FIGURE 9.47** *An example of the Add Replica function using NDS Manager*

### Checking Add Replica with DSTRACE

DSTRACE is a window to a NetWare 6 server's NDS activity. It shows what the background processes are doing. We set DSTRACE to ON in Step 2 of Phase Four to monitor the replica synchronization activity from the master while it is sending all the objects in the CAMELOT partition to CAM-SRV3. Now it is time to execute the following commands at the console prompt to stop the accumulation of trace information:

```
SET TTF = OFF (Closes the DSTRACE.DBG file)
LOAD EDIT SYS:SYSTEM\DSTRACE.DBG (Edit or view the trace
file)
```

You can also use your preferred editor to review the trace file and look for any errors that may have resulted from the Add Replica process.

> **If the state of the partition goes from new to transition, you needn't run DSTRACE because you will see the error in Partition Status of DSREPAIR.**

**TIP**

### Checking Add Replica with DSREPAIR

Using DSREPAIR or Partition Manager, first check the master partition of CAMELOT, which is stored on CAM-SRV1, by doing these things:

**1.** Choose the replica partition operation.

**2.** Choose the CAMELOT partition.

**3.** View the replica ring.

DSREPAIR should confirm that CAM-SRV3 holds a read/write replica, and the state of the replica should say ON. If the state says New Replica, the add replica operation has not finished. The states of partitions range from New Replica to Transition ON to ON. The Transition ON state means that the master replica has finished sending all the objects and CAM-SRV3 is waiting for other read/write replicas to send any other updates that the master didn't have when the operation was performed.

After confirming that the master replica has sent the updates to CAM-SRV3 as a read/write and confirming a state of ON in the replica list, you can use the DSREPAIR Report Synchronization Status option on the servers holding the master of [ROOT], CAMELOT, CHARITY, OPS, and PR to make sure that all the servers are successfully talking to CAM-SRV3.

Table 9.10 shows the replica list for the partitions in our scenario. Notice that the new replica added for the CAMELOT partition is stored on CAM-SRV3.

TABLE 9.10

*A Replica List. (M indicates a master replica, RW indicates a read/write replica, and SR indicates a subordinate reference replica.)*

| CAM- SRV1 | CAM- SRV2 | CAM- SRV3 | CAM- SRV4 | CAM- SRV5 |
| --- | --- | --- | --- | --- |
| [ROOT]-M | [ROOT]-RW | [ROOT]- RW | CHARITY- RW | PR-RW |
| NORAD-M | NORAD-RW | NORAD-RW | OPS-RW | |
| RIO-M | RIO-M | RIO-M | PR-RW | |
| CAMELOT-M | CAMELOT-RW | CAMELOT-RW | | |
| TOKYO- M | TOKYO-RW | TOKYO-RW | | |
| SYDNEY- M | SYDNEY- RW | SYDNEY- RW | | |
| CHARITY- SR | CHARITY-M | CHARITY-RW | | |
| OPS-SR | OPS-M | OPS-RW | | |
| PR-SR | PR-M | PR-RW | | |

## Deleting Replicas

For a replica to be deleted successfully:

▸ Master(s) must remove the server from the replica list(s).

▸ The server holding the deleted replica must destroy the replica.

After the replica has been destroyed, the NetWare 6 server turns all the objects on the deleted replica into external references.

**NOTE**

**The external references are removed from that server if they haven't been used by the next time the backlinker process runs. For more information on the backlinker process, refer to Chapter 8.**

For the delete replica operation, we will remove a read/write replica of CAMELOT from the server CAM-SRV4. Follow these steps to delete the replica from the server CAM-SRV4:

### Phase One

1. Run the DSREPAIR Report Synchronization Status option. The CAMELOT partition has both parent and child partitions. Therefore, removing the replica of CAMELOT from CAM-SRV4 also removes the subordinate reference replicas of CHARITY and PR from CAM-SRV4. Although the OPS partition is a child partition to CAMELOT, it is unaffected because it is a full read/write replica. The CHARITY and PR replicas are removed from the server because they are subordinate reference replicas. Subordinate reference replicas are removed after the parent replica is removed from CAM-SRV4. Therefore, we should also check the synchronization status on the parent and children using DSREPAIR.

2. Load DSREPAIR.NLM on the servers holding the CAMELOT, CHARITY, OPS, and PR partitions. You need to choose the Report Synchronization Status option.

The first phase verifies that no synchronization errors are on the partition itself and its children. You must make this determination before running the delete replica operation.

If the DSREPAIR's Report Synchronization Status option discovers any errors, you need to find out what the error is before continuing with the operation. For more information, refer to Appendix B for a listing of error codes and recommended actions.

### Phase Two

**1.** Set the DSTRACE screen on the master replica to monitor the operation.

**2.** If no errors are reported in Step 1, set DSTRACE on the server holding the master replica of the partition you intend to delete, as follows:

```
SET DSTRACE = ON     (Turn on trace screen)
SET TTF = ON     (Open DSTRACE.DBG file)
SET DSTRACE = *R     (Reset DSTRACE.DBG)
SET DSTRACE = 1     (Turn off all the switches)
SET DSTRACE = +S     (Show detailed synchronization)
```

With Phase Two, you can capture the operation that the master replica must take to finish the operation. The information is in the SYS:SYSTEM\DSTRACE.DBG file on the master.

### Phase Three

**1.** Issue the delete replica operation using NDS Manager or ConsoleOne.

### Phase Four

**1.** Verify the delete replica operation from the back end.

**2.** After issuing the call from the front end, you must check the master server that controls the back end before the operation is considered complete. You have two ways to verify the delete replica operation. You can use DSTRACE, or you can use the DSREPAIR Report Synchronization Status option. It is a good idea to use both methods.

### Checking Delete Replica with DSTRACE

DSTRACE is a window to a server's NDS activity. It shows what the background processes are doing. DSTRACE on the master shows us the process of removing CAM-SRV4 from the CAMELOT replica list. We can also capture DSTRACE on CAM-SRV2, which holds the master of CHARITY, OPS, and PR. Now you can issue the following commands at the console prompt:

```
SET TTF = OFF (Close DSTRACE.DBG file)
LOAD EDIT SYS:SYSTEM\DSTRACE.DBG
```

You can also use your preferred editor to review the trace file and look for any errors that may have resulted from the process.

### Checking Delete Replica with DSREPAIR

In this scenario, we first check the master of CAMELOT, which is stored on server CAM-SRV1, and then choose the Replica and Partition Operations option. We next choose the CAMELOT partition and then choose View Replica Ring. This approach should confirm that CAM-SRV4 has been removed from the replica list of the master. If the state says Dying Replica, the delete replica operation has not yet finished.

After you confirm that the master replica of CAMELOT has CAM-SRV4 removed from the replica list, you can use DSREPAIR on CAM-SRV2 (the master of CHARITY, OPS, and PR) to make sure that CAM-SRV4 has been successfully removed from their replica lists. It is a good idea to check the Synchronization Report Status using DSREPAIR on CAMELOT, CHARITY, OPS, and PR.

The final phase is to run DSREPAIR on CAM-SRV4 to verify that delete operation has finished. Run the DSREPAIR.NLM Advanced Options menu and then select the Replica and Partition Operations option to verify that CAMELOT, CHARITY, and PR have been removed.

The replica list for the partition in our scenario is shown in Table 9.11.

T A B L E   9.11

*A Replica List. (M indicates a master replica, RW indicates a read/write replica, and SR indicates a subordinate reference replica.)*

| CAM- SRV1 | CAM- SRV2 | CAM- SRV3 | CAM- SRV4 | CAM- SRV5 |
|---|---|---|---|---|
| [ROOT]-M | [ROOT]-RW | [ROOT]- RW | OPS-RW | PR-RW |
| NORAD-M | NORAD-RW | NORAD-RW | | |
| RIO-M | RIO-M | RIO-M | | |
| CAMELOT-M | CAMELOT-RW | CAMELOT-RW | | |
| TOKYO- M | TOKYO-RW | TOKYO-RW | | |
| SYDNEY- M | SYDNEY- RW | SYDNEY- RW | | |
| CHARITY- SR | CHARITY-M | CHARITY-RW | | |
| OPS-SR | OPS-M | OPS-RW | | |
| PR-SR | PR-M | PR-RW | | |

## Changing Replica Types

Change replica type is another very important partition operation. The master replica is in charge of all the partition operations. Any synchronization errors at the time of the change replica type operation can cause confusion between replicas and prevent the operation from completing. Therefore, no more partition operations are possible on that partition while it is in the change replica state.

To successfully change the read/write replica to a master, the old master changes the replica type in two stages and synchronizes the changes to the other replicas, including the new master.

This example changes the master of CAMELOT from CAM-SRV1 to CAM-SRV2.

### Phase One

1. Run the DSREPAIR's Report Synchronization Status option. Change Replica Type is the only partition operation that requires a replica synchronization check of the partition itself. This operation affects only the CAMELOT partition in this example.

2. Load DSREPAIR.NLM on the master of CAMELOT partition. Choose the Report Synchronization Status option.

The first phase verifies that no synchronization errors are on the CAMELOT partition before you issue a change replica type operation.

If any errors are on DSREPAIR's Report Synchronization Status, you need to find out what the errors are before continuing with the operation. For more information, refer to Appendix B for a listing of error codes and recommended actions.

### Phase Two

1. Set the DSTRACE screen on the master replica to monitor the operation.

2. When you have resolved any errors discovered in Phase One, you can set DSTRACE on the master of the partition as follows:

```
SET DSTRACE = ON      (Turn on trace screen)
SET TTF = ON      (Open DSTRACE.DBG file)
SET DSTRACE = *R      (Reset DSTRACE.DBG)
SET DSTRACE = 1      (Turn off all the switches)
SET DSTRACE = +S      (Show detailed synchronization)
```

Phase Three captures the operation that the master replica must take to finish the operation. The information is in the SYS:SYSTEM\DSTRACE.DBG file on the master.

### Phase Three

**1.** Issue the change replica type operation using NDS Manager or ConsoleOne.

### Phase Four

**1.** Verify the change replica type operation from the back end.

**2.** You have two ways to verify the change replica operation: DSTRACE and the DSREPAIR Report Synchronization Status option. It is a good idea to use both methods.

### Checking the Change Replica Type with DSTRACE

DSTRACE is a window to a server's NDS activity. It shows what the background processes are doing. DSTRACE on the master shows us the process of changing the master replica type from CAM-SRV1 to CAM-SRV2. Now it is time to execute the following commands at the console prompt:

```
SET TTF = OFF (Close DSTRACE.DBG file)
LOAD EDIT SYS:SYSTEM\DSTRACE.DBG
```

You can also use your preferred editor to review the trace file and look for any errors that may have turned up as a result of the change replica type operation.

### Checking the Change Replica Type with DSREPAIR

First, check the old master of CAMELOT, which is CAM-SRV1, and choose the Replica and Partition Operation options, choose the CAMELOT partition, and then select the View Replica Ring option. It should confirm that CAM-SRV2 has been assigned as the new master replica. If the state says Changed Replica Type, the operation is not yet finished.

Next, check the new master CAM-SRV2, and then use DSREPAIR's View Replica Ring option to verify the change.

After confirming that the master replica of CAMELOT has been changed to CHR-SRV1, use DSREPAIR on CAM-SRV2 to check the Report Synchronization Status option for CAMELOT and make sure the change was successful.

The replica list for the partition in our scenario now looks like this:

CAMELOT
CAM-SRV1-RW
CAM-SRV2-M
CAM-SRV3-RW

## Creating (Splitting) Partitions

Partitions are created when any container in the NDS Manager utility is marked as a new partition. In other words, the container is already part of another partition but gets split off as a new partition. This process establishes the new partition boundary. A new child partition gets created with respect to the parent. The servers that hold the copy of the parent partition receive the copy of the new child partition with the same replica ring as the parent. It makes sense because the only servers that have the real copy of all the objects in the child partition get a copy.

In a create partition operation:

▶ The master of the partition directs all the replicas in the list that a new partition is being created.

▶ The master of the parent becomes the master of the new child partition.

▶ Read/write copies of the parent establish a new boundary for the read/write replica of the new child partition.

▶ Subordinate reference replicas of the parent are not involved in the operation.

The following example creates a new partition called OPS, which is a container below the CAMELOT partition.

### Phase One

**1.** Run the DSREPAIR Report Synchronization Status option. As usual, you should check synchronization status before starting the operation. The CAMELOT partition needs to be checked. You don't need to check synchronization status on the sibling partitions to the new partition because the replicas of the sibling partitions won't get involved in the create operation.

**2.** Load DSREPAIR.NLM on the server holding the master of CAMELOT partition. Choose the Report Synchronization Status option.

The first phase verifies that no synchronization errors are on the CAMELOT partition before you carry out the create partition operation.

If DSREPAIR's Report Synchronization Status should turn up any errors, you need to find out what they are before continuing with the operation. For more information, refer to Appendix B for a listing of error codes and recommended actions.

### Phase Two

**1.** Set the DSTRACE screen on the master replica to monitor the operation.

**2.** After you've determined that no errors exist as discussed in Phase One, it is time to set DSTRACE on the master of the partition, as follows:

```
SET DSTRACE = ON      (Turn on trace screen)
SET TTF = ON      (Open DSTRACE.DBG file)
SET DSTRACE = *R      (Reset DSTRACE.DBG)
SET DSTRACE = 1      (Turn off all the switches)
SET DSTRACE = +S      (Show detailed synchronization)
```

Phase Three captures the operation that the master replica must take in order to finish the operation. The information is in the SYS:SYSTEM\DSTRACE.DBG file on the master.

### Phase Three

**1.** Issue the create partition operation using NDS Manager or ConsoleOne.

### Phase Four

**1.** Verify the create partition operation from the back end.

**2.** You have two ways to verify the create partition operation: DSTRACE and the DSREPAIR Report Synchronization Status option. It is a good idea to use both methods.

#### Checking the Create Partition with **DSTRACE**

DSTRACE shows what the background processes are doing. DSTRACE on the master shows us the process of creating the partition. Enter the following commands at the console prompt:

```
SET TTF = OFF (Close DSTRACE.DBG file)
LOAD EDIT SYS:SYSTEM\DSTRACE.DBG
```

You can also use your preferred editor to review the trace file and look for any errors that may have resulted from the Create Partition process.

#### Checking the Create Partition with **DSREPAIR**

DSTRACE shows what happened during the process. In contrast, DSREPAIR shows the state of the replicas and how they are synchronizing. First, check the master of CAMELOT, which is stored on CAM-SRV1, and choose Replica and Partition Operation to make sure that the OPS partition is listed. Then choose the CAMELOT partition and View Replica Ring option; it should confirm that all the replicas are ON. Carry out the same procedure on the OPS partition. If the state says Split State, the operation has not yet finished.

After you confirm that the OPS partition has been successfully created, you can run DSREPAIR on CAM-SRV1, which contains the master of both CAMELOT and OPS, and run the Report Synchronization Status on the two partitions to make sure that synchronization is successful after the operation.

## Merging (Joining) Partitions

In the merge partition operation, the existing child partition is merged with the parent partition. Because you cannot delete the partition, you must merge it with the parent. This process destroys the partition boundary and then removes all the partition properties. Thus, the container is simply an object in the tree that can hold other objects. Now you can delete the container object if it doesn't hold any objects.

By default, the Merge Operation option makes the replica ring the same for both the parent and child partitions, excluding the subrefs from the parent's replica ring. In other words, any server that holds the readable copy of the child or parent gets a read-only copy of either one. This is probably the most time-consuming part of the process and may possibly create network traffic if the partitions are large. The add replica operation is the first part of the process. A read-only replica of the child partition is added everywhere the parent is, and a read-only replica of the parent is added everywhere the child is.

In the merge partition operation:

▸ The master of the child partition finds the master of the parent partition to start the process.

▸ The master of the parent partition starts the first phase of the merge and the master of the child partition sets the states accordingly.

▸ The masters of parent and child compare replica rings to determine which servers they must add replicas to.

▸ The partition boundary is deleted.

▸ The parent's master replica becomes the master of the new partition. The child's master and read/write replicas become read/write copies of the new partition.

The following example merges the CHARITY partition into the CAMELOT partition.

**Phase One**

1. Run the DSREPAIR Report Synchronization Status option. As usual, you should check synchronization status before starting the operation. The CAMELOT and CHARITY partitions need to be checked.

2. Load DSREPAIR.NLM on the master of the CHARITY and CAMELOT partitions. Choose the Report Synchronization Status option.

The first phase verifies that no synchronization errors are on the CAMELOT and CHARITY partitions before you perform the merge partition operation. If any errors are on DSREPAIR's Report Synchronization Status option, you need to find out what the errors are before continuing with the operation. For more information, refer to Appendix B for a listing of error codes and recommended actions.

**Phase Two**

1. Set the DSTRACE screen on the master replica to monitor the operation.

2. After you have eliminated any errors found in Phase One, set DSTRACE on the master of both the CHARITY and CAMELOT partitions as follows:

```
SET DSTRACE = ON      (Turn on trace screen)
SET TTF = ON      (Open DSTRACE.DBG file)
SET DSTRACE = *R      (Reset DSTRACE.DBG)
SET DSTRACE = 1      (Turn off all the switches)
SET DSTRACE = +S      (Show detailed synchronization)
```

These steps shown in Phase Two capture all the operations that the master replicas must take to finish the operation. The information is in the SYS:SYSTEM \DSTRACE.DBG file on the master.

**Phase Three**

1. Issue the merge partition operation using NDS Manager or ConsoleOne.

**Phase Four**

1. Verify the merge partition operation from the back end.

2. The replica list for the partition in our scenario is shown in Table 9.12.

TABLE 9.12

A Replica List. (M indicates a master replica, RW indicates a read/write replica, and SR indicates a subordinate reference replica.)

| CAM-SRV1 | CAM-SRV2 | CAM-SRV3 | CAM-SRV4 | CAM-SRV5 |
|---|---|---|---|---|
| [ROOT]-M | [ROOT]-RW | [ROOT]-RW | CAMELOT-RW | PR-RW |
| NORAD-M | NORAD-SR | NORAD-SR | OPS-RW | |
| RIO-M | RIO-SR | RIO-SR | PR-SR | |
| CAMELOT-M | CAMELOT-RW | CAMELOT-SW | | |
| TOKYO-M | TOKYO-SR | TOKYO-SR | | |
| SYDNEY-M | SYDNEY-SR | SYDNEY-SR | | |
| OPS-M | OPS-M | | | |
| PR-SR | PR-M | | | |

You have two ways of verifying the merge partition operation: DSTRACE and DSREPAIR's Report Synchronization Status option. It is a good idea to use both methods.

### Checking the Merge Partition with DSTRACE

DSTRACE shows what the background processes are doing. DSTRACE on both master replicas shows us the process of merging the partitions. Enter the following commands at the console prompt:

```
SET TTF = OFF (Close DSTRACE.DBG file)
LOAD EDIT SYS:SYSTEM\DSTRACE.DBG
```

You can also use your preferred editor to review the trace file and look for any errors that may have resulted from the Merge Partition process.

### Checking the Merge Partition with DSREPAIR

DSTRACE shows what happened during the process. In contrast, DSREPAIR shows the state of the replicas and how they are synchronizing. First, check the master of CAMELOT, which is held on CAM-SRV1, and choose the Replica and Partition Operations option to make sure that the CHARITY partition is not listed. Then choose the CAMELOT partition and the View Replica Ring option; it should confirm that all the replicas are ON. If the state says Join State, the operation has not yet finished.

After confirming that the CHARITY partition has been successfully merged, run DSREPAIR on CAM-SRV1, which holds the master of CAMELOT, and the Report

Synchronization Status option to make sure synchronization is successful after the operation.

CHARITY should now be only an organizational unit inside the CAMELOT partition.

## Moving Subtrees or Partitions

The move subtree operation moves a partition and all its child entries as a unit to another logical location in the tree. The replicas of the partition being moved are held on the same servers on which they were held previously. In other words, NDS moves the subtree logically, not physically. However, the objects' full names in the partition change.

A move subtree operation involves a destination server and a source server:

▶ The destination server is the server holding the master replica of the parent partition under which the child partition is moving. This server prepares for the operation and signals the source server.

▶ The source server is the server holding the master replica of the partition that is moving. This server forms a list of servers that will participate in moving the subtree.

▶ Large numbers of packets are exchanged between the source server and the destination server during a move subtree operation.

The following example moves the subtree CHARITY under the PR partition.

**Phase One**

1. Run the DSREPAIR Report Synchronization Status option. As usual, you should check synchronization status before starting the operation. The PR, CAMELOT, and CHARITY partitions need to be checked.

2. Load DSREPAIR.NLM on the servers holding the master of the CHARITY, CAMELOT, and PR partitions. In this case, the servers are CAM-SRV1 and CAM-SRV2. Choose the Report Synchronization Status option.

Phase One verifies that no synchronization errors exist on the CAMELOT, CHARITY, and PR partitions before the move subtree operation.

If any errors exist on the DSREPAIR report synchronization status, you need to find out what they are before continuing with the operation. For more information, refer to Appendix B for a listing of error codes and recommended actions.

### Phase Two

**1.** Set the DSTRACE screen on the master replica to monitor the operation.

**2.** After you have resolved any errors that turned up in Phase One, set DSTRACE on the master of both the CHARITY and PR partitions as follows:

```
SET DSTRACE = ON     (Turn on trace screen)
SET TTF = ON     (Open DSTRACE.DBG file)
SET DSTRACE = *R     (Reset DSTRACE.DBG)
SET DSTRACE = 1     (Turn off all the switches)
SET DSTRACE = +S     (Show detailed synchronization)
```

Phase Three captures all the operations that the master replicas must take to finish the operation. The information is in the SYS:SYSTEM\DSTRACE.DBG file on the master.

### Phase Three

**1.** Issue the move subtree operation using NDS Manager or ConsoleOne.

### Phase Four

**1.** Verify the move subtree operation from the back end.

**2.** You have two ways of verifying the move subtree operation: DSTRACE and the DSREPAIR Report Synchronization Status option. It is a good idea to use both methods.

### Checking the Move Subtree with DSTRACE

DSTRACE shows what the background processes are doing. DSTRACE on both master replicas shows how the process of merging the partitions finished. Enter the following commands at the console prompt:

```
SET TTF = OFF (Close DSTRACE.DBG file)
LOAD EDIT SYS:SYSTEM\DSTRACE.DBG
```

You can also use your preferred editor to review the trace file and look for any errors that may have resulted from the Move Subtree process.

### Checking the Move Subtree with DSREPAIR

DSTRACE shows what happened during the process. In contrast, DSREPAIR shows the state of the replicas and how they are synchronizing. First, check the Master of PR, which is stored on CAM-SRV2, and choose Replica and Partition Operations. Make sure that the CHARITY partition's full name is under PR. Then choose CHARITY partition and the View Replica Ring option; it should confirm that all the replicas are ON. If the state says Move Subtree State, the operation has not finished. You should check the PR partition in the same way.

After confirming that CHARITY has been successfully moved, run DSREPAIR on CAM-SRV1, which holds the master of CAMELOT, and the Synchronization Report Status option to make sure synchronization is successful after the operation. Follow the same procedure for CHARITY and PR. Remember that the replica ring for CHARITY will remain the same.

## Troubleshooting Do's and Don'ts

This section describes some of the most common mistakes people make when installing and managing NetWare 6 and NDS eDirectory.

### Do Not Temporarily Change the Internal IPX or File Server Name

If a server is brought up without running AUTOEXEC.NCF for any reason, the NetWare OS requires that you enter a server name and internal IPX number. In NetWare 6, the server name and internal IPX number must be the same as what is stored in the AUTOEXEC.NCF. Otherwise, the NetWare 6 server treats the change as permanent and synchronizes the change to all the other servers in your tree. Even if the server is not connected to the network, the change happens on its database, and as soon as the server is connected to the network it sends the change. If this happens, let the system resolve the change first, and then change the name or internal IPX back to what it should be. Do not change the server name and internal IPX number back immediately because this can cause problems with NDS.

### Check Replica Ring Synchronization Before Doing a Partition Operation

Always run the DSREPAIR check Report Synchronization option before starting any partition operation. This action ensures that no synchronization errors exist and that any change you make is synchronized to other replicas.

### Do Not Change Read/Write to Master under Partition Error Conditions

If you change the master replica of a partition under error conditions, the operation can get stuck. This means that NDS has not properly or fully completed the process and NDS is in an inactive state. In this situation, no other partition operation is possible because the master replica controls all the partition operations. If you check the DSREPAIR option View Replica Ring, it should confirm that the replica states are Change Replica Type. If Change Replica Type doesn't resolve itself, you may have to call Novell technical support to resolve the issue.

### Centralize the Partition Operation Administration

Novell technical support has found that centralized management of all the partitions in the tree is critical to maintaining a healthy NDS tree. Managing NDS should be divided into two areas:

- ▸ Partition management
- ▸ User and server management

Partition management is the only area that needs to be centralized. User and server management can be decentralized. NDS is loosely connected, and it takes a while for changes to synchronize to other replicas. If the change happens to be partition information and multiple administrators are performing multiple partition operations, the replicas may not synchronize properly. Centralizing partition operations eliminates many of the related problems.

### Use NWCONFIG.NLM to Remove or Delete a Server

Always use the NWCONFIG.NLM option to remove NDS from a server object. This utility enables you to remove a server from the tree properly. Even if the server has a copy of any replica, NWCONFIG removes the copy from the server for you. Never delete a server object unless the server has been removed from the tree with the NWCONFIG.

### If You Suspect Errors, Verify the Partition Operation on the Back End from the Master Replica

After issuing the call from the front end to perform a partition operation, check the master partition on the server that is controlling the back-end process before considering the operation completed. You have two ways to verify that the operation is completed: DSTRACE and the DSREPAIR Report Synchronization option. Verifying partition operations from the servers holding the master replicas tells you whether the operation has finished or whether any errors have been generated as a result of the operation.

### Do Not Install the Same Server in More Than One Tree

Installing the same server name in multiple trees can create problems in replica synchronization. For example, if a server is down for a long period of time, do not try to reinstall the server unless the directory has been removed properly using NWCONFIG.

### Basic NDS Troubleshooting Guidelines

▸ Identify the partition that is experiencing errors by using and understanding the DSTRACE set parameters and the DSREPAIR utility.

▸ Identify the replica(s) in the partition that have errors. Identify these errors by using the DSTRACE SET commands and the DSREPAIR utility.

▸ Identify the error and take the appropriate action. Appendix B of this book lists the errors and recommended remedies.

## Using the DSDIAG Utility

The DSDIAG utility is a server-based utility that enables you to generate diagnostic reports and diagnostic information from your NDS tree using global or specific views. These reports perform checks on servers, background processes, partitions, and replica rings, and they produce information retrieved in report files.

To initiate DSDIAG, simply type DSDIAG at a NetWare 6 server console. You see the main screen appear as shown in Figure 9.48. You see two options, which are covered in the next section.

**FIGURE 9.48** *The main screen for the DSDIAG utility*

## Generate Report and Preferences

You first select Generate Report, and you receive the following list of report generation options. Be sure to select each option to define how you want the report to be created. Keep in mind that each of these options generates a separate report file and thus a separate report.

The second option is for preferences that you can set as defaults in DSDIAG. Both are explained in the text that follows.

### Generate Report

**Check NDS Versions** — Returns the NDS version for each server in your NDS tree. Selecting this option enables you to do these things:

- Specify how you want the information gathered (that is, NDS, SAP, or by address).
- Specify a starting context for the search.
- Select the replica type you want to search on.
- Specify how far you want to search down the tree.
- Specify the report file format and options such as size and filename.

**Check NDS Background Process Status** — List the status of the NDS background processes for each server found. Selecting this option enables you to do these things:

- Specify how you want the information gathered (that is, NDS, SAP, or by address).
- Specify a starting context for the search.
- Select the replica type you want to search on.
- Specify how far you want to search down the tree.
- Indicate the type of status to be retrieved. The options are All, Schema, Obituary, Xref Sync, and Limber.
- Specify the report file format and options such as size and filename.

**List Server's Partition Table** — List the partition table for each server found in the NDS tree. Selecting this option enables you to do these things:

- Specify how you want the information gathered (that is, NDS, SAP, or by address).
- Specify a starting context for the search.
- Select the replica type you want to search on.

▸ Specify how far you want to search down the tree.

▸ Specify a partition type match. The categories are All, Siblings, and Subtree.

▸ Specify a replica type. The categories are All, Readable, Writable, Master, Read/Write, Read Only, and Sub Ref.

▸ Specify the report file format and options such as size and filename.

**List Replica Rings** — Search for all partitions in the tree and report each partition's replica ring. Selecting this option enables you to do these things:

▸ Specify how you want the information gathered (that is, NDS, SAP, or by address).

▸ Specify a starting context for the search.

▸ Select the replica type you want to search on.

▸ Specify how far you want to search down the tree.

▸ Retrieve the replica ring from a single replica, every server in the first ring found, or all servers from all rings.

▸ Specify the report file format and options such as size and filename.

**Check Partition Status** — Check the synchronization status of each partition root found in the tree. Selecting this option enables you to do these things:

▸ Specify how you want the information gathered (that is, NDS, SAP, or by address).

▸ Specify a starting context for the search.

▸ Select the replica type you want to search on.

▸ Specify how far you want to search down the tree.

▸ Retrieve the replica ring from a single replica, every server in the first ring found, or all servers from all rings.

▸ Specify the report file format and options such as size and file name.

**Compare Replica Rings** — For each partition root found in the NDS tree, compare the replica ring with other replicas in the ring. Selecting this option enables you to do these things:

▸ Specify how you want the information gathered (that is, NDS, SAP, or by address).

▸ Specify a starting context for the search.

▸ Select the replica type you want to search on.

▸ Specify how far you want to search down the tree.

▸ Retrieve the replica ring from a single replica, every server in the first ring found, or all servers from all rings.

▸ Specify the report file format and options such as size and filename.

### Distributed Repair

The distributed repair option enables you to select certain repair options on portions of the directory tree that you specify. For example, an option to Remove Network Addresses enables you to scan certain parts of the directory tree for user objects. If the user objects are found, you can remove their network address properties based on a certain criteria or simply generate a report of logged-in users.

### Preferences

Selecting Preferences enables you to set up default configurations for all reports that you generate. You have the following options:

▸ **Manage Naming Conventions** — Used to set the format of input and display of NDS names in DSDIAG and the report files. The options are:

  • **File Output Context** — Set the naming conventions for file output to be the same or different from the naming conventions used for input.

  • **Base DN** — Fully qualify relative names and reduce the size of displayed names.

  • **Display Typed Relative Distinguished Name Values** — The default is ON.

  • **Escape Non-local Characters** — The default is ON. Nonlocal code page characters are accepted in escape format. Nonmappable characters are displayed using the escape character.

  • **Delimiter Set** — Specify the delimiter to be used to display NDS names. DOT is the most common between names.

▸ **Manage Identities** — Log in and out of identities and change the default identity. The only option here is the following:

  • List available identities found for this server.

▸ **Preferences** — Configure the display or report preferences to be used.

▸ **Numeric Values** — You can choose hexadecimal or decimal.

▸ **String Values** — Select string translation or ON to show actual strings.

▸ **Flags Format** — Select string translation or hexadecimal.

▶ **Time Format** — Select local, UTC, or hexadecimal.

▶ **Primary Address Types** — Select address types that are considered primary addresses during comparisons of servers, objects, and property values.

## Generating a Report

As an example, let's say you want to generate a report that checks the NDS background process status. You would follow these steps:

1. Load DSDIAG on the NetWare 6 server where you want to generate the report. You can either run this straight from the console or use RCONSOLE.

2. Select "Generate Report."

3. Select the option "Check NDS Background Process Status." You are presented with the screen shown in Figure 9.49.

**FIGURE 9.49** *The General Options screen*

4. Keep the defaults for the first five options, arrow down to Report File, and press Enter twice.

5. Accept the defaults unless you want to change the filename.

6. Press F10 to return to the General Options screen.

7. Press F10 again to start report generation. You see a status bar appear at the top of the server screen and the output shown on the screen. An example of this output is shown in Figure 9.50.

**FIGURE 9.50** *Output generated by running. a DSDIAG report*

## Summary

As a system administrator responsible for the maintenance and troubleshooting of NetWare 6 and NDS eDirectory, you need to know how to monitor and troubleshoot operations and check the health of the server and NDS tree. This chapter helps you understand first how to check the health of a server and the tree before you start any new NDS partition operations and then how to monitor the operations to completion. As discussed, the first step to properly monitor any NDS partition operation is to check the current health or status of the partition involved in the operation. It is extremely important that you perform the health check before starting the operation. If a previous partition operation has not yet completed, you never want to start a new one.

The Novell Management Portal utility is a great tool that can help system administrators and network managers troubleshoot and diagnose the hot spots that you see through Portal's traffic light icon. The Portal utility can help isolate what is causing the problem, gather appropriate data on the problem, find out which NLMs are causing problems, and then speak competently to the manufacturers of the offending program.

The iMonitor utility provides powerful diagnostic tests and information for NDS. One of its many uses is to help you perform a health check and troubleshoot the directory tree. You have also learned how to use the DSREPAIR utility and DSTRACE to monitor the status of the replicas and synchronization. In addition, new to NetWare 6 is the DSDIAG utility that helps you determine the status of each replica list and each partition. The benefit is that you can effectively track NDS operations as they proceed through several states on several different servers and know if the operation is complete or needs more time.

# NetWare 6 Features

**T**his chapter examines the new and enhanced features of NetWare 6 and NDS eDirectory version 8.6. While many of the changes are subtle and won't be noticed by many of your users, other changes are significant and require some additional understanding to implement in your network environment. In some cases you will find a topic that may also be covered in another chapter. We refer you to appropriate chapters for additional reading on that topic. In other cases the topic will be covered in the following sections. The NetWare 6 functions and features are categorized into the following sections:

▸ NDS eDirectory 8.6

▸ NetWare operating system

▸ File system

▸ Novell Directory Services (NDS)

▸ Network services

▸ Installation and upgrade

▸ Developer support

▸ Third-party add-ons

# NDS eDirectory 8.6

Novell's eDirectory is a cross-platform directory service that is not only used in an enterprise, but also for eBusiness. eBusiness functionality includes business relationship management, supply-chain management, and electronic storefronts. NDS eDirectory is Novell's latest release (at the printing of this book) and includes some key new features:

▸ Increased scalability and replication performance

▸ Hot-continuous backup

▸ Greater support of LDAP auxiliary classes

▸ Persistent searches

▸ Dynamic group management

▸ Novell Modular Authentication Services to support MD5 and SHA-1 passwords on top of the existing RSA PKI

### Increased scalability and replication performance

NDS eDirectory 8.6 includes an improved super scalable replication feature that allows a single eDirectory 8.6 server to simultaneously replicate data to multiple servers, which significantly decreases the amount of time required to replicate servers within the replica ring.

### Hot-continuous backup

eDirectory has now added a feature that allows for a hot-continuous backup of the directory. This feature allows companies to perform a backup of large directories while the directory is operational without having to lock the directory during the backup.

### Greater support of LDAP auxiliary classes

The NDS schema has been extended to allow auxiliary classes easier to use with the directory.

### Persistent searches

Persistent search allow LDAP client and applications to receive notifications of changes that are made on an eDirectory server. This feature will allow developers to create applications that will make a single query to the directory, receive the results, and receive the updates on that query.

### Dynamic group management

Most companies employ the use of group objects for various functions. eDirectory 8.6 supports a new feature known as dynamic groups. Dynamic groups allow administrators to dynamically mange group membership through the use of policies. For example, an administrator can create a group that grants administrators to particular resources. The administrator creates the group object and grants it the appropriate rights. You then set a policy to grant membership to any user who has administrator in their title.

### Novell Modular Authentication Services

Novell's Modular Authentication Services (NMAS) has been included with eDirectory to support authentication using SHA-1 and MD5 passwords. Applications that utilize MD5 and SHA-1 security can easily integrate with eDirectory with this feature.

. . . . . . . . . . . . . . . . . . . . . . . . . . . . . . . ◄

# The NetWare Operating System

NetWare 6 offers many new changes to the core NetWare operating system that offer increased speed and reliability. This section describes the operating system changes, which include an enhanced multiprocessor kernel, virtual memory, and memory protection.

## The NetWare 6 Multiprocessor Kernel

The core of the NetWare 6 operating system is an enhanced kernel that supports multiple processors out of the box. The enhanced NetWare 6 kernel is known as the *NetWare multiprocessor kernel (MPK)*. The obvious benefit of having a multiprocessor kernel is that it automatically supports machines that have more than one processor. In fact, it supports single and multiple processors from the same kernel. This means that you can utilize existing processors in your servers more efficiently or add processors as needed to help speed up specific services. Most companies have found that the optimal number of processors is two to four. An example of the use of multiple processors is shown in Figure 10.1.

The NetWare MPK can support a machine with as many as 32 processors. During installation, NetWare 6 automatically detects the number of processors by reading the multiple processor table in the machine's BIOS. It then determines which of the NetWare 6 Platform Support Modules (PSM) matches the hardware platform. The PSM is a hardware abstraction layer or interface that NetWare 6 uses to support different hardware dependencies.

The enhanced multiprocessor kernel provides many  services, including support for Java applications and the IP stack, both discussed later in this chapter. The NetWare 6 operating system kernel has the following functions: memory protection, virtual memory, preemption, and application prioritization.

**FIGURE 10.1** *NetWare 6 provides an enhanced kernel that supports multiple processors out of the box.*

### Memory Protection

The memory protection feature in NetWare 6 enables you to load server applications in their own protected address space. The applications are then shielded from other applications and the operating system itself. The result is that if one application fails, it does not affect any other applications or processing of the operating system. You can use protected address spaces to run untried or troublesome applications. Any program or module loaded into a protected address space cannot corrupt the operating system or cause server abends. The protected address space provides a safe place to run applications. All protected address spaces use virtual memory. An example of this concept is shown in Figure 10.2.

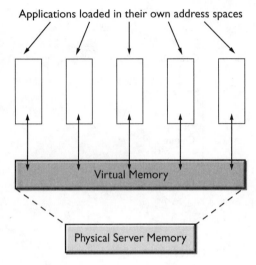

**FIGURE 10.2** *NetWare 6 enables applications to be loaded in their own memory space.*

A protected address space is a portion of cache server memory that has controlled communication with the server's operating system. The protected address space is only a portion of cache memory that can be set aside. This is sometimes called user address spaces or ring 3. In contrast, the NetWare operating system does not run in a protected address space. The operating system address space is sometimes called ring 0 or the kernel address space. The kernel cannot run in virtual address space.

In the first release of NetWare 5, only a few NLMs or applications could be loaded into the protected memory space. NetWare 6 loads Java-based applications in protected mode by default. In addition, you can optionally load GroupWise 6, Lotus Notes (except for the debugging module), Oracle 11i, and Oracle8 into protected memory spaces. However, certain types of modules and programs cannot run in protected addresses. The protected address spaces run in ring 3, and others must be loaded at ring 0 instead. Here is a list of common NLM programs and executables that cannot be loaded into a protected address space:

- ► SERVER.EXE
- ► LAN drivers
- ► Disk drivers
- ► MONITOR.NLM

### Virtual Memory

*Virtual memory* is a memory management scheme that provides the NetWare 6 operating system with the capability to allocate more than the actual physical memory of the server machine. It does this by using the disk as an extension of memory and by swapping code and data between physical memory and disk as it is needed. When the data on disk is needed again, it is moved back into physical memory. Because data is swapped in and out of disk, available memory can be used for a larger amount of data than its actual physical capacity would allow. Virtual memory provides NetWare 6 with a more efficient use of memory and lessens the likelihood that low memory conditions could cause an abend condition.

NetWare 6 moves data out of physical memory to swap files on the hard drive if the data has been used infrequently. More specifically, available memory is assessed to see which data has been used less recently than the rest. How recently data has been used is determined by a bit in each field of the translation table that indicates whether the address space has been used since the last time it was checked. Data that has not been used for some time can be moved from memory to disk, thus freeing memory for other uses.

As mentioned earlier, protected memory uses virtual memory. The reason is to allow the memory management subsystem to allocate to each process a unique protected virtual address available to run the threads of the process. Thus, each process has a separate address space, so a thread in one process cannot view or modify the memory of another process. This architecture provides the protected memory for NetWare 6. An example of this concept is shown in Figure 10.3.

As an example, the server operating system (SERVER.EXE) cannot run in virtual memory because it must always be resident in memory and cannot be swapped to disk.

### Preemption

The NetWare 6 kernel (like most previous versions of NetWare) has also been developed to support *preemption*. Preemption eliminates the problems associated with applications running on the server as NLMs that have been poorly written and monopolize too much of the processor time. In order to take advantage of preemption in NetWare 6, an application must be explicitly written or enabled by the developers to support the kernel's preemption.

**FIGURE 10.3** *Virtual memory uses the disk as an extension of physical memory.*

### Application Prioritization

The multiprocessor kernel also enables you to support what is known as *application prioritization* or *load balancing,* which ensures optimal application distribution among the processors. Application prioritization is implemented as part of the new NetWare 6 kernel, and the system administrator decides how to prioritize the applications running on the network's servers. You can specify the processor usage that you want to dedicate to each application.

The ability to adjust the usage dedicated to each application enables you to tune the quality of service provided. In addition, both single-processor and multiple-processor machines can benefit from the flexibility of application prioritization. Thus, if a single-processor machine has multiple applications, you can allow one application to have more CPU cycles than the other applications.

## The NetWare 6 GUI Console (ConsoleOne)

NetWare 5 and NetWare 6 allow the server console to appear in a graphical user interface (GUI) environment. Its appearance and operation are similar to the X Windows environment found on UNIX platforms. A GUI server environment permits the use of a graphical interface for programs, such as the Novell Installation program and Java applications at the server console.

**NOTE**

**The GUI environment requires additional server RAM. It is not recommended that you try to run the GUI environment on servers with less than 128MB of RAM.**

ConsoleOne is similar to the NWADMIN utility. Each release of ConsoleOne has been adding functionality previously found only in NWADMIN. According to Novell, ConsoleOne will completely replace NWADMIN sometime in the future, but we continue to mention both utilities throughout this book until NWADMIN is no longer used. ConsoleOne allows you to use NDS eDirectory to:

▸ Create, modify, delete objects

▸ Browse and organize network resources.

▸ Set up accounts for network users.

▸ Control access to network resources.

▸ Access remote server consoles.

## PCI Hot Plug Hardware Management

NetWare 6 provides the continued capability to upgrade or replace network interface cards while the server is up and running, easing server expansion and providing longer server uptime.

PCI Hot Plug technology allows industry-standard PCI adapters to be added or removed without disrupting operation of the NetWare 6 server. This reduces unplanned downtime for maintaining or adding disk or LAN adapters. Features of PCI Hot Plug technology include the following:

▸ **Uninterrupted service** — You can add or replace network or other I/O controller boards while a system is operating. This can be done through "hot removal" or "hot insertion."

▸ **Compatibility** — Multiple system providers, operating system suppliers, and adapter vendors can implement Hot Plug, which is compatible with existing PCI standards.

▸ **Backward compatibility** — You can use a mix of Hot Plug and non–Hot Plug components in the same system. (But non–Hot Plug components cannot be added or removed without shutting down the server.)

### Introduction to NCMCON

The Novell Configuration Manager console (NCMCON) enables you to view status information on PCI slots and to remove and add PCI Hot Plug adapters. The

NCMCON interface constantly monitors and displays the status of all slots. If there are any errors, the appropriate error message is displayed at the server.

Three menus are used in the NCMCON interface:

- ► The main menu — System Information
- ► Slot Options
- ► Slot Detailed Information

### NCMCON Interface Menus

The main menu displays a list of all PCI slots in the system, as shown in Figure 10.4.

```
Novell Configuration Manager Console          NetWare Loadable Module


                    Main Menu - System Information

  Slot  Hot Plug  Adapter Name                      Slot Status

    1     No      No adapter present                Ready
    2     No      No adapter present                Ready
    3     Yes     Compaq Netelligent 10/100 TX PCI Dual U  Active
    4     Yes     Compaq 32-Bit Fast-Wide SCSI-2/P Contro  Active
    5     Yes     Ethernet controller               Active
    6     Yes     Compaq Netelligent 10/100 TX PCI Dual U  Active
    7     Yes     Fast Ethernet Adapter with Intel 82557   Active
    8     Yes     SCSI bus controller               Active



Esc - Exit     F1 - Help
```

**FIGURE 10.4** *The main menu of NCMCON*

For each slot, the main menu displays the following information:

- ► The system board slot number
- ► Whether or not the slot is hot pluggable
- ► An adapter description field or name
- ► The status of the slot/adapter, which may have any of these states:
  - **Powered Off** — The lever is open on the slot, and power to the slot is turned off.
  - **Powered On** — The lever has been closed, power is on to the slot, and the slot is empty (this is different from Ready in that there is no card in the slot).

- **Ready** — An adapter is in the slot and ready to be used, but currently no driver is loaded for it.

- **Active** — A loaded driver is using this adapter, and the adapter is believed to be in good working order.

- **Failed** — This adapter's driver or Hot Plug driver indicated some type of device failure. The adapter can be removed, and a new one added at this time.

- **Degraded** — A device on the multidevice adapter has failed, but other devices on the adapter continue to function.

- **Processing** — An action is being performed on a slot/adapter.

Pressing Enter on a selected slot of the main menu displays the Slot Options screen, as shown in Figure 10.5. Online, context-sensitive help is available to guide you through PCI Hot Plug actions.

**FIGURE 10.5** *The Slot Options screen*

This menu lists the options available for the highlighted Hot Plug slot (selecting a non–Hot Plug slot automatically displays the Slot Detailed Information screen). An example of the detailed information is shown in Figure 10.6.

**FIGURE 10.6** *The Slot Detailed Information screen*

Items shown on the screen include the following:

**Main Chassis**

▸ Slot number

▸ Description of the adapter in the slot

**Slot Information**

▸ The bus type (PCI, EISA, or EMBEDDED)

▸ The bus number of the slot

**Hot Plug**

▸ Hot pluggable, Yes or No

**Slot Status**

▸ The status of the slot/adapter, Active or Inactive

**Device and Driver Information**

▸ The NetWare hardware instance number (HIN) of each device

This last item includes the registered device driver name and status for each HIN. Status possibilities include the following:

- **Active** — A driver is loaded for the device.
- **Inactive** — No driver is loaded for the device.
- **Failed** — The device has failed.
- **Suspended** — The driver is loaded, but activity is suspended while the adapter is being added.

Pressing F2 activates the Slot Options menu again, which allows you to take actions such as removing the card from a particular slot. Depending on the driver, the state of the slot or adapter, and the capabilities of the system, different options appear on the menu.

For example, if you want to remove a card while the system is running, you can select the Remove Adapter option after hitting F2. This option is shown in Figure 10.7.

**FIGURE 10.7** *Removing a Hot Plug adapter from your NetWare 6 system*

After selecting this option, you will be presented with a warning screen before you deactivate this card. An example is shown in Figure 10.8.

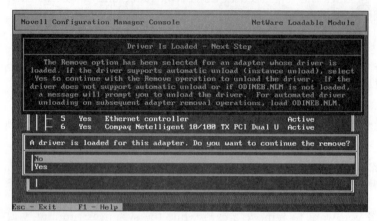

```
Novell Configuration Manager Console          NetWare Loadable Module

                    Driver Is Loaded - Next Step

     The Remove option has been selected for an adapter whose driver is
   loaded. If the driver supports automatic unload (instance unload), select
   Yes to continue with the Remove operation to unload the driver.  If the
   driver does not support automatic unload or if ODINEB.NLM is not loaded,
    a message will prompt you to unload the driver.  For automated driver
   unloading on subsequent adapter removal operations, load ODINEB.NLM.

        5   Yes   Ethernet controller                      Active
        6   Yes   Compaq Netelligent 10/100 TX PCI Dual U  Active

   A driver is loaded for this adapter. Do you want to continue the remove?

   No
   Yes

Esc - Exit    F1 - Help
```

**FIGURE 10.8** *The warning screen shown before removing a card*

**IMPORTANT** **Before powering down your adapter cards with the manual switch on the hardware, follow the previous process to remove the software driver that is bound to the card. Failure to remove the driver before powering off the card can cause your server to abend. For example, if a disk controller in slot 4 is powered off, the process abends the server to protect your data.**

Once you press Enter, the driver will be removed from the card and you will receive a message stating that the slot has been powered off, as shown in Figure 10.9.

```
Novell Configuration Manager Console          NetWare Loadable Module

                 Main Menu - System Information

   Slot  Hot Plug  Adapter Name                       Slot Status

     1    No    No adapter present                     Ready
     2    No    No adapter present                     Ready
     3    Yes   Compaq Netelligent 10/100 TX PCI Dual U  Active
     4    Yes   Compaq 32-Bit Fast-Wide SCSI-2/P Contro  Powered Off
     5    Yes   Ethernet controller                    Active
     6    Yes   Compaq Netelligent 10/100 TX PCI Dual U  Active
     7    Yes   Fast Ethernet Adapter with Intel 82557  Active
     8    Yes   SCSI bus controller                    Active

Esc - Exit    F1 - Help
```

**FIGURE 10.9** *A status message indicating that the slot has been powered off*

The interlock mechanism is one feature that can influence what appears on the Slot Options menu. The interlock is a safety mechanism that shuts off power to a slot if the slot is opened while the power is still on. Not all hardware manufacturers provide an interlock mechanism, and not all interlock mechanisms work the same way. You'll need to refer to your hardware documentation for more information.

When there is no power to the slot, the interlock mechanism is closed, and the driver supports what is known as *add functionality*. (Add functionality means that an adapter can be added to an empty slot or an existing adapter can be replaced with a different adapter.) After you remove a card from the slot, you will see the status appear on the NCMCON, screen as shown in Figure 10.10.

When there is no power to the slot, the driver supports only replace functionality, and the interlock mechanism is either closed or not supported.

**NOTE**

*Replace functionality* **means that an existing adapter can be replaced only with an identical adapter.**

**FIGURE 10.10** *The Status screen indicates that the adapter card has been powered off.*

After you replace an adapter, the Hot Plug PCI automatically detects the card, and the NCMCON utility then asks if you want to have power turned on for this slot. This message is shown in Figure 10.11.

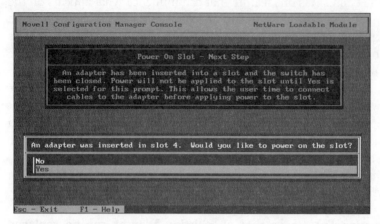

**FIGURE 10.11** *The NCMCON utility displays a message that a card has been detected in the slot.*

Once power has been applied to the card, the utility attempts to find the driver for this card and then load the driver. As you can see in Figure 10.12, the NCMCON utility initiates the NWCONFIG utility to perform this portion of the operation.

**FIGURE 10.12** *NCMCON uses the NWCONFIG utility to attempt to locate a driver for this card.*

**This utility does configure IPX automatically but does not reinstate any IP addresses you may have had bound to this card. You must take this step manually.**

NOTE

Once you have completed this step to load the driver for the card, you will see the Status screen indicate that the card is active for that slot. This is shown in Figure 10.13.

### I2O Support

I2O (Intelligent I/O) is a technology that improves I/O throughput and server performance by relieving the CPU of interrupt-intensive tasks such as memory calls and system interrupts. I2O is an industry-driven software specification designed to provide a standards-based solution to offload input/output traffic from the central processing unit and to enable hardware vendors to develop a single driver to work with all networking platforms. NetWare 6 provides I2O support for Ethernet- and SCSI-class devices and block storage, making server management easier while increasing application processing efficiency.

**FIGURE 10.13** *The Status screen indicates that the highlighted card is active.*

# The NetWare 6 File System

In addition to the changes that have been made to the operating system in NetWare 6, the file system has seen some significant changes and improvements. This section describes the changes made to the file system, which include the Novell Storage Services (NSS) and Storage Management Services (SMS).

## The Novell Storage Services

Novell Storage Services (NSS) is not new to NetWare 6, but some enhancements have been made. NSS version 3.0 is the latest software that is designed to mount large server volumes in seconds, virtually eliminating the limits on the number or size of files that can be stored in volumes and directories. You can use NSS to quickly open and update large files, such as those found in databases.

Novell Storage Services eliminates several limitations that currently exist in the NetWare file system. NSS provides an object-oriented storage with 64-bit internal and external interfaces. Without NSS, the NetWare file system supports a 32-bit interface that limits files to 2GB, directory entries to 16 million per volume, and volumes per server to 64. With NSS, the NetWare file system can host a single 8TB (terabyte) file. This capability may prove extremely useful for database applications. In addition, the NSS file system can support virtually unlimited directory entries (or number of files) per volume. During testing at Novell, a volume with a billion files was successfully created with three name spaces loaded. This demonstrates that the file system can support three billion directory entries on a single NetWare volume. Thousands of volumes can be created per server; however, the current NCP interface only supports 127 volumes per server.

In addition to larger volumes and greater numbers of files, NSS supports extremely fast volume mount times. A normal NSS volume will mount in less than one second, regardless of size or number of files stored. If the NetWare 6 server crashes and the volume is not dismounted cleanly, after the server is brought back up it is restored and mounted in approximately 15 seconds to one minute. This is the case for all NSS volumes on the server. The older FAT-based file system is organized so that the greater the number and size of files, the greater the volume mount time. For more information about the configuration and use of NSS, refer to Chapter 2.

The following enhancements are now available in NSS version 3.0:

▸ NSS version 3.0 now supports SYS: volumes in addition to the data volumes that all versions of NSS support.

▸ NSS support file compression. NetWare 6 can compress NSS files that are infrequently used or not used at all.

▸ NSS 3.0 support user and directory quotas. You can limit the space a user consumes on an NSS directory and the space a directory consumes on an NSS volume.

▸ NSS 3.0 supports the Transaction Tracking System (TTS).

ConsoleOne now provides the Menu options on the Media tab of the Server Properties page to install and configure NSS.

---

### Consulting Experience

Here's a formula that can help you calculate your memory requirements using NSS:

1. Rate your users on a scale from 1 to 10, where 1 equals *light user* and 10 equals *power user.*

2. Calculate the amount of memory required for NSS with the following formula, where R is the rating for users from step 1 and N is the number of users:

   ```
   (R × 7.5 × square root(N)) / Log10(N)
   ```

   This works for 10 to 10,000 users.

---

## Storage Management Services

Storage Management Services (SMS) is a collection of software programs loaded on a NetWare 6 server that provide backup and restore services. SMS lets you back up, restore, and verify data stored on the network and on network clients. NetWare 6 SMS includes the Enhanced SBACKUP utility, which ensures regular and complete backups of all the data on your network, including the NDS database, bindery data, GroupWise data, and client and server file systems. The SMS services are performed by a collection of components that are independent of operating systems and hardware.

## NDS eDirectory Backup and Restore

The Novell backup utility allows backups of SMS targets such as NDS, binderies, the file system, or an individual workstation's hard disk onto media that can be stored off-site. If you have a hardware failure, catastrophe, corrupted data, or incorrectly deleted or changed data, you can recover a previous version of the data.

Enhanced SBACKUP retrieves and reinstates backed-up data. The restore session produces the requested data, which is retrieved from the storage media and restored to the location you specify. During a restore session, Enhanced SBACKUP reads the backup storage media, and the Target Service Agent compares the media data set to the existing hard disk data set.

For more information on backup and restore of the NetWare 6 file system and Novell Directory Services, see Chapter 18.

# Novell Directory Services

Along with all the other exciting features of NetWare 6 comes increased functionality for Novell Directory Services (NDS eDirectory), as previously mentioned at the beginning of this chapter. Several enhancements make NDS more scalable, manageable, flexible, and secure in managing and administering a network. NetWare 6 ships with the latest version of NDS eDirectory (Version 8.6), and its release is not tied directly to the release of NetWare 6. Several features (first introduced in NetWare 5 and NetWare 5.1) help make NDS more scalable across your network servers. These features include transitive synchronization, the transitive vector, caching the replica changes, multiple objects per packet, randomized replica lists, distributive reference links, and the WAN Traffic Manager. In addition, NetWare 6's NDS reduces network traffic by restricting all outbound synchronization from all read-only replicas, and it eliminates subordinate reference replicas from normal replica synchronization.

The NDS features that enable you to more easily manage the NDS tree content include the role-based administration provided by the Inheritable ACLs, the Password Administrator property, and the Partition Administrator property. Using inheritable ACLs, you can provide role-based assignments by assigning supervisor rights to operators or help desk staff to manage specific types of objects or resources. For example, you can assign rights to a group to manage only the printers, servers, or users. Using the new Password Administrator property, you can specify a help desk group to reset only the user's password. With the Partition Administrator property, you can selectively assign rights to a specific group to perform partitioning and replication of the NDS tree without giving rights to the Supervisor for the entire tree. In addition, rights to perform partition operations can be assigned to any administrators who are lower in the tree structure without their acquiring all rights to the top.

### Inheritable ACLs

Several new NDS features enable you to more easily manage the objects and properties of the NDS tree. One of the features is the capability to inherit specific property rights down the entire tree. This feature is possible because of the new inheritable ACLs. The inheritable ACLs enable you to assign Supervisor rights to operators or help desk staff for specific types of objects or resources without giving Supervisor rights to the entire tree. For example, you can assign rights to a group to manage just the printers, servers, or users. More importantly, you can create a group to manage only user passwords. For example, a help desk group can be given only enough rights to change a user's password or to reset it. See the next section for the steps to do this.

In order to give inheritable rights to a specific property and have it flow down the NDS tree, use ConsoleOne. Inside the ConsoleOne Property Rights dialog box is a flag at the bottom of the rights list called *Inherit*. You can give specific property rights to any object that will inherit by selecting the rights and then selecting the Inherit flag.

Another new feature in NetWare 6 is the capability to display all the schema-defined properties in a single list in NWADMIN anywhere in the NDS tree. The properties that are shown are for all the objects in the schema. This gives you the ability to select any property at any level in the NDS tree to be managed. For example, you can give a group the rights to manage all users' telephone numbers from the O=Organization level on down.

### Enabling the Password Management Property

Follow these steps to enable the Password Management property and to create a Password Administration group that could be used by a help desk.

**I.** Using ConsoleOne, create a Help Desk group for Password Administration, as shown in Figure 10.14.

**FIGURE 10.14** *Creating a Password Administration group object*

**2.** Next, select the container object where you want to activate the Password Administration group and select "Trustees of This Object." Click Add Trustees and select the password group object you just created. It will appear in the trustee list. You will be presented with the dialog box shown in Figure 10.15.

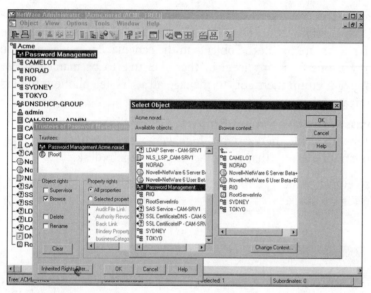

**FIGURE 10.15** *Adding trustees to the Password Group object*

**3.** Under the Property Rights category on the same page, scroll down to find the Password Management property. Select this property, mark it with the Supervisor property right and as inheritable, as shown in Figure 10.16.

**4.** Click OK, and you have completed the steps necessary to create a password administration group.

Other NDS utilities that enable you to more easily manage the overall NDS system are the DSDIAG utility and the Schema Manager utility. Using DSDIAG, you can quickly and easily determine how the partitions and replicas are synchronizing and detect errors, if any, between NetWare servers. An example of the main screen for this utility is shown in Figure 10.17. For more information on using DSDIAG, see Chapter 9.

**FIGURE 10.16** *Selecting the Password Management property in the Password group and marking it with the Supervisor right and as inheritable*

**FIGURE 10.17** *The main screen for the DSDIAG utility*

Another useful utility is the Schema Manager, which enables you to view, update, and manage the NDS schema. The NDS schema is the internal set of rules for how NDS objects and properties are created and used. An example of the Schema Manager utility is shown in Figure 10.18. For more information on using the Schema Manager utility, see Chapter 3.

**FIGURE 10.18** *The Schema Manager utility enables you to view and to modify the NDS schema.*

## Replica Synchronization

As you may know, NDS eDirectory is a loosely consistent database, which means that changes or updates can occur at various replicas, and not all the replicas may have the exact same information at the same time. However, because NDS eDirectory is loosely synchronized, an update made at one replica propagates to other replicas of the partition over time. These changes are automatically sent to the other replicas of that partition by a background process called *replica synchronization.*

The purpose of replica synchronization is to guarantee consistency of the information across all the replicas of a partition over a period of time.

The updates or modifications that affect the NDS data include adding, deleting, moving, or renaming an object, as well as changing the properties or attributes of the object. Replica synchronization passes only the data that has changed for each object or property between the replicas of the partition. Passing only the information that is updated ensures that the total amount of information sent is reduced and that network traffic for synchronization is kept to a minimum.

NetWare 6 has made changes to replica synchronization to make it even more streamlined and scalable. Remember that in NetWare 4, replica synchronization involved updating all the replicas for a specific partition with all the changes made to the partition since the last synchronization cycle. The process took the replica pointer table (replica ring) and synchronized each of the replicas one at a time with the most recent changes. The process had to contact each server in the replica ring one at a time to complete a synchronization cycle for the partition. This method of forcing the synchronization process to contact every server consumed valuable time and network resources. NetWare 6, on the other hand, makes synchronization more efficient and manageable by providing *transitive synchronization* and the *transitive vector.*

### Transitive Synchronization and Transitive Vectors

Replica synchronization in NetWare 6 uses *transitive synchronization* as a method of using the *transitive vector* during synchronization between two NetWare 6 servers. Transitive synchronization uses the transitive vector instead of the Synchronized Up To property that was used in NetWare 4.

With NetWare 6, server replication no longer happens within a replica ring or list, as it previously did, to determine whom it must contact for synchronization. Transitive synchronization works through the transitive vector. If the source server's transitive vector is more recent than a target server's vector, the source server does not need to synchronize with that target server. This procedure reduces synchronization traffic and frees up bandwidth. It also employs either the IPX or IP protocol.

The transitive vector is a structure that has been added to the Partition Root object for each partition. It is essentially a group of modification timestamps representing the values held by each replica. There is one transitive vector for each replica. The transitive vector differs from the Synchronized Up To property in that it holds a group of timestamps for each replica, whereas the Synchronized Up To property holds only one value for each replica in the partition. Another major difference between the transitive vector and the Synchronized Up To property is that the transitive vector is synchronized between servers, whereas Synchronized Up To is not synchronized. To view the status of transitive synchronization on your servers, use the NDS Manager utility, highlight a partition, right-click, and then select the Partition Continuity option. At the top of the window select the Transitive Synchronization option. You will then be shown a dialog box like the one in Figure 10.19. This dialog box indicates the status of each transitive vector for each server and reports discrepancies between servers.

**FIGURE 10.19** *The results of selecting the Partition Continuity option in NDS Manager*

You can then highlight a replica and right-click to select information. The information dialog box shows detailed information on the replica stored on a particular server. An example of this information dialog box is shown in Figure 10.20.

As previously mentioned, the transitive vector structure is kept as a vector with an attribute for each replica. By using the transitive vector, synchronization can achieve convergence among the replicas of a partition without having each replica talk to every other replica. The structure of the transitive vector consists of modification timestamps for all replicas in a given replica ring. The transitive vector has been added to the partition root object of each partition in NetWare 6, as follows:

**Server ID**   The ID of the server that holds the replica

**Timestamp vectors** A timestamp vector for each replica in the replica ring

Each time that replica synchronization is scheduled to run on the NetWare 6 server, transitive synchronization reads the transitive vector to determine which replicas it needs to synchronize with. Because each NetWare 6 server has a transitive vector, the process can immediately determine how up to date each of the other replicas is. Using transitive synchronization, a specific server does not have to contact each of the other servers in the partition to complete replica synchronization. After a successful synchronization, the target or destination server merges the transitive vector with that of the source server. In addition, the changes are guaranteed to converge across all replicas of a partition over time.

After a change occurs in an NDS object or property, replica synchronization is scheduled to run. After the synchronization starts to execute, it determines which servers need to communicate by comparing the timestamps of the source and target servers in the transitive vector. The source server is the local server that received the update, and the target server is the destination server for replica synchronization. If the time is greater for the local server, then the replica updates are sent. The local or source server does not request the target server's timestamps. The timestamps for the target server are already local in the transitive vector. After all updates are sent, then the source server sends its transitive vector values, which are merged into those of the target server.

**FIGURE 10.20** *The Information dialog box for the transitive vector*

You may be wondering how the transitive vector works if the synchronization occurs on a replica ring with NetWare 6 servers and NetWare 4 servers. If a replica ring includes a mixed-server environment, the two servers will synchronize using the NetWare 4 method of passing the synchronized up to vectors. After synchronization has completed, either the transitive vector from the NetWare 6 server or the synchronized up to vector from the NetWare 4 server is merged.

### The Replica Ring Is Randomized

In NetWare 4, after the replica synchronization started, it contacted and updated each of the replicas in the replica ring in a sequential order. Therefore, the first replica in the replica ring was updated, followed by the second one, and so on. Because the replica ring was identical on all the servers holding copies of this partition, synchronization affected all the replicas for each partition in the same order. This could have an undesirable effect if multiple servers were trying to synchronize with the same replica on the same server simultaneously. Because only one inbound synchronization was supported per partition (not per server), one of the synchronization processes would have to back off and attempt again at a later time. This situation only arose if the synchronization process tended to execute at approximately the same time on multiple servers.

To help alleviate this situation, NetWare 6 changes the sequence in which replicas are processed by randomizing the replica ring list before attempting to contact the first server. This greatly reduces the possibility that one of the servers will have to back off and attempt to resynchronize with a replica. By randomizing which replica receives the first update, transitive synchronization more quickly converges the data for each partition. As previously mentioned, transitive synchronization can converge the NDS data among all the replicas of a partition without having each replica talk to every other replica.

### Cache Object Changes

Novell Directory Services caches NDS changes to enhance the performance of replica synchronization. Remember that the changes or updates that affect the NDS objects include adding, deleting, moving, or renaming an object, as well as changing the properties or attributes of the object.

Using NetWare 4, NDS sequentially searched the entire object file, comparing timestamps to find the objects that had been updated since the last successful synchronization. Sequential searching effectively limited the size of the NDS partitions. When discussing implementation of the NDS tree in NetWare 4, we gave you a practical recommendation of 1,000–1,500 objects. In order to overcome this limitation, NetWare 6 eliminates the sequential search time by caching all changes to the objects. The capability to cache the objects in the NDS database greatly increases the speed of searching for and updating each replica and partition.

The object cache maintains a set of object IDs that have been modified since the last synchronization. The cache is populated by placing object IDs in the cache that have been modified as a result of client requests, as well as by inbound synchronization. Each cache entry has the modification time relative to the last synchronization. The cache that NDS maintains is for each partition that is stored on a server. The cache has a start time associated with it that identifies when the cache was built. Changes only need to be sent out if the transitive vector for the remote server is less than or equal to the transitive vector for the local server. The janitor process cleans up the cache periodically by removing the object IDs that have already been sent to all the replicas.

### Multiple Objects per Synchronization Packet

In order to help synchronize individual replicas faster, NetWare 6 supports more than one object in each communication packet. Formerly, NetWare 4 only allowed changes for one object in a single communication packet. By allowing multiple changes to different objects in a single packet, NetWare 6 reduces the total number of packets needed to synchronize them with other replicas. If the number of changes between two replicas is small, all the updates between two replicas may be accomplished in a single packet. Basically, this means that a partition can be synchronized in a minimum of one packet.

### Distributed Reference Links

NetWare 5 and NetWare 6 provide a method for maintaining external references called *distributed reference links (DRLs)*. These links are more efficient than backlinks when renaming, moving, and deleting external references. The distributed reference links are more efficient because, unlike backlinks, they are not tied to a specific NetWare server but instead reference the partition that stores the external reference object. Alternatively, after a backlink is created, it stores the NetWare server name and object ID for each external reference object.

As mentioned, the major downside to using backlinks is that they are tied to specific NetWare servers and not tied to the external reference object's location in the NDS tree. The result of using backlinks is that each NetWare server tends to have a connection to every other server in the NDS tree. In order to alleviate this problem, distributed reference links were added to NetWare 5 and NetWare 6 that store the partition name and object ID where each external reference object exists. By storing the partition name, they permit the individual NetWare servers to resolve the DRLs by using the NDS tree structure. An example of a distributed reference link is shown in Figure 10.21.

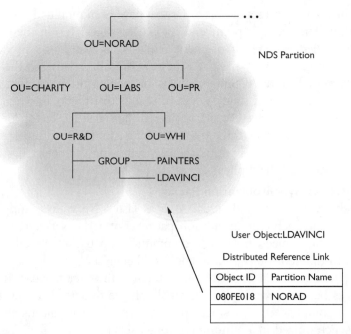

User Object:LDAVINCI

Distributed Reference Link

| Object ID | Partition Name |
|-----------|----------------|
| 080FE018  | NORAD          |
|           |                |

**FIGURE 10.21** *Distributed reference links maintain external references in NetWare 6.*

Like backlinks, the DRLs have a periodic process that checks to verify that the associated external reference still exists. This process periodically checks the DRLs and provides data integrity for the NDS database. Distributed reference links are implemented using a new "Used By" property of the object. The "Used By" property contains the distinguished name of the partition that holds the external reference and the object ID that is assigned to the object.

Although distribution reference links are fully implemented in NetWare 6, backlinks will not go away. During certain situations, backlinks will continue to be used to help maintain the external references. NetWare 6 uses both methods.

## The WAN Traffic Manager

The *WAN Traffic Manager* (WTM) allows you to manage NDS traffic across WAN links, reducing network costs and increasing performance benefits. This product would generally be used where you have slow WAN links or are using

ISDN lines. Many European sites use ISDN and will benefit from this product. This product ships with Novell Directory Services.

The WAN Traffic Manager is a policy-based tool for managing the cost and congestion of WAN traffic. Its clients (such as NDS traffic) request a policy decision before initiating WAN traffic. WTM, as a policy evaluator, checks administrator-supplied policies and attempts to match input criteria to one of them. If it succeeds, it runs the rest of the policy to see whether to allow the WAN traffic to proceed or to be delayed. WTM is a valuable tool for networks that have significant congestion on their WAN links (for example, with ISDN or slow dial-up links), enabling administrators to control and manage bandwidth use and congestion.

### How WAN Traffic Manager Works

The WAN Traffic Manager consists of three elements:

- ▸ **WTM.NLM** — WTM.NLM resides on each NetWare 6 server in the tree. Before NDS sends server-to-server traffic, WTM.NLM reads a WAN traffic policy to determine whether that traffic will be sent.

- ▸ **WAN traffic policies** — Policies are rules that control the generation of NDS traffic. WAN traffic policies are text stored as NDS property values on the NetWare Server object, the LAN Area object, or both.

- ▸ **ConsoleOne Snap-In** — This snap-in is the interface to WAN Traffic Manager. It enables you to create or modify policies, to create LAN Area objects, and to apply policies to LAN areas or to individual servers. After the WAN Traffic Manager is installed, your NDS schema will be extended to include a LAN Area object and three new detail pages for the NetWare Server object. These pages are the LAN Area Membership page, the WAN Policies page, and the Cost page.

Keep in mind that WTM enables you to control server-to-server traffic, which is defined as traffic generated from replica synchronization, schema synchronization, heartbeat, limber, backlink, connection management, and server status checking.

**NOTE**   **The WAN Traffic Manager is not the older Novell product known as PingFilt/DSFilter. PingFilt used a dirty hook into NDS and inspected every packet that NDS attempted to send. On ping packets, it recorded the values returned and used them to spoof ping packets when filtering was active. Otherwise, PingFilt either allowed packets to proceed or returned the error –625 ERR_TRANSPORT_FAILURE to NDS.**

The WAN Traffic Manager provides a policy service using WAN policy and cost attributes that are stored in NDS. After it receives a request from a client application (via the GetWanPolicy API), it selects the most appropriate policy and evaluates it. It then returns the results (SEND_NOW or DONT_SEND) to the client application.

The client application must supply WanMan with a traffic type and with optional source and destination network addresses, along with optional application-specific information in the form of named-variable and value pairs. The executed policy can modify these variables, which are returned to the client application as part of the results. This process enables a policy to tell the application more than just SEND_NOW or DONT_SEND. For example the policy might indicate to send the data at a particular time or after certain conditions (such as queue sizes) are met.

WanMan provides its services in two ways: directly and indirectly via the RollCall NLM. In the direct approach, the client application calls WanMan's exported APIs. This introduces a load order dependence — WanMan must be loaded before and while the client application is loaded. Because this usually is undesirable, WanMan also makes its APIs available via RollCall. Both WanMan and the client application will have a load order dependence on roll call, but not on each other. They can be loaded and unloaded independently. Novell anticipates that most applications will use the indirect approach via roll call.

The WAN Traffic Manager controls server-to-server traffic generated by NDS. It can restrict traffic according to cost of traffic, time of day, type of traffic, or any combination of these restrictions. Although the WAN Traffic Manager was designed to control traffic across WAN links, it can control NDS traffic between any servers in an NDS tree. The WAN Traffic Manager controls only periodic events initiated by NDS, such as replica synchronization, the janitor process, and the limber process. It does not control events initiated by administrators or users, nor does it control non-NDS server-to-server traffic such as time synchronization.

### Installing and Configuring WTM

Follow these steps to install and configure WTM:

**1.** Move the snap-in DLL WANMAN.DLL to your SYS:\Public\win32\snapins directory.

**2.** After moving the DLL to this directory, restart ConsoleOne. Once in ConsoleOne select Tools ⇨ Add WanMan Schema, as shown in Figure 10.22. This extends your NDS schema and adds the new policy pages to the server object.

**FIGURE 10.22** *Extending the NDS schema to include the WanMan policy pages*

After this operation is completed, you will have a LAN area object available in the Create Objects menu of NWADMIN, or you can select the Server object and select WAN policies. The next step is to create a LAN area object if you want to have multiple servers assigned to the same WAN policy. Using this object saves time because the policy is shared by multiple servers, and you avoid configuring multiple servers. An example of creating a LAN area object is shown in Figure 10.23.

**3.** Once you have created the new LAN area object, you can click Details and then select "Servers Belonging to LAN Area" and Add. This enables you to indicate the servers that you want to participate in this LAN area group. Adding a new server to the group is shown in Figure 10.24.

**FIGURE 10.23** *Creating a LAN area object for the WAN Traffic Manager*

**FIGURE 10.24** *Adding a server to the LAN area group*

**4.** The next step is to define a WAN policy page. We highly recommend that you use the predefined policies that are provided. Be careful if you make modifications to these policies. The WAN Traffic Manager selects and runs administrator-supplied policies to manage WAN costs and congestion. NDS uses policies to control synchronization and other background tasks based on time of day, network addresses, network costs, and so on. The WAN Traffic Manager is extensible so that clients can supply extra information to the policies. WAN Policies are stored in NDS to enable global administration, and you can use constraints such as time of day, connection cost, source and destination addresses, other connection and address specifics, and information supplied by the WTM client.

**5.** To create or enable a policy, select the WAN Policy page in the Details of the LAN area object you previously created. An example of this is shown in Figure 10.25. Notice the drop-down menu includes many predefined policies for your use. Using a predefined policy is the easiest and fastest method for using policies.

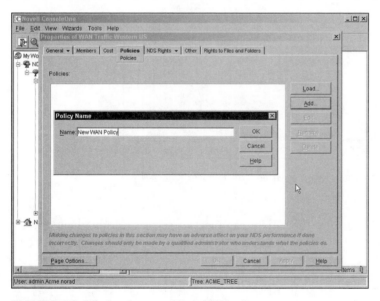

**FIGURE 10.25** *Creating or enabling a WAN policy page*

**6.** You then need to select the Load Group option to load the policy. You will see a status message, and any errors will be displayed if discovered. An example of this output is shown in Figure 10.26. If you have created your own policy, any errors in the policy will be displayed here.

**7.** The next step is to define a destination range and a cost for this range. This range can be a range of either IPX addresses or IP addresses, and the cost can be any value that you wish to measure, such as dollars or hours.

An example of selecting an IPX or IP range and a cost is shown in Figure 10.27.

**FIGURE 10.26** *Loading a policy will reveal any errors present in the policy.*

If you choose not to use the LAN area object or select an individual server to create a policy, simply highlight the server and select Details. You will notice the tabs for WANPolicies and costs on the right side of the dialog box. You also have the option of adding this server to a LANArea group by selecting the LANArea Membership tab.

**FIGURE 10.27** *Selecting an IPX or IP range and a cost for this policy*

## Catalog Services

NDS Catalog Services provides a method to store directory data in a nonpartitioned, indexed format on your NetWare 6 server for rapid access. Directory information stored in catalog or index format can be easily customized for searching, sorting, and reporting purposes. Distribution and replication of a catalog enables administrators to quickly access a "snap shot" of the complete network directory as opposed to performing a query across the entire network and walking the NDS tree.

Catalog Services enables the development of applications, which need rapid access to directory data in a centralized repository. These applications can include contextless login, NDS white pages, and fast lookup for LDAP gateways, along with many other applications. NetWare 6 provides one of these new Catalog Services applications, called *contextless login*. The contextless login leverages the NDS catalog by allowing users to authenticate from any point on the network by typing their login name and password, thus, removing the need to know the location of their user object in the NDS tree.

Catalog databases can be scoped to include data from the entire directory tree or from one or more subtrees. The attributes stored in the catalog can be filtered according to user or administrator requirements. Catalog Services includes a dredger that reads the directory to build catalogs; an NWADMIN snap-in that controls the scope, filtering, time interval, and other aspects of catalog creation; and a set of query APIs that support development of applications that can find catalogs and read data from them.

The catalog services dredger is a server-based program that creates catalogs by periodically scanning the NDS tree for the data that was previously requested by the administrator of the catalog. The dredger runs on the following platforms:

- NetWare 4.10 (NDS build 5.01 and above)
- NetWare 4.11 (NDS build 5.73 and above)
- NetWare 6 (all builds)

You can completely control scheduling of the dredger operations. You select how and when the dredger refreshes the catalogs at periodic intervals, or you can start a refresh manually at any time. Although the catalog is updated during the refresh operation, it remains available to users. In addition, dredging for multiple catalogs can occur simultaneously.

It is extremely important that after you define the Catalog Services object in the NDS object that you grant it the proper access rights. The access rights used by the dredger while creating a catalog are the rights assigned to the catalog object in NDS. The access rights are controllable through access control lists (ACLs) in the same manner that all other access rights are controlled.

In addition to controlling the rights, you can control the scope of the directory data included in a catalog by specifying a base object where dredging will begin and a tree depth of single object, subordinate objects, or full subtree. Multiple base objects can be specified, each with a corresponding tree depth. You can also create filters to control the object classes, attribute classes, and values to be included in the catalog.

Included with the Catalog Services product is a management utility that runs as a snap-in to the ConsoleOne console on Windows NT, Windows 95/98, and Windows 2000. The management utility provides the capability to create and edit filter expressions that determine what data is included in the catalog according to object classes, attribute classes, and attribute values. The management utility includes a simple browser for viewing catalog contents that is part of the Tools option.

The management utility provides a dredger server page, which enables the administrator to control certain aspects of the operation of the server on which the dredger is running. These include the number of threads allocated for dredger operation and the sync interval length at which the dredger checks its catalog list against the list on the server object in NDS. The page also displays a list of the catalogs dredged by the server. The management utility provides a summary page, which lists summary information about the dredger, including time of last dredge and log file statistics.

Catalog Services is easily installed during regular installation of a NetWare 6 server. After Catalog Services is installed, it extends the NDS schema. It also places the dredger and the management utilities on the appropriate servers. The Install Wizard provides the capability to remove SDK components and registry entries installed by Catalog Services on the local machine. It does not remove components that are installed on a file server. Components not removed include NDS schema extensions, the dredger, and the management utility.

Catalog Services consists of these components:

▶ **DSCAT.NLM** — This NetWare Loadable Module (NLM) is installed and loaded during NetWare server installation. It contains the dredger that searches the NDS database for the objects and properties that you have defined in the catalog.

▶ **DSCQRY16.DLL or DSCQRY32.DLL** — These DLLs are the query engines (16-bit or 32-bit) that the NetWare Administrator snap-in (or other applications) uses to query the directory.

▶ **NetWare Administrator Snap-In (DSCATMGR.DLL)** — This provides an interface to Catalog Services through NetWare Administrator. It lets you create, modify, query, index, and delete catalog objects.

### Creating a Master Catalog

Creating a master catalog enables you to create a place to store information extracted from the Directory database. The catalog stores only the objects and attributes you specify and lets your users find information about those objects without a time-consuming search of the entire Directory. The master catalog periodically receives updates from the catalog dredger (search engine) and distributes this information to any existing slave catalogs.

These steps will walk you through creation of a catalog:

**1.** Load the NetWare Administrator and choose the container in which you want to create the catalog object.

**2.** Choose the NDSCat:Master Catalog object icon and click OK as shown in Figure 10.28.

**FIGURE 10.28** *Creating a master catalog using NWADMIN*

**3.** In the Create Catalog dialog box, specify the catalog name, check Define Additional Attributes, and then click Create.

**4.** In the Details dialog box select a host server. The host server hosts the catalog dredger that populates and updates this master catalog. Type in the server's Complete Name (for example, CAM-SRV1.CAMELOT.ACME).

**5.** Make the catalog object security equivalent to another object so that the catalog has rights to read and browse the tree. An example of the Details dialog box is shown in Figure 10.29.

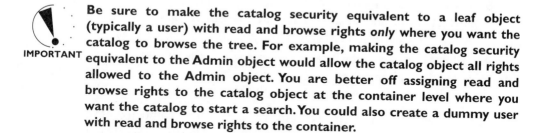

**FIGURE 10.29** *Filling in information in the Details box, including the Host Server name and security equivalency*

> **IMPORTANT**
>
> **Be sure to make the catalog security equivalent to a leaf object (typically a user) with read and browse rights *only* where you want the catalog to browse the tree. For example, making the catalog security equivalent to the Admin object would allow the catalog object all rights allowed to the Admin object. You are better off assigning read and browse rights to the catalog object at the container level where you want the catalog to start a search. You could also create a dummy user with read and browse rights to the container.**

6. (Optional) Enter a description, location, department, and organization for the master catalog.

7. Label the catalog. You need to enter both primary and secondary labels. A label is a name that is used by an application. Multiple applications can reference the same label. A primary label can be a global name, such as your company's name. A secondary label can be more specific, such as a department name. An example of creating the labels is shown in Figure 10.30.

**FIGURE 10.30** *Creating labels for your catalog*

8. Click Filter, and then enter a statement in the Filter box. The filter is an attribute name and attribute value such as "object class" = "user" and so on. An example of this box is shown in Figure 10.31.

9. Define the scope of the catalog. You can search the subtree, search immediate subordinates, or search aliases, as shown in the dialog box. You can also enter the context limits for the search.

10. Click Schedule to specify when the catalog should be updated. If you select Update Now, the dredger component on your NetWare 6 server initiates creation of the catalog. Click the Summary tab to see a summary of the catalog findings, as shown in Figure 10.32. You will see a message on your NetWare 6 server indicating the times the dredge began and completed. You can also choose to schedule a time for building the catalog by specifying an automatic time with a frequency, start time, and start date.

**FIGURE 10.31** *Specifying a filter to search NDS and to build the catalog*

**11.** Click Attributes/Indexes and then choose All Attributes or Selected Attributes. If you choose Selected Attributes, you can choose individual attributes to include in your catalog. You can select any available attributes by highlighting them and clicking Add. An example of this is shown in Figure 10.33.

**12.** Click Select Indexes on the same page to specify the attribute by which the catalog is to be indexed. You can index on any attribute that you have previously selected.

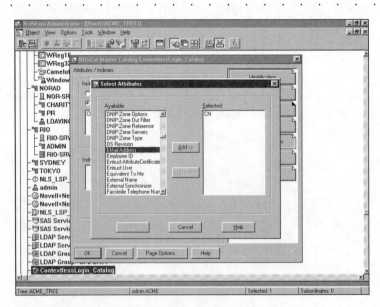

**FIGURE 10.32** *The Summary Information tab shows the results of catalog creation.*

**FIGURE 10.33** *Selecting attributes to add to your catalog*

### Installation of Contextless Login

Perhaps one of the most important features of Catalog Services is its capability to create a contextless login for your users. This feature allows users to log into the NDS tree without knowing their full context. They can simply enter their user name without knowing their location in the tree. This is a big benefit for mobile users. Follow these steps to implement contextless login:

**1.** LGNCON32.DLL is the contextless login extension that is installed as part of the NetWare Client for Windows NT install program. Verify that this file exists on your machine by examining the Windows system directory.

**NOTE**

**For Windows 95/98 this is C:\WINDOWS\SYSTEM; for NT it is C:\WINNT\SYSTEM32. For Windows 3.1, the file is LGNCON16.DLL and is in the WINDOWS\SYSTEM directory.**

**2.** Log in as a user with Administrative rights to the target tree.

**3.** If you have not already done so, install NDS Catalog Services using the NetWare 6 installation program. Select to install all except the NDS Catalog Services SDK. During the Catalog Services setup, select a tree and server to copy the dredger (DSCAT.NLM) to.

**NOTE**

**The install program modifies the server AUTOEXEC.NCF to automatically load DSCAT.NLM. You may wish to edit this file after installation completes so that you can load it manually in the future if you desire.**

**4.** Check the local WINDOWS\SYSTEM directory for a DSCQRY32.DLL. If this file does not exist, look for DSCATQRY.DLL and rename it to DSCQRY32.DLL. (Note: for Windows 3.1 this file should be renamed to DSCQRY16.DLL.) This file may also exist on the server in SYS:PUBLIC. If it does, copy it to the appropriate local Windows directory as described previously. This file is needed for contextless login to use NDS Catalog Services.

**5.** From the Start menu, run a NetWare Administration Utility program such as Z:\public\win95\NWADMN32.EXE.

**6.** Create the catalog object: Type **NDSCat:Master Catalog**, name it "usrcat" in any organizational unit or container in your tree, and save it.

**7.** Select the catalog object just created and define these additional attributes:

*Identification page:*

- Select the Browse button to the right of the Host Server field. Browse to and select the HOST server (this is the one that runs the dredger as in Step 3).
- Click the New button in the Label section. Enter **LGNCON** for the primary label and **Users** for the secondary label. *Please note that case is important.*

*Filter page:*

- Input this text in the Filter field: **"Object Class" = "User"**. *Note that case is important and be sure to include the double quotation marks.*
- Select the Search Subtree radio button and leave the Context Limits field blank, or designate the context limiting container. This will be the starting point for the dredger to fill the catalog with users; in other words, only users in this container and below will be added to the usrcat database. (When this field is blank, the entire tree will be cataloged from the [root] container down.)

*Attributes/Indexes page:*

- Select the Selected Attributes radio button.
- Select Full Name from the Available list and click the Add button. Click OK.
- Click the Select Indexes button. Select Full Name from the Available list and click Add. Click OK. Please note: This will allow the use of Full Name searching by contextless login if the administrator has included Full Name attributes for User objects in the tree.

*Schedule page:*

- Select the Manual radio button. Note: If you add more users to your tree, you'll need to update the catalog (redredge the tree), as well.

**8.** Click OK to save all changes.

**9.** Right-click on Root or the container used in Step 7 for the filter page and then select Trustees of This Object.

**10.** Click Add Trustee. Locate the catalog "usrcat" created and add it as a trustee. It should now appear in the Trustees list for this container. Verify that Browse is enabled under Object rights, and that Compare and Read are enabled under Property rights. This gives the catalog object rights to the container in order to read objects and populate the catalog.

**11.** Click OK to save changes.

**12.** Locate the catalog and right-click it to select Trustees of This Object.

**13.** Click Add Trustee. Select [Public] under the Available objects listing, and select OK. [Public] should now appear in the Trustees list for the catalog usrcat. Verify that Browse is enabled under Object rights, and that Compare and Read are enabled under Property rights. This gives contextless login the capability to open and read a catalog using [public] rights. This is necessary, as the user is not currently "Authenticated" to the tree; [public] rights are used.

**14.** Click OK to save changes.

**15.** Go to the server and load DSCAT.NLM or verify that it is loaded.

**16.** Return to the workstation and run the Administration tool again. Select the catalog object. Open the Schedule page and select the Update Now button (unless you are using automatic updating).

**17.** Return to the server and wait for a successful dredge of the catalog. After the line appears that says "USRCAT dredge is complete," you may unload DSCAT.NLM, if you wish.

**18.** Return to Administration tool and verify that the catalog has data by reselecting the USRCAT object. Select the summary page. Verify the dates and times listed on this page. Click the Query button and query this catalog. You should only see a listing of distinguished names for all users currently defined in the database (tree).

**19.** Exit the Administration tool.

**20.** Verify that the settings for contextless login are set. You may use the Registry editor or go through the Client Configuration property page for contextless login.

**21.** To use the Client Configuration property page, simply enable contextless login.

**22.** Using a Registry editor, locate the following key:

*For Win95:*

```
\\HKEY_LOCAL_MACHINE\Network\Novell\System Config\
Network Provider\Graphical Login\NWLGE\Z Xcontext
```

*For Winnt:*

```
\\HKEY_LOCAL_MACHINE\Software\Novell\Graphical Login\ NWLGE\Z
XContext
```

**23.** Under Z XContext, verify or create the following key value pairs:

| KEY NAME | KEY TYPE | KEY VALUE |
|---|---|---|
| LoginExtDesc | String | "Login Extension Contextless Login" |
| LoginExtName | String | "LGNCON32.DLL" |
| LoginExtType | Binary | 01 80 00 00 |

**24.** Save these settings and exit.

**NOTE**

**After any new users are created in the future, rerun the dredge by loading DSCAT.NLM on the server, waiting for a successful dredge, and then unloading (see Steps 14 through 16).**

**Testing the Functionality of Contextless Login**

Test if contextless login is running correctly by following these steps:

**1.** Run Loginw32.exe.

**2.** In the Tree field, enter the tree that has the catalog "usrcat," as created previously.

**3.** Input any existing user name into the Username field.

**4.** Hit the Tab key.

**5.** If the user name only exists once on the server, the user's corresponding context should now appear in the Context field.

   If the user name exists in multiple contexts in NDS, a Users dialog box should appear that states "Select your user and context from the list shown on the screen below." Click OK.

**6.** A list of all matching users and contexts should appear below the prompt.

**7.** Partial names also work but only if contextless login is configured for wild card searches.

## LDAP Services for NDS

NetWare 6 supports Lightweight Directory Access Protocol (LDAP) version 3, an industry-standard protocol that enables a user to easily access X.500-based directories including but not limited to NDS. LDAP Services for NDS is a server-based interface between NDS and any LDAP-compliant applications running optionally under Secure Sockets Layer (SSL). In NetWare 6, the performance of LDAP access to NDS has also been significantly enhanced from previous versions, allowing unlimited scalability through NDS's advanced replication and management of directory functions.

The Lightweight Directory Access Protocol (LDAP) in NetWare 6 is configured and managed using LDAP Services for NDS, a snap-in to the NetWare Administrator utility (NWADMN32.EXE). LDAP Services for NDS 3.0 is a server application that enables LDAP clients to access read and write information stored in NDS. With LDAP Services for NDS, all your NDS data is available and you define the directory information that is accessible to LDAP clients and the clients that can access the directory. You can also give different clients different levels of directory access or access the directory over a secure connection. These security mechanisms allow you to make some types of directory information available to the public, other types available to your organization, and certain types available only to specified groups or individuals.

### Installing LDAP Services for NDS

LDAP Services for NDS is installed when you install NetWare 6 and choose product options. The NetWare 6 server loads NLDAP.NLM, and a snap-in is added to NWADMIN to provide new object functionality.

### Understanding LDAP Services for NDS

LDAP Services for NDS is a NetWare server application (NLDAP.NLM) that allows LDAP clients to access information stored in NDS. With LDAP Services for NDS, you define the directory information you want to make accessible to your LDAP users and grant the rights to the LDAP clients that you want to have access to the directory. Using the NetWare Administrator utility, you can specify all the attributes of the LDAP clients and set all security information in one place.

The directory features available to LDAP clients depend on the features built into the manufacturer's LDAP server and the LDAP client. For example, LDAP Services for NDS allows LDAP clients to read and write data in the NDS database if the client has the necessary permissions. Some clients have the ability to read and write data; others can only read directory data.

### LDAP Clients

LDAP Services for NDS allows LDAP clients to access data in NDS directories. All LDAP clients bind, or connect, to NDS as one of the following types of users:

- ▸ [Public] user
- ▸ Proxy user
- ▸ NDS user

Login restrictions and password restrictions still apply; however, any restrictions are relative to where LDAP is running.

Time and address restrictions are also used, but address restrictions are relative to where the NDS login occurred — in this case, the LDAP server. Also, as LDAP does not support grace logins, it is possible to log into NetWare and yet not be able to bind to LDAP.

**[Public] User (Anonymous Bind)**    An anonymous bind is a bind that does not contain a username or password. If an LDAP client binds to LDAP Services for NDS and the service is not configured to use a proxy user, the user is authenticated to NDS as user [Public]. User [Public] is an authenticated NDS user. By default, user [Public] is assigned the Browse right to the objects and attributes in the NDS tree.

The default Browse right for user [Public] allows users to browse NDS objects but blocks user access to object attributes. The default [Public] rights are typically too limited for most LDAP clients. Although you can change the [Public] rights, this will give these rights to all users. Because of this, use of the proxy user anonymous bind is suggested.

**NOTE**

> To enable user [Public] access to object attributes, you must make user [Public] a trustee of the appropriate container or containers and assign the appropriate object and attribute rights.

**Proxy User (Proxy User Anonymous Bind)**    A proxy user anonymous bind is an anonymous bind that is linked to a normal NDS username. If an LDAP client binds to LDAP Services for NDS anonymously and the service is configured to use a proxy user, the user is authenticated to NDS as the proxy user, whose name is configured in LDAP Services for NDS and in NDS.

To implement proxy user anonymous binds, you must create the proxy user object in NDS and assign the appropriate rights to that user. Assign the Proxy User Read and Search rights to all objects and attributes in each subtree where access is needed. Use LDAP access control lists (ACLs) to restrict access as necessary. You also need to enable the proxy user in LDAP Services for NDS by specifying the same proxy username.

The key concepts of proxy user anonymous binds are as follows:

▸ All LDAP client access through anonymous binds is assigned through the proxy user object.

▸ The proxy user cannot have a password or any password restrictions (such as password change intervals) because LDAP clients do not supply passwords during anonymous binds. You should not force the password to expire or allow the proxy user to change passwords. You may want to limit the locations from which the user can log in by setting address restrictions for the proxy user object through the Network Address Restrictions page of NetWare Administrator.

▸ The proxy user object must be created in NDS and assigned rights to the NDS objects you want to publish. The default user rights provide Read access to a limited set of objects and attributes. Assign the Proxy User Read and Search rights to all objects and attributes in each subtree where access is needed. Use LDAP ACLs to restrict access as necessary.

▸ The proxy user object must be enabled on the General page of the LDAP Group object that configures LDAP Services for NDS. Because of this, there is only one proxy user object for all servers in an LDAP group.

**NOTE** **You can configure access control lists (ACLs) in the LDAP Group object to add access controls for the proxy user. For example, you can create an access control list that allows the proxy user access through one IP address or a group of IP addresses.**

**NDS User (NDS User Bind)**    An NDS user bind is a bind that an LDAP client makes using a complete NDS username and password. The NDS user bind is authenticated in NDS, and the LDAP client is allowed access to any information the NDS user is allowed to access.

After LDAP Services for NDS is installed, NDS-user-bind requests using clear-text (unencrypted) passwords are refused by default. Clear-text passwords and NDS usernames entered by LDAP clients on non–Secure Sockets Layer (SSL) connections are vulnerable to capture by network monitoring equipment. Anyone who captures an NDS username and password has immediate access through an LDAP or NDS client to all the NDS objects to which the captured username has access. NDS user binds should only be used on LDAP servers that are configured to use SSL.

**Even though clear-text passwords are not accepted by default, this does not prevent users from trying to bind with their usernames and passwords. On an unsecured connection, all attempted binds expose the username and password to eavesdropping, whether or not the bind is successful. However, not allowing clear-text passwords for NDS user binds discourages users from using their names and passwords because this method of binding will be unsuccessful.**

To support NDS user binds on non-SSL connections, you must allow clear-text passwords within the LDAP Group object.

The key concepts of NDS user binds are as follows:

▸ NDS user binds are authenticated to NDS using the username and password entered at the LDAP client.

▸ On non-SSL connections, the NDS password is transmitted in clear text on the path between the LDAP client and LDAP Services for NDS.

▸ Any NDS username and password used for LDAP client access can also be used for NetWare client access to NDS.

To support NDS user binds on non-SSL connections, you must allow clear-text passwords. To enable this feature, check the Allow Cleartext Passwords check box on the LDAP Group object using NetWare Administrator for Windows 95/98 or NetWare Administrator for Windows NT. If clear-text passwords are not enabled, all NDS-bind requests that include a username or password on non-SSL connections are rejected.

If an NDS user password has expired, NDS-bind requests for that user are rejected. The type of bind with which the user authenticates has a direct effect on the content the LDAP client can access. LDAP clients access a directory by building a request and sending it to the directory. After an LDAP client sends a request through LDAP Services for NDS, NDS completes the request for only those attributes to which the LDAP client has the appropriate access rights. For example, if the LDAP client requests an attribute value (which requires the Read right) and the username is granted only the Compare right to that attribute, the request is rejected.

LDAP Services for NDS supports the Secure Sockets Layer (SSL) protocol to ensure that the connection over which data is transmitted is secure and private. SSL is a protocol that establishes and maintains secure communication between SSL-enabled servers and clients across the Internet. To ensure message integrity, SSL uses a hashing algorithm. To ensure message privacy, SSL provides for the creation and use of encrypted communications channels. To prevent message forgery, SSL allows the server and, optionally, the client to authenticate each other during the establishment of the secure connection. This release of LDAP does not ask the LDAP client to authenticate itself.

**Key Material Object**    To implement the authentication and encryption processes, SSL uses a cryptographic mechanism called *public keys*. To establish a secure connection, the server and the client exchange their public keys to establish a session key. The session key will be used to encrypt the data for the life of the connection. A subsequent LDAP connection over SSL will result in the generation of a new session key that is different from the previous one.

Digital certificates, digital IDs, digital passports, or public key certificates are critical for verifying the identity of the contacted server. They are similar to an employee badge that identifies the wearer as an employee of a company. Each LDAP server requires a digital certificate to implement SSL. Digital certificates are issued by a Certificate Authority (CA).

Certificates are stored in a new NDS object, the key material object. Use Novell PKI Services, a snap-in of the NetWare Administrator utility (NWADMN32.EXE), to request, manage, and store certificates in NDS. Refer to the section "Installing and Using Novell's PKI Services" later in this chapter for details on setting up a certificate on a server. You can access Novell PKI Services help by selecting the Help button from any key-material-object page.

In order for the LDAP server to use a specific certificate for LDAP SSL connectivity once it is stored in NDS, you must indicate the key material object containing the certificate on the LDAP Server General page in NetWare Administrator.

**The key material object must be in the same container as the NetWare server object that will use it.**

NOTE

### SSL Configuration
Although SSL can be configured on both the client and the server to ensure the identity of both parties, clients do not require digital certificates to communicate securely. As the LDAP server listens for SSL connections on a special port, all the client needs to do is initiate the connection over that port.

Note that when you make changes to your LDAP Services for NDS configuration using NetWare Administrator, many of the changes take effect dynamically without your having to restart the LDAP server. However, most SSL configuration changes require a restart. Also note these points:

▸ If SSL is disabled, you can enable it without restarting the LDAP server, and the enabling will occur dynamically. If SSL is enabled and you disable it, you must restart the LDAP server in order for the disabling to take effect.

▸ If you make any configuration changes to the SSL port or the SSL certificate, you must restart the LDAP server for the changes to take effect.

To restart the LDAP server, type these commands at the NetWare server console prompt:

```
UNLOAD NLDAP
LOAD NLDAP
```

### Understanding Class and Attribute Mappings

A *class* is a type of object in a Directory, such as a user, a server, or a group. An *attribute* is a Directory element that defines additional information about a specific object. For example, a User object attribute might be a user's surname or phone number. In NetWare Administrator, classes are called *object types* or *classes,* and attributes are called *properties.*

A *schema* is a set of rules that defines the classes and attributes allowed in a Directory and the structure of a Directory (where the classes can be in relationship to one another). Because the schemas of the LDAP Directory and the NDS Directory are different, mapping of LDAP classes and attributes to the appropriate NDS objects and attributes is necessary. These mappings define the name conversion from the LDAP schema to the NDS schema.

LDAP Services for NDS provides default mappings. In many cases, the correspondence between the LDAP classes and attributes and the NDS object types and properties is logical and intuitive. Depending on your implementation needs, however, you may want to reconfigure the class and attribute mapping.

In most instances, the LDAP class to NDS object type mapping is a one-to-one relationship. However, the LDAP schema supports a feature called *auxiliary class support* that allows an object to be associated with more than one class. To view the mappings, select the LDAP group object you have created and select Details. You then select the Attribute Map tab to view the default settings and make changes to the mapping, if necessary. This will depend on the type of LDAP client you are using. An example of this view is shown in Figure 10.34.

**FIGURE 10.34** *The Attribute Map allows you to map LDAP attributes to NDS attributes.*

### LDAP and NDS Syntax

LDAP and NDS use different syntaxes. Some important differences are the following:

▸ Commas

▸ Typeful names only

▸ Escape character

▸ Multiple naming attributes

**Commas**   LDAP uses commas rather than periods as delimiters. For example, a distinguished, or complete, name in NDS looks like this:

CN=ALINCOLN.OU=ADMIN.OU=RIO.O=ACME.

Using LDAP syntax, the same distinguished name would be as follows:

CN=ALINCOLN,OU=ADMIN,OU=RIO,O=ACME.

**Typeful Names Only**   NDS uses both typeless (.LDAVINCI.NORAD.ACME) and typeful (CN=LDAVINCI.OU=NORAD.O=ACME) names. LDAP uses only typeful names with commas as the delimiters (CN=LDAVINCI,OU=NORAD, O=ACME).

**Escape Character**   The backslash (\) is used in LDAP distinguished names as an escape character. If you use the plus (+) character or the comma (,) character, you can escape them with a single backslash character. Following are examples:

CN=A\+EINSTEIN,OU=LABS,OU=NORAD,O=ACME (CN is A+EINSTEIN)

**Multiple Naming Attributes**   Objects can be defined with multiple naming attributes in the schema. In both LDAP and NDS, the user object has two: CN and OU. The plus symbol (+) separates the naming attributes in the distinguished name. If the attributes are not explicitly labeled, the schema determines which string goes with which attribute (the first would be CN, the second is OU for NDS and LDAP). You may reorder them in a distinguished name if you manually label each portion.

For example, here are two relative distinguished names:

SIRKAY (CN is Sirkay)
Sirkay+Charity (CN is Sirkay, the OU is Charity)

Both relative distinguished names (Sirkay and Sirkay+Charity) can exist in the same context because they must be referenced by two completely different relative distinguished names.

### Configuring the LDAP Server Object

The LDAP server object stores configuration data for one LDAP Services for NDS server. During installation, an LDAP server object named LDAP Server *servername* (where *servername* is the name of the server on which LDAP Services for NDS is installed) is created. The object is created in the same container as the NetWare server object on which the product is installed. An example of the Details dialog box is shown in Figure 10.35.

Each LDAP server object configures one LDAP Services for NDS server. Do not assign the same LDAP server object to more than one LDAP Services for NDS server. If you assign the LDAP server object to another server, it is no longer assigned to the previous server. The LDAP server object contains five property pages from which you set configuration options, which are the General (Details) page, log file options, screen options, catalog usage, and catalog schedule.

**FIGURE 10.35** *The Details dialog box for the LDAP server object*

### Using LDAP in a Wide Area Network Environment

In order to reduce network traffic when using a wide area network (WAN), you can specify exact times when you want to refresh LDAP objects in NDS.

Type one of the following three commands at the NetWare 6 server console.

**LDAP REFRESH**    This command refreshes LDAP at a specified interval. You can use the following syntax:

```
LDAP REFRESH = 'date' 'time' 'interval'
```

Use the following formats for the arguments:

▶ **Date format** — mm:dd:yyyy (If zeros are entered for all date fields, then the current date will be used.)

▶ **Time format** — hh:mm:ss (If zeros are entered for all time fields, then the current time will be used.)

▶ **Interval format in minutes** — A value greater than or equal to 1. The default is 30 seconds. If zero is entered, 30 seconds is used.

**LDAP REFRESH IMMEDIATE**   This command refreshes the LDAP objects immediately. If you have already set the LDAP REFRESH command, the set interval will be saved.

LDAP REFRESH

This command displays the time and interval of the next scheduled refresh.

**LDAP HELP**   To display help information at the server console, type the following command:

LDAP HELP

### The NetWare Time Protocol
Time synchronization in NetWare 6 always uses TIMESYNC, whether servers are using IP only, IPX only, or IPX and IP protocols. TIMESYNC.NLM is automatically installed on the NetWare 6 server installation program, but NTP.NLM must be manually loaded on your NetWare 6 server whenever the network has an IP stack in use.

NTP functionality has been built into the Timesync.NLM version 5.08 and later. Therefore, NTP is not necessary on a NetWare 6 server. This implies that TIMESYNC NLM can take time from an NTP time source and can serve time to NTP clients. Complete NTP functionality has been built into TIMESYNC.NLM. For more information on time synchronization in NetWare 6, see Chapter 7.

### Configuring TIMESYNC.NLM to Take Time from an NTP Source
The configuration is similar to obtaining time from a normal TIMESYNC NLM time source. Set the value of the Configured Source set parameter to On. Specify the IP address of the NTP time source in the Time Sources dialog box. However, an NTP time source needs to be differentiated from a TIMESYNC NLM time source by adding :123 to the front of the IP address. :123 has been chosen because it is the standard port for NTP. An example of this configuration in the MONITOR utility is shown in Figure 10.36.

In a pure timesync scenario, Single and Reference servers read time from their local clocks and serve it to time clients. They do not change their time. In other words, even if you have entered timesync time sources in Single or Reference server, they will not be used to change the time on the Single or Reference server.

However, the NTP feature now enables Single and Reference servers to obtain time from NTP time sources. This means that the Single or Reference server, if set up with NTP sources in its time sources set parameter, would poll the NTP time source and adjust its local clock to synchronize with the NTP time source.

**FIGURE 10.36** *Configuring an NTP time source in MONITOR*

# Network Services

Several new enhancements make the basic network services in NetWare 6 more flexible, manageable, and secure. The new network services included in NetWare 6 are Pure IP, Service Location Protocol (SLP), DNS/DNCP integration, ZENworks Starter Pack, Cryptographic Services, Secure Authentication Services (SAS), Public Key Infrastructure Services (PKIS), Auditing Services, NetWare Licensing Services, and Internet Connectivity.

## Pure IP

In NetWare 6, Pure IP enables NetWare to support TCP/IP in a pure sense. It does not encapsulate or tunnel IPX/SPX communications. Pure IP enables servers and clients to make NetWare Core Protocol (NCP) calls directly over the TCP/IP stack; such calls can then be routed by any IP router on the network. Although NetWare 6 maintains support for IPX/SPX protocols, you now have the option of implementing a pure TCP/IP environment or using IPX/SPX alone or as part of a mixed TCP/IP and IPX/SPX environment. This is advantageous for customers who require a Pure IP environment because it eliminates multiple protocols and frees up valuable network bandwidth, while allowing them to control IP implementation at their own pace.

Novell has severed the operating system's dependence on IPX/SPX and has rewritten IPX-only applications and utilities to support TCP/IP. As a result, NetWare 6 servers and workstations can use TCP/IP, IPX/SPX, or both. Following are the major advantages of supporting Pure IP in NetWare 6:

- ► Consolidation to one protocol in your network
- ► More efficient use of your LAN and WAN bandwidth
- ► A wider range of opportunities for remote user connectivity

Although Pure IP has major advantages, Novell is committed to remain backward-compatible to IPX/SPX. NetWare 6 is shipping with features that provide seamless compatibility between IPX- and IP-based technologies. NetWare 6's Compatibility Mode enables customers to move to an IP-only environment without having to replace valuable IPX-based applications and without having to introduce disruptions to their network operations. In addition, NetWare 6 ships an IP Compatibility Mode Migration Gateway that allows you to move to an IP-only network, incrementally if desired.

In essence, it is your choice whether to use IPX/SPX or TCP/IP as your network protocols. In order to install Pure IP, use the standard NetWare 6 installation program. During installation, select the protocols that you want your server to support. If you enable IPX/SPX, you must select an internal IPX address for the server, as you normally would. If you enable TCP/IP, you must select an IP address for the server. For more information, see Chapter 23.

### Service Location Protocol

Service Location Protocol (SLP) provides automatic resource discovery and registration over TCP/IP connections. Network resources such as servers and printers use SLP. SLP is more efficient than Service Advertisement Protocol (SAP) because it creates less ongoing network traffic than SAP. In addition, SLP allows network resources to carry extended description attributes. For example, a printer could be categorized as a "PostScript printer loaded with legal-sized paper used by Consulting." For more information on installing and configuring SLP in NetWare 6, see Chapter 23.

### DNS/DHCP

Domain Name Service (DNS) converts domain names (such as www.novell.com) to numerical IP addresses (*xxx.xxx.xxx.xxx*). NetWare 6 integrates DNS with NDS. With NDS integration, each user can automatically be assigned an appropriate DNS server upon login. For example, a mobile user in a distant location might be assigned a DNS server with a faster response time than a desktop user in a local office.

Dynamic Host Configuration Protocol (DHCP) provides unique IP addresses upon request to users and network devices. NetWare 6 uses NDS to help automate DHCP services, and this means you can store IP address in NDS. When the user logs into the network, DHCP consults NDS and provides an appropriate IP address to that user. DHCP eliminates the older methods of manually tracking and assigning IP addresses, and NDS ensures that DHCP provides managed IP addresses throughout the enterprise. For more information about DNS/DHCP, see Chapter 23.

## The ZENworks Starter Pack

NetWare 6 ships with the ZENworks Starter Pack, which includes Novell Application Launcher (NAL) and Workstation Manager as part of the NetWare 6 installation. ZENworks, which stands for Zero Effort Networking, is a bundle of management utilities that assist you in managing individual workstations in an enterprise.

The components of ZENworks enable administrators to solve a user's workstation problems without visiting the user's workstation. By adding workstation objects and workstation group objects to the NDS tree, administrators can manage the desktop configuration, distribute applications, and perform maintenance on the workstation through NDS.

With ZENworks installed, workstations are registered with NDS each time a user logs into the network. Registration enables administrators to look at a workstation object's details and centrally manage workstations through NDS.

## Features Available in the Full ZENworks Product

Additional ZENworks functionality can be obtained by purchasing the full-featured product. Once you install ZENworks and the Novell Client provided on the ZENworks CD, you can take advantage of the additional features described under the next few headings.

### The Help Requester

This application lets users send messages about a workstation problem to the administrator or Help Desk. A message automatically includes the workstation object's details stored in NDS. You can use the message and the workstation object in NWAdmin to solve the problem. This saves time and effort, especially when problem workstations are located on a WAN.

### Workstation Inventory

ZENworks allows you to easily inventory and track all the configuration data for Windows workstations on the network.

### Remote Control of Workstations

By enabling remote control access on the network's workstations, you can connect to a workstation remotely and navigate the desktop to troubleshoot workstation problems without having to visit the workstation.

For more information on installation and use of ZENworks, see Chapter 19.

# Security Features in NetWare 6

Several security features build upon NetWare 4's existing security features. For a complete description of NDS and file system security, see Chapter 13. The new security features found in NetWare 6 have been integrated with Novell Directory Services (NDS) and help simplify administration of each new feature. They also provide security for improved Internet data integrity and privacy across public networks. Novell's PKI infrastructure enables the use of public key cryptography and public key certificates on your network.

Before diving into this relatively new technology, it's important to understand the basics. Over the past couple of years we've witnessed the explosion of the Internet and its capabilities. With Internet commerce and other transactions, security has moved to the forefront of importance. Internet communications such as Web browsing or public forums lend themselves to be monitored easily by anyone with the right equipment and knowledge. However, credit card information and other sensitive data must be made secure across the Internet. Public key cryptography is the most widely used method for securing sensitive data and credit card transactions.

Public key cryptography secures data transmissions through authentication and encryption. *Authentication* is the method by which the data receiver knows that the data sender is exactly who or what it claims to be. *Encryption* is the scrambling of data such that it can only be read by the intended receiver.

Both authentication and encryption utilize the technology known as *key pairs*. Key pairs are mathematically related codes or "keys" that provide a secure method of communication. One key in each pair is publicly distributed, while the other key in the pair remains strictly private.

Therefore, during authentication, the data receiver knows that the data sender is exactly who or what the person or entity claims to be. An example of this concept is shown in Figure 10.37, in which a user authenticates to a NetWare server.

**FIGURE 10.37** *Authentication using public/private key cryptography*

Following are the basic steps of authentication:

**1.** You initiate a login request from your NetWare client.

**2.** Your client receives an encrypted private key from the server. This encrypted private key is used to generate a signature.

**3.** The public key of the NetWare server is requested by the client.

**4.** A proof is generated and encrypted with the server's public key and sent to the server.

**5.** The server decrypts the proof with the server's private key.

**6.** The server validates your signature against the request using your public key. If the results compute correctly, the signature is authenticated. Otherwise, a message is displayed that the login attempt has failed.

Encryption scrambles the data before it is transmitted across the Internet to ensure that only the intended receiver can read the data. For example, when you order a product over the Internet and enter your credit card number, encryption scrambles your credit card number so that only the intended receiver of the credit card number can read it. An example of this process is shown in Figure 10.38.

Your Workstation — Local application requests public key → NetWare 6 Server

Server responds with certificate

Application uses public key to encrypt credit card number

Encrypted message sent to store's server

Server uses store's private key to decrypt message

with a Browser application/ Credit Card Number

**FIGURE 10.38** *The process of data encryption*

Following are the basic steps of encryption process:

1. You are viewing a Web browser with the vendor's Web site and enter your credit card number in the store's application.

2. The store's application gets the store's public key directly from the store or a public directory.

3. The store's application uses this key to encrypt the message containing your credit card number.

4. The application sends the encrypted credit card information to the store's server.

5. The store's server uses the store's private key to decrypt the message.

Another important aspect of PKI is the concept of establishing trust. If a sender and receiver know and trust each other, they can exchange public keys and establish a secure data transmission, including authentication and encryption. This is accomplished through the use of each other's public keys and their own private keys. But neither party can typically trust each other, so a third party is introduced whom they both trust to provide proof of their identities.

A party needing to prove its identity in a public key cryptography environment enlists the services of a trusted third party known as a *Certificate Authority* (CA). There are commercial CAs, such as VeriSign, that provide this type of service. A CA service can also be operated by an internal organization, such as a corporate MIS department, that can issue public key certificates internally. The NDS tree CA can easily serve this purpose and enables you to save money by not using a commercial CA. A CA can also offer services such as key pair generation, key pair archival, public key certificate revocation, and public key certificate publishing services.

The CA's purpose is to verify that a party is who or what it claims to be; it then issue a public key certificate for that party to use. The public key certificate verifies that the public key contained in the certificate belongs to the party named in the certificate. After the identity of the requesting party has been established to the satisfaction of the CA, the CA issues an electronic certificate and applies to it what is called a digital signature. The digital signature verifies the authenticity of the certificate.

## Digital Signatures

A digital signature is similar to a personal signature that you would place on a document such as a check or other legal paper. Digital signatures can also be referred to as public key certificates, digital IDs, digital passports, or just certificates. A digital signature provides proof that electronic data is authentic. In order to create a digital signature, software must link the data being signed with the private key of the signer. For example, a company can request from a CA that they certify the company's public key. In this process, the company sends their public key information to the Certificate Authority for verification. Once the CA through verifies the information the CA's own rules of verification, the Certificate Authority takes a series of actions:

1. The CA creates a public key certificate containing the necessary information.

2. The CA runs a computation on the information in the public key to produce a small data string of 16 to 20 bytes.

3. The CA encrypts the small data string using the CA's private key. The encrypted string is the CA's signature for the certificate information.

4. The CA sends the public key certificate containing the requester's public key and the CA's signature to the requesting party.

Therefore, a digital signature is linked to the entity that signs it and the data. No other entity can duplicate the signature because each entity has its own private key. Even the entity that creates a signature cannot deny having signed the data. This is often referred to as nonrepudiation. So when a CA signs a public key certificate, it guarantees that it has verified the identity of the public key owner according to the CA's guidelines and policies.

The certificates generated by most commercial certificate authorities and also by Novell's NDS Tree CA are encoded using the X.509 v3 format. A public key contains the information shown in Table 10.1.

| T A B L E  10.1 |
| --- |
| *Contents of the Public Key Certificate* |
| The name of the user or organization (subject name) |
| The public key of the user or organization |
| The length of time the public key certificate is valid (typically this is one year) |
| The serial number of the public key certificate |
| The name of the CA that digitally signs the public key certificate |
| The digital signature created by the CA |
| Additional Encoded Attributes |
|     Alternative names |
|     Phone numbers |
|     E-mail addresses |
|     Key usage constraints |
|     Certification practice statements |
|     Other critical or noncritical attributes |

Now let's apply these concepts to the NetWare 6 environment. The security provided by the public key cryptography components in NetWare 6 includes the following:

▸ Novell International Cryptographic Infrastructure

▸ Public Key Infrastructure Services

▸ Secure Authentication Services

▸ The Audit system

The next four sections discuss these features and explain why they are important and how they provide NetWare 6 with advanced security services. The following section describes how you can configure Novell's PKI services in your NetWare environment.

## The Novell International Cryptographic Infrastructure

NetWare 6 includes cryptographic services known as the *Novell International Cryptographic Infrastructure (NICI)*. NICI allows developers to use the Controlled Cryptography Service (CCS) API to integrate cryptographic schemes with their applications. Therefore, an application must be written to take advantage of this service provided on NetWare 6. The big benefit is that NICI enables developers to write a single application using cryptography that can be used in different countries, regardless of the differences in countries' cryptographic laws. For example, a developer could write a single application that uses 128-bit cryptographic keys for use within the United States and 40-bit cryptographic keys when used within countries that allow only keys of that length.

NICI provides the infrastructure for network cryptographic services on a worldwide basis because it supports strong cryptography and multiple cryptographic technologies. This infrastructure has been developed in accordance with customer and internal Novell needs and at the same time abiding by the national policies and laws regarding the shipment and use of cryptography. NICI services were designed to be modular in nature, which allows for new cryptographic engines, libraries, and policy managers to be added at any time. The infrastructure is also tightly controlled, enforced through an integral OS loader that verifies modules before loading and controls access to modules only via standardized interfaces. For developers, the cryptographic services are provided via a Novell SDK.

Following are some important features that NICI offers NetWare 6:

- Developers do not have to include cryptographic code in their products. This is handled by the Controlled Cryptography Service API.

- A cryptographic library can be dynamically bound. This library delivers controlled cryptographic services to applications, regardless of the country where they are used.

- U.S. export approval is expedited for international applications.

- Integrity of key management is ensured.

- An infrastructure supports key escrow in future releases.

- A uniform cryptographic services API is included.

- Network security services are built on NICI.

NICI is the foundation for future network cryptographic services from any vendor. It ensures that your product complies with international cryptography import and export laws through enforced region-specific cryptographic laws and regulations. NICI also provides for single, worldwide commodity vendor products and supports extensible, application-specific cryptographic libraries and interchangeable cryptographic technologies.

In the past, applications had to provide their own services if they needed to employ cryptography. Because of the way the Novell cryptographic services are designed, application vendors can take full advantage of the services without having to incorporate complex and expensive cryptography inside their applications. The vendor can ship just one version of its product worldwide, instead of having multiple versions to accommodate the many and varied national cryptography regulations. Novell ensures compliance with international laws and export requirements—leaving application developers free from these concerns. Novell's PKI services for application developers are provided through Novell's SDK.

## Public Key Infrastructure Services

NetWare 6 includes *Public Key Infrastructure Services (PKIS)*, which supports public key cryptography and digital certificates in a NetWare 6 environment. Digital certificates provide a method for verifying the authenticity of keys used in a public key process. In NetWare 6, PKIS allows you to act as your own Certificate Authority or to use the services of third-party certificate authorities. Through PKIS, you can generate and sign digital certificates and store and manage these certificates within NDS.

PKIS allows any NetWare 6 administrators with Supervisor rights to the NDS tree CA to establish a Certificate Authority (CA) management domain within NDS. Additionally, PKIS allows administrators to manage certificates and keys for Secure Sockets Layer (SSL) security for LDAP servers.

Following are some important features that PKIS offers NetWare 6:

▶ Integrity of Certificate and Private Key Storage through NDS's trusted directory capabilities.

▶ The capability to manage tasks such as automated artificial certificate creation, using the local CA through the NetWare Administrator as a single point of administration.

▶ Standards Support for the PKIS-generated certificates. This is according to the X.509 v3 standard. PKIS is compatible with X.509 v1 and v2 certificates. The X.509 standard defines an internationally recognized format for providing identity and public key ownership.

▶ Standards Support for PKIS-generated PKCS #10 certificate signing requests. A PKCS #10 certificate signing request is a public key and is identity bound for certification by a signing authority. The PKCS #10 certificate request is sent to the Certificate Authority for a signature.

▶ The capability to securely manage the private keys for server applications.

▶ Worldwide exportable public key management capabilities with Novell's international cryptographic infrastructure.

PKIS helps you to build a working public key infrastructure on your network. You can create a CA specific to your organization and use the services of an external CA. You can also use a combination of both as your Certificate Authority needs dictate.

Using PKIS, you can control the costs associated with obtaining key pairs and managing public key certificates. PKIS helps you create a local CA based on NDS that signs certificates for other services on the network. With PKIS you can also generate unlimited key pairs and issue unlimited public key certificates through the local CA at no charge.

## Secure Authentication Services

Secure Authentication Services (SAS) is an infrastructure for supporting both existing and emerging authentication mechanisms, such as biometric and token-authentication systems. Through SAS, NetWare 6 supports SSL version 3. Developers can use the SAS API to write applications that can establish encrypted SSL connections. Additionally, developers can then use NICI to ensure that these SSL connections conform to the laws of each country in which the applications are used.

Authentication recognizes and protects the end user. It is how people and things identify themselves. So without authentication, you cannot secure your network. SAS security properties are attributed to applications running on the network inside of the NetWare 6 security boundary. Because SAS is a service, not a library, applications do not have access to protected authentication materials or users' secrets. It also provides worldwide exportable cryptographic services for authentication.

SAS is built entirely on NICI. SAS has the following capabilities:

▸ The SAS service is based on a single executable file. Because no cryptography is included in the SAS NLM, you can ship a single NLM worldwide. This provides easy administrator management and tracking. Also, any applications written to the SAS API can be based on a single executable file.

▸ Applications written to the SAS application can go through a one-time and usually expedited export approval process. Novell has already received export approval for SAS and NICI. This means that application developers benefit from expedited export procedures.

▸ PKIS provides key management for the SSL services. Any application written to the SAS interface inherits the capability to have PKIS manage its certificates. NDS access control lists (ACLs) manage access to the private key that enables SSL. Because SAS is a network service, it has its own network identity. ACLs are set up on the SSL key object in a way that allows only the SAS identity to read the private key. This guarantees that nonauthorized entities such as users, other server applications, and even the application built on top of SAS cannot gain access to and expose or subvert the private key.

## The Audit System

NetWare 6 includes auditing services, which allow administrators to monitor users' access to an organization's network and to record this monitoring information in audit log files. You can create NDS objects to represent audit log files, and you can then manage these objects just as you manage other objects in the NDS tree. You can also grant rights to the NDS objects representing audit log files, just as you grant rights to other objects in the NDS tree. As a result, you can assign administrators to view and manage audit log files.

The audit system now takes advantage of exposed NDS audit services in the following ways:

▸ Audit log files are represented and managed as NDS objects.

▸ Access to audit and configuration information is controlled by standard NDS rights.

▸ Auditing is configured at the container and volume levels.

▸ The audit policy for a container or volume specifies what is audited within the volume or container and which users are audited.

Auditing services are an essential element of the total NetWare security environment. You must have network audit integrity to ensure that the network is secure. As previously mentioned, the NetWare 6 auditing system can monitor and record every relevant network transaction. It detects which user performed the transaction and when the transaction occurred. This is important because businesses and other organizations, such as government agencies, often contract with independent parties to audit network transactions. These auditors review various events as requested. Generally, auditors are granted rights only to track events and activities, but they cannot open or modify network files (other than audit files).

NetWare 6 provides the highest level of audit data granularity. This includes which events are audited, control of audit configuration, and access to audit data. In order to enable auditing, you can use the AUDITCON utility. After auditing is enabled, audit-data and history files are automatically created for the volumes and containers you specify. Audit files continue to accept records until auditing is disabled or the file becomes full.

Following are some important features that Audit offers NetWare 6:

▸ The capability to assign independent auditors that are separate and distinct from administrator privileges

▸ Distributed and replicated audit information

▸ A multiple-auditors capability

▸ A high granularity of auditable events, to the user level

▸ An auditing system that the auditor can configure to meet company policies

▸ New audit events added for NetWare 6 (for example, SSL connections)

▸ Exportable audit data for use by reporting programs

## Installing and Using Novell's PKI Services

This section walks you through the steps required to set up a NetWare 6 server as a Certificate Authority to generate certificates and key pairs. Novell's PKI services are installed when you install your NetWare 6 server. When you install NetWare 6, your server installs the Novell Secure Authentication Services (SAS), the Novell PKI Services, and the NICI cryptographic modules. If these components were not installed during the installation of NetWare 6, you can use the NWCONFIG utility and select Other Installation Items/Products to complete this step.

> **The server to which a key material object is associated must be capable of communicating with at least one other server holding a writeable replica of the key material object. You must also ensure that the servers are running the same protocol (IP/IPX).**
>
> IMPORTANT

## Server and Workstation Requirements

Novell's PKI services require that your server and the workstation administering PKI services have certain basic requirement, as outlined here.

### Server Requirements

▶ NetWare 6 or NetWare 4.11 (with BorderManager installed in an NDS tree)

▶ Novell Secure Authentication Services (SAS) installed on the server that will be associated with the NDS tree CA

▶ Novell PKI services installed on the server

▶ NICI cryptographic modules installed

### Workstation Requirements

▶ A Novell client with the capability to run NWADMN32.EXE

The following objects are available in the NDS schema when you install this service:

▶ **Certificate Authority object** — This object contains the public key, the private key, the public key certificate, the certificate chain, and other information that is used by this object. This object resides in the security container. The Certificate Authority service runs on only one NetWare 6 server in your NDS tree. Be sure to choose a NetWare 6 server that is physically secure so that you don't compromise the integrity of your system.

▶ **Key material objects** — These objects contain the public key, the private key, the public key certificate, and the certificate chain. The private key is stored in the key material object in encrypted form. Any applications taking advantage of these security services will access a key material object.

▶ **Security container** — This container holds all the security-related objects for the entire NDS tree. This container, which resides at the top of your NDS tree, holds the key material objects and the Certificate Authority object. This container is installed automatically when SAS is installed on your NetWare 6 server.

The first step to enabling these security features is to create a Certificate Authority object.

### Creating a Certificate Authority Object

The Certificate Authority object should be placed on a server that is dependable and stored in a secure location. Because this server will be the centerpiece of your public key infrastructure system, you don't want to compromise the integrity of your network.

You have the option of using the NDS tree CA or an external CA as your Certificate Authority, but you must still create the NDS tree CA for rights management for PKI. Your choice of whether to use the NDS tree CA versus an external CA depends on a number of factors, including compatibility with Novell products, cost savings, and simplified management through NDS. However, an external CA can provide liability protection and availability to outside applications.

**Both types of CAs can be used simultaneously. Using one type of CA does not preclude the use of the other.**

**NOTE**

If you have already installed the security services during the NetWare 6 installation, you will see that a security container is already created in your tree below the [Root] object. You can then follow these steps to create your Certificate Authority object:

1. Launch the NetWare Administrator.

2. Set your context to [Root].

3. You will see a security container in NWADMIN. Right-click this object and select Create; a Certificate Authority object will be created as shown in Figure 10.39.

4. From the dialog box, choose the Certificate Authority object and click OK. Follow the instructions shown in the Certificate Authority Object Wizard. An example is shown in Figure 10.40.

Once this process is completed, you'll notice that the CA object will be placed in the security container. By double-clicking this object, you can view the details of this Certificate Authority object. An example is shown in Figure 10.41.

**FIGURE 10.39** *Using NWADMIN to create an NDS tree CA object*

**FIGURE 10.40** *Using the wizard to create a standard or custom Certificate Authority object*

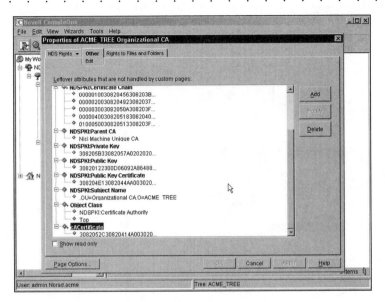

**FIGURE 10.41** *Viewing details of a certificate*

### Creating Key Material Objects

A key material object must be created in the container where the NetWare server object resides. Follow these steps to create a key material object:

1. Identify the server that is going to run your security-based applications.

2. Launch the NetWare Administrator.

3. Right-click the container object containing the server identified in Step 1 and choose Create. An example of the resulting dialog box is shown in Figure 10.42. If you select a container where no server is present, you will receive an error message.

4. Enter an key pair name and click OK. Follow the instructions shown on the Key Material Object Wizard page. You will then see a new key material object placed in that container.

Once you have configured PKI services for your network, you must configure your individual security applications so that they can use the key material objects that you established. Because the configuration procedures are unique to the individual applications, they are not discussed here. You must refer to your application's documentation for specific security information. To view the configuration information, select the key material object and select Details.

**FIGURE 10.42** *Creating a key material object*

### Installing a Public Key Certificate

Installing a public key certificate involves creating a new key material object using the Standard installation option. If you have not done so, see the previous section on how to create a key material object. You can also choose to use the NDS tree through the Custom installation option, which will automatically sign the public key certificate by the NDS tree CA.

To install a public key certificate signed by an external CA, follow these steps:

1. Launch the NetWare Administrator.

2. Double-click the key material object you have just created.

3. Select the public key certificate page. You will see a message that there is no public key certificate.

4. Select Import.

5. Choose a location of the public key certificate to install.

**6.** You can either copy and paste the certificate using any text editor or the Clipboard utility, or you can select a file option and specify the file's location.

**7.** Click Add. This will store the public key in the key material object. If you now click the Public Key Certificate page, you will see the distinguished name of the subject, the distinguished name of the issuer, and the validity period of the public key certificate, as shown in Figure 10.43.

Using the NWADMIN utility, you can also renew a public key certificate, revoke a public key certificate, or export a trusted root certificate.

**FIGURE 10.43** *The Public Key Certificate information page in NWADMIN*

## NetWare Management Agents

NetWare 6 includes NetWare management agents (NMAs) that are used to manage the operating system via the Simple Network Management Protocol (SNMP). These agents are SERVINSTR.NLM, HOSTMIB.NLM, and NWTRAP.NLM. With these agents you can use any SNMP-based console, such as ManageWise, CA UniCenter, HP Openview, IBM Tivoli, SunNet Manager, and others, to view and manage over 400 objects and 400 traps that are exposed by the NetWare Management Agents. Alerts can be set up to notify administrators of problems before end users start calling and escalating a network problem.

These agents can be installed automatically during the installation of NetWare 6. For more information on using ManageWise with NetWare 6, see your Novell documentation.

## NetWare Licensing Services

This service simplifies installation and licensing of new Novell products. It works on your NetWare 6 server to reduce the time and effort you must spend on installing and licensing. Common utilities and interfaces now standardize each of these tasks. NLS provides a single utility (NLSMANAGER.EXE) that you can use to license all future NetWare products. This new capability ensures consistent, efficient, and rapid licensing for NetWare products, and it permits licensing for any non-Novell products conforming to NLS requirements.

### Implementing NLS

When a certificate for an NLS-aware application is installed, NLS adds a license container object to the NDS tree and a license certificate object to that container object. You select the context or location in the NDS tree for that license container object. An example of a license container object is shown in Figure 10.44.

**FIGURE 10.44** *A license container object and a license object are created when you create a license certificate.*

The next section walks you through how to create a license certificate, a metered certificate, and an install envelope.

### Installing a License Certificate

If you purchase and install additional licenses, they will also be added to the NDS tree as objects in the appropriate license container object. When adding license certificates to the NDS tree, you should be aware of where in the tree you want to install the license. This location or context determines who can use the license units associated with that license certificate. You install license certificates by accessing .NLS files from the application you are installing. Installation of the license certificate can be done through either the NWADMIN utility or the NLSManager utility.

To install license certificates using the NetWare Administrator utility, follow this step: After loading NWADMIN, select Tools ➪ Install License ➪ Install License Certificate. An example of this selection is shown in Figure 10.45. You can then follow the instructions onscreen. These instructions are similar to the instructions that follow for creating a license using NLS Manager.

**FIGURE 10.45** *Installing a license certificate using NWADMIN*

The NLS Manager utility provides greater functionality for managing licenses. You can also use the NLS Manager utility by completing the following steps.

**1.** Select View ⇨ Tree View to see the dialog box shown in Figure 10.46.

**FIGURE 10.46** *The first screen of the NLS Manager utility*

**2.** Select Actions ⇨ Install License Certificate. You can also click the first license certificate icon on the toolbar. Be sure to select the tree icon before selecting Actions. If not, the option to Install License Certificate will be grayed out.

**3.** Enter the path and filename of the certificate. To locate the filename, click the folder icon next to the filename field and then navigate the directory structure. The file may be on a disk in Drive A or on a CD-ROM. The .NLS file is linked to an activation password file (key) and automatically retrieves the password.

**4.** Select the NDS context where the certificate object will be installed. To locate the context, click the tree icon next to the NDS Context field, browse the tree, and select a context. If you are installing an additional certificate in an existing license container object, select the container's parent, not the license container object.

**5.** With both fields filled, click OK to install the license certificate, OK to acknowledge the "need to update" message, and then OK to acknowledge the successful installation.

**6.** (Optional) In the Activation Key window, enter the key that you received for this license.

**NOTE**

**If the file containing the activation key is in the same directory as the license file you select, the key will be read automatically. You only see the Activation Key window when the file containing the activation key is not detected in the same directory or on the floppy disk or CD-ROM containing the file.**

A license certificate requires an activation key. If the NLS Manager utility can't find an activation key while you are installing a certificate, an Activation Key window allows you to enter a key.

An activation key is like a password. It's a sequence of numbers and letters that allows you to complete the installation of a license for a product you purchased. Software vendors provide this key at the time of purchase. During installation, you enter the activation key, which allows you to complete an installation.

With electronic purchases and distribution, activation keys allow you to install additional licenses for a product you already have. You may have purchased a product that came in a suite, or you can subsequently purchase the additional products in that suite and then use them by activating their keys. If you know the activation key, you can enter it without browsing for the file. To browse for the file containing the activation key, however, click Import.

### Creating a Metered Certificate

Metered certificates allow you to track usage of applications, even those not written to the Licensing Service Application Programming Interface (LSAPI) specifications. Most likely, you have already invested in legacy applications that are not NLS aware. By using metered certificates, you can allow users to continue using these applications while you track and manage the licenses for those applications.

You can configure ZENworks to function as the NLS client for non-license-enabled applications. ZENworks will then request licenses on behalf of the applications.

To create metered certificates using the NetWare Administrator utility, follow these steps:

**1.** Select Tools ➪ Install License ➪ Create Metered Certificate.

2. Next, use the instructions in the online help. (The steps are similar to those for the NLS Manager utility.)

You can also use the NLS Manager utility by completing the following steps:

1. Select View ⇨ Tree View.

2. Select Actions ⇨ Create Metered Certificate. You can also click the second certificate icon on the toolbar. The dialog box that appears is shown in Figure 10.47.

**FIGURE 10.47** *Creating a metered certificate using the NLS Manager utility*

3. Enter the publisher's name. This is the name of the software company, such as Novell.

4. Enter the product name. This is the name of the software package, such as GroupWise.

5. Enter the version. This is the version number, for example, 500 for NetWare version 5.00. If a period (.) is used as part of the version number, the License container object will add a backslash to its NDS name. For example, 5.00 will display in an NDS tree as "5\.00."

**6.** Choose the NDS context for the certificate. To locate the desired context, click the Browse button next to the NDS Location field. Browse by clicking the + or – symbols in the Select window. Double-click the desired context or select it and click OK.

**7.** Enter or select the number of licenses for the certificate. This is the number of licenses you have purchased. For example, if you own a 500-user version of NetWare 6, enter 500.

**8.** Enter or select the number of grace licenses you will allow. This option enables additional users to run applications until you have time to purchase additional licenses. That is, this option helps you comply with your software license agreement without interrupting users' workflow or productivity. If you don't enter a number here, users will not be allowed to open additional applications beyond the number specified in Number of Licenses. To ensure that no one is denied access to an application, enter a number that protects the users while also protecting the software vendor.

**9.** Select an update interval. This setting determines how often an application is to check whether a license is still being used and to inform the LSP of the status.

**10.** Select whether or not users use a single license when launching an application multiple times from one workstation.

**11.** Click OK twice. The first OK acknowledges that Quick View must be updated. (A new product license container for the certificate may not appear until you refresh the screen.) The second OK acknowledges that the certificate installed successfully.

You can see the license container object (for example, Novell+NetWare 6 Conn+500) and the license certificate object in the Tree view. An example is shown in Figure 10.48.

**FIGURE 10.48** *The NLS Manager view of the license container object and its contents*

### Installing an Envelope

An envelope is a file containing one or more license certificates. (It may have just one certificate because the envelope also contains other information — for example, for NIS-enabled installations — associated with the product.)

Envelopes allow you to install more than one license certificate at a time into license container objects. For example, you may have purchased three products in a suite. An envelope enables you to simultaneously install license certificates for all three products.

To install envelopes using the NetWare Administrator utility, select Tools ⇨ Install License ⇨ Install Envelope. Then use the instructions in the online help. (The steps are similar to those for the NLS Manager utility.)

You can also use the NLS Manager utility by completing the following steps:

**1.** Select View ⇨ Tree View.

**2.** Select Actions ⇨ Install Envelope. You can also click the envelope icon on the toolbar. The Envelope Installation Wizard appears, as shown in Figure 10.49.

**FIGURE 10.49** *Creating a license envelope using the Installation Wizard in NLS Manager*

**3.** Follow onscreen prompts in the Envelope Installation Wizard:

   **a.** Select an envelope. Click Next, click the folder icon, navigate to the folder containing the envelope, and then select the envelope (.NLF file).

   **b.** Choose certificates within the envelope. Click Next, select the certificates to install, and then click Next.

   **c.** Specify where in the NDS tree to install the certificates. Browse by clicking the tree icon and the + and – symbols as shown in Figure 10.50. Click the desired context and then click OK.

   **d.** Select whether or not to install all certificates in the same location or context and then click Next. Click Next for each certificate you selected.

   **e.** Verify that you selected the correct certificates and then click Finish.

   **f.** Acknowledge that the certificates installed successfully by clicking Close.

**FIGURE 10.50** *Selecting a context to install the License Certificate*

### Assigning Licenses to Users

Access to a license certificate is determined by the location of the license certificate and whether any assignments have been made to the license certificate. The owner of a license certificate is the NDS object (typically a user) that installed the license certificate. As an owner, you can assign the following objects access to the licenses:

- ▶ Users
- ▶ Groups
- ▶ Organizations
- ▶ Organizational Units
- ▶ Servers

If you assign a container object to use a certificate, all users in and below that container will be able to use the certificate through the mechanism of security equivalence. If you do not want to restrict access to licenses in this way, do not make any assignments to the license certificates.

Once you make assignments, only those objects that have been assigned to the license certificates can use the license. You can add and delete assignments to licenses through the Assignments property page.

You can assign licenses by using the NetWare Administrator utility. After you select a certificate in the Browse window, right-click Details ➪ Assignments ➪ Add.

Then browse, select an object, and click OK twice. (Steps in the online help are similar to those for the NLS Manager utility.)

You can also use the NLS Manager utility by completing the following steps:

**1.** Select View ⇨ Tree View.

**2.** Select the license certificate that you want users to access.

**3.** Select the Assignments property page as shown in Figure 10.51.

**4.** Click Add.

**5.** Locate and select the object that allows appropriate users to access the certificate's licenses and then click OK. Browse the NDS tree by clicking the + or − symbols in the Select Object(s) window.

**FIGURE 10.51** *An example of assigning the container ACME to this license*

Delete assignments to a license certificate by completing the following steps:

**1.** Navigate to the Assignments property page of the license certificate object, as explained previously.

**2.** Select the object you would like to remove from the list of assigned users, click Remove and then click Yes.

### Internet Connectivity

NetWare 6 ships with the Novell Internet Access Server (NIAS) 4.1. NIAS provides routing between local and remote LANs, remote access to all company network resources (including e-mail and Internet access) through a modem or other connection, and remote service management of all connectivity services and servers from your workstation. For more information on installing and using NIAS, see Chapter 22.

## Installation and Upgrade

Several new installation or upgrade utilities are available in NetWare 6, including new upgrade utilities that easily move your NetWare 3 or NetWare 4 server to NetWare 6. In addition, utilities also are available to help you upgrade your clients. These new installation and upgrade tools allow you to choose the options that best reflect your organization's network structure or design.

### The NetWare 6 Installation Program (NWCONFIG.EXE and -.NLM)

The NetWare 6 installation program is used either to install a new NetWare 6 server or to upgrade an existing NetWare 4 server to NetWare 6. Upgrading an existing NetWare 4 server to NetWare 6 is often called an in-place upgrade. For complete information on installing NetWare 6, see Chapter 2.

### The Novell Upgrade Wizard

The Novell Upgrade Wizard in NetWare 6 moves the NetWare 3 source server's bindery (including print information) and file system to the destination NetWare 6 server. The utility is a wizard-based interface, which ensures ease of use for across-the-wire upgrades. The wizard can also detect potential conflicts and provide options to resolve them before the upgrade begins.

### NWDEPLOY Utility

Before you start an installation of NetWare 6 you should run the NWDEPLOY utility. This utility is found on your NetWare 6 CD and does many housekeeping tasks to prepare you NetWare 5 or NetWare 4 servers for migration to NetWare 6. At the beginning of your installation of NetWare 6, the install utility will alert you at the top of the screen to run NWDEPLOY before you begin your migration or installation to NetWare 6.

The NWDEPOY provides the following processes to ensure that your server is ready to start an installation of NetWare 6:

Overview

Step 1: Back up data, A complete backup of all data is recommended before you start the install

Step 2: View and Update NDS versions, You must update NDS before you upgrade an existing server to NetWare 6 or if you are installing the first NetWar 6 server.

Step 3: Prepare for NDS 8 (required for NDS 8)

Step 4: Novell Licensing Services, You must install Novell Licensing Services prior to upgrading or installing a NetWare 6 server on your network.

Step 5: Update the Certificate Authority Object

### The Automatic Client Update

The Automatic Client Update (ACU) ships with NetWare 6. This utility is used to upgrade all types of NetWare clients. For example, you can upgrade NetWare 3 clients to NetWare 6 clients automatically from a central location. For more information on using ACU, see Chapter 17.

· · · · · · · · · · · · · · · · · · · · · · · · · · · · ·

# Developer Support

NetWare 6 caters to network developers by providing the world's fastest Java Virtual Machine (JVM) for running server-based Java applications and services. Listed here are several additional enhancements made to the NetWare 6 system.

### Java Support in NetWare 6

NetWare 6 supports Java applications running on the server. This allows a wide range of Java-developed applications to serve your network and users. Java support on NetWare 6 enables you to run Java applets on the server console, display Java applications in X Windows–style formats with full mouse and graphic support, and run multiple Java applications on the server while the server performs other tasks.

Java support in NetWare 6 is provided by JAVA.NLM. This NLM starts the Java engine, which enables Java applications to run. You can load Java support by calling JAVA.NLM at the server console prompt, and you can run Java applications using the APPLET console command.

The Java run-time environment consists of the following components:

- JVM
- Java Services Framework
- Support for GUI installation
- ORB

For more information, see your Novell documentation.

### Scripting

NetWare 6 scripting and component services offer you choice, compatibility, and speed. NetWare 6 supports the major scripting languages available, including Perl 5, NetBasic 6.0, NetBasic 7.0, and JavaScript. For more information, refer to Novell's documentation.

## Third-Party Add-Ons

There are a number of products that work with NetWare 5 and NetWare 6. Some are mentioned here for your reference.

### IBM WebSphere for NetWare

The IBM WebSphere Application Server is a Java-based application environment that enables you to build, deploy, and manage Internet and intranet applications on NetWare. This product provides you with a robust way to deploy web services on the fast, secure, and stable NetWare environment. This product (Standard Edition) is bundled for free on your NetWare 6 CD. There is a charge for the Advanced version of the software

IBM WebSpere is a standards-based suite that support Java Servlets, Java Server Pages, enterprise Java Beans and XML implementations.

Many of the Novell products such as OnDemand, iChain, Novell Portal Services, and eGuide make use of the WebSphere Application Server technology.

## Oracle8i for NetWare

NetWare 6 includes support for Oracle8i for NetWare. This version of Oracle (specifically Oracle8i) has been integrated with NDS. As a result, you can use NDS to control access to your company's Oracle database.

The five-user version of Oracle8i for NetWare in NetWare 6 includes the following:

- An intuitive installation for getting a pretuned and preconfigured Oracle8i database up and running
- Wizards to help you create databases and migrate Oracle7 server databases to Oracle8i
- HTML Web page creation based on data retrieved from Oracle8i (no knowledge of SQL or HTML syntax is required)
- The Oracle Migration Assistant for Microsoft Access for complete and easy migration from your Microsoft Access database to Oracle8i for NetWare.

Oracle8i for NetWare requires a NetWare 5 or NetWare 6 or NetWare 6 server with the following resources:

- 48MB free RAM (minimum)
- 16MB additional free RAM for the Advanced Replication option
- 200MB free disk space (minimum)

Oracle8i client software requires the following:

- A 486 or higher processor
- Windows 95/98, Windows NT Workstation version 4, or Windows NT Server version 4
- 16MB free RAM
- 25MB free disk space (minimum)

The Oracle Enterprise Manager running on an Oracle8i client requires the following:

- 32MB free RAM
- 25MB free disk space for the manager

## Btrieve

The Btrieve key-indexed record management system is designed for high-performance data handling and improved programming productivity. Btrieve enables an application to retrieve, insert, update, or delete records either by key value or by sequential or random access methods.

### Starting NetWare Btrieve 6.15

After installing Btrieve 6.15 using the NetWare installation utility, you can start it by entering this command at the server console or at a workstation running RCONSOLE:

```
bstart
```

If you have created a Btrieve server object, the BSTART.NCF command file for Btrieve 6.x automatically loads the NDS Support utility (BDIRECT.NLM). This utility checks to see whether a Btrieve server object exists, in which case the utility activates it.

**The Btrieve server object is installed at the level of the current directory context, as defined by the server's start-up script.**

NOTE

### Stopping NetWare Btrieve 6.15

To stop Btrieve 6.1x, enter this command at the server console or at a workstation running RCONSOLE:

```
bstop
```

The BSTOP command runs a NetWare command file (BSTOP.NCF) that unloads the following modules in the order shown:

1. BROUTER.NLM

2. BSPXCOM.NLM

3. BTRIEVE.NLM

**BSTOP.NCF does not unload BSPXSTUB, RSPXSTUB, or BDROUTER. To unload these modules, enter the UNLOAD command followed by the module name.**

NOTE

If you have created a Btrieve server object, the BSTOP.NCF command file for Btrieve 6.x automatically loads the NDS Support utility (BDIRECT.NLM). If an active Btrieve server object exists, it is deactivated and the NDS Support utility unloads.

**NOTE**

Before issuing the **NetWare DOWN** command on a server that has an active **Btrieve** server object, you must first issue the **BSTOP** command.

· · · · · · · · · · · · · · · · · · · · · · · · · · · · ·

## Summary

The new features and enhancements to NetWare 6 offer superior network management and control for system administrators and a more friendly and flexible interface for users. NetWare 6 is also one of the most secure and cost-effective network operating systems available, offering comprehensive security features, including cryptography, public key infrastructure, and Secure Authentication Services.

# Tuning and Optimizing the NetWare 6 Operating System

*"Good is not good, where better is expected."* — *Thomas Fuller*

Tuning and optimizing the NetWare 6 operating system is one of the responsibilities of the network administrator. These tasks can seem difficult because modifications are not always immediately perceived by the users. However, the question most people ask is, "What do I change in order to tune the operating system?"

One of the first steps in the tuning and optimizing process requires you to understand the basic characteristics of your network, servers, and user community. You should measure the baseline performance of your system during periods of both peak and off-peak production. Having a baseline beforehand enables you to gauge the changes in performance and reliability during the tuning effort.

For most implementations of the NetWare 6 operating system, the default settings for each of the internal parameters work very well. Some server implementations may make it necessary to modify some of the system settings to increase the capacity and performance of your system. These implementations may include heavy use of imaging or document retrieval types of software.

This chapter provides you with a better understanding of the vital configurable NetWare 6 system parameters. Becoming familiar with the internal system parameters helps you to make changes to increase capacity and performance without compromising the reliability of your server. This information also helps you prioritize the tuning options and reduces the trade-off between system performance and reliability.

▶ . . . . . . . . . . . . . . . . . . . . . . . . . . . ◀

## Performance versus Reliability

As most network administrators know, tuning and optimizing the operating system for performance and providing maximum reliability involve a kind of balancing act. For example, a setting in NetWare 6 allows disk writes to the NetWare volumes to be verified. This parameter is called "read after write verification" and should always be enabled on NetWare 6 volumes, which utilize disk hardware devices that do not perform write verification inherently. Turning the parameter to ON increases reliability of the data being written to disk but decreases the overall performance of the system. In this case, the reliability gained through verifying all writes to disk usually outweighs any side effects of slightly slower performance. NetWare 6 turns the read after write verification parameter ON by default.

**Consulting Experience**

For most systems with high-end (RAID 5) hardware and advanced disk drive technology, the parameter "read after write verification" is automatically enabled in the hardware. Most high-end disk drive manufacturers provide read after write verification within the hardware drive itself. The setting in NetWare is redundant and can be turned off to increase the performance.

Before you turn the "read after write verification" setting off for NetWare 6, make sure that the disk drive device is doing this process for you.

Surprisingly, for many users and administrators, performance is not the single most important issue for their NetWare 6 servers. When forced to prioritize the different functions of a network server, many users rank reliability and security as the two most important, with performance coming in a close third. Of course, each of these areas is important and each needs attention when you are the network administrator. But it's important to understand that tuning for performance's sake should not be allowed to compromise reliability and security.

Because most of the server resources or subsystems are closely tied together, changing the parameters on one subsystem can affect the performance of other subsystems. The best place to start the process of tuning the NetWare 6 operating system is with the defaults after installation. For the most part, the system will tune itself and simplify your efforts.

# NetWare 6 Is Self-Tuning

One of the key traits of Novell's NetWare operating system is its capacity to self-tune to provide your users with the best possible performance. Autotuning is NetWare's capacity to automatically increase necessary resources for the NetWare operating system. It determines workload requirements and makes enough resources, such as memory, available to provide maximum efficiencies. The procedure used to self-tune offers the capability to dynamically alter the internal system parameters and configuration in order to accommodate changing or increasing user demands.

Autotuning occurs when not enough service requests exist to handle all the incoming requests. Therefore, autotuning requests greater bandwidth by increasing some of the operating system parameters. Keep in mind that after the parameters are increased, they are never decreased automatically. For this reason, maximums are applied to all parameters, so that bandwidth allocation is very carefully controlled on the server and is not allowed to dominate all available resources. To restore these parameters to their original state, you must restart the operating system or change them manually with the SET command.

## Using the SET Parameters

For most resources on the server, the SET parameters are available to adjust the values to help fine-tune a particular resource. These parameters cover a wide variety of internal systems all the way from communications to the file system. The SET parameters enable you to set minimum and maximum limits.

NetWare 6 uses SET commands to manage the minimum and maximum values and wait times for its adjustable features. The minimum values define the number of resources that the operating system allocates immediately upon startup. The maximum values set the upper limits for resource allocations. A wait time is a specified length of time that the operating system must wait before allocating a new resource.

Also, some wait times or conditions prevent the operating system from reacting to peak loads by performing only one specific operation well. The wait time limits parameters help smooth out the peak load demands for server resources.

The SET parameters can be controlled, adjusted, or viewed using either the server console SET commands or through MONITOR.NLM, which is a server utility introduced in NetWare 6. One important note is that the SERVMAN.NLM utility is no longer available in NetWare 6. All the features and functionality that SERVMAN provided have been placed in the MONITOR utility.

The server console SET command is issued at the server prompt as follows:

SET

The SET command responds with a listing of all the server resource categories or subsystems that can be controlled or configured with the individual SET parameters. Figure 11.1 shows the category list that can be configured using the SET commands at the server console.

**FIGURE 11.1** *The server resource category list can be configured using the SET commands at the server console.*

In order to view the current settings for each of the server resources categories or subsystems listed, simply select the corresponding number and scroll through the listings. Figure 11.2 shows the screen that is displayed for the Communications category or subsystem.

**FIGURE 11.2** *Viewing the settings for the Communications category using the SET commands at the server console*

The syntax for viewing the setting for an individual SET parameter is to use this command at the server console:

```
SET PARAMETER_DESCRIPTION
```

The syntax for changing the individual SET parameter is to use this command at the server console:

```
SET PARAMETER_DESCRIPTION = NEW_VALUE
```

# Use the MONITOR Utility to Change Server Parameters

MONITOR.NLM is a server-based utility that helps you easily manage and configure each of the system SET parameters through a menu interface. The MONITOR utility enables you to view and set each parameter, as well as observe network performance statistics at a glance.

For example, the General Information screen, visible at the top when the utility is loaded, enables you to view processor utilization, server up time, processor speed, server processes, and connections used (which typically represents the number of users logged in). Figure 11.3 shows the main screen, which includes general information about server performance.

The main menu in MONITOR provides you with a menu-driven interface to the system SET parameters available on the server. From the main menu, select the menu item called Server Parameters. Other options from the main menu cover connection information, LAN configuration, storage information, volume information, and network information. After you have selected the Server Parameters, a list of categories (similar to the one displayed if you type SET at the server console) is displayed. At this point, you can select a specific category or area to view and edit.

Throughout the rest of this chapter, we use both the SET command and the MONITOR utility to show how you can change the individual parameters.

**FIGURE 11.3** *The MONITOR main screen includes general information about server performance.*

# Subsystems of the Operating System

From a performance standpoint, many of the system parameters are closely related and can be separated into specific subsystems of NetWare 6. Because of the association, we have categorized many of the most important SET parameters into the subsystems categories as follows:

- LAN communications subsystem
- Disk and file system
- The Kernel, Server Processes, and CPU Utilization
- Abend Recovery Options
- Memory Subsystem

# The LAN Communications Subsystem

The LAN communications SET parameters control the characteristics of the memory buffers used to send and receive data packets to and from the LAN. In order to tune and optimize the server for communications, you need to address several issues:

- Physical packet size
- Packet receive buffers
- Media statistics
- Packet burst
- NetWare Core Protocol (NCP) requests
- NetWare Link State Protocol (NLSP)

## Physical Packet Size

The physical size of the packet that is transmitted on the network is determined by the network topology or media access attached to the server. NetWare 6 enables you to use the SET command to set or define the maximum physical packet size that the server will support:

```
SET MAXIMUM PHYSICAL RECEIVE PACKET SIZE = n
```

The default physical packet size for Ethernet is 1,514 bytes, and the default for Token Ring is 4,202 bytes. NetWare 6 defaults the physical receive packet size to 4,224 bytes to accommodate the larger size. This is true even if the network uses only Ethernet. When a workstation makes a connection to the server, the packet size for the session is negotiated. The value set for the session with the workstation is typically established as the largest packet that the workstation can support.

Figure 11.4 shows the screen used in MONITOR, called the Communications Parameters screen, which lets you set the maximum size of the buffers for incoming and outgoing packets. You should set this size to the largest packet size on your network.

You should always make sure that the MAXIMUM PHYSICAL RECEIVE PACKET SIZE parameter is set large enough to support the protocols for the server. If the setting for the SET parameter MAXIMUM PHYSICAL RECEIVE PACKET SIZE is 1514 bytes, you should change it if you need to support Token Ring workstations as well.

**FIGURE 11.4** *The Communications Parameters screen used in MONITOR lets you set the maximum size of the buffers for incoming and outgoing packets.*

To set the value for Token Ring, you need to enter this command at the server console or in MONITOR:

```
SET MAXIMUM PHYSICAL RECEIVE PACKET SIZE = 4224
```

The parameter value ranges from 618 to 24682 (in bytes). If you want to have this value established each time the server is started, you need to place it in STARTUP.NCF. You cannot add this parameter to AUTOEXEC.NCF because the server needs to know how large each packet receive buffer should be as the server is booting. The packet receive buffers are taken from memory, and the size is not adjustable after the server is running.

## Packet Receive Buffers

The server needs to keep a certain number of packet receive buffers free to service incoming requests from clients. Having additional packet receive buffers available reduces the chance that the server will be overrun by incoming or outgoing requests that share these buffers. Each packet receive buffer is equal in size to the maximum physical receive packet size. In most cases, this is 1,514 bytes for Ethernet segments and 4,202 bytes for Token Ring.

A lack of packet receive buffers results in a "No ECB Available Count" error message, as shown in the Media Statistics section in this chapter. ECB stands for Event Control Block in NetWare. When a client sends a packet to a server that has no available packet receive buffers, the server is forced to discard the packet. The client waits for the specified time-out period and receives no reply from the server. It is then the client's responsibility to try to resend the packet. If a buffer has become available in the meantime, the incoming packet is received and the client notices no network errors — just a slightly slower response time.

Meanwhile, at the server, NetWare 6 starts a timer after the server discards the packet due to no available buffers. If no buffer is freed up after 0.1 seconds (default setting) have elapsed, the operating system allocates a new packet receive buffer for incoming and outgoing packets. You can view the current number of packet receive buffers that the operating system has allocated by using the main screen of MONITOR.NLM. Figure 11.5 shows an example of current packet receive buffers.

▶ · · · · · · · · · · · · · · · · · · · · · · · · · · · · ◀

```
NetWare 6 Console Monitor  12.00            NetWare Loadable Module
Server name: 'CAM-SRV1' in Directory tree 'ACME_TREE'
Product: Novell NetWare 6
                      General Information
        Utilization:                          2%
        Server up time:              0:01:19:34
        Online processors:                     1
        Original cache buffers:           64,668
        Total cache buffers:              19,534
        Dirty cache buffers:                   0
        Long term cache hits:                 0%
        Current disk requests:                 0
        Packet receive buffers:            2,000
        Directory cache buffers:               0
        Maximum service processes:           570
        Current service processes:             7
        Current connections:                   5
        Open files:                          231

          Kernel
          Server parameters

Tab=Next window   Alt+F10=Exit                    F1=Help
```

**FIGURE 11.5** *View the current number of packet receive buffers that the operating system has allocated using the main screen of MONITOR.NLM.*

As an administrator, you want to pay special attention to the number of current packet receive buffers on your system, especially if your users are complaining of slow response time from the server. An occasional problem is that the server receives so many packets that it runs up to the maximum packet receive buffer count. If all buffers are full, the incoming packets are dropped. This usually means that the workstations have to resend any packets to the server multiple times, slowing response time for each user.

### Setting the Packet Receive Buffer Values

Normally, NetWare dynamically allocates the packet receive buffers based on its needs. However, the operating system enables you to set both a minimum number of buffers that can be preallocated when the server boots and a maximum number or upper limit that prevents them from allocating too many resources during very high utilization.

You can adjust the settings for packet receive buffers by using the communications parameters SET commands described here:

```
SET MINIMUM PACKET RECEIVE BUFFERS = n
```

In this parameter, $n$ can be 10 to 4294967295, with the default being 128. This setting specifies the minimum number of buffers that will be immediately allocated by the operating system when it is booted. This parameter can be permanently set only in the STARTUP.NCF file:

```
SET MAXIMUM PACKET RECEIVE BUFFERS = n
```

In this parameter, $n$ can be 50 to 294967295, with the default being 500. This parameter specifies the maximum number of packet receive buffers to be used by the NetWare 6 operating system. When the maximum is reached, no more packet receive buffers will be allocated even if more are needed. If all the allocated buffers are in use, the operating system has no choice but to discard incoming packets. This parameter should be changed to meet the needs of your network environment. The parameter is set in the AUTOEXEC.NCF file.

It is extremely important to monitor the value of the current packet receive buffers to see if the value is close to the maximum value. If this is the case, you should increase the maximum to account for the increased workload performed by the server.

One of the most common errors that people encounter when using these parameters is that the current packet receive buffers become equal to the maximum and the system can no longer dynamically tune itself.

```
SET NEW PACKET RECEIVE BUFFER WAIT TIME = n
```

**Consulting Experience**

We recommend that you have at least one packet receive buffer for each client that will be attached to your server. For example, a server supporting 500 users needs the capability to allocate 500 packet receive buffers if necessary. In addition, you should allow ten packet receive buffers for each LAN adapter installed in the file server.

Thus, we recommend that you use the following formula to calculate the proper value for the MINIMUM PACKET RECEIVE BUFFERS:

MINIMUM = (1 ¥ (# of connections)) + (10 ¥ (# of LAN cards))

The proper setting for the MINIMUM PACKET RECEIVE BUFFERS parameter is the value currently in use at the file server. Using the MONITOR utility, you can compare the number configured versus the number currently in use. For example, the total number of packet receive buffers may peak at 350 after several days or weeks of continuous server operation. You can take advantage of the SET MINIMUM PACKET RECEIVE BUFFERS parameter to preallocate more than the default of 50 buffers the next time the server is rebooted. This helps overcome any sluggishness of the server after it is rebooted. Thus, we recommend that you use the following formula to calculate the proper value for the MINIMUM PACKET RECEIVE BUFFERS:

Minimum = Number of packet receive buffers in use currently

In this parameter, $n$ can be 0.1 to 20, with the default being 0.1 seconds. This setting specifies the wait time necessary before allocating any new packet receive buffers. It is recommended that you not change this setting.

## Media Statistics

The communications media statistics are reported by each LAN adapter installed in the server through the LAN driver. The statistics can be viewed using the MONITOR.NLM program at the server. These statistics can help you diagnose specific problems with the physical network media and supporting software.

For example, a lack of packet receive buffers results in a "No ECB Available Count" error message, which is reported and viewed on the media statistics screen in MONITOR. An example of the statistics screen for a LAN driver is shown in Figure 11.6.

As mentioned in the previous section, when a client sends a packet to a server that has no available packet receive buffers, the server is forced to discard the packet. Each time the server or LAN driver discards a packet, the "No ECB Available Count" is incremented.

**FIGURE 11.6** *These statistics are reported by the individual LAN driver in the server, using the MONITOR.NLM program.*

## Packet Burst

NetWare 6 automatically supports packet burst, which improves data delivery over latent links. Packet burst technology eliminates the ping-pong effect of sent/returned packets during communication. For example, using packet burst, the client sends a request to the server. The server responds to the client with multiple packets without requiring a "return receipt" for every packet. The server is content to have just one return receipt for the whole transmission. This means that the total transmission time is reduced and the "chattiness" of the NCP protocol is eliminated. This is particularly beneficial for communication across WANs where line speeds are often a bottleneck.

A SET command is available that enables a separate packet burst statistics screen to be used to see if specific workstations or clients are connected using packet burst. In order to start the packet burst statistics screen, enter this command at the server console:

```
SET ENABLE PACKET BURST STATISTICS SCREEN = ON
```

## NCP Requests

This section discusses the adjustments that you can make to the NetWare Core Protocol (NCP) requests.

`Set NCP packet signature option = `$n$

where $n$ is 0, 1, 2, or 3. The default setting is 1. The purpose of this setting is to enable Novell's packet signature security. Packet signature attaches a unique signature to each NCP packet that is transmitted between a NetWare client and a NetWare server. You use these parameters to enable or disable packet signature and to designate varying levels of security. This feature is used only where extremely high levels of security are required. Packet signature does impact performance because of the translation that must take place between receiving and sending entities on your network. What follows are the settings for packet signature at the server. The packet signature for the client is set in the user's NET.CFG file.

Server settings:

▸ 0 — Do not do packet signature.

▸ 1 — Do packet signatures only if the client requires them.

▸ 2 — Do packet signatures if the client can, but don't require them if the client doesn't support them.

▸ 3 — Require packet signatures.

For most companies packet signature is not used. If you do have a client using packet signature, the default setting of 1 is sufficient to have that client use this feature.

`SET ENABLE IPX CHECKSUMS = `$n$

where $n$ is 0, 1, or 2. The default setting is 1. The purpose of this setting is to require a checksum calculation on packets. A checksum is calculated and placed in the packet being sent across the network. After it is received, the checksum can be recalculated to ensure that the same number of bits are received as were sent. This parameter allows you to enable or disable IPX checksums. The values for the checksum have the following meanings:

▸ 0 — No checksums

▸ 1 — Checksums if enabled at the client

▸ 2 — Require checksumming

Most sites do not need to enable checksumming because this type of checking is done at the data link level of your network. Keep in mind that you will experience performance degradation with this feature enabled. Additionally, this feature is supported by only Ethernet 802.2 frame type, not 802.3.

## TCP/IP and DHCP

NetWare 6 fully supports TCP/IP and DHCP products. It does not encapsulate or tunnel IPX/SPX communications. TCP/IP enables the servers and clients to make NetWare Core Protocol (NCP) calls directly over the TCP/IP stack so that they can be routed by any IP router on the network. Novell has severed the operating system's dependence on IPX/SPX and has rewritten the IPX-only applications and utilities to support TCP/IP. As a result, the NetWare 6 servers and workstations can use TCP/IP, IPX/SPX, or both. The major advantages of supporting TCP/IP in NetWare are as follows:

- ▸ Consolidation to one protocol in your network
- ▸ More efficient use of your LAN and WAN bandwidth
- ▸ A wider range of opportunities for remote user connectivity

Although IP has major advantages, Novell is committed to remain backward-compatible to IPX/SPX. NetWare 6 ships with features that provide a seamless compatibility between IPX and IP-based technologies. NetWare 6's Compatibility Mode enables customers to move to an IP-only environment without having to replace valuable IPX-based applications and without having to introduce disruptions to their network operations. In addition, NetWare 6 ships an IP Compatibility Mode Migration Gateway that enables you to move to an IP-only network incrementally, and if desired.

In essence, you have the choice of whether to use IPX/SPX or TCP/IP as your network protocols. In order to install IP, you use either the standard NetWare 6 installation program or the INETCFG.NLM protocol configuration utility. For example, during the installation process, you select the protocols that you want your server to support. If you enable IPX/SPX, you must select an internal IPX address for the server, as you normally would. If you enable TCP/IP, you must select an IP address for the server.

NCP takes advantage of both TCP and UDP as transport protocols. Like IPX, UDP provides connectionless datagram services, which do not require a "handshake" to set up communications. TCP, on the other hand, is similar to SPX, which provides connection-oriented services. Connection-oriented services require communication partners to perform a "handshake" before exchanging data and enable these partners to acknowledge the receipt of transmitted data. Although both SPX and TCP provide connection-oriented services, TCP's windowing and streaming capabilities provide greater throughput than SPX.

Some NCP calls use UDP for its communication, whereas others use strictly TCP. For example, the "control" NCP call (which requests information for a server) uses UDP communication. TCP is used typically for large transactions, such as NCP file reads, writes, and NDS synchronization. Large transactions use TCP because TCP's streaming capability is similar to IPX's burst-mode technology. This capability provides quicker and more efficient file transfers. With IPX/SPX, the developers use sockets to define the sending or receiving process during communications. In the TCP/IP world, the Internet Registration Group assigns port numbers to vendors, thereby differentiating among the various processes on the network. For example, NetWare 6's port number is 524.

To ensure that NCP UDP packets do not become corrupted, you can control the checksumming required during the client-to-server communication. Use the following SET parameter:

```
SET ENABLE UDP CHECKSUMS ON NCP PACKETS = n
```

where $n$ is 0, 1, or 2. The default setting is 1. The purpose of this setting is to enable the use of checksumming of NCP UDP packets. A checksum is calculated and placed in the packet being sent across the network. After the packet is received, the checksum can be recalculated to ensure that the same number of bits are received as were sent. This parameter allows you to enable or disable UDP checksums. The values for the checksum have the following meanings:

- 0 — No checksums
- 1 — Checksums if enabled at the client
- 2 — Require checksumming

Most sites do not need to enable checksumming, because this type of checking is done at the data link level of your network. However, some older bridges have been known to cause packet corruption.

A workstation on an IPX/SPX network sends a SAP Get Nearest Server request to locate a NetWare server. A workstation on a TCP/IP network, on the other hand, uses the Dynamic Host Configuration Protocol (DHCP) to locate a NetWare server. After the workstation locates a server using DHCP, this workstation transmits an Address Resolution Protocol (ARP) request to find the server's hardware address. After the server's address is obtained, the workstation uses NCP calls to retrieve the server information, authenticate to NDS, and log into the server.

As mentioned, you can configure a workstation to automatically obtain an IP address from a DHCP host. Using a DHCP host can dramatically reduce the amount of time required to configure and maintain IP addressing on your network. NetWare 6 offers DHCP support through a DHCP configuration NLM (DHCPCFG.NLM). You use this NLM to configure DHCP addressing, and it performs the DHCP functions for your NetWare 6 network.

On the other hand, you can manually assign an IP address to your workstation. For example, if you wanted to manually assign an IP address to a Windows 95/98 or Windows 2000 workstation, you would define the IP address and subnetwork mask in the TCP/IP Properties window. To access the IP Address Configuration window, select Run, and then select Settings. Next, select Control Panel, select Network, and select the TCP/IP entry listed. For more information about TCP/IP and DHCP on NetWare 6, refer to Chapter 23.

# The Disk and File System

NetWare 6 optimizes the use of the server file system with several new improvements over previous versions of NetWare. These improvements enable NetWare 6 to take full advantage of the available disk space and offer speed improvements as well as savings in server memory. The specific improvements that are addressed in this chapter are as follows:

- Novell Storage Services (NSS)
- Volume block size
- Suballocation
- File compression
- Read ahead
- Prioritization of disk requests

## Novell Storage Services

Novell Storage Services (NSS) eliminates several limitations that currently exist in the NetWare file system. NSS provides object-oriented storage with 64-bit internal and external interfaces. Without NSS, the NetWare file system supports only a 32-bit interface that allows files of up to 2GB, up to 16 million directory entries per volume, and up to 64 volumes per server. With NSS, the NetWare file system can host a single 8TB (terabyte) file. This would be extremely useful for database applications. In addition, the NSS file system can support virtually unlimited directory entries (or number of files) per volume. During testing, a volume with a billion files was successfully created with three name spaces loaded. This demonstrates that the file system can support three billion directory entries on a single NetWare volume. Thousands of volumes can be created per server; however, the current NCP interface supports only 127 volumes per server.

In addition to larger volumes and more files, NSS supports very much faster volume mount times. A normal NSS volume mounts in less than one second regardless of size or number of files stored. If the NetWare 6 server crashes and the volume is not dismounted cleanly, when the server is brought back up the volume is restored and mounted in 15 seconds to one minute. This is the case for all NSS volumes on the server. The older FAT-based file system is organized so that volume mount time increases with the number of files and their size.

The amount of server memory required to support NSS is approximately 8MB. Although this is the minimum memory requirement, NSS is capable of mounting any size volume or any number of volumes in this amount of memory. This fact basically eliminates the need for any complicated server memory calculations.

Even though NSS has many new features, it is also completely compatible with the standard FAT-based file system. The server volumes running NSS look the same as the standard FAT-based volumes to the workstations and users. In addition, NSS is built to support NetWare 4, NetWare 5, and NetWare 6. NSS automatically detects which of these operating systems it is running on and loads the appropriate NLMs for that server.

In order to fine-tune NSS on each of your servers, you can adjust many parameters. To view the current parameters settings and other NSS commands, enter this command at the server console:

```
NSS HELP
```

or just

```
NSS /?
```

Figure 11.7 shows an example of the NSS help screen. Before you attempt to use the NSS commands available from the help screen, you must first load NSS.NLM.

**FIGURE 11.7** *The NSS help screen is available on the server.*

You can view the current settings for each of the NSS parameters by simply entering the command NSS STATUS. Figure 11.8 shows the screen on the server that enables you to see the current settings for the NSS parameters.

In addition to the NSS commands available at the server console, you can use the NSS Configuration Menu or utility. This utility enables you to manage and configure the NSS volumes. You can rebuild or verify specific NSS volumes or simply view the volume's information. You can load the NSS Configuration Menu by entering the following command at the server console:

    NSS MENU

**FIGURE 11.8** *The current NSS parameters can be viewed using the NSS status command at the server console.*

For more information on Novell Storage Services, refer to Chapter 21.

## Volume Block Size

One of the features in the NetWare 6 operating system is the capability to support large volume block sizes. The large volume block size increases the performance of almost every associated subsystem, such as disk channel, file cache, directory cache, directory entry table, and file allocation table (FAT). This large volume block size does not waste disk capacity when storing lots of small files because of how the files are suballocated.

In the previous versions of NetWare (including NetWare 3), the volume block size or allocation unit was typically set at 4K. In NetWare 3, larger volume block sizes were possible, but they resulted in a lot of unused disk space at the end of files. For example, if the last part of a file took up 1K of a 16K block, the remaining 15K was wasted.

With NetWare 6, the default volume block size is no longer 4K. The default volume block sizes calculated during volume creation are not based on performance criteria but on volume size to conserve server cache memory. The new defaults are listed in Table 11.1.

| TABLE 11.1 | |
| --- | --- |
| *Default Volume Block Sizes are Based on Volume Size* | |
| **VOLUME SIZE** | **DEFAULT BLOCK SIZE** |
| Less than 32MB | 4K |
| 32 to 150MB | 8K |
| 150 to 500MB | 16K |
| 500 to 2,000MB | 64K |
| 2,000MB and up | 64K |

## Suballocation

One of the greatest cost benefits to upgrading to NetWare 6 is the use of volume block suballocation. Suballocation in NetWare 6 subdivides the volume blocks, regardless of size, into smaller suballocation units of 512 bytes. This process ensures that you never waste more than 511 bytes when saving any file. You now have the flexibility to set your NetWare 6 volume block size to the recommended maximum of 64K without sacrificing valuable hard disk space. This ensures that the disk space is more efficiently used.

▶ · · · · · · · · · · · · · · · · · · · · · · · · · · · · · ◀

### Consulting Experience

We recommend a 64K volume block size for all volumes, regardless of size. The larger 64K volume block size allows NetWare 6 to use the disk channel more efficiently by reading and writing more data at once. This results in faster access to mass storage devices and improved response times for network users.

As mentioned previously, earlier versions of NetWare worked with a 4K volume block size determined at the time of installation. The block size became the smallest unit of storage on the NetWare volume and server's hard drive. Generally, the larger the block size, the better the throughput between file server hard drive and file server's RAM or cache. But the large block sizes also had the most potential of wasting disk space or creating disk slack. For example, if your volume block size is 16K (without suballocation) and you save a small file of 1K, the remaining 15K in the disk block is not used. The used space is referred to as "slack." Figure 11.9 shows a problem with large block sizes without suballocation because it creates slack.

**FIGURE 11.9** *The problem with large block sizes without suballocation is that it creates slack.*

Figure 11.10 shows the same example as the preceding one but with suballocation of the volume block to reduce the slack. Notice that the volume block size is still 16K, but the volume block has been suballocated by the NetWare 6 operating system into 512 byte blocks. FILE1.DAT (a 1K file) would ordinarily be allocated a full 16K but only takes the required 1K using two suballocated blocks. The other 15K is not wasted but can be used by other files. Another file, FILE2.DAT (3K file), is written to disk and starts in the middle of the volume block using six more suballocated blocks. This example has no slack.

Notice that new files can start in the middle of a volume block that has been suballocated. They do not have to start on the volume block boundary. This means that if you select the recommended 64K volume block size, several files can be started and stored in the middle of the 64K block.

From a performance standpoint, suballocation enhances the performance of write operations within NetWare 6 by allowing the ends of multiple files to be consolidated within a single write operation. Of course, this minor improvement is often counterbalanced by the increased overhead of managing the suballocation process. The major advantage is the optimization of the disk channel and cache around the 64K disk allocation unit.

**FIGURE 11.10** *Large block size with suballocation of the volume block reduces the slack.*

As imaging, multimedia, and other workloads involving streaming data become more prevalent, the 64K block size will become invaluable. We recommend that everyone use the 64K disk block size to realize greater efficiency, eliminate wasted space, and take advantage of read-ahead.

### File Compression

NetWare 6 provides the capability to automatically compress any files on the server that have not been used for a period of time. This compression can result in space savings of up to 50 to 60 percent in some cases for a particular file. The file listing in the directory structure (FAT table) shows the file as if no change has occurred. When the user wants to retrieve the file, the operating system automatically decompresses the file. This file compression and decompression process is completely transparent to the user.

The file compression feature in NetWare 6 is completely optional, and you can determine which servers can benefit from its use. You can choose which files, directories, or volumes to compress. The compression process runs as a background task, which means that it usually does not affect the performance of the file server. In order to enable file compression, use the following SET parameter at the server console:

```
SET ENABLE FILE COMPRESSION = ON
```

You can decide the hours during the day when you want the file compression process to start and stop scanning for files that meet the compression criteria. The default start time is 0, which represents 12:00 P.M. The possible range is 0 through 23, which represents each hour of the day. To set the hour in the day to start scanning, type the following:

```
SET COMPRESSION DAILY CHECK STARTING HOUR = 0
```

To stop scanning, type (default is 6, or 6:00 A.M.) the following:

```
SET COMPRESSION DAILY CHECK STOP HOUR = 6
```

If the COMPRESSION DAILY CHECK STARTING HOUR parameter is the same as the COMPRESSION DAILY CHECK STOP HOUR, it starts each day at that time and runs as long as necessary to finish all files that meet the criteria.

You can also set a parameter at the server that specifies the period of time that the file has not been accessed before the system compresses it. The default setting is 14 days. The parameter to specify the period of time can be set at the server console by entering the following:

```
SET DAYS UNTOUCHED BEFORE COMPRESSION = 14
```

You can control the minimum space savings that must be accomplished before the compressed file is saved. If the operating system cannot gain a given amount of space from compressing a file, it does not compress the file. The default for this parameter is 20, or 2 percent. The parameter to set the minimum space saving is entered at the server console as follows:

```
SET MINIMUM COMPRESSION PERCENTAGE GAIN = 20
```

Decompression is automatic when the user requests a compressed file. The algorithms provided are extremely fast and do not affect either the client's or the server's performance. You can also control the decompression options when the compressed file is accessed by users. The default setting is 1, but the range is 0 to 2. Enter the compression/decompression options as follows:

```
SET CONVERT COMPRESSION TO UNCOMPRESSED OPTION = 0
```
(0—means that the operating system will always leave compressed)
```
SET CONVERT COMPRESSION TO UNCOMPRESSED OPTION = 1
```

(1 — means leave compressed if it has been read only once in the last seven days or DAYS UNTOUCHED parameter; see the previous discussion)

```
SET CONVERT COMPRESSION TO UNCOMPRESSED OPTION = 2
```

(2 — means always decompress)

NetWare 6 also enables you to control the percentage of disk space that must be present before the system attempts to decompress a file. The default is 10 percent. The parameter is entered at the server console as follows:

```
SET DECOMPRESS PERCENT DISK SPACE FREE TO ALLOW COMMIT = 10
```

## Read Ahead

The read ahead feature in NetWare 6 provides the requesting workstation faster response when reading files from the server. The operating system anticipates the read requests from the workstation and caches the next volume or disk block of a file.

For example, when the workstation makes a request for a file open, the operating system opens the file and assumes that the next request from the workstation is going be a read request. In anticipation of the read request, the read ahead feature caches (places into file cache) the first block of the file.

The result is that when the request from the workstation comes in for the first block, the server already has the block available in cache. The workstation request is serviced immediately instead of waiting for a hard disk access. As the workstation reads the information out of the block in cache, the operating system fetches the next block of the file and places it in cache anticipating more read requests. When the workstation has read one-half of the current block in memory (or cache), the operating system determines that the next block is needed. Using this algorithm, the operating system can calculate when the next blocks are needed and reads them from disk before the request is made.

This read ahead feature is a low-priority task that will not be executed when the server is busy handling other processes. The greatest impact of read ahead is when accessing optical media. A CD-ROM drive, for example, is not as fast as a hard drive. Read ahead pulls the next block into cache so that it is ready when the workstation needs it.

### Prioritization of Disk Requests

In previous versions of NetWare, situations occurred when a server would start servicing heavy write requests and would seem to ignore other transactions involving read requests. For example, if a user would perform a large COPY to the file server, the other users would see poor performance for the duration of the COPY.

This condition resulted when a large number of cached writes (dirty cache buffers) hit a threshold where the server needed to switch writes from background to foreground in order to service all the requests. However, when the server switched priorities, it switched completely to foreground writes, leaving less consideration for the higher-priority read requests.

NetWare 6 includes a tiered prioritization of the disk elevator that reduces the possibility of ignored reads. It also supports lower priorities for read ahead requests. The four bins are prioritized as follows:

▶ Critical events (such as file commits and TTS log file writes)

▶ Read requests

▶ Write requests

▶ Read ahead requests

Critical events are typically guaranteed events and are always processed with greater priority. Reads are almost always generated by client foreground tasks and make up the majority of work processed by any server. Most writes can occur in the background as a write-behind process. Read ahead requests are prioritized so as not to preclude the processing of any higher priority events.

Instead of using the normal first-in, first-out (FIFO) build sequence for the disk elevators, NetWare 6 takes a percentage of requests from each priority bin. The higher the priority, the more requests are placed on the current elevator. In this way, none of the levels gets locked out due to an overabundance of requests in one of the levels.

# The Kernel, Server Processes, and CPU Utilization

The core of the NetWare 6 operating system is a new kernel that supports multiple processors out of the box. In fact, it supports single and multiple processors from the same kernel. This means that you can utilize existing processors in your servers better, or add processors as needed to help speed up specific services. In addition, the new kernel offers memory protection, virtual memory, and application prioritization.

NetWare 6 supports up to 32 processors with the new kernel, which is called the multiprocessor kernel (MPK). During installation, NetWare 6 automatically detects the number of multiple processors by reading the multiple processor table in the machine's BIOS. It then determines which of the NetWare 6 Platform Support Modules (PSM) matches the hardware platform. The PSM is a hardware abstraction layer or interface that NetWare 6 uses to support different hardware dependencies.

## Symmetric Multiprocessing

As mentioned, the core of NetWare 6 is the kernel. The kernel executes individual threads that have been placed in a queue waiting to be serviced. A *thread* is a stream of control or a unit of execution. In NetWare 6, the new kernel maintains the structure called a *run queue,* which contains all the threads that are ready to be processed. Because NetWare 6 supports multiprocessor machines, it can execute individual threads on different processors. In comparison, a uniprocessor machine or system can execute the threads only one at a time. NetWare 6 creates only one run queue for a uniprocessor machine. A machine with multiple processors creates a run queue for each processor and distributes the threads appropriately.

Threads are scheduled on the processor's run queue that they arrive on. However, an internal algorithm determines how many threads are on the queue and how long the time is from the time that the thread has been scheduled to run until it has run. If the number of threads exceeds a set threshold called the *load balance threshold,* it is determined that moving the thread to another processor will be more advantageous. Using this method, NetWare 6 can balance between processors.

NetWare 6 periodically monitors each of the processors' run queues to make sure that none of the processors become overloaded. The load balance threshold that is set in the system parameters is used to determine how much the run queues can handle before becoming overloaded. The scheduler in the kernel calculates the system-wide load and the mean load or average length of each processor's run queue against the predetermined threshold. If one processor's run queue is determined to be overloaded, any new threads targeted for that processor are moved to another processor for execution.

Figure 11.11 shows how you can configure the system threshold by using the MONITOR utility. In MONITOR, select the Server Parameters and then Multiprocessor. Next, see the setting for System Threshold. The System Threshold parameter is used in calculating load balances between server threads. Although this threshold is configurable, we strongly recommend that you keep the value at the preset or factory setting. The factory setting is optimal for every machine. If, after careful consideration, you decide to modify the threshold, experiment with a new value only in a lab environment.

**FIGURE 11.11**  *The processors in a multiprocessor machine can be automatically load-balanced using the SET parameter shown in MONITOR. The SET parameter is the System Threshold. We strongly recommend that you leave the value at the factory setting.*

To take advantage of multiple processors in a server, the server application code must be written to be multithreaded. For example, the NetWare 6 core components or processes that are enabled for multiple processors are NWPA, Media Manager, LSL, memory, Open Data-link Interface (ODI), C-library (CLIB), RSA encryption, routing functions, and the direct file system.

## Application Priorities

The new NetWare 6 kernel enables you to prioritize the applications running on your servers. You can specify the processor use that you want to dedicate to each application. More specifically, the NetWare 6 kernel applies the processor use to a collection of threads called a *share group*. Each collection of threads, or share group, tracks its use of the processor resources. The amount of processor time reserved for each share group is used only when multiple applications want the processing power simultaneously. If only one application is using the CPU at any one time, naturally it gets 100 percent of the processing power regardless of its priority. Therefore, a NetWare 6 server must have at least two share groups to benefit from the prioritization of the applications.

By adjusting the share value for each application, you can tune the quality of service provided. In addition, both single-processor and multiprocessor machines can benefit from the flexibility of the application prioritization. Thus, if a single processor machine has multiple applications or share groups, you can allow one application to have more CPU cycles than the others.

In order to set or establish the share value for each application, you use the MONITOR utility at the server console. At the main menu, select the Kernel option and then Applications. Next, select one of the specific applications running on that NetWare 6 server. Figure 11.12 shows how you use the MONITOR utility to set the share value for an application. In this example, the application is the default NetWare application. This share group represents all the NLMs loaded by the basic NetWare 6 server, which include the storage drivers, communication drivers, NDS, and others.

The default share value in NetWare 6 is 100, but share values can range from 1 to 10,000. The most important thing to remember is not the actual value of the share, but the ratio between multiple share groups. For example, for two share groups, an assignment of 200 and 100 respectively entitles the first share group to twice the amount of processing resources. The same is true if the two share groups are assigned 400 and 200, or 100 and 50. The ratio between the share groups is the key.

**FIGURE 11.12** *Using the MONITOR utility, you can set the percentage of CPU time that the operating system guarantees to one application if multiple applications request the CPU simultaneously.*

Share groups with equal values assigned to each are given the same amount of processor resources regardless of how many threads each share group has. This feature prevents applications with large numbers of threads from swamping applications with fewer threads. The share value, not the number of threads, determines the amount of processing power for each application.

When using NetWare 6 as an application server, you will find that this feature gives you more detailed control over each individual service or application. For example, if you run a Web site using the FastTrack Web Server and Oracle8 database on the same server, you can specifically establish parameters for each in sharing the CPU. You will want to give the application that is more critical a higher share value percentage.

## Preemption

The NetWare 6 kernel has also been developed to support preemption. *Preemption* eliminates the problems associated with poorly written applications running on the server as NLM and monopolizing the processor. In order to take advantage of preemption in NetWare 6, the application must be explicitly written or enabled by the developers to support the kernel's preemption.

## Service Processes

A service process is an execution thread that handles incoming service requests to the server. NetWare 6 has the capability to allocate up to 500 service processes. Typically, your NetWare 6 server will not use more than 40 service processes. In fact, most installations may never see this number rise above ten because of how well NetWare handles multiple user connections. However, you can use the server set parameters to manage this function by typing the following:

```
Set maximum service processes = n
```

where *n* can be a value from 5 to 100. The default is 40. This setting controls the maximum number of service processes available for the server.

To control the wait time for new service processes, type the following:

```
Set new service process wait time = n
```

where *n* can be 0.3 to 20 seconds. The default is 2.2 seconds. This setting specifies the wait time before the operating system can allocate any new service processes.

You can view the number of service processes in use by using the MONITOR.NLM utility and viewing the first screen, as shown in Figure 11.13.

**FIGURE 11.13** *Using MONITOR.NLM to view the number of service processes in use on a NetWare 6 server*

Changing these parameters is necessary in only a few circumstances. For example, if you are running 500 to 1,000 users on a single server, you will want to increase the maximum service processes parameter. You might also consider increasing this value if you are using this service to store imaging or other graphics-intensive data. Do not increase this value to the maximum in one single adjustment. Instead, keep raising the number of service processes in small increments until your performance improves.

## CPU Utilization

The CPU is usually the last place to look for a bottleneck on your server. But most of your tuning should be with the server's subsystems and not the CPU itself.

For example, if you were to use a bus mastering NIC in your server, you would have very little CPU activity in terms of disk read and writes. Almost all activity is handled on the NIC card itself without the intervention of the CPU. You can easily check the performance of your server's CPU through MONITOR.NLM's main screen. If you select Kernel and then select Applications, you see groups of applications. For example, all the NetWare processes are grouped in a single application called the NetWare Application. To view the individual processes or threads, select the application. If you want to see the busiest threads, press the F4 key. You see a screen similar to the one shown in Figure 11.14.

```
NetWare 6 Console Monitor  12.00              NetWare Loadable Module
Server name: 'CRM-SRV1' in Directory tree 'ACME_TREE'
Product: Novell NetWare 6
┌─────────────────────────────────────────────────────────────────┐
│          Busiest Threads and Interrupt on Processor 0             │
├─────────────────────────────────────────────────────────────────┤
│  Server 04                                           2,122,494    │
│  Server 03                                           1,789,110    │
│  WN10.1.1.25:1142                                       10,742    │
│  Java_560 N-AWT-Event                                    8,746    │
│  OS Allocated Bus Interrupt                              3,395    │
│  Checkpoint Thread                                       3,175    │
│  DB Monitor                                              1,961    │
│  OS Allocated Bus Interrupt                              1,395    │
│  MONITOR updates                                         1,254    │
│  Server 00:02                                            1,018    │
│  IPU4            1                                         927    │
│  NLS LSAPI Thread1                                        796    │
│  NLS LSAPI Thread1                                        769    │
│  CIFSPROX.NLM    1                                        517    │
│  WC10.1.1.25:1142                                         309    │
│  Java_170 Thread-2                                        279    │
│  Apache          1                                        190    │
└─────────────────────────────────────────────────────────────────┘
 Esc=Previous list    Alt+F10=Exit                         F1=Help
```

**FIGURE 11.14** *The Busiest Threads in a Share Group screen found in MONITOR.NLM*

Paging down the Processor Utilization screen displays the percentage of CPU utilization that each process on your server is using. The Idle Loop category shows the percentage of time that the CPU is sitting idle. Look carefully at this statistic to see how busy your CPU actually is. If you are using only 20 to 30 percent of the CPU time, that means 70 to 80 percent is going unused and is sitting idle. The idle loop value is the inverse of the most accurate CPU percent utilization figure available from NetWare.

Not all processes are calculated when this screen is active. Novell Directory Services, for example, uses a process known as the work-to-do process. These types of processes are not monitored by the Process Utilization screen. They are not too significant in terms of CPU power and therefore are not registered on the MONITOR screens.

Keep in mind that when you make a determination to purchase new hardware, you want to spend money where it will have the greatest impact for performance on your systems. Sometimes your money may be better spent on the subsystems of the server rather than the CPU itself.

In some cases, you may have a server experiencing high utilization and actually see the CPU reach 100 percent utilization. For brief moments, this type of activity is normal and generally does not pose a problem for your server or users. If you notice high utilization occurring for long periods of time, you have a problem that you need to investigate and solve.

# Abend Recovery Options

NetWare 6 provides recovery options for handling abends (abnormal ends) in the operating system. In addition, the NetWare 6 operating system source code has been modified to reduce the total number of abend conditions. For example, software errors in previous versions of the operating system caused the system to abend. Some of these errors could have been corrected or ignored with no adverse effect. Other errors could have been changed to be conditional based upon whether the developer option in the operating system is set to OFF. This reduces the number of events that can potentially disrupt the NetWare 6 operating system but allows them to be turned back on when the software engineers or developers are debugging a new NLM product.

You may now be wondering if abends are good or bad. The answer depends on your perspective. An abend stops the server processes before data is damaged or harmed. Although this is a positive feature, an abend disrupts or halts the entire service. This disruption in service is definitely an inconvenience. However, the abend information about the software or hardware problems helps the administrators troubleshoot the server. Thus, the abend information can decrease the troubleshooting time. One of the primary goals of the new abend recovery options is to improve the information or messages displayed on the server console. The abend recovery enhancements that are new to NetWare 6 include the following features and capabilities:

- Additional abend information is displayed on the server console.
- When an abend occurs, the header "Additional Information:" is displayed on the server console followed by the probable cause of the abend. The information displayed identifies the specific NLM or hardware problem that caused the abend so that the administrator can take immediate corrective action to prevent the problem from occurring again.

The new abend recovery options are as follows:

- The ABEND.LOG file
- The SET AUTO RESTART AFTER ABEND parameter
- The SET AUTO RESTART AFTER ABEND DELAY TIME parameter

## The ABEND.LOG File

When an abend occurs, information about the abend is automatically written to a text file called ABEND.LOG. The abend information is formatted and written to appear like a mini-core dump. The ABEND.LOG file is initially created on the DOS partition of the server. However, the next time that the SYS: volume is mounted, the information is appended to the ABEND.LOG file stored in the SYS:SYSTEM directory, and the ABEND.LOG file on the DOS partition is removed. This method provides a running history of all the abends that occur on a specific server and also provides detailed information about abends. This helps the administrators and support engineers identify and resolve server problems.

## The SET AUTO RESTART AFTER ABEND Parameter

A SET parameter called AUTO RESTART AFTER ABEND enables the NetWare 6 server to automatically recover from an abend. According to the value selected, the server will recover in a variety of ways. The three values you can set are 0, 1, or 2. The default value for this parameter is 1.

If the parameter is set to 0, the server does not try to recover from the abend. However, the server displays the standard abend information to the system console screen and writes it to the ABEND.LOG file. The server also provides the option to the user to attempt to take the server down gracefully (as if the option had been turned ON). The administrator has the option to do a core dump or simply exit to DOS at that point.

If you set the parameter to 1 (which is the default), the server attempts to recover from the abend. In order for the server to recover from the abend, it must first check the state of the SET DEVELOPER OPTION parameter. If the DEVELOPER OPTION parameter is set to OFF (which is the default), when the abend occurs, the standard abend information will be displayed on the system console screen and logged to the ABEND.LOG file. Next, if the running process is a Page Fault, Protection Fault, Invalid Opcode, or Divide Overflow Exception, or if the process can be restored to a stable state, the server continues to run and service all requests. If the SET DEVELOPER OPTION parameter is set to ON, the server is scheduled to be restarted after two minutes. When the server is scheduled to be restarted, a broadcast message is automatically sent to the system error log file and to all the users, notifying them that the server will be going down in two minutes. The server is then automatically downed and automatically restarted. The server then comes up in a clean state, reloading all the drivers and NLMs previously loaded. The clients running the new client requesters with auto-reconnect automatically reconnect to the server and continue accessing the same network files that they had open before the abend occurred.

If you set the parameter to 2, the server attempts to recover from the abend while suspending the faulting process. If the SET DEVELOPER OPTION parameter is off when the abend occurs, the standard abend information is displayed on the system console screen and logged to the ABEND.LOG. The running process, which is the faulting process, is suspended (if possible). Next, the server is scheduled to go down after two minutes. A broadcast message is sent to the system error log file and to all the users notifying them that the server will be going down in two minutes. The server is then automatically downed and restarted, and all the drivers and NLMs are reloaded. The clients running the new client requesters with auto-reconnect automatically reconnect to the server and continue accessing the same network files that they had open before the abend occurred. The faulting process continues to be suspended.

A value of 1 or 2 allows the NetWare 6 servers to automatically recover from abends and come back online rather than sitting in a halted state waiting for administrator intervention. All the error messages, conditions, and necessary information are written to a file to help the system administrator debug the problem after it occurs. These settings also allow the server to go down in a graceful fashion, which prevents both client and server file system data from being lost.

## The SET AUTO RESTART AFTER ABEND DELAY TIME Parameter

This SET parameter enables the user to configure the amount of time (in minutes) that the server will wait before going down and restarting automatically if the SET AUTO RESTART AFTER ABEND parameter is turned on (set to 1 or 2). Although the default for this parameter is 2 minutes, it can be set anywhere between 2 and 60 minutes, in one-minute intervals. It can be changed at any time after the abend has occurred but before the server actually goes down.

When you enter the SECURE CONSOLE command at the server prompt, DOS is not removed from memory automatically. To remove DOS from memory, you have to explicitly use the REMOVE DOS command. This enables abend logging and the SET AUTO RESTART AFTER ABEND functionality when the console is secured.

# The Memory Subsystem

The total amount of server memory has a larger impact on the overall performance of the operating system than any other subsystem. The memory supports the file server cache, which provides both file and directory caching. The cache memory allocates space for the hash table, the File Allocation Table (FAT), the Turbo FAT, directory caching, and finally file caching. The minimum amount of memory for NetWare 6 is 256MB.

Calculating server memory requirements for previous versions of NetWare was a common pastime; however, NetWare 5 and 6 eliminates the need to do a lengthy memory calculation. For the most part, NetWare 5 and 6 require far less memory because of the Novell Storage Services (NSS). In the past, the server memory calculations were highly dependent on the file system size, number of volumes, number of files, and name spaces wanted. For example, in NetWare 4, a server with 10GB volume needed roughly 160MB of RAM and grew with every gigabyte installed afterward. In NetWare 5 or 6, the memory requirements are more constant because NSS requires only 8MB. The 8MB requirement is minimum, but NSS guarantees that it will mount and support all volumes on the server regardless of the size. Thus, a server with 10MB, 10GB, or 100GB requires the same amount of server memory.

## Memory Protection

NetWare 6 supports several memory features that include memory protection and virtual memory. Although previous versions of NetWare had features for memory protection, NetWare 5 and 6 have complete memory protection. The memory protection in NetWare 6 enables you to load any server applications in their own protected address space. The applications are then shielded from the other applications and the operating system itself. The result is that if one application fails, it does not affect any of the other applications or processing of the operating system. You can use protected address spaces to run untried or troublesome applications. Any program or module loaded into a protected address space can't corrupt the operating system or cause server abends. The protected address space provides a safe place to run applications. All protected address spaces use virtual memory. For more information about virtual memory, see the section "Virtual Memory" later in this chapter.

## Protected Address Spaces

As mentioned, each application can be loaded into its own protected address space. A *protected address space* is a portion of cache server memory that has controlled communication with the server operating system. The protected address space is only a portion of cache memory that can be set aside. This is sometimes called user address spaces or ring 3. In contrast, the NetWare operating system does not run in a protected address space. The operating system address space is sometimes called ring 0 or the kernel address space.

Although running applications in ring 0 offers greater performance benefits, doing so can be risky. Modules or applications that are executed in ring 0 do not have protected memory. Thus, if an application has problems, it could start overwriting memory outside its own address space. As a result, the operating system could crash or abend. We recommend that you load only trusted modules in ring 0 and new or suspect modules in ring 3. This provides a layer of protection between the new module and the NetWare operating system.

Because the protected address space runs in ring 3 and the operating system runs at ring 0, there must be an interface between the two areas. This interface, in conjunction with the memory protection subsystem, prevents modules in a protected address space from having direct access to anything outside the address space, especially the server operating system. The interface prevents NLM programs in protected spaces from passing calls to the operating system address space that would corrupt or abend the core operating system.

Each protected address space has its own page translation table to provide logical memory addressing. The memory management subsystem ensures that the page translation table of each protected address space points to a different set of physical memory addresses. Only one translation table can be loaded into the memory management subsystem at a time. When you have more than one protected address space, the memory management subsystem loads one translation table for a specified time and then replaces it with another. Figure 11.15 shows how the memory management subsystem loads only one translation table for the protected address space at a time.

Loading and unloading translation tables is called a *context switch*. As you may know, context switches can be somewhat time consuming for the CPU. Thus, we recommend that you do not create more protected address spaces than you need.

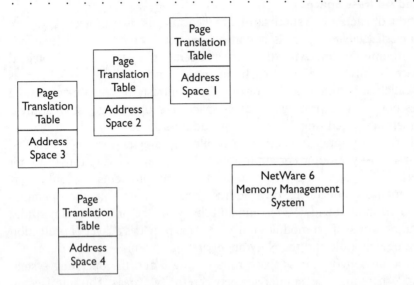

**FIGURE 11.15** *The memory management subsystem loads the translation tables one at a time.*

NetWare 6 loads Java-based applications in protected mode by default. In addition, you can optionally load enterprise software such as GroupWise, Lotus Notes, and Oracle. However, certain types of modules and programs cannot run in protected addresses. The protected address spaces run in ring 3, and others must be loaded at ring 0 instead. What follows is a list of common NLM programs and executables that cannot be loaded into a protected address space:

- ▶ SERVER.EXE
- ▶ LAN drivers
- ▶ Disk drivers
- ▶ MONITOR.NLM
- ▶ Novell Storage Services (NSS)

The server operating system (SERVER.EXE) cannot run in a protected address space because software running in a protected space is subject to being temporarily stopped and swapped to disk (see the section "Virtual Memory"). LAN and disk drivers must run in ring 0 or the operating system address space because they use physical memory addresses. Protected address spaces use logical memory addressing.

Any software modules or server applications that need to access physical memory directly or engage in direct hardware I/O (such as LAN drivers, HAM or disk drivers, and I/O services) cannot be loaded in the protected address spaces. The same is true for applications such as MONITOR that make calls directly to the operating system that are not allowed from protected address spaces. Additionally, some modules and applications aren't designed to run in protected address spaces.

### Loading Protected Address Spaces

In order to manage an application's performance and reliability, you can move it into and out of protected address space. In order to create a protected address space, you load the individual module with specific commands. Table 11.2 shows the list of commands that control creation of protected address spaces.

TABLE 11.2

*Server Console Commands for Creating a Protected Address Space*

| COMMAND | DESCRIPTION |
| --- | --- |
| [LOAD] PROTECTED module_name | Loads the module and automatically creates a new protected address space called ADDRESS_SPACE *n*, where *n* is a number. |
| [LOAD] RESTART module_name | Loads the module and automatically creates a new protected address space with restart functionality. The restart functionality means that if the protected address space abends, the operating system closes the space, cleans up its resources, restarts the space again, and reloads the modules. |
| | To prevent the server from restarting a memory space that continues to abend, the operating system uses the SET parameter called Memory Protection No Restart Interval. This parameter is found in the Miscellaneous section of the Server Parameters in MONITOR. |
| [LOAD] ADDRESS SPACE = space_name module_name | Loads modules into a new protected address space with a user-defined name. You can use this command when you want to create your own name for the space. You can also use this command when you want to load more than one module into an address space. In order to do this, repeat the command multiple times. |
| PROTECT filename. | Use this command to use an NCF file to NCF load multiple modules at once. This command creates a protected address space with the same name as the NCF file. |

*continued*

| TABLE 11.2 | |
| :-- | :-- |
| Server Console Commands for Creating a Protected Address Space (continued) | |

| COMMAND | DESCRIPTION |
| :-- | :-- |
| PROTECTION RESTART space_name | Adds restart functionality to an existing address space. Restart functionality means that if the protected address space abends, the operating system closes the space, cleans up its resources, restarts the space again, and reloads the modules.<br><br>To prevent the server from restarting a memory space that continues to abend, the operating system uses the SET parameter called Memory Protection No Restart Interval. This parameter is found in the Miscellaneous section of the Server Parameters in MONITOR. |
| PROTECTION NO RESTART space_name | Removes restart capability from an existing address space. |

You may be wondering whether the number of modules that can be run in protected mode simultaneously is limited. The answer is that no built-in limit exists to the number of protected address spaces that can be used, or to the number of modules that can be loaded into a given address space. The only limit is dictated by the amount of physical memory and disk space available.

### Unloading Protected Address Spaces

In order to unload a module or application from a protected address space, you can use the commands shown in Table 11.3. This table not only shows you each command to unload a module or application from a protected space, but it also shows you how to unload the space itself. The commands are valid only at the server console.

Under certain circumstances, a module that is being unloaded with the UNLOAD ADDRESS SPACE command will hang. The system waits a predetermined time before it displays an error message. The error message that is shown on the server console is as follows:

```
<module name> in <address space> did not unload yet. Killing
the address space is the only way to remove the NLM. Should
the address space be killed? Yes/No.
```

If you answer Yes, the system kills the address space without unloading modules from it. If you answer No, the system waits a specified time and displays the message again. You can use a SET parameter to designate the amount of time that the system waits under these conditions. The SET parameter is called Hung Unload Wait Delay and is found in the error handling section of the SET parameters. The default is 30 seconds, but you can change it to wait less time.

If you find that during an UNLOAD of an address space the server does not completely clean up all the assigned resources, a message is sent to the server console. The message may include the words "clean up failure," and you will not be able to unload the address space. In order to recover from the error and recover the resources assigned to the address space, you need to schedule a shutdown and restart of the server.

T A B L E  11.3

*Server Console Commands for Unloading Applications or Unloading the Protected Address Space*

| COMMAND | DESCRIPTION |
| --- | --- |
| UNLOAD ADDRESS SPACE = space_name module_name | Unloads the specified module or application for the specified address space, but does not remove the address space. If the module is loaded into more than one address space, this command removes only the module from the designated address space. |
| UNLOAD ADDRESS SPACE = space_name | Unloads all modules from the specified protected address space, plus removes the address space itself from memory. |
| UNLOAD KILL ADDRESS SPACE = space_name | Unconditionally removes the address space without having to unload each module first. This returns all the resources used by the protected address space to the system. You only want to use this command if you have tried and failed to unload it using the normal method. |

## Virtual Memory

Virtual memory provides the NetWare 6 operating system the capability to allocate more than the actual physical memory of the server machine. It does this by using the disk as an extension of memory and by swapping code and data between physical memory and disk as it is needed. When the data on disk is needed again, it is moved back into the physical memory. Because data is swapped in and out of disk, the available memory can be used for a larger amount of data than its actual physical capacity would allow. Virtual memory provides NetWare 6 with a more efficient use of memory and lessens the likelihood that low memory conditions will cause an abend condition.

NetWare 6 moves the data out of physical memory to swap files on the hard drive if the data has not frequently been used. More specifically, the available memory is assessed to see which data has been used less recently than the rest. How recently data has been used is determined by a bit in each field of the translation table that indicates whether the address space has been used since the last time it was checked. Data that has not been used for some time can be moved from memory to disk, thus freeing memory for other uses.

As mentioned earlier, protected memory uses virtual memory. The reason is that the memory management subsystem can allocate to each process a unique protected virtual address available to run the threads of the process. Thus, each process has a separate address space, so a thread in one process cannot view or modify the memory of another process. This architecture provides the protected memory for NetWare 6.

NetWare 6 loads a few applications or modules into virtual memory by default. One of those is the Java Virtual Machine (JVM). Any other modules that are loaded by the JVM run in virtual memory. As in the case of protected memory, however, certain types of modules and programs cannot run in virtual memory. Not surprisingly these types of programs are the same as those that cannot use protected memory. The reason is that protected memory uses virtual memory. What follows is a list of common NLM programs and executables that cannot be loaded into virtual memory:

- ▸ SERVER.EXE
- ▸ LAN drivers
- ▸ Disk drivers
- ▸ MONITOR.NLM
- ▸ Novell Storage Services (NSS)

As an example, the server operating system (SERVER.EXE) cannot run in virtual memory because it must always be resident in memory and cannot be swapped to disk. The same condition exists for all the other modules.

### Managing Virtual Memory

The memory management subsystem assesses the memory needs of all server and NLM processes and determines where the freed memory should be used. The subsystem stores freed memory in disk cache. When data is moved from memory to disk, it is stored in a swap file. Swapping the data between memory and disk requires additional system resources, but it increases the memory available for use. The availability of the additional memory can improve overall server performance.

You can manage the swapping of data by controlling the swap files where the data is stored on disk. You can use the SWAP command to create a swap file, delete a swap file, change swap file parameters, and view information about the swap file. You can also view information about the swap file in MONITOR. You can create one swap file for each NetWare 6 volume. A swap file is created for the SYS volume by default.

Table 11.4 describes each of the commands you can use to create, delete, and manage swap files that are used by virtual memory. The commands described are all executed from the server console.

### TABLE 11.4

*Server Console Commands for Creating, Deleting, and Managing the Swap Files Needed for Virtual Memory*

| COMMAND | DESCRIPTION |
|---|---|
| HELP SWAP | Learn about the SWAP command. |
| SWAP | Display a Virtual Memory Information Screen containing information about swap files. Alternatively, you can use MONITOR to view information about the swap files under the Available Options, select Virtual Memory, and then Swap Files. |
| SWAP ADD volume_name [parameter= value...] | Create a swap file on a designated volume. The optional parameters are MIN=, MAX=, and MIN FREE=. These parameters specify the minimum and maximum sizes of the swap file and the minimum free space that must be left on the volume. The values are in MB (millions of bytes). If no parameters are included, the command uses the default values of MIN=2, MAX=Free volume space, and MIN FREE=5. You generally want to place swap files on the fastest volume or the volume with the most available space. |

*continued*

TABLE 11.4

*Server Console Commands for Creating, Deleting, and Managing the*
*Swap Files Needed for Virtual Memory (continued)*

| COMMAND | DESCRIPTION |
|---|---|
| SWAP DEL volume_name | Delete a swap file from a designated volume. If you are using protected address spaces, the Java Virtual Machine, or any other application that uses virtual memory, make sure that you have at least one swap file for your system. Remember that, by default, a swap file for volume SYS is created automatically. If you do not want a swap file for SYS, place the SWAP DEL command in the STATUP.NCF file before the command to mount volumes.

If the swap file is being used when it is deleted, the swapped data is then moved to another swap file. If no other swap file exists, an error message is displayed and the file is not deleted. |
| SWAP PARAMETER volume_name parameter=value... | Change the parameter values for a swap file on a designated volume. Again, the parameters are MIN=, MAX=, and MIN FREE=. These parameters specify the minimum and maximum sizes of the swap file and the minimum free space that must be left on the volume. Values are in millions of bytes. |

When using swap files in a production NetWare 6 environment, you should be aware of several important facts. The facts about swap files are as follows:

▸ You can create one swap file per volume.

▸ The swap file for the SYS: volume is created by default; you can delete it if necessary.

▸ Data moved to disk by virtual memory will be stored in any available swap file. It does not matter which volume the swap file is on.

▸ You can add a swap file to a volume even if the volume is not mounted. When the volume is mounted, the swap file will be created.

▸ When you dismount a volume, the swap file is deleted. To keep a swap file on that volume, you must create the swap file again. Again, the only exception is volume SYS, which is created by default.

▸ You typically want to place the commands to create swap files into the AUTOEXEC.NCF file so that the files will be created each time the server is started.

▸ Swap files are dynamic; they change size as data is swapped in and out of memory.

If the overall supply of memory in the server is running low, swapping within virtual memory occurs more often. If memory is extremely low, the system may spend all its time swapping memory in and out of disk and have no time to accomplish useful work. This is called disk "thrashing."

In extremely low memory conditions, NetWare moves all the data from a protected address space into the disk swap file, temporarily stopping the modules within the space. After a period of time, NetWare moves the data back into the memory space and shuts down another space, moving its data to disk. Without virtual memory, these extremely low memory conditions would cause processes to fail. With virtual memory, the server keeps running, although very slowly.

When disk thrashing occurs, the solution is to add more RAM. Virtual memory cannot compensate for an overall lack of server memory, although it can prevent processes from failing and allow a server to continue to function. The real value of virtual memory is in using a sufficient supply of memory more efficiently, thus improving server performance.

### File Caching

NetWare 6 uses cache memory on the server to speed up file access for clients. The file cache provides a temporary data storage area (in RAM) for files that are being read or written to the server.

The most dramatic file server performance increase can be seen when the appropriate number of file cache buffers are allocated. The file cache buffers should be sufficient to keep the cache hit ratio high. The greatest performance increase is achieved when the hit ratio is between 90 and 100 percent. As a rule of thumb, the 90 percent hit ratio is achievable (in a read-intensive environment) when the cache buffers are 75 to 80 percent of total server work memory. File cache buffers are assigned from the memory that is left after the operating system is booted and the core functions and NLMs are loaded.

The most important parameter to measure cache efficiency is the LRU sitting time statistic that is updated and displayed once per second in MONITOR.NLM. LRU stands for least recently used. This statistic is found under the Cache Statistics menu as shown in Figure 11.16 and is calculated by taking the difference between the current time and the time stamp of the LRU cache block at the end of the cache list. The result is then updated every second and is displayed. The LRU sitting time measures the length of time for a most recently used (MRU) cache buffer at the beginning of the list to work its way down to the end of the list, where it becomes the LRU cache buffer. This measurement is also known as the cache churn rate.

**FIGURE 11.16** *A view of the LRU sitting time statistic in the MONITOR utility*

In environments with very large amounts of cache, the LRU sitting time will be up in the hours of time. A good rule of thumb is that your LRU sitting time should not go below 15 minutes. If your LRU value falls below 15 minutes, it usually means that you do not have enough memory to create a large enough cache for your directories. Therefore, the sitting time is very short because of the churn rate of MRUs versus LRUs. It's time to take a look at adding more memory to your server if this value remains consistently below 15 minutes. Here are some other helpful ideas for tuning your cache:

1. Estimate your server memory requirements. You can use the previous memory calculation worksheet to estimate your server memory requirements. You must first determine whether your server has adequate memory overall.

2. Observe the Cache Statistics parameter. You should monitor the LRU sitting time during peak workload periods and record that information. You should then monitor the LRU sitting time at other, slower, times of the day. Obtain an average for your LRU sitting time. Record your observations for at least one week or longer to obtain a pattern of activity on your server. Estimate a low watermark based on the information you have gained from your observations. This low watermark will help you to adjust cache if necessary.

**3.** Tune the Cache parameter by increasing its size. A simple rule of thumb is if your LRU sitting time falls below 15 minutes, you should probably increase the cache size by adding more memory to your server. You need to add memory to increase the LRU Sitting Time during your peak workloads. The added memory increases the likelihood that repeatedly used data will still be cached when the next user request is received from a client.

On the other hand, if your LRU sitting time is several hours, you have more than adequate cache resources. In this case, it is not necessary to increase your memory, and you can leave the memory in the server to support additional growth.

The point is not whether you actually add or remove memory from your server. We hope to improve your ability to interpret the LRU sitting time statistic and thereby provide you with a meaningful way to understand the efficiency and performance of NetWare 6's file cache.

### Directory Caching

*Directory caching* is the ability of NetWare to read directories and cache directory entries for faster lookup. Rather than search the disk for directory entries, the server can hold the entries in memory. Disk access performance is greatly increased with this feature. Because some directories can be extremely large, the directory cache uses what is called the least recently used (LRU) algorithm to store only the most recent directory cache blocks. By doing this, the operating system can more efficiently make use of memory. Each cache buffer is 4K and holds up to 32 directory entries. This parameter can be set as follows:

```
SET MAXIMUM DIRECTORY CACHE BUFFERS = n
```

where *n* is a number between 20 and 4000. The default is 500. This setting enables you to define the maximum number of directory cache buffers that NetWare 6 can allocate. NetWare 6 allocates extra buffers only if necessary:

```
SET MINIMUM DIRECTORY CACHE BUFFERS = n
```

where *n* is a number between 10 and 2000. The default is 20. This setting defines the minimum number of directory cache buffers that can be allocated by the NetWare 6 operating system without waiting for the directory cache allocation wait time:

```
SET DIRECTORY CACHE ALLOCATION WAIT TIME = n
```

where *n* is a value between 0.5 and 120. The default is 2.2 seconds. This parameter specifies how long the NetWare 6 operating system must wait before allocating one more directory cache buffer.

In very few circumstances do you need to adjust this parameter upward. Keep in mind that the minimum number of buffers is the number of directory cache buffers that can be set by the operating system using the wait time. If your server is functioning as a document server where many searches are being performed, you may want to increase this parameter.

Additional directory set parameters enable you to control cache functions listed here. They are also set parameters that are manipulated at your server console:

SET MAXIMUM CONCURRENT DIRECTORY CACHE WRITES = *n*

where *n* is from 5 to 10. The default setting is 10. This parameter enables you to control the number of cache writes through the disk channel. When you create a new directory addition, deletion, or other modification, a directory cache write is created. You can limit the number of cache writes through your disk channel if your disk subsystem is not extremely fast:

SET DIRECTORY CACHE BUFFER NONREFERENCED DELAY = *n*

where *n* can be 1 to 300 seconds. The default setting is 5.5 seconds. The purpose of this SET parameter is to specify the amount of time that a cache buffer can remain unreferenced before it is removed. Novell does not recommend that you make any changes to this parameter, because you can better control performance by setting the number of cache buffers:

SET DIRTY DIRECTORY CACHE DELAY TIME = *n*

where *n* can be 0 to 10 seconds. The default is 0.5 seconds. The purpose of this parameter is to reduce the likelihood of redundant cache writes. This setting causes NetWare 6 to wait for the delay time specified before performing a directory request (write) to the directory cache. The reason for the wait is to see if there are any more requests to change the same block. If duplicate requests exist, the operating system processes those requests only once with a single write. This makes writing more efficient. Only very large directory caches (hundreds of thousands of entries) realize any benefit by changing this parameter.

## Obtaining the Latest Patches

Make sure that you have the latest patches loaded for the NetWare 6 operating system and NDS eDirectory. Each Novell patch contains a readme file that explains the problems being resolved and any special loading instructions. To download the latest patches, you need to go to the Novell corporate Web site: www.novell.com/download.

## Summary

Before you can adequately tune or optimize the NetWare 6 operating system, you must first understand the basic characteristics of your network, servers, and workstations. In addition, you need to become familiar with the internal server components and processes.

A variety of SET parameters help you accomplish the task of tuning and optimizing the NetWare 6 server. These SET parameters can be adjusted either up or down to help fine-tune your system. Although the SET parameters can be manually adjusted, the default settings for each of the internal parameters work very well for most implementations. Some server implementations may make it necessary to modify some of the system settings to increase the capacity and performance of your system. These implementations may include heavy use of imaging or document retrieval types of software.

You should measure the baseline performance of your system during periods of both peak and off-peak production. Having a baseline beforehand enables you to gauge changes in performance and reliability during the tuning effort.

# NetWare 6 Administration

# Understanding and Managing Client Access

*"Good counselors lack no clients."* — *Shakespeare*

The network client provides an extension to each network user to access the corporate resources on the network servers. The network client is tasked to communicate with the desktop operating system and the network operating system and serves as a liaison between the two. If a desktop application requires the use of network services, the client redirects the output to a server. If a server application needs to communicate with a client, it directs that communication to the network client in response to the client request.

Because of the variety of clients that may exist in your network, your responsibility as a LAN administrator is to determine what type of client access is needed for a workstation to connect to NetWare 6 and to create the appropriate accessibility to meet those needs. You provide access to NDS eDirectory through the different client software components available in conjunction with NetWare login scripts. The client software provides access to NetWare 6, and the login script creates the environment for the user. The methods of client access are discussed in detail in the sections that follow. For a discussion of how to install and configure client software, refer to Chapter 17.

## NetWare 6 Network Client Software

The NetWare 6 client software is designed to support connectivity to workstations including the DOS/Windows, Windows 95/98, Windows 2000, Linux, and Solaris operating systems. Through various connections discussed in this chapter, you can connect to a NetWare 6 server and access files, applications, and NDS eDirectory.

As a network designer, you will hopefully have most of your users running on the same desktop operating system, with a few exceptions that use other systems across your departments. As you design for user access to the NDS eDirectory tree and NetWare 6 servers, you should first begin by designing access (login scripts and so on) for the majority of your user community that uses the same operating system. You can then create your access designs for the less commonly used workstations on your network. You will most likely also have mobile users that require special login scripts to give them their required access.This chapter reviews the various login scripts for setting up user environments. We review container, profile, and user login scripts and how they can be used to meet any user need. At the end of the chapter, we provide sample login scripts that can be used for Windows 95/98,Windows NT, and Windows 2000 clients. We also discuss mobile users and offer recommendations on how to best meet their needs. Figure 12.1 illustrates the different client access mechanisms and serves as the basis of our discussion. As shown in the diagram, client access can be broken down into multiple categories. Each of these categories is discussed in this chapter.

Access

| Type of Connection | Authenticated and Licensed | Not Authenticated Not Licensed | Authenticated |
|---|---|---|---|
| Workstation Software | NETX | VLM and 32-bit Client | Browser |
| Type of Service | Bindery | | NDS |
| Login Scripts | User Script in Mail Directory | System Script NET$LOG.DAT | Container L.S. Profile L.S. User L.S. |
| Type of User | Network / Remote / Mobile | | |

**FIGURE 12.1** *The components of client accessibility for NetWare 6 Networks are based on a variety of connections, workstation software, services, login scripts, and users.*

Desktop support is key to NetWare 6, as it was with all previous versions of NetWare. A server cannot serve the user community unless access is provided for the clients to communicate with NetWare servers across the entire network. This access requires speed and reliability for all users and must make good use of limited memory at each workstation. After a connection is made, the login script can set up the user's environment. Chapter 17 provides a description of currently supported clients with their latest version of software.

## Workstation Software

The newest client software is Novell's 32-bit Client architecture, which provides network connections for DOS/Windows 3.1, Windows 95/98, and Windows 2000. Novell also provides a 32-bit client for Windows NT users that also uses the 32-bit architecture, although it is slightly different than the Novell DOS/Windows client. The older DOS Requester technology is discussed first, and then the newer 32-bit client technology.

### The DOS Requester

The DOS Requester is very old technology (first introduced in NetWare 4.0) and is a group of Virtual Loadable Modules (VLMs) that work together to provide client connectivity to a NetWare 6, NetWare 5, NetWare 4, or NetWare 3 server. Using the VLM software, you can install only the VLM modules that are required for your user environment. You can create a standard configuration for the majority of your users. A drawback to this technology is that it consumes a lot of desktop memory. Some companies surprisingly still use this client technology, although very few.

An important difference between the even older NetWare 3 NETX.EXE shell and the NetWare DOS Requester is how each client handles network requests. Because NETX.EXE is a shell, all calls from an application to the workstation operating system are intercepted by the shell and then directed to either the network or to DOS.

The NetWare DOS Requester, on the other hand, receives all calls from DOS through the DOS Redirector interface known as Int2Fh. Therefore, any calls sent to this interrupt are always intended for the network. Each of these approaches has its advantages and disadvantages in terms of memory usage and performance.

A visual example of how the NETX.EXE shell works is found in Figure 12.2.

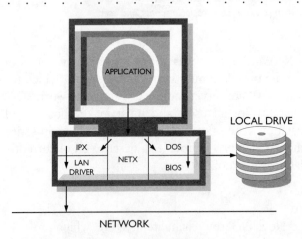

**FIGURE 12.2** *A view of NETX.EXE routing operating system requests from an application*

A visual example of how the NetWare DOS Requester receives the network requests from DOS is shown in Figure 12.3.

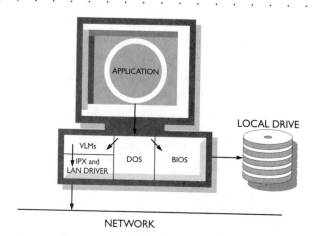

**FIGURE 12.3** *A view of the NetWare DOS Requester routing operating system requests from an application*

## Novell Client 32 Technology

The NetWare clients for Windows 95/98, Windows NT, and Windows 2000 are based on a 32-bit architecture. Installations get especially complicated in multiprotocol configurations with network connectivity using a large amount of memory. The NetWare Client 32 architecture provides a 32-bit protected-mode environment for its clients. The CPU gets switched to protected mode when the client software loads. Therefore, memory beyond 1MB is addressable as a continuous range. Figure 12.4 shows a view of the NetWare Client 32 process.

**FIGURE 12.4** *A view of the requester process of Client 32*

## Types of Service

Two types of connections exist for NetWare 6—the NDS connection and a bindery services connection. The basic difference between these two connections is that a bindery services connection is server-centric. Server-centric means that connections to multiple servers require a username and password at each server, and the login process is repeated at every server.

With the NDS eDirectory connection, on the other hand, you can have a single login to multiple NetWare 6 servers. A single login enables the user to enter a name and password once. Any additional drive mappings to other NetWare 6 servers are handled in the background by NDS. The great benefit of the NDS connection is that administrators need to manage only a single user account if they are operating completely on NetWare 6 servers.

### NDS Connections

An NDS connection requires the use of the NetWare 32-bit client software for authentication to a NetWare 6 server. An NDS connection provides a security mechanism known as RSA encryption between the client and server to provide background authentication for a single sign-on to multiple NetWare 6 servers. An NDS connection is said to be in one of three states:

- ▸ Connected but not logged in
- ▸ Authenticated
- ▸ Licensed/authenticated

Each of these states is discussed in the following sections.

**Connected but Not Logged In**    This state occurs when a user has attached to a NetWare 6 server through NETX l, the VLM client, or a NetWare 32 Client. An NDS eDirectory connection that is not logged in can exist for NetWare 3, NetWare 4, NetWare 5, or NetWare 6 users to the first attached server. If a connection is made after walking the tree, the state can exist after the first attached server.

For example, when a connection is neither authenticated nor licensed, users can navigate the NDS tree through the CX (change context) command. At this point, they have attached to a server but have not yet authenticated.

**Authenticated**    *Authentication* is a process of proving identity to a server. In NetWare 3, this meant logging in with a user id and password. In NetWare 4, NetWare 5, and NetWare 6, the authentication process happens as a "behind the scenes task" at the client.

This type of connection indicates that a NetWare 6 server has established a user's identity after the user has entered a correct name and password. When authenticated, NDS can provide connections (background authentication) to other servers on the network. Authentication occurs for NetWare 3, NetWare 4, and NetWare 6 users alike, but NetWare 4, NetWare 5, and NetWare 6 add more security to this process.

Authentication is invisible to the user. During the login sequence, the user enters a password when prompted, and the remainder of the process occurs behind the scenes. No sensitive data are transmitted across the wire for security purposes. Authentication relies on encryption algorithms that are based on a public/private key system.

After successful authentication has taken place, a process known as *background authentication* may occur if the user's login script specifies connections to other servers. A connection to another NetWare 6 server, for example, does not require the user to reenter his or her password. However, all connections are authenticated the same way; the process makes no distinction between the first and subsequent server logins.

**Licensed/Authenticated**   A connection is said to be *licensed* when a user has made a request of the server, such as mapping a drive or capturing to a printer. Each user causes the user license to decrement by one after a connection has been licensed. Only an authenticated connection can be licensed.

A combination of these states determines what level a user currently has in a NetWare 6 environment.

If users are licensed and authenticated, they can access NDS and file system information to the extent allowed by their rights.

*Additive licensing* increases the total number of licenses on any given NetWare 6 server. This feature enables administrators to more closely match the number of licensed users to their company's needs. A company that currently has a 100-user license can add a 25-user license to the NetWare 6 server to accommodate increased growth. NetWare 6 supports 5-, 10-, 25-, 50-, 100-, 250-, 500-, and 1,000-user versions in any combination.

### Bindery Services Connections

The NetWare client software provides compatibility with previous versions of NetWare through bindery services connections. This connection does not provide the capability of a single login to the network. For example, a client using the NETX.EXE shell or the LOGIN/B option with VLMs to log into a NetWare 6 server must enter a username and password for that server. Additional connections to other NetWare 6 servers would require the user to enter another username and password.

Bindery services can be enabled on any NetWare 6 server only through the MONITOR Utility. You can also make the settings directly in the STARTUP.NCF file. The administrator can select one container or multiple containers in the NDS tree to set as the bindery context. All the leaf objects in the NDS container(s) that are also objects in the NetWare 3 bindery (for example, users, groups, queues, print servers, and profiles) are seen as the bindery. For more information on the MONITOR utility, see Chapter 2.

Bindery services in NetWare 6 allows you to select up to 16 containers as the server bindery context. Bindery services requires that the server store at least a read/write replica of the partitions where the bindery context is set.

## Login Scripts

Network users execute login scripts to access NetWare 6 servers and other network resources. Traditionally, login scripts were used to establish the user's network environment. Login scripts for NetWare 6, however, are used to map network drives, map to applications, capture to printers and print queues, and set other important environment variables. Login scripts are the standard mechanism for user access and may require careful consideration.

When a user logs into the NetWare 6 network or server, login scripts associated with the user are executed. Two categories of login scripts are available to the user of the NetWare 6 network—NDS login scripts and bindery-based login scripts. NDS login scripts support the eDirectory connections, and bindery-based login scripts support the bindery services connections. Although many organizations no longer use bindery services; surprisingly, many still do.

Our focus on login scripts in this chapter is to provide information on designing access to NetWare 6, not to encompass every login script variable and command. (Definitions and functions of all variables and commands are included at the end of this chapter.) Well-designed login scripts help you create effective working environments for your users.

Login scripts execute in a specific order as shown in the following sequence of login script execution for NetWare 6:

1. The user logs into a server.
2. The user executes a container script if it is available.
3. The user executes a profile if that user's Profile property is set.
4. The user executes a user script if one is available.
5. If a user login script is not available, the user executes the default script.

Bindery-based login scripts and NDS login scripts are both discussed in the next two sections.

### Bindery-Based Login Scripts

The bindery-based login scripts that you may place in NetWare 6 are the same bindery login scripts found in NetWare 3. These login scripts can be copied onto the NetWare 6 servers to provide bindery services scripts to any NETX.EXE clients. For example, a user attaching to a NetWare 6 server with the NETX.EXE workstation software will have a bindery connection and look for the system and user login scripts on the server. The user script is in the SYS:MAIL directory, and the system login script would be placed in the SYS:PUBLIC directory as NET$LOG.DAT. Even if the user is using the VLM workstation software and selects the LOGIN/B option, that user will be attached to the server as a bindery connection.

The system login script is used for commands that affect all the bindery-based users on that server. Commands that might be placed in the system login script include the commands for displaying messages, mapping network drives and search drives, and setting environment variables. The system login script is the best place to manage the mapping and capture statements for all the bindery users that may still exist on your NetWare 6 network.

After a user successfully attaches to the server with a bindery connection, the system login script executes from SYS:PUBLIC\NET$LOG.DAT if it exists. If the user login script is present, it executes from the SYS:MAIL\USERID subdirectory. If the user login script does not exist, the default login script is executed. The default login script is hard-coded into the LOGIN.EXE program.

Figure 12.5 shows the order of execution for bindery-based login scripts. If you are familiar with NetWare 3, notice that the bindery-based login scripts for NetWare 6 are executed in the same order.

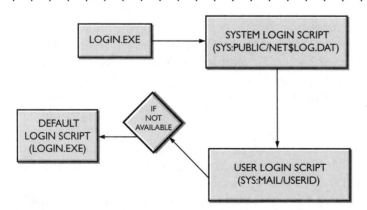

**FIGURE 12.5** *The bindery-based login scripts in NetWare 6 are executed in the same order as NetWare 3 login scripts.*

The individual user login scripts are stored in each user's mail subdirectory on the SYS: volume of any server where a bindery account exists. For example, user GWASHINGTON (with object ID of 19000023) stores the bindery-based user login scripts in the SYS:MAIL\19000023 subdirectory.

The individual user login script customizes the user environment to the specific needs of the user. The same commands placed in the system login scripts can also be placed in the individual user login scripts. It is recommended that the user login scripts be used only in situations in which the system login script will not suffice.

The bindery-based login scripts are server-centric, meaning that they are used only if a bindery user logs into the server that is holding them. Because the login scripts are server-centric, you don't have a lot of design issues to consider. However, you should try to move all the users to the NDS login scripts as soon as possible so that you have fewer scripts to support.

You can  edit the NET$LOG.DAT file (or any script) directly with any text editing program. Although the bindery-based login scripts can be edited, any changes you make to the scripts are not automatically synchronized to the corresponding NDS login scripts. You can use Novell's NETSYNC utility to synchronize login scripts if you need to maintain consistency between NetWare 3 and NetWare 6. Refer to Chapter 2 for more information on NETSYNC.

### NDS eDirectory Login Scripts

The login scripts used in NDS are different from those used by bindery services. The NDS login scripts are a property of an object and are accessible only through an NDS connection. The only NDS objects that have the login script property are the container objects (O=Organization and OU=Organizational Unit), profile objects, and user objects.

Users who obtain an NDS connection to the network and run LOGIN.EXE execute the NDS container login script in the container in which they reside. The container script is roughly equivalent to the NetWare 3 system login script. After the container login script is executed, a profile login script can be executed if the user is associated with one. The user may also have a user script, which is executed after the container and profile scripts. If no user login script exists, the user executes a default script. Again, the default login script is hard-coded into the LOGIN.EXE program and cannot be modified.

Figure 12.6 shows the order of execution for the NDS login scripts. Notice the profile login script, which falls between the container and user login scripts. Each type of login script is discussed later in this section.

In order to manage the NDS login scripts, you can use either the NWADMIN or ConsoleOne utility that ships with NetWare 6. With these utilities, you can create and edit all the login scripts, except for the default login script. You can also add a profile login script for execution by selected users. An example of editing a login script is shown in Figure 12.7. In this example, the administrator is editing a container login script for the FAC container.

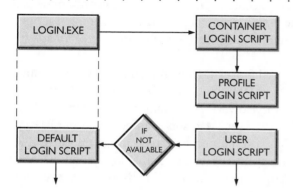

**FIGURE 12.6** *The order of execution for the NDS login scripts in NetWare 6*

**FIGURE 12.7** *You can use the NWADMIN or ConsoleOne utility to add or modify an NDS login script.*

**NDS Container Login Scripts**  Typically, the NDS users needing the same network resources are grouped together in the same NDS container. These users probably need similar drive mappings and capture statements to establish access to the network resources with which the users are grouped. You can then use the container login script to provide users access to the NDS tree in this fashion.

After the LOGIN utility has authenticated a user to the NetWare 6 network, the program checks the container login script in which the user resides. If the container login script exists, it will then be executed. NDS searches only the immediate container (O or OU) in which the user is a member. If the container login script is not defined, the system does not automatically search higher in the tree for another container login script.

For example, Figure 12.8 shows the user JMadison in the ACME tree named under the container OU=FAC.OU=ADMIN.OU=RIO.O=ACME. The container OU=FAC does not have a login script. However, a container login script is defined higher in the tree at OU=ADMIN. The user JMadison is an occupant of OU=FAC and does not execute a container login script because one is not currently in FAC. The user JMadison does not search up the tree for a container login script. In other words, no other container login scripts above the user JMadison will be executed.

**FIGURE 12.8** *Container login scripts are executed only for the immediate occupants of a container. In this example, the user JMadison does not have a container login script in FAC.*

The NDS container login script commands should establish the network environment of the users. These commands include the network drive mappings, printer and print queue captures, and other environment settings. The users in the container are best managed by using the NDS container login script.

Here is an example of a container login script that we have just added for the OU=FAC container in the RIO location of ACME tree.

```
;*********************************************************
; CONTAINER LOGIN SCRIPT EXAMPLE
; for OU=FAC.OU=ADMIN.OU=RIO.O=ACME
; Creation Date: 08/12/01
; Revisions:
;*********************************************************
REM—No default user login script
NO_DEFAULT
WRITE "Good %GREETING_TIME, %LOGIN_NAME."
MAP DISPLAY OFF
MAP ERRORS OFF
MAP *1:=%HOME_DIRECTORY
REM—Map to the e-mail and application server
;WRITE "Your E-mail server is RIO-SRV1 and the application
server is FAC-SRV1"
;PAUSE
MAP ROOT M:=RIO-SRV1\SYS:EMAIL
MAP ROOT W:=FAC-SRV1\SYS:APPS
REM—Capture to the print queue
#CAPTURE /SERVER=FAC-SRV1 /Q=HP4SI-PQ1 /L1 /NB /NFF /TI=1
```

The previous script can be created in either the NWADMIN utility or the ConsoleOne utility, as shown in Figure 12.9.

**Profile Login Scripts**   If a user has a profile script assigned, it is executed immediately after the container login script. The profile login script is optional and is used in special cases or for groups with special needs. The profile has the capability to include users that are in different containers in the tree. Its purpose is to assign additional environment settings that you may not want to assign to everyone in the profile. The scripts and the commands used in the profile login script are identical to the NDS container login scripts.

**FIGURE 12.9** *Using the NWADMIN utility to create a script for the FAC container*

Because the profile login script is a special-purpose login script, it can provide you with greater flexibility during the login process. Multiple users can be associated with the profile login script, and they can reside in different containers in your tree. Figure 12.10 shows the creation of a profile login script through the NWADMIN utility. You can enable individual users to execute the profile script by assigning them to it; make the assignments to the user objects at creation. This method can be accomplished through the NWADMIN utility, as shown in Figure 12.11.

Typically, the profile login script is used as follows:

▸ For an entire company (if the company and tree are small)

▸ To create a user environment based on location

▸ For a special group of users

The profile script is represented by the profile object, which can be placed anywhere in the Directory tree. Using the profile login script to span all the users in the entire company is recommended only for small networks. A small network consists of fewer than ten servers and is not widely distributed over wide area links. In general, we recommend using the profile login script only across small networks. Our basis for this recommendation is that using a profile script across a very large tree is expensive in terms of the amount of NDS traffic that will be generated to locate and manage this object.

**FIGURE 12.10** *Assigning an individual user to execute a profile login script*

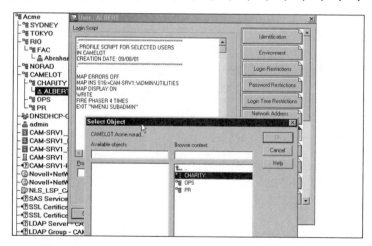

**FIGURE 12.11** *Creation of a profile login script through NWADMIN*

The profile login script is also used to create a user environment for a location. This method is similar to simply using a container script, except that you may want to create an environment for specific users within the container. Users that are organized around a particular site, building, or floor can have specific environment settings based on their particular needs. With the profile login script, it is not necessary to create floor or building containers in your tree just to have a common login script.

For example, you have a specific set of users in a building and you want them to always map to the same e-mail and applications servers. You may also have users on one floor who want to capture to the same printers. You can accomplish these tasks using the profile login script. Using the profile login script in this fashion is considered to be a *locational* use of the script.

Figure 12.12 illustrates a profile login script being used as a locational login script that includes the containers in the ACME tree below the OU=ADMIN container in the RIO location. Specifically, OU=FAC and OU=AUDIT are in the same building and need similar environment settings.

**FIGURE 12.12** *The users in both the OU=FAC and OU=AUDIT containers are using the same profile login script.*

The profile login script can also serve as a special-purpose login script for a group of users. The group members can all be in the same NDS container, or they can span across a number of OUs. If the profile login script makes assignments for users within a single OU, the profile login script is similar to a group object, with its sole purpose being to execute a script.

A more powerful use of the profile login script is to span more than one NDS container. In Figure 12.13, you see three users in a different NDS container. These users are members of a special group of administrators who need specialized access to resources in the NDS tree. When each user logs in to the network, he receives the additional drive mapping to perform various job functions. Users JMadison, ALincoln, and TJefferson are each associated with the same profile login script that gives them the extra drive mappings.

**FIGURE 12.13** *The users JMadison, ALincoln, and TJefferson are each associated with the same profile login script.*

Here is an example of a profile login script. If you have groups of users with identical login script needs, you can create a profile object and then create a profile login script. You can then assign each user to be a member of that object.

```
MAP DISPLAY OFF
MAP ERRORS OFF
MAP INS S16:=VOL1:APPL\DB
MAP *5=VOL1:ACCOUNTS\NEW
MAP *6=VOL1:ACCOUNTS\RECORDS

@GRPWISE6
MAP DISPLAY ON
MAP
WRITE
IF DAY_OF_WEEK="FRIDAY" THEN
    WRITE "WEEKLY TIME TRACKING DUE TODAY"
END
```

**NDS User Login Scripts** The NDS user login scripts are stored as a property in each of the user objects. Like the bindery-based user login script, the NDS user login script customizes the user environment to the specific needs of that user. All the login script commands and variables can be used in the individual user login scripts. However, we strongly recommend that user login scripts be used only when the commands in the container system login script are not adequate.

**TIP**

**Most, if not all, scripting can be accomplished through container login scripts. For most large NetWare environments, implementing user scripts is generally unfeasible because of the difficulty in maintaining them. As a network administrator, you don't need the extra work.**

If you decide to let your users have personal login scripts, keep in mind that maintaining all the users' login scripts will be a difficult task.

Here is an example of a user login script for JMadison in the OU=FAC container in the RIO location of the ACME tree. These users support their own user login scripts and do not request the assistance of a network administrator.

```
MAP DISPLAY OFF
MAP ERROR OFF
MAP F:=FAC-SRV1\SYS:USERS\JMADISON
;***** EMAIL *****
SET EMAILUSER = "JMADISON"
```

```
MAP M:=RIO-SRV1\SYS:POSTOFF
;***** PRINTERS *****
#capture L=1 Q=HP4SI-PQ1 NB NFF TI=1
;***** WINDOWS *****
MAP ROOT W:=FAC-SRV1\SYS:APPS\WINDOWS
;***** BRIEF EDITOR FLAGS *****
MAP S16:=FAC-SRV1\SYS:APPS\BRIEF
SET BPACKAGES = "c:t;h:t,r"
SET BPATH ="z:\\apps\\brief\\macros"
SET BHELP = "z:\\apps\\brief\\help"
SET BBACKUP = "c:\\backup"
SET BFLAGS = "-i70-u300-1200-Dega-k1 M"
SET BFILE = ""
SET BTMP = "c:\\tmp"
SET BCC = "\"cl /c %s.c\""
SET BCH = "\"cl-c-Tc %s.h\""
;***** WP *****
MAP S16:=FAC-SRV1\SYS:APPS\WP\6.1
SET WP = "/U=JM"
;***** Misc. *****
MAP S16:=FAC-SRV1\SYS:APPS\PROGRAMS\BIN
MAP
```

**Default Login Scripts**    The default login script is executed only when the user login script does not exist. The default login script is hard-coded into the LOGIN.EXE program and tries to create enough drive mappings to the server that the user can function properly. The purpose of the default login script is to serve as backup in the absence of a user login script. The default login script executes even if you have a container or profile login script.

If you do not want to run the default script, you need to place the NO_DEFAULT command in the container login script or in a profile script. The container login script can also have an EXIT command at the bottom of the script. The EXIT command prevents any other login script from running, including the default login script.

The following commands are executed as the default login script:
WRITE "Good %GREETING_TIME, %LOGIN_NAME."

```
MAP DISPLAY OFF
MAP ERRORS OFF
MAP *1:=%FILE_SERVER\SYS:
MAP *1:=%FILE_SERVER\SYS:%LOGIN_NAME
IF "%1" = "SUPERVISOR" || "%1" = "ADMIN" THEN MAP
*1:=%FILE_SERVER\SYS:SYSTEM
MAP INS S1:=%FILE_SERVER\SYS:PUBLIC
MAP INS
S2:=%FILE_SERVER\SYS:PUBLIC\%MACHINE\%OS\%OS_VERSION
MAP DISPLAY ON
MAP
```

## Mobile or Traveling Users

A newer feature found in NetWare 6 is called iFolder. The iFolder enables you to access files virtually from any desktop browser. So a user who travels to New York from San Francisco can have file available at all times and in all places. For more information on this product, refer to Chapter 20.

Additionally, NetWare 6 lets the user log in and access resources from anywhere in the network through regular client mechanisms, as well. This feature helps you to manage the mobile or traveling user more easily. In order to completely support traveling users and their specific computing requirements, you need to consider the following questions:

▸ Does the user carry a laptop computer?

▸ Where is the user geographically located?

▸ Where is the user's home office?

As users move from one location to another, they access the network and its resources differently. Knowing how each user wants to access the network helps you set up the user environments. For example, some users just want dial-in access or high-speed access through cable modems and DSL connections to the network from remote locations. These locations can range from their homes, hotel rooms, and even airplanes. Typically, this type of user dials into the network from a laptop or home computer.

### Consulting Experience

Your approach to designing access for NetWare 6 should be to first design for the majority of the non-traveling users and then design for the traveling users. In order to design the access properly, you need to know how many users in the network are traveling users. Then determine from the total number of traveling users how many are remote users and how many are true mobile users.

Some users may travel from one office to another and need full access to all the local network resources of the office they are visiting. Although the users need full access to the local resources, they still want the data from their home directory and server. Essentially, the definition of a traveling user is broken into two types: remote users and mobile users. Both types are discussed in the sections that follow.

### Remote Users

The *remote users* are the individuals who travel or carry a laptop computer and simply access the network resources through dial-in or high-speed connections. The remote user who takes a laptop on the road is usually self-contained, meaning that the laptop computer is configured with all the necessary applications software such as e-mail and word processing. The user can continue to work when on the road and merely dials into the network to transfer e-mail messages, download files, or access other resources.

Remote users require fewer design considerations for access because they access NDS eDirectory only as needed for a connection to the network. Supporting remote users does not impact the design of the eDirectory tree or require you to create any special NDS objects. Users simply dial into specific predetermined access points in the network and use their normal NDS context or location. After the normal login to the network, the users can download files and access other necessary resources.

Some remote users dial in just to transfer their e-mail messages. Typically, a company may dedicate special phone lines (and toll-free numbers) for just the remote e-mail users. These lines may have their own security and access method and would not affect the eDirectory tree access.

If a remote user travels to another office and plugs his or her laptop computer into the network and wants access to all the local resources, that user has really become a mobile user. The design considerations for the mobile users are addressed in the following section.

The speed at which these users connect to the network determines whether you attempt to have them run the ZENworks Application Launcher over the remote connection. A slow dial-up connection could take several minutes to load. You can look to use the newer remote capabilities found in ZENworks for Desktops 3. This software allows you to create an application CD and configure the ZENworks Application Launcher to run the applications from this CD.

For users who have high-speed connections, you can use the ZENworks Force Cache feature, which copies the application to a hidden cache on the remote workstation's hard drive. For more information on deploying ZENworks for Desktops 3, see Chapter 19.

### Mobile Users

The *mobile users* are individuals who travel from one office to another or from one computer to another. They expect full access to all the local network resources of the office they are visiting while maintaining the ability to access data from their home server. The mobile user may not carry around a laptop but expects to have a computer available at the other site. Some mobile users decide to carry laptop computers and plug them into the network when they arrive. Thus, the best definition of a mobile user is an individual who uses a computer on the network from a location that is away from his or her home office.

Whether the user travels thousands of miles or across the building, the issues are the same for mobile users. The user wants access to the network applications, such as word processing, spreadsheets, e-mail, and printing from the local servers, but also wants to retrieve the data from his or her home server. The user wants these capabilities to be as seamless as possible.

In order to support the needs of the mobile user, you need to answer the following questions:

▶ Where is the user geographically located?
▶ Where is the user's home office?

Several mechanisms in NetWare 6 help you answer each of these questions. These mechanisms include the NDS name context, alias objects, configuration files, login scripts, login script variables, and environment variables.

**NDS Name Context**   The *name context* in NDS helps you determine where in the NDS tree the user belongs. The name context is important because NDS requires it for every user logging into the network. The context can be set in the user's NET.CFG file or by typing the user's full name during login. Although a mobile user's physical location may change, his or her context remains constant.

If the mobile user has traveled without a laptop computer, that user expects to use any available computer in the office that he or she is visiting and log into the network. The main issue with this scenario is how to determine the user's name context for login purposes. You have several ways to work around this problem:

▸ Manually enter the context at the computer console before login.

▸ Create alias objects that point to the user in his or her normal context.

▸ Set the name context of the alias in the workstation configuration file.

**Manually Changing the NDS Name Context**   The first option involves the mobile user manually entering his or her name context into the computer that he or she is using. This option assumes that the user understands how to use the proper utilities and is familiar with their complete context in the NDS tree. The client utility is used to set the user's context before login under the Advanced Options tab.

For example, the user JMadison in the ACME tree as shown in Figure 12.14 would need to set his or her name context by typing the following in the Advanced Options tab of the client login utility:

```
.FAC.ADMIN.RIO.ACME
```

**FIGURE 12.14** *The name context for the user JMadison in the ACME tree*

▶ . . . . . . . . . . . . . . . . . . . . . . . . . . . . ◀

### Consulting Experience

Users who carry laptop computers to a new location are not considered mobile users if they do not need access to the local network resources. If the users are content to access their home resources across the network, they are simply remote users. Remote users require no special design considerations. Remember, NetWare 6 enables the users to log in from anywhere on the network. A user simply looks for a network connection and logs into the server at his or her home office.

**Using an Alias Object to Help Set the Name Context**   The second option that could help set the name context is the use of alias objects. If you have a small number of mobile users, you can create an alias object below the O=Organization for each mobile user. The alias would point to the user's primary object in the appropriate container.

The value of this strategy is that it creates a simple context for each of the mobile users. The users do not need to know where the context is or even how to set it. The users would simply enter the name of the alias object during the login process.

For example, an alias object has been created for the user JMadison in the ACME tree. Figure 12.15 shows that the alias object called JMADISON was created directly in the O=ACME container. The alias object points to the real object in the OU=FAC in the RIO location. When the user JMadison wants to log into the network from any site, he or she uses the name of the alias object as follows:

```
LOGIN .JMADISON.ACME
```

Notice the leading period in the LOGIN command line before the name of the alias object. The leading period instructs the utility to start at the [ROOT] object when looking for the alias object.

This method of using the alias object to support the mobile users works well if you have a small number of mobile users at your site. Setting up an alias object for each individual mobile user is feasible if the total number is small. This method may not work if your mobile user population is high. You need to determine how many alias objects you can manage.

**FIGURE 12.15** *An alias object called JMADISON has been created under the O=ACME container.*

**TIP**

**You can also use third-party utilities that search the tree for a user object and set the appropriate context for your mobile user. You should consider these types of utilities when you have many mobile users.**

**Using the Configuration Files to Set the Name Context**   The name context for the user can be set using the standard workstation configuration file called NET.CFG. The NET.CFG file is read during the loading of the workstation client. What follows is an example of setting the name context for the user JMadison in the ACME tree. Within the NET.CFG file, a section called the NetWare DOS Requester holds the NAME CONTEXT = "OU.FAC.OU=ADMIN.OU=RIO.O=ACME." Users traveling to different locations with their own notebooks or laptops typically have the NET.CFG file set already. When they arrive on site and connect to the network, their name context is resolved from the setting in the NET.CFG file on the laptop.

```
Link Support
    MemPool 6192
    Buffers 10 1580
    MAX STACKS 8
Link Driver NE2000
    INT 5
    PORT 300
    MEM D0000
    FRAME Ethernet_802.2
NetWare DOS Requester
    NAME CONTEXT = "OU=FAC.OU=ADMIN.OU=RIO.O=ACME"
    PREFERRED SERVER = FAC-SRV1
    FIRST NETWORK DRIVE = F
    NETWARE PROTOCOL = NDS,BIND
    SHOW DOTS = ON
    USE DEFAULTS = ON
    PB BUFFERS = 10
```

You can use the PREFERRED SERVER setting in the Windows Registry to connect the mobile user to the server that has this user's bindery context. If you force the user to connect to the proper server using the PREFERRED SERVER variable, the user can log in using bindery services. This enables users running the older NETX.EXE workstation client to participate in mobile computing if needed. For example, in the previous NET.CFG file, the variable is set as PREFERRED SERVER = FAC-SRV1. This enables the user JMadison to log in and access the server using bindery services if he is still running NETX.EXE.

### Login Scripts for Mobile Users

The two mechanisms for creating a mobile user login script are the login script variables and an environment variable that can be called NW_SITE.

What follows is an example of a container login script for mobile users. In this example, we have defined a mobile script that allows the user to easily log into the network from any of the five major sites shown in the ACME tree. The script demonstrates how a user is mapped to the local e-mail server and the local application server. This login script is used as a container login script and also requires the NW_SITE DOS environment variable to be set on the user's workstation in the CONFIG.SYS file.

```
;***********************************************************
; MOBILE CONTAINER LOGIN SCRIPT
; for OU=FAC.OU=ADMIN.OU=RIO.O=ACME
; Creation Date: 03/18/98
; Revisions:
;***********************************************************
REM Do not execute default script
NO_DEFAULT
Write "Good %GREETING_TIME, %LOGIN_NAME"
REM Map public drive to local server
MAP S16:=SYS:\PUBLIC
REM Map F drive to the user's home server
MAP F:="HOME_DIRECTORY"
REM Map NetWare Drives according to the NW_SITE variable

IF <NW_SITE> == "NORAD" THEN BEGIN
    MAP ROOT M:= NOR-SRV1\SYS:MAIL
    MAP ROOT W:= NOR-SRV1\SYS:APPS\WP
    MAP ROOT Q:= NOR-SRV1\SYS:APPS\QPRO
    END
IF <NW_SITE> == "RIO" THEN BEGIN
    MAP ROOT M:= RIO-SRV1\SYS:MAIL
    MAP ROOT W:= RIO-SRV1\SYS:APPS\WP
    MAP ROOT Q:= RIO-SRV1\SYS:APPS\QPRO
    END
IF <NW_SITE> == "CAMELOT" THEN BEGIN
    MAP ROOT M:= CAM-SRV1\SYS:MAIL
    MAP ROOT W:= CAM-SRV1\SYS:APPS\WP
    MAP ROOT Q:= CAM-SRV1\SYS:APPS\QPRO
    END
IF <NW_SITE> == "TOKYO" THEN BEGIN
    MAP ROOT M:= TOK-SRV1\SYS:MAIL
    MAP ROOT W:= TOK-SRV1\SYS:APPS\WP
    MAP ROOT Q:= TOK-SRV1\SYS:APPS\QPRO
    END
```

```
IF <NW_SITE> == "SYDNEY" THEN BEGIN
    MAP ROOT M:= SYD-SRV1\SYS:MAIL
    MAP ROOT W:= SYD-SRV1\SYS:APPS\WP
    MAP ROOT Q:= SYD-SRV1\SYS:APPS\QPRO
    END
EXIT
```

**TIP**

**In the previous script, you can specify the actual NDS volume object names instead of the server names for mapping drives. The drives M and W in our example default to searching in the bindery, which relies on SAP because we do not specify the NDS volume object names in the login script.**

### A Container Script Using Additional SET Parameters

For even greater flexibility, you can use the %NETWORK and %NETWORK_ADDRESS variables to point the user to the nearest application server or printer in your company. This variable is used in the script because all resources that reside on the network have a network address. This basic script makes use of the user's context and the network context. Therefore, you can assign a resource such as an application server to every network. When users execute their container login scripts, you can use the %NETWORK_ADDRESS variable to determine their location and "map" them to the closest application server. What follows is a sample container login script emphasizing this method.

```
;********************************************************
; MOBILE CONTAINER LOGIN SCRIPT
; for OU=FAC.OU=ADMIN.OU=RIO.O=ACME
; Creation Date: 03/18/98
; Sample login script for nearest Application Server
; Revisions:
;********************************************************
; Login script for users physically located in the office
IF NETWORK_ADDRESS ="0101C9DA"
        SET LOCATION= "ATLANTA OFFICE"
        SET APPSRV =  "ATL-APP-1"
        SET DEFPRNT = \\ATL-PS-1\HP4SI-Q
        GOTO COMMON
```

```
END
; Start script for users from same office on the road
IF NETWORK_ADDRESS<>"0101C9DA" THEN BEGIN
        INCLUDE .TRAVEL.NOVELL
        GOTO COMMON
END
; Start Common info for all users
COMMON:
        WRITE "SUBNET: %NETWORK_ADDRESS"
        WRITE "LOCATION: %<LOCATION>"
        WRITE "APP SERVER: %<APPSRV>"
        WRITE "DEFAULT PRINTER: %<DEFPRNT>"
        MAP INS S1:="%FILE_SERVER\SYS:PUBLIC"
        MAP H:="%HOME_DIRECTORY"
        WRITE ""
END
EXIT
EXIT
```

As you can tell in the previous example, if a user is away from his or her home office, the network number will be different. This implies that you must maintain a network number for each office or segment in the login script. These numbers (hopefully) remain static, so this shouldn't present much of an administrative problem for you. You would duplicate the preceding script for each location by changing the network address for each location.

Next, you need to create the Profile script that we have called TRAVEL.PROFILE. An example of this script is shown here:

```
;TRAVEL PROFILE
; NOTE: The administrator must configure this file. For best
performance configure this script so that the most frequently
accessed network addresses are at the top of this list where
they will be found first. This form is parsed from top to
bottom until the correct network number is found. For example,
if you have many users going to the same office on business,
then you should have the network address for that office at
the top of the list of network addresses.
START:
```

```
;************************************************************
IIF NETWORK_ADDRESS ="0101D9CB" THEN BEGIN
     SET LOCATION = "NEW YORK OFFICE"
     SET APPSRV = "NYC-APP-1"
     SET DEFPRNT = \\NYC-PS-1\HP4SI-Q
     GOTO EXIT
END
;************************************************************
IF NETWORK ADDRESS = "0101D9CD" THEN BEGIN
     SET LOCATION = "LOS ANGELES"
     SET APPSRV = "LAX-APP-2"
     SET DEFPRNT = \\LAX-PS-2\HP5SI-Q
     GOTO EXIT
END
: NOTE: CONTINUE THIS SEQUENCE FOR EACH NETWORK ADDRESS
REMEMBERING TO PLACE THE MOST WIDELY USED LOCATIONS FIRST IN
YOUR LIST.
; ERROR GENERATION
Write "Contact your network administrator to add the
following network address to the Travel Profile Script."
Write "Network = %NETWORK_ADDRESS"
PAUSE
GOTO ERROR1
END
;************************************************************
ERROR1
     Write "Has the administrator updated the script?"
     GOTO START
END
EXIT:
EXIT
```

### Login Script Conventions

The conventions shown in Table 12.1 should be followed when implementing any login script.

**TABLE 12.1**

*Login Script Conventions*

| SCRIPT CONVENTIONS | CONVENTION DESCRIPTIONS |
| --- | --- |
| Minimum login script | No minimum. All types of login scripts are optional except the default login script, which executes unless turned off. |
| Case | Either uppercase or lowercase is acceptable. The exception to this is that identifier variables enclosed in quotation marks and preceded by a percent sign (%) must be uppercase |
| Character per line | Maximum 512 characters per line, including any variables after they are replaced by their values; 78 characters per line (common screen width) is recommended for readability. |
| Punctuation and symbols | Type all symbols (#, % ", _) and punctuation exactly as shown in examples and syntax. |
| Command per line | Use one command per line. Start each command on a new line; press Enter to end each command and start a new command. |
|  | Lines that wrap automatically are considered one command. |
| Sequence of Commands | Enter commands in the order that you want them to execute, with the following restrictions: |
|  | ATTACH commands (NetWare 3 only) must precede related MAP commands to avoid prompting the user for a username/password during login. |
|  | If you use # or @ to execute an external program, the command must follow any necessary MAP commands. If your sequence is not important, group similar commands, such as MAP and WRITE, together to make the login script easier to read. |
| Blank lines | Blank lines don't affect login script execution, Use them to visually separate groups of commands. |
| Remarks | Lines beginning with REMARK, REM, an asterisk, or a semicolon are viewed as comments, which are not displayed when the login script executes. |
| Identifier variables | Type identifier variables exactly as shown. To display the value of an identifier variable as part of a WRITE command, enclose the identifier in quotation marks and precede it by a percent sign (%). |

*continued*

| TABLE 12.1 | | |
| :--- | :--- | :--- |
| Login Script Conventions (continued) | | |
| **SCRIPT CONVENTIONS** | **CONVENTION DESCRIPTIONS** | |
| NDS Attribute Values | NDS eDirectory attribute values can be read from a login script, including extended names. The syntax for accessing NDS eDirectory attribute values is identical to common script variables with a few exceptions: | |
| | The NDS attribute must be at the end of the string. | |
| | If multiple variables are required, they must be in separate strings. | |
| | You must use the actual NDS attribute value names. You cannot use localized names or nicknames. | |
| | You must have Read rights to read the value of objects other than values associated with your own User object. | |
| NDS Object Mappings | NDS objects such as cluster-enabled volumes can be mapped in the login script using the object's fully distinguished name and context preceded by a leading dot (.). | |
| | To map a cluster-enabled volume, you would use the following syntax: MAP N:= .<NDS object's fully distinguished name including context>. | |
| | For example: MAP N:= .cluster2_vol1.xyz.provo.novell | |

### Login Command Switches

Table 12.2 lists the NetWare general login command switches and their syntaxes. Keep in mind that these command switches are for the DOS-based LOGIN.EXE only and do not apply to the Windows-based graphical login.

| TABLE 12.2 | | |
| :--- | :--- | :--- |
| NetWare Login Commands | | |
| **COMMAND** | **COMMAND SYNTAX** | **PURPOSE** |
| General Login Commands | LOGIN [File Server\] username [options] | Logs clients into a NetWare server with a bindery or NDS connection. |
| /NS (No Script option) | LOGIN /NS | Executes a login without a login script. |

| COMMAND | COMMAND SYNTAX | PURPOSE |
|---|---|---|
| /CLS (Clear Screen option) | LOGIN /CLS | Clears screen before execution of the login script. |
| /S (Script option) | LOGIN /S filename or LOGIN /S object name | Executes a login script contained in the text filename or NDS object name. |
| /B (Bindery option) | LOGIN /B | Logs into a server using bindery services. |
| /TR (Tree option) | LOGIN /TR treename | Specifies a certain NDS tree by its tree name for logging in. |
| /SWAP | LOGIN /SWAP | Swaps LOGIN.EXE into extended RAM if you use external commands from inside the login script. |
| /? (help option) | LOGIN /? | Provides a help screen. |

### Login Script Commands

Many login script commands can be used in any of the login scripts. Table 12.3 lists each login script command and its function.

TABLE 12.3

*Login Script Commands*

| COMMAND | FUNCTION |
|---|---|
| ATTACH | The ATTACH command allows you to attach workstations to other NetWare servers. The ATTACH command only provides a bindery services connection to the selected server. This command enables you to have login scripts that are compatible and coexist with previous versions of NetWare (specifically NetWare 2 and NetWare 3). This command no longer works on the command line for NetWare 6 but is still provided in login scripts as a means of backward compatibility with NetWare 3 scripts that may be migrated into NetWare 6. |
| BREAK | The BREAK command has two settings, either ON or OFF. The ON setting enables you to execute your login scripts by pressing Ctrl+C or Ctrl+Break. The default setting is always OFF. |

*continued*

**TABLE 12.3**

*Login Script Commands (continued)*

| COMMAND | FUNCTION |
|---------|----------|
| # CHARACTER | The # character provides external program execution. For example, to execute the capture program from within a login script, type: #program name |
| #CAPTURE L=1 Q=HP4SI NB NFF TI=1 | You can enter a complete pathname/ filename for the external program or make sure that the proper drive mapping and search drives have been set. The # character must be the first character on the line. |
| CLS | The CLS command clears the workstation screen or display. It is functionally similar to the CLS command that you can execute from DOS. |
| COMSPEC | The COMSPEC command specifies the subdirectory where DOS should load the command line processor called COMMAND.COM. |
| CONTEXT | The CONTEXT command is a smaller version of the CX.EXE command line utility that enables you to set the workstation context in the NDS tree. An example of using the CONTEXT command is as follows:<br><br>CONTEXT .R&D.NORAD.ACME |
| DISPLAY | The DISPLAY command enables you to show the contents of any file on the screen. The following syntax is used:<br><br>DISPLAY [pathname]\filename The difference between this command and the DISPLAY command discussed later in this section is that this command shows all the characters in the file including control codes and ESC sequences. |
| DOS BREAK | The DOS BREAK command has two settings, either ON or OFF. The ON setting enables you to terminate any DOS program that has been executed from the login script by pressing Ctrl+C or Ctrl+Break. The difference between this command and the BREAK command is that this command enables Ctrl+Break checking for DOS. The BREAK command checks only Ctrl+Break within the login script itself. |

| COMMAND | FUNCTION |
|---------|----------|
| DOS SET, TEMP SET, | These commands can be used to establish the DOS environment variables for the workstation and user. The syntax is as follows: [OPTION] [DOS] SET name = "value" The [OPTION] parameter can be used or replaced with an optional keyword. The keywords are TEMP, TEMPORARY, and LOCAL, which means that the variable is set only during the processing of the login script. The variable is not set in DOS. |
| DOS VERIFY | The DOS VERIFY command has two settings, either ON or OFF. The ON setting means that the data copied to the local drive is written without errors. |
| DRIVE | The DRIVE command specifies which network drive will be used as the default drive. |
| EXIT | The EXIT command tells the login script to terminate the processing of the login script and exit immediately. You can use the EXIT command in conjunction with the following program name: EXIT [filename] The login script passes control to the program specified. You should place the EXIT command statement as the last line in the individual login script. The EXIT command can be placed in system or container login scripts to guarantee that no individual user login scripts are executed. |
| FDISPLAY | The FDISPLAY command shows the contents of the specified text file on the screen. The following syntax is used: FDISPLAY [pathname]\filename Only the text or characters in the file are displayed. The control characters in the file are not shown. |
| FIRE PHASERS | The FIRE PHASERS command produces blasts that sound like you are firing a toy weapon. You can fire 1 to 9 phasers as dictated in the following syntax: FIRE PHASERS n TIMES (where n is the number of times) You typically use this command for special effects during the login process. |

*continued*

T A B L E   12.3

*Login Script Commands (continued)*

| COMMAND | FUNCTION |
| --- | --- |
| GOTO | The GOTO command enables you to program the login script and jump or repeat specific locations in the login script. You can place labels in the login script to control the GOTO statements. |
| IF ... THEN ... ELSE | The IF ... THEN ... ELSE command enables you to build conditional logic into the login scripts. This command lets you execute certain portions of the login scripts conditionally. |
| INCLUDE | The INCLUDE command enables you to direct the login script to specific files that you have predefined. The following syntax is used:<br><br>INCLUDE [pathname]\filename<br><br>The contents of the file specified in the INCLUDE statement are the next lines processed in the script. After the file has been processed, control is returned to the statement immediately following the INCLUDE statement in your login script. |
| LASTLOGINTIME | The LASTLOGINTIME command checks or displays the last date and time of login. |
| MACHINE | The MACHINE command sets the hardware machine type. This variable receives its value from the LONG MACHINE TYPE variable in the NET.CFG. The default value is IBM_PC. |
| MAP and MAP DISPLAY | The MAP command is equivalent to the MAP.EXE program. The command enables you to establish network drive mappings. The MAP DISPLAY command can be set to either ON or OFF. The ON setting shows all the drive mappings during the login process. The default is ON. The OFF setting does not show the drive mapping during the login procedure. |
| NO_DEFAULT | The NO_DEFAULT command disables the execution of the default login script, which is part of the LOGIN.EXE program. Disabling the default login script can be useful when you want to control all the drive mapping for the user. This includes the drive mapping to the SYS:PUBLIC subdirectory. |

| COMMAND | FUNCTION |
|---|---|
| PAUSE or WAIT | The PAUSE or WAIT commands cause the login script to stop execution until a key is pressed. This command permits long messages to be read without scrolling off the screen. This command can also be helpful when debugging the login script. |
| PCCOMPATIBLE | The PCCOMPATIBLE command indicates that the workstation hardware is compatible with an IBM PC. For some workstations, if you do not use this command, some NetWare utilities such as NETADMIN and FILER will not work. |
| REMARK or REM | The REMARK command documents the lines or place comments in the login script file. The use of comments always improves the readability and maintenance of the scripts. To place comments in the login scripts, the following syntax is used:<br><br>REM [text]<br><br>Or<br><br>* text<br><br>or<br><br>; text |
| WRITE | The WRITE command displays text messages to the workstation screen during the login process. The following syntax is used:<br><br>WRITE [text]<br><br>You can use the semicolon (;) to join together text messages. |

**Login Variables**

NetWare 6 has always had the capability to use login variables in login scripts to help you manage the login scripts and make them more efficient and flexible. Table 12.4 lists the login script variables and their definitions that can be used to enhance your login scripts. These variables can be used in the login script to help you do the following:

- Build conditional statements
- Provide date and time functions
- Establish DOS environment and workstation settings
- Provide NDS properties to the user

TABLE 12.4

*Conditional Statement Login Script Variables*

| VARIABLE | FUNCTION |
|---|---|
| %ACCESS_SERVER | Displays or checks whether the access server is functional (TRUE=functional, FALSE=not functional). |
| %ERROR_LEVEL | Displays or checks the DOS error level. A value of 0 indicates that no DOS errors have occurred. For example, this variable can be used to see whether a drive mapping was successful. |
| %MEMBER OF "group" | Tests to see whether the user is a member of the "group." Returns TRUE or FALSE. |
| %NOT MEMBER OF "group" | Returns TRUE if the user is *not* a member of the "group." |

Most of the variables can be displayed using the WRITE login script command preceding the variable. Some examples are also provided in the use of these variables. In Table 12.3, note that some of the variables have underscores in them and some do not. This is perhaps due to inconsistencies in coding these parameters.

Table 12.5 lists the date and time login variables.

TABLE 12.5

*Date and Time Login Script Variables*

| VARIABLE | FUNCTION |
|---|---|
| %AM_PM | Displays time as day or night, using A.M. or P.M. |
| %DAY | Displays the current day value ranging from 01 to 31. |
| %DAY_OF_WEEK | Displays the written day of the week. |
| %GREETING_TIME | Displays the time of day as morning, afternoon, or evening. |
| %HOUR | Displays the time of day in hours ranging from 1 to 12. |
| %HOUR24 | Displays the hour in 24-hour time ranging from 00 to 23. |
| %MINUTE | Displays the minutes ranging from 00 to 59. |
| %MONTH | Displays the month (from 01 to 12). |
| %MONTH_NAME | Displays the name of the month. |
| %NDAY_OF_WEEK | Displays the number of the week day. |

| VARIABLE | FUNCTION |
|---|---|
| %SECOND | Displays the seconds ranging from 00 to 59. |
| %SHORT_YEAR | Displays the year in short format (92, 93, 94, 95, 96, 97, and so on). |
| %YEAR | Displays the year in full format (1992, 1993, and so on). |

Any DOS environment variable can be used in a login script if you place angle brackets (< and >) around the variable. A common example of a DOS variable used in login scripts is as follows:

```
<COMSPEC>
```

In order to use a DOS environment variable with login script commands, you need to add a percent sign (%) in front of the variable. For example, to map a drive to the COMSPEC DOS environment variable, type this:

```
MAP S16:=%<COMSPEC>
```

The list of DOS environment and workstation variables in Table 12.6 helps to set up the workstation for the specific network users. Some variables have more than one keyword, which is shown in parentheses.

TABLE 12.6

*DOS Environments and Workstation Variables*

| VARIABLE | FUNCTION |
|---|---|
| %LAST_NAME | Displays the user's last name (surname) in Novell Directory Services, or full login name in bindery-based NetWare. This value returns the same result as the SURNAME variable in the user properties. |
| %LOGIN_ALIAS_ CONTEXT | Displays the context of the alias object that the user logged in with. This variable is valid only with NDS. |
| %LOGIN_CONTEXT | Displays the context for the user. Returns the context where the user exists in the NDS tree. This variable works only with NetWare 6. |
| %LOGIN_NAME | Displays the user's login name. This returns the same result as the CN variable in the user property list, although CN is multivalued. |

*continued*

T A B L E   12.6

*DOS Environments and Workstation Variables (continued)*

| VARIABLE | FUNCTION |
| --- | --- |
| %MACHINE | Displays the machine type of a workstation (IBM_PC, and so on). |
| %NEW_MAIL | Displays the status of the variable. |
| %OS | Displays the type of operating system on the workstation (MSDOS, OS2, and so on). |
| %OS_VERSION | Displays the operating system version on the workstation (3.30, and so on). |
| %P_STATION (PHYSICAL_STATION) | The workstation's node number is shown as a 12-digit hexadecimal. |
| %PASSWORD_ EXPIRES | Displays the number of days before the user password will expire. |
| %REQUESTER_VERSION | (optional names: NETWARE_REQUESTER, REQUESTER) Displays the version of the VLM requester. |
| %REQUESTER_ CONTEXT | Displays the context that is found in the workstation's NET.CFG file at the time of login. |
| %SHELL_TYPE (SHELL_VERSION) | Displays the version of the workstation's DOS shell (1.02, and so on); supports NetWare 2 and 3 shells and NetWare 4 Requester for DOS. |
| %STATION (CONNECTION) | Displays the workstation address for that user. |

NetWare 6 extends the list of login variables, as shown in Table 12.7, through the use of the user properties found in NDS. If the property includes a space, enclose the name in quotation marks or replace the spaces with an underscore.

T A B L E   12.7

*NDS User Properties Variables*

| VARIABLE | FUNCTION |
| --- | --- |
| %ACCOUNT_BALANCE | Displays account balance information if being used. |
| %ALLOW UNLIMITED CREDIT | Displays whether unlimited credit has been assigned for that user. The value returned is "Y" or "N." |

| VARIABLE | FUNCTION |
| --- | --- |
| %BACKLINK | Established for any user object in which there is an associated external reference on a different server. |
| %BINDERY PROPERTY | Used to emulate the bindery properties that are not represented by the other user properties. |
| %CN | Displays the login name of the user who logs in to the network. |
| %DESCRIPTION | Displays any value contained in the description property for the user. |
| %EMAIL ADDRESS | Displays the first value in the e-mail address property for the user. |
| %EQUIVALENT TO ME | Displays only the first value in the list. |
| %FACSIMILE TELEPHONE NUMBER | Displays the first number in the fax number property for the user. |
| %FULL NAME | Displays the user's full name value. This value is the property stored in NDS and the bindery if the server is bindery-based NetWare. Spaces are replaced with underscores. |
| %GROUP MEMBERSHIP | Displays the values of the membership attributes. |
| %HOME DIRECTORY | Displays the complete path for the home directory property set for the user who has logged in. |
| %INITIALS | Displays the value of the user's middle initial property. |
| %L | Displays the first value of the location property for the user. |
| %LANGUAGE | Displays the current language being used by the user. |
| %LOCKED BY INTRUDER | Displays the status of the locked by intruder property. The value returned is "Y" for yes or "N" for no. |
| %LOGIN DISABLED | Displays the account disable status. The value returned is "Y" for yes or "N" for no. |
| %LOGIN GRACE LIMIT | Displays the value of the login grace limit property. |
| %LOGIN GRACE REMAINING | Displays the number of remaining grace logins for the user. |

*continued*

TABLE 12.7

*NDS User Properties Variables (continued)*

| VARIABLE | FUNCTION |
|---|---|
| %LOGIN INTRUDER ATTEMPTS | Displays the number of incorrect login attempts for the user. |
| %LOGIN MAXIMUM SIMULTANEOUS | Displays the value of the maximum simultaneous connections for the user. |
| %LOGIN TIME | Displays both the date and time of the login time for the user. |
| %MAILBOX ID | Displays the mailbox ID for the user. |
| %MAILBOX LOCATION | Displays the mailbox location for the user. MHS can, but does not have to, be installed in order to have a value for the mailbox location. |
| %MESSAGE SERVER | Displays the default server or message server name. |
| %MINIMUM ACCOUNT BALANCE | Displays the value of the minimum account balance or low balance limit. |
| %NETWORK ADDRESS | Displays the physical network address, node, and socket number for the workstation. |
| %OBJECT CLASS | Displays the base class for the user object. |
| %OU | Shows the first value defined in the Department list for the user. |
| %PASSWORD ALLOW CHANGE | Shows the value of this user property, "Y" or "N." |
| %PASSWORD EXPIRATION INTERVAL | Displays the time in total seconds before the user password will expire. |
| %PASSWORD MINIMUM LENGTH | Displays the minimum password length setting for the user. |
| %PASSWORD REQUIRED | Displays the value of the password required. Displays or returns "Y" or "N." |
| %PASSWORD UNIQUE REQUIRED | Displays the property value of unique password required. Displays or returns "Y" or "N." |
| %PHYSICAL DELIVERY OFFICE NAME | Displays the value of the city property for the user. |
| %POSTAL CODE | Displays the value of the user's postal zip code, if any. |
| %POSTAL OFFICE BOX | Displays the user's postal office box value, if any. |

| VARIABLE | FUNCTION |
|---|---|
| %PROFILE | Displays the name of the profile object if the user is associated with a profile. |
| %REVISION | Displays the value of the revision property for the user. The revision increments each time the user is accessed. |
| %S | Displays the value of the state or province property for the user. |
| %SA | Displays the value of the street address for the user. |
| %SECURITY EQUALS | Displays security equivalence assignments made for that user. Only displays the first value in the list. |
| %SEE ALSO | Displays the first value in the see also property for the user. |
| %SERVER HOLDS | Displays the number of accounting charges pending while the server performs a chargeable action. |
| %SURNAME (LAST_NAME) | Displays the user's surname property value, if any — the user's last name (surname) in NetWare Directory Services, or full login name in bindery-based NetWare. |
| %TELEPHONE NUMBER | Shows the user's phone entered in his phone number property. Only displays the first value in the list. |
| %TITLE | Displays the title for the user if one has been entered as a user property. Only shows the first value in the list. |
| %UID | Displays a unique user ID assigned to the user for use by UNIX clients. |

# Additional Login Scripts for Your Desktops

The following scripts provide a sample script for Windows 95, Windows NT, and mixed environments.

## LOGIN Script Information for Windows 95

The file locations are as follows:

| NET$LOG.DAT | SYS:PUBLIC |
|---|---|
| *.BAT files | SYS:PUBLIC\CLIENT\WIN95\IBM_ENU |
| *.REG files | SYS:PUBLIC\CLIENT\WIN95\IBM_ENU |

The *.BAT and *.REG files reflect the user location in the NDS tree to set up the proper context on the workstation. If you place the client update information at the end of the login script, you do not affect any other clients using that script, provided you have not made any typing errors. For this reason, you may want to create a TESTC32 user ID and use the "%LOGIN_NAME" variable. After the script is tested, you may then use "IF MEMBER OF GROUP" to automate multiple client upgrades without having to touch the workstations.

### NET$LOG.DAT

```
Write "Good %GREETING_TIME, %FULL_NAME"
IF "%LOGIN_NAME" = "TESTC32" THEN GOTO UPDATE
IF MEMBER OF GROUP "TESTC32" THEN GOTO UPDATE
Write "This is the Bindery Login Script"
END
EXIT
UPDATE:
Write "This will update the MS Client to Client 32"
IF "%LOGIN_NAME" = "TESTC32" BEGIN
IF MEMBER OF "GROUP1" THEN BEGIN
MAP Y:=DEMOSRVR\SYS:PUBLIC\CLIENT\WIN95\IBM_ENU
DRIVE Y:
EXIT "GROUP1.BAT"
END
IF MEMBER OF "GROUP2" THEN BEGIN
MAP Y:=DEMOSRVR\SYS:PUBLIC\CLIENT\WIN95\IBM_ENU
DRIVE Y:
EXIT "GROUP2.BAT"
END
```

### GROUP1.BAT

```
SETUP.EXE /ACU /N /U:Y:DEMOSRVR\SYS:PUBLIC\CLIENT\WIN95\
IBM_ENU\GROUP1.TXT
REGEDIT /S GROUP1.REG
```

## GROUP1.REG

```
REGEDIT4

[HKEY_LOCAL_MACHINE\Network\Novell\System Config\Network
Provider\Graphical Login]
"Tree Login"=dword:00000001
"Server Login"=dword:00000000
"Connection Tab"=dword:00000001
"Bindery Connections"=dword:00000000
"Clear Connections"=dword:00000001
"Script Tab"=dword:00000000
"Display Results"=dword:00000001
"Close Results"=dword:00000001
"Login Script"=dword:00000001
"Script Variable Tab"=dword:00000000
"Save On Exit"=dword:00000000
[HKEY_LOCAL_MACHINE\Network\Novell\System Config\Network
Provider\Graphical Login\Scripts]
[HKEY_LOCAL_MACHINE\Network\Novell\System Config\Network
Provider\Graphical Login\Scripts\1]
@=""

[HKEY_LOCAL_MACHINE\Network\Novell\System Config\Network
Provider\Graphical Login\Profiles]
[HKEY_LOCAL_MACHINE\Network\Novell\System Config\Network
Provider\Graphical Login\Profiles\1]
@=""

[HKEY_LOCAL_MACHINE\Network\Novell\System Config\Network
Provider\Graphical Login\Variables]
[HKEY_LOCAL_MACHINE\Network\Novell\System Config\Network
Provider\Graphical Login\Variables\2]
@=""

[HKEY_LOCAL_MACHINE\Network\Novell\System Config\Network
Provider\Graphical Login\Variables\3]
@=""

[HKEY_LOCAL_MACHINE\Network\Novell\System Config\Network
Provider\Graphical Login\Variables\4]
@=""
```

```
[HKEY_LOCAL_MACHINE\Network\Novell\System Config\Network
Provider\Graphical Login\Variables\5]
@=""
[HKEY_LOCAL_MACHINE\Network\Novell\System Config\Network
Provider\Graphical Login\NWLGE]
[HKEY_LOCAL_MACHINE\Network\Novell\System Config\Network
Provider\Graphical Login\NWLGE\Z XContext]
"LoginExtType"=hex:01,80,00,00
"LoginExtName"="LGNCON32.DLL"
"LoginExtDesc"="Login Extension Contextless Login"
"AllowWild"=hex:00,00,00,00
"RunContext"=hex:00,00,00,00
[HKEY_LOCAL_MACHINE\Network\Novell\System Config\Network
Provider\Graphical Login\Results Pos]
"Left"=dword:0000014f
"Top"=dword:0000011d
"Right"=dword:000002b0
"Bottom"=dword:000001e1
"XRes"=dword:00000400
"YRes"=dword:00000300
"State"=dword:00000000
[HKEY_LOCAL_MACHINE\Network\Novell\System Config\Network
Provider\Graphical Login\Trees]
[HKEY_LOCAL_MACHINE\Network\Novell\System Config\Network
Provider\Graphical Login\Trees\2]
@="TREE_NAME"
[HKEY_LOCAL_MACHINE\Network\Novell\System Config\Network
Provider\Graphical Login\Context]
[HKEY_LOCAL_MACHINE\Network\Novell\System Config\Network
Provider\Graphical Login\Context\2]
@="GROUP1.DALLAS.NOVELL"
[HKEY_LOCAL_MACHINE\Network\Novell\System Config\NetWare DOS
Requester]
[HKEY_LOCAL_MACHINE\Network\Novell\System Config\NetWare DOS
Requester\Preferred Server]
"0"=""
```

```
[HKEY_LOCAL_MACHINE\Network\Novell\System Config\NetWare DOS
Requester\First Network Drive]
"0"="F"
[HKEY_LOCAL_MACHINE\Network\Novell\System Config\NetWare DOS
Requester\module]
@="C:\\NOVELL\\CLIENT32\\CLIENT32.NLM"
[HKEY_LOCAL_MACHINE\Network\Novell\System Config\NetWare DOS
Requester\init order]
@="A0010100"
[HKEY_LOCAL_MACHINE\Network\Novell\System Config\NetWare DOS
Requester\Preferred Tree]
"0"="TREE_NAME"
[HKEY_LOCAL_MACHINE\Network\Novell\System Config\NetWare DOS
Requester\Preferred Tree\Trees]
"TREE_NAME"="GROUP1.DALLAS.NOVELL"
[HKEY_LOCAL_MACHINE\Network\Novell\System Config\NetWare DOS
Requester\Name Context]
"0"="GROUP1.DALLAS.NOVELL"
[HKEY_CURRENT_USER\InstallLocationsMRU]
"a"="\\\\DEMOSRVR\\SYS\\DESKTOPS\\WIN95\\"
"MRUList"="a"
[HKEY_USERS\.Default\InstallLocationsMRU]
"a"="\\\\DEMOSRVR\\SYS\\DESKTOPS\\WIN95\\"
"MRUList"="a"
```

The last six lines on this page were added simply to assist in pointing the desktop machines to a location where the Windows 95/98 install files (*.CAB) are located.

## An NDS Container Login Script for Windows 95 Clients

After Client 32 is installed, the container login scripts need to be updated to reflect the information that these clients were getting in the NET$LOG.DAT file. Also, any necessary changes to a Windows 95 Client 32 configuration can be made via the container login script or a profile login script. To do this, simply add these lines to the end of the login script:

```
REM The Novell Login Interpreter will read the %OS variable
and the Microsoft interpreter will not
```

```
REM and continue to the next line
IF "%OS" = "WIN95" THEN
    IF ERRORLEVEL = "0"
        WRITE "You are currently using Novell Client 32 for
Windows 95"
        ELSE
            GOTO NOC32
        END
        GOTO WIN95C32
END


NOC32:
IF <OS> ="WIN95" THEN
    IF ERRORLEVEL = "0"
        WRITE "You are currently using Microsoft Client for
Novell Networks"
        ELSE
            GOTO NOT95
        END
        GOTO MAPLE
END


WIN95C32:
    REM This Win95 client is currently using Client 32 and
will automatically update if needed
    REM If the client is up to date no changes are made. To
make a change edit the
    REM  NWSETUP.INI and change the version number. This file
is located in the
    REM SYS:PUBLIC\CLIENT\WIN95\IBM_ENU directory.
    @\\DEMOSRVR\sys\public\client\win95\ibm_enu\setup.exe /
acu /n
    MAP K:=DEMOSRVR\SYS:
    END
EXIT
```

```
    REM You may also use NCIMAN.EXE to create an update file
and use the following line:
    @\\DEMOSRVR\sys\public\client\win95\ibm_enu\setup.exe /acu
/n /U:\\DEMOSRVR\sys\public\client\win95\ibm_enu\update.txt
    END
EXIT
NOT95:
    REM Clients that are NOT Win95 will now EXIT
    Write "You are seeing this because you are not using a
recognizable Desktop OS"
    Write "Please call your network administrator or the help
desk"
    PAUSE
    END
EXIT
```

## An NDS Container Login Script for Windows NT Clients

Windows NT clients are handled a bit differently than in the Windows 95 script. The Microsoft Client for NetWare on NT reads the container login script. To update the NT workstations, change the login script by adding these lines to the end:

```
IF "%OS" = "WINNT" THEN
    GOTO WINNTC32
END
IF <OS> = "Windows_NT" THEN
    GOTO WINNTMS
END
WINNTC32:
    REM This WINNT client is currently using Client 32 and
will automatically update if needed
    REM If the client is up to date no changes are made. To
make a change edit the
    REM UNATTEND.TXT and change the version number. This file
is located in the
    REM SYS:PUBLIC\CLIENT\WINNT\I386\NLS\ENGLISH directory.
```

```
@\\DEMOSRVR\sys\public\client\winnt\i386\setup.exe /acu /u:\\
DEMOSRVR\sys\public\client\winnt\i386\nls\english\unattend.txt
    END
EXIT
WINNTMS:
    WRITE "This is an NT Client and the current seen is %OS"
    Write "This is MS Client  section for Windows NT"
    IF <COMSPEC> = "C:\WINNT\COMMAND.COM"  OR  <COMSPEC> =
"C:\WINNT\SYSTEM32\CMD.EXE" THEN BEGIN
    Write "The IF COMSPEC Worked and the next 2 lines will
execute"
REM If the next 2 lines are NOT read than check the COMSPEC
on the NT Workstation and edit
REM the login script to reflect additional COMSPEC.
MAP M:=DEMOSRVR\SYS:PUBLIC\WINNT
#\\DEMOSRVR\sys\public\client\winnt\i386\setupnw.exe /acu
/u:\\DEMOSRVR\sys\public\client\winnt\i386\nls\english\
unattend.txt
END
EXIT
```

## A Login Script for Mixed Environment of Windows Clients

NCIMAN.EXE is a new 32-bit GUI tool that provides an easy way to automatically update the clients using Novell Client 32.

### Using NCIMAN.EXE

The Win95.TXT file looks like this:

```
[Novell_Client_Install_Manager]
Novell_Client=95

[Novell_Client_Parameters]
Preferred_Server=DEMOSRVR
Preferred_Tree=NOVELL_INC
Name_Context=OU=NORAD.O=ACME
```

```
Clear_Current_Connections=NO
Close_Script_Results_Automatically=NO
Save_Settings_When_Exiting_Login=NO
Show_Location_List=YES
Show_Clear_Connections=NO
Log_File=C:\Novell\Client32\LOG.TXT
Preferred_Server_Distribute=Always
Preferred_Tree_Distribute=Always
Name_Context_Distribute=Always
Clear_Current_Connections_Distribute=Always
Close_Script_Results_Automatically_Distribute=Always
Save_Settings_When_Exiting_Login_Distribute=Always
Show_Location_List_Distribute=Always
Show_Clear_Connections_Distribute=Always
Log_File_Distribute=Always


Windows NT file


[Novell_Client_Install_Manager]
Novell_Client=NT


[SetupNWInstallOptions]
!DisplayInitialScreen=NO
!AskReboot=NO


[NovellNetWareClientParameters]
!AcceptLicenseAgreement=YES
!Preferred_Server=DEMOSRVR
!Preferred_Server_Distribute=Always
!Preferred_Tree=KP_DEMO_TREE
!Preferred_Tree_Distribute=Always
!Tree_List1=KP_DEMO_TREE
!Tree_List_Distribute=Replace
```

```
!Default_Context_List1=Norad.Acme
!Default_Context_List_Distribute=Replace
!Welcome_Screen_Caption=Novell Consulting
!Welcome_Screen_Caption_Distribute=Always

[RemoteControlParameters]
!DoInstall=YES

[WorkstationManagerParameters]
!Workstation_Manager_Tree=KP_DEMO_TREE
!Workstation_Manager_Tree_Distribute=Always

[Unattended]
OemPreinstall=YES

[Network]
InstallServices=ServicesList

[ServicesList]
NWFS=NovellNetwareClientParameters, \$OEM$\NET\NTCLIENT\I386
WM=WorkstationManagerParameters, \$OEM$\NET\NTCLIENT\I386
WUA=RemoteControlParameters, \$OEM$\NET\NTCLIENT\I386
```

## Summary

In this chapter, we reviewed the Novell Client 32 architecture and the basic methods for client access, including types of NDS scripts and sample login scripts. Designing for network access is an important step in your NDS design, and this chapter highlighted the different types of access available with the Novell clients and the benefits of using an NDS connection. We also presented sample login scripts for Windows 95 and Windows NT users.

# Managing NetWare Security

> *"Even in the common affairs of life, in love, friendship, and marriage,*
> *how little security have we when we trust our happiness*
> *in the hands of others!"* — *William Hazlitt*

As networks become increasingly more distributed, the exposure of information has also increased. Therefore, it makes sense that in large networked environments, you have to pay more attention to security and take measures to ensure that your data is protected.

Securing your network actually encompasses many areas of security including physical access, login, NDS, and file system restrictions. Other areas that can be classified within the physical access category include natural disasters and hardware failures. Another area of security violations is caused unintentionally by users who have authorized access and simply make mistakes. Computer viruses also pose a threat to security and can be caused intentionally or unintentionally.

Although each of these areas is important, the goal is to secure your important data from theft, eavesdropping, or destruction. Every organization may place greater emphasis on a particular aspect of security depending on the sensitivity of the data. Some organizations may attempt to enforce all available aspects of security, while other companies may concentrate on only a few areas. As a network administrator, you must decide along with your other managers what is an acceptable level of security versus risk for your department or company's data. Any level of security that you implement is more than what your users will want because of additional burdens placed on their ability to freely work on the network.

Some companies may be especially prone to disasters because of their geographical location and natural weather conditions. Other companies may be at a greater hardware risk because they are running their network in a factory or plant where the possibility of fire or other damage is greater.

This chapter discusses these topics including securing physical access to hardware, understanding the authentication and login process, and applying NDS restrictions. NDS restrictions include security for objects and properties as well as for the file system. These various levels of security are represented in Figure 13.1.

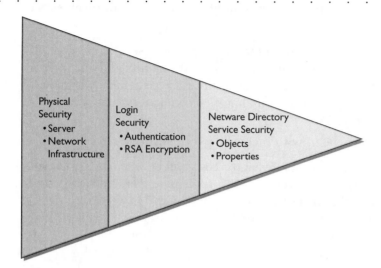

**FIGURE 13.1** *Security can be broken down into the categories of physical security, login security, and NDS security.*

# Designing a Security Policy

One of the first steps to implementing security for your environment is to design what is commonly referred to as a security policy. A *security policy* is basically your own company's road map for implementing security. Consider the following questions when implementing your security plan:

**What security threats do you have at your company?**

▶ You must evaluate all aspects of threats, including your building's age and entrance policies, the geographic location, the experience level of your users, the number of users, the age of your server hardware, and access points to your network from locations outside your company. *Access points* refer to gateways or other routing devices connected to the Internet or other wide-area links.

**What security do you currently have in place and what improvements can be made?**

▸ Most companies usually have some form of network security in place. If your network is growing or if you have recently connected to the Internet, you should consider increasing your security. If your company is in the process of relocating to a new building, you should reevaluate your security measures.

**What costs are associated with increasing your security?**

▸ You have to take into account what the costs will be when increasing your security. Will your added security measures require more staff to assist with this aspect? Will the changes require the purchase of newer, more expensive hardware such as tape backups and virus protection software? How much more administration time is needed to service each user? What is the cost of your downtime if your network should have a failure?

**Are you reviewing your security processes on a continual basis?**

▸ Each network administrator should perform a regular security check on the network to determine if new workstations or any other new devices have been added to the network. A review will also determine if any security policies need to be modified based on any other changes that may have occurred on the network.

# Controlling Physical Access to Your Hardware

One of the most basic aspects of providing a secure network is to physically secure your servers and workstations. If possible, your servers should be protected in a locked room such as a data center or wiring closet. Many large companies already place servers in their data centers. Smaller companies may not have this option, but other steps can be taken to help safeguard your servers, as explained in the next section.

## Network Hardware Security

Network administrators can secure their physical networks by encasing their network wiring in conduit to prohibit intrusion. Again, your company and administrators must determine if such an enormous expense is needed to secure your particular data.

You also should consider taking the following steps to secure your servers:

▸ Keep all servers in a data center or an air-conditioned locked room and limit access to these areas.

▸ Provide a tape backup for all servers on your network to back up files as well as NDS. Restore data to a test directory to periodically check that the restore procedure is working properly.

▸ Remove DOS from the file server by typing **REMOVE DOS** at the server console.

▸ Use an auditing tool such as Novell's AUDITCON or another third-party utility to track server events on highly sensitive servers.

▸ Lock the file server console using MONITOR.NLM and do not store the password in the AUTOEXEC.NCF file.

▸ Require passwords for print servers that need to log into the NetWare 6 servers.

▸ Periodically check containers that are under your responsibility for new objects. Investigate all new objects added to your containers.

▸ Carefully control the use of RCONSOLE and its password. You can encrypt the RCONSOLE password for your AUTOEXEC.NCF by following these steps:

**1.** At a NetWare 6 console type **REMOTE ENCRYPT**.

**2.** You are then prompted for an RCONSOLE password to be encrypted.

**3.** After you enter the password, the file LDREMOTE.NCF is created.

**4.** You can call this file in your AUTOEXEC.NCF or copy the contents out of the file into your AUTOEXEC.NCF.

## Controlling Physical Access to Workstations

Workstations are more problematic to secure because some of your employees may use notebook computers that are transported away from the office each day. Also, very few companies ever go to the bother of physically securing workstations to desks or tables. Even if your users have stationary computers, the possibility always exists that unauthorized individuals will have access to your data.

You can limit access to your servers through Novell's station restriction and time restrictions procedures, which can be accomplished with the ConsoleOne or NWADMIN utility. These procedures limit a user to a particular workstation for logging in and also limit access to specific times of the day.

You should consider taking the following steps to secure your workstations:

▶ Encourage users not to leave their workstations unattended while logged into the network unless they are using password-protected screen saver software.

▶ Always log out of the network before leaving your work location for the day.

▶ Keep office doors locked when not in use and workstations powered off if possible.

▶ Administrators especially should not leave their workstations unattended while logged in with Supervisor rights to the tree, its containers, or servers.

▶ At a minimum, you should have an asset tag for each piece of hardware on your network in case of theft or other damage.

▶ Use an antivirus product for your network that is loaded from the container login script.

▶ Carefully monitor the use of the ADMIN or any tree administrator user object. Change the password frequently.

▶ Require periodic changes in users' passwords. Do not allow them to use the same password twice.

▶ Have a company policy that no floppy disks are to be brought into the workplace unless they are scanned for viruses first.

▶ Closely monitor dial-in access and employ automatic callback features built into remote dial software.

## Understanding the Login and Authentication Process

After you have physically secured your servers, the NetWare 6 login security is the next line of defense in network security. The authentication procedure verifies that any requests that the server receives are from legitimate clients. The authentication process consists of the login and the authentication. NetWare 6 uses its own authentication process. This process is extremely secure and is known as encryption (which is discussed later in this section).

### Password Security and Verification

The purpose in having a password is to prevent unauthorized access to your network resources. The directory security must be reinforced by all network users and administrators practicing good password security. Any disclosure of passwords allows a user to access that account to the extent of that user's rights. Therefore, you can take numerous precautions to secure your network, but the human factor is always the biggest threat to your security. You can take some steps to help minimize the threat of a password breach in your security:

▸ Without exception, require user passwords for all users.

▸ Always require periodic changes of passwords for mobile users dialing into your network or users who work from home.

▸ Users should never post their passwords anywhere.

▸ Users should be encouraged to avoid easy passwords such as family member names, and so on.

Through the NetWare utilities, you can do the following:

▸ Require a minimum password length of five to eight characters.

▸ Enforce periodic changes of passwords.

▸ Enforce unique passwords.

▸ Frequently change the password for your ADMIN or tree administrator user objects.

## RSA Encryption/Decryption

NDS uses encryption to secure authentication information that is being sent across the network from one server to other servers or from a workstation to a server for authentication purposes. NetWare 6 uses the RSA encryption technology to provide public and private key encryption. The encryption process produces transmissions across the network that are unreadable except to the receiving entity.Public and private key encryption is also known as *asymmetrical cryptography* because the two keys have a mathematical relationship. If data is encrypted with the object's public key, the receiving object uses its private key to decrypt the information. The public key can be read by any requesting object. The receiving object holds the private key but never discloses it. Figure 13.2 shows the relationship between the public and private keys during transmission of authentication data. Keep in mind that only server objects keep their own private keys. Users obtain their encrypted private keys during the login process. These keys are then decrypted, used to generate a signature, and discarded.

**FIGURE 13.2** *The use of public and private key encryption of authentication data*

NDS eDirectory uses encryption to ensure that authentication information is secure while it is being transmitted on the wire. There is always a public key/private key pair for each encrypted transaction. To prevent intrusion during a transmission by capturing and replaying encrypted messages, the NetWare authentication process uses what is known as a nonce value. A *nonce value* is a random value that is generated for each encrypted transaction. The nonce value is associated only once with each encrypted message. Because the nonce is used only once, it will not do an intruder any good to capture an encrypted message and attempt to impersonate the sender.

Each transaction uses the network layer infrastructure to send and receive packets. This means that for authentication, TCP/IP and NCP requests are made between client and server, but for NDS eDirectory authentication, the data is encrypted before transmission on the wire. Keep in mind that the term *client* can mean a server holding part of the directory communicating with another server in the directory.

## The User Login

The first step to authenticating in a NetWare 6 environment is the identification phase, also known as the login phase. When the user first logs into a NetWare 6 server, the user must establish his identity with the server and then proceed through the authentication phase. This is accomplished by the client broadcasting a service request, with the broadcast type 0x0278 if the preferred tree is set on, or the broadcast type 0x0004 if the preferred server is set. A server or router that receives this request replies with a response. The client examines the response and accepts the first response with the correct tree/server being sought. This gets the client a connection to begin the tree walking (resolve name operation). NDS then searches the tree to find a writeable replica of the user's object. At that point, the login and authentication phases that are discussed next occur.

### Login Phase

The following steps occur during the login phase:

1. After a writeable replica is found with the user object, the user is prompted for a name and password.
2. After successfully proving knowledge of the password, the client receives the encrypted private key from the server.
3. The private key of the client is used to generate a signature.
4. The public key of the client is used to generate a credential.
5. The signature and credential are used to build a proof that is used later in this sequence.

### Authentication Phase

The following steps occur during the authentication phase:

1. The public key attribute of the server is read by the requesting client.
2. The proof previously generated is encrypted with the server's public key and sent to the server.
3. The server decrypts the proof with the server's private key.
4. The proof is verified by the server through a mathematical computation of the client's public key and the client key stored on the server.
5. If the proof is correct, authentication is successful.
6. The finished authentication request then calls the directory for the user's security equivalence vector.
7. The login process is then passed back to the directory to execute the applicable login script and apply NDS access controls.

Keep in mind that the client's password is never transmitted across the wire. Therefore, it is not possible for anyone to capture a password packet on the wire. In addition, the authentication data is valid only during the current login session. If a user terminates the session and then reconnects, the authentication process is repeated.

**NOTE** **Another feature, known as *packet signing*, requires each packet to have a valid signature in order to be executed by the server. Packet signing makes it far more difficult for someone to forge NCP packets and send them on to the server for processing.**

## Background Authentication

During the initial login process, a NetWare client identifies a hosting server. Although the login process in NetWare 6 is performed only once, the authentication process may occur throughout the entire session in order to enable services from other servers.

*Background authentication* is the ongoing identification process that occurs after the initial login. If a connection needs to be made to other network services, authentication is done through the process of background authentication. Background authentication can occur because the NetWare 6 servers can verify the proof provided by the client from the client's public key without additional user intervention. A server making a request of another server is also considered a client. Keep in mind that the proof is constructed at the client using the signature, credential, and public key.

When a user logs out of the network, the NetWare 6 license manager is notified and makes the license available to any other validated user needing a license. The logout includes destroying the service connection to all but one server along with all bindings that were part of the user connection. The authentication data is also destroyed on the workstation at logout.

## Other Login and Authentication Security Features in NetWare 6

Several other important security features in NetWare 6 have been integrated with NDS eDirectory. These features also provide security for improved Internet data integrity and privacy across public networks. The security features include Public Key Infrastructure Services (PKIS), Novell International Cryptographic Infrastructure (NICI), Secure Authentication Services (SAS), and the audit system. This section briefly discusses these features and explains why they are important and how they provide NetWare 6 with advanced security services.

### Public Key Infrastructure Services (PKIS)

NetWare includes Public Key Infrastructure Services, which supports public-key cryptography and digital certificates in the NetWare environment. Digital certificates provide a method for checking the authenticity of keys used in a public-key cryptographic session. In NetWare 6, PKIS allows you either to act as your own certificate authority or to use the services of third-party certificate authorities. Through PKIS, you can generate and sign various types of digital certificates and store and manage these certificates within NDS.

PKIS enables any designated NetWare 6 administrators to establish a Certificate Authority (CA) management domain within NDS. PKIS allows administrators to manage certificates and keys for Secure Sockets Layer (SSL) security for LDAP servers.

Certificate management includes services such as establishment of a CA local to your organization, certificate renewal, simplified certificate revocation with certificate suspension (without complex certificate revocation lists), creation of certificate signing requests (for use with external CAs), unlimited certificate minting services for applications, and using SSL in the NetWare environment (such as Novell LDAP Services for NDS eDirectory).

Using PKIS, you can control the costs associated with obtaining key pairs and managing public key certificates. PKIS helps you create a local CA based on the directory that signs certificates for other services on the network. With PKIS, you can also generate unlimited key pairs and issue unlimited public key certificates through the local CA at no charge.

NDS eDirectory stores all keys and certificates that are generated by PKIS or obtained from external CAs. NDS's trusted directory features means that public keys can be openly published, while private keys are securely protected.

### Novell International Cryptographic Infrastructure (NICI)

NetWare includes cryptographic services named Novell International Cryptographic Infrastructure (NICI). NICI enables developers to use the Controlled Cryptography Service (CCS) API to integrate cryptographic schemes with their applications. NICI also enables developers to write a single application that can be used in several countries, regardless of the differences in countries' cryptographic laws. For example, a developer could write a single application that uses 128-bit cryptographic keys when used within the United States and 40-bit cryptographic keys when used within countries that allow only keys of that length.

NICI is an infrastructure of network cryptographic services for worldwide consumption that supports strong cryptography and multiple cryptographic technologies. The NICI infrastructure has been developed in response to customer and internal Novell needs while complying with various national policies on the shipment and use of cryptography. Cryptography services on the NetWare platform provide fundamental security features such as confidentiality, integrity, authentication, and nonrepudiation.

The services are modular in nature, which allows new cryptographic engines, libraries, and policy managers to be dynamically added. The infrastructure is also tightly controlled, enforced through an integral OS loader that verifies modules before loading, and controls access to modules only via standardized interfaces. Available cryptographic services are provided via a Novell SDK.

NICI is the foundation for future network cryptographic services. It ensures that your product complies with international cryptography import and export laws through enforced region-specific cryptographic policies. NICI also provides for single, worldwide commodity vendor products and supports extensible, application-specific cryptographic libraries and interchangeable cryptographic technologies.

### Secure Authentication Services

NetWare 6 includes Secure Authentication Services (SAS), an infrastructure for supporting both existing and emerging authentication mechanisms, such as biometric and token-authentication systems. Through SAS, NetWare 6 also supports SSL version 3. Developers can use the SAS API to write applications that can establish encrypted SSL connections. (Developers can then use NICI to ensure that these SSL connections conform to the laws of each country in which the applications are used.)

Authentication is a fundamental component of a robust network service — it is how you identify yourself. Without authentication, you cannot secure a network. Novell's Secure Authentication Services (SAS) provides next generation authentication services, as well as serving as an evolving industry authentication mechanism for the future. In NetWare 6, SAS provides Secure Sockets Layer (SSL) support. Server applications use the SAS API set to establish encrypted SSL connections.

SAS is built entirely on NICI. This means that the SAS service itself is based on a single executable file. Because no cryptography is included in the SAS NLM, you can ship a single NLM worldwide. This provides easy administrator management and tracking. Also, any applications written to the SAS API can also be based on a single executable file.

In addition, applications written to the SAS application can go through a one-time and usually expedited export approval process. Novell has already received export approval for SAS and NICI. This means that application developers benefit with expedited export procedures.

PKIS also provides key management for the SSL services. Any application written to the SAS interface inherits the ability to have PKIS manage its certificates. NDS access control lists (ACLs) manage access to the private key that enables SSL. Because SAS is a network service, it has its own network identity. ACLs are set up on the SSL key object in such a way that allows only the SAS identity to read the private key. This guarantees that nonauthorized entities such as users, other server applications, and even the application built on top of SAS cannot gain access to and expose or subvert the private key.

### Auditing Services

NetWare 6 includes auditing services, which enable administrators to monitor users' access to an organization's network and to record this monitoring information in audit log files. You can create NDS objects to represent audit log files, and you can then manage these objects just as you manage other objects in the NDS tree. You can also grant rights to the NDS objects representing audit log files, just as you grant rights to other objects in the NDS tree. As a result, you can assign administrators to view and manage audit log files.

The audit system now takes advantage of exposed directory audit services in the following ways:

- ► Audit log files are represented and managed as NDS objects.
- ► The access to the audit information and configuration is controlled by the standard NDS rights.
- ► Auditing is configured at the container and volume levels.
- ► The audit policy for a container or volume specifies what is audited within the volume or container and which users are audited.

The audit system is an essential element of the total NetWare security environment. You must have network audit integrity to ensure that the network is secure. Additionally, some industries such as banking require auditing to be done as part of business operations. The NetWare auditing system can monitor and record every relevant network transaction, which user performed the transaction, and when the transaction occurred.

# NDS eDirectory Access Control

NDS security actually consists of two parts known as file system security and object security. Both aspects of NetWare 6 security work together to provide a flexible and effective method for controlling access to your network. *File system security* provides access control to files and directories. *Object security* provides access control to NDS objects and associated operations. You must determine to what extent you want to enable the many file system and NDS security features at your disposal. NetWare is well regarded for providing a high degree of network security, and much of the security administration happens by default, as explained later in this chapter.

The first step to understanding NetWare security is to begin with file system security. File system security consists of the security that was introduced in previous versions of NetWare. Your familiarity with the security concepts in NetWare 3 will be a great help to you in understanding security in NetWare 6.

## Understanding File System Security

Very little has changed in file system security since the original versions of NetWare. All the rules governing rights administration are the same in NetWare 6 as in previous versions. As an administrator, you don't have to learn any new concepts to manage your NetWare 6 file system. However, if you are new to NetWare, you will want to read this section and refer to Novell's documentation on managing the file system.

File system security basically consists of assigning trustee rights and file/directory attributes. The trustee rights assignments can be applied to any NDS object, including containers, user objects, group objects, and organizational roles. Table 13.1 shows the file system rights available in NetWare 6. The rights are in order as typically seen in most of the NetWare applications.

TABLE 13.1

*File System Rights*

| RIGHT | DEFINITION |
| --- | --- |
| Access Control | Adds/modifies rights to files and directories. |
| Supervisor | Enables all file and directory assignments to be made and grants all rights listed in this table. |
| Read | Enables the trustee to open, read, and execute application files. |
| Write | Enables the trustee user to open, write to, and modify a file. |
| Create | Enables the trustee to create subdirectories and files. |
| Erase | Enables the trustee to delete directories and files. |
| Modify | Enables the trustee to modify and rename directories and files, and to change file attributes. |
| File Scan | Enables the trustee to view file and directory names in the file system. |

NetWare 6 file system security includes the capability to manage access at file and directory levels just as it did in previous versions of NetWare. Attributes control what actions can or cannot be taken on a file or directory. For certain files, such as application files on the network, you may want to make sure they are flagged as Read Only and Sharable so that no unintentional or intentional deletions occur.

Additional file and directory attributes have been added when the directory was added to the NetWare file system to provide more functionality. These new file system attributes are listed in Table 13.2. For a complete list of all attributes associated with NetWare 6 files and directories, refer to Novell's documentation. The attributes are in order as normally seen in the NetWare utilities.

TABLE 13.2

*File System Rights That Have Been Added to Support the Directory in Netware Versions 4, 5, and 6*

| ATTRIBUTE | ABBREVIATION | DEFINITION |
|---|---|---|
| Compress | Co | Status attribute that indicates the file is compressed. |
| Can't Compress | Cc | Status attribute that indicates the file cannot be compressed because of limited space savings. |
| Don't Compress | Dc | Added to a directory, this attribute keeps all files within the directory from being compressed. This attribute can also be added to a specific file. |
| Immediate | Ic | Added to directories or files, this Compress attribute alerts the file system to compress a file as soon as the operating system can handle the action. |
| Migrated | M | This status attribute indicates that the file has been migrated. |
| Don't Migrate | Dm | Added to a directory, this attribute will not allow files within the directory to be migrated to secondary storage. This attribute can also be added to a specific file. |

For more information on administering file system security, refer to Novell's documentation.

## Understanding Object Security

If you have previous knowledge of how the file system security works in NetWare, this will help you understand the security used for the objects in the directory. First, the security used for objects and properties in the directory is the same terminology and the same rules as in the NetWare file system. The rules for file system security in all versions of NetWare are identical. In addition, the same rules apply to the objects and properties in the directory. The directory extends the security environment by adding access controls to all objects and properties found in your tree. The access controls are similiar to those used in the file system.

As shown in Figure 13.3, security features in the NetWare 6 environment are similar to those in NetWare 3.

| NetWare 3 | NetWare 6 |
|---|---|
| BINDERY | NOVELL DIRECTORY SERVICES |
| FILE & DIRECTORY RIGHTS FILE ATTRIBUTES | FILE & DIRECTORY RIGHTS FILE ATTRIBUTES |
| SUPERVISOR OPERATOR OBJECT RIGHTS ONLY | OBJECT & PROPERTY RIGHTS |
| SUPERVISOR USER | ADMIN USER AND BINDERY SUPERVISOR |
| EVERYONE GROUP | O=ORGANIZATION |
| GUEST USER | [PUBLIC] TRUSTEE (NOT THE SAME AS GUEST) |
| INHERIT RIGHTS MASK (IRM) | INHERITED RIGHTS FILTER (IRF) |
| DIRECTORY ENTERY TABLE (DET) | DET, ACL (ACCESS CONTROL LIST) |

**FIGURE 13.3** *Security feature similarities between the version of NetWare that did not support NetWare and one that does*

The exceptions between NetWare 3 (representative version of NetWare that does not support NDS) and NetWare 6 (version of NetWare that fully supports the directory) are as follows:

▸ Inherited rights filter (IRF) terminology is used instead of inherited rights mask (IRM) language. In NetWare 6, the term IRF describes the operation of filtering out rights for a particular object. IRFs are explained in detail later in this chapter.

▸ NetWare Object classes have been expanded from four objects in NetWare 3 to more than 50 in NetWare 6.

▸ The SUPERVISOR user is used only for bindery requests in NetWare 6. Another NDS user object (typically called ADMIN) is granted Supervisor object rights at the [ROOT] of the tree. This user object is the functional equivalent of the Supervisor found in NetWare 3 and has default Supervisor rights over all NDS objects in the tree as well as the file system for any NetWare server installed. One other major difference is that you cannot filter Supervisor rights in the NetWare 3 file system. However, you can filter Supervisor rights in the NDS tree.

▸ Guest is not automatically created in NetWare 6. The [PUBLIC] Trustee is similar to Guest in enabling users to see the NDS tree before logging into a server. However, Guest is a real object and [PUBLIC] is not, so the similarities are few.

▸ Group Everyone is not automatically created in NetWare 6. However, an equivalent feature is available by using either the [ROOT] object or O=Organization object. For example, O=ACME includes every object in the NDS tree, and rights can be assigned to O=ACME, which all users receive automatically.

▸ Operators for print queues found in NetWare 3 are now an attribute of the Queue object found in the directory.

▸ Directory entry tables are still used to store file system trustees in NetWare 6. In addition, NetWare 6 uses the access control list to store NDS trustee information.

## Object Rights Defined

*Object rights* are simply rights granted to a particular object to access or manage another object. In NetWare 3 servers, the Supervisor object has rights to manage all other bindery objects on the server. NetWare 6 has expanded on this concept by allowing all NDS objects rights to other objects. As shown in Table 13.3, NDS objects can receive many different rights. The NDS objects rights are in order as seen in the ConsoleOne or NWADMIN utility.

| | |
|---|---|
| **TABLE 13.3** | |
| *An Object Can Receive Many Different Object Level Rights to Manage Other Objects in the Directory.* | |

| NDS OBJECT | OBJECT LEVEL RIGHTS |
|---|---|
| Supervisor (S) | Grants full privileges to the trustee over an object and has complete access to all the object's property rights. |
| Browse (B) | Enables a trustee to see an NDS object in the tree during a browse of the tree. |
| Create (C) | Enables a trustee to create objects below this object (applies to container objects only). |
| Delete (D) | Enables a trustee to delete an object. Subordinate objects must be deleted first if you are deleting a container. |
| Rename (R) | Enables a trustee to rename an object. |

An example of how object rights appear in the NWADMIN utility is shown in Figure 13.4.

**FIGURE 13.4** *An example of object rights as they are displayed in the NWADMIN utility is shown. These rights can also be seen using ConsoleOne.*

## Property Rights Defined

*Property rights* enable a trustee to view or change the values of a particular object's properties. You can have rights to certain properties (selected property rights) or to all properties (all property rights) for a particular object. For example, the Supervisor right over an NDS object also grants Supervisor privileges for all properties in that object. All other rights assignments made at the object level do not affect the properties. In fact, Supervisor rights at the property level do not grant Supervisor rights at the object level. Only the reverse is true. Table 13.4 shows a list of the available property rights in NetWare 6. The NDS property rights are in order as seen in the ConsoleOne or NWADMIN utility.

TABLE 13.4

*NetWare 6 Property Rights*

| PROPERTY RIGHT | FUNCTION |
|----------------|----------|
| Supervisor (S) | Grants all rights to the object's properties. |
| Compare (C) | Enables a test for a value match and returns a true or false. Compare is a subset of read. If you have Read/Write rights, you automatically have Compare rights at the property level. |
| Read (R) | Returns a value (contents) of a property. Read contains the Compare right. |
| Write (W) | Enables you to modify, add, change, and delete a property value. |
| Add/Remove Self (A) | Enables you to add or remove yourself as a value of a property. It is a subset of the Write right. If you have Write rights to a property, you automatically have the Add/Remove Self right. |

An example of how property rights are displayed in NWADMIN is shown in Figure 13.5.

## The Access Control List

The access control list is a special property of every object. It can actually be considered the most important mechanism for determining NDS access. The access control list contains trustee assignments for an object and its properties. A user object, for example, with the Write right to the ACL of another user object has what is known as *managed rights* over that user object. This means that an object with the Write right to any object's ACL can make any rights assignments to that object.

**FIGURE 13.5** *Property rights in the NWADMIN utility*

Each object can have an ACL. The ACL is a property value and contains three entries: the trustee ID, the type of access (object or property), and the actual rights assignment. This concept is shown in Figure 13.6.

ACCESS CONTROL LIST (ACL)

| TRANSFER OBJECT ID | TYPE OF ACCESS (OBJECT OR PROPERTY) | RIGHTS ASSIGNMENT |
|---|---|---|
| 07721429 | OBJECT | [S    ] |
| 07618424 | OBJECT | [ CR ] |
| 01099600 | PROPERTY | {S    } |

**FIGURE 13.6** *Every object may have an access control list as one of its properties.*

**NOTE**

**The ACL is extremely powerful, and its access should be closely controlled for every object on your network. Because the ACL is a property of an object, it can be modified by anyone who has Write rights to the ACL property for the object. This means that someone with the Write rights to the ACL can make rights assignments for that object.**

The ACL has three categories:

▶ Object rights

▶ [All Properties]

▶ Selected properties

The [All Properties] category is a property under the ACL, and if given the Write right to the ACL, you can modify the object's trustee assignments. As a security rule, be careful how you grant the Write right to ordinary users under the ACL. Selected property rights overwrite those rights assigned by [All Property] — they are not cumulative.

By default, users do not receive Write rights to their own ACL. In the NDS schema, some of the object classes specify a default ACL template. The default ACL template grants basic access control to newly created objects. If the object (for example, the organizational unit object) contains a default ACL template when created, it would have information in its ACL as shown in Table 13.5.

**TABLE 13.5**

*The Container Object Default ACL*

| OBJECT NAME | DEFAULT RIGHTS | AFFECTED |
| --- | --- | --- |
| [ROOT] | Read | Login script and print job configuration |

When a container object is created, the [ROOT] object automatically obtains the Read property right to the container's login script and print job configuration.

The user class is another example of an object that receives a default ACL during initial creation. Its default ACL would appear as shown in Table 13.6.

| | TABLE 13.6 | |
| --- | --- | --- |
| | *The User Object Default ACL* | |
| OBJECT NAME | DEFAULT RIGHTS | AFFECTED ATTRIBUTES |
| [PUBLIC] | Read | Message server |
| [ROOT] | Browse | Object rights |
| [ROOT] | Read | Group membership |
| [ROOT] | Read | Network address |
| [self] | Read | All attributes |
| [self] | Read/Write | Login script |
| [self] | Read/Write | Print job configuration |

Therefore, as was mentioned earlier, access control is limited, and your default security is a closed-door approach. As a NetWare administrator, you must open up security doors (granting additional rights) only when necessary. Otherwise, the majority of your users receive by default sufficient access rights when they are created.

**NOTE**

**As we have stated earlier, an object may or may not have an ACL. If an object already has the effective right, the ACL is not created. For example, all objects have the default ACL that specifies that the ADMIN (or appropriate object) has object Supervisor rights to the user object. If the ADMIN already has the Supervisor object right (and it does if it creates a user object), the default ACL is not created when the NDS user object is created.**

## Inheritable ACLs

The Inheritable ACLs are a feature in NetWare 6 that enables you to more easily manage the objects and properties of the NDS tree. This feature gives you the ability to inherit specific property rights down the entire tree. The NDS inheritable ACLs enable you to assign Supervisor rights to operators or help desk staff for specific types of objects or resources without giving Supervisor rights to the entire tree. For example, you can assign rights to a group to manage just the printers, servers, or users.

You need to use ConsoleOne or NWADMIN in order to give inheritable rights to a specific property and have it flow down the NDS tree. In the ConsoleOne or NWADMIN object and property rights screen are two new buttons at the bottom of the rights list called Inherit. By selecting the Inherit button when giving specific object or property rights to any other object, you are making them inherit down the NDS tree. Figure 13.7 shows an example of using the Inherit button to grant rights to a specific property and have those rights flow down to the NDS tree.

**FIGURE 13.7** *The NDS inheritable ACLs have been implemented in ConsoleOne and NWADMIN as the Inherit button for either object or property rights. You can have specific property rights flow down the NDS tree by selecting the Inherit button when assigning the rights.*

You may be wondering how specific property rights can be assigned using the inheritable ACLs if ConsoleOne or NWADMIN only displays the property for the object in use. For example, in NetWare 4 versions, if you wanted to grant a group (TELE-GROUP) rights to manage all users' telephone numbers at the O=ACME level, you would select the O=ACME object. However, using NetWare 4 you would see only the properties that are associated with the O=ACME object, and thus the users' telephone number could not be selected. To overcome this limitation, NetWare 5 and 6 offers a feature that allows ConsoleOne or NWADMIN to list all the schema-defined properties in a single list. This means that regardless of the location in the NDS tree, the properties listed for the object are all properties defined in the schema.

The ConsoleOne or NWADMIN feature that lists all schema-defined properties gives you the ability to select any property at any level in the NDS tree. As mentioned, if you wanted to grant a group (Telephone_Group) rights to manage all users' telephone numbers at the O=ACME level, you would select the O=ACME object. The new feature lists the users' telephone numbers as a property, and you can grant specific property rights that will inherit. Figure 13.8 shows how you can use NWADMIN to grant the group, Telephone_Group, the rights to manage all users' telephone numbers at the O=Organization level.

**FIGURE 13.8** *In order to grant a group, Telephone_Group, rights to manage all users' telephone numbers at the O=ACME level, you use NWADMIN. Select the O=ACME container object and grant the group the Supervisor rights to manage all users' telephone numbers.*

## The Password Management Property

In addition to the NDS Inheritable ACLs feature, NetWare 5 and 6 supports a user property called Password Management. The Password Management property enables you to assign rights to manage just the users' passwords.

Using the Password Management property, you can grant a specific group, PASSWORD-GROUP, the ability to reset just the users' passwords and accounts. To accomplish the same thing using NetWare 4, you had to give all rights or Supervisor rights to the individual user objects or to the entire container or tree. Using the Password Management property, in combination with the new Inherit button, you can grant rights that will flow down the entire tree. Figure 13.9 shows the example of granting the group, PASSWORD-GROUP, the rights to manage all users' passwords and accounts for the entire ACME tree.

**FIGURE 13.9** *Using the Password Management property in NWADMIN, you can grant a specific group, PASSWORD_GROUP, the Supervisor rights to manage the users' passwords and accounts at O=ACME. Select the Inherit button so that these rights flow down the entire NDS tree.*

# Learning the Rules of NDS Security

Every network manager should be aware of a number of security rules when setting up a secured NetWare 6 system or network. These rules affect both the file system security and directory security.

NetWare does a very good job with security (out of the box) just using the defaults that are implemented during installation. NetWare security is not an open door system. The NetWare 6 installation process closes all the necessary doors and gives you default security settings for servers, for users, and for directory access. Then if users need additional access, the administrator can grant those additions to them.

For example, the installation process creates the Admin user object. Install creates the [Public] trustee, and each user receives rights to the [Public] trustee through security equivalence. The [Public] trustee is granted Browse rights to the [Root] object during initial installation. The install process also gives user objects the appropriate rights that they need for themselves, such as to read and modify their login scripts, to log in, and so forth. System administrators can give additional file and object rights when they are needed.

The first step in understanding NDS security is to understand the rules that govern it. This section outlines the concepts and rules for each area of security. With the groundwork in place, we then focus on some specific examples and explain how security is implemented for each.

NDS security uses the same terminology as file system security. In fact, your familiarity with NetWare 3 file system security provides you with a great foundation for understanding NetWare 6 security. The following concepts will be discussed and are shown in Figure 13.10:

- ▶ Trustee assignments
- ▶ Security equivalence
- ▶ Inheritance
- ▶ The inherited rights filter
- ▶ Effective rights

## Trustee Assignments

A *trustee assignment* indicates the rights granted to an object for a specific file, directory, object, or property. An object that has been granted rights to manage another object is said to be a *trustee* of that object. Trustee assignments for the file system are stored in the directory entry table, whereas trustee assignments for NDS objects and properties are stored in the ACL.

A trustee assignment is a direct, explicit assignment of rights to a particular object. Sometimes you hear the term *explicit trustee assignment*, which means the same thing. Trustee assignments are listed first in our pyramid diagram because it is the first point at which rights assignments are made. It is the basis for all subsequent security assignments, such as security equivalence and inheritance. In fact, a trustee assignment is the lowest level where you can make assignments. Security always begins with a trustee assignment. For example, the use of a group object requires you to grant the group a trustee assignment that the members of the group receive through security equivalence.

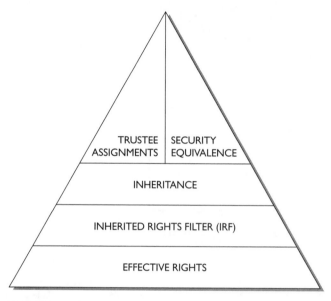

**FIGURE 13.10** *The NDS security pyramid serves as a visual basis for understanding the order and concepts of NDS security.*

The installation of NetWare 6, as another example, causes some default trustee assignments (templates) to be made for user and server objects. As an administrator, you will most likely make additional trustee assignments for groups, containers, and other administrators, as explained in the following section.

### Default Trustee Assignments for Users

During the installation of your first NetWare 6 server, the ADMIN user object (if you've named it that) receives an explicit assignment of object Supervisor at object [ROOT], as shown in Figure 13.11.

**NOTE**

**The ADMIN object is just a user object like any other object, but it has been granted object Supervisor rights at [ROOT]. It can be renamed, deleted, and moved like any other user object. Be careful.**

This assignment is the first trustee assignment made by the NetWare 6 installation software and initially is the only object in the tree with object Supervisor rights at [ROOT].

[Root]

[Public]
Admin

O=ACME

Admin

OU=NORAD

OU=LABS

| | Object Rights | Property Rights | File System Rights |
|---|---|---|---|
| [Public] | [ B ] | | |
| Admin | [S ] | | |

**FIGURE 13.11** *This diagram shows the default trustee assignments made at the installation of NetWare 6.*

Also during installation of NetWare 6, [PUBLIC] receives an object trustee assignment of object Browse at object [ROOT]. With this right, all users can browse the tree after attaching to a server before logging in. This enables users to use the CX command to browse the tree and discover object names after they have loaded the NetWare client software and have attached to a NetWare 6 server. Figure 13.11 shows a graphic representation of the PUBLIC rights received at the time of installation of NetWare 6.

### NetWare 6 Server Default Trustee Assignments

The NetWare 6 installation utility also makes trustee assignments at the file system level. The ADMIN object has object Supervisor rights to the tree. The server object is in the tree and therefore has rights to your servers. Because the ADMIN object has object Supervisor rights to the server object, the ADMIN object also receives Supervisor rights to the NetWare file system of that server. This is the only instance in NetWare 6 security where object rights have an impact on file system rights. In fact, any object with Write rights on a server's ACL has Supervisor rights on the file system of that server.

[PUBLIC] receives the Read property right to the server object's Messaging Server property right so that if the server is being used as the default login server, its property can be located. This assignment is in the template for the server object.

The container object that the new server is installed into receives Read and File Scan rights to the server's \PUBLIC directory. This default access enables all users in the container to execute any files stored on the server's \PUBLIC directory.

The container also receives Create rights to the server's \MAIL directory.

Figure 13.12 shows how these trustee assignments are made when a server object is first created.

**FIGURE 13.12** *This example shows how trustee assignments are made for a server object during installation of NetWare 6.*

### Default Trustee Assignments for Users

When user objects are created, they also receive some default trustee assignments (refer to the section "The Access Control List," earlier in this chapter, which discusses ACLs and default ACLs). These assignments greatly reduce the amount of work required by a NetWare administrator to set up user accounts and provide for their access. The following access is automatically granted during creation of a user object.

For our purposes, let's assume that a new user object has been created in the TOKYO container. The newly created user object receives the Read and Compare rights to All Properties by default. All Properties is a category that is visible using either ConsoleOne or NWADMIN by selecting Rights to Other Objects, as shown in Figure 13.13. Having the Read right to All Properties enables the user to read the values of his or her own user properties. The Compare right is a subset of Read and enables the value of the property to be compared with another value.

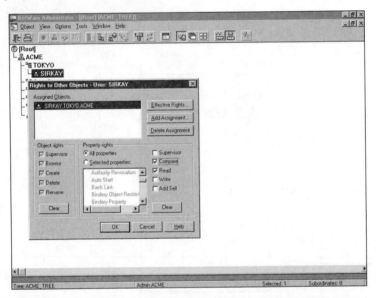

**FIGURE 13.13** *The user object SIRKAY.TOKYO.ACME receives by default the Read and Compare rights to All Properties for its own object.*

The user object is granted Read and Write rights to its own login script and print job configuration. These rights permit the users to change their own login scripts and print job configurations if they want. Figure 13.14 shows these rights assigned along with the others when a user object is created.

The table within the figure reads:

| | Object Rights | Property Rights | File System Rights |
|---|---|---|---|
| User | [ B ] | { R }<br>All Property Rights<br>{ RW }<br>Login_Script<br>Print_Job_Configuration | |
| [ROOT] | | \|{ R }\|<br>Network_Address<br>Group_Membership | |
| [PUBLIC] | [ B ] | { R }<br>Default_Server | |

**FIGURE 13.14** *Rights assignments are made when a user object is created.*

### Understanding the Rules of Trustee Assignments

As mentioned earlier, some rules govern the functionality of trustee assignments. Learning these rules can make understanding and using NetWare security much easier for you.

▸ **Trustee assignments flow down the tree** — A trustee assignment for objects and [All Property Rights] flows down the tree unless it is blocked by an inherited rights filter. (The IRF is explained later in this chapter.) For example, if user SIRKAY were granted Supervisor rights to the TOKYO container, these rights would flow down to any subsequent containers and objects below TOKYO unless an object has an inherited rights filter.

▸ **An explicit trustee assignment at a lower level in the tree replaces all previous trustee assignments** — As shown in Figure 13.15, user SIRKAY has been granted explicit Create and Rename rights beginning at object TOKYO. This trustee assignment flows down until it is blocked by an IRF or reassigned by another explicit assignment. In this example, we reassign the object the Browse right at the OU=CRIME. This explicit assignment replaces all other higher assignments at the OU=CRIME level in the tree.

| | Object Rights | Property Rights | File System Rights |
|---|---|---|---|
| [ROOT] ← SIRKAY | [ CR ] | | |
| | [ CR ] | | |
| O=ACME | | | |
| SIRKAY | [ CR ] | | |
| SIRKAY | [ B ] | | |

**FIGURE 13.15** *An explicit rights assignment made at a lower level in the tree replaces any previous explicit assignment made to that object.*

▶ **Selected property rights override any assignment made in the All Properties category** — At the time of user creation, a user object receives the Read property right to all of its own properties. Any selective assignment of a property right using the Selected Properties category overrides anything assigned through the All Properties category. For example, by default, all users have the Read property right to all of their own user object properties. Notice also that a user receives by default the Read and Write rights to his or her login script and print job configuration. The fact that the Read write is given again in the selected properties assignment indicates that it has overridden the previous assignment made in the All Properties category.

▶ **The access control list property of every object stores trustee assignments to that object** — Each object can contain a property known as the ACL. A user by default does not have Write rights to the user's own ACL or to that of any other object. Keep in mind that some objects may not have ACLs if they already have received the explicit right.

**Do not grant users Write rights to any ACL, including their own user objects, because the Write right to the ACL controls all access to those particular objects.**

IMPORTANT

For example, a user possessing the Write right to a container ACL has the ability to make any changes to that object's ACL. The user could assign Supervisor object rights to that container to anyone and could modify the object as well.

## Understanding Security Equivalence

*Security equivalence* simply means that one object can be equivalent in rights to another object. The majority of rights assignments should be made by administrators through the use of security equivalence. Using security equivalence is quick and easy because you can deal with a large number of users rather than a single user at a time. Time is always a factor for network administrators, and we recommend that you assign security equivalence to groups or containers as the best way to make rights assignments to large numbers of people.

To meet the needs of many users requiring the same rights to a directory or file, you can create a group, assign rights to the newly created group, and add members to the group. The members of the group are security equivalent in rights to the group object. Therefore, any assignment made to a group will be received by its members through security equivalence. An example of this process is shown in Figure 13.16.

**FIGURE 13.16** *An example of creating a group and granting rights to the group is shown. The users receive rights through security equivalence.*

In addition, a container functions much the same way as a group except that the group is used in your login scripts and a group can span multiple containers. If all users in a container access the same resources, using groups may not be necessary. However, if you want to further differentiate your environment setting within a container, the group object is an effective way to go.

Because the use of security equivalence will be so common on your network, understanding how NetWare 6 security functions is very important. You will save time as a network administrator if you understand the rules that govern security equivalence.

▸ **Security equivalent rights cannot be masked** — If you receive a security equivalence, this assignment cannot be masked by an IRF.

▸ **Every object is security equivalent to all container objects that are part of its distinguished name** — This security is known as *implied security* equivalence. For example, the user GUINEVERE.FIN.OPS.CAMELOT in the ACME tree is security equivalent to every object in its name. Therefore, if you were to grant the container FIN rights to a particular e-mail server, user GUINEVERE would receive those rights through security equivalence.

**NOTE**

**You cannot use an IRF to single out users to be denied rights granted to a container. If you grant rights to a container, *all* users in or subordinate to that container always receive those rights.**

▸ **Every object is security equivalent to [ROOT]** — When a user has successfully logged into a server, that user is security equivalent to [ROOT].

▸ **Every object is security equivalent to [PUBLIC]** — [PUBLIC], with the default rights of Browse, enables users to browse the tree before logging into a server. Each user is security equivalent to [PUBLIC], and [PUBLIC] has been granted Browse rights at object [ROOT]. This assignment can be changed if you like.

▸ **An object is security equivalent to all objects listed in its Security Equals property** — An NDS object keeps a list (known as the Security Equals property) of all objects that it equals in rights.

▸ **Security equivalence is not transitive** — This means that Object A can be security equivalent to Object B, but if Object B is security equivalent to Object C, Object A won't be security equivalent to Object C through Object B.

**Consulting Experience**

Be very careful with assigning rights to the [PUBLIC] trustee to make use of its security equivalence with all users, because they do not need to be authenticated to receive those rights. The assignment of file system rights is nonfunctional when using the [PUBLIC] trustee. This means that you cannot grant access to files before the user has successfully logged into the server. Generally, the use of the [PUBLIC] trustee for granting rights should be avoided.

As mentioned in the rules, security equivalence enables an object to be equivalent in rights to another object. Every object is security equivalent to [ROOT]. Every object is security equivalent to all container objects that are a part of its name. This is known as implied security equivalence; you don't see this equivalence listed in ConsoleOne and NWADMIN utilities.

This means that the users are security equivalent to every object above them that is a part of their context name. If you grant rights to an OU that contains the user's name, you have given that individual rights to that context. Conversely, if you are at an Organizational level (O = Novell) and you grant rights to that Organization, any user located in that Organizational level is going to receive whatever rights were granted to O = Novell by virtue of security equivalence. Those rights cannot be revoked because users are security equivalent to every object that is contained in their context name.

Keep in mind that when a user logs into a NetWare 6 server and authenticates to the directory, the directory creates what is known as a *security equivalence vector* that is stored in the connection table on the server. The security equivalence vector contains a list of that object's security equivalencies and is created on every server to which the client authenticates.

## Inheritance

*Inheritance* is the method by which rights to objects and files flow down to subordinate levels of the tree. Only two types of rights are inherited: trustee assignments and security equivalence. Rights given through these two methods can flow downward. This is called inheritance.

As previously stated, explicit trustee assignments at a higher level in your tree flow down. The rights you receive at lower levels without assignment are known as *inherited rights*. Inherited rights include only the object rights and the All Properties rights. Selected property rights are not inherited.

An important rule to note here is that trustee assignments and security equivalence rights flow down independently. Many think that a trustee rights reassignment affects security equivalence, but that is not the case. For example, suppose you have security equivalence rights flowing down, as well as trustee assignments flowing down at Level A. If you reassign trustee rights at Level B, that affects the trustee rights on that level and below (unless you explicitly reassign trustee assignments again).

But the security equivalence rights continue to flow down and are not affected by the change. If you have an explicit Browse trustee assignment but you still have Read and Write rights through security equivalency, those rights continue to flow down unless they are affected by an inherited rights filter at that level.

 **Sometimes people confuse security equivalence and inheritance. Keep in mind that inheritance is simply the way that previously granted rights flow down the tree to subordinate levels.**

**NOTE**

The following rights can be inherited: Object rights, File and Directory rights, and [All Property Rights]. Individual or selected property rights are not inherited.

Through trustee assignments and inheritance, you can make a user as powerful as Admin by assigning the user the Supervisor object right to the [ROOT] object. By virtue of inheritance, the user is supervisor at all subordinate levels unless filtered by an IRF.

Earlier in our discussion we mentioned that explicit rights, such as the ADMIN user object possessing the Supervisor right at the [ROOT] object, flow down the tree. As shown in Figure 13.17, the Supervisor assignment continues to flow down the tree unless it is otherwise blocked or reassigned. Therefore, at each subsequent level in the tree, the ADMIN object's rights are being received through inheritance.

Inherited rights also flow down independently of other rights assignments, such as those obtained through security equivalence. This means that the rights received through inheritance are not affected by actions you may take on other explicit rights assignments. The two operate under separate rules. Do not mix up your security rules. Figure 13.18 shows how explicit rights assignments flow down independently of security equivalence rights.

**FIGURE 13.17** *Inheritance of the Supervisor right at the second and third levels of the tree*

**FIGURE 13.18** *The explicit assignment of the Supervisor right flows down the tree independently of the Browse right, which was received because user ALincoln is security equivalent to the [PUBLIC] trustee.*

### Understanding Inherited Rights Filters (IRFs)

The filter known as the inherited rights filter is used to block inheritance. In reality, the inherited rights filter can only revoke inherited rights and is an inclusive filter. The IRF can be applied to object rights, the All Properties category, and the Selected Properties category.

An IRF exists for every file, directory, object, and property.

**As mentioned earlier, you cannot place an IRF on rights received through security equivalence. You can apply the IRF only to object rights, the All Properties category, and the Selected Properties category.**

NOTE

The IRF enables the NetWare administrator to specify which rights can be inherited from an object. It is easier to understand the concept of the IRF if you compare it to a shell around an object. When you place an IRF on an object, you are placing an imaginary shell around the object. The rights that are enabled in the IRF are the only rights that users will have to an object. For example, you could place an IRF of Browse on a server object in a container. One user must maintain Supervisor rights over the object, however. All other users can inherit only the Browse right because of the IRF that is placed around the server object.

Many are confused between security equivalence and inheritance. You can block inheritance through the IRF, but you cannot block security equivalence or trustee assignments through the IRF.

The main difference between directory security and file system security is that the Supervisor right granted in the file system can never be blocked at the file and directory level. This works the same in NetWare 4, 5, and 6 as it does in NetWare 3. In NDS, however, the Supervisor object and the property Supervisor right can be blocked with an IRF.

Another rule is that you don't inherit the container's rights — you are security equivalent to the OU container object to which you belong. For example, if you are a member of an OU (OU = ABC) and rights are explicitly assigned to ABC, you receive those rights through security equivalency. Many think they can place an IRF on the container and block all rights, but this is not so.

Also, if you assign explicit trustee assignments directly to users (underneath the IRF), the users still have rights to the objects through the trustee assignments. Again, the IRF only blocks inherited rights.

**The ACL is both the trustee assignments made and the filters applied. The same attribute (property) name is used for both.**

NOTE

### Rules that Govern the IRF

The following rules govern the inherited rights filter:

▸ **The IRF cannot grant rights** — It only revokes previously assigned rights. Keep in mind that the IRF is an imaginary shell wrapped around an object.

▸ **You can enable an IRF for every object, property, file, and directory** — In most cases, you will not need to use that many IRFs, because the user's default rights are limited to begin with. As shown in the scenarios at the end of the chapter, most IRFs are used to protect servers and to separate file system and NDS administration.

▸ **The Supervisor object/property rights can be revoked by an IRF** — An IRF can be applied to all objects, including the server object. Therefore, you can limit a person's Supervisor access to a NetWare 6 file server by applying an IRF to the server object. Remember that a user possessing the managed right (Write right to the ACL) to a server object has rights to the file system volumes for that server as well.

▸ **The Supervisor file/directory rights cannot be revoked by an IRF** — This feature is identical to NetWare 3 Supervisor rights in that any user that has Supervisor rights to a file system directly cannot have file system rights masked on that file server.

### Inherited ACLs

Each partition [ROOT] object contains a property known as the inherited access control list. For more information on the partition [ROOT] object, refer to Chapter 6. The inherited ACL property contains the summation of ACLs from parent containers. Unless an IRF is in effect, all objects in the partition will receive the rights contained in the inherited ACL. NDS can then calculate rights for objects in its partition without having to walk the Directory tree. As changes to ACLs are made to the tree, NDS updates the multivalued inherited ACL property.

The NDS janitor process has the responsibility to maintain the inherited ACLs by recalculating inheritance if any changes are made to the inherited ACLs. For more information on the janitor process, refer to Chapter 8.

## Understanding Effective Rights

The last step in the security pyramid is the calculation of effective rights. *Effective rights* are what an object can actually do after all other security factors are calculated against the object. The following sources are used in the calculation of effective rights of one object to another:

▸ The object's ACL

▸ The object's explicit assignments

▸ All security equivalent access privileges

For example, consider an object A with access to object B using security equivalence calculated at the time of authentication. The rights would be calculated as follows:

1. Calculate the sum of explicit assignments back to the partition root. Object B would be calculated back to object B's partition root. Of course, an IRF would negate some assignments.

2. Add in the inherited ACLs from the partition root.

3. Object A receives all explicit and inherited ACLs to which A is security equivalent.

As mentioned, effective rights are what an object can actually do at a particular level in the tree. You may have explicit trustee assignments at the Organizational level, but when you get down to a lower OU, an IRF may be placed there and you end up with different effective rights.

For example, at the OU=ABC level, you may have Admin rights, but at O=TOPGUN level, you may have only Browse rights. What your effective rights are depends on where you are in the directory tree. If you look at your effective rights through some of the utilities, know that those rights are calculated for the context in the tree where you currently are.

The effective rights for specific NDS objects can be viewed using ConsoleOne or NWADMIN utility in the "Trustee of this object" screen. The effective rights are the summation of all rights, and objects can receive them through explicit assignments, inheritance, and security equivalences.

## Understanding Managed Rights

*Managed rights* (or management rights) is a term used to describe an object (ADMIN, for example) that has the Write right to an object's ACL. Managed rights means that the trustee has all power over an object and can modify anything pertaining to that object. For some operations in NDS, you must have managed rights to perform that operation. Here is a list of NDS operations and the managed rights that are required to perform them:

▶ All partition operations including Create, Merge, Add Replica, and Move Subtree require the trustee to have Write rights to the target partition server object. The Merge operation requires managed rights to the [ROOT] objects of both trees.

▶ A schema modification requires the trustee to have Write rights to the ACL of the Directory's [ROOT] object.

▶ Any modifications to the following properties require Write rights to that object's ACL:

- Security Equals
- Group Membership
- Profile Membership

▶ Backup requires managed rights on the object(s) being backed up.

▶ The Add/Remove replica operation requires:

- Managed rights on the partition root
- Managed rights on the target server

*Managed rights* is a term that is used to signify all rights to a specific NDS object. Managed rights are not viewed using any utility; rather, this is a concept, not an actual assignment of rights.

## Implementing NDS Security

With an understanding of the basic concepts of security, we can now begin a discussion of how to use and implement NDS security for your network. Refer back to Figure 13.10 as the basis for our security discussion. As stated earlier, the pyramid shown in this figure shows a very logical approach to understanding NetWare 6 security. Each section of the pyramid will now be explained with examples on how you can implement security in your environment for the greatest benefit. First, let's consider some general security guidelines or tips.

**I.** When implementing security, you want to give rights to objects at the highest level possible in your environment, such as at the O or OU levels. If you have a small shop and you want to assign rights to the Mail directory, it may make sense to do this at [Root] or O=TOPGUN. But in large-scale networks, an OU level is probably a better place to assign the more global rights, because not all users need the same kind of rights. For example, if you want everyone to have file system rights to an APPS directory on a specific file server, you can grant those rights at the O or OU container level through a trustee assignment. Then everybody gets those rights to that file system by virtue of security equivalence, and it won't be blocked by an IRF.

**2.** Understand how to use the [Public] trustee. You don't want to give the [Public] trustee broad rights because users get those rights before they log in.

**3.** If you have the Supervisor object right to a file server object, you get all file system rights. This is the only place where NDS rights cross over to the file system rights. If you have the Supervisor object right to the volume object, you do not get all file system rights.

For the specific examples that follow, we refer to the ACME tree for the model to implement security. The following scenarios are discussed in terms of NetWare security. All scenarios make the assumption that you are an administrator and object Supervisor rights at the [ROOT] of your tree are assigned.

### Server-Level Security

First, consider the security required to install a NetWare 6 server under the OU=NORAD center in our example system.

It is important to understand the following security concepts:

- ▸ Trustee assignments
- ▸ Security equivalence

As a temporary administrator, you are asked to install a NetWare 6 server in the NORAD container into the ACME tree. Currently, no administrators are in your location, and this server must be brought up immediately. You would begin by contacting your main administrator to obtain Create rights for the NORAD container. Supervisor rights at your container are needed to install a NetWare 6 server into your own container or to add a partition replica to partition root. This can be accomplished in several ways as described in the following steps:

1. The first way is to simply have the administrator explicitly grant you Supervisor rights to the NORAD container. This method is difficult to track if many similar requests are made to the main NDS administrator. The administrator soon forgets who has been granted rights.

2. The second and recommended way is to use ConsoleOne or NWADMIN to create an organizational role in the NORAD location and grant the role Supervisor rights to the NORAD container known as NORAD_ADMIN.

3. The main administrator can then move you into the role temporarily as an administrator so that you can install the NetWare 6 server. A NetWare 6 installation with an add replica will *not* complete unless you have Supervisor rights to the container in which the server is being installed.

An example of this entire scenario is shown in Figure 13.19.

**FIGURE 13.19** *Rights necessary to install a server in the NORAD container*

An example of an organizational role being created with NWADMIN is shown in Figures 13.20, 13.21, and 13.22.

**FIGURE 13.20** *Creating an organizational role*

**FIGURE 13.21** *Assigning the necessary rights*

**FIGURE 13.22** *Moving a user into the role as an occupant*

The necessary rights for installing servers into the NDS tree are essentially the Supervisor rights at an NDS-specific container that is also the top object in an NDS partition. The rights needed can be assigned using the ConsoleOne or NWADMIN utility.

## Application-Level Security

The next step in our example scenario is to consider the security required to install an application on your NetWare 6 server in the CAMELOT container and grant application access to your users.

It is important to understand the following security concepts:

▶ File system trustee assignments

▶ Supervisor rights to a server object

You are a file system administrator in the LABS location responsible for installing all new applications on the location's file servers.

1. You must have, at a minimum, the Create right to the APPS subdirectory on your NetWare 6, for example. In most cases, you use Supervisor trustee rights to perform these operations.

**2.** If you have Supervisor object rights over the file server object, you also have Supervisor rights over the file system.

**3.** Install your application according to the directions.

**4.** Make sure that all executable files related to this application are flagged as sharable read-only. Most application installations automatically do this for you, but it doesn't hurt to check.

**5.** Create any supporting objects that may be needed, such as groups or directory maps. This requires Create rights at the container. You may also need file system rights as well.

**6.** Consider using Novell's ZENworks to launch applications as NDS objects from a user's desktop. For more information on ZENworks, refer to Chapter 19.

An example of this entire scenario is shown in Figure 13.23.

The rights for creating and assigning application into the NDS tree have been detailed. In addition, the assigned user will want to use ConsoleOne or the NWADMIN utility to grant the appropriate access rights to the network users.

**FIGURE 13.23** *Using NWADMIN to assign rights necessary to install an application on a NetWare 6 server in the LABS container*

## Security on the Level of Individual Rights

Consider security procedures for granting an individual rights to manage a help desk center at the CAMELOT location.

It is important to understand the following security concepts:

- ▸ Trustee assignments
- ▸ Security equivalence

Your responsibility is to assist in managing a help desk at the CAMELOT location.

1. Using ConsoleOne or NWADMIN, create a series of specialized organizational roles for your help desk administration, such as user administrators, server administrators, and tree administrators. Although currently Directory Services does not enforce rights to a specific object class, you can create organizational roles that designate these types of administrators.

2. Assign Create, Delete, and Rename rights to the user administrator's role.

3. Assign Supervisor file system rights to the server administrator's role for each server in the container to be managed.

4. Create an organizational role at the top of your tree with explicit Supervisor rights at [ROOT]. Move the top help desk administrators into the organizational role as occupants.

5. Make IRF assignments where appropriate to limit administrator access to certain areas of your system.

Examples of this entire scenario are shown in Figures 13.24, 13.25, and 13.26. The necessary rights for creating a help desk for your organization have been detailed. You will want to use the ConsoleOne or NWADMIN utility to make the rights assignments.

## Security on the Level of Subadministrators

Next, we turn to the creation of subadministrators for each major location in the ACME tree.

It is important to understand the following security concepts:

- ▸ Trustee assignments
- ▸ Security equivalence
- ▸ Inheritance

**FIGURE 13.24** *Creating an organizational role for the user administrator*

**FIGURE 13.25** *Creating an organizational role for the server administrator*

**FIGURE 13.26** *Creating an organizational role for the tree administrators*

You have been given the assignment to create subadministrators for each major location in the ACME network and assign individuals to manage the network from that level down. You currently manage the network with only the ADMIN user object.

1. Using ConsoleOne or NWADMIN, create organizational role objects in the containers NORAD, RIO, TOKYO, CAMELOT, and SYDNEY.

2. Using ConsoleOne or NWADMIN, grant the newly created organizational role objects Supervisor rights to their respective containers.

3. Choose an administrator or administrators to participate in the organizational role and add them as role occupants using ConsoleOne or NWADMIN.

4. Assign the ADMIN user explicit Supervisor rights to each of the organizational role objects.

5. Using ConsoleOne or NWADMIN, place an inherited rights filter of Browse (and possibly Read) on each of the organizational roles to prohibit management of the role by the occupants.

**6.** These new administrators will have the power to create additional objects, including subordinate containers, in their respective locations. The administrators have Supervisor rights at these lower levels in the tree through inheritance.

An example of this entire scenario is shown in Figure 13.27.

**FIGURE 13.27** *Creating organizational roles for each location in the ACME tree*

If you need to decentralize the administration of NDS eDirectory for your company, the rights for doing so have been detailed. In order to assign the appropriate rights to the specific users or groups of users that will become the subadministrators, you want to use the ConsoleOne or NWADMIN utility.

## Administrator-Level Security

Next, create a file system administrator and an administrator in the OU=TOKYO location.

It is important to understand the following security concepts:

- ▸ Trustee assignments
- ▸ Security equivalence
- ▸ Inherited rights filter

Administration in the TOKYO container is being broken out into two responsibilities. One individual will handle only the file system administration, while the other administrator will handle the directory administration. Each must have separate rights.

1. Using ConsoleOne or NWADMIN, create two organizational roles. Name the first role NDS_ADMIN and the second role FILE_ADMIN.

2. Using ConsoleOne or NWADMIN, assign the NDS_ADMIN role Supervisor rights to the TOKYO container.

3. Using ConsoleOne or NWADMIN, assign the FILE_ADMIN role Supervisor rights to the server objects TOK-SRV1 and TOK-SRV2.

4. Using ConsoleOne or NWADMIN, place an inherited rights filter of Browse (and possibly Read) on the server objects TOK-SRV1 and TOK-SRV2.

An example of this entire scenario is shown in Figure 13.28.

**FIGURE 13.28** *Separating NDS and file system administration*

Using NDS rights, you can separate the administration of the NDS tree from the NetWare file system. This method is helpful if you need to decentralize the administration of either the NDS tree or your file system and then make those assignments to other administrators in your company. In order to assign the appropriate rights to the specific users or groups of users that will become the subadministrators, you want to use the ConsoleOne or NWADMIN utility.

### Security in Partitioning Operations

As a final step in our scenario, consider the rights necessary to perform partitioning operations at different levels in the NDS tree.

You have been made responsible for partitioning operations on the ACME network. You want to prohibit all partitioning operations except those performed by you and another administrator.

1. Using ConsoleOne or NWADMIN, grant the other administrators in their organizational roles all rights to their respective containers except the Supervisor object right. Grant Read and Create rights on the container ACL also. (Keep in mind that other administrators will not be able to install NetWare 6 servers into the tree without the Supervisor right to the container if they are adding a replica. You can grant them the right temporarily to handle this situation or add the replica for them.)

2. Create an organizational role for yourself and other tree administrators for partitioning operations called OR_PARTITIONS.

3. If you have not already done so, grant the organizational role explicit object Supervisor rights to each container immediately subordinate to [ROOT].

An example of this entire scenario is shown in Figure 13.29.

By using NDS rights, you can separate the administration of the partitioning and replicas for the NDS tree from the administration of the objects and properties in NDS. This method is helpful if you need to decentralize the administration of the NDS tree. In order to assign the appropriate rights to the specific users or groups of users that will become the subadministrators, you want to use the ConsoleOne or NWADMIN utility.

| | Object Rights | Property Rights | File System Rights |
|---|---|---|---|
| **[ROOT]** | | | |
| O=ACME ◄— OR_PARTITIONS | [S     ] | | |
| OR_PARTITIONS | | | |
| NORAD_ADMIN | [ BCRD] | [  R  ]  ACL | |
| OU=NORAD | | | |
| NORAD_ADMIN | | | |
| RIO_ADMIN | [ BCRD] | [  R  ]  ACL | |
| OU=RIO | | | |
| RIO_ADMIN | | | |
| CAMELOT_ADMIN | [ BCRD] | [  R  ]  ACL | |
| OU=CAMELOT | | | |
| CAMELOT_ADMIN | | | |
| TOKYO_ADMIN | [ BCRD] | [  R  ]  ACL | |
| OU=TOKYO | | | |
| TOKYO_ADMIN | | | |
| SYDNEY_ADMIN | [ BCRD] | [  R  ]  ACL | |
| OU=SYDNEY | | | |
| SYDNEY_ADMIN | | | |

**FIGURE 13.29** *Rights needed to perform partitioning operations on the ACME tree*

## Summary

This chapter has presented you with an understanding of NDS object and file system rights. As an administrator, you can assign rights to other administrators to perform specific tasks such as managing the users in their part of the tree or performing certain operations such as doing server backups or creating new NDS users. NetWare 6 provides expanded security functions including Public Key Infrastructure (PKI) and Secure Authentication Services (SAS).

# NetWare 6 Print Services

*"Learning hath gained most by those books by which the printers have lost."*
*— Thomas Fuller*

NetWare 6 enables a printer to be shared by any or all network users and Internet users. In order to print, an entire print job must be created and placed in a print queue on the server; then the print job must wait until a print server can process it and send it to the network printer.

NetWare 6 print services uses a new approach to enable Internet users to use printers that are not physically connected. This approach is called *Internet printing*. Internet printing is based on Novell Distributed Print Services (NDPS). NDPS has been created by Novell joining forces with the leaders of printer hardware technologies, including Hewlett-Packard, Xerox, Lexmark, Ricoh, and many others.

In this chapter, we discuss these concepts and demonstrate how to design and implement NetWare 6 print services in either a queue-based printing environment or the NDPS print environment. In addition to NDPS printing, NetWare 6 supports the traditional queue-based services. The major difference between the two versions lies in the TCP/IP protocol support in NetWare 6, which enables easier setup for Internet printing.

In the first several sections of this chapter, we exclusively address setting up the traditional queue-based print services for NetWare 6. Next, we discuss the NDPS printing environment and Internet printing, which greatly increases the availability of the printers and allows network printing to be completely bidirectional, giving users and administrators complete control.

# The NDS Print Objects for Queue-Based Printing

The print objects are the building blocks for the NetWare 6 print services architecture. These print objects define the network's printing infrastructure. In NetWare 6, these objects are stored in NDS as these three separate objects:

- ▶ Print queue
- ▶ Print server
- ▶ Printer

The NetWare 6 print services infrastructure is created by the association or relationship you set up between these three objects. The print queue should be assigned to represent a specific network printer or group of printers. The printer, in turn, is assigned to a print server, and the print server is assigned to service specific print queues. With these structures, a user creates a print job that is stored in a print queue until a print server can service the print job and send it directly to a printer. The print server waits until the printer is ready to accept the print job before sending it. This relationship is shown in Figure 14.1.

**FIGURE 14.1** *The relationship between the print objects in the NetWare 6 print services infrastructure.*

Users using NetWare 6 print services redirect their print jobs to network printers or to printers attached to the network workstations. The user's data (or print job) is not sent directly from the workstation to the printer. Instead, the data is captured and redirected to a file in a print queue, where it is stored while waiting to be sent to the printer. The data is first sent to a print queue to avoid multiple print jobs contending for the same shared printer. Multiple print jobs from different network users may stack up in the print queue until the print server is able to send them to the printer. The print server services the print jobs in the order they are received unless otherwise stipulated by the network administrator or print server operator.

## The Print Queue

The *print queue* is a key object or component in NetWare 6 printing. When a network user sends a print job to a network printer, NetWare temporarily stores the print job as a file in a directory on the server called a print queue. The print jobs wait in the print queue until the print server is able to process them and send them to the waiting printer. The print queue objects represent the directories where the print jobs are sent to be serviced.

The print queues store print jobs in subdirectories on server volumes that you specify when you create them. In NetWare 6, the print queue subdirectory can be created on any server volume. The print queue is then located in a default root subdirectory, called QUEUES, of that selected server volume. This subdirectory name can also be changed if you like.

You can create print queues using the NWADMIN or ConsoleOne utility. When you define a print queue using this utility, you give it a descriptive name. This name should follow your naming convention and identify the kind of printer that the print queue is associated with, where the printer is located, or the type of print jobs that can be sent. For example, the print queue associated with a Hewlett-Packard Laser Jet 4si could be called HP4SI-PQ1.

### Consulting Experience

Print queues and printers in the NDS tree should be placed with the users who will use their print services. For example, place print queues and printers in the same OUs as their users. If you have users in different OUs in the tree who want to use these print objects, you can either alias the print objects or place them at upper levels in the tree to support the greatest number of users.

► · · · · · · · · · · · · · · · · · · · · · · · · · · · · · · ◄

**Consulting Experience**

It is a good idea to take advantage of the NetWare 6 feature that enables you to create the print queues on server volumes other than SYS:SYSTEM. We recommend that you leave extra space on the SYS: volume because NDS files are stored on the SYS:SYSTEM in a hidden directory. NDS stops accepting changes if the SYS: volume fills up.

The print queue name is used by the users and should be as clear and convenient as possible. Internally, NetWare 6 assigns a print queue a server-centric ID number, which is an eight-digit hexadecimal number. For example, the print queue named HP4SI-PQ1 might have an ID with the value of 8034D4CF. You can view this ID number in the utilities. This number is important because it is used as the corresponding subdirectory name under the QUEUES directory.

The use of print queues provides an orderly method for multiple users to send print jobs to a single printer device. Queuing print jobs at the NetWare 6 server ensures that the printer deals with only one print job at a time.

The print jobs are stored as files in the print queue subdirectory. Their filenames always start with a "Q$" and include the last four digits of the print queue ID, plus a three-digit job number as the file extension. For example, the seventh print job in the print queue with the ID of 8034D4CF would have a filename of Q$D4CF.007.

When a user creates a print job and forwards it to the print queue, the print job passes through several states before being printed. These states are outlined in Table 14.1.

► · · · · · · · · · · · · · · · · · · · · · · · · · · · · · · ◄

**Consulting Experience**

Although you can set up a print queue associated with multiple printers, we recommend that for simplicity and manageability you set up only one print queue for each printer on your network.

T A B L E  14.1

*Print Job States in the Print Queue*

| STATE | DESCRIPTION |
|-------|-------------|
| Adding | The print job is being added to the print queue by the workstation. |
| Ready | The print job is waiting to be serviced by the associated print server. |
| Active | The print job is being sent to the appropriate printer. |
| Removed | The print job is finished and is removed from the print queue. |

## Print Servers

Another key software component of NetWare 6 printing is the print server, which binds the print queues to the network printers. A print server takes print jobs from the print queue and sends them to the assigned network printer. The print server software program can either be loaded as a NetWare Loadable Module on a NetWare 6 server or run as firmware in a network-attached printer.

In NetWare 6, PSERVER.NLM supports up to 256 printers, a fact that can help you consolidate or reduce the total number of print servers you have in the network. In order to start the print server on the server, type this at the server console prompt:

```
LOAD PSERVER PrintServerName
```

Substitute the name of the specific print server for PrintServerName. You can place this command in the AUTOEXEC.NCF file if you want the print server to load automatically during server bootup. Figure 14.2 displays the main screen for the print server software.

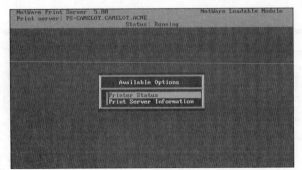

**FIGURE 14.2** *The main screen for the print server software running on the NetWare 6 server*

**Consulting Experience**

For ease of administration and use, we recommend that you configure the network printers as queue servers. This configuration requires that you connect the printers directly to the network cable system.

The print server software running at the network attached printer is often referred to as a *queue server* because the printer is set up to service the print queue directly. The queue server software logs into the server where the print queue is stored and polls the print queue to see if it has any print jobs ready for the printer. In this configuration, the printer device performs both functions of the print server and printer.

## Printers

If you use the NLM-based print server, you need to use the NPRINTER printer program that enables the print server to send jobs to a network printer. This printer can either be physically attached to the back of the NetWare 6 server, to a workstation, or directly to the network itself. Each printer requires the NPRINTER program to attach to the printer server and service print jobs.

Several different versions of the NPRINTER printer program can be loaded in several different situations. For instance, NPRINTER can be loaded as a terminate-and-stay resident (TSR) program, as a NetWare Loadable Module, or in the memory of the printer device itself. NPRINTER can be loaded in the following three ways according to the printer configuration:

- ▶ Workstations with printer devices connected should run NPRINTER.EXE to support the network printer. The printer is cabled to the parallel or serial port of the workstation. Now, a 32-bit version of NPRINTER called NPRINTER Manager is available for use on Windows 95/98/NT/2000 machines.

- ▶ Printer devices that are connected to a NetWare 6 server use the NPRINTER.NLM. The printer is cabled to the parallel or serial port of the NetWare 6 server.

- ▶ Printer devices connected directly to the network run the NPRINTER program from firmware or flash memory.

With NPRINTER loaded on a workstation, the user of that workstation can run applications and function normally. The user can even access the printer device as a local printer in stand-alone fashion, as well as a network printer. However, users are not encouraged to use the printer as a local printer because it might conflict with network printing activities. Naturally, the type of workstation and CPU speed will affect printing performance. For most large network sites, this type of configuration is not used.

NetWare 6 enables users to specify the printer object instead of a print queue when sending their print jobs. Users no longer have to know anything about print queues; they can simply send their print jobs to a printer by specifying the printer name. The network takes care of all print queue and print server activities. Sending a print job to a printer instead of a print queue is more intuitive to the user.

## NetWare 6 Print Utilities

In order for you to create and manage NetWare 6 print services, you should become familiar with several utilities that help you set up, control, and monitor network printing. One major change that you may notice immediately is that NetWare 6 no longer supports the DOS-based print utilities, such as PCONSOLE, PRINTCON, PRINTDEF, PSERVER, PSC, PUPGRADE, MIGPRINT, and ENDCAP. Instead of using the DOS-based utilities, you can use ConsoleOne or NWADMIN to create the printing objects and establish their relationship. The DOS-based utilities still available are CAPTURE, NPRINT, and NPRINTER. In addition, the server-based print utilities, PSERVER.NLM and NPRINTER.NLM, are also still supported.

The NetWare 6 print utilities and their functionality are described in the sections that follow.

### ConsoleOne

ConsoleOne is a Java-based administration tool that you can use to manage the printing components within NDS eDirectory. With ConsoleOne, you can also browse, create, modify, and grant rights to printing objects that build the printing environment. ConsoleOne also enables you to manage the server hardware components such as the server memory, hard drives, volumes, and network adapters.

### NWADMIN (NetWare Administrator)

The NetWare Administrator is a Windows-based program that enables you to manage NDS objects, including the printing objects. You can browse, create, modify, and grant rights to the printing objects. This utility offers the graphical interface for managing objects.

### NPRINTER.EXE (NetWare Printer)

The free-standing form of the NetWare printer program runs at a DOS workstation and connects the printer to the print server. With NPRINTER.EXE, the workstation printers wait to receive the print jobs passed to it. The workstation can run any application while printing takes place in the background. This program must be used in conjunction with the PSERVER program running at the server.

### NPRINTER.NLM (NetWare Printer)

The NetWare 6 printer program can also be loaded at the server as NPRINTER.NLM. This utility supports printers attached directly to the server and must be used in conjunction with the PSERVER program running at the server.

### PSERVER.NLM (Print Server)

The Print Server utility loads and runs on a NetWare 6 server that can act as a print server. The print server supports the remote and local printers running NPRINTER. The print server runs as an NLM called PSERVER.NLM. The print server can support up to 256 printers.

## Queue-Based Print Services Configurations

You should plan your printing needs in advance to determine which users need certain kinds of printers. For example, some users need strictly laser printers, whereas others may need dot matrix printers, plotters, and color printers. The type of printer has a significant effect on overall printing speeds. Where performance is a necessity, choose printers with a high page-per-minute (PPM) rating.

You need to consider five printer configurations or relationships when planning the printing infrastructure for your network. These five configurations are as follows:

- ▶ Non-network workstation printers
- ▶ Network workstation printers
- ▶ Network server printers
- ▶ Network-direct printers (remote printer mode)
- ▶ Network-direct printers (queue server mode)

## Non-Network Workstation Printers

A non-network workstation printer is connected to a workstation but is not set up as a network printer. This means that the workstation is not running the NPRINTER program, which shares the printer among all network users. Without the network software NPRINTER, the users of this workstation are the only ones that can print to the local printer. The users simply send the print jobs from the workstation to the stand-alone printer. Figure 14.3 illustrates this configuration.

▶ · · · · · · · · · · · · · · · · · · · · · · · · · · · · · · ◀

FIGURE 14.3 *The printer is set up as a non-network workstation printer. This is a stand-alone printer configuration.*

This configuration is simple for the user to set up and understand but is limited in a network environment. Because the printer is not shared by the other network users, the only person who can use the printer is the user sitting at the workstation.

You may want to consider setting up the printer in this fashion when the user requires a special-purpose workstation/printer combination. For example, the user who is responsible for printing invoices or checks may have a dedicated printer with all the forms preloaded and, therefore, may need a separate printer that should not be used by everyone on the network.

## Network Workstation Printers (Remote Printers)

A printer that is connected to a workstation can be a network printer if the proper network software is loaded. The NetWare 6 printer software NPRINTER.EXE needs to be loaded at the workstation, and the PSERVER.NLM software needs to be running at the server to communicate with the printer. The PSERVER is configured with the setup for the printer at the workstation.

The workstation that has the printer attached always needs be powered on (but not necessarily logged in) and running the NPRINTER.EXE program. The NPRINTER.EXE program connects the workstation printer to the print server and waits to receive the print jobs passed to it. Figure 14.4 illustrates the network workstation printer or remote printer configuration.

**FIGURE 14.4** *A network workstation printer, also called a remote printer*

This configuration is also called a *remote printer configuration* because the printers are not physically attached to the server running the print server. Instead, the printers are connected to the workstations in the network so that all the network users can print to them. You must start NPRINTER.EXE for each remote printer you defined for the print server. Run NPRINTER.EXE on the workstation to which the remote printer is physically attached. If you have more than one remote printer attached to the same workstation, you need to run NPRINTER once for each printer.

The easiest way to execute NPRINTER is by using the AUTOEXEC.BAT file for the PC. In this way, the NPRINTER software is running when the workstation is booted and even before a user logs in. Here is an example of loading the NPRINTER software using an AUTOEXEC.BAT file:

```
ECHO Off
PATH C:\DOS;C:\WINDOWS
PROMPT $P$G
LOADHIGH C:\NWCLIENT\LSL
LOADHIGH C:\NWCLIENT\NE2000
LOADHIGH C:\NWCLIENT\IPXODI
LOADHIGH C:\NWCLIENT\VLM
F:
NPRINTER PrintServer N
PAUSE
LOGIN...
```

Remember that NPRINTER doesn't have to be logged in to run, but it does need to be attached to the network, meaning that the NetWare shell or VLMs need to be loaded at the workstation. In order to execute the NPRINTER program before the user has logged in, you should copy it to the SYS:LOGIN directory of each server.

The remote printer configuration is a good option because the printing resources can be easily distributed around the network and placed close to the users that need them. One downside to this setup is that if the workstation is ever turned off or fails, the network printer becomes unavailable.

## Network Server Printers

A printer that is connected directly to the server can be a network printer if you load the NPRINTER.NLM software on the server. The PSERVER.NLM software also needs to be loaded to communicate with the NPRINTER software and printer.

Using this configuration, network users have the option to print to printers that are connected directly to the server. As with the network workstation printer, the users' print jobs are redirected to print queues that are serviced by the print server or PSERVER. Figure 14.5 illustrates the network server printer configuration.

Because the printer is connected directly to the server, this configuration becomes less flexible in most large network environments. Typically, in large networks the servers are placed in the computer room and may not be close to the network users. The printer cable can extend only a limited distance, thus making access for the users difficult, if not impossible.

**FIGURE 14.5** *The network server printer configuration*

This configuration is very popular in networks or remote office configurations in which the number of users is small. The server in this case can be situated close to the network users, and access to the printers is not limited. An important issue to remember when placing printers is that the users should not have to walk too far to pick up their print jobs. Printers should be placed in convenient locations.

Another issue with connecting printers directly to the server is that the printing load could slow the performance of the server. A printer connected to a server will demand CPU interrupts to process the print jobs. In a high-traffic environment, it is not wise to connect printers directly to the server.

### Network-Direct Printers (Remote Printer Mode)

A network-direct printer in remote printer mode is connected directly to the network using a special hardware device. These special hardware printing devices provide the connectivity to the network and are supplied by vendors such as Compaq, Eagle Technologies, Hewlett-Packard, Intel, and Lexmark. Depending on the hardware, this device is either connected to the port of the printer and then to the network or is installed in a slot in the printer.

In the remote printer mode, the printer functions much like a network workstation running NPRINTER.EXE. The NPRINTER program resides in the firmware or flash memory of the printer device. This configuration requires that the PSERVER.NLM be loaded on a NetWare server. The printer device then logs into the NetWare 6 server. It connects to the NetWare print server and polls print jobs. Figure 14.6 illustrates a network-direct printer running in remote printer mode.

**FIGURE 14.6** *A network-direct printer running in remote printer mode*

Using this configuration, you can distribute the printers around the network and place them close to the network users who use them. The printers running in remote printer mode under NetWare 6 run considerably faster than they did under

NetWare 4. The increased speed and flexibility of NetWare 6 makes remote printer mode a very effective way of providing network print services with these devices.

NetWare 6 can still use the NetWare SPX communication protocol between the print server and network-direct devices running in remote printer mode. This means that your existing network-direct devices can attach and receive print jobs from a NetWare 6 print server. In general, setting up a network-direct print device in remote printer mode involves the following steps:

1. Use the printer configuration utility supplied by the vendor to set up specific assignments.

2. Start NWADMIN to create your print service objects.

3. Create one or more print queues to be associated with the printer.

4. Select Other/Unknown and assign it to the print queue(s) previously created.

5. Create the print server object to service the printer and assign the printer to the print server object. If you already have an existing print server, you can use it for this purpose. Simply assign to it the printer to be serviced.

6. Run the network-attached printer configuration software supplied by the vendor.

7. Select the printer to be configured.

8. Configure the printer as a remote printer.

9. Select the print server and printer number to represent this printer.

One possible inconvenience in this process is that some printer devices require the print server to be running in order to be configured. Typically, this is not a problem, because the print server is running and servicing other printers. The new assignments made to the print server take effect immediately, and you do not need to recycle (take down and bring back up) the print server.

### CONSULTING EXPERIENCE

Some of the printer configuration utilities supplied by the vendors of the hardware can be operated only with explicit SUPERVISOR rights to the server; these utilities do not recognize a Supervisor equivalent. As a result, you need to log in using the SUPERVISOR account in bindery mode rather than logging in as ADMIN or another administrative user under NDS.

Another possible inconvenience comes with some of the older varieties of network-direct devices. These devices need to be configured on the print server with a 16-printer limitation. (This 16-printer limitation was introduced in the NetWare 3 print servers.) You should reserve printer connections 0 to 15 for these printer devices. The remaining slots (16 to 255) can then be used for your other, newer network printers.

## Network-Direct Printers (Queue Server Mode)

A network-direct printer is set up in queue server mode much as in the preceding case, in which the printer is connected directly to the network using a special hardware device. The difference with this configuration is that the printer in queue server mode acts like a special-purpose print server.

The queue server logs into the NetWare 6 server and services the associated print queue directly. The network-direct printers set up as queue servers are created and displayed in the NDS tree as print server objects.

In general, setting up a network-direct print device in queue server mode involves the following steps:

**1.** Use the printer configuration utility supplied by the vendor to set up specific assignments.

**2.** Start NWADMIN to create your print service objects.

**3.** Create one or more print queues to be associated with the printer.

**4.** Create a printer object for the network-direct printer. Configure the printer object as Other/Unknown and assign it to the print queue(s) previously created.

**5.** Create the print server object to service the printer, and assign the printer to the print server object. This name must be unique on the network. A new print server object is created for each network-direct printer set up in queue server mode.

**6.** Run the network-attached printer configuration software supplied by the vendor.

**7.** Select the printer to be configured.

**8.** Configure the printer as a queue server.

**9.** Type in the name of the print server.

**10.** Select the file server where the print queues are located.

The network-direct printer setup in queue server mode is the most popular printing solution in the industry. In many cases, it offers a fast, effective, and low-cost method for printing. This configuration also offers a good distribution of the printers across the network because the printers are placed next to the network users. This configuration is also not dependent on any external software or hardware systems such as PSERVER.NLM or a workstation. Figure 14.7 illustrates the network-direct printer running in queue server mode.

**FIGURE 14.7** A network-direct printer running in queue server mode

Several issues need to be considered when you implement this configuration:

▶ One common drawback of this configuration is that the queue servers are required to log into the network or server where the print queue resides. The queue server logs in using the normal user connection slots and takes one of the server's license connections, leaving you fewer connections for the network users. You should plan the distribution of the print queues accordingly. Of course, the PSERVER does the same thing.

▶ Some older print hardware devices are not yet NDS aware. This means the queue servers log into the NetWare 6 servers using bindery services mode and cannot read the print server configuration files from NDS.

▶ In order for the queue server to log in using bindery services, the NDS object definitions for the print queues must be in the server's bindery context. Any additional print queues serviced by the network-direct printers should also exist in the server's bindery context.

▶ NetWare 3 creates the group EVERYONE by default. Many network-direct print devices assume that this group exists and do not function properly in its absence. For these devices running in NetWare 6, you may need to manually create a group called EVERYONE in the context where the print server is defined. This way, the print server or queue server will be able to communicate with the network. Users do not have to be in the Group EVERYONE to print.

# NetWare 6 Queue-Based Printing Setup

In order to set up NetWare 6 print services, you should start by defining the print queues, print server, and printers using the NWADMIN utility. The following list outlines the steps necessary to install NetWare 6 print services:

1. Create network print queues on the file server by using NWADMIN.

2. Assign queue operators and queue users to the printer queue through NWADMIN.

3. Create a print server definition.

4. Specify the file servers that have the print queues that the print server will service.

5. Create printers to be associated with the print server.

6. Assign the print queues to the appropriate printers.

7. Optionally, set up printing for additional file servers.

8. Load PSERVER.NLM on the server.

9. If a remote printer was assigned to the print server, run NPRINTER.EXE at the appropriate workstation or run NPRINTER.NLM at the server.

10. Network printing should now be ready.

## The Quick Setup Option

The Quick Setup option is a quick way to create and set up each of the three print objects (print queue, printer, and print server) and automatically establish the appropriate relationships. This option is the simplest way to set up NetWare 6 print services, especially if you are starting without existing printing objects. Quick Setup is available in NWADMIN.

In order to run the Quick Setup option, perform the following steps:

1. Log into the network as an ADMIN user with the Create object right to the specific NDS container.

2. Load NWADMIN and change to the appropriate context.

**3.** Select the Quick Setup menu under the Tools menu.

**4.** Enter the information required on the screen by selecting names for each of the printing objects.

**5.** After saving the configuration, load the PSERVER.NLM software at a server console with the new print server object's name.

**6.** Load NPRINTER.EXE at the workstation with the printer or NPRINTER.NLM if the printer is attached directly to the server.

**7.** Network printing should now be ready.

We recommend that you use the Quick Setup option in NWADMIN if you are setting up NetWare 6 print services for the first time. Figure 14.8 shows the Quick Setup option screen in NWADMIN.

After a print queue is created, the user who created the queue is automatically assigned as a queue operator, and the users that exist in the same container in the NDS tree are assigned as print queue users. This is the default setup, and it works well for most networks.

If you want to delegate the responsibility for managing the print queues to other users, you can assign the other users to be queue operators through the NWADMIN utility.

**FIGURE 14.8** *The Quick Setup option screen in the NWADMIN utility*

Only users designated as queue users can submit print jobs to the print queue. In larger networks, delegate responsibility to queue operators for a location or department, and make only the members of the location or department queue users. The queue operators can then manage the print jobs for their areas.

## Novell Distributed Print Services

Novell Distributed Print Services is the next generation of print services. NDPS is designed to simplify access and administration of the network print services. Novell Distributed Print Services is a distributed service that consists of the client, the server, and the connectivity software components to seamlessly connect the applications to the network printers.

In NetWare 6, NDPS is included as the primary print services for the operating system. If you are currently satisfied with your current NetWare printing infrastructure, however, NetWare 6 will continue to support it. Then you can incrementally deploy NDPS at your own pace to gain the features and benefits.

NDPS gives users and administrators greater control over their printing. Features such as bidirectional feedback, print job status, automatic driver downloading, and event notification for printer status help simplify and streamline the usability and administration of the network printing. NDPS provides the following major benefits, features, and printing capabilities:

- NDPS enables the network administrator to centrally manage printing services from a single location.
- Users submit print jobs directly to the printers; no print queues need to be created.
- NDPS supports bidirectional communications with the printers.
- Administrators can move, copy, delete, prioritize, and pause print jobs.
- Network administrators are able to monitor and control print jobs, and they can receive print alerts or event notifications through e-mail, pop-up windows, event logs, and other methods, such as beepers and faxes.
- Users can determine whether a printer is available or busy and can copy or move print jobs between network printers as necessary.
- Plug-and-print option enables you to quickly install printers that can be immediately used by everyone with setup rights.

► NDPS reduces the network traffic associated with SAP broadcast because direct-connect printer devices no longer require SAP.

► Any NDPS printer can be managed through a standard SNMP console using the standard printer Management Information Base (MIB).

► NDPS completely supports the current NetWare queue-based printing environment and thus enables you to upgrade to NDPS as quickly or slowly as necessary.

NDPS uses a snap-in to NWADMIN to provide a single comprehensive management utility that enables and controls network printing for all major brands and models of printers. In the queue-based print services, the initial setup currently requires creating print queues, printer objects, and print servers, and then establishing a relationship between them. NDPS eliminates the need to create and configure print queues, printers, and print server objects. In fact, NDPS doesn't require you to manage print queues at all. Instead, using an NDPS-aware printer, you simply connect the printer to the network; users can begin sending print jobs to it at once. The printer indicates which driver it needs, and the driver is automatically downloaded to the users. This eliminates the need for the administrator to configure the users' workstations with drivers for specific printers and other devices.

## Simple Printer Access

When the client software is installed, a list of available printers (called a *short list*) is immediately available. The printers are created and configured as NDS printers, which enables users to browse the NDS tree for new printers based on a printer's properties, such as location, type, and supported languages. Because NDPS allows bidirectional information to be passed between the client and printers, users can match print jobs with the printer's capabilities. Users can also query and receive the status of the individual printers. This enables the users to know whether a printer is available, to get information about the status of the print jobs, and to receive notification that the paper tray is empty. One of the favorite features for many users is notification when the print job has been completed.

Users also have the flexibility to indicate that a print job or document needs to be printed on a special paper type. The printer then notifies the user when the paper needs to be loaded or inserted and then prints only that document on the special paper. For example, if the user specifies that a letter needs to be printed on single sheets of letterhead, the printer prompts the user to insert the letterhead and then prints only that letter or document on the letterhead.

## Easier Setup and Administration

New printers that are added to the system automatically register with NDPS, a feature that reduces the initial administrative setup and installation costs. For example, using the queue-based print services, when a new printer (set up as a queue server) is added to the network, the printer immediately starts advertising its availability, which results in increased network traffic. This advertising continues as long as the printer is turned on. Using NDPS, when a new printer is added to the network, it registers with a single registration agent. The agent then notifies all the appropriate clients of the printer's availability and advertises all the printers. This greatly reduces the overall network traffic caused by network printers.

Using NWADMIN, administrators have a centralized, simplified, and common interface to manage print services. Because NDPS is completely integrated with Novell Directory Services, administrators can create a printer object in the NDS tree and manage printers even if they come from different vendors. Because printer objects appear as NDS objects, they can easily monitor and control the printer. Figure 14.9 illustrates how the printer object in NDS can be used to monitor and control the features of the network printer directly from NWADMIN.

**FIGURE 14.9** Using NWADMIN and the printer object in NDS, you can easily monitor and control the features of the network printer.

## NDPS Architecture

The components that make up the Novell Distributed Print Services architecture are independent of any single operating system. Thus, the architecture is designed to be portable to different environments. The major components of NDPS are as follows:

▸ **Broker** — The Broker provides several network support services to NDPS. These services are the Service Registry Service, the Event Notification Service, and the Resource Management Service. When you first install NDPS, a Broker is automatically created and added to the NDS tree.

▸ **Client software** — All printing starts when the user sends print jobs to the network printers. Thus, in order to take full advantage of NDPS, you must upgrade the NetWare client software to the NetWare 6 client. The print client's responsibility is to send network print jobs from the workstation to the appropriate network printer on the network. The print clients communicate with a printer agent using the Novell Distributed Print Service Protocol (DPSP).

▸ **Gateway** — The gateways allow NDPS clients to send jobs to network printers that are not NDPS aware. They also allow non-NDPS clients in a pure NDPS environment to continue to access printers and send jobs to print queues just as they always have in the past. There are two types of gateways: third-party gateways developed by the printer manufacturer and the Novell standard gateway, which is used to support any non-NDPS-aware printers.

▸ **NDPS Manager** — The NDPS Manager is an NLM loaded on the NetWare server that enables you to create and manage the printer agents in the system.

▸ **Physical printer** — The physical printer is the actual printer device that is attached to the network to service the print jobs sent by the users. In order for the physical printer to be involved with the Novell Distributed Print Services, it must either have the Printer Agent component embedded or be able to communicate to such a component running on a NetWare 6 server.

▸ **Print device subsystem** — The print device subsystem (PDS) is part of the Novell standard gateway. It is a driver that is implemented and customized to control feedback and send it to the physical print device.

▸ **Printer agent** — A printer with an embedded printer agent is called an NDPS-enabled printer. It performs all the tasks of the current print server, spooler, and print queue. These tasks are combined into a logical print management agent that maintains information about the specific physical printer, such as printer availability, status, and other factors.

▸ **Port handler** — The port handler is part of the Novell standard gateway, which ensures that the print device subsystem can communicate with the printer no matter what type of physical port is being used (such as a parallel port, serial port, or network port).

Physical printer devices that are attached as network printers can become NDPS printers in two different ways. The printer can have an embedded printer agent, which enables the printer to become an NDPS-aware printer. The other method, used for printer hardware that does not have an embedded printer agent, must have the printer agent running on the NetWare 6 server to represent it to NDPS. However, the printer agent running at the server must communicate to a printer gateway, which in turn talks directly to the printers. The printer agents running on the NetWare 6 server are controlled and managed by the NDPS Manager. Figure 14.10 illustrates how all of these components work together to provide the printing solution.

**FIGURE 14.10** *The NDPS components work together to provide the network printing solution.*

In addition to all the components for NDPS, several utilities help you manage the printing environment. These software utilities are the snap-in to NWADMIN, Novell Printer Manager, and NDPS Remote Workstation Printer Management. Next, we discuss each of these components and software utilities in more depth.

## Printer Agents

Administrators create printer objects in the NDS tree, which represents a physical printer and enables users to submit print jobs to the printers. The printer agent represents the printer object to NDPS, and thus, the printer agent becomes the heart of NDPS. The printer agent acts as the major liaison between the network users and the physical printer devices. The printer agent receives information about the printer devices and resources that it is managing. It validates security information and provides direct notification and feedback to the appropriate client. The information received by the printer agent can be viewed using NWADMIN by selecting the individual printer object in NDS. Figure 14.11 shows the NWADMIN printer control screen for the printer object SFO-HPSI in the NDS tree. This screen enables you to manage and control the physical printer through the printer agent.

**FIGURE 14.11** *Using NWADMIN, you can manage the physical printer through logical representation of the NDS printer object and print agent.*

Before you can add a specific printer device into NDPS, you are required to represent the printer using a printer agent. The printer manufacturer typically develops these print agents. In addition, only one instance of the printer agent can represent a single physical printer, and no physical printer can be represented by more than one printer agent.

The printer agent may reside in several places on the system. The printer agent may be embedded within the physical printer device that is connected directly to the network. Or the printer agent may be run on the NetWare server as an NLM, which represents a printer that is either connected directly to the network or attached to a server or workstation. Figure 14.12 illustrates how the printer agent can be loaded and running on the NetWare 6 server and still represent the physical printer device or be embedded in the physical printer itself.

NetWare 6 Client

Printer Agent NDPS Aware Printer

Print Jobs / Feedback

**FIGURE 14.12** *The printer agent may be embedded in the physical printer or loaded on the NetWare 6 server, and it may represent either a printer connected directly to the network or one attached to a server or workstation.*

## An NDPS-Aware Printer

As mentioned, a physical printer device with an embedded printer agent is called an NDPS-aware printer. This is typically a physical printer that is attached directly to the network. The printer agent is the NDPS component that receives and processes the print job requests, providing a standard NDPS communication with the users. The physical printer device communicates with the printer agent in its native printer language.

The strength of this type of configuration is that it enables users to directly interact with the printer. They can send prints jobs directly to the printer and receive notifications and feedback from it. In this setup, the client and printer will have full bidirectional communication and feedback capabilities. Other major benefits of this configuration are that you get true plug and print, peer-to-peer printing, simple management, automatic driver download, and exceptional feedback and control. These benefits are gained because of the embedded printer agent, which maintains information about the specific physical printer. The printer agent also performs all the tasks of the current print server, spooler, and print queue. If a user queries the printer for status information or other attributes, the printer agent responds to the user on behalf of the physical device. In addition, the printer agent manages processing of all print jobs and other operations typically performed by the printer device itself. The printer agent also generates event or error notification for job completion, printing problems, or changes in printer status. Finally, the printer agent ensures scalability of the printing environment by supporting a wide range of devices, such as dot matrix, laser, and large-scale printers.

## The NDPS Manager

If the printer agent is loaded on the NetWare 6 server, it is created and managed by the NDPS Manager. The NDPS Manager is an NLM, called NDPSM.NLM, which enables you to load the printer agent entities on the system. The NDPS Manager is an object that is created in the NDS tree. In fact, you must create the NDPS Manager object before you can create or manage the printer agents. Figure 14.13 shows the main screen for the NDPS Manager in NWADMIN. You can load this screen by selecting or double-clicking the NDPS Manager object in the NDS tree.

**FIGURE 14.13** *The NDPS Manager screen can be viewed through the NWADMIN utility. To activate the screen, double-click the NDPS Manager stored in the NDS tree.*

A user wanting to create an NDPS Manager object in the NDS tree must have at least Create rights for the container in which it will be created. In addition, the user must have at least file system rights of Read, Write, Modify, Create, and File Scan at the root of the volume. Although you can perform some configuration and maintenance tasks directly through the NDPS Manager software running on the server, you will want to mainly use the NWADMIN utility to manage the different printer agents.

Because the NDPS Manager is an object in the NDS tree, you must create the NDPS Manager object before you can create or manage the printer agents. This NDPS Manager object stores information used by NDPS.NLM. A printer agent that has been created by the NDPS Manager but not officially registered as an NDS object in the tree can advertise its presence and availability as a *public access printer*, which is a network printer that is available to anyone attached to the network (even if they are not NDS users). On the other hand, printer agents that have been represented in the tree as NDS objects are called *controlled access printers* because this configuration does take advantage of the security.

As mentioned, the NDPS Manager enables you to create and manage the printer agents. Figure 14.14 illustrates how the NDPS Manager controls and manages the printer agents in the system.

**FIGURE 14.14** *The NDPS Manager enables you to create and manage the printer agents stored on the NetWare 6 server.*

After the printer agents have been created to represent the physical printer device, the users need to install the printer on their workstations and be given access to the printer. Both of these tasks can be easily accomplished by the administrators, using NWADMIN. The administrators can select the specific printer in the NDS tree and grant users access to use it. Figure 14.15 illustrates how the administrators can grant rights to the print object in NDS using NWADMIN through the printer Access Control page.

**FIGURE 14.15** *The administrators can use NWADMIN and the Access Control page to grant rights to users, managers, and operators.*

## NDPS Remote Workstation Printer Management

Although users may have rights to a printer, in order for them to access it using NDPS, the printer needs to be installed on the users' workstations. With NDPS, you can remotely change the configuration of the workstation to add, delete, or change printer configurations. These tasks are performed remotely using the remote workstation management software that comes with NDPS. The software is called the NDPS Remote Workstation Printer Management. Figure 14.16 illustrates how you can add a specific printer to the user's workstation configuration remotely using the NDPS Remote Printer Management page in NWADMIN. This example is for the specific printer SFO-HPSI.

**FIGURE 14.16** *An NDPS printer can be added to the user's workstation configuration remotely using the NDPS Remote Printer Management page in NWADMIN. This example is specific to the printer SFO-HPSI.*

The NDPS Remote Workstation Printer Management software can be executed as a stand-alone utility from the Tools menu in NWADMIN. Running it from the Tools menu enables you to make changes for multiple printers at the same time. Figure 14.17 illustrates the interface for the utility after it has been executed from the Tools menu.

In order to support the NDPS Remote Workstation Printer Management from the workstation or client side, you must be running the NetWare 6 client. The

NetWare 6 client is also required to print directly to the printer agents either embedded in the printer device itself or on the server. Some of the major advantages of the NetWare 6 client with NDPS are as follows:

- ► Automatic driver download
- ► Remote workstation management
- ► Public access printing
- ► Print queues no longer needed
- ► Event notification

**FIGURE 14.17** *The NDPS Remote Workstation Printer Management software can be executed from the Tools menu in NWADMIN, which enables you to make changes for multiple printers at the same time.*

## Novell Printer Manager

After users have an NDPS printer defined on their workstations, they can use the Novell Printer Manager to view the printer status, print jobs, and other information. In addition, they can move print jobs between printers. Figure 14.18 shows the main screen of the Novell Printer Manager, which shows the list of printers available to users. In this case, the printer shown is SFO-HPSI with its print jobs.

Figures 14.19 and 14.20 illustrate how the Novell Printer Manager can be used by users to receive status information from the printer. In Figure 14.19, the printer is reporting a caution status symbolized by the yellow icon with an exclamation mark in it. In Figure 14.20, the printer is reporting a critical error, which has halted or stopped the printer from functioning.

**FIGURE 14.18** *The Novell Printer Manager can be used by the users to view the list of printers available. In this case, the printer shown is SFO-HPSI. In addition, the print jobs that are currently placed at the printer are shown.*

**FIGURE 14.19** *Using the Novell Printer Manager, the user has received a caution status report from the printer. The caution status is symbolized by the yellow icon with an exclamation mark in it.*

**FIGURE 14.20** *Using the Novell Printer Manager, the user has received a critical error from the printer. The critical error has halted or stopped the printer.*

## NDPS Printer Gateways

As mentioned previously, a physical printer device that does not have an embedded printer agent must have the printer agent running on the NetWare 6 server to represent it to NDPS. However, the printer agent running at the server must communicate to a printer gateway, which in turn talks directly to the printers. The printer gateway communicates to the printer device in its native language to provide complete bidirectional feedback to the users. Thus, in order to support network printers that are not NDPS aware, you need to use NDPS printer gateways.

The NDPS printer gateway allows NDPS clients to send jobs to network printers that are not NDPS aware. It also allows non-NDPS clients in a pure NDPS environment to continue to access printers and send jobs to print queues just as they always have in the past. In the absence of true NDPS-aware printers, it is important that you know and understand how to support non-NDPS-aware printers in your network. To accomplish this, you need to set up the appropriate gateway and printer agent running on the server. Figure 14.21 illustrates how the printer gateway communicates directly to the printer device and then passes the information on to the printer agent. Print jobs are handled by the printer agent, which passes them to the gateway and then on to the printer itself.

**FIGURE 14.21** *The printer gateway enables the users to print to printers that are not NDPS aware, meaning that the printer agent is not embedded in the printer device itself.*

NDPS supports two different categories of printer gateways, third-party gateways and the Novell gateway.

### Third-Party Printer Gateways

The third-party gateways are developed by printer manufacturers to support printers directly attached to the network. Printer manufacturers may provide utilities that can be configured to automatically create printer agents using their gateways to support one of their non-NDPS printers. Currently, the Hewlett-Packard and Xerox gateways are included with the NDPS software. For example, the Hewlett-Packard gateway is called HPGATE.NLM.

You can also download the latest copies of a third-party gateway from the appropriate Web site. For example, the Xerox gateway is available for download at `www.xerox.networkprinters.com`. Gateways from other printer vendors will be available soon.

### The Novell Printer Gateway

The Novell gateway supports printers connected as remote printers, such as those using NPRINTER to support queue-based print services. This gateway provides the functionality to be backward-compatible with the queue-based services. The Novell gateway enables you to support not only remote printers in the network but also local printers (printers connected directly to the server ports) and printers connected to a PSERVER. Figure 14.22 illustrates how the Novell gateway supports network printers connected as remote printers and local printers.

**FIGURE 14.22** *The Novell gateway supports network printers connected as remote printers and local printers. The gateway provides backward compatibility with the queue-based services.*

The Novell gateway is implemented through the print device subsystem and the port handler. These two components of NDPS are unique to the Novell gateway and are not used for the third-party gateways.

**The Print Device Subsystem**    The print device subsystem is a driver that can be implemented and customized to control feedback and send it to the physical print device. The PDS retrieves printer-specific information and stores it in a database. A port handler can then use the information that is stored in the database to communicate with the physical printer. Normally, the print device subsystem is developed by original equipment manufacturers (OEMs) and independent software vendors (ISVs) to take advantage of the functionality of each of the physical printer devices.

The PDS is implemented as a NetWare Loadable Module and is automatically loaded when a printer agent is created using the PDS configuration utility. You should use the Novell PDS when you are creating a printer agent for either of the following situations:

▶ A network printer that is not connected directly to the network, which includes local printers and remote printers

▶ A printer that is directly connected to the network but whose manufacturer has not provided a proprietary NDPS gateway

**The Port Handler**    The port handler ensures that the print device subsystem can communicate with the printer no matter what type of physical port is being used (such as a parallel port, serial port, or network port).

## The Broker

When you first install the NDPS software on your network, a Broker is automatically created and added into your NDS tree. For performance purposes, an additional Broker is created if NDPS is installed on a server that is more than three hops away from the existing Broker. The Broker provides three services that are distinct from one another. These services are called the Service Registry Service (SRS), the Event Notification Service (ENS), and the Resource Management Service (RMS).

### The Service Registry Service

The Service Registry Service allows public access printers to advertise themselves so that users can find them. This service maintains information about the printer type, printer name, and printer address, as well as printer-specific information (such as manufacturer and model number). Figure 14.23 shows the SRS screen found in NWADMIN under the Broker object in NDS.

**FIGURE 14.23** *You can use the NWADMIN utility to manage the Service Registry Service in the Broker object in NDS.*

SRS helps reduce the network traffic and overhead problem created when printers connected directly to the network advertise using SAP. Before NDPS, all printers set up in queue server mode periodically advertised their availability through the Novell Service Advertising Protocol (SAP). This method caused an inefficient use of the network. Now, when an NDPS printer is set up on the network, it registers with SRS. In turn, when users request the use of a printer, they contact SRS and retrieve a list of registered printers on the network.

### The Event Notification Service

The Event Notification Service allows printers to send customizable notifications to users and operators about printer events and print job status. This service supports a variety of notification delivery methods including log files, pop-up windows, e-mail, and other third-party interfaces (such as pagers). Figure 14.24 shows the screen in NWADMIN for the Event Notification Service, which is included in the Broker.

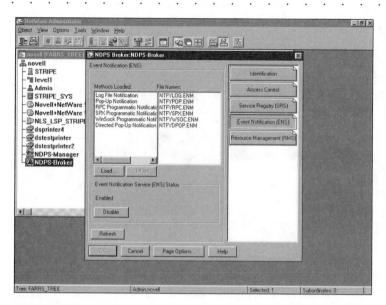

**FIGURE 14.24** *The Event Notification Service is managed by the Broker and can be seen in the NWADMIN utility.*

ENS not only enables the administrators to configure event notification, but it also enables non-job owners who wish to be notified of the existence of a defined printer event that occurs during the processing of the job. For example, the boss requests a print job but wants the secretary to pick it up for him. At the workstation, individual users can use the Novell Printer Manager to configure event notification pertaining to their own print jobs.

### The Resource Management Service

The Resource Management Service enables resources to be installed in a central location and then have those resources downloaded to the individual workstations or printers. The RMS supports adding, listing, replacing, and deleting resources including printer drivers, printer definition files (PDFs), banners, and fonts. Figure 14.25 shows the Resource Management Service screen found in NWADMIN under the Broker NDS object.

**FIGURE 14.25** *You can use the NWADMIN utility to manage the Resource Management Service in the Broker NDS object.*

# Internet Printing

Novell Internet Printing (often referred to as iPrint) is a printing solution based on the industry-standard Internet Printing Protocol (IPP) that eliminates the complexities of printing over the Internet. The Internet Printing Protocol is a new protocol that defines an open standard for client/server print operations such as job submission, printer capabilities, job status, and so on. Novell Internet Print is built on top of the Novell Distributed Print Services and inherits the manageability, scalability, reliability, and ease of use. Internet Printing exposes the printer whether it is on your desk or in Australia. The print job will be spooled, managed, and printed securely.

Novell iPrint can work with any printer as long as it is connected to the network. Within iPrint, a Web Administration Tool makes it possible to manage iPrint from anywhere in the world, with no dependence upon the Novell Client 32. The administrator could manage the printers from work, home, or (heaven forbid) even on vacation.

Internet printing has been developed to provide the following features:

- ▶ Global access to printers through a Web browser.
- ▶ No Novell or NDS client is required, but if present it will be utilized.
- ▶ No NDPS RPC or Library component.
- ▶ IPP Client must be modular and have the capability of being used with a browser as a Plug-in.
- ▶ Flexible print deployment configurations.
- ▶ Secure printing.
- ▶ Unified management through single administration of components.
- ▶ Customized viewing of printers.

The system requirements for Internet printing are broken into server, workstation, and administrator's workstation requirements, as follows:

- ▶ Server:
  - • NetWare 6
  - • NetWare 5.1 with support pack 2 or higher
  - • NetWare 5.1 printing enhancement pack
- ▶ User workstation:
  - • Windows 2000, Windows NT, or Windows 95/98
  - • Internet Explorer 5.0 or higher, Netscape Navigator 4.7 or higher
- ▶ Administrator's workstation:
  - • Microsoft's Internet Explorer 5.0 or higher
  - • iPrint Web Management Tool (included with iPrint)
  - • Novell Client 32 (optional)

Novell iPrint also provides all the tools needed to create custom Web pages for location based printing. It is as easy as dragging and dropping printer icons on an image of a floor plan. The tool saves the map as a Web page with the printers ready to be installed. Figures 14.26, 14.27, 14.28, 14.29, and 14.30 illustrate an example of selecting a printer from a Web page. This example has been put together only to demonstrate the Internet printing capability and how you can select a printer from the Web and print to it. The example is called DigitalAir and demonstrates how to select a printer and install the printer driver from the Web site.

**FIGURE 14.26** *From the Digital Air Web site, you start the selection process.*

System administrators can use the server hosting the Novell IPP back-end, or any other Web Server, to dish up Web pages offering a customized view of their print environment, as shown here in the Digital Air example. As shown in Figure 14.27 and Figure 14.28, the Web page helps users navigate through available locations and services.

Figure 14.28 shows how you can pick a printer icon from the Web site. The Web page can access the IPP workstation components to interact with the IPP printers in real time.

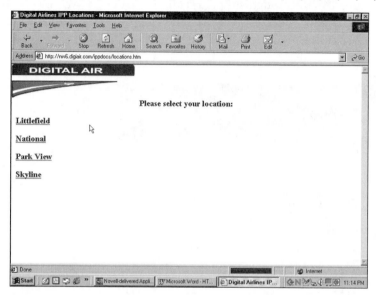

**FIGURE 14.27** *From the Digital Air example, you need to select the location from which you want to pick your printer.*

**FIGURE 14.28** *From the Digital Air Web site, you view and pick a printer from the location that you have selected.*

As shown in Figure 14.29, through simple HTML constructs, a Web page can query the printer's status and characteristics, list pending jobs, or cause the printer to be installed on the user's workstation.

**FIGURE 14.29** *From the Digital Air example, you are presented a custom Web page that enables you to view printer specific information for the printer that you previously selected.*

Figure 14.30 illustrates how you can download the appropriate print driver from the Web page that has been created to support the printer. Through IPP, the driver that matches the user's operating system and default natural language can be selected without the user's intervention. Printer driver files are compressed to expedite their download and may be signed to guarantee their integrity. Making printer driver downloads transparent to users removes most of the limitations encountered at various ASPs and Internet print shops today, while ensuring the quality and fidelity of the printed document.

**FIGURE 14.30** *If needed, you can quickly download the printer driver directly from the Web page with specifics about the selected printer.*

As shown in the last few figures, a user can find a map or list of printers through a browser. Users don't need the printer drivers because they are automatically downloaded or installed from the Web page. Users don't need to know the printer's URL because the appropriate printer can be picked from a list or map from the Web. For example, simply open your Internet browser, log on to the corporate intranet, select a printer in the desired area of the building, and print from within any application. Other examples could be a user at home printing to the printer at the office. If at a hotel, the user can print to the lobby, the local corporate office, or the copy shop across the street.

Internet printing solves a big problem for mobile employees that found it difficult to locate and install printers as they traveled from office to office. By utilizing the power of Novell Distributed Print Services, iPrint secures, simplifies, and accelerates document printing, and it provides access to all your printing resources through a Web browser. Novell Internet Printing can IPP-enable any NDPS printer with one click. You don't need to upgrade hardware. Figure 14.31 shows how you can IPP-enable any NDPS printer with one click.

**FIGURE 14.31** *Using NWADMIN, you can IPP-enable any NDPS printer. Select the IPP Client Support under details for a printer and click the "Enable IPP access to this printer" checkbox.*

## Novell IPP Printing Solution

The Novell IPP implementation is in full compliance with IPP v1.1; as such, it interoperates with any third-vendor IPP-compliant component. The capabilities of Novell IPP, however, require that Novell IPP support be present both on the server and on the user's workstation. To meet this requirement, Novell IPP uses the Web's download-on-demand software distribution model. In turn, system administrators only need to set up the server components, and users download the capabilities that they need to interact with the system on the fly.

The Novell IPP server components transform an NDPS printer into an IPP printer and give it presence on the Internet. These components are seamlessly integrated with Novell's native HTTP stack. This relationship is important because IPP communication travels as HTTP packets and because Novell IPP relies on Web pages for bootstrapping users into the system. The end result is a low-maintenance service back-end that supports the following functionality:

► **IPP communication** — With Novell IPP, system administrators can enable IPP access to any NDPS printer. IPP is the ideal protocol for submitting print jobs and communicating printer-related information over the Internet. Under the IETF scrutiny, IPP was defined with Internet security and firewall safety in mind. Recent industry-wide IPP information confirm that IPP's standard use of IANA-registered port numbers and mime types greatly improve IPP's interoperability with network firewalls and proxies. This level of Net awareness is essential for B2B and C2B print solutions and solutions that support hosted data centers and remote Internet branches.

▸ **IPP printers Web page** — Novell IPP dynamically generates a Web page that lists the IPP printers hosted on a given server. The page includes the status of each printer and a link that users can follow to install each printer on their workstations. If a user's workstation doesn't have the Novell IPP workstation components needed to install the printer, the browser can automatically download the necessary files after getting user confirmation.

▸ **Printer driver download** — Through a standard IPP extension, users can download the printer driver needed to format documents for a specific printer. The driver can be transparently downloaded to users.

▸ **Novell IPP workstation components download** — All the Novell IPP workstation components can be downloaded on demand through a Web browser. If users visit the generated printer Web page mentioned above, these components are downloaded automatically when users first try to install or communicate with a printer. System administrators may also wish to customize a Web page that enables users to explicitly download these files. The Novell IPP workstation components do not require the presence of Novell's Client32.

▸ **Security management and enforcement** — Novell IPP supports the standard security mechanisms prescribed by IPP: namely, HTTP Basic Authentication and SSL3 encryption. It uses existing NDS user accounts to perform the Internet authentication so that system administrators don't have to manage two separate security schemes. Novell IPP uses the NDPS printer roles specified in NDS to control the type of access a user can have to a given IPP printer. Novell IPP security does not require users to be logged in to a NetWare server.

▸ **Customized Web pages** — System administrators can use the server to dish up Web pages offering a customized view of their print environment, as shown in the Digital Air example.

The Novell IPP client components enable a user's workstation to have the richest interaction with the Novell IPP server components but the components are not required. The client components are packaged with security in mind. The Novell

IPP client components can coexist with Novell's Client32 but work independently of it (if needed). The following list summarizes the key functionality of the Novell IPP client components:

▶ **Security** — The Novell IPP client components can communicate with IPP printers using the following secure schemes: HTPP Basic Authentication, Digest (MD5) Authentication, SSL3 Encryption, and TLS.

▶ **HTML and Java** — The Novell IPP client components support can be accessed by any Web page via JavaScript, Java, or HTML. Through this interface, Web pages can be customized to communicate with a printer using IPP. The Web page can specify how it wishes the result of a request to come back: as an HTML page, browser cookies, Message (Pop-up) Window, or parameterized URL.

▶ **IPP Print Provider** — The Novell IPP client components implement a Windows print provider that uses IPP as its print protocol. This enables users to print directly to IPP printers and print servers from any Windows application. Printers installed via the Novell IPP HTML API appear to users as any other printer installed through the Add Printer Wizard. The Novell IPP workstation components also support installing a printer using the Add Printer Wizard. In this case, the user must type in the IPP URL of the printer. When users interact with Novell IPP printers using the Windows Printers Folder, the Novell IPP workstation components satisfy the OS requests by issuing IPP queries to the appropriate printer or print server. The end result is identical user experiences for interacting with a local printer and a printer across the Internet.

## Novell IPP Printer Setup

This section describes the steps for a system administrator to implement a working Novell IPP printer. The following assumes NDPS printers are properly configured to front-end the print devices to be shared throughout the network. This configuration includes assigning printer drivers to the NDPS printers in question. In this release of Novel IPP, you need NWADMIN to enable IPP access to an NDPS printer. Future versions may include a Web tool to accomplish this task.

The first step in the process of setting up a printer is to install the desired NDPS components and printer in NWADMIN. As you know, you must first create or define a NDPS Broker object for NDS tree. In this case, we have defined the CAM-BROKER1 in NWADMIN to be held in OU=CAMELOT. Figure 14.32 shows the setup for this object.

**FIGURE 14.32** *The first step in setting up an IPP printer is to create the NDPS Broker required to support NDPS. In this case, we have defined the CAM-BROKER1 in NWADMIN to be held in OU=CAMELOT.*

After you have created the NDPS Broker, you need at least one NDSP Manager. The NDPS Manager supports the printer agents that are tied to each printer. Figure 14.33 shows how to create the CAM-NDPS-MANAGER1 object on the CAM-SRV1.

After you have created the NDPS Broker and at least one NDPS Manager, you need to start the broker on the selected server. You can start the broker by typing the following at the server console:

```
LOAD BROKER CAM-BROKER1.CAMELOT.ACME
```

After the broker is running on the server, you see a screen similar to the one shown in Figure 14.34.

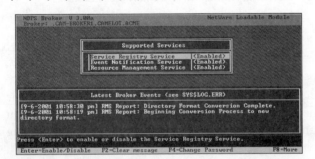

**FIGURE 14.33** *After you have created the Broker, you need at least one NDPS Manager to support the printer agents. In this case, we have defined the CAM-NDPS-MANAGER1 object on the CAM-SRV1.*

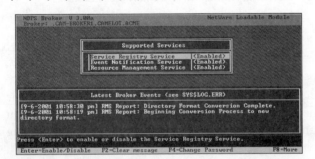

**FIGURE 14.34** *An NDPS broker called CAM-BROKER1.CAMELOT.ACME is running on the server as an NLM.*

Because the broker is running and is assigned to at least one NDPS Manager, you can now add NDPS Printers to your NDS tree to support the physical printers that you have. Figure 14.35 shows how you can create a printer called CAM-NDPS-Printer1 with a new printer agent.

**FIGURE 14.35** *After the NDPS Broker and Manager, you can create NDPS printers. In this case, we are creating an NDPS printer called CAM-NDPS-Printer1.*

The next step in defining the NDPS printer called CAM-NDPS-Printer1 is defining the printer agent. The printer agent acts as the liaison between the network users and the physical printer devices. The printer agent receives information about the printer devices and resources that it is managing. Figure 14.36 shows the setup for the printer agent for the CAM-NDPS-Printer1.

**FIGURE 14.36** *To complete the setup for the NDPS printer called CAM-NDPS-Printer1, you need to define a printer agent.*

During the setup of the printer agent, you are asked to associate it to an NDPS Manager and select the type of gateway that the printer agent will use. Next, the setup of the NDPS printer enables you to select the type of printer that CAM-NDPS-Printer1 is. Figure 14.37 shows the screen that enables you to select the printer type and port handler.

**FIGURE 14.37** *During the setup of the NDPS printer, you are asked to provide the printer type and select the port handler type.*

The next step in setting up an NDPS printer is to configure the port handler for the printer. Figure 14.38 shows the options that you have to configure the port handler for the printer. You have two options that include the connection type and port type. In order to set up an NDPS printer to support Internet Printing, you have to select the "Remote (LPR on IP)" communication option. You do not need to select a port type.

To support Internet printing, you need to select the "Remote (LPR on IP)" communication option. The next screen enables you to configure the Host IP address for the printer. Make sure that you provide the correct address for the printer, or Internet printing will not work correctly. Figure 14.39 shows the screen that enables you to provide the Host IP address for the NDPS printer that will support Internet printing.

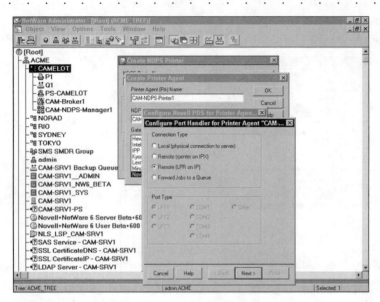

**FIGURE 14.38** *During the step to the NDPS printer, you need to configure the port handler for the printer. This includes configuring the connection type and port type.*

**FIGURE 14.39** *To support Internet printing, provide a Host IP address for the NDPS printer.*

After you have completed each of these steps to create an NDPS printer, the NDPS printer agent loads itself automatically. Figure 14.40 shows the dialog box that appears during the time that the printer agent is loading.

**FIGURE 14.40** *The printer agent loads after you have completed the steps of creating the new NDSP printer to this point.*

Next, you are asked to provide the print drivers for the NDPS printer for each of the operations systems that the users will use. Figure 14.41 shows the printer driver screen. You can associate a printer driver for each type of operating system. This allows the Internet Printer to be used by all types of users and operating systems. This screen is important to configure to support Internet Printing, regardless of the operating system that will use it.

**FIGURE 14.41** *To finish the NDPS printer setup, you are asked to supply the print driver. If you anticipate that the users have multiple operating systems, you need to supply the printer driver for each system.*

After the NDPS printer has been created, you can view the details from NWADMIN by double-clicking the new printer. The view that appears is shown in Figure 14.42. You use this screen to configure the Internet printing under the IPP Client Support tab.

**FIGURE 14.42** *After the NDPS printer is created, open details view.*

From the details dialog box for the new NDPS printer, you need to select the IPP Client Support tab. From the IPP Client Support dialog box, select "Enable IPP access to this printer" to configure this printer for Internet printing. No other steps are needed. This means that if you already have an existing NDPS printer, you need to simply select "Enable IPP access to this printer" and click the Apply button, as shown in Figure 14.43.

The dialog box displays the IPP URLs through which that printer can be accessed. You can also specify that only secure IPP communication should be allowed, by checking the Require Security checkbox. The printer is now ready to accept IPP requests.

The Novell IPP server components automatically generate a Web page listing all the NDPS printers hosted at a given NDPS Manager with IPP access enabled. Through this page, users can install any listed printers using their browsers. The URL of this page is the IP address or DNS name of the NetWare server hosting the printer with "/IPP" appended. For example, to access a printer, use the Web address HTTP://CAMSRV1-PRINTSERVER1.ACME.COM/IPP.

**FIGURE 14.43** *In order to configure Internet printing on an NDPS printer, simply select the "Enable IPP access to this printer" check box on the IPP Client Support dialog box.*

Though the previous steps are all that is required to enable users to install and use IPP printers, system administrators and system integrators have the option of setting up customized views of their printing environment. These customized views should guide users in their selection of printing services. By avoiding the common mistakes that users make when selecting and installing a printer, a Novell IPP-based solution can offer unprecedented printing reliability and user satisfaction. The following section provides a glimpse of the type of custom print solutions possible through Novell IPP.

### Novell IPP User Solutions

One of the best-selling points of Novell IPP is the power that it gives system administrators and system integrators to implement custom Internet printing solutions. Thus, with Novell IPP, the user's experience can be very different from one implementation to another. This section describes a few possible Novell IPP custom solutions, from the user's perspective. The user scenarios are as follows:

▶ The first example covers installing a printer from the Novell IPP generated page. This example uses the default printer page and does not require Web customization. A corporate user receives a memo indicating that printers are available for use at HTTP://CAMSRV1-PRINTSERVER1.ACME.COM/IPP.

When the user uses the browser to visit this site, the user is presented with the list of IPP printers hosted at CAMSRV1-PRINTSERVER1.ACME.COM. The list is automatically generated by the system and shows the status of each listed printer and whether communication to that printer is secure. Next to each printer is a link that reads Install. After clicking on one of these links, the user is asked to confirm that she wishes to install the printer onto her workstation. She okays the transaction, so the printer driver that matches the printer's make and model and the operating system on the workstation is downloaded. The printer is then installed on the workstation without any further user intervention. The next time the user tries to print from an application, she can select that printer from the available list of installed printers.

▶ The next example shows how you can quickly set up a newly hired employee. A newly hired employee logs into his company's internal site. He is presented with a personalized page containing corporate news, links to employee's benefits, and links to traditional productivity application available for downloading. Under the heading "Remote User Workstation Setup," he finds a link that reads "Install my assigned printers." He clicks on the link and is taken to a page that informs him that four different printers have been installed on his workstation along with a description of each printer's capabilities and location.

▶ Another user example covers a commercial printing application. A guest at a hotel room with Internet access needs to print a set of documents for an upcoming meeting. The user connects her laptop to the room's Internet link device and launches her browser. She is automatically taken to the hotel's home page where a number of hotel services and local shops are listed. She logs in and selects a link that reads "Available Printers," which takes her to a page listing four different printers: one located at the hotel's front desk and three others at a nearby print shop. By each printer, she finds whether the printer supports color, the cost per printed page, and a link to install the printer. She clicks on the link to install the printer that seems right for the job and is informed that the printer is now available on her workstation and will be automatically removed after her checkout date. She is also informed that she may now print to that printer from within her application and that any incurred costs will be automatically charged to her room account.

▶ This user example describes location-based or remote printing. A sales rep is visiting a branch office to pick up promotional materials and print a few documents. Using the browser on his laptop, he visits his company's internal home page and follows the link to "Corporate global print services." This takes him to a map of the United States with links placed at the regions of the country where his company has branch offices. By clicking on the state he is visiting, he is taken to a page showing the two branches located in that state. He continues to follow a few more links until he is presented with a floor plan of the building he is at with icons representing the different printers available on that floor. By positioning the cursor over a printer icon the browser displays information about the printer. He clicks on the icon nearest his current location. This causes the printer to be installed on his workstation. He runs his application and prints the documents.

▶ This final example describes an administrator who has the responsibility of a printer operator. A printer operator is responsible for making sure a set of printers in an organization are always operational. He needs to know when a printer is out of paper, low on toner, jammed, and so on. He implements a Web page that shows the printers he's responsible for as icons located on a floor plan. Healthy printers are shown with a green background, and printers that need attention are shown with a red background. The page updates itself automatically every three minutes. When you click on a printer with a red background, a separate browser page pops up, displaying five different printer attributes that, he has learned, give him enough information to know how to fix most error conditions.

## Modules of Internet Printing

The goals of Internet printing are to eliminate the use of the current Novell client and remove the dependency on the current RPC mechanism found in NDPS. To meet this objective means that the IPP transport protocol is required to communicate with servers. The IPP protocol provides a documented and ratified specification for this communication path and uses the widely known HTTP protocol as the underlying transport.

The design of print services uses a modular approach so that in the event that this code is ported to other platforms, it can be easily modified and compiled for the given environment. This modular design produces three different modules: IPP module, Print Provider module, and Browser Plug-in module. Each of these modules is described in the following sections.

## IPP Module

The Novell Internet printing solution uses the IETF-ratified Internet Printing Protocol [RFC 2910-1] to provide the over-the-wire transport or communication. The IPP module from Novell is responsible for transporting all IPP 1.0/1.1 requests and responses. The IPP specification provides a standard data-encoding structure for each of its operations, and each of the IPP-encoded operations must be sent/received to the remote IPP printer or server.

This implementation provides an IPP module that contains three separate components. All of these components are compiled into a single Windows DLL. The three components of the IPP module are as follows:

1. TCP/IP transport mechanism — The TCP/IP transport mechanism is built using the Winsock 2.0 specification. TCP/IP transport mechanism provides the raw data transfer over the wire.

2. HTTP request/response protocol — The HTTP protocol builds upon the TCP/IP transport to provide the HTTP request/response headers.

3. PP protocol — The IPP protocol builds upon the previous two components to provide the data-encoding and data-structure protocol.

This layered approach is being used so that it will be possible to call directly into each layer to make different kinds of transactions. For example, calling directly into the TCP/IP layer enables the user to make simple connections and raw data transmissions, whereas calling into the IPP layer enables the user to perform only IPP operations. This approach also eliminates the use of the current Novell client and removes the dependency on the current RPC mechanism found in NDPS. Table 14.2 shows the layered approach to the IPP module.

TABLE 14.2

*The IPP module within Internet printing provides three layers that perform specific functions.*

| LAYER | PURPOSE |
| --- | --- |
| TCP/IP Component (Winsock 2.0) | Perform raw I/O with the remote endpoint |
| HTTP Component (HTTP 1.1) | Create/Interpret HTTP request/response headers |
| IPP Component (IPP 1.0/1.1) | Encode/decode the IPP operations |

By building on the IPP module using Internet protocols such as TCP/IP and HTTP, this print solution inherits the worldwide connectivity and redundancy of the Internet. It also becomes suitable for configurations that rely on the use of firewalls, network proxies, and other components of the WWW infrastructure.

### TCP/IP Transport Component

This component makes use of the Winsock 2.0 API to provide the raw data transfer for all operations using the TCP/IP protocol suite. It passes only ready-made information to and from the remote party without paying any attention to the data that is being sent or retrieved.

### HTTP 1.1 Transport Component

The HTTP protocol is a text-based Internet protocol that specifies the request/reply frameworks for communication between a server and client. Text-based means that the request header and status header are written in understandable English. In a typical non-secure request the HTTP protocol normally uses port 80 to communicate. The client initiates a TCP/IP connection to the server, specifying port 80 and the server accepts/rejects the request. Upon acceptance, the client is now able to send/receive HTTP requests to/from the server.

The HTTP 1.1 specification defines the concept of *chunked encoding*. Chunking is a mechanism for sending/receiving information when the actual length of the information is unknown (like a print job). It is a protocol feature that allows the connection to be maintained while the remote endpoint is processing and sending the pieces. Each of the chunks that crosses the wire has a length-value in the header. This length value is used so that the remote endpoint can determine the size of the information in each chunk. The last chunk to cross the wire specifies a length of zero to end the transmission. This allows the server to tally the amount of data sent so that it can begin processing the data.

The HTTP protocol is also a non-secured protocol, which means you must perform additional steps if you want to secure your communications. The Netscape Navigator browser and Microsoft's Internet Explorer browser use the SSL (HTTPs) protocol for protection of data across the wire. Each of these browsers has support for stepping up the protection if the server is capable. Because this component may be running outside the scope of a browser, it must perform its own security and authentication.

### Consulting Experience

As a side note, Windows (Internet Explorer 4.0+) does provide an SSL implementation in its WININET implementation for performing SSL-encoded HTTP requests/responses. This implementation requires an installation of Internet Explorer 4+ to get the WININET.DLL.

The IPP Protocol component provides the assembling/disassembling of the IPP data encodings and transmitting/receiving of the requests. The IPP specification defines the operations and sequences of attributes that make up the well-documented protocol. The specification calls for mandatory operations and attributes and also provides provisions for optional operations and attributes.

This implementation provides support for all mandatory IPP operations and also includes the optional Print-URL operation. The Print-URL operation is a defined method for submitting a reference such as an address (http, ftp, and so on) so that the server can pull the data at a later time. The client is responsible for generating the address and also for providing the means to transfer the data to the server when the server asks for it.

### Print Provider Module

The Print Provider Module is the heart and soul of the print engine. This module provides the mechanism through which all applications make API calls to perform print-related requests. Behind the scenes, the print spooler is the Print Provider that is implemented as a snap-in to the spooler. The spooler gets the requests and then chains through the installed print providers to find someone who can carry out the request. Basically, the print provider is a support DLL for the spooler that provides support for remote printers and network printers. The print provider module is being built to specifically support IPP printers.

The print spooler has two interfaces. The first interface is the Windows Print API. This is a programmatic interface for other applications to make print requests. The second interface is the Printer Folder. This interface is a visual interface for installing printers and drivers, viewing installed printers, and getting job status and information. The print provider implementation provides the following support for each of the interfaces.

### Browser Plug-in Module

The Browser Plug-in Module has a programmatic API interface that is present to allow other applications to make requests of the print subsystem. This API makes it easy for applications to perform print requests and have the spooler carry them out. When using a browser on the desktop (Netscape or Internet Explorer), this application provides a viewer for information taken from a Web server. This viewer is highly customizable in that each page it reads from the Web server can be completely different. By creating Web pages and allowing the browser to view them, users or administrators can present their own customized views of printing.

The customizable viewer or browser also introduces the concept of plug-ins. Plug-ins are modules that can be added to the browser to carry out special requests. They can have their own window or they can be windowless. These plug-ins can be loaded and called by simply inserting the HTML Embed or Object tags in the Web page. The embed tag also provides the capability of supplying parameters. This feature makes the embed tag capable of performing multiple tasks based on the input parameter.

Both Netscape and Internet Explorer provide the capability to supply plug-ins for performing specific duties. These plug-in modules provide an interface so that users and/or administrators can provide custom user interfaces for IPP printer installation and management.

## Summary

The printing solution for NetWare 6 includes both traditional queue-based, NDPS-based printing, and the new Internet printing that uses the NDPS print architecture. Queue-based printing is well known; it requires users to know which physical printers are associated with each print queue. On the other hand, NDPS is easy to set up and use because users can send their print jobs directly to the physical printers. In addition, the Internet printing solution enables the user to select printers remotely using only Web browsers. This solution requires no previous knowledge of what the printers support or what they look like. It is a true printing revolution for the users.

# Preparing to Upgrade
to NetWare 6

*"If you want things to stay as they are,*
*things will have to change." — Giuseppe di Lampedusa*

**T**his chapter will help you prepare for and begin to upgrade your current system (which is either NetWare 3, NetWare 4, or NetWare 5), to NetWare 6. In order to prepare to upgrade your servers and workstations to NetWare 6, you will want to organize and educate your NetWare 6 project team, create an implementation schedule, set up a testing lab, and perform the pilot system.

# Organizing and Educating the NetWare 6 Project Team

Your first objective is to organize the NetWare 6 project team with one individual assigned as the project manager. The project manager should choose the members of the project team, matching the network responsibilities needed with the individuals' skills.

The project team will create the master schedule to manage all of the implementation tasks. In order to accomplish the individual tasks, the team members can be assembled into functional areas, with each individual presiding over a functional area and being responsible for seeing that task to completion. Here is a list of some suggested functional areas:

- ▸ Training
- ▸ Novell Directory Services
- ▸ Servers
- ▸ Clients
- ▸ Protocols
- ▸ Printing
- ▸ Applications
- ▸ Administration

## Project Team Assignments

The size of the NetWare 6 project team will vary depending on the size of the corporation or the overall project. Groups within the project team may consist of only one person performing all the tasks and functional assignments or of dozens of people helping the project to succeed. Again, each group within the project team can include one individual or many people, depending on the size or scope of the project. You must determine the scope of your project and how many people are needed to complete and maintain the installation of NetWare 6.

The primary responsibility of the entire project team is to determine the overall scope of the project, which includes a list of deliverables that the project team will create and accomplish for the company or steering committee. Depending on the demands of the project, the deliverables might also include a list of milestones, critical paths, success factors, risk analyses, and tracking mechanisms.

After assignments are made for the entire project team, you should consider the responsibilities and areas of focus for each group within the project team and their members.

## Training

One person or a group is responsible for providing the other members of the project team, the network administrator, and the users with the proper NetWare 6 training. This includes a lab environment for hands-on training, which is discussed in the "Lab Experience" section.

Several methods and sources of training are available for your network personnel. The training includes formal Novell education, Novell-sponsored workshops or conferences, lab experience, white papers, Novell AppNotes, user groups, related books, and other available media.

### Formal Education

Instructor-led courses are available through Novell Authorized Education Centers (NAECs) and Novell Education Academic Partners (NEAPs) worldwide. Computer-based training (CBT) products, videos, and self-study workbooks are available through NAECs and Novell resellers. For more information on Novell's education programs, or to find the NAEC or NEAP nearest you, in the United States and Canada call 1-800-233-EDUC. Outside the United States and Canada, call 1-801-429-5508, or contact your nearest Novell office.

Another quick 24-hour-per-day tool for information is the Novell Education FaxBack. Call 1-801-429-5363 for access to FaxBack. Ask for document 1448 for current courses.

### Novell-Sponsored Workshops and Conferences

Novell develops and delivers various workshops throughout the year at its local sales offices. You should contact your local office account teams for the scheduled workshops in your area. Novell presents several BrainShare Conferences throughout the world. BrainShare is a conference for developers, consultants, and system integrators. Currently, BrainShare conferences are held in the United States, Europe, Australia, Japan, China, South Africa, Russia, and China.

### Lab Experience

There is no substitute for hands-on experience. Hands-on experience teaches skills that transfer to your system administrators in the lab environment. A test upgrade of the servers from a copy of a production server in the lab, for example, will give your personnel valuable experience, as well as an understanding of the upgrade issues before an actual upgrade is attempted in a production environment.

### Application Notes

Novell AppNotes is published monthly by Novell. The material in AppNotes is based on actual field experience and technical research performed by Novell personnel, covering topics in the following main areas:

▶ Network design and optimization strategies

▶ Network management tactics

▶ NetWare internals and theory of operations

▶ Novell product implementation guidelines

▶ Integration solutions for third-party products

▶ NetWare programming techniques

### NetWare User International (NUI) Group

We also recommend that you join a NetWare User International Group (NUI) in order to share information and experiences with other NetWare 6 users. They also periodically invite speakers from Novell to speak on topics of interest.

### Online Support Services

Novell provides online support through Novell's corporate Web site at www.novell.com on the Internet. The Web page provides customers with the latest Novell information, which includes fixes and patches, questions and answers, technical documentation, and support knowledge.

## Novell Directory Services

One person or a group is responsible for designing Novell Directory Services. The design includes design of the NDS tree, NDS partitions and replicas, and time synchronization. This team also will work closely with other company personnel to establish the NDS naming standards. This team should have a good understanding of NDS objects and properties, as well as a good understanding of administration of the network. This team will also help manage and monitor the NDS system once it is moved into production.

## Servers

One person or a group is responsible for upgrading the file servers from your current network operating system to NetWare 6. This group will work closely with or be a part of the NDS design group and will also assist in setting up the lab for testing and staging upgrades. This includes the first pilot servers and all the additional servers added into the NDS tree. This group will also be responsible for operational issues, such as protocol support, backup and restore, and performance tuning of the NetWare 6 servers.

If you are upgrading from NetWare 3, the server team should spend some time cleaning up and preparing the NetWare 3 servers. This team can create guidelines for cleaning up the files in the file system, as well as in the NetWare 3 binderies. Cleaning up the files ensures that only files and objects you need are transferred during the upgrade process.

The server team may also want to consider upgrading the server hardware to newer and faster machines because NetWare 6 requires more resources to load and operate than previous NetWare operating systems. The server team should work with your company's hardware vendor to procure the optimal hardware for NetWare 6.

### Minimum Server Hardware Requirements

The hardware requirements for NetWare 6 have increased over those for earlier versions of NetWare. As a minimum, a NetWare 6 server must have the following:

- Pentium II-class processor
- 256MB of RAM
- 250MB minimum DOS partition
- 1GB SYS volume
- Network cards with Host Adapter Module (.HAM) drivers

NetWare 6 specifies a minimum of 250MB of space in a DOS partition. An install works with as little as 100MB of space, but this is not recommended. In addition, we recommend that the DOS partition include enough additional space to cover core dumps from server RAM. For example, a 512MB RAM system should have 512MB + 50MB = 562MB for the DOS partition.

One of the major changes in the server hardware for NetWare 5 and NetWare 6 is the replacement of the .DSK drivers with the .HAM drivers. NetWare 6 includes .HAM drivers for most adapters on the installation CD-ROM. If the adapter in your system is not available on the CD-ROM, please check `http://developer.novell.com/infosys/mastr_02.htm` for a list of all NetWare-certified adapters and drivers.

### NetWare 3 to NetWare 6 Server Preparations

If you have NetWare 3 servers that need to be upgraded to NetWare 6, the server team should also consider performing the following functions in preparation for the upgrade of each server:

▶ Apply the corporate NDS naming standard while the objects are still in the bindery.

NDS does not support different object types having the same name. By contrast, the binderies in previous versions of NetWare do support different object types with the same name. For example, in NetWare 3, a group object called HP4SI and a print queue called HP4SI can have the same name because they are different object types. In NetWare 6 you cannot have any leaf object with the same name in the same container. This conflict needs to be resolved before the upgrade of the server to NetWare 6. If there are duplicate object names, the upgrade utilities need to know how to handle the duplication. Should the objects be merged or brought over as a second occurrence of the same object name, several utilities that can help you find duplicate object names in the NetWare 3 bindery, for example, the DUPBIND (found on `www.novell.com`), among others. This utility displays the duplicate object names in the binderies so that they can be changed before an upgrade begins.

▶ Clean up the binderies and delete users and other objects that are no longer in use.

Take this opportunity to remove security and access privileges that are no longer required. The SECURITY.EXE program in NetWare 3 helps you find and expose the detailed security information for each object in the bindery. Users who have left the company or who are no longer using that server should be removed.

▶ Make a complete backup of your servers before beginning an upgrade.

Some companies have individuals in an operations group that are responsible for backups. The server team should work with this group to ensure that a recent backup has been performed on any server that is about to be updated.

- ▶ Run the BINDFIX utility in NetWare 3 to remove any objects that are corrupted in the bindery.

  If you are upgrading multiple NetWare 2 or NetWare 3 servers into a single NetWare 6 server, the server team should check for users with accounts on the multiple servers.

- ▶ Decide on a strategy for upgrading multiple servers and duplicate users, a process that presents you with several challenges during the upgrade process to NetWare 6. First, you need to determine how you want to handle the duplicate users. You can merge the users into the same NDS user object, or you can create separate objects. By default the upgrade utility merges the user objects that have the same name into a single NDS object with cumulative rights. This may or may not be what you had intended.

  If each one of the multiple NetWare 2 or NetWare 3 servers is moved into different containers in the NDS tree (OUs), the duplicate usernames will be moved to each individual container that has the same relative distinguished name but a different context. In most cases you do not want to manage the same user twice in the tree.

- ▶ Delete old files and applications from the file system. This will free up disk space for other purposes. You will discover many old, unused, and duplicated applications that are wasting disk space.

- ▶ Determine which protocols you want loaded on your servers. There are a variety of protocol configurations, namely IP, IPX, or IPX Compatibility. In addition, ensure that your network uses the NetWare 6 default Ethernet frame type of 802.2.

  Although NetWare 6 supports both the 802.3 raw and IEEE 802.2 frame types, 802.2 is the preferred standard, and it provides automatic checksumming of packets to ensure greater communications reliability.

The server team should understand how to install a new NetWare 6 server from scratch and should have experience in the upgrade of your current servers to NetWare 6.

In order to perform a new installation of NetWare 6, run the INSTALL.BAT program from the NetWare 6 CD-ROM. The NetWare 6 CD-ROM can be mounted as a DOS device on the server machine, or it can be mounted as a NetWare volume where the server is logged in as a client. The CD-ROM can also be completely copied to a server volume; this method is referred to as server-to-server installation.

**Consulting Experience**

Always try to use the 802.2 frame type and begin phasing out the 802.3 raw frame type if it is in use at your site. Choosing just one frame type will eliminate additional network traffic.

Installing a new NetWare 6 server on new hardware is simple and can be accomplished by referring to Chapter 16.

The server team needs to become familiar with the upgrade options available to them. In upgrading an existing network server to NetWare 6, you have several utilities available to you. These include the normal In-Place (using the installation program) and Across-the-Wire (using the Novell Migration Wizard) utilities. The installation program offers support for upgrading from NetWare 3, NetWare 4, and previous versions of NetWare 5. The Novell Migration Wizard upgrades NetWare 3, NetWare 4, NetWare 5, and even previous installations of NetWare 6. The DS Migrate program that was shipped in previous versions of NetWare is no longer available. However, the Novell Migration Wizard is a graphical upgrade utility that enables you to upgrade NetWare 3, NetWare 4, or NetWare 5 server binderies by upgrading modeled bindery information to an existing NetWare 6 tree. For more detailed information on the Novell Migration Wizard, refer to Chapter 16. The In-Place upgrade method is the fastest way to upgrade because it does not move any data or files. This method is also recommended when you are upgrading an existing NetWare 3 server to NetWare 6 on the existing hardware device.

The other upgrade methods are slower because the workstation has to move all the data across the network. It is recommended that you use the Novell Migration Wizard method when you want to upgrade an existing network server from one machine to another. These methods enable you to replace or upgrade the server hardware.

### Clients

One person or a group is responsible for upgrading the workstations or clients to the latest client software for the preferred desktop operating system. If there are several different types of operating systems, then the team can be divided to support each desktop operating system. For example, DOS/Windows, Windows 95/98,

Windows 2000/NT, and Linux desktops can be supported by different people within the client team. This team would be responsible for optimizing, configuring, and updating or migrating the workstations.

Upgrade at least one workstation to the latest version of Client 32 for use by the system administrator. You should do this for both new installations of NetWare 6 or for installations of NetWare 6 into an existing NDS tree. NetWare 6 includes the latest version of the Client 32 software. The new client software for NetWare 6 is found on the Client CD-ROM included with the operating system or can be downloaded from the Novell web site.

It is recommended that the client team upgrade the workstations to the latest client software before upgrading any servers to NetWare 6. For example, the NetWare Client 32 can provide your workstation with more conventional memory. Once the server is upgraded to NetWare 6, the user will have immediate support for single login and other services unique to the NetWare 6 operating system.

## Protocols

The responsibilities of the protocol team include determining which protocols will be used in the network. Large companies, however, typically have an entire organization called Router Engineering or Telecommunication, which manages and controls the network infrastructure. This group usually mandates the specific protocols and frame types for the networking teams.

NetWare 6 defaults to an IP installation. This means that if it were installed into an existing tree with only IPX, it would essentially be invisible to the servers and clients in that tree. However, you can load and bind both IP and IPX on the same NetWare 6 server to make the servers visible in an IPX environment. NetWare 6 also includes a middle-of-the-road solution called IPX Compatibility Mode.

When you select to install IP, passive support for IPX is also automatically provided. If an IPX request arrives at the server, NetWare 6 will process the IPX request. This passive support for IPX is called Compatibility Mode and is automatically enabled to provide service for applications that require IPX.

In Compatibility Mode, the server responds to IPX-based applications without having IPX bound to one of its LAN boards. The server listens for IPX requests on a specific network number and responds. Compatibility Mode provides a way to migrate easily to IP without having to reconfigure every client and server to support IP immediately.

The protocol team is responsible for determining how to implement or migrate from the current IPX segments to IP. Several options or configurations use various degrees of Pure IP, such as IP-only, IP and IPX both, or IP/CMD (which is the IPX compatibility). In order to implement the protocol solution, this team must be familiar with the following technologies:

- Migration Gateway (links the logical IPX and IP worlds)
- Compatibility Mode (CMD)
- IPX to NetWare 6
- NetWare IP (NWIP) to IP Migration
- Service Location Protocol (SLP) Agents (UA, SA, DA)
- SLP Design

## Printing

One person or a group is responsible for designing the printing strategies for NetWare 6. The strategies may include installation and configuration of the NPDS and Internet printing products. All the print software and hardware should be tested for compatibility, which includes connections greater than 255 users. The printing strategies could encompass printing in a mixed environment from both bindery-based and NDS-based configurations. This team should address how and when to implement the Novell Distributed Print Services (NDPS) strategy, as well as the following issues for both methods of printing:

- Setup for an NDS-based printing strategy
- Quick setup
  - Default Print Queue for printers
  - Workstations running VLMs
  - Workstations running NETX
  - Workstations running Client 32 for Windows and Windows 95
- Support for a mixed bindery-based and NDS-based printing strategy
  - Queues on NetWare 6, with the Print Servers on NetWare 3
  - Queues on NetWare 3, with the Print Servers on NetWare 6
  - Queues and Print Servers on NetWare 3, with Client on NetWare 6, VLMs, and Client 32 for Windows and Windows 95

► Support for Novell Distributed Print Services (NDPS) and Internet Printing (iPrint)

- Install NDPS-aware printers. This could be as simple as upgrading the flash memory of the printer hardware.
- Install and manage Printer Agents with printer-specific gateways using the NDPS Manager to support non-NDPS-aware printers.
- Install and manage the NDPS Broker.
- Set up the Novell printer gateway to support NDS- and bindery-based print jobs to non-NDPS-aware printers.
- Set up IP printing (LPR/LPD) using the Novell printer gateway, if needed.
- Load compatibility support for RPRINTER and NPRINTER printers using the Novell printer gateway.
- Install Internet printing client on workstations
- Establish Internet Printer web pages using iPrint and iManage
- Assign NDS rights for users and administrators.

The print team should test all the possible printing configurations and help with the upgrade of the printing infrastructure to NetWare 6, Internet Printing, and NDPS.

## Applications

One person or a group is responsible for performing compatibility testing for applications running on the servers and clients. Some of the issues to consider during compatibility testing are the following:

► Directory-based software programs

► ZEN-aware software programs

► Enterprise applications

► NetWare Client 32 compatibility

This group is also responsible for upgrading and implementing the applications into the NetWare 6 production environment and for testing the server and workstation applications to make sure that they will run properly.

### Administration

One person or a group is responsible for assigning system administrators and users access to both the network and NDS. This includes login scripts, bindery services, mobile users, security, and the administration of NDS. This team will determine and establish the auditing requirements for the corporation.

These team members with their assignments perform NetWare 6 design and installation. Some or all of these tasks may be performed by one person or by a team of people with specific assignments. After you have selected your project team, you are now ready to define the implementation tasks and schedule.

## Implementing Tasks and Schedules

Following are key objectives and tasks that need to be accomplished to implement NetWare 6. These key objectives are further described in the implementation schedule.

- ▸ Set project scope.
- ▸ Determine training needs.
- ▸ Understand NetWare 6 core OS enhancements.
- ▸ Conduct NDS design or review.
- ▸ Design security and audit strategy.
- ▸ Server upgrades.
- ▸ Change over protocols from IPX to IP.
- ▸ Perform Upgrade clients.
- ▸ Upgrade the printing environment and setup Internet Printing.
- ▸ Convert applications and other services.

From these objectives you can create specific tasks and associated schedules that will provide you with the time line for accomplishing the various upgrade and installation tasks. The implementation schedule should provide detailed tasks that you will accomplish or perform during the installation or upgrade of your network servers. The implementation schedule should also include the time line and the individuals or team members assigned to complete the tasks. The schedule can also provide specific guidelines and recommendations necessary to properly perform the assigned tasks.

The objective of the NetWare 6 implementation schedule is to establish and perform the implementation tasks in the proper order. The individual tasks also need to provide a continual process for the upgrade to NetWare 6. This objective can be met only if all the network administrators work together using the same goals, schedules, and task lists.

The schedule helps you track the status of the project and can provide immediate feedback or reports to your staff and management. A well-planned implementation schedule will not only help you manage and track the status of the NetWare 6 design and implementation project, but it can be used to set the deadlines for each task. For each task you should lay out a chart or schedule that includes a description, guidelines, duration, start and end date, team or person assigned, and the percentage of the task completed. If possible, the schedule can also show the interdependencies of the tasks, measure team members' progress in completing tasks, review the work, and produce reports for management.

The main responsibility of the project team as a whole is to create and lay out the implementation schedule to determine the overall scope of the project. This schedule should define what the end result of your upgrade will be.

The purpose for the implementation schedule is to provide the project team with a consistent set of tasks and objectives for the NetWare 6 upgrade and roll out. The final goal of the project team is to establish a NetWare 6 network that provides a single point of login for the users and simplifies network administration. You are also trying to enhance your network services by increasing the capacity of existing systems.

For example, in the ACME tree, we need to define an implementation schedule to accomplish the upgrade of 40 NetWare 5 servers. The schedule should outline each task, which includes the description, guidelines, duration, start and end dates, team or person assigned, and the percentage of the task completed. The implementation schedule presented in this section may be changed or customized to more closely meet the needs of your company. Table 15.1 outlines the ACME implementation schedule.

T A B L E  15.1

*A Proposed ACME Implementation Schedule*

| TASK DESCRIPTION | DURATION | START DATE | END DATE | TEAM ASSIGNED | PERCENT COMPLETE |
|---|---|---|---|---|---|
| 1. Set Project Scope | 12w | 1/1/02 | 2/1/02 | Project Team | |
| 1.1 Determine Roles and Responsibilities | | | | | |
| 1.2 Determine Milestones | | | | | |
| 1.3 Determine Critical Path | | | | | |
| 1.4 Determine Success Factors | | | | | |
| 1.5 Conduct Risk Analysis | | | | | |
| 1.6 Establish Reporting and Tracking | | | | | |
| 1.7 Establish Documentation Procedures | | | | | |
| 1.8 Design Test Strategies and Acceptance Testing | | | | | |
| 2. Determine Training Needs | 20w | 1/1/02 | 6/1/02 | Training | |
| 2.1 Determine Training Needs | | | | | |
| 2.2 Design Training Strategies | | | | | |
| 2.2.1 Administrative | | | | | |
| 2.2.2 NDS Design | | | | | |
| 2.2.3 Server Installation and Upgrades | | | | | |
| 2.2.4 Etc. | | | | | |
| 2.3 Set Up Formal Training Courses or Classes | | | | | |
| 2.4 Obtain Training | | | | | |
| 2.5 Set Up the Lab | | | | | |

| TASK DESCRIPTION | DURATION | START DATE | END DATE | TEAM ASSIGNED | PERCENT COMPLETE |
|---|---|---|---|---|---|
| 3. Understand NetWare 6 Core OS Enhancements | 4w | 1/1/02 | 2/1/02 | | |
| 3.1 iFolder | | | | | |
| 3.2 Cluster Services | | | | | |
| 3.2.1 Hardware Requirements for Cluster Services | | | | | |
| 3.3 Internet Printing | | | | | |
| 3.4 iFolder | | | | | |
| 3.5 NetWare Remote Manager (Portal) | | | | | |
| 3.6 New Debuggers | | | | | |
| 3.6.1 Assembly Level | | | | | |
| 3.6.2 Source Level | | | | | |
| 3.6.3 Virtual Level | | | | | |
| 4. Conduct NDS Design or Review | 6w | 3/1/02 | 4/15/02 | NDS Team | Training |
| 4.1 Understand New NDS Features | | | | | |
| 4.1.1 Transitive Synchronization | | | | | |
| 4.1.2 Multiple Objects per Packet | | | | | |
| 4.1.3 Distributive Reference Links | | | | | |
| 4.1.4 WAN Manager | | | | | |
| 4.1.5 Inheritable ACLs | | | | | |
| 4.1.6 Password Administrator | | | | | |
| 4.1.7 Partition Administrator | | | | | |

continued

T A B L E   1 5 . 1

A Proposed ACME Implementation Schedule (continued)

| TASK DESCRIPTION | DURATION | START DATE | END DATE | TEAM ASSIGNED | PERCENT COMPLETE |
|---|---|---|---|---|---|
| 4.1.8 Schema Manager | | | | | |
| 4.1.9 Catalog Services | | | | | |
| 4.1.10 WAN Traffic Management | | | | | |
| 4.1.11 LDAP | | | | | |
| 4.1.12 DSDIAF | | | | | |
| 4.2 If Upgrading from NetWare 4 to NetWare 6, Review NDS Design | | | | | |
| 4.2.1 NDS Health Check | | | | | |
| 4.2.2 NDS Tree Design Review | | | | | |
| 4.2.3 Coexistence Issues | | | | | |
| 4.2.4 NDS Versions | | | | | |
| 4.2.5 Synchronization Issues | | | | | |
| 4.2.6 Upgrade Issues | | | | | |
| 4.3 If Upgrading from NetWare 3 to NetWare 6, Design New NDS | | | | | |
| 4.3.1 Understand Basic NDS Concepts | | | | | |
| 4.3.2 Understand New NDS Features | | | | | |
| 4.4 Incorporate NDS Naming Standard | 2w | 3/1/02 | 3/15/02 | NDS Team | |
| 4.4.1 Identify Existing Standards | | | | | |

| TASK DESCRIPTION | DURATION | START DATE | END DATE | TEAM ASSIGNED | PERCENT COMPLETE |
|---|---|---|---|---|---|
| 4.4.2 Create NDS Naming Documents | | | | | |
| 4.4.3 Create File System Standard Structure | | | | | |
| 4.4.4 Deliver Standards Documents | | | | | |
| 4.5 Design NDS Tree | 5d | 3/15/02 | 3/20/02 | NDS Team | |
| 4.5.1 Review WAN Maps | | | | | |
| 4.5.2 Review Campus Maps | | | | | |
| 4.5.3 Design Top of the Tree | | | | | |
| 4.5.4 Review Organization | | | | | |
| 4.5.5 Review Resource List | | | | | |
| 4.5.6 Design Bottom of the Tree | | | | | |
| 4.5.7 Place Network Resources in Containers | | | | | |
| 4.5.8 Apply Design Considerations | | | | | |
| 4.5.8.1 Administration | | | | | |
| 4.5.8.2 Partitioning | | | | | |
| 4.5.8.3 Login Scripts | | | | | |
| 4.5.8.4 Bindery Services | | | | | |
| 4.5.9 Test NDS Tree Design | | | | | |
| 4.6 Design Partitions and Replicas | 5d | 3/21/02 | 3/26/02 | NDS Team | |
| 4.6.1 Review WAN Map | | | | | |
| 4.6.2 Partition Top of the Tree | | | | | |

*continued*

TABLE 15.1

A Proposed ACME Implementation Schedule (continued)

| TASK DESCRIPTION | DURATION | START DATE | END DATE | TEAM ASSIGNED | PERCENT COMPLETE |
|---|---|---|---|---|---|
| 4.6.3 Devise Replica Strategy | | | | | |
| 4.6.3.1 Replicate Locality | | | | | |
| 4.6.3.2 Replicate for Fault Tolerance | | | | | |
| 4.6.4 Partition Bottom as Needed | | | | | |
| 4.6.5 Develop Partition and Replica Guidelines | | | | | |
| 4.6.6 Test Partitions and Replica Strategy | | | | | |
| 4.7 Design Time Synchronization | 1d | 3/27/02 | 3/28/02 | NDS Team | |
| 4.7.1 Evaluate TimeSync Options | | | | | |
| 4.7.1.1 Single Reference (Default) | | | | | |
| 4.7.1.2 Time Provider Group | | | | | |
| 4.7.2 Choose Option Based on WAN | | | | | |
| 4.7.3 Evaluate TimeSync Communications | | | | | |
| 4.7.3.1 Service Advertising Protocol (SAP) | | | | | |
| 4.7.3.2 Configured List | | | | | |
| 4.7.4 Develop Time Synchronization Strategy | | | | | |
| 4.7.5 Test Time Synchronization Strategy | | | | | |
| 4.8 Design NDS Accessibility Plan | 4d | 3/30/02 | 4/4/02 | NDS Team | |
| 4.8.1 Analyze Existing Login Scripts | | | | | |

| TASK DESCRIPTION | DURATION | START DATE | END DATE | TEAM ASSIGNED | PERCENT COMPLETE |
|---|---|---|---|---|---|
| 4.8.2 Move System Login Script to Container Login Script | | | | | |
| 4.8.3 Test Login Scripts | | | | | |
| 4.8.3.1 Container Login Scripts | | | | | |
| 4.8.3.2 Profile Login Scripts | | | | | |
| 4.9 Establish Access with ZENworks | | | | | |
| 4.10 Establish Access with NDS for NT | | | | | |
| 4.11 Develop Mobile User Strategy | | | | | |
| 4.11.1 Test Mobile User Access | | | | | |
| 4.12 Deliver Accessibility Plan | | | | | |
| 5. Design Security and Audit Strategy | 10d | 4/5/02 | 4/15/02 | Administration | |
| 5.1 Server Security | | | | | |
| 5.1.1 Server Settings | | | | | |
| 5.2 NDS Security | | | | | |
| 5.2.1 Object Security | | | | | |
| 5.2.2 Property Security | | | | | |
| 5.2.3 Develop NDS Security Strategy | | | | | |
| 5.3 Test Security Strategy | | | | | |
| 5.4 File System Security | | | | | |
| 5.4.1 Develop File System Strategy | | | | | |
| 5.4.2 Test File System Strategy | | | | | |

continued

T A B L E   15.1

*A Proposed ACME Implementation Schedule (continued)*

| TASK DESCRIPTION | DURATION | START DATE | END DATE | TEAM ASSIGNED | PERCENT COMPLETE |
|---|---|---|---|---|---|
| 5.5 Audit | | | | | |
| 5.5.1 Define Audit Procedures | | | | | |
| 5.5.2 Understand Audit Utilities | | | | | |
| 5.5.3 Develop Audit Strategy | | | | | |
| 5.5.4 Test Audit Strategy | | | | | |
| 6. Server Upgrades | 20w | 5/1/02 | 10/1/02 | Server Team | |
| 6.1 Server Installation | | | | | |
| 6.1.1 Preparatory Steps | | | | | |
| 6.1.2 Impact Study | | | | | |
| 6.1.3 Planning the Upgrade Process | | | | | |
| 6.1.4 Develop Schedule | | | | | |
| 6.1.5 Determine Minimum Hardware Requirements | | | | | |
| 6.1.6 Set Recommendations for Hardware Requirements | | | | | |
| 6.2 Perform Server Upgrade from NetWare 5 to NetWare 6 | | | | | |
| 6.2.1 Evaluate In-Place Utility (INSTALL) | | | | | |
| 6.2.2 Conduct Mass Upgrades and Run Automated Scripts | | | | | |
| 6.2.3 Evaluate Enterprise Upgrade Utility | | | | | |
| 6.3 Perform Server Upgrade from NetWare 3 to NetWare 6 | | | | | |
| 6.3.1 Evaluate Across-the-Wire Utility | | | | | |

| TASK DESCRIPTION | DURATION | START DATE | END DATE | TEAM ASSIGNED | PERCENT COMPLETE |
|---|---|---|---|---|---|
| 6.3.2 Evaluate Upgrade Utilities | | | | | |
| 6.3.3 Evaluate Upgrade Wizard | | | | | |
| 6.3.4 Evaluate Third-Party Upgrade Solutions | | | | | |
| 6.4 Perform Mock Upgrade in the Lab | | | | | |
| 6.5 Test Server Upgrade Strategy | | | | | |
| 6.6 Develop and Establish File System Standards | | | | | |
| 6.7 Determine Cleanup Procedures | | | | | |
| 6.8 Develop Backup and Restore Strategy | | | | | |
| 6.9 Upgrade Volumes to NSS | | | | | |
| 6.9.1 Volume Conversions to NSS issues | | | | | |
| 6.9.2 NSS Conversion Utilities | | | | | |
| 6.10 Incorporate New Backup Utilities | | | | | |
| 6.10.1 New GUI Backup Utility | | | | | |
| 6.10.2 NDS Backup Utility | | | | | |
| 6.11 Prepare Server Pilot and Rollout | | | | | |
| 6.11.1 Server Preparation | | | | | |
| 6.11.2 Perform Cleanup (Objects and Files) | | | | | |
| 6.11.3 Back up the Server | | | | | |
| 6.11.4 Install or Upgrade Server to NetWare 6 | | | | | |
| 6.11.5 Test Server (Production-Like) | | | | | |

continued

T A B L E   15.1

*A Proposed ACME Implementation Schedule (continued)*

| TASK DESCRIPTION | DURATION | START DATE | END DATE | TEAM ASSIGNED | PERCENT COMPLETE |
|---|---|---|---|---|---|
| 6.11.6 Document Any Problems | | | | | |
| 6.11.7 Modify Procedures Based on Results | | | | | |
| 6.11.8 Perform Acceptance Testing | | | | | |
| 6.11.9 Provide Daily Support to User | | | | | |
| 6.11.10 Validate Functionality of the Servers | | | | | |
| 7. Protocol Change Over (IPX to IP) | 4w | 3/1/02 | 4/1/02 | Protocol Team | |
| 7.1 Determine Migrate Method | | | | | |
| 7.1.1 IP only | | | | | |
| 7.1.2 IP and IPX | | | | | |
| 7.1.3 IP/CMD (IPX Compatibility) | | | | | |
| 7.2 Migration Gateway /g (IP to IPX) | | | | | |
| 7.3 Migration Gateway /bs (IPX to IP to IPX) | | | | | |
| 7.4 Compatibility Mode (CMD) | | | | | |
| 7.5 NWIP to IP Migration | | | | | |
| 7.6 SLP Agents (UA, SA, DA) | | | | | |
| 7.7 SLP Design | | | | | |
| 7.8 DNS/DHCP | | | | | |

| TASK DESCRIPTION | DURATION | START DATE | END DATE | TEAM ASSIGNED | PERCENT COMPLETE |
|---|---|---|---|---|---|
| 8. Perform Client Upgrade | 10w | 3/1/02 | 5/15/02 | Client Team | |
| 8.1 Undertake Preparatory Steps | | | | | |
| 8.1.1 Develop Schedule | | | | | |
| 8.1.2 Impact Study | | | | | |
| 8.1.3 Determine Hardware Requirements | | | | | |
| 8.1.4 Set Hardware Recommendations | | | | | |
| 8.2 Evaluate Client Upgrade Options | | | | | |
| 8.3 Determine Client Upgrade Strategy | | | | | |
| 8.4 Test Client Upgrade Strategy | | | | | |
| 8.4.1 Functional Testing for Each Desktop | | | | | |
| 8.5 Plan the Upgrade Process | | | | | |
| 8.6 Conduct Client Implementation | | | | | |
| 8.6.1 IP-enabled Windows 95/98 | | | | | |
| 8.6.2 IP-enabled Windows 2000/NT | | | | | |
| 8.6.3 IP-enabled DOS/Windows | | | | | |
| 9. Printing Environment Upgrade | 5w | 3/1/02 | 4/15/02 | Print Team | |
| 9.1 Identify Existing Printing Environment | | | | | |
| 9.1.1 Bindery-Based | | | | | |
| 9.1.2 NDS Queue-Based | | | | | |
| 9.2 Design NDPS Printing Environment and Internet Printing | | | | | |

*continued*

T A B L E   15.1

*A Proposed ACME Implementation Schedule (continued)*

| TASK DESCRIPTION | DURATION | START DATE | END DATE | TEAM ASSIGNED | PERCENT COMPLETE |
|---|---|---|---|---|---|
| 9.2.1 Printer Agent and Client | | | | | |
| 9.2.2 Management Console | | | | | |
| 9.2.3 Queue-Based Printing Upgrade | | | | | |
| 9.3 Determine NDPS Gateway Placement | | | | | |
| 9.4 Evaluate Direct Print Cards and Printers | | | | | |
| 9.5 Design Printing Upgrade Strategy | | | | | |
| 9.5.1 Bindery-Based to NDPS-Based | | | | | |
| 9.5.2 NDS Queue-Based to NDPS-Based and Internet Printing | | | | | |
| 9.6 Test Printing Upgrade Strategy | | | | | |
| 10. Upgrade Applications | 5w | 3/1/02 | 4/15/02 | Applications | |
| 10.1 Identify All Server-Based and Client-Based Applications | | | | | |
| 10.1.1 Identify and Create Application Objects in NDS | | | | | |
| 10.2 Upgrade from NetWare 4 to NetWare 6 | | | | | |
| 10.2.1 Differences in Utilities | | | | | |
| 10.2.2 DOS Utilities Not Supported | | | | | |
| 10.3 Identify and Create Application Objects in NDS | | | | | |

| TASK DESCRIPTION | DURATION | START DATE | END DATE | TEAM ASSIGNED | PERCENT COMPLETE |
|---|---|---|---|---|---|
| 10.4 For Internally Written Applications | | | | | |
| 10.5 Install | | | | | |
| 10.6 Test on a Desktop | | | | | |
| 10.7 Test on Server | | | | | |
| 10.8 Test Printing | | | | | |
| 10.9 Test Document Compatibility | | | | | |
| 10.10 Deliver Applications in Production Using NAL | | | | | |
| 10.11 Upgrade Other Services | | | | | |
| 10.11.1 Oracle version 8+ | | | | | |
| 10.11.2 Netscape Enterprise Server | | | | | |
| 10.11.3 BTRIEVE | | | | | |

# Setting Up a Testing Lab

You can gain valuable experience with a product such as NetWare 6 by creating a lab environment. The lab experience provides the opportunity to understand how NetWare 6 operates at your particular site with your particular network characteristics. We recommend a lab for any company or organization that can afford the additional resources or may already have a lab in place. At a smaller site without a lab or the resources for a lab, you can obtain hands-on experience with NetWare 6 through educational training or perhaps through your integrator.

The lab is a safe environment where you can make changes and view the impact of those changes on the NDS tree. You can test many of the features and functions of NetWare 6 and become acquainted with the product. This section will first discuss the components of a lab. Next, it will cover the areas that you should test in your lab. Keep in mind that the lab experience can be short, yet productive. After reading this section you should be able to define the areas of lab testing that fit your needs. You can create a checklist of these items to help you focus on a completion date for the lab process.

## Evaluating the Need for a Lab

The decision to have a lab is dependent upon your circumstances. Although most small sites do not have the resources to install a lab, they can benefit by gaining hands-on experience through their integrator or education center. For a small site where you plan to use the default configurations, the lab is not as crucial, but it can provide you with valuable administrative experience. If your site is small and you do have a lab, we recommend a brief testing period in the lab to familiarize yourself with NetWare 6, especially from an administrative standpoint. Setting up a lab and installing NetWare 6 also instills confidence in your project team because they learn about the features and capabilities of NetWare 6. It also gives you time to work with the operating system, to perform diagnostics, and to test utilities and applications.

Implementation of a NetWare 6 lab is recommended for any site that will install or upgrade more than 30 NetWare 6 servers. Many customers will move from the default settings of NetWare 6 to configurable parameters at approximately this number of servers. Therefore, the lab gives you the opportunity to adjust and test various configuration parameters.

If you have a larger site with a wide area network (WAN) in place, we recommend that you follow, where applicable, the lab procedures presented in this section. Network administrators of large sites should fully familiarize themselves with the functions and features of NetWare 6 before beginning a full-scale upgrade to NetWare 6.

For the ACME site, lab testing is being handled at the NORAD facility in the LABS department. All new software and hardware is evaluated at this facility before being deployed onto the production network. Therefore, the new operating system being deployed in the ACME tree has gone through the lab process.

## The Lab Setup

Many large organizations have a permanent lab for testing all new software and hardware that may be placed into production at their site. Others may be considering the creation of a temporary lab for this project. In either case, you need to dedicate some hardware for use as NetWare 6 servers and workstations for the duration of your lab project.

Your lab should consist of a minimum of four nodes: two NetWare 6 servers and two workstations. The servers and adapter cards should be similar to the hardware that will be used in your network environment. If you are planning to upgrade your hardware, then use the new hardware in your lab environment. Each NetWare 6 server should exceed the minimum recommendations provided by Novell. You want to duplicate your actual environment as closely as possible. In addition, you want to duplicate your LAN topology, where possible.

Figure 15.1 shows the ACME lab for testing NetWare 6 for the entire ACME tree installation. This lab has four dedicated NetWare 6 servers and three workstations to run the Novell and third-party utilities. In addition, because the ACME network is primarily a token ring, we have a token ring concentrator in the lab to connect the servers and workstations together. All file servers have a CD-ROM drive, as well as sufficient disk and memory capacity. The lab ring also has a connection to the corporate backbone located in the labs division of NORAD.

ACME Lab Configuration

Workstation

IntranetWare                    IntranetWare

Connection to          LAN
Corporate backbone    NETWORK

                                    Workstation

CD-ROM

IntranetWare           IntranetWare

Workstation

**FIGURE 15.1** *The ACME lab consists of four NetWare 6 servers and three workstations.*

Your lab can be smaller than ACME's lab; it can even consist of only three nodes. A three-node network would consist of two NetWare 6 file servers and a single workstation. One of the servers must have a CD-ROM device for installing NetWare 6. Also, if possible, have a network connection to your backbone so that you can access any servers currently in operation on your network. Figure 15.2 shows a minimal configuration.

Minimal Lab Configuration

IntranetWare

IntranetWare

Workstation

**FIGURE 15.2** *A minimal lab configuration would have two NetWare 6 servers and a single workstation.*


## The Lab Process

The lab process simply provides order and direction to help you accomplish your objectives in the lab. Without such direction, a lab simply becomes a bunch of PCs that are not utilized, and the lab experience wears on until people lose interest in what they are trying to accomplish. With some specific objectives, you can provide a thorough test of NetWare 6 and obtain experience before beginning a large-scale upgrade.

Your network administrators can put into practice the information presented in this book, such as NDS tree design, partitioning and replication strategies, and security procedures. You can evaluate these areas in your lab, which are discussed in the sections that follow:

- ▶ Lab installation
- ▶ Hardware and required components
- ▶ Mounting a CD-ROM as a NetWare volume
- ▶ Installing NetWare 6

▸ Creating the NDS tree

▸ Creating partitions and replicas

▸ Configuring time synchronization

▸ Designing and testing container login scripts

▸ Designing and testing administration/security procedures

▸ Testing applications

▸ Gaining experience with your utilities

▸ Backing up and restoring

▸ The NetWare 6 pilot system

### Lab Installation

If your site already has a lab in place, you can simply designate a group of servers for your test along with a few workstations. You will want to follow the NetWare 6 installation procedures discussed in Chapter 16, as well as the procedures discussed in the "Installing NetWare 6" section later in this chapter.

Companies creating a lab from scratch can follow the procedures outlined in the following text.

### Hardware and Required Components

Perhaps the most time-consuming aspect of installing NetWare 6 is installing and connecting a CD-ROM drive. Your job will be much simpler if you obtain the latest CD-ROM drivers because you will spare yourself hours of frustration when mounting your CD-ROMs if you have the latest drivers running on your hardware.

For most hardware products, you can obtain their latest drivers by connecting to their bulletin boards. All drivers that are contained on the Novell NetWare 6 CD-ROM have been tested with NetWare 6.

### Mounting a CD-ROM as a NetWare Volume

Mounting a CD-ROM as a NetWare volume has become extremely easy compared to the method that was needed in NetWare 4. The following steps illustrate how to install your CD-ROM as a NetWare volume:

**1.** From the server console type:

```
LOAD CDROM.NLM
```

**2.** The LOAD command is optional and no longer required in NetWare 6. The effect of the command is that the CD that is placed in your server machine will automatically be mounted as a NetWare volume.

**3.** After loading the CDROM.NLM, type this command at the console to verify that the CD-ROM was mounted:

```
VOLUMES
```

**4.** The CD should be mounted as a NetWare 6 volume and available.

With a NetWare volume mounted you can then map a drive to this volume and access the CD-ROM.

### Installing NetWare 6

You can refer to Chapter 16 for detailed information on installation procedures. For the lab exercise you can install the NetWare 6 operating system on each of your lab servers. Loading the software is not difficult, but you should familiarize yourself with the different installation options. For example, new to NetWare 6 is a graphical user interface (GUI) installation utility with an intuitive, graphical interface.

You should also practice removing NDS from the server. On occasion you may have to remove a server from the tree because of hardware repairs or shipment to another location, and you can use NWCONFIG and the Directory Services options to remove a server from the tree. In order to remove a server from the tree you must have ADMIN rights to the directory and server that is being removed. Familiarize yourself with the new NWCONFIG utility, which replaces the INSTALL utility from NetWare 4. You may have to add new NLMs or additional licenses, and the NWCONFIG utility handles these procedures.

If you are upgrading from NetWare 3 to NetWare 6 and you have the hardware, you can perform an upgrade of a current NetWare 3 server to a lab NetWare 6 server. This approach enables you to upgrade your hardware to a new platform for NetWare 6, and it does not endanger your current NetWare 3 server.

### Creating the NDS tree

The creation of your NDS tree in your lab should be based on the information discussed in the other chapters in this book. For modeling your lab tree, you can use the Rexxware Migration Toolkit to simplify this process. In addition, refer back to Chapter 5 for information and design strategies.

The lab tree that you install will eventually become your production tree, so take the necessary time to define the appropriate levels and placement of resources. If you have a successful and functional lab tree, you do not need to re-create another tree unless you want to maintain separate trees for testing purposes.

### Creating Partitions and Replicas

The first partition created is the default [ROOT] partition. After your lab servers are up and running, you can use the NDS Manager utility to further partition each of your sites into separate partitions subordinate to [ROOT]. Use your lab to learn how to create replicas as well. Because the size of your lab may be somewhat limited, you still should learn how the partition utilities place replicas on servers. You can also learn how to identify the locations of the replicas by viewing them with the utilities.

### Configuring Time Synchronization

Your lab servers will initially have time synchronization set up with the defaults. Your first NetWare 6 server is installed as a Single Reference server. All other servers are Secondary.

The first step in configuring time synchronization is to familiarize yourself with the TimeSync SET parameters that can be accessed and to view using the MONITOR utility. You can change the default settings through the MONITOR utility. For example, you can create a small-time provider group by changing your Single Reference server to a Reference server. Then change the other two or three lab servers to Primary servers. With a LANalyzer or other equipment, you can view the packets sent and received for each time synchronization interval.

Use other commands, such as SET TIMESYNC DEBUG=7, to enable the time synchronization screen on your NetWare 6 server. This screen will show you the status of time synchronization and the adjustments being made if this server's time is not synchronized.

### Designing and Testing Container Login Scripts

The lab is a great place to design and test your container login scripts. Populate one of your containers with actual user objects from your company. Test the container login script for errors and to verify that all necessary environment variables have been defined.

If you are planning to use Profile scripts as well, the lab is the perfect place to test the functionality of these scripts.

### Designing and Testing Administration/Security Procedures

The lab testing facility is an excellent place to test your security and administrative policies and procedures. NetWare 6 includes several new security and administrative features that you may want to test, for example, the capability to inherit specific property rights down the entire tree. This feature is possible because of the new inheritable access control lists (ACLs). The inheritable ACLs enable you to assign supervisor rights to operators or help desk staff for specific types of objects or resources without giving supervisor rights to the entire tree. For example, you can assign rights to a group to manage just the printers, servers, or users.

Before making these types of rights assignments, you will want test and determine which specific property you want to have flow down the NDS tree. In order to establish the rights, use the Inherit button, a new button at the bottom of the rights list on the NWADMIN property rights screen. You can give specific property rights to any object that will inherit by selecting the rights and then selecting the Inherit button.

In addition to the inherited ACL feature, NetWare 6 provides you with the ability to assign rights to manage just the users' passwords or NDS partitions. NetWare 6 provides you with two properties called Password Administrator property and Partition Administrator property. Again, test implementation of these rights before rolling them directly into you production tree.

### Testing Applications

Not all applications need to be tested for NetWare 6 compatibility. Some applications, however, especially those written inside your corporation, may require testing. The following points should be considered when you test applications:

▸ Is the application bindery based? Bindery-based applications require bindery services to be enabled on that server, as well as on a read/write replica of the defined context.

▸ Were the applications written specifically for the NetWare 3, NetWare 4, or NetWare 5 operating system(s)? If so, they should be tested with the software. Following are some basic and easy tests that you can perform:

   • Run the application to completion or proper termination.

   • Print a document with the application.

   • Using the application, do a file save of your work onto the NetWare 6 server.

   • Run the application on the new IP client software, if applicable. Test your tape backup application support for NetWare 6 and NDS.

   • Keep your application testing procedure short and simple. You will never be able to test every feature and function of every product. Concentrate your efforts on the specialty applications that are not in the mainstream.

Administer network applications using ZENworks, which stands for Zero Effort Networking. ZENworks enables you to represent applications and workstations as objects in the Novell Directory. You can manage the application and workstation objects as Directory objects the same way you manage other objects, using the NWADMIN utility. Using application objects you can do the following:

▸ Define an application's directory, icon, command line parameters, and other properties in one place.

▸ Use trustee assignments to manage access to an application.

▸ Define startup scripts that establish the appropriate network environment for the application (drive mappings, print captures, and so on) and clean up scripts that restore the workstation's environment.

### Gaining Experience with Your Utilities

Installing a lab automatically gives you experience with Novell and NetWare and, most likely, third-party utilities. You will be exposed to the following utilities with a lab in place:

▸ ConsoleOne

▸ NDS Manager

▸ NWADMIN

▸ MONITOR.NLM

▸ NWCONFIG.NLM (formerly INSTALL.NLM)

▸ DSREPAIR.NLM

▸ DSTRACE (not really a utility, but a group of set commands)

▸ Novell Migration Wizard

▸ NetWare Remote Manager

▸ iMonitor

Review and work through each utility to gain experience and confidence with the operation of these tools.

### Backing Up and Restoring

Perform a full backup and restore of a NetWare 6 server. This backup includes files, as well as NDS tree information. Always have a clear understanding of backup procedures related to your specific backup product. The lab is the best place to gain experience in backup and recovery procedures. For more information on backup and restoration of NDS, refer to Chapter 18.

### The NetWare 6 Pilot System

A *pilot system* is the first NetWare 6 server placed into production on your network. A pilot system will be the baseline system you will use to test all the operational procedures that you have developed for the upgrade to NetWare 6. You can use either the In-Place or Across-the-Wire upgrade to perform the upgrade of users and data, depending on the previous network operating system from which you are upgrading.

If you can use separate hardware for an upgrade, you can safely move a server without affecting the production server. Once you have successfully performed the upgrade, you can redirect the actual users or group of users to the new NetWare 6 server. The server you choose to upgrade as the pilot system should probably be a server that is used by the technical staff at your facility. This way the staff members will become familiar with the operation of the NetWare 6 server in production.

Use the pilot system to optimize your workstation configurations including AUTOEXEC.BAT, CONFIG.SYS, NET.CFG, and any other files required for your installation.

The pilot system process for NetWare 6 does not require an enormous amount of time. The purpose of the pilot system is to provide adequate experience for you and your staff with the NetWare 6 server in your production environment. If you feel you have reached that point after only a couple of weeks, then the pilot system has most likely served its purpose.

## Summary

This chapter covers the major features and options that are available for preparing you to upgrade your current NetWare servers and environment to NetWare 6. Depending on the size of your organization, you may need to create an in-depth implementation schedule or just have a couple of basic tasks. The individual tasks, which include NDS design, training, understanding the new features, upgrading servers and clients, and upgrading the printing infrastructure, may be accomplished by different teams or all by the same person. Again, the number of people involved in the process depends on the overall size of the company and its number of servers.

# Migrating Data from NetWare 4 and NetWare 5 to NetWare 6

*"A permanent state of transition is man's most
noble condition." — Juan Ramon Jimenez*

This chapter explores the many methods for migrating and upgrading your NetWare 4 and NetWare 5 servers to NetWare 6. Each method has its merits, and you can choose the method that most closely meets your needs and circumstances. You face many considerations when determining which upgrade method to use. These considerations are discussed here in each upgrade section. Some network upgrades may require multiple methods depending on the circumstances of the upgrade. For example, some sites may decide to purchase new hardware to support NetWare 6 and use one upgrade utility for the entire process. Other companies may have multiple departments, each responsible for its own upgrade and each with its own budgetary constraints. They may choose to keep their existing hardware, and hence a different upgrade process may be used. This chapter focuses on upgrades from previous versions of NetWare only. NetWare 6 provides you with the following upgrade methods:

▶ In-place upgrades for NetWare 4 and NetWare 5 to NetWare 6

▶ In-place NetWare 4 or NetWare 5 to NetWare 6 mass upgrades

▶ The Across-the-Wire Upgrade using NetWare Migration Wizard 6

NetWare 6 includes an important new feature that helps you upgrade your servers. This feature enables you to boot your server from a CD-ROM. Booting from the CD automatically creates a DOS partition and installs NetWare 6 from the CD. This includes automatic install and loading of the DOS CD-ROM drivers. The previous versions of NetWare forced you to manually create the DOS partition and to locate and configure the DOS drivers and server installation. For more information on actual installation steps and procedures for NetWare 6, see Chapter 2.

▶ · · · · · · · · · · · · · · · · · · · · · · · · · · · · · ◀

### Consulting Experience

Take some time to review and practice the migration or upgrade options in your lab if you can. If you do not have the additional hardware to create a new server, make sure that you take all the necessary precautions to back up your current servers before beginning an upgrade. Our experience has shown that those who can practice upgrades in a lab will have fewer problems during an actual upgrade to NetWare 6.

# Basic Hardware Requirements

Novell's success over the years has been the capability of its products to operate on a large variety of hardware at either the server or workstation levels. As with the earlier versions of NetWare, NetWare 6 and its associated client products operate well on a variety of hardware platforms. The speed of your server hardware, however, has become much more important when you are using NetWare 6 servers to interoperate on the network. Obviously, the faster your hardware, the better performance you will have with NetWare 6. Enhanced performance not only increases the speed of access for your clients, but it also improves the speed of NDS synchronization operations and the associated NDS background processes. So look closely at your current hardware and understand that your most heavily utilized servers should be your fastest and most powerful. What follows is a list of the server hardware required to operate NetWare 6.

## Recommended Hardware Configuration

- A Pentium III 700mhz processor
- 512MB RAM
- 20GB hard disk space (SYS volume requires 2GB)
- PCI LAN card
- CD-ROM device installed in the server
- 3.5-inch floppy drive
- Monitor with supporting VGA card

We highly recommend that you back up your server before you start a migration or installation process. To accomplish this task, you can use Storage Management Services (SMS), which is a set of files and NLM programs that enables you to back up and restore data (using SBACKUP) for legacy NetWare network servers as well as workstations or other services that you select. SBACKUP can take a snapshot copy of data that you select, store the data on a tape, and retrieve the data later in case of data or hardware failure. In addition to NetWare 5, you may also need to back up and restore NetWare 4 data and NDS and NetWare 3 data.

## Back Up and Restore NetWare 5 Data and NDS

The prerequisites and system requirements for backing up and restoring (if needed) NetWare 5 and NDS are as follows:

- ▶ SMS installed with NetWare 5 on a server
- ▶ 3MB RAM
- ▶ Host server with memory to run NetWare 5
- ▶ Target server
- ▶ Backup device
- ▶ Memory to run the clients

To run SMS at the server, complete the following steps:

1. Load the drivers for controller and storage devices. Note: See "Before Running the Backup Software" in the Storage Management Services manual at the NetWare 5 Documentation Web site (http://www.novell.com/documentation/lg/nw5/docui/index.html).

2. Load the device drivers. If you loaded HAM drivers, or if you added an external device, type **LIST DEVICES** at the server console prompt.

3. Load the Target Service Agents (TSAs) and load the Storage Management Engine and backup software on the server. The TSAs for NetWare 5 are TSA500 and TSA550 for later versions.

4. Type **LOAD SMDR** and press enter to accept the default or add a new SMDR context.

5. Next, enter an Administrator username and password with the full context.

6. Enter the following commands:
   - LOAD TSA500
   - LOAD SMSDI
   - LOAD QMAN
   - LOAD SBSC
   - LOAD SBCON

7. (Optional) You can also load Enhanced SBACKUP at a workstation. See "Load Enhanced SBACKUP at a Workstation" in the Storage Management Services manual at the NetWare 5 Documentation Web site (http://www.novell.com/documentation/lg/nw5/docui/index.html).

8. Select main menu ⇨ Job Administration ⇨ Backup and then select Target Service to choose the NetWare server running your backup or restore Target Service Agent. Enter the target username and password (if prompted) for the target.

9. Select the volumes and files that you want to back up from the NetWare server screen, and then press Esc.

10. Type a descriptive name for the backup session in the Description field.

11. Select Device/Media name.

12. Select Advanced Options and select Append Session. Press Enter to save your options and continue with the backup.

13. To return to the main menu, press Esc repeatedly.

## Restoring a NetWare 5 Server

If necessary, you can restore backed up data from a server. To perform a NetWare 5 restore from a previous backup, complete the following steps:

1. Load the device drivers for your specific device and controller board.

2. Load the appropriate Target Service Agents.

3. Load Enhanced SBACKUP and select main menu ⇨ Job Administration ⇨ Restore.

4. Next, select Target Service ⇨ NetWare Server Running Your Backup and Restore Target Service Agent. When prompted for the target username, enter an Administrator username and password for the target server.

5. Type a descriptive name for the restore session in the Description field.

6. Select the device and media to restore. Press Enter at the Device/Media Name field and decide where you want to restore from.

7. Select the session to restore and select Advanced Options to make the selective restore.

8. Press Esc and answer the prompt at the Submit Job screen to begin the restore session. Press Alt+Esc to view the activity log screen.

9. To return to the main menu, press Esc repeatedly.

## Back Up and Restore Data from a NetWare 4 Server

You can use NetWare 4 SMS Backup and Restore (SBACKUP) to back up and restore data for NetWare 4 on network servers as well as workstations or other services you select. SBACKUP can take a snapshot copy of data that you select, store the data on a tape, and retrieve the data later in case of data or hardware failure. The prerequisites and system requirements for backing up and restoring (if needed) NetWare 4 and NDS are described as follows in the list:

▶ SMS installed with NetWare 4 on a server

▶ 3MB RAM

▶ Host server

▶ Target server

▶ Backup device

To run SBACKUP at a server, complete the following steps:

**1.** Load the device drivers for controller and storage devices.

**2.** Load SBACKUP.NLM and the appropriate TSA files. See "Loading the File You Need to Run SBACKUP" at the NetWare 4 Documentation Web site (`http://www.novell.com/documentation/lg/nw42/docui/index.html`). If you want to back up a NetWare 3.11 server, make sure you use the TSA_311.NLM file shipped with NetWare 4.

**3.** Load SBACKUP on the host server and select main menu ➪ Backup.

**4.** Select a target for the data you want to back up. Select Backup/Restore Target Services Running on Targetname listing, and then select the TSA you want to use.

**5.** Enter an Administrator username and password for the target you want to back up.

**6.** Select the device you want to back up to and select Type of Backup. Then select the type of backup you want to perform. Type a description of the backup session.

**7.** Press F10 to save the description and continue with the backup, and then specify when you want the backup to start. For example, set the date and time for the backup to begin.

**8.** Press F10. Press Enter to save your changes. See the NetWare 4 Documentation Web site (`http://www.novell.com/documentation/lg/nw42/docui/index.html`) for more information.

## Restoring a NetWare 4 Server

If necessary, you can restore backed up data from a server. In order to perform the restore, you need to be Supervisor/Administrator or have equivalent rights and know the file structure of the data you're restoring. The steps for a NetWare 4 restore from a previous backup are as follows (to restore data to a different location from the backup, know the full path of the restored data and the path to the area to restore to):

**1.** Load SBACKUP. From the main menu, select Restore and select the target that you want to restore the data to. Enter the Administrator username and password for the target that you want to restore to.

**2.** Specify how you want to select the data to restore. See "Restoring from Session Files" or "Restoring without Session Files" at the NetWare 4 Documentation Web site (`http://www.novell.com/documentation/lg/nw42/docui/index.html`) for more information.

**3.** Press F10 to start the restore. View the error log to determine if any files were not restored.

## Backing Up and Restoring NetWare 3 Servers

SBACKUP is a NetWare Loadable Module (NLM) that enables you to back up and restore data for NetWare 3.1x, NetWare 4.0, and OS/2 network servers as well as workstations or other services you select. SBACKUP can take a snapshot copy of data that you select, store the data on a tape, and retrieve the data later in case of data or hardware failure. The prerequisites and system requirements for backing up and restoring (if needed) NetWare 3 are described as follows in the list:

▶ SBACKUP installed with NetWare 3.12 on a server

▶ 3MB RAM

▶ Host server

▶ Target server

▶ Backup device

To run SBACKUP, complete the following steps:

1. Load TSA312.NLM on the target server to be backed up by entering LOAD TSA312.

2. Load SBACKUP and the correct driver software on the host server.

3. Enter a Supervisor username and password for the host server.

4. Select a target or device driver.

5. From the main menu, select Target to Backup/Restore and select a target. Enter the Supervisor username and password for the host server.

6. Verify that the target's name is in the screen header, and insert a pathname.

7. At the entry box, press Insert and select an entry. Repeat step until the entire path name appears in the entry box. Exit the list by pressing Esc.

To perform the back up procedure using the SBACKUP utility, use the following steps:

1. From the main menu, select Backup menu and then select the Working Directory. Type the pathname, and then press Enter or press Insert and select the path.

2. From the Backup menu, select Backup Selected Target.

3. From the Backup Options screen, select the Options field by selecting See List, and then press Enter.

4. Select the backup type.

5. Perform the backup. From the Start Backup menu, select Start Backup Now.

6. Insert or label the media.

7. Start the backup session by pressing Enter. Select View Error Log to view the error log to determine if any files were not backed up. See the NetWare 3.12 Server Backup manual for more information.

## Restore NetWare 3 Server Data

If necessary, you can restore backed up data from a NetWare 3 server. In order to perform the restore, you need to be Supervisor or have equivalent rights and know the file structure of the data you're restoring. The steps for a NetWare 3 restore from a previous backup are as follows:

**1.** From the main menu, select Restore menu.

**2.** Select options from the Restore Options screen. Save your restore options by pressing Esc.

**3.** Start the restore by selecting Yes from the Start Restore box.

**4.** Insert the source media cartridge into the storage device and press Enter.

**5.** From the Restore Session menu, select a session to restore. View the error log to determine if any files were not restored.

## The In-Place Upgrade Method

The in-place upgrade method occurs when you use the NetWare 6 CD-ROM and install it on an existing NetWare 4 or NetWare 5 server. This in-place method is used primarily for upgrading servers from either NetWare 4 or NetWare 5 to NetWare 6 using the same hardware. For example, Figure 16.1 shows the process of upgrading a NetWare 4 or NetWare 5 server to NetWare 6 on the same server hardware device.

NetWare 3, NetWare 4
or
Netware 5

In-Place Upgrade

Same
Physical
Server

NetWare 6

**FIGURE 16.1** *Upgrading a NetWare 3 or NetWare 4 server to NetWare 6 using the same server hardware device*

Because the file server hardware stays the same, the data volumes remain the same. Only new files are added to the SYS: volume in the system subdirectories and the DOS partition during the in-place upgrade process. The data files on the other volumes on the existing NetWare server are not moved or changed. The files that do get upgraded include LOGIN, SERVER.EXE, LAN drivers (*.LAN), disk drivers, and other NetWare Loadable Modules (*.NLM).

The NetWare 6 INSTALL utility installs or upgrades NDS onto the existing NetWare server. The in-place upgrade process also upgrades the NDS schema and objects found that already exist in NDS.

The in-place method is the fastest upgrade method because it does not move the data files to another server. The other upgrade methods, such as across-the-wire and file copy, are slower because all the user data must be upgraded across the LAN or WAN networks.

The upgrade to NetWare 6 is accomplished by running the NetWare 6 INSTALL. EXE program. The NetWare 6 installation program can be started in DOS on the device being used as the server hardware by accessing the NetWare 6 CD-ROM. The main menu for the installation program appears as shown in Figure 16.2. From the main menu, select the NetWare Server Installation option.

```
NetWare Installation

Welcome to the NetWare server installation.

    Select the type of installation and specify the directory
    where the server startup files will be installed.

    A new installation will destroy data on existing NetWare partitions.

    Use the Tab or arrow keys to move between windows.
    To learn more about the installation, press F1.

    ┌─────────────────────────────────────────────────────┐
    │  Is this a new server or an upgrade?  New server     │
    │                                                       │
    │  Startup directory              C:\NWSERVER           │
    └─────────────────────────────────────────────────────┘

                    ┌─────────────────┐
                    │    Options       │
                    ├─────────────────┤
                    │ Continue         │
                    │ Modify           │

Alt+F10=Exit   F2=Advanced settings   F3=Response file   Esc=Back   F1=Help
```

**FIGURE 16.2** *The main menu for the NetWare 6 installation program INSTALL.EXE*

When making your decision on the type of upgrade method to use, keep in mind the following advantages and disadvantages of the in-place upgrade process.

## Advantages of the In-Place Upgrade

This list gives the advantages of the in-place upgrade method:

- It uses the same physical server hardware, thus eliminating the cost of a new server hardware system just to perform the upgrade. Look carefully at your hardware at this point, however. That older NetWare server buried in your wiring closet somewhere may not pass muster with NetWare 6. You may still have to upgrade your hardware. For hardware and system requirements for NetWare 6, refer to Chapter 2.

- It preserves passwords. Once on NetWare 6, your users will not need to enter a new password when they initially log in.

- It preserves the original NDS tree and associated information. For example, it upgrades the existing object and security information, meaning that all the users, groups, and trustee assignments are preserved on NetWare 6.

- It upgrades the server faster than any other method available. The data in the file system or volumes remain unmodified.

- It maintains name spaces. Because the data files are not changing the name spaces (MAC, NFS, and so on), they are fully supported.

## Disadvantages of the In-Place Upgrade

Disadvantages of using the in-place upgrade method are as follows:

- It does not allow the volume block size of the server to be changed. Whenever possible, we recommend that each NetWare 6 server have 64K volume blocks, which provide for the greatest performance of disk reads and writes. But because the file system remains intact during the in-place upgrade, you will have the original volume block size set for your existing NetWare servers.

- It does not allow suballocation for the file system to be turned on before the upgrade begins. Suballocation can easily be turned on after the upgrade, but the suballocation affects only the subsequent writing of files to the disk. Therefore, any file that is rewritten to the disk will be suballocated.

- It may require a restoration from a tape backup if a failure occurs during the upgrade process.

**Consulting Experience**

If you use the In-Place Upgrade utility, you can still change your volume block size after upgrade, but only with some effort. In order to change the volume block size, follow these steps:

1. Back up the data to tape.

2. Delete the NetWare volume.

3. Create the volume and specify the 64K block size.

4. Restore data from the tape.

5. Bring the NetWare 6 server back up.

**The in-place upgrade process is restartable if a failure occurs. However, windows of vulnerability exist that may cause a failure and still require you to restore from tape.**

NOTE

# The In-Place NetWare 4/NetWare 5 to NetWare 6 Mass Upgrade

You can use any of several different methods to upgrade your NetWare 4 or NetWare 5 server to NetWare 6. The method discussed in this section is used for automatically upgrading your NetWare 4 server to NetWare 6 and can be used in a mass rollout.

Although the INSTALL.NLM program does a great job upgrading a server, it is a manual process designed to upgrade one server at a time. For example, in order to do the upgrade, you first connect to the existing NetWare server, start the install process, select a few options, answer a few questions, and then finish by bringing the server down and back up. This same sequence needs to happen for each server that you wish to upgrade. This works well if you have only a few servers and they are all local. If you have hundreds of servers and some of them are remote, you may need a better option.

In this section, we explore an option to automate large-scale or mass server upgrades both for local and remote servers across your network. This upgrade option uses Novell's CDWARE scripting language and other commonly available utilities. The greatest advantage of this solution is the ability to automate the upgrade process so that it can be accomplished quickly. This solution shows you how to automatically upgrade hundreds of remote servers in just a few hours.

An upgrade script (based on CDWARE) is included in the "Creating the Upgrade Script" section that enables you to move your servers from NetWare 4 or NetWare 5 to NetWare 6. In addition, this same solution can be used to apply service packs, patches, drivers, and application updates to the NetWare operating system as needed.

In the simplest terms, you can think of an in-place upgrade from NetWare 4 or NetWare 5 to NetWare 6 as a bunch of newer files that replace older files on your server. For example, CLIB.NLM resides in the SYS:\SYSTEM subdirectory on NetWare 4, and it is in exactly the same place for NetWare 6. Thus if the upgrade process updates or replaces the CLIB.NLM, the new version of CLIB copies over the old version of CLIB in the SYS:\SYSTEM directory. Although the files in NetWare 4, NetWare 5, and NetWare 6 are basically in the same location, a few files need to have their context changed. These files are the configuration files that require different information. These configuration files include STARTUP.NCF, AUTOEXEC.NCF, NETINFO.CFG, TIMESYNC.CFG, and a few others.

The upgrade process involves these six steps:

1. Create an image for the upgrade.
2. Store the upgrade image on a file server's directory structure.
3. Compress the upgrade image into one single file.
4. Create an upgrade script using CDWARE.
5. Move the upgrade image and script to the destination servers to be updated.
6. Schedule and launch upgrade process.

In order to create the upgrade script, you should use the CDWARE scripting language, which is native to the NetWare operating system. CDWARE is the name of the product that Novell uses to script its installation processes. As mentioned, CDWARE is built into the operating system and is not a product that you need to buy. CDWARE scripting is a very powerful scripting tool, but it is cryptic. The CDWARE scripting interpreter is provided by INSTALL.NLM for NetWare 4 or earlier and NWCONFIG.NLM in NetWare 5 or NetWare 6. Because CDWARE is built into the operating system, to use it you simply need to obtain the documentation from Novell. The CDWARE documentation can be found on the Novell corporate Web site at www.novell.com.

## Creating an Upgrade Image

In order to create an upgrade image, start by creating or building a blank directory structure on a server or workstation that looks like the NetWare 6 directory structure. This is where you will construct the upgrade image. In other words, create subdirectories that match the subdirectories structure on the NetWare 6 server. The best way to create the upgrade image for NetWare 6 is to simply install the NetWare 6 operating system on a new server using the standard installation process. Then just copy the entire image to the blank directory that you have created.

The upgrade image should include such directories as SYSTEM, PUBLIC, LOGIN, and others. The content of these directories and subdirectories then replaces the files on the existing NetWare server. For example, the files under the subdirectory NetWare6\SYS\PUBLIC that you create will replace the files in SYS:\PUBLIC on your destination server. Remember to include the files found in the COMMON and SYS directories as needed.

Next, select the products that need to be upgraded and copy the files and subdirectories to the upgrade image. If you have specific products that need to be installed on the NetWare 6 server, create a specific product subdirectory with the product installed in it. For example, if you want to have DHCP installed on your destination servers, you want to create the subdirectory in your local area under NETWARE6\PRODUCTS\DHCP\SYSTEM. These files are then moved or replace the appropriate files in SYS:\SYSTEM.

Create a SYS:\NWSERVER directory on the upgrade image. This directory corresponds to the DOS boot directory where SERVER.EXE resides, usually C:\NWSERVER. Place any files that need to be updated on the DOS boot directory in this directory. This directory should include disk and LAN drivers and other NLMs. To get an idea of what type of files are placed in this directory, look at any server's C:\NWSERVER directory. As part of the upgrade script, the files from SYS:\NWSERVER get copied to the C:\NWSERVER directory.

The nice thing about having and keeping an upgrade image of your servers is that you can now add any patches, utilities, and applications that you want to download to your servers. For example, now that you have built an upgrade image for NetWare 6, as patches become available for different products or the operating system itself, you can add them to your upgrade image. This enables you to run only one additional upgrade process on each server, instead of one upgrade for one product and then one for another. You can also customize your upgrade image to include any needed NCF files, any custom NLMs or drivers, and even application files. In addition, you can also remove unneeded files from the upgrade image. For example, if you don't need Unix Print Services, don't include the UXP files.

## Compressing the Upgrade Image

After you have built the upgrade image for NetWare 6 that can be used to upgrade a NetWare 4 or NetWare 5 server, the next step is to compress the entire image into one single file. In order to accomplish this, you can use any type of compression program. For example, you can use the PKZIP.EXE program in either DOS or Windows. If you use the DOS PKZIP program to compress your upgrade image, use this command:

```
PKZIP -~ -r -p UPGRADE.ZIP driveletter:\*.*
```

This command stores all the files and directories from the upgrade image into one file UPGRADE.ZIP. Using PKZIP.EXE, you can expect about 50 percent compression of the original file image.

In order to uncompress the UPGRADE.ZIP file after it has been downloaded to the destination server, you can use the UNZIP.NLM file found on the NetWare 5 or NetWare 6 operating systems or at `http://support.novell.com.`. This NLM is used to uncompress UPGRADE.ZIP on the destination server. UNZIP.NLM can uncompress the files in UPGRADE.ZIP and keep the correct directory structure. It can even overwrite read-only files. You will want to copy UPGRADE.ZIP and UNZIP.NLM to the SYS: volume on the destination server. Then, in order to uncompress the upgrade file image manually, enter the following command:

```
LOAD SYS:\UNZIP.NLM -o -$ SYS:\UPGRADE.ZIP
```

After the image is uncompressed, the files from SYS:\NWSERVER need to be copied to the DOS boot directory at C:\NWSERVER. This can be accomplished using NetWare Remote Manager and the access to the C:\ (or local) drive.

## Creating the Upgrade Script

After you have created an upgrade image and compressed it, you need to develop an upgrade script. The upgrade script should end in an .ILS extension. An example script, called UPGRADE.ILS, for upgrading a NetWare 4 or NetWare 5 server to NetWare 6 follows. Notice that the CDWARE code for the upgrade process includes support for making backup copies of SYS:\SYSTEM and C:\NWSERVER on the destination server. This enables you to back out of the procedure more gracefully, if need be. In addition, notice that the display command pauses execution of the script for debugging purposes. This upgrade script is called UPGRADE.ILS and is only an example; the upgrade script you develop for your production servers may be different.

The following listing, UPGRADE.ILS, is the CDWARE script that you can use to migrate your NetWare 4 or NetWare 5 servers to NetWare 6:

```
; This is a sample CDWARE Script to upgrade a NetWare 4 or
NetWare 5 server to NetWare 6.
; Server 4 upgrade to netWare 6.
; Script Version 1.00 10-15-01

Command ICMD.NLM

; The steps for upgrading a server are:

; 1. Minimize the processes that are running on the server
; 2. Make any backup copies of files if needed
; 3. Copy files to backup directories
; 4. Erase system files to avoid conflict with new operating
system
; 5. Uncompress the upgrade image on the destination server
; 6. Restore files for backup directory
; 7. Move new drivers and SERVER.EXE to C: or boot drive
; 8. Reboot the server
;
; 1) Unload Running Programs on Server
  Display 1,"Unload Running Programs."
  console 'UNLOAD MONITOR',5
  console 'UNLOAD SERVMAN',5
; 2) Make Backup Copy of Important Directories
Display 1,"Make Backup Directories for SYS:SYSTEM and
C:NWSERVER"
; Make the BACKUP Directories on SYS: and C:
GetPath Source, 1,'SYS:\\',""
SetDir Source,BACKUP,'','',10,0,0
GetPath Source, 1,'C:\\',""
```

```
SetDir Source,BACKUP,'','',10,0,0
; 3) Copy files to the Backup Directories on SYS: and C:
Display 1,"Backup Directories of SYS:SYSTEM and C:NWSERVER"
GetPath Source, 1,'SYS:\\SYSTEM\\',""
GetPath Target, 1, 'SYS:\\BACKUP',''
CopyFile 1,1,1,1,0,Source,'','','',Target,'','',''
GetPath Source, 1,'C:\\NWSERVER\\',""
GetPath Target, 1, 'C:\\BACKUP',''
CopyFile 1,1,1,1,0,Source,'','','',Target,'','',''
console 'SEARCH ADD SYS:\\BACKUP',1
; 4) Erase files on SYS:\SYSTEM and C:\NWSERVER
Display 1,"Erase File on SYS:SYSTEM and C:NWSERVER"
GetPath Source, 1,'SYS:\\SYSTEM',""
EraseFile 2,Source,'','',''
GetPath Source, 1,'C:\\NWSERVER',""
EraseFile 2,Source,'','',''
GetPath Source, 1,'SYS:\\NWSERVER',""
EraseFile 2,Source,'','',''
; 5) UNZIP the compressed file to sys: volume.
Display 1,"UNZIP File UPGRADE.ZIP Image"
NLMexec 1,'sys:\\unzip.nlm -o -$ sys:\\upgrade.zip'
; 6) Restore Files from the backup subdirectory
Display 1,"Restore NCF files from backup directories."
GetPath Source, 1,'SYS:\\BACKUP\\',""
GetPath Target, 1, 'SYS:\\SYSTEM',''
CopyFile 0,0,0,1,0,Source,'*.NCF','','',Target,'','',''
GetPath Source, 1,'C:\\BACKUP\\',""
GetPath Target, 1, 'SYS:\\NWSERVER',''
CopyFile 0,0,0,1,0,Source,'*.NCF','','',Target,'','',''
; 7) Move the files to the C: drive
Display 1,"Move Server Files to C: Drive."
```

```
GetPath Source, 1,'SYS:\\NWSERVER\\',""
GetPath Target, 1, 'C:\\NWSERVER',''
CopyFile 1,1,1,1,0,Source,'','','',Target,'','',''
; 8) Reboot the file server and exit
Display 1,"Reboot Server Now."
console 'REMOVE DOS',5
console 'DOWN',2
console 'Y',5
console 'EXIT',5
END;
```

## Launching the Upgrade Script

In addition to developing the upgrade script, you also need to create an NCF that enables you to launch the upgrade script. The NCF is for your convenience and is not required. To launch the upgrade CDWARE script, load INSTALL.NLM and point it to the script file. To launch this upgrade script, you can use this example for an UPGRADE.NCF:

```
LOAD INSTALL
B=SYS:\UPGRADE.ILS,S=C:\DOS,E=SYS:\ERR.FIL,NOSTATUS
```

As mentioned previously, the INSTALL.NLM program provides the interpreter for the CDWARE scripting for NetWare 4.11. The NWCONFIG.NLM program provides the interpreter for the CDWARE in NetWare 6. However, because we are running the upgrade script on the NetWare 4.11 server (soon to be upgraded to NetWare 6), the command to launch the script should LOAD the INSTALL program.

## Distributing the Upgrade Image

After you have created the upgrade image, compressed the upgrade image, and developed the upgrade script, you need to distribute the files to the destination servers. You should now have at least four files that you want to distribute to the server that are used to upgrade to NetWare 6. Table 16.1 shows the files that you need to download or distribute to each NetWare 4.11 server that you want to upgrade.

| T A B L E   1 6 . 1 | |
| --- | --- |
| Files to distribute to each NetWare server to be upgraded to NetWare 6 | |
| **FILE NAME** | **DESCRIPTION** |
| UPGRADE.ZIP | Compressed upgrade image |
| UNZIP.NLM | NLM that uncompresses the upgrade image |
| UPGRADE.ILS | CDWARE script to move files and reboot server |
| UPGRADE.NCF | File to launch the UPGRADE.ILS script (optional) |

As mentioned, each of the files needs to be downloaded to the destination NetWare server that you will be upgrading to NetWare 6. According to the upgrade script example, these files need to be copied to the root directory of the SYS: volume on the destination server. Choose from a variety of methods for copying these files. You can use NCOPY, COPY, or FTP. If you are copying the files across the WAN to remote servers and your network WAN is running TCP/IP, we recommend that you use FTP, because it will be the fastest.

## Performing the Upgrade

After you have successfully completed your upgrade image and script file and your files have been moved to the appropriate destination servers, you are ready to perform the upgrade process. You can manually launch the upgrade process by simply running UPGRADE.NCF. The process just described to upgrade a NetWare server to NetWare 6 takes approximately 15 minutes to complete. In addition to running the process manually, you can launch the upgrade process automatically using a scheduling program for the NetWare servers.

One scheduling program available is CRON.NLM, which is available for no cost from the Novell support Web site at http://support.novell.com. With the CROM NLM loaded or running on your servers, you can launch any NLM, NCF, or script file at a specified time or a specified interval. This enables you to perform the upgrade process automatically from any number of servers. For example, you can set all your servers to upgrade themselves at 2:00 A.M. on Friday night, or have all your servers in a specific location be upgraded at 1:00 A.M. Then the next day or week, you can upgrade another location or site automatically. The CRON.NLM program comes with documentation.

Make sure you test your upgrade process and image thoroughly before applying it to a production network. It is also important that you check compatibility issues with NDS and other applications running on the server. After your servers are upgraded to NetWare 6, you may want to revisit each server and clean up the server by deleting the zip file and the SYS:\NWSERVER directory.

As stated earlier, this upgrade process works well on a large enterprise network and has many advantages, including standardizing the operating system on all the servers while minimizing network impact during upgrade of the servers.

## Applying Patches

You can also use this process to automatically apply patches to the operating system, as they become available. Using this process, you will find that applying patches can almost be a nonevent. The following listing is an example of a CDWARE script for applying patches, called PATCHES.ILS.

This is a sample CDWARE script to apply patches to your NetWare server:

```
; Server upgrade to NetWare 6.
; Script Version 1.01 10-12-01


Command ICMD.NLM


; 1.) Unload Running Programs on Server.
console 'UNLOAD MONITOR',5
console 'UNLOAD SERVMAN',5
; 2.) Unzip the Upgrade File image to server.
NLMexec 1,'SYS:\UNZIP.NLM -o -$ SYS:\\UNGRADE.ZIP'
; 3.) Move the files to the C: drive.
GetPath Source, 1,'SYS:\\NWSERVER\\',""
GetPath Target, 1, 'C:\\NWSERVER',''
CopyFile 0,1,1,1,0,Source,'','','',Target,'','',''
; 4.) Now reboot the file server and exit.
console 'REMOVE DOS',5
console 'DOWN',2
console 'EXIT',5
; END
```

Again, to launch the CDWARE script, load INSTALL.NLM and point it to the script file. To launch or apply this patch, enter this command at the server prompt:

```
LOAD INSTALL
B=SYS:\UPGRADE.ILS,S=C:\DOS,E=SYS:\ERR.FIL,NOSTATUS
```

## The Across-the-Wire Upgrade Using the Novell Migration Wizard

The across-the-wire upgrade method moves your server data and files from NetWare 4 and NetWare 5 to NetWare 6. The Novell Migration Wizard is a utility that enables you to move NDS (or bindery) and the file system across the wire and place them in a destination server in an existing NDS tree. This utility supports only NetWare 5 and NetWare 6 destination servers. This utility comes free with NetWare and is run on a Windows 98 or Windows NT/2000 workstation that facilitates the transfer of the files and other information. Windows 95 workstations are not supported.

The workstation running the Novell Migration Wizard utility reads the server information and data files from the source server and writes them to either the NetWare 5 or NetWare 6 destination server. The connected workstation running the Migration Wizard utility must be logged into the destination and source servers with Supervisor or Administrative access on both servers.

Before you start the migration process, you need to consider a couple of prerequisites. For example, because the Novell Migration Wizard can be run from either a Windows 98 or Windows NT/2000 workstation, verify that you are running the latest NetWare Client 32 for each. Thus, any version of the client software that is equal to or greater than these values will be valid. The NetWare client software for both Windows 98 and Windows NT/2000 can be downloaded from the Novell main Web site at novell.com/download.

In addition, you should make accommodations for SAP filtering if any of the servers involved are running the IPX protocol. You should ensure that SAP filtering is disabled on each server involved in the upgrade. SAP filtering must be disabled for all servers running the IPX protocol because the servers need to be invisible and accessible. If SAP filtering cannot be disabled, you should ensure that the default server (preferred server) for the client is on the same LAN segment as the other servers you are upgrading to and from.

▶ . . . . . . . . . . . . . . . . . . . . . . . . . . . . . . . ◀

**Consulting Experience**

If you need to know the current version of the client software and have Windows 98/2000, you can select the Start button, the Settings menu, and the Control Panel, and then double-click the Network icon. Next, choose Novell NetWare or IntranetWare Client and then click the Properties button. The client page appears with the client version at the bottom. If the client version number does not appear, you have an older client that definitely needs to be updated.

## Advantages of the Novell Migration Wizard

Choosing and running the Novell Migration Wizard over the in-place method has several advantages. For example, a major advantage of choosing the Migration Wizard is that it supports migrations from NetWare 3. Listed below are more advantages:

- ▸ If you are migrating from NetWare 3, this utility upgrades all the bindery information into NDS (bindery services mode). The users, groups, and trustee assignments are maintained.

- ▸ The source NetWare server being upgraded is read-only, and the data files remain intact, thus preserving your original server if the upgrade cannot be completed because of any problems.

- ▸ It consolidates multiple source servers into a single NetWare 6 server. The source servers can be upgraded into a single, larger NetWare 6 server.

- ▸ It gives you the opportunity to replace or upgrade the server to newer, more powerful hardware.

- ▸ Passwords are preserved or moved from the source NetWare server to NetWare 6.

- ▸ Multiple Windows 98/2000 workstations can upgrade the same server with different volumes at the same time, meaning that you can have more than one workstation processing the information and upgrading it.

- ▸ You can change the volume block size on the new server volumes. You can select the volume block size during the installation of the NetWare 6 server to the recommended 64K.

- ▸ It enables file suballocation before the upgrade of the data files.

- ▸ All name spaces are supported. Specifically, the DOS, MAC, NFS, and LONG (or OS2.NAM) name spaces are supported.

### Disadvantages of the Novell Migration Upgrade

The Novell Migration Wizard method has just a couple of disadvantages:

▶ The procedure is slower than the in-place upgrade method. Because all data files are transferred across the network, the selected data being copied could disrupt other network traffic. For this reason, the across-the-wire upgrade process may need to be executed during off-peak hours.

▶ Two separate servers are required. If you have limited hardware or budget, buying a new machine just for the upgrade may not be possible.

# Preparing for Your Migration

If you choose to use the Novell Migration Wizard, you must accomplish some basic preparations before you start the migration. For example, you need to prepare a workstation (in the case of NetWare Migration Wizard) and the source and destination NetWare servers. The task of preparing your server for the migration will vary depending on the versions of NetWare that you will be migrating from.

### Preparing the Workstation

Preparing the Workstation is needed only if you plan to use the NetWare Migration Wizard 6 to perform the migration from source server to destination server. We recommend that you make sure the workstation has the following:

▶ Windows 98 or Windows NT/2000 software with at least 50MB of available disk space.

▶ Windows workstation must be running the Novell Client for Windows 98 version 3.3 or later.

▸ Windows NT/2000 must be running the Novell Client for Windows NT version 4.8 or later.

▸ If migrating from NetWare 4, the IPX protocol should be configured on your Novell Client workstation.

▸ For better performance, it is strongly recommended that the source server, destination server, and client workstation be running on a common LAN segment.

### Preparing the Source Server

The source server is the NetWare server that contains the files, volumes, and NDS data files that will be copied to the NetWare destination server. When using the NetWare Migration Wizard, the source server can be running NetWare 4.11, NetWare 4.2, NetWare 5.0/5.1, or NetWare 6. In order to prepare the source server, complete the following steps (refer to Chapters 15 and 18 for more information regarding the following preparations):

**1.** Use NWADMIN or ConsoleOne to verify that you have Supervisor or Admin rights to the source server, NDS, and file system.

**2.** Update the source server with the latest patches or Support Pack for the version of NetWare it is running. You can find the NetWare Support Pack at www.novell.com/support.

**3.** If you are migrating data from NetWare 4, you need to verify that the source server's volumes (all volumes) support long name space. To add long name space support to a NetWare 4.11 or NetWare 4.2 volume, enter the following at the server console:

```
LOAD LONG
```

and then enter:

```
ADD NAME SPACE LONG TO <volume_name>
```

**4.** Load DSREPAIR and run the following three options (and make sure there are no errors):

```
Unattended Full Repair
Time Synchronization
Report Synchronization Status
```

**5.** Back up your server before beginning an upgrade. Always make sure that you have tested the restoration of a tape backup as well. If the version of NetWare supports NDS, make sure that you include the NDS data files.

**6.** Delete unneeded files and directories before beginning an upgrade. Your upgrade will be shortened if you have fewer files to move. Besides, this is a good time to perform that long-overdue cleanup of your volumes.

**7.** Prepare your bindery by deleting unnecessary objects. Keep in mind that duplicate user names upgraded into the same container will have their trustee assignments combined into one user with the same name. For other duplicate objects, the first object upgraded is accepted, whereas the second duplicate is discarded. Therefore, if you have a group and a print queue with the same name, the first is upgraded and the second is discarded.

**8.** If you are migrating data from NetWare 3, you may want to run the BINDFIX utility to clean up your bindery and discard entries for users that no longer exist on that server.

## Preparing the Destination Server

The destination server is the new server that will receive the data from the source server. This server must be installed into a temporary or new NDS tree. When using the NetWare Migration Wizard, the source server can be running either NetWare 5 or NetWare 6. It does not support NetWare 4 destination servers. If using the NetWare Migration Wizard, the destination server automatically reboots after the data is migrated. The reboot automatically modifies the destination server AUTOEXEC.NCF file to include the source server's name and internal IPX number/server ID. You will not have to modify these manually.

Before you install the NetWare operating system and migrate data to the destination server, you need to review the following tasks on the destination server:

### Consulting Experience

The temporary server name and NDS tree must not be the same as the source server's name or current NDS name. If the destination server name and temporary NDS tree name are the same, the destination server will not assume the identity of the source server after migration.

**Consulting Experience**

NetWare Migration Wizard migrates compressed volumes. If you are migrating compressed volumes from the source server to uncompressed volumes, Migration Wizard decompresses the volume on the fly during migration. You need to make sure that you have enough room to hold the compressed volume data from the source server on the destination volumes that are uncompressed.

**1.** Use NWADMIN or ConsoleOne to verify that you have the Supervisor or Admin rights to the destination server and its file system.

**2.** You need to create a temporary server name and NDS tree to hold the destination server and migrated NDS objects.

**3.** During installation of the NetWare operating system, create volumes on the destination server that are the same size or larger than the source server. The volume names on the destination server also need to be the same as the source server.

**4.** If migrating from NetWare 4, install and configure the IPX protocol. The IPX protocol must be bound to the destination server for the migration to work. After the migration is complete, you can remove or unbind IPX.

## Running the Novell Migration Wizard

Because the utility runs on the workstation and has the responsibility to move all the data, the faster the workstation's CPU, the faster the upgrade. The workstation needs at least a 32-bit card. Figure 16.3 illustrates conceptually how the Novell Migration Wizard runs as an across-the-wire upgrade process, which means it runs on a Windows 98 or Windows NT/2000 workstation between the servers being upgraded.

To start the upgrade process at the Windows workstation, you are asked to first connect to both the source and destination (NetWare 6) servers with Admin or equivalent access rights. You can run the Migration Wizard from the location where you installed it on the workstation. The installation program by default installs the Migration Wizard at Start ➪ Programs ➪ Novell ➪ NetWare Migration Wizard ➪ NetWare Migration Wizard. After the utility is started the Novell Migration Wizard utility displays a welcome screen, as shown in Figure 16.4.

▶ • • • • • • • • • • • • • • • • • • • • • • • • • • • • ◀

## Novell Upgrade Wizard Utility

**FIGURE 16.3** *The Novell Migration Wizard utility is run on a Windows 98 or Windows NT/2000 workstation between the source NetWare server and a destination NetWare 6 server.*

▶ • • • • • • • • • • • • • • • • • • • • • • • • • • • • ◀

**FIGURE 16.4** *Immediately after starting the Novell Migration Wizard from where you installed it, the welcome screen appears.*

After the utility is launched and you are past the welcome screen, a dialog box appears that enables you to select between creating a new project or selecting an existing project. A *project* is a model that the utility uses to save the settings and options that will be used during the migration process. The project is created and completed before the actual migration takes place. In this dialog box, you are asked to select or create a project. If this is the first time you have executed the Novell Migration Wizard, you need to choose the "Create a new Project" option and click OK. Next, the wizard displays a dialog box that enables you to select the version of NetWare that the migration will use as a source. The choices that are displayed are NetWare 3; NetWare 4, 5 or 6; and Microsoft Windows NT 3.51/4 Server. Figure 16.5 shows the dialog box that enables you to choose the version of NetWare or NT that will be the source server for the migration process.

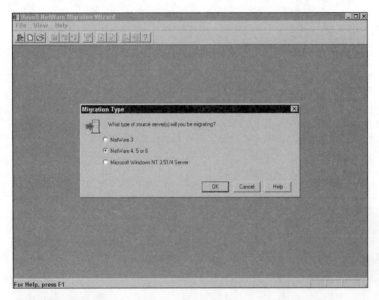

**FIGURE 16.5** *The Novell Migration Wizard enables you to select the source server. The utility supports source server options of NetWare 3, 4, 5, or 6 and Windows NT 3.51/4. In this example, we have chosen to migrate NetWare 5 to NetWare 6.*

After you select a project and a source server, the utility shows a Setup Tasks dialog box that enables you to click to view the setup tasks. When you click the

View Setup Tasks button, your default Web browser launches and takes you to the Novell Migration Wizard 6 online documentation. The documentation explains the prerequisites and requirements for each of the different source servers.

Next, you are given a dialog box that enables you to name the project. Using the Browse button to indicate the location where you want the project file to be saved, you simply and easily name the project. To continue, click the Next button at the bottom of the screen. A new page appears, asking you to select or indicate the destination NDS tree name server that you will migrate to. For this dialog box, you need to elect the name of the NDS tree where you will place (migrate) the information. The selected NDS tree is referred to as the *destination tree*. Figure 16.6 shows an example of this screen.

**FIGURE 16.6** *The Novell Migration Wizard asks you to define the destination NDS tree where the migrated objects will be placed. This step must occur before starting the migration process.*

## Copy Volumes in the Novell Migration Wizard

After you select the destination NDS tree, click Next to save your project and access the project window. You need to click Create to have the project window appear. In the project window, click Copy Volumes. Before the Migration Wizard starts copying files from the volumes, it backs up your directory and file trustees and saves them in files located on the source and the destination server. After the NDS migration is complete, Migration Wizard restores the trustees from the files it stored on the destination server.

You do not need to copy all volumes at once. You can select volumes to copy now and then copy other volumes later by reopening the project file. You also need to remember that files open at the time of migration are not migrated. If you choose to copy your volumes in phases, at the final volume copy, make sure you select all volumes that you previously copied and then click Cancel. Otherwise, Migration Wizard will restore trustee assignments only to the last volumes that were copied.

If you have big volumes or slow LAN connections, you may want to reconfigure your data by putting existing directories into different folders on the destination server. You should consider using a backup tape to copy your volumes.

**WARNING**

**If you use tape backup, do not restore the source server's standard SYS: directories to the destination server if you are upgrading your NetWare operating system to a higher version. The standard SYS: directories, such as SYS:SYSTEM and SYS:PUBLIC, were created for you during the NetWare installation and contain version specific data. If you are only migrating your existing data to new hardware and keeping the same version of NetWare, you can restore the source server's standard SYS: directories to the destination server.**

If you decide to use tape backup, select No for all volumes on the Select Volumes to Copy screen. Decide whether you want to copy the source server's SYS: directories to the destination server's SYS:MIG directory, and then click Next.

Migration Wizard never overwrites the SYS: directories on the destination server. If you choose to migrate the source server's SYS: directories, Migration Wizard migrates them to the SYS:SYS.MIG directory on the destination server. If the source server's SYS: directories include files that you want to utilize on the destination server, after the NDS migration is completed copy the files from the SYS:SYS.MIG directory into the appropriate SYS: directory on the destination server. Remember that any applications that have NLM programs in this directory need to be reinstalled after the migration.

Before you start the migration process, you need to decide how you want to handle any duplicate filenames between the source server and the destination server.

You next need to determine how you would like to process the migration from the source server to the destination server. You have the following two choices:

- Copy volumes with users logged in
- Disable login

Because Migration Wizard does not copy open files, you need to decide whether you want users on the server while it is being migrated. If you disable user login, you can be sure that no other users will log in to the network and open files during the file copy portion of the migration. After you have determined how the objects and volumes will be migrated, you can launch the Novell Upgrade Wizard utility by simply following the remainder of these steps:

1. Enter the passwords for the source and destination server or trees. If prompted, resolve any critical errors or warnings.
2. Start the migration of the server and file system to the destination NDS tree by simply clicking on the Migrate button.
3. Review the error and success logs, and then click Done.

## Edit Configuration Files on the NetWare Server

The Migration Wizard lets you modify any .NCF or .CFG files on the destination server. These configuration files contain default LOAD statements and parameters that affect the way the server responds. In order to edit the configuration files, you need to click Edit Configuration Files in the Project Window. You select the configuration file that you want to edit and then click Edit File.

**WARNING**

**If you are editing your AUTOEXEC.NCF, make sure that the file is closed before you migrate your NDS database.**

Having the ability to edit the configuration files for the Migration Wizard enables you to copy and paste pertinent commands from a configuration file on the source server to the corresponding configuration file on the destination server. For example, if you intend to change the IP address on your destination server to be the same as the IP address of your source server, you must edit your configuration files and change the IP address in two places: AUTOEXEC.NCF and

SYS:ETC/HOSTS. For example, copy the source server's IP address and paste it into the destination server's AUTOEXEC.NCF file. (This works only if your IP LOAD and BIND statements are located in the AUTOEXEC.NCF.) You also need to go to the server console of the destination server and change the IP address in the SYS:ETC\HOSTS file. Look for the original name of the destination server. If you use INETCONFIG to assign IP addresses, change the IP addresses after the migration is complete.

## NDS Migration Using the Migration Wizard

After you have selected the volumes to migrate and made the appropriate changes to the configuration files that exist on the destination server, you are ready to set up NDS for the migration process. But first make sure that you back up all volumes that you are not planning to migrate.

The first step in preparing NDS for the migration is to make sure that the servers in your source NDS tree are currently together in time synchronization and that NDS is completely up to date with all synchronizations. Next, you need to insert the licensing diskette, and browse to or enter the path to the licensing file. If you have an MLA, you also have the option of selecting the MLA instead of inserting the licensing diskette.

Select Yes or No to update the source server's schema. Migration Wizard updates the source server's schema to include the NDS classes of the default applications that are installed on the destination server. If you select No, by default the Yes radio button is enabled, which causes Migration Wizard to compare the source and destination schemas. This comparison helps you determine how to extend your schema in preparation for the migration.

Before continuing, run the DSREPAIR option to verify that the NDS tree containing the source server is functioning correctly. Migration Wizard does not prevent you from continuing if you have not run DSREPAIR to verify the health of your tree. However, if your tree is unhealthy before you begin the migration, the migration might fail.

If you are migrating from NetWare 4 running Border Manager, NetWare 5, or NetWare 6, you are prompted to copy and transfer the NICI configuration files from the source server to the destination server. Just follow the on-screen instructions and when the NICI configuration is complete, continue with the next step. If you are getting NICI errors when NDS is trying to load or when you are copying the NICI files, you should first check whether PKI.NLM will load on the destination server. If PKI.NLM won't load, see NICI Errors.

After you have completed these steps, you can click Migrate to begin the NDS migration. At the end of the migration process, the source server is brought down and the destination server reboots and takes over the name and identity of the source server. Migration Wizard automatically modifies the following items in the destination server's AUTOEXEC.NCF file:

- ▶ The file server name is changed to the name of the source server.
- ▶ The time zone is changed to the time zone stored in the source server's AUTOEXEC.NCF file.
- ▶ The server ID is changed to the IPX internal net value or server ID stored in the source server's AUTOEXEC.NCF file.
- ▶ The default time server type is changed to the value stored in the source server's AUTOEXEC.NCF file.
- ▶ The bindery context is changed to the bindery context stored in the source server's AUTOEXEC.NCF file.

## Summary

When upgrading your current NetWare servers to NetWare 6 you can use any of several different methods. Each method has its strengths or weaknesses depending on the type of upgrade that you want to perform. This chapter focused on upgrades from previous versions of NetWare only and provided details about several different options. For example, when upgrading from NetWare 4 or NetWare 5 to NetWare 6, you can either perform the in-place upgrade using the NetWare INSTALL program or use the across-the-wire program. The Novell Upgrade Wizard supports migration from NetWare 3, NetWare 4, and NetWare 5 to NetWare 6. It can be a simple process when you follow the guidelines in this chapter.

If you are upgrading your NetWare 4 or NetWare 5 servers to NetWare 6, you need to use the in-place upgrade method using the INSTALL utility that can be executed directly from the NetWare 6 CD-ROM. If you have a great number of NetWare servers that you want to upgrade rapidly, you may want to develop or use the CDWARE scripts as outlined in the previous sections.

After you have decided on an upgrade method for your servers, you will want to immediately start thinking about upgrading the workstation or client software to the latest NetWare 6 client. The next chapter addresses how to best upgrade your workstation clients to the latest software.

# Installing and Configuring Novell Clients

*"Change must be measured from a known base line." — Evan Shute*

The Novell Client 32 allows workstations to take advantage of all features in NetWare 6, and Novell provides a set of utilities to upgrade from NETX and Virtual Loadable Modules (VLMs) to Novell Client 32 and from older versions of Client 32. Once these utilities are in place, there is no need to visit individual workstations for future updates, as this can all be managed centrally, and updates can take place in an unattended mode.

Novell Client 32 works with DOS, Windows 3.x, Windows 95/98, and Windows NT/2000, providing a common network client base for all workstation types in many organizations today. Microsoft Client for Novell Networks workstations can attach to servers running NetWare but cannot take full advantage of NetWare 6, as this client operates in "bindery emulation" mode. Therefore, in order to take advantage of utilities such as ZENworks, your Microsoft Client for Novell Networks workstations need to be upgraded to Novell Client 32 software.

For simplicity, many companies are standardizing the majority of their workstations on a common desktop OS to provide for easier administration, updates, and support of their end users. Many larger organizations have selected Windows 2000. Others have standardized on Windows 98 as their desktop. In this chapter, you will find the necessary information for installing, configuring, or migrating to the Novell Client that corresponds to the desktop or desktops you deploy at your site.

**NOTE**   If you are using an older version of the Novell Client software, you should upgrade your client software. Additional features have been added that are not available in earlier versions. You can download the Novell clients free of charge from Novell's Web site at www.novell.com.

## Installation and Configuration of Novell Clients

This chapter discusses the features, installation options, and configuration options for the following clients:

- ▶  Windows 95/98
- ▶  Windows NT/2000
- ▶  DOS/Windows 3.x

## General Installation Instructions

These instructions can be used to install any Novell client software on your workstations. This includes the Novell Client for Windows 3.*x*, Windows 95/98, and Windows NT/2000. For small installations with few workstations, you can install from the *Novell Client* CD-ROM or you can download the software from Novell's Web site at www.novell.com.

Be sure to run through the following checklist before beginning any client installation on your network:

1. Understand what protocols you are running on your file servers. Have you moved completely to IP? Or are you running a combination of IP and IPX? You can install the Novell Clients to IP-Only (NetWare 5 or 6), IP with IPX compatibility mode (NetWare 5 or 6), IP and IPX (default), or IPX-Only.

2. Make sure the long filename support is installed on your NetWare 3.*x* or NetWare 4.*x* servers by typing **ADD NAME SPACE XXXX TO 'VOLUME'**. NetWare 5 and NetWare 6 servers automatically support long filenames.

3. The continuation of these instructions assumes that you have already installed and configured your network boards and have connectivity to your servers.

4. The following hardware prerequisites are assumed:

   ▶ Windows 95/98

     • 486 processor or higher

     • Minimum 28 MB free disk space

     • Minimum 16MB RAM

   ▶ Windows NT/2000

     • Minimum hardware requirements of windows NT 4.0 (server pack 3 or later) or Windows 2000

     • Minimum 24MB RAM

   ▶ DOS and Windows 3.1*x*

     • 386 processor or higher

     • Minimum 15MB free disk space

     • Minimum 8 MB RAM

     • A memory manager

The Novell Client Setup utility installs the Novell Client software on workstations running Windows. This utility lets you select the client that you want to install from the list of available clients. To install the workstation software, perform the following steps:

1. Do one of the following:

   ▶ Insert the *Novell Client*. If the Novell Client Setup utility does not automatically launch, run Winsetup.exe from the root of the CD-ROM.

   ▶ Download the latest Novell Client software from Novell's Web site.

   You will be prompted with the screen, as shown in Figure 17.1.

   Note: you can also use the ZENworks Starter Pack CD to install clients, however, you should check Novell's Web site for the latest client software for the platforms you need.

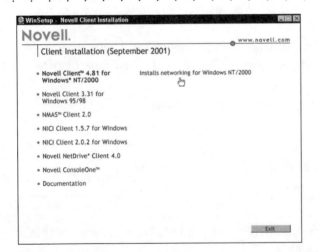

**FIGURE 17.1** *Novell Client for Windows Main Install screen*

2. Select a language.
3. Choose a platform.
4. Click the software to install. This begins installation of the client software.
5. Follow the onscreen instructions.
6. Right-click on Network Neighborhood, select the protocol that you want to configure, and click on properties, as shown in Figure 17.2.

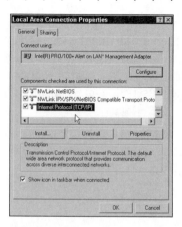

**FIGURE 17.2** *Configuring the Network Protocol for the Novell Client*

**7.** Configure the protocol options in each tab and click OK. You'll want to configure either a specific IP address for this workstation or select DHCP for automatic IP addressing, as shown in Figure 17.3.

**FIGURE 17.3** *Selecting the DHCP option for this workstation*

**8.** Click OK to make the changes.

## Performing a Network Install

You can also install the Novell Client software on multiple workstations from the network by precopying files to a file server and then modifying the login script to download the new client files when the user logs in. This installation has also been referred to as the Automatic Client Update (ACU). You can install and upgrade the client software on all platforms when users log in. The process basically requires six tasks:

► Creating a folder on the server.

► Copying Novell Client files to the new folder. Workstations can then read the files during login.

► Granting Modifyrights to the new folder.

► Modifying the ACU configuration file.

► (Optional) Creating or update the platform-specific configuration files.

► Creating or modifying the login script. (A sample login script is included.)

When the login script runs, ACU.EXE determines if the client needs to be upgraded. Users are only updated once, the first time they log in after you have set up the new client software.

### Create a Folder

Follow these steps in order to create a folder:

**1.** Log in to a server as Supervisor or as a user with Admin equivalent rights. Make sure that you have rights to copy files to a network folder that all users can access, as well as rights to modify login scripts on your server.

**2.** Create a folder in SYS:PUBLIC. For example, SYS:\PUBLIC\CLIENTS or SYS:\PUBLIC\WINNT.

### Copy Files

Choose one of the following steps in order to copy files:

► From the PRODUCTS directory on the *Novell Client* CD-ROM, copy the WINNT or WIN95 directories to the new folder you created in the previous step. If you are installing only one platform, you need only copy the platform directory for the platform you want to install. For example, copy only WINNT directory if you are only installing Windows NT on your workstations. You can also go to Novell's Web site to obtain the latest client software by client type if you are only installing one platform.

▶ If you are installing *Novell Client for Windows 95/98*, copy the Windows 95 and/or Windows 98 .CAB files to the WIN95 directory. The files are on the *Microsoft Windows 95* or *Windows 98* CD-ROMs (and *Upgrade* CD-ROM) in the respective WIN95 or WIN98 folders.

### Grant User Rights

Follow these steps in order to create a Group object in the NDS tree:

1. Place into the group users whose workstations need to be installed or upgraded. An example of this is shown in Figure 17.4

**FIGURE 17.4** *Moving the workstation users into a group that will have access to the new client files*

2. Make sure that the group has Read and File Scan rights to the folder that you created.

### Modify the ACU Configuration File

Follow these steps in order to customize an ACU:

1. Open the ACU.INI file located in the folder that you created on the server.
2. Modify the configuration options that are available to you, as shown in Table 17.1.

| TABLE 17.1 | | |
| --- | --- | --- |
| ACU Install Parameters | | |
| OPTION | DECRIPTION | SETTINGS |
| LAUNCHINSTALL] | Specifies whether the platform-specific setup utility will be launched once ACU.EXE determines that the installation is necessary. | Launch=Yes \| No {default:yes} |
| [DISPLAYDIALOG] | Specifies whether users will be prompted to begin the upgrade. | Display=Yes \| No {default:Yes} |
| [UNATTENDFILE] | Specifies whether a platform-specific configuration will be used and where it is located. | Use=Yes \| No {default:no} |
| [STATUS LOGGING] | Specifies whether a status log will be created where it will be located. | Use=Yes \| No {default:No} |
| [ADMINISTRATORMESSAGE] | Specifies additional text that will appear when the user to appear is prompted to start an ACU. | Message=the message you want |
| [CLIENTLOCALINSTALL] | Specifies whether the installation will be copied to a specified local directory and {default:no} run locally. | LocalInstall=Yes \| No |

To customize your ACU, simply open the ACU.INI file located in the folder you've created on the server. You can then easily modify the configuration options.

**We recommend that you use the ACU.INI file rather than the command line switches used in previous versions of Novell Client. ACU.INI simplifies the installation process. If you choose to use IMPORTANT switches, they will override ACU.INI options.**

### Update the Platform-Specific Configuration Files

Each platform-specific installation utility reads a configuration file generated by Novell Client Install Manager in order to configure the client properties. This file provides information such as where to copy drivers during installation and the most recent version number. This file must be placed in the same folder as the installation utility. If you are configuring Windows 95/98 workstations, options that were set in the NWSETUP.INI file or on the command line in previous versions of Novell Client (such as Display First Screen or CAB FIX) are now set up in Novell Client Install Manager.

To create a configuration file, do the following:

1. Start Novell Client Install Manager (NCIMAN.EXE). For Windows 95/98, Novell Client Install Manager is located in the WIN95\IBM_language \ADMIN folder that you copied to the server. For Windows NT/2000, Novell Client Install Manager is located in the WINNT\I386\ADMIN folder that you copied to the server. An example of the NCIMAN utility is shown in Figure 17.5.

**FIGURE 17.5** *Use the Novell Client Install Manager (NCIMAN) to create a client configuration file.*

2. Select File ➪ New, select the platform, and then click OK.
3. Modify the installation options as needed in the following ways:
   - In the Installation Options list box, double-click the configuration option that you want to modify.
   - In the property pages, set the parameters and then click OK. The values that you set appear in the right list box, as shown in Figure 17.6.

**FIGURE 17.6** *Setting the property pages in the NCIMAN install option*

**4.** Select File ⇨ Save. You can use any filename, for example, UNATT_95.TXT or UNATT_NT.TXT.

**5.** Copy this file to one of the following directories:

- WIN95\IBM_language (for Windows 95/98)
- WINNT\I386 (for Windows NT/2000)

**NOTE**

**If you install the client with the default settings, you do not need to create or to modify the configuration files. If you use a platform-specific configuration file to configure Novell Client, you must change the [UNATTENDFILE] option to Yes. The path to the text file cannot contain long filenames.**

### Create or Modify the Login Script

You need to modify login scripts for all users whose workstations will be upgraded. To upgrade workstations for users in a particular container, modify that container's login script. To upgrade workstations for users in a profile, modify that profile's login script. To upgrade specific users' workstations, modify those users' login scripts. To upgrade a workstation running bindery-based client software (such as Microsoft Client for NetWare Networks, which ships with Windows 95 or Windows 98), edit the system login script (SYS:PUBLIC\NET$LOG.DAT) with the appropriate bindery commands.

### Using ConsoleOne to Modify Login Scripts

To create or modify a login script using ConsoleOne, follow these steps:

**1.** Double-click the object whose login script you want to create or modify.

**2.** Click Login Script.

**3.** Enter the login script commands and information into the login script text box, as shown in Figure 17.7.

**4.** To save the login script and close the Details dialog box, click OK. If the login script that you just created was a container or user login script, you're finished and the client software will be installed or updated the next time users log in. If the login script that you just created was for a Profile object, you must associate the User object with the Profile object and make the User object a trustee of the Profile object.

**FIGURE 17.7** *Making changes to a login script using the ConsoleOne Utility*

### Sample Client Installation Login Script

The following sample script shows the commands that you add to the login script in order to install the client software from the network. The sample includes sample text for installing across an internal network.

```
REM ***** Windows 95/98 *****
If PLATFORM = "W95" or PLATFORM = "W98" THEN
   WRITE "Updating Novell Client for Windows 95/98."

#\\server1\sys\public\client\win95\ibm_enu\acu.exe

   I "%ERROR_LEVEL" = "1" THEN

    EXIT
   END
END

REM ***** Windows NT/2000 *****
```

```
IF PLATFORM = "WNT" THEN
   WRITE "Updating Novell Client for Windows NT/2000."
   #\\server1\sys\public\client\winnt\i386\acu.exe
   IF "%ERROR_LEVEL" = "1" THEN
      EXIT
   END
END
```

The next time your user logs in to the network, their workstation will be upgraded to the latest client software.

### Upgrading a Client Workstation to Windows 2000

You can also upgrade a Windows 95/98 or Windows NT 4.0 workstation that is running the Novell Client software to Windows 2000 quite easily without uninstalling the client software.

▶ **Windows 95/98 to Windows 2000** — Installs Novell Client version 4.51 from the *Windows 2000* CD-ROM.

▶ **Windows NT to Windows 2000** — Detects the version of Novell Client software installed and does one of the following:

If the Novell Client version is 4.6 or earlier, Windows 2000 installs the Novell Client version 4.51 from the *Windows 2000* CD-ROM.

If the Novell Client version is 4.7 or later, Windows 2000 leaves it intact but removes all installed components and changes the protocol selection.

After the migration to Windows 2000 is complete, the Novell Client will reinstall the previously installed components and restore the previously selected protocols.

**In order to complete the reinstallation of the components and protocols, the user who logs in must have Administrator rights to the workstation after the migration.**

**WARNING**

Novell Client version 4.51 on the *Windows 2000* CD-ROM has limited functionality. Therefore, you will want to upgrade to the latest Novell Client version once you have completed the upgrade. You can go back to the section above that describes how to install the latest Novell Client software. You can either access the latest client software from a product CD-ROM or download it from www.novell.com/download. Once you have set up the Automatic Client Update, the Novell Client will run an ACU from one of the following places:

▸ The path pointed to by the NWCLIENTDIR environment variable in the login script or at the command line

▸ The path were Novell Client was installed from

▸ Drive Z: on the network

You may choose to skip the Automatic Client Upgrade by setting the NWCLIENTDIR environment variable to NULL in the login script.

## Creating Login Scripts

After a user successfully logs in to the network, the login process executes one or more login scripts that automatically set up the workstation environment. You can use login scripts to map drives and search drives to directories, display messages, set environment variables, and execute programs or menus.

Login scripts are properties of specific NDS objects.

There are four types of login scripts:

▸ **Container** — Sets the general environments for all users in that container. Novell Login executes container login scripts first. Container login scripts can be associated with Organization or Organizational Unit objects but a user can use only one container login script. A container login script replaces the system login script from NetWare 3.

▸ **Profile** — Sets environments for several users at the same time. Novell Login executes a profile login script after the container login script. Profile login scripts are associated with profile objects. A user can be assigned only one profile login script but can choose other profile login scripts.

▸ **User** — Sets environments (such as printing options or an e-mail username) specific to a single user. Novell Login executes the user login script after any container and profile login scripts have executed. User login scripts are associated with User objects. A user can have only one user login script.

▸ **Default** — Contains only essential commands, such as drive mappings to NetWare utilities, and cannot be edited. It runs if a user (including user Admin) doesn't have a user login script, even if a container or profile login script exists.

**If you don't want to create any user login scripts and you don't want the default login script to execute for any users, you can disable the default login script by including the NO_DEFAULT command in the container or profile login script.**

NOTE

Maintaining many user login scripts can be time-consuming. Therefore, you should try to include as much customization information as possible in the container and profile login scripts, which are fewer in number and easier to maintain.

For example, if all users need access to the NetWare utilities in the same volume, put the search drive mapping to that volume in a single container login script rather than in every user login script.

Create profile login scripts if several users have identical login script needs. Profile login scripts are sometimes thought of as group login scripts.

Only include in user login scripts those individual items that can't be included in profile or container login scripts.

Because up to three login scripts can execute whenever a user logs in, conflicts can occur and drive mappings can be overwritten by consecutive login scripts. The last login script to execute (usually the user login script) overrides any conflicting commands in a previous login script.

In Windows NT and Windows 2000, all drive mappings made using the NetWare login are root mapped. Because of this, programs cannot access directories above the directory that the drive is mapped to. If necessary, you can turn off the default by adding SET MAPROOTOFF="1" as the first line in the login script. This will globally force all NT workstations using the login script to not map root drives.

**Don't delete the login directory (SYS:LOGIN) created during network installation. It contains the Novell Login and command line utilities. Users can use the available utilities, such as NLIST, to view a list of available NetWare servers.**

WARNING

### Where to Locate Login Scripts

Login scripts are properties of objects. Therefore, only certain objects can contain login scripts. This, in turn, largely determines where login scripts can be located. We recommend that you avoid implementing User login scripts. Unless the user can maintain their own login script, you, as an administrator, will be responsible to maintain and modify those scripts when needed. Most users can gain sufficient access to the network through the container login script. You can also use a Profile script for smaller groups of users that need separate and unique access.

### Creating or Modifying Login Scripts

You can use ConsoleOne to create login scripts or use a sample login script that is provided for you with the software. Using a sample login script can help reduce syntax errors and thus reduce the time it takes to create login scripts. All four types of login scripts use the same conventions, commands, and variables.

The main difference in creating container, profile, and user login scripts is the object that you select to contain the login scripts. The default login script is not assigned to any object.

Container login scripts are assigned to container objects (Organization or Organizational Unit objects).

Profile login scripts are assigned to Profile objects. In order for a User object to use a profile login script, you must select that User object and assign it to the Profile object.

User login scripts are assigned to User objects.

**Before you create or modify login scripts, you must have the Write property right to the object that will contain the login script. In addition, the Organization, Organizational Unit, Profile, or User object IMPORTANT that you plan to assign the login script to must already exist.**

To create or modify a login script using ConsoleOne, follow these steps:

**1.** Double-click the object whose login script you want to create or modify.

**2.** Click Login Script.

**3.** Enter the login script commands and information into the login script text box.

**Make sure that you edit the sample login script to match the server names, directory paths, and specifications of your own network.**

IMPORTANT

**4.** To save the login script and close the Details dialog box, click OK.

If the login script that you just created was a container or user login script, you're finished and the client software will be installed or updated the next time users log in. If the login script that you just created was for a Profile object, you must associate the User object with the Profile object and make the User object a trustee of the Profile object.

### Associating the User Object with a Profile Object

Follow these steps to associate the User object with a Profile object:

1. In ConsoleOne, double-click the User object that needs to use the profile login script.

2. Click Login Script.

3. Enter the name of the Profile object in the Default Profile field located under the login script text box and then click OK.

4. To add the User object as a trustee of the Profile object, double-click the Profile object.

5. Click NDS Rights ⇨ Trustees of this Object ⇨ Add Trustee.

6. Enter the name of the User object that uses this Profile object.

7. Make sure that the Browse object and the Read property check boxes are checked and then click OK to assign these rights to the User object.

The User object is now a trustee of the Profile object and has the rights necessary to run the profile login script. Repeat these steps for all additional users who need to use this script.

### Getting Around the One Profile Login Script Restriction

Users can belong to only one profile login script and so, as a rule, only one profile login script can be executed for any user. There are ways to run the equivalent of different or multiple profile login scripts by specifying other profile login scripts.

For example, to specify a different profile login script for a user at the command line, use the following command:

```
LOGIN username /p profile_object
```

You can also specify a different profile login script using ConsoleOne. On the user's Login Script page, browse until you find the profile login script that you want to associate with the user, select it, and then click OK. For more information on associating a profile login script with a user, see the ConsoleOne help.

You can also assign users to more than one Group object. Use the MEMBER OF group identifier variable to execute different parts of a login script, depending on the Group objects that the user belongs to. To accomplish this, use the IF...THEN command and the MEMBER OF group identifier variable To view an example of the IF...THEN command used with the MEMBER OF group identifier variable, see the sample login script shown earlier in this chapter.

### Creating Login Scripts from a Sample or Existing Login Script

To create a login script from an existing login script, complete the following steps:

**1.** Locate the sample or existing login script that you want to modify.

**2.** Copy the sample or existing login script as shown in Figure 17.8.

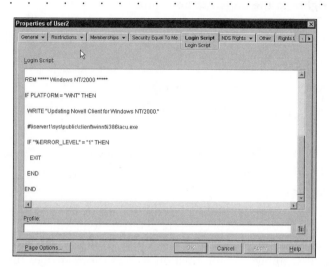

**FIGURE 17.8** *Copying an existing login script using the ConsoleOne Utility*

**3.** In ConsoleOne, open the login script, copy and then paste the sample into the login script.

**4.** Make necessary changes to the sample login script to customize it for your network.

**Make sure that you edit the sample login script to match the server names, directory paths, and specifications of your own network.**

**IMPORTANT**

**5.** Click OK to save the new login script.

If the login script that you just created was a container or user login script, you're finished. If the login script that you just created was for a Profile object, you must associate the User object with the Profile object and make the User object a trustee of the Profile object.

### Printing Login Scripts

To print a login script from the command line, use the NLIST command and redirect the output to a file or a printer. You must be in an object's parent container to see and print the login script of that object.

> **You must have a workstation running DOS 3.30 or later and Read and File Scan property rights to the object to be printed.**

**IMPORTANT**

To print a user's login script, enter the following:

```
NLIST user=username show "login script"@@> LPT1
```

To print a container's login script, enter the following:

```
NLIST "organizational unit"="ou name" show "login script"@@>
LPT1
```

Keep in mind that any option in the NLIST command that includes a space in its name must be enclosed in quotes.

### Setting Up Location Profiles

Location profiles allow you to save the information from a user's specific login into a location profile. When the user selects this profile during login, the profile automatically sets up login information such as the user's name, server, tree, context, login script, and other applicable information so that the user does not have to type this information.

Location profiles are especially powerful for users who log in from multiple locations. Users can have separate profiles for the office, home, laptop, or any other workstation they use. This simplifies the login process so that users do not have to remember their login information for each workstation. Using multiple location profiles also gives you control over what users can access from each workstation.

You can create a location profile on a single workstation or you can create location profiles for multiple workstations by using the ZENworks Workstation Configuration policy packages.

> **To create and then distribute location profiles that will be used by multiple workstations, use the Novell Client Configuration policy created in the Workstation Configuration policy package in ConsoleOne (ZENworks for Desktops 3) or NetWare Administrator (ZENworks for Desktops 2).**

**TIP**

For more information on using ZENworks for Desktops policy packages, see the ZENworks for Desktops information in Chapter 19. If you have questions while setting up a policy package, click Help.

To create a location profile on a specific workstation, follow these steps:

**1.** Open the Client property pages by right-clicking the N icon in the system tray and click Novell Client Properties and then select the Location Profiles tab as shown in Figure 17.9.

**FIGURE 17.9** *Location Profile Configuration for a single workstation*

**2.** Type the name of the profile that you want to add and then click Add.

**3.** From the Location Profile Properties menu, select one of the following:

Login Service to configure login settings, *or*

Connection Service to configure your dial-up connection settings

**4.** From the Service Instance menu, do one of the following:

Select an existing service instance, *or*

Enter a name for a new service instance and then click Add to specify the settings for this service in the Novell Client Login window or Connection Services window.

**5.** When you have finished creating the location profile, click OK.

**TIP**

When storing the profile through an **NDS** login, you can use a File System Pointer. This allows multiple users to use the same profile, provided they all use the same path as the file system pointer.

**IMPORTANT**

When storing the profile from a Windows NT 4.0 workstation on a NetWare server, that server volume must support long filenames. In versions of NetWare earlier than NetWare 4.11, the OS/2 name space was required for long filename support. In NetWare 4.11 and NetWare 5, the **LONG.NAM** name space is required on the server.

### Removing a Location Profile

You may need to remove a location profile once it has been created. If you are removing a location profile created on an individual workstation, take the steps below. If you want to remove a location profile created in a Client Configuration policy, you can either delete the Client Configuration policy or change the associations of specific users with this policy.

Follow these steps to remove a location profile:

**1.** Open the Client property pages by right-clicking the N icon in the system tray and click Novell Client.

**2.** Select the name of the profile that you want to remove and then click Remove.

### Setting Up Login Restrictions

Login restrictions are limitations on user accounts that control access to the network. These restrictions can be set in ConsoleOne for each user and include the following:

▶ Require a password (you can specify its minimum length, whether it must be changed and how often, whether it must be unique, and whether the user can change it)

▶ Set the number of logins with expired password and the number of incorrect login attempts allowed

▶ Set account limits, such as an account balance or expiration date

▶ Limit disk space for each user by specifying the maximum blocks available for each user on a volume

- Specify the number of simultaneous connections a user can have
- Specify by node address, which workstations users can log in on
- Restrict the times when users can log in (you can assign all users the same hours, or you can restrict users individually)

When a user violates login restrictions, the account is disabled and no one can log in using that username. This prevents unauthorized users from logging in.

### Customizing the Novell Login Dialog Box

The Novell Login dialog box can be customized to show the features that you want users to have access to. Customizing gives you control over the following:

- **The choice of NDS or bindery connection** — Typically, most users use the NDS connection, but you can also select a bindery connection if an old bindery-based application requires this.

- **The Location field at the top of the dialog box** — Hiding the Location field is especially useful if you have set up only one location profile for a workstation. In this case, the Location field is not useful and might confuse or distract the user.

- **The Advanced button** — If you have set up several location profiles and do not want users to change the data in various login fields (such as tree, context, server, run scripts, etc.), you can hide the Advanced button.

- **The Variables button on the Script tab** — If you use %2, %3, %4, or %5 in the login script, you might want to set these values in the location profile but not allow the user to change them. In this case, it might be helpful to hide the Variables button.

- **The Clear Connections check box on the NDS and Bindery tabs** — If you want all connections to be cleared every time the user logs in, or if you don't want any connections to be cleared, you can set the value in the location profile and then hide the Clear Connections check box.

**NOTE**

**The Clear Connections check box is never visible during initial login, because an initial login automatically clears all connections.**

- The Workstation Only check box that appears under the Password field during an initial NT/2000 login — If you do not want to allow workstation-only logins — for example, if you want to require that the user log in to NetWare in order to use the workstation — you can hide the Workstation only check box.

▸ **The Run, Display, and Automatically Close properties check box —**
For use with login scripts RAS options, if RAS is installed on the
workstation.

These additional features of the Novell Login dialog box should also be
considered:

▸ If Dialup is not installed on the workstation, the fields on the Dialup tab
are disabled.

▸ If the Novell Login dialog box is being used to log in to a specific tree, the
Tree field is disabled to prevent the user from changing the tree.

▸ If the Novell Login dialog box is being used to log in to a specific NDS
server, the Server and Tree fields on the NDS tab are disabled to prevent
the user from changing them.

▸ If the Novell Login dialog box is being used to log in to a specific bindery
server, the Server field on the Bindery tab is disabled to prevent the user
from changing the server.

The Novell Login dialog box can be customized to control the availability of
certain login options. This gives you control over how users log in.

**TIP**

**You can also customize the Novell Login dialog box for multiple
workstations using the Novell Client Configuration policy created in the
Workstation Configuration policy package in ConsoleOne (ZENworks
for Desktops 3) or NetWare Administrator (ZENworks for Desktops 2).**

For more information on using ZENworks for Desktops policy packages, see
the ZENworks for Desktops information found in Chapter 19. If you have
questions while setting up a policy package, click Help.

To show or hide any login dialog box options. Follow these steps:

**1.** Open the Client property pages by right-clicking the N icon in the system
tray and click Novell Client Advanced Login tab.

**2.** In the Show On Login section of the Advanced Login property page, check
the check boxes for the items that you want to appear, and clear those that
you do not want to appear as shown in Figure 17.10.

**FIGURE 17.10** *Showing or Hiding Login Dialog Box Options*

### Uninstalling Novell Client

You can uninstall the Novell Client by using the uninstall utility or by selecting Remove in Network Properties. For Windows 95/98, double-click the uninstall utility (UNC32.EXE) located in the PRODUCTS\WIN95\language_directory\ ADMIN directory. For Windows NT/2000, in the Network Properties, click Services ➪ Novell Client for Windows NT/2000 ➪ Remove and then click Yes.

### Native File Access

The Novell Native File Access Pack overcomes the need to install Novell client software on Windows, Macintosh, and Unix systems for access to storage on NetWare 5 and NetWare 6 servers. This server-based solution enables a broad range of clients to access NetWare storage right out of the box. Virtually any client can securely access their data from any location, and user management for disparate client operating systems is simplified through eDirectory.

## Installing Novell Native File Access Pack

Follow these steps to install the Novell Native File Access Pack:

**1.** Obtain the *Novell Native File Access Pack* CD-ROM from a dealer or from the Internet.

**2.** Make sure that your NetWare 6 server meets the minimum hardware requirements.

**3.** From the Administrator Workstation, log in to the destination server that will run the Novell Native File Access Pack software.

**4.** Create a temporary directory on the destination server.

**5.** Unzip the Novell Native File Access Pack files to the temporary directory on the destination server.

**6.** At the server console, enter **STARTX** to launch the graphical server console.

**7.** Click Novell ⇨ Install. An example of this screen is shown in Figure 17.11.

**FIGURE 17.11** *Getting ready to Install Native File Access*

**8.** From the Installed Products screen, click Add.

**9.** Enter the path to the temporary directory and select the PRODUCT.NI file.

**10.** Accept the License Agreement.

**11.** Select to install Macintosh and/or Windows components. An example of this install screen is shown in Figure 17.12.

**FIGURE 17.12** *Installation Screen for native file access*

**12.** Click Next.

**13.** (Conditional) If you choose to install the Windows component (CIFS), complete the following steps:

   **a.** Log in as a user with the Supervisor right.

   **b.** You must specify the full context for the user, for example .kbeck.b2b.sfi.

**14.** Enter the Server Name and Server Comment that will appear in Network Neighborhood as shown in Figure 17.13

**FIGURE 17.13** *Server Properties for native file access*

**15.** The Server Name must be 11 or fewer characters and must be different from the actual NetWare server name. The Server Comment is optional.

**16.** Specify whether to enable UNICODE. When checked, this option enables Unicode characters used in double-byte languages.

**17.** To specify "no-map" cases in the UNINOMAP.TXT file, enter the first Unicode value to watch for and then the second value representing the ASCII replacement code. For example:

```
0178 98
20AC CC
```

**18.** Save the values in the UNINOMAP.TXT file. If an unmappable character is encountered, the system uses the ASCII substitution character specified in the file.

**19.** Select one of the following and click Next.

- If users will authenticate using NDS, select Local.
- If users will authenticate using a Domain, select Domain.

For Windows users, there are two types of authentication methods available with Novell Native File Access: Local and Domain. Local authentication requires a simple password to log in to a NetWare server, but a simple password is not required for Domain authentication. When Novell Native File Access Pack is configured for domain authentication, it is not possible to change the simple password or the NetWare password using Windows' native Change Password feature. To change the password, you must use Windows' domain management utilities.

**20.** (Optional) Specify the IP address to be attached to the Windows (CIFS) protocol. The default is to bind all IP addresses to the CIFS protocol.

**21.** (Optional) Specify additional NetWare volumes or folders that you want to appear as share points in Network Neighborhood.

**22.** To specify a new share point, click New and then enter the path to the directory, a name, and a description. The directory name must end with a backslash (\). For example, SYS:\SYSTEM\.

**23.** Specify the NDS contexts for all Windows users who need access to the server. An example of this is shown in Figure 17.14.

**FIGURE 17.14** *Specifying the contexts to be searched by CIFS users*

If you choose to install the Macintosh component (AFP), complete the following steps:

**1.** From the Administrator Workstation, log in as a user with the Supervisor right.

**2.** Open the SYS:ETC\CTXS.CFG file in a text editor.

**3.** Enter the contexts of each Macintosh user that requires access to the server. For example:

```
crime.norad.acme
whi.labs.acme
pr.rio.acme
```

**TIP**
**The Native File Access Pack software will search each context in order until it finds the User object.**

**4.** Save the file.

**5.** (Optional) Rename a volume by editing the SYS:ETC\AFPVOL.CFG file.

**6.** Read the Summary Window as shown in Figure 17.15 and then click Finish.

**FIGURE 17.15** *Native file access install summary list*

**7.** The last step is to restart the server.

### Starting and Stopping Services

Each time the server starts, Novell Native File Access protocols are loaded from commands in the AUTOEXEC.NCF file. You can also load and unload the service from the server console.

**Starting and Stopping the Macintosh (AFP) Protocols**   Follow these steps to start and stop the Macintosh (AFP) protocols:

**1.** At the server console, enter **AFPSTRT** to load the Macintosh (AFP) protocols on the server. Any changes in the configuration files are applied when the protocols are loaded.

**2.** At the server console, enter **AFPSTOP** to unload the Macintosh (AFP) protocols.

**Starting and Stopping the Windows (CIFS) Protocols**   Follow these steps to start and stop the Windows (CIFS) protocols:

**1.** At the server console, enter **CIFSSTRT** to load the Windows (CIFS) protocols. Any changes in the configuration files are applied when the service is loaded.

**2.** At the server console, enter **CIFSSTOP** to unload the Windows (CIFS) protocols.

# Using Novell's Management Portal for File Access

Because Novell provides the NetWare Management Portal, you can also configure your servers in such a way that users can gain access to their files via a regular browser. The management portal offers file-access functionality. This section explains the steps for configuring servers so that they can gain access to their files via a regular browser.

To provide browser access to files from inside your network, you first need to provide a URL for your users that points to the Server, Volume and Subdirectory in the following form:

```
http://server-ip-address:8008/VOL/SUBDIR/
```

Port 8008 is the default for the HTTP stack in the NetWare Management Portal.

Users will be directly taken to the server/volume/subdirectory specified and will be prompted to login using their NDS user IDs and passwords. The users will then need to enter their full-context user IDs. The NetWare Management Portal then grants access to files as based on the usual NetWare file rights and will build HTML pages listing the directory contents. The users will not be able to see anything that they normally do not have rights to. An upload button is provided automatically if "write" rights exist in a directory, and it has a feature to search text files.

## Summary

This chapter has outlined the steps necessary to install, configure, or upgrade to the Novell Clients. These clients provide you with a secure and reliable desktop that can take advantage of Novell's ZENworks product to manage your desktop environment. This chapter also includes information on how to install the Native File Access on servers to eliminate the need to install Novell clients on desktops.

# Backing Up and Restoring NDS eDirectory

*"Put all thine eggs in one basket and — watch that basket." — Mark Twain*

**B**ecause NDS eDirectory is a global and distributed name service, it requires a specialized approach to backup and restore processes. Not only must you back up your files and directories, but you should have a backup of your NDS tree for all situations that may occur, including catastrophes. In most cases, you may simply need to restore a few objects or a subtree. Because NetWare 6 is not server-centric, NDS information may be stored on multiple servers. Therefore, you must have a backup solution that can read the NDS information across multiple servers and store it properly. The backup solutions for NetWare 6 must be able to read the entire NDS tree by communicating with the other servers. A restore solution must also have the same capability.

This chapter refers frequently to NDS objects and partitions. Proper partitioning and replication can provide you with a greater degree of fault tolerance. For more information on these topics, see Chapters 3 and 6 of this book.

This chapter describes how to perform NDS backup and restore using the various components of Storage Management Services (SMS). The text also covers how to devise a backup procedure through the use of replication, your first (and easiest) line of defense against NDS data loss. First, you'll learn about the components of the NetWare 6 backup architecture.

## Understanding the Basics

Before backing up and restoring NDS information, you should understand the basic components and architecture of NDS backup solutions. The process of backing up and, especially, restoring NDS information is complex, and you can always first rely on your replicas for NDS fault tolerance. For more information on NDS replicas and their placement, refer to Chapter 6.

**NOTE**

**Replication, however, is not sufficient protection for a single-server network or when all copies of the replicas are destroyed or corrupted. In these instances, if the NDS data has been backed up regularly, the NDS tree structure can be restored using backup and restore procedures.**

When you perform a Storage Management Services (SMS) backup of NDS eDirectory, you are backing up the NDS file information that is stored on each server. You do not back up information regarding the partition boundaries of the NDS tree. Instead, you back up every server that contains a portion of the NDS database. You basically have an image of your entire NDS tree that appears as a single partition on a tape backup.

Consequently, during a restore of NDS, the image partition is split into its appropriate partitions as they exist on your actual tree. Some backup solutions also let you restore subtrees or individual objects. Novell's TSANDS.NLM, which ships with NetWare 6, supports this capability, as discussed later in this chapter. If no partition information is on your tree because of a total loss of NDS, the entire image is restored to a single ([ROOT]) partition.

During a restore, you often see unknown objects or objects that are lacking a mandatory attribute. When you use the NWADMIN utility, unknown objects appear with a "?" icon. During a restore, any number of your objects have pointers to attributes of other objects that do not yet appear in your tree. For example, one user object may have been granted rights to another user object. Because the process restores only one object at a time, you may see a whole series of unknown objects until the restore is completed and these discrepancies are resolved.

## Storage Management Services

Storage Management Services (SMS) is a collection of software programs by Novell that provides backup and restore services. These services are performed by a collection of components that are independent of operating systems and hardware. SMS is an open architecture for interfacing storage management engines with NDS eDirectory. Third-party developers can develop backup solutions with their own functions and features written to the SMS standard interface. This platform provides a consistent architecture for storing, accessing, and managing data on many different client platforms, including NetWare servers, Windows 95/98, and Windows NT/2000 clients. Although the file systems may be different, SMS provides a consistent view of this data.

The SMS architecture was developed with the assistance of third-party developers, and many backup products now comply with the SMS standard. In fact, you should not purchase any NetWare 6 backup product that is not SMS compliant.

The SMS architecture actually consists of these components:

▶ Storage Management Engine (SME) backs up and restores operations. Enhanced SBACKUP (SBCON) is a basic SME for NetWare 6.

▶ SMDR (Storage Management Data Requester) communicates between the backup program and Target Service Agent (TSA) software.

- ▶ Storage device interface communicates between the SME and the storage devices.

- ▶ Device drivers are used to control the behavior of the storage devices.

- ▶ Target Service Agents (TSAs) pass requests and commands between the SME and server or NDS database, and they prepare the data for the SME. The TSA600 must be loaded on the server where the file system data is to be backed up.

- ▶ TSAProxy (TSADOS for DOS workstation) is used to register the workstation with the host server. TSAProxy also identifies and keeps track of the stations waiting to be backed up. It receives "I am here" messages from workstations available to be backed up. The TSAProxy keeps the names of these workstations in an internal list and displays the list, enabling you to select a target for a backup or restore procedure.

### The Storage Management Engine

One of the key components of the SMS architecture is the Storage Management Engine (SME). The SME is software that communicates with network clients through a common interface. The software provides cross-platform support and is easily modified to add new features or support. Novell's SBACKUP utility is an SME. Most third-party developers provide functions and features to support NetWare 6 backups by including an SME with their product. The most common use of the SME is a backup and restore application.

The SME operates on a NetWare 6 server as a NetWare Loadable Module (NLM). The SME manages all user requests and interaction between the Target Service Agents, discussed next, and the device driver for your tape backup system.

### The Target Service Agent

The Target Service Agent (TSA) is software that can scan, read, and write data found on a target file system. A target can be any item on the network that needs backing up; in most cases, this means a file server or group of file servers and NDS. Targets can also be SQL database engines or print servers or even workstations.

A TSA must understand the file structure for the particular platform that it is accessing. Therefore, the TSA is specifically written for each type of platform that you need to back up. The TSA understands all the unique features of the platform you are backing up, such as name spaces, file and directory attributes, and security rights. The TSA can also present the data to the SME in a common format. For this reason, the SME can interact with many different types of TSAs, as shown in Figure 18.1.

**FIGURE 18.1** *Each TSA can talk to its operating system platform. The TSA then presents this information to the SME in a common format.*

Because the SMS components are very modular in nature, they make supporting many operating systems easy. A vendor releasing a new version of an operating system only needs to provide a TSA to support that operating system. That way all vendors selling an SMS-compliant backup solution can support the new operating system. Novell, for example, currently provides TSAs for the following operating systems:

- ▸ NetWare 3.11 and 3.12
- ▸ NetWare 4.11 and 4.2
- ▸ NetWare 5.0 and 5.1

- ▸ NetWare 6
- ▸ NDS eDirectory
- ▸ DOS
- ▸ Windows 98/2000 clients
- ▸ OS/2 clients
- ▸ Macintosh clients
- ▸ Unix clients

SMS TSAs are loaded as NLMs on the host or target server. You can also load them as memory-resident modules on your client workstations. The latest version of the TSA600.NLM supports NetWare 6 and is backward-compatible with NetWare 5. The TSA module provides the capability to back up server-specific resources or information. This resource is provided in the SME's Resource list. The SYS: volume and other volumes are major resources that can be selected from most backup utilities and backed up.

Select Server Specific Info packages contain critical data for recovery purposes. SERVDATA.NDS, DSMISC.LOG, STARTUP.NCF, AUTOEXEC.NCF, and VOLSINFO.TXT are all backed up by selecting Server Specific Info. You have two ways to back up server specific information. The first way is to select a full file system backup on your NetWare Server. The second way is to select the Server Specific Information option from the resource list for a file system backup.

Table 18.1 lists each TSA version that you need to load for a particular operating system.

### Consulting Experience

In addition to using the traditional backup utilities to backup NDS eDirectory, you can use the DSREPAIR utility. By loading DSREPAIR –RC (where –RC is used as a parameter to DSRPAIR at the server console prompt), you can perform a backup of a particular server's Directory Information Base (DIB). The DIB of the directory for that server enables you to restore the directory database in case of disaster.

**TABLE 18.1**

*TSA Version Requirements by Operating System*

| BACKUP/RESTORE | ENTER THIS COMMAND |
| --- | --- |
| NetWare 6 | LOAD TSA600 |
| NetWare 5.0 or 5.1 | LOAD TSA500 or LOAD TSA550 |
| NetWare 4.11 or 4.2 | LOAD TSA411 or TSA420 |
| NetWare 3.11 or 3.12 | LOAD TSA311 or TSA312 |
| NDS eDirectory | LOAD TSANDS |
| DOS Partition on NetWare | LOAD TSADOSP |
| Windows 95 and Windows 98 | W95TSA.EXE and W98TSA.EXE |
| Windows NT/2000 | TSAPREFS.EXE, TSAMAIN.EXE, NT TSA |
| Unix | TSAPROXY.EXE |
| OS/2 | OS2TSA.EXE |
| Macintosh | MACTSA.EXE |

When the server-specific information is restored, it places the files in the SYS:\SYSTEM\SOURCE_SERVER_NAME directory on the target server (by default). The SOURCE_ SERVER_NAME directory is created using the 8.3 naming convention. If your backed-up server name is SMS600_S1 and you restore the Server Specific Info to server S2, the source server name in the path just given will be SMS600_S1. The new directory on S2 will be SYS:SYSTEM\SMS600_S1. All the Server Specific Info files will be put into this directory (SERVDATA.NDS, DSMISC.LOG, AUTOEXEC.NCF, STARTUP.NCF, and VOLSINFO.TXT). The following is a description of the server-specific files that are backed up.

SERVDATA.NDS contains server-specific NDS information. This file is used by INSTALL to recover from an unplanned SYS: volume failure. The restore procedures show how to use this file to recover from a SYS: volume failure in a multiserver environment with existing replicas on other servers that will be used to provide a complete recovery.DSMISC.LOG is a text file that contains the replica list and replica types that the backed-up server held at the time of backup. This file is used in the restore procedures to provide helpful information needed to prepare NDS for recovery of the failed server. It also provides a list of the other servers that were in the failed server's replica ring. Here is a sample DSMISC.LOG:

```
Wednesday, August 28, 2001   2:30:21 pm
Backing up server-specific NDS data
Successfully read addresses of the local server object.
Current partition/replica list
Partition OU=NORAD.O=ACME, current replica list:
    CN=SMS600_S5.O=ACME, type read/write
    CN=SMS600_S4.O=ACME, type read/write
    CN=SMS600_S3.O=ACME, type master
Partition OU=LABS.OU=RIO.O=ACME, current replica list:
    CN=SMS600_S5.O=ACME, type read/write
    CN=SMS600_S4.O=ACME, type read/write
    CN=SMS600_S3.O=ACME, type master
Partition OU=CHARITY.OU=NORAD.O=ACME, current replica list:
    CN=SMS600_S5.O=ACME, type read/write
    CN=SMS600_S4.O=ACME, type read/write
    CN=SMS600_S3.O=ACME, type master
Partition OU=PR.O=ACME, current replica list:
    CN=SMS600_S5.O=ACME, type subordinate reference
    CN=SMS600_S4.O=ACME, type read/write
    CN=SMS600_S3.O=ACME, type master
Partition [Root], current replica list:
    CN=SMS600_S5.O=ACME, type read/write
    CN=SMS600_S4.O=ACME, type read/write
    CN=SMS600_S3.O=ACME, type master
```

AUTOEXEC.NCF is the NetWare server executable batch file located in the NetWare partition of the server's disk. This file is used to load modules and set the NetWare operating system configuration.

STARTUP.NCF is the NetWare server boot file that loads the NetWare server's disk driver and name spaces and various SET parameters.

VOL$INFO.TXT is a text file that contains needed information about the volumes on the server at the time of backup, including name spaces, compression, and migration information. This file can be used during restore procedures to provide helpful information in preparing volumes correctly for a restore. A sample VOL$INFO.TXT is given here:

```
SMS600_s123456789
Current File System Information by Volume
Wednesday, August 28, 2001 2:15:25 pm
SYS:
Supported Name Spaces:
    DOS
    MACINTOSH
    NFS
    LONG
Extended File Formats:
    Compression is enabled.
VOL1:
Supported Name Spaces:
    DOS
    MACINTOSH
Extended File Formats:
    Compression is enabled.
VOL2:
Supported Name Spaces:
    DOS
```

A special TSA known as TSANDS.NLM supports the backup and restoration of NDS eDirectory, including objects and trustee assignments. The backup includes NDS partitions and other crucial information. TSANDS can walk the entire NDS tree to access the appropriate NDS files for backup. Novell's SBACKUP utility and the other third-party SMS-based backup solutions use this TSA.

The TSANDS.NLM has a number of features covered in the following sections.

## Extended Schema Backup

Extensions to the NDS base schema are included in the backup and restore function set of TSANDS.NLM. Backup and restore of the NDS schema are handled by TSANDS.NLM as a complete data set. A new target service resource schema is now exported by TSANDS.NLM. The backup of the schema resource consists of the packaging of all attributes followed by all class definitions from the working NDS schema. A restore of the schema data set consists of the addition of all attributes from the backup that are not part of the current working schema. After the additions of the backup attribute set have been restored, the class definitions are restored by updating the current classes with missing attributes from the backup or by the addition of a complete class when none is present.

Selecting the Full Directory Backup option includes the schema resource in its backup by default. If the backup application enables selection of resources, the schema resource can be selected and backed up separately. The schema resource can be handled the same way for restores.

### Error Handling

TSANDS.NLM now has the capability to log objects to an error log when an object cannot be backed up for whatever reason. For example, you are backing up a big tree with thousands of objects and by chance one or more of the replicas are off line so that no referrals can be found, or an object is corrupt and cannot be read properly. The object name or container name will be logged to the backup error log file. The TSANDS.NLM then continues to get the next object and continues the backup if possible. This enables TSANDS.NLM to discover and back up all the objects that are resolvable in the tree. After the backup is complete, you can view the error log file and see what objects or container objects have not been backed up.

### The Resource Configuration Option

The following options ("How to scan what you are backing up:" and the TSANDS.CFG configuration file) are included to improve the scaling of the TSANDS.NLM. These options enable administrators to back up subsections of NDS trees by assigning rights to backup users. Supervisor rights are required to back up NDS objects. It is the tree administrator's responsibility to assign Supervisor rights to any additional backup administrators. Backup administrators should be assigned supervisory rights to the subsection of the NDS tree that they will be responsible for backing up. For example, suppose you have five containers, NORAD, RIO, CAMELOT, TOKYO, and SYDNEY, that need to be backed up. You can create five backup administrators — BAdmin1, BAdmin2, BAdmin3, BAdmin4, BAdmin5 — and give each backup administrator Supervisor rights to his respective container.

This enables the backup administrator to back up only the objects for which he has been given Supervisor rights. If BAdmin1 has been given Supervisor rights to container NORAD, he can back up objects in only the container NORAD and below as long as his Supervisor rights are not filtered at a subordinate level to NORAD.

Because BAdmin1 has not been given Supervisor rights to organization ACME, he cannot start the backup from ACME context. The TSANDS.CFG file can be created to help identify the starting context for each backup administrator. The TSANDS.CFG resides in SYS:SYSTEM\TSA\ directory. The context is shown here:

```
.OU=NORAD.O=ACME
.OU=RIO.O=ACME
.OU=CAMELOT.ACME
.OU=TOKYO.ACME
.OU=SYDNEY.ACME
```

You need to create this .CFG file and enter the starting context for each backup administrator that you have in your tree. The starting context shows up in your backup utility as a selection item that each backup administrator can select as his or her starting context and initiate the backup from that point. This eliminates walking down a deep tree to select the correct starting context each time a backup needs to be performed. This also provides a starting context if browse rights are removed from each backup administrator and he cannot see below the [ROOT] object to start walking the tree down to the assigned container starting context. The backup administrator that possesses the Supervisor right to ACME does not need an entry in the TSANDS.CFG because that starting context is visible from the selection resource list.

In addition, the Supervisor rights are assigned by a tree administrator and can be assigned or filtered either at partition boundaries or at a container level. Depending on how you design and administer your tree backup procedure, these new options can help in effectively and efficiently improving your backup and restore of your NDS tree. More about using the SBACKUP utility is discussed in the section "Using the SBACKUP Utility," later in this chapter.

## The Storage Management Data Requester

The Storage Management Data Requester (SMDR) is the link between a vendor's backup application engine (SME) and the SMS TSAs. Its job is to locate and provide instructions to the TSAs on your network. The SMDR also provides the link to the storage device interface. For example, during a backup sequence, the SME receives from the TSAs data processed into the correct format. This information is communicated through the storage device interface to the backup device.

Figure 18.2 shows all of the components of the SMS architecture.

For data restoration, the SME talks to the device driver to tell it which data to restore from tape. After receiving the data, the SME passes it back to the TSA, which writes the data to the target. Again, the target could be a NetWare server, an SQL database, a print server, and so on.

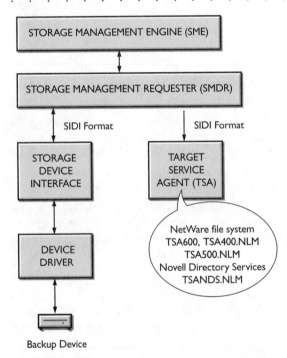

FIGURE 18.2 *The SMS architecture consists of multiple components, including the Storage Management Engine, the Target Service Agent, and the Storage Management Data Requester.*

# Backing Up Novell Directory Services

An NDS replica is generally your first mechanism for fault tolerance in NDS because of the time-sensitive nature of NDS. The replica can maintain the most recent event information about its objects and properties. You can use replicas to restore or rebuild information from a replica of the same partition that has been damaged. In contrast, a tape backup is like a snapshot in time and will become out of date, unlike the actual replica.

Nonetheless, you should have a tape backup of NDS for increased fault tolerance of your NetWare 6 network. In some cases, such as single-server environments, tape backup provides fault tolerance for NDS. In addition, a tape backup protects data and NDS information in the event of a catastrophe such as a fire or flood. Novell highly recommends that you always have a tape backup of NDS and maintain this copy by performing regular backups.

A replica is a copy of a partition. Having multiple copies of replicas increases fault tolerance for your system. As discussed in Chapter 6, too many replicas can result in a performance decrease. Typically, three replicas are sufficient for fault tolerance. This would include a Master Replica and two Read/Write replicas. Figure 18.3 shows an example of the replication process.

**FIGURE 18.3** *Using replication as a means of avoiding NDS data loss*

## Object IDs and the Backup Process

An object ID is generated for each NetWare 6 object created in your tree. SMS-compatible backup products store an object's distinguished name in typeful format. Each object has a distinguished name that serves as the object's unique identifier. For example, the user object LDAVINCI.R&D.LABS.NORAD.ACME is backed up in its typeful format:

```
CN=.LDAVINCI.OU=R&D.OU=LABS.OU=NORAD.O=ACME
```

For more information on distinguished names, refer to Chapter 4.

NetWare 6 objects have only one distinguished name that is unique across the entire tree. However, when a replica of a partition is placed on a server, NDS generates a unique object ID for the same object. Therefore, each NDS object has one distinguished name with possibly many object IDs, depending on the number of replicas created for that partition. Each server uses the object IDs to coordinate activity on the local server between the local object and, for example, file services. During a tape restore, if an object ID already exists for that object, the server receiving the restore does not create a new object ID. If the object on the tree were deleted and you subsequently did a restore, a new object ID would be created on the server receiving the restore. Figure 18.4 shows an example of this process.

**FIGURE 18.4** *A restore of an object creates a new object ID if the object does not currently exist on the tree.*

Trustee assignments for the file system are backed up along with the file system. The SMA TSA uses the object's distinguished name to back up the trustee rights from the file system in order to preserve an object's trustee assignments during restoration. For example, suppose a user object is deleted from the tree and subsequently re-created. If you then restored the user's files from tape, the TSA could match the file system assignments to the user because of the distinguished name. This also assumes that when you re-created the user, you used the same name that was in use before.

**NOTE** **The preceding paragraph explains why you must restore your objects to NDS *before* you can restore file system information. The file system restore attempts to match the file assignments to the user object's distinguished names. If they are not on the server first, the files will not be assigned back to the users.**

Choose a backup approach that fits your needs. Whenever possible, you should have a centralized approach to the backup of your NDS tree. Ideally, a single administrator will have rights to all servers in the tree in order to perform backup functions. However, this may not always be possible because of the size of some corporate networks and the geographic nature of the network. In large environments, you may want to designate a site administrator who is responsible for backups in his or her portion of the tree. Keep in mind that each administrator must have Supervisor rights to the servers for which he or she needs to perform backups. If several people are responsible for backups, it takes more coordination and organization to ensure that each location backs up their portion of the NDS tree consistently. Figure 18.5 shows an example of centralized backup approach.

You can follow these guidelines when backing up your tree:

▶ Perform backups regularly — once a week, for example. The number of backups you perform depends on how many changes are made to your tree. (Examples of changes are adding new users, moving subtrees, and so on.) If your tree does not change much, backups can be performed weekly. If it changes a great deal, backups should be more frequent.

▶ Create a company policy stating how often NDS backups should be performed. You may simply want to have your administrators perform the NDS backup each time they do a full server backup.

▶ Load TSANDS.NLM on one NetWare 6 server in your tree. Choose the server containing a replica of the largest partition in your tree. For more complex networks, TSANDS.NLM can be loaded on more than one server.

▸ Keep a written record of your partitions and replicas. If you need to do a total restoration of NDS, you may need to know where to create your partitions and replicas.

▸ Create an alternative administrative type user if you decide to reduce your ADMIN user rights. Typically, when you install the first NetWare 6 server, you call the first user ADMIN, and this user has Supervisor rights at the [ROOT] of your tree. If you subsequently reduce the rights of the ADMIN (or equivalent) user and perform a tape backup on that object, the object is backed up with the reduced rights. Subsequently, when you restore the ADMIN (or equivalent) object, it is restored with the reduced rights, which does not allow you to complete your restore.

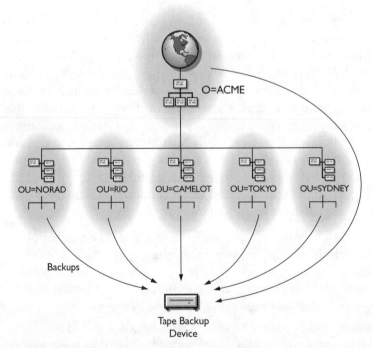

**FIGURE 18.5** *You should use a centralized backup approach for NDS whenever possible.*

## Using the Enhanced SBACKUP Utility

Enhanced SBACKUP allows backup of SMS Targets such as NDS eDirectory, binderies, the file system, or an individual workstation's hard disk onto a media that can be stored offsite. If you have a hardware failure, natural catastrophe, corrupted data, or incorrectly deleted or changed data, you can recover a previous version of the data.

Enhanced SBACKUP retrieves and reinstates backed up data. The restore session produces the requested data, which is retrieved from the storage media and restored to the location you specify. During a restore session, Enhanced SBACKUP reads the backup storage media and the Target Service Agent compares the media data set to the existing hard disk data set.

Backup services is an essential piece of SMS, a collection of services that provide backup, restore, and data migration. These services are performed by various components and are independent of operating systems and hardware. Backup is grouped according to the following topics:

- ▶ **Backup services** — Provide information on supported devices, the SMS architecture, memory requirements, types of backup offered, customizable options, schedules, how to back up NDS, how to back up the file system (both legacy NetWare file system and Novell Storage Services), and how to use Target Service Agents.

- ▶ **Restore services** — Provide information on how SMS restores data from NDS, volume sys and other volumes, single servers, multiple servers, and the NDS tree structure.

- ▶ **Error and log files** — Discuss the files that are created during backup.

In this section, we discuss the steps to launching and using the SBACKUP utility. This utility can be launched from a NetWare 6 server or from a Windows 95/98 or Windows NT/2000 workstation. This utility is run from a server through the command line prompt. It is run from a workstation through a graphical interface. Both methods are discussed here.

The NetWare 6 version of the Enhanced SBACKUP utility supports 0.25-inch, 4mm, and 8mm storage devices. If you are using 4mm tape, use only DDS (Digital Data Storage)-certified, computer-grade tapes. We recommend that you pretest your storage devices before you begin backup. To ensure reliable operations, pretest all media storage devices that are not Novell certified with the appropriate NetWare device driver and Enhanced SBACKUP backup and restore utility.

The first step is to load the necessary modules at the NetWare 6 server. To load the Storage Management Engine, follow these steps:

1. Type **LOAD SMDR**. If this is the first time you have loaded the modules, you have to select a name resolution mechanism.

2. Select a name resolution mechanism. You can select NDS, SLP, or SAP. If you choose NDS, the SMDR Configuration dialog box displays the default SMDR Group context, where the SMDR group is located.

3. Press Enter to accept the default, or add a new SMDR context. If you are loading the modules for the first time, enter the SMDR Context name. This registers the local submitter with the group submitter. You can change the context if necessary.

4. Enter the full context of your user name. This is the name of the person who will be performing the backups and restore. The person should have administrator rights to the selected contexts. The name must begin with a period (.): for example, .ADMIN.ACME.

5. Enter your password.

6. Type **LOAD TSA600**.

7. Type **LOAD SMSDI**.

8. Type **LOAD QMAN**. If this is the first time you have loaded the module, the queue is created automatically after you enter the following information:

   • Queue Context is the context that will be used for the job queue. You need this when you create backup or restore jobs.

   • Queue Name is the name of the job queue. You need this when you create backup or restore jobs.

   • User Name is the name of the person who will be submitting the jobs.

   • Password is the password of the person who will be submitting the jobs.

9. If you reload the QMAN.NLM, type **LOAD QMAN NEW** to modify the queue information specified while loading the module for the first time.

10. Type **LOAD SBSC**.

11. Type **LOAD SBCON**. If you use backup and restore on the server, load sbcon. If you use NWBACK32 on a client, you do not need to load this module.

When this module is loaded, you will see a startup screen as shown in Figure 18.6.

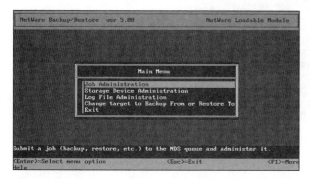

**FIGURE 18.6** *The SBACKUP utility running from a NetWare 6 server console*

### Backup Options at the Server

From the main menu, the following options are available:

- ▶ Job Administration
- ▶ Log/Error File Administration, which contains the session and error files
- ▶ Storage Device Administration, which contains the options to monitor the properties of a device
- ▶ Change Target to Back Up From or Restore To, which contains the options to change your target

From the main menu at the prompt Job Administration, the following options are available:

- ▶ Backup
- ▶ Restore
- ▶ Verify

When you select Backup Options, you are prompted to fill in the information screen as shown in Figure 18.7. You need to log in with Supervisor rights to the server you have selected as the target.

**FIGURE 18.7** *The Job Administration Backup screen*

The Target Service is the server that you wish to back up or restore to. The "What to Back Up?" screen enables you to select the entire server, SYS: volume, individual files, and so on to be backed up. An example of selecting individual files for backup is shown in Figure 18.8.

Other options on this screen include selecting the media type that you are using. Press Insert to be shown a list of the installed backup media on your server. You must have at least one option appearing in the list in order to run a successful backup. You can also give the backup job a name such as NDS Weekly Backup.

**FIGURE 18.8** *Selecting individual files for backup*

**Backup Types**

Enhanced SBACKUP has three types of backup sessions:

▶ **Full backup** — Backs up the entire file system of the selected target, regardless of whether the data has changed since the last backup, and clears the Modify bit after the backup.

▶ **Differential backup** — Available only for the file system; backs up only data that has been changed since the last full or incremental backup. When you perform a differential backup, the modify bit is not cleared after the backup. All files modified since the last full backup are included in the backup (unless they have been deleted). Each differential backup uses more media and is slower than an incremental backup because it backs up more files. Do not interchange differential backups and incremental backups. If you do, the differential backup will not contain all changes since the last full backup. Use full backups interspersed with differential backups or full backups interspersed with incremental backups.

▶ **Incremental backup** — Available only for the file system; backs up only data that has been changed since the last full or incremental backup (whichever was last). Incremental backup sessions back up only files that have the modify bit set (that is, files that changed since the last full or incremental backup session when the modify bit was cleared).

The Advanced Backup Options screen is shown in Figure 18.9. This screen enables you to specify with greater detail how and when you want a backup to occur. For example, you can specify a Full, Incremental, or Differential backup. You can also specify the time and date when you want the backup to begin.

**FIGURE 18.9** *The Advanced Backup Options screen of the SBCON utility*

After you have completed these screens, you can exit by hitting Esc. You are then asked whether you want to submit the backup job for processing. If you say Yes, the job is then scheduled for processing based on the criteria you have previously defined for that job.

An example of the job submission screen is shown in Figure 18.10.

**FIGURE 18.10** *The job submission screen for SBCON*

### SBACKUP Guidelines

Before you set up and begin backups, follow these guidelines to make backups easier and to avoid problems later:

▸ **Log in** — You will have limited success backing up and restoring if you log in without supervisor rights. For security reasons, many Enhanced SBACKUP options are limited to the network administrator.

▸ **Reserve disk space for temporary files** — Make sure you have disk space available (1 to 2 MB) on the target server's volume SYS to accommodate log and error files. Enhanced SBACKUP creates temporary files on the target server during backup. If you have linked UNIX files or files with extended attributes, the temporary files might be larger than 1 MB.

▸ **Do not mount or dismount volumes during a backup or restore session** — The data might be corrupted or an abend might occur at the host server.

▸ **Use the correct name space and name space formats** — If you do not use the correct name space and name space formats when entering paths and file names, files can't be restored. Name spaces: DOS, FTAM, Macintosh, NFS, and OS/2. Name space formats:

```
For Macintosh, use Volume::directory:directory:filename
For all others, use Volume:/directory/directory/filename
```

▸ **Exit Enhanced SBACKUP before unloading drivers** — If you unload a manually loaded driver (such as aha1740.dsk or aspitran.dsk) before exiting Enhanced SBACKUP, you might cause the host server to abend.

▸ **Use original case for non-DOS names** — Non-DOS pathnames and filenames are case-sensitive. NetWare recognizes DOS pathnames and filenames in uppercase, lowercase, or mixed case. If you're not sure of the original case, refer to your log file.

### SBACKUP from a Workstation

You can also load the SBACKUP utility at a Windows 95/98 or Windows NT/2000 workstation by doing the following steps. The workstation backup utility is stored on the SYS:Public directory and is known as NWBACK32.EXE. It accomplishes the same tasks as the SBCON utility on your NetWare 6 server but uses a graphical interface:

1. Log into your NDS tree structure. Be sure to log into the desired tree if you have more than one tree on your network.

2. Click Network Neighborhood ⇨ novell ⇨ sys:public.

3. If this is the first time you have used NWBACK32, you are prompted to configure the SMDR information, including tree name, SMDR context, and the SMDR group context. Enter the name of the NDS tree you will use to back up and restore data. Enter the context you created during the server configuration. Check the SAP (IPX) box if you want to use IPX. Uncheck the box for IP. An example of this dialog box is shown in Figure 18.11.

The application then launches, and you see a dialog box, as shown in Figure 18.12. You can then select an option. Keep in mind that the same options exist in both the SBCON (server-based utility) and NWBACK32.EXE (workstation-based utility).

**FIGURE 18.11** *The SMDR configuration dialog box is initialized the first time you run NWBACK32 from a workstation.*

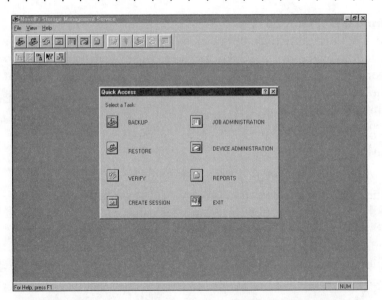

**FIGURE 18.12** *The main dialog box for NWBACK.EXE*

If you select the Backup task, you are presented with the What to Backup dialog box.

Double-click What to Backup. Click to back up NDS, NetWare Servers, or Workstations. A list of servers appears. Double-click to select the server that you want to back up. An example of this window is shown in Figure 18.13.

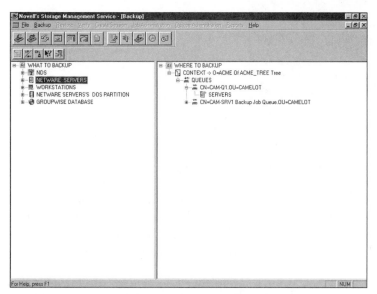

**FIGURE 18.13** *Selecting what you want to back up through the NWBack32 Utility*

You are then prompted to enter the username and password to authenticate to the server. A list of resources to back up appears, such as volumes and files. You can then click the resources to back up.

Next, select where you want your backup data to go. Double-click Where to Backup.

Change to the correct NDS tree structure and context by clicking the Change to Context button on the toolbar. Double-click Queues; a list of Queue objects appears. Click to highlight a Queue object. Right-click to open the drop-down box.

You are now ready to submit the backup job as shown in Figure 18.14.

This step enables you to submit the job to a queue, on the chosen server, or on the chosen media type.

**FIGURE 18.14** *Submitting a backup job for processing*

### Backing Up Your Windows 95/98 Workstations

To back up the workstation (the target), a TSA must be loaded on the workstation. You can select the individual directories to back up or back up the entire workstation. For Windows 95/98, make sure that W95TSA.EXE or W98/TSA.EXE is installed and configured. It is a part of the Novell Client modules (check box for Target Service Agent for Windows 95 or Windows 98).

> **NOTE**
>
> **To configure W95TSA, refer to Help that comes with the Novell Client modules. If it is installed and registered, a shield-like icon appears in the shell tray and indicates "Novell TSA (Listening)" when the mouse pointer reaches the icon. You also see an SMS window pop up when you log in to NetWare.**

To prepare for a backup on a Windows 95/98 workstation, follow these steps:

1. At the target workstation, register with W95TSA by double-clicking the shield-like icon that appears in the shell tray. The Novell Target Service Agent for Windows 95 Properties box appears. You then must follow these steps:

   a. Enter your user name and password for the TSA.

   b. Enter the server name that will be servicing this Windows 95/98 client.

   c. Choose the disk drive you want to register.

   d. (Recommended) Check Auto Register. This automatically registers your workstation with the server.

   e. Click OK.

   f. Restart your workstation.

**2.** The TSA must be installed and registered with the host server, along with the TSA username and password. At the host server, type **TSAPROXY**. You can then select or click the NetWare server running the target service agent.

**3.** Next, select or click the target workstation that you want to back up and enter the username and password when prompted. Follow the steps in the procedures to back up data to complete your backup.

### Backing Up a Windows NT/2000 Workstation

Make sure that the NT TSA is installed and configured. It is a part of the Novell Client modules (check box for Novell Target Service Agent). The Windows NT TSA has two parts:

▸ The TSA Service (TSAmain.exe) is a service that waits for and acts when there is a request from the backup engine.

▸ The TSAPrefs (TSAPrefs.exe) enables an NT administrator to set preferences and monitor the activities of the TSA Service.

The first step is to configure the NT TSA on your Windows NT client. To configure, follow these steps:

**1.** In Windows NT, click the Properties page. The TSAPrefs page appears with tabs for Preferences, Registration, Connections, and Event Logs.

**2.** Click Preferences.

**3.** Fill in the following fields:

   **a.** Workstation: Enter the name of the workstation.

   **b.** Preferred Server: Enter the name of the server on which you want to connect. This server must have TSAProxy installed.

   **c.** Protocol: Select SPX/IPX or TCP/IP.

   **d.** Events to Log: Check the items you want to log: Connection, Registration, Security, or Service.

   **e.** Allow Backup User: This grants the backup user rights depending on the group.

   **f.** Auto Register: This automatically registers the Windows NT workstation with the server.

**4.** Click Registration.

5. Check the fields in the Registration page and click Register if the fields are correct. If information in any of the fields is incorrect, click Withdraw and return to the Preferences page to change the information; then repeat Steps 4 and 5.

6. Click Connections.

7. Check the fields in the Connections page and click OK. If you need to add or change information, click Apply. You can delete connections in this page under Current Connections if preferred. Click Apply.

# Restoring NDS eDirectory and File System

Use Enhanced SBACKUP to retrieve and reinstate data that you have backed up to storage media. You restore data if it has been lost or corrupted since a backup was made. A restore session restores data from a backup. The restore session produces the requested data, which is retrieved from the storage media and restored to the location you specify. If an error occurs during the restore session, an error message is appended to the error file on the host server.

Before doing a tape backup restore of NDS, you should attempt to restore NDS information through replicas and repair operations. For more information on these processes, refer to Chapter 9. If you have to restore NDS information, an active replica is faster and more up to date than a tape backup. Remember that two or three replicas are adequate for fault tolerance. Your particular circumstances may require more or fewer replicas.

Take the following steps or precautionary measures before you begin your restoration. These measures use Enhanced SBACKUP as the SME:

1. Make sure that your current tree is functioning properly in terms of replica synchronization. Use NDS Manager or DSTRACE to verify that all partitions are error-free. Doing a restore when you still have replica synchronization errors only compounds your problems.

2. Always restore NDS information first, and then restore file system data and trustees. Failure to do so may result in the loss of trustee assignments for your user objects.

3. Know the username and password for the target server or workstation to which you want to restore data.

4. Know the session description that you want to restore. You can get this information from your session log and error files.

5. For an Advanced Options restore session, ensure that you know the file system structure of the data you are restoring. You are prompted for specific paths and filenames while setting the restore options.

6. If you restore the server-specific information from the file system backup of the failed server to a functioning server or location, you can use the VOL$INFO.TXT file as a reference for this information.

7. If you want to restore data to a new location (different from where the original data was located), you must specify the full path to both the original data and the new location. If the new location does not exist, Enhanced SBACKUP creates a new file system structure.

8. You can get the original path from your backup logbook or from the session log files if you noted the path at the time that the backup was performed.

9. Replace faulty hardware or correct the problems that caused data loss (if applicable).

10. Ensure that media is inserted in your storage device.

11. You can restore data either from the command line or from a Windows 95/98 or Windows NT/2000 workstation using the graphical interface NWBACK32.EXE.

## Restore Data from a Server

To restore your data, do the following:

1. Load the drivers for your specific device and controller board.

2. Load the appropriate Target Service Agents.

3. Load Enhanced SBACKUP by typing **SBCON**.

4. Select Main Menu ⇨ Job Administration ⇨ Restore.

5. Select Target Service ⇨ NetWare server running your backup and restore Target Services Agent. This is the name of the server or workstation on which you want to restore your data. Before selecting it, you must load the correct TSA. If you do not see the target you want on the list, check for these possible causes:

    a. The proper TSA is not loaded on the target.

    b. Network traffic is heavy. In these circumstances, it might take Enhanced SBACKUP a few moments to detect all the targets. Press Esc to return to the Main Menu, and then press Enter again. Your target should now be listed. From the Target Services list, choose a target.

    **c.** If the target you select has more than one TSA loaded, Enhanced SBACKUP shows you a list of their full names in the Backup/Restore Target Services on This Server.

**6.** Choose what you want to restore.

    **a.** If you are restoring the file system, select the server whose file system you want to restore.

    **b.** If you are restoring the NDS database, select the server with TSANDS loaded.

    **c.** If you are restoring server-specific information, select the server whose server-specific information you want to restore, and then choose the file system to restore.

**7.** When prompted for the target username, enter your username (and context if required) as the network administrator for the target. If Enhanced SBACKUP rejects the username you entered, you probably need to include the context of where the user object is located. For example, instead of entering ADMIN as the username, enter a complete name such as .CN=ADMIN.O=ACME or .ADMIN.ACME. You must include the context in the username at this point if the username exists in an NDS container that is different from the context set on the server running Enhanced SBACKUP.

**8.** If a password is requested, enter the password for the target. Enhanced SBACKUP takes a few moments to attach to the target. Wait for the confirmation box, and then press any key to continue.

**9.** Type a descriptive name for the restore session in the Description field. The descriptive name of the job helps you identify the session.

**10.** Select the device and media for restore. Press Enter at the Device/Media Name field and decide where you want to restore from. A list of objects available is displayed in the Select a Device screen. If you enter *.* (DEVICE NAME.MEDIA NAME), the engine selects the device and media that it encounters first. If your device has more than one storage device attached, choose an available device from the list. If the device contains multiple media, select the media for the backup. If the storage media does not have a label, Enhanced SBACKUP displays a message indicating that the media cannot be identified. You should set the label before selecting it for a backup job.

**11.** Select the Session to Restore. Select Choose a Session to Restore if you want to select a session from a list of session log headers that is displayed in

Select a Session. TSA600 backs up files in compressed or uncompressed format as specified by the user. However, if you try to restore a compressed file to a volume without compression, the file is corrupted and no error message is displayed.

**12.** Select Advanced Options to make the selective restore.

**13.** The Advanced Restore Options screen appears. You can perform the advanced restore, specify the execution time, reschedule the job, and so on, using this form. Complete the Advanced Restore Options form.

**14.** Press Esc and answer the prompt at the Submit Job screen to begin the restore session.

**15.** Press Alt + Esc to view the activity log screen. If the job execution starts and is not successfully completed, the error messages appear on this screen. The activity log file ACTIVITY.LOG is located at the server's SYS:\SYSTEM\TSA\LOG directory.

**16.** To view the Run Time Status of a job, select Job Administration ➪ Current Job List ➪ *job name*.

**17.** When the restore session finishes, your screen display reads:

```
The restore process was completed normally.
```

**18.** To return to the Main Menu, press Esc as required. The Esc key enables you to exit Enhanced SBACKUP one screen at a time until you reach the main menu. If you want to exit Enhanced SBACKUP, answer the confirmation prompt.

## Performing a Partial NDS Restore

NetWare 6 provides SMS TSAs that enable you to selectively restore objects and groups of objects from your tape backup. This is known as a partial restore.

You need to determine whether a partial restore is the fastest solution to your particular problem. For example, if you are trying to restore a single object, it might be quicker to simply re-create the object using NWADMIN than to perform a partial restore. Remember that you must understand how the restore process works in terms of object IDs and dependent objects to successfully carry out a partial restore. A full or partial restore can be done with either the SBCON or NWBACK32 utilities by selecting Job Administration/Restore and entering the same information as was entered for the backup. Keep in mind that you must have created a previous backup session to restore from.

### Object IDs

If you are restoring an object that no longer exists in your NDS tree, a new object ID is created when you restore the object. Any (old) object ID associated with the file system trustees, such as directories for user mail, is affected in this situation. The new object ID will not match the old file system ID assignments. If an object already exists in the tree and you do a restore, you copy the object's properties from tape backup over the existing object's properties. This may or may not be what you intended to do.

### Dependent Objects

Dependent objects are dependent upon other objects to exist in your tree. A print queue object, for example, maintains directory and host server properties to determine where the queue is stored and on what server. Without this information, the print queue object cannot function. Therefore, if you restore any dependent objects, they will not be functional in your tree without the other supporting objects.

You may restore some dependent objects, including Directory Map objects, print queue objects, and any schema extension objects you have created. After they are restored, these types of objects are nonfunctional. The best way to resolve this problem is to restore the supporting objects for the dependent object, delete the previously restored dependent object, and re-create it with NWADMIN. After you re-create the object, it will make use of the supporting objects.

### Unknown Objects

Restoring the NDS may create unknown objects. If a restored object is dependent on other objects in the tree that do not currently exist, the object will be designated as unknown. NDS creates an unknown object until the real object is restored. If the actual object is restored during the restore, the unknown category is replaced by the actual object name.

You will always see unknown objects during a restore until all the resources — servers, volumes, users, and so on — are in place in your tree. Most objects should be cleaned up after the restore is completed. If not, you can delete the unknown objects and re-create the actual objects, or you can attempt to selectively restore the actual objects and overwrite the unknown objects. Again, you have to determine whether it's easier to restore the objects or to re-create them with NWADMIN.

### Bindery Objects and Applications

As mentioned, new object IDs are created for restored objects that do not exist in the tree. Bindery-based applications such as printing, e-mail, and others probably will not function because they use object IDs to communicate. If the bindery application has one list of object IDs and you restore the objects with new

IDs, these applications will not function properly. In most cases, you need to reinstall and reconfigure these applications after you restore the tree.

The login scripts of bindery-based user objects are stored in their mail subdirectories if the scripts were created with a utility such as SYSCON. These subdirectories are based on an object ID. Therefore, when you restore the user objects with a new object ID, the mail subdirectories are not automatically renamed.

### Print Services

After restoring NDS, you have to restore print services objects from your tape backup if you are using queue server mode printing. You also have to run any setup software from your third-party print package to reconfigure your printing environment. Because your queue ID has changed during the restore, you have to re-create the queue to allow for a reassignment of the queue ID to the new print server object ID. You most likely will need to reset your printers after reconfiguration as well.

For remote printing mode, your printing should be fully functional after a tape restore of NDS.

## Performing a Full NDS Restore

You would need to perform a full NDS tree restore if all servers in the tree suffered a catastrophic failure. In large, geographically dispersed networks, this situation is all but impossible. Some smaller companies in a single building or a few buildings in the same location are more likely to experience this situation.

Follow these steps to carry out a full NDS restore:

1. Reinstall NetWare 6 on your file servers to regain a [ROOT] partition of your network on the first server. Be sure to specify the exact tree structure organization (Organization and Organizational Unit objects) that was present in your first tree. Now is not the time to make changes to your tree.

2. Reinstall additional NetWare 6 servers as you had them before the failure. Any servers that you cannot install before the restore may cause some errors due to dependent objects that do not restore properly. This may require you to go back with NWADMIN and re-create objects.

**IMPORTANT** Be sure to re-create the **ADMIN** or equivalent user with the same name, same container, and same password that was used to create the original backup. If you made and backed up extensions to the schema, you need to make those extensions again. Extensions to the default schema are not backed up, but the objects created with these extensions are. Therefore, you must extend the schema on your tree before restoring your objects. Failure to do so will result in an incomplete restoration.

3. If you have reinstalled more than one NetWare 6 server, you should remove the default replicas of [ROOT] before beginning the restoration. Having a single copy of the [ROOT] partition will simplify the restore process. This process assumes that you have a server holding [ROOT] with enough disk space to restore the entire NDS tree.

4. Install your tape backup drivers and bring up your backup software. Restore the entire NDS backup to your server. The NDS tree is placed in your [ROOT] partition.

5. Restore the file information to each NetWare 6 server in your tree. When performing a restore, be sure to set your backup software to delete any existing trustees before restoring the data. This purges any existing trustees before the tape backup; its trustee assignments are restored to the server.

6. Re-create your partition boundaries using your written record of the partition boundaries. Alternatively, you can designate and place replicas of your partitions where they are needed.

7. Run DSREPAIR on each server to verify the accuracy of your database.

## Server/SYS Volume Failure

It's common to have a single server fail in your NDS tree. Often this occurs because of a SYS: volume failure. Such a failure is serious because your SYS: volume contains all or portions of the NetWare Directory and can affect other servers in your tree that participate in the same partition as the failed server.

If your SYS: volume fails on a single-server network, the situation is similar to a total tree failure of many servers. The restore procedure is basically the same as a full NDS restoration, with the addition of a few steps:

1. Replace or resolve the problem that caused your SYS: volume to fail. This usually means replacing the hard drive unit itself.

2. Reinstall NetWare 6 on your file servers to regain a [ROOT] partition of your network on the first server. Be sure to specify the exact tree structure organization (Organization and Organizational Unit objects) that was present in your first tree. Now is not the time to make changes to your tree. Specify 64K for your volume block size. Have INSTALL mount all volumes during the installation process. Make sure that you install all the patches and updates to the operating system and utilities as well.

**IMPORTANT**

**Again, be sure to re-create the ADMIN or equivalent user with the same name, same container, and same password that was used to create the original backup. If you made and backed up extensions to the schema, you need to make those extensions again. Failure to do so will result in an incomplete restoration.**

3. Run DSREPAIR on any volumes other than SYS on the server to purge invalid trustees contained on those volumes. Run the option UNATTENDED FULL REPAIR to purge any invalid trustee information.

4. Install your tape backup drivers and bring up your backup software. Load TSANDS and TSA500 NLMs.

5. Restore the entire NDS backup to your server. The NDS tree will be placed in your [ROOT] partition.

6. Restore the file system information to your NetWare 6 SYS: volume from your tape backup. You need to choose an option for restoring without session files.

7. Restore any trustee assignments (without data streams) for any other volumes that existed before the failure.

**IMPORTANT**

**If you restore data on volume SYS, you will no longer have trustee assignments for the other volumes because you ran DSREPAIR in Step 3. You can restore only the directory without data streams on these volumes. Because the data files already exist, you only need the directory structure to obtain the trustee assignments. Consult the instructions for your third-party backup program for details on how to accomplish this task.**

8. Run DSREPAIR on each server to verify the accuracy of your NDS database.

### Consulting Experience

In addition to using the traditional restore utilities to recover NDS eDirectory, you can use the DSMAINT utility that comes with NetWare 6. Using DSMAINT –PSE, you can restore NDS on a server that has lost its SYS: volume due to hardware problems or other problems.

When a multiserver environment is in a partition, it's also extremely common to have a single server fail for whatever reason, including the failure of the SYS: volume. This does not mean, however, that you have lost all your replicas of that partition. This situation requires a slightly different approach:

1. Remove this server from the NDS by using the NDS Manager utility. Start by deleting the failed server's Server object and volume objects from the tree. If your failed server holds a master replica, you must run DSREPAIR or NDS Manager to designate another active replica in the partition as the master. Verify through NDS Manager or DSREPAIR that the server has been removed from the replica list and that your tree is functioning properly. If the server is not returning for use in your tree, this is all you need to do. If your server is returning to the tree, continue reading the following steps.

**Only follow these procedures if your server has failed and is completely inoperable. If you have a functioning NetWare 6 server that you want to remove from the tree, instead load INSTALL and use the option**
IMPORTANT **Remove Directory Services from that server.**

2. After you have repaired the failed server hardware, you can reinstall NetWare 6 on that server. Make sure that your install includes all the latest patches and versions of the operating system and utilities that you were using before the failure.

3. Restore the replica(s) that were present on the server before the failure. Allow the synchronization process to place the objects on the server. You do not need to use your SMS tape backup to restore NDS information. Verify through DSREPAIR and Partition Manager that the replicas are synchronizing properly on the restored server hardware.

4. Use your SMS backup to restore the data and trustee assignments for the SYS: volume that was lost during the server failure.

5. Restore any other volumes besides SYS that were not affected by the failure. Again, you can only restore the trustee assignments without the data streams for those volumes.

6. Be sure to delete existing trustees before restoring. This option purges existing trustees before restoring the backed up trustee assignments from the backup. You can simply restore the directory structure without data streams on these volumes. Because the data files already exist, you only need the directory structure to get the trustee assignments back. Follow your backup vendor's guidelines to accomplish this task.

# Devising a Disaster Recovery Plan

You should have a disaster recovery plan to protect your system and your data in case of an emergency. Your disaster recovery plan can include redundant hardware along with proper replication and tape backup.

For some sites requiring a high degree of redundancy, you can consider using disk mirroring or disk duplexing, which provide you with varying degrees of safety.

Always maintain at least two to three replicas of your partitions as one of your strongest backup defenses for NDS. Some sites create one or two NDS servers that contain all replicas of all partitions for backup purposes. If you use an NDS server for replica storage, consider these recommendations:

- Have a centralized NDS server across the fastest WAN link possible.

- Use only fast hardware (Pentium III+–class machines) for your NDS replica server.

- If you have more than 100 replicas, distribute the replicas on two servers for greater synchronization performance.

- The synchronization process on these servers should complete in 30 minutes or less. If the server cannot complete a synchronization cycle (synchronizing all replicas on the server) in this amount of time, place some of the replicas on a second replica server. This recommendation is based on the fact that the background NDS synchronization interval occurs each 30 minutes.

- Make sure that you have a regular tape backup of your entire NDS tree, as discussed in this chapter.

# Summary

This chapter has provided you with the basics of the backup and restore mechanism for NetWare 6 and NDS. We have covered the architecture of the Storage Management Services, including the Storage Management Engine, the Target Service Agent, and the Storage Management Data Requester. Additionally, we have covered the SBACKUP utility for NetWare 6. This utility enables you to perform file system and NDS backups with greater flexibility and reliability.

# Integrating Additional Services with NetWare 6

# Integrating Novell ZENworks with NetWare 6

This chapter provides you with information to install and configure Novell's Zero Effort Networks (ZENworks) products on your NetWare 6 servers and network. Two products comprise the ZENworks bundle: ZENworks for Servers 2 and ZENworks for Desktops 3. ZENworks for Servers 2 provides an intelligent and secure distribution layer for moving application files and objects through your network. ZENworks for Desktops 3 simplifies and automates many aspects of desktop management. ZENworks is a combination of Novell products that provide you with application management, workstation management, and desktop maintenance of your Windows 3.1, Windows 95/98, and Windows NT/2000 desktops. This chapter discusses the installation and configuration of both products, beginning with ZENworks for Desktops 3 followed by ZENworks for Servers 2. These products can be purchased as a bundle or separately. Included in the ZENworks for Servers/ZENworks for Desktops bundle is the functionality of ManageWise, a server management product that enables you to monitor the entire network from a single location. This book does not discuss ManageWise.

## ZENworks for Desktops 3

ZENworks for Desktops 3 enables the network administrator to reduce the overall cost and complexity of configuring and maintaining workstation desktops on the network. ZENworks for Desktops 3 is ideal for automatically installing software on your Windows workstations. This product also includes the capability to create a workstation inventory and to store this inventory as a workstation object in NDS eDirectory. Inventory information can include operating information, hard disk space, workstation memory, and versions of software.

Desktop management features also enable an administrator to store and to configure Windows 95/98, Windows NT, and Windows 2000 desktop policies in NDS eDirectory. These policies can then follow a user from desktop to desktop. Because the policies are stored in NDS, the users can easily move from one desktop to another and have their associated policies follow them. Printer drivers can also be delivered to the desktop via ZENworks, so that users can easily print from any desktop to any printer.

Novell's Desktop Management software (previously known as Workstation Manager) enables all user account and desktop information for Windows NT, Windows 95/98, and Windows 2000 to be centrally managed within NDS eDirectory using a single administrative utility, ConsoleOne. For NT environments, it also eliminates the need for NT domains or for a large number of NT user accounts to reside in the local SAM of each workstation.

Configuration information is stored in policy package objects that are particular to the platform. For example, for Windows NT/2000 and Windows 95/98, there are NT/2000 package objects and Windows 95 package objects. Each package contains policies that can be enabled, configured, and scheduled for downloading to the workstations. Note that most of the examples in this chapter use the NT/2000 desktop. The same concepts can be applied to the other previously mentioned desktops as well.

ZENworks provides you with these features:

▸ **NDS eDirectory policy support** — Enables you to customize import of workstation object information into NDS and to set rules on how the remote-control feature and the end-user help request system can be used.

▸ **Hardware and software inventory** — Automatically stores the hardware and software inventory in NDS for tracking and troubleshooting.

▸ **Dynamic print configuration** — Provides dynamic distribution and updating of print drivers from a single location.

▸ **Profile management** — Provides centralized location and administration of user profiles.

▸ **Client configurations stored in NDS** — Enables you to view and update client configurations without visiting the workstation.

▸ **Update clients on workstations** — Enables you to update during off hours or when users are not logged in.

▸ **NDS-authenticated remote control of a workstation or NT server** — Enables you to solve user problems without visiting the workstation or NT server.

▸ **Administrative control of an end-user help request system** — The Help Requester is an end-user program that helps users provide pertinent information on themselves and their workstation to the help desk through e-mail or phone. This can mean faster problem resolution.

▸ **Applications Delivered via NDS eDirectory** — Using the Novell
Application Launcher within ZENworks for Desktops 3, you can create
and configure application objects that can be delivered to the user's
desktop via NDS.

▸ **Manage Windows 2000 without Active Directory** — ZENworks can
manage policies and profiles for Windows 2000 without the need for
Active Directory

▸ **Automatically install operating systems across your entire
enterprise** — Installation of an operating system across an entire
network is made easy through ZENworks.

▸ **Manage this application through ConsoleOne** — ConsoleOne can
manage all aspects of ZENworks for Desktops.

▸ **Software metering** — ZENworks can keep track of who is using software
on your network.

## Hardware Requirements

In order to run ZENworks for Desktops 3, you need the following minimum
hardware. Keep in mind that these are minimums, and depending on the size of
your network, you may need to have a more powerful desktop:

▸ 486 33MHz processor or higher

▸ 40MB of available memory

▸ 175MB of available hard disk

▸ 125MB of server disk space

## Software Requirements

Your server needs to have the following software to run ZENworks for
Desktops 3:

▸ NetWare 4.11 or above (NetWare 5.x includes the ZENworks Starter
Pack 2.0, which does not include the complete functionality found in
ZENworks for Desktops 3)

▸ Windows 2000 or Windows NT 4.0 running NDS eDirectory

Your workstation must be running the following:

- Windows 2000, Windows NT 4.0, or Windows 95/98
- Novell Client for Windows NT/2000 or Novell Client for Windows 95/98
- ZENworks client software on all participating workstations

## Installing ZENworks for Desktops

The following are three methods for installing the ZENworks for Desktops product:

- Typical install
- Product install
- Custom install

This chapter discusses only the typical installation. The product install and custom install enable you to select specific programs or groups of programs to install and can speed your installation. The typical install enables you to install all the product components, one at a time, on the servers you select. The following products are installed during the typical install:

- Application Management
- Automatic Workstation Import
- Workstation Management
- Workstation imaging with Preboot Services
- Remote Management
- Workstation Inventory
- Sybase Database (optional)

### Running the Install

You can use the following steps to perform a typical install of ZENworks for Desktops 3:

1. Select an appropriate workstation to run the install routine. The workstation should be either a Windows 2000 workstation or server.

2. At the workstation or server, insert the ZEN for Desktops CD. The autorun feature should start the install routine automatically. You see an install screen, as shown in Figure 19.1.

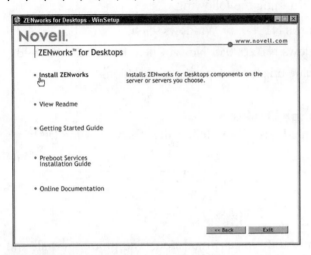

**FIGURE 19.1** *Installation Screen for ZENworks for Desktops 3*

**3.** Click English ⇨ Install ZENworks to launch the NIS setup program.

**4.** Read the notes and cautions in the Product install dialog box.

**5.** Read the license agreement and then click Accept to move on with the install.

**6.** From the Install Prerequisites dialog box, verify that your servers to which you are installing this product meet the minimum hardware requirements and click Accept.

**7.** In the ZENworks Install Types, select Typical and click Next.

**8.** Select the NDS tree where you want to install ZEN for Desktops and click Next. If this product is being installed onto a previous version of the ZEN for Desktops workstation Inventory or the Inventory Database, you will be prompted with an upgrade notice. You can select upgrade or Full install. If you choose upgrade only, ZEN for Desktops 3.2 Inventory enhancements will be installed on the ZEN for Desktops 3 servers. If you choose Full install, the servers you select later will have the Sybase Database and the policies and configurations overwritten.

**9.** Within the ZENworks List of Servers dialog box, choose the server where you want to install ZEN for Desktops and click Next, as shown in Figure 19.2.

**FIGURE 19.2** *Select the servers where you want to install ZENworks.*

**10.** From the Inventory Database Server Selection dialog box, select the server where you want to install the ZENworks inventory database and click Next. You can also opt to not install the database at this time. If you choose to install the database, another dialog box appears, enabling you to select the server volume where you want to install the database. Avoid choosing Vol SYS so that you don't fill up that volume.

**11.** Click Next on the Languages dialog box. English is the default.

**12.** In the Automatic Workstation Import Management dialog box, select the import (or import/removal) role for at least one of the servers and click Next. An example of this is shown in Figure 19.3.

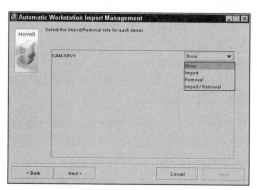

**FIGURE 19.3** *Selecting the import/removal role for the Automatic Workstation Import*

**13.** In the Inventory Server Roles dialog box, select the assignment you want to give each of the inventory servers you have created, and click Next.

**14.** In the ScanDir Volume dialog box, select the server volume where you want to scan the data files to be stored. If you have chosen to install the database, you are prompted to enter a unique site ID and name on the Site ID for the Database dialog box.

**15.** Click Next to continue.

**16.** The next screen is the Summary dialog box. Review your list of products to be installed and the amount of disk space required; then click Finish to begin the copy process. An example of this Summary dialog box is shown in Figure 19.4.

**FIGURE 19.4** *The Summary dialog box, shown before beginning the copy process*

**17.** If you have chosen the ZEN for Desktops Preboot Services, you see the Preboot Services dialog box to remind you that you have to insert the Preboot Services CD into the drive.

**18.** The Preboot Services Source Location dialog box prompts you to select the location where the ZFDPXE file is located. Click OK.

After the installation has completed, you can use the ConsoleOne Schema Manager to verify that your NDS eDirectory schema has been extended. You see the following attributes if ZENworks has been installed properly:

```
ZENLOCZfD3InstalledZENLOCZfD3SP1InstalledZENLOCZfD332Installed
```

### Setting Up Desktop Policies

A desktop policy contains the rules of use and configurations for users or their workstations. ZEN for Desktops requires policy package objects in the tree for the types of users and desktops that you wish to manage. You are also required to create and associate one Search Policy that allows the system to find the other policies that you've created.

We recommend that you create an Organization Unit (OU) to hold your policy packages. To minimize tree walking, you should create the policy package container at the root partition that contains the objects with which the policy package will be associated.

You can also create multiple policy packages OUs where it makes sense. You can copy policy package objects (for example, alias objects) from one OU to another OU in order to reduce resolve name traffic

To create a policy package, follow these steps:

1. Bring up ConsoleOne and right-click on the container where you want the container for the policy packages to be placed. Click New and then click Object. Be sure to use a short, yet descriptive name — for example, ZEN for Desktops policies. An example of this is shown in Figure 19.5.

**FIGURE 19.5** *Creating a ZEN for Desktop policy package*

**2.** Right-click the newly created policy package's container, click New, and click Policy Packages. Select one of the following packages:

- Container Package
- Server Package
- Service Location Package
- User Package
- Workstation Package

**3.** Click Next and give the package a short and descriptive name. Click Next to create another policy package, or click Finish if you are done creating packages.

A search policy is used to instruct ZEN for Desktops where to find the other policies. You can set up a search policy by doing the following:

**1.** Using ConsoleOne, right-click the Container Package and click Properties.

**2.** Check the box under the Enabled column for the Search policy. This selects and enables the policy. An example of this is shown in Figure 19.6.

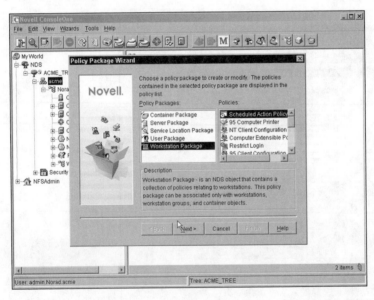

**FIGURE 19.6** *Creating a search policy*

**3.** Click on Properties. The Search level tab is displayed.

**4.** Select the level to search up to:

- [Root]: Search to the root of the tree.
- Object Container: Search to the parent container.
- Partition: Search to the partition root.
- Selected Container: Search to the selected container.

An example of selecting a search level is shown in Figure 19.7.

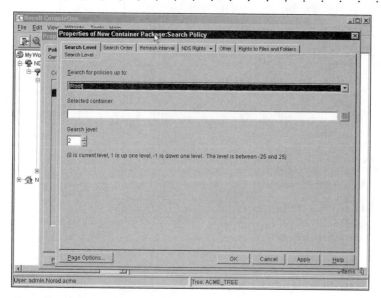

**FIGURE 19.7** *Selecting a search level*

**5.** If you choose Selected Container, browse your tree to select the desired container.

**6.** You can limit searching either up or down by specifying a number:

- 0 — Limits the search to the selected level.
- 1 — Limits the search to one level above the selected level.
- -1 — Limits the search to one level below the selected level.

**7.** Click the Search Order tab and select the policy searching order. Use the arrow keys, the Add button, and the Remove button as necessary to create your search order.

**8.** Click on the Refresh Interval Tab and select the frequency for how often the policy should be refreshed. The default is set to hourly. Setting both time increments to zero causes the policies to never be refreshed. An example of setting the Refresh Interval is shown in Figure 19.8.

**FIGURE 19.8** *Setting the Refresh Interval*

**9.** Click on the Associations tab and choose Add.

**10.** Browse to select the container object for association to the Search Policy, as shown in Figure 19.9.

**11.** Click OK to finish.

The last step is to associate the container package with the search policy. You can do this with the following easy steps:

**1.** Using ConsoleOne, right-click the container Package and click Properties.

**2.** Click on the Associations tab and then select Add.

**3.** Browse for the container (which should be placed high in the tree) and click OK. An example of this is shown in Figure 19.10.

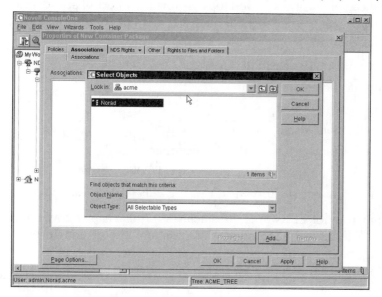

**FIGURE 19.9** *Associating a container with a search policy*

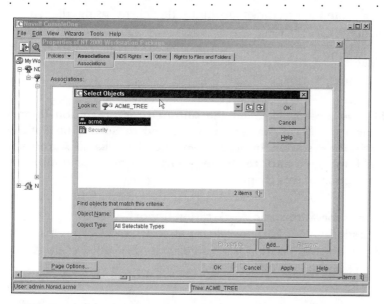

**FIGURE 19.10** *Associating a container package with the search policy*

After it is installed, ZENworks for Desktops 3 provides a host of services that can assist you in managing your network desktops. You can perform the following operations using ZEN for Desktops:

- ▶ Setting up Automatic Workstation Import
- ▶ Installing Application Management
- ▶ Preparing an Imaging Server
- ▶ Installing the Remote Management Component
- ▶ Installing Workstation Inventory to a NetWare Server
- ▶ Installing Workstation Inventory to Windows NT/2000 servers
- ▶ Installing Workstation Inventory in an Existing ZEN for Desktops 3 setup

Due to the immensity of ZENworks documentation, this chapter covers only the first two topics, Setting up Automatic Workstation Import and Installing Application Management. For more information on the other topics, please refer to your Novell documentation or visit www.zenworks.com.

## Setting Up Automatic Workstation Import

One of the useful features in ZEN for Desktops is Automatic Workstation Import. This feature allows management of users' workstations and enables you to push software and computer settings down to the client using the Novell Application Launcher (NAL) software.

You must install Automatic Workstation Import before you set up user and workstation policy packages, workstation inventory, imaging, or remote management.

**NOTE**

**You should have already installed the Automatic Workstation Import during a Typical Install, so that you can proceed to Setting up Policies for Automatic Workstation Import. If you need to install Automatic Workstation Import, go back to the ZENworks Install steps outlined in the previous section of this chapter.**

### Setting Up Policies for Automatic Workstation Import

Setting up policies for the Automatic Workstation Import takes two steps. First, you need to configure the Workstation Import Policy for ZEN for Desktops, and second, you need to associate it with a Server Package.

Follow these steps to configure the Workstation Import Policy for ZEN for Desktops:

1. If you have not done so already, create a Server Package using ConsoleOne by right-clicking the server container where your server object is found. Click Policy Package and select Server Package. Select Workstation Import and click Next. Then name the package and click Finish.

2. Right-click the Server Package and select Properties. The policies tab with a General page is displayed, as shown in Figure 19.11. General policies apply to all valid platforms, including NetWare and Windows NT/2000.

**FIGURE 19.11** *Selecting General Policies for a server package*

3. On the General page, check the box under the Enabled column for the Workstation Import policy.

4. Click Properties.

5. On the Containers tab, click Add.

6. Select a valid workstation container where rights are needed to create workstations and click OK. An example of this is shown in Figure 19.12.

**FIGURE 19.12** *Selecting a workstation container*

7. Click the Platforms tab. The General page with its Location tab is displayed. Again, use these settings, which apply to all platforms.

8. To select where to create workstation objects, click the Create Workstation Objects in the drop-down list and select one of the following, as shown in Figure 19.13:

   • **Selected Container** — The selected path is displayed.

   • **Server Container** — Uses a server container, or enter a relative DS path.

   • **User Container** — Uses a user container, or enter a relative DS path.

   • **Associated Object Container** — Uses an associated object container, or enter a relative DS path.

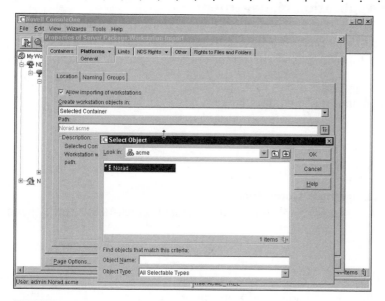

**FIGURE 19.13** *Selecting where to create workstation objects*

**9.** Click on the Naming tab.

**10.** If you wish to change the default naming syntax, you can do the following:

- Click Add to add name field items. The default is Computer+MAC address. You can select User, Container, DNS, Server, OS, CPU, IP Address, or user-defined.

- Click an item and then click the up-arrow or the down-arrow to change the item's position in the syntax.

**11.** Click OK.

Follow these short steps to associate the Server Package:

**1.** Using ConsoleOne, right-click on Server Package and then click Properties.

**2.** Click on the Associations Tab and select Add.

**3.** Browse for the server container or server object for associating the package and then click OK.

## Setting Up Application Management

Using ZEN for Desktop application management, you can distribute and install applications to workstations and uninstall the applications that have been distributed. The following are the components required for application management:

- Application management components
- Application distribution
- Application uninstall
- Application caching

### Application Management Components

The ZEN for Desktops application management consists of three main components:

- Application objects
- snAppShot
- Novell Application Launcher and Application Explorer

**Application Objects**  In order to have an application be distributed to a workstation, the application must first have an NDS object that defines the information required to distribute it. ZEN for Desktops includes a ConsoleOne snap-in that enables you to create application objects in NDS. Application objects define critical information, including the following:

- The physical location of application source files on the network
- The target location for installation of the application on a workstation
- Registry settings, .INI files, text configuration files, application files, icons, shortcuts, and other settings that support the application
- The users or workstations associated to the application
- Additional settings such as availability scheduling, granting of rights, fault tolerance, load balancing, application site lists, and folders

Application objects allow control over how applications are distributed. For example, you could create an application object that installs an application to the user's workstation and then immediately runs the application. Additionally, you could create an application object that automatically installs files when the user logs in to a workstation. You can even create application objects that are available for a certain period of time or only on specific days.

In addition to adding application objects to NDS, the application management snap-in adds new attribute pages to the following objects: User, Group, Workstation, Workstation Group, Organizational Unit, and Organization. These attribute pages let you associate applications with a specific user, a specific workstation, groups of users, groups of workstations, entire organizational units, or entire organizations.

**snAppShot**     Distributing an application to a workstation can require various changes to the workstation, such as modifying the workstation's settings and installing the application's source files. All these changes must be recorded in the application object.

To help you create application objects that contain the correct distribution information, ZEN for Desktops application management provides the snAppShot utility. SnAppShot creates application installation packages that consist of two types of files: an Application object template (.AOT) file and one or more application source (.FIL) files.

The .AOT file contains information about the application source (.FIL) files that will be installed and the workstation settings that will be modified to support the application. When you create an application object, you can specify the .AOT file to use as the template for the application object, in which case the .AOT information is used to populate the application object's information fields (source files location, installation target directory, Registry settings, .INI files, shortcuts, and so forth).

To use snAppShot to create an installation package for an application, start snAppShot on a workstation that does not have the application installed. SnAppshot records the changes that occur on the workstation as the application is installed. As the installation proceeds, snAppShot captures the differences between the workstation's preinstallation configuration state and the workstation's post-installation state, compares the two pictures, and records any differences in the .AOT file. SnAppShot also tracks all of the files that are installed to the workstation. These files, which become the application source files, are copied to a network source location, renamed numerically, and given a .FIL file extension.

SnAppShot can be used on Windows 95/98 and Windows NT/2000 workstations.

**Novell Application Launcher and Application Explorer**     Novell Application Launcher and Application Explorer are workstation applications that display Application object icons on users' workstations and perform various application management functions, such as distributing (installing) applications, uninstalling applications, and caching applications. Application Launcher and Application Explorer display only the Application objects to which the user or workstation has been associated.

Application Launcher is a standalone desktop window. With Application Launcher, users can create personal folders (if you've given them the appropriate rights), refresh applications, change views, and get information about folders and applications.

Application Explorer also provides a standalone desktop window. However, while Application Launcher limits you to displaying Application objects in the Application Launcher window only, Application Explorer lets you display Application objects in the Application Explorer window, the Start menu, the Quick Launch toolbar, the system tray, and the desktop.

Both Application Launcher and Application Explorer can be used on Windows 95/98 and Windows NT/2000 workstations. The main difference is that Application Launcher can be used to replace the Windows desktop, providing greater administrative control of users' workstations, while Application Explorer extends the desktop and enables users to access Application objects from multiple locations.

You control whether users run Application Launcher/Explorer by including the appropriate executable commands in users' login scripts.

### Application Distribution

ZEN for Desktops application management provides the capability to distribute applications to Windows 95/98 and Windows NT/2000 workstations. You can do the following:

- Distribute applications to workstations whose users are authenticated to NDS.

- Distribute applications to workstations whose users are not currently authenticated to NDS. Workstations that have been disconnected from the network (NDS) can continue to run, install, and verify applications. To run, the applications must have already been installed. To install or verify applications, the applications must reside in a local cache (hidden directory). The applications can be distributed from the network (prior to disconnecting) or from a portable storage medium, such as a CD or Jaz drive (after disconnecting).

- Distribute MSI-based applications. Application objects can be created using Microsoft Windows Installer (.MSI) packages and distributed to users.

- Distribute applications to newly imaged workstations as part of the imaging process.

### Application Uninstall

Any application (including MSI-based applications) distributed through ZEN for Desktops 3 application management can now be uninstalled. The uninstall includes the deletion of all files, INI entries, and registry entries associated with the application. Shared DLL references are observed.

Each user's workstation has a local cache that contains information about applications installed on the workstation. When you uninstall an application, this cache is used to ensure that the appropriate files and settings are removed from the workstation.

By default, ZEN for Desktops 3 does not enable users to uninstall applications themselves; however, a system administrator can enable users with this capability, or you can limit application uninstall to system administrators only.

### Application Caching

Application caching enables users to install, run, and verify (repair) applications while they are disconnected from NDS.

ZEN for Desktops application management creates a hidden cache directory (NALCACHE) on the root of each user's workstation. This cache directory contains the NDS information required to run an application when the workstation is disconnected from NDS. If the application has already been installed to the workstation and the user disconnects from NDS, the application continues to run just as if the user were still connected.

The cache directory also can contain the application source files and other information required to install the application or verify (repair) problems that may occur with the application while in disconnected mode. For example, if a user does not install the application before disconnecting from NDS, he or she can still install it, provided the application has been cached to the workstation's cache directory.

To ensure that users always have mission-critical applications when disconnected, you can configure Application objects to be cached automatically when you associate the Application objects with users. In addition, you can configure Application Launcher/Explorer to display the Application Management dialog box. This dialog box, which is turned off by default, enables users to select which applications they want to cache to their workstations' local drives.

To save disk space, application files are compressed before being stored in the cache directory.

## Starting Application Launcher and Application Explorer

Application Launcher/Explorer must be running on each workstation to which you want to distribute applications. Perform the steps in the following sections to start Application Launcher/Explorer on users' workstations:

- ▶ Starting Application Launcher
- ▶ Starting Application Explorer

### Starting Application Launcher

To manually start Application Launcher on a workstation, run NAL.EXE from the SYS:\PUBLIC directory on the server where you installed ZEN for Desktops.

To automatically start Application Launcher each time the user logs in to NDS, enter the following line in the user's login script:

```
@\\servername\sys\public\nal.exe
```

where *servername* is the actual name of your network server.

### Starting Application Explorer

To manually start Application Explorer on a workstation, run NALEXPLD.EXE from the SYS:\PUBLIC directory on the server where you installed ZEN for Desktops Application Management.

To automatically start Application Explorer each time the user logs in to NDS, enter the following line in the user's login script:

```
@\\servername\sys\public\nalexpld.exe
```

where *servername* is the actual name of your network server.

## Distributing an Application

Distributing applications is one of the main tasks that you perform using ZEN for Desktops. The following sections provide instructions for distributing an application, Microsoft CD Player, from the network to a user's workstation. After you've distributed CD Player, you will better understand the process required to distribute more complex applications that use snAppShot packages or Microsoft Windows Installer packages.

- ▶ Copying CDPLAYER.EXE to a network directory
- ▶ Creating the CDPLAYER Application object

▸ Specifying CDPLAYER.EXE as the application file to install

▸ Defining the application's operating system requirement

▸ Associating the application object with a user

▸ Running CDPLAYER on the user's workstation

### Copying CDPLAYER.EXE to a Network Directory

An application's source files must be kept in a network directory so that Application Launcher/Explorer can access the files from the user's workstation to install them. We recommend that you create separate directories for each application's source files.

**1.** Create a CDPLAYER directory in the network location where you want the application source files to be stored.

**2.** Copy CDPLAYER.EXE from a workstation's Windows directory (for example, C:\WINDOWS or C:\WINNT) to the CDPLAYER directory.

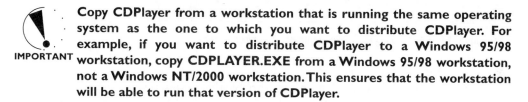

**IMPORTANT** **Copy CDPlayer from a workstation that is running the same operating system as the one to which you want to distribute CDPlayer. For example, if you want to distribute CDPlayer to a Windows 95/98 workstation, copy CDPLAYER.EXE from a Windows 95/98 workstation, not a Windows NT/2000 workstation. This ensures that the workstation will be able to run that version of CDPlayer.**

### Creating the CDPlayer Application Object

Follow these steps to create the CDPlayer application:

**1.** In ConsoleOne, right-click the container in which you want to create the Application object and then click New ⇨ Object.

**2.** Click App:Application in the list and then click OK.

**3.** Click Create a Simple Application Object (No .AOT/.AXT or .MSI File) and then click Next.

**4.** In the Object Name field, enter CDPLAYER. This is the name that will be given to the Application object.

**5.** In the Path to Executable field, type **%*windisk%\cdplayer\cdplayer.exe**. An example of this is shown in Figure 19.14.

**FIGURE 19.14** *Creating the CDPlayer Application object*

%*windisk% is a Windows macro variable that represents the disk drive where the Windows directory is located (typically C:). The path specified above causes CDPLAYER.EXE to be run from the workstation's C:\CDPLAYER directory.

Application Launcher/Explorer supports a variety of macros, including Windows macro variables, environment variables, NDS macro variables, login script variables, and Application object macros.

**6.** Click Finish to create the Application object.

### Specifying CDPLAYER.EXE as the Application File to Install

CDPlayer is run from the workstation's %*windisk%\CDPLAYER directory. You need to configure the Application object to copy CDPLAYER.EXE from the network to the workstation's %*windisk%\CDPLAYER directory, as follows:

**1.** Right-click the CDPLAYER Application object and then click Properties.

**2.** Click the Distribution Options tab and then click Application Files.

**3.** Click Add ➪ File to display the Edit Files dialog box. An example of this is shown in Figure 19.15.

**FIGURE 19.15** *Selecting CDPLAYER as the application file to install*

**4.** In the Source File field, enter the UNC path for the CDPLAYER.EXE file you copied to the network. For example:

`\\NOVELL\APPS\CDPLAYER\CDPLAYER.EXE.`

**5.** In the Target File field, type **%*windisk%\cdplayer\cdplayer.exe**.

**6.** Click OK to add CDPLAYER.EXE to the Application Files list. Only files in this list are copied to the workstation.

**7.** Leave the Application object properties open and continue with the next section.

### Defining the Application's Operating System Requirement

Before Application Launcher/Explorer can distribute the Application object to a user, it must verify that the user's workstation meets the application's requirements for the operating system.

By default, when you create an Application object, the operating system requirements are defined as any version of Windows 95/98 or Windows NT/2000. These requirements are sufficient for distributing CDPLAYER.EXE. If you want to see where the operating system requirements are set, you can follow the steps below to verify the requirements. If not, you can skip to the next section, "Associating the Application Object with a User. "

To verify the application's operating system requirements, follow these steps:

**1.** Click the Availability tab and then click System Requirements.

**2.** Verify that the list contains an OS Version requirement (Windows NT/2000 or Windows 95/98) for the workstation to which you want to distribute the application. If the correct OS version is not listed, click Add ⇨ Operating System and then enter the requirements for the operating system and click OK to add it to the list. An example of this is shown in Figure 19.16.

**FIGURE 19.16** Defining operating system requirements

**IMPORTANT**

**An OS Version requirement must be defined before an application will be distributed.**

**3.** Leave the Application object properties open and continue with the next section.

### Associating the Application Object with a User

Follow these steps to associate the Application object with a user:

**1.** Click the Associations tab.

**2.** Click Add and then browse and select a user to whom you want to distribute the application, and click OK to add the user to the Associations list.

**3.** Select the locations where you want the Application object icon to display as shown in Figure 19.17.

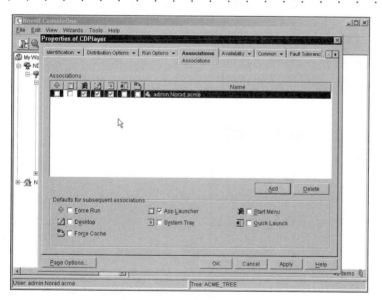

**FIGURE 19.17** *Associating the Application object with a user*

Application Launcher can display the icon in the Application Launcher window. Application Explorer can display the icon in the Application Launcher window, the Start menu, the system tray, the Quick Launch toolbar, and the desktop. Click the Help button for more information about each location.

4. Click OK (or Apply) to save the Application object information.

### Running CDPLAYER on the User's Workstation

Follow these steps to run CDPLAYER on the User's Workstation:

1. At the user's workstation, make sure the user is logged in to NDS.

2. If Application Launcher/Explorer is not running, start it. See the "Starting Application Launcher and Application Explorer" section.

   *or*

   If Application Launcher/Explorer is already running, right-click the Application Launcher/Explorer icon and then click Refresh.

3. The Application object icon should appear in the locations you specified when associating the Application object with the user.

4. Double-click the Application object to install CDPlayer to the workstation and run the application. See Figure 19.18.

**FIGURE 19.18** *Running the application*

**5.** You can verify that CDPlayer was installed to the workstation by looking in the C:\CDPlayer directory.

## Complex Application Installation

When a complex application is installed to a workstation, it is possible that the application's Setup program makes changes to the workstation including the Windows registry, .INI files, system files, CONFIG.SYS and AUTOEXEC.BAT files, and any other configurations that support the application.

The information gathered by NAL snAppShot is to be used when creating and setting up application objects using the NetWare Administrator and the NAL snap-in component.

### Using snAppShot

The following steps explain how to use the Novell Application Launcher snAppShot component, including how to compare the pre- and post-installation states of a workstation, how to create Application Object Template (.AOT) and .FIL files, and how to make those files available to the NetWare Administrator using the NAL snap-in.

Use NAL snAppShot to make the .AOT and .FIL files available to the NAL snap-in. The following steps walk you through an example of using snAppShot to make this happen:

**1.** Find a workstation that is representative of the ones on your network to which you will distribute applications. This workstation should be configured the same as the workstations you use on your network.

Although no two workstations are exactly the same, find a workstation that is configured similarly to the other target workstations. The more representative the workstation is, the fewer manual setup procedures you need to do during and after distribution.

**2.** For best results, close all other applications on the workstation you have chosen to use.

**3.** Run NAL snAppShot by executing the SNAPSHOT32.EXE file from the directory where you installed it (most likely SYS:\Public\Snapshot\); then read the introductory window, and choose the appropriate option. An example is shown in Figure 19.19.

**FIGURE 19.19** *Using the snAppShot utility*

4. You can choose among these discovery options:

   - **Standard** — Performs the discovery process using the factory default settings.

   - **Custom** — Enables you to specify the drives, files, folders, registry hive, and shortcuts you want to include or exclude in the discovery process.

   - **Express** — Quickly scans for changes on the desktop using a snAppShot Preferences file created during a previous discovery process.

   Be sure to read the Getting Started option before choosing a discovery option; it gives you a good overview of snAppShot.

   For example purposes, we will describe the Standard installation here. Select the Standard option to be presented with an information dialog box. Fill in a name for the NDS application object and an application icon title, and then click Next. An example of this is shown in Figure 19.20.

5. Specify the application file location for the .FIL files that will be created as a result of running NAL snAppShot. Also specify the Windows Drive and Boot Drive. Click Next. An example of this procedure is shown in Figure 19.21.

**FIGURE 19.20** *The snAppShot Information dialog box*

**FIGURE 19.21** *Specifying the network or workstation directory of the .AOT*

The next dialog box asks you to enter the filename and location that you want to use for the Application Object Template (.AOT) file. In our example, the name will default to WordApplicationObject.AOT. You can change this if you desire another name.

**IMPORTANT** **If you are going to use NAL snAppShot again to discover the changes of additional application installations, we recommend creating unique directories on the network for each application. If you don't use unique source directories, .AOT and .FIL files could be overwritten and cause you problems.**

**6.** Specify the drives that you want snAppShot to scan. If you select the custom option, specify which files, directories, .INI Files, .TXT files, and Registry keys you want to include or exclude during the NAL snAppShot discovery process, and then click Next. For example, because you might not want to record the changes to the Windows 95/98 Recycle Bin as a result of installing an application, you can exclude this directory from the discovery process.

**7.** After reviewing the snAppShot settings summary, you are ready to take the preinstallation snapshot of the workstation. Click Next or click Back to check or change a previous setting.

The preinstallation discovery process records all current files and configurations on the workstation and stores the information in a hidden file. When NAL snAppShot finishes the preinstallation discovery, it is ready for you to run the application's Setup program. An example of this information gathering is shown in Figure 19.22.

When the process is completed, the utility displays a dialog box stating that it's time to install the application. Click the button that says Run Application Install. An example of this is shown in Figure 19.23.

**FIGURE 19.22** *The snAppShot utility first does a scan of the workstation.*

**FIGURE 19.23** *After scanning the workstation, snAppShot displays this dialog box to install your application.*

**8.** Complete the installation of the application. Your application installation files can reside anywhere and can be located by browsing.

**9.** When the application is installed, the snAppShot utility automatically goes to the post-installation discovery. This step notes any changes made to the files and configurations on the workstation as a result of the application's Setup program. An example of the post-application install scan is shown in Figure 19.24.

**FIGURE 19.24** *A post-application install scan of the workstation*

You are then shown a dialog box that notifies you that an AOT template is being generated. This takes a few minutes, depending on how many files you have on your workstation (see Figure 19.25).

**FIGURE 19.25** *The final stage in the snAppShot process is to generate the template file.*

After the generation is complete, a dialog box (shown in Figure 19.26) is displayed, showing that the process is finished. The template is stored as both an .AOT file and an .AXT (text) file in the locations that you've previously specified.

**FIGURE 19.26** *The SnAppShot Completion dialog box*

### Creating an Application Object Using the .AOT and .FIL Files That You Generated

Now that you have successfully completed the creation of the .AOT files for an application, you are ready to create an application object that will represent the application to your NDS users. Follow these steps:

1. Start ConsoleOne.

2. Right-click the organization or organizational unit object under which you want to create an application object and click Create. Select Application and then click OK.

3. The resulting dialog box is shown in Figure 19.27.

**FIGURE 19.27** *Creating an application object*

4. You can create an application object with or without an associated .AOT/.AXT file.

**5.** Browse for the .AOT files, if necessary, and then click Next to see the dialog box shown in Figure 19.28.

**FIGURE 19.28** *Selecting a predefined .AOT file to associate with an application object.*

**6.** Check (and change, if necessary) the target and source directories of the application object, and then click Next.

**7.** Review the information about the application object, and then click Create to see the dialog box shown in Figure 19.29.

**8.** Associate the application object with a user, group, organization, or organizational unit object. To associate an application, right-click the application object, click Details, and then click the Associations button found on the right side of the dialog box. Use this property page to assign other objects to the application object. An example of creating associations is shown in Figure 19.30.

**FIGURE 19.29** *You can review the settings for the application object before its creation.*

**FIGURE 19.30** *Associating the application object with users in NDS*

## Customizing Application Objects

For your reference, all configuration options for an application object are listed in the next section. You can view these options by selecting the application object and double-clicking it or by right-clicking Details. An example of the Details dialog box is shown in Figure 19.31.

**FIGURE 19.31** *Customizing the application object through the Details dialog box*

The next section lists each section of the Details dialog box.

### The Identification Page

Use the Identification property page to control the application icon that the user sees at the workstation. For example, you can select a different icon picture, write the icon's title, and give the icon a display and run priority. You can also specify the path to the application's executable file and set up the application to run just one time.

**Application Icon Title** The text you type here appears as the caption beneath the application icon in the Application Launcher window or Application Launcher Explorer software. The application icon title, which is mandatory, can be different from the application object name (that is, the name that NDS uses to identify the application) and can contain periods and other special characters. Use the Description property page for longer descriptions of the application.

**Path to Executable File**    The path you specify here is to the executable that is run when an Application Object icon is double-clicked in the Application Launcher window or Application Launcher Explorer. You can type the path as a UNC path or a file directory path. Use the Browse button to browse the file directory structure and find the executable you want. Refer to the following example syntax when mapping a drive:

```
SERVER\VOLUME:PATH
\\SERVER\VOLUME\PATH
\\TREE\.DIRECTORY_MAP_OBJECT_NAME\PATH
VOLUME_OBJECT_NAME:PATH
DIRECTORY_MAP_OBJECT_NAME:PATH
DRIVELETTER:\PATH
```

**Install Only (No Executable Needed)**    Use this option if no application is supposed to run. For example, this application object's purpose might be to just update some files on the workstation. When you select the Install Only option, the software is installed but not run.

**Application Icon**    This option lets you assign an icon to an application object. The icon you choose appears in the Application Launcher window or Application Launcher Explorer, depending on what you have specified on the Applications property page. If you do not specify an icon, a default Application Launcher icon is used.

**Order Icons**    This option performs two useful functions. First, it organizes the icons in the Application Launcher window and Application Launcher Explorer. Second, it dictates the order in which application objects set as Force Run will run.

▶ · · · · · · · · · · · · · · · · · · · · · · · · · · · · ◀

### Consulting Experience

You should use the variable %TARGET_PATH% wherever possible. Example: Start Netscape Communication with %TARGET_PATH%\Program\Netscape.EXE where %TARGET_PATH% is equal to C:\Program Files\Netscape\Communicator. If you don't want to run an application (for example, this application object's purpose might be to just update some files on the workstation), use the Install Only option and do not specify a path.

Ordering is left to right or top to bottom, depending upon the way the user views icons in the Application Launcher window and Application Launcher Explorer. You achieve ordering by entering a numeric value into the Icon Order text box. All application objects you wish to order must have a numeric value. The value of zero gives the icon the highest priority and thus the highest prominence in the list. The maximum value is 999. If you do not order application objects, they will be ordered alphabetically (the default).

Example: Suppose that you have ten icons that you want to organize in the Application Launcher window. In each of those ten application objects, select Order Icons on the Identification property page and type the icon's order number. If you want the icon to be the sixth icon in the list, type 5. If you want it to be the first one, type 0.

If two application objects have the same Icon number, they will be arranged alphabetically. This works well if you want to order sets of Application Object icons.

Example: Suppose you are distributing, in order of highest priority, a productivity suite with five icons, a set of utilities with seven icons, and a set of tools with four icons. You want the group of highest priority (the suite) to display most prominently.

To achieve this, give all icons in the first group a value of zero. Give the next set a value of one, and the third set a value of two. When users (who have been associated with the application objects of the three groups) run the Application Launcher window or Application Launcher Explorer, they see three sets of icons, arranged alphabetically within each set. The very top set is the suite applications.

**Run Once**  When an application object's purpose is to install software to a workstation, it can be confusing to users if the icon remains on their workstations after the software has been installed. Use the Run Once option if you want the application to run just once and then have its icon disappear, so as to not cause confusion. You can choose from a variety of ways to use Run Once in combination with other object properties. For example, if the application is specified as a Force Run on the Applications property page (meaning that the user is not involved, and the application runs when Windows starts), the application is forced to run one time.

### The Environment Property Page
Use the Environment property page (shown in Figure 19.32) to identify the environment that might be required for an application object. Some applications require custom configuration parameters to function properly. Before launching the application, the Application Launcher window or Application Launcher Explorer software configures the workstation to properly run the application. The

parameters, directories, mappings, and printer ports associated with the application automatically execute (mappings and captures don't actually happen until the user launches the application). After exiting the application, the application's post-termination script removes any drive mappings or port captures it created during execution.

**FIGURE 19.32** *The NAL Environment page*

To set up the application's environment, follow these steps:

**1.** Right-click the application object and click Details.

**2.** Click the Environment button.

**3.** Change the following Environment properties as needed, and then click OK.

**Command Line Parameters**   Some applications require application-specific parameters to run in a desired mode or view. You can place one or more parameters here. See your application's documentation for more information about the types of parameters that you can use.

**Working Directory**   This option can be designated for any application object and might be required by some applications (your application's documentation describes the working directories it needs). You can look for the working directory by using the Browse button to the right of the Working Directory field.

▶ · · · · · · · · · · · · · · · · · · · · · · · · · · · · · · · · · · · · ◀

### Consulting Experience

Users running this application object must be given rights to write to this file for this option to work correctly.

**Run**    This group box sets the application's initial window size. Choose whether you want to run the application in Normal, Minimized, or Maximized mode.

To run on Windows NT (a 32-bit operating system), 16-bit applications must run in a Virtual DOS Machine (VDM) that emulates Windows 3.1 functionality. The 16-bit Windows emulator called WOW (for Win16-on-Win32) isolates 16-bit application errors from the rest of the 32-bit operating system.

Sixteen-bit Windows applications can run in their own separate WOW sessions, or they can share a WOW session with other 16-bit applications. Sharing a WOW session saves memory and enables applications to use DDE or OLE to communicate with other applications in the same WOW session. Running an application in its own separate WOW session allows for more robust operation because the application is isolated from other 16-bit applications. Because some applications do not run properly in a separate WOW session, the default option is to run the 16-bit Windows application in a shared WOW session.

**Enable Error Logging to File**    Specify the path to a file where any errors are logged if the application fails to install or launch. No status is tracked here except for errors.

**Clean Up Network Resources**    The process of "cleaning up" means that the license for a particular network connection is removed. This prevents users from using a network connection when they don't need it.

If the Clean Up Network Resources option is selected, drive mappings and printer ports associated with the applications launched by the Application Launcher window or Application Launcher Explorer are cleaned up. If this check box is not selected, drive mappings and printer ports established earlier remain in effect.

**Monitor Module Name**    When an application is launched, the Application Launcher window or Application Launcher Explorer monitors the executable of the application. When the executable terminates, the process of cleaning up network resources begins. However, the executable filename may actually be a *wrapper* that sets up environments, runs other executables, and then terminates. If the Application Launcher window or Application Launcher Explorer monitors the wrapper executable, it might prematurely start cleaning up network resources before the application has terminated.

Consult your application documentation about whether the application uses a wrapper executable. If it does, find out the name of the module that remains running. Type this name (without the extension) in the text box provided.

### The Drives/Ports Page

Because the applications that users see in the Application Launcher window or Application Launcher Explorer are linked directly to application objects, users do not need drive mappings established through their login scripts.

However, each application object can map additional drives and capture printers as needed. Use the settings on the Drives/Ports property page to set up drive mappings and port captures for printers for an application. Such drive mappings and port captures are set up before the Application Launcher window or Application Launcher Explorer software executes the application.

If the Clean Up Network Resources option is selected on the Environment property page, the drive mappings and port captures that the Application Launcher window or Application Launcher Explorer creates are released when the user exits all applications that use the resources.

### Consulting Experience

If the resource (a connection, map, or capture) is already in use when the Application Launcher window or Application Launcher Explorer is started, the Application Launcher window or Application Launcher Explorer uses it and does not clean it up. Otherwise, the resource is created and cleaned up when all other Application Launcher window or Application Launcher Explorer applications are finished using it. The connection to the server containing the resource is removed as well. If the applications that the Application Launcher window or Application Launcher Explorer launched are still running when the Application Launcher window or Application Launcher Explorer is terminated, the allocated resources remain intact.

**Consulting Experience**

The paths to executable files, drive mappings, and port captures are stored as strings and not as NDS object names. Therefore, if a subtree is moved, some application objects might still point to the previous, but possibly invalid, objects.

For example, suppose you are configuring a word processing application that requires a specific mapped drive. This application is installed and runs from the same drive letter. You choose to map drive w: for this application and specify w:\apps\word1\word1.exe in the Path to Executable File text box on the Identification property page. Then, in the Drives/Ports property page, you map drive W: to the server where the application exists. When the Application Launcher window or Application Launcher Explorer runs the application, it checks for a mapping of drive w:. If w: is mapped to the correct volume and server, the drive is used. If w: is mapped to some other server or volume, it is not used, and the application does not run. If w: is not mapped at all, the Application Launcher window or Application Launcher Explorer maps it. In the case where the Application Launcher window or Application Launcher Explorer actually maps the drive, it cleans up the mapping after the application terminates. If several applications use the same drive mapping, drive mappings aren't cleaned up until the last application terminates.

### The Description Property Page
Use the Description property page to give your users more complete information than the application icon caption allows. Users can right-click an application object in the Application Launcher window or Application Launcher Explorer to see details containing both the descriptive name of the application and the more lengthy description that you provide using the Description property page.

For example, suppose you are creating an application object that installs a word processor to the user's workstation. The description you type, which is longer than the icon's title can contain, might include a description and any special instructions you'd like your users to see. The description is also used with the function "Prompt before distribution."

### The Fault Tolerance Property Page
Use the Fault Tolerance property page to make sure your users can access the applications they need even if the server containing those applications becomes inaccessible.

An application object pulls application source files from a specific server. If that server is inaccessible, you can set up alternative servers from which the application files can be accessed. By doing this, you keep the applications running with no disruptions in availability to your users. You can use two methods for setting up alternative servers: load balancing and fault tolerance. Both of these are discussed in the sections that follow.

**Load Balancing**   Load balancing lets the Application Launcher window or Application Launcher Explorer software spread the user load across multiple application objects. Ordinarily, you use load balancing when all the servers that the application objects use are located in a single site on a local area network. If a particular server goes down, rendering that application object inoperable, the application object is removed from the list of available applications, the list is randomized again, and a server is selected.

**Fault Tolerance**   Fault tolerance lets the Application Launcher window or Application Launcher Explorer search the specified servers in the order in which you have set them up. If the first server specified is too busy or is not available, the Application Launcher window or Application Launcher Explorer tries each server in the order listed until it comes to a server that is available; it accesses the application from that server. Ordinarily, you use fault tolerance when the servers are located at various sites throughout a wide area network. However, the servers that you are using for fault tolerance must reside in the same NDS tree.

**Combining Both Methods**   You can set up your applications to take advantage of both load balancing and fault tolerance. If you do so, the Application Launcher window or Application Launcher Explorer first attempts to locate an available server among those designated for load balancing. If none of those is available, the Application Launcher window or Application Launcher Explorer then goes in order through the servers listed for fault tolerance.

To set up load balancing, follow these steps:

**1.** Right-click the application object and click Details.

**2.** Click the Fault Tolerance button.

**3.** Choose the Enable Load Balance check box.

**4.** Click the Add button (below the Load Balancing text box).

After the Select Object window is displayed, find the next application to launch by using the browser in the panel on the right. The applications are contained in the object you created for them. Your current context is shown above the Browser text box. To change your current context, click the Change Context button below the Browser text box.

The application now appears in the Load Balancing text box.

To set up fault tolerance, follow these steps:

1. Right-click the application object and click Details.
2. Click the Fault Tolerance button.
3. Choose the Enable Fault Tolerance check box.
4. Click the Add button.

After the Select Object window is displayed, find the next application to launch by using the browser in the panel on the right. The applications are contained in the object you created for them. Your current context is shown above the browser panel. To change your current context, click the Change Context button located below the browser text box.

The application now appears in the Fault Tolerance text box.

To delete an application object from the load balancing or fault tolerance lists, follow these steps:

1. Right-click the application object and click Details.
2. Click the Fault Tolerance button.
3. Choose the load balanced- or fault tolerant-enabled application that you want to remove from the list, and then click the Delete button.
4. Click OK to save changes.

### The System Requirements Page

Use the System Requirements property page as a filter to display application icons only on workstations that meet certain criteria that you specify, such as the specific version of an operating system, the amount of RAM, or the amount of free disk space. If workstations do not meet the criteria you specify, the icons do not appear on that workstation.

For example, suppose you want a word processing application icon to appear only on Windows 95/98 workstations that have at least 32MB of RAM, a Pentium processor, and 500MB of free disk space on the C: drive. Using the options on the System Requirements property page, you can tailor the requirements in this way.

**Display Applications on a Particular Operating System** Because you might have a mixture of platforms on your network, you can select one or more platforms, such as Windows 3.x, Windows 95/98, and Windows NT/2000.

For example, suppose you want the application to run only Windows NT 4.0 or later workstations. To specify this configuration, select Windows NT, and then type **4** in the Major text box and type **0** in the Minor text box. If you leave the Major and Minor text boxes empty, only the operating system is verified.

**Display Applications on Machines That Have at Least**   Use the options in this group box if you need further filtering. For example, if the application object sets up a suite of applications, minimum disk space and memory requirements may need to be met.

**MB of RAM**   This field is valid only for Windows 95/98 and Windows NT/2000 workstations (Windows 3.x is ignored). Use it by entering the minimum amount of total installed RAM that the workstation must have to see and run this application.

For example, if the application requires 8MB of RAM ), you type **8** in this text box. If you leave this text box blank, no memory checking is done.

**Processor**   This field shows the minimum processor needed to run this application. The choices are 386, 486, or Pentium. For example, if you select 486 and the user has a 386 workstation, the application object is not displayed on the workstation.

**Free Disk Space**   Use this group box to check three different drives for available disk space. For example, you can check the workstation for 20MB free on the Windows directory drive, 10MB free on the TEMP drive, and 80MB free on the D: drive. As with the other settings, if you leave these text boxes blank, no checking is done for available disk space.

▶ . . . . . . . . . . . . . . . . . . . . . . . . . . ◀

### Consulting Experience

If the drives selected for any of the three fields happen to be the same drive, Application Launcher adds those minimum requirements together to determine available space. For example, if you specify 20MB free on the Windows directory drive (which happens to be the C: drive), 10MB free on the TEMP drive (which is also the C: drive), and 50MB free on the D: drive, Application Launcher only shows the application object as if 30MB were available on the C: drive and 50MB were free on the D: drive.

### The Scripts Property Page

Use the Scripts property page to set up scripts that are executed automatically each time the application is launched and closed. Unlike environment parameters, scripts can overwrite existing drive mappings and printer ports. You can use these options when running these scripts:

- ▶ Run Before Launching (or Startup) scripts are executed after the environment is set and before the application is launched.

- ▶ Run After Termination (or post-termination) scripts are executed after the application is closed and before the network resources are cleaned up. The Scripts property page uses the same syntax as a NetWare login script. Refer to your NetWare documentation for more syntax descriptions and examples.

**Examples of What You Can Do with Application Scripts** An application script can provide extra mappings beyond those defined on the Drives/Ports property page. For example, you can take any of these actions with an application script:

- ▶ Provide a mapping to override another mapping.

- ▶ Run other applications.

- ▶ Log into other servers or NDS trees.

- ▶ Terminate applications under certain circumstances.

**Create Application Object Scripts** To enable an application object script, type the appropriate commands in either the Run before Launching or Run after Termination text box.

Commands for cleaning up the changes made by the prelaunch script should be placed in the post-termination script. The post-termination script is run after Application Launcher detects that the application has terminated. Both scripts follow the login script language syntax, and all login script variables are allowed (that is, %FULL_NAME, %LOGIN_NAME, <PATH>, and so on).

The Application Launcher supports these scripting commands:

- ▶ DAY

- ▶ FILESERVER or FILE_SERVER

- ▶ FULL_NAME

- ▶ HOUR24 (24HOUR)

- ▶ HOUR (HOURS)

- ▶ LAST_NAME

- ▶ LOGIN_NAME

- MINUTE (MINUTES)
- MONTH
- NDAY_OF_WEEK
- NETWORK (NETWORK_ADDRESS)
- OS_VERSION
- OS
- PLATFORM
- PHYSICAL_STATION (P_STATION)
- REQUESTER_CONTEXT
- SECOND (SECONDS)
- SHORT_YEAR
- TERM
- WINVER
- YEAR

The Application Launcher currently does not support these scripting commands:

- ACCESS_SERVER
- AM_PM
- CLS
- DAY_OF_WEEK
- DIALUP
- DISPLAY
- ERROR_LEVEL
- EXIT
- FDISPLAY
- GREETING_TIME
- INCLUDE
- LASTLOGINTIME
- LOCATION
- LOGIN_ALIAS_CONTEXT
- LOGIN_CONTEXT
- MACHINE

- ▸ MONTH_NAME
- ▸ NEW_MAIL
- ▸ NO_DEFAULT
- ▸ NOSWAP
- ▸ OFFLINE
- ▸ PASSWORD_EXPIRES
- ▸ PAUSE
- ▸ PCCOMPATIBLE
- ▸ REQUESTER_VERSION
- ▸ SCRIPT_SERVER
- ▸ SET_TIME
- ▸ SHELL_VERSION
- ▸ SMACHINE
- ▸ STATION
- ▸ SWAP
- ▸ USERID
- ▸ WRITE

The Application Launcher scripting does not pause or output display errors to the screen.

### The Contacts Property Page

Use the Contacts property page to add, delete, and list the users who are resources or support contacts for specific application objects. This information is displayed in the properties of each application icon on a user's workstation through the Application Launcher window or Application Launcher Explorer.

The Help information can be tailored so that users are directed to the support group at their locations. Designating a user support contact helps channel problems to knowledgeable people and alleviate your workload.

A user can find out who is assigned to what application by choosing File ⇨ Properties and clicking the Contacts tab from the Application Launcher window or Application Launcher Explorer. The user can contact the assigned contact in person, by phone, or by using the Application Launcher window or Application Launcher Explorer to send an e-mail.

---

**Consulting Experience**

Using the Applications property page, you can assign user, group, organizational unit, organization, or country objects to multiple application objects. For example, if you create several application objects, you can use the Applications property page for a given user object to assign those applications to the user. Furthermore, you can specify how applications are displayed on the workstation (that is, through the Application Launcher window, Application Launcher Explorer, Windows Explorer, Start menu, Desktop, and System Tray).

---

### The Associations Property Page

Use the Associations property page to grant multiple users, groups, organizations, or organizational units the right to see and use the application object. If you do not associate applications with these objects, they are not available to users in the Application Launcher window or Application Launcher Explorer.

When the association is complete, the object and application contain information about each other. The user, group, organizational unit, organization, or country object shows which applications it can use, and the application shows what other objects can access it. Only direct associations appear. For example, if a user is a member of a group and the group is associated with an application, viewing the user object does not show the application association and viewing the application does not show the user association. However, the group object shows both the user and the application associations.

### The Administrator Notes Property Page

Use the Administrator Notes property page to create a section of notes that only you, as the administrator, can view and edit.

For example, you might want to remind yourself about some special settings for a particular application. Or if your system is managed by several administrators, you could use the Administrator Notes property page to provide a history of application upgrades and file changes.

### The System Requirements Page

Use the System Requirements property page as a filter to display application icons only on workstations that meet certain criteria that you specify, such as the specific version of an operating system, the amount of RAM, or the amount of free disk space. If workstations do not meet the criteria you specify, the icons do not appear on that workstation.

> · · · · · · · · · · · · · · · · · · · · · · · · · · · · ◀

**Consulting Experience**

Before any change on this property page goes into effect, you must change the version stamp value on the Distribution property page. Changing this value signals Application Launcher to redistribute the application.

For example, suppose you want a word processing application icon to appear only on Windows 95/98 workstations that have at least 32MB of RAM, a Pentium processor, and 500MB of free disk space on the C: drive. Using the options on the System Requirements property page, you can tailor the requirements in this way.

### The Macros Property Page

Use the Macros property page to manage the macros that are used on other property pages of the application object. You can use macros in these application object locations:

- Full path
- Command line
- Working directory
- Mapping path
- Capture port path
- Registry property page: key, name, value (string only)
- .INI Files property page: group, name, value
- Application Files property page: source/target, directory
- Text Files property page: find and add string
- Icons/Shortcuts property page: all locations

For example, suppose that you have a complex application object that uses the %SOURCE_PATH% macro throughout numerous property pages. What if the path that %SOURCE_PATH% points to changes? Rather than change each case, you can change the value of %SOURCE_PATH% one time on the Macros property page; the change will be reflected on all other property pages where the macro is used.

### The Registry Settings Property Page

Use the Registry Settings property page to add, change, delete, and import Registry keys, names, and values as if you were working with the actual Windows Registry. You specify whether these settings are created or removed in the Windows Registry when the application runs or distributes.

### The Application Files Property Page

Use the Application Files property page to make changes to application-related files on the target workstation when the application is distributed.

The easiest way to use the Application Files property page is to run the snAppShot first. Application Launcher snAppShot compares the configuration settings on a representative workstation before and after you install an application on it. These differences are recorded in an Application Object Template (.AOT) file. If files are copied during the installation, the changes are imported to the Application Files property page when you create the application object. Giving you a point of reference, the .AOT file method takes the guesswork out of knowing which files and settings are required to run an application. If you need to upgrade an application and you have new files to copy, you import a new .AOT file into the Application Files property page. These application files can be conditionally installed:

- ► Always Copy
- ► Copy If Does Not Exist
- ► Copy If Exists
- ► Copy If Newer
- ► Copy If Newer and Exists
- ► Request Confirmation or deleted

### The Text Files Property Page

Use the Text Files property page to add, change, or delete workstation text files (such as CONFIG.SYS and AUTOEXEC.BAT). Text file changes go into effect after you change the application object's version stamp.

For example, suppose that users are experiencing problems due to an incorrect text string found in their workstation's CONFIG.SYS file. Rather than visit and change each workstation or run the risk of users incorrectly and inconsistently implementing a change, you can set up a Text File template that finds, deletes, modifies, or adds text strings to the text file of your choice. The Text File template implements the changes the next time the application runs.

The easiest way to use the Text Files property page is to use snAppShot first, which compares the configuration settings on a representative workstation before and after you install an application on it. These differences are recorded in an Application Object Template (.AOT) file. If changes are made to text files during the installation, the changes are imported to the Text Files property page when you create the application object. Giving you a point of reference, the .AOT file method takes the guesswork out of knowing which files and settings are required to run an application. If you need to upgrade an application and you have new text file changes, you import a new .AOT file into the Text Files property page.

Use the Text File Edit dialog box to find, delete, and add text strings to the text file template that is used to change text files when related applications are run.

### The Schedule Property Page

Use the Schedule property page to define when you want a particular application to run or how long you want an application's icon to appear in the Application Launcher window or Application Launcher Explorer.

For example, suppose you want users to have access to a particular application for only five days. After that, you want to remove the application from their view. Using the settings on the Schedule property page, you can automatically remove the icon from users' workstations.

Or suppose that you want to run a virus detection application on users' workstations at a certain time, and only one time. The Schedule property page contains settings that make this possible as well.

### The Icons/Shortcuts Page

Use the Icons/Shortcuts property page to control the icons of application objects that appear in Program Manager (Windows 3.x) and Shortcuts in Windows Explorer (Windows 95/98 and Windows NT 4.x). The items that appear in the Icons/Shortcuts list control the Program Group, Program Group Item, and Shortcuts.

Example: Suppose that your company uses special icons for the applications that users run on their Windows 95/98, Windows NT, and Windows 3.x workstations. Using the Icons/Shortcuts property page for this application object, you can change the icons for the other applications.

### The Distribution Property Page

Use the Distribution property page to configure general distribution behavior when an application object distributes.

To access the Distribution Property Page, follow these steps:

**1.** Right-click the application object and click Details.

**2.** Click the Distribute button.

**3.** Use the options to change settings, and then click OK.

### Show Distribution Progress to User

The Show Distribution Progress option displays an easy-to-read progress bar to users the first time they distribute an application to their workstations. Turn off this option if you are distributing only a small change to the application, such as a Registry modification. Turn it on if you are distributing a large application and want to give the user a general idea of how long to expect the distribution to take.

### The Folders Property Page

Use the Folders property page to create Custom or Linked folders in which to organize application objects. A Custom folder is tied to one application object. A Linked folder might contain many application objects. All folders appear in the Application Launcher window or Explorer browser view and also in the Start Menu. Using folders, you can achieve *subfoldering*, or the placing of folders within folders.

Use the Folders property page on the application object to create both Custom and Linked folders. Use the folder object to create one Linked folder to which you link other application objects.

### The Create a Folder for an Application Object

Follow these steps if you want to create a folder for an application object:

**1.** Right-click the application object.

**2.** Click the Folders button.

**3.** Click Add and select Custom to create a folder exclusively for this application object or choose Linked to create a separate folder object that can be shared by this and other application objects.

**4.** If you want to change or delete the name of a folder, highlight it and use the Modify or Delete buttons.

**5.** Select Launcher Window and/or Start Menu, depending on whether you want to display the folders in the Application Launcher window, in the Application Launcher Explorer browser view, or on the Start menu.

### The .INI Settings Property Page

Use the .INI Settings property page to create or change the .INI files on the target workstation when the application runs. The easiest way to use the .INI Files property page is to run the Novell Application Launcher snAppShot component first. Application Launcher snAppShot compares the configuration settings on a representative workstation before and after you install an application on it. These differences are recorded in an Application Object Template (.AOT) file. If changes are made to .INI files during the installation, the changes are imported to the .INI Files property page when you create the application object. Giving you a point of reference, the .AOT file method takes the guesswork out of knowing which files and settings are required to run an application. If you need to upgrade an application and you have new .INI file changes, you import a new .AOT file into the Text Files property page.

### The File Rights Property Page

Use the File Rights property page to grant rights to files, directories, and volumes when this application object is associated to a user object or a group, organizational unit, organization, or country to which the user is already associated. Such rights are removed when the application object is unassociated.

The file rights are stored in the NetWare file system. The file page eases the administration of the file rights and synchronizes these to the associated users, groups, organizational units, organizations, or countries.

If two separate application objects give file rights to the same file, directory, or volume and just one of them is unassociated with the user, the user loses all rights even though the user might still be associated with the other application object.

File rights are not dynamic. For example, the file rights you set up are not dependent on whether or not the user is actually using the application.

### The Termination Property Page

Use the Termination property page to terminate an Application Launcher–delivered application. You can choose from several methods to terminate the application, ranging from simple requests for users to exit an application on their own, all the way to revoking the application without warning. To terminate an application object, follow these steps:

1. Right-click the application object and click Details.

2. Click the Termination button.

3. Choose one of the termination behaviors from the drop-down list.

### The Application Site List Property Page

Use the Application Site List property page to set up a site *ring* or *chain* of applications to ensure that users who travel from site to site always access applications from the server that is geographically closest to them. An application site list gives users faster access to their applications and reduces WAN traffic and associated costs. A site list must include application objects located within the same NDS Tree.

To set up an application site list, follow these steps:

1. Right-click the application object.
2. Click the Application Site List button.
3. Click Link To and specify the application objects that would be geographically close to the user should that user travel to a different site.
4. To unlink a site, highlight its name and click Unlink This Site.

# Installing and Setting Up ZENworks for Servers 2

Novell ZENworks for Servers (ZEN for Servers) Policy and Distribution Services is a directory-enabled distribution, configuration, and behavioral management system for servers. It provides the means to manage Policy and Distribution Services for all servers from one workstation using ConsoleOne.

This section provides instructions on installing and setting up the Policy and Distribution Services components of the ZEN for Servers product. Because this service enforces policies and distributes software throughout a network environment, we strongly recommend against a first-time installation of Policy and Distributions Services in a production environment. Instead, first install and test this product in a lab environment.

## Distribution Services in a Production Environment

Before deploying to your production environment, you should understand the current Tiered Electronic Distribution (TED) architecture, carefully plan your implementation, and set up a test environment. For information on understanding and planning your ZEN for "Servers Policy and Distribution Service" implementation, see Novell's product documentation.

Only the basic information you will need to install and set up Policy and Distribution Services to a test system is provided in this section. For more advanced setup and administration information, see Novell's product documentation.

## Installing Policy and Distribution Services Software

Detailed planning is necessary for a full deployment to a production environment. Therefore, we suggest that you perform your first installation to a test environment.

To install ZEN for Servers Policy and Distribution Services, perform the steps in each of the following sections:

- ▸ Beginning the ZEN for Servers Installation
- ▸ Configuring the Distributor Objects
- ▸ Configuring the Subscriber Objects

### Beginning the ZEN for Servers Installation

Before you start the install, make sure your display resolution is $1024 \times 768$ or higher, because the Install Wizard does not work on smaller screens and cannot be resized.

To install ZEN for Server Policy and Distribution Services, perform the following steps:

1. If any management and monitoring services are running on the server, stop these processes now. See Stopping and Starting Management and Monitoring Services for information.

2. If Sybase is running on the server on which the database will be installed, quit the Sybase engine now.

3. If Java has not been unloaded on the target servers, unload JAVA.NLM. For example, at each server's console prompt, type the following:

   ```
   java -exit
   ```

4. Insert the ZEN for Servers Software CD in the CD of the workstation.

   The startup screen appears. If the startup screen is not automatically launched after you insert the CD, you can launch it by running WINSETUP.EXE at the root of the CD. An example of the startup screen is shown in Figure 19.33.

5. If you have not extended the NDS schema, do so now through the install.

6. On the ZEN for Servers Software CD, click ZENworks for Servers ⇨ Install Policy and Distribution Services.

7. If you agree with the license agreement, click Accept ⇨ Next.

**FIGURE 19.33** *ZEN for Servers installation screen*

**8.** Browse and select the tree to which you will be installing and click Next.

**9.** If you have previously installed ZEN for Servers 1.0 to the tree, click No for the Warning message and perform the steps under "Upgrading to ZEN for Servers Management and Monitoring Services from ManageWise 2.7," found in Novell's online product documentation; otherwise, continue. An example of this screen is shown in Figure 19.34.

**FIGURE 19.34** *Selecting the tree in which to install ZENworks for Servers*

**10.** Check the Install Licenses check box and then click Add.

> **IMPORTANT** Because Policy and Distribution Services and Management and Monitoring Services use different licensing models, they each require their own licenses. Even if you installed a license during the Management and Monitoring Services installation, you still need to install a Policy and Distribution license.

**11.** Browse to select the NDS container in which to create the NLS license object for the service, click Select, click OK, and then click Next. An example of selecting an NDS container is shown in Figure 19.35.

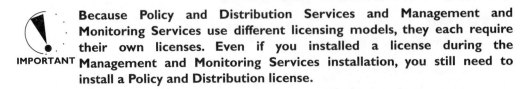

**FIGURE 19.35** *Selecting an NDS container for the NLS license object*

The Distributor and Policy Package agents (ZEN for Servers agents) check the NLS object as they are loaded and will not load unless an NLS object exists.

> **IMPORTANT** If you are installing ZEN for Servers from an evaluation CD, you can install the license object in the NDS tree only once. If you install more than one copy of the Evaluation License, every server will display an error message every two minutes. For valid licenses installed from a product CD, installation to multiple locations in the NDS tree is allowed.

**12.** Click Add Server and browse NDS to select the servers.

We recommend that you have at least three servers for an ample test environment. Also, cross-platform servers require eDirectory for their platform to be available when you browse the directory to select servers.

> **IMPORTANT** **A local installation option for Windows NT servers eliminates the need for a cross-platform directory. If eDirectory is not installed, a SYS Share must be set up and the installation run locally. For instructions, see "Installing ZEN for Servers Locally to a Windows NT Server," found in your Novell online documentation.**

**13.** If you installed ConsoleOne to your workstation, check the ConsoleOne Snap-ins check box for the Local Machine entry.

**14.** If you installed ConsoleOne to any of your servers, check the ConsoleOne Snap-ins check box for each of those servers. Note that the wizard enables you to make multiple selections per column.

(Optional) For the NetWare 5.x server where you have SSL installed, check the box in the Remote Web Console (RWC) column. RWC needs to be installed on a single server only to make Policy and Distribution Services accessible from the Remote Web Console.

**15.** Determine which server will be the Distributor and then click the radio button for this server in the Distributor column. If you have enough servers, you may designate as many Distributors as needed.

**16.** For this test system, to install the Database to the same server as the Distributor, click the radio button in its Database column. For more information on database issues, see the "Policy and Distribution Services" section in your Novell online documentation.

**17.** For all NetWare servers, check their check boxes in the Server Policies column. To select all, right-click the column. This component is required for all servers being managed by Policy Packages or any server receiving software packages.

**18.** For all other servers that are not a Distributor, check the boxes for these servers in the Subscriber column, and then click Next.

**19.** Click Next without making any changes to this page to accept the defaults.

For your first installation, you want to accept the defaults here so that the proper files will be copied, the AUTOEXEC.NCF file will be modified, and the installation will be able to pause if you didn't unload Java on a target server. You can customize these settings when you do a full deployment to your production environment. This page is shown in Figure 19.36.

**FIGURE 19.36** *The default installation page*

If you want to make changes to this page, follow these steps:

**1.** Select the Copy Files and Create Objects for the Selected Components radio button. If this option is not selected, software will not be installed and NDS objects will not be created in the tree. This is enabled by default.

**2.** If you want to load Policy and Distribution Services each time the server is started, check the Modify AUTOEXEC.NCF To Load ZENworks For Servers Components On Startup check box. This is the default.

**3.** If you want the installation to pause and give you the opportunity to unload Java before continuing the install, check the Pause Installation If JAVA.NLM Is Loaded On Target Server check box. This is the default.

If this is not checked, the installation program skips any servers where Java is loaded and does not install Policy and Distribution Services. An error is logged to C:\WINDOWS\ZEN FOR SERVERSSETUP.LOG.

**4.** Select a volume for the database and then click Next. SYS: is not recommended because the database file can become large. It is used for logging report information on Server Policies and TED usage.

**5.** To define the Distribution routes, click the Distributor in the Distribution Routes box, click a Subscriber in the Subscribers box, and then click Add.

This page is where you create the routes that the Distributions will follow to get from a Distributor to an end-node Subscriber. A route represents the most efficient path to any given segment of your WAN. The route is a list of Subscribers that relay a distribution to other Subscribers. Subscribers can minimize the workload for the Distributor by being able to pass on Distributions.

**TIP**

**To create the Distribution routes, consider your WAN design and the number of Subscribers on each LAN, and build the routing table to mimic your network topology. If your test system does not have a WAN, make sure that you implement the parent Subscriber functionality by having one Subscriber assigned as a parent so that you can verify your routing goals and design.**

You can select to move multiple Subscribers at a time. You do not need to move all Subscribers to the Distribution Routes box, just the ones that you want to use as intermediaries to pass distributions on to other subscribers.

You can also define distribution routes by clicking Subscribers in the Distribution Routes box and adding subscribers below them.

**6.** Repeat Step 5 until you have structured the routing table to include all desired paths that the distribution will take to get to all the subscribers in your WAN.

**TIP**

**The routing table can be modified after installation by modifying the properties of each Distributor object.**

**7.** When you finish moving Subscribers, click Next.

**8.** Click Add to create at least one Channel. You can name your Channels according to the Distributions you intend for them. However, for testing purposes, you can simply name the Channels by appending sequential numbers to each Channel.

If you are installing multiple Distributors, they can all use the same Channel for their Distributions. You may want to create several Channels. In ZEN for Servers2, Distributors do not own Channels, and Subscribers can receive Distributions from any Distributor through any Channel that a Subscriber is subscribed to. All these channels should be created in the same container, such as TED.for_Server.ZENworks.

**9.** Click Next when you finish creating Channels. The Distributor Object page is displayed next and is shown in Figure 19.37.

**FIGURE 19.37** *The Distributor Object page*

## Configuring the Distributor Objects

To configure the Distributor objects, do the following:

**1.** To configure the same attributes for all Distributors, select multiple Distributors and then change any of the attributes displayed. Use Shift or Ctrl to select multiple servers.

**2.** To change the OU for the Distributor that is displayed, click the server's name in the left list box and browse for a container. Locate and select the OU for the Distributor. For example, TED.for_Servers.ZENworks. If you have multiple Distributors, be sure to select the correct OU for each. You can click the browse button to the right of the OU field to select an OU.

**3.** To change any attributes for any of the Distributors from those displayed, click a Distributor and then change any of the attributes displayed.

**4.** Repeat Step 3 for each Distributor, as needed.

**5.** Click Next when you finish configuring the Distributors. The Subscriber Object page is displayed next and is shown in Figure 19.38.

**FIGURE 19.38** *The Subscriber Object page*

### Configuring the Subscriber Objects

Follow these steps to configure the Subscriber objects:

**1.** To configure the same attributes for all Subscribers, select multiple Subscribers and then change any of the attributes displayed.

**2.** To select the OU for a Subscriber object, click a Subscriber's name in the left list box and then browse for a valid container name. For example, locate and select the TED.for_Servers.ZENworks OU for the Subscriber object. If the OU field is disabled, that means the Subscriber's OU was established when you selected the OU for a Distributor on that server.

3. Repeat Step 2 for each Subscriber or set of Subscribers until they all have the correct OUs assigned.

4. To change the attributes for any of the Subscribers from those displayed, select multiple Subscribers and then change any of the attributes displayed.

5. Repeat Step 4 for each Subscriber or set of Subscribers where you want to create specific attributes.

6. To assign a parent Subscriber, select from the drop-down list box. Parent Subscribers serve two purposes:

   • To minimize WAN traffic. If all Subscribers on the other side of a WAN link from the Distributor have the same parent Subscriber, a Distribution crosses the WAN link once.

   • To minimize the Distributor's workload in sending Distributions. A Distributor needs to send a Distribution on to only a few parent Subscribers that in turn can send the Distribution to many other Subscribers.

7. For each Subscriber that you want to receive Distributions from a parent Subscriber rather than directly from the Distributor, click the down-arrow on the Parent field and then select a Subscriber. You may want to leave one Subscriber without a parent Subscriber so that you can see how that relationship works.

8. To associate each Subscriber to a Channel, select a Subscriber and then check all boxes for the Channels from which you want this Subscriber to receive Distributions, as shown in Figure 19.39.

   All available Channels are displayed with disabled check boxes. Checking a Channel's check box enables the Subscriber to receive all of the Distributions associated with that Channel.

9. Repeat Step 8 for each Subscriber.

10. When finished configuring Subscriber objects, click Next. The Summary page is displayed.

11. Review your selections and then click Finish. The installation program now copies files and installs the ZEN for Servers objects.

You have now completed the installation of ZEN for Servers Policy and Distribution Services; proceed with the section "Setting Up Policy and Distribution Services."

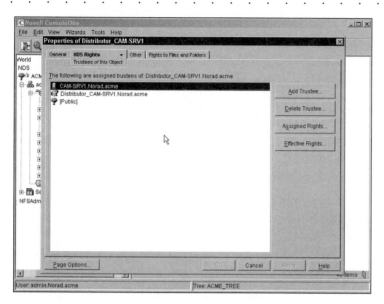

**FIGURE 19.39** *Associating a subscriber to a channel*

### Installing ZEN for Servers Locally to a Windows NT Server

If you do not have NDS for NT installed to the Windows NT server, you must install ZEN for Servers locally on the NT machine. If NDS for NT is not installed, a SYS Share must be set up and the installation run locally.

Follow these steps to install ZEN for Servers locally:

1. If you have not installed the JRE1_1_8 from the ZEN for Servers Companion CD, do so now.

2. Insert the ZEN for Servers Software CD in the CD drive of the Windows NT server. The startup screen appears. If the startup screen is not automatically launched after inserting the CD, you can launch it by running WINSETUP.EXE at the root of the CD.

3. On the ZEN for Servers Software CD, click ZENworks for Servers ⇨ Install Policy and Distribution Services.

4. If you agree with the license agreement, click Accept ⇨ Next.

**5.** Browse and select the tree to which you will be installing and then click Next.

**6.** Click Next on the Licenses page. Do not check the Install Licenses check box.

**7.** Click the Subscriber column for Local Machine and then click Next.

**8.** Click Next without making any changes to this page to accept the defaults. You want to accept the defaults here so that the proper files will be copied. You can customize these settings when you do a full deployment to your production environment.

**9.** Click Next to skip adding Channels.

**10.** To select the OU for the Subscriber object, browse for a valid container name. For example, locate and select the TED.for_Servers.ZENworks OU for the Subscriber object.

**11.** As needed, change any of the attributes that are displayed. You can select a parent Subscriber and make Channels associations after installing.

**12.** When you finish configuring the Subscriber object, click Next. The Summary page is displayed.

**13.** Review your selections and then click Finish. The installation program now copies files and creates the ZEN for Servers objects.

## Setting Up Policy and Distribution Services

Before ZEN for Servers Policy and Distribution Services can begin to perform distribution and management functions for your servers, you must create and configure the NDS objects in ConsoleOne. These objects include Server Policies and Packages, Server Software Packages and Components, and TED objects.

To set up ZEN for Servers for your system, complete the following procedures:

▶ Creating and Configuring the ZENworks for Servers Policy

▶ Creating and Configuring the License Location Policy

▶ Creating and Configuring the Search Policy

▶ Creating and Configuring the ZENworks Database Policy

▶ Configuring the Remote Web Console

▶ Starting the ZEN for Servers Java Processes

### Creating and Configuring the ZENworks for Servers Policy

Follow these steps to configure the required attributes for the ZENworks for Servers policy:

1. In ConsoleOne, click through the NDS tree structure to access a Policies container object.

2. Right-click the Policies container and then click New ⇨ Policy Package. The Policy Package Wizard opens.

3. Under Policy Packages, select Server Package and then click Next.

4. Name the package and then click Next ⇨ Finish to create the package. You can accept the default name of Server Package.

5. Right-click the Server Package and then click Properties ⇨ Policies ⇨ General ⇨ NetWare.

6. Click the box under the Enabled column for the ZENworks for Servers policy to enable it.

7. Click the ZENworks for Servers policy name and then click Properties.

8. Click the ZENworks for Servers tab and then enter a console prompt on the Configuration page. You may customize the prompt using plain text and/or variables. The default is as follows:

   `%SERVER_NAME% - ZEN for Servers>`

   You can use any of the predefined or user-defined variables.

9. Enter a working path. This is for the Server Policies temporary and backup files. SYS:\SMANAGER\WORKING will be created if you do not enter a working directory. We recommend that the working directory not be on the SYS: volume.

10. To determine how old database information should be before it is purged, enter the number of days and then click OK. All ZEN for Servers information older than the number of days entered will be purged when ZEN for Servers is running on the same server where the database file resides.

**WARNING**

**The database can be purged only if the Policy Package component (ZEN for Servers agent) is installed on the same server where the Sybase database is located.**

**11.** Click Associations ⇨ Add, and then browse back up to the ZENworks container. Click OK.

**12.** Click Associations ⇨ Add, and then browse to an OU containing servers running ZEN for Servers (Policy Package) Java processes. Click OK.

**13.** Repeat Step 11 and Step 12 for each OU containing servers running ZEN for Servers (Policy Package) Java processes.

**14.** Click OK to close the Server Package Properties page.

**15.** Repeat Step 1 through Step 14 for each Policy container in the tree.

### Creating and Configuring the License Location Policy

Policy and Distribution Services uses the NLS licensing model. The License Location policy is part of the Service Location Package. Each time a Distributor or Policy Package agent (ZEN for Servers agent) is loaded, it checks the License Location policy for the location of the nearest NLS License object.

Follow these steps to create and configure the Service Location Package and the License Location policy:

**1.** In ConsoleOne, click through the NDS tree structure to access the Policies container object where you will create a Service Location package.

**2.** Right-click the Policies container and then click New ⇨ Policy Package. The Policy Package Wizard opens.

**3.** Under Policy Packages, select Service Location Package ⇨ Next.

**4.** Name the package and then click Next ⇨ Finish. You can accept the default name.

**5.** Right-click the package you just created and click Properties.

**6.** Select ZENworks for Servers License Location Policy.

**7.** Check the Enabled check box to enable the license and select Properties. You can accept the default name.

**8.** Click the Browse button to the right of the ZENworks License DN field; then browse to the NLS Policy object to find the NLS License object created when you installed Policy and Distribution Services. Click OK twice.

**9.** To associate the Service Location Package, click the Associations tab, click Add, and then browse to the parent container to the OUs containing servers running ZEN for Servers Java processes and OUs containing Distributor objects. Select these containers and click OK.

**10.** Click Apply ⇨ Close.

### Creating and Configuring the Search Policy

The Search policy determines how a tree is read to locate effective policies. The ZEN for Servers agent uses it to locate all effective policies. The Distributor agent uses it to locate the ZEN for Servers License policy.

Follow these steps to configure the required attributes for the Search policy:

1. In ConsoleOne, click through the NDS tree structure to access the Policies container object where you will create a Search policy.

2. Right-click the Policies container and then click New ⇨ Policy Package. The Policy Package Wizard opens.

3. Under Policy Packages, select Container Package ⇨ Next.

4. Name the package. Click Next ⇨ Finish. You can accept the default name of Container Package.

5. Right-click the Container Package. Click Properties ⇨ Policies.

6. Click the box under the Enabled column for the Search policy to enable it.

7. Click the Search policy name ⇨ Properties ⇨ Search Level.

8. To determine the upper limits of the search policy, select Object Container from the drop-down list. This sets the search to the parent container of each server object.

9. Click Refresh Interval. Set an interval and click OK. This tab contains the frequency with which the ZEN for Servers agent rereads the DS for changes to existing policies and for new policies. The refresh interval should reflect how often you expect to be adding and modifying policy packages.

10. Click Associations ⇨ Add.

11. Browse to the parent container to the OU containing servers running ZEN for Servers Java processes and OUs containing Distributor objects. Select these containers and click OK.

12. Repeat Step 1 through Step 11 for each container containing servers running ZEN for Servers Java processes.

13. Click Apply ⇨ Close.

### Creating and Configuring the ZENworks Database Policy

Follow these steps to create and configure the ZENworks Database policy:

1. In ConsoleOne, click through the NDS tree structure to access a Policies container object.

**2.** Right-click the Policies container and click New ➪ Policy Package. The Policy Package Wizard opens.

**3.** Under Policy Packages, select Service Location Package ➪ Next.

**4.** Name the package. Click Next ➪ Finish. You can accept the default name of Service Location Package. You can also use the existing Service Location Package created when you configured the ZEN for Servers License Location policy.

**5.** Right-click the Service Location Package and click Properties ➪ Policies.

**6.** Click the box under the Enabled column for the ZENworks Database policy to enable it.

**7.** Click the ZENworks Database policy name ➪ Properties ➪ ZEN for Servers Database.

**8.** Click the Browse button to the right of the ZEN for Servers Database DN. Browse for the ZEN for Servers Database object. Click OK ➪ Apply ➪ Close. This object was created during install and is located in the same container as the server object on which you installed the database. For example, the Database object might read:

```
ZEN for Servers Database.Chicago.XYZCorp
```

**9.** To associate the Service Location Package, click the Associations tab and then click Add. Browse to the parent container to the OUs containing servers running ZEN for Servers Java processes and OUs containing Distributor objects. Select these containers, click OK, click Apply, and then click Close.

You may have already performed this association when creating the NLS License Location policy.

### Configuring the Remote Web Console

To configure the Remote Web Console (RWC), follow these steps:

**1.** Map a drive to the SYS: volume of the server where RWC was installed.

**2.** Browse to the SYS:\JAVA\LIB directory.

**3.** Create a text file named NSSL.PROPERTIES, containing the following line:

```
nssl.keystore = SSL_Certificate_object_name
```

Make sure you use a space before and after the = symbol. For example:

```
nssl.keystore = SSL CertificateIP - server_name
```

where *server_name* is the name of the server as displayed in ConsoleOne for the SSL Certificate name.

The SSL Certificate object is created automatically when SSL is installed and is located in the same container as the Server object.

**4.** Save the NSSL.PROPERTIES file to the SYS:\JAVA\LIB directory.

For instructions on using the Remote Web Console, refer to Policy and Distribution in your Novell online documentation.

### Starting the ZEN for Servers Java Processes

Follow these steps to start the ZEN for Servers (Policy Package) Java processes:

**I.** At the main console prompt of each server where the Server Policies component was installed, start the ZEN for Servers policies Java process by entering:

```
SYS:\SMANAGER\ZEN FOR SERVERS.NCF
```

If the ZEN for Servers Java process does not load, the ZEN FOR SERVERSINIT.TXT file (under SYS:\SMANAGER) contains information about what happened. This file is used to log ZEN for Servers information until ZEN for Servers reads NDS to know where and at what level the information should be logged to ZEN FOR SERVERSLOG.TXT (or whatever you have named the log file in the ZENworks for Servers policy).

 **IMPORTANT** **You should include the full path to the Java process the first time you run it. This sets the path during the current session for restarting the Java process. After you have started the Java process for the first time using the full path, or you have rebooted the server, you need to type only the Java process's name, such as DIST, at the server console prompt to restart a Java process during a session.**

**2.** At the Distributor server's main console prompt, start the Distributor's Java process by entering the following:

```
SYS:\TED2\DIST.NCF
```

This process also creates the security certificates for the Distributor that are used by any Subscribers that will receive Distributions from the Distributor.

See "Sending Your First Distribution" in your Novell online product documentation to complete setting up ZEN for Servers Policy and Distribution Services.

## Sending Your First Distribution

The purpose of this section is to help you create and send your first Distribution. To send your first Distribution, perform the following procedures:

- Configuring Subscriber Properties
- Scheduling the Channel
- Creating a Distribution Object
- Configuring the Distribution
- Sending the Distribution

### Configuring Subscriber Properties

Follow these steps to configure the Subscriber properties:

1. In ConsoleOne, right-click a Subscriber object and click Properties.
2. Click Channels ⇨ Add. Browse for the Channel and click OK. Make sure the Channel is listed as Active in the Channels list.
3. Click the Schedule tab. Click the arrow for the drop-down box. Click Run Immediately ⇨ OK. This schedule type causes the Subscriber to extract the Distribution as soon as it is received.
4. Repeat these steps for each Subscriber in your test system.

### Scheduling the Channel

Follow these steps to schedule the Channel:

1. In ConsoleOne, right-click the Channel object and click Properties.
2. Click Schedule. Click the arrow for the drop-down box. Click Interval and make the interval every 5 minutes. Click OK. This causes the Distributor to send the Distributions that are in the Channel every five minutes.

### Creating a Distribution Object

Follow these steps to create a Distribution object:

1. In ConsoleOne, right-click the container where the TED objects were created. Click New ⇨ Object ⇨ TED Distribution ⇨ OK.
2. Enter a Distribution name.
3. To give the Distributor ownership of the Distribution, browse and select the Distributor object.
4. Check Define Additional Properties and click OK.

### Configuring the Distribution

The following steps assume that you selected to define additional properties for the Distributor object when you created it in the "Creating a Distribution Object" section.

Follow these steps to configure the Distribution:

1. Click the Agent tab.

2. In the Agent Type field, click the arrow for the drop-down list and select File Agent.

3. Click the New Target button.

4. In the Text field that is created, replace %DEST_VOLUME% with SYS: and then press Enter. Be sure to press Enter, or your change will not be made.

5. Click the Add Folder button. Enter Test1 as the folder name and press Enter. Be sure to press Enter, or your entry will not be made.

6. Click the Add Files button, double-click the server's SYS: volume to browse the volume, locate and click the \README directory, click Select, and then click OK.

7. Click the Channels tab and then click Add.

8. Browse to select the Channel created during installation. Click Select ➪ OK.

9. Click Schedule. Click the arrow for the drop-down list. Click Run Immediately. This causes the Distributor to gather (or build) the distribution as soon as it rereads the Distribution information from NDS.

10. Click OK and then click Yes (to resolve certificates). This copies the security certificates from the Distributor to the Subscribers that are subscribed to the Channel. For more information on certificates, see "Policy and Distribution Services" in your Novell online product documentation.

### Sending the Distribution

Follow these steps to send the Distribution:

1. Make sure all NDS replicas are in sync on your test tree.

2. At the main console prompt of each server where a Subscriber was installed, start the Subscriber's Java process by entering the following:

```
SYS:\TED2\SUB.NCF
```

On a Windows NT server, change to the SYS Share directory (created by the NDS for NT installation). Change to the TED2 directory and run SUB.BAT.

**3.** At the console prompt of the Distributor server, enter the following:

REFRESH

This causes the Distributor to reread NDS and get all of the changes that were made in NDS.

The building of the Distribution happens immediately (per the Distribution's schedule), and the Distribution is in five minutes (per the Channel's schedule). You already set both of these schedules in earlier steps.

As soon as the Subscriber receives the entire Distribution, it extracts the contents to the Test1 subdirectory that you previously specified.

You are now ready to use your ZEN for Servers test system. For instructions on using ZEN for Servers, see "Policy and Distribution Services" in your Novell online product documentation.

## Summary

This chapter has presented the basics of using ZENworks for Desktop and ZENworks for Servers with NetWare 6. We have discussed installation of the ZENworks components, including the creation of workstation objects to manage desktops and application objects to manage your NDS applications. NDS provides a powerful system for delivering applications to your users, managing their desktops, and managing your servers.

# Understanding and Using Novell's iFolder and eGuide

**N**ovell's iFolder allows mobile users the ability to access files flexibly and securely via a Web browser. Novell's eGuide enables you to search any directory (via LDAP) for content information. This chapter discusses installation and use of both iFolder and eGuide.

Novell iFolder enables you to create and publish a personal folder on a Novell iFolder server. You can then download and install the Novell iFolder client on every computer you use regularly. Novell iFolder also ensures that the latest version of your files is always where you need it, when you need it. These files are secure and hidden from all except you, on the server and over the wire. Novell iFolder is software that simplifies, accelerates, and secures access to your data across the Internet. There has never been an easier way to manage your data.

When you install the Novell iFolder client on your clients, the contents of your personal iFolder exist both on the Novell iFolder server and on these client computers. Each client basically subscribes to your published iFolder. Novell iFolder automatically and transparently updates the contents of your personal iFolder between the server and all of the subscribing computers.

You access and manage your personal iFolder from these subscribing computers just as you access and manage any folders located on these computers' hard drives.

IFolders are accessible even when you're not using one of your own computers. Through the use of a Java-enabled browser you can access and manage your personal iFolder files.

## Installing Novell iFolder on NetWare 6

Novell iFolder uses the Apache Web server version 1.3.20. The Apache server uses port 80, which is also the same port that NetWare Enterprise Web server (the default NetWare Web server) uses. In order to run the Apache Web server, you must unload the NetWare Enterprise Web server before you can install iFolder.

If you want to run both the Apache Web server and the NetWare Enterprise Web server, you must set the secondary IP address prior to the iFolder installation and assign either the Apache or Enterprise Web server to that secondary IP address. To install iFolder, perform the following steps:

1. On your workstation, map a Novell drive to the SYS: volume on the server where you plan to install iFolder and Apache.

**NOTE** Apache must be installed on the **SYS:** volume.

2. Locate the iFolder software that you downloaded from your product CD-ROM and double-click the iFolder Apache server executable (ApacheiFolderServer.EXE) for NetWare. An example of the install screen is shown in Figure 20.1.

**FIGURE 20.1** *The install screen for the Apache iFolder Server*

3. Read the Welcome screen and click Next.
4. Click Yes to accept the licensing agreement.
5. Enter your username and the name of your company, and then click Next.
6. Browse to the drive letter that you mapped in Step 1 and then click Next.

**TIP** In order to install Novell iFolder on multiple servers from the same workstation, you must delete the directory that represents your last installation. To do this, go to C:\Program Files\Installshield Installation Information. If you have multiple directories, look at their creation timestamps and delete the one that was created at the time that you performed your last installation. After you delete this directory, you should be able to install Novell iFolder on another server from the same workstation.

If Apache is already installed on your server, the iFolder install shield asks you to choose one of the following options (as shown in Figure 20.2) and then click Next:

▶ Overwrite the existing Apache installation on your server and install Apache *and* iFolder.

▶ Leave the existing Apache installation on your server and install only iFolder.

▶ Exit the install.

**FIGURE 20.2** *Apache Install Options*

If you chose to overwrite an existing Apache installation, or if Apache is not installed on your server, you are prompted to enter the DNS name of the server, the IP address of the server, and your e-mail address, and then click Next.

**1.** Enter the IP address of your LDAP server in the LDAP Host field.

**2.** Enter the LDAP port you want to use. An example of this is shown in Figure 20.3.

If you are using port 389, the LDAP Group object must be marked to Allow Clear Text Passwords. To verify this, launch ConsoleOne and locate the context where your server resides, right-click the LDAP Group object, click Properties, and make sure the Allow Clear Text Passwords check box is checked, as shown in Figure 20.4.

**FIGURE 20.3** *Apache configuration screens*

**FIGURE 20.4** *Verifying that the LDAP group object allows clear text passwords*

Choose port 636 if you want to use SSL, which provides your network with encryption and security when data is transferred across the wire. If you choose port 636, make sure you have copied the ROOTCERT.DER file from your LDAP server's SYS:PUBLIC directory to your iFolder server prior to the iFolder installation.

If you have chosen port 636, enter the path to the LDAP Root Certificate. This is the path to the place where you copied the ROOTCERT.DER prior to the installation.

Enter the LDAP login DN context. This is the context of the container where your User objects are located. iFolder enables you to enter multiple contexts. After each context, insert a semicolon. Do not put any spaces between the contexts. An example of entering multiple contexts is shown in Figure 20.5.

**FIGURE 20.5** *Entering multiple contexts where user objects are located*

If you want iFolder to search all subcontainers below the specified LDAP login DN context, make sure you check the Subcontainer Search check box.

If you are doing a subcontainer search, you must assign the CN property to the Public object or create an LDAP proxy user.

---

**Consulting Experience**

Any rights assigned to the Public object are automatically inherited by all other objects in the NDS tree. You might not want to assign the CN property to the Public object if these rights will cause a security risk. If your iFolder server is outside the firewall and you do not want the CN property assigned to all objects in your NDS tree, you can also use an LDAP Proxy Username to search the subcontainers of your tree.

---

To assign the CN property to the Public object, follow these instructions:

1. Launch ConsoleOne.
2. Right-click your NDS Tree object and then click Properties.
3. Click NDS Rights ⇨ Public object ⇨ Assigned Rights ⇨ Add Property.
4. Check the Show All Properties check box, select the CN property from the list, and then click OK. See Figure 20.6 for an example.

**FIGURE 20.6** *Assigning rights to Public for all users*

5. Check the Inheritable check box. Then click Apply.
6. Click Apply and then click OK.

To create an LDAP proxy user, follow these instructions:

1. Launch ConsoleOne.
2. Create a user without a password.
3. Right-click your NDS tree object and then click Properties ⇨ NDS Rights ⇨ Add Trustee.
4. Browse to your NetWare server, select the LDAP Group object, and click Apply ⇨ OK. An example of this is shown in Figure 20.7.

**FIGURE 20.7** *Creating an LDAP proxy user*

**When you add this user as a trustee of the tree, just accept the default Browse, Compare, and Read rights.**

TIP

5. Right-click the LDAP Group object and then click Properties ⇨ General.

6. Click the Browse button next to the Proxy Username field and browse to the user to whom you just gave trustee rights.

7. Double-click the user so that the name appears in the Proxy Username field.

8. Click Apply and then click OK.

9. Click Next in the iFolder setup.

10. If you are using a secondary LDAP server, enter the LDAP information for that server.

11. Fill in this information only if you have two LDAP directories that contain usernames that need iFolder accounts. For example, suppose you have one LDAP directory that contains all your employee usernames and another LDAP directory that contains all your vendor usernames and you want the users from both directories to have iFolder accounts. You would enter the information for a secondary LDAP server.

**12.** Enter the path to the directory where you want the iFolder user data to be stored on the server.

**13.** Enter the names of all the administrators who need rights to modify iFolder user account information via the Server Management Console, and then click Next.

**14.** If you are entering more than one name, separate the usernames with a semicolon. For example, if you wanted users alincoln and admin to have rights to administer the Server Management Console, you would enter:

```
alincoln;admin
```

**15.** If prompted, enter the IP address or the DNS name of your server and then click Next.

**16.** Click Finish to complete the installation.

You can then do one of the following:

▶ If you are using only one IP address, to start Novell iFolder, you can reboot your server (this runs the edited AUTOEXEC.NCF) or enter the following commands at the server console:

```
search add sys:\Apache
search add sys:\Apache\iFolder\Server
STARTIFOLDER
```

▶ If you are using two IP addresses, edit the AUTOEXEC.NCF file and enter the following lines after the search add sys:\Apache\iFolder\Server command line:

```
set command line prompt default choice=on
set command line prompt time out=60
```

Also enter **?** in front of the STARTIFOLDER command line.

After you edit the AUTOEXEC.NCF, to start Novell iFolder, you can reboot your server (this runs the edited AUTOEXEC.NCF) or enter the following commands at the server console:

```
search add sys:\Apache
search add sys:\Apache\iFolder\Server
STARTIFOLDER
```

Novell iFolder is now installed on your NetWare 6 server. To learn more about Novell iFolder, go to the "Using iFolder" section.

## Client Installation Instructions

Install the iFolder Client on every computer that you use regularly. From a browser, go to the URL of the Web server where iFolder is installed (get this from your network administrator) and download the iFolder client (IFOLDERCLIENT.EXE) to a temporary directory.

Go to the temporary directory, double-click IFOLDERCLIENT.EXE, and follow the onscreen instructions.

1. Reboot your computer if it is running Windows NT or 2000.

2. If your computer is running Windows 95 or 98, click the check box next to Start iFolder and continue with Step 4.

3. Click Continue after reading the short introductory message to iFolder.

4. Enter your user ID and password.

5. Your user ID and password will be the same as your network user ID and password.

6. Click the Login button.

7. Click OK to place a shortcut to your personal iFolder files on your desktop.

8. When you install the iFolder client, a personal folder is created for you on the hard drive of your computer and the iFolder Web server. By default, this personal folder is installed in C:\Program Files\NovelliFolder.

9. Enter your pass phrase and confirm it.

   This phrase is used to create the encryption keys that are used when files are uploaded or downloaded between your computer and the iFolder server. This encryption occurs on your computer, which means that you can store your confidential files on an untrusted server and you can protect your iFolder files on your hard drive from being accessed by someone other than you.

After iFolder is installed, an icon representing your personal iFolder files appears on your desktop. This is where you will keep all the files that you want to share among your multiple computers.

## Using iFolder

A few important tasks are associated with your personal iFolder files. By right-clicking the iFolder icon that appears on the system tray of your workstation, you can do the following tasks:

### Log In and Log Out

You can be logged in to only one iFolder server at a time. To log in, right-click the iFolder icon in your system tray and then click Login. To log out, right-click the iFolder icon and then click Logout. An example is shown in Figure 20.8.

**FIGURE 20.8** *iFolder login*

### Synchronize Your Files

The iFolder client lets you specify how often you want the changes that you've made to your personal iFolder files uploaded to the iFolder server. To set these parameters, right-click the iFolder icon on your system tray and then click Account Information ⇨ Preferences as shown in Figure 20.9. To implement the changes, click Apply.

You can instantly synchronize your files by right-clicking the iFolder icon and then clicking Synch Now.

**FIGURE 20.9** *Synchronizing your files*

## View Your Account Information

Double-click the iFolder icon in your system tray. The Account Information screen captures all the activity occurring between your iFolder server and your iFolder clients. See Figure 20.10.

**FIGURE 20.10** *Viewing account information*

## Access iFolder through a Browser

You also have the option of accessing your iFolder account through a Web browser. This means that from a browser you can see your personal iFolder files that are located on the iFolder server, access them, and make changes to them. In fact, you don't even need the iFolder Client installed on the workstation; you need only an Internet connection.

With iFolder Web access, you have the flexibility to download only the files that you need instead of the whole directory. It also frees you from becoming dependent on a certain computer to access your files. With the iFolder Web access, you can get to your files from any computer that has Internet access.

To access your iFolder files through a Web browser, follow these steps:

1. Open a browser and go to the URL of your iFolder Web server (get this URL from your network administrator).

2. Click Login.

3. Enter your username, password, and pass phrase, and then click Connect.

When you are logged in, you see your personal iFolder files. See Figure 20.11. They appear in a directory structure. To expand the folder and view the files, double-click the Home folder.

**FIGURE 20.11** *Logging in to iFolder via a Web browser*

From the browser, you can download and upload files to the server or delete, create, and rename them. Only the changes are then uploaded to the iFolder Web server and synchronized out to all the other computers where you have the iFolder client installed.

### View Your Account Information

Double-click the iFolder icon in your system tray. The Account Information screen captures all the activity occurring between your iFolder server and your iFolder clients.

### Managing Novell iFolder Accounts

After Novell iFolder is installed and running, you have access to the following two Web sites:

▶ The default iFolder Web site at `www.yoursite.com`.

▶ The Server Management Console at www.yoursite.com.

The default iFolder Web site contains the *iFolder Client Quick Start Guide* and other important information about Novell iFolder. It is also where users will download the iFolder client and access their iFolder files via a browser. You can modify this page to fit your company's internal needs. To access the default iFolder Web site, enter the IP address or the DNS name of your server into a browser.

The Server Management Console lets you manage your users' iFolder accounts. From this site, you perform administrative tasks and manage the activity between the server and the iFolder clients. The Server Management Console URL is case sensitive. Access the Server Management Console by opening a browser and entering

```
https://ifolderserverip/iFolderServer/Admin.
```

## Using the Server Management Console

In order to access the iFolder user account information, you must log in to the Server Management Console with your administrative username and password. After you are logged in, you can view and modify iFolder accounts as well as set specific policies for your iFolder clients and server.

You can perform the following tasks in the Server Management Console:

▸ View general server information

▸ View LDAP settings

▸ View user account information

As an administrator, you can remove a user account, change a user's disk storage quota on the iFolder server, and set specific policies for individual users. Use the following menu options to perform this activity:

▸ View iFolder client connections

▸ Configure user policies

You can determine what policies will be applied to the iFolder clients. For example, you can enforce policies so that your iFolder users do not have the option to change them. You can also hide certain iFolder client options. For example, if you enforce and hide the option to request encryption of the iFolder data, the data will be encrypted and the user will be unaware of the transaction. Things that are hidden do not appear in the iFolder client dialog boxes.

### Configure server policies

You can regulate server behavior, such as how much disk space will be allotted to each iFolder client or how much time will pass before a session times out. To perform server functions, see the following sections.

#### Removing an iFolder Account

Follow these steps to remove an iFolder account:

**1.** Click User Accounts.

**2.** Select the user ID that you want to remove and then click Remove.

### Restoring a User's Folder

Follow these steps to restore a user's folder:

1. At the Server Management Console, click User Accounts.
2. Roll your mouse over the user's ID and look at the ID that appears in the bottom of your browser.
3. Restore this folder from a backup tape to a secondary iFolder server that the user can attach to and restore the files.

### Changing LDAP Settings

In order to change LDAP settings in either NetWare 6 or Windows NT 4/2000, follow these paths:

- **NetWare 6** — Modify the HTTPD_NW_ADDITIONS.CONF file located in SYS:Apache\iFolder\Server directory.
- **Windows NT 4/2000** — Go to the registry ⇨ HKLM ⇨ System ⇨ CurrentControlSet ⇨ Services ⇨ W3SVC ⇨ iFolderServer.

### Optimizing Your iFolder Server

You can optimize the performance of your iFolder server by taking the following steps:

- Add more RAM to your server.
- Increase the threads. (This applies to only Apache Web Servers running on NetWare.)

  For optimal performance, one thread per client is recommended; however, in terms of scalability, iFolder has been tested up to 25 clients per thread.
- Change the amount of disk space allotted to your iFolder users. Be careful; allotting large amounts of disk space to users could decrease the iFolder server's performance.
- Change the default sync delay parameters to much higher numbers if you have thousands of users and you need to improve the iFolder server performance. Otherwise, use these current defaults:
  - 5-second delay after file activity
  - 20-second delay after server polling interval
- To improve performance, make the following changes:
  - 30-second delay after file activity
  - 1-minute delay after server polling interval

# Novell's eGuide Installation and Use

Novell's eGuide is a Web-based application that lets users query a variety of data sources and retrieve information about other users. Novell eGuide can run on any server with Java 1.1.4 or higher. Novell recommends that you install the latest Java virtual machine available from your browser vendor.

When combined with NDS eDirectory, your organization can implement a complete out-of-the-box address book solution. By leveraging the user information stored in NDS eDirectory, you do not need to enter address book information into a separate application or database. With an intuitive and easy-to-use interface, users can create their own eGuide profiles containing their personal preferences.

Based on open standards, the default protocol used to retrieve user information is Lightweight Directory Access Protocol (LDAP), which gives users access to multiple public directories that exist on the Internet today.

Novell eGuide is a Web-based application that makes it easy for users to search multiple directories for other users. It is very easy to install, configure, and administer. The following is a list of some of eGuide's features:

- 100% Web-based.
- Compatible with any Java 1.1-compliant browser.
- For basic functionality, does not require users to install anything on the client. Novell eGuide is delivered to users through the browser.
- Comprised of HTML and Java applets. Both the client and server pieces run on all platforms that have a Java 1.1 virtual machine. Tested platforms include Windows 95/98, Windows NT, Linux, and Solaris.
- Installs and configures in minutes.
- Architecture based on open protocols.
- LDAP protocol supported out of the box.
- Requires no directory schema modifications.

eGuide is configurable by both end-users and administrators. Administrators can create default profiles (directories and authentication information) that are available to all users. In addition, users can create their own graphical look by selecting themes and adding their own directories. Organizations can create their own themes, complete with their own logos.

**Consulting Experience**

If you are upgrading an existing eGuide installation and you have configured that installation using property files (as explained in the section "Configuring the Novell eGuide Server," later in this chapter), make sure you back up those property files before completing the installation procedure below. After completing the installation procedure, you can restore the property files to preserve your previous configuration.

eGuide retrieves information from multiple directories and merges the information into a single view. Each entry indicates which directory it came from. eGuide also displays query results as soon as they begin to come in. As more results come in, they are added to the view.

This product also integrates with popular messaging platforms. For example, you can send an e-mail message to a user by clicking his or her e-mail address. If an AOL screen name exists for a Novell eGuide entry, you can send an Instant Message simply by clicking the AOL screen name.

## Product Requirements

Novell eGuide requires a server (such as NetWare, Solaris, Linux, or Windows NT) with the following installed:

- Web server
- Java 1.1.4 (or later) virtual machine
- LDAP server

You can download a Java virtual machine from the Sun Java Technology site or from the Microsoft Web site.

## Installing Novell eGuide

Follow these steps to install Novell's eGuide:

1. Download eGuide from Novell's Web site at www.Novell.Com/downloads.
2. Make sure your Web server and LDAP server are up and fully functional.

**3.** The LDAP server must be accessible to the Web server. Typically, it will be on the same machine as the Web server, but this is not required.

**4.** If you will install the product to a NetWare server, map a drive to the root of the SYS: volume.

**5.** Extract the eGuide files that you downloaded and then run the installation executable file.

**6.** Follow the instructions on the screen to complete the installation.

The eGuide server files are copied to a directory named SERVER off of the primary installation directory (the HTML documents directory).

After the installation is complete, the default LDAP server to be searched will be the server that the eGuide server was installed on. To change this server, edit the ABSERVER.PROP file in the directory where you installed the eGuide server. For detailed information on this and other configuration options, see the section "Configuring the Novell eGuide Server," later in this chapter.

### Starting the eGuide Server, by Platform

The following are instructions on how to start the eGuide server after this installation completes. See the appropriate section, depending on which platform you are using.

#### NetWare

At the server console prompt, type **eGuide** and then press Enter. Note that an EGUIDE.NCF file is placed in the SYS:SYSTEM directory on the NetWare server during installation.

#### UNIX/Linux

**1.** At the console prompt, change to the eGuide server directory (HTMLDOCS/SERVER).

**2.** Type **chmod +x eguide.sh**.

**3.** Type **./eguide.sh** and then press Enter.

#### Windows

**1.** At the DOS prompt, change to the eGuide server directory (HTMLDOCS/SERVER).

**2.** Type **eguide** and then press Enter.

**Consulting Experience**

You will be prompted for a Primary Installation Directory. This directory is the directory to which the HTML documents will be installed. This directory must be accessible from your Web server and will become the root of the eGuide Web page. If this directory does not already exist, you will be prompted to create it.

## Using eGuide to Look up Someone

Type in a portion of someone's last name and click the search button. By default, anyone whose last name starts with the text you entered will be found. If photos exist in the directory, they are displayed in the eGuide detail frame.

▶ Experiment with searches. You can search for people by a variety of attributes. For instance, you can look up people by Last Name, First Name, Company, and so on. You can also include qualifiers such as STARTS WITH, CONTAINS, and ENDS WITH. Click on any of the down arrow buttons to get to the selection qualifier menus. An example of this is shown in Figure 20.12.

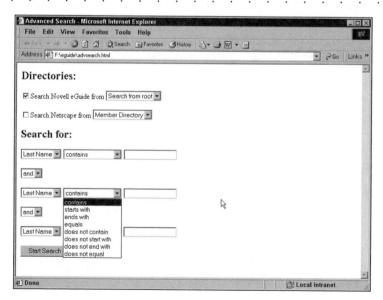

**FIGURE 20.12** *Doing a search with eGuide*

▸ Change the look of the eGuide interface. Click the settings button and select the themes tab. Next, select the look you desire. Choose from Connecting Points, Japan, or Novell. Click OK and the new theme takes effect. It is also easy to create your own themes with Novell eGuide.

▸ Get Addressbook system information. Click on the settings button and then select the System Information tab. You can see a variety of information about your local machine and the machine on which the eGuide server is running.

▸ Login to the eGuide and update your information. If you know your username and password, click on the Login button and enter them. Click login. You see a "Me" entry in eGuide. Click on the Edit button in the "Me" detail page. Add, Delete, or Change your information and click update. This updates your information on the eGuide LDAP server.

▸ Add a new data source. If you know of an LDAP accessible directory on the Internet, you can have eGuide search it. Click on the settings button and select the Data Source tab. Next, click the New button. Enter the information for the LDAP directory you want to add and click OK. Your next search includes the directory you just entered.

## Configuring the Novell eGuide Server

Novell eGuide is easy to configure to meet the needs of your organization and to optimize performance. You configure eGuide by editing the following property (.PROP) files in a text editor, such as Notepad. Some of the property files have variables in their names relating to language or IPaddress.

▸ ABFILTER.PROP

▸ ABSERVER.PROP

▸ ATTRMAP-RESOURCES-*language*.PROP

▸ LDAPSEARCHKEY-*language*.PROP

▸ ATTRMAP.PROP

▸ ABFILTER.PROP

You can define which attributes your users will see in the entries they find with an eGuide search. A list of the attributes that will be filtered by Novell eGuide is found in the ABFILTER.PROP file. In other words, an attribute listed in ABFILTER.PROP will *not* be displayed by eGuide. This file is located where the

Novell eGuide server was installed. The contents of the file might look like this:

```
objectClass=true
objectclass=true
networkAddress=true
groupMembership=true
uid=true
privacylevel=true
objectClass=true
```

**1.** To modify the ABFILTER.PROP file, follow these steps:

**2.** Open the file in a text editor.

**3.** To filter out an attribute, type the name of the attribute and then type **=true**.

**4.** Save the file.

### ABSERVER.PROP

You can set up additional LDAP directories that can be accessed by your users through eGuide. This is done with settings defined in the ABSERVER.PROP file. The ABSERVER.PROP file contains the following settings:

```
MailFromAddress=user@domain.com
MailHost=mail.domain.com
MailUser=anonymous
MailPassword=nothing
ProtocolsKey=LDAP
#DefaultContextKey=
AuthenticationServerKey=localhost
#BlockFunctions=login,settings,mail,instantmessage,netmeeting,
export,help
AuthenticationNamingAttribute=cn
searchObjectClass=inetOrgPerson,person
NamesReturnIncrement=50
MaxPhotos=1
MaxPhotoSize=250K
```

Each setting defines a specific operation of eGuide. For example, the ProtocolsKey defines the protocol used (LDAP).

To add a new directory, simply add a new directory section to the file:

**1.** Open ABSERVER.PROP in a text editor.

**2.** Copy the attributes from an existing book.

**3.** Fill in the attributes with values. (See the attribute explanation earlier in this section.)

**4.** Save the file.

### Authentication Settings

Three of the keys in the ABSERVER.PROP properties file are used for user authentication. The advantage of authentication is that it allows users' preferences to be stored in the directory so that the preferences will be used each time the user logs in.

In order to enable authentication, you must extend the schema in NDS to add the preferences attribute, and then create an LDAP mapping for that attribute. After completing those tasks, you can use the new preferences attribute to define the PrefsAttrKey in the ABSERVER.PROP file. To extend the schema, follow these steps:

**1.** In ConsoleOne, select the NDS tree whose schema you want to extend, and then click Tools ⇨ Schema Manager.

**2.** Click the Attributes tab, and then click Create ⇨ Next.

Type a name in the Attribute Name field. (You can type any name you like, but remember this name must match the PrefsAttrKey in the ABSERVER.PROP file.)

**3.** Leave the ASN1 ID field blank.

**4.** Click Next and then select Stream for the Attribute Syntax.

**5.** Click Next ⇨ Next ⇨ Finish.

**6.** Click the Classes tab, and then select a User object.

Click Add, and then select the attribute you just created from the Available Attributes list. Click the right-arrow to add the attribute to the User object.

**7.** Click OK and then click Close.

To create an LDAP mapping for the attribute, follow these steps:

**1.** In ConsoleOne, select the OU object where the LDAP Group object resides, and then double-click the LDAP Group object.

**2.** Verify that Allow Clear Text Passwords is checked. This setting must be turned on if you want to use authentication for any LDAP servers that your users will access.

**3.** Click the Attribute Map tab and then click Add. The Attribute Mapping dialog box appears. Next, follow these steps:

   **a.** Select the preferences attribute that you already created from the drop-down list and then type a name for the LDAP class.

   **b.** Click OK ⇨ OK.

   **c.** Exit ConsoleOne.

The following keys can be used to define server preferences or to set up a default context in eGuide:

- **AuthenticationServerKey** — Defines the server to which your users will be able to log in and have their preferences saved.

- **DefaultContextKey** — Defines the context in which your users reside on the server specified with the AuthenticationServerKey. If this key is blank or commented out, users will be presented with the context browser.

Directory Definition Settings

- **BookNameKey=eGuide List** — The name of the book, as it is displayed in Settings ⇨ Data Sources in eGuide.

- **BookProtocolKey=ldap** — The protocol key.

- **BookServerKey=255.255.255.255** — The IP address of the server.

- **BookSearchBaseKey=o=novell** — You can make users log in to a data source and provide a password through this key.

- **BookUserNameKey=** — The username used to log in to the data source.

- **BookPasswordKey=** — The password used to log in to the data source.

- **BookSearchSubsKey=true** — Search all subcontainers for the criteria specified.

- **BookSearchActiveKey=true** — Search the key of focus within the book.

- **BookMaxEntriesKey=1000** — Defines the maximum number of hits eGuide returns. This number can also be defined at the LDAP server itself. If the LDAP server is defined to return fewer entries than the eGuide configuration, the LDAP setting overrides the eGuide configuration.

- **searchObjectClass=inetOrgPerson,person** — Defines the object class to search on.

### Personal Information Layout Settings

System administrators can customize the Edit Personal Information dialog box. They can choose which attributes get edited, which editors get used, the heights of the fields, the widths of the fields, and the order of fields. This is defined in EDITLAYOUT-EN-US.DEF in the LANGUAGES directory off the root of where the server is installed. This is a language-related file because the field labels need to be localized for each language.

Below is a sample extraction from the default EDITLAYOUT file that is shipped with eGuide:

```
General
Photo:|PHOTO|PhotoEditor|true|500|8|
Given Name:|FIRSTNAME|TextField|true|120|1|
Initials:|INITIALS|TextField|false|30|1|
Description:|DESCRIPTION|TextArea|true|300|3|
Contact
```

Phone #s: |PHONE|MultiTextField|true|220|1| Two types of entries appear:

▶ Section entries

▶ Field entries

Section entries are just text. In the Personal Information dialog box, these appear as section headings with an underline, which sets them apart with the fields below.

Field entries are for editing users' attributes. They have the following format:

▶ Label text

▶ Attribute mapping name (as defined in ATTRMAP.PROP in the root of the eGuide server directory)

▶ Edit control type; the types are:

   • TextField

   • MultiTextField

   • TextArea

   • PhotoEditor

▶ Whether or not this field is to start a new line (true or false)

▶ The width of the field in pixels

▶ The height of the field in lines (based on the font at runtime)

► The size of the dialog box adjusts dynamically to fit the height and width of the layout within certain reasonable limits and bounded by the screen resolution at runtime.

More editors will likely be added in the future.

### Function Blocking Settings

The system administrator can block certain functions from being available in eGuide. If these functions are blocked, the corresponding button does not appear on the toolbar; menu items in pop-up menus are not added; and mouse clicks, highlights, and key combinations that may otherwise expose the functionality are hidden. The configuration of this blocking is done in the ABSERVER.PROP file as just another entry in the header. The format of the line is the following:

```
BlockFunctions=login, netmeeting, etc.
```

The seven functions that can be blocked and their exact wording are the following (case doesn't matter):

► login

► settings

► mail

► instantmessage

► netmeeting

► export

► help

More flexibility will be forthcoming with future releases of eGuide.

### Directory Edit Panel Blocking Setting

Some companies may feel that the ability for users to define their own Directory Search Definitions (accessed via the first tab in the Settings dialog box) may be too complex for their users and may just want to allow such configurations to be done by the system administrator. If this is the case, you can prevent that capability from being exposed to users by setting the AllowDirectoryEdit field in ABSERVER.PROP. The default installation sets it to True.

### E-mail Information Settings

Novell eGuide has the ability to send system information via e-mail for support purposes. To expose this functionality, the following keys in the ABSERVER.PROP file must be set with valid values. The shipping ABSERVER.PROP file includes placeholder values for these keys. They are as follows:

```
MailFromAddress=user@domain.com
MailHost=mail.domain.com
MailUser=anonymous
MailPassword=nothing
```

▸ MailFromAddress should be set to an e-mail return address.

▸ MailHost should be set to a valid SMTP host.

▸ MailUser should be set to a generic username that has a valid e-mail account for your organization.

▸ MailPassword should be the mail password for the generic e-mail user.

### Authentication Server Attribute Mapping

For users' Personal Information editing functions to operate properly, you must make sure that you add an entry in the ATTRMAP.PROP file for authentication server. This entry defines attribute mappings to be used for user attributes such as application state and photos.

### Photo Administration Settings

Two administrator definable settings control photos that users may add to their personal profiles. These are both defined in the ABSERVER.PROP file in the eGuide server directory. The two entries are MaxPhotos and MaxPhotoSize.

▸ MaxPhotos defines the maximum number of photos that a user may store in his or her profile.

▸ MaxPhotoSize defines the maximum size of stored photos. The value is defined in bytes by default but can contain an appended K or M, which specifies kilobytes and megabytes, respectively.

As an example, if you wanted to allow a maximum of three photos to be stored with a maximum size of 1 megabyte each, you would enter the following values:

```
MaxPhotos=3
MaxPhotoSize=1M
```

Photos may be stored in the Authentication Server's directory in two ways. The first way is to map the attribute key PHOTO to an LDAP binary attribute. The second way photos can be stored is to store them in a mapped preferences attribute. The preferences attribute is used as a catch-all for any attribute that eGuide has knowledge of but is not mapped by the administrator. Note that on most LDAP servers, binary attributes are single-valued. Because of this, the eGuide server does not allow more than one photo to be stored in a mapped binary attribute. If, however, a photo attribute is not mapped, multiple photos can be stored in the preferences attribute.

### Authentication Server Naming Attribute Setting

Because not all LDAP servers use CN (Common Name) as the naming attribute for user authentication, the eGuide server allows this setting to be overridden. The key that allows for the naming attribute to be overridden is as follows:

```
AuthenticationNamingAttribute=cn
```

For example, if your server's naming attribute is uid, you would enter the following key and value:

```
AuthenticationNamingAttribute=uid
```

Thus, authentication requests sent to the server are in the form of uid=username,ou=xyz,o=organization.

### Search Object Class Settings

Because not all LDAP servers use the same base object for defining user objects, a key in ABSERVER.PROP may be overridden to allow the user to select from a different key. This key is searchObjectClass. Multiple values for this key may be separated by commas. Note that this value, when defined in the main ABSERVER.PROP section, is used only to populate the objectclass menu in the Edit Directory user interface. Administrators can predefine objectClass(es) to search for on a per directory basis by adding this key to a directory definition in the ABSERVER.PROP file. For example, if an administrator wanted to allow users to select from predefined objectClasses of person and inetOrgPerson and set up a predefined search directory that searches for myCompaniesUser, the administrator could add the following to the ABSERVER.PROP file:

```
AuthenticationServerKey=ip-address
SearchObjectClass=person,inetOrgPerson
[myDir]
kNameKey=My Company
searchObjectClass=myCompaniesUser
ld enter the following value
```

### Server Preferences Attribute Setting

For complete eGuide functionality, including the ability for users to change their own personal information, the only attribute that must be mapped is a binary preferences attribute. Some preferences are stored in the form of cookies on the local workstation in the absence of a preference attribute being mapped. Administrators must make sure that an entry for the Authentication Server is in the ATTRMAP.PROP file in the eGuide server directory. The preferences attribute is defined in the Authentication Server attribute mapping entry with a key named ABPREFS. The value of this key is the name of the binary preferences attribute. For example, if an administrator wanted to set up an Authentication Server with an IP address of 137.65.139.111 with a preferences attribute of abprefs, the following entry would need to be added to the ATTRMAP.PROP file:

```
[137.65.139.111]
USERNAME=userName
DN=dn
EMAIL=mail|
ABPREFS=abprefs
```

### ATTRMAP-RESOURCES-*language*.PROP

The ATTRMAP-RESOURCES-*language*.PROP file lets you assign more user-friendly names to attributes. Many attributes are not easily known or guessed by name (such as DN, CN, or IMID).

In this configuration file, you can assign more user-friendly names to these attributes, so that users can understand them more easily. In the example, DN becomes Distinguished Name, CN becomes Network Name, and IMID becomes Instant Messenger ID. For example:

```
#Wed Aug 18 15:34:12 MDT 1999
cn=Network Name
alias=Also Known As
businesscategory=Business Category
seealso=See Also
areaofinterest=Interests
experience=Experience
personalstatement=Personal Statement
favoriteforum=Favorite Forum
INITIALS=Initials
USERNAME=User Name
DN=Distinguished Name
EMAIL=E-Mail Address
INITIALS=Initials
FIRSTNAME=First Name
LASTNAME=Last Name
FULLNAME=Full Name
TITLE=Title
FAX=Fax
```

```
PHONE=Phone
STREET=Street
STATE=State
POBOX=P.O. Box
ZIPCODE=Zip
POSTALADDRESS=Address
CITY=City
COMPANY=Company
LOCATION=Location
DESCRIPTION=Description
COUNTRY=Country
KEYWORDS=Key Words
ABPREFS=Addressbook Preferences
IMID=Instant Messenger ID
HOMEPAGE=Home Page
PHOTO=Photo
NETMEETING=NetMeeting ID
NICKNAME=Nick Name(s)
```

To modify the ATTRMAP-RESOURCES-*language*.PROP file, follow these steps:

**1.** Open the file in a text editor.

**2.** In the line of the attribute to which you want to assign an alternative name, type the alternative name after the equals sign (=).

**3.** Save the file.

The ATTRMAP-RESOURCES-*language*.PROP file also lets you map the definitions of specified attributes to a particular language. The languages are defined in the first lines of the file:

```
es-LanguageKey=Spanish
```

These files are located in the SERVER/LANGUAGES/ATTR-MAP directory. Languages are defined by a two-character code, such as DE for German, JA for Japanese, and so on. Some languages, such as English, have a sub-definition, such as EN - US for U.S. English.

Below the language definitions are the language equivalents for the attributes, listed in the following syntax:

```
attribute=language equivalent
```

For example, the Spanish equivalents for some selected attributes would be as follows:

```
email=email
city=ciudad
phone=telefono
```

To modify the ATTRMAP-RESOURCES-*language*.PROP file, follow these steps:

**1.** Open the file in a text editor.

**2.** To add an attribute mapping, type the name of the attribute mapping, and then type the equivalent of the attribute in the specified language.

**3.** Save the file.

### LDAPSEARCHKEY-*language*.PROP

When users submit a query to the server for a search, eGuide must convert this query into search keys that the server will understand. These search keys are defined on Novell eGuide in the LDAPSEARCHKEY-*language*.PROP file. For example, in the file example below, the default attribute default=) represents the attribute that is initially selected for qualified searches. This is initially set to surName.

```
####
#
#   The key is the LDAP name and the value is the UI String
#
#   Every attribute in this list is searchable, to remove
#   or add an entry will remove or add that entry to/from
#   the searchable attributes.
#
####
default=surName
surName=Last Name
givenName=First Name
mail=E-Mail
description=Description
title=Title
cn=Common Name
keywords=Keyword
```

For example, when a user starts a search by Last Name, eGuide reads the LDAPSEARCHKEY-EN-US.PROP file for a server equivalent to Last Name and finds the following line in the file:

```
surName=Last Name
```

It converts the Last Name part of the query into *surName=query value* and sends it to the LDAP server, which interprets it, searches for it, and returns it to eGuide, which in turn reconverts the attribute into Last Name.

To modify the LDAPSEARCHKEY-*language*.PROP file, follow these steps:

**1.** Open the file in a text editor.

**2.** In the line of the attribute to which you want to assign a search key to the server equivalent, type the new search key after the equals sign (=).

**3.** Save the file.

### ATTRMAP.PROP

You can modify the ATTRMAP.PROP file to map attributes by the IP Address of a directory. This file contains the mappings for all IP addresses. These IP address mappings are separated by .INI style headers.

Often, attribute names are not consistent across LDAP servers. Novell eGuide uses standard attribute keys that provide consistency across directories. These keys cannot be changed. The value (to the right side of the equals sign) should be replaced with the actual attribute name for the specified directory. If one server calls one's last name surName, another calls it Name, and a third calls it LASTNAME, you can set up a ATTRMAP.PROP file for each LDAP server and modify a line to state that for entries coming from each server

```
surName=Last Name
Name=Last Name
LASTNAME=Last Name
```

where Last Name is the eGuide attribute for Last Name. This way, the last name of each entry will be displayed with the Last Name attribute, regardless of what it is called in the originating LDAP server.

For example,

```
[127.0.0.1]
PHOTO=photo
USERNAME=userName
DN=dn
EMAIL=mail
INITIALS=initials
FIRSTNAME=givenName
LASTNAME=sn
FULLNAME=fullNam
TITLE=title
FAX=facsimileTelephoneNumber
```

```
PHONE=telephoneNumber
STREET=street
STATE=st
POBOX=postOfficeBox
ZIPCODE=postalCode
POSTALADDRESS=postalAddress
CITY=physicalDeliveryOfficeName
COMPANY=ou
LOCATION=l
DESCRIPTION=description
KEYWORDS=keywords
ABPREFS=abprefs
#COUNTRY=c
#IMID=
#HOMEPAGE=
#NETMEETING=
#NICKNAME=
[Next IP ADDRESS]
PHOTO=picture
USERNAME=uid
DN=dn
EMAIL=electronicmailaddress
INITIALS=in
FIRSTNAME=firstName
LASTNAME=lastName
FULLNAME=myname
TITLE=title
FAX=faxnumber
PHONE=telNumber
STREET=street
STATE=st
POBOX=box
ZIPCODE=zip
POSTALADDRESS=address
CITY=city
COMPANY=company
LOCATION=site
DESCRIPTION=description
KEYWORDS=keywords
ABPREFS=userpreferences
COUNTRY=country
IMID=aolscreenname
```

```
HOMEPAGE=homepage
NETMEETING=netmeetingid
NICKNAME=alias
```

To modify the ATTRMAP.PROP file, open the file in a text editor. To enter an attribute of the server, type the attribute name, type =, type the attribute name to which you want to map the other server's attribute, and then save this file.

## Automating Novell eGuide with JavaScript

You can automate, or script, some behavior of eGuide within your HTML document using the JavaScript APIs that ship with eGuide. To include the APIs and make them accessible, you need to add the following statement to your HTML:

```
<SCRIPT SRC="eGuide.js"></SCRIPT>
```

This is about a 2 KB file. If you want only a subset of the APIs, you are free to edit that file and remove the APIs that you don't need. If you do so, and you are using APIs that return a result, you should not remove the following two first lines (which allow results to get easily passed back):

```
var egRetValue = "";
function egResult(retValue) {egRetValue = retValue;}
```

The APIs are the following:

- ▸ enableDirectory(dirName)
- ▸ disableDirectory(dirName)
- ▸ disableAllDirectories( )
- ▸ enableAllDirectories( )
- ▸ setDirectoryName(dirName, name)
  - • Example: "Netscape Member Directory", "Netscape"
- ▸ setDirectoryHostName(dirName, hostName)
  - • Example: "Netscape", "memberdir.netscape.com"
- ▸ setDirectoryMaxEntries(dirName, maxEntries)
  - • Example: "Netscape", "1000"
- ▸ setDirectorySearchBase(dirName, searchBase)
  - • Example: "Novell", "ou=people,o=novell"
- ▸ setDirectoryUserName(dirName, userName)
- ▸ setDirectoryUserPassword(dirName, password)

- setDirectorySearchSubContainers(dirName, searchSubContainers)
  - Example: "Novell", "true"
- startSearch(filter)
  - Example: "(surname=jack*)"
- isDirectoryEnabled(dirName)
- isSubContainerSearchOn(dirName)
- getDirectoryMaxEntries(dirName)
- getDirectoryHostName(dirName)
- getDirectorySearchBase(dirName)
- getDirectoryUserName(dirName)
- getDirectoryPassword(dirName)

## Client Configuration Options

The following are client configuration options. For additional client configuration and usage information, see the online help.

### Cookies

The following Novell eGuide settings are saved as a cookie:

- **Theme Selection** — If the user changes a theme, the next time he or she runs eGuide, that theme will be the default theme.
- **Directory State** — If the user adds his or her own directory entries via the Settings dialog box, all of that information is saved in a cookie and the next time eGuide is run, all of that information is restored, except for the password. The user needs to retype the password every time he or she reloads eGuide. However, if the user logs in to eGuide, all of this information is stored in the directory, including the password, and that user never needs to type it in again.

Any predefined directory that comes from the network always takes precedence over information a user may have in the cookie. For example, if an administrator defined a Directory in ABSERVER.PROP that has a Maximum Search Entries of 1000, but the user changes it to 500, the next time the user runs eGuide, that value comes from the network and is restored to 1000. However, the one exception is the active state of the directory. If a user toggles a directory active state as On or Off, the next time he or she runs eGuide, it defaults to what the user last chose, even if the definition in the network has a different default.

### Photos

Users can upload their photos into the directory by logging in and clicking the Edit Personal Information button in the Details View. A photo editor enables users to add, edit, remove, and swap photos. The supported image formats are GIF, JPEG, and Windows Bitmap (noncompressed, using the RGB color model). The system administrator can configure the size limit and number of photos limit that users are allowed to upload to the directory.

The Add button lets users browse to an image file either on the local hard drive or on a mapped network drive. eGuide copies the selected file into the directory, at which point it becomes visible in the Details View to anyone who looks that user up.

- ▶ The Remove button removes the photo from the directory.
- ▶ The Edit button enables users to change the selected photo.
- ▶ The Swap button lets users change the order of photos.

### Name Display Order

For the Name List, you can choose whether or not you want last or first names to appear first. You can do this by right-clicking the Name header bar of the Name List and selecting from the two-item pop-up menu. If you select to view by first names first, the list still sorts by last names.

### Object Class Selector

In editing the definition of Directories, you can specify which object classes are to be searched. This allows three capabilities:

1. The ability to make accurate name mappings tailored to your installation and configuration of LDAP (for example, in some companies, InetOrgPerson may be mapped to people; others may have different mappings).

2. The ability to look for any object (you are not limited to just people; you can look up virtually any type of conceivable object in your directory, such as printers, volumes, and so on).

3. The ability to look up multiple object types simultaneously.

Most of the user interface to eGuide is focused around presenting and editing users and user information. So, if you look up a printer, you currently cannot edit the printer's properties and many of the values in the second column of the name list do not have values.

If you don't specify an object class, it defaults to looking up all objects of every class in the given directory as the specified searchbase.

## Summary

This chapter has covered the installation and use of Novell's iFolder and eGuide products. With iFolder, you can access your files from any location, simply by using a Web browser. With eGuide, you can search Novell's eDirectory or any LDAP server for directory information. You can search user information, send messages, and do advanced queries on valuable directory-stored information.

# Novell Storage Services (NSS)

**N**ovell Storage Services (NSS) enables you to attach very large storage systems to NetWare 6. It installs on a NetWare server as a set of NLM programs. NSS is ideal for systems with large files and volumes or large numbers of volumes, directories, and files. NSS allows up to an 8 Terabyte file size and holds up to 8 trillion files on any NSS volume. You can also mount up to 256 NSS volumes on a server. To accomplish this, NSS uses a 64-bit interface to all storage systems. In contrast, a NetWare server without NSS using the traditional NetWare file system can support only a 32-bit interface that allows hard disk storage of up to 2GB, up to 16 million directory entries per volume, and up to 64 volumes per server.

NSS and the traditional NetWare file system run side-by-side. You can create up to 64 NetWare volumes or 256 NSS and NetWare volumes combined, including SYS. As an administrator, you decide how the volumes are deployed as long as you have at least one NetWare volume called SYS on each server. NSS is also now the default method for mounting CD-ROMs as volumes, offering much faster access to individual and multiple CD-ROM drives installed in CD-ROM towers.

Having NSS support very large storage systems is extremely useful for Web and database applications. During testing of NSS, a volume with a billion files was successfully created with three name spaces loaded. This demonstrates that the file system can support three billion directory entries on a single NetWare volume.

In addition to larger volumes and more files, NSS supports much faster volume mount times. A normal NSS volume mounts in less than one second regardless of size or number of files stored. If the NetWare server abends and the volume is not dismounted cleanly, when the server is brought back up, the volume is restored and mounted in 15 seconds to 1 minute. This is the case for all NSS volumes on the server. The traditional NetWare FAT-based file system is organized so that volume mount time increases with the number of files and their size.

The total amount of server memory required to support NSS is 8MB. Although this is the minimum memory requirement, NSS is capable of mounting any size volume or any number of volumes in 1MB of memory. This fact basically eliminates the need for any complicated server memory calculations.

Even though NSS has many new features, it is also completely compatible with the traditional FAT-based file system. The server volumes running NSS look the same as the traditional FAT-based volumes to the workstations and users. In addition, NSS has been built to support NetWare 4.11, NetWare 5, and NetWare 6. NSS automatically detects which of these two operating systems it is running on and loads the appropriate supporting NLMs for that server.

· · · · · · · · · · · · · · · · · · · · · · · ◄

# Benefits and Advantages of NSS

The following describes the major benefits or advantages that Novell Storage Services (NSS) offers. The benefits and advantages are as follows:

- The capability to store larger files (up to 8 terabytes).

- The capability to store large numbers of files on an NSS volume (up to 8 trillion).

- The capability to have up to 1,000,000 files open simultaneously.

- Rapid access to data regardless of file size. Any size file can be opened in the same amount of time.

- The capability to mount many NSS volumes on a server — up to 256 depending on the NetWare Loadable Module and physical limitations.

- NSS volumes that mount and verify themselves rapidly. Any size volume can be recovered and mounted in under a minute if cleanly dismounted.

- NSS reduces data recovery time after a file system crash. Instead of scanning an entire volume for corruptions, NSS quickly replays the latest set of changes to make sure they are written correctly, and brings the NSS volume back online shortly.

- Full CD-ROM support for ISO9660 and Macintosh HFS formats that includes automatic mounting using CDROM.NLM. The new CDROM.NLM along with NSS makes mounting your CD-ROM much faster and easier.

- DOS FAT partitions that can be made available dynamically as NSS volumes.

- The capability to mount NSS volumes with only 1MB available RAM.

- The capability to define name spaces (in addition to DOS, Macintosh, LONG, and UNIX/NFS).

- NSS uses a smaller amount of space to support name spaces because multiple name spaces share the same storage space. In contrast, the traditional NetWare file system creates individual name space storage for each name space in an object's name. For example, the traditional NetWare file system can support up to 16 million directory entries. But each name space requires an entry on the volume for each file. So if you have four name spaces, your traditional NetWare file system maximum is 4 million files. In NSS, the maximum number of files is 8 trillion regardless of how many name spaces are loaded.

▶ The capability to define new media formats through the Loadable Storage Subsystem (LSS) interface. Future formats could include Universal Digital Format (UDF) for use with Digital Video Discs (DVD) and others.

▶ The capability to store a large object or large numbers of objects without degrading system performance. No matter how large a volume, directory, or file is, NSS still performs well.

## Advantages Over the NetWare File System

NSS and the traditional NetWare file system differ in structure and behavior. Table 21.1 is a synopsis of the advantages and differences between NSS and the traditional NetWare file system.

TABLE 21.1

Advantages and Differences between Novell Storage Services and the Traditional NetWare File System

| TOPICS AND FEATURES | NETWARE FILE SYSTEM | NOVELL STORAGE SERVICES |
|---|---|---|
| Backup | Uses TSA, SMS, and Enhanced SBACKUP. | Larger files (over 2 GB) need the current version of TSA (TSA600) shipped with NetWare 6. SMS and Enhanced SBACKUP are supported. |
| CD-ROM support | Used old CD-ROM.NLM with slow indexing and manual mounting. | New CD-ROM.NLM that mounts CD-ROMs immediately. Supports both ISO9660 and Macintosh HFS formats. |
| Characters used | ASCII double-byte. | UNICODE. Allows for more complete internationalization |
| Data access/ volume mount time | If a server goes down, data may take hours to repair and retrieve. | If a server goes down, NSS volumes recover and mount quickly for faster file retrieval. |
| Directory tree depth | Allows 100 directory levels. | Limited only by the workstation client that runs the directory structure. |
| DOS FAT partitions | Supported. Can't be added as a mounted volume. | Anyone who has NetWare administrator rights can mount a DOS FAT partition as an NSS volume. Java programs can access DOS FAT partitions. |

| TOPICS AND FEATURES | NETWARE FILE SYSTEM | NOVELL STORAGE SERVICES |
|---|---|---|
| Extended attributes | Supports 16 attributes and 10 data streams. | Unlimited. |
| Files | 32-bit file system that limits a file's size to 4 GB. Supports up to 16 million files per server. Allows 100,000 open files per server. | 64-bit file system that allows a file size up to 8 Terabytes. Supports up to 8 trillion files per volume (depending on file size, the limit in data capacity is 8 Terabytes). Allows 1,000,000 open files per server. |
| Objects (volumes, files, etc.) | Object size is limited. Number of objects is limited. | Can handle almost any size object. Can handle almost any number of objects. |
| Retrieve deleted files | SALVAGE turns on or off for the whole file system. | SALVAGE can be turned on or off at the NSS volume level or for the whole file system. |
| Resource use | More memory may be needed as the network grows. | Memory and disk space usage are improved. Software needs no more RAM than what NetWare requires. In fact, NSS requires only 1-8MB. |
| Storage administration | Provides storage capacity limited by physical storage on a device. May require you to administer volumes from several geographical locations. May require you to configure storage for one device at a time. | Provides more storage availability (not limited to free space on one physical device). Recognizes space on various devices for storage pools so that free space is not wasted. Administers NSS volumes from one location even though the NSS volumes reside on different devices. Configures many devices from one storage pool. |
| Volumes | Supports up to 64 mounted volumes. Supports up to 8 segments or 8 volumes per partition. Supports 1 Terabyte volume size. | 256 volumes can be mounted and visible to existing clients simultaneously. No limit on volumes per partition. Supports an 8 Terabyte volume size. |

# NSS Server Requirements

NSS requires the following:

▶ A server running NetWare 5 or NetWare 6.

▶ A minimum of 11MB space free for an NSS volume. If you have only one hard drive and you did not allocate enough free space in your NetWare partition and NetWare volume for NSS, reconfigure your drive to allow the required 10MB space.

▶ 1.5MB minimal memory (300 cache buffers) for installing or loading the modules.

▶ 2MB memory (500 cache buffers) for testing of NSS volumes.

▶ 8MB memory (2,000 cache buffers) for running NSS in production.

When NSS loads, it typically consumes 10 percent of the cache buffers by default, so you need to make sure that you have sufficient cache buffers before you create any NSS volumes. If the NSS modules load and consume more cache than the NSS default, NSS compensates for it by raising or lowering the cache buffers. For more information about view and managing cache buffers, see the "Set the NSS Cache Buffers Commands" section, later in this chapter.

## Loading NSS

If the NSS modules are not currently running, you can enter the following command at the server console:

```
LOAD NSS
```

In NetWare 6, the NSS modules are loading automatically and by default. During installation, the NSS NLMs or modules are copied to your DOS partition and the server's SYS:SYSTEM. If you have already loaded NSS, you do not need to load it again unless your server goes down.

After the NSS modules are installed and loaded and you configure NSS (create your storage pools and NSS volumes), your NSS volumes are ready to use.

You may need to mount an NSS volume before you can use it. In order to mount a newly created NSS volume, enter the following command at the server console:

```
MOUNT VOLUME_NAME
```

Where VOLUME_NAME is the name of the new NSS volume. You can also use the MOUNT ALL command at the server console, if preferred. If you use the MOUNT ALL command, you see the new NSS volume and an additional NSS_ADMIN volume that is a read-only volume, containing configuration information describing NSS objects.

**NOTE**    **CD-ROMs recognized by NSS are mounted automatically. In NetWare 6, this occurs when the NetWare 6 version of the CDROM.NLM is loaded. The CD and CD-ROM utilities used in previous releases of NetWare are no longer supported.**

## Configuring NSS

The NSS configuration process, prepares blocks of storage so that files created in or moved to NSS can be located easily. Hard disk space on any number of storage devices can be fully optimized. Unused free space that exists on all hard disks and NetWare volumes on your server can be combined into a storage pool and then used to create NSS volumes. This pooling enables you to have better control of your unused storage free space. NSS can even use any free space that is available on your SYS: volume.

In order to configure and manage NSS, you can use ConsoleOne and NSS Disk Management on either the NetWare server or your workstation. The first step when using ConsoleOne and the NSS Disk Management tool is to select an NDS tree and server. Figure 21.1 shows how you select the NDS tree and server using ConsoleOne.

In previous versions of NetWare, you could use the NWCONFIG and an NSS Menu utility to manage NSS. In NetWare 6, the NWCONFIG and NSS Menu utility are no longer supported. In NetWare 6, ConsoleOne is the only supported utility for NSS.

**FIGURE 21.1** *You need to use ConsoleOne and the NSS Disk Management tools to configure and manage NSS.*

## NSS Components

During file system operation, the traditional NetWare file system makes use of NetWare partitions, volumes, directories, and files. On the other hand, NSS makes use of NSS partitions, storage groups or pools, NSS volumes, directories, and files. Before you start the configuration of NSS on your server, you need to understand the NSS components that are used. The first step in understanding and using NSS is to understand components and new terms that are used for NSS. The following is a list of components in NSS:

▶ **Storage Deposit** — The free space on the server is called storage deposit. In NSS, it is identified by an NSS provider and deposited in the NSS object bank.

▶ **Object Bank** — The object bank is responsible for registration of storage managers and storage data objects. Storage free space is recognized by NSS and deposited into the object bank for NSS use.

▸ **Storage Pool** — The storage pool is the free space that is gathered from various media and that is deposited in the object bank. Free space from the pool can be owned by NSS and used to create storage groups and NSS volumes.

▸ **Storage Group** — The storage group is a pool of storage free space that represents logical space owned by NSS. After free space is claimed by NSS, the free space becomes a managed object that can be divided into other storage groups and NSS volumes.

▸ **NSS Volume** — A NetWare volume that has been created and owned by NSS.

▸ **NSS Admin Volume** — The NSS Admin volume is a read-only volume that is automatically created when a storage group and NSS volume are created on a NetWare server. This volume contains a dynamic list of objects that NSS uses. It cannot be deleted.

Figure 21.2 shows how the NSS Disk Management tool in ConsoleOne enables you to view the NSS components for the hard drives in the server.

**FIGURE 21.2** *Using ConsoleOne and the NSS Disk Management tool, you can manage many NSS functions on the server's hard drives.*

## Storage Deposits and Object Banks

NSS scans each of your hard disk devices to find free space for NSS to use and lists the free space as a separate storage deposit. From this pool of storage deposits, you can select how much space you want NSS to claim ownership of. When NSS claims the free space on a device, it becomes an NSS managed object. From NSS managed objects, you can create storage groups and NSS volumes.

In NetWare 6, the hard disk free space is recognized in two forms:

▸ Unpartitioned free space on a hard disk

▸ Available free space inside an existing NetWare volume

We suggest that you do not mix NetWare volume free space with unpartitioned free space when creating your NSS volumes, because unpredictable results may occur. When you create an NSS volume from NetWare volume space, NSS creates an NSS volume within the NetWare volume. When NSS claims ownership of unpartitioned free space, it creates an NSS partition on each device. Figure 21.3 shows how the NSS Disk Management tool in ConsoleOne enables you to view free space on the hard drives in the server.

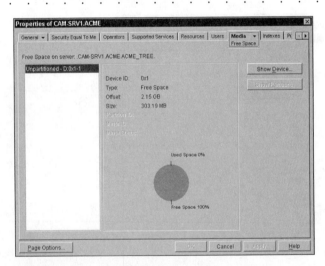

**FIGURE 21.3** *Using ConsoleOne and the NSS Disk Management tool, you can view free space on the server's hard drives.*

---

**Consulting Experience**

IBM partitions defined on hard disks can contain only four partitions. An NSS partition is considered a different operating system type than a NetWare partition. If a disk already contains four partitions, NSS cannot acquire any free space on that disk because it cannot have its own partition. If the number of partition areas exceeds four, an error message appears.

---

NSS can use up to 100 percent of available free space inside a NetWare volume. NSS cannot use free space in a NetWare partition unless the free space is inside an existing NetWare volume. After NSS takes free space out of a NetWare volume and owns it, the traditional NetWare file system recognizes the NSS-owned space as a file. NSS takes the free space in 2 GB segments or less, depending on how much space is available in the NetWare volume. NetWare then acknowledges the reduced amount of free space available in the NetWare volume. With the NSS-owned space, NSS creates an NSS volume within the NetWare volume. Both volumes must be mounted to use the NSS volume.

## NSS Storage Pools and NSS Volumes

After NSS has claimed ownership of free space, you can create NSS volumes and/or storage pools. NSS gives you three ways to create NSS volumes:

- ▶ Automatically creating a single NSS volume comprising all the free space claimed by NSS from hard disk NSS partitions only

- ▶ Manually creating one or more NSS volumes from the list of managed objects

- ▶ Mounting CD-ROMs and DOS FAT partitions as NSS volumes

The option for automatically creating a single NSS volume occurs when you install the NetWare 6 server. All available NSS space can be configured automatically from a pool as a single NSS volume. Figure 21.4 shows how an NSS volume named SYS was created during the NetWare 6 installation. Only unpartitioned free space is used to create a single NSS Volume.

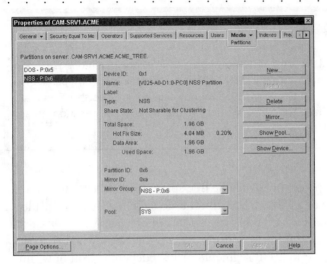

**FIGURE 21.4** *The NetWare 6 installation program automatically creates an NSS volume called SYS.*

Available NSS free space can also be manually divided into one or more NSS volumes. To accomplish this, you first create NSS partitions, storage pools, or NetWare volumes with available NSS space. One or more NSS volumes can be created out of a storage pool. Figure 21.5 shows how you can manually create an NSS volume from unpartitioned free space.

**FIGURE 21.5** *You can manually create another NSS volume from the unpartitioned free space using ConsoleOne.*

When you create NSS volumes, you are setting up access to NSS data. Use the ConsoleOne utility that can be loaded on the server or your workstation to set up new NSS volumes. As mentioned, the NSS providers first scan your devices to find free space for NSS to own, and include any devices that have been hot swapped in and out of the server. For example, one IBM-specific provider searches for free space on devices for IBM partitions. Other providers search for free space on NetWare volumes. Figure 21.6 shows the devices on the server and the free and used space for each.

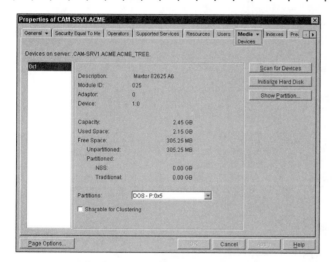

**FIGURE 21.6** *From ConsoleOne, you can see the hardware devices that are currently installed in the server. For each device, you can see the capacity, used space, and free space.*

The provider also deposits free space on storage devices into the object bank. Not all deposits can be used by NSS for data input (such as a Read-Only CD-ROM), but the free space that can be used appears in a managed objects list after NSS takes ownership.

You select assign ownership to have NSS own the available free space you want from the storage deposits. The free space then becomes an NSS partition. When you assign ownership, it means that NSS gathers the amount of free space you designate and initializes it for NSS use.

You choose to create an NSS volume using the free space or unpartitioned space. You select or enter the size you want the volume to be (to create two volumes, you enter an amount less than that shown, so that you have enough space to add the second volume), and name the NSS volume. NSS then creates the NSS volume. You then create the second NSS volume using the same storage group and following the same procedure. Figure 21.7 shows the screen in ConsoleOne that enables you to create a new NSS volume from the free space that is available. The tab that enables you to create a new volume is called Create a New Partition.

**FIGURE 21.7** *Using ConsoleOne, you can create new volumes on your server from free space on the hard drives.*

## CD-ROMs as NSS Volumes

When NSS recognizes free space on the devices attached to your server, it also recognizes CD-ROMs and creates a read-only NSS volume for that CD-ROM. In NetWare 6, this is done automatically when the CD-ROM NLM is loaded. The CDROM.NLM is now an NLM that loads the CD9660, CDHFS, and NSS modules. The CD9660.NSS and CDHFS.NSS modules load the ISO9660 and Macintosh Hierarchical File System (HFS) file formats. This means you can map to both formats from the same client if you have a Macintosh CD drive and an ISO9660 CD drive.

The CD9660.NSS LSS makes the contents of the standard ISO9660 CD-ROM available as a read-only NSS volume. If the CD-ROM is in the drive when CD9660 loads, it mounts as an NSS volume immediately. No longer do you have to wait for lengthy index generations with CD9660 as was done with the previous version of CDROM.NLM. This is also true for the CDHFS.NSS module.

**NOTE**

**The earlier versions of CDROM.NLM should not be loaded when the CD9660.NSS or CDHFS modules are loaded. The previous version of CDROM.NLM is now called CDINST.NLM and is used only for NetWare installation. The CD.NLM module is no longer supported.**

The volume name displayed by the NetWare volumes command is the CD-ROM volume label if one exists. Otherwise, a volume name of the form CDXXXXXX is generated (where X is a number). The behavior of this volume is the same as any other NetWare volume, except that it allows only read-only access.

To load the CD-ROM and NSS modules (CD9660.NSS, CDHFS.NSS, and NSS), first make sure that NSS is loaded, and then launch CD-ROM.NLM at the server console. To load CD9660.NSS alone, enter the following at the server console:

LOAD CD9660.NSS

To load CDHFS alone, enter the following at the server console:

LOAD CDHFS.NSS

To unload these modules, enter UNLOAD CDROM, and enter UNLOAD CD9660 or UNLOAD CDHFS. You can use an earlier version of CD-ROM when NSS is loaded, as long as you do not load the new version of CD-ROM at the same time.

**NOTE**

**CD-ROMs generate NSS volumes and are not added to NDS automatically because the CD-ROM volumes are typically temporary. If you want the CD-ROM volumes added, use ConsoleOne to add them.**

## DOS Partitions as NSS Volumes

When the DOSFAT.NSS module is loaded, DOS FAT partitions are dynamically made available as NSS volumes and mounted. In NetWare 6, the DOSFAT.NSS module is automatically loaded. Having the DOS partition mounted means you can perform tasks such as use DOS commands, change DOS attributes, use NetWare utilities such as the MAP command, access DOS FAT partitions from Java, and access local partitions. The volume name displayed by the NetWare volumes command is DOS-P:X, where X is the hard drive number — for example, DOS-P:0x5, as shown in Figure 21.8.

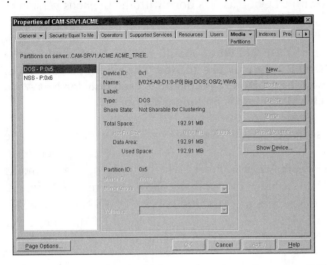

**FIGURE 21.8** *Using ConsoleOne, you can view and mount the DOS partition on your server.*

You can bring the server down and use the DOS label command to rename the volume. The behavior of this volume is the same as with any other NetWare volume, allowing controlled access to the data on DOS FAT partitions.

Some of the benefits provided by the DOSFAT.NSS module are as follows:

▸ **Standard DOS commands** — If you have the proper NetWare rights, you can create or manage files and directories in DOS. You can perform DOS commands such as DIR, COPY, and many others.

▸ **Long filenames as well as DOS filenames for other file systems** — This uses the Windows 95/98/2000 method for placing long names onto a DOS FAT partition.

▸ **NetWare trustee rights** — An administrator with Supervisor rights can only access the DOS volume.

▸ **NetWare utilities** — Any client or server utility that accesses or manages NetWare volumes can do the same with DOS FAT partitions.

▸ **MAP command** — NetWare clients can map to the volume and use it as any other NetWare mapping.

▸ **DOS for Java** — This allows Java programs that run on the server to access DOS FAT partitions.

▸ **Local partition** — This allows access to the local partition.

# Managing NSS

In order to manage your NSS implementation, you can use ConsoleOne and the Disk Management tools. In this section, we review how to manage and change an existing Novell Storage Services configuration for NetWare 6. This section assumes that you have installed a server and created at least one NSS volume. Items that we address in this section are as follows:

- ▸ View and manage NSS pools
- ▸ View and manage NSS volumes
- ▸ Add an NSS volume to NDS
- ▸ Rebuild an NSS pools and volumes
- ▸ Command-line NSS utility at the server console
- ▸ Use In-Place to Upgrade Volumes

## View and Manage NSS Pools

Using ConsoleOne, you can view current NSS pools that have been previously created. Figure 21.9 shows the current NSS pool called SYS using the Disk Management tools in ConsoleOne. This volume was created automatically from the NetWare 6 installation program. Notice that this screen references "Pools on server: .CAM-SRV1.ACME.ACME_TREE."

From the NSS pools screen, you have several options that include add new pools, rename current pools, increase size, deactivate, delete, show segments, show volumes, and more. Because NSS volumes are associated to storage pools, changes to the NSS pools could affect the NSS volumes as well. For example, when you remove a storage pool, any NSS volumes that were created with that pool will also be deleted. If the NSS volume has been added to NDS, it will not automatically be removed if the pool is removed. You must remove the NDS volume object manually.

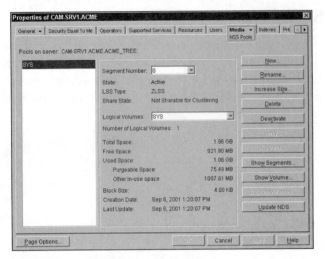

**FIGURE 21.9** *You can view current pools on the server using ConsoleOne. In this case, the volume is called SYS.*

The following includes some of the reasons you might want to make changes to NSS:

▶ When you add a new hard drive, you may want to create a new NSS volume. NSS scans your new devices for free space so that you can create the volume.

▶ You may find that an NSS volume is too small and you need to increase its size. If you create a storage pool and then an NSS volume, you can increase the size of the storage pool while the volume is mounted.

▶ If you do not have enough space to create a new NSS volume, you either have to add a new drive or free up space on one of your existing hard drives. This may include deleting another NSS volume (be sure you back it up first) to free up the space.

▶ If you want to merge two NSS volumes together, create a storage pool and then an NSS volume.

The New button enables you to add new storage pools to NSS. This task is dependent on how much free space is available. If you have no unpartitioned free space, you must free up storage space by adding another storage device, deleting an existing pool, deleting an NSS volume, deleting a traditional NetWare volume, or using free space from an existing NetWare volume. Figure 21.10 shows the new dialog box that appears when you select the new options from the NSS pools screen.

**FIGURE 21.10** *You have the option to define new NSS storage pools to the server with this dialog box.*

The NSS pool screen enables you to grow the capacity of the pool by using the increase size option. Using this feature, you can increase the size of an NSS volume by adding free space to the NSS pool.

The next option available from the NSS pools screen is Rename. If you select the rename option, you are presented with a dialog box that enables you to perform the task. But, first, you are presented with a warning message that indicates that renaming the pools deactivates all logical volumes assigned and closes all open files. Obviously, we recommend that you perform this activity only during off-peak hours when the impact is minimal. Figure 21.11 shows the warning message that appears when you select the rename option for the NSS pools screen. In this case, the pool is called SYS.

Likewise when deleting an NSS pool, you are provided a warning message in a separate dialog box. This message warns you of the impact that will occur if you proceed with the delete. Figure 21.12 shows the warning message that appears during the delete of an NSS pool.

**FIGURE 21.11** *If you choose to rename the NSS pool, you are warned that all logical volumes are deactivated and all open files are closed.*

**FIGURE 21.12** *If you choose to delete an NSS pool from the server, you are presented with a warning message that details the impact of the delete.*

Using ConsoleOne, you can also view the associated segments for the NSS storage pool that has been defined on the server. From the NSS pool screen, you can select the Show Segments button and view the segments. Figure 21.13 shows the segments screen that appears when you select Show Segments. In this case, one segment is associated with SYS.

**FIGURE 21.13** *You can view the segments for an NSS pool by choosing the Show Segments button.*

## View and Manage NSS Volumes

Using ConsoleOne, you can view current NSS volumes that have been previously created. To show the current volumes for the NSS pools screen, you can select the Show Volumes button that appears to the right. Figure 21.14 shows a current NSS volume called SYS. This volume was created automatically from the NetWare 6 installation program. Notice that this screen references "NSS Logical Volumes on server: .CAM-SRV1.ACME.ACME_TREE."

**FIGURE 21.14** *You can view the NSS volumes from ConsoleOne. This option displays information about the NSS volumes, such as the volume name, state, size, creation date, and supported name spaces.*

From the NSS Logical Volume screen, you have several options that include add new volumes, rename current volumes, delete, deactivate, properties, and update NDS. The command line NSS console utility provides a few utilities that ConsoleOne does not support, such as REBUILD or VERIFY. We address the command-line NSS utility later in this chapter.

Using the NSS logical volume screen, you can add new volumes to the server. If you do not have space to create the new volume, you must obtain free space from NetWare, delete another NSS volume or traditional NetWare volume and partition, or add a new hard drive. When you select this option, you need to perform the following steps to add a volume:

1. Enter a name for your NSS volume or accept the default. The default volume name is typically NSS. A maximum of 15 characters is allowed. We recommend that you use the standard NetWare volume naming conventions.

2. Select Yes to confirm your decision and press Enter.

3. Mount your NSS volume.

4. If needed, add your NSS volume to NDS.

After you create the NSS volumes, you can check your NSS configuration. If no NSS volumes appear here, your setup probably was not successful or NSS is not loaded. If your setup was not successful, return to the NSS logical volumes using ConsoleOne and make a quick check to see if something is wrong.

Using ConsoleOne, you can delete an existing NSS volume by selecting the Delete button. This task deletes an NSS volume from a particular NSS pool. You might want to use this option so that the free space from the deleted volume can be added to another NSS volume. Removing an NSS volume destroys the volume and all data in it. After you complete these tasks, free space becomes available to increase another pool or NSS volume. You can also use the free space for a traditional NetWare volume.

Using the ConsoleOne and Disk Management tools for NSS, you can also view traditional NetWare volumes. Traditional NetWare volumes are FAT-based volumes that have been used with previous versions of NetWare. NetWare 6 supports traditional volumes mounted on the server. Figure 21.16 shows the Traditional Volumes screen in ConsoleOne that enables you to view and manage traditional volumes. In this case, the screen is called "Traditional Volumes on server: .CAM-SRV1.ACME.ACME_TREE."

### Consulting Experience

We recommend that before you delete an existing NSS volume from your system that you first make a backup of the data on the NSS volume and verify that it is valid to restore.

In addition to adding new volumes, deleting current volumes, or deactivating volumes, you can use ConsoleOne to view the selected volume's attributes or properties. By selecting the Properties button of the NSS logical volume screen, you can view and set attributes for the volume. Figure 21.15 shows how you can view the current attributes and set new attributes to fine-tune the volume.

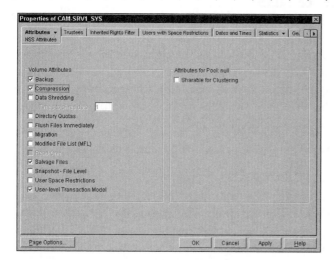

**FIGURE 21.15** *ConsoleOne enables you to view the current attributes or properties for the selected volume. You can also set or change the attributes as needed.*

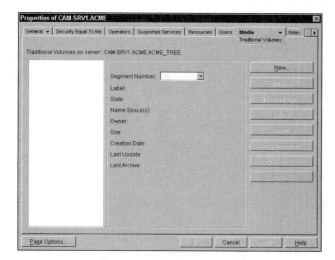

**FIGURE 21.16** *Using the Traditional Volume screen in ConsoleOne, you can view and manage the FAT-based volumes on the server.*

## Add an NSS Volume to NDS

If you do not want to view NSS volumes in ConsoleOne, you may need to add your NSS volumes to NDS and view them using NWADMIN. You can accomplish this task by selecting the Update NDS button on the right side of the NSS logical volume screen. The update NDS option registers the NSS logical volume as an NDS volume object associated to the current server. In most cases, you want to add your NSS volume to the NDS tree. The NSS volumes are automatically added to the NDS tree if the following conditions are met:

1. The NSS volume exists, having been previously created using ConsoleOne.

2. NDS is installed and loaded.

Otherwise, you must add your NSS volume to NDS using NWCONFIG or NetWare Administrator (NWADMIN) manually. This means if you chose to create your NSS volumes using ConsoleOne, you must still use NWCONFIG or NWADMIN to add the NSS volumes to NDS. The following items are instances where you may not want to add an NSS volume to NDS:

▶ You want the NSS volume to be for local server use only.

▶ You created the NSS volume temporarily and you will destroy it soon.

▶ You want to use the NSS volume for test purposes.

▶ You are using a readable CD-ROM and you want to read the NSS volume locally rather than from the network.

When an NSS logical volume is created, the volume automatically registers itself into NDS. You need to use this selection only if there is a problem or the directory was down when the volume was built. Figure 21.17 shows the message that appears when you select the Update NDS button and the volume has already been registered in the directory tree.

**FIGURE 21.17** *You can use the Update NDS button in the NSS logical volume screen to register the selected volume in the directory. However, if the volume had been previously added, you receive this warning message.*

You can verify that the NSS volume has been added to the NDS tree by logging in to the directory and launching NWADMIN. From NWADMIN, select the container object that holds the target server and view associated NSS volumes. If the volume does not appear in NWADMIN, repeat the steps to add the NSS volumes.

If needed, you can add NSS volumes using NWADMIN, instead of ConsoleOne. To add an NSS volume to NDS using NetWare Administrator, first mount your volume, and then do the following:

1. At a Windows client, log in to the directory.

2. Change to directory SYS:\PUBLIC\WIN32.

3. Double-click NWADMIN32.EXE.

4. In NetWare Administrator, place the cursor where you want the NSS volume in the NDS tree.

5. Right-click Create.

6. At the New Object dialog box, select Volume and click OK.

7. At the Create Volume box, perform the following steps:

    a. In the Volume name field, add the NSS volume name, including the server name.

    b. In the Host server, choose the server on which the NSS volume resides.

    c. In the Physical volume field, choose the NSS volume to add.

    d. Click Create.

    You can also remove an NSS Volume from the NDS tree by using NetWare Administrator.

## Rebuild an NSS Volume

NSS volumes do not use the VREPAIR utility as traditional NetWare volumes do. Instead, NSS provides a utility that is used to rebuild corrupted NSS volumes. The Rebuild option from the NSS pools screen salvages the data it finds on a corrupted NSS volume and rebuilds the NSS volume. This option protects against only software failures, not hardware failures.

NetWare users may be used to repairing traditional NetWare volumes with VREPAIR. The VREPAIR utility is used only for traditional NetWare volumes, and the Rebuild option is used only for NSS volumes. It takes much less time to recover an NSS volume than a NetWare volume.

Rebuild verifies and uses the existing leaves of an object tree to rebuild all the other trees in the system. While NSS volumes are being verified and rebuilt, they are placed in maintenance mode. This means the NSS volumes are unusable until this process is finished, and the volume is remounted.

Rebuild also copies rebuild information such as errors and transactions into an error file called VOLUME_NAME.RLF at the root of the SYS: volume on your server. Every time you rebuild a particular NSS volume, the previous error file is overwritten. If you want to keep old error files, move them to another location. You can check the error file whenever an NSS volume will not come up in active mode after a rebuild.

NOTE

**Always back up your data before you perform a rebuild. If an NSS volume becomes corrupted, use the Rebuild option first. You might have to create a new NSS volume or restore your old NSS volume from backup.**

You can rebuild volumes using either ConsoleOne or the NSS command-line utility on the server console. See the next section called NSS Server Command-Line Utility for more details on rebuilding the volumes using the NSS commands on the server console.

## NSS Server Command-Line Utility

In order to fine-tune NSS on each of your servers, you can use the NSS command-line utility that is available on the server console. To view a complete list of NSS commands, enter this command at the server console:

```
NSS, NSS HELP, or NSS/?
```

Figure 21.18 shows an example of the NSS help screen. Before you attempt to use the NSS commands available from the screen, you must first load NSS.NLM on the server.

The NSS command-line utility enables you to provide the following type of information about NSS on the server:

- ► NSS Informational Commands
- ► NSS Load Commands
- ► Set the NSS Cache Buffers Commands
- ► DOS FAT Commands

▸ NSS Tunable Parameters

▸ Rebuild NSS Volumes

▸ Salvage NSS Deleted Data

**FIGURE 21.18** *The NSS help screen is available on the server console.*

### NSS Informational Commands

Several NSS server console commands are available to provide in-depth information on your NSS configuration. To use the commands, enter the following at the server console:

▸ **NSS STATUS** — This command lists the current status of the more important tuneable parameters in NSS.

▸ **NSS MODULES** — This command lists the providers, loadable storage subsystems, and semantic agents.

▸ **NSS VERSION** — This command enables you to view the module name, version, build number, and snap date for each NSS module. This information can help you keep track of versions for NSS.

▸ **VOLUMES** — This command lists all the NetWare and NSS volumes that are mounted and should include the NSS_Admin volume.

▸ **NSS VOLUMES** — This command lists all the NSS volumes including NSS_Admin.

▸ **NSS EXIT** — This command is used to unload the NSS modules.

You can view the current settings for each of the NSS parameters by entering the following command on the server: NSS STATUS. Figure 21.19 shows the screen on the server that enables you to see the current settings for the NSS parameters.

**FIGURE 21.19** *The current NSS parameters can be viewed using the NSS STATUS command at the server console.*

In addition to viewing the current NSS parameters and status, you can also view the current NSS version. The NSS VERSION command enables you to view the module name, version, build number, and snap date for each NSS module. This information can help you keep track of versions for NSS. Figure 21.20 shows the view you receive when you execute the NSS VERSION command.

**FIGURE 21.20** *The current version for all NSS modules can be viewed by executing the NSS VERSION command on the server console.*

### NSS Load Commands
Use these NSS load commands at the server console to retrieve more information about each command:

▶ **NSS HELP** — This command enables you to access the NSS help screen and learn more information about each of the NSS commands.

- ▶ **NSS /(NO)SKIPLOADMODULES** — This command prevents autoloading of all the NSS modules. This lets you load only the NSS modules you need.

### Set the NSS Cache Buffers Commands

A cache buffer is a block (4 K) of NetWare server memory that temporarily stores data. To tune your server to support NSS, you can change the default cache buffers as follows:

- ▶ You can set a maximum of 1048576 cache buffers.

- ▶ You can set the buffers in percentages rather than integers.

Use these commands at the server console to set or check your cache buffers as follows:

- ▶ **NSS /MINBUFFERCACHESIZE** — This command sets the minimum buffer size. The default is 512. The range is 256 to 1048576. When NSS is loaded, it requires at least 512 cache buffers.

- ▶ **NSS /MINOSBUFFERCACHESIZE** — This command sets the minimum size for NetWare. The default is 1024. The range is 1024 to 1048576. We do not recommend that you set this value below 1024.

- ▶ **NSS /NAMECACHESIZE** — This command sets the number of Name Cache entries. NSS keeps a cache of file and directory entry names that it has recently looked up. This speeds up opening files and path searches. The default is 2111. The range is 3 to 65521.

- ▶ **NSS /(NO)NAMECACHE** — This command sets Name Cache to ON or OFF. The default is ON.

- ▶ **NSS /(NO)CACHEBALANCE** — This command sets the buffers to percentages rather than integers for dynamic balancing of free memory for the buffer cache. The default is ON. Use this switch with /MinBufferCacheSize.

- ▶ **NSS /CACHEBALANCE** — This command sets the percent balance of free memory that NSS uses for its cache buffer. The CacheBalance percentage determines how many cache blocks NSS takes from the traditional NetWare file system for its own cache. If this number is too large, some NLMs may be difficult to load. If you use NSS extensively, the default should be changed. The default is 10 percent. The range is from 1 to 99 percent.

▸ **NSS /CACHEBALANCETIMER** — This command sets the cache balance timer in seconds. NSS checks the total number of cache buffers in the system and determines whether the CacheBalance percentage is met. NSS then gives or takes the appropriate number of cache buffers. The default is 30. The range is 1 to 3600.

▸ **NSS /AUTHCACHESIZE** — This command sets the number of Authorization Cache entries. If many trustees have been set on different files and directories, we recommend that you increase this number. The default is 1024. The range is 16 to 50000.

▸ **NSS /BUFFERFLUSHTIMER** — This command sets the flush time for modified cache buffers in seconds. The default is 1 second. The range is 1 to 3600 seconds.

▸ **NSS /CACHESTATS** — This command shows the buffer cache statistics.

## DOS FAT Commands

You can use the following NSS commands at the server console to view and manage the DOS FAT partition and configuration:

▸ **NSS /(NO)FATINMEMORY** — This command loads the entire File Allocation Table into memory for faster access, regardless of its size. The default is OFF.

▸ **NSS /(NO)FATLONGNAMES** — This command enables long filenames on FAT volumes. The default is ON.

▸ **NSS /(NO)FATLAZYWRITES** — This command performs lazy writes of FAT. If set to ON, data that is written will be kept in memory for a specified period of time before it is also written to FAT. This increases performance. The default is ON.

▸ **NSS /FATLAZYWRITEDELAY=VALUE** — This command sets the FAT lazy write delay (in seconds). When (No)FATLazyWrites is set to ON, you specify how many seconds you want data kept in memory before it is written to FAT. The default is 60. The range is 5–180.

▸ **NSS /FATPARTITION=PARTITION_TYPE_NUMBER** — This command supports up to three additional partition types containing 16-bit FATs, such as /FATPartition=12,13.

## NSS Tuneable Parameters

Use these NSS commands at the server console to manage NSS:

▸ **NSS /ACTIVATE=VOLUME_NAME** — This command activates an NSS volume.

▸ **NSS /DEACTIVATE=VOLUME_NAME** — This command deactivates an NSS volume.

▸ **NSS /MAINTENANCE=VOLUME_NAME** — This command switches the specified NSS volume to maintenance mode.

▸ **NSS /FORCEACTIVATE=VOLUME_NAME** — This command forces an NSS volume to become active.

▸ **NSS /VERIFYVOLUME=VOLUME_NAME** — This command verifies the specified NSS volume's physical integrity.

▸ **NSS /REBUILDVOLUME=VOLUME_NAME** — This command rebuilds the specified NSS volume.

▸ **NSS /VERIFYVOLUME** — This command enables you to select an NSS volume from the menu to verify the volume's physical integrity.

▸ **NSS /REBUILDVOLUME** — This command enables you to select an NSS volume from the menu for rebuild.

▸ **NSS /AUTOVERIFYVOLUME=VOLUME_NAME** — This command enables you to verify an NSS volume at startup.

▸ **NSS /STORAGEALARMTHRESHOLD=VALUE** — This command enables you to set the threshold for a low storage space warning. The default is 10. The range is 0 to 1000000.

▸ **NSS /STORAGERESETTHRESHOLD=VALUE** — This command enables you to reset the threshold for a low storage space warning. The default is 10. The range is 1 to 1000000.

▸ **NSS /(NO)STORAGEALERTMESSAGES** — This command turns ON or OFF the low storage message to users. The default is ON.

▸ **NSS /NUMWORKTODO=VALUE** — This command sets the number of WorkToDo entries, which may be concurrently executing. NSS uses WorkToDo entries for tasks such as flushing file metadata to disk in the background. Increasing the number of WorkToDo entries might be useful on a system that is heavily used. NSS always reserves 20 WorkToDo entries. The default is 40. The range is 5 to 100.

▶ **NSS /FILEFLUSHTIMER=VALUE** — This command sets the flush time for modified open files in seconds. Increasing this number might reduce the number of writes to disk; however, it increases the amount of data that will be lost if the system crashes. The default is 10 seconds. The range is 1 to 3600 seconds.

▶ **NSS /OPENFILEHASHSHIFT=VALUE** — This command sets the size of the Open File hash table (in powers of 2). If many files are used concurrently on the server, we recommend that you increase this number. The default is 11. The range is 8 to 20.

▶ **NSS /CLOSEDFILEHASHSHIFT=VALUE** — This command sets the number of closed files that can be cached in memory. The default is 512. The range is 1 to 100000.

▶ **NSS /MAILBOXSIZE=VALUE** — This command sets the size of your mailbox. The default is 228. The range is 64 to 256.

### Rebuild NSS Volumes

You can use the NSS server command-line to perform a rebuild of an NSS volume. In order to accomplish this task, you need to execute the NSS /REBUILDVOLUME command from the server. The rebuild command from the NSS command-line utility salvages the volume data it finds on a corrupted NSS volume and rebuilds it.

This option is available only for NSS volumes. Traditional NetWare volumes cannot be rebuilt using this command. Instead, NetWare users can repair traditional NetWare volumes with VREPAIR.

Rebuild verifies and uses the existing leaves of an object tree to rebuild all the other trees in the system. While NSS volumes are being verified and rebuilt, they are placed in maintenance mode. This means the NSS volumes are unusable until this process is finished and the volume is remounted.

The NSS command-line utility includes two methods to launch the rebuild process. The first option is to use the following command:

```
NSS /REBUILD
```

This option enables you to see a list of volumes that you can rebuild, and you can pick one or select a volume to rebuild. The second option is the following command:

```
NSS /REBUILD=VOLUME_NAME
```

This option enables you to specify the NSS volume that you want to rebuild as a parameter of the command. If you want to rebuild more than one volume at a time and specify the volumes, you need to use the following command:

```
NSS /REBUILD=VOLUME_NAME, VOLUME_NAME
```

You can rebuild as many NSS volumes as you want, but NSS rebuilds only five at a time. To switch screens and view other NSS volumes that are being rebuilt, press Alt + Esc. The screen indicates the time elapsed, the time remaining, the total elapsed time, the number of objects processed, and so on, so that you know how long the rebuild will take.

It is recommended that you verify the volume that has completed being rebuilt. To verify an NSS volume, you need to use the NSS /VERIFY or NSS /VERIFY=VOLUME_NAME. The verify command is used similar to the rebuild command.

The verification process verifies accounts for all blocks on the volume. If errors are found, they are reported to the screen. After the verify process is complete, check to see if the NSS volume has been left in maintenance mode; otherwise, it is placed back to the active state.

### Salvage NSS Deleted Data

Salvaging deleted files is supported and behaves almost the same in NSS as in previous versions of NetWare. The SALVAGE feature in the traditional NetWare file system was either turned on or off for the whole file system using the Immediate Purge of Deleted Files set parameter. In NSS, you turn SALVAGE on or off for each NSS volume using the following commands:

- **NSS /SALVAGE=ALL** — This command enables SALVAGE on all NSS volumes.

- **NSS /SALVAGE=VOLUME_NAME** — This command enables SALVAGE on the NSS volume you specify.

- **NSS /NOSALVAGE=ALL** — This command disables SALVAGE on all NSS volumes.

- **NSS /NOSALVAGE=VOLUME_NAME** — This command disables SALVAGE on a specific NSS volume.

If SALVAGE is turned off for an NSS volume by using NSS /NOSALVAGE or by using the set parameter, all deleted files are automatically purged from the NSS volume and can no longer be salvaged.

The SALVAGE utilities used in NWADMN32 recognize and list deleted NSS directories and files. After directories are salvaged, they reappear as directories with all attributes and trustees intact. Files in a directory must be salvaged separate from the directory because they are separate objects. If deleted directories contain other deleted directories and files, these contained directories and files can be salvaged after their parent is salvaged. If, however, a deleted directory contains no deleted subdirectories and files, it is automatically purged and cannot be salvaged.

## Use In-Place to Upgrade Volumes

You can use an In-Place Upgrade to copy or move traditional NetWare files from a NetWare volume to a new NSS volume without losing trustee rights, attributes, resource forks, or name spaces. In order to perform an In-Place Upgrade, the following requirements and guidelines should be met:

▶ A server running NetWare 5.

▶ Identify the NetWare volumes you want to convert to new NSS volumes.

▶ Back up your data before you copy or move your NetWare volume to NSS.

▶ Make sure you have enough free space for the NSS volume.

During In-Place Upgrade, an NSS volume is created inside an existing NetWare volume. Because an NSS volume is created inside the NetWare volume, if you delete the NetWare volume, you also delete the NSS volume and its contents.

When you move or copy a NetWare volume to a new NSS volume, the NSS volume is created automatically. The commands for transferring NetWare volumes to NSS volumes are as follows:

```
IPCU (NetWare) VOLUME_NAME
```

Where VOLUME_NAME is the name of the traditional NetWare volumes. This command moves an existing NetWare volume to a new NSS volume. The old NetWare volume still exists, but the contents are empty except for the NSS volume (the NetWare volume recognizes it as a file). The new NSS volume resides inside the old NetWare volume.

```
IPCU (NetWare) VOLUME_NAME (NSS) VOLUME_NAME
```

This command copies a NetWare volume to a new NSS volume. The contents in the NetWare volume remain intact. The name of the new volume is VOLUME_NSS. For example, if the NetWare volume is named users, the new NSS volume will be named USERS_NSS.

```
IPCU -D (NetWare) VOLUME_NAME (NSS) VOLUME_NAME
```

This command moves a NetWare volume from a specific location to the new NSS volume. The old NetWare volume still exists, but the contents are empty except for NSS. Mount the NetWare volume and the NSS volume before you attempt to use them.

## The NSS Architecture

To gain more of an understanding of how the underlying structure of Novell Storage Services is laid out, review the following sections. This section is not required reading for NSS setup and maintenance. The NSS architectural layers, from the media (device) connection to the interface (client) connection, are as follows:

- Media Access Layer (MAL)
- Loadable Storage Subsystem (LSS)
- Object Engine
- Common Layer Interface (CLI)
- Semantic Agents (SA)

### Media Access Layer

The Media Access Layer (MAL) provides the connection to and communication with storage devices such as hard drives and CD-ROMs. The MAL lets network administrators create NSS storage groups and NSS volumes through the MAL managers (providers and consumers) that view and manage the storage capabilities of servers as a quantity of storage deposits.

The MAL frees administrators from having to enable large numbers of storage devices individually. The modular design allows new devices and new technologies to be added easily as required for productivity.

The storage object bank is the central layer of the MAL that is responsible for storage manager and storage object registration. The registered provider in the MAL deposits usable free space, called the storage deposit, into the object bank. Each registered storage object in the object bank has a deposit type. Each storage deposit type is tagged with attributes — for example, media such as read-only disks.

Two types of storage managers are in the MAL: consumers and providers. Consumers and providers are the managers you select when you set up or change your NSS configuration. After a consumer claims free space, input/output then proceeds to and from the device on which the free space (now owned by NSS) resides. Because the MAL provides an abstraction of system storage media, NSS could be portable to other operating systems such as UNIX or Linux. This means potentially any type of device could be supported on any system.

Providers interface and manage the physical system resources (devices) used by the MAL. They are installed with NSS and query the server's storage devices for free space. Providers find, manage, and register storage objects, such as DOS partitions, NetWare volumes, or CD-ROMs in the object bank. Providers understand and can recognize various partition types such as NetWare or DOS.

Providers allow the following functions:

▸ Locate partitions or NetWare volumes.

▸ Determine whether they are in use.

▸ Construct storage objects if they are not.

▸ Deposit the storage objects as storage deposits in the object bank.

If you add new media such as a hard disk, you choose a provider (through the Update Provider Information option) to scan and recognize the device for NSS configuration.

Consumers are similar to other applications installed in NetWare. Consumers are attached to the file system and help build the file input and output path. They configure and claim (or take) ownership of the storage deposit that has been combined from various media types by the provider. Consumers register themselves with the object bank so that they can control any deposited media objects (storage deposits) they own. Consumers take NSS ownership of the file system free space or free space on physical partitions for storage group and NSS volume creation. NSS consumers cannot own NetWare partition space, but they can consume free space inside a NetWare volume.

## Loadable Storage Subsystem

The Loadable Storage Subsystem (LSS) contains the loadable file system types that various devices understand. Currently, the LSS supports file system types for CD-ROM (using ISO9660 and Hierarchical File System or Macintosh HFS), DOS FAT (for local hard drives and DOS FAT partitions), and the NSS file system for rapid restart and scalability. If you enter the volumes command at the server console, and you use DOS or CD-ROM formats, the LSS recognizes both of them and displays them as NSS volumes. The LSS gathers information from the Media Access Layer (MAL) about the storage devices it recognizes (for this release, hard drives and CD-ROMs). The MAL lets the LSS know what storage devices it identifies and registers an existing NSS volume on the storage devices with NSS. The LSS then obtains information from the MAL about the NSS volume on which the data resides and passes the information up to the semantic agent (SA) so that the volume can be viewed at the client workstation.

## Object Engine

The object engine layer is the NSS object store. The design of this layer differs from the traditional NetWare file system by providing much higher levels of volume, directory, and file object efficiency. The NSS object engine uses sophisticated and efficient mechanisms to manage the objects it stores, achieving high levels of performance, scalability, robustness, and modularity.

- **Performance** — The NSS object engine stores objects on disks in balanced trees (called B-trees) to improve performance. The compact B-tree structures guarantee that the system can retrieve an object from disk in no more than four input and output cycles. This provides more speed per cache block. B-trees also improve memory management by allowing the system to locate an object anywhere in storage without loading the entire directory entry table (DET) into memory. The capability to share name space also improves disk space usage. Instead of storing a name for each name space in a single stored object as is the case in the traditional NetWare file system, NSS uses one name for DOS and another name for NFS. The name spaces in an object share a common name if no naming conflicts exist.

- **Scalability** — The object engine uses 64-bit interfaces to let network administrators create a much greater number of objects (volumes, files, and eventually HTML pages, and so on) and individual objects much larger than in the traditional NetWare file system.

- **Rapid recovery** — To enable rapid NSS volume mounts after a system crash, the LSS maintains a log that records all transactions written and waiting to be written to disk. The object engine defines interfaces for any LSS to implement journaled management recovery. If a server crashes, the traditional NetWare recovery procedure uses the VREPAIR utility to check and repair inconsistencies in the DET, which might take hours to complete. By contrast, NSS locates an error on a disk by referencing the journal, noting the incomplete transaction, and correcting the error by either reprocessing the incomplete transaction or by backing it out. Consequently, the NSS volume does not have to be thoroughly searched.

▶ **Modularity** — The modularity of the object engine lets network administrators define new storage objects and plug them into the storage system whenever they are needed. In the near future, new storage technologies such as the Digital Video Disc (DVD) could be plugged into the engine transparently without affecting other pieces of the software.

## Common Layer Interface

The Common Layer Interface (CLI) contains a set of Application Protocol Interfaces (APIs) that define the interfaces that the NSS semantic agents (covered in the next section, "Semantic Agents") use to access the object engine for NSS naming, object, and management services.

▶ Naming services include basic object naming and lookup operations as well as name space and context management services.

▶ Object services provide the creation, deletion, storage, and definition of objects.

▶ Management services provide other underlying types of NSS management, such as registration, file locking, transactions, and management of storage pools and NSS volumes.

## Semantic Agents

The Semantic Agent (SA) layer contains loadable software modules that define client-specific interfaces available to stored NSS objects.

For example, the traditional NetWare file system Semantic Agent interprets requests received from a NetWare client, passes the requests to the Common Layer Interface, and onward to the object engine for execution.

In the future, another semantic agent may implement an HTTP interface, allowing Web browsers to access data also stored by the object engine. This modular approach means administrators no longer need separate storage solutions for their various storage systems. New semantic agents can be created and loaded on the server as NetWare modules at any time without interrupting other loaded semantic agents.

## Architecture Example

The following example illustrates what happens to a file owned by NSS that is requested from the client machine. A user wants to access a word processing file called AGENDA.DOC. The user is logged in to the network from a Novell client. The request for a file moves through the NSS structure to the NSS volume found in the NDS tree. The following sequence illustrates each step that the user request follows:

**1.** At the client, the user makes a request to retrieve and open a word processing document called AGENDA.DOC from a workstation. The user has already logged in to the network and directory.

**2.** The request for the file passes from the workstation to its Semantic Agent. The semantic agent interprets the request as a file system operation from the NetWare Core Protocol (NCP). The semantic agent then translates the request into the set of common layer calls required to execute the NetWare file system operation. The SA then passes the request to the Common Layer Interface.

**3.** After the request is received from the SA, the Common Layer Interface (CLI) routes the request into its proper naming, object, and management services, and then it passes the request to the object engine layer for execution.

**4.** The Object Engine is passed the file request from the CLI. The object engine then identifies the NSS volume on which the file resides and sends notification to the object engine layer (MAL) to retrieve the file.

**5.** The request to retrieve the file AGENDA.DOC is sent from the object engine to the Media Access Layer (MAL). The MAL managers notify the physical media (the specific hard drive or CD-ROM) on which the data is written.

**6.** The physical media finds the requested file from a hard drive in the server. The file is retrieved and the request is sent back to the workstation for the user.

# Troubleshooting NSS Problems

The following items help you identify and fix NSS problems that may occur. This list contains only the most common NSS problems. The items are as follows:

▶ **NSS Doesn't Recognize a Device** — NSS does not recognize free space on a device.

  • NSS only recognizes what the Media Manager recognizes. For this release, the NSS providers only recognize hard drives, CD-ROMs, and NetWare partitions.

▶ **Free Space Doesn't Show Up** — You think you have free space on your server, but you don't or can't view it.

  • You may need to free up NetWare space or add a new hard drive.

  • If you deleted your NSS volumes and storage pool to create free space and you can't reconfigure NSS, you may need to exit and reload the ConsoleOne utility to become aware of the changes you have made.

  • Rescan your media devices and then go to view free space to check the free space.

▶ **Cannot Use the Free Space That Appears** — You can see the free space, but you can do nothing with it.

  • Check to make sure you have no more than four partitions on your hard drive. Free space cannot be utilized in NSS with more than four partitions.

▶ **NSS In-Place Upgrade Problems** — There is not enough memory to run the In-Place Upgrade utility and you cannot convert NetWare files to NSS files because you don't have enough memory.

  • In-Place Upgrade requires 300 K of RAM to run. Make sure you have at least this much RAM available.

▶ **Not Enough Free Space to Run In-Place Upgrade** — You cannot convert NetWare files to NSS files because you don't have enough space.

  • In-Place Upgrade requires at least 2MB of free space to run.

▶ **Cannot Complete the Setup Procedure** — NSS will not allow you to create your storage groups or NSS volumes.

  • You may not have enough free space. Check the amount of free space on your physical media. To allocate free space, remove unwanted files in NetWare or add more unpartitioned free space.

  • NSS may not own the free space you used to try to create a new storage pool.

▸ **Cannot Create an NSS Partition** — You may have tried to create an NSS volume in a NetWare partition and you cannot create NSS volumes in NetWare partitions unless you use available free space inside a NetWare volume. For example, you have installed NetWare on a 4 GB drive and have created a NetWare partition using 4 GB. You then create a 1 GB NetWare volume. You want to create NSS volumes with the 3 GB available on the NetWare partition.

  • Reinstall NetWare and create a 1 GB NetWare partition. Leave 3 GB unpartitioned space for NSS to use.

  • Reinstall NetWare and create a 4 GB NetWare partition. Create a 4 GB NetWare volume (NSS can use up to 100 percent of the NetWare volume space).

  • Create a 3 GB NetWare volume in the remaining portion of the 4 GB partition. NSS can use up to 100 percent of that 3 GB.

▸ **Cannot Delete the NSS_Admin volume** — You tried unsuccessfully to remove the NSS_Admin volume.

  • The NSS_Admin volume is a virtual volume that exists in RAM. It is used for read-only purposes and cannot be deleted.

▸ **The NSS Volume on My Server Will Not Load** — Your NSS volume has become corrupted and needs to be rebuilt.

▸ **An NSS Volume Won't Mount** — You created an NSS volume and now you cannot mount it. This is probably because the NSS volume you created is corrupted.

  • Your NSS volume may be corrupt and needs to be rebuilt. Use the REBUILD utility to rebuild your NSS volume. If the rebuild utility does not fix the problem, try the options below.

  • The following procedure destroys your NSS volume and all data contained within the volume. We recommend that you back up your data first. At the server console, enter **NSS /SKIPLOADMODULES**. Manually load the modules MBCOMN.NSS and MAL.NSS and the provider you want, such as MMPRV.NSS. Release or delete the volume. Reconfigure and mount the NSS volume.

# Summary

Novell Storage Services enables you to attach and manage a new type of storage system to NetWare 6. The value of NSS is that it enables you to mount very large disk systems to the server. For example, NSS supports 8 trillion files on an NSS volume and you can mount 256 volumes on the server. It also enables you to have a single file size of 8 Terabytes. And, all these features are supported with under 10MB of memory on the server.

# Installing the Novell Internet Access Server and FTP Services

In this chapter we look at the installation and configuration of the Novell Internet Access Server. We'll first discuss how you install the software and then how you manage the components.

## Installing and Managing Novell Internet Access Server Components

In this section we discuss how to install and configure the components of the Novell Internet Access Server.

▶ To install the Novell Internet Access Server components on the server, use INSTALL.NLM, select Product Options, and choose Install a Product Not Listed. Then specify the path to the *Novell Internet Access Server 6* CD-ROM.

▶ To configure the IPX/IP gateway on the server, use INETCFG.NLM.

▶ To install the client support for the IPX/IP gateway on workstations, install NetWare Client 32 and choose Additional Options on Windows 95/98 or Windows 2000.

▶ To work with the IPX/IP gateway object in NDS and to configure access rights, add the IPX/IP gateway snap-in utility to the NetWare Administrator utility by editing the NWADMN3X.INI file.

## Installing and Managing FTP Services for NetWare 6

In this section we review the steps to install FTP Services for NetWare 6.

▶ To install FTP Services for NetWare 6, use INSTALL.NLM, select Product Options, and choose Install a Product Not Listed. Then specify the path to the *FTP Services for NetWare 6* CD-ROM.

▶ To configure FTP Services for NetWare 6 and to create an Anonymous FTP user account, use UNICON.NLM.

Just when we were beginning to get comfortable with Internet technology, intranet technology appeared. From a technical standpoint, an *intranet* is simply a Web server that is confined to a private internal network and publishes files to a private audience, such as the employees of a corporation. A true Web server is connected to the Internet and publishes files to the world.

The reason that intranet technology is so popular is that people can use their Web browsers to view private information. An intranet server publishes shared information in HTML files that can be created with almost any word processor or text editor and can be viewed with Internet browsers on almost every operating system.

NetWare 6 is Novell's comprehensive operating system for a modern, full-service intranet. It starts with the NetWare 6 operating system and then adds the following intranet and Internet features:

- **IPX/IP Gateway** — This gateway enables administrators to allow IPX-based workstations to access TCP/IP-based resources, such as FTP and the World Wide Web, without having to install or configure TCP/IP on those workstations. The gateway also lets administrators implement access control — they can limit users by TCP port number, IP address or target host, and time of day.

- **MultiProtocol Router** — This feature provides WAN connectivity, routing multiple protocols over leased lines, frame relay, or ISDN lines. This capability allows you to connect network users to an Internet service provider (ISP).

- **Netscape Navigator** — This is the Web browser that lets you locate and read information stored on the Internet or on an intranet.

- **FTP Services for NetWare 6** — FTP services let you configure FTP access for your intranet.

In your NetWare 6 package, you'll find the following CD-ROMs:

- The *NetWare 6 Operating System* CD-ROM, which contains the regular NetWare 6 product software and the NetWare Web server. The NetWare Web server also contains the Netscape Navigator Web browser (and a single-user license for the browser).

- The *NetWare 6 Online Documentation* CD-ROM, which contains HTML documentation for NetWare 6.

- The *Novell Internet Access Server 6* CD-ROM, which contains most of the NetWare 6 features: the IPX/IP gateway, MultiProtocol Router for WAN connectivity, and the Netscape Navigator Web browser (multiuser license). This CD-ROM also contains HTML-formatted documentation for the IPX/IP gateway.

▸ The *FTP Services for NetWare 6* CD-ROM, which contains the FTP services and configuration utilities.

**NOTE**

**To read the HTML-formatted documentation for the Novell Internet Access Server product, use a Web browser from a workstation.**

For instructions on installing the Netscape Navigator browser that comes with the NetWare Web server on the *NetWare 6 Operating System* CD-ROM, see Chapter 14. For instructions on installing the browser from the *Novell Internet Access Server* CD-ROM, see the *Internet Access Server 4 Quick Reference Guide*, which comes with the NetWare 6 kit. The two browsers are identical, and they are placed on both CD-ROMs primarily for convenience.

**NOTE**

**If you have NetWare 6, you are allowed to use as many copies of the Web browser as your NetWare 6 user license permits. In other words, if you bought a 50-user version of NetWare 6, you can let 50 users use the browser. If you have NetWare 6 alone, you have only a single-user license to the browser.**

## Installing the Novell Internet Access Server Software

Before installing the Novell Internet Access Server software, which provides the software necessary to run the routing, WAN connectivity, and IPX/IP gateway, you must first install a NetWare 6 server as usual. Then you can install the Novell Internet Access Server software. During the installation, the Netscape Navigator browser will be copied to SYS:NETSCAPE so that you can later install it on workstations.

To install Novell Internet Access Server components on the NetWare 6 server, complete the following steps.

**1.** Insert the *Novell Internet Access Server 6* CD-ROM in a drive on the server and mount the CD-ROM as a NetWare volume.

**2.** At the server console, load INSTALL.NLM.

**3.** From the Installation Options menu, choose Product Options, and then choose Install a Product Not Listed.

**4.** To specify a path to the installation software, press F3 and type the following:

```
NIAS6:\NIAS\INSTALL
```

**5.** Choose Install Product. The Install to Servers list displays the local server name. The value in the title reflects the number of servers to be installed. If you want to install Novell Internet Access Server software on a remote server, press Insert to add the server to the list. If an expected server is not displayed, ensure that the latest version of RSPAWN.NLM is loaded on that server. To remove a server from the Install to Servers list, select the server, press Delete, and select Yes at the prompt.

**6.** From the Install to Servers menu, press Enter and select Yes to begin the installation. Servers are installed in alphabetical order. If you are installing to a remote server, you will be prompted to log in as an administrator. Enter the administrator's full login name and password.

**7.** When the prompt "Install previously created configuration files?" appears, select No.

**8.** When prompted for the Novell Internet Access Server license diskette, insert the NetWare 6 license diskette in the specified drive and press Enter. Once the login, license, and configuration file information for each server is provided, the installation begins copying files to the destinations.

**9.** When the installation is completed, you can read the installation log file if you desire. Choose Display Log File. When you're finished reviewing the log, press Esc to return to the Installation Options menu.

**10.** To verify that the Novell Internet Access Server software installed correctly, choose Product Options from the Installation Options menu and then select Configure ⇨ View ⇨ Remove Installed Products. The Currently Installed Products list appears, showing entries for the NetWare MultiProtocol Router software, WAN Extensions 3.1, and Novell Internet Access Server 6. Press Esc to return to the Installation Options menu.

**11.** From the Installation Options menu, select NCF Files Options and then choose the Edit STARTUP.NCF file. Modify the STARTUP.NCF file for each installed server to include the following line at the end of the file if you are using the NetWare 6 server to make a WAN connection:

```
SET MINIMUM PACKET RECEIVE BUFFERS=400
SET MAXIMUM PACKET RECEIVE BUFFERS=1000
```

The value of the second parameter can be increased as needed.

**12.** To exit the installation screen, press Esc and then select Yes to save the changes.

**13.** Bring down and restart the server to make sure all the correct NLMs are loaded. At the server's console, type the following:

```
DOWN
RESTART SERVER
```

# The IPX/IP Gateway

NetWare 6 includes an IP Compatibility Mode feature that provides much of the same functionality as the IPX/IP gateway. You can either install this gateway or use the functionality provided by NetWare 6. For more information on IP Compatibility Mode, see Chapter 23.

The IPX/IP gateway is an important part of the Novell Internet Access Server components of NetWare 6. With this gateway, IPX-based clients can access the Internet and other IP-based resources without having to install TCP/IP on the workstations themselves. The IPX/IP gateway gets installed on the server as part of the Novell Internet Access Server installation. To take advantage of the gateway, you must install IPX/IP gateway support on each workstation. Client gateway support is included as an option in the NetWare Client 32 installation.

Not having to use TCP/IP on each workstation is a benefit in many cases because significant management tasks are associated with maintaining TCP/IP workstations. With TCP/IP, you have to manually keep track of and configure many items for each individual workstation, such as the unique IP address, subnet mask, IP addresses of the default router and the domain name servers, and the domain name.

An IPX/IP gateway removes many of the individual management problems that occur with maintaining TCP/IP workstations by letting you retain IPX on those workstations.

When the IPX/IP gateway is installed on the NetWare 6 server, the server runs IPX to communicate with the IPX workstations on the network and TCP/IP so that it can communicate with the Internet. From the viewpoint of a remote host on the Internet, all traffic through the gateway seems to originate from the IP address assigned to the gateway server. Because the IPX/IP gateway uses only a single IP address, regardless of the number of users it supports, the private network is safe from outside interference. Using the Novell IPX/IP gateway alleviates the difficulties of administering a TCP/IP environment by providing ease of management and centralized control over Internet access.

By using Novell's IPX/IP gateway, you can run only IPX on the network workstations. Compared to IP, IPX is simple to manage. It assigns user connections dynamically, eliminating the need for a registered address to be configured at each desktop. Because IPX addresses are assigned dynamically, workstation IPX address conflicts do not occur. Users can move transparently between IPX networks, and traveling IPX users can roam between multiple networks within an enterprise.

The Novell IPX/IP gateway enables you to limit access to Internet services by the type of traffic (for example, Web browsing or FTP) and by remote host. Either type of restriction can be limited to specific times during the day to reduce "rush hour" traffic on an Internet connection.

## Configuring the IPX/IP Gateway

After you've installed Novell Internet Access Server on the server, you can configure the IPX/IP gateway by following these steps:

1. At the server console, load INETCFG.NLM. If you are asked if you want to transfer your LAN driver, protocol, and remote access commands, choose Yes. What this really means is that you will move the LOAD and BIND commands from the AUTOEXEC.NCF file to INETCFG's startup files.

2. From the main menu, select Protocols, choose TCP/IP, and then choose IPX/IP Gateway Configuration.

3. Specify "enabled" in the "Enabled for the IPX/IP Gateway" field so that the gateway will become operational.

4. If you want to record when clients access a service over the gateway, enable the Client Logging field. The log is stored in a field called GW_AUDIT.LOG in the SYS: volume.

5. In the Console Messages field, specify the type of messages you want to display on the gateway logging screen and the gateway status log file (GW_INFO.LOG in the SYS volume). You can choose "Informational, warning, and errors" (the default), "Warnings and errors only," or "Errors only."

6. To enforce access restrictions (which you set using the NetWare Administrator utility), enable the Access Control field.

**7.** In the Domain Name field, specify the name of the domain in which the gateway is installed. Your Internet service provider may provide you with this name.

**8.** In the Name Server fields, specify the IP addresses of any active domain name servers. Your Internet service provider may provide these addresses.

**9.** Press Esc twice and then log in as user Admin when prompted.

**10.** If you want to configure the gateway to use leased lines, frame relay, or ISDN lines, complete the following steps (see the documentation that came with the Novell Internet Access Server for more specific details about parameters):

   **a.** Choose Boards from the INETCFG.NLM main menu. Then specify the appropriate WAN driver and configure any necessary parameters.

   **b.** Choose Network Interfaces from the INETCFG.NLM main menu. Then configure the appropriate WAN interfaces.

   **c.** Choose WAN Call Directory from INETCFG's main menu and press Insert to configure a new WAN call destination. Then configure any necessary parameters.

   **d.** Choose Bindings from INETCFG's main menu, press Insert, and bind TCP/IP to the appropriate board or driver.

**11.** Exit INETCFG.NLM and save the changes you made.

**12.** Reboot the server to make the changes take effect.

After you've enabled and configured the gateway, a gateway server NDS object appears in the NDS tree in the same context as the server on which it is installed. The gateway object's name is the same as the server's name, with -GW added to the end of the name. This gateway object assists gateway clients in locating active IPX/IP gateway servers.

### Adding IPX/IP Gateway Tools to the NetWare Administrator Utility (NWADMIN)

To add the IPX/IP gateway support to the NetWare Administrator utility, complete the following steps:

**1.** If you haven't yet opened the NetWare Administrator utility, open it and close it.

**2.** From the Windows File Manager on your workstation, double-click on the NWADMN3X.INI file (located in the WINDOWS directory) to open it for editing.

**3.** Under the heading [Snapin Object DLLs WIN3X], add the following line:
`IPXGW3X=IPXGW3X.DLL`

**4.** Save and close the file. Now the NetWare Administrator utility will recognize the IPX/IP gateway object.

## Controlling Access to the IPX/IP Gateway

To control the IPX/IP gateway object, you'll need to add the gateway's snap-in utility to the NetWare Administrator (NWADMIN) utility. This will enable NetWare Administrator to recognize the new gateway object and the new access-control property that was added to certain objects. The IPX/IP Gateway snap-in should be automatically installed so that NWADMIN will recognize the snap-in when it launches.

After the IPX/IP gateway server is fully installed and configured, you can use the NetWare Administrator utility to give the IPX/IP gateway server access-control information for the various objects in the NDS tree. Then you can use NetWare Administrator to set restrictions for users, groups, or containers.

To give the gateway server access-control information, use the NetWare Administrator utility to make the following changes to the NDS tree:

▸ Make the Public object a trustee of the gateway object, with browse object rights and read and compare property rights (for all properties).

▸ Make the Public object a trustee of the File Server object that is running the IPX/IP gateway, with browse object rights and read and compare property rights for the Network Address property only (under selected properties).

▸ Make the gateway object a trustee in the Root object, with browse object rights and read and compare property rights (for all properties).

You control user access through the IPX/IP gateway by using the NetWare Administrator utility. As the point of connection between a NetWare network and a TCP/IP network, an IPX/IP gateway is in an ideal position to enforce restrictions on traffic between the two networks.

These access restrictions can be stored in two properties that are added to the User, Group, Organization, or Organizational Unit objects after the gateway is enabled:

▸ **Service Restriction** — Tells the gateway object which applications may be used by the object and which are restricted. These restrictions are based on the port number.

▶ **Host Restriction** — Tells the gateway which remote hosts are restricted from the object. These restrictions are based on the IP address.

Storing access restrictions in the NDS objects provides a single database of restrictions that all gateway servers share. You do not need to configure access control separately on each gateway. Restrictions are active on all gateways, regardless of whether they are applied to an entire organization or created individually for each user.

To place access restrictions on a User, Group, Organization, or Organizational Unit object, use the NetWare Administrator utility and select the object in question. Then choose Details under the Object menu and open the IPX/IP Gateway Service Restrictions page. On this page, you can enter restrictions for this object.

To restrict access to a specific Internet site, place a host restriction on the IP address of that site. To prevent certain types of traffic from being forwarded by the server, create a service restriction for the appropriate port number. For example, you might restrict Web browser access to certain hours during the day but allow FTP or Telnet access during those same hours. You could also place the remote host www.games.com off-limits. To prevent newsreaders from operating across the gateway, you might place a restriction on traffic to port number 119 (News) at any site.

## Installing the IPX/IP Gateway Client

The IPX/IP gateway support is installed as an option in the NetWare Client 32 workstation software. The following instructions explain how to install the support on Windows 95/98 and Windows 2000 workstations:

1. Click Customize to customize the client.

2. Choose Add.

3. In the "Type of Network Component You Want to Install" box, double-click on Protocol.

4. In the Manufacturers box, choose Novell and then double-click on Novell NetWare IPX/IP Gateway.

5. Choose OK to exit the Network configuration screen.

6. If you receive a prompt to select a preferred gateway server, click Yes, enter the name of your preferred IPX/IP gateway server, and then select OK. If a preferred gateway server is configured, the gateway task will attempt to locate that gateway server through NDS and connect to it. If the preferred gateway

server is not available, the gateway client will search for other gateway servers, first in the user's NDS context, then in the bindery of the attached server, and then finally by querying for a SAP broadcast of any gateway server.

**7.** If you are asked for additional files, type the location of those files in the Copy Files From box. If you are asked for Client 32 files, type in the path to the directory from which you ran SETUP.EXE.

**8.** Click Yes to restart the computer. The IPX/IP Gateway Switcher program runs automatically during the first restart after installation. This switcher program switches the client from gateway operation to native TCP/IP operation (if TCP/IP is available on the client).

**9.** To enable the gateway, click the Enable IPX/IP Gateway button and then click OK.

# Installing FTP Services for NetWare 6

In addition to the Novell Internet Access Server components, NetWare 6 also includes FTP Services. This feature, which is a subset of the NetWare UNIX Print Services product, enables NetWare clients to use FTP to work with files on the Internet or on an intranet.

To install FTP Services for NetWare 6 on your server, complete the following steps:

**1.** Mount the *FTP Services for NetWare 6* CD-ROM as a volume on the NetWare 6 server.

**2.** Load INSTALL.NLM on the server.

**3.** Choose Product Options and then choose Install a Product Not Listed.

**4.** Press F3 and then type in the following path to the FTP Services files on the CD-ROM:

NWUXPS:\NWUXPS

**5.** If you are asked to specify a host name, press Enter to accept the default name displayed or enter the correct host name.

**6.** Accept the default boot drive (or specify the correct drive from which the server boots).

**7.** To install the online documentation for FTP Services, choose Yes. This documentation is separate from the regular NetWare online documentation and describes how to install and use FTP Services.

**8.** If you have already installed the NetWare 6 Online Documentation viewer, choose No when asked if you want to install a new one.

**Note:** If you receive the message "hosts.db does not exist," ignore it.

**9.** When prompted for a user name, enter the ADMIN name and password.

**10.** Choose the name service option you want to use on this server and answer any prompts necessary for the name service you choose. If you choose to use a local name service, the database that holds the name service information will be stored on this server and will be the master database. You can use the UNICON.NLM utility to work with the master database on a local server. If you choose to use a remote name service, that database will reside on another server. You can use UNICON.NLM only to view the database information but not to modify it. You can choose one of the following options:

- **Local DNS and Local NIS** — This option stores both master databases on this server.

- **Remote DNS and Remote NIS** — This option uses the master databases stored on another server.

- **Remote DNS and Local NIS** — This option stores the master NIS database on this server and the DNS database on another server.

- **No DNS and Remote NIS** — This option stores the master NIS database on another server and does not provide DNS service at all.

**11.** Follow any prompts necessary to initialize the name service and the product.

**12.** To start FTP Services, press Insert and choose FTP Server. FTP Services will start running and will appear in the Running Services menu.

**13.** To exit the installation program, press Esc as many times as necessary.

**14.** Restart the server to make the new settings take effect by typing the following:

```
DOWN
RESTART SERVER
CONFIGURING FTP SERVICES
```

With FTP Services, users can use FTP to access and transfer files from an intranet or the Internet. If you desire, you can create an Anonymous FTP account for users to use. With an Anonymous account, any user can access the FTP service by typing in any password. (Any password will work; the FTP service doesn't actually authenticate the password.)

To configure an Anonymous FTP account, complete the following steps:

**I.** At the server console, load UNICON.NLM.

**2.** When prompted, enter the ADMIN user name and password.

**3.** Choose Manage Services, then choose FTP Server, and then choose Set Parameters.

**4.** Choose Default Name Space and enter NFS. This action installs the NFS name space on the server, which enables the server to store UNIX files.

**5.** Change the Anonymous User Access field to Yes so that the Anonymous account will be enabled.

**6.** Choose Anonymous User's Home Directory and change the path from the SYS: volume (displayed as /sys) to a directory you prefer to use as the login directory for Anonymous FTP users.

**7.** When finished, press Esc to exit the installation program and to save the changes you've made.

**8.** Return to the main menu by pressing Esc twice, then choose Perform File Operations, and then choose View ⇨ Set File Permissions.

**9.** Enter the path to the Anonymous user's home directory (specified in Step 6) and press F9 to see the permissions (the UNIX equivalent of trustee rights) that have been set for this directory. If the permissions are not correct, modify them on this screen. The permissions should be as follows:

```
[U = rwx] [G =---] [o =---]
```

**10.** Press Esc multiple times to exit UNICON and to save the changes you've made.

**11.** Even though you specified the NFS name space in Step 4, you still need to add it to the volume. (You only need to add the name space to the volume once. To see if you've already added NFS name space to a volume, type **VOLUMES** at the server console — the display will show which name spaces are supported on each volume.) If you need to add the name space, type the following command, replacing "volume" with the name of the volume:

```
ADD NAME SPACE NFS TO volume
```

## Summary

This chapter has discussed how to install the Internet Access Server component for NetWare 6 and FTP services. The Novell Internet Access Server provides the software necessary to run routing, WAN connectivity, and the IPX/IP gateway on a NetWare 6 server. The IPX/IP gateway is an important part of the Novell Internet Access Server components because IPX-based clients can access the Internet and other IP-based resources without having to install TCP/IP on the workstations themselves. The FTP Services enables users to transfer files from an intranet or the Internet.

# TCP/IP in NetWare 6

**N**etWare 6 completely supports the TCP/IP protocol, which provides the capability to access NetWare services through the use of the IP networking protocol instead of only IPX/SPX as in previous versions of NetWare (prior to version 5). This means that the NetWare Core Protocol (NCP) services can run over the TCP/IP stack. The NetWare Core Protocol services that run over TCP/IP are file reads and writes, user login and authentication, and NDS eDirectory synchronization.

TCP/IP support has frequently been called pure IP. The term *pure* implies that IPX encapsulation is not required. In NetWare 6, TCP/IP services allows NCP to sit directly on top of User Datagram Protocol (UDP) or Transmission Control Protocol (TCP) headers and use IP services for discovery, addressing, and data-transfer operations. The IP port for the NetWare Core Protocol was registered by IANA as port 524. The NetWare system implements the IP connection as a TCP connection.

## Support for TCP/IP in NetWare 6

The TCP/IP services feature makes NetWare 6 protocol-independent. One of the advantages of a protocol-independent system is that the system can support TCP/IP, IPX/SPX, or both concurrently. Although traditional NetWare networks have primarily used IPX as the network protocol, a TCP/IP network is more easily integrated with other systems such as Windows NT/2000, UNIX, and the Intranet. Thus, you have significant opportunity for mixing and matching the multiple protocols to achieve migration goals.

### NetWare 6 Client Support

The foundation of TCP/IP services lies in the protocol-independent communication for both the server and the NetWare client. Like the NetWare 6 server, the NetWare client also can use either IP or IPX, or both. This is the case for NetWare clients running on Windows 95/98 and Windows NT/2000. Thus, both the NetWare 6 client and NetWare 6 server enable the user to implement dual protocol stacks. As mentioned, the system is designed to prefer IP, if an IP connection can be made. IPX is available for communication with the remaining IPX network. Such an approach minimizes the risk of discontinuity because most network clients already use both IP and IPX stacks.

### NDS eDirectory Support

NDS eDirectory has been modified in NetWare 6 to support the IP protocol suite in addition to the IPX protocol suite. The Novell Directory Access Protocol (NDAP) is able to provide NDS communications via UDP or TCP. This support extends to the partition level, where an NDS tree can support some partitions that are located on IPX-based machines, other partitions that are located on IP-based machines, and yet other partitions that are based on machines that support both IP and IPX stacks concurrently.

**It is important to remember that all servers in a tree must be able to talk to all the other servers in a tree to handle NDS backlink obituaries and external references.**

NOTE

### Winsock Support

Within the NetWare 6 server, the WinSock 2 API is used as the portal to the communications infrastructure. The developer is able to write to a single API and gain access to UDP, TCP, IPX, and SPX. Additionally, the WinSock API provides a single interface to naming services. Novell has implemented name service providers for NDS, DNS, DHCP, SLP, and SAP. NetWare 6 still supports the existing BSD Sockets and TLI interfaces to the protocol stacks.

In addition to those mentioned, NetWare 6 uses an array of IP-related protocols, services, and tools to make migrating to a TCP/IP network manageable. These services and tools allow migration of your network from IPX to IP without losing connectivity or IPX application support. Before we consider all the different options for upgrading or migrating your network protocols to TCP/IP, we must first introduce some of the migration components and IP-related services.

## Migration Components in TCP/IP

As previously mentioned, NetWare 6 provides the option to run the TCP/IP protocol on your network. However, if IPX applications are required, you need to bind the IPX protocol or the Compatibility Mode. In order to help you migrate to TCP/IP or to configure your network to support both IPX/SPX and TCP/IP, NetWare 6 offers several possible IP and IPX configurations. These configurations are dependent upon the IP-related services and are as follows:

- ▸ IPX Compatibility Mode (CMD)
- ▸ Client Compatibility Mode driver

- Server Compatibility Mode driver
- Migration agent with gateway support
- Migration agent with backbone support

To allow flexibility in migrating an IPX-based network to an IP-based network, these migration components have been integrated into NetWare 6 rather than placed in a separate migration tool. The migration components and, more specifically, the IPX Compatibility Mode drivers are used by the server only when an IPX application requires them. And because an IPX stack is loaded on the server, some IPX symbols may persist. This does not mean, though, that the system is using IPX on the wire, only that the system is compatible with IPX if it is needed by an IPX application. If there are no requests for IPX services, the IPX stack is not used.

The following description of each key component in TCP/IP is intended to give you just enough information to understand the migration options and strategies mentioned in this chapter. For more detailed information about each component, refer to the associated information found later in this chapter.

## The IPX Compatibility Mode Driver (CMD)

The IPX Compatibility Mode driver (CMD) has two parts, one for the server and one for the client. At the server, the Compatibility Mode driver is viewed as a network adapter. When it functions in this capacity, you can bind both IPX and IP protocols to the CMD adapter and it acts like a router. The CMD at the server is called the *Server Compatibility Mode driver.*

At the workstation, the CMD is invisible because it is an integral part of the new client. It provides the IP communications link required by an IP client. Because NetWare 6 is IP, you have no need for IPX at the client. The Compatibility Mode driver at the workstation or client is called the *Client Compatibility Mode driver.*

## The Client Compatibility Mode Driver

The NetWare 6 client automatically supports the Compatibility Mode driver, which ensures that IPX-dependent applications running on the NetWare 6 clients transmit only IP communications. This means that any IPX application will be able to communicate to other IPX services across the IP-Only network. For example, if a printer driver were IPX dependent and required a SAP broadcast to locate a print server (PSERVER.NLM), the Client Compatibility Mode driver would change this SAP query to an SLP query. Figure 23.1 shows how a SAP request or query is redirected to SLP.

**FIGURE 23.1** *When the client needs to discover services from SAP and you have an IP-Only network, the client request for SAP services will be redirected to SLP.*

The Service Location Protocol (SLP) is introduced in this section. For more detailed information on SLP, please refer to the later sections.

### The Server Compatibility Mode Driver

By default, the Server Compatibility Mode driver (SCMD.NLM) runs on every NetWare 6 server to support any server-based applications that are IPX dependent. SCMD is often referred to as the Compatibility Mode server process, which allows all IPX applications to communicate in a TCP/IP network. This server component supports IPX-based applications without having to bind IPX to the wire. A virtual IPX network is created to support the IPX applications.

Although the Server Compatibility Mode driver is loaded by default, you can manually load and unload the process using its name (SCMD.NLM). For example, to load the Server Compatibility Mode driver manually at the server console, type the following:

```
LOAD SCMD ( the LOAD keyword is optional)
```

To remove or unload the Compatibility Mode server, type the following:

```
UNLOAD SCMD (the UNLOAD keyword is mandatory)
```

The SCMD process translates IPX communications — such as Service Advertising Protocol queries, SAP broadcasts, and IPX packets — into the TCP/IP format. For example, suppose that a NetWare Loadable Module such as PSERVER.NLM needs to broadcast its presence on the network using SAP broadcasts. SCMD redirects the SAP broadcasts to the Service Location Protocol process running on the NetWare 6 server. The SLP process registers the IPX-dependent NLM, enabling workstations to discover this NLM just as they discover IP services. PSERVER.NLM is unaware that its service announcement has been redirected. Figure 23.2 shows how SAP broadcasts from the PSERVER.NLM program are redirected to SLP.

The IPX compatibility driver treats the IP Network as a virtual IPX network segment (CMD network segment), by encapsulating IPX datagrams inside UDP datagrams, and by resolving RIP and SAP requests through the use of the Service Location Protocol. To run IPX applications in your IP network or to connect IP systems with IPX systems, Service Location Protocol must be enabled across the network, because the IPX compatibility drivers are dependent upon the capabilities of SLP. Additionally, at least one migration agent must be used on the network if you interconnect IPX and IP systems.

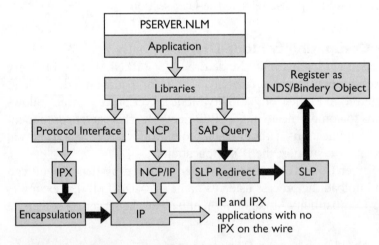

**FIGURE 23.2** *PSERVER.NLM sends SAP broadcasts to announce its presence on the network. If you have an IP-Only network, the SAP broadcasts are redirected to SLP, which enables discovery of services through IP.*

The default IPX network number (CMD network number) assigned to the virtual IPX network created by the IPX compatibility drivers is 0xFFFFFFFD. Migration agents that interconnect IP Systems with IPX systems must have a CMD network number that does not conflict with the internal IPX network number of a server or the IPX network number of a network segment. Be aware that IPX routers should not filter this address.

If a system or a segment conflicts with the CMD network number, you can either override the default CMD network number by modifying the configuration of the IP-Only clients and servers, or you can change the network number of the conflicting system or segment.

## The Migration Agent with Gateway Support

The migration agent (MA) is a migration component that enables communication between the IPX stack and the IP stack. It can run only on the NetWare 6 server because it is a special condition of the SCMD.NLM program, and it is enabled by loading the SCMD /G or /GATEWAY option. The migration agent is often referred to as the SCMD with gateway support. The terms *migration agent* and *SCMD /G* are equivalent.

The SCMD.NLM provides both the Server Compatibility Mode driver and the migration agent with gateway service. Although the Server Compatibility Mode driver is enabled by default, you must manually enable and configure the migration agent to get gateway support. To enable the migration agent, you load SCMD.NLM re-entrantly by entering the following commands:

```
LOAD SCMD.NLM /G (the LOAD keyword is optional)
```

The migration agent allows access between IPX and IP networks and vice versa: It enables users on a TCP/IP network to access services located on an IPX network. Likewise, the migration agent enables users on an IPX network to access services located on a TCP/IP network. Figure 23.3 illustrates how the migration agent using the SCMD /G option is used as a router between the services on the IPX network and the virtual IPX network segment created by the IPX compatibility drivers. The migration agent with gateway support resides on the server that acts as a gateway between the existing IPX network and the newer TCP/IP network. The server running as the gateway should be accessible to all the nodes from both the IPX and IP networks so that the services provided by each are fully accessible.

**FIGURE 23.3** *The migration agent using the SCMD /G is set up as a router between the IPX network and nodes and the IP services. All TCP/IP servers and clients use the gateway to the IPX segments and vice versa.*

In this example, the servers named SYD-SRV1 and TOK-SRV1 are both configured to support only IP. The servers called NOR-SRV1 and RIO-SRV1 are configured with the IPX stack only. To enable these two networks to communicate with one another, you can load the migration agent on the NetWare 6 server, CAM-SRV1. To accomplish loading the gateway, load SCMD /G to allow the server on the TCP/IP network to communicate with the servers on the IPX network. The servers on the IPX network may be running NetWare 2, NetWare 3, NetWare 4, NetWare 5, or NetWare 6 but are configured to support only IPX.

The migration agent provides protocol translation services, changing IPX-based queries into IP–based queries. As a result, any workstation or clients on the IPX network could access services that resided on the TCP/IP network.

You should use the /G option only if you want to configure a migration agent to connect one IPX network and one TCP/IP network. When configuring the migration agent, you can set it up to use one or two network boards. Figure 23.4 shows how you run the migration agent on a NetWare 6 server with only one network board. The IP and IPX stacks are bound to this single network card.

**FIGURE 23.4** *The migration agent supports the gateway service on a NetWare 6 server that only has one network board with both the IP and IPX stacks bound to it.*

In addition to the single network board support, the migration agent can provide the gateway service on a NetWare 6 server with two network boards. In this configuration, both the IP and IPX stacks are bound to the separate network cards. Figure 23.5 shows how the migration agent can be run on a NetWare 6 server with two network boards with IP and IPX bound to each card.

**FIGURE 23.5** *The migration agent with gateway support can be run on a NetWare 6 server with two network boards. In this configuration, both the IP and IPX stacks are bound to the separate network cards.*

## The Migration Agent with Backbone Support

As mentioned previously, SCMD.NLM provides both the Server Compatibility Mode driver and the migration agent with gateway service. In addition, SCMD.NLM provides the backbone support that allows the IPX services to connect to other IPX services across an IP-Only communication link.

The migration agent with backbone support is a migration component that enables IPX services to communicate across an IP-Only segment. The migration agent with backbone support can run only on the NetWare 6 server because it is a special condition of the SCMD.NLM program. The migration agent with backbone support is enabled by loading the SCMD /BS option.

The backbone support allows access between IPX services connected with only an IP network. The backbone support is used if you want two disconnected IPX networks to communicate through a TCP/IP network. Figure 23.6 shows how you can use the migration agent with backbone support to allow two remote IPX networks to communicate over an IP-Only network.

Although SCMD.NLM is typically loaded automatically when the server is booted, you must manually enable and configure the migration agent to get backbone support. To enable the migration agent, you load SCMD.NLM re-entrantly by entering one of the following commands:

```
LOAD SCMD.NLM /BS (the LOAD keyword is optional)
```

By enabling the /BS option, you have configured the migration agent to forward IPX packets through the IP network bound to the server. This allows the migration agents to exchange SAP and Routing Information Protocol (RIP) information about the disconnected IPX networks.

**FIGURE 23.6** *Two disconnected IPX networks are communicating through an IP-Only WAN link. If you load the SCMD.NLM with the /BS option, the migration agent encapsulates IPX packets inside IP, thus enabling these disconnected IPX networks to communicate.*

## Comparison of the SCMD Options

You may be wondering what the similarities and differences are among the SCMD options. For example, how does the Server Compatibility Mode driver differ from the migration agent with gateway support (SCMD /G)? Or how does SCMD /G differ from SCMD /BS? For the most part, the options are very similar. They can be viewed or considered as concentric circles, with each option adding functionality. This means that when you load SCMD /G, it loads all the features of SCMD (Compatibility Mode) plus the gateway function. When you load SCMD /BS, you get the SCMD /G and SCMD features, plus the backbone support. Figure 23.7 shows how each of the options available for SCMD.NLM adds functionality.

The least functionality is SCMD, with SCMD /G adding the gateway support. The most functionality comes with the SCMD /BS option, which provides features for each of the other options.

**FIGURE 23.7** *The SCMD.NLM options are Compatibility Mode, gateway support, and backbone support. The options can be viewed or considered as concentric circles with each option adding functionality.*

The two migration agent options have many similarities; for example, they each perform the following five functions:

- Registers migration agent services with an SLP service agent. (An SLP service agent works on behalf of a service to respond directly to queries for specific services. For more information about SLP service agents, see the section on Service Location Protocol later in this chapter.)

- Registers SAP services with an SLP service agent.

- Unencapsulates and forwards SAP queries to an IPX network.

- Unencapsulates and forwards RIP queries to an IPX network.

- Encapsulates and unencapsulates IPX traffic that is coming from or going to a TCP/IP network.

**Registering Migration Agent Services with an SLP Service Agent**
Migration agents register their services with a local SLP service agent, making the services available to devices on the TCP/IP network. Sometimes a NetWare 6 client running the Compatibility Mode client process might require the services of

the migration agent. In this case, the NetWare 6 client would use SLP to discover the migration agent.

### Registering SAP Services with an SLP Service Agent

As the translator between an IPX network and a TCP/IP network, a migration agent receives SAP broadcasts from the IPX network. For example, a server would send a SAP broadcast every 60 seconds on the IPX network, announcing the server's file, directory, and other services. After receiving this SAP broadcast, the migration agent would send an SLP packet to the SLP service agent, registering the server's services.

If a NetWare 6 client running the Compatibility Mode client process wants to use an IPX service, this client sends an SLP query to the SLP service agent. The SLP service agent then returns the network address of the device providing the requested IPX service.

### Unencapsulating and Forwarding SAP Queries to an IPX Network

If a NetWare 6 client running the Compatibility Mode client process queries an SLP service agent for an IPX service and that service is not registered with the SLP service agent, this client can encapsulate a SAP query inside IP and send the query directly to the migration agent. The migration agent, in turn, unencapsulates the SAP query and forwards it to the IPX network. The migration agent then encapsulates the SAP reply inside IP and sends this reply to the requesting NetWare 6 client.

### Unencapsulating and Forwarding RIP Queries to an IPX Network

After a NetWare 6 client running the Compatibility Mode client process locates an IPX service, this client encapsulates a RIP query inside IP and sends the query directly to the migration agent. Next, the migration agent unencapsulates the RIP query and forwards it to the IPX network. The migration agent then encapsulates the RIP reply inside IP and sends this reply to the requesting NetWare 6 client.

### Encapsulating and Unencapsulating IPX Traffic

If a NetWare/IP client exists on a TCP/IP network, the migration agent can unencapsulate IPX packets and forward them in native IPX format to the IPX network. For example, if a NetWare/IP client resided on a TCP/IP network, this client would encapsulate IPX packets within a UDP/IP header.

When a NetWare/IP client needs to locate a service on an IPX network, the client sends a SAP request to the migration agent. The migration agent then unencapsulates the SAP request and sends it in its native IPX format onto the IPX network.

# IP Migration Options and Strategies

Migrating a NetWare network from IPX to IP reduces administrative costs, especially if you are already supporting both protocols, or if you are expending a significant portion of your Information Services budget managing IPX. Because of the flexibility of TCP/IP, there is no single migration utility or method. Anyone wanting to migrate from IPX to IP needs to implement the newer technology while providing continued access to all existing network services.

The client and server can be installed to support several different configurations. In some cases, the customer may want to mix and match IP and IPX. Certainly, the migration process requires compatibility of both protocols during the transition period. NetWare 6 provides tremendous flexibility in configuring the IPX and IP protocols. The following configuration options are supported within NetWare 6:

▸ IP-Only (no legacy IPX application support)
▸ IP and IPX dual stack (assumes both IP and IPX protocols routed everywhere)
▸ IP with IPX application support (SCMD)
▸ IP with IPX connected segment (SCMD /G, assumes IPX filtering)
▸ IP backbone with IPX linked segments (SCMD /BS)

Although NetWare 6 fully supports the IPX/SPX stack as a protocol option, it will not be discussed in this section. For obvious reasons, it is not a migration strategy to IP. However, IPX remains 100 percent supported in NetWare 6 with native support for all the current IPX applications and services.

Typically, the protocol installation screen determines the binding between protocol stacks and the network adapters. It does not determine which protocol stacks are loaded in the system. For example, if the IP-Only installation option is selected, only the TCP/IP stack is attached to the network adapter. Figure 23.8 shows the Protocol Installation window that enables you to choose the protocols that you want the server to run.

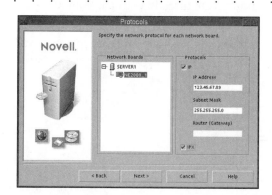

**FIGURE 23.8** *This protocol installation window that appears during server installation enables you to select which protocols the server will have available to requesting services.*

## IP-Only

NetWare 6 can be configured to support a TCP/IP network. Systems installed using the IP-Only installation option have both the TCP/IP and IPX stacks loaded by default, but only the TCP/IP stack is bound to the network adapter. If a TCP/IP network in the strictest sense is required, the IPX stack loaded as the CMD driver that helps support IPX application compatibility needs to be unloaded (because it is loaded by default). Figure 23.9 shows the layout for the IP-Only protocol architecture.

**The IP-Only migration strategy or option assumes that no legacy IPX applications will be supported on the client or the server.**

**NOTE**

As mentioned, during installation of the NetWare 6 server, the IPX stack is loaded on the system with the IP-Only option to give those systems the capability to execute IPX applications and to connect with IPX services through a migration agent. Any NetWare 6 servers installed with the IP-Only option have the following capabilities:

▶ Establish NCP connections with clients installed with one of the install options that include IP.

▶ Establish NCP connections through migration agent with pre–NetWare 6 clients whose clients only support NCP connections over IPX or with NetWare 6 clients installed with the IPX-only option.

> ▸ Execute IPX applications and communicate directly with NetWare 6 systems installed with the IP-Only option.

> ▸ Execute IPX applications and communicate through a migration agent with IPX nodes.

| Applications (APIs) | | |
|---|---|---|
| SPX/IPX | NCP | TCP/IP |
| IPX Compatibility Mode | | |
| | | |
| Network Adapters | | |

**FIGURE 23.9** *The IP-Only protocol architecture layout*

## IP and IPX Dual Stack

NetWare 6 allows both native IPX and IP protocols to be bound to the server. This configuration can be very useful where bandwidth and administration issues are not relevant. Systems installed with the IP and IPX option are configured to establish NCP connections over the TCP/IP stack or over the IPX stack. The NetWare 6 server, by default, seeks to transmit on the IP network whenever possible. Figure 23.10 shows the relationship between the protocol stacks for the IP and IPX protocol stacks.

**The dual stack approach assumes that both protocols are freely routed — thus providing global access for either IPX or IP clients.**

NOTE

**FIGURE 23.10** *The IP and IPX protocol relationship and architecture layout*

With both the IPX and IP stacks bound, NDS eDirectory communicates to appropriate partitions depending on local protocol communications. In a dual-stack environment, the NCP engine selects an IP connection before an IPX connection, if available. If an IP connection is made, all of the NCP packets use the TCP transport for communication between the client and server. Any NetWare 6 servers installed with both the IP and IPX protocol stacks have the following capabilities:

▸ Establish NCP connections with NetWare clients that are previous to NetWare 6 or with NetWare 6 clients without regard for the option used to install them.

▸ Execute IPX applications and communicate directly with other IPX services or nodes.

▸ Execute IPX applications and communicate through a migration agent with NetWare 6 systems installed with the IP-Only option.

Having a NetWare client installed with the IP and IPX option does not guarantee that the client will be able to establish an NCP connection with a server installed with the IP-Only option without the use of a migration agent. The type of address obtained by the client when trying to connect to a server determines the protocol stack utilized to establish the connection.

Applications that obtain address information from the bindery will not be able to connect with servers installed with the IP-Only option if no migration agent is installed and if the client is installed with both the IP and IPX stacks. This is not the case if the client has been installed with the IP-Only option.

## IP with IPX Application Support (SCMD)

If IP with the IPX Compatibility Mode (SCMD) is loaded, the NetWare 6 server can communicate with existing IPX services. The IPX Compatibility Mode driver's job is to provide IPX connectivity over the IP network. In other words, applications using the IPX stack for communications will still be able to function properly. The IPX Compatibility Mode driver also allows IP systems to communicate with IPX systems by utilizing the services of migration agents. The IPX Compatibility Mode driver achieves its job by treating the IP network as a virtual IPX network segment (CMD network segment), by encapsulating IPX datagrams inside of UDP datagrams, and by resolving RIP and SAP requests through the use of the Service Location Protocol.

The services of the IPX compatibility drivers are utilized only when the user wishes to execute an IPX application or wishes to establish connections between IP and IPX systems. If the IPX Compatibility Mode is not used, it does not affect network communications.

Figure 23.11 shows how you can install and configure the IP and IPX Compatibility Mode (SCMD). In the figure, the server called SERVER1 is upgraded from 4.11 to NetWare 6, whereas the server called SERVER 2 is a new NetWare 6 server, with one IP printer and two workstations. The clients have Compatibility Mode enabled, although they are sitting on an IP segment.

**FIGURE 23.11** *Installing and configuring a NetWare 6 server and clients with the IP and Compatibility Mode*

### Installation to Support IP with the IPX Compatibility Mode Option

In order to install and configure the servers and clients to support IP with the IPX Compatibility Mode option, follow these steps:

**I.** After your server has been upgraded to NetWare 6, you need to unbind and remove IPX from the network board. To accomplish this task, you want to load the Internetworking Configuration utility at the server console by typing INETCFG. From the Internetworking Configuration utility's startup screen, select Protocols. From the Protocol Configuration screen, select IPX and press Delete. Select Yes to disable IPX. Then exit INETCFG and down and reinitialize the server. Figure 23.12 shows an example of removing the IPX protocol using the Internetworking Configuration utility.

**FIGURE 23.12** *You can remove the IPX protocol from the upgraded server using the Internetworking Configuration utility.*

**2.** Now you need to bind the TCP/IP protocol stack to the appropriate board using the Internetworking Configuration utility. Type **INETCFG** to enter the utility and view the first screen. Select the Protocols option from the main menu. From the Protocol Configuration screen, enable TCP/IP and then press Esc to save the settings. Next, from the main menu, select Bindings. Press Insert. Select TCP/IP from the List of Protocols. Select the first interface board and press Enter. Enter the IP address and Subnet mask, as shown in Figure 23.13. Then exit INETCFG and restart the server.

**NOTE**

**If you need to have static routing enabled, you can select the Protocol option for the INETCFG menu. Select TCP/IP, enable static routing, and configure the static routing table.**

**3.** Next, you need to load the Compatibility Mode driver (SCMD.NLM) on the upgraded NetWare 6 server. This can be accomplished by entering the following command at the NetWare 6 server console:

```
LOAD SCMD (the LOAD keyword is optional)
```

**FIGURE 23.13** *You can install and bind the TCP/IP protocol stack on the upgraded server using the Internetworking Configuration utility.*

4. Finally, you want to verify the installation and configuration settings that you have made by typing the **CONFIG** command at the server console. You need to make and verify that SCMD is loaded with the board name as CMD Server. If it was installed and configured correctly, you should see information similar to the screen shown in Figure 23.14.

Compare this list with the information in Figure 23.14:

▶ **Hardware setting** — CMD server uses a reserved UDP port 2645 (A55 H).

▶ **Node address** — 7E01< IP address of the first interface bound>; the node address starts with 7E01 to distinguish from NWIP nodes.

▶ **Frame type** — Signifies Compatibility Mode driver.

▶ **Board name** — Signifies SCMD is functioning as the CMD server.

▶ **LAN protocol** — This is the IPX CMD network number.

In order to have SCMD.NLM loaded as the CMD server, the IPX protocol stack should not be bound to any network card. If IPX is bound, it comes out with the following error message: "SCMD: Could not set the router in CMD Mode routing. Unbind IPX network(s) from IPX stack/router if bound."

When you install a new NetWare 6 server and configure it for IP-Only support, it automatically loads the SCMD.NLM module as CMD server. To verify that the CMD server is functioning correctly, at the server console, type **DISPLAY SERVERS**, which shows the SAP services of the IPX servers on the network. The DISPLAY SERVERS command is a good test because it is an IPX application on the server and will not run if SCMD is not set up correctly.

```
File server name: RIO-SRV1
IPX internal network number: 0F2AC1AE
Server Up Time: 18 Hours 46 Minutes 55 Seconds

Novell NE2000
    Version 3.65a December 27, 1997
    Hardware setting: I/O ports 30 Ch to 31FH, Interrupt 3h
    Node address: 008029E1D27F
    Frame type: ETHERNET_II
    Board name: NE2000_1_II
    LAN protocol: ARP
    LAN protocol: IP Address 147.87.206.134 Mask
                  FF.FF.FF.0(255.255.252.0) Interfaces 1

Compatibility Mode Driver
    Version 1.04c August 13, 1998
    Hardware setting: I/O ports A55h
    Node address: 7E00C04FBFFE73
    Frame type: CMD
    Board name: CMD Server
    LAN protocol: IPX network FFFFFFD

Tree Name: ACME_TREE
Bindery Context(s): .acme.rio.
```

**FIGURE 23.14** *After you have changed the settings from the previous steps, you want to verify that the installation and configuration settings are correct. You can do this by typing* **CONFIG** *at the server console.*

### CMD Server Configuration Parameters

The current implementation of SCMD.NLM provides several different configuration parameters that enable you to control the features of the program. The configuration parameters are the following:

▶ Changing the CMD network number

▶ Configuring the preferred migration agent

▶ Setting the CMD preferred IP address

**Changing the CMD Network Number**    By default, the CMD network number is set to FFFFFFFD, but this can be changed through the MONITOR utility or by using the SET parameter as follows:

```
SET CMD NETWORK NUMBER=XXXXXXXX
```

The SCMD module has to be loaded before you can change the SET parameter value. Subsequently, you can unload and reload the module in order to make the change take effect permanently. Optionally, the CMD network number can be changed dynamically as the module is loaded. To do this, at the console prompt, type the following:

```
LOAD SCMD /NET=XXXXXXXX
```

**Configuring Preferred Migration Agent**    The CMD server, when configured on the network, registers itself with the SLP, learns all the available registered SLP services, and builds a link list in memory. It queries the SLP server agent or directory agent every five minutes to refresh its records. CMD clients attached to this server can access all the services learned by this server.

If a registered migration agent is available on the network, CMD Server discovers the migration agent from the SLP database and registers it with the MA. The CMD server, once registered with MA, subsequently gets its updates from MA through an event-driven delta transfer. The CMD server algorithm discovers the best MA registered with SLP. However, we can statically set the list of MAs by typing the following:

```
SET PREFERRED MIGRATION AGENTS LIST = xxx.xxx.xxx.xxx/
```

The IP address for the preferred MAs needs to be entered in decimal notation separated by periods. You can create a list of preferred migration agents. This list has a maximum of five elements. Each element in the list needs to be separated by a semicolon. You can specify the end of the list with a backslash character (/) . To make the changes effective, unload and reload SCMD.NLM.

**Setting the Preferred IP Address**    If the server is configured with multiple-interface IP-bound boards, you can specify on which IP address CMD (all modes of operation) should advertise its services and availability. To do this, type the following at the console prompt:

```
SET CMD PREFERRED IP ADDRESS = xxx.xxx.xxx.xxx
```

The IP address for the preferred IP address needs to be entered in decimal notation. To make the change take effect, unload and reload SCMD.NLM.

## IP with an IPX Connected Segment (SCMD /G)

The SCMD /G option for IP services provides a gateway to IPX services. The SCMD /G option is also called a migration agent. Having the migration agent with a gateway on the IPX network builds up the SAP/RIP list for the CMD servers on the IP network registered with the SLP and generates the SAP on the local IPX segments. On the other hand, all IPX services available on the IPX segments are provided to all the CMD servers registered with MA. The CMD server provides service and route visibility between IPX and TCP/IP networks.

**This scenario assumes that IPX has been filtered (not allowed on the IP network).**

In order to install and configure the NetWare 6 server to support IP with the SCMD /G option, follow these steps:

1. Install the NetWare 6 server as the CMD server.
2. Unload the SCMD.NLM module.
3. Bind IPX to the network adapter.
4. Load the SCMD module with the /G or /Gateway option by typing **SCMD /G**.
5. Type **CONFIG** at the server console to ensure that the settings are correct. Make sure that both IP and IPX are bound to the interface.
6. To verify that SCMD /G is advertising its services, type the command **DISPLAY SERVERS** at the server console prompt of the CMD server. You should see all of the IPX services of the IPX servers on the IPX segment. On the other hand, when you type **DISPLAY SERVERS** on the IPX servers, you should see the SAPs of the CMD servers on the IP segment.
7. If multiple MAs are on the network segment, to distribute the load you can configure CMD servers to register with the specific MA by setting the preferred migration agent list, as discussed previously in this chapter.
8. To view the list of migration agents on the network that have been registered with the SLP database, type the following at the console:
   ```
   DISPLAY SLP SERVICES mgw.novell
   ```

If you wonder why the command DISPLAY SLP SERVICES mgw.novell uses the name of Novell on the end, the reason is that SLP is an open standard and each type of service needs to register. In this example, the Novell migration agents are a specific type of service provided in SLP.

## IP Backbone with IPX Linked Segments (SCMD /BS)

The SCMD /BS option for IP services enables you to connect network IPX segments over an IP-Only segment. This type of situation can occur during the migration from IPX networks to TCP/IP networks. In such scenarios, the IPX networks must be able to see and access each other's services. Because the service discovery mechanisms in IPX and IP are different, such access is not possible directly. The feature that facilitates visibility and accessibility between disconnected IPX segments connected via CMD is referred to as *IP backbone support*.

For instance, consider a network that has two different IPX segments, as shown in Figure 23.15. Furthermore, suppose that they are connected via an IP-Only link. Because the link between the two segments is IP-Only, they cannot communicate with each other in IPX. The feature that facilitates communication between the two IPX segments is referred to as IP backbone support.

**FIGURE 23.15** *Two separate IPX network segments are connected via an IP-Only WAN link. SCMD /BS provides the support to forward the IPX communication packets across the IP link.*

### The IP Backbone Feature in CMD

The IP backbone component in CMD achieves the functionality of providing visibility and accessibility between disconnected IPX segments, as mentioned previously. The IP backbone component resides on the different migration agents at the IPX/IP network borders and helps them exchange information. The migration agents exchange information about the services and routes they are aware of and thus connect the different IPX segments. Figure 23.16 shows how the NetWare 6 servers with the module SCMD /BS loaded provide the IPX packet forwarding capabilities. In the figure are two IPX networks (IPX1 and IPX2), which are connected by a TCP/IP network. The two NetWare 6 servers each have the SCMD /BS or migration agent loaded. These migration agents provide service and route visibility between the IPX segments and the TCP/IP network.

If a client in IPX1 wants to access a service in IPX2 (or vice versa), the migration agent called MA1 should be aware of the services in IPX2. In turn, the migration agent called MA2 should be aware of services in IPX1. This is possible only if MA1 and MA2 exchange information about the respective IPX networks to which they are connected.

Such an information exchange has to be reliable and efficient, and it should not generate much traffic. To achieve all this and still keep the implementation simple enough, the IP backbone component uses the NetWare Link Services Protocol (NLSP) as a carrier for this information exchange. NLSP takes care of reliability, load balancing, efficient routing, and other such desirable features.

**FIGURE 23.16** *The NetWare 6 servers with the module SCMD /BS loaded provide the IPX packet forwarding capabilities. The NetWare 6 servers are positioned at each end of the IP link.*

### Usage of the IP Backbone Component

The IP backbone feature can be activated only on a migration agent. Because this component may not be required on all migration agents, it can be enabled or disabled according to the requirement with a command line load option. By default, when CMD is loaded in the MA mode, this component is switched off. To enable it, SCMD.NLM should be loaded with the /BS (backbone support) option, as shown here:

```
LOAD SCMD /BS (the LOAD keyword is optional)
```

In order for this feature to work, the IPXRTR.NLM has to be loaded in the server with Routing = NLSP option. This is transparent to the user because IPXRTR is loaded automatically by SCMD if not already loaded. Apart from this option, the IPX Router should be configured to use NLSP as its routing protocol.

A migration agent that has been loaded with the /BS option (on which the IP backbone feature has been enabled) exchanges data about the IPX networks only with other migration agents on which this component is enabled.

### How to Set Up the IP Backbone Feature

In order to set up or configure the IP backbone feature, follow these steps:

1. At the borders between the IPX networks and the IP-Only link, place two NetWare 6 servers having two network interface cards each.

2. Bind IPX on the interfaces connecting the server(s) with the IPX network(s).

3. Bind IP on the interfaces connecting the server(s) with the IP-Only link.

4. Check to make sure that the Service Location Protocol is loaded on the servers.

5. Check whether SLP is able to communicate between the two servers. This can be done by issuing the command DISPLAY SLP SERVICES, which should display all the SLP services visible to that server.

6. Load SCMD.NLM with the /BS option on both the NetWare servers as shown later.

After you have set up the IP backbone feature, you need to check or verify that it is working. You can check whether the IPX server in one of the IPX networks is able to see the IPX server in the other IPX network and vice versa by using the command DISPLAY SERVERS, which displays all the services that the server is aware of. If the DISPLAY SERVERS command does not work, you can perform the following checks to determine the problem with the IP backbone feature:

1. Check to make sure that both migration agents have the same CMD network number.

2. Check to make sure that the IP link between the migration agents is OK.

3. Check whether SLP is loaded on both migration agents.

4. Check whether SLP is communicating properly between the migration agents. You can use the DISPLAY SLP SERVICES command as described previously.

### Filter Issues with the IP Backbone Component in CMD

The IP backbone feature uses the NLSP protocol to achieve its functionality. One of the issues with NLSP is that SAP/RIP filtering is not applicable to NLSP; that is, if any SAP/RIP filtering is applied on the migration agents, this filtering is overridden, because the filtering does not apply to NLSP. The filter issue is illustrated in Figure 23.17. In the figure, the two IPX networks are connected via an IP-Only link. The migration agents MA1 and MA2 help the IPX networks to see and access services across the two networks. If there is a need to filter some of the services in IPX1 from IPX2, any kind of SAP/RIP filtering on the migration agents will not work. This is because the two migration agents exchange service/route information using NLSP, and NLSP overrides SAP/RIP filtering. To achieve filtering in such a situation, do the following on all the migration agents' IPX interfaces:

**1.** Load the INETCFG utility.

**2.** Select Bindings.

**3.** Select IPX.

**4.** Select Expert Bind Options.

**5.** Select RIP Bind Options and change the RIP State to ON.

**6.** Select SAP Bind Options and change the SAP State to ON.

**7.** Select NLSP Bind Options and change the NLSP State to OFF.

**FIGURE 23.17** *The two separate IPX segments communicate through an IP-Only link. Two migration agents with the backbone feature support the communication.*

### Configuration Issues with the IP Backbone Component in CMD

The IP backbone feature uses the NLSP protocol for its functionality. The IPX router (IPXRTR.NLM) is auto-loaded in this mode of operation of CMD if it is not already loaded. If IPXRTR is already loaded, CMD does not ensure that the routing protocol used is NLSP. In such a case, the user has to configure IPX to use NLSP as its routing protocol. This can be done using the INETCFG utility in the server as follows:

**1.** Load the INETCFG utility.

**2.** Select Protocols.

**3.** Select IPX.

**4.** Select Routing Protocol.

**5.** Select NLSP with RIP/SAP Compatibility.

**6.** Reinitialize the system.

If this configuration is not present, the IP backbone feature will not work.

### Dependence on the Service Location Protocol

For different migration agents to exchange information, they must discover each other in the first place. This discovery is achieved using the Service Location Protocol. Thus, in a way, the IP backbone feature in CMD is dependent on SLP. The following issue with the usage of SLP affects functioning of this feature.

### Multicasting over WAN

SLP uses multicasting as its mechanism for communication. Multicasting may not be supported over a WAN link. As a result, SLP cannot communicate over the WAN link. This, in turn, affects the IP backbone feature, because it depends on SLP to discover the services across the WAN link. This issue can be overcome by using an SLP DA (directory agent) on the migration agents on either side of the IP-Only link.

### An Issue with the CMD Clients (Split Horizon)

When using the IP backbone feature, you can create a situation in which clients requesting the services will have a split horizon. The split-horizon issue happens if you set up the migration agents as shown in Figure 23.18. The migration agents MA1 and MA2 are using the backbone support with MA1, MA2, and the CMD client in the same CMD network. The CMD client is configured to contact MA1 to get all IPX service/route information. If the CMD client wants to know the route to the IPX server in IPX2, it queries MA1 for it. But because MA1 has obtained the service/route information about IPX2 from the interface over which it is connected to the client, it does not respond to the client query, due to the split-horizon algorithm. Thus, the CMD client is unable to access services in IPX2 in such a scenario.

The split-horizon issue can be resolved by installing a new migration agent as shown in Figure 23.19. In this figure, MA1 and MA2 are still using the backbone support mode, but they now have a different CMD network number. MA3 is the new migration agent, which has a different CMD network number. The CMD client is also in the CMD network that the new migration agent is in. Thus, the client contacts MA3 to get the IPX service/route information.

In such a configuration, MA1 and MA2 achieve the MA-MA functionality. MA1 thus populates IPX1 with the service/route information of IPX2. MA3 gets all the service/route information about IPX1 and IPX2 through the IPX interface only. So when the client queries MA3 about IPX2, the split horizon does not apply, because it gets the information from a different interface.

**FIGURE 23.18** *A situation can arise in which clients cannot access desired services because of the split horizon among migration agents.*

**FIGURE 23.19** *The split-horizon issue can be resolved by installing a new migration agent with a different CMD network number.*

# Your Migration Strategy Depends upon Your Goals

The migration options that we have discussed do not take into account your goals or needs in migrating your network protocols. The most common goals for changing your IPX networks to IP are the following:

▶ Migrate to obtain Internet connectivity.

▶ Migrate to cut administrative costs associated with IPX networking.

▶ Migrate to have an IP-Only network.

### Migrate to Obtain Internet Connectivity

In order to add Internet connectivity to NetWare systems, simply upgrade your network servers to NetWare 6 using the IP and IPX option, as described previously. Although this upgrade path requires administration of both the IP and IPX networking protocols, you do not have to worry about setting up any migration agents to maintain connectivity to IPX as you upgrade your systems.

### Migrate to Cut IPX Administrative Costs

If you want to migrate your networks from IPX to IP to maximize your return on your investment, you will probably want to take advantage of the functionality provided by the IPX compatibility drivers and migration agents. The IPX compatibility feature is critical in this scenario because it allows migration without losing connectivity and without forcing you to upgrade existing applications. When utilizing the IPX compatibility feature to migrate, start the migration with the leaves of the network and finish with the backbone of the network or vice versa.

Administrators wanting to migrate networks using the IPX compatibility feature must understand that the IPX compatibility drivers are dependent upon the functions of SLP and that costs are associated with setting up an SLP infrastructure. On the other hand, setting up an SLP infrastructure is an investment in the future because SLP is an emerging Internet standard that will be leveraged by future applications and devices.

# Migrate to Have an IP-Only Network

The choice to migrate your network to IP-Only on both servers and workstations depends completely on whether you have to support IPX applications anywhere in the network. If you do not have any applications that need IPX, you can configure your servers and workstations to use IP. The definition of an IP segment is one that does not pass IPX through the router to the other network segments.

By using the Compatibility Mode drivers, you can configure your network segments to run only IP but still support IPX applications. The Compatibility Mode drivers can be loaded on both servers and workstations. Using the Compatibility Mode drivers, you ensure that IPX applications are 100 percent supported without having to bind IPX to the network.

Applications are considered IPX applications if they use the interfaces provided by the IPX stack or they specify IPX addresses when trying to establish NCP connections. The best way to screen out IPX applications is to run them on a test network on which IPX is absent (no IPX stacks loaded). Many applications let you specify the networking protocol to use when communicating.

In order to convert all services on a network segment from IPX to IP, you typically need to configure the Compatibility Mode to support IPX applications and then turn IPX routing off at the router. These steps are as follows:

1. Place a migration agent in a central location within the network topology. Because the rest of the network will still have IPX, the migration agent must be placed outside of the segment being converted so that it can collect the SAP/RIP information for clients and servers in the IP area.

2. Before you start upgrading clients to IP/CMD, you should upgrade all the servers in the IP area to NetWare 6 with IP and IPX bound. IPX clients and IP clients will then be able to access these servers while you are converting the clients from IPX to IP/CMD.

3. Before you start upgrading clients in the IP area to IP/CMD, you may want to convert the printers in the area to NDPS and configure NDPS to print via IP.

4. To avoid upgrading the clients twice (IPX/IP and later to IPX/CMD), you must place migration agents in a central location within the network topology. During the client upgrade, you can configure the clients to use the migration agents to access IPX services.

5. After the clients have been upgraded to IP/CMD, you can remove IPX from the NetWare 6 servers and load SCMD (which provides IPX application support).

6. After the clients, servers, and printers in the IP area have been upgraded to IP/CMD, you can shut off IPX routing to the IP segment.

Sometimes, IP-Only is the final goal but you have an immediate need to remove IPX from the network. The following migration path requires migration of all applications from IPX to IP before IPX is disabled on the network.

In order for this migration method to function properly, the NetWare clients must be configured twice during the course of this migration. Taking advantage of the Automatic Client Update (ACU) feature of NetWare 6 and the Workstation Manager feature can minimize the cost of modifying client configurations.

If you later discover that your applications require IPX, you must switch to one of the migration strategies outlined in this chapter. The steps that follow describe how to migrate a network from IPX to IP without relying on the IPX Compatibility Mode feature:

1. Identify IPX applications and make sure that they can be configured/upgraded/replaced to run over the TCP/IP stack.

2. Start upgrading/installing your servers and clients using the IP and IPX option.

3. Start migrating applications from IPX to IP.

4. Turn off IPX networking at the routers when all the IPX applications have been migrated and all the NetWare clients and servers have been upgraded/installed using the IP and IPX option.

5. Modify the configuration of the NetWare servers and clients to be IP-Only servers and clients.

## Migrating a Section of the Network

In order to successfully convert your network protocols, you need to know how to migrate just a portion of the network. You have the option to first migrate your networks starting with the leaf nodes or with the backbone. In order to migrate only a section of your network at a time, follow the steps outlined here. In order to complete these steps successfully, you must ensure that the network section being migrated is not used to interconnect other sections of the network using IPX. Figure 23.20 shows the setup for migrating a segment of your network.

**FIGURE 23.20** *The IPX segment can be migrated to IP.*

Using this example, you can follow these steps to convert the IPX segment in your network to IP:

1. Upgrade Server 1 to NetWare 6 as a migration agent.
2. Upgrade Server 2 to NetWare 6 using the IP and IPX install option.
3. Upgrade clients to NetWare 6 using the IP-Only install option.
4. Unbind IPX from the network adapters in Server 1 and load SCMD.NLM. Unbind IPX from the network adapters in Server 1 and reload SCMD.NLM without the migration agent option.
5. Turn off IPX routing at the router.

### Migrating Leaf Networks First

Migrating leaf networks first reduces the impact of the migration on the IPX routing infrastructure of the network, and it allows the administrator to focus efforts on specific sites. Because the backbone is the last portion of the network migrated, however, administrative costs may not be offset as quickly.

These steps describe how to migrate a network from IPX to IP, starting with the leaf networks first:

1. Identify the nodes and links that form the backbone of the network.

2. Select and Upgrade/Install some servers in the backbone to serve as migration agents.

3. Select the leaf portion of the network to be migrated. This may be a group of segments connected to the backbone via a WAN link. Migrate the selected portion of the network following the steps outlined previously in the section called "Migrating a Section of the Network."

4. Repeat Step 3 until all networks connected to the backbone are migrated.

5. Migrate the backbone section using the steps outlined in the section called "Migrating a Section of the Network."

Figure 23.21 shows an example of converting the leaf segments in your network before you convert the backbone segment.

The segment marked C is the backbone in the network. You want to upgrade or install two servers on this segment to NetWare 6. These two servers should also be running as migration agents. After you have set up the migration agents, you want to select the portion of the network consisting of leaf segments to perform the migration. In the example, the segments marked A and B are the ones that you want to target. Next, follow the migration instructions as outlined in the section called "Migrating a Section of the Network." Make sure that you first upgrade or install servers in both segment A and segment B as NetWare 6 migration agents to minimize performance degradation while each segment is being migrated. After you have successfully installed the migration agents on the segments, turn off IPX routing in routers A and B when all the nodes in the section have been migrated to IP-Only. After all the leaf segments have been converted or migrated to segment C, use the steps outlined in the section called "Migrating a Section of the Network."

**FIGURE 23.21** *An example of migrating a leaf segment of the network before the backbone*

## Migrating the Backbone First

Migrating the backbone first alleviates administrative costs associated with maintaining IPX over the backbone. This migration path requires migration agents at each of the segments connected to the backbone and the backbone support feature of the migration agents before IPX routing is disabled on the backbone. The migration agents with the backbone support feature enabled are able to interconnect IPX segments by exchanging RIP and SAP information and by routing encapsulated IPX datagrams.

These steps describe how to migrate a network from IPX to IP starting with the backbone:

**1.** Identify the nodes and links that form the backbone of your network.

**2.** Select and upgrade or install some servers to NetWare 6 in each one of the segments connected to the backbone. These servers should serve as migration agents with the backbone support feature enabled.

**3.** Migrate the nodes on the backbone section using the steps outlined in the section called "Migrating a Section of the Network."

**4.** Select all leaf segments of the network to migrate. These may consist of a group of segments connected to the backbone via a WAN link. Migrate the selected portion of the network following the steps outlined in the section called "Migrating a Section of the Network." Repeat this step until all networks connected to the backbone are migrated.

Figure 23.22 shows an example of converting the backbone segment in your network before you convert the leaf segments.

**FIGURE 23.22** *An example of migrating the backbone segment before migrating the leaf networks*

The segment marked B is the backbone in the network. You want to upgrade or install servers on each leaf segment to NetWare 6. The leaf networks are marked as segment A, segment C, and segment D. You need to run the migration agent with backbone support on each of the leaf segments. After you have set up the migration agents (SCMD /BS), you want to convert or migrate the nodes on the backbone segment, which is marked as segment B. Follow the migration instructions outlined in the section called "Migrating a Section of the Network." After you have successfully migrated the backbone segment, you then need to turn off IPX routing in routers A, C, and D. Finally, migrate segments A, C, and D.

### NetWare/IP Networks Rely on Migrating Leaf Segments First

Migrating a NetWare/IP network to IP relies heavily on the IPX Compatibility Mode feature to maintain connectivity. This typically means that you want to migrate the leaf segments or networks first. In addition, you want to upgrade or install the NetWare 6 servers with the IP and IPX protocols.

**NOTE**

**Migrating a NetWare/IP network to IP-Only using the migrate backbone (first) method is not recommended because it will seriously disrupt the NetWare/IP infrastructure.**

The workstation and servers that utilize NetWare/IP to communicate are viewed as IPX nodes to clients running IP-Only, They are reached through the migration agents. Workstations and servers using the IP-Only protocol are viewed as IPX nodes by NetWare/IP. This implies migration agents also need to function as NetWare/IP gateways, which allows the NetWare/IP clients to communicate with machines using IP-Only.

Migrating NetWare/IP to IP without using the migration agents (Compatibility Mode) is accomplished by simply installing the IPX or IP network protocol that you wish. However, be aware that you are removing the NetWare/IP component for the workstation or server and replacing it with either IPX or IP. Be aware that, without using the migration agent at the server, a disruption in service between NetWare/IP and IPX or IP may result.

### Other Migration Considerations

In addition to the normal issues, you may need to understand several miscellaneous migration issues. These issues are not presented in any specific order.

#### SAP/RIP Filters and the Migration Agent Backbone Support Feature

If the backbone support feature of the migration agents is enabled, the RIP/SAP information exchange between these agents may bypass the RIP/SAP filters that you may have set up in your routers. Refer to the migration agent documentation to learn how to set up RIP/SAP filters using the migration agents.

### Turning Off Microsoft IPX Networking

Clients may be set up to do Microsoft Networking using IPX and/or IP. If clients are set up to do Microsoft Networking over IPX and you want to migrate them from IPX to IP, you may want to enable Microsoft Networking over TCP/IP and then disable Microsoft Networking over IPX. This may be necessary to reduce the demand on the services provided by the IPX Compatibility feature.

### IPX-, Bindery-, and SAP-Based Applications and Utilities

Most networks have evolved slowly over the years and are generally a combination of old and new software and hardware. Legacy software and legacy network infrastructure remain necessary for many years after newer replacements have been made available. Sometimes these applications and infrastructure elements limit the ease of migration. The situations described here might present such limitations when migrating from an IPX to an IP network.

Many of the DOS utilities that were released in the NetWare 4 release were modified to work with both NDS and the older bindery. These utilities make their first attempt at discovery by going to the bindery context of NDS. If the discovery attempt fails, these utilities attempt to use SAP and bindery calls to use the older technology.

Many of the scripts that IS&T staffs use to run their daily operations are based on both NCP and DOS batch processing files. In both cases, the NetWare-specific elements are generally command-line versions of NetWare DOS utilities or NetWare NLMs. The reasons for continuing to use these commands should be reevaluated in light of the newer technology shipped with NetWare 6.

### The Filtered Network

The first question that needs to be addressed with regard to filtering is whether it remains necessary in the IP environment. Filtering in the IPX environment sought to address congestion control and service access. With an IP-based system, the SAP that created congestion no longer exists. Service visibility is a different issue.

The real solution for this issue is the use of NDS rather than the SAP/bindery infrastructure. The filtering capability within the IP routers can still be used to replace the IPX routing. But in the IPX environment, SAP was just a special packet type that could be easily managed at the routing level. SLP, DHCP, DNS, NCP, NDS, and other protocols are just data within the IP packet and not so easily managed at the router.

# The Service Location Protocol

The *Service Location Protocol* is an Internet standard protocol as defined by the Request for Comments (RFC) 2165. SLP is defined as a discovery method for TCP/IP-based communications. It is not a name resolution service like NDS or DNS. The main purpose or function of SLP is discovery. SLP discovers infrastructure services such as NDS servers, DNS servers, DHCP servers, NDPS registration servers, and various protocol gateways. In addition, SLP encapsulates SAP broadcasts in IP packets if you have IPX Compatibility Mode running.

The Service Location Protocol basically provides the same type of information in IP networks as SAP provides in IPX networks. It registers information in a database and allows clients to query the database to find services. However, the following are two principal differences between SAP and SLP:

▶ SLP does not maintain a global database of services. It registers services only in the local area. It discovers services in the local area via multicast requests, which are forwarded using NDS replication from network to network within a site.

▶ SLP assumes that the client is able to locate services themselves or a database server representing those services using these pan-network multicasts.

If a global database of services is required for your network, you can configure SLP to store its information in the NDS tree. Using this method, local SLP information is compiled to provide a global representation of all available services on the network. This provides dynamic discovery of services locally and scalability in large networks.

**NOTE**

**SLP and IP require that NetWare 6 be running on at least one NetWare server in the network.**

The Service Location Protocol provides a method for registering and discovering network services dynamically in IP networks. The Novell Client for Windows 95/98 and Windows NT/2000 can use SLP to dynamically discover NDS trees and NetWare servers, providing plug-and-play capabilities similar to what Novell customers have enjoyed for many years with their IPX networks. Figure 23.23 shows how the Service Location Protocol provides a method to register and discover network services.

**FIGURE 23.23** *The Service Location Protocol provides IP with a method to register and discover network services.*

SLP is not router-based. It uses standard UDP and TCP packets to register and discover network services. Network routers are not involved in maintaining SLP service information. This feature eliminates the need for constant router synchronization traffic (for example, once-a-minute SAP broadcasts in IPX networks).

If you do not use IPX Compatibility Mode (in other words, if your network does not include any IPX applications or services), or if you are not planning on using SLP for NDS tree or NetWare server discovery, SLP does not need to be enabled for your IP network.

### SLP Agents

The three types of agents that NetWare 6 SLP uses are the following:

▶ User agents, which acquire service handles for user applications

▶ Service agents, which advertise service handles

▶ Directory agents, which collect service handles in internetworked enterprises

Applications running on a computer are represented by a user agent that understands the service and resource needs of the application. Each network service is represented by a service agent, which makes it available to user agents. SLP dynamically maintains service attributes, so that a user agent can obtain current information.

NetWare 6 includes a Compatibility Mode feature, which enables SLP to register services that are SAP dependent. When a service that relies upon service discovery is loaded on a NetWare 6 server, the server reroutes the SAP broadcast to SLP. The service can then be registered by a service agent or by a directory agent, and a user agent can locate this service.

### User Agents

A *user agent* initiates a discovery on behalf of an application. The NetWare 6 client software contains a user agent that is enabled by default and is launched during the bootup process. In an IP environment, SLP is the client software's preferred method to locate an NDS tree and server when this client software does not support DHCP.

### Service Agents

A *service agent* works on behalf of a service to respond directly to a user agent's query for specific services. You can also configure a service agent to register the service with one or more directory agents. A user agent queries a service agent directly if no directory agent exists or if a directory agent does not respond to discovery queries.

### Directory Agents

A *directory agent* collects and maintains information about service agents. A directory agent responds to a user agent's query only if the directory agent maintains information about the requested service.

If you use directory agents on a NetWare 6 network, the NetWare 6 client software queries the directory agent for service information during the bootup process. To configure a NetWare 6 server as a directory agent, you load an optional NetWare Loadable Module. However, you do not configure every server as a directory agent. You configure one local server as a directory agent, which provides service information for many other NetWare 6 servers.

The point of interface between SLP and NDS is the SLP directory agent. The directory agent provides common data storage of network service information collected through SLP. The directory agent uses NDS as its database for network service information that is distributed globally. NDS adds significant value to SLP by leveraging existing NDS standards for configuring NDS tree structures, for providing a central point of administration, and for enabling NDS to replicate service information. NDS replication services allow directory agent-to-directory agent communication. This is unique in SLP implementations, and it facilitates global distribution of SLP database information. NDS replica services give the directory agent the capability to access global services from a local replica.

### Scopes

A *scope* can be thought of as a collection of services within a logical group. You might want to implement a scope for a very large installation to create a group of directory agents and services registered with these directory agents.

## SLP NDS Objects

SLP in NetWare 6 has several new NDS objects. These objects are represented by SLP:

- ▶ Scope container object
- ▶ SLP service object
- ▶ SLP directory agent object

The SLP scope container object represents an SLP scope and is the container in which SLP service objects are stored. SLP service objects represent a network service discovered through the Service Location Protocol. They contain all of the SLP information about the network service, including its network address and attributes. The SLP Directory agent object represents the actual SLP directory agent.

### The SLP Scope Container Object

The SLP scope container object is the storage container for SLP service information. Each object contains all the SLP service objects for the specific scope. The NDS administrator can replicate the container into other partitions within the tree or within federated trees. The object is a stand-alone entity within the NDS tree, and there is no relationship between its distinguished name, the tree name, and the scope name. When a Service agent forwards a service record to a directory agent within a specific scope, the scope name is mapped to the scope object by using the name attribute within the container object. The SLP scope object must contain rights to read, write, and browse the container because the access rights of the directory agent object access are equivalent to the access rights of the scope object. Because the scope object uses distinguished name syntax, the scope object can be moved to a different location in the tree and NDS automatically changes all values to reflect the new location.

### The SLP Service Object

The SLP service object is a leaf object that represents a service registration. SLP service objects are subordinate to the SLP scope object and contain all information supplied by a service registration. SLP service objects are stored in the appropriate SLP scope object according to their scope.

### The Directory Agent Object

The SLP directory agent object is a leaf object that represents a single instance of a directory agent. Multiple directory agents cannot share a single object. This object defines the directory agent's configuration, scope, and security. The directory agent uses this object to log into the server and operate under the access control requirements assigned to the NCP server object.

## Major Features of SLP

As mentioned, IP uses Service Location Protocol, which is a service discovery mechanism that allows NetWare 6 clients to locate servers and services that are Service Advertising Protocol-dependent during the bootup process.

NetWare 6 provides several methods to discover services, including the following:

- ▸ **NDS eDirectory query** — The preferred method for an application to locate a service is through NDS, which provides authentication and security services for devices that can be registered as NDS objects.

- ▸ **Domain Naming System (DNS) lookup** — An application that is not NDS aware can use DNS to locate a service.

- ▸ **Dynamic Host Configuration Protocol (DHCP) query** — The NetWare 6 client software uses DHCP to locate an NDS tree and server when the client is configured to use DHCP services. DHCP offers three new options for obtaining NDS tree, server, and context information from a NetWare DHCP server daemon (a DHCP server process running on a NetWare 6 server).

- ▸ **Lightweight Directory Access Protocol (LDAP) lookup** — NetWare 6 provides LDAP support when an application specifically sends an LDAP query.

- ▸ **SLP query** — NetWare 6 clients in an IP environment use SLP to discover the preferred NDS tree and server when the clients are not configured to use DHCP services. Although SLP can be used as a more fully functional mechanism to discover services, the best implementation is to use SLP only during the bootup process.

The application itself determines which discovery method to use. For example, an NCP-based application queries NDS directly to locate a service. However, another application could use an LDAP query to locate a service.

The NetWare 6 client software has two options for locating an NDS tree and server in an IP environment: DHCP or SLP. The NetWare 6 client software uses DHCP if you have configured the client to use DHCP services. For example, you can configure the client to obtain an IP address from a DHCP server. The NetWare 6 client software uses SLP if you have not configured the client to use DHCP services.

**NOTE**

**In NetWare's IPX/SPX-based communications architecture, the NetWare client software issues a SAP broadcast (also known as a Get Nearest Server request) during the bootup process to locate services. When a NetWare 6 network is configured to support only IP, however, the NetWare 6 client software cannot use SAP to locate services. (Of course, losing SAP is not really a bad thing because devices that use SAP continually broadcast their services on the network.)**

### Discovery of Infrastructure Service Providers

SLP works with NDS to help bring together the IP infrastructure services, which include NDS trees, DNS servers, NCP servers, NDPS service registries, and some of the protocol gateways. Doing so allows NetWare clients to discover services by querying one database rather than the whole network. The NetWare Client uses this information to gain access to infrastructure services. The SLP system does not create end user–accessible NDS objects from these infrastructure services. Instead, it uses NDS to collect and replicate knowledge of these services for the benefit of the client.

In previous IPX-based versions of NetWare, this kind of global distribution of infrastructure knowledge was accomplished through the SAP/bindery architecture. SAP was global, and each machine had a bindery. Consequently, any service that could place a SAP packet on the wire could be globally known. Unfortunately, there was a price to be paid for this global distribution. Bandwidth was consumed and network administrators had to engage in significant filtering to regulate line congestion and service visibility. With the advent of NDS, this began to change. Newer applications were able to forego SAP, register themselves directly with NDS, and take advantage of the NDS replication to attain global visibility.

Many administrators, however, wanted not one but many NDS trees to service their companies. So how was the network client to find these trees? Each tree generated a SAP advertisement that was saved in the router tables of each NetWare server. The client had only to make it to an initial server to find this global infrastructure information.

SAP was created in the early days of networking with a worst-case scenario in mind. The system refreshed itself every 60 seconds, regardless of whether anything had changed. This was advantageous for plug-and-play in the LAN but impractical across WAN links. Services are registered in SLP with a lifetime that defines the amount of time the service will be available. If the service goes away before the lifetime has elapsed, a request to that service fails.

NDPS makes significant use of SLP in the IP environment. The presence of SLP allows a degree of automated management in the IP environment that is equivalent to that found in the IPX environment. NDPS will function without SLP, but automated management is reduced.

### Where to Place the Directory Agents

A small network may not need SLP configuration. The user and service agents on both client and server are automatically loaded and require no configuration. In a small network (up to 25–30 servers), you probably have no need to implement a directory agent. For larger networks, a directory agent is needed to provide scaling and enterprise visibility of services. Placement and frequency of directory agents in the network depends on several factors:

- ▶ Is the company centralized, or is it distributed, or does it support many small branch offices?
- ▶ Should IP multicast be routed outside the local segment?
- ▶ What does the existing NDS replication infrastructure look like?
- ▶ Will there be a need to use SLP scoping for congestion control?
- ▶ What degree of fault tolerance is desired in the system?
- ▶ Will every network segment need to work with every other network segment?
- ▶ How many services will be represented on the network?
- ▶ What is an acceptable response time for service discovery?

If you set up the SLP infrastructure using directory agents, and if you rely on the IPX Compatibility Mode feature to accomplish the migration, you must place directory agents so as to minimize the round-trip distance between the IP-Only nodes and their closest directory agent. This is necessary to avoid having IPX applications timing out when they perform RIP or SAP requests.

Finally, within the corporate LAN, the administrator could easily use any of the technologies presented as well as IP multicast for SLP directory agent synchronization. A mixture of technologies could work concurrently in the LAN environment. The following issues should be considered.

**IP Multicast**    The advent of IP multicast technology creates an additional factor that the system administrator must consider. On a local segment, multicast is manageable. But when routers are configured to enable multicast, the multicast packet enters the router, which checks to determine whether any other local segments have registered to listen to multicast. Upon finding a registered listener, the router moves the multicast packet into another segment. With the wrong configuration, multicast takes on characteristics of broadcast, consuming bandwidth. Properly configured, however, IP multicast can provide a global distribution of critical information.

In its default mode in a local network segment environment, the SLP user agent uses IP multicast to access the several SLP service agents. Or IP multicast can be configured and made available across the networks. Then SLP will utilize the available bandwidth to continue seeking service agents. If you decide to restrict multicast traffic, you can implement DHCP to help the user agents find service and directory agents that are not local and cannot be discovered through multicast.

**NDS Replication**    NDS replication can be used to synchronize the data in numerous SLP directory agents across the enterprise. Synchronization traffic across a WAN link can be expensive, though, and consumes bandwidth. Within the LAN, however, this replication service is a viable alternative. System administrators should consult the existing literature on NDS deployment to understand the administrative requirements and network impacts of NDS replication.

**Fault Tolerance**    While a single SLP directory agent could provide service for a fairly large company, that would create a single point of failure. The presence of multiple directory agents provides a degree of fault tolerance so that the failure of a single DA will not impact the network. Once again, consider the issue of synchronizing the multiple directory agents. Each of the alternatives previously presented carries both costs and benefits.

**Service Visibility**    Services do not necessarily have to be provided to the whole network. For many years, NetWare administrators have been regulating network congestion and service visibility through IPX packet filtering at the routers. Not every user of the network saw every service that SAP advertised in the network. A similar situation can be achieved by disabling IP multicast. A network can be configured to use multiple SLP directory agents, each containing different data and servicing a different region of the network.

# SLP Design

In a large network, the system administrator has to use the SLP directory agent to achieve scalability across the network. The directory agent may be installed with system defaults that make it immediately usable. On installation, the directory agent extends the NDS NCP object schema and creates an SLP-DA record within the NCP server object. It also creates a default container in the NDS name base for SLP entries. This container may be replicated at the discretion of the system administrator.

In the largest networks, however, the use of a flat SLP implementation may prove inadequate for scalability and traffic management. SLP scopes subdivide services. For example, some services may be regularly registered on the machines in the engineering department and have no use to anyone outside of that department. Thus, the administrator could configure the system to attach a scope attribute of "ENG" to each service in that area. These services would then be seen only by requests that included the attribute of SCOPE=ENG. Such subdividing of services provides a kind of filtering that administrators are used to in both IP and IPX environments. SLP implementations that don't utilize scopes are said to be *unscoped*.

You may not use every SLP option on your company's network. The set of processes you use depends on which SLP network design you choose. The SLP network design you choose, in turn, depends on the size and complexity of your company's network. Essentially, you determine the number of services running on the network, and you choose the best SLP network design to handle these services. You can choose one of the following SLP network designs:

▶ Small service radius
▶ Medium service radius
▶ Large service radius

## Small Service Radius

You can use the small service radius design for an installation that supports 50 servers or less. In this design, user agents query service agents to locate services. If you use a small service radius design on a NetWare 6 network, you simply keep the default settings for NetWare 6 and the NetWare 6 client software. Figure 23.24 shows a small network with fewer than 25 servers. This size network gains no advantage from an SLP directory agent. All SLP communication can be handled by the SLP service and user agents with local segment IP multicast. With this simple system, the network client is able to have dynamic discovery of NDS trees, NCP servers, the NDPS Service Registry, and other infrastructure services such as gateways. NDS-aware services could register themselves with NDS.

**FIGURE 23.24** *You can implement the small service radius SLP design when you have fewer than 25 NetWare 6 servers.*

## Medium Service Radius

In a large installation, however, you may not want hundreds of service agents replying to queries from user agents. In this case, you can load the directory agent on one NetWare server. When service agents for NetWare 6 servers discover that a directory agent is available, these service agents register with the directory agent. The directory agent then replies to queries from user agents. By default, the NetWare 6 client software can locate and use a directory agent if one exists on the NetWare 6 network. You do not have to reconfigure the NetWare 6 client software to use a directory agent.

As shown in Figure 23.25, a medium network using Service Location Protocol requires SLP directory agents to provide scaling and WAN support. If the network is architected to be a rather flat network, a single directory agent might be sufficient. Unlike on the smaller systems, there may be no IP multicast in this network. In that case, the directory agent can be found by the user agents through the use of DHCP. Also, with the directory agent, information can be stored in an NDS container that can be replicated through the corporate network and have information that can be made available to other directory agents. Classification of service information would not normally be necessary in this environment.

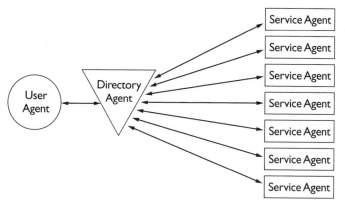

**FIGURE 23.25** *When you implement the medium service radius SLP design, you want to implement the SLP agents to provide scaling and WAN support.*

## Large Service Radius

You can use the large service radius design for a very large installation that has services spanning WAN links. In this design, you group services in scopes. For example, if your company had two offices — one in London and one in Paris — you could configure two scopes: a London scope and a Paris scope. When a user in the London office requested a service, the request would indicate which scope contained the requested service. In this way, you would prevent SLP queries from being sent over a WAN link, which is typically a low-bandwidth, high-latency link that is not designed to handle excessive traffic.

You can also use the large service radius design to reduce the load on a particular directory agent: You separate services into scopes and set up a directory agent for each scope, ensuring that a single directory agent does not have to handle all SLP queries.

Large-scale implementation of Service Location Protocol will most likely require a combination of SLP directory agents, NDS eDirectory, DHCP, and local IP multicast. Figure 23.26 illustrates the role that NDS would play in such an environment. The SLP directory agent would collect service information from the local service agents. That information would then be loaded to a container in NDS. That container would then be replicated as necessary with other SLP directory agents feeding in information from different parts of the network and retrieving information collected from other directory agents. Thus, the local service can receive global distribution (at the system administrator's discretion).

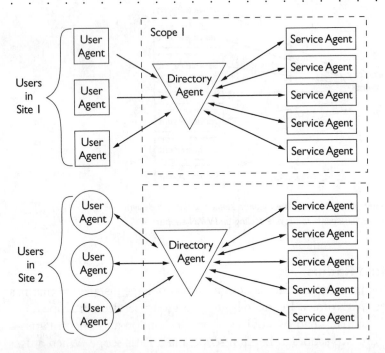

**FIGURE 23.26** *In the large service radius design, you can assign several scopes to a particular directory agent, and you can assign several directory agents to one scope.*

# SLP Communications

SLP communications can use the User Datagram Protocol (UDP) or Transmission Control Protocol (TCP) with registered port 427. Although most SLP communications use UDP, TCP can be used for bulk information transfer—that is, traffic generated by a single request with multiple replies. (If you use an access filter or a security filter on routers or gateways, you must remove the filter on port 427 to enable SLP communications to work properly.)

SLP uses a combination of several types of communications:

- Directory agent discovery multicast packets (147.85.1.35)
- SLP general multicast packets (147.85.1.22)
- Internet Group Message Protocol (IGMP) multicast packets
- Unicast packets (station address)

### Locating a Directory Agent

During the bootup process, an SLP device sends a directory agent discovery multicast packet, looking for a directory agent. If the service agent locates a directory agent, the service agent uses unicast packets to communicate with that directory agent.

If your company's network doesn't support multicast packets or DHCP services, broadcast communications or static configurations can be used to discover directory agents. For example, if your company has a large network, you might have disabled multicast forwarding on routers to control traffic. In addition, you might have manually assigned IP addresses, eliminating the need for DHCP services.

Broadcast communications are, however, an undesirable way to implement SLP because a broadcast is considered a local operation and typically isn't allowed to propagate throughout an entire internetwork. As a result, using a broadcast reduces the radius in which services can be discovered to the local network only. A device cannot discover services on the other side of a router, unless the router forwards broadcast packets.

If no directory agent exists, the user agent sends an SLP general multicast packet to locate the requested service (rather than the directory agent).

### Joining a Multicast Group

SLP devices join a multicast group during the bootup process by sending an IGMP multicast packet on the network. Based on the IGMP multicast packets that IP routers receive from SLP devices, these routers decide whether or not to forward multicast packets to particular subnetworks. IP routers forward multicast packets only to subnetworks in which other devices have joined the multicast group. In this way, SLP uses multicast groups to reduce traffic.

To get a better idea of how SLP works, let's take a look at the NetWare 6 client software's bootup process. If the NetWare 6 client software is using SLP to discover services on a network that does not use directory agents or scopes, this client software completes the following bootup process:

▸ The client software's user agent sends an SLP directory agent discovery multicast packet.

▸ The client software's user agent sends an SLP general multicast packet for the migration gateway. (The migration gateway offers a gateway service between IP and IPX configurations on a NetWare 6 network.)

▸ The client software's user agent sends an SLP general multicast packet to discover the preferred NDS tree and server.

▸ The client software's DHCP stack sends DHCP attempts.

▸ The service agent replies.

## SLP Service Types

The services that register in SLP have specific types associated with them. The service types are used as categories for the services and are used for query and display purposes. The service types in SLP appear with URLs to define the specific resource that registered. This method of defining resources creates more flexible communications and naming mechanisms that take advantage of existing technology. For example, when a user agent sends an SLP query to find the preferred NDS tree and server, either a service agent or a directory agent replies with the following information:

```
service:ndap.novell:///CAMELOT.ACME.ACME_TREE
```

The information displayed shows the CAMELOT.ACME.ACME_TREE information that has registered with SLP. An example of the CAM-SRV1 server registering with the SLP would appear as follows:

```
service:bindery.novell:///CAM-SRV1
```

The IP address of the service provider (the NDS server, in this example) is located in the attributes of the reply. Devices can also use SLP to discover other types of services. The following list shows some of the most common Novell SLP service types and what they are used for:

▸ The MGW.NOVELL service type is used for migration agents that register with SLP.

▸ The NDAP.NOVELL service type is used by the NDS partitions. A NetWare 6 server that has IP bound with a replica for a given partition in an NDS tree registers with SLP on behalf of that NDS partition.

▸ The BINDERY.NOVELL service type is used by NetWare 6 servers. Every NetWare 6 server with an IP stack registers with SLP as a BINDERY.NOVELL server.

▸ The SAPSRV.NOVELL service type is used for NetWare5 servers with IPX Compatibility Mode, which redirects all the IPX SAP requests to SLP as SAPSRV.NOVELL objects.

▸ The RMS.NOVELL service type is used by the NDPS brokers. The Resource Management Service of NDPS registers with SLP.

▸ The RCONSOLE.NOVELL service type registers the new NetWare 6 rconsole with SLP.

▸ The DIRECTORY-AGENT service type is used to send an SLP multicast packet to rediscover the directory agents on the network.

## SLP Console Commands

Many SLP commands have been made available to you at the server console. These commands enable you to display, query, monitor, debug, and set up the Service Location Protocol information.

### DISPLAY SLP SERVICES <SERVICE TYPE> [<RESTRICTION CLAUSE>]

The console command to display SLP services enables you to display or view all the IP services that have been registered. You can restrict the display of services by providing the specific service type or using a restriction clause. An example of using the Display SLP Services console command is shown in Figure 23.27.

In order to restrict the view using a service type, you can use some of the most common Novell SLP service types, such as the following:

▸ MGW.NOVELL

▸ NDAP.NOVELL

▸ BINDERY.NOVELL

▸ SAPSRV.NOVELL

▸ RMS.NOVELL

▸ RCONSOLE.NOVELL

▸ DIRECTORY-AGENT

**FIGURE 23.27** *An example of using the Display SLP Services console command*

## DISPLAY SLP ATTRIBUTES [<RESTRICTION CLAUSE>]

The console command to display the SLP attributes for a specific service enables you to display or view all the SLP attributes for the services that have been registered. You can restrict the display of attributes for a specific service by providing a restriction clause. An example of using the Display SLP attributes console command is shown in Figure 23.28.

**FIGURE 23.28** *An example of using the Display SLP Attributes console command*

SLP query restrictions are in parentheses at the end of the SLP query string. The format for restriction clauses is as follows (<slp attribute>==<value>). Also, <=, >= can be used in place of ==. For example, if you want to list all the migration agents servicing the CMD network number 01010000, enter the following SLP query from the server console:

```
DISPLAY SLP SERVICES MGW.NOVELL (CMD NETWORK==01010000)
```

### DISPLAY SLP DA

This console command displays the list of SLP directory agents and their current status. You can use the command SLP DEBUG LEVEL = 8 to display all the requests made to the DA, including the type of SLP request and the IP address of the UA or SA sending the request. In order to log this information to a file for a period of time, you can use SLP OPEN and SLP CLOSE. The SLP trace file can then be GREPed to find any UAs or SAs that are requesting more from the DA than they should. In addition, you may also use the following command:

```
DISPLAY SLP SERVICES DIRECTORY-AGENT
```

This command enables you to discover and view the status of all the directory agents that exist in the network. You can also change the status of the directory agents from inactive to active using the following SET SLP DEBUG command:

```
SET SLP DEBUG = <numeric option>
```

The numeric options are defined as 0x01=COMM, 0x02=TRAN, 0x04=API, 0x08=DA, 0x010=ERR, 0x020=SA. These bits can be OR'd together for multiple values. For example, the COMM and API could be 5, or the COMM, API, and DA could be 13.

### SLP OPEN <FILENAME.LOG>

You can enable a trace file to track the information for SLP. When you specify the filename for the trace file, it will be created in the root of SYS: volume.

### SLP CLOSE

You can close the SLP trace file that was active or open. The SLP trace file must be open before you can close it. You can use SLP DEBUG LEVEL = 8 to display all the requests made to the DA, including the type of SLP request and the IP address of the UA or SA sending the request. Log this information to a file for a period of time using SLP OPEN and SLP CLOSE. The SLP trace file can then be GREPed to find any UAs or SAs that are requesting more from the DA than they should.

## SLP Set Parameters

Several SLP SET parameters and commands enable you to monitor and control many of the features and activities of the Service Location Protocol. Table 23.1 outlines each of the SLP SET parameters and describes their purpose or use.

T A B L E  23.1

*SLP SET Parameters Used to Monitor and Control the Features and Activities of the Service Location Protocol.*

| SET PARAMETER | DESCRIPTION |
| --- | --- |
| SLP DA Discovery Options = *value* | The SLP DA discovery uses multicast DA advertisements. The settings for the options value are:<br>0x01 = Use multicast directory agent advertisements<br>0x02 = Use DHCP discovery<br>0x04 = Use static file SYS:ETC\\SLP.CFG<br>0x08 = Scopes required<br>These bits can be ordered together for multiple values. The supported values are 0 to 8, with the default set at 3. This parameter can be set in the STARTUP.NCF file |
| SLP TCP = *value* | Use TCP packets instead of UDP packets when possible. The supported values are ON or OFF, with the default set at OFF. This parameter can be set in STARTUP.NCF. |
| SLP Debug = *value* | You can use the SLP debug command to enable debugging or change the mode. The common settings are called:<br>0x01 = COMM<br>0x02 = TRAN<br>0x04 = API<br>0x08 = DA<br>0x10 = ERR<br>0x20 = SA<br>The supported values are 0 to 4294967255, with the default of zero. This parameter can be set in STARTUP.NCF. |
| SLP Multicast Radius = *value* | This parameter is used to specify an integer describing the multicast radius. The supported values are 0 to 32, with the default of 32. This parameter can be set in STARTUP.NCF. |
| SLP Broadcast = *value* | This parameter enables you to use broadcast packets instead of multicast packets for SLP. The supported values are ON and OFF, with the default being OFF. This parameter can be set in STARTUP.NCF. |
| SLP MTU Size = *value* | Use this parameter to specify an integer describing the maximum transfer unit size. The supported values are 0 to 4294967255, with the default set at 1472. This parameter can be set in STARTUP.NCF. |

| SET PARAMETER | DESCRIPTION |
|---|---|
| SLP Rediscover Inactive Directory Agents = *value* | This parameter enables you to specify the minimum time period in seconds that SLP will wait to issue service requests to rediscover inactive directory agents. The supported values are 0 to 4294967255, with the default of 60. This parameter can be set in STARTUP.NCF. |
| SLP Retry Count = *value* | Using this parameter, you can specify an integer value describing the maximum number of retries. The supported values for this parameter are 0 to 128. The default for this parameter is set to 3. This parameter can be set in STARTUP.NCF. |
| SLP Scope List = *value* | This parameter allows you to specify a comma-delimited scope policy list. The maximum length value for this parameter is 1023, with the default set at 1023. This parameter can be set in STARTUP.NCF. |
| SLP SA Default Lifetime = *value* | This parameter specifies an integer value describing the default lifetime in seconds of service registers. The supported values for this parameter are 0 to 4294967255. The default for this parameter is set to 900. This parameter can be set in STARTUP.NCF. |
| SLP Event Timeout = *value* | This parameter specifies an integer value describing the number of seconds to wait before timing out multicast packet requests. The supported values for this parameter are 0 to 4294967255. The default for this parameter is set to 53. This parameter can be set in STARTUP.NCF |
| SLP DA Heart Beat Time = *value* | This parameter enables you to specify an integer value describing the number of seconds before sending the next directory agent heartbeat packet. The supported values for this parameter are 0 to 4294967255. The default for this parameter is set to 10800. This parameter can be set in STARTUP.NCF. |
| SLP Close Idle TCP Connections Time = *value* | Using this parameter, you can specify an integer value describing the number of seconds before idle TCP connections should be terminated. The supported values for this parameter are 0 to 4294967255. The default for this parameter is set to 300. This parameter can be set in STARTUP.NCF. |

| T A B L E   23.1 | |
| --- | --- |
| SLP SET Parameters Used to Monitor and Control the Features and Activities of the Service Location Protocol. (continued) | |
| SET PARAMETER | DESCRIPTION |
| SLP DA Event Timeout = *value* | This parameter enables you to specify an integer value describing the number of seconds to wait before timing out directory agent packet requests. The supported values for this parameter are 0 to 429. The default for this parameter is set to 5. This parameter can be set in STARTUP.NCF. |

## SLP Client Configuration Settings

In addition to Server SLP SET parameters that enable you to fine-tune the configuration, the NetWare 6 Client and SLP interaction can be configured from the client property pages in NWADMIN. The client settings are as follows.

- ► SLP Active Discovery
- ► SLP Cache Replies
- ► SLP Default Registration Lifetime
- ► SLP Maximum Transmission Unit
- ► SLP Multicast Radius

### SLP Active Discovery

This parameter specifies that SLP is required to look up services from a directory agent and not use IP multicasting directly to SLP service agents for services. During normal operation of SLP, it first checks directory agents. If no directory agent is found, SLP multicasts to service agents.

> *Property Page:* Novell Client Configuration
> *Tab:* Advanced Settings
> *Parameter Group:* SLP General
> *Default:* On

### SLP Cache Replies

When SLP receives a service request from a User Agent, the SLP reply is saved for the amount of time specified by the SLP Cache Replies parameter. If SLP receives a duplicate of this request, the cached reply is sent, so the same reply does not have to be generated again. The default value for this parameter is one minute. Setting this value higher consumes more memory to retain replies longer. We recommend that you not change the default setting, because any duplicate requests should occur within the first minute.

> *Property Page:* Novell Client Configuration
> *Tab:* Advanced Settings
> *Parameter Group:* SLP Times
> *Range:* 1 to 60 (minutes)
> *Default:* 1

### SLP Default Registration Lifetime

This parameter specifies the lifetime of a service registration that is registered by a service provider requesting the default lifetime value. If the service provider specifies a lifetime value when the service is registered, this value is not used.

The directory agent deletes the service when the lifetime expires, if it hasn't been specifically renewed or unregistered before then. This prevents the directory agent's information from becoming too stale if the server agent registering the service goes down. The server agent automatically renews the service so that the application doesn't need to.

The default value for this parameter is 10,800 seconds, which is three hours. Using a smaller value makes the directory agent's information less stale at the expense of more network traffic to renew services more frequently. This parameter does not affect how long the service is registered by the server agent.

> *Property Page:* Novell Client Configuration
> *Tab:* Advanced Settings
> *Parameter Group:* SLP Times
> *Range:* 60 to 60000 (seconds)
> *Default:* 10800

### SLP Maximum Transmission Unit

This parameter specifies the maximum transmission unit (UDP packet size) for the link layer used. Setting this parameter either too large or too small adversely affects performance of SLP. For this reason, we recommend that you leave the parameter with the default setting of 1,400.

> *Property Page:* Novell Client Configuration
> *Tab:* Advanced Settings
> *Parameter Group:* SLP General
> *Range:* 576 to 4096
> *Default:* 1400

### SLP Multicast Radius

SLP uses IP multicasting to dynamically discover other SLP service agents and directory agents. This parameter specifies the maximum number of subnets (number of routers plus 1) that SLP's multicasting should traverse. A value of 1 confines multicasting to the local segment (no routers).

> *Property Page:* Novell Client Configuration
> *Tab:* Advanced Settings
> *Parameter Group:* SLP General
> *Range:* 1 to 32 (number of routers plus 1)
> *Default:* 32

# DNS/DHCP Services

Because NetWare 6 provides IP capabilities, your clients will most likely use IP at the desktop as well. Therefore, your users will take advantage of IP for their applications and their software and will need an IP address at their workstation. Because assigning an IP address to every user is cumbersome and time consuming, NetWare 6 provides Dynamic Host Configuration Protocol services and a Domain Name Service. These two features provide an administrator with the capability to supply IP addresses quickly and easily to the user community.

The support for DHCP addresses is stored in the directory. You should create an individual OU=DHCP high in the NDS tree to handle the sheer number of DHCP IP objects that can be created. This design is simple and enables you to manage the IP addresses from one point.

## Domain Name Services

A Domain Name Service is a database that matches computer names to their corresponding IP address. The DNS is broken into two categories: the hierarchy and the name service. The hierarchy specifies a host's domain in relation to other hosts on the domain. As in NDS, the domain is considered an upside-down tree with a root at the top followed by the top-level domains such as .com, .edu, and .org. Following these are the subdomains, which would include the name of your company, if registered (for example, novell.com).

The name service component of DNS maps the host name to an IP address. Clients known as *resolvers* can query the name server for host address information. If one name server does not contain the information in the query, the request is sent on to other servers up and down the domain hierarchy until a response to the query is received.

## The Dynamic Host Configuration Protocol

In order for a computer or any other device to function on an IP network, the device must be configured with the appropriate IP information, including the client's own domain name and IP address, the DNS server's IP address, and the subnet mask. Dynamic Host Configuration Protocol servers provide the capability to automatically hand out IP addresses and other network information to your network's workstations.

A client that is using DHCP initializes and contacts a DHCP server on your network. The server responds to the client with an IP address that it has selected from a pool. The server also sends the client any necessary DHCP information. The server also includes a lease time of how long the IP address is valid for this client. Clients periodically ask for a renewal of the lease, and the DHCP server grants it. If the client does not renew, the IP address goes back into the pool of IP addresses available to other users.

## Dynamic DNS

The nature of DHCP is dynamic because users are constantly obtaining new and different IP addresses each time they log into the network. Because DNS has the responsibility of providing a current address for any host name sent to it by a resolver, DNS would constantly be out of sync with the devices on its network. Dynamic DNS (DDNS) allows a DNS database to be notified immediately of address assignments made by DHCP servers. Through NDS, DNS can easily be updated when a change is sent over from DHCP, because all information is maintained in the Directory.

## NDS-Enabled DHCP

In the previous versions of NetWare, DHCP was provided by using a flat text file to track distributed IP addresses. Because networks have grown considerably with IP, Novell has introduced NDS-enabled DHCP in NetWare 6. NDS is now used as the database to store all DHCP objects. Also new to NetWare 6's DHCP is its capability to *ping ahead*. This process pings the network before allocating an IP address to the client. This ensures that a duplicate IP address will not be issued. As shown in Figure 23.29, you can enable the ping option using the DNS/DHCP Management Console utility when you create a DHCP server for your tree. The

DNS/DHCP utility can be run in stand-alone mode or inside of the NWADMIN utility. Installation of this utility is discussed in a later section.

**FIGURE 23.29** *Check the box Ping Enabled at the bottom of this screen to have the server ping the network before allocating an IP address.*

## DNS/DHCP in a Mixed NetWare Environment

NetWare 6 works well in a mixed environment with other versions of NetWare servers. You can use the NetWare 6 DHCP server to issue IP addresses to any client, such as Windows 95/98, Windows NT/2000, UNIX, or Macintosh in a mixed NetWare 5 and NetWare 6 environment.

## NDS Objects for DNS and DHCP

Five objects are created when you enable DHCP on your NetWare 6 server. The schema in your NDS tree is extended to support these new DNS/DHCP objects. The new objects for DHCP are as follows:

▸ **DHCP server object** — This object contains the configuration information for a DHCP server with a multivalued attribute listing all subnet ranges that the DHCP server is servicing. This object is created for you when you install DNS/DHCP services on your NetWare 6 server for the first time.

▸ **Subnet object** — This object represents a subnet and can be contained in an O, OU, C, or L object. The subnet object is a container object for the IP address and address range objects.

▸ **Subnet pool object** — This object provides support for multiple subnets through a DHCP or BOOTP forwarder on a router and by identifying a pool of subnets for remote LAN address assignments. This object can be contained in O, OU, C, or L containers.

▸ **Address range object** — This object is used to denote a range of addresses to create a pool of addresses for dynamic address assignment. It's also used to identify a range of addresses to be excluded from address assignment.

▸ **IP address object** — This object represents a single IP address. This object must include an address number and an assignment type. This address can be assigned manually, automatically, or dynamically, and it can be excluded from DHCP address assignment.

Additionally, the following three new objects are also created for DNS:

▸ **DNS zone object** — This object is a container object to hold all data for a single DNS zone. A zone object is the first level of the DNS zone description. A zone object can be contained under an O, OU, C, or L object.

▸ **DNS resource record set object** — This object is an NDS leaf object that is contained in a DNS zone object. This object represents an individual domain name within a DNS zone.

▸ **DNS name server object** — This object is different from the regular server object in NDS. A DNS server has configuration information about DNS such as a list of forwarders and a list of zone servers. This object can be contained in an O, OU, C, or L container.

## Design Guidelines for DNS and DHCP Objects

As we've mentioned at many points throughout this book, NDS eDirectory is a distributed database and, therefore, updates are exchanged with other servers at periodic intervals. Unless you are only managing a few IP objects, we recommend that you create a separate container to maintain the DNS and DHCP objects in your tree.

Create an OU near the top of the tree. You can then locate the DNS/DHCP Group and Locator objects under the container object. You can also create an administrator group object in this container. The administrator group should have

Read and Write rights to all DNS/DHCP locator object attributes except the global and data options fields. Members of this group can use the Management Console to modify and create DNS and DHCP objects.

Try to place your DNS and DHCP servers at locations where they are geographically close to the hosts that require their services. You can have one DHCP server in each partition of your network to minimize any WAN communications problems caused by normal load, configuration changes, or replication.

The location of group and locator objects is also very important. Each NDS tree has only one set of group and locator objects. Try to keep these objects no more than two or three levels deep in the tree. The NDS Group object is created automatically during installation and has DNS/DHCP servers as members of the group. Servers gain rights to DNS and DHCP data within the tree because of their security equivalence to the group object. An example of the group object as seen at the management console in NWADMIN is shown in Figure 23.30.

**FIGURE 23.30** *Create a group object for DNS/DHCP servers*

The locator object is used for DNS/DHCP operation. This object contains global defaults; DHCP options; and all DNS and DHCP servers, subnets, subnet pools, and zones in the tree. You create only one locator object per NDS tree. This object is created automatically during the installation of the DNS/DHCP software. An example of how this object is placed in your NDS tree is shown in Figure 23.31.

**FIGURE 23.31** *An example of using the DHCP objects in your NDS tree*

## Using DHCP Over Routers

Novell's DHCP allows a NetWare client to traverse a router and obtain an IP address from the Novell DHCP server. Obtaining an IP address is done by using the subnet pool object to provide an address to a router that is running a BOOTP forwarder. The subnet pool identifies a pool of subnet address assignments and forwards an address to a DHCP or BOOTP forwarder. You must configure your BOOTP forwarder with your DHCP server's address so that the requests are relayed from the clients.

In many situations, you may have more than one subnet. Using the subnet pool object in NDS, you can define multiple numbers of subnets.

## Using the DNS/DHCP Management Console

The DNS/DHCP Management Console runs on Microsoft Windows 95/98 and Windows NT/2000 client workstations with the Novell Client software delivered with NetWare 6. The DNS/DHCP Management Console provides the following management functions from the client's desktop:

▸ Importing and exporting DNS/DHCP configuration to and from NDS
▸ Creating, updating, reading, or browsing configuration information
▸ Viewing DNS and DHCP server status, events, and alerts
▸ Viewing audit trail logs

After the software installation, existing DNS information is converted to master file format and can be imported to the server where NetWare 6 has been installed. You must use the DNS/DHCP Management Console to import any existing DHCP information. If you have no existing configuration information to import, you must use the DNS/DHCP Management Console to create the necessary objects to support your network. If you have imported configuration information, use the DNS/DHCP Management Console to create the DNS and DHCP server objects prior to operation.

### Installing the DNS/DHCP Management Console

Installation of the DNS/DHCP Management Console software on a client workstation requires the following:

▸ 20MB of free disk space
▸ 64MB of memory (recommended), 32MB minimum
▸ Novell NetWare 32-bit Client (or higher) software installed

The installation process uses Install Shield to install the DNS/DHCP Management Console on the client's hard disk. Exit all Windows programs before beginning the software installation.

To install the DNS/DHCP Management Console on a client workstation, complete the following steps:

1. Map a drive to the SYS: volume on a server on which you have installed NetWare 6.
2. Click Start and then select Run.
3. Use the Browse button to select the drive mapped to the SYS: volume on the selected server. Then select the Public and DNSDHCP folders.
4. Double-click Setup and then click OK in the Run dialog box.

You can also begin the installation from the DOS prompt by entering:

```
X:\PUBLIC\DNSDHCP\SETUP.EXE
```

where *x* is the drive mapped to volume SYS on the server on which NetWare 6 has been installed. A welcome window is displayed, and you are reminded to exit all Windows programs before running the Setup program. After the installation has completed, you must restart your computer before attempting to use the DNS/DHCP Management Console.

After the DNS/DHCP Management Console has been installed on a workstation, a DNSDHCP icon is added to the client's desktop and the DNSDHCP folder. Double-click the DNSDHCP icon to launch the DNS/DHCP Management Console. The DNS/DHCP Management Console can also be launched from NetWare Administrator by selecting DNS/DHCP Management Console from the Tools menu.

### Using the DNS/DHCP Management Console

You must first log into the tree you want to administer before launching the DNS/DHCP Management Console. Additionally, you must have sufficient rights to use the DNS/DHCP Management Console. All network administrators must have Read and Write rights to the container where the DNS/DHCP Locator and Group objects are located.

Administrators also must have Read and Write rights to the specific containers they manage. For example, if your company has offices in Sydney, Tokyo, and Norad, all administrators would require Read and Write rights to the container storing the Locator and Group objects. However, the administrator in Sydney would require Read and Write rights only to the Sydney part of the tree for the following objects:

- ▸ DNS and DHCP server objects
- ▸ DNS zone object
- ▸ Subnet container object
- ▸ Subnet pool object

It is convenient to create an NDS group object for administrators and grant that object the necessary rights as explained in the previous section.

Managing DNS is managing primary and secondary zones. When beginning configuration, it might be better to import the data, especially if you have a large zone. Doing so reduces the chances of error.

If you are using Dynamic DNS, when a client receives an address assignment from the DHCP server, a request is made to update NDS. The only way to override DDNS is by using the DNS/DHCP Management Console.

After you have installed and configured your zones, you must still use the DNS/DHCP Management Console to assign a DNS server to service the zones.

### Managing DHCP

After configuring your DHCP servers and beginning to provide DHCP services, you can also perform auditing or generate SNMP traps. Deciding which DHCP options to use depends on your implementation. Managing DDNS is complicated because each Subnet Address Range type requires a different configuration.

It is important to understand the difference between static (or manual) and dynamic address assignment. If you use static address assignment, you must use the DNS/DHCP Management Console to assign permanent IP addresses to the clients in your tree. If you are using dynamic address assignment, the DHCP server assigns the address to a client when it starts. You can deny address assignment to clients based on hardware address-based exclusion.

### Events and Alerts

You can configure the DNS and DHCP servers to maintain a history of server activity in the events log. Events are activities that are considered significant, such as loading or unloading the server or problems that the server encounters. The events logged depend on parameters set on the server's Options tab page.

You can configure DNS and DHCP servers to log major events, all events, or none (the default). Event logs can be saved for future reference. When you are logging events, it is important to pay attention to the event log size. Event logs grow rapidly, especially if you are experiencing or researching problems. Event logs should be maintained or purged regularly to control the amount of disk space used. You can launch the CSAUDIT management utility by typing CSAUDIT at the server console.

## Configuring DHCP

To manage an organization's IP address database, you must define the global address pool in the form of Class A, B, and C network addresses. The addresses available to a network are managed by the DNS/DHCP Management Console and logically organized into the following types of objects:

- ▶ Subnet
- ▶ Subnet address range
- ▶ IP address
- ▶ DHCP server
- ▶ Subnet pool

The Novell DHCP server views an organization's network as a collection of DHCP objects.

### Importing DHCP Configuration Information

You can use the DNS/DHCP Management Console to import existing DHCP configuration information. The DHCP information should be in DHCP version 2.0 or 3.0 file format. To import existing DHCP configuration information, complete the following steps:

1. Launch the Management Console by double-clicking the icon.
2. Click the DHCP Service tab.
3. Click Import. The Import-File Input dialog box is displayed, requesting the location of the DHCP database file.
4. Enter the drive and path to the DHCP database file, or use the Browse button to navigate your way to the file. After you select the file to import, the path to that file is displayed in the DHCP File dialog box.
5. Click Next. The Import DHCP - Subnet List dialog box is displayed, listing each subnet found in the configuration file.
6. Select the desired subnet or subnets and click Add, or click Add All to import all the subnets on the list.
7. Select the Subnet Context and click Next.
8. The Import dialog box is displayed, indicating the subnet context and the subnets to import. (The subnet address and name are displayed on the list.)
9. Click Import.
10. The Server Input dialog box is displayed, prompting you to select a default NCP server to manage the newly imported subnet.
11. Use the Browse button to select the target server and click OK.

If an error occurs during the importing process, an error message will be displayed, and the Details button will be enabled, allowing you to display more information.

### Setting Up DHCP

This section provides basic information about the steps required to set up DHCP. This section does not describe how to enable all the available features. The following steps must be completed prior to setting up DHCP:

1. Load NetWare 6 on the selected server or servers.
2. Load the Novell Client software delivered with NetWare 6 on client computers that will be used to administer DNS and DHCP.

**3.** Install the DNS/DHCP Management Console on client computers that will be used to administer DNS and DHCP.

### Logging into the Tree

To complete the steps required to set up DHCP, you must first log into the tree where NetWare 6 has been installed. To log into the server, complete the following steps:

**1.** Right-click Network Neighborhood and select NetWare Login on a NetWare 6 client workstation on which you have installed the DNS/DHCP Management Console.

The NetWare Client login dialog box is displayed.

**2.** Under the Login tab, enter your user name and password, and then click Connection.

**3.** Under the Connection tab, enter the Tree, Server, and Context of the server on which you have installed NetWare 6, and then click OK.

### Launching the DNS/DHCP Management Console

Launch the DNS/DHCP Management Console by double-clicking its icon. The DNS/DHCP Management Console can be installed on a client workstation, or it can be accessed from the Tools menu of the NetWare Administrator utility. When the DNS/DHCP Management Console loads, you are prompted to enter the NDS Tree Name where you want to set up DHCP.

**Setting Global DHCP Options**   You use the DNS/DHCP Management Console to set global DHCP options. Setting global DHCP options is not required to set up DHCP, however. To set global DHCP options, complete the following steps:

**1.** Click the DHCP Service tab of the DNS/DHCP Management Console.

**2.** Click Global Preferences on the toolbar. The Global DHCP Options tab of the Global Preferences dialog box is displayed, listing code, name, and value of any global DHCP options selected. Two other tab pages are available. One shows any global DHCP defaults set for the selected object; the other is the DHCP Options table. An example of this dialog box is shown in Figure 23.32.

**3.** Click the Global DHCP Defaults tab and then click Add. The Add Exclude Hardware Address dialog box is displayed. Any devices or addresses you configure here will be excluded from any global defaults or global options.

An asterisk (*) can be used as a wildcard character to select a range of
addresses to exclude. The asterisk can be used only as a trailing character,
however. It cannot be used as a prefix or in the middle of a hardware
address. The default delimiter for hardware addresses is a colon (:), but a
dash (–) or a period (.) can also be used. Only one type of delimiter can be
used within an address.

**FIGURE 23.32** *Setting global preferences for DHCP*

**4.** Click in the Hardware Type field to select a type of hardware to exclude,
and enter an address in the Exclude Hardware Address field. An example
of this is shown in Figure 23.33. You can use the wildcard character (*)
and a different delimiter if you choose.

**FIGURE 23.33** *Excluding hardware in the Global Preferences section*

**5.** Click the DHCP Options Table tab. A list of DHCP options is displayed, listing all available DHCP options including codes, data syntax, and the option name.

**6.** Select a desired option from those listed and then click Add. When you select a DHCP option, if any additional information is required to support the option, you are prompted to provide that information. For example, if you select option 85 for NDS Server, you are prompted to supply the IP address of the NDS Server.

**7.** Provide any requested information specific to the selected option (as in Figure 23.34) and then click OK. The Global Preferences dialog box is redisplayed, listing the global options that have been set.

**8.** When you have completed selecting global DHCP options, click OK.

**FIGURE 23.34** *Selecting DHCP options from the Options table*

## Creating a DHCP Server Object

You use the DNS/DHCP Management Console to create and set up a DHCP server object. A DHCP server object can be created or located under any of the following objects:

- ▶ Organization (O)
- ▶ Organization unit (OU)
- ▶ Country (C)
- ▶ Locality (L)

To create and set up a DHCP server object, complete the following steps:

**1.** Click the DHCP Service tab of the DNS/DHCP Management Console. The Our Network object is the only object displayed on the DNS/DHCP Management Console's left pane.

**2.** Click Create on the toolbar. The Create New DHCP Object dialog box is displayed, enabling you to create a DHCP server object, a subnet object, or a subnet pool object. An example of this dialog box is shown in Figure 23.35.

**FIGURE 23.35** *Creating a DHCP server object*

**3.** Select DHCP Server and click OK. The Create DHCP Server dialog box is displayed, prompting you to select a server object.

**4.** Use the Browse button to select a server within the context and then click Create. The DHCP server object is created and displayed in the lower pane of the DNS/DHCP Management Console. An example of selecting a DHCP server is shown in Figure 23.36.

**FIGURE 23.36** *Selecting a DHCP server object to be created*

## Creating a Subnet Object

You use the DNS/DHCP Management Console to create and set up a DHCP subnet object for each of the subnets to which you will assign addresses. To create and set up a subnet object, complete the following steps:

1. Click the DHCP Service tab of the DNS/DHCP Management Console. The Our Network object is the only object displayed on the DNS/DHCP Management Console's left pane.

2. Click Create on the toolbar. The Create New DHCP Object dialog box is displayed, enabling you to create a DHCP server, a subnet, or a subnet pool object.

3. Select Subnet and click OK. The Create Subnet dialog box is displayed. For each subnet you create, enter the following information in the fields provided: subnet name, NDS context, subnet address, and subnet mask. If you have set up a default DHCP server, its name is displayed and can be changed. You can click the Define Additional Properties check box to provide more detailed configuration, including DHCP options specific to each subnet. An example of this dialog box is shown in Figure 23.37.

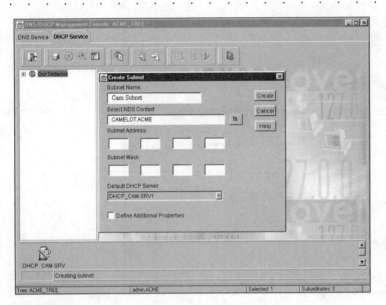

**FIGURE 23.37** *Creating a new subnet for DHCP*

**4.** Enter the required information and then click Create. The DHCP subnet object is created and displayed in the left pane of the DNS/DHCP Management Console.

### Creating Subnet Address Ranges

You also use the DNS/DHCP Management Console to create and set up subnet address range objects for each pool of addresses you want to be dynamically assigned by DHCP. To create and set up a subnet address range object, complete the following steps:

**I.** Click the DHCP Service tab of the DNS/DHCP Management Console.

**2.** Select the subnet object under which you want to create the subnet address range object, and then click Create. The Create New DHCP Record dialog box is displayed, as shown in Figure 23.38.

**FIGURE 23.38** *Creating a subnet range in the DNS/DHCP utility*

**3.** Select Subnet Address Range and click OK. The Create New Subnet Address Range dialog box is displayed.

**4.** Enter a name for the subnet address range, specify the range's starting and ending address, and then click Create. If you click the Define Additional Properties check box, the range's detailed information dialog box is displayed, enabling you to provide more detailed configuration information. An example of the Create Subnet Address Range dialog box is shown in Figure 23.39.

**FIGURE 23.39** *Specifying a subnet address range*

## Creating IP Address Objects

You use the DNS/DHCP Management Console to create and set up any IP address objects to be assigned to specific devices or to be excluded from dynamic assignment. Create an IP address object for each such device or address. Assigning a specific address to a client requires you to specify the client's media-access control (MAC) address or Client ID.

If you have set up subnets and subnet address ranges, you are not required to set up individual IP addresses unless you want to perform manual address assignment or exclude addresses from assignment. To create and set up an IP address object, complete the following steps:

1. Click the DHCP Service tab of the DNS/DHCP Management Console.

2. Select the subnet object of the target IP address and then click Create on the toolbar. The Create New DHCP Object dialog box is displayed.

3. Select IP Address and click OK. The Create IP Address dialog box is displayed.

4. Enter the IP address to be assigned or excluded, select the assignment type, and then click Create as shown in Figure 23.40.

**FIGURE 23.40** *Creating an IP address for a single user*

If you choose Manual Assignment Type, you must provide information for either the Client Identifier or MAC Address fields. You can also specify the MAC type by clicking in the field; the default is FF, Any.

### Starting the DHCP Server

After you have created and set up a DHCP server and configured the NDS objects required for DHCP, enter the following command at the DHCP server console:

```
LOAD DHCPSRVR
```

After you load DHCPSRVR.NLM, the DHCP server can respond to client requests and assign IP addresses.

### Configuring Clients to Use DHCP

Configuring clients to use DHCP is performed at the client workstation. To configure Windows 95/98 and Windows NT/2000 client workstations to use DHCP, complete the following steps:

**1.** At the client desktop, select Start ⇨ Settings ⇨ Control Panel, and then double-click Network. The Network dialog box is displayed, listing the network components installed on the client workstation.

**2.** Select TCP/IP for this adapter card and click Properties. The TCP/IP Properties dialog box is displayed, usually showing the IP Address tab page.

**3.** Select Obtain an IP Address Automatically, and then click OK. The next time the client starts up, it sends a request to the DHCP server for an IP address.

**NOTE**

**Any client configuration settings override the configuration received from a DHCP server. The only exception is the hostname parameter set on the DNS Configuration tab of TCP/IP Properties dialog box.**

### Detailed DHCP Configuration

This section provides detailed information about configuring DHCP objects using the DNS/DHCP Management Console. All the procedures in this section assume that you have already launched the utility and that you have selected the DHCP Service tab.

**Modifying a DHCP Server Object**    After a DHCP server object has been created, you can double-click the server icon to display and modify detailed information about the DHCP server object. The DHCP server object's detailed information dialog box displays two tab pages, Server and Options.

On the Server tab page, you can view the Subnet Address Ranges Serviced by This Server and Subnets Serviced by This Server. You can enter comments (up to 256 characters) about the server in the comments field.

On the Options tab page, you can configure policies specific to this DHCP server. You can configure the Set SNMP Traps Option parameter for None (default), Major Events, or All. You can configure the Set Audit Trail and Alerts Option parameter for None (default), Major Events, or All. You can also set the Enable Audit Trail Log on this page (the default is not enabled).

You can also configure the Mobile User Options parameter on the Options tab page to the following:

- No mobile users allowed.
- Allow mobile users, but delete a previously assigned address (default).
- Allow mobile users, but do not delete a previously assigned address.

Another option available on the DHCP Server Options tab page is Ping Enable. Click this check box to have the server ping an address before the address is assigned to a device. Doing so ensures that the address is not already in use; however, pinging the address also increases network traffic.

### Modifying an Existing Subnet Object

After a subnet object has been created, you can use the DNS/DHCP Management Console to display three tab pages of detailed information about the subnet object that include Address, Subnet Options, and Other DHCP Options.

The Address tab page displays Subnet Address, Mask, and Type attributes from information entered when the object was created. If changes are required to these attributes, you must delete the subnet object and re-create it. If you are going to use Dynamic DNS, this is the page where you configure the DNS zone for dynamic updating (DDNS) and domain name.

You can modify the subnet pool reference from the default (none) to the subnet pool to which this subnet object is assigned. You can also modify the subnet's default DHCP server on the Address tab page and enter up to 256 characters of information in the Comments field.

You can configure lease types on the Subnet Options tab page. A lease type can be permanent or timed. If you specify leases to be timed, specify the lease duration in days, hours, and minutes. You can also specify the settings for Set Boot Parameter Options on the Subnet Options tab page.

DHCP options can be configured from the Other DHCP Options tab page. Any options that are set for this subnet are displayed here. You can set additional DHCP options by clicking Modify, which displays the Modify DHCP Options dialog box. You pick a DHCP option from the Available DHCP Options list and then click Add.

Click Default to display the Default DHCP Options dialog box listing all DHCP options and values configured for a subnet.

### Modifying a Subnet Address Range Object

To modify a subnet address range object, you must first select the object, which displays in the left pane of the DHCP Service dialog box. Clicking on the subnet address range object displays its detailed information in the right pane and enables modifications. The following range type options are available:

- Dynamic BOOTP
- Dynamic DHCP with Automatic Host Name Generation
- Dynamic DHCP
- Dynamic BOOTP and DHCP (the default)
- Excluded

You can also specify a DHCP server other than the default server for this subnet address range object.

### Modifying an Existing IP Address Object

After an IP address object has been created, its detailed information dialog box displays three tab pages:

- ▶ Address
- ▶ Usage
- ▶ Other DHCP Options

On the Address tab page, the IP address field of the object is displayed in read-only format. You can set the Assignment Type parameter to Manual or Excluded, and you can specify a client identifier. You can change the MAC type from the default (FF, Any) to any of the following:

- ▶ 15, Frame Relay
- ▶ 16, Asynchronous Transfer Mode (ATM)
- ▶ 17, HDLC
- ▶ 18, Fibre Channel
- ▶ 19, Asynchronous Transfer Mode (ATM)
- ▶ 20, Serial Line
- ▶ 21, Asynchronous Transfer Mode (ATM)

You can enter the IP address's MAC address, hostname, and DNS domain suffix, and you can identify an NDS object to use a specific IP address on the Address tab page. The Usage tab page displays the IP Address Lease Expiration option, which can be either Permanent or Timed. If Timed is selected, the year, month, day, hour, and minute that the lease expires are displayed.

DHCP options can be configured from the Other DHCP Options tab page. Any options that are set for this IP address object are displayed here. You can set additional DHCP options by clicking Modify.

### Creating a Subnet Pool Object

A subnet pool object is a logical group of related subnet objects of the same type. A subnet pool object can be created or located under any of the following objects:

- ▶ Organization (O)
- ▶ Organization unit (OU)

▸ Country (C)

▸ Locality (L)

To create a new subnet pool object, complete the following steps:

**1.** Click Create on the toolbar.

**2.** Select Subnet Pool and click OK.

**3.** Enter a unique name for the subnet pool object.

**4.** Use the Browse button to select the NDS context in which to create the subnet pool object.

After a subnet pool object has been created, you can select it and check the Define Additional Properties check box to display the detailed information dialog box and to add subnet objects to and remove them from the subnet pool object. Only subnet objects with the same range type can be added to a subnet pool object.

### Modifying a Subnet Pool Object

Click Add to bring up a dialog box with a list of available subnet objects (either LAN or WAN) to be added to the list. After a subnet object has been added to the subnet pool object, its NDS distinguished name is updated in the subnet object's subnet pool list attribute.

## Using DNS

Plan to install and operate a primary name server and at least one secondary name server on your NDS tree. The secondary name servers provide load balancing and fault tolerance to your DNS implementation.

When you configure your zone, the primary name server is considered authoritative for the zone, meaning that it contains the most up-to-date information about the zone and all the hosts within it.

A secondary name server receives its zone data from the primary name server. When it starts up and at periodic intervals, the secondary name server queries the primary name server to determine whether the information it contains has been changed. If the zone information in the secondary name server is older than the zone information in the primary name server, a zone transfer occurs and the secondary name server receives the zone information from the primary name server.

### Planning and Implementing Zones

If you are running a primary name server and providing DNS service for a zone, the size or geography of your network might require creating subzones within the zone. Keep the zone data as a separate partition, and replicate the partition to all places on your network where you have a name server for the zone. Doing so enables independent replication of the zone data and also provides a degree of fault tolerance in the case of server downtime.

### The Novell DNS Server as a Primary Name Server

You must install the Novell DNS server as a primary name server to have authoritative control over your zone and to take advantage of Dynamic DNS, the dynamic updating of DNS by DHCP.

When operating the Novell DNS server as a primary name server, you use the DNS/DHCP Management Console to make configuration changes. When you operate a primary name server, the zone data can receive dynamic updates from DHCP servers. Non-Novell secondary name servers can transfer data in from the Novell primary name server.

## Configuring DNS

The DNS/DHCP Management Console provides similar interfaces for configuring both DNS and DHCP. The left pane of the DNS Service dialog box displays all DNS resources, the right pane displays detailed information about the object selected in the left pane, and the lower pane displays all DNS servers.

The view in the left pane of the DNS Service dialog box is similar to the DNS hierarchical structure, with the virtual All Zones object as the root of the three hierarchical levels shown. The first level contains the zone objects, the second level contains the Resource Record Set (RRSet) objects, and the third level contains the individual resource records. An example of this is shown in Figure 23.41.

The view in the right pane of the DNS Service dialog box provides detailed information about DNS objects selected in the left pane. The detailed information varies, depending on the type of object selected. For example, a zone object's detailed information includes tab pages for Attributes and Start of Authority, whereas the detailed information for resource records provides only an Attributes page.

The lower pane of the DNS Service dialog box displays all currently existing DNS server objects in the NDS tree and a description of their operational status.

**FIGURE 23.41** *A view of the attributes for the DNS Service window*

## Importing DNS Configuration Information

You can use the Novell DNS/DHCP Management Console to import existing DNS configuration information. The DNS information should be in DNS BIND Master file format. To import existing DNS configuration information using the Management Console, complete the following steps:

**1.** Launch the DNS/DHCP Management Console by double-clicking the icon, or load it through NWADMIN.

**2.** Click the DNS Service tab.

**3.** Click Import DNS Database. The Import-File Input dialog box is displayed, requesting the location of the DNS BIND Master file, as shown in Figure 23.42.

**4.** Enter the drive and path to the DNS database file, or click the Browse button to navigate your way to the file. After you select the file to import, the path to that file is displayed in the DNS File dialog box.

**5.** Click Next. The Import DNS - Zone List dialog box is displayed, listing each zone found in the configuration file.

6. Select the Zone Context and click Next.

7. The Import dialog box is displayed, indicating the zone context and the zones to import. The subnet address and name are displayed in the list.

8. Click Import.

9. The Server Input dialog box is displayed, prompting you to select a default NetWare server to manage the newly imported zone.

10. Use the Browse button to select the target server, and then click OK.

**FIGURE 23.42** *Importing an existing DNS configuration information file*

## Setting Up DNS

This section describes how to set up DNS for a common environment. Your situation may vary from this description depending on your network configuration. The following steps must be completed before setting up DNS:

1. Install Novell NetWare 6 on the selected server or servers.

2. Load the Novell Client software delivered with NetWare 6 on client computers that will be used to administer DNS and DHCP.

3. Install the DNS/DHCP Management Console on client computers that will be used to administer DNS and DHCP.

## Creating a DNS Server Object

Use the DNS/DHCP Management Console to create and set up a DNS server object for each DNS server you plan to operate. To create and set up a DNS server object, complete the following steps:

1. Click the DNS Service tab of the DNS/DHCP Management Console, if necessary. The All Zones object is the only object displayed on the DNS/DHCP Management Console's left pane.

2. Click Create on the toolbar. The Create New DNS Object dialog box shown in Figure 23.43 is displayed, enabling you to create a DNS server object or a zone object.

3. Select DNS Server and click OK. The Create New DNS Server dialog box is displayed, prompting you to select a DNS server object.

4. Enter the desired server's name or use the Browse button to select the server.

5. Enter the server's domain name and then click Create. The DNS server object is created and displayed in the lower pane of the DNS/DHCP Management Console.

**FIGURE 23.43** Creating a DNS server object

### Creating a Primary DNS Zone Object

After you create a DNS server object, use the DNS/DHCP Management Console to create and set up a primary DNS zone. To create a primary DNS zone object, complete the following steps:

1. Click the DNS Service tab of the DNS/DHCP Management Console. The All Zones object and the Root Server Info zone object are displayed in the DNS/DHCP Management Console's left pane.

2. Click Create on the toolbar, select Zone, and then click OK. The Create Zone dialog box is displayed. The default setting is to create a new, primary zone. An example of this dialog box is shown in Figure 23.44.

**FIGURE 23.44** *Creating a new primary DNS Zone*

3. Use the Browse button to select the NDS context for the zone.
4. Enter a name for the zone object in the Zone Domain Name field.
5. In the Assign Authoritative DNS Server field, select a DNS server. After you have selected an authoritative DNS server, the Name Server Host Name field is filled with the name of the authoritative DNS server.

**6.** Click Create. A message is displayed indicating that the new zone has been created, and you are reminded to create the Address record for the host server domain name and corresponding Pointer record in the IN-ADDR.ARPA zone (if you have not already done so).

### Starting the DNS Server

After you have created and set up a DNS server object and a DNS zone object, enter the following command at the DNS server console:

```
LOAD NAMED
```

After NAMED.NLM is loaded, the DNS server can respond to queries for the zone.

### Configuring Clients to Use DNS

Clients are configured to use DNS at the client workstation. To configure Windows NT/2000 or Windows 95/98 client workstations to use DNS, complete the following steps:

**I.** At the client desktop, select Start ⇨ Settings ⇨ Control Panel, and then double-click Network. The Network dialog box is displayed, listing the network components installed on the client workstation.

**2.** Select TCP/IP, and then click Properties. The TCP/IP Properties dialog box is displayed, usually showing the IP Address tab page.

**3.** Click the DNS Configuration tab.

**4.** Provide a hostname and domain name for each client.

**5.** Enter the IP address of DNS servers for this client in the search order of preference, and then click OK. The client can now send DNS queries to the DNS name server.

### Creating a Zone Object

The DNS zone object is an NDS container object that comprises Resource Record Set (RRSet) objects and resource records. This section provides information about how to create a Secondary DNS zone object and an IN-ADDR.ARPA zone object.

### Creating a Secondary DNS Zone Object

After you create a DNS server object, you can use the DNS/DHCP Management Console to create and set up a Secondary DNS zone object. To create a Secondary DNS zone object, you must provide the IP address of the DNS server that will perform zone-in transfers for the secondary zone.

1. Click the DNS Service tab of the DNS/DHCP Management Console.

2. Click Create on the toolbar, select Zone, and then click OK.

3. Use the Browse button to select the NDS context for the zone.

4. Enter a name for the zone object in the Zone Domain Name field.

5. Under Zone Type, select Secondary. When you select a secondary type zone, the Assign Authoritative DNS Server field and the Name Server Host Name field entries are optional.

6. Enter the IP address of the DNS server that will provide zone-out transfers for this secondary zone. You can optionally select to assign an authoritative DNS server.

7. Click Create. A message is displayed indicating that the new zone has been created, and you are reminded to create the Address record for the host server domain name and corresponding Pointer record in the IN-ADDR.ARPA zone (if you have not already done so).

**Creating an IN-ADDR.ARPA Zone Object**

After you create a DNS server object, you can use the DNS/DHCP Management Console to create and set up an IN-ADDR.ARPA zone object. To create an IN-ADDR.ARPA zone object, complete the following steps:

1. Click the DNS Service tab of the DNS/DHCP Management Console.

2. Click Create on the toolbar, select Zone, and then click OK. The Create Zone dialog box is displayed. The default setting is to create a new, primary zone.

3. Select Create IN-ADDR.ARPA.

4. Use the Browse button to select the NDS context for the zone.

5. Enter an IP address in the Zone Domain Name field. After you enter the IP address, it is reversed and prepended to .IN-ADDR.ARPA and reflected in the box below the Zone Domain Name field.

6. Under Zone Type, select Primary or Secondary. If you select Secondary, you must enter the IP address of the DNS Name Server that will provide zone-out transfers to this zone.

7. In the Assign Authoritative DNS Server field, select a DNS server. After you have selected an authoritative DNS server, the Name Server Host Name field is filled with the name of the authoritative DNS server.

8. Click Create, and then click Save.

### Creating an IP6.INT Zone Object

After you create a DNS server object, you can use the DNS/DHCP Management Console to create and set up an IP6.INT zone object. Only one IP6.INT DNS zone object can exist in an NDS tree. To create an IP6.INT zone object, complete the following steps:

1. Click the DNS Service tab of the DNS/DHCP Management Console.

2. Click Create on the toolbar, select Zone, and then click OK. The Create Zone dialog box is displayed. The default setting is to create a new, primary zone.

3. Select Create IP6.INT.

4. Use the Browse button to select the NDS context for the zone.

5. Under Zone Type, select Primary or Secondary. If you select Secondary, you must enter the IP address of the DNS Name Server that will provide zone-out transfers to this zone.

6. For a Primary zone, click in the Assign Authoritative DNS Server field to select a DNS server to service the zone.

7. Click Create, and then click Save.

### Modifying a Zone Object

After you have created a zone object, you can modify it and provide more detailed configuration information. To modify a new zone object's attributes, complete the following steps:

1. Select the zone object you want to modify.

2. To change a Primary zone to a Secondary zone, click the Secondary check box and provide the Primary DNS Server's IP address in the Zone Master IP Address field.

3. To designate a DNS name server to be an Authoritative DNS Server, select one or more entries from the Available DNS Servers list and click Add. The selected DNS name server's name is moved from the list of Available DNS Servers to the list of Authoritative DNS Servers. If only one server is available, that server automatically becomes the designated server.

4. To select a server from the list of Authoritative DNS Servers to become the designated server, click the Dynamic DNS Server field.

5. Type any relevant comments about the zone directly into the Comments field.

To view or modify a new zone object's Start of Authority information, click the SOA Information tab. The following information is displayed:

- ▸ Zone master
- ▸ E-mail address
- ▸ Serial number
- ▸ Interval values:
    - • Refresh (default is 180 minutes)
    - • Retry (default is 60 minutes)
    - • Expire (default is 168 hours)
    - • Minimal caching (default is 24 hours)

### Creating Resource Records

A *resource record* is a piece of information about a domain name. Each resource record contains information about a particular piece of data within the domain. To create a new resource record, complete the following steps:

1. Select the zone object under which you want to create a new resource record. The Create New DNS Object dialog box is displayed.

2. Select Resource Record and click OK. The Create Resource Record dialog box is displayed, prompting you for the domain name of the resource record you want to create. You can select the A record (the default) to create an Address record or the CNAME record to create a canonical name, or you can check the Others box to create a resource record from the displayed list of supported resource record types.

3. Enter the domain name you want to associate with this resource record. The name you select is prepended to the domain name of the zone under which the resource record will be created.

4. Enter any additional information required for the resource record type, and then click Create. After you have created a resource record, its type cannot be modified. If changes are required, you must delete the resource record and create a new one.

**NOTE**  **Start of Authority (SOA) is defined as part of a zone object's attributes, and a Pointer (PTR) record is created automatically when any new A resource record or IPv6 (AAAA) resource record is created if the IN-ADDR.ARPA zone exists.**

If you are creating a new resource record within an existing RRSet object, the Domain Name field is displayed in read-only format in the Create Resource Record dialog box. The domain name was defined for the RRSet object and must be the same for subordinate resource record objects.

## Summary

One of the notable features in NetWare 6 is pure TCP/IP. Pure IP enables you to run the TCP/IP protocol stack on both the client and the server and have only one protocol for your entire network. NetWare 6 offers several options to help you migrate your company's network from IPX to IP. The Compatibility Mode processes enable you to run IPX-dependent NLMs and applications on a TCP/IP network. The migration agent translates protocols between a TCP/IP network and an IPX network. As a result, you can continue to use IPX-dependent NLMs and applications, and you can migrate some segments of your company's network to IP while maintaining IPX on other segments. Users on the IPX network can then continue to use services on the TCP/IP network, and vice versa.

# Appendixes

# The CD-ROM Set Included with This Book

This appendix includes information and installation instructions for the contents of the three CD-ROMs included with this book. The CD-ROMs contain the following:

**Disc 1:**

▸ NetWare 6 Operating System — 5-User Demo

**Disc 2:**

▸ Digital Airlines Demo

**Disc 3:**

▸ Complete NetWare 6 Online Documentation

# NetWare 6 Operating System — 5-User Version

The NetWare 6 Operating System CD-ROM (Disc 1) that comes with this book contains a 5-user version with the NetWare 6 license embedded in the NetWare 6 code. No separate license disc is required to install this software. During installation, the license will be loaded from the CD itself. Additionally, this software has no expiration date, so you can install it at any time.

### NetWare 6 Minimum Requirements

Here are the minimum requirements for server hardware in order to run NetWare 6:

▸ Server-class PC with a Pentium processor

▸ VGA display adapter

▸ 64MB of RAM

▸ 600MB available disk space (50MB for the boot partition, 550MB for the NetWare partition)

▸ Network board

▸ CD-ROM drive

▸ PS/2 or serial mouse recommended

### Installing NetWare 6

The following steps guide you through the installation of NetWare 6 on your system:

**1.** Create a 50MB DOS boot partition.

**2.** Install a CD-ROM drive and drivers according to your hardware vendor's instructions.

**3.** Insert the NetWare 6 Operating System CD-ROM (Disc 1) and type **INSTALL.**

**4.** Accept the License Agreement.

**5.** Choose the server language, if prompted.

**6.** Select New Server.

**7.** Confirm computer settings.

**8.** When prompted for the License Diskette, select the license located in the \LICENSE directory on the NetWare 6 Operating System CD-ROM. *Please note that there is no separate license diskette.*

**9.** Complete the installation by following the onscreen instructions.

**For more in-depth instructions on the installation of NetWare 6, refer to Chapter 2.**

**X-REF**

## Digital Airlines Demo

The Digital Airlines demo contains a preconfigured demonstration of the NetWare 6 operating system based on a fictitious company called Digital Airlines.

Digital Airlines is a fully configured image of a NetWare 6 Server. The installation will completely destroy any existing partitions on the machine on which you install it. *The image should not be used in a production environment!* Before testing the Digital Airlines image, you should isolate the server and clients on a hub or use a crossover cable.

**WARNING**

For instructions on setting up the Digital Airlines Demo, click on the Digital Airlines Setup link in the Index PDF on Disc 3.

## NetWare 6 Online Documentation

Complete NetWare 6 Online Documentation is included on Disc 3 of the CD-ROM set that accompanies this book. To install the documentation on your hard drive, follow these steps:

1. Insert Disc 3 of the CD-ROM set included with this book. If your CD-ROM supports autorun programs, then the autorun.inf file will launch the Index PDF file.

2. You can also browse to the Index PDF and launch it. The file exists in the root directory of Disc 3. Click on chapter links to view documentation on various subjects of interest.

# NDS Error Codes and Definitions

**T**his appendix provides a list of the NDS error codes and, where appropriate, any action that should be taken to resolve each error condition. You can use this appendix as a reference when troubleshooting NDS or other operating system problems on NetWare 6 servers. For more information on troubleshooting NDS and related problems, refer to Chapter 10 in conjunction with this appendix.

## Novell Directory Services Error Codes

This section provides information on the NDS error codes and provides a description of the error and any client action that needs to be taken to remedy the problem. In some cases you will not see an explanation or action. This is because the error is internal to NDS, and in most cases you will neither see it, nor can you take any action on it. We include these error codes, though, to provide you with a complete listing.

### NO_SUCH_ENTRY   –601   0xFFFFFDA7   FDA7

**Explanation:** This error on a NetWare 6 server during DSTRACE usually means that an entry is missing from the entry record table on the source server.

**Client Action:** Check the context specified for the object name entered. If the command line input was the object name, check the workstation's context. Make sure that it points to the correct level of the Directory for the object name specified. If the input includes the object's full or partial context, make sure that the leading and trailing dots are specified appropriately and that the types are correct. This error is common if you are trying to delete bindery type objects through NWADMIN or the 4.02 version of NETADMIN. Use the 4.01 version of NETADMIN to delete bindery type objects from a 4.0x server. This error should not occur in NetWare 6.

**Server Action:** Do a SET DSTRACE=+SYNC on both the source and the target server (and any other servers in the replica list) to see which object is returning the –601 error and what errors the target server is getting in return. If the object is not a server object, try deleting it. If the object with the error is a server object, see if DSTRACE returns any other errors besides –601 and attempt to resolve them. If there are no additional errors, do a Send All Objects from the server reporting the error (the source server), or Receive All Objects from the target server using DSREPAIR. (This method helps only if the source server is the master.) Send All Objects causes a lot of network traffic!

### NO_SUCH_VALUE   –602   0xFFFFFDA6   FDA6

**Explanation:** The requested property value could not be found. If this error is encountered during login or authentication, it usually means that either the user's or the server's public keys could not be located. If this is the case, regenerate the user's key pair by changing the password with utilities.

An occurrence of this error during synchronization between servers means that a value of an object being synchronized is missing from the target server. This error may be a temporary condition that exists because of the loosely consistent nature of Directory Services.

**Server Action:** What error are you seeing on the target server? You may see one of the following messages without an error code:

▸ **Error unable to communicate** — Look in DSTRACE for the object with the problem (SET DSTRACE=+SYNC). The problem is either the public key or the remote ID. Run DSREPAIR to verify remote server IDs. If errors appear there, run this same option once more to verify remote server IDs. If you get a –602 or –603 in DSREPAIR when verifying remote server IDs, call a Novell Authorized Service Center for support. Be aware, however, that a public key cannot be repaired unless at least one server in the tree is authenticating without problems to the target server. The server authenticating OK to the target server must also have a real copy of the target server object, so it must have a replica (other than a subordinate reference) of the partition holding the target server object. If this is only a two-server tree, the target server will need to be removed from the tree and reinstalled.

▸ **Error sending updates** — Look in DSTRACE for the object with the problem (SET DSTRACE=+SYNC) and try deleting the object.

### NO_SUCH_ATTRIBUTE   –603   0xFFFFFDA5   FDA5

**Explanation:** The requested property could not be found. In the Directory, if a property does not contain a value, then the property does not exist for the specific object.

**Client Action:** Ensure that the property being requested is a valid DS property (check spelling and syntax). Use NLIST.EXE to determine if the property exists for the specified object. For example, NLIST *user=username* /d will show all of the properties and their values for the specified user name. (To see all of the properties associated with the object requires supervisor rights to the object in question. Browse rights are given by default.) We have seen this error occur when users try to edit properties that are grayed out in the utilities (properties that are not supported in the current DS schema). This error can also occur when schema synchronization problems are in a mixed tree (4.0x and NetWare 6 servers in the same tree).

**Server Action:** This error is basically the same as a –602 error except that you get a –602 on a multivalued property and a –603 on a single-valued property. What error are you seeing on the target server? You may see one of the following messages without an error code:

▸ **Error unable to communicate** — Look in DSTRACE for the object with the problem (SET DSTRACE=+SYNC). This problem is either the public key or the remote ID. Run DSREPAIR to verify remote server IDs. If errors appear there, run this same option once more to verify remote server IDs. If you get a –602 or –603 in DSREPAIR when verifying remote server IDs, call a Novell Authorized Service Center for support. Be aware, however, that a public key cannot be repaired unless at least one server in the tree is authenticating without problems to the target server. The server authenticating OK to the target server must also have a real copy of the target server object, so it must have a replica (other than a subordinate reference) of the partition holding the target server object. If this tree is only a two-server tree, the target server will need to be removed from the tree and reinstalled.

▸ **Error sending updates** — Look in DSTRACE for the object with the problem (SET DSTRACE=+SYNC) and try deleting the object. If a mixed environment currently is in the tree or if NetWare 6 servers were ever in a now completely 4.0x tree, this could be a schema problem. Run the Global Schema Update option in DSREPAIR on a NetWare 6 server. If no NetWare 6 servers are in the tree, or if the Global Schema Update does not fix the problem, bring the server down with the master replica of the partition returning the error and then bring the server back up. Upon startup, the server will force a schema update. The schema problem should now be resolved.

**NO_SUCH_CLASS    –604    0xFFFFFDA4    FDA4**

**Explanation:** An object class that does not exist in the Directory is being referenced by a utility. An object class in NDS is similar to the object type in the bindery. For example, object type 1 in the bindery is a user object, and in the Directory the object class is USER. The class indicates the kind of object to be created.

**Action:** NetWare 6 utilities access only Novell's base schema, which must be present for the Directory to operate. Determine which utility is being used to create the object. This utility is attempting to use an object class that is currently not defined in NDS. The NetWare 6 utilities only display valid object classes. NetWare 6 enables the schema to be extended, so this error in NetWare 6 may point to schema synchronization problems.

### NO_SUCH_PARTITION   –605   0xFFFFFDA3   FDA3

**Explanation:** A partition with the specified name does not exist.

**Action:** Ensure that the partition name requested is valid and is a valid object name.

### ENTRY_ALREADY_EXISTS   –606   0xFFFFFDA2   FDA2

**Explanation:** An attempt was made to add an object at the same level as a preexisting object of the same name but not necessarily of the same class.

**Action:** Specify a different name for the object being added or rename the existing object.

### NOT_EFFECTIVE_CLASS   –607   0xFFFFFDA1   FDA1

**Explanation:** This error indicates that the class being used to create the specified object is a noneffective class and cannot be used when creating an object. Two types of object classes are in the Directory — effective and noneffective. All effective classes can be used to create objects. (The class being used to create the specified object is referred to as the "base class" of the object.) *User* would be one example of an effective class. Noneffective classes are used as superclasses to define information associated with various effective classes.

**Action:** The standard Novell utilities that ship with NetWare 6 only allow effective classes to be used when creating objects. Find out what utility is being used to create the object. This may mean that your non-Novell utility is not following the rules of the specified object.

### ILLEGAL_ATTRIBUTE   –608   0xFFFFFDA0   FDA0

**Explanation:** An attempt was made to add a property that is illegal to an object. The NDS schema determines which properties an object class can inherit. (Refer to the Directory Services Schema documentation in Chapter 3.) This error can also occur in mixed trees (4.0x and NetWare 6 servers in the same tree) or in upgraded trees (4.0x servers that have been upgraded to NetWare 6) when a server does not have the correct schema.

**Client Action:** You cannot add the specified property to the specified object.

**Server Action:** Do a SET DSTRACE=+SYNC and then SET DSTRACE=*H to see the object causing the error. If the object is not a server object, try deleting it.

In the case of a schema problem, run Global Schema Update in DSREPAIR from a NetWare 6 server. If no NetWare 6 servers are in the tree or if Global Schema Update does not correct the problem, bring the server down containing the master replica of the partition showing errors and then bring the server back up. Upon startup, the server will force a schema update, which usually corrects these schema problems. If the problem persists, call a Novell Authorized Service Center for support.

### MISSING_MANDATORY   –609   0xFFFFFD9F   FD9F

**Explanation:** This error indicates that one or more of the mandatory properties for the object being created are missing. Each object class in the Directory has a set of mandatory properties (properties that must contain a value before the object can be created). For example, a USER object in the Directory is required to have a Common Name (CN) and a Surname. Without these properties the object will not be created. A property exists only if a value has been supplied for the given property. This error can also occur in mixed trees (4.0x and NetWare 6 servers in the same tree) when a server does not have the correct schema.

**Client Action:** Input the required information when creating the object.

**Server Action:** Do a SET DSTRACE=+SYNC and then SET DSTRACE=*H to see the object causing the error. If the object is not a server object, try deleting it. In the case of a schema problem, run Global Schema Update in DSREPAIR from a NetWare 6 server. If no NetWare 6 servers are in the tree or if Global Schema Update does not correct the problem, bring the server down with the master replica of the partition showing errors and then bring the server back up. Upon startup, the server will force a schema update, which usually corrects these schema problems. If the problem persists, call a Novell Authorized Service Center for support.

### ILLEGAL_DS_NAME   –610   0xFFFFFD9E   FD9E

**Explanation:** Illegal Directory Names are those that are too long (more than 255 characters) or ones that contain illegal character combinations. The backslash (\) may be followed only by a period (.), an equal sign (=), a plus sign (+), or a backslash (\).

### ILLEGAL_CONTAINMENT   –611   0xFFFFFD9D   FD9D

**Explanation:** The containment rules of the Directory specify where an object class may appear in relation to other objects in the Directory tree. For example, the object class Country can only be created at the top of the Directory, and the object class User can only be created under Organizations and Organizational Units. The Schema enforces the containment rules for NDS.

**Action:** Go to the appropriate container to create the object.

### CANT_HAVE_MULTIPLE_VALUES   −612   0xFFFFFD9C   FD9C

**Explanation:** This error indicates that the specified property is single valued. All properties are either single or multivalued. For example, the Group Membership property is multivalued. A user can be a member of multiple groups. The Group Membership property exists once and contains multiple group names (values).

**Action:** For this property (information category in the utility), only one value (piece of information) can be supplied.

### SYNTAX_VIOLATION   −613   0xFFFFFD9B   FD9B

**Explanation:** An attribute value being added to an object is incorrect. This error is most often encountered if that value is the name of another object that does not exist. This error is also seen during the installation or upgrade to NetWare 6.

**Client Action:** For most cases, verify that the object name being added as a value is correct.

**Server Action:** If a new NetWare 6 server being installed hangs while copying over the Directory Services objects, check the DSTRACE screen of the server with the master replica of the partition where the new NetWare 6 server is being installed. If the master is giving errors, run DSREPAIR on the master. If problems persist, do a SET DSTRACE=+SYNC to find the object returning the error and check the description field (and any other field that accepts a string) for any unusual ASCII characters. Correct the corruption or delete the object, and the replica should complete copying to the new server.

We have also seen this error occur when a bindery-type object (usually created by a third-party program) becomes corrupt. If the −613 errors are on these objects, delete all objects created by the program and then reinstall the program.

### DUPLICATE_VALUE   −614   0xFFFFFD9A   FD9A

**Explanation:** An attempt was made to add a duplicate value to the specified property.

**Action:** Enter a different value.

### ATTRIBUTE_ALREADY_EXISTS   −615   0xFFFFFD99   FD99

**Explanation:** An attempt was made to add a property that already exists.

**Action:** If the attribute is multivalued, just add the specified value to the existing property. If the property is single valued, you will need to delete the property in order to create it again with the new value.

### MAXIMUM_ENTRIES_EXIST   −616   0xFFFFFD98   FD98

**Explanation:** This error indicates that the maximum number of entries (objects) exists in the Directory tree. The maximum number of objects that can be created in the Directory is FFFFFF (3 bytes of FF), which equal 16,777,215 decimal. Some of these entries are used by the Directory itself.

**Action:** For the current version of the Directory, you have reached the maximum number of objects that can be created. You need to delete objects that are no longer needed.

**DATABASE_FORMAT    –617    0xFFFFFD97    FD97**

**INCONSISTENT_DATABASE    –618    0xFFFFFD96    FD96**

**Explanation:** This error indicates that an error has been encountered in the database itself. Usually this error means that the number of entries in a container does not match the number stored in the container's entry. When this error occurs during synchronization, the target server has a corrupted database.

**Action:** Run DSREPAIR only once.

**TIP**

> If you run **DSREPAIR** a second time, the original .OLD database files will be overwritten after 72 hours, and it will not be possible to restore their former Directory Information Base (DIB).

If the error persists after running DSREPAIR the first time, consult a Novell Authorized Service Center.

**INVALID_COMPARISON    –619    0xFFFFFD95    FD95**

**Explanation:** An attempt was made either to compare two properties that are not comparable or to use an invalid compare syntax.

**Action:** Check the syntax and verify that the properties are comparable.

**COMPARISON_FAILED    –620    0xFFFFFD94    FD94**

**TRANSACTIONS_DISABLED    –621    0xFFFFFD93    FD93**

**Explanation:** This error indicates that Transaction Tracking has been disabled for the server on which the Directory operation is taking place. When TTS is disabled, NDS operations, which require modifying the database on that server, also are disabled.

**Action:** At the console prompt of the file server type **ENABLE TTS**. If TTS was disabled because the SYS volume is full, log into the file server, delete unnecessary files from the SYS volume, and type **ENABLE TTS** at the file server. If you are unable to log into the file server, try running VREPAIR on volume SYS and selecting Purge Deleted Files from the VREPAIR menu. If there still is not enough space, put another drive into the server and span the SYS volume across both drives to give SYS more space.

**INVALID_TRANSPORT    −622    0xFFFFFD92    FD92**
**SYNTAX_INVALID_IN_NAME    −623    0xFFFFFD91    FD91**
**REPLICA_ALREADY_EXISTS    −624    0xFFFFFD90    FD90**

**Explanation:** This error indicates that a replica of the specified partition already exists on the server.

**Action:** Select a different server.

### TRANSPORT_FAILURE    −625    0xFFFFFD8F    FD8F

**Explanation:** This error occurs when a client and a server or two servers cannot communicate with each other across the network.

**Action:** Check for SAP filtering of the DS SAP types of 26B and 278. Check cabling, the LAN card, and the LAN driver. Make sure they can RCONSOLE to the target server. Does typing **DISPLAY SERVERS** on the source server show the target server? Are other servers also showing this −625 error to the same target server? Can workstations attach and log into the target server from the same segment as the source server? Type **RESET ROUTERS** and then type **SET DSTRACE=*U** at the source server to flag all servers as UP and retry communicating with them. This error is almost always a LAN communication issue. Occasionally a change of the server's name, a move of the server object, or a change to the internal IPX number can also cause this error to occur. Run DSREPAIR with the option to Repair Network Addresses on the Source Server to check the internal IPX number of the target server. The change may not complete successfully. This error can also occur when trying to communicate with servers that have locked databases (that is, with DSREPAIR).

### ALL_REFERRALS_FAILED    −626    0xFFFFFD8E    FD8E

**Explanation:** The object could not be found. It is still possible that the object does exist but that a server could not communicate with the server holding a copy of the object. The target server tried to walk the tree by contacting all other servers in the replica ring and was unable to do so. This error commonly occurs when partition management is requested and the requested operation cannot take place because a key server is inaccessible. Invalid creation timestamps can also return this error.

**Server Action:** Run DSREPAIR with the options to Repair Network Addresses and verify remote server IDs. Check the replica rings to verify that there is one master replica for the partition in question. Check the replica states and make sure they are all ON. Resolve whatever problems you find in the DSREPAIR.LOG file. Look in DISPLAY SERVERS to see if the tree name is present. If not, check the issues with −625 errors (including SAP filtering). If creation timestamps are invalid, running the NetWare 6 DSREPAIR with the option to Check External References under Advanced Options (only available in newer DSREPAIRs) should repair this problem.

### CANT_REMOVE_NAMING_VALUE   –627   0xFFFFFD8D   FD8D

**Explanation:** This error indicates that an attempt was made to delete the naming property, but the naming value cannot be removed.

**Action:** Rename the object and then delete the property.

### OBJECT_CLASS_VIOLATION   –628   0xFFFFFD8C   FD8C

**Explanation:** An object class violation has occurred.

**Server Action:** This error can occur when the source server's objects are unknown but are fine on the target server. Isolate the bad replica by either locking the databases with DSREPAIR and then running NETADMIN or NWADMIN to view the objects or by using DSVIEW (available on NetWire). Then delete the bad replica and add it back again through Partition Manager (verifying first that the master is a good copy).

A schema synchronization problem can also generate this error. Run the Global Schema Update option in DSREPAIR on a NetWare 6 server. If no NetWare 6 servers are in the tree, or if the Global Schema Update does not fix the problem, bring the server down with the master replica of the partition, which returns the error and then brings the server back up. Upon startup, the server will force a schema update, which usually corrects a schema problem.

### ENTRY_IS_NOT_LEAF   –629   0xFFFFFD8B   FD8B

**Explanation:** This error indicates that the object being deleted or modified is not a leaf object. A container object that does not contain any objects is considered a leaf object. Therefore, it can be deleted. If you attempt to delete a container object that does contain objects of any class, the following error message is returned: "The utility can't delete <object class>=<object name> because it is not a leaf object." A container object that is a partition root cannot be deleted.

**Action:** Delete all objects under the container object that are being deleted or modified. If the object is a partition root, merge the partition with the parent partition and then delete the object.

### DIFFERENT_TREE   –630   0xFFFFFD8A   FD8A
### ILLEGAL_REPLICA_TYPE   –631   0xFFFFFD89   FD89

**Explanation:** This error indicates that a request was made of a replica, but the replica was the wrong type. Therefore, the request could not complete.

**Server Action:** This is usually seen at the file server console when attempting to set the bindery context. The bindery context requires a writeable replica (either a read/write or a master) in order to be set. Verify that the server has a writeable replica of the partition containing the container to which you are attempting to set the bindery context.

### SYSTEM_FAILURE   −632   0xFFFFFD88   FD88

**Explanation:** This error indicates that unexpected results have occurred. For example, the client requested that the Directory return a network address attribute, and the Directory actually returned a public key attribute. This condition may be temporary. While the client usually returns errors in the −301 to −399 range, the client, as well as the server, returns this error during authentication. A server may return a −632 during synchronization because authentication could not complete due to an error in the public key—the key is the right key, but it is corrupt (not the right format). This error can also be returned in DSTRACE if the server is unable to open the local database. However, −632 is just a general error, which means that the process being attempted failed because the server(s) being contacted was busy or down, or the source server could not authenticate to it.

**Symptom:** After upgrading a server, the DS is unable to open the database. SET DSTRACE=ON and then SET DSTRACE=+MISC. Then dismount and remount the SYS volume. Check the DSTRACE screen and confirm that a −632 error is returned when DS tries to open the database. If so, the database is corrupted. DS needs to be removed from the server and reinstalled (either from another replica in the tree or, if a single-server environment, from backup).

**Server Action:** Run DSREPAIR with the option to verify remote server IDs on every server in the replica list. Then go back and run DSREPAIR a second time with the option to verify remote server IDs on every server in the replica list. If the remote server ID check returns a −632 after running it the second time, call a Novell Authorized Service Center. Otherwise, try to resolve the process that failed.

### INVALID_ENTRY_FOR_ROOT   −633   0xFFFFFD87   FD87

**Explanation:** An attempt was made to either restore or move an object that is flagged as a partition root but whose base class is not a container, or to perform a split at an object whose base class is not a container.

### NO_REFERRALS   −634   0xFFFFFD86   FD86

**Explanation:** This means that the target server does not have a copy of what the source server is requesting. In other words, the source server has no objects that match the request and no referrals to search for the object.

**Action:** None required. This is not a serious error, just a response.

### REMOTE_FAILURE    –635    0xFFFFFD85    FD85

**Explanation:** In order to complete certain operations, a server will need to contact another server. If this is not possible (because of a link being down, for example), this error will be returned.

**Action:** The target server does not have the correct information about the source server. This error is often caused by a problem with local to remote IDs or the server object. Run DSREPAIR with the option to verify remote server IDs on every server in the replica list. Then go back and run DSREPAIR a second time with the option to verify remote server IDs on all servers in the replica list. Resolve any errors found after the second run of DSREPAIR.

### UNREACHABLE_SERVER    –636    0XFFFFFD84    FD84
### PREVIOUS_MOVE_IN_PROGRESS    –637    0XFFFFFD83    FD83

**Explanation:** Once an object has been moved from one context in the Directory to another, the Directory will not allow that object to be moved again until all replicas of that object have been updated. The length of time for a move to complete varies depending on the size of the replica, the number of replicas, and condition of the communication links between all the servers holding the replicas. This error can be caused by a moved object that lost the original object (the primary obituary) or by a broken partition.

**Action:** Leave the object in its current context until it can be moved again. This may require that the object be left in its new context for several minutes. If the object still cannot be moved, load the NetWare 6 DSREPAIR with –m (LOAD DSREPAIR –M) and then run Repair Local Database. (For 4.0x DSREPAIR, type **LOAD DSREPAIR –A**, Select Options, and toggle A until it reads "Find obituaries for move and move-inhibit.") View the DSREPAIR.LOG file, which displays objects that have move obituaries. Verify that the problem objects and all their attributes have been successfully moved to the new location by running NWADMIN or NETADMIN and viewing the objects. If the objects have been moved, load the NetWare 6 DSREPAIR with –MR (load the 4.0x DSREPAIR with –A, Select Options, and then toggle A until it reads "Purge obituaries for move and move-inhibit"), which will delete the move obituaries for those problem objects. Use SET DSTRACE=+J and SET DSTRACE=*F to verify that the purger ran successfully.

**NO_CHARACTER_MAPPING   −638   0xFFFFFD82   FD82**
**INCOMPLETE_AUTHENTICATION   −639   0xFFFFFD81   FD81**
**INVALID_CERTIFICATE   −640   0xFFFFFD80   FD80**
**INVALID_REQUEST   −641   0xFFFFFD7F   FD7F**

**Explanation:** The server did not understand the request. For example, a client workstation could have sent an incorrect verb.

**Server Action:** A nonsynchronized schema can cause this error. Run the NetWare 6 DSREPAIR and do a Global Schema Update. This error can also be a response error, so check for errors on the target server and resolve any that you may find there first.

**INVALID_ITERATION   −642   0xFFFFFD7E   FD7E**

**Explanation:** A client workstation sent an invalid iteration handle.

**SCHEMA_IS_NONREMOVABLE   −643   0xFFFFFD7D   FD7D**

**Explanation:** An attempt was made to delete an NDS structure or configuration.

**SCHEMA_IS_IN_USE   −644   0xFFFFFD7C   FD7C**

**Explanation:** An attempt was made to delete an NDS configuration or structure (such as a container object) that still contains an object using that structure.

**Action:** First delete the object or property and then delete the structure.

**CLASS_ALREADY_EXISTS   −645   0xFFFFFD7B   FD7B**

**Explanation:** This error indicates that the object class being created already exists as a class in the schema of the Directory. (See also NO_SUCH_CLASS −604 0xFFFFFDA4.)

**Action:** This error should occur only in a utility that updates the schema of the Directory. Determine the utility that is causing the error.

**BAD_NAMING_ATTRIBUTES   −646   0xFFFFFD7A   FD7A**
**NOT_ROOT_PARTITION   −647   0xFFFFFD79   FD79**

**Explanation:** An attempt was made to execute a function that is required on the root partition. Either the client did not pass on the root partition name or the client attempted to perform the function somewhere other than the root partition.

**INSUFFICIENT_STACK   −648   0xFFFFFD78   FD78**
**INSUFFICIENT_BUFFER   −649   0xFFFFFD77   FD77**

**Explanation:** The server ran out of memory. The operating system will self-correct this error.

**Action:** Be patient. Check the "Resolving Server Memory Problems" in Novell's manual *Supervising the Network*.

**AMBIGUOUS_CONTAINMENT**   −650   0xFFFFFD76   FD76
**AMBIGUOUS_NAMING**   −651   0xFFFFFD75   FD75
**DUPLICATE_MANDATORY**   −652   0xFFFFFD74   FD74
**DUPLICATE_OPTIONAL**   −653   0xFFFFFD73   FD73
**PARTITION_BUSY**   −654   0xFFFFFD72   FD72

**Explanation:** Another partition operation is currently taking place. For example, if a request has previously been issued to split a partition, a second request for a split (even at another point in the same partition) will result in this error.

**Server Action:** This is a normal error immediately after a partition operation has been initiated. If this error does not go away, in the 310 build of the DS this error can indicate that the target server does not think that the source server has a copy of that partition. Confirm this through DSREPAIR.LOG or by watching DSTRACE. Try running PTEST (4.0x) or Cancel Partition Operation (NetWare 6) to abort the partition operation on the source server. You can also remove the source server from the tree or call a Novell Authorized Service Center for support.

**MULTIPLE_REPLICAS**   −655   0xFFFFFD71   FD71

**Explanation:** This error is an internal error that appears as a result of a programming discrepancy, not a system inconsistency.

**CRUCIAL_REPLICA**   −656   0xFFFFFD70   FD70

**Explanation:** An attempt was made to perform one of the following illegal operations on a master replica: remove it, change its replica type (the correct way to change a replica type is to change the replica type of another server's replica to the master, which indirectly forces the master to become a read/write), or request that it receive all updates from the master. This error can also be caused by trying to add a replica to the server where the master of that replica already exists.

**SCHEMA_SYNC_IN_PROGRESS**   −657   0xFFFFFD6F   FD6F

**Explanation:** The function could not be completed because Directory synchronization is in progress.

**Action:** Wait awhile and try again.

**SKULK_IN_PROGRESS**   −658   0xFFFFFD6E   FD6E

**Explanation:** The function could not be completed because replica synchronization is in progress.

**Action:** Wait awhile and try again.

**TIME_NOT_SYNCHRONIZED**   −659   0xFFFFFD6D   FD6D

**Explanation:** NDS uses timestamps to determine the order of events that take place in the Directory. Time Synchronization services have been implemented to maintain a consistent time across the network. Modification operations require the issuance of a timestamp. If a replica on a server has issued a timestamp and the time on that server is set back, in 4.0x no further modification operations may take place until the time on the server moves past the last modification time on the partition. This applies only to operations that modify, not to those that just read information. In other words, users will be able to log into the Directory, but no objects can be edited through the utilities. In NetWare 6, the Directory will issue synthetic timestamps on objects, enabling those objects to be modified, yet still not allow illegal timestamps. The server console will display a synthetic time error when the server time is behind the NDS time.

**Action:** Check DSTRACE for other errors first and resolve any you find. Then run Repair Timestamps (found in the NetWare 6 DSREPAIR), which will reset the timestamps to the current server time. The 4.0x equivalent of Repair Timestamps is Rebuild Replicas and is performed from the Partition Manager. This action deletes the objects from all replicas except the Master and then recopies all objects from the Master copy to all other replicas. BEWARE! If the Master copy was corrupt in any way, the other replicas will also be corrupt when a Repair Timestamps or Rebuild Replicas action is performed. Repair Timestamps or Rebuild Replicas can also cause considerable traffic on the network. You may have to perform this action on a partition-by-partition basis.

**RECORD_IN_USE    –660    0xFFFFFD6C    FD6C**
**DS_VOLUME_NOT_MOUNTED    –661    0xFFFFFD6B    FD6B**
**DS_VOLUME_IO_FAILURE    –662    0xFFFFFD6A    FD6A**
**DS_LOCKED    –663    0xFFFFFD69    FD69**

**Explanation:** The Directory database is locked on the server. This error will be seen in DSTRACE when the source server is trying to synchronize with the target server, which has a locked database. There will be no activity in the TRACE screen on the server with the locked database. The server with the problem often receives an error when it tries to open the Directory while mounting the SYS volume. We have seen this error occur when DSREPAIR is loaded on the server, when DSDUMP has the Directory locked, when the hard drive on the server is going bad, and when a new 4.02 server installation does not complete properly.

**Action:** Try running DSREPAIR on the server.

**TIP**

**Run DSREPAIR. If DSREPAIR is run more than once, keep in mind that the .OLD database files will be overwritten after 72 hours. If DSREPAIR doesn't fix the problem, try bringing the server down and bringing it back up again. If running DSREPAIR and bringing the server down do**

not fix this error, the server may need to be removed from the tree. If this is a new server with no replicas on it, remove DS from the server. If you don't want to remove DS from the server, escalate the call. When the DS is locked, the normal removal of DS on a 4.02 server may not complete properly. You may need to load install with the –dsremove switch (LOAD INSTALL -DSREMOVE) and then try to remove DS through install. This will most likely return an error about being unable to remove DS but will perform the removal anyway. Try loading install with the –dsremove switch again and try the removal a second time. DSI should report that DS was already removed from the server. Don't use –DSREMOVE unless the normal removal process won't work! The –dsremove switch will ignore errors and warnings and may not perform all the steps necessary to do a clean removal.

### OLD_EPOCH   –664   0xFFFFFD68   FD68

Explanation: This is an NDS timestamp error.

### NEW_EPOCH   –665   0xFFFFFD67   FD67

Explanation: This is an NDS timestamp error.

### INCOMPATIBLE_DS_VERSION   –666   0xFFFFFD66   FD66

Explanation: This error occurs when performing operations that require the same schema, but servers are involved in the operation with dissimilar schemas.

Symptom: Partition Manager returns this error when a partition operation is requested and the server with the Master replica is a NetWare 6 server, but other 4.0 servers are on the replica list (including servers holding subordinate reference replicas). DSREPAIR for NetWare 6 may also return this error during a remote to local ID check.

Server Action: Most partition operations involving a NetWare 6 server as the server holding the Master will be unable to complete to 4.0x servers. The 4.0x servers on the replica list must be upgraded to NetWare 6 before the partition operation can be completed. If the Master replica were on a 4.02 server, you would not have this particular problem. If this error is seen in DSREPAIR during a remote-to-local ID check, do a SET DSTRACE=!V on the NetWare 6 server. This check resets the list of restricted versions (DS versions that are restricted from synchronization) to the default, which is DS 290 and above.

### PARTITION_ROOT   –667   0xFFFFFD65   FD65

Explanation: This error indicates that the object being manipulated is the root of a Directory Services partition. This error would most commonly occur when you attempt to delete a container object that is a partition root.

Action: Using the partition management tools, merge this partition into the parent partition.

### ENTRY_NOT_CONTAINER    –668    0xFFFFFD64    FD64

**Explanation:** An illegal function was attempted on a leaf object.

### FAILED_AUTHENTICATION    –669    0xFFFFFD63    FD63

**Explanation:** An invalid password was sent. Authentication failed. This error is seen in DSTRACE when one server tries to synchronize with another server. The most likely problems are either the remote ID or the public key.

**Server Action:** Try running DSREPAIR with the option to verify remote server IDs on the source server and all other servers on the replica list. If the DSREPAIR.LOG file has errors, run DSREPAIR with the option to verify remote server IDs once more on every server in the replica list. This should resolve the problem with incorrect remote IDs. The other scenario is when the source server is either using or looking at the wrong public key (the key is the right format, but is for the wrong object). If the problem is the public key and if the source server has a REAL copy of the target server object (a Master, R/W, or R/O replica of the partition containing the target server object), check to see if the other servers on that replica list (for the partition containing the target server object) can authenticate to the target server. If another server can authenticate, do a Send All Objects from the good server, or a Receive All Objects on the target server (but only if the server with the "good" copy has the Master).

Also, remember that Send All Objects generates a lot of traffic. If no servers can authenticate to the target server, remove DS from the target server and reinstall it back into the tree, or call a Novell Authorized Service Center for support.

If the source server has a subordinate reference replica or no replica of the partition containing the target server object, the external reference to that object will need to be rebacklinked. Call a Novell Authorized Service Center for support.

### INVALID_CONTEXT    –670    0xFFFFFD62    FD62
### NO_SUCH_PARENT    –671    0xFFFFFD61    FD61
### NO_ACCESS    –672    0xFFFFFD60    FD60

**Explanation:** The client does not have sufficient results to complete the requested operation. This error in DSTRACE means that the target server's replica list doesn't match the source server's replica list.

**Server Action:** Compare the replica ring information for all the servers on the replica list (available though Display Replica Information). If you confirm that the target server doesn't have the source server on its replica list, then either remove DS from the target server or call a Novell Authorized Service Center for support.

**REPLICA_NOT_ON    −673    0xFFFFFD5F    FD5F**

**Explanation:** The replica is being created on a server. Until all the object information has been received on that server, the replica is "off" (not available for use by Directory clients).

**Server Action:** Wait. If the replica is stuck, look for the error that is preventing the replica from turning "on" and address that problem.

**INVALID_NAME_SERVICE    −674    0xFFFFFD5E    FD5E**

**INVALID_TASK    −675    0xFFFFFD5D    FD5D**

**INVALID_CONN_HANDLE    −676    0xFFFFFD5C    FD5C**

**INVALID_IDENTITY    −677    0xFFFFFD5B    FD5B**

**DUPLICATE_ACL    −678    0xFFFFFD5A    FD5A**

**PARTITION_ALREADY_EXISTS    −679    0xFFFFFD59    FD59**

**TRANSPORT_MODIFIED    −680    0xFFFFFD58    FD58**

**ALIAS_OF_AN_ALIAS    −681    0xFFFFFD57    FD57**

**AUDITING_FAILED    −682    0xFFFFFD56    FD56**

**INVALID_API_VERSION    −683    0xFFFFFD55    FD55**

**SECURE_NCP_VIOLATION    −684    0xFFFFFD54    FD54**

**MOVE_IN_PROGRESS    −685    0xFFFFFD53    FD53**

**NOT_LEAF_PARTITION    −686    0xFFFFFD52    FD52**

**CANNOT_ABORT    −687    0xFFFFFD51    FD51**

**CACHE_OVERFLOW    −688    0xFFFFFD50    FD50**

**INVALID_SUBORDINATE_COUNT    −689    0xFFFFFD4F    FD4F**

**INVALID_RDN    −690    0xFFFFFD4E    FD4E**

**MOD_TIME_NOT_CURRENT    −691    0xFFFFFD4D    FD4D**

**INCORRECT_BASE_CLASS    −692    0xFFFFFD4C    FD4C**

**MISSING_REFERENCE    −693    0xFFFFFD4B    FD4B**

**Explanation:** A required reference is missing from the object. This error is frequently seen in the NetWare 6 utilities if you are trying to delete an object with a zero creation timestamp.

**Server Action:** Run the latest version of the NetWare 6 DSREPAIR on the server. This gives objects with missing creation timestamps a valid timestamp. If the object continues to give a −693 error during deletion, a server in that partition's replica list still has a zero creation timestamp for that object. Run the latest DSREPAIR on each server on that partition's replica list.

**LOST_ENTRY    −694    0xFFFFFD4A    FD4A**

**AGENT_ALREADY_REGISTERED    −695    0xFFFFFD49    FD49**

**DS_LOADER_BUSY    −696    0xFFFFFD48    FD48**

**DS_CANNOT_RELOAD    −697    0xFFFFFD47    FD47**

**REPLICA_IN_SKULK    −698    0xFFFFFD46    FD46**

**Explanation:** The replica is busy skulking, and no other replica processes will be done until the skulk has completed.

**Server Action:** Usually this error occurs as a normal part of a partition operation and will resolve itself. If this error does not go away, check for other errors that may be preventing the partition operation from completing. Remember that the master replica is controlling all partition operations.

**FATAL    −699    0xFFFFFD45    FD45**

**Explanation:** An unrecoverable error has occurred and the operation cannot be completed. A variety of problems can cause this error.

**Server Action:** Go to the target server and look for a response TRACE error. (Turn off the DSTRACE filters by using a setting like FFFF6FF7 or 8164B19 in 4.0x or an 8164B91 in NetWare 6.) Sometimes you will see an error without an error code (such as "skulk lost entry"), which can also be important. Resolve the error on the target server. Treat a "skulk lost entry" error the same as a −601 error.

**Error −709 (Hex: FFFFFD3B)**

**Explanation:** Invalid response. A DS client makes an invalid request and receives an invalid response.

**Error −715 (Hex: FFFFFD35)**

**Explanation:** A checksum error has occurred.

**Error −716 (Hex: FFFFFD34)**

**Explanation:** An error was received because checksumming is not supported.

**SERVER IN SKULK    -6015 FFFFE881**

**Explanation:** The local server can't outbound to another server because some other thread in the local server is already outbounding to that server.

**Possible Cause:** A server can only receive inbound NDS replica synchronization from one server at a time. When two servers in the same replica ring try to synchronize to the NDS server before one of them completes the synchronization, this error occurs.

**Action:** Consider this error transitory. NDS replica synchronization will resolve the error.

### RETURNING PARTIAL RESULTS    -6016 FFFFE880

**Explanation:** An error has occurred during a search or read operation, and the entry being returned as the result contains partial values. This is a nonfatal error. The client might attempt to retrieve and use the partial results that have been returned.

**Possible Cause:** The operation being performed computes the attribute values of an entry dynamically and has encountered an internal error during the computation. This usually means that a search was performed internally across multiple servers and one or more of the servers could not be contacted. Specifically, this error can occur during a listing of dynamicgroup members. When the members of the dynamicgroup are expanded using a search and if the search fails, the results are returned as members along with this error code.

**Action:** Make sure that the memberquery attributes of the dynamicgroup objects involved are correct and the scope in the attribute covers servers that are contactable.

Remove and reinstall the third-party schema and re-create the extension.

### NO SUCH SCHEMA    -6017 FFFFE87F

**Explanation:** The schema definition being requested was not found. Therefore, the operation that was requested could not be completed.

**Possible Cause:**  Third-party schema is not synchronized.

**Action:** Contact third-party for assistance. Schema may not have been extended properly or at all.

### SERIAL NUM MISMATCH    -6018 FFFFE87E

**Explanation:** A serial number does not match the database's serial number.

**Possible Cause:** This error is reported when an incremental backup is being restored and the serial number of the database stored in the incremental backup's header does not match the serial number of the database. Generally, this means that an attempt is being made to restore an incremental backup from another database.

**Action:** Locate the correct roll-forward log (RFL) file and retry the operation.

### BAD RFL DB SERIAL NUM    -6019 FFFFE87D

**Explanation:** A serial number does not match the database's serial number.

**Possible Cause:** This error is reported when the database's serial number, recorded in the header of a RFL, does not match the current database's serial number. Generally, this means that an attempt is being made to replay an RFL file from another database during a database restore operation.

**Action:** Locate the correct RFL file and retry the operation.

### BAD RFL SERIAL NUM    -6020 FFFFE87C

**Explanation:** A serial number in the RFL does not match either the RFL serial number stored in the database or in the prior RFL file.

**Possible Cause:** This error usually means that an attempt is being made to replay an RFL from another database during a database restore operation.

**Action:** Locate the correct RFL file and retry the operation.

### INVALID FILE SEQUENCE    -6021 FFFFE87B

**Explanation:** An incorrect file number has been detected while traversing a file set.

**Possible Cause:** This error is reported when an incremental backup is being restored and the sequence number (or incremental backup number) does not match the expected number recorded in the database.

**Action:** Locate the correct incremental backup and retry the operation. Run DSRepair.

### RFL TRANS GAP    -6022 FFFFE87A

**Explanation:** The database has detected that transactions are missing from the RFL.

**Possible Cause:** This error is reported during recovery (after a server crash) or during a database restore operation if one or more RFL files have been damaged, resulting in a gap in the transactions recorded in the log.

**Action:** No action can be taken.

### BAD RFL FILE NUMBER    -6023 FFFFE879

**Explanation:** The RFL file number does not match the file number recorded in the RFL file's header.

**Possible Cause:** This is reported during a database restore operation if the wrong RFL file is provided.

**Action:** Locate the correct RFL file and retry the operation.

### RFL FILE NOT FOUND    -6024 FFFFE878

**Explanation:** A RFL file, needed for database recovery, could not be found.

**Possible Cause:** This error could occur if any of the required RFL files in the NDS.RFL directory have been deleted.

**Action:** Restore the missing RFL files from backup.

### BACKUP ACTIVE    -6025 FFFFE877

**Explanation:** An operation has been requested during a database backup that cannot be performed while the backup is running.

**Possible Cause:** This error will be returned if more than one concurrent backup of the database is requested.

**Action:** Wait until the backup operation has completed and then retry the operation.

### RFL DEVICE FULL    -6026 FFFFE876

**Explanation:** The volume hosting the RFL files is full.

**Possible Cause:** No more space is available on the RFL volume.

**Action:** Free up some disk space on the volume hosting the RFL files.

### UNSUPPORTED VERSION    -6027 FFFFE875

**Explanation:** The file format used by a backup set or the database is not supported by the current code revision.

**Possible Cause:** This error may be returned when a prior version of Novell eDirectory is used to restore a backup set made with a newer version of eDirectory.

### MUST WAIT CHECKPOINT      -6028 FFFFE874

**Explanation:** An operation has been requested at a time when the database must force a checkpoint.

**Possible Cause:** An error has occurred (for example, out-of-disk) that requires the database to flush all dirty cache buffers to disk.

**Action:** Retry the operation once the checkpoint has completed. Because this error is frequently the result of an out-of-disk condition, verify that free disk space is available on the volumes hosting the database and RFL files.

## Other Error Codes

This section describes additional error codes that, for the most part, are internal to NDS and would not be seen by a network administrator unless they are coding to NDS.

| | | |
|---|---|---|
| −1 | FFFFFFFF | "DSERR_INSUFFICIENT_SPACE" |
| −19 | FFFFFF89 | "DSERR_BUFFER_TOO_SMALL" |
| −120 | FFFFFF88 | "DSERR_VOLUME_FLAG_NOT_SET" |
| −121 | FFFFFF87 | "DSERR_NO_ITEMS_FOUND" |
| −122 | FFFFFF86 | "DSERR_CONN_ALREADY_TEMPORARY" |
| −123 | FFFFFF85 | "DSERR_CONN_ALREADY_LOGGED_IN" |
| −124 | FFFFFF84 | "DSERR_CONN_NOT_AUTHENTICATED" |
| −125 | FFFFFF83 | "DSERR_CONN_NOT_LOGGED_IN" |
| −126 | FFFFFF82 | "DSERR_NCP_BOUNDARY_CHECK_FAILED" |
| −127 | FFFFFF81 | "DSERR_LOCK_WAITING" |
| −128 | FFFFFF80 | "DSERR_LOCK_FAIL" |
| −129 | FFFFFF7F | "DSERR_OUT_OF_HANDLES" |

| −130 | FFFFFF7E | "DSERR_NO_OPEN_PRIVILEGE" |
| −131 | FFFFFF7D | "DSERR_HARD_IO_ERROR" |
| −132 | FFFFFF7C | "DSERR_NO_CREATE_PRIVILEGE" |
| −133 | FFFFFF7B | "DSERR_NO_CREATE_DELETE_PRIV" |
| −134 | FFFFFF7A | "DSERR_R_O_CREATE_FILE" |
| −135 | FFFFFF79 | "DSERR_CREATE_FILE_INVALID_NAME" |
| −136 | FFFFFF78 | "DSERR_INVALID_FILE_HANDLE" |
| −137 | FFFFFF77 | "DSERR_NO_SEARCH_PRIVILEGE" |
| −138 | FFFFFF76 | "DSERR_NO_DELETE_PRIVILEGE" |
| −139 | FFFFFF75 | "DSERR_NO_RENAME_PRIVILEGE" |
| −140 | FFFFFF74 | "DSERR_NO_SET_PRIVILEGE" |
| −141 | FFFFFF73 | "DSERR_SOME_FILES_IN_USE" |
| −142 | FFFFFF72 | "DSERR_ALL_FILES_IN_USE" |
| −143 | FFFFFF71 | "DSERR_SOME_READ_ONLY" |
| −144 | FFFFFF70 | "DSERR_ALL_READ_ONLY" |
| −145 | FFFFFF6F | "DSERR_SOME_NAMES_EXIST" |
| −146 | FFFFFF6E | "DSERR_ALL_NAMES_EXIST" |
| −147 | FFFFFF6D | "DSERR_NO_READ_PRIVILEGE" |
| −148 | FFFFFF6C | "DSERR_NO_WRITE_PRIVILEGE" |
| −149 | FFFFFF6B | "DSERR_FILE_DETACHED" |
| −150 | FFFFFF6A | "DSERR_NO_ALLOC_SPACE" |
| −150 | FFFFFF6A | "DSERR_TARGET_NOT_A_SUBDIR" |
| −150 | FFFFFF6A | "ERR_INSUFFICIENT_MEMORY" |
| −151 | FFFFFF69 | "DSERR_NO_SPOOL_SPACE" |
| −152 | FFFFFF68 | "DSERR_INVALID_VOLUME" |
| −153 | FFFFFF67 | "DSERR_DIRECTORY_FULL" |
| −154 | FFFFFF66 | "DSERR_RENAME_ACROSS_VOLUME" |
| −155 | FFFFFF65 | "DSERR_BAD_DIR_HANDLE" |
| −156 | FFFFFF64 | "DSERR_INVALID_PATH" |
| −156 | FFFFFF64 | "DSERR_NO_SUCH_EXTENSION" |
| −157 | FFFFFF63 | "DSERR_NO_DIR_HANDLES" |
| −158 | FFFFFF62 | "DSERR_BAD_FILE_NAME" |
| −159 | FFFFFF61 | "DSERR_DIRECTORY_ACTIVE" |
| −160 | FFFFFF60 | "DSERR_DIRECTORY_NOT_EMPTY" |
| −161 | FFFFFF5F | "DSERR_DIRECTORY_IO_ERROR" |
| −162 | FFFFFF5E | "DSERR_IO_LOCKED" |
| −163 | FFFFFF5D | "DSERR_TRANSACTION_RESTARTED" |
| −164 | FFFFFF5C | "DSERR_RENAME_DIR_INVALID" |
| −165 | FFFFFF5B | "DSERR_INVALID_OPENCREATE_MODE" |

· · · · ·

| −166 | FFFFFF5A | "DSERR_ALREADY_IN_USE" |
| −167 | FFFFFF59 | "DSERR_INVALID_RESOURCE_TAG" |
| −168 | FFFFFF58 | "DSERR_ACCESS_DENIED" |
| −190 | FFFFFF42 | "DSERR_INVALID_DATA_STREAM" |
| −191 | FFFFFF41 | "DSERR_INVALID_NAME_SPACE" |
| −192 | FFFFFF40 | "DSERR_NO_ACCOUNTING_PRIVILEGES" |
| −193 | FFFFFF3F | "DSERR_NO_ACCOUNT_BALANCE" |
| −194 | FFFFFF3E | "DSERR_CREDIT_LIMIT_EXCEEDED" |
| −195 | FFFFFF3D | "DSERR_TOO_MANY_HOLDS" |
| −196 | FFFFFF3C | "DSERR_ACCOUNTING_DISABLED" |
| −197 | FFFFFF3B | "DSERR_LOGIN_LOCKOUT" |
| −198 | FFFFFF3A | "DSERR_NO_CONSOLE_RIGHTS" |
| −208 | FFFFFF30 | "DSERR_Q_IO_FAILURE" |
| −209 | FFFFFF2F | "DSERR_NO_QUEUE" |
| −210 | FFFFFF2E | "DSERR_NO_Q_SERVER" |
| −211 | FFFFFF2D | "DSERR_NO_Q_RIGHTS" |
| −212 | FFFFFF2C | "DSERR_Q_FULL" |
| −213 | FFFFFF2B | "DSERR_NO_Q_JOB" |
| −214 | FFFFFF2A | "DSERR_NO_Q_JOB_RIGHTS" |
| −214 | FFFFFF2A | "DSERR_UNENCRYPTED_NOT_ALLOWED" |
| −215 | FFFFFF29 | "DSERR_Q_IN_SERVICE" |
| −215 | FFFFFF29 | "DSERR_DUPLICATE_PASSWORD" |
| −216 | FFFFFF28 | "DSERR_Q_NOT_ACTIVE" |
| −216 | FFFFFF28 | "DSERR_PASSWORD_TOO_SHORT" |
| −217 | FFFFFF27 | "DSERR_Q_STN_NOT_SERVER" |
| −217 | FFFFFF27 | "DSERR_MAXIMUM_LOGINS_EXCEEDED" |
| −218 | FFFFFF26 | "DSERR_Q_HALTED" |
| −218 | FFFFFF26 | "DSERR_BAD_LOGIN_TIME" |
| −219 | FFFFFF25 | "DSERR_Q_MAX_SERVERS" |
| −219 | FFFFFF25 | "DSERR_NODE_ADDRESS_VIOLATION" |
| −220 | FFFFFF24 | "DSERR_LOG_ACCOUNT_EXPIRED" |
| −222 | FFFFFF22 | "DSERR_BAD_PASSWORD" |
| −223 | FFFFFF21 | "DSERR_PASSWORD_EXPIRED" |
| −224 | FFFFFF20 | "DSERR_NO_LOGIN_CONN_AVAILABLE" |
| −232 | FFFFFF18 | "DSERR_WRITE_TO_GROUP_PROPERTY" |
| −233 | FFFFFF17 | "DSERR_MEMBER_ALREADY_EXISTS" |
| −234 | FFFFFF16 | "DSERR_NO_SUCH_MEMBER" |
| −235 | FFFFFF15 | "DSERR_PROPERTY_NOT_GROUP" |
| −236 | FFFFFF14 | "DSERR_NO_SUCH_VALUE_SET" |

| | | |
|---|---|---|
| −237 | FFFFFF13 | "DSERR_PROPERTY_ALREADY_EXISTS" |
| −238 | FFFFFF12 | "DSERR_OBJECT_ALREADY_EXISTS" |
| −239 | FFFFFF11 | "DSERR_ILLEGAL_NAME" |
| −240 | FFFFFF10 | "DSERR_ILLEGAL_WILDCARD" |
| −241 | FFFFFF0F | "DSERR_BINDERY_SECURITY" |
| −242 | FFFFFF0E | "DSERR_NO_OBJECT_READ_RIGHTS" |
| −243 | FFFFFF0D | "DSERR_NO_OBJECT_RENAME_RIGHTS" |
| −244 | FFFFFF0C | "DSERR_NO_OBJECT_DELETE_RIGHTS" |
| −245 | FFFFFF0B | "DSERR_NO_OBJECT_CREATE_RIGHTS" |
| −246 | FFFFFF0A | "DSERR_NO_PROPERTY_DELETE_RIGHTS" |
| −247 | FFFFFF09 | "DSERR_NO_PROPERTY_CREATE_RIGHTS" |
| −248 | FFFFFF08 | "DSERR_NO_PROPERTY_WRITE_RIGHTS" |
| −249 | FFFFFF07 | "DSERR_NO_PROPERTY_READ_RIGHTS" |
| −250 | FFFFFF06 | "DSERR_TEMP_REMAP" |
| −251 | FFFFFF05 | "DSERR_UNKNOWN_REQUEST" |
| −251 | FFFFFF05 | "DSERR_NO_SUCH_PROPERTY" |
| −251 | FFFFFF05 | "ERR_REQUEST_UNKNOWN" |
| −252 | FFFFFF04 | "DSERR_MESSAGE_QUEUE_FULL" |
| −252 | FFFFFF04 | "DSERR_TARGET_ALREADY_HAS_MSG" |
| −252 | FFFFFF04 | "DSERR_NO_SUCH_OBJECT" |
| −253 | FFFFFF03 | "DSERR_BAD_STATION_NUMBER" |
| −254 | FFFFFF02 | "DSERR_BINDERY_LOCKED" |
| −254 | FFFFFF02 | "DSERR_DIR_LOCKED" |
| −254 | FFFFFF02 | "DSERR_SPOOL_DELETE" |
| −254 | FFFFFF02 | "DSERR_TRUSTEE_NOT_FOUND" |
| −255 | FFFFFF01 | "DSERR_HARD_FAILURE" |
| −255 | FFFFFF01 | "DSERR_FILE_NAME" |
| −255 | FFFFFF01 | "DSERR_FILE_EXISTS" |
| −255 | FFFFFF01 | "DSERR_CLOSE_FCB" |
| −255 | FFFFFF01 | "DSERR_IO_BOUND" |
| −255 | FFFFFF01 | "DSERR_NO_SPOOL_FILE" |
| −255 | FFFFFF01 | "DSERR_BAD_SPOOL_PRINTER" |
| −255 | FFFFFF01 | "DSERR_BAD_PARAMETER" |
| −255 | FFFFFF01 | "DSERR_NO_FILES_FOUND" |
| −255 | FFFFFF01 | "DSERR_NO_TRUSTEE_CHANGE_PRIV" |
| −255 | FFFFFF01 | "DSERR_TARGET_NOT_LOGGED_IN" |
| −255 | FFFFFF01 | "DSERR_TARGET_NOT_ACCEPTING_MSGS" |
| −255 | FFFFFF01 | "DSERR_MUST_FORCE_DOWN" |
| −255 | FFFFFF01 | "ERR_OF_SOME_SORT" |

| | | |
|---|---|---|
| −301 | FFFFFED3 | "ERR_NOT_ENOUGH_MEMORY" |
| −302 | FFFFFED2 | "ERR_BAD_KEY" |
| −303 | FFFFFED1 | "ERR_BAD_CONTEXT" |
| −304 | FFFFFED0 | "ERR_BUFFER_FULL" |
| −305 | FFFFFECF | "ERR_LIST_EMPTY" |
| −306 | FFFFFECE | "ERR_BAD_SYNTAX" |
| −307 | FFFFFECD | "ERR_BUFFER_EMPTY" |
| −308 | FFFFFECC | "ERR_BAD_VERB" |
| −309 | FFFFFECB | "ERR_EXPECTED_IDENTIFIER" |
| −310 | FFFFFECA | "ERR_EXPECTED_EQUALS" |
| −311 | FFFFFEC9 | "ERR_ATTR_TYPE_EXPECTED" |
| −312 | FFFFFEC8 | "ERR_ATTR_TYPE_NOT_EXPECTED" |
| −313 | FFFFFEC7 | "ERR_FILTER_TREE_EMPTY" |
| −314 | FFFFFEC6 | "ERR_INVALID_OBJECT_NAME" |
| −315 | FFFFFEC5 | "ERR_EXPECTED_RDN_DELIMITER" |
| −316 | FFFFFEC4 | "ERR_TOO_MANY_TOKENS" |
| −317 | FFFFFEC3 | "ERR_INCONSISTENT_MULTIAVA" |
| −318 | FFFFFEC2 | "ERR_COUNTRY_NAME_TOO_LONG" |
| −319 | FFFFFEC1 | "ERR_SYSTEM_ERROR" |
| −320 | FFFFFEC0 | "ERR_CANT_ADD_ROOT" |
| −321 | FFFFFEBF | "ERR_UNABLE_TO_ATTACH" |
| −322 | FFFFFEBE | "ERR_INVALID_HANDLE" |
| −323 | FFFFFEBD | "ERR_BUFFER_ZERO_LENGTH" |
| −324 | FFFFFEBC | "ERR_INVALID_REPLICA_TYPE" |
| −325 | FFFFFEBB | "ERR_INVALID_ATTR_SYNTAX" |
| −326 | FFFFFEBA | "ERR_INVALID_FILTER_SYNTAX" |
| −328 | FFFFFEB8 | "ERR_CONTEXT_CREATION" |
| −329 | FFFFFEB7 | "ERR_INVALID_UNION_TAG" |
| −330 | FFFFFEB6 | "ERR_INVALID_SERVER_RESPONSE" |
| −331 | FFFFFEB5 | "ERR_NULL_POINTER" |
| −332 | FFFFFEB4 | "ERR_NO_SERVER_FOUND" |
| −333 | FFFFFEB3 | "ERR_NO_CONNECTION" |
| −334 | FFFFFEB2 | "ERR_RDN_TOO_LONG" |
| −335 | FFFFFEB1 | "ERR_DUPLICATE_TYPE" |
| −336 | FFFFFEB0 | "ERR_DATA_STORE_FAILURE" |
| −337 | FFFFFEAF | "ERR_NOT_LOGGED_IN" |
| −338 | FFFFFEAE | "ERR_INVALID_PASSWORD_CHARS" |
| −339 | FFFFFEAD | "ERR_FAILED_SERVER_AUTHENT" |
| −340 | FFFFFEAC | "ERR_TRANSPORT" |

· · · · ·

| | | |
|---|---|---|
| –341 | FFFFFEAB | "ERR_NO_SUCH_SYNTAX" |
| –342 | FFFFFEAA | "ERR_INVALID_DS_NAME" |
| –343 | FFFFFEA9 | "ERR_ATTR_NAME_TOO_LONG" |
| –344 | FFFFFEA8 | "ERR_INVALID_TDS" |
| –345 | FFFFFEA7 | "ERR_INVALID_DS_VERSION" |
| –346 | FFFFFEA6 | "ERR_UNICODE_TRANSLATION" |
| –347 | FFFFFEA5 | "ERR_SCHEMA_NAME_TOO_LONG" |
| –348 | FFFFFEA4 | "ERR_UNICODE_FILE_NOT_FOUND" |
| –349 | FFFFFEA3 | "ERR_UNICODE_ALREADY_LOADED" |
| –350 | FFFFFEA2 | "ERR_NOT_CONTEXT_OWNER" |
| –351 | FFFFFEA1 | "ERR_ATTEMPT_TO_AUTHENTICATE_0" |
| –352 | FFFFFEA0 | "ERR_NO_WRITABLE_REPLICAS" |
| –353 | FFFFFE9F | "ERR_DN_TOO_LONG" |
| –354 | FFFFFE9E | "ERR_RENAME_NOT_ALLOWED" |

# NetWare Server Console Commands

The NetWare server console commands and utilities enable you to change server parameters, monitor the load on the server, and control its allocation of resources. This appendix lists and describes the most significant console commands for the NetWare server. You can also view the console online help screen, which describes how to use each of the commands. You can access the help screen at the server prompt by typing the following:

```
HELP
```

You can enter the server console commands only at the server prompt or command line. These commands can also be used in the AUTOEXEC.NCF file but not in the STARTUP.NCF file. A few commands are available only in the AUTOEXEC.NCF file and will not function at the server prompt. For example, the commands FILE SERVER NAME and IPX INTERNAL NET are available only in the AUTOEXEC.NCF file.

The server console commands can also be placed in NetWare command files other than the AUTOEXEC.NCF file. The NetWare command files have .NCF file extensions and are used to group the server console commands together to perform specific tasks. The command files should be stored in the SYS:SYSTEM directory. You can execute a command file by typing the command filename (without the .NCF extension) at the server prompt.

## Server Console Commands

The following section presents the NetWare server console command, gives its syntax, and provides examples.

### ABORT REMIRROR

This command stops the remirroring of a NetWare file system partition. By default NetWare automatically begins remirroring a mirrored partition that is out of synchronization. The partition can fall out of synchronization if one-half of the mirror is disabled or damaged. The remirror process starts automatically after the pair is back up and running. The syntax for this command is

```
ABORT REMIRROR partition_number
```

You can selectively stop the remirroring process for any of the NetWare partitions.

**Example:** ABORT REMIRROR 3
**See also:** REMIRROR PARTITION

## ADD NAME SPACE

This command enables you to add and support non-DOS files, such as Macintosh, NFS (UNIX), OS/2 HPFS, and FTAM on the NetWare volume. The command is executed only once for each name space on each NetWare volume. The syntax for this command is

```
ADD NAME SPACE name [TO [volume_name]]
```

The name parameter can be replaced with one of these terms:

- ▸ **Macintosh** — Used for Apple Macintosh files
- ▸ **NFS** — Used for UNIX files
- ▸ **OS/2** — Used for IBM OS/2 HPFS files

The name space support module (file with .NAM file extension) must be loaded on the server before you can execute this command. For example, to support the Macintosh files, the MAC.NAM name space module must be loaded first.

After a volume is configured for name space support, the appropriate name space NLMs must be loaded prior to mounting the volume. Therefore, you must copy the .NAM name space file to the DOS partition of the server and include the statement to load the file in the STARTUP.NCF file. After a volume is set to store a non-DOS file system, the setting cannot be reversed unless the volume is deleted.

To display the name space support currently loaded on the server, you can enter the ADD NAME SPACE command without the other parameters. A list of all the loaded name spaces is displayed.

**Example:** ADD NAME SPACE MAC TO SYS
**See also:** VMVOLUMES

### Alert

This command enables you to specify what form an event should generate. For example, you can have the event sent to a log file or to the console or to everyone, and so on. For more information and help, type **HELP ALERT** at the server console prompt.

**Syntax:** ALERT nmID {Commands} {ON | OFF}, ALERT #50019 ALL OFF
**Commands:**

| | |
|---|---|
| **EVENT** | Description: Generate Event BIT(s) |
| **LOG** | Description: Log to File BIT(s) |
| **EVERYONE** | Description: Send to Everyone BIT(s) |
| **CONSOLE** | Description: Display on Console BIT(s) |
| **BELL** | Description: No Ring the Bell BIT(s) |
| **ID** | Description: Display ID BIT(s) |
| **LOCUS** | Description: Display LOCUS BIT(s) |
| **ALERT** | Description: No Alert BIT(s) |
| **NMID** | Description: No Display nmID BIT(s) |
| **ALL** | Description: Toggle (LOG, CONSOLE, EVERYONE,BELL) |

## ALIAS

This command creates an alias command that is used in place of an original command. For example, you can type **ALIAS V VOLUME**. Typing V is now equivalent to typing the whole command VOLUME at the server prompt.

After you type ALIASES, a list of current aliases is displayed on the server. Here is an example of an alias displayed on the server:

```
1. V ALIAS FOR <VOLUME>
```

## BIND

This command assigns or connects a specific communication protocol to a LAN driver loaded on the server. A communication protocol must be linked to the network board, or it will not be able to send and receive packets to and from the network. The syntax to connect a protocol to the network board is

```
BIND protocol [TO] board_name [protocol_parameter . . .]
```

or

```
BIND protocol [TO] LAN_driver [driver parameters . . .]
     [protocol_parameter . . .]
```

NetWare supports multiple communication protocol stacks in the server. The LAN driver and protocol stack modules must be loaded before this command can be used. The BIND command can be used to connect multiple protocol stacks to a single LAN adapter, or a single protocol can use multiple LAN adapters.

**Example:** BIND IPX TO NE3200 SLOT=3 FRAME=ETHERNET_802.2 NET=12345678

**See also:** UNBIND

## BINDERY

This command adds or removes a bindery context to or from the list of all bindery contexts for this server.

**Examples:**

BINDERY ADD CONTEXT = OU=DEPARTMENT OU=DIVISION O=CORPORATION

BINDERY DELETE CONTEXT = OU=DEPARTMENT OU=DIVISION O=CORPORATION

## BROADCAST

This command enables you to send a message to all the users that are currently logged in or attached to the server. You can also broadcast to a list of users or connection numbers. The syntax for the broadcast message is as follows:

```
BROADCAST "message" [[TO] user_name | connection_number]
    [[and | ,] username | connection_number . . .]
```

**Example:** BROADCAST "PLEASE LOG OUT OF THE SERVER. SERVER GOING DOWN IN 5 MINUTES" OR "HELLO TO SUPERVISOR 5 10 11 23."

**See also:** SEND

## CLEAR STATION

This command clears the connection for a specific connection number. After this command is issued against the user, the workstation is no longer attached to the server and all the allocated resources at the server are removed. The syntax for this command is

```
CLEAR STATION station_number
```

You can use the MONITOR program to determine connection numbers or match the connection number with the user.

**Example:** CLEAR STATION 5

## CLS

This command clears the console screen.
**Example:** CLS
**See also:** OFF

## CONFIG

This command displays the current status of the following information:

- ▶ File server name
- ▶ Internal network number for the server
- ▶ NDS tree name
- ▶ Hardware settings on all the network boards installed
- ▶ Network address for each network board
- ▶ LAN drivers loaded
- ▶ Communication protocol bound to the network board
- ▶ Frame type assigned to the protocol
- ▶ Board name assigned
- ▶ Effective bindery services context

**Example:** CONFIG

## CSET

Category SET enables you to view or set SET parameters by a particular category. For example, cset MEMORY. Hitting any key other than ESC causes you to scroll down through all the memory SET parameters. Hitting Y enables you to change a parameter as you scroll through them.

## DISABLE LOGIN

This command prevents additional clients from logging into the server but does not log out the clients that are already logged in. This command applies to all clients of the server whether they are users trying to connect to the server or another NetWare server authenticating to support replica synchronization for NDS.
**Example:** DISABLE LOGIN
**See also:** ENABLE LOGIN

## DISABLE TTS

This command manually turns off the transaction tracking system (TTS) feature. During normal operation, there is no reason for you ever to turn TTS off. In fact, NDS eDirectory depends on TTS, and you should not disable it. TTS automatically becomes disabled when the TTS backout volume is full or when server memory is insufficient.

The DISABLE TTS command is primarily a tool for application developers who need to test transactional applications with TTS disabled.

After you have manually disabled TTS, you should enable TTS using the ENABLE TTS command or reboot the server.

**Example:** DISABLE TTS
**See also:** ENABLE TTS

## DISMOUNT

This command causes the selected volume to be dismounted. If you have open files on that volume, the server prints a warning on the server console screen and prompts you for confirmation before it dismounts the volume. The syntax for this command is

```
DISMOUNT volume_name
```

You can use DISMOUNT to make a volume unavailable to your users. This enables you to do maintenance on the volume while the server is up. If you have a volume that is not used very often, such as a CD-ROM, you can dismount it until you need to use it again. Mounted volumes take up memory.

If the volume being dismounted is the SYS: volume, which contains the NDS eDirectory data files, the directory is closed for that server. All requests that require the directory are directed to another server in the network, which has another copy of the same NDS partition information.

**Example:** DISMOUNT SYS
**See also:** MOUNT

## DISPLAY ENVIRONMENT

This command displays the current search paths and the current values of the set parameters for the server. The name of the set parameter is highlighted in white with the current value in yellow. This command displays only set parameters that are not marked as hidden. When each set parameter is displayed, it includes the limits (min and max) values, as well as the default setting of the set parameter, if applicable. For more information about this command, type **HELP DISPLAY ENVIRONMENT** at the server console prompt.

**Example:** DISPLAY ENVIRONMENT

## DISPLAY INTERRUPTS

This command displays the interrupt handler and interrupt statistics information. This command shows you the current hardware interrupts that have been assigned. For more information about this command, you can type **HELP DISPLAY INTERRUPTS**.

**Examples:**

| | |
|---|---|
| DISPLAY INTERRUPTS | (Displays interrupts currently in use) |
| DISPLAY INTERRUPTS 3 10 | (Displays interrupts 3 and 10) |
| DISPLAY INTERRUPTS ALL | (Displays all system interrupts) |
| DISPLAY INTERRUPTS PROC | (Displays per processor interrupt information) |

## DISPLAY MODIFIED ENVIRONMENT

This command displays only the persistent set parameters that have been changed from their default value. It displays the current setting and the default setting. For more information about this command, you can type **HELP DISPLAY MODIFIED** at the server console prompt.

**Example:** DISPLAY MODIFIED ENVIRONMENT

## DISPLAY NETWORKS

This command displays the server's list of all the network numbers that the internal router is aware of. The list shows the IPX network number (which includes the internal network number of the server), the number of hops (networks that must be crossed) to reach the network, and the estimated time in ticks for a packet to reach the network. A tick is 1/18th of a second. The total number of networks is displayed at the end of the list.

**Example:** DISPLAY NETWORKS

**See also:** DISPLAY SERVERS

## DISPLAY PROCESSORS

This command displays the processor status for any or all processors you have running in your server. For more information about this command, you can type **HELP DISPLAY PROCESSORS** at the server console prompt.

**Examples:**
DISPLAY PROCESSORS [P# P# P#]
DISPLAY PROCESSORS (Displays the status of all processors)
DISPLAY PROCESSORS 1 3 (Displays the status of processors 1 and 3)

## DISPLAY SERVERS

This command displays the list of all the devices that send out a Service Advertising Protocol that the internal router is aware of. This command shows all servers regardless of type; for example, print servers, queue servers, and others are displayed.

The list shows the advertising name (typically a server) and the number of hops (networks that must be crossed) to reach the server. The total number of servers is displayed at the bottom of the list.

**Example:** DISPLAY SERVERS
**See also:** DISPLAY NETWORKS

## DOWN

This command brings down the server. The server going down means that all the connections are cleared, all volumes are dismounted, and IPX packet routing is suspended. If files are in use by a workstation when the DOWN command is issued, the server displays a warning on the console screen and asks for confirmation before it goes down.

You should always type the DOWN command before turning off the power to the server. The DOWN command ensures data integrity by writing all cache buffers to disk, closing all files, and updating the appropriate directory and file allocation table.

**Example:** DOWN
**See also:** EXIT, and RESTART SERVER

## ECHO OFF

This command tells the server not to echo or display the commands in the NetWare Command File to the screen when they are executed. This command is valid for use in only the .NCF files. ECHO OFF is the default.

**Example:** ECHO OFF
**See also:** ECHO ON

## ECHO ON

This command tells the server to echo the commands in the NetWare Command File to the screen as they are executed. This command is valid for use in only the .NCF files. The default is not to echo.

**Example:** ECHO ON
**See also:** ECHO OFF

## ENABLE LOGIN

This command enables clients to connect and log in to the server. This command is the default when the server is booted. You should use this command only if you have disabled login using the DISABLE LOGIN command. This command does not affect users that are already connected.

The ENABLE LOGIN command prevents the supervisor account from being locked out by the intruder detection.

**Example:** ENABLE LOGIN
**See also:** DISABLE LOGIN

## ENABLE TTS

This command manually turns on the transaction tracking system feature of NetWare. During normal operation, TTS is always enabled.

When volume SYS is mounted, TTS is automatically enabled if enough disk space and memory is available to allow transaction tracking. NDS eDirectory depends on TTS, and you should always leave it enabled. If a problem occurs that disables TTS automatically, you must fix the problem before you can enable TTS.

The server automatically disables TTS if one of the following events occurs:

- ▸ Volume SYS becomes full
- ▸ Insufficient memory to operate TTS

**Example:** ENABLE TTS
**See also:** DISABLE TTS

## EXIT

After the server has been taken down, the EXIT command leaves the server program and returns to DOS. This enables you to access the DOS files or rerun the SERVER.EXE program.

The DOWN command must always be issued before the EXIT command. If the REMOVE DOS command was issued, the server performs a reboot.

After you bring down the server, it is still connected to the network and receiving packets. You can still execute console commands that deal with packets such as TRACK ON and TRACK OFF.

**Example:** EXIT

**See also:** DOWN, and RESTART SERVER

## FILE SERVER NAME

This command sets the server name when the server boots up. The file server name is used to identify the server on the network. The file server name is distributed throughout the network using the SAP. The name chosen should be a unique value on the network because it does have the SAP. The syntax for this command is

```
FILE SERVER NAME server_name
```

The clients find the server by knowing the name of the server. The file server name for NetWare 6 is also widely used by NDS eDirectory for many of its services.

This command is available only in the AUTOEXEC.NCF file and cannot be used at the server prompt.

**Example:** FILE SERVER NAME CAM-SRV1

## HELP

This command displays the help screen at the file server console. The help screen lists all the server console commands with examples of how to use them. You can specify an individual command with HELP. The HELP ALL command lists all the server console commands in alphabetical order and pauses between each command.

**Example:** HELP, HELP BIND, OR HELP ALL

## IPX INTERNAL NET

This command sets the internal network number that the router uses to identify all services/clients that reside in the same machine as the router. For NetWare, the internal network number is very important and is used in NDS eDirectory. The syntax for this command is

```
IPX INTERNAL NET network_address
```

The internal IPX network number chosen should be a unique number on the network. This command is available only in the AUTOEXEC.NCF file.

**Example:** IPX INTERNAL NET 370DC321

## LANGUAGE

This command sets the server console to use the language specified. The server console command and server utilities or NLM programs use the appropriate language message files. The syntax for this command has several options:

- ▶ **Language** — Displays current NLM language
- ▶ **Language list** — Displays list of available languages
- ▶ **Language name|number** — Sets language by name or number
- ▶ **Language add number name** — Adds a new language name and number
- ▶ **Language rename number new_name** — Renames the language specified

**Example:** LANGUAGE SPANISH

## LIST DEVICES

This command displays all the physical device information for the server.
**Example:** LIST DEVICES

## LOAD

This command executes a NetWare Loadable Module file and links it to the operating system. The file executed is named with one of the following extensions: .NLM (server utilities), .DSK (disk driver), and .LAN (LAN driver). The LOAD command searches the SYS:SYSTEM directory by default for the files. The SYS: volume must be mounted. The syntax for the LOAD command is

```
LOAD [path] load_module [parameter . . .]
```

You can also specify a complete path name for the file to be loaded or set up additional paths to search for the file by using the SEARCH command.
**Example:** LOAD MONITOR
**Note:** Typing load before loading an NLM is no longer necessary in NetWare 6.
**See also:** UNLOAD, SEARCH

## MAGAZINE INSERTED

This command acknowledges the insertion of the specified media magazine in response to the "Insert Magazine" console alert.
**Example:** MAGAZINE INSERTED

## MAGAZINE NOT INSERTED

This command acknowledges that the insertion of the specified media magazine was not performed.

**Example:** MAGAZINE NOT INSERTED

## MAGAZINE NOT REMOVED

This command acknowledges that the removal of the magazine was not performed.

**Example:** MAGAZINE NOT REMOVED

## MAGAZINE REMOVED

This command acknowledges the removal of a magazine from the specified device in response to the "Remove Magazine" console alert.

**Example:** REMOVE MAGAZINE

## MEDIA INSERTED

This command acknowledges insertion of the specified media in response to the "Insert Media" console alert.

**Example:** MEDIA INSERTED

## MEDIA NOT INSERTED

This command acknowledges that insertion of the specified media was not performed.

**Example:** MEDIA NOT INSERTED

## MEDIA NOT REMOVED

This command acknowledges that removal of the media was not performed.

**Example:** MEDIA NOT REMOVED

## MEDIA REMOVED

This command acknowledges removal of the media from the specified device in response to the "Remove Magazine" console alert.

**Example:** REMOVE MEDIA

## MEMORY MAP

This command displays a map of server RAM.
**Example:** MEMORY MAP

## MEMORY

This command displays the total memory installed that the NetWare operating system can address.
**Example:** MEMORY
**See also:** REGISTER MEMORY

## MIRROR STATUS

This command displays all mirrored logical disk partitions and the status of each.
**Example:** MIRROR STATUS

## MODULES

This command displays names and descriptions for all the NetWare Loadable Modules currently loaded on the server.
**Example:** MODULES

## MOUNT

This command causes the specified volume to be mounted as a NetWare volume. The syntax for the MOUNT command is

```
MOUNT volume_name or MOUNT ALL
```

**Example:** MOUNT SYS, MOUNT ALL

## NAME

This command displays the server's name. The NAME command is still supported in NetWare 6 but is not very useful because the server prompt includes the server name.
**Example:** NAME
**See also:** FILE SERVER NAME

## NCP ADDRESSES

This command displays the currently registered NCP service addresses. For more information about this command, type **HELP NCP ADDRESSES** at the server console prompt.

**Example:** NCP ADDRESSES

## NCP DUMP

This command dumps the NCP standard deviation statistics to a specified file.

**Example:** NCP DUMP FILENAME.EXT

## NCP STATS

This command displays the NCP statistics on incoming NCP requests. The command can also be used to reset counters.

**Example:** NCP STATS {RESET}

## NCP TRACE

This command decodes the incoming NCP packets to the screen or to a file if specified. The syntax for this command is as follows:

```
NCP TRACE ON {filename.ext}
NCP TRACE OFF
```

## OFF

This command clears the server console screen and is equivalent to the CLS command.

**Example:** OFF
**See also:** CLS

## PAUSE

This command causes the screen and processing to stop and waits for a key to be pressed while in a NetWare Control File (NCF).

**Example:** PAUSE

## PROTECT

This command is used when you have an NCF file that is used to load NLM(s) and you would like to load them in a protected address space.

**Example:** PROTECT (NCF FILE NAME); FOR EXAMPLE, PROTECT GRPWISE

## PROTECTION

This command displays the information about the protected memory address spaces in the system. It also provides the ability to enable and disable the restart feature for a protected address space. For more information about this command, type **HELP PROTECTION** at the server console prompt.

**Examples:**
PROTECTION
PROTECTION ADDRESS_SPACE1
PROTECTION RESTART ADDRESS_SPACE1
PROTECTION NO RESTART ADDRESS_SPACE1

## PROTOCOL

This command displays the protocol identification numbers registered with the server. These numbers are based on the server's communication protocol and media type. The PROTOCOL command can also be used to register new protocol IDs and numbers with the server. The proper syntax for this command is

```
PROTOCOL or PROTOCOL REGISTER protocol_name frame id_number
```

If you load a communication protocol module and try to bind it, you may get an error message stating that the module is not loaded. The error message probably means that the communication protocol or the media type contained in the driver is not registered with NetWare. In this case, you should use the PROTOCOL REGISTER to register the new protocol.

**Example:** PROTOCOL REGISTER IP ETHERNET_II 800

## PROTOCOL REGISTER or PROTOCOL

This command enables you to view registered protocols or register additional protocols and frame types.

**Example:** PROTOCOL REGISTER IP ETHERNET_II 800

## PSM

This command executes a Platform Support Module (PSM) console command. To display a list of supported PSM commands, you can type **PSM ?**. For more information, you can type **HELP PSM** at the server console prompt.

**Example:** PSM ?

## REGISTER MEMORY

For some hardware systems, NetWare does not recognize more than 16MB of RAM. In these situations, you must use the REGISTER MEMORY command at the console. This command uses the following syntax:

```
REGISTER MEMORY memory_start memory_length
```

You can replace the `memory_start` with a value in hexadecimal representing a memory address beyond 16MB. In most cases, this is the value 0x1000000 (which equates to 16MB). The `memory_length` is the value of the memory installed that is beyond 16MB. This number must be an even paragraph boundary that is divisible by 0x10. For example, to add 4MB of memory above 16MB (for a total of 20MB RAM), you need to enter the following command:

```
REGISTER MEMORY 1000000 1250000
```

This command can be added to the AUTOEXEC.NCF file for automatic registration of memory when the server is booted. For EISA-based machines, memory above 16MB is registered automatically.

**See also:** MEMORY

## REM or ; or #

Each of these commands is used to specify a comment line or a remark in the AUTOEXEC.NCF, or NCF.

**Example:** REM This line will load the LAN driver for the NE3200 network board.

## REMIRROR PARTITION

This command starts the remirroring of a logical disk partition. Partition remirroring typically consumes upward of 70 percent of the CPU's time, so you might want to delay the remirroring process until activity on the server is reduced. The syntax for this command is

```
REMIRROR PARTITION partition_number
```

**Example:** REMIRROR PARTITION 4

## REMOVE DOS

After the server is running, the memory being used by DOS can be released and given to the server cache memory. After this command is issued and the server is brought down, the EXIT command will not be able to return to DOS. You must power off the machine to reboot.

By removing DOS from the server's memory, you are providing an additional 1MB of memory for the server cache memory. However, because DOS is no longer residing in memory of the server, the files located on the DOS drives are no longer accessible. This can be implemented as a security step because the NLMs cannot then be loaded from the DOS drivers.

You can also use the REMOVE DOS command to enable warm booting of the server using the EXIT command.

**Example:** REMOVE DOS

**See also:** EXIT

## RESET ENVIRONMENT

This command displays and prompts for every set parameter that has been changed from its default value, querying the console user whether to change the value back to its default value or to skip to the next modified set parameter. For more information about this command, type **HELP RESET ENVIRONMENT** at the server console prompt.

**Example:** RESET ENVIRONMENT

## RESET ROUTER

This command clears the information stored in the internal router tables of the server. The RESET ROUTER command erases all known servers and networks. The router automatically rebuilds the tables as SAP and RIP advertising information is received.

This command is useful when you want to debug communication problems that you may have in the network or the server itself. By resetting the router, you can tell whether the server is receiving the routing information.

For example, if several servers or bridges on your network go down, any packets sent to or through their routers will be lost. If you reset routers in the server that are still up, the router sends a request to the nearest server to verify any other networks or routes it knows about. From this information, the router builds a new, accurate router table.

**Example:** RESET ROUTER

## RESTART SERVER

This command reloads the SERVER.EXE software after the DOWN command has been issued. This command is valid only if the server has not been exited. The following options are available with the RESTART SERVER command:

- ▸ **-ns** — Do not use the STARTUP.NCF file.
- ▸ **-na** — Do not use the AUTOEXEC.NCF file.
- ▸ **-d** — Break into the internal debugger.

**Example:** RESTART SERVER

## SCAN FOR NEW DEVICES

This command checks for storage devices and hardware that have been added since the server was last booted. This command causes the operating system to look for and add new devices on the system.

**Example:** SCAN FOR NEW DEVICES

## SEARCH

This command dictates where the server should automatically search for the NetWare Loadable Module (.NLM) files and the NetWare Command File (.NCF). The directory that the server searches by default is SYS:SYSTEM. You can use this command to add additional search paths and to display the current setting for the search paths on the server. The proper syntax for the SEARCH command is

```
SEARCH [ADD [number]] path
```

or

```
SEARCH DEL [number]
```

**Example:** SEARCH ADD 4 C:\NWSERVER\NLMS OR SEARCH DEL 1

## SECURE CONSOLE

This command enables you to restrict access to the server console by

- ▸ Restricting the loading of NLMs from every place but the current search path
- ▸ Preventing keyboard entry into the internal NetWare debugger

▶ Preventing anyone except the console operator from changing the date and time

▶ Removing DOS from the server

**Example:** SECURE CONSOLE

## SEND

This command enables you to send a message to all users logged in or attached to the server or a list of users or connection numbers. The syntax for the SEND command is

```
SEND "message" [[TO] user_name | connection_number] [[and |,]
    username | connection_number . . .]
```

**Example:** SEND "PLEASE DELETE SOME FILES" TO JACK AND JILL

## SET

This command displays and changes the server's configuration information. Many configuration parameters can be adjusted by using this command. Typing the SET command without a configuration parameter name displays a small menu of configuration parameters. The display shows the configuration parameter name, its current setting, the limits that it can be set to, and a description of what the configuration parameter controls. The syntax for this command is

```
SET [parameter_name] [=parameter_value]
```

The SET command can be used in the STARTUP.NCF and AUTOEXEC.NCF files. The following three configuration parameters can be set in the STARTUP.NCF (they cannot be set from the server console command line):

▶ Minimum Packet Receive Buffers

▶ Maximum Physical Receive Packet Size

▶ Cache Buffer Size

**Example:** SET BINDERY CONTEXT = OU=NORAD.O=ACME

## SET TIME

This command sets the server date and time; it accepts a variety of formats. You can set just the date, just the time, or both. The syntax for the SET TIME command is

```
SET TIME [month/day/year] [hour:minute:second]
```

This command assumes that if the time is specified, a colon separates the hours and minutes. If "am" or "pm" is not specified, the server assumes that the time has been entered during working hours. Working hours are 7:00 to 12:00 A.M. and 1:00 to 6:00 P.M.

The month can be entered as a number or a name. If the month is entered as a number, the command assumes that the month precedes the day or year number.

**Example:** SET TIME APRIL 6 1999 3:45:00 PM

**See also:** TIME, and SET

## SET TIME ZONE

This command sets the server time zone using the specific time zone strings in NetWare. The SET TIME ZONE command is also used to display the current setting of the time zone on the server. The syntax for this command is

```
SET TIME ZONE zone [hour[daylight]]
```

**Example:** SET TIME ZONE MST7MDT

## SPEED

This command displays the CPU speed rating for the server hardware. The speed is a processor-relative value in which a 386-based machine has a slower rating than a 486-based machine. The Pentium class of machines is faster or has a higher speed rating for the processor.

**Example:** SPEED

## SPOOL

This command enables you to create, change, or display spooler mappings. These mappings are needed to set up default print queues for NPRINT and CAPTURE. They also support applications that make calls to printer numbers rather than to queues. The syntax for the SPOOL command is

```
SPOOL
```

or

```
SPOOL number [TO] [QUEUE] queue_name
```

**Example:** SPOOL 1 TO QUEUE HP4SI

## START PROCESSORS

This command starts all secondary processors on your server.

**Examples:**

START PROCESSORS [P# P# P#...]

START PROCESSORS (Starts all secondary processors)

START PROCESSORS 1 3 (Starts secondary processors 1 and 3)

## STOP PROCESSORS

This command stops all secondary processors on your server.

**Examples:**

STOP PROCESSORS [P# P# P#...]

STOP PROCESSORS (Starts all secondary processors)

STOP PROCESSORS 1 3 (Starts secondary processors 1 and 3)

## SWAP

This command adds or removes the swap file from a volume and sets MIN, MAX, and MIN Free. If no parameters are given, all swap file information is displayed. The following constraints apply:

▶ All values are in millions of bytes.

▶ MIN or MINIMUM = Minimum swap file size, with a default of 2.

▶ MAX or MAXIMUM = Maximum swap file size with a default = Free volume space.

▶ MIN FREE or MINIMUM FREE = Minimum free space to be left on volume not occupying the swap file, with a default of 5.

**Examples:**

SWAP

SWAP ADD VOL2

SWAP ADD VOL3 MIN = 5 MAX = 100 MIN FREE = 10

SWAP DELETE VOL3

SWAP PARAMETER VOL1 MIN = 2 MAX = 1000 MIN FREE = 100

## TIME

This command displays the current server date, time, and time synchronization status.

**Example:** TIME

**See also:** SET TIME

## TRACK OFF

This command closes the Router Tracking Screen on the server that views the activity on the server caused by sending and receiving advertising packets from the Service Advertising Protocol and Routing Information Protocol.

**Example:** TRACK OFF
**See also:** TRACK ON

## TRACK ON

This command starts the Router Tracking Screen and makes it active on the server console. The screen displays the activity caused by sending and receiving advertising packets from the Service Advertising Protocol and Routing Information Protocol.

**Example:** TRACK ON
**See also:** TRACK OFF

## UNBIND

This command disconnects the specified communication protocol stack from a LAN adapter. The LAN adapter is specified by the LAN driver name if the driver is servicing only one adapter. If the LAN driver is servicing more than one adapter, the optional parameters indicate the hardware settings of the adapter to be unbound. If either the LAN driver or the protocol stack is unloaded using the command, the protocol stack is automatically unbound from the LAN adapter. The syntax for the UNBIND command is

```
UNBIND protocol [FROM] LAN_driver [driver parameters . . .]
```

or

```
UNBIND protocol [FROM] board_name
```

**Example:** UNBIND IPX FROM NE3200 SLOT=3 FRAME=ETHERNET_802.2
**See also:** BIND

## UNLOAD

This command removes or unlinks the NetWare Loadable Module from the operating system. The NLM, which was previously loaded, is removed from the server memory. You can use the UNLOAD command to upgrade or change any of the NLMs loaded on the server.

**Example:** UNLOAD PSERVER
**See also:** LOAD

## VERSION

This command displays the server's version information and copyright notice.
**Example:** VERSION

## VOLUME

This command displays a list of all the volumes currently mounted on the server.
**Example:** VOLUME
**See also:** MOUNT

## VMDISMOUNT

This command allows volume maintenance or repairs while the file server is up by making a volume unavailable to the users temporarily.
**Example:** VMDISMOUNT SYS OR VMDISMOUNT 0

## VMMOUNT

This command makes a volume available to users.
**Example:** VMMOUNT SYS OR VMMOUNT 0

## VMVOLUMES

This command displays a list of the currently mounted volumes including the number, status, and name.
**Example:** VMVOLUMES

# NetWare 6 Debugger Commands

The NetWare 6 operating system includes an internal assembly language debug utility. This debugger enables you to execute the commands listed in this appendix. You can use the debugger to help determine the cause of a server abend or simply to become more familiar with the internal structure of NetWare 6. The NetWare 6 debugger features color-coded data that helps you more easily identify the more important information and make it quicker and easier to use.

After the debugger is entered, it displays the following: a screen with a # as the prompt; default information, including the location in code at which the server abended or was manually interrupted; and the cause of the abend or trap. The general registers and flags are also presented.

# Invoking the NetWare 6 Debugger

Four methods are available to invoke the debugger: two from the server console, one from a program, and one from hardware.

## From the Server Console

▸ Press Alt+Left-Shift+Right-Shift+Esc simultaneously at the server keyboard. You can enter this key combination either while the server is running or after an abend. This method will not work if the server is hung in a tight infinite loop (some infinite loops are not too tight), if it has interrupts disabled, or if the server console has been locked.

▸ If the server abends or GPIs (General Power Interrupts), you can type **386debug** to invoke the debugger. The characters you type do not appear onscreen, but the # prompt immediately appears. Remember, the # prompt indicates that you are in the debugger.

## From an NLM Program

▸ If the NLM program supplies an INT 3 in the desired code segment, the program will invoke the debugger. If the programmer is using C and the CLIB interface, the programmer can call a Breakpoint() function.

## With Hardware or Manually

▸ You can break into a server by using an NMI board. After the server has abended, you can use either of the steps for invoking the debugger from the server console. This method seems abrupt but may be required if the software program being debugged is in a tight infinite loop with interrupts disabled.

# Debugger Commands

Once you have entered the debugger, you can display a great deal of information. The debugger commands and their functions are listed in Tables D.1 through D.4.

TABLE D.1

*Debugger Commands*

| COMMAND | FUNCTION |
|---|---|
| Q | Quits the debugger and returns to DOS. |
| G | Continues server execution (go) from the current position. |
| G [address(es)] | Begins execution at the current position and then sets a temporary breakpoint at the address or several temporary breakpoints at the addresses. |
| P | Proceeds with the next instruction. Using this command, you can trace or single step each of the following instructions. One limitation is that this command will not single step through loops in the code or trace into a subroutine call. You can repeat this command by simply pressing Enter at the prompt. |
| T or S | Enables you to trace or single step through the program code, through loops, and into subroutine calls. |
| U address | Enables you to unassemble instructions from a specific address, which can be done for count instructions. You can repeat this command by simply pressing Enter at the prompt. |
| V | Enables you to switch over and view the server console screens. You will be able to step through the screens sequentially. |

*continued*

TABLE D.1

*Debugger Commands (continued)*

| COMMAND | FUNCTION |
|---------|----------|
| ? address | Displays the closest symbols to the address if symbolic information has been loaded. By default, this command is the EIP register. |
| N symbol | Enables you to assign a symbol name to a specific name address. |
| N –symbolname | Removes the specific symbol name. |
| N— | Removes all defined symbols. |
| Z expression | Evaluates the expression. This command is useful as a calculator in the debugger. Zd will evaluate the expression in decimal. |

TABLE D.2

*Help Commands*

| COMMAND | FUNCTION |
|---------|----------|
| H | Displays help for general commands. |
| .H | Displays help for the "." Commands. |
| HB | Displays help for breakpoints. |
| HE | Displays help for expressions. |
| H3 | Displays help for SFT III commands. |

TABLE D.3

*Dot "." Commands*

| COMMAND | FUNCTION |
|---------|----------|
| .a | Displays the reason for an abend or a break. |
| .c | Does a diagnostic memory dump to a floppy or hard disk. |
| .d | Displays a page directory map for the current debugger domain. |
| .d | Displays a page entry map for the current debugger domain. |
| .f | Toggles the developer option flag ON/OFF. |
| .g | Displays the GDT. |

| COMMAND | FUNCTION |
|---|---|
| .h | Displays help for the "." commands. |
| .l | Displays the IDT. |
| .l2 | Displays the IDT for Processor 2. This command defaults to the math coprocessor on a single-processor system. |
| .l offset[offset] | Displays the linear address given to page map offsets. |
| .la[linear address] [<cr3>] | Finds all aliases of a linear address. |
| .lp[physical address] [<cr3>] | Finds all linear mappings of a physical address. |
| .lx address | Displays page offsets and values used for translation. |
| .m | Displays loaded module names and addresses. |
| .p | Displays all process names and addresses. |
| .p address | Displays *address* as a process control block. |
| .r | Displays the running process control block. |
| .s | Displays all screen names and addresses. |
| .? | Displays the server state. |
| .s address | Displays *address* as a screen structure. If no address is specified, this command displays all screen names and addresses. |
| .t address | Displays *address* as a TSS structure. |
| .ts [segnum] | Displays GDT *[segnum]* as a TSS structure. |
| .v | Displays the server version. |

**T A B L E   D . 4**

*Memory Commands*

| COMMAND | FUNCTION |
|---|---|
| C address | Interactively changes the contents of a memory location. |
| C address = number(s) | Changes the memory contents beginning at *address* to the specified number(s). *Number* is a hexadecimal value. |
| C address = "text string" | Changes the memory contents starting at *address* to the text string value. |

*continued*

| TABLE D.4 | |
|---|---|
| Memory Commands (continued) | |
| **COMMAND** | **FUNCTION** |
| D address [count] | Dumps the contents of memory, starting at *address*, for *count* number of bytes. The address and count are in hexadecimal values. *Count* is an optional value; if it is not supplied, one page (100h bytes) will be displayed. This command can be repeated continually by pressing Enter after each dump of contents. |
| M address [L length] bytepattern(s) | Searches memory for a byte pattern match, starting at the location *address* and continuing until *L length* is reached. If a match is found, 128 bytes (starting with the pattern) are displayed. This command can be repeated by pressing Enter at the # prompt. |

# Registers

Tables D.5 through D.7 list the NetWare6 debugger commands used on a microprocessor's internal registers. These registers are both the general and flag registers.

| TABLE D.5 | |
|---|---|
| Netware 6 Debugger Commands Used on a Microprocessor's Internal Registers | |
| **COMMAND** | **FUNCTION** |
| R | Displays the EAX, EBX, ECX, EDX, ESI, EDI, ESP, EBP, EIP, and flag registers. |
| Name of Register = value | Enables you to change a specific register to a new value. This command affects the EAX, EBX, ECX, EDX, ESI, EDI, ESP, EBP, EFL, and EIP registers. |
| Name of F flag = value | Enables you to change a specific flag register to a new value. The value has to be 0 or 1 because these are the only values the flag register can hold. This command affects the CF, AF, ZF, SF, IF, TF, PF, DF, and OF flag registers. |

T A B L E D.6

*Input/Output Commands*

| COMMAND | FUNCTION |
|---------|----------|
| I[B,W,D] port | Inputs a (B)yte, (W)ord, or (D)ouble word from a port. The default is byte O[B,W,D] port = value. Outputs a (B)yte, (W)ord, or (D)ouble word value to a port. |

T A B L E D.7

*Breakpoints Commands*

| COMMAND | FUNCTION |
|---------|----------|
| B | Displays all breakpoints that are currently set. |
| B = address | Sets an execution breakpoint at *address*. The break will occur if EIP = address is changed and the condition evaluates to TRUE. |
| BC number | Clears the breakpoint specified by *number*. |
| BCA | Clears all breakpoints. |
| BI = address | Sets an I/O read/write breakpoint at address. This breakpoint occurs when the specified I/O port address is accessed with either a read or a write. |
| BR = address {condition} | Sets a read/write breakpoint at the address specified when the indicated condition is true. |
| BW = address {condition} | Sets a write breakpoint at the address specified when the indicated condition is true. |

# Debug Expressions

In Table D.8, all the numbers in the debug expressions are entered and shown in hex format. In addition to the numbers, the following registers, flags, and operators can be used in the debug expressions:

Registers — EAX, EBX, ECX, EDX, ESI, EDI, ESP, EBP, EIP

Flags — FLCF, FLAF, FLZF, FLSF, FLIF, FLTF, FLPF, FLDF, FLOF

TABLE D.8

*Debug Expressions and Their Numbers*

| SYMBOL | DESCRIPTION | PRECEDENCE |
|--------|-------------|------------|
| ( ) | (Expression) Causes the expression to be evaluated at a higher level. | 0 |
| [ ] | [Size Expression] Causes the expression to be evaluated at a higher precedence and then uses the value of the expression as a memory address. | 0 |
| { } | {Size Expression}Causes the expression to be evaluated at a higher precedence and then uses the value of the expression as a port address. | 0 |
| ! | Logical Not | 1 |
| - | 2's Complement | 1 |
| ~ | 1's Complement | 1 |
| * | Multiply | 2 |
| / | Divide | 2 |
| % | Mod | 2 |
| + | Add | 3 |
| - | Subtract | 3 |
| > | Bit Shift Right | 4 |
| << | Bit Shift Left | 4 |
| > | Greater Than | 5 |
| < | Less Than | 5 |
| >= | Greater Than or Equal To | 5 |
| <= | Less Than Or Equal To | 5 |
| == | Equal To | 6 |
| != | Not Equal To | 6 |

| SYMBOL | DESCRIPTION | PRECEDENCE |
|--------|-------------|------------|
| & | Bitwise AND | 7 |
| ^ | Bitwise XOR | 8 |
| \| | Bitwise OR | 9 |
| && | Logical AND | 10 |
| \|\| | Logical OR | 11 |

## Conditional Evaluation

```
expression1 ? expression2, expression3
```

If `1expression1` is true, then the result is the value of `expression2`. Otherwise (if `expression1` is not true), the result is the value of `expression3`.

# *Index*

*continued*

*continued*

*continued*

## G

## H

## I

*continued*

*continued*

*continued*

*continued*

## O

*continued*

*continued*

*continued*

continued

## U

*continued*

# Wiley Publishing, Inc.
# End-User License Agreement

**READ THIS.** You should carefully read these terms and conditions before opening the software packet(s) included with this book "Book". This is a license agreement "Agreement" between you and Wiley Publishing, Inc. "WPI". By opening the accompanying software packet(s), you acknowledge that you have read and accept the following terms and conditions. If you do not agree and do not want to be bound by such terms and conditions, promptly return the Book and the unopened software packet(s) to the place you obtained them for a full refund.

1.  **License Grant.** WPI grants to you (either an individual or entity) a nonexclusive license to use one copy of the enclosed software program(s) (collectively, the "Software" solely for your own personal or business purposes on a single computer (whether a standard computer or a workstation component of a multi-user network). The Software is in use on a computer when it is loaded into temporary memory (RAM) or installed into permanent memory (hard disk, CD-ROM, or other storage device). WPI reserves all rights not expressly granted herein.

2.  **Ownership.** WPI is the owner of all right, title, and interest, including copyright, in and to the compilation of the Software recorded on the disk(s) or CD-ROM "Software Media". Copyright to the individual programs recorded on the Software Media is owned by the author or other authorized copyright owner of each program. Ownership of the Software and all proprietary rights relating thereto remain with WPI and its licensers.

3.  **Restrictions On Use and Transfer.**

    **(a)** You may only (i) make one copy of the Software for backup or archival purposes, or (ii) transfer the Software to a single hard disk, provided that you keep the original for backup or archival purposes. You may not (i) rent or lease the Software, (ii) copy or reproduce the Software through a LAN or other network system or through any computer subscriber system or bulletin- board system, or (iii) modify, adapt, or create derivative works based on the Software.

    **(b)** You may not reverse engineer, decompile, or disassemble the Software. You may transfer the Software and user documentation on a permanent basis, provided that the transferee agrees to accept the terms and conditions of this Agreement and you retain no copies. If the Software is an update or has been updated, any transfer must include the most recent update and all prior versions.

4.  **Restrictions On Use of Individual Programs.** You must follow the individual requirements and restrictions detailed for each individual program in Appendix A of this Book. These limitations are also contained in the individual license agreements recorded on the Software Media. These limitations may include a requirement that after using the program for a specified period of time, the user must pay a registration fee or discontinue use. By opening the Software packet(s), you will be agreeing to abide by the licenses and restrictions for these individual programs that are detailed in Appendix A and on the Software Media. None of the material on this Software Media or listed in this Book may ever be redistributed, in original or modified form, for commercial purposes.

5.  **Limited Warranty.**

    **(a)** WPI warrants that the Software and Software Media are free from defects in materials and workmanship under normal use for a period of sixty (60) days from the date of purchase of this Book. If WPI receives notification within the warranty period of defects in materials or workmanship, WPI will replace the defective Software Media.

**(b) WPI AND THE AUTHOR OF THE BOOK DISCLAIM ALL OTHER WARRANTIES, EXPRESS OR IMPLIED, INCLUDING WITHOUT LIMITATION IMPLIED WARRANTIES OF MERCHANTABILITY AND FITNESS FOR A PARTICULAR PURPOSE, WITH RESPECT TO THE SOFTWARE, THE PROGRAMS, THE SOURCE CODE CONTAINED THEREIN, AND/OR THE TECHNIQUES DESCRIBED IN THIS BOOK. WPI DOES NOT WARRANT THAT THE FUNCTIONS CONTAINED IN THE SOFTWARE WILL MEET YOUR REQUIREMENTS OR THAT THE OPERATION OF THE SOFTWARE WILL BE ERROR FREE.**

**(c)** This limited warranty gives you specific legal rights, and you may have other rights that vary from jurisdiction to jurisdiction.

6. **Remedies.**

   **(a)** WPI's entire liability and your exclusive remedy for defects in materials and workmanship shall be limited to replacement of the Software Media, which may be returned to WPI with a copy of your receipt at the following address: Software Media Fulfillment Department, Attn.: *Novell's Guide to NetWare 6 Networks*, Wiley Publishing, Inc., 10475 Crosspoint Blvd., Indianapolis, IN 46256, or call 1-800-762-2974. Please allow four to six weeks for delivery. This Limited Warranty is void if failure of the Software Media has resulted from accident, abuse, or misapplication. Any replacement Software Media will be warranted for the remainder of the original warranty period or thirty (30) days, whichever is longer.

   **(b)** In no event shall WPI or the author be liable for any damages whatsoever (including without limitation damages for loss of business profits, business interruption, loss of business information, or any other pecuniary loss) arising from the use of or inability to use the Book or the Software, even if WPI has been advised of the possibility of such damages.

   **(c)** Because some jurisdictions do not allow the exclusion or limitation of liability for consequential or incidental damages, the above limitation or exclusion may not apply to you.

7. **U.S. Government Restricted Rights.** Use, duplication, or disclosure of the Software for or on behalf of the United States of America, its agencies and/or instrumentalities "U.S. Government" is subject to restrictions as stated in paragraph (c)(1)(ii) of the Rights in Technical Data and Computer Software clause of DFARS 252.227-7013, or subparagraphs (c) (1) and (2) of the Commercial Computer Software - Restricted Rights clause at FAR 52.227-19, and in similar clauses in the NASA FAR supplement, as applicable.

8. **General.** This Agreement constitutes the entire understanding of the parties and revokes and supersedes all prior agreements, oral or written, between them and may not be modified or amended except in a writing signed by both parties hereto that specifically refers to this Agreement. This Agreement shall take precedence over any other documents that may be in conflict herewith. If any one or more provisions contained in this Agreement are held by any court or tribunal to be invalid, illegal, or otherwise unenforceable, each and every other provision shall remain in full force and effect.